Lecture Notes in Computer Science

Edited by G. Goos and J. Hartmanis

71

Automata, Languages and Programming

Sixth Colloquium, Graz, Austria, July 16–20, 1979

Edited by Hermann A. Maurer

Springer-Verlag
Berlin Heidelberg New York 1979

Editor
Hermann A. Maurer
Institut für Informationsverarbeitung
Technische Universität Graz
Steyrergasse 17
8010 Graz/Austria

AMS Subject Classifications (1970): 68-XX
CR Subject Classifications (1974): 4.1, 4.2, 5.2, 5.3

ISBN 3-540-09510-1 Springer-Verlag Berlin Heidelberg New York
ISBN 0-387-09510-1 Springer-Verlag New York Heidelberg Berlin

Library of Congress Cataloging in Publication Data.
Colloquium on Automata, Languages and programming, 6th, Graz, 1979. Automata, languages and programming. (Lecture notes in computer science ; 71) Includes index.
1. Sequential machine theory--Congresses. 2. Formal languages--Congresses,
3. Programming languages (Electronic computers)--Congresses. I. Maurer, Hermann A., 1941- II. Title. III. Series.
QA267.5S4C63 1979 001.6'42 79-15859

Printing and binding: Beltz Offsetdruck, Hemsbach/Bergstr.
2145/3140-543210

PREFACE

The Sixth Colloquium on Automata, Languages and Programming (ICALP 79) was preceded by similar colloquia in Paris (1972), Saarbrücken (1974), Edinburgh (1976), Turku (1977) and Udine (1978), all sponsored by EATCS (European Association for Theoretical Computer Science).

Of a total of 139 papers submitted to ICALP 79, fifty papers were selected. Together with three invited presentations they are contained in this volume.

The program committee of ICALP 79 consisted of G.Ausiello, W.Brauer, K.Culik II, J. de Bakker, E.Engeler, S.Even, M.Harrison, I.M.Havel, J.Hopcroft, G.Hotz, W.Kuich, H.Maurer (chairman), M.Nivat, M.Paterson, Z.Pawlak, A.Salomaa, D.Wood, H.Zima.

As conference chairman, I would like to thank the members of the program committee for their hard work in evaluating the submitted papers. Special thanks are also due to the following referees who helped in the refereeing process: A.Aho, J.Albert, G. Andrews, K.R.Apt, J.Archer, E.A.Ashcroft, L.Banachowski, G.Baron, C.Batini, J.C.Beatty, J.Becvar, D.Bini, A.Blikle, C.Böhm, R.Book, S.Breidbart, A. de Bruin, J.Brzozowski, R.Cartwright, L.M.Chirica, R.S.Cohen, A.B.Cremers, P.Dembinski, K.Ecker, H.Ehrig, M. Furst, G.Gati, G.Goos, J.Gorski, M.Grabowski, D.Gries, J.Gruska, J.Grzymala-Busse, V. Haase, M.Hofri, M.Jazayeri, J.Karhumäki, O.Kariv, M.Karpinski, C.Keleman, B.Konilcowska, A.Krecmar, H.P.Kriegel, F.Krieger, M.Lao, R.Leipälä, M.Linna, F.Luk, G.Mahr, T.S.E. Maibaum, J.Maluszynski, A.Marchetti-Spaccamela, A.Mazurkiewicz, L.G.L.T.Meertens, R. Milner, A.Moura, T.Müldner, K.Müller, E.J.Neuhold, A.Obtulowicz, J.Opatrny, Th.Ottmann, D.M.R.Park, A.Paz, M.Penttonen, A.Pettorossi, F.Plášil, H.Prodinger, V.Rajlich, P.Raulefs, J.C.Reynolds, J.L.Richier, M.Rodeh, W.P.de Roever, F.Romani, D.Rotem, P. Ruzicka, A.Salwicki, G.Schlageter, F.Schneider, E.Shamir, J.Simon, M.Steinby, W.Stucky, S.Termini, J.W.Thatcher, F.J.Urbanek, V.K.Vaishnavi, P.van Emde Boas, J.van Leeuwen, J.Weglarz, L.Wegner, K.Weihrauch, J.Winkowski, C.K.Yap.

Finally, the support of the Austrian Federal Ministry for Science and Research, the Province of Styria, the City of Graz, the Research Center Graz, IBM Austria, Sperry Univac, the Institut f. Angewandte Informatik und Formale Beschreibungsverfahren - Universität Karlsruhe and the Technical University of Graz is gratefully acknowledged. Last not least, I want to thank the members of the organizing committee and my secretary Mrs. A.Kleinschuster for their help in organizing the conference, and Springer-Verlag for excellent cooperation concerning the publication of this volume.

Graz, April 1979

Hermann Maurer

CONTENTS

SHARING IN NONDETERMINISM

Egidio ASTESIANO - Gerardo COSTA

Istituto di Matematica dell'Università di Genova
Via L.B.Alberti, 4 - 16132 Genova - Italy

ABSTRACT. *We consider a language of typed λ-expressions with primitives including nondeterministic choice operators. Starting from the natural idea that a first order nondeterministic procedure should define a one-many function, we give a reduction system in which ground arguments are shared, in order to avoid some unnatural consequences due to unrestricted application of the copy-rule. This is achieved by extending the language and modifying the usual β-rule. Then we discuss how to define a corresponding denotational semantics, establishing in particular the existence of a model which is fully abstract w.r.t. the operational semantics.*

1. INTRODUCTION

Consider the usual language of first order deterministic recursive procedures, enriched with a binary choice operator <u>or</u> and extend the usual evaluation mechanism by letting t <u>or</u> t' evaluate to either t or t'. Then consider the following example /HA1/ where x ranges over the domain of non-negative integers $\mathbb{N}$:

$$\begin{cases} F(x) \Leftarrow \text{ if } x=0 \text{ then } 0 \text{ else } G(x \underline{\text{ or }} x-1) \\ G(x) \Leftarrow \text{ if } x=0 \text{ then } 0 \text{ else if } x=1 \text{ then } 1 \text{ else } 2 \end{cases}$$

Evaluation of F(1), <u>using an outermost strategy</u>, yields, as possible values, 0, 1 and 2. Hennessy and Ashcroft point out that in a functional model corresponding to this evaluation strategy F and G cannot denote functions f and g from $\mathbb{N}$ into $2^{\mathbb{N}}$. Indeed we would have: $f(1) = g(\{0,1\}) = g(0) \cup g(1) = \{0,1\}$, in contrast with the operational result. This motivates in /HA1,HA2/ the choice of a model in which the meanings for F and G are functions from $2^{\mathbb{N}} \setminus \{\emptyset\}$ into itself. From a mathematical point of view, however, it seems perfectly reasonable to take a different approach: the equation for G is deterministic and by itself defines a function from $\mathbb{N}$ into $\mathbb{N}$, it should then define the "same" (see below) function when considered together with the equation for F. In general, it is mathematically sound to say that <u>nondeterministic recursive procedures define one-many functions</u>. In this framework, deterministic procedures, like the one for G, define one-singleton functions and the result of applying a function f to a set A is given by $\cup \{f(a), a \in A\}$. This is the approach we shall take here (the same choice is made in /AN1,AN2/, though in a different setting).

Looking for an operational semantics corresponding to this (intuitive) model, we remark that the point in the above example is that G makes two copies of its argument, which then behave independently; hence we have to inhibit this possibility. There are essentially three solutions.

a) Innermost derivations (innermost w.r.t. choices as well as w.r.t. unknown function symbols.

b) Derivations in which choices have the precedence over replacement of unknown function symbols (this implies the problem of detecting "implicit choices", see below).

c) Outermost derivations together with sharing techniques.

In the example above, the three strategies yield the same result (e.g. F(1) evaluates to 0 or 1) but this is not true in general. For instance, consider the following system, where x and y range over $\mathbb{N}$:

$$\begin{cases} F(x,y) \Leftarrow G(x,K(y)) \\ G(x,y) \Leftarrow \text{if } x=0 \text{ then } 0 \text{ else } G(x-1,H(y)) \\ H(x) \Leftarrow H(x) \ \underline{\text{or}}\ H(x-1) \\ K(x) \Leftarrow 1 + K(x) \end{cases}$$

According to a) : F(m,n) obviously diverges, any m and n.

According to b) : F(0,n) evaluates to 0, any n, but F(m+1,n) evaluates to G(m,H(K(n))), which diverges, any m and n, because of H(K(n)); notice that we have to derive H(K(n)) first, because H implies a choice.

According to c) : F(m,n) evaluates to 0, any m and n.

Actually, there is a strict hierarchy: strategy a) is less powerful then strategy b) which is less powerful then strategy c); where "less powerful" means that the computed functions are less defined. Moreover it seems that there are some difficulties in defining precisely an operational semantics based on strategy b) and the corresponding functional model. This has been attempted in /HA2/ for this language of first order recursive procedures over flat domains (the evaluation mechanism is called "call-time choice"), but the results are rather unsatisfactory.

Strategy c) seems the one which better corresponds to our purpose of preventing duplication of arguments, without introducing unwanted non-terminations. Therefore it is the one we analyze here, using a nondeterministic language of typed λ-expressions, NDLS, derived from PCF (see /P2/ and also /HA1,AC2/).

It turns out that to be consistent with the mathematical model we have in mind, we have to consider sharing only w.r.t. arguments of ground type. Indeed, consider an higher type version of the relevant part of our first example.

$\Theta(X)(n) \Leftarrow$ if X(n)=0 then 0 else if X(n)=1 then 1 else 2 ;

where n and X range over $\mathbb{N}$ and $\mathbb{N} \dashrightarrow 2^{\mathbb{N}}$, respectively, and so we want Θ to denote a function θ in $(\mathbb{N} \dashrightarrow 2^{\mathbb{N}}) \dashrightarrow \mathbb{N} \dashrightarrow 2^{\mathbb{N}}$. Now, in a call like Θ(F or G)(1) , where F and G are the procedures $F(n) \Leftarrow n$, $G(n) \Leftarrow n-1$, we regard F or G as a procedure itself; hence it must denote a function, say h, from $\mathbb{N}$ into $2^{\mathbb{N}}$ and, quite naturally, h is defined by h(n) = {n,n+1} . So we get:

θ(h)(1) = if h(1)=0 then 0 else if h(1)=1 then 1 else 2 = {0,1,2} (by definition of natural extension to sets of one-one functions such as = and if-then-else).

It is clear that this result is obtained, operationally, with the usual evaluation mechanism (call-by-name with copy-rule), assuming that F or G may evaluate to either F or G.

Using sharing at higher level (apart from the technical problems, see /W/) would correspond to an intuitive setting quite different from the one we have outlined here. For example, it seems that the meaning of F or G should be a set of functions; this would pose several problems, like finding a suitable powerdomain structure. We think, however, that this point deserves further investigation.

The discussion above explains also why in our language NDLS we do not have or symbols of higher type (they are not needed as we can define them in terms of ground type or's) and why in our models we must consider domains of sets at ground level only.

Having defined the intuitive setting of our work, we are faced with two problems: the first one is that of finding a suitable description for the sharing of ground arguments (suitable w.r.t. both the operational and the denotational semantics); the second concerns the mathematical models.

In the language of the first two examples, sharing can be described very naturally by using graphs or labeled terms /V, PMT/; but also in a neater way (neater mathematically speaking) using derived algebras (see for instance /AC1/) or magmoids /A/. In λ-calculus the description is much more involved. The classical approach is that of Wadsworth /W/ using graphs. Another approach /L/ makes use of a precise notion of duplication of redexes and of simultaneous contraction of duplicated redexes; but an evaluation mechanism corresponding to this strategy has not yet been given.

The use of graphs has two drawbacks in our case. First of all, we want our operational semantics to be given by a formal reduction system and this seems rather difficult to obtain on graphs. Secondly, when both an operational and a denotational semantics are given it is useful (mainly in proving invariance of the semantics through evaluation) to associate a denotational meaning not only to programs and results, but also to each entity which represents an intermediate step in the evaluation process. Now if these intermediate steps are represented by graphs, one is faced with the problem of transferring the sharing relations into the denotational semantics.

The solution we propose is that of extending the language of λ-expressions by introducing terms of the form M {N/x} and modifying the β-rule by having (λxM)N reduce to M {N/x}, when x is of ground type. In other words we suspend the substitution of N in M and keep x bound to its actual value; the idea is similar to that of the association list of the LISP interpreter (but suitable renamings of bound variables prevent from the fluid variables phenomenon).

Modifying the β-rule requires that we give an explicit reduction algorithm. We do this by a reduction system which is monogenic (but for the choice rule) and which follows a kind of call-by-need strategy /W,V/. In this system the concept of critical variable is central: roughly speaking, a variable is critical in a term if we need to know the value of the actual argument associated to it to proceed in our evaluation (notice the obvious connection with the concept of sequentiality /V,B/; at this point we rely on the kind of interpretations we consider).

As for the functional semantics of the terms M {N/x} , it is given following the usual style of the denotational semantics (this does not came to light here, since proofs have been omitted; see however section 7).

The second problem concerns the models for our language. It is rather easy to give a model, $\mathcal{S}$, for NDLS by modifying the usual Scott-Milner continuous functions model. However what one finds is a model which is "too large" and therefore not intrinsicly fully abstract (i.f.a. for short) in the sense of /M2/. We show in /AC3/ that the technique used by Milner in /M2/ can be adapted to obtain an i.f.a. model for typed λ-calculi with sharing at ground level. Here we simply state the main result and apply it to show the (constructive) existence of an i.f.a. model, $\overline{\mathcal{M}}$, for NDLS. Finally, following a pattern already outlined in /AC2/, we discuss the relationships between the operational semantics defined by the reduction system and the denotational semantics associated to the models $\mathcal{S}$ and $\overline{\mathcal{M}}$. In particular, the semantics defined by $\overline{\mathcal{M}}$ is shown to be equivalent to the operational one (i.e. $\overline{\mathcal{M}}$ is fully abstract w.r.t. the operational semantics, according to the well known definition in /M1/).

2. THE LANGUAGE NDLS

We consider two ground types, o and ι ; then T, σ and τ , κ will denote, respectively: the set of functional types generated from o and ι, arbitrary types, a general ground type. We shall call first order type any type of the form $\kappa_1 \to \kappa_2 \to \dots \kappa_n \to \kappa$ for $n \geq 1$.

The set of terms of the language NDLS is the set generated, by using typed λ-abstraction and application, from :

1) a set of ground constant symbols (typical element c) namely: tt, ff, of type o : 0, 1, ..., n,.... of type ι ;
2) a set of first order constant symbols, namely: Z , of type $\iota \to o$; (+1) and (-1) , of type $\iota \to \iota$; IF_κ , of type $o \to \kappa \to \kappa \to \kappa$;
3) the special combinators or_κ , of type $\kappa \to \kappa \to \kappa$;
4) the sets $VAR = \{ X_i^\sigma , \sigma \in T , i \geq 1 \}$ and $FIX = \{ Y_\sigma , \sigma \in T \}$, where X_i^σ and Y_σ have type σ and $(\sigma \to \sigma) \to \sigma$ respectively.

We adopt the usual conventions for suppressing redundant parenthesis in writing terms and we shall often omit subscripts in primitive symbols and variables. We use letters M and N to denote arbitrary terms, adding sometimes subscripts to indicate their type. Closed terms of ground type will be called programs.

We shall need later on Ω_σ and $Y_\sigma^{(n)}$, defined as follows: $\Omega_\kappa = Y_\kappa(\lambda X_1^\kappa X_1^\kappa)$, $\Omega_{\sigma\to\tau} = \lambda X_1^\sigma \Omega_\tau$, $Y_\sigma^{(0)} = \Omega_{(\sigma\to\sigma)\to\sigma}$ and $Y_\sigma^{(n+1)} = \lambda X(X(Y_\sigma^{(n)} X))$, where X stands for $X_1^{\sigma\to\sigma}$.

Finally, $M^{(n)}$, $n \geq 0$, will denote the term obtained from M by replacing all occurrences of Y_σ by $Y_\sigma^{(n)}$, for all σ, and we shall call finite any term which contains Y only in the combination for Ω_κ (e.g. $M^{(n)}$ is finite).

3. OPERATIONAL SEMANTICS

We now define the language ENDLS, extension of NDLS, in which we are able to express sharing of ground arguments. We shall define our reduction system w.r.t. this extended language, but we are only interested in giving an operational semantics for programs in NDLS.

Let ENDLS be the language defined by all the rules for NDLS plus the following one: if M_σ and N_κ are terms, then $(M_\sigma \{N_\kappa / X_i^\kappa\})$ is a term of type σ, any σ, κ, i. For example $(((((\text{IF}_\iota\ X_1^o)\ X_1^\iota\ )\ \{((+1)\underline{2})\ /\ X_1^\iota\}\ )\ X_2^\iota\ )\ \{\underline{tt}\ /\ X_1^o\ \}\ )$ is a term of type ι in ENDLS. We shall extend to terms in ENDLS the conventions on round brackets and subscripts, so the term above would usually be written as
$\text{IF}_\iota\ X\ X_1\ \{\ (+1)\underline{2}\ /\ X_1\}\ X_2\ \{\underline{tt}\ /\ X\ \}$.

For terms in ENDLS the definition of free variable is obtained by adding to the usual definition the following clause: $\text{Free}(M\{N/X\}) = (\text{Free}(M) - X) \cup \text{Free}(N)$, where Free(M) is the set of variables having a free occurrence in M. Hence, if M[N/X] denotes the result of substituting N for all free occurrences of X in M (with suitable renamings) then, for example, $(X^o\{X^o/X^o\})\ [\underline{tt}/X^o] = X^o\{\underline{tt}/X^o\}$. The definition of open (closed) term is the usual one (but w.r.t. the new definition of free variable).

We now define a reduction algorithm for terms in ENDLS by means of a (partial) relation $\dashrightarrow$ between terms, which is given by the rules below.

1) $\underline{or}\ M\ N \dashrightarrow M$; $\underline{or}\ M\ N \dashrightarrow N$;
2) $(+1)\underline{n} \dashrightarrow \underline{n+1}$; $(-1)\underline{n+1} \dashrightarrow \underline{n}$; $(-1)\underline{0} \dashrightarrow \underline{0}$;
3) $Z\ \underline{0} \dashrightarrow \underline{tt}$; $Z\ \underline{n+1} \dashrightarrow \underline{ff}$;
4) $\text{IF}\ \underline{tt}\ M\ N \dashrightarrow M$; $\text{IF}\ \underline{ff}\ M\ N \dashrightarrow N$;
5) $Y\ M \dashrightarrow M(YM)$;
6a) $(\lambda X^\sigma\ M)N \dashrightarrow M\ [N\ /\ X^\sigma]$, for non ground σ ;
6b) $(\lambda X^\kappa\ M)N \dashrightarrow M\ \{N\ /\ X^\kappa\}$, where we perform in M all the renamings of bound variables which would be required by the application of the usual β-rule;
7a) $\dfrac{M \dashrightarrow M'}{MN \dashrightarrow M'N}$; 7b) $\dfrac{N \dashrightarrow N' ,\ f \in \{(+1), (-1), Z, \text{IF}\}}{fN \dashrightarrow fN'}$;
8) $\dfrac{M \dashrightarrow M'}{M\ \{N/X\} \dashrightarrow M'\{N/X\}}$;
9) $\gamma\ \{N/X\} \dashrightarrow \gamma$, where γ is a primitive symbol (i.e. $\underline{c}$, (+1), Y, $\underline{or}$,...);
10) $(\underline{or}\ M)\ \{N/X\} \dashrightarrow \underline{or}\ (M\ \{N/X\})$;
11a) $(\text{IF}\ \underline{b})\ \{N/X\} \dashrightarrow \text{IF}\ \underline{b}$
11b) $(\text{IF}\ \underline{b}\ M)\ \{N/X\} \dashrightarrow (\text{IF}\ \underline{b})(M\ \{N/X\})$, for $\underline{b} = \underline{tt}, \underline{ff}$;

12) $(\lambda X_i^\sigma M)\{N/X_j^\kappa\} \dashrightarrow \lambda\tilde{X}_i^\sigma(\tilde{M}\{N/X_j^\kappa\})$, where ~ indicates renamings, to be performed if $\sigma = \kappa$ and $i = j$, or if X_i^σ is free in N;

13a) $\dfrac{X \in CR(M)}{M\{\underline{c}/X\} \dashrightarrow M[\underline{c}/X]}$; 13b) $\dfrac{X \in CR(M)\ ,\ N \dashrightarrow N'}{M\{N/X\} \dashrightarrow M\{N'/X\}}$;

where CR(M) is defined as follows (in a PASCAL-like language):

```
CR(M) := case M            of
             X_i^κ           : {X_i^κ} ;
             M1M2            : case M1  of
                                   (+1),(-1),Z,IF  : CR(M2) ;
                                   "else"          : CR(M1) ;
                               end
             M1{M2/X}        : if X ∈ CR(M1) then CR(M2) else CR(M1);
             "else"          : ∅
         end
```

Notice that CR(M) is a subset of Free(M) and it is either a singleton or the empty set; we call it the <u>critical set of M</u> and if $CR(M) = \{X_i^\kappa\}$, then we say that <u>X_i^κ is critical in M</u>.

<u>LEMMA 2.1</u> For any term M in ENDLS, if M' in ENDLS exists s.t. $M \dashrightarrow M'$, then $CR(M)=\emptyset$. We omit the proof, which can be easily done by induction on the structure of terms. Remark that the reverse of the implication is false (just consider $M = X^{\iota\to\iota}$). □

The three examples below should illustrate the non standard features of our rewriting system; the last one embeds the translation of the first example in section 1 and emphasizes the differences between rules 6a) and 6b) in relation to <u>or</u> (we thank one of the referees for suggesting it). Here we symplify our notation by using x,y,w as names for variables and, in the third example, by using infix form for ($\underline{+}$)1, <u>or</u> and IF. Side comments should help understanding why Theorem 2.2 below is true, i.e. no freedom is permitted except when using rule 1.

<u>EX.1</u> ((λx (λx x)) M) (<u>or</u> <u>1</u> <u>2</u>) --→ (both x's are ground here)
((λy y) {M/x}) (<u>or</u> <u>1</u> <u>2</u>) --→ (by rule 12, if y is not free in M)
(λy (y {M/x}) (<u>or</u> <u>1</u> <u>2</u>) --→
(y {M/x}) {<u>or</u> <u>1</u> <u>2</u> /y} --→ (CR(y{M/x}) = CR(y) = {y})
y{M/x}{<u>n</u>/y} --→ <u>n</u>{M/x} --→ <u>n</u> (<u>n</u> is either <u>1</u> or <u>2</u>).

<u>EX.2</u> (λx (((λx (IF_o x))x) <u>tt</u> x)) (<u>or</u> <u>tt</u> <u>ff</u>) --→
(((λx (IF_o x)) x) <u>tt</u> x) {<u>or</u> <u>tt</u> <u>ff</u> /x} --→
((IF_o x){x/x} <u>tt</u> x) {<u>or</u> <u>tt</u> <u>ff</u> /x} --→ (CR(IF_o x{x/x}<u>tt</u> x)=CR(IF_o x{x/x})= {x} ; note it is the x above /)
((IF_o x) {x/x} <u>tt</u> x) {<u>b</u>/x} --→ (<u>b</u> is either <u>tt</u> or <u>ff</u>)
((IF_o x) {<u>b</u>/x} <u>tt</u> <u>b</u>) --→
IF_o <u>b</u> <u>tt</u> <u>b</u> --→ <u>b</u> .

EX.3 Let: $M = \lambda x N$; $Q = \lambda w(M(w \text{ or } w-1))$;

N = if Zx then $\underline{0}$ else if $Z(x-1)$ then $\underline{1}$ else $\underline{2}$. Then:

(λy (λx(if Zx then y(x+1) else yx))) Q $\underline{1}$ ---> (by rule 6a)

(λx (if Zx then Q(x+1) else Qx)) $\underline{1}$ ---> (by rule 6b; notice that Q contains or)

(if Zx then Q(x+1) else Qx) {$\underline{1}$ / x} ---> (CR(if...) = {x})

if Z$\underline{1}$ then Q($\underline{1}$+1) else Q$\underline{1}$ --->

(λw (M(w or w-1))) $\underline{1}$ --->

M(w or w-1) {$\underline{1}$/w} --->

N {w or w-1 /x} {$\underline{1}$/w} ---> (by rule 8; notice that CR(N{w or w-1/x}) = ∅)

either into (a) or into (b) below:

(a) N {w/x}{$\underline{1}$/w} ---> N {$\underline{1}$/x} --->

if Z$\underline{1}$ then $\underline{0}$ else if Z($\underline{1}$-1) then $\underline{1}$ else $\underline{2}$ ---> .... ---> $\underline{1}$

(b) N {w-1/x}{$\underline{1}$/w} ---> N {$\underline{1}$-1/x} ---> .... ---> $\underline{0}$.

The following proposition takes the place of a Church-Rosser and normal reduction result, stating that our reduction system is monogenic (but for the choice rule).

THEOREM 2.2 For every closed term of ground type (ctg for short) M in ENDLS, one and only one of the following conditions hold:

i) M is a constant;

ii) a unique ctg M' exists such that M ---> M' without using rule 1 ;

iii) two ctg's M' and M'', uniquely determined, exist such that M ---> M' and M ---> M'' , using rule 1 .

Proof. See Appendix. □

If we denote by $\xrightarrow{*}$ the reflexive and transitive closure of ---> , the proposition above allows us to define the set of all (possible) results of a program P in our original language NDLS, Eval(P), using the special symbol ∞ as an abbreviation, by:

- $\underline{c}$ ∈ Eval(P) iff P $\xrightarrow{*}$ $\underline{c}$;
- ∞ ∈ Eval(P) iff there is an infinite sequence, $P = P_0, P_1, \ldots, P_n, \ldots$ such that $P_i \longrightarrow P_{i+1}$ (we say then that P may diverge or simply diverges).

Notice that this last clause makes sense because we consider individual data and results which belongs to flat domains; for a more general approach, in a different setting, see /AN1,AN2/.

4. INTERPRETATIONS

We assume that the reader is familiar with the notions of: (flat) cpo, finite (= isolated) element, (ω-) algebraic cpo, consistently complete cpo, monotonic and continuous function (see for ex. /P2,B/).

Given a flat cpo D, the (Egli-Milner) ordering between nonempty subsets of D is given by:

$A \sqsubseteq B$ iff ($\forall a \in A, \exists b \in B$ s.t. $a \sqsubseteq b$) and ($\forall b \in B, \exists a \in A$ s.t. $a \sqsubseteq b$)
iff either $A = B$ or ($A \ni \bot$ and $A \setminus \{\bot\} \subset B$).

Then the powerdomain of D, $\mathbb{P}(D)$, is defined as the set $\{ A \mid \emptyset \neq A \subset D , |A| = \infty \Longrightarrow A \ni \bot \}$, together with the above order (see /P1,Sm/).

It is well known that for any denumerable flat cpo D, $\mathbb{P}(D)$ is an ω-algebraic, consistently complete cpo, whose finite elements are the finite nonempty sets, and that the binary union function on $\mathbb{P}(D)$ is continuous.

Following Milner, we consider a first order interpretation (see /M2/ for motivations); moreover, because of sharing, it turns out to be handier that the interpretation be deterministic.

Hence the (standard) interpretation for NDLS, $\mathfrak{J}$, is given by:

- basic domains: $B_o = \mathbb{T}$; $B_\iota = \mathbb{N}$, where $\mathbb{T}$ and $\mathbb{N}$ are the flat cpo's of truth values and nonnegative integers, respectively;
- ground constants: $\mathfrak{J}(\underline{c}) = c$, for each ground constant symbol $\underline{c}$;
- first order functions: $\mathfrak{J}((+1))$, $\mathfrak{J}((-1))$, $\mathfrak{J}(Z)$ and $\mathfrak{J}(IF_\kappa)$ which are, respectively, the usual successor, predecessor, test-for-zero functions on $\mathbb{N}$ and the usual sequential conditional function on B_κ (but $\mathfrak{J}((-1))(0) = 0$).

We have not interpreted Y's and or's; their meaning will be given in the model(s).

5. FUNCTIONAL MODEL

We shall present here a functional model for NDLS and $\mathfrak{J}$, that we call $\mathfrak{S}$, derived from the usual Scott-Milner model for typed λ-calculus and which corresponds to the ideas about the semantics of nondeterministic procedures we have previously discussed. In a similar fashion one could modify the model given in /HA1/. In the following section we shall axiomatize what we mean by a model for a calculus with sharing (s-model). To make the reference more transparent, the definition of $\mathfrak{S}$ follows the general pattern. The model $\mathfrak{S}$ is given by i), ii) and iii) below.

i) Domains. In the light of our previous discussion we see that, when defining functional spaces we have to distinguish, at first order level, between the source (a basic domain) and the target (a powerdomain). This leads to the following definition (recalling that $B_o = \mathbb{T}$ and $B_\iota = \mathbb{N}$).

Let: $D_\kappa = \mathbb{P}(B_\kappa)$; $D_{\sigma\to\tau} = B_{\sigma\to\tau} = [B_\sigma \longrightarrow D_\tau]$, i.e. the cpo of all continuous functions from B_σ into D_τ;

then the domains for $\mathfrak{S}$ are the D_σ (notice they are ω-algebraic consistently complete cpo's).

ii) Application maps. For all types σ and τ we have the continuous map

$-.-: D_{\sigma\to\tau} \times D_\sigma \longrightarrow D_\tau$, defined below.

Let $-(-): D_{\sigma\to\tau} \times B_\sigma \longrightarrow D_\tau$ be the usual functional application; then $-.-$ is precisely $-(-)$ when σ is not ground, while for $\sigma = \kappa$ is such that, if g is in $D_{\kappa\to\tau}$,

$\tau = \sigma_1 \to \sigma_2 \to \ldots \to \sigma_n \to \kappa'$, then:

$$(\dagger) \begin{cases} g.\{c\} = g(c) \text{ , for any } c \text{ in } B_\kappa \text{ ;} \\ g.(d \cup_\kappa d').d_1.d_2.\ldots.d_n = g.d.d_1.d_2.\ldots.d_n \cup_{\kappa'} g.d'.d_1.d_2.\ldots.d_n \text{ , for any } \underline{\text{finite}} \\ \qquad d,d' \text{ in } D_\kappa \text{, any } d_i \text{ in } D_{\sigma_i} . \end{cases}$$

Notice that (†) amounts to require that $g.(d \cup_\kappa d') = g.d \cup_\tau g.d'$, where the continuous binary function $\cup_\sigma : D_\sigma \times D_\sigma \dashrightarrow D_\sigma$ is defined by:

$\cup_\kappa$ is the usual set-union function;

$\cup_{\sigma\to\tau}$ is such that $(h \cup_{\sigma\to\tau} h')(a) = h(a) \cup_\tau h'(a)$, any h,h' in $D_{\sigma\to\tau}$ and a in B_σ.

Moreover, (†) completely specifies -.- because the D_κ are algebraic (and we have imposed that -.- be continuous).

iii) Meanings. Let Env be the cpo of type preserving maps from VAR into $\bigcup\{D_\sigma, \sigma \in T\}$. Then to each term M in NDLS we associate the continuous function $[\![M_\sigma]\!] : Env \dashrightarrow D_\sigma$, such that, for each ρ in Env:

$[\![X_i^\sigma]\!](\rho) = \rho(X_i^\sigma)$;

$[\![\underline{c}]\!](\rho) = \{\mathfrak{I}(\underline{c})\} = \{c\}$;

$[\![f]\!](\rho)$ = the one-singleton function associated to $\mathfrak{I}(f)$; any first order constant symbol f (e.g. $[\![(+1)]\!](\rho) = \lambda n\,\{n+1\}$);

$[\![\underline{or}_\kappa]\!](\rho)$ = the function $\lambda c\, \lambda c'\, \{c\} \cup \{c'\}$;

$[\![Y_\sigma]\!](\rho) = \bigsqcup\{[\![Y_\sigma^{(n)}]\!](\rho) , n \geqslant 0\}$ setting: $[\![\Omega_\kappa]\!](\rho) = \bot_\kappa$;

$[\![MN]\!](\rho) = [\![M]\!](\rho) . [\![N]\!](\rho)$;

$[\![\lambda X_i^\sigma M]\!](\rho).d = [\![M]\!](\rho[d/X_i^\sigma])$, any d in D_σ and $\sigma \neq \kappa$, where $\rho[d/X_i^\sigma](y) =$ if $y = X_i^\sigma$ then d else $\rho(y)$;

$[\![\lambda X_i^\kappa M]\!](\rho).\{c\} = [\![M]\!](\rho[\{c\}/X_i^\kappa])$, any c in B_κ .

Remarks. a) Because of the properties of -.- the last clause completely specifies $[\![\lambda X_i^\kappa M]\!]$ (in terms of $[\![M]\!]$).

b) Due to the asymmetry in $D_{\kappa\to\kappa}$, $[\![Y_\kappa]\!](\rho)$ is not directly a fixpoint operator. However, $[\![Y_\kappa]\!](\rho).g$ can be interpreted as $fix_\kappa(\hat{g})$, where fix_κ is the least fixed point operator on $[D_\kappa \dashrightarrow D_\kappa]$ and $\hat{g}$ is the natural extension to subsets of g (i.e. $\hat{g}(A) = \bigcup\{g(a) , a \in A\}$).

We have thus defined our functional model $\mathfrak{S}$.

As a last remark about this definition, we point out that we could have exploited the nature of $\mathfrak{S}$ and define $-.- : D_{\kappa\to\tau} \times D_\kappa \dashrightarrow D_\tau$ by (††) below.

(††) for each g in $D_{\kappa\to\tau}$ and d in D_κ : $g.d = \bigcup_\tau\{g(c) , c \in d\}$;

where $\bigcup_\tau$ is defined inductively on types starting from $\bigcup_\kappa$ which is denumerable union ("big union" to be more precise, see /Pl,Sm/).

It is not hard to show that (††) gives a good definition, i.e. the right hand side belongs to D_τ .

We now proceed in discussing models in a more general way; for the relation between the semantics derived from $\mathfrak{S}$ and the operational semantics defined by Eval, see section 7.

6. FULLY ABSTRACT MODEL

The functional model of the previous section gives an insight of what a model for a calculus with sharing should be. We collect now the fundamental properties in a formal definition.

Consider a set of ground types (typical element κ) and the associated set of functional types (typical elements σ and τ) and let Λ be the language of typed λ-expressions built from: ground constant symbols from C, first order function symbols from F, typed variables, Y_σ and $\underrightarrow{or}_\kappa$ combinators.
Moreover, let $\mathcal{A}$ be a first order deterministic interpretation which associates : a flat cpo B_κ to each κ , an element in B_κ to each $\underline{c}$ in C and a function f (of the appropriate type) on the B_κ to each $\underline{f}$ in F. We shall consider denumerable B_κ's only.

Then an (ω-algebraic, order-extensional) s-model $\mathcal{M}$ for Λ and $\mathcal{A}$ is given by i), ii) and iii) below (see also /M2,B/ for the "standard" case).

i) Domains. For each σ, an ω-algebraic cpo D_σ , where D_κ is (isomorphic to) $\mathbb{P}(B_\kappa)$.

ii) Application maps. For each σ and τ , a continuous map

$-.- : D_{\sigma\to\tau} \times D_\sigma \longrightarrow D_\tau$ such that:

- if d is in D_σ , then $\bot_{\sigma\to\tau} . d = \bot_\tau$;
- (for every d in D_σ , $g.d \sqsubseteq g'.d$) $\Longrightarrow$ $g \sqsubseteq g'$, any g,g' in $D_{\sigma\to\tau}$;
- if $\sigma = \kappa$, then, if $\tau = \sigma_1 \to \sigma_2 \ldots \to \sigma_n \to \kappa'$ and g is in $D_{\kappa\to\tau}$:

$$(\dagger)\begin{cases} g.(d \cup_\kappa d').d_1.d_2.\ldots.d_n = g.d.d_1.d_2.\ldots.d_n \cup_{\kappa'} g.d'.d_1.d_2.\ldots.d_n , \\ \text{for any } \underline{\text{finite}}\ d, d' \text{ in } D_\kappa \text{ , any } d_i \text{ in } D_{\sigma_i} . \end{cases}$$

iii) Meanings: as iii) of section 5, replacing: Λ for NDLS, $\mathcal{A}$ for $\mathfrak{I}$ and "it is possible to associate a" for "we associate the" .

The model preorder on Λ associated to $\mathcal{M}$, $\sqsubseteq_\mathcal{M}$, is given by: $M \sqsubseteq_\mathcal{M} N$ iff $[\![M]\!] \sqsubseteq [\![N]\!]$. $\mathcal{M}$ is intrinsicly fully abstract (i.f.a.) /M2/ whenever, for any M and N:

(††) $M \sqsubseteq_\mathcal{M} N$ iff $C[M] \sqsubseteq_\mathcal{M} C[N]$ for every context C[ ] such that both C[M] and C[N] are programs (a context is simply a term with one or more holes).

For instance, the functional model outlined in the last section is an s-model for NDLS and $\mathfrak{I}$ (a natural one), but it is not i.f.a.. Indeed, while the only if part of (††) holds (actually, this can easily be proved for any s-model), the if part does not. This happens because there are (finite) elements in the domains of $\mathcal{S}$ which are not definable in NDLS (see /P2,AC2/ for proofs in similar situations).
To get full abstraction, one should attempt to restrict the functional spaces; however this has proved to be a very hard (and, to our knowledge, yet unsolved) problem, even in the deterministic case, see /B/. The best we can do for the present is to show that we can adapt the powerful techniques used by Milner in /M2/. The s-model that we shall obtain is i.f.a. but its domains are characterized in a syntactic way, rather than defined as sets of functions satisfying suitable conditions. The main steps of the construction follow closely Milner's paper, but the proofs are much more involved as a

consequence of sharing, which forces us to consider more complex reduction rules and to take care of the distinction between basic domains of individual elements and the induced powerdomains. Here we only state the result, referring to /AC3/ for the proof and to /M2/ for the general philosophy of this technique.

Recall that a finite projection on a cpo D is a continuous function $\psi : D \dashrightarrow D$ such that: $\psi \circ \psi = \psi$, $\psi \sqsubseteq id_D$ and $\psi(D)$ is a finite set. Consider now B_κ; as it is flat and denumerable, it is well known that there exists a sequence $\{\psi_i^\kappa\}$ of finite projection on $\mathbb{P}(B_\kappa)$ whose lub is the identity on $\mathbb{P}(B_\kappa)$ (i.e. $\mathbb{P}(B_\kappa)$ is an SFP object, see /P1,B/).

THEOREM 6.1 /AC3/ There exists an (ω-algebraic, order-extensional) s-model for Λ and $\mathcal{A}$ in which all finite elements are λ-definable in terms of $\{f\}$, $\{\psi_i^\kappa\}$, $\{\cup_\kappa\}$ and the finite elements of the B_κ. Moreover the s-model is intrinsicly fully abstract, provided the ψ_i^κ are λ-definable (in terms of $\{f\}$,$\{\cup_\kappa\}$ and the elements of the B_κ). □

Going back to NDLS and $\mathfrak{J}$, we remark that it is easy to define projections for the interpretation $\mathfrak{J}$. So,as an application of Theorem 6.1, we get

THEOREM 6.2 There exists an intrinsicly fully abstract s-model, $\overline{\mathcal{M}}$, for NDLS and $\mathfrak{J}$. □

At this point it could be interesting to compare the situation here with the one found in /AC2/ for a similar language and w.r.t. a call-by-name rule. But we have no room for that here and in particular we avoid any discussion on the uniqueness of the fully abstract s-model; the interested reader is referred to /M2/ (of course) for general results and to /AC2/ for application of these results to non deterministic languages, in a call-by-name regime.

7. THE RELATION BETWEEN OPERATIONAL AND DENOTATIONAL SEMANTICS

We want to relate here the operational semantics of NDLS given by Eval to the (denotational) semantics deduced from the models $\mathcal{S}$ and $\overline{\mathcal{M}}$. This can be achieved following a very general pattern of proof, already outlined in /AC2/ : establish the equivalence of the two semantics on finite programs, then extend it to all programs and finally obtain (full/partial) equivalence on general terms. In this process, the last two steps rely just on general properties of the reduction relation $\dashrightarrow$ and of the models.

Recall that finite terms, Ω_κ , $Y^{(n)}$, $M^{(n)}$ have been defined at the end of section 2 and notice that here Ω_κ is treated just as a symbol of ground constant (and a syntactic equivalent for $\bot_\kappa$).

Let $\xrightarrow[F]{}$ be the relation obtained from $\dashrightarrow$ by suppressing rule 5 (about Y) and adding some obvious Ω-rules relative to Ω_κ , such as $(+1)\Omega_\iota \xrightarrow[F]{} \Omega_\iota$.

Then if P is a finite program, $Eval^F(P)$ is defined as follows:

$Eval^F(P) \ni \underline{c}$ iff $P \xrightarrow[F]{*} \underline{c}$; $Eval^F(P) \ni \Omega_\kappa$ iff $P \xrightarrow[F]{*} \Omega_\kappa$.

PROPOSITION 7.1 For any finite program P, the following holds w.r.t. both $\mathcal{S}$ and $\overline{\mathcal{M}}$:
$\underline{c} \in [\![P]\!](\rho)$ iff $\underline{c} \in Eval^F(P)$; $\perp \in [\![P]\!](\rho)$ iff $\Omega_\kappa \in Eval^F(P)$, any ρ in Env.
The proof is omitted; its strategy however deserves some comments. In the case of $\mathcal{S}$, we carry out our proof (though rather painfully in some parts) by extending the model to ENDLS. This is done by setting (see section 5 for $\bigcup_\sigma$):
$[\![M_\sigma \{N/X_i^\kappa\}]\!](\rho) = \bigcup_\sigma \{ [\![M_\sigma]\!](\rho[\{c\} / X_i^\kappa]) \mid c \in [\![N]\!] (\rho) \}$.
The same strategy could be applied in the case of $\overline{\mathcal{M}}$. But (and we think this is easier) we have preferred to exploit an essential feature of Milner's technique: the meaning of finite programs is given through reduction rules which can parallel the ones defining $\xrightarrow[F]{}$, but for the lack of simplifications and rules about critical variables (which are not needed when considering finite programs). □

To extend the above result to arbitrary programs, we need two lemmas. In what follows, let P be any program.
LEMMA 7.2 In any s-model, for any ρ : $[\![P]\!](\rho) = \bigsqcup\{[\![P^{(n)}]\!](\rho) \quad , \quad n\geq 0 \}$.
Proof. This fact follows from the property: $[\![Y]\!](\rho) = \bigsqcup \{[\![Y^{(n)}]\!](\rho) \quad , \quad n\geq 0\}$.
LEMMA 7.3 $P \xrightarrow{*} \underline{c}$ iff ($\exists\, n_0$ s.t. $P^{(n)} \xrightarrow[F]{*} \underline{c}$, $\forall\, n \geq n_0$) ;
P diverges iff $P^{(n)} \xrightarrow[F]{*} \Omega_\kappa$, $\forall\, n\geq 0$.
The proof of this lemma is rather long and we omit it; it uses a syntactical pre-order on terms /P2/, a notion of computation tree for P and $P^{(n)}$ and König's lemma. □
THEOREM 7.4 For both $\mathcal{S}$ and $\overline{\mathcal{M}}$, for any ρ :
$[\![P]\!](\rho) \ni c$ iff $Eval(P) \ni \underline{c}$; $[\![P]\!](\rho) \ni \perp$ iff $Eval(P) \ni \infty$.
Proof. This follows easily from Proposition 7.1, Lemma 7.2 (and the definition of the order between subsets) and Lemma 7.3. □

Let us now consider general terms.
The operational preorder, $\lessapprox_{op}$, is defined as follows:

- if P and Q are programs, $P \sqsubseteq_{op} Q$ iff $\begin{cases} \text{either } Eval(P) = Eval(Q) \\ \text{or } Eval(P) \ni \infty \text{ and } Eval(P)\setminus\{\infty\} \subset Eval(Q) \end{cases}$
- if M and N are terms, $M \lessapprox_{op} M$ iff $C[M] \sqsubseteq_{op} C[N]$, for all contexts C[ ] s.t. both C[M] and C[N] are programs.

THEOREM 7.5 a) $\lessapprox_{op}$ strictly contains $\sqsubseteq_{\mathcal{S}}$; b) $\lessapprox_{op}$ and $\sqsubseteq_{\overline{\mathcal{M}}}$ coincide.
Proof. Consider (1) and (2) below.
(1) $C[M] \sqsubseteq_{\mathcal{M}} C[N]$ for all contexts C[ ] s.t. both C[M] and C[N] are programs.
(2) $C[M] \sqsubseteq_{op} C[N]$ for all contexts C[ ] s.t. both C[M] and C[N] are programs.
Then, if $\mathcal{M}$ is either $\mathcal{S}$ or $\overline{\mathcal{M}}$ (1) and (2) are equivalent because of Theorem 7.4 and the definitions of $\sqsubseteq_{op}$ and order in powerdomains. Now: for any s-model $\mathcal{M}$, $(M \sqsubseteq_{\mathcal{M}} N)$ $\Longrightarrow$ (1), because of the homomorphic definition of $[\![\ ]\!]$; if $\mathcal{M}$ is i.f.a. , then $(M \sqsubseteq_{\mathcal{M}} N) \Longleftrightarrow$ (1). We have thus proved b) and half of a). Strictness in a) can be proved by utilizing the fact that $\mathcal{S}$ is not i.f.a. (see /P2/ for a similar proof). □

ACKNOWLEDGEMENT The autors would like to thank one of the referees for his valuable remarks and suggestions.

REFERENCES

A A.Arnold, Schémas de programmes récursifs non déterministes avec appel syncrone, Proc. 3e Colloque International sur la Programmation, Paris 1978, Dunod, 126-140.

AC1 E.Astesiano, G.Costa, On algebraic semantics of polyadic recursive schemas, Proc. 2e Colloque sur les Arbres an Algèbre et en Programmation, Lille 1977, Université de Lille, 29-83.

AC2 = = = Nondeterminism and fully abstract models, 1978, submitted for publication.

AC3 = = = Fully abstract semantics for nondeterministic typed λ-s-calculi, 1989, to appear.

AN1 A.Arnold, M.Nivat,Non deterministic recursive program schemas, Proc. FCT 1977, Lecture Notes in C.S. 56, Springer, 12-21.

AN2 = = = Interpretations métriques des schémas de programme, Proc. 1er Colloque AFCET-SMF de Math. Appliquées, Ecole Polytechnique, 1978, Vol.1, 191-208.

B G.Berry, Stable models of typed λ-calculi, Proc. 5th ICALP, Udine 1978, Lecture Notes in C.S. 62, Springer, 72-89.

HA1 M.Hennessy, E.A.Ashcroft, The semantics of nondeterminism, Proc. 3rd ICALP, Edinburg 1976, Edinburg University Press, 478-493.

HA2 = = = Parameter-passing mechanism and nondeterminism, Proc. 9th ACM Symp. on the Theory of Comput. , 1977, 306-311.

L J.J.Lévy, Le problème du partage dans l'évaluation des λ-expressions, Proc. 1er Colloque AFCET-SMF de Math. Appliquées, Ecole Polytechnique, 1978.

M1 R.Milner, Processes, a mathematical model for computing agents, Logic Coll. 1973, Studies in Logic and the Foundations of Mathematics 80 , North-Holland & American Elsevier, 1975, 157-174.

M2 = = = Fully abstract models of typed λ-calculi, T.C.S. 4 (1977) 1-22.

P1 G.Plotkin, A powerdomain construction, Siam J. Comput. 5 (1976) 452-487.

P2 = = = LCF as a programming language, T.C.S. 5 (1977) 223-255.

PMT G.Pacini, C.Montangero, F.Turini, Graph representation and computation rules for a typeless recursive language, Proc. 2nd ICALP, Saarbrücken, 1974, Lecture Notes in C.S. 14 , Springer, 157-169.

Sm M.B.Smyth, Power domains, JCSS 16 (1978) 23-36.

V J.Vuillemin, Correct and optimal implementation of recursion in a simple programming language, JCSS 9 (1974) 332-354.

W C.P.Wadsworth, Semantics and pragmatics of the λ-calculus, Ph.D. Thesis, University of Oxford, 1971.

APPENDIX

Proof of Theorem 2.2

We use the predicate Red over ENDLS defined as follows (cgt = closed ground term):

- a cgt is Red iff the thesis holds for it;
- a term M which is not a cgt, is Red iff all its Red-closures are Red, where

a Red-closure of M is any cgt $\tilde{M}$ (in NDLS) of the form $M'\xi_1\ldots\xi_m$, $m \geq 1$, where:

- $M' = M[N_1/u_1]\ldots[N_n/u_n]$, $n \geq 0$; if $n = 0$ then $M' = M$;
- ξ_i is a string either of the form $N_{i1}\ldots N_{in_i}$ or of the form $\{N'_{i1}/v_{i1}\}\ldots\{N'_{in_i}/v_{in_i}\}$, $n_i \geq 0$; if $n_i = 0$ then ξ_i is the empty string;
- the u's are non-ground variables and the v's are ground variables;
- the N's are Red-terms of appropriate type in NDLS.

For example, if $M = X_1^{o\to o\to o}$ then $\tilde{M}$ may be $\underline{or}_o\{\underline{1}/X_1^{\iota}\}X_1^{o}\{\underline{2}/X_2^{\iota}\}\underline{tt}\{\underline{ff}/X_1^{o}\}$, where as usual the missing round brackets associate to the left.

We prove by structural induction that all terms in ENDLS are Red.

Case M=c. Trivial.

Case $M=X^{\sigma}$, $\sigma \neq o, \iota$. Any Red-closure of M has the form $\tilde{N}_{\sigma}$ (i.e. is a Red-closure of N_{σ}) where N_{σ} is Red, hence it is Red.

Case $M=X^{\kappa}$. Any $\tilde{M}$ has the form $\tilde{M} = X^{\kappa}\{N_1/v_1\}\ldots\{N_n/v_n\}$, $n \geq 1$. It is clear that $\tilde{M}$ can be reduced only by using rule 13a) or rule 13b), possibly together with rule 8); so we restrict our attention to how those rules can be applied to $\tilde{M}$.

We have: $CR(\tilde{M}) = \emptyset$, as $\tilde{M}$ is closed, and $CR(X^{\kappa}) \neq \emptyset$; hence it is easy to see that, if M_i stands for $X^{\kappa}\{N_1/v_1\}\ldots\{N_i/v_i\}$, there exists j s.t.: $CR(M_i) \neq \emptyset$ if $1 \leq i < j$, $CR(M_i) = \emptyset$ if $j \leq l \leq n$, and $CR(N_j) = \emptyset$ (indeed we must have: $CR(M_{j-1}) = \{v_j\}$).

By Lemma 2.1, M_i cannot be reduced, if $1 \leq i < j$, hence $\tilde{M}$ is reducible only by working on one of the M_i, for $i \geq j$. On the other hand, consider $N_{j,p} = N_j\{N_{j+1}/v_{j+1}\}\ldots\{N_p/v_p\}$, $j \leq p \leq n$. We have: $N_{j,n}$ is Red and cgt (it is a Red-closure of N_j), so the thesis holds for it, and $CR(N_{j,p}) = \emptyset$ for $j \leq p \leq n$; hence rules 13a) and 13b) cannot be applied for reducing $N_{j,n}$. Then three cases arise.

i) $N_j = \underline{c}$ and n=j. Then $\tilde{M}$ reduces (uniquely for what seen above) to $M_{j-1}[\underline{c}/v_j]$, using rule 13a).

ii) $N_j = \underline{c}$ and $n > j$ (so $N_{j,n}$ is reduced by using rule 9). Then $\tilde{M}$ reduces (uniquely) to $(M_{j-1}\ [c/v_j])\{N_{j+1}/v_{j+1}\}\ldots\{N_n/v_n\}$ by rule 13a), together with rule 8).

iii) $N_{j,n}$ is reduced by reducing N_j (and no other reductions apply to $N_{j,n}$). If N' unique exists s.t. $N_j \longrightarrow N'$, then $\tilde{M} \longrightarrow M_{j-1}\{N'/v_j\}\ldots\{N_n/v_n\}$; similarly if $N \longrightarrow N'$ and $N \longrightarrow N''$. Uniqueness of the reduction for $\tilde{M}$ derives, in both cases, from the hypothesis on $N_{j,n}$ and the arguments above about the critical sets.

Case M=(+1). We distinguish two subcases.

i) $\tilde{M}$ is of the form $(+1)N\{N_1/v_1\}\ldots\{N_n/v_n\}$, $n \geq 0$. Then, either $N=\underline{m}$, and so clearly $\tilde{M} \longrightarrow \underline{m+1}\{N_1/v_1\}\ldots\{N_n/v_n\}$ (and this is the only possibility), or $N \neq \underline{m}$. In this case, notice that the thesis of the Theorem holds for $\tilde{N} = N\{N_1/v_1\}\ldots\{N_n/v_n\}$. Then : either $\tilde{N}$ is reduced by reducing N and then the same applies to $\tilde{M}$, by rule

7b), possibly together with rule 8), and no other reduction is possible; or $\tilde{N}$ is reduced by using 13a) or 13b). But: $CR((+1)N) = CR(N)$ and $CR((+1)N\{N_1/v_1\}\ldots\{N_i/v_i\}) = CR(N\{N_1/v_1\}\ldots\{N_i/v_i\})$, for $1 \leq i \leq n$; so we can argue as for the case $M=X^K$.

ii) $\tilde{M}$ is of the form $(+1)\{N_1/v_1\}\ldots\{N_m/v_m\}N\{N_1'/v_1'\}\ldots\{N_n'/v_n'\}$, $m \geq 1$, $n \geq 0$. Then we apply rule 9) together with 7a), and possibly 8); no other reduction is possible (notice that the critical set of $\tilde{M}$ and of any of its initial "segments" is empty).

Case M = (-1), Z. We argue as for the case above.

Case M=or. We simply sketch this part of the proof, by indicating the reduction rules which are applied; as for uniqueness one can use arguments similar to those developed above. There are three subcases.

i) $\tilde{M}$= or{N/v} ....; then $\tilde{M}$ ---→ or..... , by rule 9);

ii) $\tilde{M}$= or N_1\{N/v\}.... ; then $\tilde{M}$ ---→ or(N_1\{N/v\}).... , by rule 10) ;

iii) $\tilde{M}$= or N_1 N_2 ..... ; then: either $\tilde{M}$ ---→ N_1.... or $\tilde{M}$ ---→ N_2.... , by rule 1).

Notice that the rules mentioned above are applied, possibly, together with rule 7a) and/or rule 8) .

Case M=IF. We proceed as above and distinguish five subcases.

i) $\tilde{M}$= IF{N/v}..... ; then we use rule 9);

ii) $\tilde{M}$= IF b{N/v}....; then we use rule 11a);

iii) $\tilde{M}$= IF b N_1\{N/v\} ..... ; then we use rule 11b) ;

iv) $\tilde{M}$= IF b N_1N_2 .... ; then we use rule 4).

As before it is understood that the rules above are applied, possibly, together with rule 7a) and/or rule 8). As for uniqueness of the reductions, this is seen by remarking that in each case no other rule can be used; in particular notice that $CR(\tilde{M}) = CR(\tilde{M}') = \emptyset$ for any 'initial segment' $\tilde{M}'$ of $\tilde{M}$.

v) $\tilde{M}$= IF $N_1\xi_1N_2\xi_2N_3\xi_3$, where ξ_i stands for $\{N_{i1}/v_{i1}\}\ldots\{N_{in_i}/v_{in_i}\}$, $n_i \geq 0$, and and $N_1 \neq$ c . Then we know by hypothesis on N_1 that $\tilde{N}_1=N_1\ \xi_1^i\xi_2\ \xi_3^i$ is Red. As it is a cgt and not a constant, either ii) or iii) of the Theorem apply to it.

Two possibilities arise.

- $\tilde{N}_1$ reduces as N_1 reduces; then the same applies to $\tilde{M}$ by rule 7b), together with rules 8) and 7a).
- $\tilde{N}_1$ reduces by rule 13a) or 13b); then the corresponding reduction applies to $\tilde{M}$ as we have:

$CR(\text{IF } N_1\{N_{11}/v_{11}\}\ldots\{N_{1j}/v_{1j}\}) = CR(N_1\{N_{11}/v_{11}\}\ldots\{N_{1j}/v_{1j}\})$;

$CR(\text{IF } N_1\ \xi_1\ N_2\{N_{21}/v_{21}\}\ldots\{N_{2j}/v_{2j}\}) = CR(N_1\xi_1\{N_{21}/v_{21}\}\ldots\{N_{2j}/v_{2j}\})$;

$CR(\text{IF } N_1\xi_1N_2\xi_2N_3\{N_{31}/v_{31}\}\ldots\{N_{3j}/v_{3j}\}) = CR(N_1\xi_1\xi_2\{N_{31}/v_{31}\}\ldots\{N_{3j}/v_{3j}\})$.

Case M=Y. It is very simple and we omit the details.

Case M= λXM_1. If $\tilde{M}=(\lambda XM_1')\{N/v\}\ldots$ then we use rule 11) together with 7a) and possibly 8). Otherwise $\tilde{M}=(\lambda XM_1')N\ldots$ and then either 6a) or 6b) are used. Uniqueness is proved by the usual arguments.

Cases $M=M_1M_2$, $M=M_1\{M_2/X\}$ (where M_1 and M_2 are Red). Any $\tilde{M}$ is also a Red-closure of M_1 hence it is Red by inductive hypothesis. □

SUR LES MOTS SANS CARRÉ DÉFINIS PAR UN MORPHISME

par

Jean Berstel

Institut de Programmation, Université Paris VI
Laboratoire d'Informatique Théorique et Programmation, CNRS

Abstract : A word w is called repetitive if it contains two consecutive equal factors ; otherwise w is nonrepetitive. Thus the word abacacb is repetitive, and abcacbabcbac is nonrepetitive. There is no nonrepetitive word of length 4 over a two letter alphabet ; on the contrary, there exist infinite nonrepetitive words over a three letter alphabet. Most of the explicitly known infinite nonrepetitive words are constructed by iteration of a morphism. In this paper, we show that it is decidable whether an infinite word over a three letter alphabet obtained by iterating a morphism is nonrepetitive. We also investigate nonrepetitive morphisms, i.e. morphisms preserving nonrepetitive words, and we show that it is decidable whether a morphism (over an arbitrary finite alphabet) is nonrepetitive.

1. Introduction.

La construction de mots sans carrés, c'est-à-dire de mots ne contenant pas deux facteurs consécutifs égaux, a fait l'objet de nombreux travaux depuis le premier article consacré à ce sujet par Thue [15], il y a maintenant plus de 70 ans. L'existence de mots arbitrairement longs sans carré est en effet surprenante et constitue une propriété combinatoire remarquable des mots. De plus, ces mots interviennent en dynamique symbolique (cf. Gottschalk, Hedlund [7]), et dans la preuve de l'existence de groupes infirmant la conjecture de Burnside (voir Adjan [1]). Enfin, la question de savoir si l'ensemble des mots contenant un carré est un langage algébrique ("context-free") est un problème ouvert dont la résolution permettrait de mieux savoir quand un langage algébrique est rationnel [3].

Les seuls mots sans carré sur un alphabet à deux lettres x et y sont x , y , xy , yx , xyx , yxy . Pour un alphabet à trois lettres, la situation change ; il existe alors des mots arbitrairement longs, donc aussi des mots infinis, sans carré. Le premier mot infini sans carré a sans doute été décrit par Thue en 1906 [15]. Depuis, d'autres mots infinis sur un alphabet à trois ou quatre lettres ont été trouvés ou retrouvés entre autres par Thue [16], Arson [2], Morse, Hedlund [11], Leech [10], Zech [17], Dean [4], Dejean [5], Pleasants [12], Shyr [14], Istrail [9]. (Ainsi, un des mots sans carré décrits par Istrail a déjà été obtenu, mais d'aune autre manière, par Morse et Hedlund et est aussi donné par Thue. Le mot sans carré de Pleasants, repris dans le livre de Harrison [8], est lui aussi décrit par Thue ([16], Satz 18, page 30).) On sait maintenant, grâce à une construction de Kakutani (cf. Gottschalk, Hedlund [7]) que l'ensemble des mots infinis sans carré sur un alphabet à trois lettres a la puissance du continu.

Dans la plupart des cas, la construction explicite d'un mot infini sans carré se fait itération d'un morphisme donné $\alpha : X^* \to X^*$. Partant d'une lettre fixée x , on construit la suite de mots

$$x , \alpha(x) , \alpha^2(x) , \ldots , \alpha^n(x) , \ldots. \qquad (1)$$

dont chacun est facteur gauche du suivant, ce qui permet, en passant à la limite dans un sens que nous préciserons, de définir un mot infini $\underline{\underline{a}}$ qui est sans carré ssi les mots $(\alpha^n(x))_{n \geq 0}$ sont sans carré. La preuve de ce que les $\alpha^n(x)$ sont sans carré est en général assez pénible et utilise des propriétés spécifiques du morphisme α considéré.

Nous donnons, dans cet article, un algorithme pour décider si un mot infini $\underline{\underline{a}}$ sur un alphabet à trois lettres est sans carré, lorsque $\underline{\underline{a}}$ est donné comme limite d'une suite (1) . Plus précisément, nous montrons que $\underline{\underline{a}}$ est sans carré si et seulement si le mot $\alpha^p(x)$ est sans carré, où p est une constante explicite ne dépendant que du morphisme α (Théorème 2). Toutefois, la majoration que nous avons pu obtenir pour p (Proposition 4) est encore trop élevée pour qu'un calcul concret soit facile ; de plus, notre résultat ne s'applique que pour un alphabet à trois lettres. Même si ce cas est le plus intéressant et le plus étudié, il est utile d'examiner les mots sur un alphabet de taille quelconque.

Pour cela, nous définissons les <u>morphismes sans carré</u>, qui sont les morphismes tels que l'image d'un mot sans carré est elle aussi un mot sans carré. On voit facilement que si α est un morphisme sans carré, les mots de la suite (1) sont sans carré, mais la réciproque est fausse (voir l'exemple 2 ci-dessous).

Nous prouvons qu'un morphisme est sans carré si et seulement s'il préserve les mots sans carré de longueur N , où N est une constante ne dépendant que du morphisme (Théorème 1). La constante N est facile à calculer et n'est pas trop grande ; de plus, ce résultat est vrai sans restriction sur la taille de l'alphabet. Enfin, il étend un résultat analogue de Thue [16] qui, lui, n'est valable que pour des morphismes vérifiant une condition supplémentaire assez restrictive.

2. <u>Notations et définitions</u>.

Soit X un alphabet. On note X^* le monoide libre engendré par X , $|w|$ la longueur d'un mot w , $|w|_x$ le nombre d'occurrences de la lettre x dans w , ε le mot vide et $X^+ = X^* - \{\varepsilon\}$.

Un <u>mot infini</u> sur X est une application $\underline{\underline{x}} : \underset{\sim}{N} \to X$. On l'écrit

$\underline{\underline{x}} = x_0 x_1 \dots x_n \dots \qquad x_i \in X$

et on note

$$\underline{\underline{x}}^{[k]} = x_0 x_1 \ldots x_{k-1}$$

le facteur gauche de longueur k de $\underline{\underline{x}}$. Tous les morphismes considérés ici sont propres ("ε-free") ; ceci n'est pas une restriction essentielle, mais facilite l'exposé.

Un morphisme $\alpha : X^* \to X^*$ est prolongeable en $x_0 \in X$ si $\alpha(x_0) = x_0 b$ pour un mot $b \in X^+$. Alors chaque mot $\alpha^n(x_0)$ est facteur gauche propre de $\alpha^{n+1}(x_0)$ et le mot infini $\underline{\underline{a}}$ déterminé par la condition

$$\underline{\underline{a}}^{[k]} = \alpha^n(x_0) \quad \text{pour } k = |\alpha^n(x_0)| \ , \quad n \geq 0$$

est la limite de la suite $(\alpha^n(x_0))_{n \geq 0}$. On écrit alors

$$\underline{\underline{a}} = \alpha^{\omega}(x_0) \ .$$

$\underline{\underline{a}}$ est le mot obtenu par itération de α en x_0.

Un mot (fini ou infini) est sans carré s'il ne contient pas de facteur de la forme uu, avec $u \neq \varepsilon$. Clairement, le mot $\alpha^{\omega}(x_0)$ est sans carré ssi $\alpha^n(x_0)$ est sans carré pour tout $n \geq 1$. Un morphisme $\alpha : X^* \to X^*$ est sans carré si $\alpha(w)$ est sans carré pour tout mot (fini) sans carré w.

Si $w \in X^*$, on note $F(w)$ l'ensemble des facteurs non vides de w. Si $\underline{\underline{a}}$ est un mot infini, alors de même $F(\underline{\underline{a}})$ est l'ensemble des mots finis non vides qui sont facteurs de $\underline{\underline{a}}$. Enfin $F_N(w) = \{u \in F(w) \mid |u| \leq N\}$ et de même pour $F_N(\underline{\underline{a}})$.

Exemple 1. - Soit $X = \{0,1,2\}$ et $\alpha_1 : X^* \to X^*$ défini par

$$\alpha_1(0) = 01201$$

$$\alpha_1(1) = 020121$$

$$\alpha_1(2) = 0212021 \ .$$

Le mot infini

$$\alpha_1^{\omega}(0) = 012010201210212021012\ldots\ldots \qquad (2)$$

est sans carré. En effet, Thue [16] a prouvé que α_1 est un morphisme sans carré. Ce mot infini a été retrouvé par Pleasants [12].

Exemple 2. - Soit X comme ci-dessus, et $\alpha_2 : X^* \to X^*$ donné par

$$\alpha_2(0) = 012 \quad , \quad \alpha_2(1) = 02 \quad , \quad \alpha_2(2) = 1 \ .$$

On obtient

$\alpha_2^{\omega}(0) = 012021012102.....$

Le morphisme α_2 est dû à Istrail [9], le mot infini a été donné aussi sous une forme différente par Thue [16] et Morse, Hedlund [11]. Bien que $\alpha_2^{\omega}(0)$ soit sans carré, le morphisme α_2 n'est pas sans carré, puisque 010 est un mot sans carré, alors que $\alpha(010) = 01202012$ contient le carré 2020 .

3. Résultats.

Soit $\alpha : X^* \to X^*$ un morphisme (propre). Le paramètre de base pour les résultats de décidabilité est la notion d'écart. Posons

$$\max(\alpha) = \max \{|\alpha(x)| \ : x \in X\} \quad ;$$

$$\min(\alpha) = \min \{|\alpha(x)| \ : x \in X\} \ .$$

L'<u>écart</u> de α est le nombre

$$e(\alpha) = \frac{\max(\alpha)}{\min(\alpha)} \ .$$

Soit $N(\alpha) = 2 + [2e(\alpha)]$. Alors on a :

<u>Théorème</u> 1. - Un morphisme $\alpha : X^* \to X^*$ est sans carré si et seulement s'il est propre et si $\alpha(w)$ est un mot sans carré pour tout mot w sans carré de longueur $|w| = N(\alpha)$.

Ce résultat permet de tester assez rapidement si un morphisme est sans carré. Thue ([16], Satz 17, page 28) a prouvé un résultat analogue, mais qui ne s'applique qu'à des morphismes satisfaisant une condition supplémentaire assez restrictive.

<u>Exemple</u> 1(suite). - Pour cet exemple, on a $e(\alpha_1) = \frac{7}{5}$, donc $N(\alpha_1) = 4$, et la vérification sur les mots de longueur 4 montre que α_1 est sans carré.

Comme le montre l'exemple 2, un morphisme peut définir un mot infini sans carré sans être un morphisme sans carré. Il n'existe, à ma connaissance, pas de caractérisation de ces morphismes. Toutefois, on peut donner une réponse dans le cas d'un alphabet à 3 lettres.

Soit donc X un alphabet à 3 lettres, $\alpha : X^* \to X^*$ un morphisme prolongeable en x_0, et soit $\underline{\underline{a}} = \alpha^{\omega}(x_0)$ le mot infini obtenu par itération de α en x_0.

<u>Théorème</u> 2. - Il existe un entier $p = p(\alpha)$ effectivement calculable tel que $\underline{\underline{a}}$ est sans carré si et seulement si le mot $\alpha^p(x_0)$ est sans carré.

Ce résultat est une conséquence de la proposition ci-dessous. On pose :

$$\bar{N}(\alpha) = \max\{5 , N(\alpha)\} , \quad M = M(\alpha) = \bar{N}(\alpha) . \max(\alpha) .$$

<u>Proposition</u> 3. - Le mot $\underline{\underline{a}}$ est sans carré ssi les deux conditions suivantes sont vérifiées :

(i) $\underline{\underline{a}}^{[31]}$ est sans carré ;

(ii) l'ensemble $F_M(\underline{\underline{a}})$ est constitué de mots sans carré.

Pour déduire le Théorème 2 de la Proposition 3, il faut prouver que l'ensemble $F_M(\underline{\underline{a}})$ est calculable. Or, ceci est un cas particulier d'un théorème de Reutenauer [13]. Plus précisément, on peut calculer un entier p tel que $|\alpha^p(x_0)| \geq 31$ et

$$F_M(\underline{\underline{a}}) \subset F_M(\alpha^p(x_0)) . \qquad (3)$$

Une majoration du plus petit entier p vérifiant (3) s'obtient par des résultats de Ehrenfeucht, Lee et Rozenberg [6], montrant que $p = O(M^3)$. En fait, on peut profiter de la situation très particulière étudiée ici ; on obtient alors la

<u>Proposition</u> 4. - Le mot $\underline{\underline{a}}$ est sans carré ssi $\underline{\underline{a}}^{[31]}$ est sans carré et $\alpha^p(x_0)$ est sans carré, où $p \leq n_0 + c.\log M(\alpha)$, avec $c^{-1} = \log \frac{5}{4}$ et n_0 une constante calculable.

Malheureusement, la constante n_0, qui est le plus petit entier n tel que $F_5(\underline{\underline{a}}) \subset F_5(\alpha^n(x_0))$, est encore trop élevée pour que la Proposition 4 permette un calcul aisé. Il est plus commode de calculer directement $F_M(\underline{\underline{a}})$.

Ainsi, pour le morphisme d'Istrail, on obtient $p(\alpha_2) \leq 19$.

4. Esquisse des preuves.

Les preuves reposent sur un lemme technique dont la vérification est assez longue et délicate, même si elle ne fait pas intervenir de technique nouvelle.

Lemme 5. - Soit $\alpha : X^* \to X^*$ un morphisme propre, tel que $\alpha(xy)$ est sans carré pour $x,y \in X$, $x \neq y$. Soit d'autre part w un mot sans carré tel que $\alpha(w)$ contienne un carré, et supposons w minimal ayant cette propriété, en ce sens qu'elle n'est satisfaite par aucun facteur propre de w . Si $|w| > N(\alpha)$, alors il existe des lettres x , y , z telles que $x \neq y$, $z \neq y$, et

(i) $w = xvyvz$ pour un mot $v \in X^+$;

(ii) il existe des factorisations

$\alpha(x) = hb$, $\alpha(y) = cb$, $\alpha(z) = ch'$, avec $b,c \in X^+$, $h,h' \in X^*$.

Le Théorème 1 se déduit sans peine de ce lemme : c'est pourquoi nous n'en donnons pas la preuve ici.

Preuve de la Proposition 3. - Supposons l'énoncé faux, donc que $\underline{\underline{a}}$ contient un carré. Alors il existe un plus petit n tel que $\alpha^n(x_0) = \alpha(w_n)$, avec $w_n = \alpha^{n-1}(x_0)$, contienne un carré, et il existe un facteur w de w_n tel que w soit sans carré et $\alpha(w)$ contienne un carré uu . Choisissons w de longueur minimale. En vertu des hypothèses, $uu \notin F_M(\underline{\underline{a}})$, donc $|uu| > M$, et $|\alpha(w)| \geq |uu| > M$. Comme d'autre part, $|\alpha(w)| \leq \max(\alpha)|w|$, on a donc $|w| > \bar{N}(\alpha)$. Appliquons donc le lemme ci-dessus. Il en résulte que le mot $\bar{w} = xyz$ n'appartient pas à $F_3(\underline{\underline{a}})$, car sinon $\alpha(xyz)$ serait sans carré, alors que $\alpha(xyz) = hbcbch'$.

Maintenant intervient de manière essentielle le fait que X est composé de trois lettres. Comme l'a vérifié Thue ([16], page 30), si h est un mot sans carré de longueur ≥ 31 , alors tous les mots de longueur 3 formés des trois lettres de l'alphabet sont facteurs de h . En vertu de l'hypothèse (i), le mot $\bar{w}$ ci-dessus s'écrit donc $\bar{w} = xyx$, avec $x,y \in X$, $x \neq y$.

Examinons maintenant la factorisation $w = xvyvx$. Comme $|w| > 5$, on a $|v| \geq 2$, donc $v = tv't'$ pour $t,t' \in X$. Alors

$$w = xtv't'ytv't'x$$

et comme w est sans carré, on a $t = t' = z$, où z est la troisième lettre de l'alphabet X . Ceci montre que $v' \neq \varepsilon$. Si t'' est la dernière lettre de v' , alors $t''t'yt = t''zyz$ est facteur de w , donc $t'' = x$. De même, la première lettre de v' est x . Donc $xzyzx$ est facteur propre de w , et en vertu du choix de w , le mot $\alpha(xzyzx)$ est sans carré. Or $\alpha(xzyzx) = hb\alpha(z)cb\alpha(z)ch'$, d'où la contradiction. ∎

Revenons sur le caractère effectif de la Proposition 3. Le calcul de $F_M(\underline{\underline{a}})$, où $\underline{\underline{a}} = \alpha^{\omega}(x_0)$ et où M est donné, peut se faire de la manière suivante. On considère le graphe $G = (S,U)$ dont l'ensemble S des sommets est constitué des mots de longueur $\leq M$, et ayant un ensemble d'arcs U défini par

$$(u,v) \in U \text{ ssi } v \text{ est facteur de } \alpha(u) .$$

Ce graphe est fini et calculable. De plus, il y a un chemin de longueur n de u vers v dans G ssi v est facteur de $\alpha^n(u)$. Ainsi, $F_M(\underline{\underline{a}})$ est l'ensemble des sommets de G accessibles à partir de x_0 . Le fait que α est prolongeable en x_0 implique que $F_M(\underline{\underline{a}}) = F_M(\alpha^p(x_0))$, où p est la profondeur en x_0 de G ,c'est-à-dire le maximum des distances de x_0 à ses descendants. Ce nombre p est fini parce que G est fini, ce qui montre le caractère effectif du Théorème 2.

Jusqu'alors, nous n'avons pas utilisé, dans cette discussion, le fait que l'alphabet est composé de 3 lettres. On peut tirer profit de cette contrainte à travers le lemme que voici.

Lemme 6. - Si u est un mot sans carré, alors $|u| \leq 3 + 4 \cdot |u|_{x_0}$.

Ce lemme découle immédiatement de l'observation que les mots sans carré sur un alphabet à deux lettres ont une longueur au plus 3 . On en déduit le

Corollaire 7. - Soit w un mot sans carré, et soit v un mot de longueur minimale tel que w est facteur de $\alpha(v)$. Alors $|w| \geq \frac{5}{4} (|v| - 1)$.

Dans le graphe G défini plus haut, ce corollaire s'interprête comme suit : Soient v,w des mots sans carré sommets de G, et soit n la longueur du plus court chemin de v à w. Si $|v| > 5$, et si w n'est descendant d'aucun facteur de v, alors $|w| - 5 \geq (\frac{5}{4})^n (|v| - 5)$. La Proposition 4 s'en déduit alors par des arguments standards.

Remerciement. - Je remercie J.E. Pin pour des discussions très fructueuses au début de la préparation du présent travail.

Références.

1 S.I. Adjan, Burnside groups of odd exponents and irreducible systems of group identities, in : Boone, Cannonito, Lyndon (eds), "Word Problems", North-Holland 1973, p 19-38.

2 S. Arson, Démonstration de l'existence de suites asymétriques infinies, Mat. Sb. 44 (1937), p 769-777.

3 J.M. Autebert, J. Beauquier, L. Boasson, M. Nivat, Quelques problèmes ouverts en théorie des langages algébriques, RAIRO, Informatique théorique, à paraître.

4 R. Dean, A sequence without repeats on x, x^{-1}, y, y^{-1}, Amer. Math. Monthly 72 (1965), p 383-385.

5 F. Dejean, Sur un théorème de Thue, J. Combinatorial Theory, Series A, 13 (1972), p 90-99.

6 A. Ehrenfeucht, K. Lee, G. Rozenberg, Subword complexities of various classes of deterministic developmental languages without interaction, Theor. Comput. Sci. 1 (1975), p 59-75.

7 W. Gottschalk, G. Hedlund, "Topological Dynamics", Amer. Math. Soc. Colloq. Publ. Vol. 36, 1955.

8 M. Harrison, "Introduction to Formal Language Theory", Addison-Wesley 1978.

9 S. Istrail, On irreductible languages and nonrational numbers, Bull. Soc. Math. Roumanie 21 (1977), p 301-308.

10 J. Leech, Note 2726 : A problem on strings of beads, Math. Gazette 41 (1957), p 277-278.

11 M. Morse, G. Hedlund, Unending chess, symbolic dynamics and a problem in semigroups, Duke Math. J. 11 (1944), p 1-7.

12 P.A. Pleasants, Non-repetitive sequences, Proc. Cambridge Phil. Soc. 68 (1970), p 267-274.

13 C. Reutenauer, Sur les séries associées à certains systèmes de Lindenmayer, Theor. Comput. Sci., à paraître.

14 H.J. Shyr, A strongly primitive word of arbitrary length and its applications, Intern. J. Comput. Math., Section A 6 (1977), p 165-170.

15 A. Thue, Über unendliche Zeichenreihen, Norske Vid. Selsk. Skr. I. Mat.-Nat. Kl., Christiania 1906, Nr. 7, p 1-22.

16 A. Thue, Über die gegenseitige Lage gleicher Teile gewisser Zeichenreihen, Vidensk. Skr. I. Mat.-Naturv. Kl., 1912, Nr. 1, p 1-67.

17 T. Zech, Wiederholungsfreie Folgen, Z. Angew. Math. Mech. 38 (1958), p 206-209.

A CHARACTERIZATION OF ABSTRACT DATA AS MODEL-THEORETIC INVARIANTS

A. Bertoni - G. Mauri - P.A. Miglioli

Istituto di Cibernetica - Università di Milano

1. INTRODUCTION

The problem of abstract data specification has been seriously taken into account in a lot of recent papers, and one of the most accredited approaches is the algebraic one, as developed by Liskov and Zilles [9] , Zilles [15], Guttag [5] and ADJ [4], that hinges on the following theses:

a) a data type is a many-sorted equational algebra;
b) an abstract data type is an isomorphism class of initial many-sorted equational algebras.

This approach gives rise to various difficulties, as pointed out by Majster [11], Klaeren [7], ADJ [14] and by the authors in [1]. In particular, the authors believe that the improvements proposed by ADJ [14] are not sufficient to overcome all the technical difficulties connected with the initialalgebra approach, and in [1] they proposed, by means of some examples, a more general approach based on model-theoretic concepts and techniques. In this frame, not only equational axioms are to be taken into account in order to specify abstract data types, but the full expressive power of first order languages can be conveniently used. Furthermore, the model-theoretic point of view has clearly shown the need of requiring something more than initiality: the main thesis of [1] is that an abstract data type is an isomorphism class of models of a first order theory which are at the same time initial and prime.

The present paper is a further development of [1]: here we want not only to work out our ideas by examples and theses, but to revise, in a model theoretic frame, the notion itself of "abstract datum" and, on the basis of an intuitive analysis of this concept, to provide an adeouate formalization of it.

Our starting point is any first order theory T of general kind (i.e. a set of first order sentences, not necessarily equivalent to a set of universally ouantified equations), where, in order to simplify the treatment, we require that the language of T contains only functional symbols (together with, of course, the relational symbol =).

In this frame, an abstract datum on T can be defined starting from a particular formula Δ provable from T, in such a way that, in every model $\mathfrak{M}$ of T, there is a unique element (the concrete datum) satisfying the formula Δ. Here the difference between the concrete datum and the abstract datum (independent from any model of T) is that the latter turns out to be the formula Δ itself (to be more precise, an appropriate equivalence class of formulas to which Δ belongs), that defines a model-theoretic invariant in the sense of Kreisel [8].

As a consequence, the notion of abstract data type follows in a natural way from our definition of abstract datum: under appropriate requirements, the set of all the abstract data can be structured as an algebra $\mathfrak{A}$; when this algebra turns out to be a model of T, we say that T admits an abstract data type, and call $\mathfrak{A}$ the abstract data type on T.

A strong semantical characterization of the theories which admit abstract data types is then provided. As a consequence of a theorem of Kreisel [8], we can prove that a theory T admits an abstract data type if and only if there is a model $\mathcal{A}$ of T such that, for every model $\mathcal{M}$ of T, there is a unique monomorphism from $\mathcal{A}$ to $\mathcal{M}$: we will refer to this property as monoinitiality of $\mathcal{A}$, as opposed to initiality, that requires the existence of a unique morphism, mono or not.

We remark that monoinitiality captures abstractness for data types just as initiality; furthermore, we show that monoinitiality is a weaker property than initiality plus primeness, but it is independent (i.e. there are no implications) of initiality: so, our approach, based on monoinitiality, is essentially different from the one of ADJ [4].

As a second result, we are able to show that if a theory T is recursively axiomatizable and admits an abstract data type $\mathcal{A}$, then there is $\mathcal{A}' \simeq \mathcal{A}$ whose defining operations are recursive: so an essential adequacy requisite for an abstract data specification technique, i.e. to capture recursiveness, is fulfilled.

Finally, we point out that the concept of monoinitiality often critically depends on the presence in the theory of axioms with unequalities; an example presented by Oppen [12] shows that the explicit assignment of such negative" axioms in the theory of LISP list structures leads to efficient decision algorithms.

2. FUNDAMENTAL DEFINITIONS

The basic notions we need are those of relational structure (generalizing that of algebra) and of first order language.

We start with a many-sorted alphabet A, that consist of:

a) a set S of sorts;

b) a set Σ of operation symbols, together with an arity function

$$\nu_\Sigma : \Sigma \longrightarrow S^+ xS ;$$

c) a set R of relation symbols, together with an arity function

$$\nu_R : R \longrightarrow S^+;$$

d) a set C of constant symbols, together with a sort function ν_C: C $\longrightarrow$ S.

Def.2.1 - A structure for A is a pair $\mathcal{M} = \langle M, i_M \rangle$ where $M = \{M_s / s \in S\}$ is a class of non empty sets indexed by S, called the carriers of the structure, and i_M is the interpretation function, that associates:

i) with every $\sigma \in \Sigma$ such that $\nu_\Sigma(\sigma) = \langle s_1 \ldots s_k, s \rangle$ a function

$$i_M(\sigma) = \sigma_M : M_{s_1} x \ldots x M_{s_k} \longrightarrow M_s \quad ;$$

ii) with every $r \in R$ such that $\nu_R(r) = s_1 \ldots s_k$ a relation

$$i_M(r) = r_M \subseteq M_{s_1} x \ldots x M_{s_k} \quad ;$$

iii) with every $c \in C$ such that $\nu_C(c) = s$ an element $i_M(c) = c_M \in M_s$.

Def.2.2 - Let $\mathfrak{M}$ and $\mathfrak{M}'$ be two structures for A; a <u>morphism</u> h: $\mathfrak{M} \longrightarrow \mathfrak{M}'$ is a class $\{h_s : M_s \longrightarrow M'_s \;/\; s \in S\}$ of maps such that relations, functions and constants are preserved.

Fact: The class of structures for a given many-sorted alphabet A, together with their morphisms, is a category [10].

Now, we can construct expressions to describe the structures by using the symbols of A and:

e) a class $\{X_s / s \in S\}$ of infinite sets of <u>variables</u>;

f) the <u>logical connectives</u> $\wedge$ (and), $\vee$ (or), $\sim$ (not), $\rightarrow$ (implies), the <u>equality symbol</u> =, the <u>quantifiers</u> $\forall$ (for all) and $\exists$ (there exists).

Def.2.3 - The set T_s of <u>terms</u> of sort $s \in S$ is the smallest set containing X_s, all constant symbols of sort s, and such that if $\sigma \in \Sigma$, $\nu_\Sigma(\sigma) = \langle s_1 \ldots s_k \rangle$ and $t_i \in T_{s_i}$, then $\sigma(t_1,\ldots,t_k) \in T_{s_i}$.

The set AF of <u>atomic formulas</u> is the smallest set such that if $t_1, t_2 \in T_{s_i}$, then $t_1 = t_2 \in AF$, and if $r \in R$, $\nu_R(r) = \langle s_1 \ldots s_k \rangle$ and $t_i \in T_{s_i}$ then $r(t_1,\ldots,t_k) \in AF$.

The set F of <u>first order formulas</u> is the smallest set such that $AF \subseteq F$ and if $\varphi, \psi \in F$, $x \in X$, then $\varphi \wedge \psi$, $\varphi \vee \psi$, $\varphi \rightarrow \psi$, $\sim\varphi$, $\exists x\varphi$, $\forall x\varphi \in F$.

In the formulas $\forall x\varphi$ and $\exists x\varphi$, the variable x is called <u>bounded</u> (by the quantifier). A formula that contains only bounded variables is called a <u>sentence</u>.

Def. 2.4 - Let T be a set of sentences, and $\mathfrak{M}$ a structure such that all the sentences in T hold on $\mathfrak{M}$. We say that T is a <u>theory</u> and $\mathfrak{M}$ a <u>model</u> for T, and write $\mathfrak{M} \models T$.

Fact: The class of models of T forms a subcategory of the category of structures.

Finally, we define the notions of initiality, primeness and monoinitiality.

Initiality is a general category-theoretical notion that has been assumed by ADJ [4] to characterize abstract data types.

Def.2.5- An object O in a category $\mathcal{C}$ is said to be <u>initial</u> iff for every other object O' there is an unique morphism h: O $\longrightarrow$ O'.

The fundamental theorem, that guarantees the "abstractness" (independence of any representation) of initial objects is the following [10].

Th.2.1 - If O is an initial object in a category, then an object O' is initial iff it is isomorphic to O.

In the particular case where $\mathcal{C}$ is a category of equational algebras (i.e. of models of a theory without relation symbols and containing only equations) the existence of an initial object is guaranteed by a well known theorem of universal algebra [2]. These theorems are the basis for the ADJ's thesis that an abstract data type is the unique (up to isomorphisms) initial object in a category of many sorted equational algebras.

Now, let $\mathcal{C}_m$ be the subcategory of $\mathcal{C}$ containing only the monomorphisms of $\mathcal{C}$.

Def.2.6 - An object O in a category $\mathcal{C}$ is said to be monoinitial iff it is initial in the category $\mathcal{C}_m$.

Def.2.7 - Let $\mathfrak{M}$ and $\mathfrak{N}$ be two structures on the same alphabet. An embedding of $\mathfrak{M}$ in $\mathfrak{N}$ is a morphism $h: \mathfrak{M} \longrightarrow \mathfrak{N}$ such that for every atomic formula φ and every assignment s in $\mathfrak{M}$

$$\mathfrak{M} \models \varphi(s) \quad \text{iff} \quad \mathfrak{N} \models \varphi(h \circ s)$$

Def.2.8 - A model $\mathfrak{M}$ of a theory T is called prime iff for every model of T, $\mathfrak{N}$, there is an embedding $h: \mathfrak{M} \longrightarrow \mathfrak{N}$

This definition has its category-theoretical counterpart as follows:

Def.2.9 - An object O in a category $\mathcal{C}$ is said to be prime iff for every other object O' there is a monomorphism $h: O \longrightarrow O'$.

3. INITIALITY, MONOINITIALITY AND PRIMENESS.

The first thing we want to prove is that monoinitiality captures the notion of abstractness just as initiality.

Th.3.1 - If O is monoinitial in a category $\mathcal{C}$, then O' is monoinitial iff it is isomorphic to O.

Proof - Obvious corollary of Th.2.1, applied to the category $\mathcal{C}_m$.

More interesting is the following theorem, that gives a weaker condition for the only if part:

Th.3.2 - If O is monoinitial and, for an object O', there is a monomorphism $m: O' \longrightarrow O$, then O' is monoinitial.

Proof - Let m' the (unique) monomorphism from O to O'. Then

$$m \cdot m' = 1_O$$

the unique monomorphism from O to O.

Furthermore,

$$m' \cdot m = m''$$

is a monomorphism, and

$$m'' \cdot m'' = (m'm)(m'm) = m'(m \cdot m')\, m = m'm = m'' = 1_O\, m'' \Rightarrow m'' = 1_{O'}$$

Thus we have $m^{-1} = m'$. This implies that O' is isomorphic to O, and hence, by Th.3.1, it is monoinitial.

We turn now to the analysis of the relations existing among the concepts of initiality, monoinitiality and primeness; these relations can be summarized as follows.

Th.3.3 - a) monoinitiality $\not\rightleftarrows$ initiality;

b) monoinitiality $\overset{\rightarrow}{\not\leftarrow}$ primeness;

c) monoinitiality $\not\leftrightarrows$ primeness and initiality

Proof - a) Two counterexamples will show that monoinitiality and initiality are independent concepts.
First, we consider the theory T with $C = \{a\}$, $\Sigma = R = \emptyset$ and the only axiom $\exists! x(x \neq a)$. The set $\{a,b\}$ is a model of T monoinitial, but not initial. For, $f: \{a,b\} \longrightarrow \{a,b\}$ with $f(a) = f(b) = a$ is a morphism (not mono) different from the identity.
The second counterexample refers to the theory of natural numbers with constant 0, operation S and without axioms. In this case, the obvious initial object is not monoinitial; for, if we consider the model with carrier 0 and operation $S(0) = 0$, the unique morphism from the initial object to this model is not mono.
b) By definition, it is obvious that monoinitiality implies primeness. To show that primeness does not imply monoinitiality, it suffices to quote a counterexample: as discussed in [13], the theory of the dense linear orderings without first and last element admits infinitely many prime models which are not monoinitial.
c) Quite obvious.

To complete our analysis, we finally prove the following:

Th.3.4 - If a category admits an initial object 0 and a monoinitial object 0', then $0 \simeq 0'$.
Proof - We first prove that the unique morphism $f: 0 \longrightarrow 0'$ is mono. For, let $h,k: C \longrightarrow 0$ such that $fk = fh$. Thus, we have:

$$mfk = mfh \Longrightarrow (mf)k = (mf)h \Longrightarrow 1_0 k = 1_0 h \Longrightarrow k = h$$

where m is the unique monomorphism from 0' to 0. This means that f is a monomorphism; hence, by Th.3.2, $0 \simeq 0'$.

4. ABSTRACT DATA ON A THEORY

In the preceding approaches, the primitive notion was that of abstract data type, and an abstract datum was defined as an element of the carrier of an abstract data type. On the contrary, we start with a definition of the concept of abstract datum on a (consistent) theory T whose axioms specify the properties that must hold for abstract data.

For sake of simplicity, in this section we restrict our attention only to theories on a one-sorted language without relational symbols: the treatment of the general case would be very cumbersome, even if not substantially different from the conceptual point of view.

Def.4.1 - An <u>abstract datum</u> on a theory T is a quantifier-free formula $\Delta(x,\underline{y})$ such that:

$$T \vdash \exists! x \exists \underline{y}\, \Delta(x,\underline{y})$$

From the semantical point of view, this means that the formula $\Delta(x,y)$ identifies a unique element in every model of T, and this fact agrees with the intuitive meaning of "abstract datum' as an object independent of any representation.

We remark that, for every constant c (if any), the formula $x = c$ is an abstract datum.

So, we obtain a set $\{..\Delta..\}$ of abstract data on T. On this set, we want to introduce an algebraic structure, where the functional symbols of T can be interpreted. This is possible only under particular conditions, that are specified as follows.

Def.4.2 - Let Δ_1 and Δ_2 be two abstract data. We say that Δ_1 is equal to Δ_2, $\Delta_1 = \Delta_2$, if and only if:

$$T \vdash \exists x_1 \exists x_2 \exists \underline{y}_1 \exists \underline{y}_2 \, (\Delta_1(x_1,\underline{y}_1) \wedge \Delta_2(x_2,\underline{y}_2) \wedge x_1 = x_2)$$

We say that Δ_1 is strongly different from Δ_2, $\Delta_1 \neq_s \Delta_2$, if and only if:

$$T \vdash \exists x_1 \exists x_2 \exists \underline{y}_1 \exists \underline{y}_2 \, (\Delta_1(x_1,\underline{y}_1) \wedge \Delta_2(x_2,\underline{y}_2) \wedge x_1 \neq x_2)$$

These definitions mean, respectively, that the elements identified by Δ_1 and Δ_2 are equal, or are different, in every model of T.

Two abstract data being not equal are not necessarily strongly different for an arbitrary theory: it is quite possible that there exists some model $\mathfrak{M}$ of T and a couple of abstract data Δ_1 and Δ_2 such that:

$$\exists ! x \exists \underline{y}_1 \exists \underline{y}_2 (\Delta_1(x,\underline{y}_1) \wedge \Delta_2(x,\underline{y}_2))$$

even if $\Delta_1 \neq \Delta_2$ (where $\neq$ has the usual meaning of "not equal"); in the latter case, however, there is necessarily some other model $\mathfrak{M}'$ of T such that:

$$\mathfrak{M}' \models \exists x_1 \exists x_2 \exists \underline{y}_1 \exists \underline{y}_2 \, (\Delta_1(x_1,\underline{y}_1) \wedge \Delta_2(x_2,\underline{y}_2) \wedge x_1 \neq x_2)$$

We want to avoid such situations by requiring that the theory T satisfies the following property.

Def.4.3 - A theory T almost admits an abstract data type iff for every two abstract data Δ_1, Δ_2:

$$\sim \Delta_1 = \Delta_2 \iff \Delta_1 \neq_s \Delta_2$$

(remark, on the other hand, that $\Delta_1 \neq_s \Delta_2$ always implies $\sim \Delta_1 = \Delta_2$).

We can now construct the algebra $\mathcal{A}$ of abstract data on a theory T almost admitting an abstract data type.

i) the elements of the carrier A of the algebra are the equivalence classes of abstract data with respect to the relation = :

$$A = \{..\Delta..\}/=$$

ii) the operations on A are defined in the following way. Let f be any n-ary functional symbol in T; we set:

$$f([\Delta_1],\ldots,[\Delta_n]) = [\Delta(x,x_1,\ldots x_n,\underline{y}_1,\ldots,\underline{y}_n)]$$

where $\Delta = (x=f(x_1,\ldots,x_n) \wedge \Delta_1(x_1,\underline{y}_1) \wedge \ldots \wedge \Delta_n(x_n,\underline{y}_n))$

is an abstract datum, because

$$T \vdash \exists ! x \exists x_1,\ldots,x_n,\underline{y}_1,\ldots,\underline{y}_n \Delta(x,x_1,\ldots,x_n,\underline{y}_1,\ldots,\underline{y}_n).$$

Def.4.4 - A theory T admits an abstract data type iff it almost admits an abstract data type and the algebra is a model of T, i.e. $\mathcal{A} \models T$. In this case, we call $\mathcal{A}$ the abstract data type generated by T.

Of course, there are theories that almost admit, but do not admit, an abstract data type. A very trivial example is the theory T with $C = \{a\}$, without relational or functional symbols and with the axiom $\exists x(x \neq a)$. Here, the only abstract datum is the formula $\Delta \equiv x=a$. Hence, the carrier of the algebra contains exactly one element, so $\mathcal{A}$ cannot be a model of T.

5. A CHARACTERIZATION OF THEORIES WHICH ADMIT ABSTRACT DATA TYPES

In this section, we give the main result of the paper, that strongly characterizes the theories which admit abstract data types.

Th.5.1 - A theory T admits an abstract data type if and only if the category of models of T contains a monoinitial object.
This object is precisely the abstract data type generated by T.

Proof - a) The "only if" part is proved by defining a special morphism m: $\mathcal{A} \longrightarrow \mathcal{M}$ where $\mathcal{M}$ is any model of T: with every equivalence class $[\Delta]$ belonging to the carrier of $\mathcal{A}$ we associate the unique element of $\mathcal{M}$ simultaneously satisfying all the formulas of the form $\exists \underline{y}\, \Delta'(x,\underline{y})$, with $\Delta' \in [\Delta]$.
As a consequence of the condition of Def.4.3, one easily sees that:
1) m is a monomorphism.
We also have:
2) if m': $\mathcal{A} \longrightarrow \mathcal{M}$ is a monomorphism, then m' = m.
To prove this fact, let us assume that m' ≠ m. Thus, there is $[\bar{\Delta}]$ such that $a = m([\bar{\Delta}]) \neq m'([\bar{\Delta}]) = b$. Now, let $\mathcal{M}_{m'}$ be the image of $\mathcal{A}$ in $\mathcal{M}$ under the morphism m'; since $\mathcal{A}$ is a model of T, $\mathcal{M}_{m'}$ is a model T too, and is isomorphic, under m', to $\mathcal{A}$. Hence, we have

$$\mathcal{M}_{m'} \models \exists \underline{y}\, \bar{\Delta}'(b,\underline{y})$$

with $\bar{\Delta}'$ any element of $[\bar{\Delta}]$; a fortiori,

$$\mathcal{M} \models \exists \underline{y}\, \bar{\Delta}'(b,\underline{y}).$$

On the other hand,

$$\mathcal{M} \models \exists \underline{y}\, \bar{\Delta}'(a,\underline{y})$$

with a ≠ b. This contradicts our hypothesis that

$$T \vdash \exists ! x \exists \underline{y}\, \bar{\Delta}'(x,\underline{y}).$$

b) For the "if" part, a consequence of the fact that T has a monoinitial model $\bar{\mathcal{A}}$ is that T almost admits an abstract data type. For, let Δ_1 and Δ_2 be two abstract data on T and let $\Delta_1 \neq \Delta_2$; then we can prove:

1) $\bar{\mathcal{A}} \models \exists x_1 \exists x_2 \exists \underline{y}_1 \exists \underline{y}_2 (\Delta_1(x_1,\underline{y}_1) \wedge \Delta_2(x_2,\underline{y}_2) \wedge x_1 \neq x_2)$;

2) if 1) holds, then

$$\mathcal{M} \models \exists x_1 \exists x_2 \exists \underline{y}_1 \exists \underline{y}_2 (\Delta_1(x_1,\underline{y}_1) \wedge \Delta_2(x_2,\underline{y}_2) \wedge x_1 \neq x_2)$$

for every model $\mathcal{M}$ of T.

To prove 1), let us assume the contrary; then,

$$\bar{\mathcal{A}} \models \exists ! x \exists \underline{y}_1 \exists \underline{y}_2 (\Delta_1(x,\underline{y}_1) \wedge \Delta_2(x,\underline{y}_2)).$$

Let $\mathcal{M}$ be any model of T, and let $\mathcal{M}_m$ be the image of $\bar{\mathcal{A}}$ into $\mathcal{M}$ under the (unique) monomorphism m: $\bar{\mathcal{A}} \longrightarrow \mathcal{M}$; then $\mathcal{M}_m$ is isomorphic to $\bar{\mathcal{A}}$, so that

$$\mathfrak{M}_m \models \exists! x \exists \underline{y}_1 \exists \underline{y}_2 (\Delta_1(x,\underline{y}_1) \wedge \Delta_2(x,\underline{y}_2));$$

a fortiori, we have

$$\mathfrak{M}_m \models \exists x \exists \underline{y}_1 \exists \underline{y}_2 (\Delta_1(x,\underline{y}_1) \wedge \Delta_2(x,\underline{y}_2)),$$

so that, being $\mathfrak{M}_m \subseteq \mathfrak{M}$, and being Δ_1 and Δ_2 quantifier-free,

$$\mathfrak{M} \models \exists x \exists \underline{y}_1 \exists \underline{y}_2 (\Delta_1(x,\underline{y}_1) \wedge \Delta_2(x,\underline{y}_2)).$$

But Δ_1 and Δ_2 are abstract data on T, so that

$$\mathfrak{M} \models \exists! x \exists \underline{y}_1 \Delta_1(x,\underline{y}_1) \quad \text{and} \quad \mathfrak{M} \models \exists! x \exists \underline{y}_2 \Delta_2(x,\underline{y}_2)$$

and we necessarily have

$$\mathfrak{M} \models \exists! x \exists \underline{y}_1 \exists \underline{y}_2 (\Delta_1(x,\underline{y}_1) \wedge \Delta_2(x,\underline{y}_2));$$

since $\mathfrak{M}$ is any model of T, this contradicts the hypothesis $\Delta_1 \neq \Delta_2$.
The proof of 2) is similar.

The above points 1) and 2), according to the completeness theorem for the first order theory T, immediately implies that $\Delta_1 \neq_s \Delta_2$, so that T almost admits an abstract data type: hence, the algebra $\mathfrak{A}$ can be defined for T.
Now, we have to prove the crucial part of the theorem, i.e. that $\mathfrak{A}$ is indeed a model of T, as required by Def.4.4. To show this, we will use the following lemma, whose proof is an immediate consequence of a theorem in [8].

<u>Lemma</u> - For every element d of the carrier of the monoinitial model of T there is a quantifier-free formula $\Delta_d(x,\underline{y})$ such that $T \vdash \exists! x \exists \underline{y}\, \Delta_d(x,\underline{y})$ and $\overline{\mathfrak{A}} \models \exists \underline{y}\, \Delta_d(d,\underline{y})$.

The lemma allows us to conclude that $\overline{\mathfrak{A}}$ is isomorphic to $\mathfrak{A}$, i.e. that $\mathfrak{A}$ is a model of T. For, one defines an application $\overline{m}$: $\overline{\mathfrak{A}} \rightarrow \mathfrak{A}$, which associates with every $d \in \overline{\mathfrak{A}}$ the equivalence class $[\Delta_d]$; then, one shows:

α) $\overline{m}$ is a monomorphism;

β) $\overline{m}$ is bijective.

The easy proof of α) is omitted; to prove β), let $[\Delta]$ be any element of the carrier of $\mathfrak{A}$ and let $d \in \overline{\mathfrak{A}}$ be such that

$$\overline{\mathfrak{A}} \models \exists \underline{y} \Delta(d,\underline{y})$$

Then, as it is easy to see, $\Delta \in [\Delta_d]$, i.e. $[\Delta] = [\Delta_d]$.
This concludes the proof of the "if" part and of the theorem.

6. MONOINITIALITY AND RECURSIVENESS

The monoinitiality property, which strongly characterizes an abstract data type, is a model-theoretic notion which directly leads to recursiveness; as a matter of fact, under a quite reasonable requirement on the theory T, an abstract data type on T turns out to be recursive up to isomorphisms. To explain what we mean, the following definitions are in order.

Def.6.1 - A (one-sorted) structure $\mathfrak{M}$ for the alphabet A (whithout relational symbols different from =) is said to be <u>recursive</u> if either:

a) the carrier of $\mathfrak{M}$ is finite; or

b) the carrier of $\mathfrak{M}$ is the set of the natural numbers, and all the functions defined on $\mathfrak{M}$ are general recursive functions.

Remark - The requirement made in b) on the carrier of $\mathfrak{M}$ has the only purpose of defining a "canonical form' for the recursive structures.

Def.6.2 - A model $\mathfrak{M}$ of a theory T is said to be recursive iff $\mathfrak{M}$ is isomorphic to a recursive structure $\mathfrak{M}'$.

Remark - The essential feature of the structure $\mathfrak{M}'$ is that all the functions defined on $\mathfrak{M}'$ are recursive: if one defines as recursive any structure whose carrier is the set of the natural numbers without any further requirement, then, as a trivial consequence of the downward Lowenheim-Skolem theorem, every theory T has a recursive model.

Def.6.3 - A theory T is said to be axiomatizable iff T is a recursively enumerable set of sentences.

The following result is well known.

Fact - A theory T is axiomatizable iff all the formulas provable from T can be proved starting from a recursive set of axioms..

Now we can state the main result of this section:

Th.6.1 - If an axiomatizable theory T admits an abstract data type, then the abstract data type $\mathfrak{A}$ on T is recursive.

Proof - Let us exclude the trivial case, i.e. let us assume that the carrier of $\mathfrak{A}$ is infinite. First of all, by the axiomatizability of T, one can define a recursive enumeration

$$e_1: \Delta_o, \Delta_1, \ldots, \Delta_n, \ldots$$

of all the abstract data on T.

Secondly, since $\Delta_i \neq \Delta_j$ implies $\Delta_i \neq_s \Delta_j$ for every Δ_i and Δ_j, one can prove or disprove that $\Delta_i = \Delta_j$; hence, using the enumeration e_1, one can define an enumeration

$$e_2: \Delta'_o, \Delta'_1, \ldots, \Delta'_n, \ldots.$$

such that:

1) for every abstract datum Δ on T, there is a n such that

$$e_2(n) = \Delta'_n$$

2) if $i \neq j$, then $e_2(i) = \Delta'_i \neq \Delta'_j = e_2(j)$.

Now, let f_k be any function defined on $\mathfrak{A}$ and let $\Delta'_{i_1}, \ldots, \Delta'_{i_K}$ be elements of the range of e_2: if one considers the abstract datum

$$\Delta \equiv \quad x = f_k(y_1,\ldots,y_k) \wedge \Delta'_{i_1}(y_1,\underline{z}_1) \wedge \ldots \wedge \Delta'_{i_K}(y_k,\underline{z}_k)$$

then there is some $\Delta'_n = e_2(n)$ such that $\Delta \in [\Delta'_n]$; hence, since $\Delta \neq \Delta'_1$,..., $\Delta \neq \Delta'_{n-1}$, $\Delta = \Delta'_n$ can be proved in a finite number of steps, one can recursively find such a Δ'_n . As a consequence, the function f_k is transformed, according to the enumeration e_2, into a partial recursive function f'_k defined on the set of all the k-tuples of the range of e_2.

Let $\mathfrak{A}'$ be the structure whose carrier is the range of e_2, and containing, for every f_K defined on $\mathfrak{A}$, the corresponding function f'_K ; of course,

$\mathfrak{A}'$ is isomorphic to $\mathfrak{A}$. On the other hand, e_2 is a bijection of the set of the natural numbers N into the carrier A of $\mathfrak{A}'$ and, for every f'_k of $\mathfrak{A}'$, the function f^N_k defined by the commutative diagram

$$\begin{array}{ccc} A^k & \xrightarrow{f'_k} & A \\ e_2^k \uparrow & & \downarrow e_2^{-1} \\ N^k & \xrightarrow[f^N_k]{} & N \end{array}$$

is general recursive. We can therefore devise a recursive structure isomorphic to $\mathfrak{A}$.

The above theorem 6.1. does not say, on the other hand, that the range of the enumeration function e_2 is recursive in the (recursive) set of all the quantifier-free formulas of the language of T: to obtain a recursive structure, an isomorphism is essential. In other words, if one wants to consider as the data type exactly the algebra and not a structure isomorphic to (having a "non intuitive" carrier), then the meaning of Th.6.1 is the following: the algebra $\mathfrak{A}$ is locally recursive, i.e. once one knows that the object $\Delta'_1, \ldots, \Delta'_k$ are abstract data, then he can effectively compute the function $f'_k(\Delta'_1, \ldots, \Delta'_k)$ and be sure that the result is again an abstract datum; but to be sure that $\Delta'_1, \ldots, \Delta'_k$ are abstract data, one needs an enumeration.

Now, we analyze how to impose the stronger condition that the carrier of $\mathfrak{A}$ is recursive (i.e. the isomorphism in Th.6.2 is a recursive function): our goal is to give, by using some classical model-theoretic techniques, some properties of the axiom system T sufficient to warrant that the generated abstract data type admits a recursive carrier.

Def.6.4 - A theory T is $\exists$-complete iff, for every quantifier-free formula $\varphi(\underline{y})$ we have:

$$T \vdash \exists \underline{y}\, \varphi(\underline{y}) \quad \text{or} \quad T \vdash \sim\exists \underline{y}\, \varphi(\underline{y})$$

The fundamental point is that for a $\exists$-complete theory any system of equalities and unequalitie has a solution in every model of T iff it has a solution in at least a model. The main consequence is the following

Th.6.2 - Let T be a recursively axiomatizable theory that admits an abstract data type $\mathfrak{A}$; if T is $\exists$-complete, then the carrier of $\mathfrak{A}$ is recursive.

The proof, similar to that of Th.6.1, is obtained observing that the set of formulas $\{\varphi \,/\, T \vdash \exists \underline{y}\, \varphi(\underline{y})\}$ is recursive, for the $\exists$-completeness hypothesis, and that: $\exists ! x \exists \underline{y}\, \Delta(x,\underline{y}) \leftrightarrow \exists x \exists \underline{y}\, \Delta(x,\underline{y}) \wedge \sim\exists x_1 x_2 \underline{y}_1 \underline{y}_2 (\Delta(x_1,\underline{y}_1) \wedge \Delta(x_2,\underline{y}_2) \wedge x_1 \neq x_2)$.

7. FINAL REMARKS

The aim of this section is to informally point out some differences between our approach and the one of ADJ [4] with respect to the implementation problems.

As we pointed out in [1] for the STACK structure, monoinitiality implies the explicit assignment of an infinity of axioms of the type $t_1 \neq t_2$, where t_1 and t_2 are terms; these axioms are equivalent to the induction axiom schema. As a consequence of such an axiomatization, we obtain the completeness and the decidability of the theory of STACKS .

A second example, explicitly discussed by Oppen [12], is the theory RDS (Recursive Data Structures). In this theory, the defining operations are a "constructor" function c and k "selectors" $s_1, \ldots, s_k$; the unioue relations is = and the axioms are:

1) (Construction)

$$c(s_1(x),\ldots,s_k(x)) = x$$

2) (Selection)

$$s_i(c(x_1,\ldots,x_k)) = x_i \qquad (1 \leq i \leq k)$$

3) (Acyclicity)

$$s_1(x) \neq x$$

....

$$s_1(s_2(x) \neq x$$

....

The category of the models of this theory admits a monoinitial object, and the monoinitiality is obtained from the acyclicity axioms.

The main result in [12] is the description of an efficient procedure which determines the satisfiability of a conjunction φ of the form:

$$v_1 = w_1 \wedge \ldots \wedge v_n = w_n \wedge \; x_1 \neq y_1 \wedge \ldots \wedge x_m \neq y_m$$

This procedure determines the satisfiability of φ in linear time, and therefore the (full) ouantifier-free theory of RDS is NP (hence NP-complete). We remark that the linearity of the decision procedure is obtained by using in an essential way the axioms of type 3), that cannot be reduced to equations.

REFERENCES

[1] Bertoni,A., Mauri,G., Miglioli,P.A., Model-theoretic aspects of abstract data specification, Colloquium on Mathematical Logic in Programming, Salgotarjan, 1978

[2] Cohn,P.M., Universal Algebra, Harper and Row, New York, 1965

[3] Eklof,P.C., Ultraproducts for algebraists, in 'Handbook of Mathematical Logic' (J. Barwise ed.), North-Holland, Amsterdam, 1977

[4] Goguen,J.A., Thatcher,J.W., Wagner,E.G., An initial algebra approach to the specification, correctness and implementation of abstract data types, IBM Res. Rep. RC6487, Yorktown Heights, 1976

[5] Guttag,J.V., Abstract data types and the development of data structures, SIGPLAN Notices 8, 1976

[6] Hardgrave,W.T., A technioue for implementing a set processor, SIGPLAN Notices 8, 1976

[7] Klaeren,H., Datenraume mit algebraischer struktur, Bericht Nr.43, Technische Hochschule Aachen, 1978

[8] Kreisel,G., Model-theoretic invariants: applications to recursive and hyperarithmetic operations, Proc. Symp. on the theory of models, North-Holland, Amsterdam, 1965

[9] Liskov,B.H., Zilles,S.N., Programming with abstract data types, SIGPLAN Notices 6, 1974

[10] Mac Lane,S., Categories for working mathematician, Springer, Berlin, 1971

[11] Majster,M.E., Limits of the algebraic specification of abstract data types, SIGPLAN Notices 9, 1977

[12] Oppen,D.C., Reasoning about recursively defined data structures, Res. Rep. STAN-CS-78-678, Stanford University, 1978

[13] Robinson,A., Introduction to model theory and metamathematics of algebra, North-Holland, Amsterdam, 1963

[14] Thatcher,J.W., Wagner,E.G., Wright,J.B., Data type specification: parameterization and the power of specification techniques, Proc. SIGACT 10th Symp. on theory of computing, 1978

[15] Zilles,S.N., Algebraic specification of data types, Project MAC Progress Report 11, MIT, Cambridge, Mass., 1974

This research has been developed in the frame of the Communication and Programming Project of Università di Milano and Honeywell Information Systems Italia, and supported by CNR.

INHERENT AMBIGUITIES IN FAMILIES OF GRAMMARS *

EXTENDED ABSTRACT

Meera Blattner
Rice University
Houston, Texas 77001/USA

I. Introduction

A (context-free) grammar form G is a master grammar from which we obtain a family of grammars by "interpretations" of the production rules of G. Each grammar in the family has structural properties similar to G. In particular, the production rules in an interpretation grammar "look like" the rules of G.

In this paper it is shown that grammar form theory provides a natural way of describing how certain types of ambiguities arise in grammars. Every grammar form whose grammatical family (the set of languages generated by interpretation grammars) is neither the regular sets nor the set of context-free grammars contain structural weaknesses with respect to the sets they generate. These weaknesses are based in the fact that regular sets may be introduced by any nonterminal that generates more than a finite set of strings. By generating such regular sets we may create overlapping sets in a language that cannot be separated by any interpretation grammar in a particular family of grammars. We can then regard L as being inherently ambiguous with respect to that family even though there are grammars in this same family that generate L. Since L is not inherently ambiguous we may with respect to all context-free grammars find another grammar with "more structure" that generates L unambiguously.

An example is $L = \{a^n b^n c^i d^j \mid n,i,j \geq 1\} \cup \{a^i b^j c^m d^m \mid i,j,m \geq 1\}$. Clearly L is linear but cannot be generated by any linear grammar unambiguously. Yet it is simple to find a context-free grammar that generates L unambiguously.

II. Preliminary Definitions and Concepts

Definition: A (context-free) grammar form $G = (V,\Sigma,P,S,)$ is a context-free grammar together with an associated universe of infinite symbols $\mathcal{V}$ that contain an infinite set of terminal symbols $\mathcal{S}$. In this paper G may be regarded either as a grammar or a grammar form. $\mathcal{V}$ and $\mathcal{S}$ are understood. An interpretation grammar G_I of G is a grammar obtained from a substitution (or interpretation) μ on V such that $\mu(a)$, $a \in \Sigma$, is a finite set of strings of symbols in $\mathcal{S}^*$ and $\mu(X)$, is a finite set of symbols in $\mathcal{V} - \mathcal{S}$ with the condition that if $X \neq Y$, for $X,Y \in V - \Sigma$, then $\mu(X) \cap \mu(Y) = \emptyset$. A finite set of rules from $\{\mu(X) \to \mu(a) \mid X \to \alpha \in P\}$ are the productions of G_I and S', the start symbol in G_I, is in $\mu(S)$. The family of grammars of G is $\mathcal{G}(G) = \{G_I | G_I$ is an interpretation grammar of $G\}$ while the gramatical family of G is $\mathcal{L}(G) = \{L(G_I) | G_I$ is an interpretation grammar of $G\}$. If $\mathcal{L}(G_1) = \mathcal{L}(G_2)$ then G_1 and G_2 are equivalent.

It is known from [CG] that $\mathcal{L}(G)$ is a full semi-AFL, $\hat{\mathcal{M}}(L(\tilde{G}))$, where $\tilde{G}$ is in $\mathcal{G}(G)$. Also we may select a grammar G' which is sequential and reduced and $\mathcal{L}(G) = \mathcal{L}(G')$. It is also known that if a reduced grammar form is expansive, that is, if $X \stackrel{+}{\Rightarrow} u_1Xu_2Xu_3 \stackrel{+}{\Rightarrow} u_1u_4u_2u_5u_3$ for some u_1,u_2,u_3 in Σ^* and u_4,u_5 in Σ^+ then $\mathcal{L}(G)$ is the entire set of context-free languages designated as $\mathcal{L}_{cf}$. The regular languages, $\mathcal{L}_{reg}$, are contained in every grammatical family $\mathcal{L}(G)$ unless $\mathcal{L}(G)$ is a set of finite or empty languages.

All grammars used in the following material are assumed to be context-free. Since the grammars discussed in this paper are nonexpansive, if $X \to \alpha X \beta$ is a production rule then α,β are in $(V - \{X\})^*$.

Definition: A production is repeating if $X \to \alpha X \beta$ and branching if $X \to \gamma$, $\alpha,\beta \in V^*$ and $\gamma \in (V - \{X\})^+$. Given a grammar $G = (V,\Sigma,P,S)$, then $G_X = (V,\Sigma,P,X,)$, where X is in $V - \Sigma$, and $L_X = L(G_X)$. If $\alpha \in V$ then $G_\alpha = (V\cup\{S_0\},\Sigma,P\cup\{S_0\to\alpha\},S_0)$. An X-production is a production with a nonterminal X on the left.

The convention that capital Latin letters are nonterminals, small Latin letters are strings of terminals, and small Greek letters are strings of mixed symbols will be used. Capital Greek letters will be saved for special purposes.

III. Separated Grammars and Matched Languages

Our objective in this section is to find a canonical form G_{SM}, called a separated matched grammar, for every derivation bounded grammar form G. The grammar form G_{SM} will be considered a canonical form for G if $\mathcal{L}(G_{SM}) = \mathcal{L}(G)$ and the grammar of G_{SM} is in some particular form. The canonical form we desire is one that reveals the "cyclic" structure of G. The construction of G_{SM} is begun by taking G', the sequential grammar equivalent to G, and forming a "separated" grammar G_S. Intuitively, a separated grammar G_S is one whose rules are divided into separate grammars G_i, $1 \leq i \leq j$, so that $G = G_1 \cup G_2 \cup \ldots \cup G_j$ and each nonterminal in G_i has exactly one repeating production and one branching production. The sequentialness of G' is vital to this construction. From G_S we construct G_{SM} by:

1) removing nonterminals that generate only regular sets,
2) replacing terminal symbols in production rules in G_S by "matched" pairs of a's and b's.

Regular sets contribute nothing to the analysis of G however, matched pairs can only be generated by nonterminals with nonregular production rules (Ogden's Lemma). Our final results on ambiguity come about because G_{SM} with its matched symbols has not enough nonterminals to generate a particular language L_0 unambiguously. The language L_0 is described in Section IV.

More formally, let $G = (V,\Sigma,P,S,)$ be a derivation bounded grammar form. By identifying nonterminals X_1 and X_2 such that $X_1 \overset{+}{\Rightarrow} \alpha_1 X_2 \beta_1$ and $X_2 \overset{+}{\Rightarrow} \alpha_2 X_1 \beta_2$ we may construct a grammar $G' = (V',\Sigma,P',S')$ such that $G \in \mathcal{G}(G')$, $\mathcal{L}(G) = \mathcal{L}(G')$ and G' is sequential. A grammar G' is <u>sequential</u> if every nonterminal in V' has an index X_i for some $i \geq 0$, and if $X_i \to \alpha X_j \beta$ then $i \leq j$. This construction was described in [CG]. Note the fact that in a sequential grammar if $X \overset{+}{\Rightarrow} \gamma \overset{+}{\Rightarrow} \alpha X \beta$ then X must occur in γ. For each nonterminal X let $X \to \alpha_i X \beta_i$, $1 \leq i \leq m$, and $X \to \gamma_\ell$, $1 \leq \ell \leq n$, be the set of a X-productions where γ_ℓ contains no occurrence of X. Then let $G'' = (V',\Sigma,P'',S')$ be the grammar where $P'' = \{X \to \alpha_1\alpha_2 \ldots \alpha_m X \beta_m \beta_{m-1} \ldots \beta_1, X \to \gamma_\ell \mid X \to \alpha_i X \beta_i, X \to \gamma_\ell$ is in P', $1 \leq i \leq m$, $1 \leq \ell \leq n\}$. In other words, all repeating X-productions are combined into one production. We may assume S appears only on the left without loss of generality.

<u>Lemma 1</u>: $\mathcal{L}(G) = \mathcal{L}(G'') = \mathcal{L}(G)$.

<u>Proof</u>: The nonrepeating productions $X \to \gamma_\ell$ of P' and P'' are the same. Any repeating production $X \to \alpha_k X \beta_k$ for some $k \in \{1,\ldots,m\}$, in P' can be "simulated" by an interpretation of $X \to \alpha_1\alpha_2 \ldots \alpha_m X \beta_m \ldots \beta_1$ where α_k, β_k are interpreted as themselves and all other α_i, β_i can derive only e, the empty string. This shows $\mathcal{L}(G') \subseteq \mathcal{L}(G'')$. To show the converse we note that $X \to \alpha_1 \ldots \alpha_m X \beta_m \ldots \beta_1$ can be "simulated" by applying the rules $X \to \alpha_i X \beta_i$, $1 \leq i \leq m$, in a chain so that $X \to \alpha_1 X_1 \beta_1$, $X_1 \to \alpha_2 X_2 \beta_2, \ldots, X_{j-1} \to \alpha_j X \beta_j$. So $\mathcal{L}(G'') \subseteq \mathcal{L}(G')$.

Let $G''' = (V''',\Sigma,P''',S')$ be the grammar such that $\mathcal{L}(G'') = \mathcal{L}(G''')$ and each rule in P''' has the property that if $X \to \alpha U \beta V \gamma$ then $U \neq V$. Also, if $X \to \eta$ and $Y \to \nu$ are different rules in P''' and $\nu = \pi Z \delta$ then $\eta = \mu Z \gamma$ only if $Y = Z$ or if $X = Z$. Put differently, a nonterminal may not appear twice on the right side of a production and a nonterminal Z may appear in two different productions on the right only if one of those productions is a Z-production. This construction is given in [BG]. The grammar G''' is also sequential.

Let $\mathcal{T} = \{T \mid T$ is a derivation tree in G''' and no path in T has a production appearing more than once$\}$. Clearly $\mathcal{T}$ is a finite set of trees. Since each nonterminal has at most one repeating production and one branching production that means a nonterminal may appear on any path at most twice and, by our construction of G''', at most twice in a tree. Now we rename all nonterminals on a tree T except S'. Each tree $T_i \in \mathcal{T}$ in G''' $1 \leq i \leq h$, has associated with it a grammar $G_i = (V_i,\Sigma, P_i,S')$ where $V_i = \Sigma \cup \{X \mid X$ is a label of a node in the T_i tree$\}$. More formally, let $\mathcal{T}$ be the trees, as above in G''' and $\lambda(\bar{n})$ the label on node $\bar{n}$ then $V_s =$

$\{X_i | \bar{n} \in T_i, \lambda(\bar{n}) = X, T_i \in \mathfrak{T},$ for each $i, 1 \leq i \leq h,$ and $X \neq S'\} \cup \Sigma \cup \{S'\}$,
$P_s = \{X_i \to w_1(Y_1)_i\ w_2(Y_2)_i \ldots w_n(Y_n)_i\ w_{n+1} | X \to w_1Y_1w_2Y_2\ldots w_nY_nw_{n+1}$ is a production on the T_i tree in $\mathfrak{T}$, $X_i = S'$ if $X = S'\}$. Then $G_s = (V_s, \Sigma, P_s, S')$ and G_s is called a separated grammar because each production rule in G_s can be found on one and only one node of a tree in $\mathfrak{T}$. Hence each production is "separated" from the others. Note that G_s is sequential and $G_s = \bigcup_{i=1,h} G_i'$, where G_i' is the grammar of the ith tree in G_s.

Definition: A separated matched language (SML) L is a subset of $\{a,b\}^*$ such that:

1) $L_e = \{e\}$ is a SML.
2) $L_0 = \{a^nb^n | n \geq 1\}$ is a SML.
3) If L_1 and L_2 are SML's then L_1L_2 is a SML and L_1^* is a SML.
4) If L_1, L_2, L_3 are SML's then

   $\{w_1^k w_2 w_3^k | w_1 \in L_1, w_2 \in L_2, w_3 \in L_3, k \geq 1\}$ is a SML and

   $\{a^n w_2 b^n, a^n w_2 w_3^n, w_1^n w_2 b^n | n \geq 1, w_1 \in L_1, w_2 \in L_2, w_3 \in L_3, L_2 \neq \{e\}$ and $L_1 \neq \{e\}\}$.

In the section below we show that each separated grammar G_S has a grammar G_{SM} such that $\mathcal{L}(G_{SM}) = \mathcal{L}(G_S) = \mathcal{L}(G)$ and $L(G_{SM})$ is a union of separated matched languages. We rely heavily upon the fact that G_S is sequential and has at most one repeating production, that is, a production of the type $X \to \alpha X \beta$.

In [CG] it was shown that for any grammar form G it is decidable if $\mathcal{L}(G)$ is empty, finite, contains only the empty string, or is regular. Also if $\mathcal{L}(G)$ is infinite we may find an interpretation of G which is either finite or contains only the empty string. This construction is trivial and will not be described.

Let $G_{S_1} = (V_S \cup \{c\}, \Sigma \cup \{c\}, P_{S_1}, S')$ be the grammar:

$$P_{S_1} = \left\{X \to \alpha c \beta | X \to \alpha Y \beta,\ \mathcal{L}(G_Y) \subseteq \mathcal{L}_{reg} \text{ but } \mathcal{L}(G_Y) \neq \{\{e\}\}\right\}$$

Then G_{S_1} has a c replacing each nonterminal Y in G where $\mathcal{L}(G_Y) \subseteq \mathcal{L}_{reg}$ but $\mathcal{L}(G_Y) \neq \{\{e\}\}$. An example of why a c must replace a nonterminal Y is shown by the equivalent grammar forms:

$$G_A = (\{S,B,a\}, \{a\}, \{S \to aSB, B \to a, S \to e\}, S) \text{ and}$$

$$G_B = (\{S,a\}, \{a\}, \{S \to aSa, S \to e\}, S).$$

Equivalence is only maintained if B is replaced by a terminal symbol and not e.

Lemma 2: $\mathcal{L}(G_S) = \mathcal{L}(G_{S1}) = \mathcal{L}(G)$.

Proof: We may easily construct a $G'_{S1} \in \mathcal{G}(G_S)$ such that $L(G'_{S1}) = L(G_{S1})$ and $\mathcal{L}(G'_{S1}) = \mathcal{L}(G_{S1}) \subseteq \mathcal{L}(G_S)$. Specifically if $\mathcal{L}(G_Y) \subseteq \mathcal{L}_{reg} - \{\{e\}\}$, then $Y \stackrel{+}{\Rightarrow} c$ (only). Conversely, let G''_{S1} be the generator of the full semi-AFL of $\mathcal{L}(G'_{S1})$. The symbols c_i will replace c in this construction and $\mathcal{L}(G'_{S1}) = \mathcal{L}(G''_{S1})$. To complete the proof we need only run $L(G''_{S1})$ through an a-transducer that replaces each c_i with a regular set. So $\mathcal{L}(G_S) \subseteq \mathcal{L}(G'_{S1}) = \mathcal{L}(G_{S1})$.

The next grammar G_{S2} replaces strings in Σ^+ in production rules in G_{S1} with the letters e and c.

Let $G_{S2} = ((V_{S1} - \Sigma) \cup \{c\}, \{c\}, P_{S2}, S')$ be a new grammar where:

$P_{S2} = \{X \to Y_1Y_2\ldots Y_n | n \geq 1, X \to w_1Y_1w_2\ldots w_nY_nw_{n+1}$ for all branching productions in $P_{S1}\} \cup \{X \to \mu_1Y_1\mu_2Y_2\ldots\mu_nY_n\mu_{n+1} |$

$X \to w_1Y_1w_2\ldots w_nY_nw_{n+1}$, $\mu_i = e$ if $w_i = e$, $\mu_i = c$

if $w_i \in \Sigma^+$ in P_{S1}, and $X = Y_k$ for some k, $1 \leq k \leq n\} \cup \{X \to c | X \to w \in P_{S1}\}$.

Lemma 3: $\mathcal{L}(G_{S1}) = \mathcal{L}(G_{S2}) = \mathcal{L}(G)$.
The techniques used to prove the above are straightforward and in the literature.

Finally, we are ready to "match" letters in repeating productions whose derivations reveal the cyclic structure of G. We take out the c and replace terminal symbols with matched a's and b's.
Define $G_{SM} = (V_{S2} - \{c\} \cup \{a,b\}, \{a,b\}, P_{SM}, S')$
where for all $X \to \alpha X \beta$ in P_{S1}:

$S_1 = \left\{X \to aXb | \text{ if } \mathcal{L}(G_\alpha) \subseteq \mathcal{L}_{reg} - \{\{e\}\}, \mathcal{L}(G_\beta) \subseteq \mathcal{L}_{reg} - \{\{e\}\}\right\}$.

$S_2 = \{X \to \Delta_1\Delta_2\ldots\Delta_n X\eta | \mathcal{L}(G_\alpha) \not\subseteq \mathcal{L}_{reg}, \mathcal{L}(G_\beta) \subseteq \mathcal{L}_{reg}$

$\alpha = \gamma_1Y_1\gamma_2\ldots\gamma_nY_n\gamma_{n+1}$, $\Delta_i = e$ if $\mathcal{L}_{Y_i}(G) = \{\{e\}\}$,

$\Delta_i = Y_i$ otherwise, $\eta = b$ if $\mathcal{L}(G_\beta) \neq \{\{e\}\}$, $\eta = e$ otherwise$\}$.

$S_3 = \{X \to \eta X\Delta_1\Delta_2\ldots\Delta_n | \mathcal{L}(G_\beta) \subseteq \mathcal{L}_{reg}, \mathcal{L}(G_\alpha) \subseteq \mathcal{L}_{reg}$,

$\beta = \gamma_1Y_1\gamma_2Y_2\ldots\gamma_nY_n\gamma_{n+1}$ $\eta = a$ if $\mathcal{L}(G_\alpha) \neq \{\{e\}\}$

$\eta = e$ otherwise, $\Delta_i = Y_i$ if $\mathcal{L}_{Y_i}(G) \neq \{\{e\}\}$, $\Delta_i = e$ otherwise$\}$

$S_4 = \{X \to \phi_1\phi_2\ldots\phi_j X\Delta_1\ldots{}_k | \mathcal{L}(G_\alpha) \not\subseteq \mathcal{L}_{reg}, \mathcal{L}(G_\beta) \not\subseteq \mathcal{L}_{reg}$,

$\alpha = w_1Y_1\ldots w_nY_nw_{n+1}$, $\phi_i = Y_i$ if $\mathcal{L}(G_{Y_i}) \neq \{\{e\}\}$,

$\phi_i = e$ otherwise. Similarly for $\Delta_1\ldots\Delta_k$.$\}$

$S_5 = \{X \to \Delta_1\ldots\Delta_n | X \to w_1Y_1\ldots w_nY_nw_{n+1}$ in P_{S_2}

$\Delta_i = Y_i$ if $\mathcal{L}(G_{Y_i}) \neq \{\{e\}\}$,

$\Delta_i = e$ otherwise$\}$.

$$S_6 = \{X \to e | X \to w \in P_{S_2}\} \cup \left\{X \to X | X \to \alpha X \beta,\ \mathcal{L}(G_\alpha) = \mathcal{L}(G_\beta) = \{\{e\}\}\right\}$$

$$P_{SM} = S_1 \cup S_2 \cup S_3 \cup S_4 \cup S_5 \cup S_6$$

Lemma 4: $\mathcal{L}(G_{SM}) = \mathcal{L}(G)$

The proof techniques used are similar to those in the literature and in the previous Lemmas.

Definition: A derivation in G_{SM} is sequential if $\alpha \Rightarrow \beta$ implies that $\alpha = \gamma X_i \eta$, $\beta = \gamma \delta \eta$, $p_i : X_i \to \delta$ and X_i is the nonterminal of lowest index in α. Note that if p is the production $X \to uXv$ then $X \overset{+}{\Rightarrow} u^k X v^k$, $k \geq 1$.

If each repeating production is written this way then a nonterminal will appear at most once in the generated expression and furthermore each tree in G_{SM} generates one and only one expression of a string expressed in powers of k.

Example:

$X_1 \to aX_1b \qquad X_2 \to aX_2b,\ X_2 \to e$

$X_1 \to X_2X_3 \qquad X_3 \to aX_3b,\ X_3 \to e$

$$X_1 \overset{+}{\Rightarrow} a^{k_1}X_1b^{k_1} \overset{+}{\Rightarrow} a^{k_1}X_2X_3b^{k_1}$$

$$\overset{+}{\Rightarrow} a^{k_1}a^{k_2}b^{k_2}a^{k_3}b^{k_3}b^{k_1}$$

Lemma 5: $L(G_{SM})$ is a union of separated matched languages.

Proof: Apply productions sequentially to the initial symbol S'. For each grammar G_k in G_{SM} we have a set of productions $p_1, \ldots, p_n$ and nonterminals $X_1, \ldots, X_m$, where X_m is the nonterminal of highest order. Observe that X_m has only branching production $X_m \to e$ and if X_m has a repeating production it can only be $X_m \to aX_mb$ so $L(G_{X_m})$ is a SML. Inductively it can be shown that if L_{X_j} is a SML then $L_{X_{j-1}}$ has a repeating production $X_{j-1} \to uX_{j-1}v$ then $X_{j-1} \overset{+}{\Rightarrow} u^kX_{j-1}u^k$. By induction L_u and L_v SML's and X_{j-1} has a branching production: $X_{j-1} \to Y_1 \ldots Y_\ell X_h Y_{\ell+1} \ldots Y_q$. By induction the L_{Y_i}'s are SML's and L_{X_h} is a SML.

Definition: Let $L(G_k)$ be a separated matched language. Let a^nb^n, $n \geq 1$, be a pair in the expression obtained from $L(G_K)$. Then $L(G_K)$ may be written as $\{\phi a^nb^n\psi | n \geq 1\}$ or as $\phi a^nb^n\psi$. Note that $\phi a^nb^n\psi$ does not imply the concatenation of ϕ and ψ to a^nb^n but rather ϕ represents the right side and ψ the left side in the particular expression generated by G_k.

Examples: 1) $L(G_k) = \{a^nb^n | n \geq 1\}$ then

$L(G_k) = \{\phi a^n b^n \psi \mid \phi = \psi = e\} = \phi a^n b^n \psi$

2) $L(G_k) = \{a^{n_1} a^{n_2} b^{n_2} a^{n_3} b^{n_3} a^{n_4} b^{n_4} b^{n_1} \mid n_i \geq 1,\ 1 \leq i \leq 4\}$ then

$L(G_k) = \{\phi a^{n_3} b^{n_3} \psi \mid n_3 \geq 1,\ \phi = a^{n_1} a^{n_2} b^{n_2},\ \psi = a^{n_4} b^{n_4} b^{n_1}\}$

$= L(G_k) = \phi a^{n_3} b^{n_3} \psi.$

IV. Results

Definition: A non trivial language L_0 is inherently ambiguous with respect to grammar form G if L_0 is in $\mathcal{L}(G)$ but for all G' in $\mathcal{G}(G)$ if $L_0 = L(G')$ then G' is ambiguous.

In this section we show how to construct a language L_0 in $\mathcal{L}(G_{SM})$ (hence in $\mathcal{L}(G)$) where L_0 is inherently ambiguous with respect to G_{SM}. In order to show L_0 is inherently ambiguous with respect to G we need an additional argument. The construction of a derivation bounded grammar G'' such that $L_0 = L(G'')$ and G'' is unambiguous is not difficult.

Let $G_{SM} = G_1 \cup G_2 \cup \ldots \cup G_j$ be a separated matched grammar (as previously defined) and each $G_k \subseteq G_{SM}$ is the separated matched grammar obtained from the finite derivation trees $T_k \subseteq \mathcal{T}$ used in the construction of separated grammars.

Definition: A subgrammar $G_i \subseteq G_{SM}$ is maximal if $\mathcal{L}(G_i) \subseteq \mathcal{L}(G_\ell)$ implies $\mathcal{L}(G_i) = \mathcal{L}(G_\ell)$, $1 \leq \ell \leq j$. If G_i is maximal then $L(G_i)$ is a maximal language.

In order to construct L_0 we begin with a maximal subgrammar G_m of G_{SM} and insert pairs $\{a^n b^n a^+ b^+ \mid n \geq 1\}$ and $\{a^+ b^+ a^n b^n \mid n \geq 1\}$ into $L(G_m)$. We select a nonterminal U and add productions $P_{m_1}: U \to X,\ X \to aX,\ X \to bY,\ Y \to bY,\ Y \to aZb,\ Z \to aZb,\ Z \to e$ to G_m to form G_{m_1} and productions $P_{m_2}: U \to X',\ X' \to X'b,\ X' \to Y'a,\ Y' \to Y'a,\ Y' \to aZ'b,\ Z' \to aZ'b,\ Z' \to e$ to G_m to form G_{m_2}. Then $L_0 = L(G_{m_1}) \cup L(G_{m_2})$. These productions need to be added to G_m to replace $U \to e$. If U is not a correctly chosen nonterminal then the addition of the productions above may not have the desired effect. Below is an algorithm to select a nonterminal U such that adding $P_{m_1} \cup P_{m_2}$ to P_m will create an ambiguous grammar.

Definition: Let T_m be the derivation tree (with one production per path) for G_m as described in the definition of separated grammar. Let $\bar{n}$ be a node on this tree. Then $G_{\bar{n}} = \{V_m, \Sigma_m, \tilde{P}_m, \lambda(\bar{n})\}$ where $\tilde{P}_m$ is the set of productions in G_m that are (labels) on nodes and descendents of $\bar{n}$. The reason we can't use the notation $G_{\lambda(\bar{n})}$ is because $\lambda(\bar{n})$ may appear on two distinct nodes in T_m. The maximal path algorithm

<u>to construct</u> L_0: Let $G_m \subseteq G_{SM}$ be a maximal separated matched subgrammar. G_m is sequential so we may consider the nonterminals of G_m to be ordered: $X_1, \ldots, X_\ell$. T_m is the corresponding derivation tree of G_m.

1. Let $X_1 \to u_1 X_{i_1} u_2 X_{i_2} \ldots u_n X_{i_n} u_{n+1}$ be the first production on T_M and $\lambda(\bar{n}_{i_k}) = X_{i_k}$, $1 \leq k \leq n$. Select some $\bar{n}_{i_k}$ such that $L(G_{\bar{n}_i})$ is maximal.
2. Using $\bar{n}_{i_k}$ as the starting node repeat the process selecting a node with a maximal language from the immediate descendents of $\bar{n}_{i_k}$. Continue until the last node which generates only terminals (in its associated production rules) is reached.
3. Let the last node obtained by this procedure be $\bar{n}_t$ where $\lambda(\bar{n}_t) = X_t$. The nonterminal X_t can only have productions of the type: $X_t \to aX_tb$, $X_t \to e$ (or $X_t \to X_{t_1}X_{t_2} \ldots X_{t_r}$, $X_{t_i} \to e$; $1 \leq i \leq r$, but this case is similar to $X_t \to e$ so we will only concern ourselves with the case $X_t \to e$). Add the following productions to P_m to get G_{m_1}:

$$G_{m_1} = (V_m \cup \{Y_1, Y_2, Y_3\},\ \Sigma_m, (P_m - \{X_t \to e\})$$
$$\cup \{X_t \to aY_1,\ Y_1 \to aY_1,\ Y_1 \to bY_2,\ Y_2 \to bY_2,$$
$$Y_2 \to aY_3b,\ Y_3 \to aY_3b,\ Y_3 \to e\}, X_1).$$

The language generated by G_{m_1} is $L(G_{m_1}) = \{\phi a^n a^+ b^+ a^i b^i b^n \psi \mid n,i \geq 1$

$a^n b^n$ is the pair generated by X_t, $L(G_m) = \phi a^n b^n \psi\}$.

To get G_{m_2} we generate the pair a^+b^+ on the other side of a^ib^i:

$$G_{m_2} = (V_m \cup \{Z_1, Z_2, Z_3\},\ \Sigma_m,\ (P_m - \{X_t - e\}) \subset \{X_t \to Z_1b,\ Z_1 \to Z_1b,\ Z_1 \to Z_2a,$$
$$Z_2 \to Z_2a,\ Z_2 \to aZ_3b,\ Z_3 \to aZ_3b,\ Z_3 \to e\}, X_1).$$ Now $L(G_{M_2}) =$ $\{\phi a^n a^i b^i a^+ b^+ b^n \psi \mid n,i \geq 1$, $a^n b^n$ generated by X_t in P_m and $L(G_m) = \phi a^n b^n \psi\}$.

<u>Definition</u>: A <u>maximal</u> <u>path</u> in T_m is a sequence of nodes $\bar{n}_1, \bar{n}_2, \ldots, \bar{n}_t$ where $\bar{n}_1$ is the root and $\bar{n}_2, \ldots, \bar{n}_t$ are nodes obtained (in that sequence) by using the maximal path algorithm.

<u>Theorem I</u>: L_0 is inherently ambiguous with respect to G_{SM}.

The proof of this Theorem depends directly on the two lemmas below.

<u>Lemma 6</u>: L_0 is inherently ambiguous with respect to G_m.

Proof (Outline): Using Ogden's Pumping Lemma it is easy to show that $L_p = \{a^n b^n a^+ b^+ \mid$

$n \geq 1\} \cup \{a^+b^+a^nb^n | n \geq 1\}$ cannot be generated unambiguously by a linear grammar. See [AU] and [Ha] for similar arguments. So if $G' \in \mathcal{G}(G_{\bar{n}_t})$ and $L(G') = L_p$ then G' is ambiguous. (The node $\bar{n}_t$ is the last node obtained by the maximal path algorithm hence has linear rules.) Assume there is some $\bar{n}_t'$ such that $G_{\bar{n}_t'}$ is unambiguous and $L_p = L(G_{\bar{n}_t'})$. Then $\mathcal{L}(G_{n_t}) \subseteq \mathcal{L}(G'_{n_t})$ since $\mathcal{L}(G'_{\bar{n}_t'})$ is not a linear family. Using the fact that $\bar{n}_t$ is on a maximal path and every node on the maximal path generates a maximal language we arrive at a contradiction when we consider the language families $\mathcal{L}(G_{\bar{n}_{t-1}})$, $\mathcal{L}(G_{\bar{n}_{t-2}})$, ... , $\mathcal{L}(G_{\bar{n}_1})$ by an inductive procedure.

The last case occurs if two different nodes generate strings in L_p. Using Ogden's Pumping Lemma once more we find there are strings $\phi w \psi = \phi a^\ell a^\ell b^\ell a^\ell b^\ell b^\ell \psi$ where $\ell = K + K!$ where K is as in Ogden's Lemma. But now w is generated by two different nodes so a grammar generating these strings is ambiguous.

Lemma 7: Let $G_{SM} = G_1 \cup G_2 \cup \dots \cup G_S$ and $L_0 = L(G_0)$ where $G_0 = (G_1' \cup G_1' \cup \dots \cup G_s'$, G_i' is in $\mathcal{G}(G_i)$, $1 \leq i \leq s$, and G_0 is unambiguous then $L_0 = L(G_0')$ where G_0' is in $\mathcal{G}(G_m)$ for some i, $1 \leq i \leq s$, and G_0' is unambiguous. Put in other words, if L_0 is generated unambiguously by a union of grammars in $\mathcal{G}(G_{SM})$, then L_0 is generated unambiguously by a grammar which is an interpretation of one $G_i'' \in \mathcal{G}(G_i)$.

Proof (Outline): First we consider the case where $G_0 = G_i' \cup G_k'$, G_i' in $\mathcal{G}(G_i)$ and G_k' in $\mathcal{G}(G_k)$ and $i \neq k$. Since the productions $P_i' \cap P_k' = \phi$ it can be shown that $L_0 = L(G_0')$ where G_0' is in $\mathcal{G}(G_i)$ or $\mathcal{G}(G_k)$ (and G_0' is unambiguous). Let $L = L_i' \cup L_k' = L(G_i') \cup L(G_k')$. Three cases must be considered:

i) If L_i' or L_k' is finite the result follows quickly.

ii) If $L_i' \subseteq L_k'$ or $L_k' \subseteq L_i'$ the result also follows quickly.

iii) If $L_i' - L_k'$ and $L_k' - L_k'$ are infinite then a more complicated argument needs to be made.

Rather than introducing the technical machinery needed to formally prove the lemma let

$$L_0 = \{a^na^mb^ma^ib^jb^n | n,i,j,m \geq 1\} \cup \{a^na^ib^ja^mb^mb^n | n,i,j,m \geq 1\} = L_1 \cup L_2$$

serve as an example of how the proof is done. The underlying grammar G_m generates $L(G_m) = \{a^nb^n | n \geq 1\}$ so if $L_0 = \{\phi_1 a^ib^j \psi_1 | i,j \geq 1\} \cup \{\phi_2 a^ib^j \psi_2\}$ where a^ib^j as above, then the substrings a^ib^j could only be generated by regular production rules (Ogden's Pumping Lemma) creating ambiguity in the grammar. But we still must consider the case where either L_1 or L_2 or both have infinite pairs generated by different grammars. Let Z be the integers greater than 0. So we have sets of the type:

$L_i'' \cup L_j'' = \{a^{n_1}a^{m_1}b^{m_1}a^{i_1}b^{j_1}b^{n_1},\ a^{n_2}a^{i_2}b^{j_2}a^{m_2}b^{m_2}b^{n_2} \mid n_q \in N_q,\ m_q \in M_q,\ i_q \in I_q,\ j_q \in J_q,$ $q \in \{1,2\}$, and $N_1 \cup N_2 = M_1 \cup M_2 = I_1 \cup I_2 = J_1 \cup J_2 = Z\}$, for either L_1 or L_2. Let L_i'' be the first and L_j'' be the second of the sets in the expression above. It can be shown that L_i'' and L_j'' are generated using productions of the type $X \to a^tXb^t$, $X \to a^tX$, $X \to Xa^t$, $X \to b^tX$, $X \to Xb^t$, where t is not always 1. However, such productions have interpretations that do allow $t = 1$, hence the grammar that generates L_i'' or L_j'' unambiguously will also generate $L_i'' \cup L_j''$ unambiguously.

To conclude the proof of Theorem 1 we must show that if $L_0 = L(G_0')$ and G_0' is unambiguous then G_0' is not in $\mathcal{G}(G_0)$, where G_0 is in $\mathcal{G}(G_i)$, G_i is a maximal subgrammar of G_{SM}. But the pair a^ib^j in L_1 and L_2 requires an additional nonterminal that generates a nonregular set by Ogdon's Pumping Lemma. This violates the maximality of G_0 so G_0' is not in $\mathcal{G}(G_{SM})$.

At this point we note that the construction of an unambiguous grammar by adding an additional nonterminal and for L_0 using the maximal path algorithm is very easy. From G_m we construct three unambiguous grammars $G_{m_3}, G_{m_4}, G_{m_5}$, for the sets

$$\{\phi a^{n_1}a^{n_2}b^{n_2}a^{n_3}b^{n_3}b^{n_1}\psi \mid n_1,n_2,n_3 \geq 1,\ \ \phi,\psi \text{ as in } L_0\},$$

$$\{\phi a^{n_1}a^{n_2'}b^{n_2}a^{n_3}b^{n_3}b^{n_1}\psi \mid n_1,n_2,n_2',n_3 \geq 1,\ \ n_2 \neq n_2',\ \ \phi,\psi \text{ as in } L_0\}$$
$$\cup \{\phi a^{n_1}a^{n_2}b^{n_2}a^{n_3}b^{n_3'}b^{n_1}\psi \mid n_1,n_2,n_3,n_3' \geq 1,\ \ n_3 \neq n_3',\ \ \phi,\psi \text{ as in } L_0\},$$

again by adding an additional nonterminal. That is, $X_t \to e$ is now replaced by $X_t \to T_1T_2$ and $T_1 \to aT_1b$, $T_1 \to e$, $T_2 \to aT_2b$, $T_2 \to e$.

Finally in the last theorem we reach our objective: The proof that L_0 is inherently ambiguous with respect to G.

<u>Theorem 2</u>: Let G be a grammar form such that $\mathcal{L}_{reg} \subsetneq \mathcal{L}(G) \subsetneq \mathcal{L}_{cf}$. Then there is an L_0 such that $L_0 = L(G')$ where G' is in $\mathcal{G}(G)$ and L_0 is inherently ambiguous with respect to G, but L_0 is not inherently ambiguous.

<u>Proof</u> (Outline): If $\mathcal{L}(G) \subsetneq \mathcal{L}_{cf}$ then G is derivation bounded. We now reexamine the proof of Theorem 1. The ambiguity of a $G_0, L_0 = L(G\ )$ and $G_0 \in \mathcal{G}(G_{SM})$ depends on the <u>positions</u> of terminals and nonterminals in productions. The grammar G is an interpretation of the sequential grammar G' used to obtain G_{SM}. Only nonterminals that generated regular sets in G' were removed to form G_{SM}. L_0 is ambiguous with respect to G_{SM} because certain nonterminals generating nonregular sets do not exist in positions in G_{SM} and G'. We can show L_0 is ambiguous with respect to G' so it follows that any grammar in $\mathcal{G}(G)$ that generates L_0 is

ambiguous.

V. Associated Research Problems and Conclusions.

Theorem 2, and its proof, show that inherent ambiguity in grammar forms is a direct result of the generating power of particular nonterminals. Some additional research should provide us with an answer as to how any possible structural ambiguity can arise with a family of similar grammars.

In general, the classification and description of types of ambiguities and degrees of ambiguity is a problem that should be studied by using grammatical families.

Acknowledgment: The subject was selected and the theorems formulated with the help of Professor Seymour Ginsburg of The University of Southern California. I wish to thank Professor Ginsburg for his help and suggestions.

References:

[AU] Aho, A., Ullman, J., The Theory of Parsing, Compiling and Translation, Vol. I, Prentice-Hall (1972).

[BG] Blattner, M., and Ginsburg, S., "Position Restricted Grammar Forms." Submitted.

[CG] Cremers, A. B., Ginsburg, S., "Context-free grammar forms." JCSS 11, (1975), pp. 86-117.

[Ha] Harrison, M., Formal Languages, Addison Wesley (1978).

[Og] Ogden, W., "A helpful result for proving inherent ambiguity." Math. Systems Theory 2:3 (1968), pp. 191-194.

* This research was supported in part by NSF Grant No. MCS 77-02470.

REPRESENTING COMPLEXITY CLASSES BY EQUALITY SETS†

(Preliminary Report)

Ronald V. Book and Franz-Josef Brandenburg

Department of Mathematics
University of California at Santa Barbara
Santa Barbara, Ca. 93106, U.S.A.

Recently there have been a number of new results regarding the decidability or undecidability of certain combinatorial questions about formal languages, grammars, L-systems, homomorphisms, and other types of mappings [2,5,7]. These results are based on three related characterizations of the class of recursively enumerable sets.

Let h_1, h_2 be homomorphisms with a common domain in Σ^*. Define the <u>equality set</u> $Eq(h_1,h_2)$ <u>of</u> h_1, h_2 as $Eq(h_1,h_2) = \{w \mid h_1(w) = h_2(w)\}$. A <u>DGSM mapping</u> $g : \Sigma^* \to \Delta^*$ is a function computed by a deterministic generalized sequential machine with accepting states. For any function $f : \Sigma^* \to \Sigma^*$, the <u>fixed-point language</u> $Fp(f)$ <u>of the function</u> f is defined to be $Fp(f) = \{w \in \Sigma^* \mid f(w) = w\}$. For any language L, let $MIN(L) = \{x \in L \mid$ there is no nonempty y such that $xy \in L\}$.

<u>Proposition</u>. Let L be a language. The following are equivalent:

(i) L is recursively enumerable;

(ii) there exist a pair (h_1,h_2) of homomorphisms and a DGSM mapping g such that $g(Eq(h_1,h_2)) = L$ [7];

(iii) there exists a DGSM mapping g and a homomorphism h such that $h(Fp(g)) = L$ [5];

(iv) there exist homomorphisms h_0, h_1, h_2 such that $h_0(MIN(Eq(h_1,h_2))) = L$ [2].

In each case the proof proceeds by showing that the set of accepting computations of a Turing machine or the set of proper derivations of a phrase structure grammar can be encoded in the appropriate way. The fact that certain questions are undecidable follows immediately from the fact that the system under study forms a basis for the class of all recursively enumerable sets.

In this paper we approach equality sets as part of the study of complexity classes of formal languages and exploit the equality

---

† This research was supported in part by the National Science Foundation under Grant MCS77-11360. The work of the second author was also supported by the German Academic Exchange Service under Grant No. 430/402/777/9.

mechanism in its purest and simplest form. Using the basic encoding strategy employed by Salomaa [7], we pay strict attention to the amount of time and space used in the accepting computations of a Turing machine, and we show that many classes such as NP, the Grzegorcyzk classes, and PSPACE can be represented in terms of equality sets of pairs of homomorphisms.

Culik [3] and Engelfriet and Rozenberg [5] have studied a specific equality set with very interesting properties. Let $0, 1, \bar{0}, \bar{1}$ be four symbols. Let g be the homomorphism determined by defining $g(0) = \bar{0}$ and $g(1) = \bar{1}$. Let $L_{\{0,1\}} = \{x_1y_1 \ldots x_ny_n \mid x = x_1 \ldots x_n, g(x) = y_1 \ldots y_n, x \in \{0,1\}^*\}$. The language $L_{\{0,1\}}$ is called the <u>complete twin shuffle</u> language. For homomorphisms h_1, h_2 determined by defining $h_1(a) = h_2(\bar{a}) = a$ and $h_1(\bar{a}) = h_2(a) = e$ for $a \in \{0,1\}$, it is the case that $L_{\{0,1\}} = Eq(h_1,h_2)$. It is shown in [3,5] that $L_{\{0,1\}}$ is a full principal semiAFL generator for the class of all recursively enumerable sets.

While $L_{\{0,1\}}$ is the equality set for a pair of homomorphisms, it is shown here that $L_{\{0,1\}}$ cannot be the equality set for a pair of homomorphisms if either is nonerasing. On the other hand, we show that equality sets of pairs of nonerasing homomorphisms can be used to represent accepting computations of Turing machines and that this power is sufficient to enable us to represent complexity classes when we use the notion of "balance" of homomorphisms.

The results presented in Sections 2 and 3 are closely related to those in [2-5]. However, by considering both the time and the space used by a Turing machine, our representations for the language recognized by a Turing machine are very tight. Further, these representations lead to characterizations of a wide variety of complexity classes of formal languages specified by time-bounded or space-bounded machines.

Let h_1, h_2 be homomorphisms. Define the <u>equality set of</u> h_1, h_2 by $Eq(h_1,h_2) = \{w \mid h_1(w) = h_2(w)\}$. A language L such that for some pair (h_1,h_2) of homomorphisms $Eq(h_1,h_2) = L$ is an <u>equality set</u>.

Note that there are equality sets that are regular, or context-free and nonregular, or non-context-free. For example, if $L_1 = \Sigma^*$ and for each $a \in \Sigma$, $h_1(a) = h_2(a)$, then $Eq(h_1,h_2) = L_1$; if $L_2 = \{w \in \{a,b\}^* \mid$ the number of a's in w equals the number of b's in $w\}$ and $g_1(a) = g_2(b) = a$ and $g_1(b) = g_2(a) = e$, then $Eq(g_1,g_2) = L_2$; if $L_3 = \{cb^2a^4b^8 \ldots a^{2^{n-2}}b^{2^{n-1}}d^{2^n} \mid n \geq 1\}$ and $f_1(a) = f_1(d) = a$,

$f_1(b) = b$, $f_1(c) = c$, $f_2(a) = b^2$, $f_2(b) = a^2$, $f_2(c) = cb^2$, $f_2(d) = e$, then $Eq(f_1,f_2) = L_3$.

It is clear that every equality set is recursive. In fact, every equality set can be recognized in linear time by a deterministic Turing machine with one work tape. Also, every equality set can be recognized by a deterministic Turing machine that uses only $\log n$ work space.

Let $L \subseteq \Sigma^*$ be a language and let $h : \Sigma^* \to \Delta^*$ be a homomorphism. If f is a function such that for some $k > 0$ and for all but finitely many $w \in L$, $|w| \leq kf(|h(w)|)$, then we say that h _is_ f-_erasing_ _on_ L.

Theorem 1. Let M be a Turing machine, let T be the function that measures M's running time and let S be the function that measures the space M uses. Then there exist homomorphisms h_0, h_1, h_2 and a regular set R such that $h_0(Eq(h_1,h_2) \cap R) = L(M)$ and h_0 is $T \cdot S$-erasing on $Eq(h_1,h_2) \cap R$.

While Theorem 1 uses equality sets, regular sets, and homomorphisms instead of fixed points of DGSM mappings or minimal subsets of equality sets, the essential difference between Theorem 1 and the Proposition stated earlier is the attention paid to the time and space bounds and the amount of erasing allowed.

It is important to note that Theorem 1 allows us to represent the set of accepting computations of a Turing machine in a simple way. If the running time and the work space of a Turing machine are unbounded, then a nonrecursive set may be accepted. In this case the actual running time and the actual work space used are bounded by partial recursive functions. Since each set of the form $Eq(h_1,h_2) \cap R$ is clearly recursive, we see that the class of all such sets forms a "basis" for the class of recursively enumerable sets since each recursively enumerable set is the homomorphic image of a set of the form $Eq(h_1,h_2) \cap R$. Thus all of the "usual" questions such as finiteness, emptiness, equality are undecidable [8]. This will be true for the class of fixed points of DGSM mappings, etc., for exactly the same reason.

For a time bound T, let $NTIME(T) = \{L(M) \mid M$ is a nondeterministic multitape Turing machine that runs in time $T\}$. If $\mathcal{B}$ is a class of time bounds, then let $NTIME(\mathcal{B}) = \bigcup_{T \in \mathcal{B}} NTIME(T)$. Similarly, for a space bound S, let $NSPACE(S) = \{L(M) \mid M$ is a nondeterministic Turing machine that uses space $S\}$, and if $\mathcal{B}$ is a class of space bounds, then let $NSPACE(\mathcal{B}) = \bigcup_{S \in \mathcal{B}} NSPACE(S)$. As special cases, let NP be the class of languages accepted by nondeterministic Turing machines that run in polynomial time and let PSPACE be the class of languages accepted by Turing machines that use polynomial space.

Let $\mathcal{B}$ be a class of functions that serve as time bounds. Such a class $\mathcal{B}$ is said to be a good class if it has the following properties:

(i) there exists a function t in $\mathcal{B}$ such that for all $n \geq 0$, $t(n) \geq n^2$;

(ii) $\mathcal{B}$ is closed under composition.

Notice that each of the following classes of times bounds is good: the class of polynomials; for each $k \geq 3$, the Grzegorzcyk class ξ^k; the class of primitive recursive functions; the class of total recursive functions. We will provide new characterizations of classes of languages of the form NTIME($\mathcal{B}$) for good classes $\mathcal{B}$. To do so we must make certain definitions.

Let $\mathcal{B}$ be a class of functions. Let $L \subseteq \Sigma^*$ be a language and let $h : \Sigma^* \to \Delta^*$ be a mapping. The mapping h is $\mathcal{B}$-erasing on L if for some function $f \in \mathcal{B}$, h is f-erasing on L. A class $\mathcal{B}$ of languages is closed under $\mathcal{B}$-erasing homomorphisms (DGSM mappings) if for every $L \in \mathcal{L}$ and every homomorphism (DGSM mapping) h that is $\mathcal{B}$-erasing on L, $h(L) \in \mathcal{L}$.

Theorem 2. Let $\mathcal{B}$ be a good class of time bounds. The class NTIME($\mathcal{B}$) is the smallest class containing all equality languages and closed under $\mathcal{B}$-erasing homomorphisms and intersection with regular sets.

Theorem 2 provides representations for each of the following classes of languages:

(a) NP;

(b) for each $k \geq 3$, the class ξ_*^k of languages accepted by Turing machines that run within time bounds in the Grzegorcyzk class ξ^k;

(c) the class of primitive recursive sets;

(d) the class of recursive sets.

Now we turn to representations of PSPACE.

Let R be a binary relation on strings over an alphabet Σ.

The relation R is length-preserving if for all x, y, when R(x,y) holds, then $|x| = |y|$. Let R^* be the transitive reflexive closure of R. If # is a symbol not in Σ, then let $SE_\#(R) = \{x \# y \mid x, y \in \Sigma^*$ and $R(x,y)$ holds$\}$. If $L \subseteq \Sigma^*$ and $a \in \Sigma$, let $R_a(L) = \{\langle x,y \rangle \mid x, y \in (\Sigma - \{a\})^*$ and $xay \in L\}$.

A class $\mathcal{L}$ of languages is weakly transitively closed [1] if the following condition holds: Let $L \in \mathcal{L}$, let Σ be a finite alphabet such that $L \subseteq \Sigma^*$, and let $a \in \Sigma$. If $R_a(L)$ is length-preserving, then $SE_a(R_a^*(L)) \in \mathcal{L}$.

Theorem 3. The class PSPACE is the smallest weakly transitively closed class containing all equality languages and closed under intersection with regular sets and polynomial-erasing homomorphisms.

Theorem 3 follows immediately from Theorem 2 and the techniques of [1]. It should be noted that the representation given in Theorem 3 can be generalized to other classes of languages specified by space-bounded machines. However, as soon as a class $\mathcal{B}$ of space bounds contains a function that majorizes 2^n and is closed under composition, then NSPACE($\mathcal{B}$) = NTIME($\mathcal{B}$) as long as the class $\mathcal{B}$ is suitably well behaved. Thus no new information is gained from generalizing Theorem 3.

In [5] a "hardest" equality set is introduced. For strings $x, y \in \Sigma^*$, let $\text{shuffle}(x,y) = \{x_1y_1x_2y_2 \ldots x_ny_n \mid x = x_1\ldots x_n, y = y_1\ldots y_n\}$ and let $L_\Sigma = \cup\{\text{shuffle}(w,\bar{w}) \mid w \in \Sigma^*\}$. Note that $L_\Sigma = Eq(h_1,h_2)$ where $h_1(a) = h_2(\bar{a}) = a$ and $h_1(\bar{a}) = h_2(a) = e$ for $a \in \Sigma$. In [5] it is shown that the class of all equality sets is the smallest class containing $L_{\{0,1\}}$ and closed under inverse homomorphism. This means that Theorems 1-3 can be reformulated in terms of $L_{\{0,1\}}$ and closure under inverse homomorphism. In this form Theorem 1 yields as a corollary the fact that $L_{\{0,1\}}$ is a full principal semiAFL generator (and also a cylinder generator) for the class of all recursively enumerable sets.

Let us point out a combinatorial property of sets of the form L_Σ.

Lemma 4. For any finite alphabet Σ with at least two elements, the language L_Σ cannot be represented as the equality set of two homomorphisms if either homomorphism is nonerasing, i.e., if $L_\Sigma = Eq(h_1,h_2)$, then both h_1 and h_2 are erasing.

In contrast to Lemma 4, notice that for homomorphisms h_1, h_2 from Σ^* to $\{a\}^*$, where a is a single symbol, the set $Eq(h_1,h_2)$ is a context-free language [7], in fact, it is a deterministic one-counter language. Further, for every pair (h_1,h_2) of homomorphisms mapping Σ^* to $\{a\}^*$, there exists a pair (h_1',h_2') of nonerasing homomorphisms such that $Eq(h_1',h_2') = Eq(h_1,h_2)$--for every $b \in \Sigma$ define $h_1'(b) = h_1(b)a$ and $h_2'(b) = h_2(b)a$.

We will show that, in contrast to Lemma 4, equality sets of nonerasing homomorphisms have the power to represent accepting computations of certain restricted Turing machines and that this power is sufficient to enable us to represent complexity classes. To accomplish this we need the notion of "balance" of homomorphisms.

Consider a pair of homomorphisms (h_1,h_2) from Σ^* to Δ^* and a word x in Σ^*. Then, the <u>balance of</u> x is defined by $bal(x) = |h_1(x)| - |h_2(x)|$.

Let $f : N \to N$ be a bounding function. A <u>pair of homomorphisms</u> (h_1,h_2) has <u>f-bounded balance on a language</u> L if for every x in L and each prefix y of x, $abs(bal(y)) \leq f(|x|)$, where for any integer i, $abs(i)$ is the absolute value of i.

If the pair (h_1,h_2) has f-bounded balance on $Eq(h_1,h_2)$, then (h_1,h_2) is said to have f-bounded balance and $Eq(h_1,h_2)$ is called an <u>equality set with f-bounded balance</u>.

Let $\hat{EQ}(f)$ $(EQ(f))$ denote the <u>family of equality sets</u> $Eq(h_1,h_2)$ <u>with f-bounded balance</u> (where h_1, h_2 are nonerasing homomorphisms), and for a family $\mathcal{F}$ of bounding functions, let $\hat{EQ}(\mathcal{F}) = \bigcup_{f\in\mathcal{F}} \hat{EQ}(f)$ and $EQ(\mathcal{F}) = \bigcup_{f\in\mathcal{F}} EQ(f)$.

For every $x \in \Sigma^*$ and every pair (h_1,h_2) of homomorphisms on Σ^*, $abs(bal(x)) \leq k|x|$ where $k = \max\{abs(|h_1(a)| - |h_2(a)|) \mid a \in \Sigma\}$. Thus every pair of homomorphisms has linear-bounded balance on every language in the domain of the homomorphisms. Also, notice that for every f, $Eq(f) \subseteq \hat{Eq}(f)$, and if f and g are functions such that for all $n \geq 0$, $f(n) \leq g(n)$, then $\hat{Eq}(f) \subseteq \hat{Eq}(g)$ and $Eq(f) \subseteq Eq(g)$.

It is known [2,3,7] that for any pair (h_1,h_2) of homomorphisms, the set $Eq(h_1,h_2)$ is regular if and only if $Eq(h_1,h_2)$ has f-bounded balance for some function f such that there exists k with the property that for all $n > 0$, $f(n) \leq k$. In [11] it is shown that if M is a deterministic Turing machine that reads its input in only one direction and is f-space bounded, then $L(M)$ non-regular implies that $\liminf \frac{f(n)}{\log n} > 0$.

<u>Theorem 5</u>. If L is an equality set with f-bounded balance and L is not regular, then $\liminf \frac{f(n)}{\log n} > 0$.

Bounds on the balance can also be obtained for equality sets that are of the form L_Σ.

<u>Lemma 6</u>. For every alphabet Σ containing at least two elements, if h_1, h_2 are homomorphisms such that $Eq(h_1,h_2) = L_\Sigma$, then (h_1,h_2) has f-bounded balance where f is such that $\limsup \frac{f(n)}{n} > 0$.

Thus we conclude that for any alphabet Σ with at least two elements, the language L_Σ can be represented as $Eq(h_1,h_2) = L$ only if both h_1 and h_2 are erasing (and one-to-one) and the pair (h_1,h_2) has linear bounded balance.

Now we return to the representation of complexity classes by considering pairs of nonerasing homomorphisms.

Theorem 7. Let M be a Turing machine, let T be the function that measures M's running time, and let S be the function that measures how much space M uses. Then there exist a pair (α,β) of nonerasing homomorphisms, a homomorphism γ, and a regular set R such that $\gamma(Eq(\alpha,\beta) \cap R) = L(M)$, γ is g-erasing on $Eq(\alpha,\beta) \cap R$, where $g(n) = S(n)T(n)$, and (α,β) has S-bounded balance on $Eq(\alpha,\beta) \cap R$.

As in Theorem 1, we have considered only single-tape Turing machines. However, results similar to both Theorem 1 and also Theorem 7 can be obtained for multitape Turing machines by using a parallel encoding.

Note that in Theorem 7 the balance of (α,β) on $Eq(\alpha,\beta)$ is bounded by $f(n) = n^{1/2}$. For any Turing machine M there is a constant $k > 1$ such that if M operates within space bound S and time bound T, then for all $n > 0$, $n \leq S(n) \leq T(n) \leq k^{S(n)}$. Clearly the representation technique of Theorem 7 can be extended in order to represent complexity classes, and when doing so the balance bounds for equality sets of pairs of homomorphisms must range between "log-bounded balance," i.e., $\log n$-bounded balance, and "root-bounded balance," i.e., $n^{1/2}$-bounded balance.

Theorem 8. For every $L \in NTIME(n)$, there is a pair of nonerasing homomorphisms (h_1,h_2) with square-root-bounded balance, a regular set R and a homomorphism h, such that $L = h(Eq(h_1,h_2) \cap R)$, and h is n^3-erasing on $Eq(h_1,h_2) \cap R$.

In the last result the bound of n^3 on the amount of erasing allowed can be reduced to n^2 when the version of Theorem 7 for multitape machines is used.

Theorem 9. If $\mathcal{B}$ is a good class of time bounds, then $NTIME(\mathcal{B})$ is the smallest class containing all equality sets of nonerasing homomorphisms with root-bounded balance and closed under intersection with regular sets and under $\mathcal{B}$-erasing homomorphisms.

Theorem 10. For every (deterministic) context-sensitive language L, there is a pair of nonerasing homomorphisms (h_1,h_2) which have log-bounded balance, a regular set R and an exponential erasing homomorphic mapping h such that $L = h(Eq(h_1,h_2) \cap R)$.

Theorem 11. For every language $L \in PSPACE$ there is a pair of nonerasing homomorphisms (h_1,h_2) with log-bounded balance, a regular set R, and a homomorphism h such that $L = h(Eq(h_1,h_2) \cap R)$ and for some constants $c > 1$, $k > 0$, h is c^{n^k}-erasing on $Eq(h_1,h_2) \cap R$.

Notice that L_Σ is neither an equality set of a pair of nonerasing homorphisms nor an equality set with f-bounded balance for any function f with $\limsup \frac{f(n)}{n} = 0$. On the other hand, the class $\{L \cap R \mid L \in \mathrm{Eq(log)},\ R \text{ is regular}\}$ is a basis for the class of recursively enumerable sets, as well as many complexity classes.

Note that results similar to those in this section can be obtained by considering fixed-point languages and DGSM mappings.

Theorems 8-11 are similar to some results of Culik [3].

To see the relationship between the bounds on the balance and the bounds on the amount of erasing allowed, consider the following facts.

(1) A language L is regular if and only if there exist a (nonerasing) homomorphism h, an integer k, a language $L_0 \in \mathrm{Eq}(k)$, and a regular set R such that $h(L_0 \cap R) = L$.

(2) A language L is in NP if and only if there exist a homomorphism h, a language $L_0 \in \mathrm{Eq(root)}$, and a regular set R such that $h(L_0 \cap R) = L$ and h is polynomial-erasing on $L_0 \cap R$.

(3) A language L is in PSPACE if and only if there exist a homomorphism h, a language $L_0 \in \mathrm{Eq(log)}$, and a regular set R such that $h(L_0 \cap R) = L$ and h is f-erasing on $L_0 \cap R$, where for some $c > 1$, $k \geq 1$, and all n, $f(n) = c^{n^k}$.

(4) A language L is recursively enumerable if and only if there exist a homomorphism h, a language $L_0 \in \mathrm{Eq(linear)}$ (Eq(log)) and a regular set R such that $h(L_0 \cap R) = L$.

References

1. R. Book, Polynomial space and transitive closure, SIAM J. Computing, to appear.

2. K. Culik II, A purely homomorphic characterization of recursively enumerable sets, J. Assoc. Comput. Mach., to appear.

3. K. Culik II, On homomorphic characterization of families of languages, unpublished manuscript.

4. K. Culik II and H.A. Maurer, On simple representations of language families, RAIRO - Informatique Theorique, to appear.

5. J. Engelfriet and G. Rozenberg, Fixed point languages, equality languages, and representation of recursively enumerable languages, J. Assoc. Comput. Mach., to appear. An extended abstract appears in the Proceedings of the 19th IEEE Symposium on Foundations of Computer Science (1978), 123-126.

6. J. Hopcroft and J. Ullman, Formal Languages and Their Relation to Automata, Addison-Wesley, Reading, Mass., 1969.

7. A. Salomaa, Equality sets for homomorphisms of free monoids, Acta Cybernetica, to appear.

8. R. Smullyan, Theory of Formal Systems, Annals of Mathematics Studies, No. 47, Princeton University Press, 1961.

9. R. Stearns, J. Hartmanis and P. Lewis, Hierarchies for memory limited computations, Conference Record 6th IEEE Symp. on Switching Circuit Theory and Logical Design (1965), 179-190.

10. C. Wrathall, Remarks on languages and relations, in preparation.

SUPERCOUNTER MACHINES

B.v.Braunmühl
Institut für Informatik
Universität Bonn
Wegelerstraße 6
5300 Bonn

E.Hotzel
Gesellschaft für Mathematik
und Datenverarbeitung
Postfach 1240
5205 St.Augustin 1

Introduction. A pushdown automaton, deterministic or not, which recognizes a language L can always be replaced by a pushdown automaton that works in real-time, and therefore halts and uses at most a linear amount of tape in any computation. Moreover, a pushdown automaton can always be simulated by a deterministic Turing machine in $\log^2$-tape. It is an open question whether every context-free language can be recognized by a deterministic, or at least by a nondeterministic Turing machine in log-tape. It has been conjectured that not even an arbitrary deterministic pushdown automaton can be simulated deterministically in log-tape [9, 10].

From a different angle one may ask whether there are automata structures more general than the pushdown which can be simulated deterministically or nondeterministically in $\log^2$-tape. It is to be expected that the deterministic two-way pushdown automaton and, equivalently, the two-way pushdown automaton with auxiliary log-bounded tape are not within the nondeterministic $\log^k$-space complexity class for any k [1, 10, 6, 7], although the deterministic two-way pushdown automaton works on linear tape. It seems likely that the (one-way) nondeterministic stack automaton can also not be simulated nondeterministically in $\log^k$-tape. Only the nondeterministic one-way log-tape auxiliary pushdown automaton and the nondeterministic two-way log-tape auxiliary pushdown automaton working in polynomial time can be shown to be simulatable nondeterministically in $\log^2$-tape.

It remains to be seen whether there are natural types of automata which in contrast to the log-tape auxiliary pushdown automaton are not just defined by way of tape complexity conditions, and which are stronger than the one-way nondeterministic pushdown automaton, but are still in the nondeterministic complexity class of $\log^2$ space. There are several ways to find new automata types by formal means not involving complexity (cf. [8, 12]). One way, which occasionally has been indicated in the past (e.g. [1]), consists in considering automata as Turing machines with an input tape and with one or more working tapes together with restrictions on the form of the Turing machine instructions (cf. [11] for an investigation of one-way Turing machines with two strongly restricted working tapes). The instructions of a one-way Turing machine with one working tape can be given as 7-tuples (q,a,A,q',B,d_o,d_1) where A, B, and d_1 concern the working tape. Conditions which concern the working tape alone and can be verified on every instruction separately must then be formulated in terms of A, B, and d_1 by means of the formal constants □ (blank), 1, 0, -1 (right, remain, left) and propositional logic (together with the equality sign). It is well known that the condition

$$d_1 = -1 \Longrightarrow B = \square$$

can be used to define a pushdown machine (= automaton). Another example is the condition

$$(**) \quad A \neq \square \Longrightarrow (B \neq \square \text{ and } d_1 = -1).$$

A study of the corresponding 2^{12} (formally different) automata types has shown that there are exactly three maximal types one of which is the nonerasing stack automaton (the usual stack automaton is not found in this way) [13].

One of the three maximal types, which is just the one given by the above condition (**), will be investigated in this paper. We call these automata supercounter machines (SCM) since they are strictly more powerful than counter automata (in both the deterministic and the nondeterministic case) although they may be restricted to one non-blank working tape symbol. Nondeterministically a pushdown automaton can always be simulated by a supercounter machine but deterministically the supercounter is incomparable to the pushdown. A supercounter machine can always be nondeterministically simulated in $\log^2$-tape; it can also be shown that this simulation runs in polynomial time so that a deterministic simulation in $\log^3$-space can be achieved. With most of the known one-way automata and with the deterministic two-way pushdown automata the (one-way) SCMs have in common that they work on linear tape; in contrast to most of the known cases the halting SCMs are less powerful than arbitrary SCMs.

For the two-way SCMs (which are not considered in this paper) it can be shown that they can be nondeterministically $\log^2$-tape simulated as long as they work on polynomial tape. It is to be expected that the nondeterministic two-way SCMs cannot generally be restricted to polynomial tape since otherwise the deterministic polynomial-time languages would be recognizable in $\log^2$-tape [7].

<u>1. Definitions and basic properties.</u> We consider nondeterministic Turing machines with a one-way read-only input tape and with one working tape (which is infinite in both directions). A situation (instantaneous description) is defined to be a 5-tuple (q,w,W,i,j) which describes the state, the input word, the inscription on the working tape and the positions of the heads on the two tapes at some point of a computation. An instruction is a 7-tuple (q,a,A,q',B,d_o,d_1) from a set $Q\times\Sigma\times\Gamma\times Q\times\Gamma\times\{-1,0,1\}\times\{-1,0,1\}$. By such an instruction a Turing machine is allowed to turn from a situation (q,w,W,i,j) with w(i) = a, W(j) = A to a situation (q',w,W',i',j') with W'(j) = B, W'(l) = W(l) if $l \neq j$, $i' = i + d_o$ and $j' = j + d_1$. A sequence of situations, pairwise connected by way of an instruction, will be called a run. If such a sequence begins with $(q_o,w,\varepsilon,1,0)$ where q_o is the distinguished starting state (ε is an abbreviation to

indicate that the working tape is empty) and is maximal insofar it is not extendible by further situations then it is called a w-run. An input phase of a run R is a maximal connected subsequence of R whose situations have one and the same reading position on the input tape. If a is read by the input head we speak of an a-phase. We formally define an input change of a run R to be a situation with which an input phase begins; we also say that an input change takes place on the working tape cell which is scanned in such a situation. An empty segment of the working tape surrounded by non-blank symbols (A □ ... □ B) will occasionally be called a gap.

A word w is accepted by a Turing machine if there is a w-run that is finite and halts in a situation with a final state, i. e. a state belonging to the distinguished subset of accepting states. As usually, the set of all words accepted by a Turing machine M is called the language recognized by M, and two machines are called equivalent if they recognize the same language.

Occasionally we shall consider deterministic Turing machines whose characteristic property is that two instructions are equal if they are equal in each of the first three components. A halting Turing machine is a Turing machine whose w-runs are all finite.

Definition. A Turing machine is called a supercounter machine (SCM) if all instructions (q,a,A,q',B,d_o,d_1) of M satisfy

$$A \neq \square \Longrightarrow (B \neq \square \text{ and } d_1 \neq 1).$$

Without loss of generality we may require the sharper condition

$$A \neq \square \Longrightarrow (B = A \text{ and } d_1 \neq 1)$$

(even $d_1 = -1$ may be required) which will tacidly be done in the following. Intuitively, a supercounter machine is a Turing machine with a working tape on which every cell can be altered at most once and no non-empty cell can be traversed from left to right. The following fact is easily proved.

Proposition 1. For every SCM there is an equivalent one with just one non-blank working tape symbol (the property of being halting or deterministic can be preserved).

Hence a supercounter machine may be compared with a counter automaton which is allowed at times to print a new bottom symbol. Formally a counter machine may be defined by the conditions

$$A \neq \square \Longrightarrow B \neq \square$$

and

$$B \neq \square \Longrightarrow d_1 \neq -1.$$

The connection to the pushdown automata is given by the following statement.

<u>Theorem 1.</u> For every pushdown machine M there is an equivalent SCM M'.

Hint: if M prints a symbol then M' also prints that symbol and moves to the right over an arbitrary number of cells. If M is erasing then M' moves left across the next non-empty cell and goes some number of cells farther but possibly not as far as the following non-empty cell (otherwise M' rejects). M' always rejects if a non-empty cell is reached from the left.

That the (non-deterministic) SCMs are strictly more powerful than the pushdown automata is seen by the following fact:

$$\{ a^{n^2} \mid n \geq 0 \} \quad \text{is a supercounter language.}$$

In fact, considering $n^2 = 1 + 3 + \ldots + (2n-1)$, we may construct a supercounter machine for this language which nondeterministically works as follows:

(1) M prints # on the working tape, and then goes an arbitrary but odd number of cells to the right while synchronously reading the input tape, then prints *, (2).

(2) M arbitrarily moves left on the working tape, rejecting if # or an A is read. Then M prints A whereupon M moves right while synchronously reading the input tape until * is reached. If then (but not earlier) □ is read on the input tape (3), else (2).

(3) M moves left until # is reached while checking whether the A's are from the left onward on every second cell; if so, M accepts, if not, M rejects.

Observe that the SCM just described is halting. We shall see that there are deterministic pushdown languages that cannot be recognized by halting SCMs (Proposition 4). Therefore the halting SCMs are incomparable to the pushdown automata. The same holds in the deterministic case for we shall see that every deterministic SCM is equivalent to a halting deterministic SCM and we have the following example:

$$L_h = \{a_1^n a_2^n \ldots a_h^n \mid n \geq 0\} \quad \text{is a deterministic supercounter language}$$

(for every $h \geq 0$). We omit the proof of this and of the following fact.

<u>Proposition 2.</u> Every deterministic supercounter language over a one-symbol alphabet is regular.

We summarize the inclusion properties mentioned so far in the following diagram:

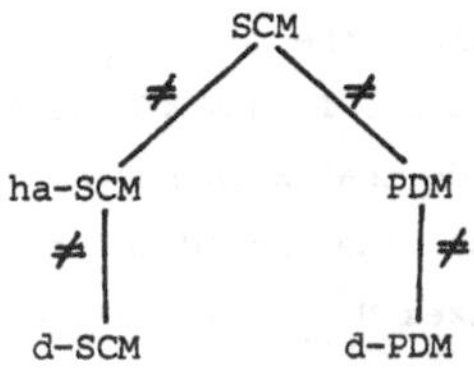

2. Halting supercounter automata. The following facts are repeatedly used in the proofs of some subsequent assertions. Observe that we are mostly dealing with non-deterministic machines.

Lemma 1. Let M be a one-way machine with k states. Let S be an a-phase of M which starts in state r on cell 1 of the working tape and ends in state t on the same cell and which is such that on the working tape precisely the cells from 1 up to n are read and that all of these cells are empty from beginning to end. Then there exists an a-phase S' of M which is not longer than S and which has the same data as S except that on the working tape precisely the cells from 1 up to n' are read for some $n' \leq k^2$. The corresponding holds if the input head does not remain on one cell during S but always reads the same input symbol a (the number of input cells scanned during S' may be smaller).

Lemma 2. Let M be a one-way machine with k states and let d be the least common multiple of {1,2,...,k}. There exists a number K with the following property:

Let $N^a_{r,t}$ be the set of numbers $n \geq 1$ such that there exists an a-phase of M which

(1) starts in state r on cell 1 of the working tape,

(2) ends in state t on cell n of the working tape,

(3) does not reach any cell to the left of cell 1 or to the right of cell n,

(4) has all cells from 1 up to n empty in all situations.

Then there exist numbers $r_1, r_2, \ldots, r_l \leq d$ with $l \leq d$ such that

$$\{n \mid n \in N^a_{r,t} \text{ and } n \geq K\} = \{n \mid n = jd + r_i \text{ for some } j \text{ and some } i,\ n \geq K\}.$$

Moreover, if S is an a-phase with properties (1) - (4) for some $n \in N^a_{r,t}$, $n \geq K + d$, then there is an a-phase S' with properties (1) - (4) for $n' = n - d$ which is strictly shorter than S. The corresponding holds if $N^a_{r,t}$ is defined with respect to runs of M during which the input head possibly reads different input cells but always finds the same symbol a (the number of input cells scanned may vary).

To prove the first of these lemmas we assume that the a-phase S is as short as possible and associate with every cell i, i = 1, 2, ..., n-1, the pair (p_i,q_i) where p_i is the state in the last situation of S in which cell i is read before cell n is reached whereas q_i is the state in the first situation in which cell i is reached thereafter; with cell n we associate the pair (p_n,p_n) where p_n is the state in which cell n is reached for the first time. If $n > k^2$ there must be two cells having the same pair which allows to conclude that S is not as short as possible. To see that the second lemma is at least plausible one should observe that a two-way finite automaton can be constructed which recognizes $N^a_{r,t}$. We shall use this lemma in the form of the following argument: An empty segment of the working tape of length $l \geq K + d$ $(l \geq K)$ which is entered and left only during single input phases (alternatively: during phases in which the same input symbol is read in all situations) can arbitrarily be replaced by a segment of length $l - d$ $(l + d)$ as long as none of these cells is printed upon and the changes of the lengths of the input phases are appropriate. We assume $K \geq k^2$ (k the number of states) so that by lemma 1 an input phase entering and leaving on the same side may be assumed to reach only k^2 cells.

A Turing machine is called strongly linear tape-bounded if the number of cells used in an arbitrary w-run (accepting resp. finite or not) is linearly bounded by the length of the input word w.

Proposition 3. Every strongly linear tape-bounded SCM is equivalent to a halting SCM, and conversely.

For the proof of the first part of the assertion it is suitable to deduce that in an input phase in which after a certain number of steps (depending on k^2) no non-blank symbol has been printed a further possibly successful movement may essentially retain one direction until a non-blank symbol is printed or the next lower non-empty cell is reached. The global movement can then be directed towards a cell with a non-blank symbol. Any gap is successively filled with non-blank symbols until it is left or acception or rejection can be foreseen. The converse part of the assertion is deduced by a consideration of states on consecutive empty cells outside of gaps.

Corollary. Every deterministic SCM is equivalent to a halting deterministic SCM.

Clearly every deterministic SCM can be so modified that it is strongly linear tape-bounded.

It has already been remarked that the deterministic SCMs are not less powerful than pushdown automata. We now show that they do not recognize all deterministic pushdown languages.

Proposition 4. $L = \{a^m b^n a^n b^m a^p b^q a^q b^p \mid m,n,p,q \geq 0\}$ cannot be recognized by any halting SCM.

Proof. Suppose that M is a halting (nondeterministic) SCM recognizing L. Let M have k states and just one non-blank working tape symbol A. We consider all words $w = a^m b^n a^n b^m a^p b^q a^q b^p$ with

$$m > k\cdot(k+K+d+k^2)^2, \quad n \geq m, \quad p > k^4\cdot(m+n+n+m)^3,$$

$$q > k\cdot(k\cdot(m+n+n+m+p+k\cdot(k\cdot(m+n+n+m+p)+K+d)^3)+k^2)^3 \quad \text{and (say)} \quad q \leq m^{100}$$

(here K and d are taken from lemma 2). The conditions imply that for every m satisfying the first inequality at most finitely many words $a^m b^n a^n b^m a^p b^q a^q b^p$ are considered (at least one). For every w under consideration an accepting w-run R is singled out which is as short as possible. In R the first A appears on the working tape after at most k steps; otherwise two among the first k+1 situations had the same state and an empty working tape so that either R could be made shorter or a word $a^{m'}b^n a^n b^m a^p b^q a^q b^p$ with $m' < m$ would also be accepted. Without loss of generality we may assume that the first A is printed on cell 0 while the input head still remains on the first input symbol. We shall distinguish whether or not in the first situation after $a^m b^n a^n b^m$ has been read (so that an a is read in this situation) all A's appear properly on the left side of the working tape head (case 1 and case 2, respectively).

Case 1. Let h_1 (h_2) be the working tape cell which is scanned in the first situation after a^m ($a^m b^n$) has been read. By lemma 1 the rightmost cell which is reached while a^m is read is at most h_1+k^2. Then $k\cdot(h_1+k^2)^2 \geq m$ for otherwise there would not be enough different situations (the number of working tape inscriptions, combined with head positions, that appear after the first A is printed and before b is read on the input tape is at most $h_1+k^2 + h_1-1+k^2 + \ldots + k^2$). We shall see that after $a^m b^n$ has been read at least one cell $C \geq h_1-(K+d)$ bears an A. If this was wrong we first distinguish whether or not h_2 is smaller than h_1. If h_2 is smaller than h_1 we observe that no cell greater than h_1+k^2-1 has been reached so far. Therefore, since $k\cdot(2k^2+K+d) < n$ we have $h_2 < h_1-(K+d)$. By lemma 2 we may change the run R by taking out d cells from the section from $h_1-(K+d)$ up to h_1 in the phase during which a^m is read as well as in the phase during which b^n is read (h_1 is replaced by h_1-d, h_2 remains and $a^m b^n$ is possibly replaced by $a^{m'}b^{n'}$ with $a^{m'}b^{n'} \neq a^m b^n$). Thereby a shorter run is obtained so that either R is not as short as possible or a word $a^{m'}b^{n'}a^n b^m a^p b^q a^q b^p$ with $a^{m'}b^{n'} \neq a^m b^n$ is also accepted. If h_2 is not smaller than h_1 we observe that no cell smaller than h_1-k^2 can be reached while b^n is read. Since $k\cdot(2k^2+K+d+1) < n$ we have $h_2 > h_1+(K+d)$. Now we take out d cells from the section from h_1 up to h_2 in the phase during which b^n is read (h_2 is replaced by h_2-d) and insert d cells in the section from $h_1-(K+d)$ to h_1 in the phase during which a^m is read (h_1 is replaced by h_1+d, h_2 receives the former value). We iterate these replacements until $h_2 \leq h_1+(K+d)$. Then we have obtained a new run which accepts a word $a^{m'}b^{n'}a^n b^m a^p b^q a^q b^p$. Now we modify this run in such a way that during the reading of the subword $a^{m'}$ and again during the reading of the subword $b^{n'}$ no tape inscription, together with head position, appears twice. Then $n' = n$ is impossible since $k\cdot(2k^2+K+d+1) < n$. Hence we arrive at a contradiction under both assumptions.

Let C be the smallest cell greater or equal to $h_1-(K+d)$ that is imprinted with an A while $a^m b^n$ is read. Let $\overline{m}$ be such that the input head is on cell $\overline{m}+1$ when A is printed on C but only in case the input symbol a is read at that point; let $\overline{m} = m$ otherwise and put $a^m = a^{\overline{m}}a^{\overline{\overline{m}}}$. Then $\overline{m} \geq m - k\cdot(K + d+1+k^2)^2$ since at most $K+d+1+k^2$ working tape cells are available while the remaining subword $a^{\overline{\overline{m}}}$ is read.

By the general assumption of case 1 cell C is not reached again before $a^m b^n a^n b^m$ has been read and the next input symbol a is under scan. Certainly

C must be reached again in the course of R for otherwise, since $C + K + d \geq h_1$ and $k\cdot(h_1+k^2)^2 \geq m$, so that $C > k$, a shorter run could be obtained by leaving out some cells in the section from 1 to C in the phase during which a^m is read - observe that in this phase the working tape head is always to the right of every A and that after any k steps a state is found which has appeared before. We now distinguish five cases according to whether C is reached again while (1a) a^p is read, (1b) b^q is read, (1c) a^q is read, (1d) b^p is read, or (1e) the blank behind the input has been reached.

Before turning to case 2 we want to show how a contradiction is obtained if there are infinitely many words satisfying the initial conditions to which case 1 applies. Then to infinitely many one of the cases (1a) - (1e) applies, e.g. case (1c). For any of these words, in the last situation in which cell C is empty either a or b is under scan on the input tape; we assume that for infinitely many words a is under scan (the other case is similar). There are two states of M, say r and t, such that infinitely many of these words have the property that the specified cell C is scanned in state r just before A is printed on it, and is finally reached again in state t. Let W be the set of just these words. We choose a word $w_1 = a^{m_1}b^{n_1}a^{n_1}b^{m_1}a^{p_1}b^{q_1}a^{q_1}b^{p_1}$ from W (with specified cell C_1 in the distinguished w_1-run R_1). The initial conditions on m_1, n_1, p_1, q_1 allow us to find a second word $w_2 = a^{m_2}b^{n_2}a^{n_2}b^{m_2}a^{p_2}b^{q_2}a^{q_2}b^{p_2}$ from W (with specified cell C_2 in the distinguished w_2-run R_2) such that $m_2 > m_1 + k\cdot(K + d + 1 + k^2)^2$. From the initial phase of R_2 which ends with the situation before A is printed on C_2 (after $a^{\overline{m}_2}$ has been read), the middle phase of R_1 which begins after A has been printed on C_1 and ends when C_1 is reached again, and the final phase of R_2 which begins after C_2 has been reached we construct a run of M that accepts $a^{\overline{m}_2}a^{\overline{\overline{m}}_1}b^{n_1}a^{n_1}b^{m_1}a^{p_1}b^{q_1}a^{q_3}b^{p_2}$ for some q_3. Since $\overline{m}_2 + \overline{\overline{m}}_1 \geq \overline{m}_2 \geq m_2 - k\cdot(K + d + 1 + k^2)^2 > m_1$ we have obtained a contradiction.

<u>Case 2</u>. Let h_1 (h_2) be the working tape cell which is scanned in the first situation after $a^m b^n a^n b^m a^p$ $(a^m b^n a^n b^m a^p b^q)$ has been read. Now for the first time in the proof we use the assumption that M is halting. We see that the rightmost cell of the working tape which is reached while $a^m b^n a^n b^m$ is read is not above $k\cdot(m+n+n+m)$. Otherwise the number of working tape cells used up to an instant of R would increase by more than k in some input phase so that a non-halting run of M could be obtained. Furthermore, by the same argument, h_1 is not smaller than $-k\cdot(m+n+n+m+p)$. On the other hand, since $p > k\cdot(k\cdot(m+n+n+m))^3$ (an upper bound for the number of working tape inscriptions, combined with head positions, on $k\cdot(m+n+n+m)$ cells during R), h_1 is smaller than 0. After $m+n+n+m+p + k(k(m+n+n+m+p)+K+d)^3$ input symbols have been read (so that the input head is within the subword b^q) a cell below $h_1-(K+d)$ must have been reached. At this point, similarly to what happened in case 1, an A must have been printed on a cell smaller than or equal to $h_1+(K+d)$. Let C be the smallest cell bearing an A in this situation. Because of the halting property we have $C \geq -k\cdot(m+n+n+m+p + k(k(m+n+n+m+p)+K+d)^3)$, hence $q > k\cdot(C + k^2)^3$. We conclude

that the cell C-1 is reached in R in a situation where C bears an A before m+n+n+m+p+q input symbols have been read. On the other hand, this cannot happen before m+n+n+m input symbols have been read. Now we let $\overline{p}$ be such that the input head is on cell $m+n+n+m+\overline{p}+1$ when cell C-1 is reached after C has been printed upon but only in case an a is read at that point; let $\overline{p} = p$ otherwise and put $a^p = a^{\overline{p}}a^{\overline{\overline{p}}}$. Now $\overline{p} \geq p - k\cdot(K+d+1+k^2)$. We distinguish whether an a is read on the input tape in the first situation in which cell C-1 is reached after C has been printed upon (case 2a; then $\overline{p} < p$) or whether b is read in that situation (case 2b). Now by the conclusion arrived at in the discussion of case 1 there are infinitely many words w satisfying the initial conditions and being such that one of the cases (2a) and (2b) applies. A contradiction is now obtained in the same way as in case 1, which ends the proof.

In a similar way it can be shown that the language $L = \{a^m b^n a^m b^n \mid m \leq n\}$ cannot be recognized by any (non-halting) SCM. On the other hand it is easily seen that the language $\{a^m b^n a^m b^n \mid n < m\}$ is even a deterministic supercounter language. The complement of L is well known to be a nondeterministic counter language. We conclude that the class of supercounter (halting supercounter) languages is neither closed under complement nor under reversal.

It is not difficult to infer from the definition of a supercounter machine that the class of all supercounter languages is a full AFL. The halting supercounter languages form a semi-AFL, but not a full semi-AFL or an AFL as can be deduced from proposition 4.

3. Linear boundedness. We shall see that the SCMs have the following property in common with the pushdown automata: they all work on linear-tape insofar as for every word that is accepted there exists an accepting w-run using an amount of space that is linearly bounded by the length of the input word. We first need the following consequence of lemma 2.

Lemma 3. Let R be a run of a one-way machine M (with k states) which consists of r consecutive input phases and begins in a state p on the leftmost or rightmost cell of the empty segment $[1,m]$ of the working tape and ends in a state q just after this segment has been left. Assume that no non-blank symbol is printed during R. Let $g = K + d$ (where K and d are as in lemma 2 and K is assumed to be greater than k^2). Suppose $m \geq rg$. Then, for any $n \geq rg$ with $n \equiv m \mod d$, there exists a run R' of M consisting of r consecutive input phases which begins in state p and ends in state q and moves over the empty segment $[1,n]$ in correspondence to R (i.e. beginning and leaving on corresponding sides); also no non-blank symbol is printed during R'.

Intuitively: If a supercounter machine goes in r input phases across an empty tape segment $[1,m]$ without printing then it behaves in the same way on an empty segment $[1,n]$ provided that $n \equiv m \mod d$ and both are large enough. The central argument of this section is summarized in the following statement.

Lemma 4. Let M be a supercounter machine with k states and γ working tape symbols. Let $0 \leq e < d$ and let

$$\mathbb{L}_{t'} = \mathbb{L}(A,A',B',B;q,a,q';p,b,p';e,t')$$

be the set of all $t \in \mathbb{N}$ such that

(1) $t \equiv e \mod d$,

(2) $t \geq g(16k^3\gamma^2)^{2k^2\gamma d+1} + t'$,

(3) there exists a run R leading from $(q,\check{a}ub,A\underbrace{\check{\square}\ldots\square}_{t}B)$ to $(p',au\check{b},\check{A}U'A'WB'VB)$ for some pieces of tape inscriptions U',W,V (the positions of the heads are indicated by $\vee$) having a subrun R_1 leading from $(q,\check{a}ub,A\underbrace{\check{\square}\ldots\square}_{t}B)$ to $(q',\check{a}ub,AUA'\underbrace{\check{\square}\ldots\square}_{t'}B'VB)$ for some U and a subrun R_2 leading from $(p,au\check{b},AU\check{A}'WB'VB)$ to $(p',au\check{b},\check{A}U'A'WB'VB)$.

Suppose $\mathbb{L}_{t'}$ is non-empty. Let $\lambda_o = \min\{t - e' \mid t \in \mathbb{L}_{e'}\}$ where

$$e' = \begin{cases} t', & \text{if } t' \leq g \\ \min\{\varepsilon \mid \varepsilon \equiv t' \mod d,\ g \leq \varepsilon,\ \mathbb{L}_\varepsilon \neq \emptyset\}, & \text{if } t' > g. \end{cases}$$

Then there exists, for every $\sigma \geq t'$, a $t \in [\sigma, \sigma + d\lambda_o]$ such that $t \in \mathbb{L}_{t'}$.

Intuitively: If M starts on a gap $A\underbrace{\check{\square}\ldots\square}_{t}B$ and prints on it in an input phase so that A—$A'\underbrace{\check{\square}\ldots\square}_{t'}B'$—$B$ is arrived at and if M after later on having reached the A' arrives at A again within one input phase then the parts of the gap which eventually hold A—A' and B'—B can be made smaller or larger without changing the essential behaviour of M on the gap $A'\underbrace{\square\ldots\square}_{t'}B'$.

Sketch of proof. We shall show that the gap $A\underbrace{\square\ldots\square}_{\lambda_o+e'}B$ can be made larger.

Let i_o be the cell bearing the A and $i'_o = i_o + \lambda_o + e' + 1$ the cell bearing the B.

1. All cells between i_o and i'_o (i_o included) which during R_1 at one moment appear as the rightmost non-empty cell are called r-cells.

a) If there are more than $k^2 \cdot \gamma$ r-cells to the left of A' (resp. to the right of B') then there are two that get imprinted with the same symbol in the same state and the cells immediately to the left are later on reached in the same state. The tape segment between these cells can repeatedly be inserted d times without essentially affecting the behaviour of M.

b) An empty tape segment of length a multiple of d can be inserted if the rightmost r-cell is at least $g+1$ cells to the left of B.

c) If neither a) nor b) apply there are two neighbouring r-cells with a distance $\geq \frac{\lambda_o - g}{2k^2 - 1} > \lambda_o/4k^2$, say j_o and j_o'. If they surround the gap $A'\Box\ldots\Box B'$ we only count the number of cells outside the gap.

2. All cells between j_o and j_o' which during R after the printing on j_o' appear at one moment as the leftmost non-empty cell are called l-cells.

a) If there are more than $k\cdot\gamma$ l-cells to the left of A' (resp. to the right of B') then two of them are imprinted with the same symbol and the cells immediately to the left are later on reached in the same state, hence the tape segment between these cells can repeatedly be inserted d times without essentially affecting the behaviour of M.

b) An empty tape segment of appropriate length can be inserted if the leftmost l-cell is at least $g+1$ cells to the right of j_o.

c) If neither a) nor b) apply then there are two neighbouring l-cells with a distance $\geq \frac{1}{4}\text{distance}(j_o, j_o')/k\gamma \geq \lambda_o/16k^3\gamma^2$, say i_1 and i_1'.

We now repeat these considerations from 1. on until (after at most $2k^2\gamma d$ iterations) we have pairs (i_ν, i_ν') and (i_μ, i_μ') with $B_\nu = B_\mu$, $p_\nu = p_\mu$, $q_\nu = q_\mu$ and $\lambda_\nu \equiv \lambda_\mu \mod d$ (A_ν the symbol on i_ν, B_ν the symbol on i_ν', p_ν the state immediately before the printing of A_ν, q_ν the state immediately after the reading of A_ν, $\lambda_\nu = \text{distance}(i_\nu, i_\nu')$). Therefore, if the gap $A\underbrace{\Box\ldots\Box}_{\lambda_o+e'}B$ is increased by $|\lambda_\nu - \lambda_\mu|$ M behaves in essentially the same way.

<u>Proposition 5</u>. Suppose that R is a w-run of a supercounter machine M having a subrun R_1 leading from $(q, u\check{a}v, XA\underbrace{\check{\Box}\ldots\Box}_{t}BY)$ to $(q', u\check{a}v, XAUA'\underbrace{\check{\Box}\ldots\Box}_{t'}B'VBY)$ and another subrun R_2 (beginning after the end of R_1) leading from $(p, u'\check{b}v', XAU\check{A}'WB'VBY)$ to $(p', u'\check{b}v', X\check{A}U'A'WB'VBY)$. Suppose that there are r input changes that take place on cells of the gap indicated by $A\Box\ldots\Box B$ before the beginning of R_1, including the cell bearing B, excluding the cells of the gap indicated by $A'\Box\ldots\Box B'$ (also the cell bearing B').

Then there is an $s \leq t' + (r+1)g + c$ where c is a constant depending on M alone, and a w-run $\overline{R}$ having a subrun $\overline{R}_1$ leading from $(q, u\check{a}v, XA\underbrace{\check{\Box}\ldots\Box}_{s}BY)$ to $(q', u\check{a}v, XA\overline{U}A'\underbrace{\check{\Box}\ldots\Box}_{t'}B'\overline{V}BY)$ and a subsequent subrun $\overline{R}_2$ leading from $(p, u'\check{b}v', XA\overline{U}\check{A}'WB'\overline{V}BY)$ to $(p', u'\check{b}v', X\check{A}\overline{U}'A'WB'\overline{V}BY)$ such that the situations appearing in $\overline{R}$ outside $\overline{R}_1$ and $\overline{R}_2$ correspond in turn to the situations appearing in R outside R_1 and R_2 (excepting the working tape segments on which M works in the subruns considered in each case).

Proof by lemmas 3 and 4. Remark: The assertion includes the case $t' = 0$, $u = u'$, $v = v'$, $a = b$ ($AUA'\square\ldots\square B'VB$ should be replaced by $A'VB$, i.e. $A = A' = B'$, so that R_2 disappears), and also holds if R_1 begins with $(q, u\check{a}v, XA\underbrace{\square\ldots\check{\square}}_{t}BY)$.

Proposition 6. Let R be a w-run of a supercounter machine M which has a subrun R' leading from $(q, u\check{a}_1\ldots a_n v, XA\underbrace{\check{\square}\ldots\square}_{s}BY)$ to $(q', ua_1\ldots\check{a}_n v, X\check{A}WBY)$ $(n \geq 1)$.

Suppose that r input changes take place on the tape segment indicated by $A\underbrace{\square\ldots\square}_{s}B$ before R' begins.

Let $A\underbrace{\square\ldots\square}_{H(n,r)}B$ be the smallest gap which may replace $A\underbrace{\square\ldots\square}_{s}B$ without affecting R outside R' (in the sense of proposition 5).

Then $H(n,r) \leq \max\{(n + r - 2)\cdot z, \frac{z}{4}\}$ for some constant z.

The analoguous assertion holds if R starts with $(q, u\check{a}_1\ldots a_n v, XA\underbrace{\square\ldots\check{\square}}_{s}BY)$.

Sketch of proof (induction by n). Let $z = 4(2g + 4c)$. By proposition 5, if $n = 1$, we may replace the gap by a gap of length $H(1,r) \leq (r+1)g + c \leq \max\{(1+r-2)\cdot z, \frac{z}{4}\}$. Assume that the assertion is valid for all $\nu < n$. At the end of the first input phase within R' the tape inscription is as follows:

$$XA \text{———————} A_1 \overset{1}{\downarrow} B_1 \text{———} BY$$

Let M reach A_1 in the j_1th input phase. This input phase ends with a tape inscription

$$XA \text{———————} A_2 \overset{j_1}{\downarrow} B_2 \text{———} A_1 \overset{1}{\downarrow} B_1 \text{———} BY$$

The gap indicated by $A_2 \quad B_2$ may be left in the j_2th input phase thereafter, i.e. in the (j_1+j_2)th input phase, etc. At the end of R' we have a tape inscription of the form

$$\underbrace{\overset{n=j_1+\cdots+j_t}{\downarrow} XA \text{——} A_t}_{s_t}\underbrace{\overset{j_1+\cdots+j_{t-1}}{\downarrow}}_{r_t} B_t \text{——}\ldots\text{——} \underbrace{A_3 \overset{j_1+j_2}{\downarrow} B_3}_{r_3} \underbrace{\text{——————}}_{s_2} \underbrace{A_2 \overset{j_1}{\downarrow} B_2}_{r_2} \underbrace{\text{——}}_{s_1} \underbrace{A_1 \overset{1}{\downarrow} B_1}_{r_1} \text{——} BY$$

Here r_i is the number of input changes occurring on the segment $A_i \ldots B_i$ before R' begins and s_i the corresponding number for B_{i+1}——A_i together with a piece of B_1——B. By proposition 5 one can deduce

$$H(n,r) \leq H(j_1,r_1) + H(j_2+1,r_2) + \ldots + H(j_t+1,r_t) + (s_1+1)g + c + \ldots + (s_t+1)g + c\ .$$

Theorem 2. Every (nondeterministic) SCM is linear-tape bounded.

4. The tape complexity of supercounter languages. We shall now indicate how a supercounter machine M can be simulated by a nondeterministic two-way Turing machine T on $\log^2$-tape. For this we describe a nondeterministic algorithm which simulates an arbitrary run of M that begins and remains on the interior cells of an initially given gap (beginning with an arbitrary state and on an arbitrary input cell). The algorithm operates on a list of blocks, each of the form

$$((p_1,i_1,k_1,C_1),(q_1,j_1,h_1,A),(q,j,h),(q_2,j_2,h_2,B),(p_2,i_2,k_2,C_2)),$$

which we imagine being printed on the working tape of T. Such a block is meant to indicate a situation in a run of M in the following way: (q,j,h) specifies the state, the input cell and the working tape cell of the present situation, h_1 is the nearest non-empty cell to the left of h , k_1 is the nearest non-empty cell to the left of h_1 (for the initial situation we take $k_1 = h_1$), h_2 is the nearest non-empty cell to the right of h_1, whereas k_2 is the nearest non-empty cell to the right of k_1 - not in the present situation but in the first situation of the run in which cell k_1 is non-empty. The other data give further information about these cells, e.g. (q_1,j_1,h_1,A) specifies that cell h_1 bears an A and that state and input cell in the situation immediately before this A appeared were q_1 and j_1, respectively. We shall speak of the gap of the block, given by the second and fourth component of the block, and of the overgap of the block, given by the outer components; the middle component will be called the pointer. We distinguish M-blocks and H-blocks and the "working block", in addition the "initial block" (holding the information about the initial situation) is distinguished among the M-blocks. Working block and initial block exist at every step of the algorithm.

All changes within a run of M are represented in the pointer of the working block as long as no new symbol is printed and the bottom cell of the present gap is not reached. If a symbol is printed and the head moves right then the working block is made an M-block and a new working block is formed (all necessary information is immediately available from the old working block). If a symbol is printed and the head moves left or stays on the same cell then the working block is suitably modified (only the third and fourth component need be changed). If the bottom cell of the gap is reached the working block can only be modified directly if the overgap of the present working block coincides with the gap of an M-block (the last that has been printed); otherwise the information for the overgap of the new working block cannot immediately be obtained. In this case the necessary information is recalculated: The working block is made an H-block, a new working block is formed from that M-block which describes the most recent situation before the present point (possibly the initial block); then the algorithm proceeds (possibly with other recomputations being inserted) until the working cell has reached the gap which coincides with the overgap of an H-block (necessarily the former working block). At any step of the algorithm

M-blocks (with the exception of the initial block) can arbitrarily be erased (which together with the eventual nondeterminism of M accounts for the nondeterminism of the simulation).

It is well possible (since M may be nondeterministic) that during a recomputation a different run of M is simulated. However, it can be shown that every situation arrived at by the algorithm (especially an accepting situation) can also be reached from the initial situation by a run of M.

By a simulation of a given run R we understand a run of the algorithm in which all steps in the main computation and in the recomputations are made as in R. We say that the run R has a block need of c if there exists a simulation of R in which the maximal number of blocks appearing in the list is c whereas there is no simulation of R with a smaller maximal number of blocks.

Lemma 5. Let R be a run of M with a block need of $c \geq 3$. Let r be the initial situation of R, let t be the first situation such that the subrun from r to t has a block need of c, and let s be the first situation in which the working tape head is within the gap whose bottom cell is the rightmost non-empty cell (properly) to the left of the working tape head in t. Then $r \neq s$ and the subruns of R from r to s and from s to t both have a block need of $c-1$.

Sketch of proof. Let t^- be the situation just before t. Since the subrun from r to t^- has a block need of at most c-1 we see that in t the working tape head has just reached the lower boundary of a gap and that a recomputation becomes necessary. But no recomputation is necessary if s is described by the initial block since this is always available, hence $r \neq s$. There is a simulation of the subrun from r to t^- with a list of at most c-1 blocks. From this a simulation of the subrun from s to t^- with a list of at most c-1 blocks can be derived. By the argument used before the subrun from s to t has a block need of at most c-1. This block need cannot be smaller than c-1 since otherwise R could be simulated with a list of at most c-1 blocks: s could be reached with a list of at most c-1 blocks, and then s could be kept in an M-block which takes the place of the initial block of a simulation of the run from s to t. The block need of the subrun from r to s cannot be smaller than c-1 since otherwise a recomputation from r to s with a list of at most c-2 blocks together with a single H-block would suffice to simulate the step from t^- to t.

Corollary. If a run R has a block need of $c \geq 3$ then the number of non-empty working tape cells is increased by at least 2^{c-2} during R.

Since for any SCM M there exists a constant c_M such that for every accepted word w of length $n > 1$ there exists a w-run needing at most $c_M \cdot n$ working tape cells (Theorem 2) every such word w can be accepted by a run with a block need of at most

$\log(c_M \cdot n) + 2$. Hence we have the following statement.

Theorem 3. Every SCM M can be simulated by a nondeterministic two-way Turing machine on $\log^2$-tape.

The theorem also holds for two-way supercounter machines provided that they work on polynomial tape. It can be shown that the above algorithm needs at most n^2 steps in order to simulate an accepting w-run of a word w of length n. Hence with the aid of Savitch's method it can be deduced that any SCM can be simulated by a deterministic two-way Turing machine on $\log^3$-tape.

REFERENCES

1. P. C. Fischer, Turing machines with restricted memory access, Inf. and Control 9, 364 - 379, 1966

2. S. Ginsburg, S. A. Greibach, M. A. Harrison, One-way stack automata, JACM 14, 389 - 418, 1967

3. J. E. Hopcroft, J. D. Ullman, Nonerasing stack automata, JCSS 1, 166 - 186, 1967

4. J. D. Ullman, Halting stack automata, JACM 16, 550 - 563, 1969

5. S. A. Cook, Characterisations of pushdown machines in terms of time-bounded computers, JACM 18, 4 - 68, 1971

6. S. Cook, R. Sethi, Storage requirements for deterministic polynomial time recognizable languages, JCSS 13, 25 - 37, 1976

7. Z. Galil, Two-way deterministic pushdown automaton languages and some open problems in the theory of computation, IEEE-SWAT, 170 - 177, 1974

8. S. Ginsburg, Algebraic and Automata-Theoretic Properties of Formal Languages, Amsterdam, New York, 1975

9. I. H. Sudborough, A note on tape-bounded complexity classes and linear contextfree languages, JACM 22, 499 - 500, 1975

10. I. H. Sudborough, On deterministic contextfree languages, multihead automata, and the power of an auxiliary pushdown store, 8th ACM-STOC, 141 - 148, 1976

11. B. v. Braunmühl, Zwei-Zähler-Automaten mit gekoppelten Bewegungen, Berichte der Gesellschaft für Mathematik und Datenverarbeitung Nr. 116, München, Wien, 1977

12. E. Ginsburg, E. Spanier, Pushdown acceptor forms, TCS 5, 307 - 320, 1977

13. B. v. Braunmühl, E. Hotzel, A classification of one-way automata, in preparation

14. B.. v. Braunmühl, E. Hotzel, Some remarks on pushdown automata, in preparation

Existential Quantifiers in Abstract Data Types *)

M. Broy, W. Dosch, H. Partsch, P. Pepper, M. Wirsing
Technische Universität München
Institut für Informatik
Postfach 2o 24 2o
D-8ooo München 2

Abstract

Hierarchies of abstract data types are specified by axioms which are positive formulas consisting of universally and existentially quantified disjunctions and conjunctions of equations. Necessary and sufficient conditions for the existence of terminal algebras are investigated. Furthermore, some advantages of disjunctions and existential quantifiers whithin the laws are discussed and the usefulness of terminal algebras is demonstrated by a few examples.

*) This research was carried out within the Sonderforschungsbereich 49, Programmiertechnik, Munich.

1. Introduction

Abstract data types are used to specify the basic functions and properties of computation structures. In contrast to formal specifications using first order logic, abstract data types include a "generation principle" for the abstract objects : The computation structures only contain objects that can be computed by a finite number of applications of the basic functions. This generation principle has important consequences:

First, it implies the validity of the "data type induction" which is a very powerful proof method. Second, a partial order can be defined on the set of models of a data type. By restricting the form of the axioms the existence of minimal (terminal) or maximal (initial) models can be guaranteed.

Conditions for the existence of initial models were investigated by /Thatcher et al. 77/. Roughly speaking, the form of the axioms must be restricted to universally quantified conditional equations (implications). To guarantee the existence of terminal models the negations of equations, i.e. inequalities, have to be forbidden and therefore implications between equations have to be avoided, too. In this paper we show that terminal models exist, if all axioms are positive formulas, i.e. if they consist of universally or existentially quantified disjunctions and conjunctions of equations.

In general, types are hierarchically based on (more) primitive types. If all these types are specified by positive formulas, their terminal models comprise only one-element carrier sets. However, if we allow e.g. the basic type BOOL of the truth values to be one of the primitive types, then types with nontrivial terminal models can be specified by positive formulas.

In this case, where an abstract data type is based on primitive types, a supplementary but necessary condition is required: the type must be t-complete. This condition is comparable to the notion of "sufficient completeness" of Guttag. We show that - roughly speaking - each sufficiently complete type is t-complete, too.

Therefore, if sufficient completeness can be proved for a type - a condition necessary to avoid pathological models and to guarantee that all "visible" properties of abstract objects are completely determined - then this approach provides a great freedom to define formal specifications and assures simultaneously the existence of an appropriate standard model: the terminal algebra.

To give a first example for the use of existential quantifiers and positive formulas in the specification of abstract data types (for the notation cf. / Partsch, Broy 79/) we consider the type MULTIPLES specifying certain subsets of $\mathbb{N}$: With any number all its multiples belong to the subset, too.

```
type MULTIPLES ≡ (type BOOL, type NAT) multi, empty, incorp, contains:
        sort multi,
        funct multi empty,
        funct (multi, nat) multi incorp ,
        funct (multi, nat) bool contains ,

  ∀ multi m, nat i, nat j :
        law contains(empty, i) ≡ false ,
        law contains(incorp(m,i),j) ≡ ∃ nat k :  eq(i × k, j) ∨ contains(m, j)

                                                               end of type
```

This type can be used e.g. as a basis for a program similar to the "sieve of Eratosthenes" computing the set of all prime numbers less or equal to a given natural number n .

```
funct primenumbers ≡ (nat n) set nat : sieve(n, 2, empty) ,

funct sieve ≡ (nat n, nat p, multi s) set nat :
      if p > n              then ∅
    elif ¬ contains(s, p) then sieve(n, p+1, incorp(s, p)) ∪ {p}
                            else sieve(n, p+1, s)                  fi
```

2. Definitions and Basic Properties

A *(data) structure* D is a heterogeneous algebra (cf. /Birkhoff, Lipson 70/) consisting of a finite family of *carrier sets*, a finite (possibly empty) family of *primitive data structures* [1] (different from D) and a finite set of total functions [2], called *operations*, between the carrier sets of D and the primitive structures.

---

[1] Note that data structures and abstract data types are inductively defined starting with structures (types) without primitive structures (types). Thus, one has hierarchies of structures (types).

[2] The extension of these notions and of the following theorems to partial functions makes no specific problems (cf. /Broy et al. 79/), if a definedness predicate is introduced and sufficiently completely specified to indicate the domain for which the function is total.

All elements of the carrier sets have to be generatable by a finite number of applications of the functions of D or of the primitive structures.

This *"generation principle"* distinguishes the data structures as a special subclass of the heterogeneous algebras of some type. A *signature* $\Sigma = (S, F)$ consists of a set S of symbols for carrier sets, called *sorts*, and of a set F of symbols for functions. Every symbol $f \in F$ has a *functionality*, i.e. a (possibly empty) string $(s_1, \ldots, s_n)$ of sorts, called *domain*, and a sort s_{n+1}, called *range*.

An *(abstract data) type* T consists of a signature $\Sigma = (S, F)$, a finite (possibly empty) family $\mathbb{P}$ of *primitive types* (different from T) and a set E of *laws*. Note that the functionalities of the symbols $f \in F$ many contain sorts of T and of the primitive types.

A data structure D is called *model of type* T, iff

(D1) there is a fixed correspondence between the sorts, function symbols and primitive types of T and the carrier sets, operations and primitive structures of D .

(D2) the primitive structures of D are models of the corresponding primitive types of T and

(D3) the laws of T hold in D .

The carrier sets, operations or primitive structures of D that correspond to a sort s , a function symbol f or a primitive type P are denoted by s^D, f^D or P^D, resp.

Note that all elements of primitive carrier sets have to be finitely generatable by operations of the respective primitive structure only.

If a heterogeneous algebra A satisfies (at least) condition D1 , it is called a $(\Sigma, \mathbb{P})$-*algebra*; if it satisfies D1 and D3 it is called a $(\Sigma, \mathbb{P}, E)$-*algebra*. If, in addition, A is a data structure, it is called a $(\Sigma, \mathbb{P})$-*structure* or a $(\Sigma, \mathbb{P}, E)$-*structure*, resp.

For any Σ and $\mathbb{P}$ there exists a particular $(\Sigma, \mathbb{P})$-structure, the *term algebra* $W_{\Sigma,\mathbb{P}}$. Its carrier sets consist of all "syntactially well-formed terms [1]".

---

[1] For a more detailed and formal definition cf. /Birkhoff, Lipson 70/ and /Goguen et al. 78/.

Such a term is called to *be of sort* s , if its outermost function symbol has range s.

For a type $T = (\Sigma, \mathbb{P}, E)$ we also write W_T instead of $W_{\Sigma,\mathbb{P}}$. We often need a special subset of the terms of W_T , viz. those terms which are of a primitive sort: For $P \in \mathbb{P}$ the restriction $W_T|P$ denotes the set of all terms which are of a sort s of P[1] .

The *interpretation* t^D of a term $t \in W_{\Sigma,\mathbb{P}}$ of sort s in some $(\Sigma, \mathbb{P})$-algebra D denotes that object of the carrier set s^D which is obtained by substituting all function symbols f by the corresponding operations f^D and by evaluating the resulting expression.

A type T is understood to be the set Mod_T of all models T . T is called *consistent*, if there exists at least one model for T .

Introducing homomorphisms between data structures we obtain a categorical structure on Mod_T (cf. /Goguen et al. 78/):

Let A and B be $(\Sigma, \mathbb{P})$-structures. A function $\varphi: A \to B$ is called a *homomorphism* if φ is a homomorphism for the primitive structures and if for all operation symbols f of Σ and for all arguments $(x_1, \ldots, x_n)$ of f^A

$$\varphi(f^A(x_1, \ldots, x_n)) = f^B(\varphi(x_1), \ldots, \varphi(x_n))$$

holds. A homomorphism φ is called *epimorphism* if φ is surjective.

For every $(\Sigma, \mathbb{P})$-structure D there exists (exactly) one epimorphism from $W_{\Sigma,\mathbb{P}}$ onto D (cf. /Birkhoff, Lipson 7o/). If φ is a homomorphism between two $(\Sigma, \mathbb{P})$-structures A and B , then for all terms $t \in W_{\Sigma,\mathbb{P}}$ $\varphi(t^A) = t^B$ holds.

A model Z of a type T is called *terminal*, if for every model D of T there exists an epimorphism $\varphi_D: D \to Z$ from D onto Z . For every type T there exists (up to isomorphism) at most one terminal model (cf. /Wand 78/).
The (model theoretic) equality = in a terminal model Z of T can be characterized as follows: For all terms $s, t \in W_T$

$$s^Z = t^Z \iff \text{there exists a model } D \text{ of } T \text{ with } s^D = t^D .$$

---

[1] Note that in general $W_P \subsetneqq W_T|P$, as the restriction only concerns the outermost function symbol of the terms.

An *initial model* A of T is defined analogously using an epimorphism $\varphi_D: A \to D$. The equality is characterized here by

$$s^A = t^A \Leftrightarrow \text{for all models } D \text{ of } T \quad s^D = t^D \text{ holds} .$$

For a type $T = (\Sigma, \mathbb{P}, E)$ a term $t \in W_T$ is called *reducible* to a term $s \in W_T$, iff there is a finite reduction sequence $t \equiv t_1 \equiv \ldots \equiv t_{n-1} \equiv s$ using the laws of E (and of the primitive types) as well as the rules and axioms of first order predicate logic, including reflexivity, symmetry, transitivity, substitution for $\equiv$.

T is called *sufficiently complete with respect to a primitive type* P (cf./Guttag 75/), iff every term $t \in W_T|P$ (being of a sort P) is reducible to some $p \in W_P$. T is called *sufficiently complete* iff it is sufficiently complete for all $P \in \mathbb{P}$.

Sufficient completeness guarantees that no terms $t \in W_T|P$ exist the interpretations of which add new elements to primitive carrier sets.

In contrast to this "deduction theoretic" notion we employ a "model theoretic" condition:

A type T is *t-complete* iff for all primitive types P of T , for all $t \in W_T|P$, for all $u, v \in W_P$ and for all models A , B of T the following holds:

If $t^A = u^A$ and $t^B = v^B$ then there exists a model C of T (which is an epimorphic image of A and of B) such that $t^C = u^C = v^C$ holds.

t-completeness is a necessary but not sufficient condition for the existence of terminal algebras. If each primitive type has only isomorphic models, then sufficient completeness implies t-completeness.

To ensure the existence of terminal (initial) models we concentrate on types the laws of which have a special syntactic form:

A *positive formula* (cf. /Shoenfield 67/) has the form

$$Q_1 x_1 \ldots Q_n x_n A \quad (n \geq 0)$$

where $Q_1, \ldots, Q_n$ are universal ($\forall$) or existential ($\exists$) quantifiers and where A is built from disjunctions and conjunctions of equations.

According to the laws of the propositional calculus this also includes implications like

$$s_1 \not\equiv t_1 \wedge \ldots \wedge s_k \not\equiv t_k \Rightarrow s_{k+1} \equiv t_{k+1} \quad .$$

Of course, two laws of the form

$$b \equiv \text{false} \;\vee\; t \equiv s_1$$
$$b \equiv \text{true} \;\vee\; t \equiv s_2$$

may be abbreviated by

$$t \equiv \underline{\text{if}}\ b\ \underline{\text{then}}\ s_1\ \underline{\text{else}}\ s_2\ \underline{\text{fi}} \quad .$$

3. Existence of Terminal Models

First of all we show that t-completeness is a necessary condition for the existence of terminal models.

Lemma

If there exists a terminal model for a type T, then T is t-complete.

Proof

Let Z be a terminal model of type T. Let P be a primitive type in T and let $t \in W_T | P$, $u, v \in W_P$ and let A, B be models of T. Assume $t^A = u^A$ and $t^B = v^B$. Since there is an epimorphism from A onto Z we have $t^Z = u^Z$ and analogously $t^Z = v^Z$. Thus $t^Z = u^Z = v^Z$ holds. Therefore T is t-complete. •

But t-completeness is not sufficient for the existence of terminal models. Consider the following type TRIPLE describing triples of elements at least two of which are different:

```
type TRIPLE ≡ triple, f, g, h :

        sort triple ,
        funct triple f ,
        funct triple g ,
        funct triple h ,
        law f ≢ g
                              end of type
```

Since TRIPLE has no primitive types it is t-complete. But TRIPLE has (up to isomorphism) two different two-element models between which no homomorphism exists. Hence TRIPLE has no terminal model.

If a type is not t-complete or if there are inequalities in the laws of a type, the existence of terminal models is not guaranteed, otherwise terminal models exist:

Theorem

If T is a consistent, t-complete abstract data type the axioms of which are positive formulas, then there exists a terminal model of type T.

Sketch of the Proof

For the construction of a terminal model we define the following relation $\sim$ in the term algebra W_T :

For all $s, t \in W_T$

$$s \sim t \underset{\text{def}}{\Longleftrightarrow} \text{there exists a model } D \text{ of } T \text{ with } s^D = t^D .$$

Then the transitive closure $\sim^*$ of $\sim$ is a congruence relation and we can define an algebra $Z = W_T/\sim^*$.

For each model D of T the homomorphism φ defined by $\varphi(t^D) = t^Z$ $(t \in W_T)$ is well-defined, since for all terms $s, t \in W_T$ with $s^D = t^D$ we have $s \sim^* t$ and thus $\varphi(s^D) = s^Z = t^Z = \varphi(t^D)$.

Therefore, if Z is a model of T then Z is terminal. So the proof is complete if we are able to show that Z is a model of T. By definition Z is finitely generated by T and has the same signature as T. Therefore it suffices to show that

(1) each primitive structure of Z is a model of the corresponding primitive type and

(2) the laws of T hold in Z.

The proof of (1) can be done by contradiction using the t-completeness of T, the proof of (2) uses the positive form of the laws. •

Corollary

Let T be a consistent type with the primitive types $P_1, \ldots, P_n$.
Assume that for some $l \leq n$

(1) $P_1, \ldots, P_l$ have only isomorphic models,
(2) $T, P_{l+1}, \ldots, P_n$ have only positive formulas as axioms and are sufficiently complete with respect to $P_1, \ldots, P_l$.

Then there exists a terminal model for T .

Proof

Let U be the type which has as signature and axioms the union of the signatures and axioms of $T, P_{l+1}, \ldots, P_n$. Let $P_1, \ldots, P_l$ be the primitive types of U . Since T is consistent, U is consistent, too. Because of (1) and (2) U is sufficiently complete and its primitive types have only isomorphic models. Each such type is t-complete (cf. /Broy et al. 79/). Therefore the theorem guarantees the existence of a terminal model Z of U . Every model of T is a model of U , too. Since T is consistent and Z terminal, there exists an epimorphism from a model of T onto Z . Hence, since Z fulfills the axioms of T , Z is a model of T , too.
From $Mod_T \subseteq Mod_U$ we obtain that Z is a terminal model of T . •

One might expect that sufficient completeness of a type T together with the existence of terminal models for the primitive types could be sufficient to guarantee the existence of terminal models for T . Unfortunately, this conjecture is wrong as the following example shows:

```
type COUNTEREXAMPLE ≡ (type PRIMITIVE) c , inject , project :
          sort c ,
          funct (p) c inject ,
          funct (c) p project ,
       law  project(inject(p0)) ≡ p0 ,
       law  project(inject(p1)) ≡ p1 ,
       law  project(inject(p2)) ≡ p0

                                          end of type ,
```

type PRIMITIVE ≡ <u>p</u>, <u>r</u>, p_o, p_1, p_2, r_o, r_1, r_2 :

<u>sort</u> <u>p</u> ,
<u>sort</u> <u>r</u> ,
<u>funct</u> <u>p</u> p_o, <u>funct</u> <u>p</u> p_1, <u>funct</u> <u>p</u> p_2,
<u>funct</u> <u>r</u> r_o, <u>funct</u> <u>r</u> r_1, <u>funct</u> <u>r</u> r_2,

<u>law</u> $p_o \neq p_1$,
<u>law</u> $p_o \neq p_2$,
<u>law</u> $p_1 \neq p_2 \Rightarrow r_1 \neq r_2$

<u>end of type</u>

The type PRIMITIVE has a terminal model Z (characterized by $p_1^Z = p_2^Z$ and $r_o^Z = r_1^Z = r_2^Z$), an initial model I (in which p_o^I, p_1^I, p_2^I and r_o^I, r_1^I, r_2^I are pairwise different) and two non-isomorphic models Y, characterized by $p_1^Y \neq p_2^Y$ and $r_o^Y = r_1^Y \neq r_2^Y$ resp. $r_1^Y \neq r_2^Y = r_o^Y$.

Using the laws of COUNTEREXAMPLE we obtain

$$\text{project}(\text{inject}(p_1)) \equiv p_1 \neq p_o \equiv \text{project}(\text{inject}(p_2)) .$$

Therefore in all models G of COUNTEREXAMPLE $p_1^G \neq p_2^G$ and $r_1^G \neq r_2^G$ which excludes Z as primitive structure.

A simple further study of COUNTEREXAMPLE shows that this type has no terminal models, although being consistent and sufficiently complete. Of course, COUNTER-EXAMPLE is not t-complete. ∎

In the next sections we are going to give some less artificial examples to show the usefulness of the discussed specification means.

4. Aspects of Terminal Models

Most approaches to abstract data types, e.g. /Zilles 74/, /Goguen et al. 78/, /Thatcher et al. 77/ deal with the initial models. This choice is motivated by the idea that all equalities which hold in the model can be deduced from the laws of the type.

When using abstract data types in program development one usually is not interested in the objects themselves and their equality but in their behaviour, i.e. in the properties that can be talked about or asked for using the functions of the abstract type. As it seems not meaningful to distinguish elements of some sorts of an abstract type, which behave the same way under all functions, it is sufficient to take the roughest equality, i.e. a terminal model. In addition, all algebras A for which there exists an epimorphism $\varphi: A \to B$ can be used to represent the algebra B, viz. by setting up the quotient structure induced by φ on A. Therefore, one usually has a greater choice of possible representations for terminal models than for initial ones. In particular, any representation for an initial model can be used for a terminal model too (by taking a suitable quotient structure) but not vice versa (cf. /Wand 78/).

Existential quantifiers often allow a short and clear description of certain abstract data types. Note that for boolean functions <u>funct</u> ($\underline{m}_1, \ldots, \underline{m}_n$) <u>bool</u> p even equations of the form

$$\forall\, \underline{m}_1 t_1 \ldots \forall\, \underline{m}_n t_n \;:\; p(t_1, \ldots, t_n) \equiv \exists\, \underline{m}\; x : (t[x] \equiv \text{true})$$

are allowed, since they are equivalent to (let x, y be identifiers not occurring free in $t_1, \ldots, t_n$ or in t) :

$$\forall\, \underline{m}_1 t_1 \ldots \forall\, \underline{m}_n t_n : (p(t_1, \ldots, t_n) \Rightarrow \exists\, \underline{m}\; x : t[x] \equiv \text{true}) \;\wedge$$
$$((\exists\, \underline{m}\; x : t[x] \equiv \text{true}) \Rightarrow p(t_1, \ldots, t_n))$$

We eliminate the symbol $\Rightarrow$ and one existential quantifier using

$$(\exists\, x\, A \to B) \Longleftrightarrow \forall\, x\, (\neg A \vee B)$$

and obtain the following normal forms:

$$\forall\, \underline{m}_1 t_1 \ldots \forall\, \underline{m}_n t_n\; \exists\, \underline{m}\; x \;\; \forall\, \underline{m}\; y :$$
$$(p(t_1, \ldots, t_n) \equiv \text{false} \;\vee\; t[x] \equiv \text{true}) \;\wedge$$
$$(p(t_1, \ldots, t_n) \equiv \text{true} \;\vee\; t[y] \equiv \text{false})$$

The above form can be used as a shorthand in the laws of the following type SUBSPACE :

<u>type</u> SUBSPACE ≡ (<u>type</u> BOOL, <u>type</u> INT) <u>subspace</u>, nullspace, incorp, iselem:

<u>sort</u> <u>subspace</u> ,
<u>funct</u> <u>subspace</u> nullspace ,
<u>funct</u> (<u>subspace</u>, <u>int</u>) <u>subspace</u> incorp ,
<u>funct</u> (<u>subspace</u>, <u>int</u>) <u>bool</u> iselem ,

∀ <u>subspace</u> s , <u>int</u> i , <u>int</u> j :

<u>law</u> : iselem(nullspace, i) ≡ iszero(i) ,
<u>law</u> : iselem(incorp(s, j), i) ≡ ∃ <u>int</u> k : iselem(s, i + k * j)

<u>end of type</u>

In the type SUBSPACE the equality of objects of sort <u>subspace</u> is not fully determined, i.e. there exist nonisomorphic models, in particular a terminal model and an initial one. In any initial model neither the law

incorp(incorp(s, i), j) ≡ incorp(incorp(s, j), i)

nor the law

incorp(incorp(s, i), i) ≡ incorp(s, i)

holds, whereas in terminal models both equations are satisfied. When using the initial algebra approach one is either forced to include the laws above as axioms of the type or one has to distinguish elements although they behave the same way under all applications of the function iselem . Thus the set of possible representations is drastically reduced.

The abstract type SUBSPACE represents all linear subspaces of the modul $\mathbb{Z}$. As stated above in the initial model of SUBSPACE the ordering in which the elements are incorporated into the subspace is considered to be relevant, although this is not intended for the corresponding mathematical structure, which is characterized by the terminal algebra. A formulation without existential quantifiers requires the introduction of additional (hidden) functions, which makes the presentation inconvenient (e.g. Skolem-functions with three arguments for the three universal quantifiers).

Our last example specifies graphs (binary relations) with finite numbers of edges based on a type NODE with an equality function eq .

The function isnpath tests whether a path has length n , and trans tests whether two nodes are connected in the transitive closure of the graph.

<u>type</u> GRAPH ≡ (<u>type</u> BOOL, <u>type</u> NODE, <u>type</u> PNAT)[1] <u>graph</u>, em, connect, isnpath, trans :

<u>sort</u> <u>graph</u> ,
<u>funct</u> <u>graph</u> em ,
<u>funct</u> (<u>graph</u>, <u>node</u>, <u>node</u>) <u>graph</u> connect ,
<u>funct</u> (<u>graph</u>, <u>node</u>, <u>node</u>, <u>pnat</u>) <u>bool</u> isnpath ,
<u>funct</u> (<u>graph</u>, <u>node</u>, <u>node</u>) <u>bool</u> trans ,

∀ <u>graph</u> g, <u>node</u> x, <u>node</u> y, <u>node</u> z, <u>node</u> v, <u>pnat</u> n :

<u>law</u> isnpath(em, x, y, n) ≡ false ,
<u>law</u> isnpath(connect(g, x, y), z, v, 1) ≡
 <u>if</u> eq(x, z) ∧ eq(y, v) <u>then</u> true
 <u>else</u> isnpath(g, z, v, 1) <u>fi</u> ,

<u>law</u> isnpath(g, x, y, n+1) ≡
 ∃ <u>node</u> p : (isnpath(g, x, p, n) ∧ isnpath(g, p, y, 1)) ,
<u>law</u> trans(g, x, y) ≡ ∃ <u>pnat</u> n : isnpath(g, x, y, n)

<u>end of type</u>

A specification of graphs with the functions isnpath and trans without using existential quantifiers is possible, but leads to the introduction of notions like "weight-function for nodes" or "minimal path" and hence to further laws in order to obtain a sufficiently complete specification. During a further development of the data type these notions may become necessary, but e.g. for correctness proofs, for the understandability of the axioms and for studying the models of the type their very technical content is a considerable ballast.
Assume that the type NODE has only ismorphic models. Then our theorem guarantees the existence of a terminal model Z for the type GRAPH. Moreover there exists an initial model I which is not isomorphic to Z , since e.g. the law

connect(connect(g, x, y), x, y) ≡ connect(g, x, y)

does not hold in I but in Z .

In a specification one often wants to express the surjectivity and/or totality of a function symbol f . With the help of existential quantifiers we get for the

---

1) PNAT denotes the natural numbers greater than zero.

surjectivity: $\forall\ \underline{m}_{n+1} x_{n+1} : \exists\ \underline{m}_1 x_1, \ldots, \underline{m}_n x_n : f(x_1, \ldots, x_n) \equiv x_{n+1}$

or (if we consider partial functions)

totality: $\forall\ \underline{m}_1 x_1, \ldots, \underline{m}_n x_n : \exists\ \underline{m}_{n+1} x_{n+1} : f(x_1, \ldots, x_n) \equiv x_{n+1}$

Injectivity, however, cannot be expressed by positive formulas, but it can be formulated by universally quantified conditional equations:

$$\forall\ \underline{m}_1 x_1, \ldots, \underline{m}_n x_n, \underline{m}_1 y_1, \ldots, \underline{m}_n y_n :$$
$$f(x_1, \ldots, x_n) \equiv f(y_1, \ldots, y_n) \Rightarrow x_1 \equiv y_1 \wedge \ldots \wedge x_n \equiv y_n$$

If a boolean operation eq for the equality of objects is introduced by a sufficiently complete specification, then surjectivity, totality and injectivity can always be expressed in terms of eq and therefore written as positive formulas.

5. Concluding remarks

Since all elements of a data structure can be represented by a term of the term algebra, existential quantifiers may be considered as infinite disjunctions. Disjunctions and conjunctions of equations do not destroy minimal models (if the type remains consistent). Therefore, existential quantifiers do not lead to specific problems for the existence of terminal models - in contrast to the situation for initial algebras.

Often types including existential quantifiers can also be specified by universal quantifiers only, since the introduction of Skolem-functions or the use of the operation " $\vee$ " in the type BOOL may help to avoid existential quantifiers. But this often leads to specifications which are not sufficiently complete and require additional axioms. Moreover, we believe that a specification mechanism should be as flexible as possible for the sake of convenience, shortness and clearness.

Acknowledgement

We wish to thank Prof. F.L. Bauer and Prof. K. Samelson for stimulating discussions.

References

/Birkhoff, Lipson 70/

G. Birkhoff, J.D. Lipson: Heterogeneous Algebras. Journal of Combinatorial Theory 8, 115-133 (1970).

/Broy et al. 79/

M. Broy, W. Dosch, H. Partsch, P. Pepper, M. Wirsing: Abstract Data Types: Some Theoretical Aspects and their Practical Consequences. To appear.

/Goguen et al. 78/

J. Goguen, J.W. Thatcher, E.G. Wagner: An Initial Algebra Approach to the Specification, Correctness and Implementation of Abstract Data Types. In: R.T. Yeh (ed.): Current trends in programming methodology, 4, Data Structuring, N.J.: Prentice-Hall, 1978.

/Guttag 75/

J.V. Guttag: The Specification and Application to Programming of Abstract Data Types. Ph. D. Th., Univ. of Toronto, Dept. of Comp. Sci., Rep. CSRG-59, 1975.

/Guttag et al. 76a/

J.V. Guttag, E. Horowitz, D.R. Musser: Abstract Data Types and Software Validation. USC/Information Sciences Institute, RR-76-48 (1976).

/Guttag et al. 76b/

J.V. Guttag, E. Horowitz, D.R. Musser: The Design of Data Type Specifications. USC/Information Sciences Institute, RR-76-49 (1976).

/Majster 77/

M. Majster: Data Types, Abstract Data Types and their Specification Problem. Technische Universität München, Institut für Informatik, TUM-INFO-7740, 1977.

/Partsch, Broy 79/

H. Partsch, M. Broy: Examples for Change of Types and Object Structures. In: F.L. Bauer, M. Broy (eds.): Proc. of the International Summer School on Program Construction, Marktoberdorf 1978, LNCS, Springer Verlag 1979. To appear.

/Thatcher et al. 77/

J.W. Thatcher, E.G. Wagner, J.B. Wright: Specification of Abstract Data Types Using Conditional Axioms. IBM Research Report RC-6214, 1977.

/Wand 78/

M. Wand: Final Algebra Semantics and Data Type Extensions. Indiana University, Comp. Science Department, Technical Report No. 65, 1978.

/Zilles 74/

S. Zilles: Algebraic Specification of Data Types. Computation Structures Group Memo 119, MIT, Cambridge, Mass., 1974.

A GENERALIZATION OF GINSBURG AND ROSE'S CHARACTERIZATION OF G-S-M MAPPINGS

C.CHOFFRUT

Université Paris VII, Département de Mathématiques

Tour 55-56, 2, Pl. Jussieu - 75221 PARIS CEDEX 05

Abstract: *We generalize Ginsburg and Rose's characterization of g-s-m mappings to the broader family of so-called subsequential functions, introduced by M.P.Schützenberger*

INTRODUCTION

Let A^* (resp. B^*) be the free monoid generated by the finite non empty set A (resp. B)..For each integer $n \geq 0$ let A_n (resp. B_n) be the set of all words of length not greater than n. The empty word shall be denoted by 1.

Consider a partial function $f : A^* \longrightarrow B^*$. We shall set $xf = \emptyset$ whenever xf is undefined, where $\emptyset$ is the zero of the $\mathbb{Z}$ - algebra of B^*. Let $\equiv$ be the right congruence over A^* defined by: $u \equiv v$ iff there exist a partial function $h : A^* \longrightarrow B^*$ and two words $x, y \in B^*$ such that the following holds for each $w \in A^*$: $uwf = x\,(wh)$ and $vwf = y\,(wh)$. With Schützenberger we say that f is *subsequential* iff the right congruence $\equiv$ has finite index (cf. [Sch]).

The main result of this paper is the following characterization of the partial functions which are subsequential:

Main Theorem. *Let* $f : A^* \longrightarrow B^*$ *be a partial function. Then itis subsequential iff it satisfies the two following conditions:*

i) There exists an integer $k > 0$ *such that for all* $u \in A^*$ *and all integer* $n \geq 0$ *there exists* $x \in B^*$ *verifying:* $uA_nf \subseteq xB_{k.n}$.

ii) For each rational subset $L \subseteq B^*$, Lf^{-1} *is a rational subset of* A^*.

When f is a function (not just a partial function) and when x equals uf , we obtain - apart from the irrelevant condition $1\,f = 1$ - Ginsburg and Rose's characterization of g-s-m mappings (cf. [Gi Ro]). In order to precise which partial functions are concerned with the theorem, let us recall that a partial function $h : A^* \longrightarrow B^*$ is *rational* iff its *graph* $h_{\#} = \{(u, v) \in A^* \times B^* \mid v = uh\}$ is a rational subset of the monoid $A^* \times B^*$. Then it is not hard to show that *a partial function* $f : A^* \longrightarrow B^*$ *is subsequential iff there exist a g-s-m mapping* $g : A^* \longrightarrow B^*$ *and a rational partial function of finite image* $h : A^* \longrightarrow B^*$ *such that the following holds for all* $u \in A^*$: $u f = u g \, u h$. (cf. [Ch1] , Proposition VI,1.2.). An example of subsequential partial function is given in section III, §1.

As a consequence of this last remark, every subsequential partial function is rational (cf. [Ei] , Proposition XI,3.1. and Theorem IX,4.1.). The family of subsequential partial functions possesses remarkable properties. To quote only two of them: 1) the composition of two subsequential partial functions is subsequential - obvious from the theorem - and 2) given any rational subset of $A^* \times B^*$, it is decidable whether it is the graph of a subsequential partial function (cf. [Ch2]). The notion of subsequential partial function thus provides an interesting class of rational partial functions and it is very likely that its study will benefit the theory of rational partial functions as a whole.

This paper is divided into three sections. Section 1 dispenses some basic notions, slightly altered so that they suit our purpose. For example our sequential transducers are obtained from Ginsburg's generalized sequential machines by introducing final states (a quite natural generalization, now widely accepted, see e.g. [Sa]) and by leaving the possibility for the output function to be into any free monoid but also into any free group. In doing this we can work in more pleasant structures. These machines "realize" in the usual way, sequential partial functions of a free monoid into a free monoid or a free group, which are considered in section2. We verify that these partial functions are rational and we give a characterization of all partial functions of a free monoid into a free group which are sequential. This last result is formal but it makes some verifications easier, as illustrated in section 3.

Subsequential partial functions of a free monoid into another were introduced two years ago in a paper of M.P.Schützenberger (cf. [Sch]). A systematic approach of the problem can be found in [Ch2] Chap.III and VI. In section 3, we recall their definition in terms of "subsequential" transducers and we prove that for each subsequential partial function there exists a subsequential transducer of a standard type (called "normalized") which realizes it. We show that the subsequential partial functions of A^* into B^* are exactly the sequential partial functions of A^* into $B^{(*)}$ whose image is in B^* (we assume B^* embedded into the free group $B^{(*)}$ generated by B). We solve the problem of determining under which conditions a rational partial function of A^* into B^* is the restriction of a sequential function of A^* into B^* . Finally we prove the Main Theorem.

I.PRELIMINARIES

1.Free monoids

Let A^* be the free monoid generated by the set A and 1 its unit - or *empty word* -. An element x of A^* is called a *word*. The length of x is denoted by $|x|$. We set $A^+ = A^* \setminus \{1\}$. As usual we shall denote by Rat A^* the family of all rational subsets of A^* (cf. [Ei], Chap.VII).

2.Free groups

Let A^{-1} be a copy of A and denote by a^{-1} the element corresponding to $a \in A$ in the bijection. Denote by $\equiv$ the congruence over the free monoid $(A \cup A^{-1})^*$ generated by all relations : $a a^{-1} = a^{-1} a = 1$, where $a \in A$. The *free group* $A^{(*)}$ generated by A is equivalent to the quotient $(A \cup A^{-1})^* \setminus \equiv$ (cf. [MKS]).

We shall make no distinction between A^* and its image in the canonical morphism of $(A \cup A^{-1})^*$ onto $A^{(*)}$. In other words we shall consider A^* as a submonoid of $A^{(*)}$.

All free monoids and free groups considered in the sequel will be supposed finitely generated. As many definitions and properties apply at the samme time to free monoids and free groups, we shall designate by M any free monoid or free Group.

3. Sequential transducers

Definition A *sequential transducer* T consists of:

- a finite non empty set Q, the set of *states*
- an element $q_- \in Q$, the *initial* state
- a subset $Q_+ \subseteq Q$, the subset of *final* states
- a function $\theta : Q \times A \to Q$, the *next state* function
- a function $\lambda : Q \times A \to M$, the *output* function

Observe that the four first data define a finite deterministic automaton which we shall refer to as the *automaton of* T.

For all $q \in Q$ and all $a \in A$ we shall write $q.a$ and $q*a$ instead of $(q,a)\theta$ and $(q,a)\lambda$ respectively. With this convention, and as long as no confusion may arise, we shall write : $T = (Q, q_-, Q_+)$.

The next state and the output functions are extended to $Q \times A^*$ in the usual way, by induction with respect to the length of the words:

For all $q \in Q$ we set : $q.1 = q$ and $q*1 = 1$.

For all $q \in Q$, all $u \in A^*$ and all $a \in A$ we set:

$$q.(ua) = (q.u).a \quad \text{and} \quad q*(ua) = (q*u)((q.u)*a)$$

Then for all $q \in Q$ and all $u, v \in A^*$ the following identity holds:

$$(1) \qquad q*uv = (q*u)((q.u)*v)$$

Practically allproofs in this paper involve constructions on sequential transducers. Proposition III.1 asserts that these constructions can be made on standard sequential transducers which are more easily manipulated than the general ones and whose definition is given now:

Definition A sequential transducer $T = (Q, q_-, Q_+)$ is *normalized* iff the following conditions hold:

i) For all $q \in Q$ there exists $u \in A^*$ such that : $q_-.u = q$

ii) For all $q \in Q$ and all $a \in A$ we have : $q.a \neq q_-$

iii) There exists at most one state $q_0 \in Q$ such that : $q_0.A^* \cap Q_+ = \emptyset$

iv) For all $q \in Q$ and all $a \in A$ we have : $q*a = 1$ if $q.a = q_0$.

II. SEQUENTIAL PARTIAL FUNCTIONS

Given any partial function f of a set X into M we write $x f = \emptyset$ whenever $x f$ is undefined, where $\emptyset$ is the zero of the $\mathbb{Z}$-algebra of M.

1. Basic definitions and properties

Definition A partial function $f : A^* \longrightarrow M$ is *sequential* iff there exists a sequential transducer T verifying for all $u \in A^*$: $u f = q_- * u$ if $q_-.u \in Q_+$ and $\emptyset$ otherwise. We say that T *realizes* f.

The usual notion of g-s-m mapping corresponds to the case when $M = B^*$ and when f is a function (cf. [Gi], p.93).

We give two elementary propositions on sequential partial functions (abbreviated *s.p.f.*). We recall that a partial function $f: A^* \longrightarrow M$ is *rational* if its *graph* $f\#= \{(u, v) \in A^* \times M \mid v = u f\}$ is a rational subset of the product monoid $A^* \times M$ (cf. [Ei], IX,8.). We first determine which partial sequential functions are sequential partial functions :

Proposition 1. *A partial function* $f : A^* \longrightarrow M$ *is sequential iff it is the restriction of a sequential function* $f' : A^* \longrightarrow M$ *to a rational subset of* A^*.

Proof. Let $T = (Q, q_-, Q_+)$ be a sequential transducer realizing f. Denote by f' the sequential function of A^* into M realized by the sequential transducer T' obtained from T by considering every state as final, i.e. by setting : $Q_+ = Q$. Then f is the restriction of f' to the subset $L \subseteq A^*$ recognized by the automaton of T.

Conversely, let $f' : A^* \longrightarrow M$ be a sequential function and $T' = (Q, q_-, Q_+)$ a sequential transducer realizing f'. Let $L \subseteq A^*$ be the rational subset recognized by a finite automaton (P, p_-, P_+). Denote by $T = (Q \times P, (q_-,p_-), Q_+ \times P_+)$ the sequential transducer whose next state and output functions are defined for all $(q,p) \in Q \times P$ and all $a \in A$ by: $(q,p).a = (q.a,p.a)$ and $(q,p)*a = q*a$. Then the s.p.f. realized by T is the restriction of f' to L □

The family of s.p.f. is a subfamily of all rational partial functions :

<u>Proposition 2.</u> *Every sequential partial function* $f : A^* \longrightarrow M$ *is rational.*

<u>Proof.</u> Let $T = (Q, q_-, Q_+)$ be a sequential transducer realizing f. Let j be a bijection of a set D over the (finite) set of all triples $(q,a,u) \in Q \times A \times M$ such that $q * a = u$. Define a next state function $Q \times D \longrightarrow Q$ as follows: $q.d = q'$ if $d\,j = (q,a,u)$ and $q.a = q'$. The resulting automaton (Q, q_-, Q_+) recognizes a rational subset L of D^*. Let h be the morphism of D^* into $A^* \times M$ defined by $d\,h = (a,u)$ if $d\,j = (q,a,u)$. Then in view of Proposition VII,2.4. of [Ei], the subset $L\,h = f^\# \subseteq A^* \times M$ is rational □

<u>2.The case when M is a free monoid B^*</u>

When in the previous definition, f is supposed to be a function (not just a partial function) and when M is supposed to be a free monoid B^*, we obtain the important case of what is known in the literature as g-s-m mappings. Certainly one of the most striking results on these functions is the following characterization (see for ex. [Ei], Theorem XI,6.3.):

<u>Theorem 3.</u>(Ginsburg and Rose) *Let* $f : A^* \longrightarrow B^*$ *be a function such that* $1\,f = 1$. *Then it is sequential iff the two following conditions are satisfied :*

- *i) There exists an integer* $k > 0$ *such that for all* $u \in A^*$ *and all* $a \in A$ *we have :* $u\,a\,f \in u\,f\,(B^* \setminus B^* B^{k+1})$
- *ii) For each* $L \in \text{Rat}\, B^*$, *we have :* $L\,f^{-1} \in \text{Rat}\, A^*$.

As mentionned in the introduction, our main result is a generalization of this theorem to a family of partial functions (the subsequential ones) defined in section 3.

<u>3.The case when M is a free group $B^{(*)}$</u>

Given any partial function $f : A^* \longrightarrow B^{(*)}$ consider the right congruence $\underset{f}{\equiv}$ over A^* defined by : $u \underset{f}{\equiv} v$ iff there exists $x \in B^{(*)}$ such that for all $w \in A^*$ we have : $u\,w\,f = x\,(v\,w\,f)$. The following result generalizes Theorem XII,4.2. of [Ei] :

<u>Proposition 4.</u> *Let* $f : A^* \longrightarrow B^{(*)}$ *be a partial function such that* $1\,f = 1$ *or* $\emptyset$. *Then it is sequential iff* $\underset{f}{\equiv}$ *has finite index*

Proof.

Necessity: Let $T = (Q, q_-, Q_+)$ be a sequential transducer realizing f. Denote by $\equiv$ the right congruence over A^* defined by : $u \equiv v$ iff $q_-.u = q_-.v$. Then by identity (1) of I.3., $u \equiv v$ implies for all $w \in A^*$: $u w f = (q_- * u)((q_-.u) * w$ and $v w f = (q_- * v)((q_-.v) * w)$, i.e. $u w f = x(v w f)$ with $x = (q_- * u)(q_- * v)^{-1} \in B^{(*)}$. Since $\equiv$ has finite index and is a refinement of $\equiv_f$, the latter right congruence has finite index too.

Sufficiency: For each $u \in A^*$ denote by $[u]$ the class of the right congruence $\equiv_f$ to which it belongs. Denote by Q the set consisting of all $[u]$'s where $u \in A^+$ and of a distinct element q_-. Let Q_+ be the subset of Q consisting of q_- if $1 f \neq \emptyset$ and of all $[u]$'s such that $u \in A^+$ and $u f \neq \emptyset$. Since $\equiv_f$ is a right congruence, we may define as usual a next state function $Q \times A \longrightarrow Q$ by setting :

$$q.a = \begin{cases} [a] & \text{if } q = q_- \\ [ua] & \text{if } [u] = q \quad \text{otherwise} \end{cases}$$

Let q_o be the unique state of Q (if such a state exists) such that $q_o.A^* \cap Q_+ = \emptyset$. We can suppose $q_- \neq q_o$ since otherwise f is nowhere defined and hence trivially sequential. Assign to every state $q \in Q \setminus \{q_o\}$ two words $v_q, w_q \in A^*$ as follows:

$$v_q = \begin{cases} 1 & \text{if } q = q_- \\ \text{otherwise choose an arbitrary} \\ v \in A^* \text{ such that } [v] = q \end{cases} \qquad w_q = \begin{cases} 1 & \text{if } q \in Q_+ \cup \{q_-\} \\ \text{otherwise choose an arbitrary} \\ w \in A^* \text{ such that } q.w \in Q_+ \end{cases}$$

Define now an output function $Q \times A \longrightarrow B^{(*)}$ by setting :

$$q * a = \begin{cases} 1 & \text{if } q_o = q.a \\ (a w_{q_-.a}) f & \text{if } q = q_- \\ ((v_q w_q) f)^{-1} (v_q a w_{q.a}) f & \text{otherwise} \end{cases}$$

In order to prove that the resulting transducer $T = (Q, q_-, Q_+)$ realizes f, we shall verify by induction on the length of $u \in A^+$, that $q_- * u = (u w_{q_-.u}) f$ holds whenever $q_-.u \neq q_o$.

Since the previous equality holds trivially when $u \in A$, we consider the case $u \in A^+$ and $a \in A$ and we set $q_-.u = q$. By hypothesis of induction we have $q_- * u = (u w_q) f$ and therefore $q_- * ua = (u w_q) f ((v_q w_q) f)^{-1} (v_q a w_{q.a}) f$. Since $u \equiv v_q$ we have $(u w_q) f ((v_q w_q) f)^{-1} = (u a w_{q.a}) f \; ((v_q a w_{q.a}) f)^{-1}$ which implies $q_- * ua = (u a w_{q_-.ua}) f$.

If we observe that $1 f = 1$ holds iff $q_- \in Q_+$, for all $u \in A^*$ we have $q_-.u \in Q_+$ iff $q_- * u = u f \neq \emptyset$, which completes the proof □

III. SUBSEQUENTIAL PARTIAL FUNCTIONS

1. Basic definitions

For all subset $\emptyset \neq X \subseteq B^*$ we denote by $X\wedge$ the greatest left common factor of all words in X and we set $\emptyset\wedge = \emptyset$.

Definition. A *subsequential transducer* is a pair (T, s) where:

- $T = (Q, q_-, Q_+)$ is a sequential transducer
- $s : Q \longrightarrow B^*$ is a partial function whose domain is Q_+

Further (T, s) is *normalized* if T is a normalized sequential transducer and if for all $q \in Q \setminus \{q_-\}$ the following holds:

(2) $\{q*u((q.u)s) \in B^* \mid q.u \in Q_+\}\wedge = 1$ or $\emptyset$

Definition. A partial function $f : A^* \longrightarrow B^*$ is *subsequential* iff there exists a subsequential transducer (T, s) such that the following holds for all $u \in A^*$: $u f = q_- * u((q_-.u)s)$. We say that (T, s) *realizes* f.

Obviously every p.s.f. is subsequential (take for s the partial function whose image is $\{1\}$). The converse is false:

Example: Let $A = \{a, b\}$ and consider the function $f : A^* \longrightarrow A^*$ defined for all $u \in A^*$ by : $u f = ua$. Then f is subsequential but not sequential.

From now on we shall drop the adjective "partial": by subsequential function we mean subsequential partial function.

Proposition 1. *Any subsequential function can be realized by a normalized subsequential transducer.*

Proof. Let us first verify that the subsequential function $f : A^* \longrightarrow B^*$ can be realized by a subsequential transducer (T, s) where T is normalized. We shall proceed as follows. Starting with any subsequential transducer (T, s) realizing f, we shall assume that the i-th of the four conditions of a normalized transducer may not be satisfied, but that the precedent are. Then we shall prove that there exists a subsequential transducer (T', s') satisfying all i first conditions and realizing f.

i) Denote by $Q' \subsetneq Q$ the subset of all elements $q \in Q$ for which there exists $u \in A^*$ with : $q_-.u = q$. Since $Q'.A \subsetneq Q'$ we can define a next state function $Q' \times A \longrightarrow Q'$ as the restriction of the next state function of T to $Q' \times A$. Further define an output function $Q' \times A \longrightarrow B^*$ as the restriction of the output function of T to $Q' \times A$. Then $T' = (Q', q_-, Q' \cap Q_+)$ is a sequential transducer satisfying condition i) of the definition of a normalized transducer.

ii) Suppose condition ii) is not satisfied. Consider $Q' = Q \cup \{q'_-\}$ where $q'_- \notin Q_+$ and $Q'_+ = Q_+$ if $q_- \notin Q_+$ and $Q'_+ = Q_+ \cup \{q'_-\}$ if $q_- \in Q_+$. Extend the next state and the output functions of T to $Q' \times A$ by setting: $q'_-.a = q_-.a$ and $q'_- * a = q_- * a$. The resulting sequential transducer $T' = (Q', q'_-, Q'_+)$ satisfies conditions i) and ii). If we denote by $s' : Q' \longrightarrow B^*$ the partial function obtained by extending s by setting $q'_- s' = q_- s$, (T', s') is the desired subsequential transducer satisfying i) and ii).

iii) and iv) Suppose condition iii) or iv) is not satisfied. Consider the equivalence $\sim$ over Q defined by : $q_1 \sim q_2$ iff $q_1 = q_2$ or $q_1.A^* \cap Q_+ = q_2.A^* \cap Q_+ = \emptyset$

Then $\sim$ is a congruence of the automaton of T and we can define a next state function $Q/\!\sim \times A \longrightarrow Q/\!\sim$ and an output function $Q/\!\sim \times A \longrightarrow B^*$ by setting:

$$[q].a = [q.a] \text{ where } [q] \text{ designates the class of } q \text{ in } \sim$$

and
$$[q] * a = \begin{cases} 1 & \text{if } q.A^* \cap Q_+ = \emptyset \\ q * a & \text{otherwise} \end{cases}$$

Then $T' = (Q/\!\sim, q_-, Q_+/\!\sim)$ is normalized. If $s' : Q/\!\sim \longrightarrow B^*$ is the partial function defined by $[q]\, s' = q\, s$, the subsequential transducer (T', s') realizes f and is therefore the desired one.

We shall verify now that condition (2) at the beginning of this paragraph, may as well be satisfied. Assume f is realized by (T, s) where T is normalized. Let $h : Q \longrightarrow B^*$ be defined by :

$$q\, h = \begin{cases} 1 & \text{if } q = q_o \text{ or } q_- \\ \bigwedge\{q * u((q.u)s) \in B^* \mid q.u \in Q_+\} & \text{otherwise} \end{cases}$$

Let T' be the normalized sequential transducer obtained from T by defining a new output function $\circ$ as follows:

$$q \circ a = \begin{cases} 1 & \text{if } q.a = q_o \\ (qh)^{-1} q*a\,(q.a)h & \text{otherwise} \end{cases}$$

We have : $q*a\,\{(q.a)*u((q.au)s) \in B^*\mid q.au \in Q_+\} = \{q*au((q.au)s) \in B^*\mid q.au \in Q_+\}$

$\subseteq \{q*u((q.u)s) \in B^* \mid q.u \in Q_+\}$, which shows that qh is a left factor of $q*a(q.a)h$. This implies : $(qh)^{-1}q*a(q.a)h \in B^*$. Let $s' : Q \to B^{(*)}$ be defined by : $qs' = (qh)^{-1}(qs)$. As qh is a left factor of qs , s' applies Q into B^*. Since (T', s') is a normalized subsequential transducer, it suffices to prove that it realizes f . But this follows from the equalities:

$$q_- \circ u(q_-.u)s' = q_- * u\,(q_-.u)h\,((q_-.u)h)^{-1}(q_-.u)s = uf \;\square$$

The following proposition is a verification that subsequential functions constitute a subfamily of all rational partial functions.

<u>Proposition 2.</u> *Each subsequential function is rational*

<u>Proof.</u> Let (T, s) be a subsequential transducer realizing the subsequential function $f : A^* \to B^*$, and set $T = (Q, q_-, Q_+)$. For every $q_+ \in Q_+$ denote by f_{q_+} the sequential partial function realized by the transducer obtained from T by considering q_+ as unique final state. Then by Proposition II.2., the graph $f\#$ is rational since we have: $f\# = \bigcup_{q_+ \in Q_+} f_{q_+}\# .\{(1, q_+s)\}$ $\square$

<u>2. Subsequential functions and sequential partial functions into a free group</u>

The relationship between the family of subsequential functions of A^* into B^* and the family of sequential partial functions of A^* into $B^{(*)}$ is given by the following result which justifies our extension of the classical notion of sequential transducer to the free group.

<u>Proposition 3.</u> *Let* $f : A^* \to B^{(*)}$ *be a partial function such that* $A^* f \subseteq B^*$. *Then it is sequential iff there exists a subsequential function* $g : A^* \to B^*$ *such that* $ug = uf$ *holds for each* $u \in A^+$.

<u>Proof.</u>

<u>Sufficiency</u>: Let (T, s) be a nomalized subsequential transducer realizing g . According to Proposition 1., we may suppose that $q_-s = 1$ or $\emptyset$. Denote by h the

function of Q into B^* defined by :

$$qh = \begin{cases} qs & \text{if } qs \neq \emptyset \\ 1 & \text{otherwise} \end{cases}$$

Let $T' = (Q, q_-, Q_+)$ - where $Q_+ = \text{Dom } s \subseteq Q$ - be the sequential transducer obtained from T by replacing the output function $*$ by the new output function $\circ$ defined for all $q \in Q$ and $a \in A$ by: $q \circ a = (qh)^{-1} q * a(q.a)h \in B^{(*)}$. Then one easily verifies by induction on the length of $u \in A^*$ that the following holds: $q_- \circ u = q_- * u(q_-.u)h$. In other words, the partial function $f : A^* \longrightarrow B^{(*)}$ such that for all u A , $uf = ug$ holds, is sequential □

<u>Necessity:</u> Let $T = (Q, q_-, Q_+)$ be a normalized sequential transducer realizing f . Without loss of generality, we may suppose that for all $u \in A^*$ the following holds : (3) $q_- * u \in B^*$. Indeed assign to every $q \in Q' = Q \setminus (Q_+ \cup \{q_-\} \cup \{q_0\})$, any word $w_q \in A^*$ such that $q.w_q \in Q_+$ and consider the function h of Q into B^* defined by :

$$qh = \begin{cases} q*w_q & \text{if } q \in Q' \\ 1 & \text{otherwise} \end{cases}$$

Denote by T' the (normalized) sequential transducer obtained from T by replacing the output function $*$ by the new output function $\circ$ defined for all $a \in A$ and all $q \in Q$ by:

$$q \circ a = \begin{cases} (qh)^{-1} q * a(q.a)h & \text{if } q.a \neq q_0 \\ 1 & \text{otherwise} \end{cases}$$

For all $u \in A^*$ we have:

$$q_- \circ u = \begin{cases} 1 & \text{if } q_-.u = q_- \\ q_- * u(q_-.u)h = q_- * u((q_-.u) * w_{q_-.u}) = q_- * uw_{q_-.u} \in B^* & \text{if } q_-.u \in Q' \\ q_- * u = uf \in B^* & \text{if } q_-.u \in Q_+ \end{cases}$$

Since $q_-.u = q_0$ implies $u = u'a$ with $u' \in A^*$ and $a \in A$, and $q_-.u' = q \neq q_0$, we have $q_- \circ u = q_- \circ u' \in B^*$. Thus, in all cases, equality (3) holds.

From now on we shall assume that (3) holds. For every $q \in Q \setminus \{q_-\}$ denote by $x_q \in B^*$ the longest right common factor of all words of the set $\{q_- * w \in B^* \mid w \in A^*, q_-.w = q\}$, and set $x_{q_-} = 1$. Let T' be the (normalized) sequential transducer obtained from T by replacing the output function $*$ by the new output function $\circ$ defined for all $a \in A$ and $q \in Q$ by : $q \circ a = 1$ if $q.a = q_0$ and $x_q (q*a)(x_{q.a})^{-1}$ otherwise. One easily verifies by induction on the length of

$u \in A^*$ that $q_- \circ u = q_- * u\, (x_{q_-.u})^{-1}$ holds, i.e. that (3) still holds. Let us verify now that for every $q \in Q$ and every $a \in A$, $q \circ a$ belongs to B^*.

Let $q \in Q$ and $u, v \in A^*$ be two words satisfying $q_-.u = q_-.v = q$ and such that $q_- \circ u$ and $q_- \circ v$ have no right common factor different from the empty word. If $q.a \neq q_o$ we have: $q_- \circ ua = (q_- * u (x_{q_-.u})^{-1})\, x_{q_-.u}\, ((q_-.u) * a)\, (x_{q_-.ua})^{-1} = y \in B^*$

and $q_- \circ va = (q_- * v (x_{q_-.v})^{-1})\, x_{q_-.v}\, ((q_-.v) * a)\, (x_{q_-.va})^{-1} = y' \in B^*$

Setting: $q_- * u\, (x_{q_-.u})^{-1} = z \in B^*$ and $q_- * v (x_{q_-.v})^{-1} = z' \in B^*$ we obtain:

$z\, (q \circ a) = y$ and $z'\, (q \circ a) = y'$ i.e. $z\, z'^{-1} = y\, y'^{-1}$. Since z and z' have no right common factor different from 1, the word $z\, z'^{-1}$ is reduced and there exists a word $t \in B^*$ such that $y = zt$ and $y' = z't$ hold. Thus: $q \circ a = t \in B^*$.

Let $s : Q \longrightarrow B^*$ be the partial function defined by $q\, s = x_q$ if $q \in Q_+$ and $\emptyset$ otherwise. If we denote by $g : A^* \longrightarrow B^*$ the subsequential function realized by the subsequential transducer (T', s), for all $u \in A^+$ we have $uf = ug$ □

3. The problem of the extension of a rational partial function to a sequential function

As another application of Proposition 1., we characterize all rational partial functions $f: A^* \longrightarrow B^*$ which are the restriction of a sequential function.

Proposition 4. *Let* $f : A^* \longrightarrow B^*$ *be a rational partial function such that* $1\, f = 1$ *or* $\emptyset$. *It can be extended to a sequential function iff the following conditions hold:*

i) f *is subsequential*

ii) For every $u, v \in A^*$ *such that* $uf \neq \emptyset$ *and* $uvf \neq \emptyset$ *we have:* $uvf \in uf\, B^*$.

Proof.

Necessity: Condition ii) is necessary since it is implied by the identity (1) of I.3. Further, if f is rational, then $\mathrm{Dom}\, f = (f^{\#})p$ (where p is the natural projection of $A^* \times B^*$ over A^*) is rational in view of Proposition VII,2.4. of [Ei]. It suffices now to use Proposition II.2.

Sufficiency: Let (T, s) be a normalized subsequential transducer realizing f. We have for each $q_-.u = q \in Q_+$: $q_- * u(qs) = uf = \{ uvf \in B^* | q.v \in Q_+ \} \wedge$

$= q_- * u \{ q * v((q.v)s) \in B^* | q.v \in Q_+ \} \wedge = q_- * u$ which implies

$qs = 1$. Consider now all states of T as final and denote by $g : A^* \longrightarrow B^*$ the sequential function realized by the new sequential transducer. Then g is the desired extension of f □

4. A characterisation of subsequential functions: proof of the Main Theorem

We can now turn to the proof of the Main Theorem. We recall that given any integer $n \geq 0$, A_n (resp. B_n) denotes the set of all words of A^* (resp. B^*) of length less or equal to n.

Theorem 5. *Let* $f : A^* \longrightarrow B^*$ *be a partial function. Then it is subsequential iff it satisfies the two following conditions:*

i) There exists an integer $k > 0$ *such that for all* $u \in A^*$ *and all integer* $n \geq 0$ *there exists* $x \in B^*$ *with :* $uA_n f \subseteq x B_{k.n}$

ii) For each rational subset $L \subseteq B^*$, Lf^{-1} *is a rational subset of* A^*.

Proof.

Necessity. Let (T , s) be a subsequential transducer realizing f and $k > 0$ an integer greater than all $|q*a|$ and $|qs|$ where $q \in Q$ and $a \in A$. For every $u \in A^*$ and every $v \in A_n$ we have: $uvf = q_-*u((q_-.u)*v)((q_-.uv)s) \subseteq q_-*u\, B_{2k.n}$. This proves condition i). In view of Proposition 2., f is rational. Then by Theorem IX,3.1. of [Ei], for each $L \in \mathrm{Rat}\, B^*$ we have $Lf^{-1} \in \mathrm{Rat}\, A^*$, which proves condition ii).

Sufficiency: Condition ii) implies that: $B^*f^{-1} = \mathrm{Dom}\, f \in \mathrm{Rat}\, A^*$. Let n be the number of states of an automaton recognizing $\mathrm{Dom}\, f$. We set $m = k.n$ (where k is as in condition i)), $F = A^* \setminus A^*A^{n+1}$ and $G = B^* \setminus B^*B^{m+1}$. We denote by R the set of all partial functions $r : F \longrightarrow G$ such that $(Fr)\wedge = 1$ or $\emptyset$. We shall prove the following facts:

A) there exists a function ρ assigning with each $u \in A^*$ an element $u\rho \in R$.

B) for each $r \in R$, $r\rho^{-1}$ is a rational subset of A^*. As a consequence, since R is finite, there exists a finite automaton $\mathcal{A}$ recognizing each $r\rho^{-1}$ (with $r \in R$)

C) the right congruence associated with the automaton $\mathcal{A}$ is a refinement of the congruence $\equiv_f$ defined in II.4.

A) Let $g : A^* \longrightarrow B^*$ be the partial function defined by: $ug = (uFf)\wedge$. To each $u \in A^*$ assign the partial function $u\rho = r : F \longrightarrow B^*$ defined by:

$$xr = \begin{cases} \emptyset & \text{if} \quad Fr = \emptyset \\ (ug)^{-1}uxf & \text{otherwise} \end{cases}$$

In view of condition i) we have $Fr \subseteq G$. Since $ug = (uFf)\Lambda$, we have $(Fr)\Lambda = \emptyset$ or 1 and therefore $r \in R$.

B) For each $z \in G$ and $|y| \leqslant 3m$ we set:

$$L_z^y = \begin{cases} yzf^{-1} & \text{if} \quad |y| < m \\ (B^{2m+1})^* yzf^{-1} & \text{if} \quad m \leqslant |y| \leqslant 3m \end{cases}$$

It is convenient to write $L_\emptyset^y = A^* \setminus B^*f^{-1}$ for all $|y| \leqslant 3m$.

For each $x \in A^*$, the partial function $t_x : A^* \longrightarrow A^*$ which to every $ux \in A^*$ associates $u \in A^*$ is rational since its graph is $(\bigcup_{a \in A} (a,a))^*(x,1)$. By theorem IX,3.1. of [Ei], for all $r \in R$ we have: $X_r = \bigcup_{|y| \leqslant 3m} (\bigcap_{x \in F} L_{xr}^y t_x) \in \text{Rat } A^*$. In order to prove B) it suffices to verify: $r\rho^{-1} = X_r$.

1) $r\rho^{-1} \subseteq X_r$

If $u\rho = r \in R$, then for all $x \in F$ we have $uxf = ug(xr)$. In particular, if $r = r_o$ where $r_o \in R$ is the partial function of F into G which is nowhere defined, for all $x \in F$ we have: $ux \in A^* \setminus B^*f^{-1}$. By defintion of $L_\emptyset^y$, this implies: $u \in \bigcap_{x \in F} (A^* \setminus B^* f^{-1})\, t_x = \bigcap_{x \in F} L_\emptyset^y\, t_x \subseteq X_{r_o}$ with $|y| \leqslant 3m$ arbitrary.

If $r \neq r_o$, two different cases must be distinguished:

<u>Case 1.</u> $|ug| < m$. This implies for all $x \in F$:

$ux \in L_{xr}^{ug}$ i.e. $u \in \bigcap_{x \in F} L_{xr}^{ug}\, t_x \subseteq X_r$.

<u>Case 2.</u> $m \leqslant |ug|$. Let $s \geqslant 0$ be the unique integer such that $(2m+1)s \leqslant |ug| - m < (2m+1)(s+1)$. There exist two words $b \in (B^{2m+1})^*$ and $y \in B^*$ such that we have: $ug = by$ and $m \leqslant |y| \leqslant 3m$. Thus, for all $x \in F$ we have $ux \in L_{xr}^y$ which implies: $u \in \bigcap_{x \in F} L_{xr}^y\, t_x \subseteq X_r$.

2) $X_r \subseteq r\rho^{-1}$

Let $u \in \bigcap_{x \in F} L_{xr}^y\, t_x$ where $|y| \leqslant 3m$. If $r = r_o$ then for each $x \in F$ we have $uvf = \emptyset$ i.e. $ug = \emptyset$ and therefore $u\rho = r_o$. We shall assume now $r \neq r_o$

Two different cases must be considered:

Case 1. $|y| < m$. For every $x \in F$ we have $uxf = y(xr)$. Since $(Fr)\Lambda = 1$ holds, we obtain $y = ug$ and thus: $u\rho = r$.

Case 2. $m \leqslant |y| \leqslant 3m$. Let $x_1, x_2 \in \text{Dom}\, r$. According to condition i) there exist $b_1, b_2 \in (B^{2m+1})^*$, $z, t_1, t_2 \in B^*$ with $|t_1| \leqslant m$ and $|t_2| \leqslant m$ such that the following equalities hold: $\{t_1, t_2\}\Lambda = 1$, $ux_1f = b_1y(x_1r) = zt_1$ and $ux_2f = b_2y(x_2r) = zt_2$. For $i = 1, 2$ we have: $|z| - m \leqslant |b_iy| \leqslant |z| + m$, which implies $||b_2y| - |b_1y|| \leqslant 2m$ and consequently $|b_1| = |b_2|$ since $||b_2y| - |b_1y|| = 1.(2m+1)$ where $1 \geqslant 0$ is an integer. Further we have $b_1 = b_2$, since $b_1 \neq b_2$ implies $|z| < |b_1|$ and thus $|z| + m < |b_1y|$, which contradicts the previous inequalities. As a consequence, there exists a word $b \in B^*$ such that $uxf = by(xr)$ holds for all $x \in \text{Dom}\, r$. This signifies precisely that: $u\rho = r$.

C) Let $\mathcal{Q} = (Q, q_-)$ be a finite deterministic automaton recognizing each $r\rho^{-1} \in \text{Rat}\, A^*$, where r ranges over R , and let $\equiv$ be the right congruence over A^* defined by: $u \equiv v$ iff $q_-.u = q_-.v$. Thus $u \equiv v$ implies $u\rho = v\rho$.

Given any integer $1 > 0$, consider the following predicate:

P_1: For each $u, v \in A^*$ such that $u \equiv v$ there exists an element $x \in B^{(*)}$ satisfying for all $w \in A_1$: $uwf = x\,(vwf)$.

Assume there exists a greatest integer $L > 0$ for which P_1 is true. Then certainly $L \geqslant n$. For every $a, b \in A$ and $u, v \in A^*$ satisfying $u \equiv v$, there exist $x, y \in B^{(*)}$ such that for all $w \in A_L$ we have: $uawf = x\,(vawf)$ and $ubwf = y\,(vbwf)$. We may suppose that there exist $w_1, w_2 \in A_L$ such that $uaw_1f \neq \emptyset$ and $ubw_2f \neq \emptyset$ since otherwise x or y or both x and y may be chosen arbitrarily and therefore x and y may be chosen equal. Then there exist two words $t_1, t_2 \in A_{n-1}$ (because $\text{Dom}\, f = B^*f^{-1}$ is recognized by an automaton having n states) such that $uat_1f \neq \emptyset$ and $ubt_2f \neq \emptyset$. Since we have $at_1, bt_2 \subsetneq A_n \subsetneq A_L$ there exists $z \in B^*$ with: $uat_1f = z\,(vat_1f)$ and $ubt_2f = z\,(vbt_2f)$ i.e. $x = y$. This shows that P_{L+1} is true, which contradicts the fact that L is maximal.

Since $\equiv$ is a refinement of $\equiv_f$, by Propositions 3. and II.4., the proof is completed □

<u>Corollary 6.</u> *If* $f : A^* \longrightarrow B^*$ *and* $g : B^* \longrightarrow C^*$ *are subsequential functions, then the composition* $f\,g : A^* \longrightarrow C^*$ *is subsequential*

<u>Proof.</u> For all $L \in \mathrm{Rat}\ C^*$ we have $Lg^{-1} \in \mathrm{Rat}\ B^*$ and therefore $(Lg^{-1})f^{-1} = L(fg)^{-1} \in \mathrm{Rat}\ A^*$ which proves that condition ii) of the theorem is satisfied.

Let $k, l > 0$ be the integers satisfying condition i) for f and g respectively. For each $u \in A^*$ and each integer $n > 0$ there exists $x \in B^*$ with $uA_n f \subseteq xB_{k.n}$. Applying the same condition to $x \in B^*$ and $k.n$, we have: $xB_{k.n}\, g \subseteq tC_{l.k.n}$ where $t \in C^*$. Thus: $uA_n fg \subseteq tC_{l.k.n}$ □

REFERENCES

[Ch 1] CHOFFRUT C., Contribution à l'étude de quelques familles remarquables de fonctions rationnelles, Thèse Sci. Math. Université Paris VII, Paris,1978.

[Ch 2] CHOFFRUT C., Une caractérisation des fonctions séquentielles et des fonctions sous-séquentielles en tant que relations rationnelles,Theoret. Comput. Sci., <u>5</u>,(1977), 325-337.

[Ei] EILENBERG S., " Automata, Languages and Machines", Vol. A, Academic Press, New York, N.Y., 1974.

[Gi] GINSBURG S., "The Mathematical Theory of Context-Free Languages", Mac Graw-Hill, New York, 1966.

[Gi Ro] GINSBURG S. & G.F.ROSE, A characterization of machine mappings, Can. J. Math. <u>18</u>,(1966), 381-388.

[MKS] MAGNUS W., KARRASS A. & D. SOLITAR," Combinatorial Group Theory", Interscience Publ., New York,1966.

[Sa] SALOMON K., The Decidability of a Mapping Problem for Generalized Sequential Machines with Final States, J. Comput. System Sci.,<u>10</u>,(1975),200-218.

[Sch] SCHUTZENBERGER M.P., Sur une variante des fonctions séquentielles, Theoret. Comput. Sci.,<u>11</u>,(1977),47-57.

STRICT DETERMINISTIC LANGUAGES AND CONTROLLED REWRITING SYSTEMS

by

Laurent CHOTTIN
Université de Bordeaux I
Mathématiques et Informatique
Laboratoire associé au C. N. R. S. n°226
33405 Talence, FRANCE

ABSTRACT. -

A controlled rewriting system over an alphabet X is a finite set of rules $v_i \to w_i$ $(1 \leq i \leq n)$ with v_i, w_i in X^* such that $|v_i| < |w_i|$, each rule being associated with a regular language $R_i \subseteq X^*$. Given such a system, $f \Rightarrow g$ means that $f = \alpha v_i \beta$ and $g = \alpha w_i \beta$ for some i, α in R_i, β in X^*. The system is said to be injective if and only if $f \Rightarrow g \Leftarrow f'$ implies $f = f'$. Controlled rewriting systems are a special case of finite relations with computable left context (P. Butzbach [5], 1973), which can be defined as above, with the R_i's recursive instead of regular. P. Butzbach proved [5] that every simple deterministic language [11] is generated by some finite relation with computable left context iterating from a finite set of words. Here we improve this result with our THEOREM 1 : "Every strict deterministic language is generated by some injective controlled rewriting system iterating from a finite set of words". Moreover, let A be a deterministic pushdown automaton and $\Rightarrow$ be the rewriting relation associated with A by the above theorem. Let $\theta : X^* \to X^*$ defined by $\theta(u) = v$ if $v \overset{*}{\Rightarrow} u$ and $\nexists\, w, w \Rightarrow v$ (v is unique, for $\Rightarrow$ is injective) ; in some sense, θ generalizes the semi-Dyck simplification. We state :

THEOREM 2 : "If $R \subseteq X^*$ is regular then so is $\theta(R)$". This extends a result of M. Benois [1], also obtained by M. Fliess [10] (using quite different methods).

THEOREM 3 : "Let L be a language accepted by A by some accepting states. Then $\theta(L)$ is regular and $L = \{f \,/\, \exists\, g \in \theta(L),\ g \overset{*}{\Rightarrow} f\} = \theta^{-1}(\theta(L))$."

This is a reformulation of a result recently obtained by J. Sakarovitch [18] with a different method.

INTRODUCTION. -

Among the devices used to define formal languages, we find automata, equations, grammars and congruences. The first three devices are strongly related, and the results about their mutual relations are numerous in the litterature. On the other hand, the relations between congruences and other devices are much less known, and the existing results about these relations are never exact characterizations but only inclusions. One reason of this fact is that automata usually read from left to right, but congruences work from any point in a given word ; for instance it is well known that the reverse of a deterministic context-free language is not necessarily deterministic. This remark is one of the motivations which have lead us to define a class of relations in the free monoïd which generalize the semi-Thue systems by the addition of a control over the use of the rules $v_i \to w_i$; this control consists in allowing to rewrite $\alpha v_i \beta$ in $\alpha w_i \beta$ only if the prefix (or "left context") α is in a given regular language R_i associated with the rule $v_i \to w_i$. Such a definition intentionally brings something like a left-to-right orientation.

A very similar notion (called finite relation with computable left context) was introduced in 1973 by Butzbach [5] in connection with the equivalence problem for simple deterministic languages [12]. The definition of Butzbach differs from ours by allowing the R_i's to be arbitrary recursive sets.

The present work is originated in papers of M. Nivat and Y. Cochet about basic systems, which are defined as finite sets of length-increasing rules $v_i \to w_i$ such that :

(i) no w_i is a proper factor of any w_j ;

(ii) there is no non-empty word which ends some v_i and begins some w_j ;

(iii) there is no non-empty word which begins some v_i and ends some w_j .

These systems are strongly related with simple and very simple deterministic languages. A context-free language L is said to be simple deterministic [12] iff it is generated by a context-free grammar in Greibach normal form in which for each pair (x, ξ) (where x is a terminal letter and ξ a non-terminal letter) there exists at most one rule $\xi \to a u$. L is said to be very simple iff it is generated by a grammar as above with the stronger condition that each terminal letter x determines at most one rule $\xi \rightarrow au$. The main results about these systems are the following :

THEOREM A (Nivat [13]) - Every language generated by a basic semi-Thue system with a finite set of axioms is context-free.

THEOREM B (P. Butzbach [4]) - Every very simple language is generated by a basic Thue system with a finite set of axioms ; moreover this system has the Church-Rosser property.

Remark. In the preceding statement, "Thue system" can be replaced by "semi-Thue system", because of the Church-Rosser property (a system $\{(v_i, w_i) / 1 \leq i \leq n\}$ with $|v_i| \leq |w_i|$ is said to have the Church-Rosser property iff the corresponding rewriting relation $\Rightarrow$ satisfies the condition $\overset{*}{\Leftrightarrow} = \overset{*}{\Rightarrow}\overset{*}{\leftrightarrows}$ where $\Leftrightarrow$ is $\Rightarrow \cup \Leftarrow$ and $\leftrightarrows$ is the relation defined by the lenght-preserving rules).

Recently, J. Sakarovitch [19] has considered "left-basic" systems (i. e. systems satisfying the conditions (i) and (ii) above) with the additional conditions that :

(iv) no w_i is a proper factor of any w_j

(v) $w_i = w_j$ implies $v_i = v_j$.

About these systems, he has proved the following :

THEOREM A'. - Every language generated by a left-basic semi-Thue system satisfying (iv) and (v), with a regular set of axioms, is deterministic.

Let's also quote the following result of P. Butzbach [5] :

THEOREM B'. - Every simple language is generated by a relation with computable left context with a finite set of axioms.

Remark : In fact, when inspecting the proof of Butzbach, we can see that the control languages R_i's which determine the "left context" in the above theorem are deterministic languages. The theorem 1 in the present paper says that (a) theorem B' holds for every strict deterministic language and (b) the R_i's can be choosen regular.

For more information concerning languages defined by congruences, see Y. Cochet [6, 7, 8] and M. Nivat [14, 15, 16]. A more complete bibliography is given in the survey of J. Berstel [2]. This paper is divided into four sections : the first one is devoted to the definition of controlled rewriting systems and to some technical definitions about iterative pairs associated with a pushdown automaton (the systematic use of iterative pairs was settled by L. Boasson [3] ; our definitions are essentially the same). In section 2 we associate various languages with a pushdown automaton A ; some of them are finite ; the others are regular. In section 3, we use these languages to build a controlled system S and a finite set D associated to A, and we show that if A is deterministic then (i) S is injective and (ii) the language generated by S with the set D of axioms is precisely the language accepted by A with empty store. In section 4, we focus on the properties of the above system S ; this leads us to the result that the simplification θ associated to S preserves regularity (this generalizes a result of M. Benois [1], also proved by M. Fliess [10] via quite different tools). Moreover we obtain the following result : let L be any language recognized by A by final state ; then $\theta(L)$ is regular. This is a reformulation of a result recently obtained by J. Sakarovitch [18] with a different method.

In a forthcoming paper, we shall examine under what conditions an injective controlled rewriting system does generate a deterministic language.

I - NOTATIONS AND TERMINOLOGY.

a) Controlled rewriting systems.

Let X be an alphabet. A controlled rewriting system over X is a finite set of triples

$$S = \{(R_i, u_i, v_i) \;/\; 1 \leqslant i \leqslant n\}$$

such that, for each i, u_i and v_i are two distinct words over X and R_i is a regular language over X.

A binary relation $\underset{S}{\Rightarrow}$ on X^* is associated with S as follows : let f, g be words over X ; then

$$f \underset{S}{\Rightarrow} g \quad \text{iff} \quad f = \alpha u_i \beta \text{ and } g = \alpha v_i \beta \text{ for some } i, \text{ with } \alpha \in R_i .$$

If the context makes S clear, $\underset{S}{\Rightarrow}$ is written $\Rightarrow$.

A word g is in normal form w. r. t. S if there is no g' such that $g \Rightarrow g'$. If $f \overset{*}{\Rightarrow} g$ with g in normal form then g is a normal form of f (w. r. t. S).

S is functional if $\underset{S}{\Rightarrow}$ is a functional relation. In this case, every f in X^* has at most one normal form, denoted by $\rho_S(f)$ if it does exist. If the context makes S clear, ρ_S is written ρ.

For S as above, let us define $S^{-1} = \{(R_i, v_i, u_i) / 1 \leq i \leq n\}$. Then S^{-1} is also a controlled rewriting system and $\underset{S^{-1}}{\Rightarrow} = (\underset{S}{\Rightarrow})^{-1}$, i.e. $f \underset{S^{-1}}{\Rightarrow} g$ iff $g \underset{S}{\Rightarrow} f$.

S is <u>injective</u> iff S^{-1} is functional. In this case we denote by θ_S the partial function $\rho_{S^{-1}}$; θ_S is the <u>simplification associated with</u> S.

S is <u>decreasing</u> if $|v_i| < |u_i|$ for all i. In this case, $\Rightarrow$ is noetherian, i.e. there is no infinite sequence $f \Rightarrow f_1 \Rightarrow f_2 \Rightarrow \ldots$ of rewritings. We obtain immediately :

PROPOSITION. - <u>If</u> S <u>is functional and decreasing, then every word</u> f <u>in</u> X^* <u>has a unique normal form</u> w. r. t. S. <u>In other words,</u> ρ_S <u>is a total mapping.</u>

<u>Remark.</u> Every functional controlled rewriting system has in an obvious way the Church-Rosser property.

<u>Example</u> : Let $T = \{(u_i, v_i) / 1 \leq i \leq n\} \subset X^* \times X^*$ be a semi-Thue decreasing system with the conditions (iv) and (v) (cf. introduction). We can associate with T a functional controlled rewriting system $L(T) = \{(R_i, u_i, v_i) / 1 \leq i \leq n\}$ which simulates the leftmost computations of T, i.e. : $f \underset{L(T)}{\Rightarrow} g$ iff $f = \alpha u_i \beta$ and $g = \alpha v_i \beta$ for some i and, for every decomposition of f in $\alpha' u_j \beta'$, either (a) $|\alpha| < |\alpha'|$ or (b) $\alpha = \alpha'$ and $|u_i| < |u_j|$; (b) never occurs because (iv) holds for T, and the leftmost restriction is obtained by taking $R_i = X^* - X^* A X^*$ for each i, with $A = \{u_j / 1 \leq j \leq n\}$. Because of condition (v), $L(T)$ is guaranteed to be functional. Moreover, g is in normal form w. r. t. T iff it is in normal form w. r. t. $L(T)$. For such a word, if we assume T to have the Church-Rosser property, then $f \overset{*}{\underset{T}{\Rightarrow}} g$ iff $f \overset{*}{\underset{L(T)}{\Rightarrow}} g$.

b) <u>Pushdown automata</u> ; <u>iterative pairs</u> ; <u>iterative factors</u>.

A pushdown automaton is a 6-tuple $A = (X, Y, Q, d, q_o, y_o)$ where X is the input alphabet, Y is the pushdown-store alphabet, Q is the finite state set (assumed to be disjoint from Y), d is the transition mapping from $YQ(X \cup \{1\})$

into the finite subsets of Y^*Q, q_0 is the initial state and y_0 is the initial pushdown symbol (we do not consider terminal states).

Given such an automaton, we define a binary relation $\vdash$ in Y^*QX^* by its graph

$$\{(uyqxf\,,\ uvq'f)\ /\ u, v \in Y^*,\ q, q' \in Q,\ f \in X^*,\ x \in X \cup \{1\},\ y \in Y \text{ and } vq' \in d(yqx)\}.$$

Let f be in X^*, u, u' in Y^*, q, q' in Q;

$$uq \xrightarrow{f} u'q'$$

means that $uqf \overset{*}{\vdash} u'q'$.

The language accepted by A (<u>by empty store</u>) is

$$L(A) := \{f \in X^* \ /\ y_0 q_0 \xrightarrow{f} q \ , \quad \text{for some } q \text{ in } Q\}.$$

A is said to be <u>deterministic</u> if

$$|d(yqx)| + |d(yq)| \leq 1 \quad \text{for all } y \text{ in } Y,\ q \text{ in } Q,\ x \text{ in } X.$$

Now, given a pushdown symbol y and a state q, we define the notions of yq-<u>iterative pair</u> and yq-<u>iterative factor</u> (with respect to A) as follows :

(1) <u>A</u> yq-<u>iterative pair of a word</u> $f \in X^*$ <u>is a</u> 5-<u>tuple</u> (f', u, v, w, f'') <u>of words over</u> X, <u>such that</u> :

$$\begin{cases} f = f'uvwf'', \\ yq \xrightarrow{f'} \alpha y'q' \ \underline{\text{with}}\ \alpha\ \underline{\text{in}}\ Y^*,\ y'\ \underline{\text{in}}\ Y,\ q'\ \underline{\text{in}}\ Q, \\ y'q' \xrightarrow{u} \beta y'q' \ \underline{\text{with}}\ \beta\ \underline{\text{in}}\ Y^+, \\ y'q' \xrightarrow{v} q'' \ \underline{\text{with}}\ q''\ \underline{\text{in}}\ Q, \\ \beta q'' \xrightarrow{w} q''. \end{cases}$$

Note that, if A is deterministic, the condition "β non empty" implies "u non empty". The integer $|\beta|$ is said to be the <u>width</u> of the pair.

(2) <u>A</u> yq-<u>iterative factor of</u> f <u>is a triple</u> (f', u, f'') <u>such that</u> :

$$\begin{cases} f = f'uf'' \text{ with } u \text{ non empty}, \\ yq \xrightarrow{f'} \alpha y'q' \text{ with } \alpha \text{ in } Y^*,\ y' \text{ in } Y,\ q' \text{ in } Q, \\ y'q' \xrightarrow{u} y'q'. \end{cases}$$

<u>Terminology</u>. - We say that f is yq-<u>prime</u> if it has neither yq-iterative pair nor yq-iterative factor. We say that f is yq-<u>primary</u> if it has only one yq-iterative pair and no yq-iterative factor, or only one yq-iterative factor and no yq-iterative pair.

II - SOME SETS ASSOCIATED WITH A PUSHDOWN AUTOMATON.

Let y be in Y, q, q' in Q ; we define the sets $D(yqq')$, $F(qy)$, $P(yqq')$, $R(yq)$ as follows :

$D(yqq') = \{f \in X^* \,/\, yq \overset{f}{\curvearrowright} q'$ and f is yq-prime $\}$,

$F(yq) = \{f \in X^+ \,/\, yq \overset{f}{\curvearrowright} yq$ and f is yq-primary $\}$,

$P(yqq') = \{(u, v, w) \in (X^*)^3 \,/\, yq \overset{u}{\curvearrowright} \alpha yq,\ yq \overset{v}{\curvearrowright} q',\ \alpha q' \overset{w}{\curvearrowright} q'$ for some α in Y^+ and $u v w$ is yq-primary$\}$;

for u in X^* we define :

$R(yq, u) = \{f \in X^* / y_o q_o \overset{f}{\curvearrowright} \alpha y q$ for some α in Y^* and $f u$ is $y_o q_o$ - prime $\}$;

$S(yq) = F(yq) \cup \{u v w \,/\, (u, v, w) \in P(yqq')$ for some $q' \in Q\}$.

PROPERTY 1. - <u>The sets</u> $D(yqq')$, $F(yq)$, $P(yqq')$ <u>are finite</u> ; <u>if</u> $u \in S(yq)$ <u>then</u> $R(yq, u)$ <u>is regular.</u>

<u>Proof</u> : Claiming that $D(yqq')$, $F(yq)$ and $P(yqq')$ are finite is nothing else than stating the classical pumping lemma for pushdown automata [17]. Let's consider the sets $R(yq,u)$ with u in $S(yq)$; in order to show they are regular, we build a <u>finite automaton</u> A' as follows : the states of A' are the words αq where q is in Q and α is a word over Y of length $\leq m$, with $m = card(Y \times Q \times Q)$. Now let's define the moves of A' : say that A' acts like A with the clause that, after each move, if the length of the pushdown store exceeds m, we preserve only its m topmost letters. Formally :

if $d(y q x) = u q'$ (in A), then

for each α in Y^* with length $< m$, the triple $(\alpha\, y q,\ x,\ (\alpha\, u)^{(m)}\, q')$ is a transition-rule of A' ($v^{(m)}$ denotes v if $|v| \leq m$, and the last m letters of v elsewhere). Of course, $y_o q_o$ is the initial state of A'.

Now, it is easy to check that every word f which has a $y_o q_o$ - iterative pair has a $y_o q_o$ - iterative pair of width $\leq m$ ("width" is defined in section 1). Thus every word f for which A' blocks before ending to read it, is guaranteed to have at least one $y_o q_o$ - iterative pair. So $R(yq, u)$ is included in the set $R'(yq)$ recognized by A' with $\{\alpha y q \,/\, \alpha \in Y^*,\ |\alpha| < m\}$ as set of accepting states. Now it is straightforward to show that if u is in $S(yq)$, then :

$R(yq, u) = R'(yq) \cap \{f \,/\, \forall y'q' \in YQ,\ fu \notin R'(y'q')\, S(y'q')\, X^+\}$;

the regularity of $R(yq, u)$ follows.

A more detailed proof will be given in a forthcoming version of this paper.

III - CONTROLLED REWRITING SYSTEM ASSOCIATED WITH A PUSHDOWN AUTOMATON.

Now we set $S = S' \cup S''$ with :

$$S' = \{(R(yq, uvw), v, uw / y \in Y,\ q \in Q,\ (u, v, w) \in P(yqq'),\ q' \in Q\},$$

$$S'' = \{(R(yq,u), 1, u) / \ y \in Y,\ q \in Q,\ u \in F(yq)\}.$$

Let $D = \bigcup_{q \in Q} D(y_o q_o q)$; clearly, D is a finite prefix-free language ; let $\Rightarrow$ be the rewriting relation associated to S (as defined in section 1). Then :

THEOREM 1. - If A is deterministic then the associated controlled rewriting system S is injective, and :

$$L(A) = \{ f \in X^* \ / \ g \overset{*}{\Rightarrow} f \quad \text{for some} \quad g \in D\}.$$

Proof : The fact that A is deterministic implies the following facts :

Claim 1. - Let u, u', u'' be in Y^*, q, q', q'' in Q, f in X^*, g in X^+; if $uq \overset{f}{\curvearrowright} u'q'$ and $uq \overset{fg}{\curvearrowright} u''q''$ then $u'q' \overset{g}{\curvearrowright} u''q''$.

Claim 2. - Let f in X^* be such that $f = \alpha h \beta$ with α in $R(yq, h)$ and h in $F(yq)$ or in $\bigcup_{q' \in Q} \{uvw / (u, v, w) \in P(yqq')\}$, for some yq in YQ. Then such a factorization of f is unique (this claim says that S is injective).

The proof of claim 1 is immediate.

Proof of claim 2 : Suppose $f = \alpha' h' \beta'$ with α', h', β' as above. Since α and α' are $y_o q_o$-prime, neither αh is a prefix of α' nor $\alpha' h'$ is a prefix of α. Thus either $|\alpha'| < |\alpha h| \leqslant |\alpha' h'|$ or $|\alpha| < |\alpha' h'| \leqslant |\alpha h|$. Let's treat the first case (the second is quite analogous) ; we have two subcases :

case (i) : $|\alpha| \leqslant |\alpha'|$ we can write $\alpha' = \alpha f_1$, $h = f_1 f_2$, $h' = f_2 f_3$; we must again treat separately four cases according to the possibles forms of h and h' ; here we shall just consider the case $h = uvw$, $h' = u'v'w'$ with (u,v,w) in $P(yqq')$, (u', v', w') in $P(y_1 q_1 q'_1)$, and $\alpha' \in R(y_1 q_1, h')$; in this case we have (according to the definitions of R and P :

$$y_o q_o \overset{\alpha}{\curvearrowright} a y q \overset{f_1 f_2}{\curvearrowright} a q' \quad \text{with } a \text{ in } Y^*,$$

$$y_o q_o \overset{\alpha f_1}{\curvearrowright} b y_1 q_1 \overset{f_2 f_3}{\curvearrowright} b q'_1 \quad \text{with } b \text{ in } Y^*.$$

If f_1 and f_3 are nonempty, then claim 1 allows to write :

$$y_o\, q_o \xrightarrow{\alpha} a\, y\, q \xrightarrow{f_1} b\, y_1\, q_1 \xrightarrow{f_2} a\, q' \xrightarrow{f_3} b\, q'_1 .$$

But by the definition of $P(y\,q\,q')$, $a\,y\,q \xrightarrow{f_1 f_2} a\,q'$ comes from $y\,q \xrightarrow{f_1 f_2} q'$, so $|b| \geq |a|$; for the same reason we have $y_1 q_1 \xrightarrow{f_2 f_3} q'_1$, so $|a| \geq |b\, y_1|$; here we have a contradiction. Thus, either $f_1 = 1$ and $a\,y\,q = b\,y_1\,q_1$ or $f_3 = 1$ and $a\,q' = b\,q'_1$; in both cases, the fact that $f_1 f_2$ is yq-primary and $f_2 f_3$ is $y_1 q_1$-primary implies that $h = h'$, $\alpha = \alpha'$ and $\beta = \beta'$. The other cases concerning h and h' lead to an analogous treatment ; we leave them to the reader.

<u>case</u> (ii) : $|\alpha| > |\alpha'|$; this case leads rapidly to a contradiction with the fact that h is yq-primary. So claim 2 is proved.

Now, we can prove the equality $L(A) = M$, where $M = \{f \,/\, g \overset{*}{\Rightarrow} f$ for some g in $D\}$.

(a) Suppose $f \Rightarrow g$ with f in L(A) ; either $f = \alpha\, v\, \beta$ and $g = \alpha\, u\, v\, w\, \beta$ with $\alpha \in R(yq, u\,v\,w)$ and (u, v, w) in $P(y\,q\,q')$, or $f = \alpha\,\beta$ and $g = \alpha\, u\, \beta$ with $\alpha \in R(yq, u)$ and u in $F(yq)$.

In the first case we have :

$$y_o q_o \xrightarrow{\alpha v \beta} q_1 ,\quad y_o q_o \xrightarrow{\alpha} a\, y\, q ,\quad y\, q \xrightarrow{v} q' ,$$
$$\text{and} \quad y\, q \xrightarrow{uvw} q' ,$$

necessarily $v\beta$ is nonempty ; thus claim 1 gives $a\, y\, q \xrightarrow{v\beta} q_1$; in the same way we have $a\, q' \xrightarrow{\beta} q_1$; hence

$$y_o\, q_o \xrightarrow{\alpha} a\, y\, q \xrightarrow{uvw} a\, q' \xrightarrow{\beta} q_1 \;;\; \text{this gives :}\;\; y_o\, q_o \xrightarrow{g} q_1 .$$

This proves that $f \Rightarrow g$ with $f \in L(A)$ implies $g \in L(A)$; knowing that $D \subseteq L(A)$, we can conclude that $M \subseteq L(A)$.

(b) Let g be in $L(A) \setminus D$; g is accepted by A and has at least one $y_o q_o$-iterative pair or one $y_o q_o$-iterative factor. Let's treat the first case (we leave the second case to the reader). Let g_1 be the shortest prefix of g which is not $y_o q_o$-prime ; necessarily every $y_o q_o$-iterative pair of g_1 has its 5th component empty, and g_1 is necessarily $y_o q_o$-primary; let $(\alpha, u, v, w, 1)$ be a $y_o q_o$-iterative pair of g_1 , with $y_o q_o \xrightarrow{\alpha} a\,y\,q$, $y\,q \xrightarrow{u} b\,y\,q$, $y\,q \xrightarrow{v} q'$, $b\,q' \xrightarrow{w} q'$, and $|\alpha|$ <u>maximum</u> ; this condition imposes $u\, v\, w$ to be yq-primary ; hence $(u, v, w) \in P(y\,q\,q')$ and we can conclude that $f = \alpha\, v\, \beta \Rightarrow g$ and $f \in L(A)$. Now we have the other inclusion, and theorem 1 is proved.

EXAMPLE. - Consider the deterministic pushdown automaton $\mathfrak{A} = (\{a, b, c\}, \{y_o, y\}, \{q_o, q\}, d, q_o, y_o)$ where d is given by the following table :

	a	b	c	1
$y_o q_o$	$y_o y q_o$	-	q	-
$y_o q$	-	-	-	q
$y q_o$	$y y q_o$	q_o	q	-
$y q$	-	-	-	q

One checks easily that $L(\mathfrak{A}) = \{wc \mid w \in \{a, b\}^*, |u|_a \geq |u|_b$ for each prefix u of w $\}$. We obtain the following controlled rewriting system :

$$S = \{(\{a\}^*, 1, ab), (\{a\}^*, c, ac)\}$$

and $D = \{c\}$ as axiom set .

IV - THE SIMPLIFICATION ASSOCIATED WITH A .

We still assume A to be deterministic ; S is the controlled rewriting system associated with A ; here we write $S = \{(R_i, v_i, w_i) \mid 1 \leq i \leq n\}$. By theorem 1 we know that S is injective and that $|v_i| < |w_i|$ for each i . Thus we can define a total mapping $\theta : X^* \to X^*$, called simplification w. r. t. A , by setting :

$$\theta(f) = g \quad \text{iff} \quad g \overset{*}{\Rightarrow} f \quad \text{and} \quad \nexists\, g' \text{ such that } g' \Rightarrow g .$$

THEOREM 2. - *If* $R \subseteq X^*$ *is regular, then* $\theta(R)$ *is regular.*

When applying theorem 2 to deterministic pushdown automata accepting the Dyck and semi-Dyck sets, we obtain a result of M. Benois [1], also obtained by M. Fliess [10] with quite different tools. This result simply says that the Dyck and semi-Dyck simplifications preserve regularity (though they are not rational transductions).

Theorem 2 is a consequence of the two following lemmas.

LEMMA 1. - *Let* i, j *be in* $\{1, \dots, n\}$, r_i *in* R_i, r_j *in* R_j. *Then*

(1. 1) $R_i w_i X^* \cap R_j = \emptyset$;

(1. 2) <u>if</u> $r_i = r_j\alpha$ <u>and</u> $w_i = \beta\gamma$ <u>with</u> $v_j = \alpha\beta$ <u>then</u> $\beta = 1$;

(1. 3) <u>if</u> $r_i = r_j\alpha$ <u>and</u> $v_i = \beta\gamma$ <u>with</u> $w_j = \alpha\beta$ <u>and</u> $v_j \neq 1$ <u>then</u> $\gamma = 1$;

(1. 4) $\nexists\ \alpha, \beta$ <u>such that</u> $v_j = \alpha\, w_i\, \beta$ <u>and</u> $r_i = r_j\, \alpha$.

The proof of lemma 1 does not present any difficulty ; it consists in examining the behaviour of automaton A , taking account of the definitions of the triples (R_i, v_i, w_i) (cf. section 2).

<u>Remark.</u> - In the above condition (1. 3), we can't conclude that $\gamma = 1$ if we dont assume that $v_j \neq 1$.

Let m be the integer $\max\{|v_i| \,/\, 1 \leqslant i \leqslant n\}$. We state :

LEMMA 2. - <u>Let</u> f, g <u>be in</u> X^* ; $f \overset{*}{\Rightarrow} g$ <u>holds iff</u> :

(2.1) $f = f_1 v_{i_1} h_1 f_2 v_{i_2} h_2 \dots f_p v_{i_p} h_p f_{p+1}$ <u>with</u> $p \geqslant 0$, $|h_j| < m$, <u>and</u>

(2.2) $g = f_1 g_1 f_2 g_2 \dots f_p g_p f_{p+1}$ <u>with, for</u> $1 \leqslant j \leqslant p$,
$f_1 v_{i_1} h_1 f_2 \dots f_j = r_j \in R_{i_j}$ and $v_{i_j} h_j \overset{*}{\underset{j}{\Rightarrow}} g_j$,
$\underset{j}{\Rightarrow}$ <u>being defined by the system</u> $\{(r_j^{-1} R_i , v_i , w_i) \,/\, 1 \leqslant i \leqslant n\}$.

In this statement $r^{-1}R$ denotes the set $\{u \,/\, ru \in R\}$. This lemma can be proved by induction over the number of rewriting steps from f to g . The words h_j's are indispensable, according to the above remark (however, if v_{i_j} is nonempty, h_j can be choosen empty).

Now, let $R \subseteq X^*$ be a regular language, accepted by some deterministic finite automaton $\mathfrak{A} = \langle X, P, \delta, p_o, F \rangle$; we can build a finite nondeterministic automaton $\mathfrak{A}' = \langle X, P^2, T, p_o p_o, PF \rangle$ (with $T \subseteq P^2 \times X \times P^2$) accepting the set $R' = \{f \,/\, f \overset{*}{\Rightarrow} g$ for some g in $R\}$.

We build $\mathfrak{A}'$ as follows : first, without loss of generality we can assume that we have n subsets $F_1, \dots, F_n$ of P such that $R_i = \{f \,/\, \delta(p_o, f) \in F_i\}$ for $1 \leqslant i \leqslant n$. Secondly, we set

$T = T' \cup T''$, with

$T' = \{(pq, x, p'q') \,/\, pq \in P^2,\ x \in X,\ p' = \delta(p, x),\ q' = \delta(q, x)\}$ and

$T'' = \{(pq, v_i h, p'q') \,/\, 1 \leqslant i \leqslant n,\ |h| < m,\ pq \in F_i P,\ p' = \delta(p, v_i h),\ q' = \delta(q, g)$
for some g such that $v_i h \overset{*}{\underset{p}{\Rightarrow}} g\}$,

where $\underset{p}{\Rightarrow}$ is defined by the system $S_p = \{(R_{i,p}, v_i, w_i) / 1 \leq i \leq n\}$ with $R_{i,p} = \{ f / \delta(p, f) \in F_i \}$.

Informally, when reading a word f, $\mathfrak{A}'$ simulates two finite automata running concurrently ; the first one reads f as $\mathfrak{A}$ would do and determines some decomposition of the form (2. 1) ; simultaneously, the second one acts as if it would be reading some corresponding decomposition of the form (2. 2). So we obtain :

$$L(\mathfrak{A}') = R' .$$

On the other hand, without breaking the results of the preceding sections, we can assume that A never blocks ; with this hypothesis, we have :

$$\theta(X^*) = \bigcup_{yq \in YQ,\, u \in S(y,q)} R(yq, u) \cup D X^* ,$$

which is regular (property 1).

Since $\theta(R) = R' \cap \theta(X^*)$, theorem 2 follows.

Moreover let us choose some subset Q' of Q (the state-set of A) and let $L_{Q'}$ be the language accepted by A with Q' as set of final states :

$$L_{Q'} = \{ f \in X^* / y_o q_o \overset{f}{\frown\!\!\!\rightarrow} \alpha q \text{ for some } \alpha \text{ in } Y^* \text{ and } q \text{ in } Q' \} .$$

We can easily check that :

$$\theta(L_{Q'}) = \Big(\bigcup_{yq \in YQ',\, u \in S(yq)} R(yq, u) \Big) \cup \Big(\bigcup_{q \in Q'} D(y_o q_o q) \Big) . \text{ So :}$$

THEOREM 3. - <u>For every language</u> L <u>accepted by</u> A , $\theta(L)$ <u>is a regular language included in</u> L .

Note that $\theta(L)$ is a rational cross-section of L (see [9]) with respect to the equivalence modulo θ . Clearly this equivalence is right-regular, i.e. $\theta(f) = \theta(g)$ implies $\theta(fh) = \theta(gh)$. Thus theorem 3 reformulates a result recently obtained by J. Sakarovitch [18] with a different method.

ACKNOWLEDGEMENTS. - I thank R. Cori, B. Courcelle, M. Nivat and J. Sakarovitch for their remarks and criticisms.

REFERENCES

1. BENOIS, M. : Parties rationnelles du groupe libre, C.R. Acad. Sci. PARIS A 269 (1969) 1188-1190.

2. BERSTEL, J. : Congruences plus-que-parfaites et langages algébriques, Séminaire d'Informatique Théorique (75/76/77) PARIS VI-VII, 123-147.

3. BOASSON, L. : Paires itérantes et langages algébriques, Thèse Sc. Math., Univ. PARIS VII (1974).

4. BUTZBACH, P. : Une famille de congruences de Thue pour lesquelles le problème de l'équivalence est décidable. Application à l'équivalence des grammaires séparées, in M. Nivat (éd.) Automata, Languages and Programming, North-Holland (1973) 3-12.

5. BUTZBACH, P. : Sur l'équivalence des grammaires simples, in J.P. Crestin et M. Nivat (éd.) Langages Algébriques, actes des journées d'informatique théorique de Bonascre 1973, ENSTA (1978), 223-245.

6. COCHET, Y. : Sur l'algébricité des classes de certaines congruences définies sur le monoïde libre, Thèse de 3ème cycle, RENNES (1971).

7. COCHET, Y. : Church-Rosser congruences on free semi-groups, Proceedings of the Colloquium on Algebraic Theory of Semi-Groups, Szeged (1976).

8. COCHET, Y. et NIVAT, M. : Une généralisation des ensembles de Dyck, Israel J. of Math. 9 (1971), 389-395.

9. EILENBERG, S. : Automata, Languages and Machines, vol. A., Acad. Press, New-York (1974).

10. FLIESS, M. : Deux applications de la représentation matricielle d'une série rationnelle non commutative, J. of Algebra 19 (1971), 344-353.

11. HARRISON, M.A. and HAVEL, I.M. : Strict Deterministic Grammars, J. of Computer and System Sciences 7 (1973), 237-277.

12. HOPCROFT, J. and KORENJAK A.J. : Simple Deterministic Languages, 7 th Annual Symposium on Switching and Automata Theory, Berkeley (1966), 36-46.

13. NIVAT, M. : On some families languages related to the Dyck language, 2nd Annual ACM Symp. on Computing (1970), 221-225.

14. NIVAT, M. : Congruences de Thue et t-langages, Studia Sci. Math. Hungarica 6 (1971), 243-249.

15. NIVAT, M. and BENOIS, M. : Congruences parfaites et quasi-parfaites, Séminaire Dubreil, 25ème Année (71/72).

16. NIVAT, M. : Congruences et théorème de Church-Rosser, Journées sur les demi-groupes : Algèbre et Combinatoire, Séminaire Dubreil (75/76).

17. OGDEN, W. : Intercalation theorems for pushdown store and stock languages, Ph. D. Thesis, Stanford (1968).

18. SAKAROVITCH, J. : Un théorème de transversale rationnelle pour les automates à pile déterministes, Proc. 4 th GI Conference on Theor. Computer Sci. (K. Weihrauch, éd.), Springer-Verlag, to appear.

19. SAKAROVITCH, J. : Thèse Sc. Math., PARIS VII (in preparation).

A String Matching Algorithm Fast on the Average

Extended Abstract[x)]

by

Beate Commentz-Walter
FB 10 - Informatik
Universitaet des Saarlandes

currently:
IBM-Germany
Scientific Center Heidelberg
Tiergartenstrasse 15
D-6900 Heidelberg

0. Introduction

In many information retrieval and text-editing applications it is necessary to be able to locate quickly some or all occurrences of user-specified words or phrases in one or several arbitrary text strings. Specifically, we consider retrieval from unformatted data, for example, a libary data base where there is for each book a record containing the signature, title, and abstract of book. Each such record we call a document. A user of the data base specifies one or several words or phrases, so called keywords, describing the information sought. The answer will be the documents which contain all or some of the user specified keywords. It takes too much time to scan each document of the data base for every user seperately. Therefore, we introduce a sort of secondary index (compare Scheck lit /12/) containing keyword fragments. Searching the index with the user specified keywords yields a superset of the documents required. This

----

x) For detailed version compare lit (4). The work reported here was done at the Heidelberg Scientific Center of IBM-Germany. It is part of a project dealing with subjects like Automatic Indexing, Clustering, and retrieval structures of unformatted data base.

superset contains documents where the fragments match but the keywords do not. These documents we want to reject. Therefore, we scan the documents of the superset for the user specified keywords.

Aho, Corasick lit /2/ describe an efficient algorithm doing this job. Their algorithm first preprocesses the keywords in time linear in the "total lengths of the keywords i. e. in the sum of the length of the keywords. Then their algorithm searches for the keyword occurrences in the document in time linear in document length (worst case).

The idea of this algorithm is based on the ideas of the Knuth-Morris-Pratt algorithm lit /10/ and those of finite state machines.

If there is only one keyword to search for in some document, Boyer, Moore lit /3/ give an algorithm the preprocessing phase of which also runs linearly and the search phase of which is faster on the average than Aho-Corasick's algorithm.

In the case of large alphabets the Boyer-Moore algorithm takes time about |D|/|W| on the average to search for all occurrences of the keyword W in document D (where |S| denotes the length of string S).

With the modification due to Galil lit /7/ the search phase of the Boyer-Moore algorithm behaves linearly in the document length even in the worst case. This is proved by Knuth, Morris, Pratt lit /10/, Guibas, Odlyzko lit /8/, and Galil lit /7/.

We give an algorithm B for a set of keywords. Its search phase behaves similar to the Boyer-Moore algorithm, sublinear on the average. It does not maintain linear search time for the worst case. Modification to B yield algorithm B1, which does maintain linear search time. But for practical purposes algorithm B is more useful. The overhead of algorithm B1 is very high.

These algorithms B and B1 combine the idea of the Aho-Corasick and Boyer-Moore algorithms.

This short paper concentrates on algorithm B .

Chapter I describes the structure of the preprocessed set of keywords.

Chapter II describes the search phase of B.

Chapter III describes the preprocessing phase of B.

Chapter IV considers B's running time.

Chapter V outlines the modification for B1.

Acknowledgement:

I want to to thank G. Jaeschke and G. Walch for stimulating discussions, hints and critical remarks, M. Zoeppritz for editing my English and R.Scherner for typing the paper.

I. The Structure of the Preprocessed Set of Keywords

To represent some given set of keywords in a useful way, we consider the data structure of a trie:

A trie is a tree T such that:

1. Each node v of T, except the root r is labeled by some character a = l(v), an element of some alphabet A.

2. The root r is labeled by ε, denoting the empty word.

3. If the nodes v' and v" are brothers (sons of the same node v), v' $\neq$ v" then l(v') $\neq$ l(v").

We say a path $v_1,\ldots.v_m$ of T where v_{i+1} is son of v_i represents the word $l(v_1)\ l(v_2)\ldots l(v_m)$.
This word we denote by $w(v_m)$ iff $v_1 = r$, the root.

Moreover, for each node we denote its depth by

$$d(v) = \begin{cases} o & \text{if } v = r, \text{ the root} \\ d(v')+1 & \text{if } v \text{ son of } v' \end{cases}$$

and by

$$d(T) = \max \{d(v);\ v \in T\}$$

we denote the depth of trie T.

Now, let $K = W_1,\ldots,W_r$ be the set of keywords on some alphabet A which we want to search for in some document D.

Similar to Aho, Corasick lit /2/ we represent K by a trie T. But in contrast, we base our trie T on the reversed keywords:

Exactly for h = 1...r there is one node v_h of T representing the reversed keyword $W_h{}^R$.

i.e.

$$w(v_h) = w_{h,1},\ldots,w_{h,|W_h|}$$

$$\text{where } W_h = w_{h,|W_h|},\ldots,w_{h,1}$$

To each node we add an output function

$$out(v) = \{\ W\ ;\ W^R = w(v),\ W \text{ in } K\ \}$$

To this trie we add the functions, shift1 and shift2, which map each trie node to an integer. Their purpose will become obvious from the description of the search phase of algorithm B. (Compare ChapterII):

The definition of shift1 and shift2 is based on sets of nodes:
For each $v \neq r$ of T:

$$\text{set1}(v) = \{v' ;\ w(v) \text{ is proper suffix of } w(v') \text{ i.e. } w(v') = u\, w(v) \text{ for some non empty word } u\}$$

and

$$\text{set2}(v) = \{ v' ;\ v' \text{ is element of set1}(v) \text{ and out}(v') \neq \emptyset \}$$

Now shift1 and shift2 are defined by:

$$\text{shift1}(v) = \begin{cases} 1 & \text{if } v = r \\ \min(\{k \,;\, k = d(v')-d(v),\ v' \text{ is element of set1}(v)\} \cup \{ \text{wmin} \}) & \text{else} \end{cases}$$

$$\text{shift2}(v) = \begin{cases} \text{wmin} & \text{if } v = r \\ \min(\{k \,;\, k = d(v')-d(v),\ v' \text{ is element of set2}(v)\} \cup \text{shift2}(v' \text{'s father}\}) & \text{else} \end{cases}$$

Let

$$\text{wmax} = \max \{|W_h|;\ l = 1,\ldots,r\}$$

$$\text{wmin} = \min \{|W_h|;\ l = 1,\ldots,r\}$$

Finally we add a function

$$\text{char: } A \longrightarrow N \text{ where}$$

$$\text{char}(a) = \min(\{d(v);\ l(v) = a\} \ \{\text{wmin} + 1\})$$

<u>Example</u>: k = { cacbaa, acb, aba, acbab, ccbab } , wmin = 3

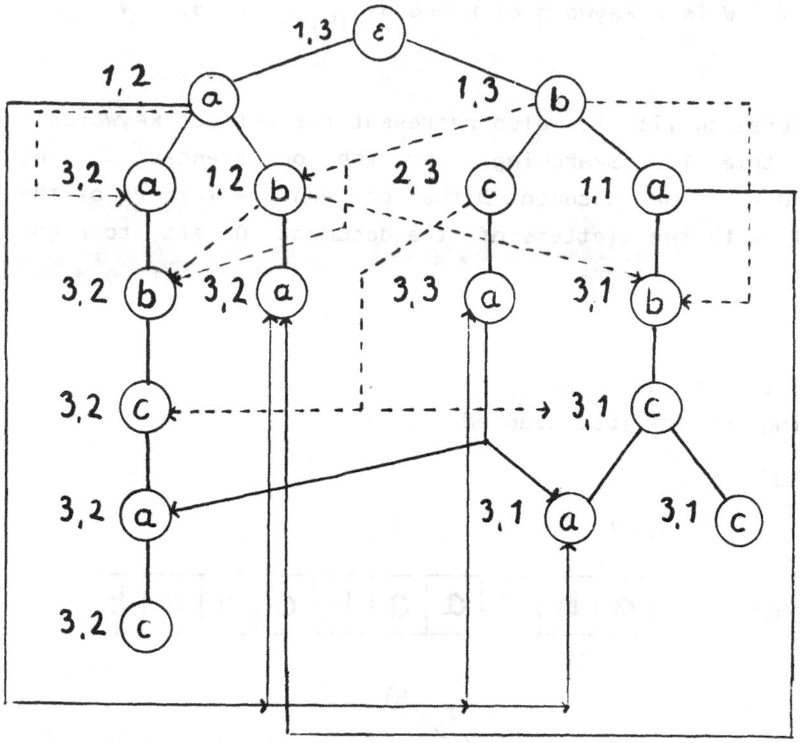

For each node v ≠ r ⇢ and → point to the nodes of set1(v) where → points to set2(v).

The two integers beside each node v denote the functions shift1(v), shift(2)v.

II. The Search Phase of Algorithm B for String Matching Fast on the Average

The input for the search phase of algorithm B is some document D and, for some keyset K, the preprocessed trie T and the functions out, shift1, shift2, and char.

The output of the search phase of algorithm B is a list of pairs (W, i) where W is a word and i is an integer representing the occurrence of W, i.e.

(W, i) element of the output of B

iff

$$W \text{ is a keyword of } K \text{ and } d_{i-|W|+1},\ldots,d_i = W.$$

Aho, Corasick lit /2/ also represent the set of keywords K by a trie T. Searching for the occurrences of any keyword W in any document D they compare the letters of the trie T with the letters of the document D left to right until mismatch occurs.

If mismatch occurs, the root is "shifted right along the document" by a number of letters calculated from the matching letters just scanned.

Example:

documents:

trie:

shift:

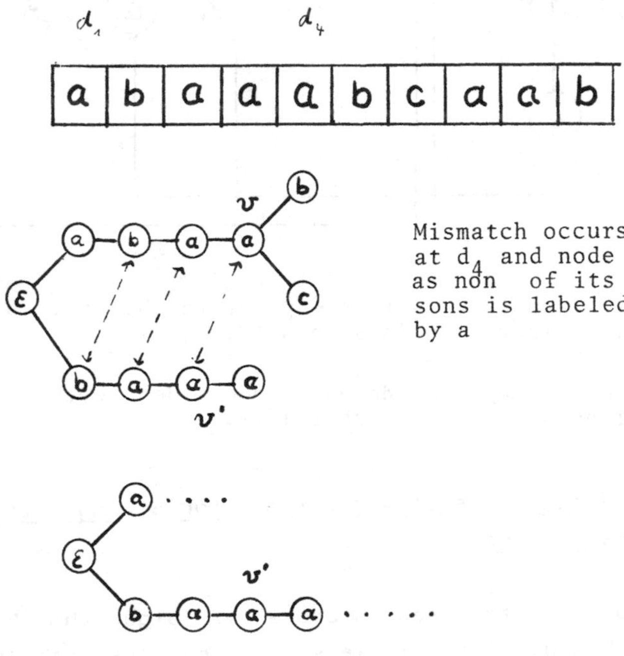

Mismatch occurs at d_4 and node v as non of its sons is labeled by a

w(v') is the maximal praefix of some keyword, which is suffix of w(v)

For detail compare lit /2/.
The Boyer-Moore algorithm lit /3/ starts putting the keyword (only one) beneath the left end of the document. It differs from the Aho-Corasick algorithm in that it compares the letters of the document with the letters of the keyword from right to left. If mismatch occurs, the keyword is shifted right by a number of letters calculated from the matching

letters and the mismatch character. This right to left scan and left to right shift yields a sublinear behaviour on the average, lit /3/, and the linear worst case behaviour is easy to preserve, lit /7,8,10/.

We combine these ideas:
We base our trie on the reversed keywords. Let wmin denote the minimal length of some keyword. The algorithm B starts putting the root r of T underneath d_{wmin+1}. Next it "scans" the document right to left until mismatch occurs. (For detail compare the algorithm mentioned below). Assuming we have just scanned the matching document letters $d_{i-m+1},\ldots,d_i$ and a mismatch occured at letter d_{i-m} we then shift the trie root right by some number of letters S calculated from the document letters $d_{i-m},\ldots d_i$.

The search phase of algorithm B in detail:

Initial phase:

```
v ← root r        (v is the "present" node of T)

i ← wmin          (i points to the document letter
                  above the nodes of depth 1 .)

j ← 0             (j indicates the depth of the
                  present node v.)

While i ≤ length document do

Scan phase:
begin
 while there is some son v' of v labeled by d[i-j] do
  begin

   v ← v'
   j ← j + 1
   output: (W,i) for each W of out(v)
  end
shift phase:
begin
 i ← i + S(v,d[i-j])
```

j ← 0
end end

where $S(v, d_{i-j})$ is the length of the shift defined by

$$S(v,d_{i-j}) = \min(\max(\text{shift1}(v),\ \text{char}(d_{i-j})-j-1),\ \text{shift2}(v)).$$

Example:

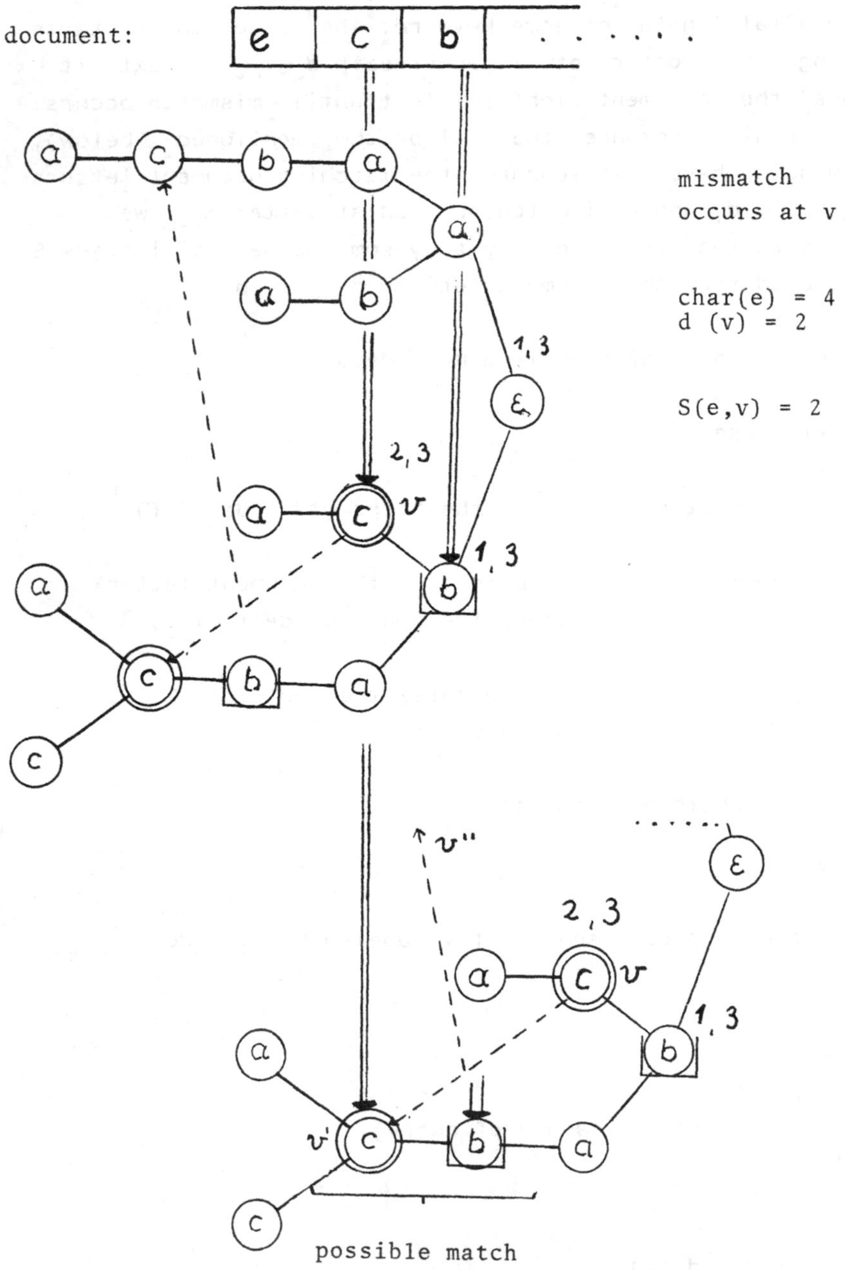

Obviously, each pair (W,i) found by B represents some occurrence of the keyword W. So it remains to show, that B finds each occurrence of some keyword in the document D.

Due to the construction of B's search phase it is sufficient to show that no shift is too long.

i. e. $d_{i-j+1},\ldots,d_i = W_t^R(v)$ for some v of T implies there is no i' such that:

1.) $i < i' < S(v, d_{i-j})$

and 2.) $d_{i'-|W|+1},\ldots,d_{i'} = W$

for some keyword W.

Due to the construction of $S(v,d_{i-j})$ this is easy to show.

III. The Preprocessing Phase of Algorithm B

The input of the preprocessing phase of B is the set of keywords $K = \{W_1,\ldots,W_r\}$. Its output is the trie T of the reversed keywords and the functions out, shift1, shift2, and char.

We shall show that the time used by the preprocessing phase is linear in the total length of the keywords i.e. in the sum of the lengths of the keywords $W_1,\ldots,W_r$.

Obviously, the time of computing the trie T and the functions out and char is linear in the total length of the keywords. It remains to analyse the computation of shift1 and shift2.

Consider some function on T's nodes:

$f(v') = v$ where $w(v)$ is maximal proper suffix of $w(v')$ in T.

This function coincides with the failure function of Aho-Corasick's pattern matching machine.

The inversion of f is given by

$$set1'(v) = \{v'; f(v') = v\}$$

Obviously set1'(v) is subset of set1(v). Moreover it contains the nodes v' of set1(v) where d(v')-d(v) is minimal. Hence due to lit /2/ the computation of shift1 is linear in the total length of the keywords.

The computation of shift2 can be done analogusly using

$$set2'(v) = \{v'; v' \text{ is element of } set1'(v) \text{ and } out(v') \neq 0\}.$$

IV. The Average and Worst Case Behavior of the Search Phases of Algorithm B

The running time of the search phase of algorithm B splits into two parts; the running time to perform the scan phase and the running time to perform the computation of the shift $S(v, d_{i-j})$ whenever necessary.

The total running time for the scan and shift phases is linear in the total number of character comparisons. Hence we measure the speed of algorithm B by the number of character inspections which are performed.

As in the Boyer-Moore algorithm lit /3/: If the size of the alphabet A is large, the search phase needs to inspect only about |D|/wmin letters of the document on the average.
Unfortunately, the search phase of algorithm B can perform |D| x wmax letter comparisons in the worst case.

Notice, the search phase of the usual Boyer-Moore algorithm with changes due to Galil lit /7/, lit /8/ and lit /10/ does at most c|D| letter comparisons in the worst case.

We did some experimental runs of algorithem B to get an estimate of its average behavior. Our experiments are based on 100 titles of English and German books on Computer Science and related subjects.These titles are our documents.

For the alphabet we took:
ALP = A B C D E F G H I J K L M N O P Q R S T U V W X Y Z 0 1 2 3 4 5 6 7 8 9 and blank.

From the set of titles we choose sets of strings to function as keyword sets.

The number of keywords in a set was to be : 2,4,8,16,32,64.

The length of a keyword in a set was to be : 3,5,7,9,11

For each possible pair of number and length we choose four sets of keywords.For each keywordset and the 100 titles the average number of references to a document letter by algorithm B is computed.

For each pair of number and length of keywords we take the average on the four different keyword probes. In the figure below this mean value is plotted against the length of the keywords for each different number of keywords. In addition, we indicate the average number of references to a document for each probe by a dot for number of keywords = 4 and by a circle for number of keywords = 16.

The results of the experiments show that the average behavior of algorithm B is sublinear.

For experimental results of other versions of algorithm B compare lit /4/.

Experimential Results:

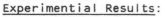

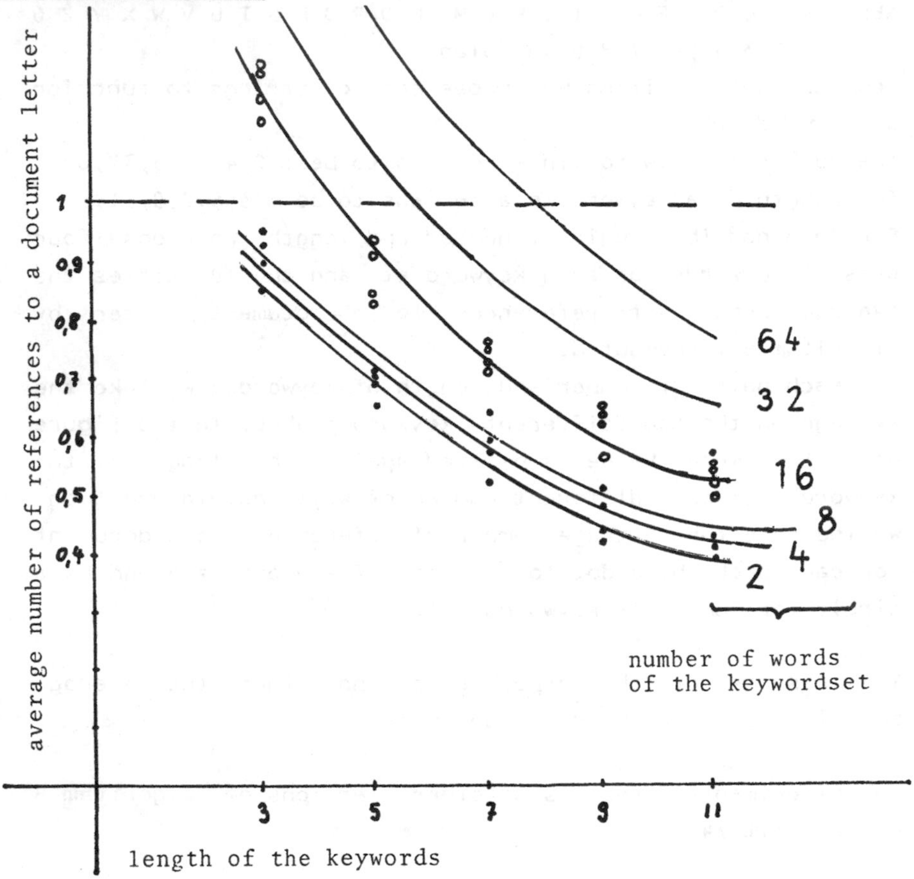

V. The Construction of Algorithm B1, Linear for the Worst Case

Algorithm B1 differs from B in "remembering" the document letters already scanned. As "memory" it uses the trie T and some additional functions.

For detailed description compare lit /4/.

Because of this "memory" the search phase of B1 behaves linear in the worst case. Moreover, on the average it is probably faster than B. Of course we have to pay a price for this improvement: Some constant increase in time and space needed for the overhead of preprocessing and search phases Anyway, B1's preprocessing phase remains linear in the total length of keywords. The proof is based on lit /11/.

Literature:

/1/ Aho, A.V., Hopcraft, J. E.and Ullman J.D.
"The Design and Analysis of ComputerAlgorithms"
Addison-Wesley Publ. Comp. Read. Mass.

/2/ Aho, A.V. and Corasick, M.
"Efficient String Matching: An Aid to Bibliographic Search"
Com. ACM, June 75, Vol. 18, No. 6

/3/ Boyer, R.S. and Moore, J.S.
"A Fast String Searching Algorithm"
Com. of the ACM, Vol. 20, No. 10, 1977, 262-272

/4/ Commentz-Walter, B.
"A String Matching Algorithm Fast on the Average"
Scientific Center Heidelberg, Technical Report, in print.

/5/ Fagin, R., Nievergelt, J., Pippenger, N. and Strong, H.R.
"Extendible Hashing - A Fast Access Method for Dynamic Files"
IBM, Research Rep. RJ 2305, 1978 (San Jose)

/6/ Galil, Z.
"Saving Space in Fast String-Matching"
IBM, Reseach Rep., RC 6670, 1977 (Yorktown Heights)

/7/ Galil, Z.
"On Improving the Worst Case Running Time of Boyer-Moore String Matching Algorithm"
Automata, Languages and Programming, 5th Colloquium
EATCS, July 1978

/8/ Guibas, L.J. and Odlyzko, A.M.
"A New Proof of the Linearity of the Boyer-Moore String Searching Algorithms"
Proceedings 18th Annual IEEE Symposium on Foundations of Computer Science, 1977

/9/ Guibas, L.J., McCreight, E.M., Plass, M.F. and Roberts, J.R.
"A new Representation for Linear Lists"
9th Annual ACM Symposium on Theory of Computing, 1977

/10/ Knuth, D.E., Morris Jr., J.H. and Pratt, V.B.
"Fast Pattern Matching in Strings"
SIAM J. on Computing, Vol. 6, No. 2, 1977, 323-350

/11/ McCreight, E.M.
"A Space Economical Suffix Tree Construction Algorithm"
Journal of the ACM, Vol. 23, No. 2, 1976, 262-272

/12/Scheck, H.-J.
"The Reference String Indexing Method" Proceedings Information System Methodology, Venice 1978 Lecture Notes in Comp. Sc. 65 Springer Heidelberg 1976

/13/ Weiner, P.
"Linear Pattern Matching Algorithm"
Proceedings 14th Annual IEEE Symposium in Switching and Automata Theory, 1973, 1-11

FUNCTIONAL CHARACTERIZATION OF SOME SEMANTIC EQUALITIES INSIDE λ-CALCULUS

M. COPPO M.DEZANI-CIANCAGLINI

Istituto di Scienza dell'Informazione

Università di Torino

Corso Massimo d'Azeglio 42 10125 TORINO (Italy)

P. SALLE'

Laboratoire Langages et Systèmes Informatiques

Université Paul Sabatier

118 Rte de Narbonne 31500 TOULOUSE (France)

Abstract - Both (operational or denotational) semantics and type theories for λ-calculus induce in a natural way equivalence relations between terms. The aim of the present paper is to show that in some cases the semantic and functional equivalences coincide.

INTRODUCTION

It is well known that λ- calculus is a formalism to represent partial recursive functions which has played a central role in the development of recursion theory.

From the beginning λ-calculus has been used to study program properties and, moreover, it has also been proposed as a programming language in itself. In this last case the interest in building a semantics for it becomes clear. One of the first approachs was that of Morris [10] which gives an operational semantics concerned with the behaviour of terms inside arbitrary contextes. A deeper approach was found successively with the discovery of lattice - theoretic models [15]. These models, moreover, build a basis for Strachey's theory of programming language semantics which is now very satisfactory and still in development.

The problem of defining a semantic for λ -calculus (or combinatory logic) was also faced, in a completely different way, by Curry [6] , [7]. One of the original motivations of Curry for the study of λ -calculus, in fact, was to give a foundation for logic but he discovered that, in the pure unrestricted system, different kinds of paradoxes were possible. To avoid them he introduced its theory of functionality in which terms of λ-calculus are associated, by means of a formal set of axioms and deduction rules, with functional characters (as Curry call them) or types. The types give an explicit and consistent representation of the range-domain properties of terms when these last are considered as functions from terms to terms. It is then implicit that any interpretation of terms which is consistent with their functional characters is a good interpretation and no paradox can arise. Also in considering λ -calculus as a programming language, it is interesting to study functional characters of terms since they could be used as a tool to prove properties of programs like termination (every terms which possesses a functional character is strongly normalizable) or correctness. No substantial effort, however, has been done until now in this direction because of some limitations of Curry's theories. Functional characters, for example, are not preserved by convertibility and the set of terms to which it can be assigned a functional character is only a subset of normalizable terms. This is inacceptable since, as it is known, some foundamental primitives as recursion operators can be represented only by terms without normal form. Both the previous limitations, however, have been overcomed by the development of new functionality theories [4], [5] , [13] , [14], which extend in a natural way the notion of functional character. Many features of Curry's functionality, however, are preserved as its purely formal aspect and the fact that functional characters are still a consistent basis for the definition of a semantics of λ-calculus. In particular normalization properties still hold and have been extended in the sense that both the set of types that can be assigned only to terms which have normal form and head normal form can be characterized. In this paper we will deal with two extended functionality theories which we will introduce as theories G [5] and T [14].

It is now natural to ask if there are any relations, and which, between the notion of semantics suggested by theories G and T and that ones introduced by other approaches such as models or Morris' operational semantics. As it will be proved in this paper, in both the theories G and T the finite nature of functional characters can be explained with the notion of approximant as introduced by Wadsworth [17] and Hyland [8] . As a consequence of this we will be able to show that the theories G and T. induce the same equality relations between terms as that ones introduced, respectively, by the model P_ω and the extensional equality of Morris [10] . This fact gives a further motivation to consider functional characters as a basis for a semantics of λ-calculus. The importance of this fact is twofold. On one side it proposes the theories G and T as formal supports for proofs inside these semantics, and, on the other hand, allows to extend some known result about P_ω or extensional equalities to theories G and T. It follows, for example, that in both theories all fixed point combinators [2] have the same functional characterizations.

1 - Presentation of systems G and T.

Both systems G and T are functionality theories for λ-calculus. Let's recall that, according to the classical work of Curry [6], a formula in a functionality theory is a statement τ X where X is a term and τ its functional character or type. So τ X means that τ is a type for X. Functional characters are build from a set of basic elements (which can be different in the various theories) and a composition operator F. If σ , τ are any types F σ τ is the type of a term which defines a function from the terms of type σ to the terms of type τ . We shall use here $[\sigma]\ \tau$ instead of F σ τ . Types are assigned to terms by means of axioms and deduction rules in a purely formal way. If we limit ourselves in the framework of natural deduction systems we must introduce the concept of basis for a deduction. A basis is a collection of statements of the shape τ X where τ is a type and X a term. $B \vdash \tau X$ will mean that from the statements of B we can deduce type τ for X.

The fundamental axioms and rules that characterize functionality theories are the following:

(Axiom Ap) If B contains τ X then $B \vdash \tau X$.

(Rule F_e) $$\frac{B \vdash [\sigma]\,\tau X \quad B \vdash \sigma Y}{B \vdash \tau (XY)}$$

(Rule F_i) $$\frac{B, \sigma x \vdash \tau X}{B \vdash [\sigma]\ \tau\ \lambda x.X}$$ if x does not occur in B.

Rules F_e and F_i give a natural functional interpretation to the formation rules for term of λ-calculus. New objects and rules can be adjoined to the previous ones leading to different systems of functionality. Also in the theories G [5] and T [14] types are build from a set of basis elements $\{\omega, \varphi_1, \varphi_2, \ldots\}$. The meanings of $\varphi_1, \varphi_2, \ldots$ are different in the theories G and T (here, in particular, we have only two basic types except ω) while ω has, in both theories, the meaning of an universal category (as in [6 p.240]) i.e. each term has type ω. Types are build from basic elements by means of two operations, one of which is the classical composition (i.e. Curry's F). The other is the operations of "sequencing" which builds a new type as a collection of types. The meaning of σ X where σ is a sequence of types is then that X possesses all types of σ (with respect to a given basis). The syntax of types is then the following:

Definition 1 - The set of types (of G and T) is defined as follows:

i) each basic type is a type

ii) if $\sigma_1, \ldots, \sigma_n$ are types then $\sigma_1, \ldots, \sigma_n$ is a type

iii) if σ and τ are types then $[\sigma]\,\tau$ is a type.

In the following $\varphi_1, \varphi_2, \ldots$ are basic types different from ω and $\sigma, \tau, \rho, \mu, \ldots$ are metavariables which range over types.

Type ω is characterized by a particular axiom which defines its property of universal type.

(Axiom A_ω) for all terms X: $\vdash \omega$ X.

In both theories G and T all properties of typed terms are proved to be invariant if we introduce the following equivalence relation between types:

$$(E_\omega) \qquad [\sigma]\,\omega = \omega \qquad \text{for all types } \sigma .$$

So we will consider here only the type with the minimum number of occurrences of basic types for each equivalence class induced by E_ω.

One can define the level of a type occurrence τ into a type σ as follows:

(i) if $\tau \equiv \sigma$ the level of τ in σ is 0

(ii) if $\sigma \equiv \sigma_1,\ldots,\sigma_n$ and τ occurs in σ_i the level of τ in σ is the level of τ in σ_i $(1 \leq i \leq n)$

(iii) if $\sigma \equiv [\rho]\mu$ the level of τ in σ is:

- one plus the level of τ in ρ if τ occurs in ρ
- the level of τ in μ if τ occurs in μ.

We will say that a type τ is proper if either τ does not contain ω or ω occurs in τ only at odd levels. A proper basis instead is a basis containing types in which either ω does not occur or the level of all occurrences of ω is even.

We introduce, lastly, some more technical definitions.

The lenght $\| \tau \|$ of a type τ is defined as the number of occurrences in it of basic types.

Let $\mathcal{D}$ be a deduction of $B \vdash \sigma X$ and $R \equiv (\lambda x.Y)Z$ a redex in X. The characteristic set of R in $\mathcal{D}$ is the set $C(R)$ of all types τ different from ω assigned to $\lambda x.Y$ in $\mathcal{D}$, i.e.

$$C(R) \equiv \{ \tau \mid \tau \neq \omega \text{ and } \tau \text{ is a type of } \lambda x.Y \text{ in } \mathcal{D} \}.$$

The height $h(R)$ of R is the maximum length of the types of $C(R)$, i.e. $h(R) = \max \{ \|\tau\| \mid \tau \in C(R) \}$.

We say that a component Y of X is meaningful in a deduction $\mathcal{D}$ of $B \vdash \sigma X$ iff there is no component Z of X such that Y is a component of Z and $\mathcal{D}$ assigns to Z only type ω.

Let's associate to any deduction $\mathcal{D}$ a pair of non-negative integers $< m(\mathcal{D}), n(\mathcal{D}) >$ (measure of $\mathcal{D}$) defined as:

$m(\mathcal{D})$ = maximum height of meaningful redexes in $\mathcal{D}$

$n(\mathcal{D})$ = number of meaningful redexes with height $m(\mathcal{D})$ in $\mathcal{D}$

We intend $m(\mathcal{D}) = 0$ if there are no meaningful redexes in $\mathcal{D}$ and $n(\mathcal{D}) = 0$ if $m(\mathcal{D}) = 0$.

Integer pairs can be ordered by the usual lexicographic order relation ($\lesssim$) defined as: $<h',k'> \lesssim <h,k>$ iff $h' < h$ or $h' = h$ and $k' \leq k$.

The theory G.

In the theory G there is a numerable set of basic types different from ω (like basic objects of Curry's theory in [6 cap.9]).

The axioms and deductions rules are Ap, A_ω, Fe, Fi with the equivalence relation E ω . $\vdash_G$ will denote a deduction in G.

The principal results which can be proved in G are the following:

Theorem 1 - A term X has a β-normal (an head normal) form iff there are some proper basis B and proper type τ (some basis B and type τ different from ω) such that $B \vdash_G \tau X$.

Theorem 2 - Any two β-convertible terms have in G the same set of types for any basis.

The following result will be used in the proof of Lemma 7 in section 3.

Lemma 1 [5] - Let D be any deduction of $B \vdash_G \tau X$ whose measure is not $< 0,0 >$. Then there is a term X' and a deduction D' of $B \vdash_G \tau X'$ such that $X \geq X'$ and the measure of D' is less than that one of D.

The theory T

In the theory T the basic types are 0 and 1 which have the following meaning (according to [4]):

- 0X means that X has a normal form
- 1X means that $X Y_1 .....Y_n$ has a normal form for all $n > 0$ and $Y_1 ,...,Y_n$ which, in their turn, have normal forms.

These meaningsof 0 and 1 justify the introduction of the following equivalence relations:

(E_0) $[1]\ 0 = 0$

(E_1) $[0]\ 1 = 1$.

In T then we will consider only types with the minimum number of occurrences of 0, 1 and ω for each equivalence class induced by E_0 , E_1 and E_ω . Therefore the lenght of a type must be computed modulo E_0 , E_1 and E_ω . $\vdash_T$ denotes a deduction in T.

The main results provable for theory T are the following:

Theorem 3 - A term X has a β- η- normal (and head normal) form iff there are some proper basis B and proper type τ (some basis B and type τ different from ω) such that $B \vdash_T \tau X$.

Theorem 4 - Any two β- η- convertible terms have in T the same set of types for any basis.

In analogy to Lemma 1 we have then:

Lemma 2 [14] - Let D be any deduction of $B \vdash_T \tau X$ whose measure is not $<0,0>$. Then there is a term X' and a deduction D' of $B \vdash_T \tau X'$ such that $X \geq X'$ and the measure of D' is less than that one of D.

2. Some equivalence relations on terms.

The theories G and T induce in a natural way the following equivalence relations between terms:

Definition 2. Let M and N be terms.

$M \sim_G N$ iff for any basis B and type τ :

$$B \vdash_G \tau M \quad \text{iff} \quad B \vdash_G \tau N$$

$M \sim_T N$ iff for any basis B and type τ :

$$B \vdash_T \tau M \quad \text{iff} \quad B \vdash_T \tau N .$$

In what follows, $M \sim_X N$ for $X = G$ or T will abbreviate $M \sim_G N$ or $M \sim_T N$.

Then $\sim_G$ and $\sim_T$ split the set of terms into equivalence classes such that all terms in the same class have the same functional characterization. It is obvious from Theorems 2 and 4 that both $\sim_G$ and $\sim_T$ extend the relation of β-convertibility. As said in the introduction, we are interested to study the relations between $\sim_G$, $\sim_T$ and other semantic equivalence relations on terms.

We give here a short review of some classical notions and results that will be used in section 3. First we introduce the definition of approximant (following Wadsworth [17] and Hyland [8], [9]) by adjoining a new constant Ω to the set of terms. Ω has the following reduction properties: for all terms M and variables x, ΩM and $\lambda x.\Omega$ are said Ω-redexes and both reduce to Ω (Ω-reductions). A term M is in β-Ω-normal form iff it contains no β-redexes and no Ω-redexes;

it is in β- Ω-η-normal form iff it is in β - Ω -normal form and it contains no η-redexes. A term A is said to be a direct approximant of a term M iff A and M are identical (modulo Ω-reductions) except at components which are occurrences of Ω in A and moreover A is in β -normal form.

For a given term M, we define its sets of approximants $A(M)$ and $A_e(M)$ as in [8] :

Definition 3 -

$A(M) = \{A \mid \exists M', A'$ such that $M' =_\beta M$, $A' =_\Omega A$,

A' is a direct approximant of M' and A is a β- Ω - normal form $\}$

$A_e(M) = \{A \mid \exists M', A'$ such that $M' =_{\beta\eta} M$, $A' =_{\Omega\eta} A$,

A' is a direct approximant of M' and A is a β - Ω - η -normal form $\}$.

As usual, a context C [ ] is a term in which one subterm is missing, C [M] denotes the result of filling the missing subterm with M.

$M =_{P\omega} N$ will mean that M , N have the same meaning in the model P_ω [12] [16] .

With $M = e\ N$ we denote the extensional equivalence of [10] :

Definition 4 - If M, N are terms, $M = e\ N$ iff for any context C [ ]:

either C [M] and C [N] reduce to the same β - η -normal form

or C [M] and C [N] do not possess any β - η - normal form.

As usual [17] we say that two head normal forms are similar iff they have the same head variable (after α-conversion, if necessary, so that bound variables agree) and the difference between the number of initial bound variables and the number of main arguments is the same for both. Two similar head normal forms are strongly similar iff they have the same number of main arguments (and therefore also the same number of initial bound variables).

Hyland [8] proofs that the equalities $=_{P\omega}$ and $= e$ may be characterized by means of the sets of approximants:

Property 1 - $M =_{P\omega} N$ iff $A(M) = A(N)$.

Property 2 - $M =_e N$ iff $A_e(M) = A_e(N)$.

It follows immediately that $M =_{P\omega} N$ implies $M =_e N$ (but not viceversa).

Lastly we recall Böhm's Theorem and its extension to head normal forms.

Böhm's Theorem [3]. If M and N are distinct β-η-normal forms, then there exists a context C[ ] such that $C[M] =_\beta I$ and $C[N] =_\beta K$.

Extension of Böhm's Theorem [9]. If M and N are non similar head normal forms then there exists a context C[ ] such that $C[M] =_\beta I$ and $C[N] =_\beta K$.

3. Type theories vs models.

In this section we will prove that the equalities induced by theories G and T coincide respectively with the equalities $=_{P\omega}$ and $=_e$.

Let's prove, firstly, that $\sim_G$ and $\sim_T$ are invariant under any trasformation that can be defined by means of contexts.

Lemma 3 - If M, N are terms and $M \sim_X N$ then for any C[ ]; $C[M] \sim_X C[N]$ where X = G or T.

Proof. Let $B \vdash_X \tau C[M]$ and D any deduction of it. To obtain $B \vdash_X \tau C[N]$ it is sufficient to replace in D each deduction σ M by the corresponding deduction σ N. □

The following two lemmas gives a first characterization of the equalities $\sim_G$ and $\sim_T$ with respect to the property of having head normal form or normal form.

Lemma 4 - If $M \sim_X N$ then either M and N are both unsolvable or they have similar head normal forms for X = G or T.

Proof - By Theorems 1 and 3 it is obvious that either M and N are both unsolvable or they have both head normal forms. Let ad absurdum M and N have non similar head normal forms. Then by the extension of Böhm's Theorem there is a context C[ ] such that $C[M] =_\beta I$ and $C[N] =_\beta K$. It is clear that $I \not\sim_X K$ and this fact is in contradiction with Lemma 3 since types are invariant by β-conversion. □

Lemma 5 - If M, N have β - η -normal forms and $M \sim_X N$ for $X = G$ or T then M and N are β - η -convertible.

Proof. The proof is the same as that of Lemma 4, by replacing normal forms for similar head normal forms and Böhm's Theorem for its extension. □

A stronger result may be proved in the case of head normal forms with the same set of types in G.

Lemma 6 - If M and N are head normal forms, i.e.

$M \equiv \lambda x_1 \dots x_n . \zeta\, M_1 \dots M_m$, $N \equiv \lambda x_1 \dots x_{n'} .\ \zeta\, N_1 \dots N_{m'}$

and $M \sim_G N$ then M and N are strongly similar and $M_i \sim_G N_i$ $(1 \leq i \leq m)$.

Proof - Let's first observe that, for all terms M and N and variables x, $M \sim_G N$ iff $\lambda x.M \sim_G \lambda x.N$ (the proof follows trivially from Lemma 3).

By Lemma 4 M and N are similar. Now suppose, for example, n' > n. From above $\zeta\, M_1 \dots M_m \sim_G \lambda x_{n+1} \dots x_{n'} .\ \zeta\, N_1 \dots N_{m'}$. But this is impossible since we have $\underbrace{[\omega] \dots [\omega]}_{n} \varphi\zeta \vdash_G \varphi\ \zeta\, M_1 \dots M_m$ while, obviously, $\underbrace{[\omega] \dots [\omega]}_{n} \varphi\zeta \not\vdash_G \varphi\ \lambda x_{n+1} \dots x_{n'} .\ \zeta\, N_1 \dots N_{m'}$, when φ is any basic type different from ω .

To prove $N_i \sim_G M_i$ $(1 \leq i \leq m)$ let's suppose that there exist B , τ such that $B \vdash_G \tau\, M_i$ and $B \not\vdash_G \tau\, N_i$. Let φ be any basic type which does not occur in B . Then

$B, \underbrace{[\omega] \dots [\omega]}_{i-1}, [\tau] \underbrace{[\omega] \dots [\omega]}_{m-i} \varphi\zeta \vdash_G \varphi\ \zeta\, M_1 \dots M_m$ but

$B, \underbrace{[\omega] \dots [\omega]}_{i-1}, [\tau] \underbrace{[\omega] \dots [\omega]}_{m-i} \varphi\zeta \not\vdash_G \varphi\ \zeta\, N_1 \dots N_m$. In fact, since φ does not occur in B , B cannot contain any statement $[\overline{\sigma}_1] \dots [\overline{\sigma}_m]\ \varphi\ \zeta$. Then we have $\zeta\, M_1 \dots M_m \not\sim_G \zeta\, N_1 \dots N_m$ against the hypothesis. □

Lastly let's consider the relations between the types of a term and those of its approximants.

Lemma 7 - For any term M, basis B and type τ , $B \vdash_G \tau\, M$ iff $B \vdash_G \tau\, A$ for some $A \in \mathcal{A}(M)$.

Proof.

If part. By induction on the measure of D , where D is any deduction of $B \vdash_G \tau\, M$.

First step. If the measure of D is $< 0,0 >$ then any redex of M is non meaningful, i.e. it occurs in a component to which only type ω is assigned in D. Then A can be obtained from M by replacing Ω for all non meaningful components. It is easy to verify that A is a β - Ω-normal form.

Inductive step. Immediate from Lemma 1.

Only if part. If $B \vdash_G \tau\ A$ and $A \in \mathcal{A}(M)$ then there exists M' such that $M' =_\beta M$ and A is a direct approximant of M', i.e. M' can be obtained from A by replacing each occurrence of Ω by suitable terms Z. Then a deduction of $B \vdash_G \tau\ M'$ can be obtained from any deduction of $B \vdash_G \tau\ A$ by replacing each $\vdash_G \omega\ \Omega$ by $\vdash_G \omega\ Z$. □

Lemma 8 - For any term M, basis B and type τ, $B \vdash_T \tau\ M$ iff $B \vdash_T \tau\ A$ for some $A \in \mathcal{A}_e(M)$.

Proof.

The proof succeds as that one of Lemma 7, if we replace $\vdash_G$ by $\vdash_T$, Lemma 1 by Lemma 2, $\mathcal{A}(M)$ by $\mathcal{A}_e(M)$ and $=_\beta$ by $=_{\beta\eta}$. □

Now we are able to prove the main results of the present paper.

Theorem 5. For any two terms M and N, $M \sim_G N$ iff $M =_{P\omega} N$.

Proof. By Property 1 it is sufficient to prove $M \sim_G$ iff $\mathcal{A}(M) = \mathcal{A}(N)$.

If part. If $B \vdash_G \tau\ M$ then by Lemma 7 there is $A \in \mathcal{A}(M)$ such that $B \vdash_G \tau\ A$. From $B \vdash_G \tau\ A$ and $A \in \mathcal{A}(N)$ it follows $B \vdash_G \tau\ N$ again by Lemma 7.

Only if part. Let $A \in \mathcal{A}(M)$. We prove by structural induction on A that $A \in \mathcal{A}(N)$. If $A \equiv \Omega$ or A is a single variable this is obvious. Else M must possess an head normal form strongly similar to A and by Lemma 6 also to that one of N. I.e. we have $A \equiv \lambda x_1 \ldots x_n . \zeta A_1 \ldots A_m$, $M = \lambda x_1 \ldots x_n . \zeta M_1 \ldots M_m$ and $N = \lambda x_1 \ldots x_n . \zeta N_1 \ldots N_m$. Then we have $A_i \in \mathcal{A}(M_i)$ $(1 \le i \le m)$ and $M_i \sim_G N_i$ by Lemma 6. By inductive hypothesis, then, $A_i \in \mathcal{A}(N_i)$ $(1 \le i \le m)$ and so $A \in \mathcal{A}(N)$. □

Theorem 6. For any two terms M and N, $M \sim_T N$ iff $M =_e N$.

<u>Proof.</u>

<u>If part.</u> The proof succeds as that one of the only if part of Theorem 5, if we recall that $M =_e N$ implies $A_e(M) = A_e(N)$ (Property 2), by replacing $\vdash_G$ by $\vdash_T$, Lemma 7 by Lemma 8, A by A_e.

<u>Only if part.</u> Let C [ ] by any context. There are two possible cases:

- C [M] has a proper type for a proper basis. By Lemma 3 also C [N] has this type for the same basis. This means that C [M] and C [N] possess the same β- η -normal form by Theorem 3 and Lemma 5.
- C [M] does not have any proper type for any proper basis. By Lemma 3 this is true also for C [N] and so C [M] and C [N] do not possess β- η-normal form by Theorem 3. □

As immediate consequence of Theorems 5 and 6 we obtain that $\sim_T$ is an extension of $\sim_G$, i.e. for any two terms M and N : $M \sim_G N$ implies $M \sim_T N$.

Conclusion

The interest of the given functional characterization lies also in the fact that equality in P_ω coincides with equality in T_ω [12] [1] and in Levy's syntactic model. Further researches will be done to define constructively for each term M of λ -calculus an unique principal type scheme in the theory G, i.e. (according to [7 p. 296]) a type τ build from basic types and type variables such that each type of M is a specialization of τ. Then the semantic properties of terms in the above models can be proved in a system which is totally formalizable.

References

[1] H. Barendregt, G. Longo, Equality of Lambda Terms and Recursion Theoretic Reducibility in the Model Tω, Preprint n. 107, University Utrecht, (1979).

[2] C. Böhm, The CUCH as a Formal and Description Language, in Formal Language Description Languages for Computer Programming, ed. T.B. Steel, North-Holland, Amsterdam, (1966), 179-197.

[3] C. Böhm, Alcune proprietà della forma β - η -normali del λ - K -calcolo, Pubbl. IAC-CNR n. 696, Roma, (1968)

[4] M. Coppo, M. Dezani-Ciancaglini, A New Type Assignment for λ -terms, in Archiv für Math. Logik und Grundlageforshung, 19, (1978), 1-17.

[5] M. Coppo, M. Dezani-Ciancaglini, B. Venneri, Functional Characters of Solvable Terms, Internal Report, Turin University.

[6] H.B. Curry, R. Feys, Combinatory Logic, Vol. 1, North-Holland, Amsterdam, (1968).

[7] H.B. Curry, R. Hindley, J.P. Seldin, Combinatory Logic, 2, North-Holland, Amsterdam, (1972).

[8] J.M.E. Hyland, A Survey of Some Useful Partial Order Relations on Terms of the λ -calculus in : λ -calculus and Computer Science Theory, ed. C. Böhm, Lecture Notes in Computer Science, 37, Springer-Verlag, (1975), 83-95.

[9] J.M.E. Hyland, A Syntactic Characterization of the Equality in Some Models of the λ -calculus, J. London Math. Soc. 12 (2), (1976), 361-370.

[10] J.H. Morris, λ -calculus Models of Programming Languages, Ph.D.thesis, MIT, Cambridge, (1968).

[11] G. Plotkin, Tω as a Universal Domain, D.A.I. Research report N.28, University of Edinburgh, (1977).

[12] G. Plotkin, A Set-Theoretical Definition of Application, School of A.I., Memo MIP-R-95, Edinburgh, (1972).

[13] P. Sallé, Une Extension de la Théorie des Types en λ-calcul, in: Automata, Languages and Programming, ed. s G. Ausiello and C. Böhm, Lecture Notes in Computer Science, 62, (1978), 398-41.

[14] P. Sallé, Une Generalisation de la Théorie des Types, to appear in R.A.I.R.O., Informatique Theorique.

[15] D. Scott, Continous Lattices, Lecture Notes in Mathematics, in : Toposes, Algebraic Geometry and Logic, ed. F.W. Lawvere, n. 274, Springer-Verlag, (1972), 97-136.

[16] D. Scott, Data Types as Lattices, SIAM J. Comput., Vol. 5, n. 3, (1976), 522-587.

[17] C.P. Wadsworth, The Relation between Computational and Denotational Properties for Scott's D_∞-Models of the λ-calculus, SIAM J. Comput., Vol. 5, n. 3, (1976), 488-521.

ARBITRATION AND QUEUEING UNDER LIMITED SHARED STORAGE REQUIREMENTS*)

(Preliminary Report)

by

Armin B. Cremers
Informatics Department
University of Dortmund
Dortmund, Fed. Rep. of Germany

and

Thomas N. Hibbard
Jet Propulsion Laboratory
California Institute of Technology
Pasadena, California, USA

Abstract: An algorithm is presented which implements mutual exclusion for a system of n processes by means of protocol-controled communication on a (n + const.)-valued shared buffer. The algorithm uses a generalized test-and-set instruction, and schedules processes into their critical sections on a first-come, first-serve basis. The method can be extended to accomodate any queueing discipline defined as a function of the system history between consecutive idle periods.

Introduction

The mutual exclusion problem in concurrent programming, as stated by Dijkstra [1], consists in the design and implementation of a mechanism whereby to control the exclusive access to a single resource R shared by several concurrently running processes. In view of the general applicability of such a mechanism, it seems worthwhile to spend some effort in devising efficient and economical solutions to

*) This research was supported in part by the Office of Naval Research under Contract No. NOOO14-77-C-0536 through the University of Southern California, Los Angeles, Calif., USA.

this problem. In addition, it turns out that when studied from the point of view of an economical design, the problem exhibits nontrivial aspects that can be interesting for people working in such diverse areas of computer science as applied combinatorics, program transformation, complexity, process communication.

In [6, 9] we have pointed out that when the only synchronization primitive available is a generalized test-and-set instruction, more powerful than the binary test-and-set underlying Dijkstra's binary semaphore solution, we are able to implement mutual exclusion in terms of a communication variable whose size (in bits) grows logarithmically with the number of participating processes. (Compare this against the linear growth of the shared variable in the most widely known solution due to Dekker.)

To be more specific, we have shown in [9] that a (2n-1)-valued shared variable is sufficient for implementing a mutual exclusion mechanism with respect to resource R for n processes, using a generalized test-and-set.

Recently, an improvement of our solution has been published [1o], which is not only more economical but also neater than our original version in [9]. There, it has been shown that a $(\lfloor \frac{n}{2} \rfloor + 9)$-valued shared variable is sufficient if lock-out-freeness is the only fairness requirement. In addition, it has been stated in [1o] that any generalized test-and-set solution "with bounded waiting" requires at least n+1 distinct values of the communication variable. (Bounded waiting means that there is a constant c such that each process, demanding access to its "critical section", succeeds before any other process executes its "critical section" more than c times. The critical section denotes the section of the process's code in which the resource R is required.)

In the present paper we study the most strict fairness requirement, first-come, first-serve, and present an algorithm which solves the mutual exclusion problem using a (n + 17)-valued communication variable. By the lower bound result of [1o], mentioned above, we know that our solution must must be optimal (within a small additive constant).

1. The Algorithm

Our solution is rather complex although the basic principle can be stated quite succintly: Every participating process has its own number i, $1 \le i \le n$. After leaving its critical section, a process becomes the "scheduler", i.e., takes on the responsibility of scheduling the next waiting process into its critical section, in a first-come, first-serve order. For this purpose, a list of chains of process identifiers is maintained which reflects the arrival history.

The list takes the form

$$n_1, \ldots, n_k,$$

where n_j denotes the identifier of the most recent arrival on chain j, $1 \le j \le k$.

Example of a chain: $3 \to 6 \to 4 \to 0$. The special identifier 0 is at the bottom of each chain. 4 is the predecessor of 6 (in arrival order), 6 is the previous (in chain order) with respect to 4.

The inverse chains concatenated from left to right give the proper order of arrivals, i.e., the least recent arrival is at the bottom of the n_1-chain. The scheduler at (practically) every time maintains the list in its local memory, and, after having determined the next scheduler, passes the list on to it. Such communication tasks become difficult when the goal is to economize on shared buffer memory. Every signal set in the buffer can get interrupted before it arrives at the receiver intended, and, analogously, every response can get intercepted before it gets back to the original sender. This is the reason why we have to deal with a list of chains instead of with a single string of arrival numbers: Whenever the scheduler notices a change of the communication variable not due to it, the scheduler starts a new chain and appends it to the local list. Arrivals that go by "unnoticed" by the scheduler put themselves on the most recent chain n_k.

The structure of the algorithm which serves as a communication protocol for every participating process, is outlined in the following diagram:

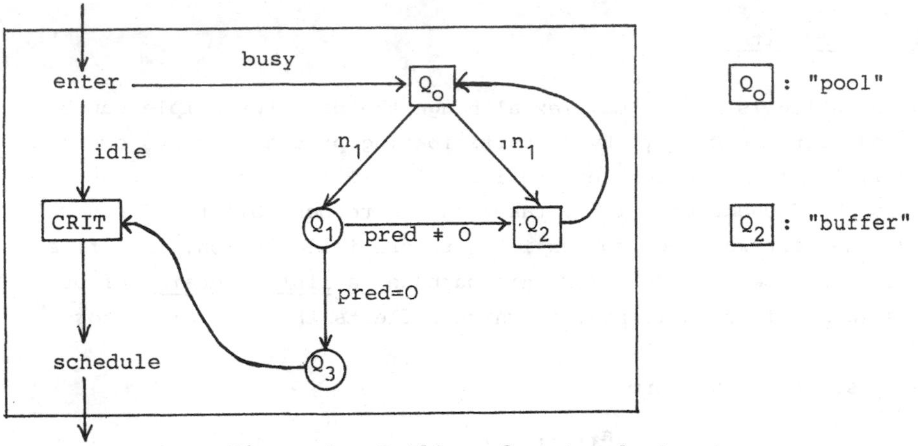

Figure 1: Outline of protocol structure (implemented entirely in terms of control structures, i.e. without using explicit data structures)

Here is a brief verbal description of the protocol: When a new process enters the system it first checks if the system is idle (i.e. if nobody is demanding or using resource R). If it is, the process simply proceeds to its critical section CRIT. After leaving CRIT, the process becomes the scheduler and now has to determine which process is to enter CRIT next (and subsequently become the new scheduler). Suppose there is just one process in the system (in CRIT) when the next arrival occurs. The latter process enters a random queueing structure Q_o(the "pool") after having left its number in the shared buffer variable v. The next arrival, before anything else happens, will take the number in v, memorize it as its predecessor, leave its own number, and wait in Q_o. - Suppose now the present scheduler leaves its critical section. If it finds the "pool" Q_o empty it simply leaves, and the system is idle again. Otherwise the present scheduler has to identify the bottom process of the n_1-chain (the one with predecessor "0"): The latter process is to become the new scheduler. - To this end, the present scheduler calls process n_1 out of the pool. Processes $\neq n_1$ that intercept this call get transferred to another auxiliary queue Q_2 (the "buffer"), and the scheduler repeats its call until n_1 has received the message. Process n_1 is then transferred to point Q_1 where it communcates its predecessor number to the scheduler. If it has a nonzero predecessor, process n_1 is transferred to the buffer from which it gets recommited to the pool along with all other members of the buffer. As soon as the buffer has been emptied, the present scheduler calls n_1's predecessor and continues this way until the bottom process of the n_1-chain has been identified. The latter, call it $\bar{n}$, will wait at point Q_3. Now the next to last process on the n_1-chain, the one which is the "previous" with respect to $\bar{n}$, has to be called out of the pool to change its predecessor to 0. Any process not intended that intercepts a signal during this procedure is (re-)committed to the pool. Now process $\bar{n}$ which is still waiting at Q_3 may enter its critical section and take over as the new scheduler as soon as it will have received the current arrival list from the old scheduler. A special signal "eol" (end of list) seems to be necessary to implement a smooth transition of control to the new scheduler. (A typical difficulty is raised by states in which the old scheduler has completed, from its point of view, all of the list transmission but the list has not yet been received in its entirety, due to interrupts by new arrivals.)

As mentioned before, the communcation buffer must be large enough to distinguish n + 17 values. These are: 0, 1,...,n, idle, eol, as well as the primed and unprimed versions of the following: a, b, c, <calling pool>, <calling buffer>, <calling prev>, <calling new scheduler>.

2. Synchronization and Communication Tools

We shall proceed to give a complete version of the algorithm. Its only synchronization tool is a generalized test-and-set operation as introduced in [9] in terms of the following scheme (in which the broken line indicates indivisibility of the test on the shared variable v and the subsequent assignment to v):

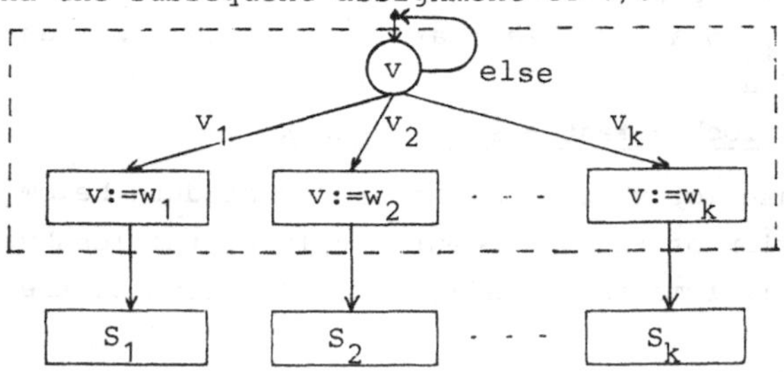

Figure 2: Generalized test-and-set instruction

When a process encounters such a construct in its protocol, it waits for v to assume one of the values $v_1, \ldots, v_k$ ("busy wait"), executes the respective assignment $v := w_i$ without interference by any other process, and continues with statement S_i.

In [1o] the following syntax has been proposed for our scheme:

<u>test</u> v <u>until</u>
v_1 <u>setto</u> w_1 : S_1;
⋮
v_k <u>setto</u> w_k : S_k
<u>endtest</u>.

Unfortunately, this elegant syntax loses some of its advantages when the continuing statements S_i get more complex and involve additional test-and-sets (as is the case with our algorithm). We thus found it sometimes more convenient to recur to primitives <u>lock</u> (v) and <u>unlock</u> (v) that only get engaged in a test-and-set fashion, i.e., a <u>lock</u> (v) can only be followed by a test on v, a subsequent assignment to v, and an <u>unlock</u> (v). Using these primitives (whose fair implementation must be guaranteed at a lower level of abstraction), the syntax of [1o] translates to:

A : <u>lock</u> (v);
<u>case</u> v <u>of</u>
v_1 : $v := w_1$; <u>unlock</u> (v); S_1;
⋮
v_k : $v := w_k$; <u>unlock</u> (v); S_k;
<u>else</u> : <u>unlock</u> (v); <u>goto</u> A
<u>end</u>.

For the sake of style and programming convenience we shall occasionally permit an assignment to a variable that is local to a process to occur in the middle of a

<u>lock</u> - <u>test</u> - <u>set</u> - <u>unlock</u>

sequence. In such a case (of which the "record"-procedure below is an example) the execution of the statement involving the local variable gets postponed until immediately after the execution of the subsequent <u>unlock</u>.

The special role of message value 0 ("neutral" state of a busy system) motivates the use of the following two procedures:

```
procedure reset;              procedure record;
begin v := 0;                 begin  lock;
     unlock                    if v = j (j integer ≠ 0) then
end.                             List := List, j
                               end.
```

Since v is the only shared variable we can omit v in the calls on lock and unlock. - The statement "List := List,j" means: process identifier j gets appended to the local arrival list (i.e., process j is the most recent arrival on a new chain).

The following two procedures are used for message transmission. Results are returned in a local variable "resp"; $v_1,\ldots,v_s,r_1,r_2$ are values of v (message values).

```
procedure send message (v1,r1,r2); {v locked when called}
begin  v := v1;  unlock;
  A :  lock;
       case v of
       integer j     : reset;  List := List,j; goto A;
       ri (i = 1,2): resp := ri;
       else : unlock; goto A
       end
end.   {v locked upon exit}

procedure send (v1...vs);  {v locked when called}
begin  for i := 1 to s do
  send message (vi, vi', vi')
end.   {v locked upon exit}
```

3. Implementation

We are now ready to specify the main protocol procedures. Throughout, integer i denotes a process identifier.

An important requirement of the entrance protocol, due to the condition of lockout-freeness, is that every process upon its arrival be able to react to any value of the shared variable v. Special precaution has to be taken when the arriving process intercepts the message "eol", i.e. the end-of-list message of the old scheduler. The eol-part of the following procedure should be (re-)read in context with the procedures "schedule" and "receive list".

```
procedure enter process(i);
begin List := empty;
  lock;
  case v of
  idle:       reset; CRIT(i); schedule;
  integer j:  v := i; unlock; pred := j; wait in pool;
  eol:        send (a^i b); reset;
              A : if List = empty then
                     lock;
                     if v = 0 then
                        v := eol; unlock; pred := 0; wait in pool
                     else
                        List := List, v; reset; goto B
                     fi
                 else
                     B: n:= first(List); List := rest(List); record;
                        send (a^n b); reset; goto A
                 fi;
  other:      v:= i; unlock; pred := 0;
              test v until
              0 setto other: wait in pool
              endtest
  end {case}
end. {proc}
```

Here and in the following, CRIT(i) denotes the critical section of process i.

Upon leaving the critical section, the process becomes the new scheduler, i.e., it calls the following procedure:

```
procedure schedule;
begin if List = empty then
        lock;
        if v = 0 then
           v := idle; unlock; {exit proc}
        else
           List := List, v; reset; goto A
        fi
      else
         A : n := first(List); buffer-size := 0; prev := 0;
             "get bottom of first chain"
         B : record; send (<calling pool>a^n);
             send message (b, a, c); reset;
             if resp = a then "get predecessor"
                count := 0;
                repeat record; send message (b, a, c);
                   reset; count := count + 1
                until resp = c
             else
                buffer-size := buffer-size + 1; goto B
             fi;
             if count > 1 then
                prev := n;  n := count - 1;
                buffer-size := buffer-size + 1;
                while buffer-size > 0 do
                  buffer-size := buffer-size - 1;
                  record; send (<calling buffer>); reset
                od;
                goto B
             fi;

             if prev = 0 then
                List := rest (List)
             else "get previous from pool"
              repeat record; send (<calling prev> a^prev);
                send message (b, a, c); reset;
                buffer-size := buffer-size + 1
              until resp = a
             fi;
```

```
        while buffer-size > 0 do
         buffer-size := buffer-size - 1;
         record; send (<calling buffer>); reset
        od;
         record; send (<calling new scheduler>); reset;
        C : if List = empty then
              lock;
              if v = 0 then
                 v := eol; unlock; {exit proc}
              else
                 List := List, v; reset; goto D
              fi
            else
              D : n := first (List); List := rest (List);
                 record; send (a^n b); reset; goto C
            fi
    fi
end. {proc}
```

It is clear from the procedures "enter" and "schedule" that when the system is not idle every new arrival will join the "pool" of waiting processes where to await its turn. There are only three occasions on which a waiting process is intended to leave the pool: (1) to identify its predecessor (in this case the process belongs to the first chain of the arrival list and returns to the pool after it has identified a nonzero predecessor),(2) to change its predecessor to 0 (after having done so the process returns to the pool, knowing that it will be the next to enter its critical section),(3) to become the new scheduler (i.e., to receive the arrival list from the old scheduler, enter the critical section, and take on the responsibility to select the next scheduler).

However, it is possible that a process leaves the pool because it has intercepted a message not intended for it. The scheduler keeps track of these interceptors in its local variable "buffer-size" and makes them return to the pool as soon as the (repeated) message has reached the receiver intended.

The tasks described above,

wait in pool
identify predecessor
receive list
wait in buffer

are specified by the following procedures.

```
[Q0]: procedure wait in pool (i);
      begin test v until
              <calling pool> setto  <calling pool>' : t := 0;
              <calling prev> setto  <calling prev>' : t := 1
              endtest;
              count := 0;
          A: if count ≠ i then
                lock;
                if v = a then
                   v := a'; unlock; count := count + 1; goto A
                else
                   if v = b then
                      v := c; unlock; wait in buffer
                   fi
                fi
             else
                lock;
                if v = a then
                   v := a'; unlock; count := count + 1; goto A
                else
                   if v = b then
                      v := a; unlock;
                      if t = 0 then
                         identify predecessor
                      else
                         pred := 0; wait in buffer
                      fi
                   fi
                fi
             fi
      end.
```

Q_1 :
```
procedure identify predecessor;
begin count := pred;
  while count > 0 do
      lock;
      if v = b then
         v := a; unlock; count := count - 1
      else
         unlock
      fi
  od;
  test v until
  b setto c : if pred = 0 then
                 receive list
              else
                 wait in buffer
              fi
  endtest
end.
```

Q_3 :
```
procedure receive list (i);
begin test v until
      <calling new scheduler> setto <calling new scheduler>':
      endtest;
      n := 0;
   A: lock;
      if v = eol then
         reset
      else
         if v = a then
            v := a'; unlock; n := n + 1; goto A
         else
            if v = b then
               v := b'; unlock; List := List,n; n:= 0;goto A
            fi
         fi
      fi;
      CRIT (i)
end.
```

| Q_2 | : **procedure** wait in buffer;

```
begin test v until
      <calling buffer> setto <calling buffer>' : wait in pool
      endtest
end.
```

Remark: A careful analysis of our algorithm shows that it is, in essence, applicable not just to first-come, first-serve queueing but to any queueing discipline defined as a function of the arrival history since the last idle period of the system. This observation lends greater generality to our optimal result.

References

1. Dijkstra, E.W., "Solution of a problem in concurrent programming control", CACM 8 (1965), 569.

2. Knuth, D.E., "Additional comments on a problem in concurrent programming control", CACM 9 (1966), 321.

3. de Bruijn, N.G., "Additional comments on a problem in concurrent programming control", CACM 1o (1967), 137.

4. Eisenberg, M.A., and M.R. McGuire, "Further comments on Dijkstra's concurrent control problem", CACM 15 (1972), 999.

5. Lamport, L., "A new solution of Dijkstra's concurrent programming problem", CACM 17 (1974), 453.

6. Cremers, A.B., and T.N. Hibbard, "An algebraic approach to concurrent programming control and related complexity problems", Symposium on Algorithms and Complexity, Pittsburgh, April 1976, (Copies available from the authors.)

7. Rivest, R.L., and V.R. Pratt, "The mutual exclusion problem for unreliable processes: preliminary report", 17th Symposium on Foundations of Computer Science, October 1976.

8. Peterson, G.L., and M.J. Fischer, "Economical solutions for the critical section problem in a distributed system", 9th Symposium on Theory of Computing, May 1977.

9. Cremers, A.B., and T.N. Hibbard, "Mutual Exclusion of N Processors Using an O(N)-Valued Message Variable", 5th ICALP, Udine, Italy, Springer Lecture Notes in Computer Science 62, 165 - 176. July 1978.

1o. Burns, J.E., M.J. Fischer, P. Jackson, N.A. Lynch, G.L. Peterson, "Shared Data Requirements for Implementation of Mutual Exclusion Using a Test-and-Set Primitive", Computer Science Tech. Rept. 3, University of Washington, Seattle, August 1978.

ON THE HOMOMORPHIC CHARACTERIZATIONS OF FAMILIES OF LANGUAGES†

K. Culik II
Department of Computer Science
University of Waterloo
Waterloo, Ontario, Canada
N2L 3G1

1. Introduction

In this paper we summarize some results obtained jointly with N. Diamond [CD] and H.A. Maurer [CM]. We refer the reader to [CD, CM] for the proofs omitted here and additional material. Most of the results discussed here are consequences or extensions of the pure homomorphic characterization of recursively enumerable sets obtained in [C3].

The main result of [C3] is that for each recursively enumerable language L there exist erasing h_0 (a homomorphism either preserving or erasing any symbol) and homomorphisms h_1, h_2 such that $L = h_0(e(h_1, h_2))$, where $e(h_1, h_2)$ is the set of minimal strings on which h_1 and h_2 are equal. In Section 3 we show that by restricting the erasing h_0 we obtain various time-complexity classes of languages (suggested by a referee of [C3]) and by restrictions on the pair h_1, h_2 we obtain various space complexity classes of languages. Thus we get very simple "machine independent" characterization of both time- and space-complexity classes of languages which are equivalent to the usual definitions using Turing machines.

The well known notion of k-limited erasing (see [HU]) is generalized as follows. For a monotone function f on the integers we say that an erasing h is f-bounded on a language L if for each w in L at most $f(|w|)$ consecutive symbols of w may be erased. For any class of "nice" functions F closed under squaring let L_F be the class of languages accepted by nondeterministic Turing machines that operate with time bounds in F. We show that L is in L_F iff there exist homomorphisms h_0, h_1, h_2 such that $h_0(e(h_1, h_2)) = L$ and h_0 is f-bounded erasing on $e(h_1, h_2)$ for some of f in F.

As special cases we have, for example, the following. A language L is in NP (is primitive recursive, recursive) iff there exist homomorphisms h_0, h_1, h_2 such that $h_0(e(h_1, h_2)) = L$ and h_0 is polynomial- (primitive recursive-, recursive-) bounded erasing on $e(h_1, h_2)$.

---

† This research was supported by the Natural Sciences and Engineering Research Council of Canada, Grant No. A 7403.

The notion of the balance of a pair of homomorphisms was introduced in [C2] and in [C3] it was shown that a language L is regular if and only if it can be written in the form $L = h_0(e(h_1, h_2))$, where h_0 is an erasing and the pair of homomorphisms h_1, h_2 has k-bounded balance on $e(h_1, h_2)$ for some constant k .

Just as we have generalized the notion of k-limited (bounded) erasing, we can similarly generalize k-bounded balance. Given a monotone function f on the integers, a language $L \subseteq \Sigma^*$ and an erasing h on Σ^* , we say that a pair of homomorphisms (h_1, h_2) has f-bounded balance on L with respect to h if for each x in L and each prefix w of x we have $||h_1(w)| - |h_2(w)|| \leq f(|h(x)|)$. We show for all classes of "nice" functions F that a language L is of space complexity F iff there exist an erasing h_0 and homomorphisms h_1, h_2 such that $L = h_0(e(h_1, h_2))$ and the pair (h_1, h_2) has f-bounded balance on $e(h_1, h_2)$ with respect to h_0 for some f in F . For example, the context sensitive languages are exactly those which can be expressed in the form $h_0(e(h_1, h_2))$ where the pair (h_1, h_2) has linear-bounded balance on $e(h_1, h_2)$ with respect to h_0 .

In the last section we consider representations of language families by "generators". We want to obtain representation theorems of the following form: For a family of languages L , there is a language U in L , called a generator, such that each L in L can be expressed as $L = f(U)$, where f is a single operation or a simple combination of basic language operations.

One example is the Chomsky-Schützenberger theorem for the family of context-free languages which asserts that a Dyck language can be chosen as U and that f can be chosen to be the intersection with a regular set followed by a particularly simple type of homomorphism. Another example is Greibach's theorem on the hardest context-free language establishing for the family of context-free languages that with a proper choice of U the mapping f can be taken to be a single inverse homomorphism. Still another example is the notion of a full principal AFL since for any such full principal AFL L there exists a U such that every L in L can be written as $L = f(U)$, where f is a finite (rational) transduction.

A number of other similar results are known in the literature. In particular, a Chomsky-Schützenberger type theorem for the families of EOL and ETOL languages was shown in [C1] and for the family of recursively enumerable languages in [ER]. We strengthen the latter result in our Theorem 4.1 and show a similar result for every principal cone (Theorem 4.2) and consequently every full principal AFL .

We then discuss the generation of language families by inverse homomorphisms, possibly followed by an erasing, from a single generator. The well known Greibach's result on the "hardest" context-free language shows that the family of context-free languages can be generated by inverse homomorphisms from a single generator. Similar results are known for context sensitive and recursively enumerable languages. However,in all cases the generator essentially encodes all languages in the given family. We will show that the family of recursively enumerable sets can be generated from a single "simple" generator if we allow an inverse homomorphism to be followed by an erasing (Theorem 4.4).

Finally, we mention that no similar characterization exists for regular sets.

2. Preliminaries

We assume familiarity with basic formal language theory (see [H]). We recall some basic definitions and some notation from [C3] and [ER].

We say that C is a class of complexity functions if C is a class of functions closed under addition of and multiplication by a constant. A language L is of time (space) complexity C if L is accepted by a nondeterministic multitape on-line Turing machine M which operates within time-bound (space-bound) f, for some f in C.

A homomorphism $h : \Sigma^* \to \Delta^*$ is called an erasing if for some subset T of Σ we have $h(a) = a$ if $a \in T$ and $h(a) = \varepsilon$, otherwise (ε is the empty string). Throughout the paper such an erasing will be denoted by Π_T.

Let h_1, h_2 be two homomorphisms, $h_1, h_2 : \Sigma^* \to \Delta^*$. The minimal equality set of h_1 and h_2, denoted by $e(h_1, h_2)$ is defined by:

$$e(h_1, h_2) = \left\{ w \in \Sigma^+ \mid h_1(w) = h_2(w) \text{ and if } w = uv \text{ where } u \in \Sigma^+, \ v \in \Sigma^+, \text{ then } h_1(u) \neq h_2(u) \right\} .$$

Throughout this paper, if Σ is an alphabet, $\bar{\Sigma}$ will denote an alphabet disjoint from Σ consisting of "barred" symbols, $\bar{\Sigma} = \{\bar{a} \mid a \in \Sigma\}$. For any word $x \in \Sigma^*$, $\bar{x}$ denotes the word obtained from x by barring each symbol.

Let Σ be an alphabet. The twin-shuffle over Σ is a language over $(\Sigma \cup \bar{\Sigma})^*$, denoted by $L(\Sigma)$ and defined by:

$$L(\Sigma) = \left\{ x \in (\Sigma \cup \bar{\Sigma})^* \mid \overline{\Pi_{\Sigma}(x)} = \Pi_{\bar{\Sigma}}(x) \right\} .$$

3. Homomorphic Characterization of Complexity Classes of Languages

As already outlined in [C3], restrictions on the erasing h_0 or on the pairs (h_1, h_2) in the formula $h_0(e(h_1, h_2))$ lead to time- or space-complexity classes of languages. The time-complexity characterization (Theorem 3.1 and its corollaries) was suggested by an anonymous referee of [C3]. For proofs and more details see [CD].

3.1 Time-Complexity Classes

We generalize the notion of k-limited erasing ([HU]) as follows.

For a function f on the integers we say that an erasing h is f-bounded on a language L if for each w in L, $w = xyz$ and $h(y) = \varepsilon$ implies $|y| \leq f(|w|)$, that is at most $f(|w|)$ consecutive symbols of w may be erased. We say that h is C-bounded, for a class C of complexity functions, if h is f-bounded for some f from C.

We get the following "machine independent" characterization of time complexity of languages.

Theorem 3.1 Let C be a class of complexity functions closed under squaring. Then for each language L, L is of time complexity C iff there exist homomorphisms an erasing h_0 and h_1, h_2 such that $L = h_0(e(h_1, h_2))$ and h_0 is C-bounded erasing on $e(h_1, h_2)$.

Note that for a recursive f, h_0, h_1, and h_2 can be found effectively (from any standard representation of L).

Corollary A language L is in NP iff there exists homomorphisms h_0, h_1, h_2 such that $h_0(e(h_1, h_2)) = L$ and h_0 is polynomial-bounded erasing on $e(h_1, h_2)$.

Corollary A language L is primitive recursive (recursive) iff there exist homomorphisms h_0, h_1, h_2 such that $h_0(e(h_1, h_2)) = L$ and h_0 is primitive recursive- (recursive-) bounded erasing on $e(h_1, h_2)$.

3.2 Space-Complexity Classes

We now give a purely homomorphic characterization of space complexity classes. We will need the notion of bounded balance defined originally in [C2].

Definition Consider two fixed homomorphisms h_1 and h_2 from Σ^* to Δ^* and a word w in Σ^*. The balance of w is defined by

$$B(w) = |h_1(w)| - |h_2(w)| \quad .$$

We say that the pair (h_1, h_2) has k-bounded balance on a given language L for some $k \geq 0$ if $|B(u)| \leq k$ holds for each prefix u of every word in L.

In [C3, Theorem 4] it was shown that a constant bound on the balance of the pair (h_1, h_2) on $e(h_1, h_2)$ in $h_0(e(h_1, h_2))$ characterizes the regular set. Just as we have generalized the notion of k-limited (k-bounded) erasing on L we now generalize in a similar way the notion of k-bounded balance. Given a monotone function f on the integers we say that a pair of homomorphisms (h_1, h_2) has f-bounded balance on a language L, with respect to an erasing h_0, if for each x in L and each prefix w of x we have $|B(w)| \leq f(|h(x)|)$. Given a complexity class C, we say that (h_1, h_2) has C-bounded balance on L with respect to h_0, if the same is true for some $f \in C$.

Theorem 3.2 Let C be any class of complexity functions. Then for each language L, L is of (nondeterministic, on-line) space complexity C iff there exist homomorphisms an erasing h_0 and h_1, h_2 such that $L = h_0(e(h_1, h_2))$ and the pair (h_1, h_2) has C-bounded balance on $e(h_1, h_2)$ with respect to h_0.

Corollary A language L is context sensitive iff there exist an erasing h_0 and homomorphisms h_1, h_2 such that $L = h_0(e(h_1, h_2))$ and the pair (h_1, h_2) has linear-bounded balance on $e(h_1, h_2)$.

4. Generation of Language Families From a Single Language

For proofs which are omitted in this section and additional material see [CM].

4.1 Generation Using Intersection with a Regular Set Followed by a Homomorphism

In this subsection we consider the problem of representing each language L of a family of languages $\mathcal{L}$ as the homomorphic image of the intersection of some (presumably simple) language D_L and a regular set.

The historically first and most widely known result of this type is the well known Chomsky-Schützenberger theorem which can be stated as follows:

<u>Proposition 4.1</u> Let T be an arbitrary alphabet. Then there exist a language D_T and an erasing Π_T such that for every context-free language L over T there exists a regular set R such that $L = \Pi_T(D_T \cap R)$.

Similar results have been established for the families of EOL and ETOL languages in [C1] and recently for the family of recursively enumerable languages in [ER]. We will now show that the latter result also follows easily from Theorem 1 in [C3].

<u>Lemma 4.1</u> For every recursively enumerable language $L \subseteq T^*$ there exist a twin-shuffle $L(\Gamma)$, a regular set R_L and an erasing Π_T such that $L = \Pi_T(L(\Gamma) \cap R_L)$.

<u>Proof</u> By Theorem 1 of [C3] we can write $L = \Pi_T(e(h_1, h_2))$ for some homomorphisms $h_1, h_2 : \Sigma^* \to \Delta^*$ and $T \subseteq \Sigma$. We may assume that $\Delta \cap \Sigma = \phi$. Moreover, it follows from the proof of the theorem that we may assume that a symbol 3 is in Σ and $e(h_1, h_2) \subseteq (\Sigma - \{3\})^*\{3\}$.

Let $\overline{\Sigma} = \{\overline{a} \mid a \in \Sigma\}$, $\overline{\Delta} = \{\overline{b} \mid b \in \Delta\}$, $\Gamma = \Sigma \cup \Delta$, $\overline{\Gamma} = \overline{\Sigma} \cup \overline{\Delta}$ and let $\overline{w}$ be the word obtained from a word w by barring each symbol, $w \in (\Sigma \cup \Delta)^*$. Let $F = \{ah_1(a)\overline{h_2(a)} \mid a \in \Sigma\}$ and let $R_L = (F \cup (\overline{\Sigma} - \{\overline{3}\}))^*\{\overline{3}\}$.

Clearly, $e(h_1, h_2) = \Pi_\Sigma(L(\Gamma) \cap R_L)$. Note in particular that only "minimal solutions" are in $L(\Gamma) \cap R_L$, since the symbol $\overline{3}$ acts as an "endmarker".

□

Lemma 4.1 can be readily strengthened by making the twin-shuffle dependent only on T but not on L . We can use the twin-shuffle $L(T \cup \{0, 1\})$ as a fixed generator for every $L \subseteq T^*$.

<u>Theorem 4.1</u> Let $L \subseteq T^*$ be an RE language. There exists a regular set $R_L \subseteq (T \cup \overline{T} \cup \{0, \overline{0}, 1, \overline{1}\})^*$ so that $L = \Pi_T(L(T \cup \{0, 1\}) \cap R_L)$, where Π_T is the erasing preserving only letters from T .

<u>Proof</u> Let $L \subseteq T^*$ be an arbitrary RE language. By Lemma 4.1 there exist an alphabet Γ , $T \subseteq \Gamma$ and a regular set $Q \subseteq \Gamma^*$ so that $L = \Pi_T(L(\Gamma) \cap Q)$. Let $\Gamma - T = \{c_1, c_2, \ldots, c_m\}$ and let $g : (\Gamma \cup \overline{\Gamma})^* \to (T \cup \overline{T} \cup \{0, 1, \overline{0}, \overline{1}\})^*$ be the homomorphism defined by:

$$g(a) = a \quad \text{for } a \in T \cup \overline{T}$$

$$\left.\begin{aligned} g(c_i) &= 01^i \\ g(\overline{c_i}) &= \overline{0}\overline{1}^i \end{aligned}\right\} \quad \text{for } i = 1,2,\ldots,m \quad .$$

Finally, let $R_L = g(Q)$. Since g is a one-to-one mapping, since $g(L(\Gamma)) = L(T \cup \{0, 1\}) \cap (g(\Gamma \cup \overline{\Gamma}))^*$ and since $\Pi_T(x) = \Pi_T(g(x))$ for every $x \in (\Gamma \cup \overline{\Gamma})^*$, we have

$$L = \Pi_T(L(\Gamma) \cap Q) = \Pi_T(g(L(\Gamma)) \cap g(Q))$$
$$= \Pi_T(L(T \cup \{0, 1\}) \cap R_L) \ .$$

□

We establish that representation theorems such as Theorem 4.1 are not restricted to a few special language families but hold for a variety of "natural" families of languages.

First we recall the notion of a principal cone.

<u>Definition</u> A family of languages $\mathcal{L}$ is a <u>principal cone</u> if there is an L in $\mathcal{L}$ such that $\mathcal{L}$ is the closure of $\{L\}$ under the operations of homomorphism, inverse homomorphism and intersection with a regular set, or equivalently $\mathcal{L}$ is the closure of $\{L\}$ under finite transducers (rational relations) c.f. [Gi].

<u>Theorem 4.2</u> Let T be an alphabet and $\mathcal{L}$ a principal cone. There exists a language L_T in $\mathcal{L}$ so that for each L in $\mathcal{L}$, $L \subseteq T^*$, there exists a regular set R_L such that $L = \Pi_T(L_T \cap R_L)$.

<u>Proof</u> We can write $L = t_L(L_0)$ where t_L is a finite transducer. We may assume that $L_0 \subseteq \Sigma^*$, $\Sigma \cap T = \phi$. Using [E, Theorem 2.5], there is an $R \subseteq (T \cup \Sigma)^*$ such that $L = \Pi_T(\Pi_\Sigma^{-1}(L_0) \cap R)$. Now, let $L_T = \Pi_\Sigma^{-1}(L_0)$. Then, for all L in $\mathcal{L}$, $L \subseteq T^*$,there is an $R \subseteq (\Sigma \cup T)^*$ such that $L = \Pi_T(L_T \cap R)$. Note, that L_T and Π_T depend only on T and not on L .

□

Since each principal full AFL is a principal cone [Gi] we have the following

<u>Corollary</u> Let T be an alphabet and $\mathcal{L}$ a full principal AFL . There exists a language L_T in $\mathcal{L}$ such that for each L in $\mathcal{L}$, $L \subseteq T^*$, there exists a regular set R_L such that $L = \Pi_T(L_T \cap R_L)$ (Π_T is an erasing).

We conclude this subsection by observing that a result similar to Theorem 4.2 holds for any countable family of languages $\mathcal{L}$, provided we do not insist that the generator is element of $\mathcal{L}$:

<u>Theorem 4.3</u> Let Σ be an alphabet and $\mathcal{L}$ a countable family of languages over (subsets of) Σ . Then there exists a language U such that for each $L \in \mathcal{L}$ there

exist an erasing Π_T and a regular set R such that $L = \Pi_T(U \cap R)$.

Proof Let $\mathcal{L} = \{L_1, L_2, L_3, \ldots\}$ and let c, d be new symbols. Let $U = \bigcup_{i=1}^{\infty} c^i dL_i$. Suppose $L = L_i \in \mathcal{L}$, $L \subseteq T^*$. Define $R = c^i dT^*$. Clearly, $L = \Pi_T(U \cap R)$.

□

Note that by restricting the choice of T in the erasing Π_T we can get a precise characterization, i.e. only languages in $\mathcal{L}$, even if U is not in $\mathcal{L}$.

4.2 Generation Using Inverse Homomorphism, Possibly Followed by Homomorphism

Greibach's result on the "hardest" context-free language, see [Gr] or [H] asserts that every context-free language can be obtained as an inverse homomorphic image of one fixed context-free language:

Proposition 4.2 There exists a context-free language U such that for each context-free language L there exists a homomorphism h such that $L = h^{-1}(U)$.

Similar results are also known ([B], [W], new proofs in [CM]) for the families of recursively enumerable languages and context-sensitive languages.

Proposition 4.3 There exists a recursively enumerable language $U \subseteq \{0, 1\}^*$ such that every recursively enumerable language L can be written as $L = h_L^{-1}(U)$ for some homomorphism h_L .

Proposition 4.4 There exists a context-sensitive language $U \subseteq \{0, 1\}^*$ such that every context-sensitive language L can be written as $L = h_L^{-1}(U)$ for some homomorphism h_L .

The above results are "trivial" in the sense that they are proved by encoding all the languages in the given family $\mathcal{L}$ into the (complicated) generator U so that every language L in $\mathcal{L}$ can be "retrieved" from U by the inverse homomorphism h_L .

We now show that every recursively enumerable language can be obtained from a "simple" generator U by some inverse homomorphism followed by an erasing. So the price for the "simplicity" of the generator is the need for an additional erasing.

Theorem 4.4 There exists a fixed recursively enumerable language $U \subseteq \{0, 1\}^*$ such that for every recursively enumerable language L there is a homomorphism h and an erasing Π_T such that $L = \Pi_T(h^{-1}(U))$.

Proof Assume $L \subseteq T^*$. By Theorem 1 in [C3] we can write $L = \Pi_T(e(h_1, h_2))$ for some homomorphisms $h_1, h_2 : \Sigma^* \to \Delta^*$ and $T \subseteq \Sigma$.

Let $\Delta = \{c_1, c_2, \ldots, c_m\}$ and $g_1, g_2 : \Delta^* \to \{0, 1\}^*$ be homomorphisms defined by $g_1(c_i) = 01^i$, $g_2(c_i) = 001^i$, for $i = 1,2,\ldots,m$. That is, g_1 and g_2 encode an arbitrary alphabet Δ into the binary alphabet $\{0, 1\}$. Observe that both g_1 and g_2 are one-to-one functions.

Let f_1, f_2 be finite transducers defined by their diagrams in Figure 1. (Shaded circles indicate final states.)

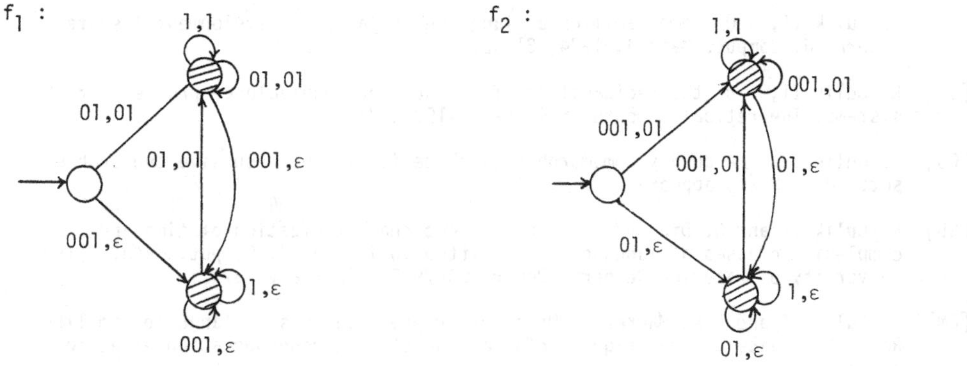

Figure 1

Using f_1 and f_2 we now define our generator U. Let

$$U = \{w \in \{0, 1\}^* \mid f_1(w) = f_2(w) \neq \phi \text{ and } f_1(v) \neq f_2(v) \text{ for each proper prefix } v \text{ of } w\}.$$

Note that U is defined independently of Δ. However, for each Δ we have:

$$U \cap (g_1(\Delta) \cup g_2(\Delta))^*$$

(1) $$= \{w \in (g_1(\Delta) \cup g_2(\Delta))^* \mid g_1^{-1}(w) = g_2^{-1}(w) \text{ and } g_1^{-1}(v) \neq g_2^{-1}(v) \text{ for each proper prefix } v \text{ of } w\}.$$

Finally, let $h : \Sigma^* \to \{0, 1\}^*$ be the homomorphism defined by $h(a) = g_1(h_1(a))$ for each $a \in \Sigma$. It follows from (1) that $e(h_1, h_2) = h^{-1}(U \cap (g_1(\Delta) \cup g_2(\Delta))^*) = h^{-1}(U)$. Hence $L = \Pi_T(h^{-1}(U))$ as desired.

□

Finally, we mention that a strictly homomorphic characterization of regular sets is not possible. For a proof see [CM].

Theorem 4.5 For every regular set R there exists a regular set R' such that $R' \neq g(h^{-1}(R))$ holds for all homomorphisms g and h.

References

[B] R.V. Book, Comparing Complexity Classes, J. of Comput. Syst. Sci. 9, 1974, 213-229.

[C1] K. Culik II, On some families of languages related to developmental systems, Intern. J. Comput. Math 4, 1974, 31-42.

[C2] K. Culik II, On the decidability of the sequence equivalence problem for DOL systems, Theoretical Computer Science 3, 1977, 75-84.

[C3] K. Culik II, A purely homomorphic characterization of recursive enumerable sets, J. ACM (to appear).

[CD] K. Culik II and N. Diamond, A homomorphic characterization of time and space complexity classes of languages. Submitted to Intern. J. Comput. Math., also University of Waterloo Research Report CS-79-07, February 1979.

[CM] K. Culik II and H.A. Maurer, On simple representations of language families, Revue Francaise d'Automatique, Informatique et Recherche Operationnelle, to appear.

[E] S. Eilenberg, Automata, Languages and Machines, Academic Press, 1976.

[ER] J. Engelfriet and G. Rozenberg, Equality languages, fixed point languages and representations of recursively enumerable languages, 19th Annual Symposium on Foundations of Computer Science, 1978, 123-126.

[Gi] S. Ginsburg, Algebraic and automata-theoretic properties of formal languages, North Holland, Amsterdam, 1975.

[Gr] S. Greibach, The hardest context-free language, SIAM J. of Comput. 2, 1973, 304-310.

[H] M.A. Harrison, Introduction to Formal Language Theory, Addison-Wesley, Reading, Mass. 1978.

[HU] J.E. Hopcroft and J.D. Ullman, Formal Languages and their Relation to Automata. Addison-Wesley, Reading, Mass. 1969.

[W] B. Wegbreit, A generator of context sensitive languages, J. of Comput. Syst. Sci. 3, 1969, 456-461.

TWO LEVEL GRAMMARS : CF-GRAMMARS WITH EQUATION SCHEMES

Piotr Dembiński
Jan Małuszyński
Institute of Computer Science
Polish Academy of Sciences
00-901 Warsaw PKiN, PO Box 22

Introduction

Two-level grammars have attracted attention as a tool for programming language specification and as another formalism for defining type 0 languages. The power of the formalism is a disadvantage from the compiler designer point of view. On the other hand, it enables a formal description of context-dependent features, and even of the semantics, of programming languages. It is doubtful however, that such a unique description of the syntax and semantics of a programming language could be useful for compiling purposes. At least none of the existing parsing methods can be directly applied.

The paper shows that any two-level grammar W can be viewed as a context-free grammar G(W) with an attached semantic mechanism S(W). The grammar G(W) is a modification of the Wegner's "skeleton grammar" and is constructed from W in a straightforward manner. It has the property that each derivation of W can be transformed into a derivation of G(W) in such a way that $L(W) \subseteq L(G(W))$. As a matter of fact one should consider standard derivations only (e.g. left-most derivations), but this is not necessary for the presentation of the idea. For each derivation of G(W) the semantic mechanism S(W) produces a set of string equations of the form

$$\alpha_0 X_1 \alpha_1 X_2 \cdots \alpha_{n-1} X_n \alpha_n = \beta_0 Y_1 \beta_1 Y_2 \cdots \beta_{k-1} Y_k \beta_k$$

with coefficients α_i, $i = 0,\dots,n$, and β_j, $j = 0,\dots,k$, being strings, and variables ranging over context-free languages. For any string s in L(G(W)), $s \in L(W)$ iff there exists a derivation of s in G(W) such that the corresponding set of equations has a solution. Any solution of that set of equations can be considered a "meaning" of s. As it was shown in [2] such an approach to the semantics of programming languages is very similar to the well-known attribute approach of Knuth [5]. The problem of the existence of a solution of such sets of string equations is recursively unsolvable. Therefore, in this paper we consider regular based two-level grammars (as called by Wegner [8] with the additional property that no metanotion occurs more than once in any hypernotion. It is known, that any type 0 language can be designed by a grammar of that kind. Let W be a two-level grammar of that type. We give an algorithm which produces all solutions of the set of equations corresponding to a derivation of G(W). It does not mean that we can solve the parsing problem for W (which is obviously recursively unsolvable): for a given string s of L(G(W)) we choose one of its derivations and check whether the corresponding set of equations has a solution or not. If yes, s is in L(W), if not - we have to choose another derivation of s in G(W) and check the existence of solutions of the other set of equations etc. But it may happen that the outlined procedure does not halt because of "empty loops" in G(W).

Two-level grammar as a CF grammar with equation schemes

The notion of two-level grammar was introduced by Van Wijngaarden and has been applied as a descriptive tool for the syntax of ALGOL 68 [9]. It was shown in [1] and [4] that using two-level grammars one can describe also the semantics of programming languages. Several other formalisms closely related to the original one have been proposed, e.g., in [6] and [7].

Any two-level grammar can be considered to be a context-free grammar with possibly an infinite number of nonterminals and productions. The following definition is similar to that given by Deussen [3] and differs slightly from the original one.

A two-level grammar W consists of:

X - a finite auxiliary alphabet;

T - a finite terminal alphabet;

M - a finite set of metanotions;

L_m - $m \in M$, a family of context-free languages over X - the domains of the metanotions;

H - the set of hypernotions: a finite subset of $\{\langle\}\{X \cup M\}^{+}\{\rangle\}$ where $\langle$ and $\rangle$ are special symbols and do not belong to any other alphabet of W;

$\mathcal{H} \subset H \times (H \cup T)^{*}$ - a finite set of hyperrules;

$\langle\sigma\rangle \in H$ - the start element; it is assumed that $\sigma \in X^{+}$.

The production rules P_W of W are derived from the hyperrules in the following way:

A <u>consistent replacement</u> ϱ of W is any homomorphism

$\varrho : H \longrightarrow \{<\} X^* \{>\}$

such that $\varrho(\alpha) = \alpha$ if $\alpha \in X \cup \{<,>\}$

$\varrho(\alpha) \in L_\alpha$ if $\alpha \in M$.

Any production rule p of W is the image $\varrho(R)$ of a hyperrule $R = h_0 \longrightarrow a_0 h_1 a_1 \ldots a_{n-1} h_n a_n$ ($h_i \in H$, $a_i \in T^*$ for $i=0,\ldots,n$) under a consistent replacement ϱ where $\varrho(R)$ is defined as $\varrho(h_0) \longrightarrow a_0 \varrho(h_1) a_1 \ldots a_{n-1} \varrho(h_n) a_n$.

The set N_W of <u>nonterminals</u> of W consists of all images of the hypernotions in H under consistent replacements. The language specified by a two-level grammar W - L(W) is the set of all terminal strings derivable from $<\sigma>$ by the production rules of W.

<u>Example 1</u>

We define a two-level grammar W which produces a regular language of bit strings and associates to each string its "semantics" - a pair of natural numbers - the length and the decimal value of the string. These numbers are coded in the unary code within nonterminals of W as the sequences of the auxiliary symbol i corresponding to the occurrences of the metanotions L and D in the hypernotions.

$X = \{a,b,\ldots,z\}$; $T = \{0,1\}$; $M = \{D, D1, L\}$

$L_D = L_{D1} = \{i\}^*$, $L_L = \{i\}^+$

$<\sigma> = <$binary$>$;

$\mathcal{H} =$

```
          h0                 h1
{R1: < binary > ---> < binary with  L  and  D >,
               h2                         h3
 R2: < binary with  i  and  D > ---> < bit with  D >,
               h4
 R3: < binary with  Li  and  DDD1 > ---
               h1                    h5
     < binary with  L  and  D > < bit with  D1 >,
           h6
 R4: < bit with  i > ---> 1,
           h7
 R5: < bit with > ---> 0 ; }
```

$H = \{h0,\ldots h7\}$ (i.e. the hypernotions are strings in the special brackets < and > as defined above).

An example of a derivation:

```
< binary >,
< binary with  ii  and  ii >,          (by  R1  with  L = ii  D = ii)
< binary with  i  and  i > < bit with >,  (by  R3  with  L = i
                                                   D = i   D1 = ε )
```

<bit with i>	<bit with>,	(by R2 with D = i)
1	<bit with>,	(by R4)
1	0	(by R5)

Let W be a two-level grammar. We are going to define a CF grammar G(W) and to sketch the proof of the following two facts:

1. $L(W) \subseteq L(G(W))$

2. For each derivation d in G(W) one can construct a set of equations E(d) such that:

if d derives a terminal string s in G(W) and E(d) has a solution then $s \in L(W)$

To show the above 1 and 2 is the same as to say that

$L(W) = \{ s$: there is d which derives s in G(W) and E(d) has a solution $\}$

We define:

$G(W) = (H.T,P, \langle \mathcal{S} \rangle)$

where H, T and $\langle \mathcal{S} \rangle$ are hypernotions, terminals and the start element of the two-level grammar W. The set of productions P of G(W) is the disjoint union of the following sets:

$P_0 = \mathcal{H}$ (hyperrules of W)

$P_1 = \{ (h_1,h_2) : h_1.h_2 \in H \}$

The disjoint union in this definition means that we want to distinguish between original hyperrules and possibly the same but "renamed" rules. This can be avoided by a more elaborated definition of G(W).

Let us consider now $w = w_0X_1 \dots X_nw_n$, where $X_i \in N_W$ and $w_i \in T^*$. We say that w is obtained from $z \in (H \cup T)^*$ by a vector of consistent replacements $\overline{\varrho} = (\varrho_1, \dots, \varrho_n)$ (for short $w = \overline{\varrho}(z)$) if

$z = w_0h_1 \dots h_nw_n$ and $\varrho_i(h_i) = X_i$, $i = 1, \dots, n$

Now, if $w \underset{W}{\Longrightarrow} v$ then it means that there is $1 \leqslant i \leqslant n$, a hyperrule $R = g_0 \longrightarrow v_0g_1 \dots g_kv_k$ and a consistent replacement ϱ such that: $\varrho_i(h_i) = \varrho(g_o)$ and $v = \overline{\varrho}''(z'')$ where:

$$z'' = w_0h_1 \dots w_i\ v_og_1 \dots g_kv_kw_{i+1}h_{i+1} \dots h_nw_n$$

$$\overline{\varrho}'' = (\varrho_1, \dots \varrho_{i-1}, \underbrace{\varrho, \dots, \varrho}_{k}, \varrho_{i+1}, \dots, \varrho_n)$$

That way $z \underset{G(W)}{\Longrightarrow} z' \underset{G(W)}{\Longrightarrow} z''$ where

$$z' = w_0 h_1 \cdots w_i g_0 w_{i+1} h_{i+1} \cdots h_n w_n$$

$$\bar{\varrho}' = (\varrho_1, \ldots, \varrho_{i-1}, \varrho, \varrho_{i+1}, \ldots, \varrho_n)$$

Note, that by the above construction one step in a derivation of W is replaced by two steps in the corresponding derivation of $G(W)$ (except the case when $h_i = g_0$). The property $\varrho_i(h_i) = \varrho(g_0)$ means that $\bar{\varrho}(z) = \bar{\varrho}'(z_1)$.

It is now clear that $L(W) \subseteq L(G(W))$ since for every derivation in W one can construct a corresponding derivation in $G(W)$.

Suppose, we have a derivation $z_1, \ldots, z_n$ in $G(W)$. This derivation corresponds (in the above sense) to a derivation in W iff one can find $\bar{\varrho}_1, \ldots, \bar{\varrho}_n$ such that either $\bar{\varrho}_i(z_i) = \bar{\varrho}_{i+1}(z_{i+1})$ or $\bar{\varrho}_i(z_i) \underset{W}{\Longrightarrow} \bar{\varrho}_{i+1}(z_{i+1})$. $i = 1, \ldots n-1$

Assume, that we have already found $\bar{\varrho}_1, \ldots, \bar{\varrho}_j$. Consider two seperate cases:

1. $z_j = z'$, $z_{j+1} = z''$ and $\bar{\varrho}_j = \varrho'$ as defined above, i.e., a hyperrule $R \in \mathcal{H} = P_0$ has been applied. Then $\bar{\varrho}_j(z_j) \underset{W}{\Longrightarrow} \bar{\varrho}_{j+1}(z_{j+1})$ where $\bar{\varrho}_{j+1} = \bar{\varrho}''$ (see above)

2. Assume $z_i \underset{G(W)}{\Longrightarrow} z_{j+1}$ by a production $h_i \longrightarrow g_0 \in P_1$. It means we have the situation where $z_j = z$, $z_{j+1} = z'$ and $\bar{\varrho}_j = \bar{\varrho}$, $\bar{\varrho}_{i+1} = \bar{\varrho}'$ are properly chosen only if the condition

(1) $\varrho_i(h_i) = \varrho(g_0)$

is satisfied.

If $h_i = \langle \alpha_0 a_1 \cdots a_m \alpha_m \rangle$ and $g_0 = \langle \beta_0 b_1 \cdots b_p \beta_p \rangle$ where $\alpha_r, \beta_s \in X^*$ and $a_r, b_s \in M$, then to decide whether the condition (1) can be fulfilled is the same as to decide whether the string equation

(2) $\alpha_0 X_1 \cdots X_m \alpha_m = \beta_0 Y_1 \cdots Y_p \beta_p$

has a solution, treating X_r and Y_s as variables ranging over the context-free domains L_{a_r}, L_{b_s} prescribed by the source two-level grammar.

In other words, to decide whether a string derived in the context--free grammar G(W) belongs to the language L(W) means to be able to solve a finite set of equations (2) linked to a derivation of this string in G(W).

Note, that in this set of equations each variable is related to a metanotion and a consistent replacement. This means that two variables representing the same metanotion have the common domain, but these are identical variables only if they are related to the same consistent replacement in possibly different equations of type (1). For example, in the above h_i and g_0, a_r may equal b_s but X_r and Y_s must differ since ϱ_i and ϱ are different.

As an example let us consider a derivation in G(W) corresponding to the derivation in Example 1.

$$h_0 \xrightarrow{R1} h_1 \longrightarrow h_4 \xrightarrow{R3} h_1 h_5 \longrightarrow h_2 h_5 \xrightarrow{R2} h_3 h_5 \longrightarrow h_6 h_5 \xrightarrow{R4} 1h_5 \longrightarrow 1h_7 \xrightarrow{R5} 10$$

$$\varrho_1 \quad \varrho_2 \quad \varrho_2\varrho_2 \quad \varrho_3\varrho_2 \quad \varrho_3\varrho_2 \quad \varrho_4\varrho_2 \quad \varrho_2 \quad \varrho_5$$

The set of string equations for this derivation is the following (indexes of the variables correspond to the indexes of the above replacements)

binary with L_1 and D_1 = binary with D_2i and $D_2D_2D1_2$

binary with L_2 and D_2 = binary with i and D_3

bit with D_3 = bit with i

bit with $D1_2$ = bit with

The only solution of this set is the following one

D_3 = i, L_2 = i, $D1_2$ = , D_2 = i, L_1 = ii, D_1 = ii.

Restricted two-level grammars and string equations.

Considering the problem of finding all solutions of a given set of string equations we can observe that in general this problem is recursively unsolvable: consider a string equation of the form

X = Y

where X and Y are variables and L_X and L_Y certain context-free languages. The set of all solutions of this equation is the intersection of the two context-free languages. Thus, in the general case even the problem of the existence of a solution is recursively unsolvable. Therefore we restrict the form of the two-level grammars under consideration.

A two-level grammar W is called <u>regular based</u> iff for each metanotion m of W the domain L_m is a regular language.

A two-level grammar W is called <u>repetition-free</u> iff each metanotion of W occurs in any hypernotion of W at most once.

These restrictions do not influence the generative power of two-level grammars. It can be shown (see e.g. Wegner [8]) that for each type 0 language L there exists a regular based and repetition-free two-level grammar W such that L(W) = L.

Let W be a regular based and repetition-free two-level grammar. Consider sets of equations obtained for the derivations of G(W) by the construction of the previous section. Each of them has the following form

$$\text{(E)} \quad \alpha_0^i X_1^i \alpha_1^i \ldots \alpha_{n_i-1}^i X_n^i \alpha_n = \beta_0^i Y_1^i \beta_1^i \ldots \beta_{k_i-1}^i Y_{k_i}^i \beta_{k_i}^i$$

$$i = 1,\ldots,m$$

$$\text{(r1)} \quad X_j^i \neq X_l^i \quad \text{for each} \quad 1 \leqslant i \leqslant m, \quad j \neq l, \quad j,l = 1,\ldots,n_i$$

$$\text{(r2)} \quad Y_j^i \neq Y_l^i \quad \text{for each} \quad 1 \leqslant i \leqslant m, \quad j \neq l, \quad j,l = 1,\ldots,k_i$$

$$\text{(r3)} \quad X_j^i \neq Y_l^i \quad \text{for each} \quad 1 \leqslant i \leqslant m, \quad 1 \leqslant j \leqslant n_i, \quad 1 \leqslant l \leqslant k_i$$

where the properties (r1), (r2) and (r3) express the repetition--free property of the grammar W. Any string equation having these properties will be called a <u>repetition-free string equation</u>.

In order to express another property of the sets of equations we deal with we introduce an auxiliary notion of the <u>dependency relation</u> D on the set of variables of (E).

Let X and Y be variables occurring in (E):

X <u>depends</u> on Y in the i-th equation of (E)

$X \, D^i \, Y$ iff X occurs in the lhs and Y occurs in the rhs of the i-th equation of (E) or vice versa

X <u>depends</u> on Y in the set (E)

$X\,D\,Y$ iff there exists such a sequence $i_1,\ldots,i_k$ that
$1 \leq i_j \leq m$ and $i_j \neq i_l$ for $j \neq l$, $j,l = 1,\ldots,k$,
and $X(D^{i_1} \circ D^{i_2} \circ \ldots \circ D^{i_k})Y$,
where $\circ$ is the composition of binary relations

A set of equations (E) is called <u>proper</u> iff for each $i = 1,\ldots,m$:

X^i_j does not depend on X^i_l in (E) for $j,l = 1,\ldots,n_i$ and

Y^i_j does not depend on Y^i_l in (E) for $j,l = 1,\ldots,k_i$.

It can be shown that for each derivation of $G(W)$ the corresponding set of equations is proper if W is repetition-free.

<u>Solving repetition-free string equations with regular domains</u>

In this section we shall try to find the set of all solutions of an arbitrary repetition-free string equation with regular domains.

Let us start with an equation

(e) $\alpha_0 X_1 \alpha_1 \ldots \alpha_{n-1} X_n \alpha_n = \beta_0 Y_1 \beta_1 \ldots \beta_{k-1} Y_k \beta_k$

where $\alpha_0,\ldots,\alpha_n,\beta_0,\ldots,\beta_k \in V^*$, $X_1,\ldots,X_n,Y_1,\ldots,Y_k$ are variables ranging over V^* (i.e., each domain equals V^*, V is a finite alphabet), $k + n > 0$, and

$X_i \neq X_j$ for $i \neq j$, $i,j = 1,\ldots,n$,

$Y_i \neq Y_j$ for $i \neq j$, $i,j = 1,\ldots,k$,

$X_i \neq Y_j$ for $i = 1,\ldots,n$, $j = 1,\ldots,k$

The first easy observation one can make is that an equation (e) certainly has no solution if α_0 and β_0 or α_n and β_k do not "agree" (see Proposition 1).

The second observation follows. Namely, if the extreme coefficients do agree then some solutions can be easily "extracted" from words in which:

- all and only coefficients α_i and β_j occur,
- α_i precedes α_{i+1} (β_j precedes β_{j+1}) and they do not overlap (note, that α_i and β_j can overlap).

For example, if we consider an equation

$$\overbrace{ab}^{\alpha_0}X\overbrace{ab}^{\alpha_1} = Y\underbrace{ba}_{\beta_1}Z \qquad (\beta_0 = \beta_2 = \varepsilon)$$

then these words are the following:

$$1.\ \overbrace{ab}^{\alpha_0}\overbrace{ab}^{\alpha_1} \qquad 2.\ \overbrace{ab}^{\alpha_0}a\overbrace{ab}^{\alpha_1} \qquad 3.\ \overbrace{ab}^{\alpha_0}b\overbrace{ab}^{\alpha_1} \qquad 4.\ \overbrace{ab}^{\alpha_0}ba\overbrace{ab}^{\alpha_1}$$

$$1.\ a\underbrace{ba}_{\beta_1}b \qquad 2.\ a\underbrace{ba}_{\beta_1}ab \qquad 3.\ ab\underbrace{ba}_{\beta_1}b \qquad 4.\ ab\underbrace{ba}_{\beta_1}ab$$

Now, in each case, everything which can be put in between α_0 and α_1, without moving β_1, may be considered as a solution for X; everything on the left (right) of β_1 is than a solution for $Y(Z)$. This way, we get four disjoint families of solutions:

1. $X = \varepsilon$	2. $X = ay$	3. $X = yb$	4. $X = y_1bay_2$
$Y = a$	$Y = a$	$Y = aby$	$Y = aby_1$
$Z = b$	$Z = yab$	$Z = b$	$Z = y_2ab$

where y, y_1 and y_2 are arbitrary strings in V^*.

In this particular case it is easy to see that these are all solutions of the equation. The example suggests that, in general, it is enough to consider the possible ways the coefficients can be arranged within a word (a finite number of possibilities) to be able to derive all solutions of the equation. In other words, this states that there is always a finite number of minimal solutions generating all other solutions. In the example these solutions are given above if we omit y, y_1 and y_2.

The remaining part of this section is devoted to formalize the outlined method of solving repetition-free string equations and to prove this method correct.

Let V be an alphabet and $\alpha_0, \ldots, \alpha_n$, $\beta_0, \ldots, \beta_k \in V^*$, $k \geq 0$, $n \geq 0$. By a <u>common denominator</u> for the sequences $\alpha_0, \ldots, \alpha_n$ and $\beta_0, \ldots, \beta_k$ we mean any string $d \in V^*$ such that:

1. $|d| \leqslant \max(|\alpha_0|, |\beta_0|) + \max(|\alpha_n|, |\beta_k|) + \sum_{i=1}^{n-1} |\alpha_i| + \sum_{j=1}^{k-1} |\beta_j|$
2. There exist $x_1, \ldots, x_n$; $y_1, \ldots, y_k \in V^*$ such that

   $d = \alpha_0 x_1 \alpha_1 \ldots \alpha_{n-1} x_n \alpha_n$ and

$d = \beta_0 y_1 \beta_1 \ldots \beta_{k-1} y_k \beta_k$.

Directly from the definition follows:

<u>Proposition 1</u>. A common denominator for the sequences $\alpha_0, \ldots, \alpha_n$ and $\beta_0, \ldots, \beta_k$ exists iff one of the following conditions holds:

either α_0 is a prefix of β_0 and α_n is a postfix of β_k
or α_0 is a prefix of β_0 and β_k is a postfix of α_n
or β_0 is a prefix of α_0 and α_n is a postfix of β_k
or β_0 is a prefix of α_0 and α_k is a postfix of α_n.

As length of a common denominator is bound, the following proposition holds:

<u>Proposition 2</u>. For given sequences $\alpha_0, \ldots, \alpha_n$ and $\beta_0, \ldots, \beta_k$ the set of all common denominators is finite.

From the condition (2) of the definition we obtain at once:

<u>Proposition 3</u>. If d is a common denominator of the sequences $\alpha_0, \ldots, \alpha_n$ and $\beta_0, \ldots, \beta_k$ then

$$|d| \geqslant \max\left(\sum_{i=0}^{n} |\alpha_i|, \sum_{j=0}^{k} |\beta_j|\right).$$

Common denominators play the role of words composed entirely from coefficients (see the informal explanation above). For the sake of the simplicity of the definition we have relaxed the assumptions for the only important thing is that the set of all common denominators is finite. In other words, we do not restrict ourselves to "minimal" solutions but we allow some other solutions to be included (always a finite number). We try now to use the notion of the common denominator for finding all solutions of (e).

Let d be a common denominator for $\alpha_0, \ldots, \alpha_n$ and $\beta_0, \ldots, \beta_k$. We find in d occurrences of the string $x_1, \ldots, x_n$ and $y_1, \ldots, y_k$ and fix them by inserting round brackets around each α_i in d for $i = 0, \ldots, n$ and square brackets around each β_j for $j = 1, \ldots, k$. In order to avoid ambiguity we adopt the following conventions:

- in the case when α_i coincides with certain β_j in d the square brackets have to be inserted around the round brackets, e.g. [(abc)] where abc $= \alpha_i = \beta_j$ but neither ([abc]) nor ([abc)] etc.

- in the case when $\alpha_i(\beta_j)$ is a substring of certain $\beta_j(\alpha_i)$ the corresponding square brackets (round brackets) occur within the round brackets (within the square brackets), e.g. [ab(c)] where abc = β_j and c = α_i but not [ab(c]):

- in the case when occurrences of α_i's and/or β_j's immediately precede each other the corresponding brackets are not mixed, e.g.

...(ab)(c)... or ...(ef)[gh]... etc.
but neither ...(ab()c)... nor ...(ef[)gh]... etc.

- the empty string ε is considered to be an additional symbol but only to denote an "empty coefficient". Otherwise, as usual, it does not occur in a given string.

Any string obtained from d using the above conventions will be called a <u>bracketed common denominator</u>.

We introduce one more auxiliary notion. Let s be a string in $(V \cup \{(,),[,]\})^*$. s is said to be <u>properly bracketed</u> iff:

- the first symbol of s is an opening bracket (or [and the last one is a closing bracket) or];
- the numbers of opening brackets and closing brackets of the same type occurring in s are equal.

Note that each bracketed common denominator is a properly bracketed string.

Let s be a properly bracketed string. By a <u>splitting sequence</u> of s we mean any such sequence $s_0,\ldots,s_p$ $p \geq 0$ of properly bracketed strings that $s_0 s_1 \ldots s_{p-1} s_p = s$. It can be shown that every properly bracketed string s has exactly one splitting sequence (called the <u>greatest splitting sequence</u> of s) $s_0, s_1,\ldots,s_p$, such that, for each $0 \leq i \leq p$, the only splitting sequence of s_i is s_i itself.

Let d be a bracketed common denominator for $\alpha_0,\ldots,\alpha_n$ and $\beta_0,\ldots,\beta_k$. Let $d_0,\ldots,d_p$, $p \geq 0$, be the greatest splitting sequence of d. Let $Z_1,\ldots Z_p$ be variable symbols that do not occur in the equation (e). Consider the string

$$d' = d_0 Z_1 d_1 \ldots d_{p-1} Z_p d_p$$

We denote by

$s_i(d')$ for $i = 1,\dots,n$, the substring of d' occurring between the i-th occurrence of (and the (i + 1)th occurrence of) in d' with all square brackets erased and by

$t_j(d')$ for $j = 1,\dots,k$, the substring of d' occurring between the j-th occurrence of [and the (j + 1)th occurrence of] in d' with all round brackets erased

Consider the following set of equations:

$$(e') \qquad X_i = s_i(d') \qquad i = 1,\dots,n$$
$$Y_j = t_j(d') \qquad j = 1,\dots,k$$

The only variables occurring in the rhs of the equations of (e') are Z_is.

Note, that for each bracketed common denominator d for the sequences $\alpha_0,\dots,\alpha_n$ and $\beta_0,\dots,\beta_k$ of the coefficients of the equation (e) the expressions $s_i(d')$, $i = 1,\dots,n$ and $t_j(d')$, $j = 1,\dots,k$, are unique up to the renaming of the variables Z_l, $l = 1,\dots,p$. It can be also shown that $0 \leqslant p \leqslant \max(n,k)$, where p is the number of "fresh variables" Z_l.

Using the above auxiliary notions one can prove the following theorems:

Theorem 1

For any valuation v of the variables Z_l, $l = 1,\dots,p$, in V^* the set of equations (e') determines a solution of the equation (e) i.e.

$$\alpha_0[s_1(d')]_v\alpha_1\dots\alpha_{n-1}[s_n(d')]_v\alpha_n = \beta_0[t_1(d')]_v\beta_1\dots\beta_{k-1}[t_k(d')]_v\beta_k$$

Theorem 2

If $x_i, y_j \in V^*$ $(i = 1,\dots,n,\ j = 1,\dots,k)$ is a solution of (e) then there exists a bracketed common denominator d for the sequences $\alpha_0,\dots,\alpha_n$ and $\beta_o,\dots,\beta_k$ and a valuation v of the variables $Z_1,\dots,Z_p$ such that

$$x_i = [s_i(d')]_v \quad \text{for } i = 1,\dots,n$$
$$y_j = [t_j(d')]_v \quad \text{for } j = 1,\dots,k$$

Corollary

The equation (e) has a solution iff there exists a common denominator for the sequences $\alpha_0, \ldots, \alpha_n$ and $\beta_0, \ldots, \beta_k$.

Example 2

We solve the equation

$$aefX_1efc = aY_1efY_2c$$

$\alpha_0 = aef$, $\alpha_1 = efc$, $\beta_0 = a$, $\beta_1 = ef$, $\beta_2 = c$

Common denominators for α_0, α_1 and $\beta_0, \beta_1, \beta_2$ are words aefxefc where $|x| \leqslant 2$. The bracketed common denominators are:

1.1 ([a][ef])↑(ef[c]) } $x = \varepsilon$
1.2 ([a]ef)↑([ef][c]) }
2.1 ([a]ef)↑[ef]↑(ef[c]) $x = ef$
2.2 ([a][ef])x(ef[c]) } $1 \leqslant |x| \leqslant 2$
2.3 ([a]ef)x([ef][c]) }

splitting "points" indicated by ↑

We introduce "fresh variables":

1.1 ([a][ef])Z_1(ef[c])
1.2 ([a]ef)Z_1([ef][c])
2.1 ([a]ef)Z_1([ef][c])
2.2 ([a][ef])x(ef[c])
2.3 ([a]ef)x([ef][c])

The solutions are:

1.1 $X_1 = s_1(d') = Z_1$
$Y_1 = t_1(d') = \varepsilon$
$Y_2 = t_2(d') = Z_1ef$

1.2 $X_1 = s_1(d') = Z_1$
$Y_1 = t_1(d') = efZ_1$
$Y_2 = t_2(d') = \varepsilon$

2.1 $X_1 = s_1(d') = Z_1efZ_2$
$Y_1 = t_1(d') = efZ_1$
$Y_2 = t_2(d') = Z_2ef$

2.2 $X_1 = s_1(d') = x$
$Y_1 = t_1(d') = \varepsilon$
$Y_2 = t_2(d') = xef$
(a particular case of 1.1)

2.3 $X_1 = s_1(d') = x$
$Y_1 = t_1(d') = efx$
$Y_2 = t_2(d') = \varepsilon$
(a particular case of 1.2)

One can notice that the bracketed common denominators 2.2 and 2.3 could have been omitted since they led to solutions being included in 1.1 and 1.2 respectively. A general rule can be formulated which decreases, in general case, the number of the bracketed common denominators to be considered.

The theorem 1 and 2 enable us to find the set of all solutions of the equation (e) also in the cases when the domains of the variables are proper regular subsets of V^*. In those cases it is necessary to find appropriate restrictions for the valuations of the variables Z_l, $l = 1,\ldots,p$, corresponding to each bracketed common denominator of the coefficients of (e). It can be shown, that in any such case the domain of each Z_l is a regular subset of V^*.

Solving sets of repetition-free string equations with regular domains

Let E be a proper set of $m > 1$ equations satisfying (r1) (r2) and (r3) defined above. Suppose we have found a set of solutions of the first equation in E (see the Theorem 1), i.e., the expressions

$$s_i^1(d'),\quad i = 1,\ldots,n,\qquad t_j^1(d'),\quad j = 1,\ldots,k$$

are defined for a chosen bracketed common denominator d of the sequences $\alpha_0^1,\ldots,\alpha_n^1$ and $\alpha_0^1,\ldots,\alpha_k^1$.

Denote by E' the set of remaining $m-1$ equations of E in which all occurrences of the variables X_i^1 and Y_j^1 are replaced by the expressions $s_i^1(d')$ and $t_j^1(d')$ respectively ($i = 1,\ldots,n$, $j = 1,\ldots,k$).

Theorem 3

If E is a proper set of $m > 1$ equations satisfying (r1), (r2) and (r3) then E' is also a proper set of $m-1$ equations satisfying (r1), (r2) and (r3).

Having the property stated in Theorem 3 one can define an effective procedure for solving an arbitrary proper set of equations satisfying (r1), (r2), and (r3). Roughly speaking we can solve equations one-by-one with respect to the subsequent choice of a bracketed common denominator, updating "fresh variables" which occur in each step (see the preceding section). Notice, that if one of the equations in the set E has no common denominator then there is no solution of the set E. Since our intention has been to show the effectiveness of the procedure and not the procedure itself, we do not present all details of the algorithm. Instead, we end this section with an example.

Example 3

Assume that the alphabet consist of the symbols {a, b, c, d, e, f} and consider the following set of equations:

$$\text{(E)}\quad \begin{aligned} aefX_1efc &= aY_1efY_2c \\ bY_1 &= W_1cd \\ afX_1c &= aW_2bc \end{aligned}$$

Having different solutions of the first equation (see Example 2) we obtain several possibilities (we omit solutions 2.2 and 2.3 being included in the other solutions):

1.1 $X_1 = Z_1$ (E.1.1) $b = W_1cd$

$Y_1 = \varepsilon$ $afZ_1efc = aW_2bc$

$Y_2 = Z_1ef$

1.2 $X_1 = Z_1$ (E.1.2) $befZ_1 = W_1cd$

$Y_1 = efZ_1$ $afZ_1c = aW_2bc$

$Y_2 = \varepsilon$

2.1 $X_1 = Z_1efZ_2$ (E.2.1) $befZ_1 = W_1cd$

$Y_1 = efZ_1$ $afZ_1efZ_2c = aW_2bc$

One can see that in the case 1.1 (E.1.1) has no solution. therefore we abandon this path.

Solving E.1.2 we solve the first equation with respect to Z_1 and W_1. We have only one bracketed common denominator

d = ([]bef)[cd()] hence d′ = ([]bef)V[cd()]

and we have a solution

$Z_1 = Vcd$ $W_1 = befV$

We follow this path updating Z_1. We obtain

$X_1 = Vcd$ $Y_1 = efVcd$ $Y_2 = \varepsilon$

and the last equation to be solved

$afVcdc = aWbc$

Again, the last equation has no solution (no common denominator) and we abandon this path.

We start with E.2.1. The solution of the first equation is the same as in the previous case. Hence, we have:

$X_1 = VcdefZ_2$ $\qquad$ $Z_1 = Vcd$

$Y_1 = efVcd$ $\qquad$ $W_1 = befV$

$Y_2 = Z_2ef$

and

$$afVcdefZ_2c = aW_2bc$$

Again we have only one bracketed common denominator:

$$d = ([a]f)(cdef)[b(c)] \qquad d' = ([a]f)V_1(cdef)V_2[b(c)]$$

The solution is:

$$V = V_1, \quad Z_2 = V_2b, \quad W_2 = fV_1cdefV_2$$

Updating again the previous results we have the set of all solutions of (E) expressed by means of the new variables V_1 and V_2 ranging over $\{a,b,c,d,e,f,\}^*$, namely

$X_1 = V_1cdefV_2b$

$Y_1 = efV_1cd$

$Y_2 = V_2bef$

$W_1 = befV_1$

$W_2 = fV_1cdefV_2$

Now suppose that each D_{X_1}, D_{Y_1}, etc. denote domains of the variables X_1, Y_1 etc. being languages over $\{a,b,c,d,e,f\}$. The problem consists in "extracting" from the general solutions of E those solutions the coordinates of which are in the prescribed domains. If the domains are regular the problem can be effectively solved since, roughly speaking, it reduces to the problem of finding the intersections of regular languages.

Conclusions

The paper gives another understanding of the two-level grammar formalism: any two-level grammar can be splitted into two parts - a context-free "syntax" and an equational "semantics". It has been shown that in the case of a repetition-free and regular based two-level grammar one can always solve the equations assigned to each derivation of the resulting CF grammar. This suggests an approach to the parsing problem of two-level grammars based on well known methods for CF grammars and the algorithm presented. The approach may occur efficient however, only if some restrictions are imposed on two-level grammars. One sort of restrictions we have discussed in the paper (repetition-free and regular based grammars). Others should result from the requirements of programming languages. For example, one obvious requirement is that two-level grammars should be (semanticaly) unambiguous, i.e., here - in terms of the corresponding CF grammars and equations - that each set of equations has at most one solution.

It could be promising to experiment with (fragments of) ALGOL 68 in order to better understand the described method, its complexity and feasibility with respect to the two-level programming language definitions.

References

[1] Cleaveland, J.C., Uzgalis, R.C.: Grammars for programming languages, Elsevier, New York 1977

[2] Dembiński, P., Małuszyński, J.: Attribute grammars and two-level grammars: a unifying approach, Proc. of the MFCS'78 Symposium, Lecture Notes in Computer Sc., 64 143-154, Springer-Verlag 1978

[3] Deussen, P.: A decidability criterion for Van Wijngaarden grammars, Acta Informatica 5(4), 353-375 , 1975

[4] Hesse, W.: Vollstaendige formale Beschreibung von Programmiersprachen mit zweischichtigen Grammetiken, Bericht 7623 TU Muenchen

[5] Knuth, D.E.: Semantics of context-free languages, Math. Systems Theory. 2(2), 127-145

[6] Koster, C.H.A.: Affix grammars, Proc. of the IFIP Working Conf. on ALGOL 68 Implementation, 95-103, North-Holland 1972

[7] Lewis, P.H.. Rosenkrantz, D.J., Stearns, R.E.: Attributed translations, JCSS 9, 279-307. 1974

[8] Wegner, L.: On parsing two-level grammars, Bericht 7/78, TU Graz Institut fuer Informationsverarbeitung

[9] Van Wijangaarden, A. et al.: Revised report on the algorithmic language ALGOL 68, Acta Informatica 5(1-3), 1-236, 1975

PROVING TERMINATION WITH MULTISET ORDERINGS

by

Nachum Dershowitz[1] and Zohar Manna[2]

Stanford University and Weizmann Institute

ABSTRACT

A common tool for proving the termination of programs is the *well-founded set*, a set ordered in such a way as to admit no infinite descending sequences. The basic approach is to find a *termination function* that maps the values of the program variables into some well-founded set, such that the value of the termination function is continually reduced throughout the computation. All too often, the termination functions required are difficult to find and are of a complexity out of proportion to the program under consideration. However, by providing more sophisticated well-founded sets, the corresponding termination functions can be simplified.

Given a well-founded set S, we consider *multisets* over S, "sets" that admit multiple occurrences of elements taken from S. We define an ordering on all finite multisets over S that is induced by the given ordering on S. This *multiset ordering* is shown to be well-founded. The value of the multiset ordering is that it permits the use of relatively simple and intuitive termination functions in otherwise difficult termination proofs. In particular, we apply the multiset ordering to prove the termination of *production systems*, programs defined in terms of sets of rewriting rules.

An extended version of this paper appeared as Memo AIM-310, Stanford Artificial Intelligence Laboratory, Stanford, California.

This research was supported in part by the United States Air Force Office of Scientific Research under Grant AFOSR-76-2909 (sponsored by the Rome Air Development Center, Griffiss AFB, NY), by the National Science Foundation under Grant MCS 76-83655, and by the Advanced Research Projects Agency of the Department of Defense under Contract MDA 903-76-C-0206.

[1]Current Address:
Department of Computer Science
University of Illinois
Urbana, Illinois 61801

[2]Current Address:
Department of Computer Science
Stanford University
Stanford, California 94305

I. INTRODUCTION

The use of well-founded sets for proving that programs terminate has been suggested by Floyd [1967]. A *well-founded set* consists of a set of elements S and a transitive and irreflexive ordering $\succ$ defined on the elements such that there can be no infinite descending sequences of elements. The idea is to find a well-founded set and a *termination function* that maps the values of the program variables into that set such that the value of the termination function is continually reduced throughout the computation. Since, by the nature of the set, the value cannot decrease indefinitely, the program must terminate.

The well-founded sets most frequently used for this purpose are the natural numbers under the "greater-than" ordering and n-tuples of natural numbers under the lexicographic ordering. In practice using these conventional orderings often leads to complex termination functions that are difficult to discover. For example, the termination proofs of programs involving stacks and production systems are often quite complicated and require much more subtle orderings and termination functions. Finding an appropriate ordering and termination function for such programs is a well-known challenge among researchers in the field of program verification. In this paper, we introduce a powerful ordering that can sometimes make the task of proving termination easier.

II. THE MULTISET ORDERING

For a given partially-ordered set $(S,\succ)$, we consider *multisets* (sometimes called "bags") over S, i.e. unordered collections of elements that may have multiple occurrences of identical elements. For example, {3,3,3,4,0,0} is a multiset of natural numbers; it is identical to the multiset {0,3,3,0,4,3}, but distinct from {3,4,0}. We denote by $\mathcal{M}(S)$ the set of all finite multisets with elements taken from the set S.

For a partially-ordered set $(S,\succ)$, the *multiset ordering* $\gg$ on $\mathcal{M}(S)$ is defined as follows:

$$M \gg M'$$

if for some multisets $X,Y \in \mathcal{M}(S)$, where $\{\} \neq X \subseteq M$,

$$M' = (M \setminus X) \cup Y$$

and

$$(\forall y \in Y)(\exists x \in X)\ x \succ y .$$

In words, a multiset is reduced by the removal of at least one element (those in X) and their replacement with any finite number - possibly zero - of elements (those in Y), each of which is smaller than one of the elements that have been removed. Thus, if S is the set N of natural numbers 0,1,2,... with the > ordering, then under the corresponding multiset ordering $\gg$ over N, the multiset {3,3,4,0} is greater than each of the three multisets {3,4}, {3,2,2,1,1,1,4,0}, and {3,3,3,3,2,2}. In the first case, two elements have been removed; in the second case, an occurrence of 3 has been replaced by two occurrences of 2 and three occurrences of 1; and in the third case, the element 4 has been replaced by two occurrences each of 3 and 2, and in addition the element 0 has been removed. The empty multiset {} is clearly smaller than any other multiset.

The multiset ordering is in fact a partial ordering, i.e. if $\succ$ is irreflexive and transitive, then $\gg$ also is. We have the

THEOREM: *The multiset ordering* $(\mathcal{M}(S),\gg)$ *over* $(S,\succ)$ *is well-founded, if and only if* $(S,\succ)$ *is.*

Proof: The "only if" part is trivial. For the "if" part, assume that $(S,\succ)$ is well-founded. Let $S' = S \cup \{\bot\}$ be S extended with a least element $\bot$, i.e. for every element $s \varepsilon S$, $s \succ \bot$ in the ordering on S'. Clearly S' is well-founded if S is. Now, suppose that $(\mathcal{M}(S),\gg)$ is not well-founded; therefore, there exists an infinite descending sequence $M_1 \gg M_2 \gg M_3 \gg \ldots$ of multisets of $\mathcal{M}(S)$. We derive a contradiction by constructing the following tree. Each node in the tree is labelled with some element of S'; at each stage of the construction, the set of all terminal nodes in the tree forms a multiset in $\mathcal{M}(S')$.

Begin with a root node with children corresponding to each element of M_1. Then since $M_1 \gg M_2$, there must exist multisets X and Y, such that $\{\} \neq X \subseteq M_1$, $M_2 = (M_1 - X) \cup Y$, and $(\forall y \varepsilon Y)(\exists x \varepsilon X) x \succ y$. Then for each $y \varepsilon Y$, add a child labelled y to the corresponding x. In addition, grow a child $\bot$ from each of the elements of X. (Since X is nonempty, growing $\bot$ ensures that even if Y is empty, at least one node is added to the tree. Since Y is finite, the nodes corresponding to X each have a finite number of children.) Repeat the process for $M_2 \gg M_3$, $M_3 \gg M_4$, and so on.

Since at least one node is added to the tree for each multiset M_i in the sequence, were the sequence infinite, the tree corresponding to the sequence would also be. But by Konig's Infinity Lemma, an infinite tree (with a finite number of children for each node) must have an infinite path. On the other hand, by our construction, all paths in the tree are descending in the well-founded ordering $\succ$ on S', and must be finite. Thus, we have derived a contradiction, implying that the sequence $M_1, M_2, M_3, \ldots$ cannot be infinite.

Remarks:

- If $(S,\succ)$ is totally ordered, then for any two multisets $M, M' \varepsilon \mathcal{M}(S)$, one may decide whether $M \gg M'$ by first sorting the elements of both M and M' in descending order (with respect to the relation $\succ$) and then comparing the two sorted sequences lexicographically.
- *If* $(S,\succ)$ *is of order type* α, *then the multiset ordering* $(\mathcal{M}(S),\gg)$ *over* $(S,\succ)$ *is of order type* ω^α.

• Consider the special case where there is a bound k on the number of replacement elements, i.e. take the (irreflexive) transitive closure of the relation $M \gg' M'$ which holds if $M'=(M \setminus X) \cup Y$ and $|Y| < k$. *Any termination proof using this bounded multiset ordering over* $\mathbb{N}$ *may be translated into a proof using* $(\mathbb{N},>)$. This may be done using, for example, the order-preserving function

$$\psi(M) = \sum_{n \in M} k^n$$

which maps multisets over the natural numbers into the natural numbers by summing the number k^n for every number n in a multiset M. □

We turn now to consider *nested multisets,* by which we mean that the elements of the multisets may belong to some base set S, or may be multisets containing both elements of S and multisets of elements of S, and so on. For example, $\{\{1,1\}, \{\{0\},1,2\},0\}$ is a nested multiset. More formally, given a partially-ordered set $(S,\succ)$, a *nested multiset over* S is either an element of S, or else it is a finite multiset of nested multisets over S. We denote by $\mathcal{M}^*(S)$ the set of nested multisets over S.

We define now a *nested multiset ordering* $\gg^*$ on $\mathcal{M}^*(S)$; it is a recursive version of the standard multiset ordering. For two elements $M,M' \in \mathcal{M}^*(S)$, we say that

$$M \gg^* M'$$

if

• $M,M' \in S$ and $M \succ M'$

(two elements of the base set are compared using $\succ$), or else

• $M \notin S$ and $M' \in S$

(any multiset is greater than any element of the base set), or else

• $M,M' \notin S$, and for some $X,Y \in \mathcal{M}^*(S)$, where $\{\} \neq X \subseteq M$,

$$M' = (M \setminus X) \cup Y$$

and

$$(\forall y \in Y)(\exists x \in X)\ x \gg^* y.$$

For example, the nested multiset $\{\{1,1\},\{\{0\},1,2\},0\}$ is greater than $\{\{1,0,0\},5, \{\{0\},1,2\},0\}$, since $\{1,1\}$ is greater than both $\{1,0,0\}$ and 5. The same nested multiset $\{\{1,1\}, \{\{0\},1,2\},0\}$ is also greater than $\{\{\{\},1,2\},\{5,5,2\},5\}$, since $\{\{0\},1,2\}$ is greater than each of the three elements $\{\{\},1,2\}$, $\{5,5,2\}$, and 5.

Let $\mathcal{M}^i(S)$ denote the set of all nested multisets of *depth* i. In other words $\mathcal{M}^0(S)=S$, and $\mathcal{M}^{i+1}(S)$ contains the multisets whose elements are taken from $\mathcal{M}^0(S)$, $\mathcal{M}^1(S),\ldots,\mathcal{M}^i(S)$, with at least one element taken from $\mathcal{M}^i(S)$. Thus, the set $\mathcal{M}^*(S)$ is the infinite union of the disjoint sets $\mathcal{M}^0(S)$, $\mathcal{M}^1(S)$, $\mathcal{M}^2(S),\ldots$. The following property holds:

For two nested multisets, M *and* M', *if the depth of* M *is greater than the depth of* M', *then* $M \gg^* M'$.

In other words, the multisets of $\mathcal{M}^i(S)$ are all greater than the multisets of $\mathcal{M}^j(S)$, under the ordering $\gg^*$, for any $j<i$.

The relation $\gg^*$ is a partial ordering; it can be shown to be both irreflexive and transitive. The following theorem gives the condition under which it is well-founded:

THEOREM: *The nested multiset ordering* $(\mathcal{M}^*(S), \gg^*)$ *over* $(S,\succ)$ *is well-founded, if and only if* $(S,\succ)$ *is well-founded.*

In order to show that $(\mathcal{M}^*(S), \gg^*)$ is well-founded, it suffices to show that each $\mathcal{M}^i(S)$ is itself well-founded under $\gg^*$. This may be proved by induction on i.

Remark: It can be shown that *if* $(S,\succ)$ *is of order type less than* ε_0, *then* $(\mathcal{M}^*(S), \gg^*)$ *is of order type* ε_0. (Gentzen [1938] used in ε_0 ordering to prove the termination of his normalization procedure for proofs in arithmetic.) □

In the following two sections, we shall apply the multiset ordering to problems of termination, first proving the termination of conventional programs, and then proving the termination of production systems.

III. TERMINATION OF PROGRAMS

In the following examples, we shall prove the termination of programs using multiset orderings as the well-founded set.

EXAMPLE 1: *Counting tips of binary trees.*

Consider a simple program to count the number of tips - terminal nodes (without descendents) - in a full binary tree. Each tree y that is not a tip has two subtrees, *left*(y) and *right*(y). The program is

```
S := (t)
c := 0
loop until S=()
     y := head(S)
     if tip(y) then S := tail(S)
                    c := c+1
               else S := left(y)·right(y)·tail(S)
               fi
     repeat.
```

It employes a stack S and terminates when S is empty. At that point, the variable c is to contain the total number of tip nodes in the given tree t. The termination of this program may be proved using the well-founded set (N,>). The appropriate termination function is

$$\tau(S) = \sum_{s \in S} nodes(s),$$

where *nodes*(s) is the total number of nodes in the subtree s - not just the tip nodes.

Using the multiset ordering over trees, we can prove termination with the simple termination function

$$\tau(S) = \{s : s \in S\},$$

giving the multiset of trees appearing in the stack. The trees themselves are ordered by the natural well-founded subtree ordering, i.e. any tree is greater than its subtrees. Thus, removal of a tree from the stack decreases τ in the multiset ordering by removing an element, and the replacement of a tree with two smaller subtrees decreases τ.

In general, any program in which elements are repeatedly removed from a stack, queue, bag, etc. and replaced with any number of smaller elements (in some well-founded ordering) can be shown to terminate with the corresponding multiset ordering. □

EXAMPLE 2: *McCarthy's 91-function*

The following is a contrived program to compute the simple function

$$f(x) = \textit{if } x>100 \textit{ then } x-10 \textit{ else } 91$$

over the set of integers Z, in a round-about manner. Though this program is short, the proof of its correctness and termination are nontrivial, and for this reason it is often used to illustrate proof methods.

The program is:

```
n := 1
z := x
loop L: assert f(x)=f^n(z), n≥1
     if z>100 then n := n-1
                   z := z-10
              else n := n+1
                   z := z+11
              fi
     until n=0
     repeat
assert z=f(x).
```

The predicates $f(x)=f^n(z)$ and $n \geq 1$ are loop invariants. The loop is exited if control reaches the until clause with $n=0$; at that point $f(x)=f^0(z)=z$.

Consider the following well-founded partial-ordering $\succ$ on the integers:

$$a \succ b \text{ if and only if } a<b<111.$$

(This is the same ordering on integers as in the familiar structural-induction proof, due to Rod Burstall, of the recursive version of this program.) As the well-founded set, we use the set $(\mathcal{M}(Z), \ggcurly)$ of all multisets of integers, under the corresponding multiset ordering. The appropriate termination function τ at L yields a multiset in $\mathcal{M}(Z)$, and is defined as

$$\tau(n,z) = \{z, f(z), \ldots, f^{n-1}(z)\}.$$

We must show that for each loop iteration this function decreases. There are three cases to consider:

1. $z>100$ at L: In this case, the then branch of the conditional is executed and both n and z are decremented. When control returns to L (assuming that the loop has not been exited), we have, in terms of the old values of n and z,

$$\begin{aligned}\tau(n-1, z-10) &= \{z-10, f(z-10), \ldots, f^{n-2}(z-10)\}\\ &= \{f(z), f^2(z), \ldots, f^{n-1}(z)\}.\end{aligned}$$

Thus, the value of the termination function τ has been decreased by removing the element z from the original multiset $\{z, f(z), \ldots, f^{n-1}(z)\}$.

2. $90 \le z \le 100$ at L: In this case, the else branch is taken and both n and z are incremented, yielding

$$\tau(n+1, z+11) = \{z+11, f(z+11), f^2(z+11), \ldots, f^n(z+11)\}.$$

Either $z+1=101$ or else $z+1 \le 100$; in both cases $f^2(z+11)=f(z+1)=91=f(z)$.
Thus, we get

$$\tau(n+1, z+11) = \{z+11, z+1, f(z), \ldots, f^{n-1}(z)\}$$

Since $z<z+1<z+11 \le 111$, we have $z \succ z+11$ and $z \succ z+1$. Accordingly, the multiset has been reduced by replacing the element z with the two smaller elements, $z+11$ and $z+1$.

3. $z<90$ at L: The else branch is taken and we have

$$\begin{aligned}\tau(n+1, z+11) &= \{z+11, f(z+11), f^2(z+11), \ldots, f^n(z+11)\}.\\ &= \{z+11, 91, f(z), \ldots, f^{n-1}(z)\}.\end{aligned}$$

Again z has been replaced by two smaller elements (under the $\succ$ relation), $z+11$ and 91. □

EXAMPLE 3: *Ackermann's function.*

The following iterative program computes Ackermann's function $a(m,n)$ over pairs of natural numbers:

```
S := (m)
z := n
loop L: assert a(m,n) = a(s_k,a(s_{k-1},...,a(s_2,a(s_1,z))...))
     y := head(S)
     S := tail(S)
     if y=0 then z := z+1
     else
     if z=0 then S := (y-1)·S
                 z := 1
            else S := y·(y-1)·S
                 z := z-1
            fi fi
     until  S=()
     repeat
assert z = a(m,n),
```

where the stack S has k elements $s_1,s_2,\ldots,s_k$.

To prove termination, consider the set $N \times N$ of lexicographically-ordered pairs of natural numbers and use the corresponding multiset ordering over $N \times N$. Let $y=head(S)=s_1$. The termination function at L is

$$\tau(S,z) = \{(s_k+1,0),(s_{k-1}+1,0),\ldots,(s_2+1,0),(y,z)\}.$$

Thus, $\tau(S,z)$ yields a multiset containing one pair per element in the stack S. Note that at L, the stack S is nonempty, and all the elements of S as well as z are nonnegative.

The proof considers three cases, corresponding to the three branches of the conditional in the loop:

1. $y=0$: If the loop is not exited, then the new value of τ at L is

$$\tau((s_2,\ldots,s_k),z+1) = \{(s_k+1,0),\ldots,(s_2+1,0),(s_2,z+1)\}.$$

This represents a decrease in τ under the multiset ordering, since the element (y,z) has been removed and the element $(s_2+1,0)$ has been replaced by the smaller $(s_2,z+1)$.

2. $y\neq 0$ and $z=0$: In this case we obtain

$$\tau((y-1,s_2,\ldots,s_k),1) = \{(s_k+1,0),\ldots,(s_2+1,0),(y-1,1)\}.$$

Thus, the element (y,z) has been replaced by the smaller element $(y-1,1)$.

3. $y\neq 0$ and $z\neq 0$: Here we have

$$\tau((y,y-1,s_2,\ldots,s_k),z-1) = \{(s_k+1,0),\ldots,(s_2+1,0),(y,0),(y,z-1)\}.$$

The element (y,z) has been replaced by the two smaller elements $(y,0)$ and $(y,z-1)$.

Remark: The previous examples suggest the following heuristic for proving termination: given a program over a domain $(D,\succ)$ that computes some function $f(x)$, if the program has a loop invariant of the form

$$f(x) = h(f(g_1(y)), f(g_2(y)), \ldots, f(g_n(y))),$$

where the g_i are the arguments of occurrences of f in the right-hand side, then try the multiset ordering $(\mathcal{M}(D), \gg)$ and use the termination function

$$\tau(y) = \{g_1(y), g_2(y), \ldots, g_n(y)\}.$$

The idea underlying this heuristic is that τ represents the set of unevaluated arguments of some recursive expansion of the function f.

IV. TERMINATION OF PRODUCTION SYSTEMS

A production system Π (also called a *term-writing system*) over a set of expressions E is a (finite or infinite) set of rewriting rules, called *productions*, each of the form

$$\pi(\alpha, \beta, \ldots) \rightarrow \pi'(\alpha, \beta, \ldots),$$

where π and π' are expressions containing variables $\alpha, \beta, \ldots$ ranging over E. (The variables appearing in π' must be a subset of those in π.) Such a rule is applied in the following manner: given an expression $e \varepsilon E$ that contains a subexpression

$$\pi(a, b, \ldots),$$

(i.e. the variables $\alpha, \beta, \ldots$ are instantiated with the expressions $a, b, \ldots$, respectively), replace that subexpression with the corresponding expression

$$\pi'(a, b, \ldots).$$

We write $e \Rightarrow e'$, if the expression e' can be derived from e by a single application of some rule in Π to one of the subexpressions of e.

For example, the following is a production system that differentiates an expression, containing + and $\cdot$, with respect to x:

Dx	$\rightarrow$	1
Dy	$\rightarrow$	0
$D(\alpha+\beta)$	$\rightarrow$	$(D\alpha + D\beta)$
$D(\alpha\cdot\beta)$	$\rightarrow$	$((\beta\cdot D\alpha) + (\alpha\cdot D\beta))$,

where y can be any constant or any variable other than x. Consider the expression

$$D(D(x\cdot x)+y).$$

We could either apply the third production to the outer D, or else we could apply the fourth production in the inner D. In the latter case, we obtain

$$D(((x\cdot Dx)+(x\cdot Dx))+y)$$

which now contains three occurrences of D. At this point, we can still apply the third production to the outer D, or we could apply the first production to either one of the inner D's. Applying the third production yields

$(D((x\cdot Dx)+(x\cdot Dx)+Dy)$.

Thus,

$$D(D(x\cdot x)+y) \Rightarrow D(((x\cdot Dx)+(x\cdot Dx))+y) \Rightarrow (D((x\cdot Dx)+(x\cdot Dx))+Dy).$$

In general, at each stage in the computation there are many ways to proceed, and the choice is made nondeterministically. In our case, all choices eventually lead to the expression

$$((((1\cdot 1)+(x\cdot 0))+((1\cdot 1)+(x\cdot 0)))+0),$$

for which no further application of a production is possible.

A production system Π *terminates* over E, if there exist no infinite sequences of expressions $e_1,e_2,e_3,\ldots$ such that $e_1 \Rightarrow e_2 \Rightarrow e_3 \Rightarrow \ldots$ and $e_1 \varepsilon E$. In other words, given any initial expression, execution always reaches a state for which there is no way to continue applying productions. The difficulty in proving the termination of a production system, such as the one for differentiation above, stems from the fact that while some productions (the first two) may decrease the size of an expression, other productions (the last two) may increase its size. Also, a production (the fourth) may actually duplicate occurrences of subexpressions. Furthermore, applying a production to a subexpression, not only affects the structure of that subexpression, but also changes the corresponding superexpressions, including the top-level expression. And a proof of termination must hold for the many different possible sequences generated by the nondeterministic choice of productions and subexpressions.

The following theorem has provided the basis for most of the techniques used for proving the termination of production systems:

THEOREM: *A production system over E terminates, if and only if there exists a well-founded set* $(W,\succ)$ *and a termination function* $\tau: E \to W$, *such that for any* $e,e' \varepsilon E$

$$e \Rightarrow e' \text{ implies } \tau(e) \succ \tau(e').$$

Several researchers have considered the problem of proving the termination of production systems. Among them: Gorn [1965] in an early work addresses this issue; Iturriaga [1967] gives sufficient conditions under which a class of production systems terminates; Knuth and Bendix [1969] define a well-founded ordering based on a weighted size for expressions; Manna and Ness [1970] and Lankford [1975] use a "monotonic interpretation" that decreases with each application of a production; Lipton and Snyder [1977] make use of a "value-preserving" property as the basis for a method of proving termination. Recently, Plaisted [July 1978, Oct. 1978] has applied two classes of well-founded orderings on terms to the termination of production systems.

In the following examples, we illustrate the use of multisets in proving termination. We begin with a very simple example.

EXAMPLE 1: *Associativity.*

Consider the set of arithmetic expressions E constructed from some set of atoms (symbols) and the single operator +. The production system

$$\boxed{(\alpha+\beta)+\gamma \rightarrow \alpha+(\beta+\gamma)}$$

over E contains just one production which reparenthesizes a sum by associating to the right. For example, the expression $(a+b)+((c+d)+g)$ becomes either $a+(b+((c+d)+g))$ or $(a+b)+(c+(d+g))$, both of which become $a+(b+(c+(d+g)))$. Since the length of the expression remains constant when the production is applied, some other measure is needed to prove termination.

To prove termination, we use the multiset ordering over the natural numbers, $(\mathcal{M}(N),\gg)$, and let $\tau:E\rightarrow\mathcal{M}(N)$ return the multiset of the lengths of all the subexpressions in e to which the production is applicable, i.e.

$$\tau(e) = \{|(\alpha+\beta)+\gamma|:(\alpha+\beta)+\gamma \text{ in } e\}.$$

For example,

$$\tau((a+b)+((c+d)+g)) = \{|(a+b)+((c+d)+g)|,|(c+d)+g|\} = \{9,5\}.$$

1. The value of the termination function τ *decreases* with each application of a production, i.e. for any possible values of α, β, and γ,

$$\tau((\alpha+\beta) \gg \tau(\alpha+(\beta+\gamma)).$$

Before an application of the production, the multiset $\tau((\alpha+\beta)+\gamma)$ includes an occurrence of $|(\alpha+\beta)+\gamma|$, along with elements corresponding to the subexpressions of α, β, and γ. With application of the production, that element is removed; the only element that may be added is $|\beta+\gamma|$ (if β is of the form $(\beta_1+\beta_2)$), which is smaller. The multiset has accordingly been decreased.

2. Since the production does not change the length of the expression it is applied to, i.e.

$$|\pi| = |\pi'|,$$

the length of superexpressions containing $(\alpha+\beta)+\gamma$ is also unchanged.

The multiset $\tau(e)$ consists of all the elements in $\tau((\alpha+\beta)+\gamma)$ plus the lengths of some of their superexpressions and other subexpressions. The only elements in $\tau(e)$ that are changed by the production are those in $\tau((\alpha+\beta)+\gamma)$ and they have been decreased by the production. Thus, $e\Rightarrow e'$ implies that $\tau(e)\gg\tau(e')$. □

EXAMPLE 2: *Differentiation.*

The following system symbolically differentiates an expression with respect to x:

$$
\begin{array}{|l|}
\hline
Dx \rightarrow 1 \\
Dy \rightarrow 0 \\
D(\alpha+\beta) \rightarrow (D\alpha+D\beta) \\
D(\alpha\cdot\beta) \rightarrow ((\beta\cdot D\alpha) + (\alpha\cdot D\beta)) \\
D(-\alpha) \rightarrow (-D\alpha) \\
D(\alpha-\beta) \rightarrow (D\alpha-D\beta) \\
D(\alpha/\beta) \rightarrow ((D\alpha/\beta) - ((\alpha\cdot D\beta)/(\beta\uparrow 2))) \\
D(\ln\alpha) \rightarrow (D\alpha/\alpha) \\
D(\alpha\uparrow\beta) \rightarrow ((D\alpha\cdot(\beta\cdot(\alpha\uparrow(\beta-1)))) + (((\ln\alpha)\cdot D\beta)\cdot(\alpha\uparrow\beta))) . \\
\hline
\end{array}
$$

We present two solutions. The first uses a multiset ordering; the second uses nested multisets.

•Solution 1.

We use the multiset ordering over sequences of natural numbers. The sequences are compared under the well-founded *stepped lexicographic* ordering $\succ$, i.e. longer sequences are greater than shorter ones (regardless of the values of the individual elements), and equal length sequences are compared lexicographically. The termination function is

$$\tau(e) = \{(d_1(x), d_2(x), \ldots): \ x \text{ is an occurrence of an atom in } e\},$$

where $d_i(x)$ is the distance (number of operators) between x and the ith enclosing D.

For example, consider the expression

$$e = DD(Dy\cdot(y+DDx)),$$

or in the tree form (with the D's enumerated for expository purposes),

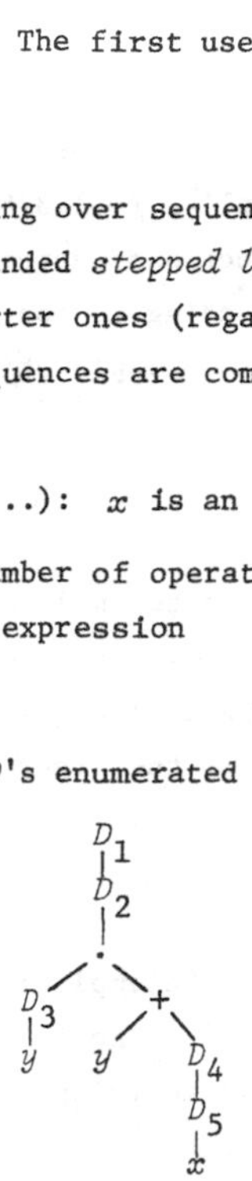

There are three atoms: y, y, and x. The left atom y contributes the element (0,2,3) to the multiset, since there are no operators between D_3 and y, there are two operators (· and D_3) between D_2 and y, and there are three operators (D_2, ·, and D_3) between D_1 and y. Similarly the other two atoms contribute (2,3) and (0,1,4,5). Thus,

$$\tau(e) = \{(0,2,3),\ (2,3),\ (0,1,4,5)\}.$$

Applying the production

$$D(\alpha\cdot\beta) \rightarrow ((\beta\cdot D\alpha) + (\alpha\cdot D\beta)),$$

to e, yields $e' = D(((y+DDx)\cdot DDy) + (Dy\cdot D(y+DDx)))$. In the tree form (with the labelling of the D's retained), we have

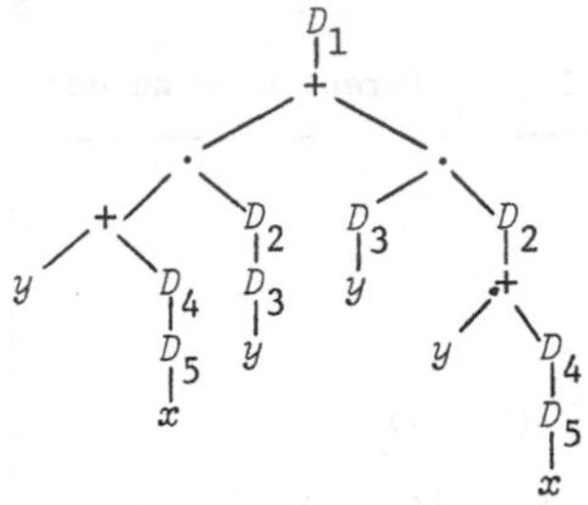

and accordingly

$$\tau(e') = \{(3),(0,1,5),(0,1,4),(0,3),(1,4),(0,1,3,6)\},$$

Thus, $\tau(e) \gg \tau(e')$, since the element (0,1,4,5) has been replaced by five shorter sequences and by the lexicographically smaller (0,1,3,6).

In general, applying any of the productions decreases τ, and the productions only affect the sequences in $\tau(e)$ corresponding to the atoms of the subexpression that they are applied to. Therefore, for any application of a production, $e \Rightarrow e'$ implies $\tau(e) \gg \tau(e')$.

• Solution 2.

For the alternative solution, we use nested multisets. Note that the arguments to D are reduced in length by each production. One would therefore like to prove termination using the well-founded set $(\mathcal{M}(N), \gg)$ and a termination function that yields the multiset containing the length of the arguments to each occurrence of D, i.e.

$$\tau(e) = \{|\alpha|: \ D\alpha \text{ in } e\}.$$

The value of this function is decreased by the application of a production, i.e. $\tau(\pi) \gg \tau(\pi')$ for each of the productions $\pi \to \pi'$. The problem is that the size of superexpressions increases, since $|\pi'| > |\pi|$; applying a production to a subexpression of e will therefore increase $\tau(e)$.

To overcome this problem, we need a termination function that takes the nested structure of the expression into consideration and gives more significance to more deeply nested subexpressions. Fortunately, this is exactly what nested multisets can do for us.

Let the well-founded set be the nested multisets over the natural numbers, $(\mathcal{M}^*(N), \gg^*)$, and let the termination function $\tau: E \to \mathcal{M}^*(N)$ yield $|\alpha|$ for each occurrence of $D\alpha$, while preserving the nested structure of the expression. For example, the arguments of the six occurrences of D in the expression $D(D(Dx \cdot Dy)+Dy)/Dx$ are $D(Dx \cdot Dy)+Dy$, $Dx \cdot Dy$, x, y, y, and x. They are of lengths 9, 5, 1, 1, 1, and 1, respectively. Considering the nested depths of the D's, the structure of the expression is

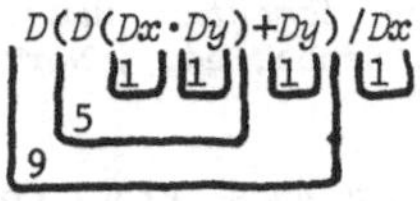

Thus, for

$$e = D\,(D\,(Dx \cdot Dy) + Dy)\,/\,Dx$$

we have

$$\tau(e) = \{\{9,\{5,\{1\},\{1\}\},\{1\}\},\{1\}\}.$$

For each production $\pi \to \pi'$, we have $\tau(\pi) \gg^* \tau(\pi')$ under the nested multiset ordering. It remains to ascertain what happens to the value of τ for superexpressions. The crucial point here is that the termination function gives greater weight to the more deeply nested D's by placing their length at a greater depth in the nested multiset. The effect of the productions on lower-level expressions is therefore more significant than their effect on higher-level expressions, and the decrease in τ for the subexpression to which the production is applied overshadows any increase in the length of a superexpression.

Consider, for example,

$$D(D(x \cdot x)+y) \Rightarrow D(((x \cdot Dx)+(x \cdot Dx))+y).$$

The value of τ for the expression on the left is $\{\{6,\{3\}\}\}$, while for the right-hand side expression it is $\{\{11,\{1\},\{1\}\}\}$. Note that this represents a decrease in the nested multiset ordering over N, despite the fact that the element 6, corresponding to the length of the top-level argument, has been increased to 11. This is the case since the production has replaced the element $\{3\}$ in the multiset $\{6,\{3\}\}$ by two occurrences of the smaller $\{1\}$, and $\{3\}$ is also greater than 11 - or any number for that matter - on account of its greater depth.

Thus, $e \Rightarrow e'$ implies $\tau(e) \gg^* \tau(e')$. □

In this section, we have illustrated the use of multiset and nested multiset ordering in proofs of termination of production systems, by means of examples. Along similar lines, using these orderings, one can give general theorems which express sufficient conditions for the termination of broad classes of production systems.

ACKNOWLEDGMENT

We thank Bob Boyer, John Doner, Chris Goad, John McCarthy, Steve Ness, Amir Pnueli, Adir Pridor, and Richard Weyhrauch for stimulating discussions.

REFERENCES

Floyd, R. W. [1967], *Assigning meanings to programs*, Proc. Symp. in Applied Mathematics, vol. 19 (J. T. Schwartz, ed.), American Mathematical Society, Providence, RI, pp. 19-32.

Gentzen, G. [1938], *New version of the consistency proof for elementary number theory*, The collected papers of Gerhart Gentzen (M. E. Szabo, ed.), North Holland, Amsterdam (1969), pp. 252-286.

Gorn, S. [Sept. 1965], *Explicit definitions and linguistic dominoes*, Proc. Conf. on Systems and Computer Science, London, Ontario, pp. 77-115.

Iturriaga, R. [May 1967], *Contributions to mechanical mathematics*, Ph.D. thesis, Carnegie-Mellon Univ., Pittsburgh, PA.

Knuth, D. E. and P. B. Bendix [1969], *Simple word problems in universal algebras*, Computational Problems in Universal Algebras (J. Leech, ed.), Pergamon Press, Oxford, pp. 263-297.

Lankford, D. S. [May 1975], *Canonical algebraic simplification in computational logic*, Memo ATP-25, Automatic Theorem Proving Project, Univ. of Texas, Austin, TX.

Lipton, R. J. and L. Snyder [Aug 1977], *On the halting of tree replacement systems*, Proc. Conf. on Theoretical Computer Science, Waterloo, Ontario, pp. 43-46.

Manna, Z. and S. Ness [Jan 1970], *On the termination of Markov algorithms*, Proc. Third Hawaii Intl. Conf. on Systems Sciences, Honolulu, HI, pp. 789-792.

Plaisted, D. [July 1978], *Well-founded orderings for proving the termination of rewrite rules*, Memo R-78-932, Dept. of Computer Science, Univ. of Illinois, Urbana, IL.

Plaisted, D. [Oct. 1978], *A recursively defined ordering for proving termination of term rewriting systems*, Memo R-78-943, Dept. of Computer Science, Univ. of Illinois, Urbana, IL.

One Abstract Accepting Algorithm for all Kinds of Parsers

P. Deussen
Fakultät für Informatik
Universität Karlsruhe

Introduction.

The techniques of syntactical analysis fill a vast amount of literature, their commonalities however are darkened by details (e.g. items, local look-ahead etc.) which are important for ultimate refinements of parsing algorithms but which should be hidden as long as possible if one is concerned with the principles of syntax analysis. Syntax analysis has three main aspects:

Semi-Thue aspect. Formal languages are generated by Semi-Thue systems (e.g. contextfree grammars) and they are accepted by Semi-Thue systems (e.g. push-down acceptors). To each generating Semi-Thue system there is at least one accepting Semi-Thue system whose accepting sequences are in one-to-one correspondence with left- (or right-)most derivations of the generating system: the accepting system yields a parse of the accepted word.

Algorithmic aspect. Special accepting Semi-Thue systems directly give rise to an abstract accepting algorithm $\mathfrak{A}$. This algorithm when started from an initial situation selects productions from the Semi-Thue system according to a predicate $\mathfrak{P}$, applies one of them and then continues. Depending on properties of $\mathfrak{P}$, $\mathfrak{A}$ turns out to be partially correct or deterministic, respectively. A recursive formulation of $\mathfrak{A}$ after one small change directly yields the off-spring of all backtracking algorithms used in syntax analysis including those of recursive descent.

Finite automata aspect. Efficiency of $\mathfrak{A}$ solely depends on that of the predicate $\mathfrak{P}$. In practically important cases, e.g. contextfree languages, $\mathfrak{P}$ is decidable by means of a finite state acceptor (which is again a special accepting Semi-Thue system). Subset construction and state reduction are consequently the main tools for improving efficiency.

This paper is mainly concerned with the algorithmic and the finite automata aspect whereas the first one is only sketched. It points out that on this level of abstraction the proof of partial correctness of $\mathfrak{A}$ is almost trivial; furthermore, that almost all parsable language classes - e.g. LL(k), SLL(k), LR(k), SLR(k), LALR(k), LC(k), SLC(k) grammars - are characterized by requiring α to be deterministic.

1. Semi-Thue system aspect.

For any contextfree production system Π with typical productions A::=r one obtains two different types of push-down acceptors which expressed in terms of accepting Semi-Thue systems are obtained according to the table:

Π	Π_{LR}	Π_{LL}	
A::=r	rq::=Aq	Aq::=r^cq	
	qt::=tq	tqt::=q	for all $t \in T$
$Z \Longrightarrow z$ $(z \in T^*)$ $\Leftrightarrow$	$qz \Longrightarrow Zq$ $\Leftrightarrow$	$Zqz \Longrightarrow q$	

Π_{LR} essentially applies A::=r in reverse direction but only if r is to the left of the marker (state) q; the second production type of Π_{LR} serves for shifting terminals from the right side of q to its left (into the stack). Π_{LR} accepts z from *L*eft to right and the sequence of reduce steps rq::=Aq in reverse order yields a *R*ightmost derivation $Z \underset{\Pi}{\Longrightarrow} z$; Π_{LR} is a bottom-up acceptor.

Π_{LL}, as opposed to the previous case, is a top-down acceptor. To the left of the marker (state) q (in the stack) a word is derived via Aq::=r^cq (r^c denotes the converse of r) which is compared via tqt::=q with the yet uninspected terminal word to the right of q. Π_{LL} accepts z from *L*eft to right and the sequence of steps Aq::=r^cq directly yields a *L*eftmost derivation $Z \underset{\Pi}{\Longrightarrow} z$.

Both types of Semi-Thue systems with set of states $Q = \{q\}$ are special cases of the general type

Π_Q with productions of type $\kappa qx::=\lambda q'y$

where V and Q are finite sets of symbols and states, respectively, $V \cap Q = \emptyset$ and $\kappa, x, \lambda, y \in V^*$, $q, q' \in Q$. For such Π_Q, the accepted language L is defined by

$$L = \{z \in T^* : aq_0 z \underset{\Pi_Q}{\Longrightarrow} f\}$$

for some $a \in V^*$, $q_0 \in Q$ and final situation $f \in V^*QV^*$. (see [4,13,15,16])

2. Algorithmic aspect.

2.1 The repetitive accepting algorithm for L.

All following considerations hold for general production systems Π_Q,

the most important cases, however, are Π_{LR} and Π_{LL}.
In the algorithm (see also [2])

$\mathfrak{A}$: <u>uqw</u> := aq_oz;
<u>while</u> uqw ≠ f <u>do</u>
  P := $\{\pi \in \Pi_Q : \mathfrak{P}(\pi, uqw)\}$;
  <u>if</u> P ≠ ∅ <u>then</u> <u>for</u> <u>some</u> $\pi \in P$ <u>do</u> uqw := π(uqw) <u>od</u>
    <u>else</u> print(z ∉ L); stop <u>fi</u>
    <u>od</u>;
print(z ∈ L)

productions $\pi \in \Pi_Q$ are collected in P according to the predicate $\mathfrak{P}$; the choice operator "<u>for</u> <u>some</u>" nondeterministically selects one π from P which then is applied to the current situation uqw yielding π(uqw).

If we assume that $\mathfrak{A}$ works well, we may regard $\mathfrak{A}$ as the core of each parsing algorithm: set e.g. Π_{LL} for Π_Q, then a simple book-keeping of the applied productions supplies us with the necessary information to obtain a parse for z; furthermore, instead of printing "z ∉ L" we may call for some error handling routine.

In order that $\mathfrak{A}$ works well, we must impose a series of conditions on the predicate $\mathfrak{P}$ which are to be discussed now.
Each $\pi \in P$ necessarily must be applicable to uqw, whence we generally require

$$\mathfrak{P}(\pi, uqw) \succ \pi | uqw \qquad \text{(i.e. } \pi \text{ is } \textit{applicable} \text{ to uqw)} \qquad (1)$$

When the algorithm $\mathfrak{A}$ is elaborated the sequence of intermediate situations uqw represents a derivation $aq_oz \Longrightarrow uqw$, but conversely, not every such derivation will be produced by $\mathfrak{A}$.

Definition. A derivation

$$aq_oz = u_1q_1w_1 \xrightarrow[\pi_1]{} u_2q_2w_2 \xrightarrow[\pi_2]{} \cdots \xrightarrow[\pi_{n-1}]{} u_nq_nw_n = uqw$$

is called a $\mathfrak{P}$-*derivation* ($aq_oz \overset{\mathfrak{P}}{\Longrightarrow} uqw$ for short), iff $n \geq 1$ and

$$\forall i \in \{1,2,..,n-1\} : u_iq_iw_i \neq f \wedge \mathfrak{P}(\pi_i, u_iq_iw_i) \quad .$$

In the sense of HOARE the following assertion holds:

$$z \in T^* \; \{\mathfrak{A}\} \; aq_oz \overset{\mathfrak{P}}{\Longrightarrow} uqw \wedge (uqw = f \vee \forall \pi \in \Pi_Q : \neg \mathfrak{P}(\pi, uqw) \quad .$$

Hence, the discussion of the algorithm $\mathfrak{A}$ essentially consists in discussing $\mathfrak{P}$-derivations.

Partial correctness of $\mathfrak{A}$.

Since each $\mathfrak{P}$-derivation is simply a derivation, $\mathfrak{A}$ prints "$z \in L$" correctly; but depending on $\mathfrak{P}$, "$z \notin L$" might be an incorrect reaction e.g. if no π exists with $\mathfrak{P}(\pi, uqw)$ although still $uqw \Longrightarrow f$ holds. Thus we require

$$uqw \Longrightarrow f \wedge uqw \neq f \quad > \quad \exists \pi \in \Pi_Q: \; \mathfrak{P}(\pi, uqw) \wedge \pi(uqw) \Longrightarrow f \qquad (2)$$

Still there might be productions π satisfying $\mathfrak{P}$ but leading $\mathfrak{A}$ into a blind alley. Therefore, we require

$\mathfrak{P}$ is *free of blind alleys:*

$$uqw \Longrightarrow f \wedge uqw \neq f \quad > \quad \forall \pi \in \Pi_Q: \; \mathfrak{P}(\pi, uqw) > \pi(uqw) \Longrightarrow f \qquad (3)$$

Both conditions, (2) and (3), now guarantee partial correctness of $\mathfrak{A}$.

Determinism of $\mathfrak{A}$.

$\mathfrak{A}$ is deterministic if the set P consists of at most one element. Thus the condition

$$\mathfrak{P} \text{ is } \textit{unique:} \qquad \mathfrak{P}(\pi_1, uqw) \wedge \mathfrak{P}(\pi_2, uqw) > \pi_1 = \pi_2 \qquad (4)$$

guarantees determinism of the algorithm $\mathfrak{A}$.

Termination of $\mathfrak{A}$.

Each $\mathfrak{P}$-derivation is at the same time a derivation in the general sense but the converse does not hold. If

$$\mathfrak{P} \text{ is } \textit{complete:} \; \pi | uqw \wedge \pi(uqw) \Longrightarrow f \quad > \quad \mathfrak{P}(\pi, uqw) \qquad (5)$$

then an easy induction yields

Lemma: If $\mathfrak{P}$ is complete then each derivation $aq_0z \Longrightarrow f$ *without repetitions of f* is a $\mathfrak{P}$-derivation.

Consequently, if $z \in L$ and $\mathfrak{P}$ is complete and unique then $\mathfrak{A}$ terminates. The case $z \notin L$ is much more difficult and can sufficiently be treated only if both Π_Q and $\mathfrak{P}$ are more specialized. In fact, termination is equivalent to the nonexistence of infinite (nonterminating) $\mathfrak{P}$-derivations.

Finally, an important though easy result should be mentioned:

$$(2) \wedge (4) > (3) \quad . \qquad (6)$$

2.1.1 Specializations of the predicate $\mathcal{P}$.

As a first but raw choice for $\mathcal{P}$ we obtain

$$\mathcal{P}_1(\pi, uqw) \quad :\Leftrightarrow \quad \pi | uqw \tag{7}$$

$\mathcal{P}_1$ meets conditions (1), (2), (5) but it is definitely not free of blind alleys. Indeed, $\mathfrak{A}$ is not partially correct. If, however, we amend $\mathcal{P}_1$ by setting

$$\mathcal{P}_2^o(\pi, uqw) \quad :\Leftrightarrow \quad \pi | uqw \wedge \pi(uqw) \Longrightarrow f \quad , \tag{8}$$

then $\mathcal{P}_2^o$, additionally, is free of blind alleys. Introducing so-called *situation classes* [10,12]

$$\mathcal{K}_\pi^o := \{uqw \in V^*QV^*: \ \pi | uqw \wedge \pi(uqw) \Longrightarrow f\} \quad ,$$

the predicate $\mathcal{P}_2^o$ now reads

$$\mathcal{P}_2^o(\pi, uqw) \quad \Leftrightarrow \quad uqw \in \mathcal{K}_\pi^o \quad .$$

Thus, the test of $\mathcal{P}_2^o$ consists in deciding wether a situation uqw belongs to some situation class $\mathcal{K}_\pi^o$.

Apart from the decision problem involved with this test, one realizes that these $\mathcal{K}_\pi^o$ are far too large: they contain a lot of situations which will never be reached from start situations aq_oz with $z \in T^*$. We therefore restrict the situation classes to

$$\Sigma := \{uqw \in V^*QV^*: \ \exists z \in T^*: \ aq_oz \Longrightarrow uqw\}$$

to obtain

$$\mathcal{K}_\pi^1 := \mathcal{K}_\pi^o \cap \Sigma \quad .$$

With these restricted situation classes we define

$$\mathcal{P}_2^1(\pi, uqw) \quad :\Leftrightarrow \quad uqw \in \mathcal{K}_\pi^1 \quad . \tag{9}$$

As a matter of fact, the decision problem uqw $\in \mathcal{K}_\pi^i$ is of similar difficulty as is the problem $z \in L$; the following heuristic considerations will give a general method to overcome this circumstance. Let $N \neq \emptyset$ be some set and let be

$$\varphi: V^*QV^* \to N \quad , \quad \Phi: \{\mathcal{K}_\pi^i : \pi \in \Pi_Q\} \to 2^N$$

arbitrary functions which are *compatible* in that sense that

$$\varphi(\mathfrak{H}^i_\pi) \subset \Phi[\mathfrak{H}^i_\pi] \tag{10}$$

holds for all $\pi \in \Pi_Q$ (i=o or 1). If we choose the functions properly, we may hope that the decision problem $\varphi(uqw) \in \Phi[\mathfrak{H}^i_\pi]$ will be easier than the previous one (see section 3).
The predicates

$$\mathfrak{P}^i_3(\pi,\ uqw) \quad :\Leftrightarrow \quad \pi | uqw \wedge \varphi(uqw) \in \Phi[\mathfrak{H}^i_\pi] \tag{11}$$

meet conditions (1), (2), and are complete because of (10). It is not very helpful to reformulate the condition of $\mathfrak{P}^i_3$ being free of blind alleys, but - and this is the key for the following considerations - uniqueness of $\mathfrak{P}^i_3$ is already sufficient for $\mathfrak{P}^i_3$ to be free of blind alleys (see (6)).

2.1.2 Determinism of the algorithm $\mathfrak{A}$.

We already saw in the preceeding section that uniqueness of the predicate $\mathfrak{P}$ is the natural condition for $\mathfrak{A}$ to be deterministic.
In this section we restrict Π_Q either to Π_{LL} or to Π_{LR} and we inspect the consequences for the underlying contextfree production system Π if we require that the predicates $\mathfrak{P}^i_2$ or $\mathfrak{P}^i_3$ are unique.
From its definition, uniqueness of $\mathfrak{P}^i_2$ can equivalently be expressed in terms of situation classes:

$$\mathfrak{P}^i_2 \text{ is unique} \Leftrightarrow \forall \pi,\pi' \in \Pi_Q\colon\ \mathfrak{H}^i_\pi \cap \mathfrak{H}^i_{\pi'} \neq \emptyset \Rightarrow \pi = \pi' \ .$$

This property of the situation classes we shall call π-*disjointness* and it is related to the unambiguity of Π by the

Theorem. Let be either

$$\Pi_Q = \Pi_{LL},\quad a = Z\ ,\quad q_o = q\ ,\quad f = q$$

or

$$\Pi_Q = \Pi_{LR},\quad a = \varepsilon\ ,\quad q_o = q\ ,\quad f = Zq \qquad \text{(see [10])}$$

then the following statements are equivalent:

1. Π is unambiguous
2. $\mathfrak{P}^1_2$ is unique (the situation classes $\mathfrak{H}^1_\pi$ are π-disjoint) and Π_Q does not allow for f-repetitions (i.e. $f \overset{+}{\Longrightarrow} f$ is impossible).

The only remarkable point as far as the proof is concerned is the pro-

perty that Π_Q must not allow for f-repetitions; the rest of the proof is a tedious induction for which careful knowledge about the derivation mechanism both of Π_Q and of Π is necessary.
In case $\Pi_Q = \Pi_{LL}$ an f-repetition were $q \overset{+}{\Longrightarrow} q$, which is impossible due to the production forms of Π_{LL}; in case $\Pi_Q = \Pi_{LR}$ however, f-repetition means $Zq \overset{+}{\Longrightarrow} Zq$ and the latter is equivalent to the existence of a proper right-most derivation $Z \overset{+}{\Longrightarrow} Z$ in Π. It should be clear now why Π_Q must have no f-repetition.
Formally however, one needs this property essentially in the proof direction 2. → 1., here the lemma from section 2.1 comes into play.

Let us turn now to the predicate $\mathfrak{P}_3^i$. Again, uniqueness of them can be expressed in terms of the sets $\Phi[\mathfrak{H}_\pi^i]$:

$$\mathfrak{P}_3^i \text{ is unique iff for all } \pi,\pi' \in \Pi_Q \text{ and } uqw \in V^*QV^*\text{:}$$

$$\varphi(uqw) \in \Phi[\mathfrak{H}_\pi^i] \cap \Phi[\mathfrak{H}_{\pi'}^i],\ \pi|uqw\ ,\ \pi'|uqw \ \succ\ \pi = \pi'$$

The latter property we shall call *weak π-disjointness (with respect to φ)*. One obtains from the assumed compatibility (10)

$$\mathfrak{P}_3^i \text{ unique } \succ \mathfrak{P}_2^i \text{ unique}$$

or

$$\Phi[\mathfrak{H}_\pi^i] \text{ weakly } \pi\text{-disjoint} \succ \mathfrak{H}_\pi^i\ \pi\text{-disjoint} \quad . \tag{12}$$

The most prominent and important choice for the function φ is given by

$$\varphi = \varphi_k \quad \text{where } \varphi_k(uqw) := uq(k{:}w) \qquad (k \geq 0) \quad .$$

$k{:}w$ indicates the first k symbols of $w\#^k$ ($\#$ serves as an endmarker). Thus, φ_k takes into account the whole stack u, the state q, but only the k-*look-ahead* $k{:}w$ of the word w.
Additionally we need the auxiliary function $\bar{\varphi}_k(uqw) := k{:}w$, which solely takes the k-look-ahead into consideration.

If we now combine φ_k and properly chosen Φ on one side with Π_{LL} and Π_{LR} on the other, the requirement of $\mathfrak{P}_3^i$ to be unique directly yields well-known classes of grammars Π.
The results are depicted in the following table rather than are stated as theorems in order to enhance the symmetries.
The proofs of these results are partly tedious inductions and partly set-theoretical reformulations. They show no new ideas and are therefore omitted here.

Π_Q =	Π_{LL}		Π_{LR}	
aq_o =	Zq		q	
f =	q		Zq	
	no f-repetition			
$\varphi(uqw)$=	$\varphi_k(uqw) = uq(k:w)$			
$\Phi[\mathfrak{H}_\pi^1]$ = weakly π-disj.	$\varphi_k(\mathfrak{H}_\pi^1)$	$\varphi_o(\mathfrak{H}_\pi^1)\cdot\bar{\varphi}_k(\mathfrak{H}_\pi^1)$	$\varphi_k(\mathfrak{H}_\pi^1)$	$\varphi_o(\mathfrak{H}_\pi^1)\cdot\bar{\varphi}_k(\mathfrak{H}_\pi^1)$
- - - iff - - -				
Π is	LL(k)	strong LL(k)	LR(k)	LA(k)
		[19]	[8,10]	

Three remarks are necessary:

1. If instead of $\mathfrak{H}_\pi^1$ we had taken $\mathfrak{H}_\pi^o$, in the Π_{LL} case we had obtained two new less known, less important and more restrictive grammar classes; in the Π_{LR} case, however, nothing new had emerged because if Π has no useless nonterminals then $\mathfrak{H}_\pi^o = \mathfrak{H}_\pi^1$.
2. For both cases of Π_Q again we assume that no f-repetitions are possible. As already discussed this assumption is vacuously true for the Π_{LL} case, whereas in the Π_{LR} case it causes differences (see [8]). Clearly, as far as the determinism of $\mathfrak{A}$ is concerned this assumption is not necessary but production systems Π whose $\varphi_k(\mathfrak{H}_\pi^1)$ are weakly π-disjoint and whose Π_{LR} allows for f-repetitions are because of the latter ambiguous (compare (12) and the theorem of this section). The difference is small the more as f-repetitions always can be avoided by introducing a new start symbol Z'. Finally it should be noted that the absence of f-repetitions is necessary for termination of $\mathfrak{A}$ (see also lemma of section 2.1).
3. This remark is concerned with the new class LA(k) ("look ahead"). Firstly, its definition is the analog counterpart to that of strong LL(k) grammars, both of which are based on the sets $\varphi_o(\mathfrak{H}_\pi^1)\bar{\varphi}_k(\mathfrak{H}_\pi^1)$. Secondly, LA(k) grammars play the central role for understanding SLR(k) and LALR(k) grammars which can be seen from the following arguments. The test for $uq(k:w) \in \varphi_o(\mathfrak{H}_\pi^1)\bar{\varphi}_k(\mathfrak{H}_\pi^1)$, i.e. for $\mathfrak{P}_3^1$, can be splitted: first look whether $uq \in \varphi_o(\mathfrak{H}_\pi^1)$, and if there is at most one such π then this is applied; only if the LR(o) information from $\varphi_o(\mathfrak{H}_\pi^1)$ is not sufficient that is, if there are more than one such π, then also

the look-ahead k:w is tested for k:w $\in \bar{\varphi}_k(\mathcal{H}_\pi^1)$. This strategy is supported by the well-known fact that in practical cases only in a small number of steps, say 10 %, the algorithm $\mathfrak{A}$ really needs the look-ahead k:w for uniquely determining the next production $\pi \in \Pi_{LR}$. Thirdly, the classes LA(1) and SLR(1) coincide. This and a systematic treatment of the SLR(k) and LALR(k) case on our basis will be presented in a forthcoming paper.

2.2 Recursive formulation of the accepting algorithm.

There is no problem to reformulate our algorithm $\mathfrak{A}$ equivalently in a recursive way:

```
proc ACCEPT(uqw);
   if uqw ≠ f then
         local P := {π∈Π_Q: 𝒫(π,uqw)};
         if P ≠ ∅  then for some π ∈ P do ACCEPT(π(uqw)) od
                   else print(z ∉ L); stop fi
            else print(z ∈ L) fi
```

Any call ACCEPT(aq_oz) evokes the same computations, i.e. $\mathcal{P}$-derivations, as does $\mathfrak{A}$, and so far this algorithm presents no new aspects. But what happens if we replace the choice operator "<u>for</u> <u>some</u>" by the (finite) quantifier "<u>for</u> <u>all</u>"?

Now, in each incarnation of the procedure systematically all elements $\pi \in P$ and their corresponding situations $\pi(uqw)$ will be pursued. It is therefore incorrect to stop if P is empty for some incarnation: its dynamic predecessor might find another way. Thus we obtain

```
proc ARIADNE(uqw);
   if uqw ≠ f then
         local P := {π ∈ Π_Q: 𝒫(π,uqw)};
         for all π ∈ P do ARIADNE(π(uqw)) od
            else print(z ∈ L) fi
```

The call ARIADNE(aq_oz) will now deterministically pursue all $\mathcal{P}$-derivations and each time the situation f is reached "z ∈ L" is printed. ARIADNE - both the above algorithm and the first female informatician who lived in Kreta approximately in the 17th century before Christ - is the mother of all backtracking algorithms.

ARIADNE is deterministic, it (she) is already partially correct if we require the weak condition (2) for the predicate $\mathcal{P}$; since ARIADNE traces all $\mathfrak{P}$-derivations it terminates iff there are no infinite $\mathfrak{P}$-derivations, i.e. iff $\mathfrak{A}$ terminates. If, additionally, $\mathfrak{P}$ meets stronger conditions then ARIADNE will do its job more efficiently: in case $\mathfrak{P}$ is free of blind alleys (3) no useless trials are made and if $\mathfrak{P}$ is unique then ARIADNE follows the single $\mathfrak{P}$-path through the labyrinth of all derivations.

This holds especially for the LL(1) case ($\Pi_Q = \Pi_{LL}$, $\mathfrak{P} = \mathfrak{P}_3^1$ where $\Phi[\mathcal{H}_\pi^1] = \varphi_1(\mathcal{H}_\pi^1)$). But now only the top symbol of the stack u of the situation uqw together with $\mathfrak{P}$ controls and selects the next production π which is to be applied. In this case ARIADNE is the origin of those algorithms which work according to the method of "recursive descent".

3. Finite automata aspect.

Let us assume throughout this section that the predicate $\mathfrak{P}$ is unique. Then

$$p(uqw) := \underline{if}\ \mathfrak{P}(\pi,uqw)\ \underline{then}\ \pi\ \underline{else}\ \emptyset\ \underline{fi}$$

is a function from V*QV* into $\Pi_Q \cup \{\emptyset\}$. The line "P := {...};" of our algorithm $\mathfrak{A}$ can now be replaced by "P:=p(uqw);" which would look like an ordinary function call if only the function p were easy to compute. The aim of this section is to inspect $\mathfrak{P}$ with respect to an efficient computability of p.

If $\mathfrak{P} = \mathfrak{P}_2^i$ then its test is as hard as that of $z \in L$. This fact gave the reason for introducing $\mathfrak{P}_3^i$ (see (11)) and we shall here restrict ourselves to $\varphi = \varphi_k$. Furthermore let us disregard the condition $\pi|uqw$ (which is implied by $\varphi_k(uqw) \in \Phi[\mathcal{H}_\pi^i]$ if $k \geq 1$, $\Pi_Q = \Pi_{LL}$ or Π_{LR} and Φ is e.g. one of the functions in the table of section 2.1.2).

Our function reads now:

$$p(uqw) := \underline{if}\ uq(k{:}w) \in \Phi[\mathcal{H}_\pi^i]\ \underline{then}\ \pi\ \underline{else}\ \emptyset\ \underline{fi}\quad .$$

Since only truncated situations uq(k:w) are tested we may assume $\Phi[\mathcal{H}_\pi^i] \subset V^*QC_k$ where $C_k = k{:}T^*$.But with respect to a later result we assume a bit more:

$$\Phi[\mathcal{H}_\pi^i] \subset \varphi_o(\mathcal{H}_\pi^i)C_k \quad . \tag{13}$$

Still the test required for computing p(uqw) remains the main difficulty. Therefore we assume that the

$$\Phi[\mathcal{H}_\pi^i] \text{ are regular sets} \quad .$$

Then there exists a finite state acceptor which written again as a Semi-Thue system with states has the following properties (compare "CFSM" in [5]; "goto graph" in [1]; [2]):

> M is a finite set of states with start state $s \in M$
>
> Π_M is a deterministic and complete set of productions of form
>
> $mv ::= m' \quad (m,m' \in M\ ,\ v \in V)$
>
> $E_{\pi,qc} \subset M$ are final sets with the property
>
> $$\langle su\rangle \in E_{\pi,qc} \Leftrightarrow uqc \in \Phi[\mathcal{H}^i_\pi]$$
>
> where $c \in C_k$ and where $\langle su\rangle$ denotes that unique state in M which is reached from s upon acception of $u \in V^*$ via Π_M.

If we define the *parsing table* by

$$T(m,q,c) := \underline{\text{if}}\ m \in E_{\pi,qc}\ \underline{\text{then}}\ \pi\ \underline{\text{else}}\ \emptyset\ \underline{\text{fi}}$$

then one easily verifies

$$p(uqw) = T(\langle su\rangle,q,k:w)$$

which fact reduces the function call $p(uqw)$ to a mere table look up T if in the algorithm $\mathfrak{A}$ we always had $\langle su\rangle$ to our disposal. This is achieved if we replace the stack $u = v_1v_2\ldots v_n$ $(n \geq o)$ by

$$s^u := s\langle sv_1\rangle\langle sv_1v_2\rangle\langle sv_1v_2v_3\rangle \ldots \langle sv_1v_2\ldots v_n\rangle \quad .$$

s^u is that unique sequence of states $m \in M$ which are traversed during the acception of u by the above finite acceptor. The last (top) symbol (state) of (the stack) s^u equals $\langle su\rangle$ which circumstance ensures an easy access to this information needed for evaluating the table T. The crucial point is that the function $u \rightarrowtail s^u$ need not be injective in which case the replacement $u \leftrightarrow s^u$ would make our $\mathfrak{A}$ incorrect or else we must keep track of both u and s^u.
Fortunately, the condition (13) implies the desired injectivity:

Theorem [20]. Call $m \in M$ an *error state* if for no $lqc \in V^*QC_k$ and π $\langle ml\rangle \in E_{\pi,qc}$ holds. Assume that condition (13) holds, then for all $v,v' \in V$, $u,u' \in V^*$, $q \in Q$:

1. If $\langle suv\rangle$ is not an error state then $\langle suv\rangle = \langle suv'\rangle$ implies $v = v'$
2. If $\langle su\rangle$ is not an error state then $s^u = s^{u'}$ implies $u = u'$ (injectivity of $u \rightarrowtail s^u$).

Proof. 1. From assumptions we get $\langle suvl\rangle, \langle suv'l\rangle \in E_{\pi,qc}$ for some π, lqc. Hence $uvlqc, uv'lqc \in \Phi[\mathcal{H}^i_\pi]$ and (13) implies $uvlqz, uv'lqz' \in \mathcal{H}^i_\pi$

for some z, z'. Thus $uvlqz \stackrel{+}{\Longrightarrow} f$, $uv'lqz' \stackrel{+}{\Longrightarrow} f$. If both v and v' are not touched in the course of the corresponding derivation, then $v = v'$. If e.g. v is touched then we can split the derivation:
$uvlqz \Rightarrow u_1u_2v\bar{l}\bar{q}\bar{z}_1\bar{z}_2 \xrightarrow{\pi_1} u_1\lambda q'y\bar{z}_2 \Rightarrow f$ where $u=u_1u_2$, $\pi_1 = u_2v\bar{l}\bar{q}\bar{z}_1 ::= \lambda q'y$.
Hence $\langle suv\bar{l}\rangle \in E_{\pi_1, \bar{q}\bar{c}}$ for $\bar{c}=k:\bar{z}_1\bar{z}_2$. By assumption $\langle suv'\bar{l}\rangle \in E_{\pi_1, \bar{q}\bar{c}}$ whence as above one concludes $uv'\bar{l}\bar{q}\bar{z} \in \mathfrak{H}^i_{\pi_1}$ for some $\bar{z}$. Thus $\pi_1 | uv'\bar{l}\bar{q}\bar{z}$ which implies $v=v'$.
2. is an easy consequence of 1.

With all this in mind we get a refinement of the algorithm $\mathfrak{A}$: replace $u \longleftrightarrow s^u$ and split the data structure s^uqw into its three components s^u, q, w where s^u is a right-stack and w is a left-stack.

```
ᾱ : rightstack s^u:=s^a , state q:=q_o , leftstack w:=z ;
    while (s^u,q,w) ≠ f̄ do
          P := T(top(1,s^u) , q , top(k,w)) ;
          if P ≠ ∅  then  (s^u,q,w) := APPLY(P, (s^u,q,w))
                    else print(z ∉ L) ; stop fi
                       od
    print(z ∈ L)
```

It is tacitly assumed that the stack operation top is defined in the usual sense. The function APPLY extends the application of π to uqw to the new data structure (s^u,q,w) and this function can be resolved into component functions top, pop, and push which operate on both stacks; but, additionally, we must be able to compute m^κ if the production $\kappa qx ::= \lambda q'y$ is applied. Thus, depending on the type of Π_Q we need a more or less complete information on Π_M, the state transition table of the finite state acceptor for the $\Phi[\mathfrak{H}^i_\pi]$.
Another problem is caused by the size of the table T: all further efforts in refining $\bar{\mathfrak{A}}$ must be directed to the reduction and compression of T. But now the specialities of the respective Π_Q come into play and therefore we end this discussion.

We conclude:
- Regularity of $\Phi[\mathfrak{H}^i_\pi]$ and (13) is the most important prerequisite for obtaining efficient parsing or accepting algorithms $\mathfrak{A}$. To the ingenuity of D. KNUTH we owe the knowledge that the $\varphi_k(\mathfrak{H}^i_\pi)$ for Π_{LR} are regular sets.
All $\Phi[\mathfrak{H}^i_\pi]$ of the table in section 2.1.2 are regular and fulfill (13); this is a consequence of far more general regularity results which will be discussed in a forthcoming paper.
- Parsing tables (T) and finite state acceptors (Π_M) for $\Phi[\mathfrak{H}^i_\pi]$ are

synonymous concepts. Thus optimization always concerns the finite state acceptor Π_M. Classical state reduction techniques known from automata theory are therefore relevant for this purpose.

4. Further results and outlooks.

There are further results which illuminate our thesis that the most natural way for defining every class of parsable languages is to require that some specialized version of the predicate $\mathfrak{P}_3^i$ is unique and, hence, the algorithm $\mathfrak{A}$ is deterministic and partially correct.

There is a transformation which transforms each ε-free contextfree production system Π into a new Π' that has no left recursions: Π is LC(k) iff Π' is LL(k). Instead of transforming Π to Π' and then constructing the system $(\Pi')_{LL}$, we also could construct directly from Π a third accepting Semi-Thue system with states, Π_{LC}, which equals $(\Pi')_{LL}$. Again, the property of Π being LC(k) is reformulated as weak π-disjointness of the $\varphi_k(\mathfrak{H}_\pi^1)$ for Π_{LC} [19].

Bounded right-context or BRC(m,k)-languages are those which can be accepted deterministically by Π_{LR} by taking k-look-ahead and only the top m symbols of the stack into account.

Hence taking

$$\Phi_{BRC}[\mathfrak{H}_\pi^1] := \{(u:m)q(k:w) \ : \ uqw \in \mathfrak{H}_\pi^1\}$$

in case of $\Pi_Q = \Pi_{LR}$, we again obtain that Π is BRC(m,k) iff the sets $\Phi[\mathfrak{H}_\pi^1]$ are weakly π-disjoint (with respect to the function $uqw \mapsto (u:m)q(k:w)$) [1,7,12].

In a current diploma thesis all types of precedence grammars are considered in order to find functions φ, Φ such that again the property of Π being a precedence grammar is equivalent to the weak π-disjointness of the $\Phi[\mathfrak{H}_\pi^1]$ for Π_{LR}.

The concept of LR-regular grammars [3] can easily be reformulated as uniqueness of an appropriate predicate $\mathfrak{P}$ where $\Pi_Q = \Pi_{LR}$. If one takes Π_{LL} or Π_{LC} or others instead, one would obtain LL-regular or LC-regular grammars a.s.f.

The mechanism of Π_{LR} can be generalized to a system Π_{LR}^o for accepting arbitrary Chomsky languages in a way that retains the main property of

Π_{LR}: Π^{O}_{LR} accepts from *L*eft to right and its reduce steps in reverse order yield a *R*ightmost derivation in the sense of [6,9,11] (see [4,13]).

Similarly, Π_{LL} can be generalized to Π^{O}_{LL} which accepts arbitrary Chomsky languages from *L*eft to right yielding a *L*eftmost derivation [13,17].

With these generalizations we can carry over all our considerations from contextfree to arbitrary Chomsky grammars. In case of contextsensitive grammars this might shed additional light on the determinism problem (compare [18]).

Finally, we mention that all considerations from sections 1. and 2. apply also to van Wijngaarden or two level grammars if we regard the latter as a means for finitely describing an *infinite* set Π of contextfree productions. This holds because nowhere the finiteness of our production systems Π and Π_Q has really been used.

References.

[1] Aho, A.V., Ullman, J.D.: The theory of parsing, translating, and compiling. Prentice Hall 1972

[2] Backhouse, R.C.: An alternative approach to the improvements of LR(k) parsers. Acta Informatica 6, 277-296 (1976)

[3] Culik II, K., Cohen, R.: LR-regular grammars - an extension of LR(k)-grammars. Journal Comp. Syst. Sc. 7, 66-96 (1973)

[4] Deussen, P.: A unified approach to the generation and acception of formal languages. Acta Informatica 9, 377-390 (1978)

[5] DeRemer, F.L.: Simple LR(k) grammars. Comm. ACM 14, 453-460 (1971)

[6] Eickel, J., Loeckx, J.: The relation between derivations and syntactical structures in phrase-structure grammars. Journ. Comp. Syst. Sc. 6, 267-282 (1972)

[7] Harrison, M.A., Havel, I.M.: On the parsing of deterministic languages. Journ. ACM 21, 525-548 (1974)

[8] Geller, M.M., Harrison, M.A.: On LR(k) grammars and languages. Theor. Comp. Sc. 4, 245-276 (1977)

[9] Hotz, G.: Eindeutigkeit und Mehrdeutigkeit formaler Sprachen. Elektron. Informationsverarb. Kybernetik 2, 235-246 (1966)

[10] Langmaack, H.: Application of regular canonical systems to grammars translatable from left to right. Acta Informatica 1, 111-114 (1971)

[11] Langmaack, H.: Zur Äquivalenz der Hotz'schen und Paul'schen Definition der Mehrdeutigkeit von Chomsky-Sprachen. in: 4. Kolloquium über Automatentheorie, Erlangen 1967

[12] Loeckx, J.: An algorithm for the construction of bounded-context parsers. Comm. ACM 13, 297-307 (1970)

[13] Loeckx, J.: The parsing for general phrase-structure grammars. Inform. Contr. 16, 443-464 (1970)

[14] Mayer, O.: Syntaxanalyse. B.I. 1978

[15] Nelson, R.J.: Introduction to automata. Wiley, New York 1968

[16] Salomaa, A.: Formal languages. Academic Press, New York 1973

[17] Szabó, P.: Der allgemeine LL-Akzeptor. Interner Bericht 3/78, Fakultät für Informatik, Universität Karlsruhe

[18] Walters, D.A.: Deterministic context-sensitive languages. Inform. Contr. 17, 14-61 (1976)

[19] Sattler, M.: Current diploma thesis

[20] Drossopoulou, S.: Current diploma thesis

STUDIES IN ABSTRACT/CONCRETE MAPPINGS IN PROVING ALGORITHM CORRECTNESS

Arthur G. Duncan
Indiana U./Purdue U. at Indianapolis

Lawrence Yelowitz
U. of Pittsburgh

ABSTRACT

This paper discusses the problem of factoring program proofs into a proof of correctness of an abstract algorithm followed by a proof of correct implementation at the concrete level. The problem of showing that diagrams commute is simplified by the introduction of a set of abstract entities that define constraints on the abstract operations. Correctness at the concrete level is then shown by exhibiting two appropriate mappings, CA (from the concrete state space to the abstract state space) and CE (from the concrete state space to the set of abstract entities).

1. INTRODUCTION.

Early efforts of proving programs correct were based on invariant assertions and path analysis (([1,2,3,4]), with the proof carried out at the same level of abstraction as the program itself.

Subsequent approaches deal with factoring proofs into levels ([5,6,7]). The underlying logic of an algorithm is demonstrated at a high level, while concrete lower level programs are shown to be correct implementations of the high-level concepts. This generally involves defining mappings between the concrete and abstract program states and then showing, via commuting diagrams, that the concrete operations correctly reflect the abstract operations. One advantage of this approach is its complete generality; however, such generality can also be a drawback in that it gives no hints on how to show that the appropriate diagrams commute.

We introduce an intermediate step in the abstract/concrete proof method. This step involves adding certain <u>constraints</u> at the abstract level, producing a family of abstract programs that are "conditionally correct," provided the abstract functions obey the constraints. At the concrete level one looks for suitable mappings that demonstrate that the concrete functions satisfy these abstract constraints.

Section 2 describes the abstract/concrete proof methodology and the notion of a "constrained functional mapping", relating the concrete program operations to the abstract constraints. Section 3 describes an abstract class of marking algorithms and the appropriate constraints on the abstract functions. Sections 4,5, and 6 apply the theory to a class of concrete marking algorithms and Section 7 offers the authors' conclusions.

2. ABSTRACT/CONCRETE MAPPINGS

Preliminaries

The following notation is used below. Each entity can be prefixed with "a-" or "c-" to identify it as an abstract or concrete entity. In practice the prefixes do not refer to absolute terms but rather to two consecutive levels in the refinement process.

The components of both abstract and concrete programs include:

(i) VEC: a set of state vectors, elements of which are denoted "vec";

(ii) f_i: functions from VEC to VEC.

(iii) inv, term-cond, in-spec, out-spec: predicates on VEC, denoting the program invariant assertion, termination condition, and input/output specifications.

In addition to these components there is a mapping function CA ("concrete-to-abstract") defined for each concrete state vector. Thus, CA(c-vec) is of type a-vec. CA is generally not 1-1 (corresponding to the fact that an abstract program state can be represented in different ways), hence CA^{-1} is generally a relation.

Levels of Verification

Consider the following program:

pgm-1:

<u>while</u> <u>not</u> term-cond (vec) <u>do</u> vec: = f(vec) <u>od</u>

(For notational ease, we use the very simple structure shown here; however, the ideas will carry through for any level of complexity of program structure.)

In our notation the abstract program would deal with a-vec, a-f, and a-term-cond, while the concrete program would involve c-vec, c-f, and c-term-cond.

We can identify the following levels of program verification.

<u>Level 1</u> (Lowest level): Standard path analysis at the "current level." The details of this level are well-known [1,2,3].

<u>Level 2</u> (Factorization of underlying logic/implementation): Let a-pgm and c-pgm denote the abstract and concrete versions of pgm-1. Proving correctness of c-pgm can be done as follows:

<u>Step 1</u>: Prove a-pgm is correct, either by standard path analysis or by some other means.

<u>Step 2</u>: Verify the following properties of the mapping CA.

(i) c-in-spec(c-vec) $\rightarrow$ a-in-spec(CA(c-vec));

(ii) CA(c-vec) = a-vec $\rightarrow$ CA(c-f(c-vec)) = a-f(a-vec)

(iii) c-term-cond(c-vec) $\rightarrow$ a-term-cond(CA(c-vec)); and

(iv) a-out-spec(a-vec) $\rightarrow$ c-out-spec(x) for all x ε CA^{-1} (a-vec).

Actually, verifications (ii), (iii), and (iv) may involve more work than is really needed as it is usually sufficient for these verifications to hold at certain check-point locations in c-pgm, (cf., [6,7]).

<u>Level 3</u> ("Constrained functional mapping"):

The basic idea is to define a relation R on a-VEC that preserves the abstract invariant. We do this by means of a set of constraints.

We begin by introducing a set E of entities. For each pair a-vec, a-vec' from a-VEC and each entity E ε E we introduce a new abstract predicate

a-constraint(a-vec,e,a-vec')

with the property that

(2.2.1) (∀<a-vec,E,a-vec'> ε a-vec x E x a-VEC)
((a-inv(a-vec) and a-constraint(a-vec,E,a-vec'))
→ a-inv(a-vec'))

Our invariant-preserving relation R would then be defined by

<a-vec,a-vec'> ε R $\triangleq$ (∀ E ε E) (a-constraint(a-vec,E,a-vec'))

At this point we introduce a mapping function CE ("concrete to entity set") from c-VEC to E. Verification of c-pgm now proceeds in the following way.

Step 1: Prove the adequacy of the abstract invariant by proving

(i) (2.2.1) and (a-inspec(a-vec) → a-inv(a-vec))

and (ii) (a-inv(a-vec) and a-term-cond(a-vec)) → a-out-spec(a-vec)

Step 2: Prove that a-inv and a-constraint capture the essence of c-pgm, i.e., prove

(i) c-in-spec(c-vec) → a-in-spec(CA(c-vec))

(ii) c-term-cond(c-vec) → a-term-cond(CA(c-vec))

(iii) a-out-spec(a-vec) → c-out-spec(x) for all x ε CA^{-1}(a-vec)

and (iv) for each concrete function c-f in c-pgm, a-inv(CA(c-vec)) → a-constraint (CA(c-vec),CE(c-vec),CA(c-f(c-vec))).

In general, there will be several mapping functions CE, since there may be more than one c-f corresponding to a particular a-f. Also we note in passing that we do not actually have a well-defined a-pgm. In a sense, we are defining a-pgm by defining each a-f(a-vec) to be CA(c-f(c-vec)) for some c-vec in CA^{-1}(a-vec). The well-definedness of a-f is not the issue, however, the main consideration being the preservation of the condition a-inv(CA(c-vec)) on the space c-VEC.

The following theorem provides the justification for the above method.

THEOREM 2.1: Suppose that all conditions in steps 1 and 2 above hold and that c-pgm is started in some state c-vec$_0$ satisfying c-in-spec(c-vec$_0$). If c-pgm terminates, it will terminate in some state c-vec$_f$ such that a-out-spec(CA(c-vec$_f$)) holds.

Proof: From steps 2(i) and 1(i) we see that a-inv(CA(c-vec)) holds upon first entering the while loop in c-pgm. From step 2(ii,iii) and step 1(ii) we see that

a-inv(CA(c-vec)) and c-term-cond(c-vec) → a-out-spec(CA(c-vec)).

From step 2(iv) and step 1(i) we have

a-inv(CA(c-vec)) and not c-term-cond(c-vec) {c-f} a-inv(CA(c-vec)),

and the proof is complete.

This method might be termed "simulation of invariants" or "simulation of verification conditions." Like program simulation ([6,7]) it assumes correctness of a-pgm

codeset = {+, a, b}

If the current data structure is γ, then $\gamma(x, ALINK) = \langle +, y \rangle$ means that x is joined to y by a <u>normal</u> A-link; whereas, $\gamma(u, BLINK) = \langle b, v \rangle$ means that b is joined to v by a <u>redirected</u> B-link.

ASSERTIONS ON DATA STRUCTURES

Assertions on multilinked structures often take the form: "There is a path of a certain type joining one particular node to another." Classes of paths through the structure can by described by defining languages over nameset codeset. If L is such a language, we define con(x, L, y, γ) to mean there exists a path of type L in γ joining x to y.

Example: The Schorr-Waite Algorithm uses a "reverse stack" of nodes joined by redirected A- and B-links in order to "back up" once it finds an atom. If T is the pointer to this reverse stack, then the assertion that x is on this stack can be expressed as

$$\mathrm{con}(T, \{\langle ALINK, A\rangle, \langle BLINK, B\rangle\}^*, x, \gamma).$$

One final detail. The operation of changing a link in the structure can be expressed by the operation:

$$\gamma' := \text{insert-arc}(node, \langle name, code\rangle, node', \gamma).$$

where

$$\gamma'(n, m) = \begin{cases} \langle code, node'\rangle, & \text{if } \langle n, m\rangle = \langle node, name\rangle \\ \gamma(n, m), & \text{otherwise} \end{cases}$$

A formal semantics of insert-arc is given in [12,13].

5. TWO CONCRETE MARKING ALGORITHMS.

We first present two fairly straightforward implementations of a-pgm, both of which can be found in Knuth [8].

<u>c-pgm-A</u>:

```
while K ≤ M do
   if MARK(n_K) then
      if ALINK(n_K) ≠ λ and not MARK(ALINK(n_K)) then
      α: (MARK(ALINK(n_K)),K) := (true, min(K+1, ADDR(ALINK(n_K))))
      fi;
      if BLINK(n_K) ≠ λ and not MARK(BLINK(n_K)) then
      β: (MARK(BLINK(n_K)), K) := (true, min(K+1, ADDR(BLINK(n_K))))
      fi
   else
   γ: K := K + 1
    fie
od
```

The specifications are as follows:

c-vec $\triangleq$ <M, N, ADDR, ALINK, BLINK, MARK, K, S_0>, where

M = a fixed positive integer

N = a set of M nodes

ADDR: $N \to \{1, \ldots, M\}$ is a 1-1 function on N

ALINK, BLINK: $N \to N \cup \{\lambda\}$ are functions of N

MARK: $N \to \{\underline{true}, \underline{false}\}$ is a function on N

K = an integer variable taking values in $\{1, \ldots, M+1\}$

S_0 = an arbitrary fixed subset of N.

The input/output specifications and termination conditions are:

c-in-spec $\triangleq$

$(S_0 = \{x \in N: MARK(x) = \underline{true}\})$ and $(K = 1)$

c-out-spec $\triangleq$

$(\forall y \in N)(MARK(y) = \underline{true} \leftrightarrow$
$(\exists x \in S_0)(con(x, \{ALINK, BLINK\}^*, y)))$

c-term-cond $\triangleq$

$K > M$

Notation: In c-pgm-A, n_K stands for $ADDR^{-1}(K)$.

We relate c-pgm-A to a-pgm by means of the mapping

$CA(M, N, ADDR, ALINK, BLINK, MARK, K, S_0)$

$= \langle N, S_0, R_0, marked, S, R\rangle$, where

$R_0 = \{\langle x, y\rangle \in N \times N: y \notin S_0$ and
$(ALINK(x) = y$ or $BLINK(x) = y)\}$

$marked = \{x \in N: MARK(x) = \underline{true}\}$

$R = \{\langle x, y\rangle \in N \times N: MARK(y) = \underline{false}$ and
$(ALINK(x) = y$ or $BLINK(x) = y)\}$

$S = \{x \in N: MARK(x) = \underline{true}$ and $ADDR(x) \geq K\}$

As for the mapping CE, we can consider the three sections of code at α, β, and γ separately and define the mapping

CE(c-vec) = <A, B, C, D>

separately for each section.

(i) For Section α, we have

$A = \{x: ADDR(x) \geq min(ADDR(ALINK(n_K)), K+1)$
and $MARK(x) = \underline{true}\}$

$B = \{n_K\} \cap \{y: ADDR(y) > ADDR(ALINK(n_K))\}$

$C = \{ALINK(n_K)\}$

$D = \{ALINK(n_K)\}$

(note: specifying D_2 is equivalent to specifying D, cf. Section 3)

(ii) For Section β, we have the same with ALINK replaced by BLINK.

(iii) For Section γ, we have

$A = C = D_2 = \{\ \}$

$B = \{n_K\}$

It is now a straightforward matter to prove partial correctness of c-pgm-A by showing that CA and CE satisfy the conditions of Theorem 3.1.

The second concrete algorithm uses a stack of addresses which we will represent by an array of positive integers indexed starting at 1.

c-pgm-B:

```
   while T ≠ 0 do
      (x,T) := (ADDR⁻¹(STACK[T]), T-1);
      if (* CONDITION A *)
            ALINK(x) ≠ λ and not MARK(ALINK(x)) then
               (STACK[T+1], T, MARK(ALINK(x))) :=
                   (ADDR(ALINK(x)), T+1, true)
   fi;
   if (* CONDITION B *)
            BLINK(x) ≠ λ and not MARK(BLINK(x)) then
                (STACK[T+1], T, MARK(BLINK(x))) :=
                    (ADDR(BLINK(x)), T+1, true)
   fi
od
```

The concrete state vector is

c-vec = <N, ADDR, ALINK, BLINK, STACK, T, MARK, S_0>, where

N, ADDR, ALINK, BLINK, MARK, and S_0 are as in c-pgm-A,

STACK = an array of (possible arbitrarily many) positive integers indexed from 1.

T = an integer variable taking non-negative values.

The specifications are:

c-in-spec $\triangleq$

$(S_0 = \{x \in N: MARK(x) = \underline{true}\})$ and

$(S_0 = ADDR^{-1}\{STACK[1], \ldots, STACK[T]\})$

c-out-spec $\triangleq$ same as in c-pgm-A

c-term-cond $\triangleq$ $T = 0$.

We can define the concrete/abstract mapping by

CA(c-vec) = <N, S_0, R_0, marked, S, R>, where

$S = ADDR^{-1}\{STACK[1], \ldots, STACK[T]\}$ and

N , S_0, R_0, marked, R are the same as in c-pgm-A.

Now, the loop body of c-pgm-B can be considered one of four different operations. depending on which combination of conditions A and B holds upon entry. Each such operation will have its corresponding CE mapping.

Case 1: Conditions A and B both true:

$A = C = D_2 = \{ALINK(x), BLINK(x)\}$

$B = \{ x \}$

Case 2: Condition A true, condition B false:

$A = C = D_2 = \{ALINK(x)\}$

$B = \{ x \}$

Case 3: Condition A false, condition B true:

$A = C = D_2 = \{BLINK(x)\}$

$B = \{ x \}$

Case 4: Conditions A and B both false:

$A = C = D_2 = \{ \ \}$

$B = \{ x \}$

As with c-pgm-A, it is a straightforward matter to use Theorem 3.1 to prove partial correctness of c-pgm-B.

6. THE SCHORR-WAITE ALGORITHM.

Algorithms A and B dealt with a fixed data structure. The Schorr-Waite Algorithm [8,9,10,11], on the other hand, varies the data structure dynamically; thus, we shall use the coded structural graph model to describe how the data structure varies.

We shall also introduce a somewhat simplified notation and a new operation select.

Notation: When there is no confusion between the abstract and concrete meanings of a symbol, we will use the abstract name in the concrete program; thus, we shall use R(x) to mean $\{y \in N : con(x,\{\langle ALINK, +\rangle,\langle BLINK, +\rangle\}, y, \gamma)$ and $(MARK(y) = \underline{false})\}$ and marked to mean $\{x \in N : MARK(x) = \underline{true}\}$.

The statement

$$\sigma \stackrel{\Delta}{=} \underline{select}\ x_1\ \underline{in}\ A_1, \ldots, x_k\ \underline{in}\ A_k\ \underline{such\ that}\ B(x_1, \ldots, x_k)$$

is defined by

$$wp(\sigma,Q) = (\forall\, x_1 \in A_1, \ldots, x_k \in A_k)\ (B(x_1, \ldots, x_k) \rightarrow Q)$$
$$\underline{and}\ (\exists\, y_1 \in A_1, \ldots, y_k \in A_k)\ (B(y_1, \ldots, y_k)).$$

We shall now present the Schorr-Waite Algorithm, followed by its specifications.

c-pgm-E (Schorr-Waite):

```
repeat
   while R(P) ≠ { } do
   α : select name in {ALINK, BLINK}, x in R(P)
           such that con(P{<name, +>}, x, γ);
       code := if name = ALINK then a else b fie;
       (γ, T, P) := (insert-arc(P, <name, code>, T, γ), P, x);
       marked := marked ∪ { x }
   od;
   repeat
     if T ≠ λ then
```

```
β : select x in N, name in {ALINK, BLINK}, code in {a,b}
      such that con(T, {<name, code>}, x, γ);
      (γ, T, P) := (insert-arc(T, <name, +>, P, γ), x, T)
   fi
  until T = λ or R(P) ≠ {  }
 until T = λ and R(P) = {  }
```

The concrete state vector is given by

$\text{c-vec} = \langle N, P_0, \text{MARK}, P, T, \gamma_0, \gamma \rangle$, where

N, MARK are as in the previous algorithms

P_0 = a particular node in N

P, T are variable pointers to nodes in N

γ_0, γ are coded structural graphs on the space $\langle N, \{\text{ALINK}, \text{BLINK}\}, \{+, a, b\} \rangle$.

The specifications can be written as:

$$\text{c-in-spec} \triangleq (\forall x \in N)(\text{MARK}(x) = \underline{\text{true}} \leftrightarrow x = P_0) \text{ and } (P = P_0) \text{ and } (T = \lambda)$$

$$\text{c-out-spec} \triangleq (\forall x \in N)(\text{MARK}(x) = \underline{\text{true}} \leftrightarrow \text{con}(P_0, \{\langle \text{ALINK}, + \rangle, \langle \text{BLINK}, + \rangle\}^*, x, \gamma_0))$$

$$\text{c-term-cond} \triangleq (T = \lambda) \ \underline{\text{and}} \ R(P) = \{ \ \}.$$

The mapping to the abstract state space is given by

$\text{CA}(\text{c-vec}) = \langle N, S_0, R_0, \text{marked}, S, R \rangle$, where

$$S_0 = \{P_0\};$$

$$R_0 = \{\langle x, y \rangle \in N \times N : \text{con}(x, \{\langle \text{ALINK}, + \rangle, \langle \text{BLINK}, + \rangle\}, y, \gamma_0) \ \underline{\text{and}}(\text{MARK}(y) = \underline{\text{false}});$$

$$S = \{ P \} \cup \{y \in N : \text{con}(T, \{\langle \text{ALINK}, a \rangle, \langle \text{BLINK}, b \rangle\}^*, y, \gamma)$$

R = same as R_0 with γ in place of γ_0;

$$\text{marked} = \{x \in N : \text{MARK}(x) = \underline{\text{true}}\}.$$

We define two mappings $\text{CE}(\text{c-vec}) = \langle A, B, C, D \rangle$, corresponding to the segments of code at α and β in c-pgm-E.

For α, we have

$$A = C = D_2 = \{ x \}$$
$$B = \{ \ \},$$

while for β we have

$$A = C = D_2 = \{ \ \}$$
$$B = \{ P \}.$$

By going through the checklist provided by the two CE mappings, we can show that the Schorr-Waite Algorithm is correct *as a marking algorithm*, i.e., we can show that it will mark all the right nodes. However, we also want to know that it will restore the original data structure, i.e., that $\gamma = \gamma_0$ at termination.

Informally stated, the auxiliary assertions needed to show restoration of the original data structure are:

1. The reversal of pointers property,

2. Each node in the "reverse stack" has exactly one of its pointers redirected.
3. If $T \neq \lambda$ then T can reach λ with penultimate node P_0; moreover, the path is unique.
4. All nodes x such that <u>not</u> con(T, {<ALINK, a>, <BLINK, b>}*, x, γ) have their links at the original value.

In the above discussion, we were able to separate the marking aspects of the Schorr-Waite Algorithm from the "bookkeeping" aspects. In fact, we could go even further and model abstractly the property of restoring the original links. We could then show that the links are restored properly by discovering new CA and CE mappings. This procedure could then be used as a basis for proving correctness of link restoration for other related algorithms.

7. <u>CONCLUDING REMARKS</u>.

In proving correctness of the concrete marking algorithms, we were not required to devise intermediate assertions, as this had already been handled in the abstract algorithm.

The goal of this approach is to reduce the proof effort by proving entire classes of algorithms. Recently, Lee and others [14] have used an abstract/concrete approach to prove a class of list copying algorithms.

Hopefully, this approach will prove useful in the development and proof of programs approaching real-world complexity.

ACKNOWLEDGEMENTS.

The authors wish to thank the referees for their many valuable and detailed comments on this paper.

BIBLIOGRAPHY.

1. Floyd, R. W., Assigning meanings to programs, Proceedings of a Symposium in Applied Mathematics, 19, (ed. Schwartz, J. T.), Providence Island: American Mathematical Society, 1967, pp. 19-32.
2. Manna, Z., Properties of programs and the first-order predicate calculus, JACM, 16, 1969, pp. 244-255.
3. Hoare, C.A.R., An axiomatic basis for computer programming, CACM 12, 1969, pp. 576-580, 583.
4. Dijkstra, E. W., A discipline of programming, Prentice-Hall, Inc., Englewood Cliffs, NJ, 1976.
5. Wulf, W. A., London, R. L., and Shaw, M., An introduction to the construction and verification of Alphard programs, IEEETSE SE-2, 4, Dec. 1976, pp. 253-265.
6. Milner, R., An algebraic definition of simulation between programs, Report No. CS-205, Computer Science Dept., Stanford University, Feb. 1971.
7. Birman, A. and Joyner, W. H., A Problem-Reduction Approach to Proving Simulation between Programs, IEEETSE SE-2, 2, June 1976.
8. Knuth, D. E., The art of computer programming, v. 1, Fundamental algorithms, Addison-Wesley Publishing Co., Reading, Mass., 1972-1973.
9. Schorr, H., and Waite, W., An efficient machine-independent procedure for garbage collection in various list structures, CACM 10.
10. Yelowtitz, L., and Duncan, A. G., Abstractions, instantiations, and proofs of marking algorithms, in Proceedings of the Symposium on Artificial Intelligence and Programming Languages, SIGPLAN Notices, 12, 8 and SIGART Newsletter no. 64, August 1977, pp. 13-21.
11. Topor, T., The correctness of the Schorr-Waite list marking algorithm, Report MIP-R-104, School of Artificial Intelligence, University of Edinburgh, July 1974.
12. Duncan, A. G., Studies in Program Correctness, Ph. D. Dissertation, University of California, Irvine, 1976.
13. Yelowitz, L. and Duncan, A. G., Data Structures and Program Correctness: Bridging the Gap, Computer Languages, v. 3, 1978.
14. Lee, S., deRoever, W. P. and Gerhart, S. L., The Evolution of List-Copying Algorithms, Proceedings of the Sixth ACM Symposium on Principles of Programming Languages, January 1979.

A CHARACTERIZATION OF A DOT-DEPTH TWO ANALOGUE OF GENERALIZED DEFINITE LANGUAGES

Faith E. Fich
Computer Science Division
University of California
Berkeley, California 94720

J.A. Brzozowski
Department of Computer Science
University of Waterloo
Waterloo, Ontario, Canada N2L 3G1

Abstract

The family of G-trivial languages is investigated. This family is a generalization of L-trivial and R-trivial languages, a relationship analogous to the one between generalized definite languages and the definite and reverse definite languages. Characterizations of G-trivial languages are given in terms of their syntactic monoids, various congruence relations, and the (finite) automata which recognize them. Finally, we examine noncounting languages and their connection to G-trivial languages.

1. Introduction

Within the family of star-free languages many interesting hierarchies have been found. Probably the most famous is the dot-depth hierarchy [2] illustrated in Figure 1(a). Here F is the set of all finite languages of a given finite alphabet A, C is the set of all cofinite languages, and for any family of languages L, $L\mathbf{M}$ and $L\mathbf{B}$ denote the concatenative closure of L and the Boolean closure of L, respectively. It has just recently been shown that this hierarchy is infinite [6].

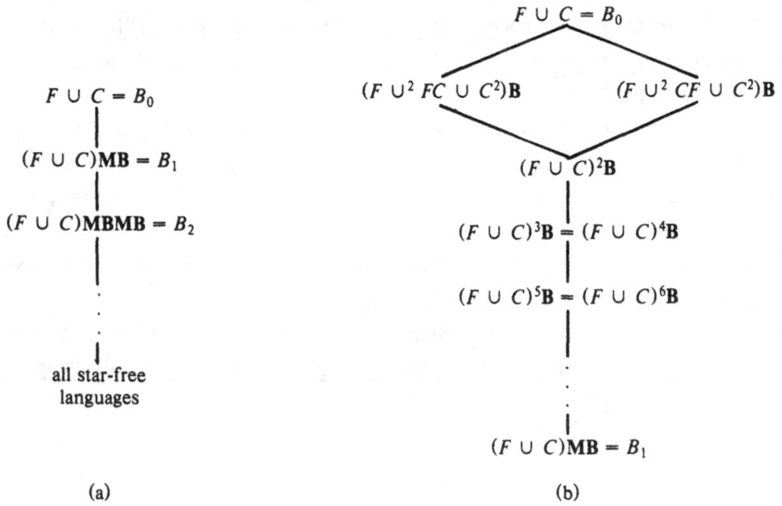

Figure 1

Another important hierarchy is the depth 1 finite/cofinite hierarchy [2]. See Figure 1(b). The families of definite, reverse definite, and generalized definite languages, which have been extensively studied [1,7,9,11,13,17,18,22,23], are just $(F^2 \cup CF \cup C^2)\mathbf{B}$, $(F^2 \cup FC \cup C^2)\mathbf{B}$, and $(F \cup C)^2\mathbf{B}$. The depth 1 finite/cofinite hierarchy plays a key role in understanding the structure of B_1, the languages of dot-depth 1.

It is natural to ask whether such a hierarchy exists for dot-depth 2 and in general for dot-depth n, $n > 2$. A starting point for such an investigation would be to find collections of languages with dot-depth 2 analogous to the finite/cofinite, definite, reverse definite, and generalized definite languages.

In semigroup theory, Green's relations (J, L, R, and H) and the monoids in which these relations are trivial (i.e. the resulting equivalence classes are all singletons) are of fundamental importance. For example, Schützenberger [19] showed that a language is star-free iff its syntactic monoid is finite and H-trivial.

The family of languages with J-trivial syntactic monoids were studied by Simon in [20] and [21]. We have examined R-trivial and L-trivial languages in a previous paper [5]. It turns out that with respect to their syntactic monoids, the congruences which represent them, and their automata, the J-trivial, L-trivial, and R-trivial languages are natural generalizations of the finite/cofinite, definite, and reverse definite languages.

In this paper we investigate a family of languages, the G-trivial languages, which, in a similar way, is a generalization of the family of generalized definite languages.

2. The Congruence Characterization

For any congruence $\sim$ on A^*, the $\sim$ languages are those which can be expressed as the finite union of congruence classes of $\sim$. The finite and cofinite languages can be described by the congruences $\underset{n}{+}$, $n \geqslant 0$, where, for $x, y \in A^*$,

$$x \underset{n}{+} y \quad \text{iff} \quad |x|, |y| \geqslant n \quad \text{or} \quad x = y \text{ and } |x| < n\,.$$

The appropriate generalization of the concept of *length* n turns out to be *n-full*.

Definition 2.1 Let $x \in A^*$ and $n \geqslant 0$.

(a) $\mu_n(x) = \{y \mid |y| \leqslant n \text{ and } y \text{ is a subsequence of } x\}$.

(b) The *alphabet* of x is $\alpha(x) = \{a \in A \mid x = uav \text{ for some } u, v \in A^*\}$, the set of all letters which occur in x.

(c) x is *n-full* if it contains all subsequences of length less than or equal to n over its alphabet; i.e. if $\mu_n(x) = \bigcup_{i=0}^{n} (\alpha(x))^i$.

(d) $x \underset{n}{\sim} y$ iff $\mu_n(x) = \mu_n(y)$.

The congruences $\underset{n}{\sim}$ are those corresponding to the J-trivial languages. In [20] the following important lemma concerning these congruences is presented.

Lemma 2.2 $u \underset{n}{\sim} uv$ iff there exists $u_1, \ldots, u_n \in A^*$ such that $u = u_1 \cdots u_n$ and $\mu_n(u_1) \supseteq \cdots \supseteq \mu_n(u_n) \supseteq \mu_n(v)$.

The congruences characterizing reverse definite languages ($\underset{n}{\overset{\cdot}{\leftarrow}}$) and R-trivial languages ($\underset{nR}{\equiv}$) are concerned with the beginning of words while those for definite ($\underset{n}{\overset{\cdot}{\rightarrow}}$) and L-trivial ($\underset{nL}{\equiv}$) languages are concerned with their endings. In particular, for $n \geqslant 0$,

$\underset{n}{\overset{\cdot}{\leftarrow}}$ is the smallest congruence satisfying $uv \underset{n}{\overset{\cdot}{\leftarrow}} u$ for all $u, v \in A^*$ such that $|u| = n$, and

$\underset{n}{\overset{\cdot}{\rightarrow}}$ is the smallest congruence satisfying $vu \underset{n}{\overset{\cdot}{\rightarrow}} u$ for all $u, v \in A^*$ such that $|u| = n$.

Informally this says that two words are in the same $\underset{n}{\overset{\cdot}{\leftarrow}}$ class ($\underset{n}{\overset{\cdot}{\rightarrow}}$ class) if their first (last) n letters are the same. Similarly, for $n \geqslant 0$,

$\underset{nR}{\equiv}$ is the smallest congruence satisfying $uv \underset{nR}{\equiv} u$ for all $u, v \in A^*$ such that u is n-full and $\alpha(v) \subseteq \alpha(u)$, and

$\underset{nL}{\equiv}$ is the smallest congruence satisfying $vu \underset{nL}{\equiv} u$ for all $u, v \in A^*$ such that u is n-full and $\alpha(v) \subseteq \alpha(u)$.

The usual congruences associated with the family of generalized definite languages are defined as follows. For $x, y \in A^*$ and $n \geqslant 0$, $x \underset{n}{\leftrightarrow} y$ iff $x \underset{n}{\overset{\cdot}{\leftarrow}} y$ and $x \underset{n}{\overset{\cdot}{\rightarrow}} y$. That is, the congruence class a word belongs to depends on its first n letters and last n letters. For purposes of generalization, we have found it more convenient to adopt the following definition.

$\underset{n}{\overset{\cdot}{\leftrightarrow}}$ is the smallest congruence satisfying $uvw \underset{n}{\overset{\cdot}{\leftrightarrow}} uw$ for all $u, v, w \in A^*$ such that $|u| = |w| = n$.

It is straightforward to verify that, for any $n \geqslant 0$, $x \underset{n}{\overset{\cdot}{\leftrightarrow}} y$ implies $x \underset{n}{\leftrightarrow} y$ and $x \underset{2n}{\leftrightarrow} y$ implies $x \underset{n}{\overset{\cdot}{\leftrightarrow}} y$.

All this serves to introduce the following congruences, which we will relate, in section 3, to the G-trivial languages.

Definition 2.3 Let $n \geqslant 0$. Then $\underset{nG}{\equiv}$ is the smallest congruence satisfying $uvw \underset{nG}{\equiv} uw$ for all $u, v, w \in A^*$ such that u and w are n-full and $\alpha(u) = \alpha(w) \supseteq \alpha(v)$.

It is also useful to consider two additional relations and another congruence.

Definition 2.4 Let $x, y \in A^*$ and $n \geqslant 1$. Then $x \underset{nG}{\overset{\cdot}{\equiv}} y$ iff there exist $z_1, z_2, u, v, w \in A^*$ such that $x = z_1 uvwz_2$, $y = z_1 uwz_2$, u and w are n-full and $\alpha(u) = \alpha(w) \supseteq \alpha(v)$. $\underset{nG}{\overset{*}{\equiv}}$ is the transitive closure of $\underset{nG}{\overset{\cdot}{\equiv}}$.

Note that $\underset{nG}{\equiv}$ is the symmetric transitive closure of $\underset{nG}{\overset{\cdot}{\equiv}}$. Exactly the same congruence is obtained if, in the above definition, the containment $\alpha(w) \supseteq \alpha(v)$ is replaced by equality.

Definition 2.5 Let $n \geqslant 0$. Then $\underset{nG}{\approxeq}$ is the smallest congruence satisfying $u \underset{nG}{\approxeq} uvu$ for all $u, v \in A^*$ such that u is n-full and $\alpha(u) \supseteq \alpha(v)$.

If u is $n+1$-full then it is also n-full. Hence $x \underset{n+1G}{\equiv} y$ implies $x \underset{nG}{\equiv} y$ and $x \underset{n+1G}{\approxeq} y$ implies $x \underset{nG}{\approxeq} y$ for all $x, y \in A^*$ and all $n \geqslant 1$.

Proposition 2.6 Let $n \geqslant 1$ and $u, v \in A^*$ be such that $\alpha(u) \supseteq \alpha(v)$. Then

(a) $u^{2n} \underset{nG}{\equiv} u^{2n+1}$,

(b) $u^{2n} \underset{nG}{\equiv} u^{2n}vu^{2n}$,

(c) $u^n \underset{nG}{\approxeq} u^{n+1}$, and

(d) $u^n \underset{nG}{\approxeq} u^n vu^n$.

Proof: (a) and (d) follow immediately from the fact that u^n is n-full. Since $u^{2n} = u^nu^n \underset{nG}{\equiv} u^nu^{2n}u^n = u^nu^nu^nu^n \underset{nG}{\equiv} u^nu^nvu^nu^n = u^{2n}vu^{2n}$ and $u^n \underset{nG}{\approxeq} u^nu^n \underset{nG}{\approxeq} u^nu^2u^n = u^{n+1}u^{n+1} \underset{nG}{\approxeq} u^{n+1}$, (b) and (c) hold.

These congruences are closely related. In fact, the two families of languages $\{ X \mid X$ is a $\underset{nG}{\equiv}$ langugage for some $n \geqslant 0\}$ and $\{ X \mid X$ is a $\underset{nG}{\approxeq}$ language for some $n \geqslant 0\}$ are the same.

Proposition 2.7 Let $x,y \in A^*$ and $n \geqslant 1$. Then $x \underset{2nG}{\approxeq} y$ implies $x \underset{nG}{\equiv} y$.

Proof: Suppose $u,v \in A^*$ are such that u is $2n$-full and $\alpha(u) \supseteq \alpha(v)$. From Definition 2.5 and Lemma 2.2 it follows that there exist $u_1, \ldots, u_{2n} \in A^*$ such that $u = u_1 \cdots u_{2n}$ and $\alpha(u_1) = \cdots = \alpha(u_{2n})$. Let $u' = u_1 \cdots u_n$ and $u'' = u_{n+1} \cdots u_{2n}$. Then u' and u'' are n-full, $u = u'u''$, and $\alpha(u') = \alpha(u'') = \alpha(u''vu')$; thus $u = u'u'' \underset{nG}{\equiv} u'(u''vu')u'' = uvu$. Since $\underset{2nG}{\approxeq}$ is the smallest congruence satisfying $u \underset{2nG}{\approxeq} uvu$ for all $u,v \in A^*$ such that u is $2n$-full and $\alpha(u) \supseteq \alpha(v)$, it follows that $x \underset{2nG}{\approxeq} y$ implies $x \underset{nG}{\equiv} y$ for all $x,y \in A^*$.

Proposition 2.8 Let $x,y \in A^*$ and $n \geqslant 1$. Then $x \underset{nG}{\equiv} y$ implies $x \underset{nG}{\approxeq} y$.

Proof: Let $u,v,w \in A^*$ be such that u and w are n-full and $\alpha(u) = \alpha(w) \supseteq \alpha(v)$. Since $\alpha(u) \supseteq \alpha(wuvw)$, $u \underset{nG}{\approxeq} uwuvwu$. But $u \underset{nG}{\approxeq} uwu$, $w \underset{nG}{\approxeq} wuw$, and $\underset{nG}{\approxeq}$ is a congruence; thus $uw \underset{nG}{\approxeq} uwuvwuw \underset{nG}{\approxeq} uvw$. Since $\underset{nG}{\equiv}$ is the smallest congruence satisfying $uw \underset{nG}{\equiv} uvw$ for all $u,v,w \in A^*$ such that u and w are n-full and $\alpha(u) = \alpha(w) \supseteq \alpha(v)$, it follows that $x \underset{nG}{\equiv} y$ implies $x \underset{nG}{\approxeq} y$ for all $x,y \in A^*$.

The following technical lemma is from [10].

Lemma 2.9 If $n \geqslant 1$ and $x,x',x'' \in A^*$ are such that $x \underset{nG}{\dot{\equiv}} x''$ and $x' \underset{nG}{\dot{\equiv}} x''$, then there exists $x_0 \in A^*$ such that $x_0 \underset{nG}{\dot{\equiv}} x$ and $x_0 \underset{nG}{\dot{\equiv}} x'$.

Proposition 2.10 Suppose $n \geqslant 1$ and $x \underset{nG}{\equiv} y$. If x is an element of its $\underset{nG}{\equiv}$ class with minimal length, then $x \underset{nG}{\overset{*}{\equiv}} y$.

Proof: If $x \underset{nG}{\equiv} y$ then there exist $m \geqslant 1$ and $z_0, z_1, \ldots, z_m \in A^*$ such that $x = z_0$, $y = z_m$ and for $i = 1, \ldots, m$ either $z_{i-1} \underset{nG}{\dot{\equiv}} z_i$ or $z_i \underset{nG}{\dot{\equiv}} z_{i-1}$.

The proof proceeds by induction on m. If $m = 1$ then either $x \underset{nG}{\dot{\equiv}} y$ or $y \underset{nG}{\dot{\equiv}} x$. In the latter case, since x is minimal, $x = y$ and thus $x \underset{nG}{\dot{\equiv}} y$ as well. Assume the result is true for $m-1$.

If $z_{i-1} \underset{nG}{\dot{\equiv}} z_i$ for $i = 1, \ldots, m$ then $x \underset{nG}{\overset{*}{\equiv}} y$ by definition. Otherwise there exists k, $0 \leqslant k \leqslant m-1$, such that $x \underset{nG}{\overset{*}{\equiv}} z_k$ but $z_k \underset{nG}{\not\dot{\equiv}} z_{k+1}$. Note that from the proof for $m = 1$, $x \underset{nG}{\dot{\equiv}} z_1$ so $k \geqslant 1$.

Since $z_{k+1} \underset{nG}{\dot{\equiv}} z_k$ and $z_{k-1} \underset{nG}{\dot{\equiv}} z_k$, it follows from Lemma 2.9 that there exists $z'_{k-1} \in A^*$ such that $z'_{k-1} \underset{nG}{\dot{\equiv}} z_{k+1}$ and $z'_{k-1} \underset{nG}{\dot{\equiv}} z_{k-1}$. Continuing inductively for $i = k-2, \ldots, 0$, since $z'_{i+1} \underset{nG}{\dot{\equiv}} z_{i+1}$ and $z_i \underset{nG}{\dot{\equiv}} z_{i+1}$, there exists $z'_i \in A^*$ such that $z'_i \underset{nG}{\dot{\equiv}} z'_{i+1}$ and $z'_i \underset{nG}{\dot{\equiv}} z_i$.

Let $z'_i = z_{i+1}$ for $i = k, \ldots, m-1$. Now $z'_0 \underset{nG}{\dot{\equiv}} z_0 = x$ and x is minimal, so $z'_0 = x$. Thus $z'_0, z'_1, \ldots, z'_{m-1}$ are such that $z'_0 = x$, $z'_{m-1} = z_m = y$, and for $i = 1, \ldots, m-1$ either $z'_{i-1} \underset{nG}{\dot{\equiv}} z'_i$ or $z'_i \underset{nG}{\dot{\equiv}} z'_{i-1}$. By the induction hypothesis, $x \underset{nG}{\overset{*}{\equiv}} y$.

Corollary 2.11 Every congruence class of $\underset{nG}{\equiv}$, $n \geqslant 1$, contains a unique element of minimal length.

Proof: Suppose $n \geqslant 1$ and $x,y \in A^*$ are such that $x \underset{nG}{\equiv} y$ and x and y are both elements of minimal length. Hence $|x| = |y|$ and by Proposition 2.10 $x \underset{nG}{\overset{*}{\dot\equiv}} y$. From Definition 2.4, if $z,z' \in A^*$ then $z \underset{nG}{\dot\equiv} z'$ implies $|z| \leqslant |z'|$, with equality if and only if $z = z'$. Since $\underset{nG}{\overset{*}{\dot\equiv}}$ is the transitive closure of $\underset{nG}{\dot\equiv}$, it follows that $x = y$.

It is interesting to note that the congruences $\underset{n}{\dot\leftarrow}$, $\underset{n}{\dot\rightarrow}$, $\underset{n}{\dot\leftrightarrow}$, $\underset{nR}{\equiv}$, and $\underset{nL}{\equiv}$ also share this last property whereas $\underset{n}{\dot-}$ and $\underset{n}{\sim}$ do not.

The following is an algorithm which, given x, transforms it into the unique minimal element of $[x]_{\underset{nG}{\equiv}}$.

Algorithm Find the unique minimal element of $[x]_{\underset{nG}{\equiv}}$.

for each $C \subseteq \alpha(x)$ such that $C \neq \varnothing$ **do**
  for each decomposition $x = z_1yz_2$ such that y is $2n$-full, $\alpha(y) = C$, z_1 does not end with a letter in C, and z_2 does not begin with a letter in C **do**
    let u be the shortest prefix of y such that u is n-full and $\alpha(u) = \alpha(y)$.
    let w be the shortest suffix of y such that w is n-full and $\alpha(w) = \alpha(y)$.
    let $v \in A^*$ be such that $y = uvw$.
    Replace x by z_1uwz_2. Note that since $uw \underset{nG}{\dot\equiv} uvw = y$, $z_1uwz_2 \underset{nG}{\dot\equiv} x$.

Note that, from Lemma 2.9, the order in which 'pieces' are removed from a word is irrelevant.

Example Let $x = abaaacbccaab$ and $n = 1$.

Consider the non-empty subsets of $\alpha(x) = \{a,b,c\}$ in the following order: $\{a,b,c\}$, $\{a,b\}$, $\{b,c\}$, $\{a,c\}$, $\{a\}$, $\{b\}$, $\{c\}$. Let z_1uvwz_2 be any decomposition of x such that uvw is 2-full.

subset	decomposition of x					replace x by
	z_1	u	v	w	z_2	
$\{a,b,c\}$	1	*abaaac*	*bc*	*caab*	1	*abaaaccaab*
$\{a,b\}$						
$\{b,c\}$						
$\{a,c\}$	*ab*	*aaac*	1	*caa*	*b*	
$\{a\}$	*ab*	*a*	*a*	*a*	*ccaab*	*abaaccaab*
	abaacc	*a*	1	*a*	*b*	
$\{b\}$						
$\{c\}$	*abaa*	*c*	1	*c*	*aab*	

Therefore the unique minimal element $\underset{1G}{\equiv}$ congruent to *abaaacbccaab* is *abaaccaab*.

Proposition 2.12 For any finite alphabet A and any $n \geqslant 1$, $\underset{nG}{\equiv}$ is of finite index.

Proof: By induction on #A.

If $\#A = 1$, say $A = \{a\}$, then the $\underset{nG}{\equiv}$ classes are $\{1\}$, $\{a\}$, ... , $\{a^{2n-1}\}$, and $\{a^i \mid i \geqslant 2n\}$ so that $\underset{nG}{\equiv}$ is clearly of finite index on A.

Now assume the result is true for alphabets with cardinality $\#A - 1$. For $a \in A$ let $y \in (A-\{a\})^*$ be such that y is the unique minimal element of $[y]_{\underset{n\,G}{\equiv}}$ and $|y| = \max\{|y'| \mid y' \in (A-\{a\})^*$ is the unique minimal element of $[y]_{\underset{n\,G}{\equiv}}\}$. Note that $|y|$ is independent of the choice of a.

Suppose $x \in A^*$ is the unique minimal element of $[x]_{\underset{n\,G}{\equiv}}$. If x is not $2n$-full then there exist $x_1, \ldots, x_{m+1} \in A^*$ and $a_1, \ldots, a_m \in A$ where $0 \leqslant m < 2n$, $x = x_1a_1 \cdots x_ma_mx_{m+1}$, $\alpha(x_ia_i) = \alpha(x)$ for all $i = 1, \ldots, m$, and $\alpha(x_i) \subsetneq \alpha(x)$ for $i = 1, \ldots, m+1$. Let $a_{m+1} \in \alpha(x) - \alpha(x_{m+1})$. Consider x_i where $1 \leqslant i \leqslant m+1$. If $|x_i| > |y|$ then there exists $x'_i \in (A-\{a_i\})^*$ such that $x'_i \underset{nG}{\equiv} x_i$ and $|x'_i| < |x_i|$. But $\underset{nG}{\equiv}$ is a congruence so $x_1a_1 \cdots a_{i-1}x'_ia_i \cdots x_{m+1} \underset{nG}{\equiv} x_1a_1 \cdots a_{i-1}x_ia_i \cdots x_{m+1} = x$. Since $|x_1a_1 \cdots a_{i-1}x'_ia_i \cdots x_{m+1}| < |x|$ this contradicts the fact that x is the minimal element of $[x]_{\underset{n\,G}{\equiv}}$. Therefore $|x_i| \leqslant |y|$ which implies $|x| \leqslant m + \sum_{i=1}^{m+1} |y| = m(1+|y|) < 2n(1+|y|)$.

Now consider the case when x is $2n$-full. Then there exist $x_1, \ldots, x_n, x'_1, \ldots, x'_n, z \in A^*$, and $a_1, \ldots, a_n, a'_1, \ldots, a'_n \in A$, such that $x = x_1a_1 \cdots x_na_nza'_nx'_n \cdots a'_1x'_1$ and $\alpha(x_i) \neq \alpha(x_ia_i) = \alpha(x) = \alpha(a'_ix'_i) \neq \alpha(x'_i)$ for $i = 1, \ldots, n$. As above, it follows that $|x_i|, |x'_i| \leqslant |y|$ for $i = 1, \ldots, n$. Since $x_1a_1 \cdots x_na_n$ and $a'_nx'_n \cdots a'_1x'_1$ are n-full and $\alpha(x_1a_1 \cdots x_na_n) = \alpha(a'_nx'_n \cdots a'_1x'_1) = \alpha(x) \supseteq \alpha(z)$, if $z \neq 1$ then $(x_1a_1 \cdots x_na_n)(a'_nx'_n \cdots a'_1x'_1) \underset{nG}{\equiv} x$. This contradicts the minimality of x. Hence $z = 1$ and $|x| = \sum_{i=1}^{n} |x_ia_i| + |a'_ix'_i| \leqslant 2n(1+|y|)$.

Since there is only a finite number of words of length less than or equal to $2n(1+|y|)$ it follows that $\underset{nG}{\equiv}$ partitions A^* into a finite number of distinct congruence classes.

This proof can be extended to show that $\max\{|y'| \mid y' \in A^*$ is the unique minimal element of $[y']_{\underset{n\,G}{\equiv}}\} = 2n\left(\dfrac{(2n)^{\#A}-1}{2n-1}\right)$. See [10] for details.

3. The Monoid Characterization

The syntactic semigroups, S, of finite/cofinite, reverse definite, definite, and generalized definite languages have been shown to be characterized by the conditions $e\,S \cup Se = e$ (every idempotent is a zero), $e\,S = e$ (every idempotent is a left zero), $Se = e$ (every idempotent is a right zero), and $e\,S = e\,S \cap Se = e$ (every idempotent is a middle zero), respectively, for all idempotents $e \in S$.

For $f \in M$, let $P_f = \{g \in M \mid f \in MgM\}$ and $M_f = P_f^*$. Then M_f is the submonoid of M generated by the elements g with which f can be written. If we replace S by M_e in the first three of the above conditions we have described the finite J-trivial, L-trivial, and R-trivial monoids. These and other equivalent properties are given explicitly in the following theorems from [3] and [20].

Theorem 3.1 Let M be a finite monoid. The following conditions are equivalent.

1. M is J-trivial (i.e. $MfM = MgM$ implies $f = g$).
2. M is R-trivial and L-trivial.
3. For all idempotents $e \in M$, $eM_e \cup M_ee = e$ (Every idempotent is a local zero).
4. There exists $n \geqslant 0$ such that, for all $f,g \in M$, $(fg)^n = (fg)^nf = g(fg)^n$.
5. There exists $n \geqslant 0$ such that, for all $f,g \in M$, $f^n = f^{n+1}$ and $(fg)^n = (gf)^n$.

Theorem 3.2 Let M be a finite monoid. The following conditions are equivalent.

1. M is R-trivial (i.e. $fM = gM$ implies $f = g$).
2. For all idempotents $e \in M$, $eM_e = e$ (Every idempotent is a local left zero).
3. There exists $n > 0$ such that, for all $f,g \in M$, $(fg)^n f = (fg)^n$.
4. For all $f,g,h \in M$, $fgh = f$ implies $fg = f$.

Theorem 3.3 Let M be a finite monoid. The following conditions are equivalent.

1. M is L-trivial (i.e. $Mf = Mg$ implies $f = g$).
2. For all idempotents $e \in M$, $M_e e = e$ (Every idempotent is a local right zero).
3. There exists $n > 0$ such that, for all $f,g \in M$, $g(fg)^n = (fg)^n$.
4. For all $f,g,h \in M$, $hgf = f$ implies $gf = f$.

This leads to the following natural generalization.

Definition 3.4 Let M be a finite monoid. Then M is *G-trivial* iff $eM_e \cap M_e e = e$ for all idempotents $e \in M$.

This is the same as saying that every idempotent is a local middle zero. As with the other three families of monoids there are various alternative characterizations for the family of G-trivial monoids.

Theorem 3.5 Let M be a finite monoid. The following conditions are equivalent.

1. M is G-trivial.
2. There exists an $n > 0$ such that for all $f_1, \ldots, f_m \in M$ and all $g \in \{f_1, \ldots, f_m\}^*$, $(f_1, \ldots, f_m)^n g (f_1, \ldots, f_m)^n = (f_1, \ldots, f_m)^n$.
3. For all $f,g,h,k \in M$, $fghkf = f$ implies $fgkf = f$.

Proof:

(1⇒2) Let $f_1, \ldots, f_m \in M$ and let $g \in \{f_1, \ldots, f_m\}^*$. Since M is finite, there exists an $n > 0$ such that $e = (f_1 \cdots f_m)^n$ is idempotent. Now $f_1, \ldots, f_m \in P_e$ so $g \in M_e$. Thus $(f_1 \cdots f_m)^n g (f_1 \cdots f_m)^n = ege = e = (f_1 \cdots f_m)^n$.

(2⇒3) Let $f,g,h,k \in M$ be such that $fghkf = f$. Then $f = (fghk)^n f$, so $fgkf = [(fghk)^n] fgk [(fghk)^n f] = [(fghk)^n (fgk)(fghk)^n] f = (fghk)^n f = f$.

(3⇒1) Suppose $e \in M$ is idempotent and let $g \in M_e$. If $g = 1$ then $ege = ee = e$. Otherwise $g = g_1 \cdots g_m$ where $m \geqslant 1$ and $g_i \in P_e$ for $1 \leqslant i \leqslant m$. Since $g_i \in P_e$ there exist $f_i, h_i \in M$ such that $e = f_i g_i h_i$.

Now $e = eee = e(f_1 g_1 h_1)e = e1f_1(g_1 h_1)e = eg_1 h_1 e$, so suppose $e = eg_1 \cdots g_i h_i e$ where $1 \leqslant i \leqslant m-1$. Then

$$e = ee = eg_1 \cdots g_i h_i ee = e(g_1 \cdots g_i)(h_i f_{i+1})(g_{i+1} h_{i+1})e = e(g_1 \cdots g_i)(g_{i+1} h_{i+1})e\,.$$

By induction, $e = eg_1 \cdots g_m h_m e$. Thus $e = e(g_1 \cdots g_m) h_m 1 e = e(g_1 \cdots g_m) 1 e = ege$.

Definition 3.6 Let M be a monoid. Then $\equiv$ is the smallest congruence such that $f \equiv f^2$ and $fg \equiv gf$ for all $f,g \in M$.

Theorem 3.7 Let M be a finite monoid. M is *G*-trivial iff M is aperiodic and for all idempotents $e, f \in M$, $e \equiv f$ implies $MeM = MfM$.

Proof:

($\Rightarrow$) Since M is finite there exists $n > 0$ such that f^n is idempotent for all $f \in M$. Let $f \in M$ and let $e = f^n$. Clearly $f \in M_e$ so $ef \in eM_e$ and $fe \in M_e e$. Since $ef = f^{n+1} = fe$, $f^{n+1} \in eM_e \cap M_e e = e$. Therefore $f^{n+1} = f^n$; i.e. M is aperiodic.

To prove that $e \equiv f$ implies $MeM = MfM$ for all idempotents $e, f \in M$ it is sufficient to show that for $g,h,k,l \in M$

1. if $e = ghk$ and $f = gh^2k$ are idempotent then $MeM = MfM$ and
2. if $e = ghkl$ and $f = gkhl$ are idempotent then $MeM = MfM$.

   1. Since e is idempotent $e = ee^2e = e(ghk)(ghk)e = e(gh)(kg)(hk)e$. But M is *G*-trivial so $e = e(gh)(hk)e = efe$. Therefore $MeM = MefeM \subseteq MfM$. Similarly, $f = fff = f(gh)hkf$ so $f = f(gh)kf = fef$ and $MfM \subseteq MeM$. Thus $MeM = MfM$.
   2. Since e is idempotent, $e = ee^2e = e(ghkl)(ghkl)e$. Because M is *G*-trivial it follows that $e = egklghkle$, $e = egkhkle$, and finally $e = egkhle = efe$. Therefore $MeM \subseteq MfM$. By symmetry $MfM \subseteq MeM$; thus $MeM = MfM$.

($\Leftarrow$) Let $e \in M$ be idempotent and $f \in eM_e \cap M_e e$. Then $f = eg = he$ for some $g,h \in M_e$. If $g = 1$ then $f = e$. Otherwise $g = g_1 \cdots g_m$ where $g_i \in P_e$ for $i = 1, \ldots, m$. For each i, $1 \leqslant i \leqslant m$, there exist $k_i, l_i \in M$ such that $e = k_i g_i l_i$. Then $f = eg = e^m g = e^m g_1 \cdots g_m \equiv (eg_1) \cdots (eg_m) = (k_1 g_1 l_1 g_1) \cdots (k_m g_m l_m g_m) \equiv (k_1 g_1 g_1 l_1) \cdots (k_m g_m g_m l_m) \equiv (k_1 g_1 l_1) \cdots (k_m g_m l_m) = e^m = e$.

M is finite; therefore there exists $n > 0$ such that k^n is idempotent for all $k \in M$. Then $f^n \equiv f \equiv e$, hence $Mf^nM = MeM$. Now $MfM \supseteq Mf^nM = MeM$ and $MfM = MegM \subseteq MeM$. Thus $MeM = MfM$.

Since $e \in MeM = MfM = MegM$, there exist $k,l \in M$ such that $e = kegl = k^n e(gl)^n$. Then $e = k^n e(gl)^n = k^n e(gl)^n (gl)^n = e(gl)^n = egl(gl)^{n-1} \in egM = fM$. This implies $eM = fM$ because $f \in eM_e \subseteq eM$. Similarly $Me = Mf$.

Because M is finite and aperiodic, it is *H*-trivial; hence $f = e$. Therefore $eM_e \cap M_e e = e$.

An alternate proof of this theorem can be found in [3].

It is now possible to identify the *G*-trivial monoids with the family of languages defined by the congruences in the previous section.

Proposition 3.8 If X is a $\sim$ language and there exists $n > 0$ such that for all $u,v \in A^*$, $\alpha(u) \supseteq \alpha(v)$ implies $u^n \sim u^n v u^n$, then the syntactic monoid, M, of X is *G*-trivial.

Proof: Let $f_1, \ldots, f_m \in M$ and let $g \in \{f_1, \ldots, f_m\}^*$. Then $g = f_{i_1} f_{i_2} \cdots f_{i_r}$ where $r \geqslant 0$ and $1 \leqslant i_j \leqslant m$ for $j = 1, \ldots, r$. Since the syntactic morphism, ψ, is surjective, there exist $u_1, \ldots, u_m \in A^*$ such that $\psi(u_i) = f_i$ for $i = 1, \ldots, m$. Let $u = u_1 \cdots u_m$ and let $v = u_{i_1} \cdots u_{i_r}$.

Now $\alpha(u) \supseteq \alpha(v)$, so $u^n \sim u^n v u^n$. Since M is the syntactic monoid of X, $(f_1 \cdots f_m)^n g (f_1 \cdots f_m)^n = \psi(u^n v u^n) = \psi(u^n) = (f_1 \cdots f_m)^n$. By Theorem 3.5, M is *G*-trivial.

Lemma 3.9 Let M be a monoid and let $\phi : A^* \to M$ be a surjective morphism. Then $\alpha(x) \supseteq \alpha(y)$ implies $\phi(y) \in M_{\phi(x)}$ for all $x,y \in A^*$.

Proof: If $y = 1$ then clearly $\phi(y) = 1 \in M_{\phi(x)}$. Otherwise $y = a_1 \cdots a_n$ for some $n > 0$ where $a_i \in A$. For $i = 1, \ldots, n$, $a_i \in \alpha(y) \subseteq \alpha(x)$ so $x = u_i a_i v_i$ for some $u_i, v_i \in A^*$. Since $\phi(x) = \phi(u_i)\phi(a_i)\phi(v_i)$, $\phi(a_i) \in P_{\phi(x)}$. Thus $\phi(y) = \phi(a_1) \cdots \phi(a_n) \in M_{\phi(x)}$.

Lemma 3.10 Let M be a finite G-trivial monoid and $\phi : A^* \to M$ be a surjective morphism. Let n be the cardinality of M and let $u,v \in A^*$. Then $u \underset{n}{\sim} uvu$ implies $\phi(u) = \phi(uvu)$.

Proof: Suppose $u \underset{n}{\sim} uvu$. By Lemma 2.2 there exist $u_1, \ldots, u_n \in A^*$ such that $u = u_1 \cdots u_n$ and $\alpha(u_1) \supseteq \cdots \supseteq \alpha(u_n) \supseteq \alpha(vu)$. Note that, since $\alpha(u) \supseteq \alpha(u_1)$, these containments are actually equalities. Let $u_0 = 1$. By definition of n, the elements $\phi(u_0), \phi(u_0u_1), \ldots, \phi(u_0u_1 \cdots u_n)$ cannot all be distinct. Hence there exist i and j, $0 \leqslant i < j \leqslant n$, such that $\phi(u_0u_1 \cdots u_i) = \phi(u_0u_1 \cdots u_iu_{i+1} \cdots u_j)$.

Let $f = \phi(u_0u_1 \cdots u_i)$, $g = \phi(u_{i+1} \cdots u_j)$, and $h = \phi(u_{j+1} \cdots u_n)$. Then $f = fg$ so $f = fg^m$ for all $m \geqslant 0$. Choose m such that g^m is idempotent. Now $\alpha(u_{j+1} \cdots u_n v u_0 \cdots u_i) \subseteq \alpha((u_{i+1} \cdots u_j)^m)$, so $h\phi(v)f = \phi(u_{j+1} \cdots u_n v u_0 \ldots u_i) \in M_{\phi((u_{i+1} \cdots u_j)^m)} = M_{g^m}$ by Lemma 3.9. Thus

$$\begin{aligned}\phi(uvu) = fgh\phi(v)fgh &= fg^m h\phi(v)fg^m h \\ &= fg^m h \quad \text{since } g^m M_{g^m} g^m = g^m \\ &= fgh \\ &= \phi(u).\end{aligned}$$

Theorem 3.11 Let M be the syntactic monoid of $X \subseteq A^*$. M is finite and G-trivial iff X is a $\underset{n\,G}{\approx}$ language for some $n \geqslant 1$.

Proof:

($\Rightarrow$) Suppose M is finite and G-trivial. Let n be the cardinality of M. Since $\underset{n\,G}{\approx}$ is the smallest congruence such that $u \underset{n\,G}{\approx} uvu$ for all $u,v \in A^*$ such that u is n-full and $\alpha(u) \supseteq \alpha(v)$, it is sufficient to show $u \underset{n\,G}{\approx} uvu$ implies u and (uvu) have the same image under the syntactic morphism. But this follows from Lemma 3.10 since $u \underset{n\,G}{\approx} uvu$ implies $u \underset{n}{\sim} uvu$. Thus X is a $\underset{n\,G}{\approx}$ language.

($\Leftarrow$) Immediate from Propositions 2.6(d) and 3.8.

4. The Automaton Characterization

In a manner similar to that discussed for the monoid and congruence characterizations, the automata of G-trivial languages are local analogues of the automata of generalized definite languages, extending the correspondences between the three other pairs of families. For the following theorems let S = <A, Q, σ> be a semiautomaton and let M be its transformation monoid.

Theorem 4.1 M is the monoid of a finite/cofinite language iff there exists an $n \geqslant 0$ such that for all $x,y \in A^*$, $|x| = n$ implies $\sigma(q,yx) = \sigma(q,x) = \sigma(q,xy)$ for all $q \in Q$.

Theorem 4.2 M is the monoid of a reverse definite language iff there exists an $n \geqslant 0$ such that for all $x,y \in A^*$, $|x| = n$ implies $\sigma(q,x) = \sigma(q,xy)$ for all $q \in Q$.

Theorem 4.3 M is the monoid of a definite language iff there exists an $n \geqslant 0$ such that for all $x,y \in A^*$, $|x| = n$ implies $\sigma(q,x) = \sigma(q,yx)$ for all $q \in Q$.

Theorem 4.4 M is the monoid of a generalized definite language iff there exists an $n \geqslant 0$ such that for all $x,y \in A^*$, $|x| = n$ implies $\sigma(q,x) = \sigma(q,xyx)$ for all $q \in Q$.

Theorem 4.5 M is J-trivial iff there exists an $n \geqslant 0$ such that for all $x,y \in A^*$, x n-full and $\alpha(y) \subseteq \alpha(x)$ imply $\sigma(q,yx) = \sigma(q,x) = \sigma(q,xy)$ for all $q \in Q$.

Theorem 4.6 M is R-trivial iff there exists an $n \geqslant 0$ such that for all $x,y \in A^*$, x n-full and $\alpha(y) \subseteq \alpha(x)$ imply $\sigma(q,x) = \sigma(q,xy)$ for all $q \in Q$.

Theorem 4.7 M is L-trivial iff there exists an $n \geqslant 0$ such that for all $x,y \in A^*$, x n-full and $\alpha(y) \subseteq \alpha(x)$ imply $\sigma(q,x) = \sigma(q,yx)$ for all $q \in Q$.

Proofs of the above theorems and alternative characterizations of the automata of these languages can be found in [1], [5], [11], [14], [17], [20], [21], and [22].

Theorem 4.8 M is G-trivial iff there exists an $n \geqslant 0$ such that for all $x,y \in A^*$, x n-full and $\alpha(y) \subseteq \alpha(x)$ imply $\sigma(q,x) = \sigma(q,xyx)$ for all $q \in Q$.

Proof:

($\Rightarrow$) The proof follows directly from Lemma 3.10.

($\Leftarrow$) Suppose $e \in M$ is idempotent. Let $f \in M_e$. If $f = 1$ then $efe = e^2 = e$. Otherwise $f = f_1 \cdots f_m$ where $m \geqslant 1$ and $f_i \in P_e$. Then there exist $g_i,h_i \in M$ such that $e = g_i f_i h_i$. Since the syntactic morphism, ψ, is surjective, there exist $x_1, \ldots, x_m, y_1, \ldots, y_m, z_1, \ldots, z_m \in A^*$ such that $\psi(x_i) = g_i$, $\psi(y_i) = f_i$, and $\psi(z_i) = h_i$ for $i = 1, \ldots, m$.

Thus $e = e^m = g_1 f_1 h_1 \cdots g_m f_m h_m = \psi(x_1 y_1 z_1 \cdots x_m y_m z_m)$ and $f = f_1 \cdots f_m = \psi(y_1 \cdots y_m)$. Let $u = x_1 y_1 z_1 \cdots x_m y_m z_m$ and let $v = y_1 \cdots y_m$. Clearly $\alpha(u^n) \supseteq \alpha(v)$ and u is n-full. Therefore $\sigma(q,u^n v u^n) = \sigma(q,u^n)$ for all $q \in Q$ so that $e = e^n = \psi(u^n) = \psi(u^n v u^n) = e^n f e^n = efe$.

Hence $eM_e e = e$ for all idempotents $e \in M$.

5. The Dot-Depth Hierarchy

In [10] it is shown that the family of G-trivial languages is contained in dot-depth 2. However this family is incomparable with B_1. For example, consider the language denoted by the expression $(ab)^* \in B_1$. The graph of its automaton is illustrated in Figure 2.

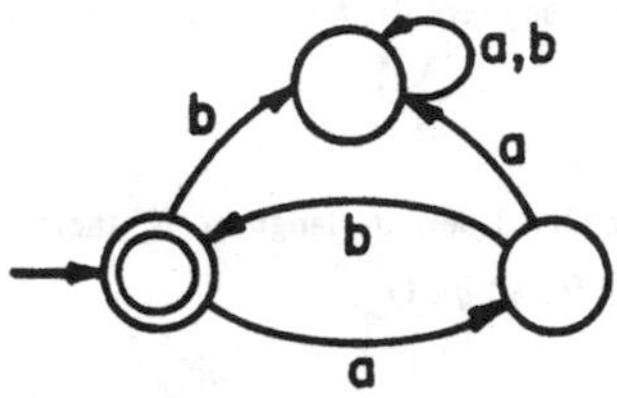

Figure 2

Let $f = \underline{ab}$, $g = \underline{a}$, $h = \underline{b}$ and $k = \underline{1}$. Then $fghkf = \underline{ababab} = \underline{ab} = f$ since $\sigma(q_0,(ab)^3) = q_0 = \sigma(q_0,ab)$, $\sigma(q_1,(ab)^3) = q_2 = \sigma(q_1,ab)$, and $\sigma(q_2,(ab)^3) = q_2 = \sigma(q_2,ab)$. But $fgkf = \underline{abaab} \neq \underline{ab} = f$ since $\sigma(q_0,abaab) = q_2 \neq q_0 = \sigma(q_0,ab)$. From Theorem 3.5 it follows that this language is not G-trivial.

Also, there exist R-trivial languages (and hence G-trivial languages) which are not in B_1. See, for example, [20] page 116.

6. Noncounting Languages

The family of noncounting languages is also important in the study of star-free languages. In [8], [15], [16], and [21] it is proved that every star-free language is noncounting and, moreover, that a regular language is noncounting only if it is star-free.

Definition 6.1 For $n \geqslant 0$ define $\underset{n}{-}$ to be the smallest congruence such that $u^n \underset{n}{-} u^{n+1}$ for all $u \in A^*$. A language is *noncounting* if and only if it is a $\underset{n}{-}$ language for some $n \geqslant 0$.

Given some alphabet, A, it is customary to denote by N_n the set of all $\underset{n}{-}$ languages over this alphabet. That is, $N_n = \{X \subseteq A^* | X \text{ is a } \underset{n}{-} \text{ language }\}$. The set of all noncounting languages is represented by $N = \bigcup_{n \geqslant 0} N_n$. Clearly N_n and N are Boolean algebras. It is immediate from the definition that $x \underset{n+1}{-} y$ implies $x \underset{n}{-} y$ for all $x,y \in A^*$ and $n \geqslant 0$. Thus $N_0 \subseteq N_1 \subseteq \cdots$. Each containment is proper; consider, for example, the languages $\{a^n\} \in N_{n+1} - N_n$ for $n \geqslant 0$.

Green and Rees [12] proved that $\underset{1}{-}$ is a congruence of finite index for any alphabet. Thus every language in N_1 is regular and hence star-free. However in [4], Brzozowski, Culik, and Gabrielian showed that for any alphabet of cardinality greater than 1, N_2 contains languages which are not even recursively enumerable.

Here we look at $\underset{1}{-}$ and investigate the relationship between N_1 and the G-trivial languages.

Definition 6.2 Let $x \in A^+$ and suppose $a \in A$ and $u,v \in A^*$ are such that $x = uav$ and $\alpha(u) \subsetneq \alpha(ua) = \alpha(x)$. Then the *initial mark* of x is $a_L(x) = a$ and the *initial segment* of x is $f(x) = u$. Symmetrically, if $x = uav$ and $\alpha(v) \subsetneq \alpha(av) = \alpha(x)$ then the *terminal mark* of x is $a_R(x) = a$ and the *terminal segment* of x is $t(x) = v$.

The initial segment of a word is just its longest prefix which does not contain every letter occurring in the word. The initial mark is the letter in the word whose first appearance occurs furthest to the right. Analogous remarks can be made concerning terminal segments and terminal marks.

The following characterization of $\underset{1}{\sim}$ from [4] provides a useful working definition.

Lemma 6.3 Let $x,y \in A^*$. Then $x \underset{1}{\sim} y$ if and only if $a_L(x) = a_L(y)$, $a_R(x) = a_R(y)$, $f(x) \underset{1}{\sim} f(y)$, and $t(x) \underset{1}{\sim} t(y)$.

Definition 6.4 Let $n \geq 0$, $m \geq 1$ and $x,y \in A^*$. Then $x \overset{(m)}{\underset{n}{\sim}} y$ if and only if for every decomposition $x = x_1 \cdots x_m$ there exists a decomposition $y = y_1 \cdots y_m$ such that $x_i \underset{n}{\sim} y_i$ for $i = 1, \ldots, m$ and vice versa. N_n^m denotes the set $\{X \subseteq A^* \mid X \text{ is a } \overset{(m)}{\underset{n}{\sim}} \text{ language}\}$.

In [4] it is shown that $(N_n)^m\mathbf{B} = \{X \subseteq A^* \mid X \text{ is a } \overset{(m)}{\underset{n}{\sim}} \text{ language}\}$. This justifies the notation N_n^m. Since $\underset{1}{\sim}$ is of finite index, $\overset{(m)}{\underset{1}{\sim}}$ is also of finite index for $m \geq 1$. Hence every $\overset{(m)}{\underset{1}{\sim}}$ language is star-free.

Proposition 6.5 For $n \geq 1$, $N_1^n\mathbf{B} \subseteq N_{2n-1}$.

Proof: Let $x \in A^*$. If $x = 1$ then $x^{2n-1} = x^{2n}$, so assume $|x| \geq 1$.

Consider any decomposition of x^{2n} into n pieces $x_1, \ldots, x_n$. Since $|x| + \cdots + |x_n| = |x_1 \cdots x_n| = |x^{2n}| = 2n|x|$ there exists i, $1 \leq i \leq n$, such that $|x_i| \geq 2|x|$. Let y be the prefix of length $2|x|$ of x_i. Then $x_i = yz$ for some $z \in A^*$. Now $x^{2n} = (x_1 \cdots x_{i-1})y(zx_{i+1} \cdots x_n)$; thus there exist $u,v \in A^*$ such that $y = uxv$ and $x = vu$. Let $x_i' = uvz$ and $x_j' = x_j$ for $j = 1, \ldots, i-1, i+1, \ldots, n$. Then $x_1' \cdots x_n' = (x_1 \cdots x_{i-1})uvz(x_{i+1} \cdots x_n) = x^{2n-1}$ and, since $x_i = uxvz = uvuvz \underset{1}{\sim} uvz = x_i'$, $x_j \underset{1}{\sim} x_j'$ for $j = 1, \ldots, n$.

Conversely, consider any decomposition $x^{2n-1} = x_1' \cdots x_n'$. Since $|x_1'| + \cdots + |x_n'| = |x_1' \cdots x_n'| = |x^{2n-1}| = (2n-1)|x| \geq n|x|$ there exists i, $1 \leq i \leq n$, such that $|x_i'| \geq |x|$. Let y be the prefix of length $|x|$ of x_i', let $x_i' = yz$ where $z \in A^*$, and let $u,v \in A^*$ be such that $y = uv$ and $x = vu$. Now, if $x_i = uxvz$ and $x_j = x_j'$ for $j = 1, \ldots, i-1, i+1, \ldots, n$, then $x_1 \cdots x_n = x^{2n}$ and $x_j' \underset{1}{\sim} x_j$ for $j = 1, \ldots, n$.

Thus $x^{2n} \overset{(n)}{\underset{1}{\sim}} x^{2n-1}$ for all $x \in A^*$. But $\underset{2n-1}{\sim}$ is, by definition, the smallest congruence satisfying this property. Hence $x \underset{2n-1}{\sim} y$ implies $x \overset{(n)}{\underset{1}{\sim}} y$ for all $x,y \in A^*$ and thus $N_1^n \subseteq N_{2n-1}$. Since N_{2n-1} is a Boolean algebra $N_1^n\mathbf{B} \subseteq N_{2n-1}$.

Proposition 6.6 For $n \geq 1$, $N_1^n \not\subseteq N_{2n-2}$.

Proof: Let $A = \{a_1, \ldots, a_n\}$, let $x = (a_1 \cdots a_n)^{2n-2}$, and let $y = (a_1 \cdots a_n)^{2n-1}$. Clearly $x \underset{2n-2}{\sim} y$. Consider the decomposition $y = y_1 \cdots y_n$ where $y_1 = a_1 \cdots a_{n-1}a_na_1 \cdots a_{n-1}$, $y_n = a_2 \cdots a_na_1a_2 \cdots a_n$, and $y_i = a_{n+2-i} \cdots a_na_1 \cdots a_{n-i}a_{n+1-i}a_{n+2-i} \cdots a_na_1 \cdots a_{n-i}$ for $i = 2, \ldots, n-1$. From Lemma 6.3 it is clear that y_i is the unique minimal element of $[y_i]_{\underset{1}{\sim}}$. Since $|x| < |y|$ there do not exist $x_1, \ldots, x_n \in A^*$ such that $x = x_1 \cdots x_n$ and $x_i \underset{1}{\sim} y_i$ for $i = 1, \ldots, n$. Therefore $x \overset{(n)}{\underset{1}{\not\sim}} y$ and $N_1^n \not\subseteq N_{2n-2}$.

We now look at the relationship between the noncounting languages and the G-trivial languages.

Proposition 6.7 A monoid M is idempotent if and only if $f\mathrm{M}_f f = f$ for all $f \in \mathrm{M}$.

Proof: Clearly, if $f\mathrm{M}_f f = f$ for all $f \in \mathrm{M}$ then M is idempotent since for any $f \in \mathrm{M}$, $1 \in \mathrm{M}_f$ and thus $f^2 = f1f = f$.

Now suppose M is idempotent, $f \in \mathrm{M}$, and $g \in \mathrm{M}_f$. Then $g \in \mathrm{P}_f^n$ for some $n \geqslant 0$. The proof proceeds by induction on n. The case $n = 0$ is trivial since $f = f^2 = f1f$ in an idempotent monoid.

Let $g \in \mathrm{P}_f$. Then $f = hgk$ for some $h,k \in \mathrm{M}$ so that

$$\begin{aligned} f = hgk &= h(gk) \\ &= h(gk)(gk) = (hgk)gk \\ &= (f)gk = (fg)k \qquad \text{(note that } f = fgk) \\ &= (fg)(fg)k = (fg)(fgk) \\ &= fg(f) = fgf. \end{aligned}$$

Assume now that the result is true for n, where $n \geqslant 1$, and suppose $g \in \mathrm{P}_f^{n+1}$. Then $g = g'g''$, where $g' \in \mathrm{P}_f^n$ and $g'' \in \mathrm{P}_f$. From the induction hypothesis, $f = fg'f$ and $f = fg''f$; hence

$$\begin{aligned} f = fg'f &= (f)g'f \\ &= (fg''f)g'f = f(g''fg')f \\ &= f(g''fg')(g''fg')f = (fg''f)g'g''(fg''f) \\ &= (f)g'g''(f) = fg'g''f = fgf. \end{aligned}$$

By induction it follows that $f = fgf$ for all $g \in \mathrm{M}_f$.

Clearly a language is in N_1 if and only if its syntactic monoid is idempotent. From the above proposition and Theorem 3.5 it follows that every idempotent monoid is G-trivial. Thus every $\frac{}{1}$ language has a G-trivial syntactic monoid.

Note that idempotent monoids are not necessarily R-trivial or L-trivial. Consider M, the free idempotent monoid on the two generators $\{a,b\}$. It is the transformation monoid of the automaton depicted in Figure 3.

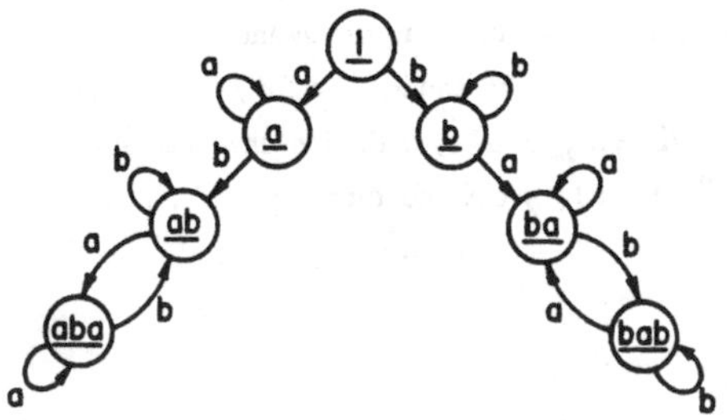

Figure 3

Here $\underline{ab}$M = $\{\underline{ab}, \underline{aba}\}$ = $\underline{aba}$M and M$\underline{ab}$ = $\{\underline{ab}, \underline{bab}\}$ = M$\underline{bab}$, but $\underline{aba} \neq \underline{ab} \neq \underline{bab}$. Thus M is neither R-trivial nor L-trivial.

By Lemma 2.6(c) $u^n \underset{nG}{\approx} u^{n+1}$ for all $u \in A^*$. But $\underset{n}{-}$ is the smallest congruence such that $u^n \underset{n}{-} u^{n+1}$ for all $u \in A^*$; thus $x \underset{n}{-} y$ implies $x \underset{nG}{\approx} y$ for all $x,y \in A^*$. In the special case when $n = 1$ the following interesting relationship holds. It follows from the fact that $\alpha(u) \supseteq \alpha(v)$ implies $u \underset{1}{-} uvu$, which is a direct consequence of Lemma 6.3.

Proposition 6.8 Let $x,y \in A^*$. Then $x \underset{1}{-} y$ if and only if $x \underset{1G}{\approx} y$.

The congruences $\overset{(n)}{\underset{1}{-}}$, for $n \geqslant 2$, do not fare as well.

Proposition 6.9 There does not exist an $n \geqslant 1$ such that $x \underset{nG}{\equiv} y$ implies $x \overset{(2)}{\underset{1}{-}} y$ for all $x,y \in A^*$.

Proof: Let $x = (ab)^n b (ab)^n$ and let $y = (ab)^{2n}$. Since $\alpha((ab)^n) \supseteq \alpha(b)$ and $(ab)^n$ is n-full, it follows that $x \underset{nG}{\equiv} y$.

Now consider the decomposition $x = x_1 x_2$ where $x_1 = (ab)^n$ and $x_2 = b(ab)^n$. Suppose $y = y_1 y_2$ where $x_1 \underset{1}{-} y_1$ Then $y_1 = (ab)^i$ for some i, $1 \leqslant i \leqslant 2n$. However this implies $y_2 = (ab)^{2n-i} \underset{1}{\not-} x_2$. Therefore there does not exist a decomposition $y = y_1 y_2$ such that $x_1 \underset{1}{-} y_1$ and $x_2 \underset{1}{-} y_2$. Thus $x \overset{(2)}{\underset{1}{\not-}} y$.

Corollary 6.10 For $n \geqslant 2$, N_1^n contains languages whose syntactic monoids are not G-trivial.

Acknowledgements

This research was supported by the National Research Council of Canada under a Postgraduate Scholarship and under grant No. A-1617 and by National Science Foundation grant MCS74-07636-A01.

References

[1] Brzozowski, J.A., *Canonical Regular Expressions and Minimal State Graphs for Definite Events,* Mathematical Theory of Automata, New York, 1962, 529-561.
[2] Brzozowski, J.A., *Hierarchies of Aperiodic Languages,* R.A.I.R.O. Information Théorique 10 (1976), 35-49.
[3] Brzozowski, J.A., *A Generalization of Finiteness,* Semigroup Forum 13 (1977), 239-251.
[4] Brzozowski, J.A., Culik, K., and Gabrielian, A., *Classification of Noncounting Events,* J. Comput. System Sci. 5 (1971), 41-53.
[5] Brzozowski, J.A., and Fich, F.E., *Languages of R-Trivial Monoids,* to appear in J. Comput. System Sci.
[6] Brzozowski, J.A. and Knast, R., *The Dot-Depth Hierarchy of Star-Free Languages is Infinite,* J. Comput. System Sci. 16 (1978), 37-55.
[7] Brzozowski, J.A., and Simon, I., *Characterizations of Locally Testable Events,* Discrete Mathematics 4 (1973), 243-271.
[8] Cohen, R.S., and Brzozowski, J.A., *Dot Depth of Star-Free Events,* J. Comput. System Sci. 5 (1971), 1-16.
[9] Eilenberg, S., *Automata, Languages, and Machines,* Volume B, Academic Press, New York, 1976.
[10] Fich, F.E., *Languages of R-Trivial and Related Monoids,* M.Math. thesis, Department of Computer Science, University of Waterloo, Waterloo, Ontario, Canada, 1979.
[11] Ginzburg, A., *About Some Properties of Definite, Reverse-Definite, and Related Automata,* IEEE Trans. Electronic Computers EC-15 (1966), 806-810.

[12] Green, J.A., and Rees, D., *On Semigroups in which $x^r = x$,* Proc. Cambridge Philos. Soc. 48 (1952), 35-40.
[13] Kleene, S.C., *Representation of Events in Nerve Nets and Finite Automata,* in Automata Studies, Annals of Mathematics Studies 34, C.E.Shannon and J.McCarthy (eds.), Princeton University Press, Princeton, N.J., 1956, 3-40.
[14] McNaughton, R., and Papert, S., *Counter-Free Automata,* The M.I.T. Press, Cambridge, Mass., 1971.
[15] Meyer, A.R., *A Note on Star-Free Events,* J. ACM 16 (1969), 220-225.
[16] Papert, S. and McNaughton, R., *On Topological Events,* in Theory of Automata, University of Michigan Engineering Summer Conference, Ann Arbor, Mich., 1966.
[17] Perles, M., Rabin, M.O., and Shamir, E., *The Theory of Definite Automata,* IEEE Trans. on Electronic Computers EC-12 (1963), 233-243.
[18] Perrin, D., *Sur Certains Semigroups Syntaxiques,* Séminaires de P.I.R.I.A. Logiques et Automates, 1971, 169-177.
[19] Schützenberger, M.P., *On Finite Monoids Having Only Trivial Subgroups,* Information and Control 8 (1965), 190-194.
[20] Simon, I., *Hierarchies of Events with Dot-Depth One,* Ph.D. thesis, Department of Computer Science, University of Waterloo, Waterloo, Ontario, Canada, 1972.
[21] Simon, I., *Piecewise Testable Events,* in Automata Theory and Formal Languages, 2nd GI Conference, H. Brakhage (ed.), Lecture Notes in Computer Science 33, Springer-Verlag, Berlin, 1975, 214-222.
[22] Steinby, M., *On Definite Automata and Related Systems,* Ann. Acad. Sci. Fenn. Ser. AI 444, 1969.
[23] Zalcstein, Y., *Locally Testable Languages,* J. Comput. System Sci. 6 (1972), 151-167.

Partitioned LL(k) Grammars.

Dietmar Friede
Fachbereich Informatik der Universität Hamburg
Schlüterstr. 70
D 2 Hamburg 13
Federal Republic of Germany

1. Introduction.

This paper reports on part of a study on extending the class of languages parsable by the method of recursive descent (without backup) to all deterministic context-free languages. This extension of a well known and simple method of syntactic analysis can be rather easily applied for compiler construction. The aim is to give a grammatical characterization of all deterministic context-free languages by only a slight variation of LL(k) grammars, namely by defining partitioned LL(k) grammars (in short PLL(k) grammars). This work was inspired by a paper on transition diagrams [Lomet73] and a paper on strict deterministic grammars [HarrisonHavel73].

The definition of PLL(k) grammars is based on strict deterministic grammars [HarrisonHavel73] and LL(k) grammars [RosenkrantzStearns69], which characterize only subsets of the deterministic context-free languages. As shown by Harrison and Havel the set of strict deterministic context-free languages are equal to the set of prefix-free deterministic context-free languages. But in general it is difficult to construct a strict deterministic grammar for an arbitrary prefix-free deterministic context-free language. To generate deterministic context-free languages which are not prefix-free one must extend the strict deterministic grammars by a lookahead, like that of LL(k) and LR(k) grammars. The main property of LL(k) grammars is the exact knowledge (with k-lookahead) of the rule by which the leftmost nonterminal in a leftderivation of a given word is to be expanded.

The PLL(k) grammars are a synthesis of both classes of grammars. First of all, when producing the left derivation of a given word with a PLL(k) grammar, a class of nonterminals is determined, which contains the leftmost nonterminal actually used in the derivation. The class is the object which is expanded in going top-down with k-lookahead. When reaching a terminal symbol, that member of the class which builds up the correct derivation tree is fixed. The equivalence class of the leftmost nonterminal defines a set of rules to continue the derivation.

The fundamental idea of partitioning the vocabulary of a grammar aims to restrict to a minimum the "sub-grammar" with which the derivation of a given word has to continue.

A similar, but more complicated way is given by [Lomet74] and [Pittl77] by the "left local precedence grammars". The advantage of PLL(k) grammars is that the analyser is only a set of finite automata and not a set of precedence analysers. The construction of transition diagrams as parsers for PLL(k) grammars is discussed in [Friede78,79].

The grammars are always assumed to be reduced. The empty word is denoted by e. The notations and definitions not given in this paper are that of Aho and Ullman [AhoUllmanI72,II73].

2. PLL(k) grammars

Definition 1 :

A context-free grammar $G = (N,T,R,S)$ (N nonterminals, T terminals, R rules, S startsymbol in N, all sets finite and nonempty, N and T disjoint, $V := N \cup T$) is a partitioned LL(k) grammar (in short PLL(k) grammar) iff there is an equivalence relation $\equiv$ on V such that:

1. $T \in V/\equiv$, i.e. T is an equivalence class under $\equiv$.
2. For any $A,B \in N$ and any $a,b,c \in V^*$ with $A \to ab$, $B \to ac$, $A \equiv B$ holds:
   If $first_k(b\ follow_k(A)) \cap first_k(c\ follow_k(B)) \neq \emptyset$
   then either
   $b \neq e$ and $c \neq e$ and ${}^{(1)}b \equiv {}^{(1)}c$
   or $b = c = e$ and $A = B$.

I.e., for any two rules $A \to u$, $B \to v$ such that $A \equiv B$ and for any possible factorisations $u = ab$ and $v = ac$ the condition given in 2. must hold.

Notation: ${}^{(n)}w$ is the prefix of w with the length $\min(lg(w),n)$.

Let $a \in V^*$:

$first_k(a) := \{{}^{(k)}w \in T^*: a \Rightarrow^* w\}$

$follow_k(a) := \{w \in first_k(c): S \Rightarrow^* bac,\ b,c \in V^*\}$

Let $X \subseteq V^*$:

$$first_k(X) := \bigcup_{a \in X} first_k(a)$$

Example: The rules of the grammar G_1 are

$S \to A \mid B \mid e$

$A \to aAb \mid ab$

$B \to aBc \mid ac$

G_1 is a PLL(1) grammar. The classes of the equivalence relation are $\{a,b,c\},\{S\},\{A,B\}$

The language generated by G_1 is $L(G_1) = \{a^nb^n, a^nc^n: n \geq 0\}$.

<u>Definition 2 :</u>

$x,y \in A^*$ are the distinguishing suffixes of $u,v \in A^*$ iff $u = wx$, $v = wy$ and ${}^{(1)}x \not\equiv {}^{(1)}y$ or $x = y = e$.

The following algorithm - similar to that given by [HarrisonHavel73] for strict deterministic grammars - determines for a given k, whether a given context-free grammar is a PLL(k) grammar or not. If G is a PLL(k) grammar the algorithm produces the (minimal strict) partition of V.

<u>Algorithm:</u>

Assume that the productions of G are consecutively numbered, i.e., $R = \{A_i \rightarrow a_i \; : \; 1 \leq i \leq |R|\}$ and all productions are distinct.

Step 1: $V/\underline{\equiv} := \{\{A\} : A \in N\} \cup \{T\}$; $i := 0$;

Step 2: $i := i + 1$; $j := i$; if $i > |R|$ then halt and G is PLL(k);

Step 3: $j := j + 1$; if $j > |R|$ go to step 2;

Step 4: if $A_i \not\equiv A_j$ then go to step 3;

Step 5: Let b,c be the distinguishing suffixes of a_i and a_j;
if $\mathrm{first}_k(b \; \mathrm{follow}_k(A_i)) \cap \mathrm{first}_k(c \; \mathrm{follow}_k(A_j)) = \emptyset$
then go to step 3;

Step 6: if $b = e$ or $c = e$ then go to step 9;

Step 7: if ${}^{(1)}b \underline{\equiv} {}^{(1)}c$ then go to step 3;

Step 8: if ${}^{(1)}b$ and ${}^{(1)}c$ are both in N
then replace the equivalence classes $[{}^{(1)}b]$ and $[{}^{(1)}c]$ in $V/\underline{\equiv}$ by one new equivalence class $[{}^{(1)}b] \cup [{}^{(1)}c]$ and restart the algorithm at step 2, i.e.
$V/\underline{\equiv} := V/\underline{\equiv} - \{[{}^{(1)}b],[{}^{(1)}c]\} \cup \{[{}^{(1)}b] \cup [{}^{(1)}c]\}$;
$i := 0$; go to step 2;

Step 9: Halt. G is not PLL(k);

The flow of control in the algorithm is schematized in the following figure:

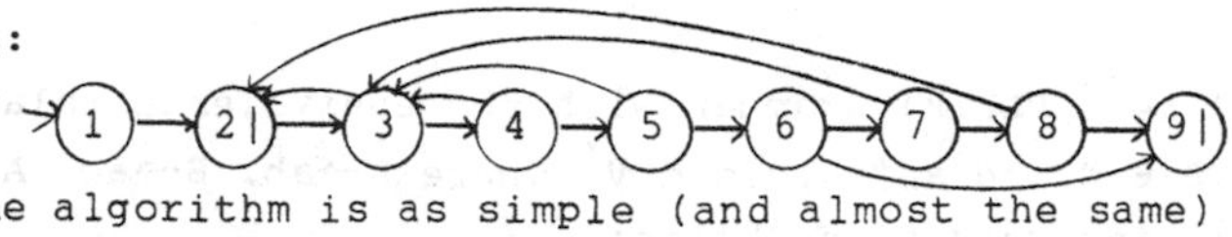

The algorithm is as simple (and almost the same) as that given by Harrison and Havel [HarrisonHavel73] for strict deterministic grammars. By almost the same way as in [HarrisonHavel73] an outline of the proof of its correctness is given:

First let us check that the algorithm always halts. We can see that all closed loops go through step 3. But step 3 always increases the value of j. Only step 2 can decrease this value but it always increases the value of i. Only step 8 can decrease the value of i but it also decreases the cardinality of $V/\underline{\equiv}$. And $\min|V/\underline{\equiv}| = 2$.

For the proof of correctness it is to investigate how a grammar may fail to be PLL(k) for a given k. Under the hypothesis and notation of definition 1 we note that if $A = B$ (in the initial stage of the algorithm) or if $A \equiv B$ (as a result of preceding stages in any subsequent stage) and if $b \neq e \neq c$ and ${}^{(1)}b, {}^{(1)}c \in N$, the definition can always be satisfied by forcing ${}^{(1)}b \equiv {}^{(1)}c$. We do not obtain a failure under these circumstances. But the following three kinds of failures are possible. Assume $A \equiv B$ (forced by preceding stages).

1. $A \rightarrow ab_1$
   $B \rightarrow a$

where $b_1 \neq e$. Taking $b = b_1$ and $c = e$ and $first_k(b\ follow_k(A)) \cap follow_k(B) \neq \emptyset$ we get a contradiction to definition 1. b and c have both to be equal e or both unequal e. The algorithm rejects a grammar with rules of this kind in step 6.

2. $A \rightarrow a$
   $B \rightarrow a$

where $A \neq B$ and $follow_k(A) \cap follow_k(B) \neq \emptyset$. The definition requires $A = B$. The algorithm halts in the same way as in the above case.

3. $A \rightarrow aCb_1$
   $B \rightarrow axc_1$

where $C \in N$, $x \in T$ and $b = Cb_1$ and $c = xc_1$ where $first_k(b\ follow_k(A)) \cap first_k(c\ follow_k(B)) \neq \emptyset$.
In this case the definition of a PLL(k) grammar requires that $x \equiv C$ which is a contradiction to the definition. A grammar with rules of this type will be refused in step 9 because none of the conditions in step 5,6,7 and 8 are fulfilled.

These are all the possible ways for a grammar to fail to be a PLL(k) grammar. If no failure occurs, G is PLL(k) and the algorithm halts in step 2.

Corollary 1 :

Let $G = (N,T,R,S)$ be a PLL(k) grammar with the equivalence relation $\equiv$ on V. Then for any $A,B \in N$ and any $a,b,c \in V^*$ where $A \rightarrow ab$, $B \rightarrow ac$, $A \equiv B$, one of the three following conditions holds:

- $b = c = e$ and ($A = B$ or $follow_k(A) \cap follow_k(B) = \emptyset$)
- $b \neq e$ and $c \neq e$ and (${}^{(1)}b \equiv {}^{(1)}c$ or $first_k(b\ follow_k(A)) \cap first_k(c\ follow_k(B)) = \emptyset$)
- (either $b = e$ and $c \neq e$ or $b \neq e$ and $c = e$) and $first_k(b\ follow_k(A)) \cap first_k(c\ follow_k(B)) = \emptyset$

Proof: Follows directly from the definition of a PLL(k) grammar.

In the following the sign $\Rightarrow$ for derivation always means left derivation.

Theorem 2 :

Let $G = (N,T,R,S)$ be a PLL(k) grammar with the equivalence relation $\equiv$ on V. Then for any $A,B \in N$, any $a,b,c \in V^*$ and any $n > 0$ if $A \Rightarrow^n ab$, $B \Rightarrow^n ac$, $A \equiv B$ and $first_k(b\ follow_k(A)) \cap first_k(c\ follow_k(B)) \neq \emptyset$

then either $b \neq e$ and $c \neq e$ and ${}^{(1)}b \equiv {}^{(1)}c$,

or $b = c = e$ and $A = B$.

Proof: By induction on n.

For $n = 1$ the theorem follows from definition 1.

Assume the assertion is true for a given $n \geq 1$ and consider the case $n + 1$. We can write

$$A \Rightarrow^n wCb_1 \Rightarrow wb_2b_1 = ab$$

and $$B \Rightarrow^n w_1Dc_1 \Rightarrow w_1c_2c_1 = ac$$

for some $C,D \in N$, $w,w_1 \in T^*$, $b_1,b_2,c_1,c_2 \in V^*$ and let, whithout loss of generality, $lg(w) \leq lg(w_1)$.

Case 1.: $0 \leq lg(a) < lg(w)$

therefore $$A \Rightarrow^n aw'Cb_1 \Rightarrow aw'b_2b_1 = ab$$

and $$B \Rightarrow^n aw_1'Dc_1 \Rightarrow aw_1'c_2c_1 = w_1c_2c_1 = ac$$

where $w = aw'$ and $w_1 = aw_1'$.

We have $w' \neq e \neq w_1'$ and ${}^{(1)}b$ and ${}^{(1)}c \in T$, thus ${}^{(1)}b \equiv {}^{(1)}c$.

Consideration:

Let $lg(a) \geq lg(w)$ and $w \neq w_1$, thus $w_1 = ww_1'$ and

$$A \Rightarrow^n wCb_1 \Rightarrow wb_2b_1 = ab$$

and $$B \Rightarrow^n ww_1'Dc_1 \Rightarrow w_1c_2c_1 = ac\ .$$

From the induction hypothesis follows:

$first_k(Cb_1\ follow_k(A)) \cap first_k(w_1'Dc_1\ follow_k(B)) = \emptyset$,

now we have $first_k(b\ follow_k(A)) \cap first_k(c\ follow_k(B)) = \emptyset$.

In the following two cases we only have to inspect the case $w = w_1$. Further we assume for both cases without loss of generality $lg(c_2) \geq lg(b_2)$.

Case 2.: $lg(w) \leq lg(a) < lg(wb_2)$

thus $$A \Rightarrow^n wCb_1 \Rightarrow wd_1d_2b_1 = ad_2b_1 = ab$$

and $$B \Rightarrow^n wDc_1 \Rightarrow wd_1d_3c_1 = ad_3c_1 = ac$$

where $w_1 = ww_1'$ and $b_2 = d_1d_2$ and $c_2 = d_1d_3$.

The induction hypothesis holds for $a' = w$, $b' = Cb_1$ and $c' = Dc_1$.

If $first_k(b'\ follow_k(A)) \cap first_k(c'\ follow_k(B)) = \emptyset$ then $first_k(b\ follow_k(A) \cap first_k(c\ follow_k(B)) = \emptyset$.

Otherwise we have $C \equiv D$, and we apply definition 1 to $C \rightarrow d_1d_2$ and $B \rightarrow d_1d_3$

Case 3.: $lg(wb_2) \leq lg(a) \leq lg(wb_2b_1)$

thus $$A \Rightarrow^n wCb_1 \Rightarrow wb_2b_1'b_1'' = ab_1'' = ab$$

and $$B \Rightarrow^n wDc_1 \Rightarrow wb_2c_2'c_1 = ac$$

where $b_1 = b_1' b_1''$ and $c_2 = b_2 c_2'$.

Assume $first_k(Cb_1\ follow_k(A)) \cap first_k(Dc_1\ follow_k(B)) \neq \emptyset$ - otherwise the proof is finished. From the induction hypothesis follows $C \equiv D$.

1. $c_2 \neq b_2$ and $C \rightarrow b_2$ and $D \rightarrow b_2c'$ with $c' \neq e$. Then by corollary 1 we get $follow_k(C) \cap first_k(c'\ follow_k(D)) = \emptyset$ and therefore $first_k(b\ follow_k(A)) \cap first_k(c\ follow_k(B)) = \emptyset$.
2. $c_2 = b_2$
   If $C \neq D$ then by corollary 1 $follow_k(C) \cap follow_k(D) = \emptyset$.
   If $C = D$ then for $a' = wCb_1'$ and $b' = b$ and $c' = c$,
   we use the induction hypothesis and after replacing the nonterminal C by b_1 (determined by the rule $C \rightarrow b_1$)
   the proof is completed.

Corollary 3 :

Let $G = (N,T,R,S)$ be a PLL(k) grammar with an equivalence relation $\equiv$ on V. Then for any $A,B \in N$, any $a,b,c \in V^*$ and any $n > 0$ if $A \Rightarrow^n ab$, $B \Rightarrow^n ac$, $A \equiv B$ one of the three following conditions holds:

- $b = c = e$ and ($A = B$ or $follow_k(A) \cap follow_k(B) = \emptyset$)
- $b \neq e$ and $c \neq e$ and ($^{(1)}b \equiv {}^{(1)}c$ or $first_k(b\ follow_k(A)) \cap first_k(c\ follow_k(B)) = \emptyset$)
- (either $b = e$ and $c \neq e$ or $b \neq e$ and $c = e$) and $first_k(b\ follow_k(A)) \cap first_k(c\ follow_k(B)) = \emptyset$

Theorem 4 :

Let $G = (N,T,R,S)$ be a PLL(k) grammar. If $A \Rightarrow^+ e$, $A \equiv B$, $A \neq B$, $A,B \in N$, then $first_k(B\ follow_k(B)) \cap follow_k(A) = \emptyset$.

Proof: Inspect all words $w \in T^*$ derivable from B:

Let $A \Rightarrow^n e$ and $B \Rightarrow^{n'} w$ where $n,n' \geq 1$.

If $n \leq n'$ then $A \Rightarrow^n e$ and $B \Rightarrow^n a \Rightarrow^* w$ and also by theorem 2 (or 3) $first_k(a\ follow_k(B)) \cap follow_k(A) = \emptyset$.

If $n > n'$ we have $A \Rightarrow^{n'} a' \Rightarrow^+ e$ and $B \Rightarrow^{n'} w$. Since $a' \in N$ we have $^{(1)}a' \not\equiv {}^{(1)}w$ therefore $first_k(a'\ follow_k(A)) \cap first_k(w\ follow_k(B)) = \emptyset$.

For any word $w \in T^*$ derivable from B one of these two cases holds and this completes the proof.

Corollary 5 :

Let $G = (N,T,R,S)$ be a PLL(k) grammar if $A \Rightarrow^+ e$, $B \Rightarrow^+ e$, $A \equiv B$, $A \neq B$, $A,B \in N$, then $follow_k(A) \cap follow_k(B) = \emptyset$.

Theorem 6 :

Let $G = (N,T,R,S)$ be a PLL(k) grammar if $A \Rightarrow^+ e$, $A \Rightarrow^+ w$, $w \in T^+$, then $first_k((first_k(A) - \{e\})\ follow_k(A)) \cap follow_k(A) = \emptyset$.

Proof: Inspect all words $w \in T^+$ derivable from $A \in N$.

$A \Rightarrow^n e$ and $A \Rightarrow^{n'} w \neq e$ and $n,n' \geq 1$.

If $n \leq n'$ we get $A \Rightarrow^n e$ and $A \Rightarrow^n a \Rightarrow^* w$, by theorem 2 we have $follow_k(A) \cap first_k(a\ follow_k(A)) = \emptyset$.
If $n > n'$ then $A \Rightarrow^{n'} a \Rightarrow^+ e$ and $A \Rightarrow^{n'} w$, must always be ${}^{(1)}w \not\equiv {}^{(1)}a$, since $a \in N^+$. Otherwise we would not derive e from the word a by one or more step(s). Now we can conclude that
$first_k(a\ follow_k(A)) \cap first_k(w\ follow_k(A)) = \emptyset$.
Since this holds for any word $w \neq e$ derivable from A this completes the proof.

Theorem 7 :

Let G be a PLL(k) grammar. Then for any $A,B \in N$ and $a \in V^*$,

$$A \Rightarrow^+ Ba \quad \text{implies} \quad A \not\equiv B.$$

Proof: Let $A \Rightarrow^+ Ba$ for some $A,B \in N$ and $a \in V^*$.
Then there is a left derivation
$A \Rightarrow a_1 \Rightarrow^* a_i = Ba \Rightarrow a_{i+1} \Rightarrow^* a_n = w$
$a_i \in V^*$, $i \geq 1$, $w \in T^*$ (G is supposed to be reduced).
Let $A \rightarrow a'b = a_1$ with $b \Rightarrow^* Ba$, ${}^{(1)}b \Rightarrow^* Ba''$, $a',a'' \in V^*$, $a' \Rightarrow^* e$, $B \rightarrow d$ and $a_{i+1} = da$.
For any j with $1 \leq j < n$ holds
$\emptyset \neq first_k(a_{j+1}\ follow_k(A)) \subseteq first_k(a_j\ follow_k(A))$
and $first_k(a_j\ follow_k(A)) \subseteq first_k(a_1\ follow_k(A))$
therefore $first_k(Ba\ follow_k(A)) \subseteq first_k(a'b\ follow_k(A))$.
As $first_k(Ba\ follow_k(A)) \subseteq first_k(B\ follow_k(B))$
and $first_k(a_{j+1}\ follow_k(A)) \subseteq first_k(Ba\ follow_k(A))$
we get $first_k(d\ follow_k(B)) \cap first_k(a_1\ follow_k(A)) \neq \emptyset$
further holds $first_k(b\ follow_k(A)) = first_k(a_1\ follow_k(A))$.
Assume for the sake of contradiction $A \equiv B$.
Let $a' = A_1 \ldots A_m$ with $m \geq 0$ and $A_i \Rightarrow^+ e$, $A_i \in V$.
From corollary 5 and the defintion of PLL(k) grammars follows if $A_1 \neq e$ that ${}^{(1)}d = A_1$ and if $A_2 \neq e$ and $d = A_1d'$ that ${}^{(1)}d' = A_2$ and so on for every $A_i \neq e$. Therefore the string d starts with a' :
$d = a'c$ and $a_{i+1} = a'ca$.
From definition 1 follows ${}^{(1)}b \equiv {}^{(1)}c$. By induction we can continue with ${}^{(1)}b \Rightarrow^j ca'_{i+1}$. We never reach an n with $a_n = w \in T^*$. It is always ${}^{(1)}a_i \in N$ and ${}^{(1)}a_i \equiv {}^{(1)}a_{i+j}$, contracticting the reducedness of G.

Corollary 8 :

No PLL(k) grammar is left recursive (i.e., for no $A \in N$ and $a \in V^*$, $A \Rightarrow^+ Aa$).

Theorem 9 :

For any PLL(k) grammar G there is an e-free PLL(k) grammar G' where $L(G) - \{e\} = L(G')$.
Proof: We use the well known algorithm which constructs for any context-

free grammar G an e-free context-free grammar G′ where L(G′) = L(G) - {e}.

<u>Algorithm</u> (similar to [AhoUllmanI72] P.148 f)

Input: A context-free grammar G = (N,T,R,S).

Output: The equivalent e-free, context-free grammar G′ = (N′,T,R′,S).

Step 1: N_e := {A ∈ N: $A \Rightarrow_G^+ e$}; N_{Te} := {A ∈ N_e: $A \Rightarrow_G^+ w$, w ∈ T^+};

Step 2: Let R′ be the set of productions constructed as follows:

If $A \rightarrow a_0B_1a_1B_2 \ldots B_na_n \in R$ and $B_i \in N_e$ $(1 \le i \le n)$
and $a_j \in (V - N_e)^*$ $(0 \le j \le n)$,
then add to R′ all rules of the form $A \rightarrow a_0X_1 \ldots X_na_n$
where X_i is either e or B_i if $B_i \in N_{Te}$, without adding
$A \rightarrow e$ to R′.

Step 3: N′ := {A ∈ N: A->a is in R′}

Step 4: G′ = (N′,T,R′,S)

It is well known that the algorithm yields an equivalent e-free context-free grammar for an arbitrary context-free grammar. We have to show that it produces an equivalent e-free PLL(k) grammar for a given PLL(k) grammar.

Let be G a PLL(k) grammar, and let be $A \rightarrow aa_{i-1}B_ia_ib \in R$, as given in the algorithm where $1 \le i \le n$, $a,b \in V^*$, $B_i \in N_e$, $a_{i-1}, a_i \in (V-N_e)^*$.
We add to R′ the rules $A \rightarrow a'a_{i-1}a_ib'$, where $a',b' \in V^*$ are constructed by the algorithm from a and b. If $B_i \in N_{Te}$ we add to R′ the rules $A \rightarrow a'a_{i-1}B_ia_ib'$, too. We get by theorem 6: if there is a $w \in T^+$ with $B_i \Rightarrow_G^+ w$ and $B_i \Rightarrow_G^+ e$, then
$first_k^G((first_k^G(B_i) - \{e\})\ follow_k^G(B_i)) \cap follow_k^G(B_i) = \emptyset$.
Then for $B_i \in G'$, we get
$first_k^{G'}(B_i\ follow_k^{G'}(B_i)) \cap follow_k^{G'}(B_i) = \emptyset$.
It is easy to see that $first_k^G(a_ib\ follow_k^G(A)) \subseteq follow_k^G(B_i)$
and then also $first_k^G(a_ib'\ follow_k^G(A)) \cap first_k^G(B_ia_ib'\ follow_k^G(A)) = \emptyset$.
Therefore both rules are possible in the same PLL(k) grammar.
Assume, there is another rule in R′ $A' \rightarrow a'a_{i-1}Bb''$ and $A' \equiv A$.
Let $a' \in V^*$ with $a' = a_1 \ldots a_j \ldots a_n$, the a_j in V or in T, $n \ge 0$.
In G and therefore in G′ then either

- for some $j \le n$ $first_k(a_j \ldots a_na_{i-1}Bb''follow_k(A'))$
 $\cap\ first_k(a_j \ldots a_na_{i-1}B_ib''\ follow_k(A')) = \emptyset$.
- or $first_k(a_{i-1}Bb''\ follow_k(A')) \cap first_k(a_{i-1}B_ib'\ follow_k(A')) = \emptyset$
- or $first_k(Bb''\ follow_k(A)) \cap first_k(B_ib''\ follow_k(A)) = \emptyset$
- or at least $a'a_{i-1} = aa_{i-1}$ and therefore a′ = a or a′ is - by the algorithm - constructed from a. Otherwise G would be no PLL(k) grammar.

Hence either $first_k(Bb''\ follow_k(A')) \subseteq follow_k(B_i)$ or $B \equiv B_i$.
If $B = B_i$, the proof is finished, otherwise use theorem 4.

Definition 3 :

L is a PLL(k) language, iff there is a PLL(k) grammar G with L(G) = L.

G is a PLL grammar, iff there is a $k \geq 0$, such that G is a PLL(k) grammar.

L is a PLL language, iff there is a PLL grammar G with L(G) = L.

Definition 4 :

[HarrisonHavel73]

A context-free grammar G = (N,T,R,S) is a strict deterministic grammar iff there is an equivalence relation $\equiv$ on V with:

1. $T \in V/\equiv$, i.e. T is equivalence class under $\equiv$.
2. For any $A,B \in N$ and any $a,b,c \in V^*$, if $A \to ab$, $B \to ac$, $A \equiv B$ then either

   $b \neq e$ and $c \neq e$ and ${}^{(1)}b \equiv {}^{(1)}c$

   or $b = c = e$ and $A = B$.

Corollary 10 :

G is PLL(0) grammar, iff G is strict deterministic context-free grammar. The PLL(0) languages are the strict deterministic context-free languages.

Theorem 11 :

Let G be a e-free PLL(0) grammar (strict deterministic grammar) and:

$G = (N, T \cup \{\$\}, R, S)$, $V = N \cup T$, $\$ \notin V$,

$R \subseteq N \times (V^* \cup V^*\{\$\})$, $L(G) \subseteq T^*\{\$\}$.

Let $G' = (N,T,R',S)$ and $R' := R_1 \cup R_2$, where

$R_1 := \{A \to a : (A,a) \in R \text{ and } a \in V^*\}$ and

$R_2 := \{A \to a : (A,a\$) \in R \text{ and } a \in V^*\}$

G′ is a PLL(1) grammar with $L(G')\{\$\} = L(G)$.

Proof: It is easy to see that the language generated by G′ is L(G) without the "endmark" \$, therefore $L(G')\{\$\} = L(G)$.

Let be $A \to ab$ and $B \to ac$ rules in G where $A \equiv B$ and $A \neq B$.

If b and c are both unequal to \$, they fulfill the conditions of a PLL(1) grammar, since they fulfill the conditions of a PLL(0) grammar.

Let (without loss of generality) $b = \$$.

Then $\$ \equiv {}^{(1)}c$ and $c \neq e$. Further we get ${}^{(1)}c \in T$ and $c \neq \$$.

By construction of G we have $\text{follow}^G(\$) = \{e\}$ and therefore always $\text{follow}^{G'}(A) = \text{follow}^G(A) = \{e\}$.

But $\text{first}^{G'}(c) = \{{}^{(1)}c\}$ and ${}^{(1)}c \neq e$.

We conclude that $\text{first}^{G'}(b\ \text{follow}^{G'}(A)) \cap \text{first}^{G'}(c\ \text{follow}^{G'}(B)) = \emptyset$.

Both rules fulfill the conditions of a PLL(1) grammar.

<u>Theorem 12 :</u>

For any deterministic context-free language L there is a PLL(1) grammar G with L = L(G).

Proof: For any deterministic context-free language L there is an e-free strict deterministic grammar G with L(G) = L{$} [HarrisonHavel74], where $ is not in the alphabet of L(G). With the preceding theorem 11 we get the assertion.

3. Summary

For PLL(k) grammars we have:

- For any PLL(k) grammar there is an e-free PLL(k) grammar generating the same language (without e).
- The given definition of PLL(k) grammars refers to rules and not to a generally infinite set of derivations.
- It is easy to test whether a grammar is PLL(k) or not - for a given k.
- The PLL(0) grammars are exactly the strict deterministic grammars.

Especially for PLL(1) grammars we have:

- They include the LL(1) grammars.
- They characterize the deterministic context-free languages.

Elsewhere [Friede78] it is shown:

- The PLL(k) languages form no proper hierarchy, i.e. the class of PLL(k) languages is equal to the class of PLL(1) languages (for k > 0);. But the PLL(0) languages are a proper subset of the PLL(1) languages.
- Parsing PLL(k) grammars (at least for k = 0 and 1) is very easy by a slightly extended recursive descent method (without backup).

There are some open questions (among others):

1. What are the relations between PLL(k) grammars and LR(k) grammars (and SLR(k) and LALR(k) grammars), especially for k = 1 ?
   Geller and Harrison in [GellerHarrison73] studied the relations between strict deterministic and LR(0) grammars.
2. How big and how quick are PLL-parsers? Especially in comparison to LR-parsing methods?

4. Acknowledgments

I am very grateful to W. Brauer, M. Jantzen and F. Schwenkel who supervised my diploma thesis. This paper is based on the second chapter of this thesis [Friede78]. I also want to thank David Cram, Gerd Friesland, Manfred Kudlek, Manuel Mall, Angelika Rudolph and Ingrid Westphal for their hints, remarks and help.

5. References

[AhoUllmanI72]: Aho, A.V., Ullman, J.D., The Theory of Parsing, Translation, and Compiling, Vol. 1: Parsing, Prentice Hall, Englewood Cliffs, New York, 1972.

[AhoUllmanII73]: Aho, A.V., Ullman, J.D., The Theory of Parsing, Translation, and Compiling, Vol. 2: Compiling, Prentice Hall, Englewood Cliffs, New York, 1973.

[Friede78]: Friede, D., Über determistisch kontextfreie Sprachen und rekursiven Abstieg, Bericht Nr. 49 des Fachbereichs Informatik der Universität Hamburg, 1978.

[Friede79]: Friede,D., Transition Diagrams and Strict Deterministic Grammars, Lecture Notes in Computer Science 67: Theoretical Computer Science 4th GI Conference, 1979.

[GellerHarrison73]: Geller, M.M, Harrison, M.A., Strict Deterministic versus LR(0) Parsing, Conference Record of ACM Symposium on Principles of Programming Languages, 1973.

[HarrisonHavel73]: Harrison, M.A., Havel, I.M., Strict Deterministic Grammars, Journal of Computer and System Sciences, Vol. 7, Nr. 3, 1973.

[HarrisonHavel74]: Harrison, M.A., Havel, I.M., On the Parsing of Deterministic Languages, Journal of the ACM, Vol.21 Nr.4, 1974.

[Lomet73]: Lomet, D.B., A Formalisation of Transition Diagram Systems, Journal of the ACM, Vol. 20 Nr 2, 1973.

[Lomet74]: Lomet, D.B., Automatic generation of multiple exit parsing subroutines. Proc. of the 2nd Colloquium on Automata , Languages and Programming. Springer-Verlag, Lecture Notes in Computer Science 14, New York, 1974, 214-231.

[Pittl77]: Pittl, Jan, Exponential Optimization for the LLP(k) Parsing Method, Lecture Notes in Computer Science 53: Mathematical Foundations of Computer Science, 1977.

[RosenkrantzStearns69]: Rosenkrantz, D.J., Stearns, R.E., Properties of Deterministic Top-Down Grammars, ACM Symposium, Marina del Rey 1969.

RECURSION SCHEMES AND GENERALIZED INTERPRETATIONS*

(Extended Abstract)

Jean H. Gallier
Department of Computer and Information Science
University of Pennsylvania
Philadelphia, PA 19104 U.S.A.

Abstract

This paper investigates some of the underlying axioms allowing the fixpoint-semantics approach to hold for tree-like recursion schemes. The notions of scheme and interpretation are generalized. The axioms satisfied by "algebraic theories" are shown to be adequate for the definition of the notion of an interpretation. It is also shown that in order to provide the semantics of arbitrary finite recursion schemes, rational algebraic theories are insufficient and it is necessary to introduce a new class of "recursion-closed" algebraic theories. Finally, free recursion-closed algebraic theories are shown to exist.

1. Introduction

The object of this paper is to study the fixpoint-semantics of recursion schemes in the sense of Courcelle and Nivat [8] (without a reserved symbol if then else) under a generalized notion of interpretation (algebraic theories [10,15,26,27]). The main contribution of this paper is to pinpoint some of the properties (axioms) that an interpretation should satisfy in order for the fixpoint-semantics approach to go through. Two such axioms (satisfied by functions) are:

(1) The operations assigned by an interpretation can be composed;

(2) they can be grouped to form vectors of operations (tupling).

We show that the axioms satisfied by an (ordered) algebraic theory are adequate.

An algebraic theory is a domain of objects (arrows) which can be thought of as functions, together with two operations, a composition operation and a "tupling" operation and satisfying some simple axioms (associativity, existence of identities, etc.).

Our investigations proceed in three steps.

(1) By extending slightly the definition of a recursion scheme, we define an operation of substitution of schemes which confers an interesting structure on the class of schemes.

(2) Exploiting a suggestion made in Goguen, Thatcher, Wagner and Wright [15], we define an extended interpretation I as a function $I : \Sigma \to T$ from the alphabet Σ from which the schemes are constructed to an ordered algebraic theory T. Then, with every scheme α is associated a functional α_I which is shown to be monotonic and the mapping which assigns the functional α_I to the scheme α is a homomorphism of algebraic theories, substitution of schemes corresponding to the composition of functionals.

(3) We investigate the minimal requirements on an interpretation I for the functional α_I associated with a scheme α to have a least fixpoint. We show that the "rational algebraic theories" of [15] are insufficient for that purpose and we define a new class of ordered algebraic theories called "recursion-closed" algebraic theories which satisfy the desired condition. It is shown that every "recursion-closed" algebraic theory is rational in the sense of [15], and we prove that for every ranked alphabet Σ there is a free "recursion-closed" algebraic theory RCT_Σ generated by Σ, generalizing results of [15]. The structure of the free "recursion-closed" algebraic theory RCT_Σ generated by Σ can be described explicitly. Indeed, its elements are n-tuples of (usually infinite) trees having the property that a suitable encoding of their set of branches is a deterministic context-free language. This result is similar to a result of Courcelle [6].

One of the features of this paper is that we generalize the notion of an interpretation, taking the notion of an algebraic theory as a key concept. Conventionally, an interpretation is a mapping assigning functions to the symbols of the base alphabet, and since functions can obviously be composed, the role played by composition is obscured. Our more general notion of an interpretation (which includes the standard notion) clarifies the role played by composition and the nature of the axioms that an interpretation should satisfy for the fixpoint approach to hold.

This paper supports the view that "algebraic theories" constitute a unifying framework for studying the semantics of recursive program schemes. Elgot [10,11] and Wagner [28,29] first recognized the importance of algebraic theories for semantics. Following Elgot [10,11,12], Ginali [13], Burstall and Thatcher [5], Goguen, Thatcher, Wagner and Wright [14,15], and Thatcher, Wagner and Wright [26,27] have used algebraic theories in semantic studies. In particular, the semantics of flowchart programs and of monadic recursion schemes is very nicely treated in [27] using the "introduction of variables construction". A brief sketch of the "introduction of variables construction", which is very closely related to our treatment, is also given in [26] for monadic recursion schemes. Related studies of schemes are those of Nivat [20], Courcelle [6,7], Courcelle and Nivat [8] and Guessarian [17]. Recent work of Arnold [1] and Arnold and Nivat [4] attacks the difficult problem of tackling nondeterminism. Nivat and Arnold [21] is noteworthy since it bases its foundations on the concept of complete metric spaces instead of partial orders. We finally point out that there seems to be very close connections between algebraic theories and the "magmoides" of Arnold and Dauchet [2].

2. Preliminaries: Labeled Trees, Algebraic Theories

In order to minimize the preliminaries, we will follow as much as possible the definitions and notations found in Thatcher, Wagner and Wright [26,27] and Goguen, Thatcher, Wagner and Wright [14,15]. We have summarized the key definitions used in this paper in an Appendix. We also warn the reader that our definition of an algebraic theory is the dual of that of [26,27]. This has the advantage of eliminating a number of confusing reversals.

3. Extended Recursion Schemes

An extended recursion scheme can be described as a system of mutually recursive definitions where the left-hand sides are distinct "undefined function symbols" F_i, and the right-hand sides are Σ-trees possibly labeled with the function symbols F_j constituting the left-hand sides. What is new in this definition is that we allow "many-sorted" trees and that these trees can be infinite.

Example 1:

F(x)<=<u>if</u> tips(x) <u>then</u> 1 <u>else</u> G (F(left(x)) ,F(right(x)))

G(m,n)<=<u>if</u> eq(n,0) <u>then</u> m <u>else</u> succ(G(m,pred(n)))

We have three "sorts": binary trees, nonnegative integers and boolean. The sorts of the functions and predicates involved are as follows: F: tree → int, left, right: tree → tree, tips : tree → bool, G: int.int → int, succ, pred : int → int, eq : int.int → bool, <u>if then else</u> : bool.int.int → int.

Given an S-sorted alphabet Σ, let $D(S)$ be the new alphabet consisting of all pairs (u,s) in $S^* \times S$. For every string $\bar{u}$ in $D(S)^+$ with $\bar{u} = (u_1,s_1)\ldots(u_N,s_N)$, let $\Phi_{\bar{u}}$ be the set of "undefined function symbols" $\Phi_{\bar{u}} = \{F_1^{\bar{u}}, \ldots, F_N^{\bar{u}}\}$. Each $F_i^{\bar{u}}$ is a symbol of sort s_i and of arity u_i (corresponding to the i-th symbol (u_i,s_i) in $\bar{u}$).

Definition 3.1

A <u>recursion scheme</u> α using undefined function symbols in the set $\Phi_{\bar{u}}$ (where $\bar{u} = (u_1,s_1)\ldots(u_N,s_N)$) is a mapping assigning a tree α_i of sort s_i to each undefined function symbol $F_i^{\bar{u}}$, and such that the only symbols besides those in Σ which may occur in the tree α_i are the function variables $F_i^{\bar{u}}$ in $\Phi_{\bar{u}}$ and the variables in the set X_{u_i} associated with the arity u_i of $F_i^{\bar{u}}$. Formally, a recursion scheme is defined as a function $\alpha : \Phi_{\bar{u}} \to \underline{\underline{CT}}_{\Sigma\cup\Phi_{\bar{u}}}$, such that each tree $\alpha_i = \alpha(F_i^{\bar{u}})$ belongs to $\underline{\underline{CT}}_{\Sigma\cup\Phi_{\bar{u}}}(u_i,s_i)$.

A scheme using undefined function symbols in $\Phi_{\bar{u}}$ is a scheme of type $\bar{u}$.

Given a scheme α, we obtain a program by assigning an interpretation I to the symbols in Σ. Then, following Scott's approach [22,23,24], we associate a functional α_I to the pair (α,I) and, provided that the functional α_I has a least fixpoint, we define the meaning of the program (α,I) as the least fixpoint of α_I.

4. Generalized Interpretations and Functionals

Definition 4.1

A <u>generalized interpretation</u> is a pair (I,T), where T is an ordered algebraic theory and $I : \Sigma \to T$ is a function assigning an arrow $I(f) : u \to s$ in T to each symbol f in $\Sigma_{u,s}$. When the theory T is fixed, we denote an interpretation (I,T) as I.

What is new in this definition is the fact that we do not necessarily assign functions to the symbols in Σ, but possibly more general operations, as long as they satisfy certain axioms (those of an ordered algebraic theory). Consequently, we are focusing on the properties that are required of the elements of an interpretation for the fixpoint-semantics approach to hold. This is also the motivation for introducinn the new class of "recursion-closed" algebraic theories.

Given a scheme α of type $\bar{u}$ (with $\bar{u} = (u_1,s_1) \ldots (u_N,s_N)$) and an interpretation (I,T), we will define a functional α_I (really $\alpha_{I,T}$). For that purpose, we note that there is a bijection between the set of N-tuples $(a_1, \ldots, a_N)$ in $T(u_1,s_1) \times \ldots \times T(u_N,s_N)$ and the set of functions $a : \Phi_{\bar{u}} \to T(u_1,s_1) \times \ldots \times T(u_N,s_N)$. We abbreviate the Cartesian product $T(u_1,s_1) \times \ldots \times T(u_N,s_N)$ as $T^{\bar{u}}$. Then, the functional $\alpha_I : T^{\bar{u}} \to T^{\bar{u}}$ associated with the pair $(\alpha,(I,T))$ is defined as follows.

Definition 4.2

For any $a \in T^{\bar{u}}$, the unique function $a : \Phi_{\bar{u}} \to T^{\bar{u}}$ corresponding to a and the interpretation $I : \Sigma \to T$ define a function $a_I : \Sigma \cup \Phi_{\bar{u}} \to T$, and a_I has a unique homomorphic ω-continuous extension $\bar{a}_I$ as in the following diagram.

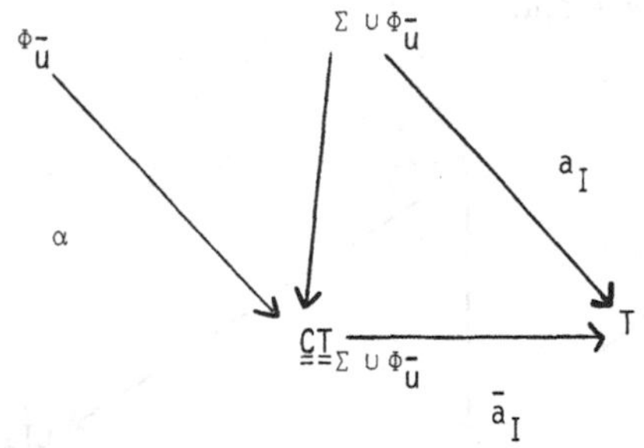

Abusing the notation slightly, we define $\alpha_I(a)$ the value of the functional α_I at a as $\alpha.\bar{a}_I$.[1]

We generalize slightly the concept of a scheme, and this generalization allows us to show that the class of (generalized) schemes has the structure of an algebraic theory. This allows us to define schemes of "higher types". We extend the definition of a scheme in the following way.

1. We denote composition from left to right, that is, $(f.g)(x) = g(f(x))$.

Definition 4.3

Given any pair of strings $\bar{u}$, $\bar{v}$ in $D(S)^+$ with $\bar{u} = (u_1,s_1) \dots (u_n,s_n)$ and $\bar{v} = (v_1,r_1)\dots(v_p,r_p)$, an extended scheme α of type $(\bar{u},\bar{v})$ is a function $\alpha : \Phi_{\bar{v}} \to \underline{\underline{CT}}_{\Sigma \cup \Phi_{\bar{u}}}$, such that each tree $\alpha_j = \alpha(F_j^{\bar{v}})$ is a tree of sort r_j in $\underline{\underline{CT}}_{\Sigma \cup \Phi_{\bar{u}}}(v_j,r_j)$ (if $\bar{u} = \lambda$ or $\bar{v} = \lambda$ then $\Phi_\lambda = \emptyset$).

This definition coincides with the previous one when $\bar{u} = \bar{v}$, in which case we say that α is a closed scheme. Also, for any interpretation (I,T), α and (I,T) define a functional $\alpha_I : T^{\bar{u}} \to T^{\bar{v}}$. The set of all extended schemes is denoted $CPRS_\Sigma$ (for Continuous Polyadic Recursion Schemes). We also have the sets PRS_Σ and $FPRS_\Sigma$ corresponding to the trees in T_Σ and FT_Σ.

The operation of scheme-substitution gives a structure of algebraic theory to the class of schemes $CPRS_\Sigma$. As a consequence, we prove that every closed recursion scheme has a least fixpoint, which can be considered as the unfoldment of the scheme.

Definition 4.4

The substitution of a scheme α into a scheme β consists in a simultaneous substitution of the trees α_i forming α for the undefined function symbols occurring in the trees β_j forming β and performed in a homomorphic fashion. (This is rather different from tree-composition.) The result of substituting a scheme α of type $(\bar{u},\bar{v})$ into a scheme β of type $(\bar{v},\bar{w})$ is the scheme $\alpha \to \beta$ of type $(\bar{u},\bar{w})$ defined in the following diagram as $\alpha \to \beta = \beta.\bar{\alpha}$.

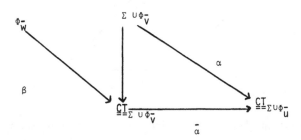

Theorem 1. The set $CPRS_\Sigma$ of extended schemes is an ω-continuous algebraic $D(S)$-theory under the operation of scheme-substitution.

Note that the complexity of the set of sorts increases. Starting with a set of sorts S, we obtain a $D(S)$-theory based on the set of sorts $D(S)$. Noticing that the set $CF(T)$ of all ω-continuous functions of the form $H : T^{\bar{u}} \to T^{\bar{v}}$ is an ω-continuous algebraic $D(S)$-theory under composition, we have the theorem:

Theorem 2. For every interpretation (I,T) where T is an ω-continuous algebraic

S-theory, the mapping $I : CPRS_\Sigma \to CT(T)$ which assigns the functional $\alpha_I : T^{\bar{u}} \to T^{\bar{v}}$ to a scheme α of type $(\bar{u},\bar{v})$ is a homomorphism of ω-continuous algebraic D(S)-theories.

Theorem 2 implies that the functionals α_I are ω-continuous and that scheme-substitution corresponds to the composition of functionals. For every pair of schemes α of type $(\bar{u},\bar{v})$ and β of type $(\bar{v},\bar{w})$, we have $(\alpha \to \beta)_I = \alpha_I . \beta_I$.

5. Fixpoint Solutions

From Theorem 2, every functional $\alpha_I : T^{\bar{u}} \to T^{\bar{v}}$ is ω-continuous. In particular, when α is a closed scheme $(\bar{u} = \bar{v})$, α_I has a least fixpoint $\alpha_I^\nabla = \bigcup_{n\in\omega} \alpha_I^n(\bot)$ (where $\bot$ is the least element of $T^{\bar{u}}$). The operation of scheme-substitution allows us to show that every closed scheme α of type $\bar{u}$ has a least fixpoint, in the sense that there is a scheme α^∇ of type $(\lambda,\bar{u})$ (which is an n-tuple of infinite trees not containing any of the symbols in $\Phi_{\bar{u}}$) which is the least solution of the "scheme equation" $\eta = \eta \to \alpha$. If $\bot$ denotes the scheme of type $\bar{u}$ composed of the trees $\bot$, $\alpha^\nabla = \bigcup_{n\in\omega} \alpha^{(n)}$, where $\alpha^{(0)} = \bot$ and $\alpha^{(n+1)} = \alpha^{(n)} \to \alpha$. α^∇ can be thought of as the unfoldment of the scheme α.

Theorem 2 yields a "Mezei-Wright" [19] type of result, namely that the identity $(\alpha^\nabla)_I = (\alpha_I)^\nabla$ holds: the least fixpoint of the functional α_I is equal to the image of the unfoldment α^∇ of the scheme α under the homomorphism $\bar{I}$.

6. Recursion-Closed Algebraic Theories

Goguen, Thatcher, Wagner and Wright [15] observed that the full power of ω-continuity was not necessary to compute fixpoint solutions and that certain difficulties stemmed from the question of ω-completeness. They introduced the notion of a rational algebraic theory: an ordered algebraic theory T is rational if every closed regular scheme has a fixpoint definition in T, that is, for every interpretation (I,T), the functional α_I has a least fixpoint in T (a scheme is regular if the undefined function symbols occurring in it are of arity λ, which implies that they can only label leaves of the tree). Unfortunately, functionals defined by non-regular schemes may fail to have a least fixpoint in some rational theories. If we choose the "free rational algebraic theory RT_Σ" generated by Σ (see [15]) as an interpretation, we claim that there exist non-regular schemes which do not have a least fixpoint in RT_Σ. This can be derived from a result due to Ginali [13]. Indeed, the elements of RT_Σ are n-tuples of infinite trees, and a suitable encoding of their sets of branches is a regular set [13]. The conclusion results from the fact that there exist recursion schemes whose least fixpoint is encoded by a non-regular language.

In order to resolve this difficulty, we have defined a new class of algebraic theories which we have termed "recursion-closed". An ordered algebraic theory T is "recursion-closed" if, for every finite closed recursion scheme α and for every interpretation (I,T), the functional α_I has a least fixpoint in T.

We now proceed with the formal definition of a "recursion-closed" algebraic theory.

Definition 6.1

Given any ordered algebraic theory T, we define the S-ranked alphabet $T\Omega = \{T\Omega_{u,s}\}_{(u,s) \in S^* \times S}$ where $T\Omega_{u,s}$ is the set of symbols $\{\hat{\phi} \mid \phi \in T(u,s)\}$ in one to one correspondance with the set of arrows in T(u,s). Every symbol $\hat{\phi}$ is a name for the arrow $\phi : u \to s$ in T(u,s). We also define the interpretation $TI : T\Omega \to T$ such that $TI(\hat{\phi}) = \phi$, that is, TI is the function assigning to each name the arrow it represents.

The reason for defining $T\Omega$ and TI is the following. For any arbitrary S-ranked alphabet Σ, any arbitrary finite recursion scheme α over Σ and any arbitrary interpretation $I : \Sigma \to T$, there is a recursion scheme over $T\Omega$ denoted $T\alpha$ such that the functionals α_I and $(T\alpha)_{TI}$ are identical. Indeed, the scheme $T\alpha$ is the scheme obtained by renaming every symbol $f \in \Sigma_{u,s}$ with the symbol $\widehat{I(f)}$ corresponding to the arrow I(f) assigned to f by I. This property yields immediately the following Lemma.

Lemma 3

Given any algebraic theory T, for every finite closed recursion scheme α (over an arbitrary S-ranked alphabet Σ) and for every interpretation $I : \Sigma \to T$, the functional α_I has a least fixpoint in T if and only if for every finite closed recursion scheme β over $T\Omega$, the functional β_{TI} (under the fixed interpretation TI) has a least fixpoint.

Noticing that for ω-continuous interpretations (I,T) the least fixpoint of a functional of the form α_I (where α is a finite closed scheme) is given by the identity $(\alpha_I)^{\nabla} = \bigcup \alpha_I^n(\bot)$ and the fact that in any ordered algebraic theory the identity $\alpha_I^n(\bot) = (\alpha^{(n)})_I$ holds (only monotonicity is needed), we see that the ω-chain $((\alpha^{(n)})_I)_{n\in\omega}$ has a least upper bound. We will require that in a recursion-closed algebraic theory, for every finite closed scheme α over $T\Omega$, the ω-chain $((\alpha^{(n)})_{TI})_{n\in\omega}$ has at least upper bound in T. We actually need the following slightly stronger conditions in order to prove the existence of free recursion-closed algebraic theories.

Definition 6.2

An ordered algebraic S-theory T is recursion-closed if the following conditions hold.

(1) (Completeness) For all finite schemes α and β over $T\Omega$, with β a closed scheme of type $\bar{u} = (w_1,s_1)\ldots(w_n,s_n)$ and α a (not necessarily closed) scheme of type $(\bar{u},\bar{v})$ where $\bar{v}$ is of the special form $(u,v_1)\ \ldots\ (u,v_p)$, the ω-chain $((\beta^{(i)} \to \alpha)_{TI})_{i\in\omega}$ has a least upper bound in T(u,v) denoted $(\beta^{\nabla} \to \alpha)_{TI}$ (with $v = v_1 \ldots v_p$).

(2) (Right continuity) For all α and β as in (1), for all ϕ: $w \to u$ in T, we have $\phi \circ (\bigcup (\beta^{(i)} \to \alpha)_{TI}) = \bigcup (\phi \circ (\beta^{(i)} \to \alpha)_{TI})$.

(3) (Left continuity) For all α and β as in (1), for all ϕ: $v \to w$ in T, we have

$(\bigcup(\beta^{(i)} \to \alpha)_{TI}) \circ \phi = \bigcup((\beta^{(i)} \to \alpha)_{TI}) \circ \phi)$.

It should be noted that for all $i \in \omega$, $(\beta^{(i)} \to \alpha)_{TI}$ is an element of $T(u,v)$, because the special form of $\bar{v}$ implies that $T^{\bar{v}} = T(u,v)$, and therefore the above compositions are meaningful.

It can be easily shown that every recursion-closed algebraic theory is rational in the sense of [15] and it is obvious that every ω-continuous algebraic theory is recursion-closed. We will also need the concept of a homomorphism of recursion-closed algebraic theories.

Definition 6.3

A homomorphism $h: T_1 \to T_2$ between two recursion-closed algebraic theories T_1 and T_2 is a homomorphism of ordered theories such that for all pairs of schemes α and β as in the previous definition we have the identity, $h(\bigcup(\beta^{(i)} \to \alpha)_{TI}) = \bigcup h((\beta^{(i)} \to \alpha)_{TI})$.

The definition of a recursion-closed algebraic theory also allows us to provide the semantics of recursion schemes having a "main procedure".

Definition 6.4

A recursion scheme with a main procedure is a pair (α,β) where β is a finite closed scheme of type $\bar{u} = (w_1,s_1) \ldots (w_n,s_n)$ and α is a finite scheme of type $(\bar{u},(u,v))$ consisting of a unique tree. The scheme α is the main procedure and it contains procedure calls to the procedure names $F_i^{\bar{u}}$ defined by the "procedure declaration" β.

Note that a scheme with main procedure corresponds to the special case where in the pair (α,β) of the definition 6.2, the scheme α consists of a single tree.

The semantics of a scheme with main procedure (α,β) under an interpretation I are defined as $(\beta^{\nabla} \to \alpha)_I = \bigcup(\beta^{(i)} \to \alpha)_I$, which is defined for any recursion-closed interpretation T.

We also prove that the set of n-tuples of trees of the form $\beta^{\nabla} \to \alpha$ where α and β are schemes as in definition 6.2, form the free recursion-closed algebraic theory generated by the S-ranked alphabet Σ. We define the free recursion-closed algebraic theory $\underline{\underline{RCT}}_\Sigma$ in the following way.

Definition 6.5

We define the subset $\underline{\underline{RCT}}_\Sigma$ of $\underline{\underline{CT}}_\Sigma$ as the set of all p-tuples of trees of the form $\beta^{\nabla} \to \alpha$, where β is a finite closed scheme of type $\bar{u} = (w_1,s_1) \ldots (w_n,s_n)$ and α is a finite scheme of type $(\bar{u},\bar{v})$ with $\bar{v} = (u,v_1) \ldots (u,v_p)$.

Example 2: A scheme with main procedure (α,β) and the unfoldment tree $\beta^{\nabla} \to \alpha$.

Scheme α (main procedure)

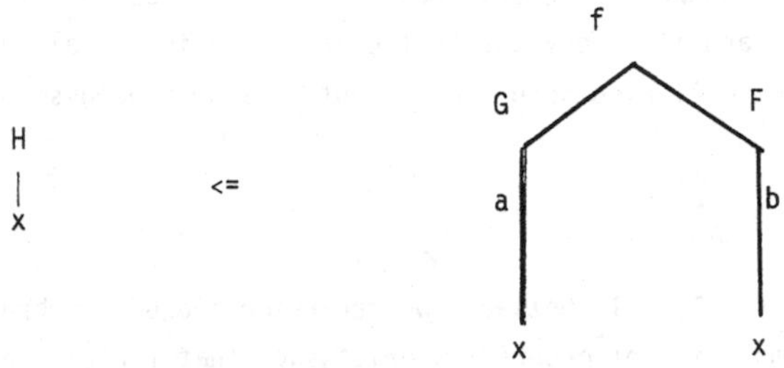

Scheme β (Prodecure declaration)

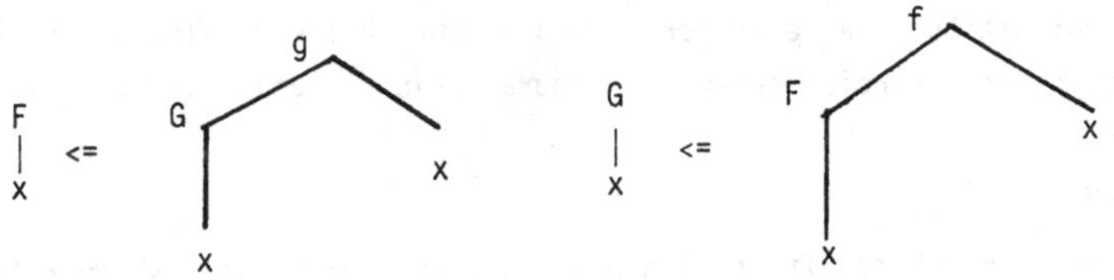

The tree $\beta^{\nabla} \to \alpha$

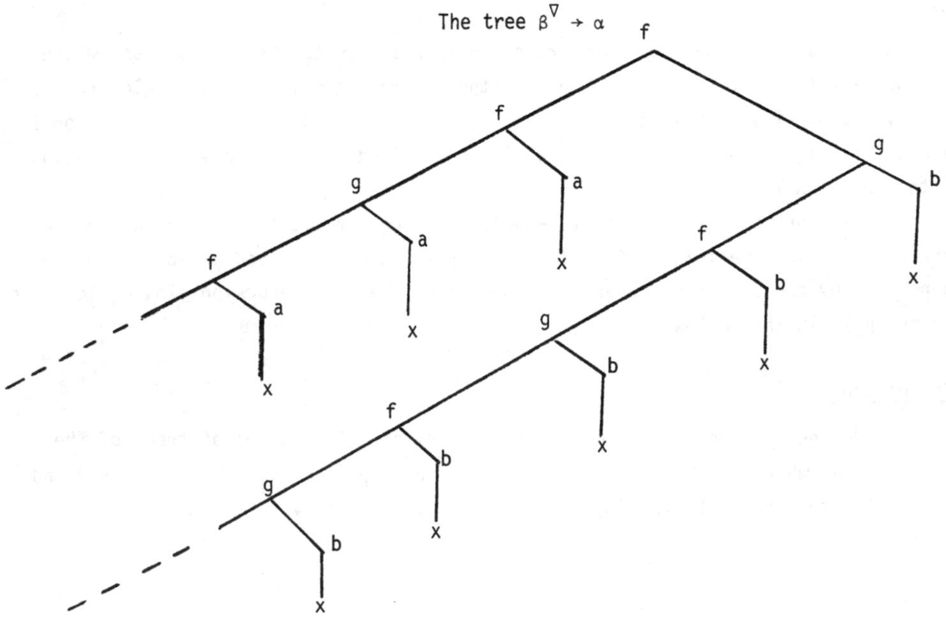

Note that β^∇ is a n-tuple of trees without undefined function symbols and that $\beta^\nabla \to \alpha$ is a p-tuple of trees without undefined function symbols and belongs to $\underline{CT}_\Sigma$ (u,v).

Theorem 4

$\underline{RCT}_\Sigma$ is the free recursion-closed algebraic theory generated by Σ. That is, for every recursion-closed algebraic theory T and for every function $h : \Sigma \to T$, there exists a unique homomorphism $\bar{h} : \underline{RCT}_\Sigma \to T$ extending h, and such that for every pair of schemes (α,β) as in definition 6.5, we have $\bar{h}(\beta^\nabla \to \alpha) = \bigcup \bar{h}(\beta^{(i)} \to \alpha)$.

The proof consists in showing that $\underline{RCT}_\Sigma$ is closed under composition, tupling, that it is recursion closed, and that it has the unique extension property stated in Theorem 4. The verification that $\underline{RCT}_\Sigma$ is closed under the desired operations is accomplished by constructing appropriate schemes and using properties of fixpoints.

Following the terminology of [15], we can say that $\underline{RCT}_\Sigma$ consists of the "behaviors" of recursion schemes defined by pairs (α,β) as in definition 6.5.

Given any program $((\alpha,\beta),I)$ where (α,β) is a scheme with main procedure and $I : \Sigma \to T$ is an interpretation with T a recursion-closed algebraic theory, the unique homomorphism $\bar{I}$: $\underline{RCT}_\Sigma \to T$ extending I gives a fixpoint semantics $(\alpha,\beta)_I = \bar{I}(\beta^\nabla \to \alpha) = \bigcup (\beta^{(i)} \to \alpha)_I$ to the program $((\alpha,\beta),I)$. This implies that two pairs of schemes (α_1,β_1) and (α_2,β_2) are equivalent in all recursion-closed interpretations, if and only if they are "tree equivalent", that is, if the trees $\beta_1^\nabla \to \alpha_1$ and $\beta_2^\nabla \to \alpha_2$ are identical. The "Mezei-Wright" result also holds, since for every finite closed recursion scheme α we have, $(\alpha_1)^\nabla = \bigcup \alpha_I^n(\bot) = \bigcup \alpha_I^{(n)} = (\alpha^\nabla)_I$ from Theorem 4.

We have also proved that there exists an encoding of the set of branches of the tree $\beta^\nabla \to \alpha$ which consists of a finite set of deterministic context-free languages. This is analogous to a result of Courcelle [6]. However, our proof is more direct and uses a different encoding due to Ginali [13]. Also, we construct a DPDA whereas Courcelle constructs a strict deterministic grammar. This last result will appear elsewhere.

Acknowledgments:

I would like to thank Professor R.V. Book for many helpful suggestions. It is also a pleasure to thank Professor J.A. Goguen for many illuminating discussions and Dr. J.W. Thatcher for his encouragement.

Appendix: Review of definitions: labeled trees, algebraic theories.

Sorts (or types). By a set of sorts (or types), we understand a set S of data types in some programming language. For example, S = {integer, real, boolean, character} is a set of sorts.

S-ranked alphabet. An s-ranked alphabet Σ is a family $(\Sigma_{u,s})_{(u,s)\in S^*xS}$ of sets $\Sigma_{u,s}$ indexed by the pairs (u,s) in S* x S. Intuitively, if $u = u_1 \dots u_n$, each symbol f in $\Sigma_{u,s}$ represents an operation taking n arguments each of sort u_i and yielding an element of sort s. Symbols in $\Sigma_{\lambda,s}$ are called constants of sort s. We say that a symbol f in $\Sigma_{u,s}$ is of sort s and has artiy u. In the rest of this paper, we will assume that a special symbol denoted $\perp$ is adjoined to every S-ranked alphabet Σ ($\perp$ is of arity λ).[1]

Σ-trees. A Σ-tree t is a (finite branching, ordered, possibly infinite) tree whose nodes are labeled with symbols from an S-ranked alphabet Σ in a way which is consistent with the sorts and arities of the symbols in Σ. By this, we mean that for any node v in the tree having exactly n successors $v_1, \dots, v_n$, the symbol f labeling v must have some arity $u_1 \dots u_n$ and each symbol f_i labeling v_i must be of sort u_i. In particular, the leaves of the tree are labeled with constants.

A tree whose root is labeled with a symbol of sort s is called a tree of sort s. The set of all trees of sort s is denoted CT^s_Σ and the set of all trees is denoted CT_Σ. A tree is total if the label $\perp$ (of arity λ) does not occur in the tree and otherwise it is partial. The set of total finite trees is denoted T_Σ and the set of partial and total finite trees is denoted FT_Σ. The tree consisting of a unique node labeled $\perp$ is also denoted $\perp$. There is a partial ordering $\leq$ defined on CT_Σ (and FT_Σ) as follows. For every pair of trees $t_1, t_2 \in CT_\Sigma$, the relation $t_1 \leq t_2$ holds if the unlabeled tree t_1 is a subtree of the unlabeled tree t_2 and for every node w in t_1 not labeled with $\perp$, the corresponding node in t_2 has the same label.

Tree-composition. The relevant operation here is that of tree-composition. We introduce for every string $u \in S^*$ the set of variables $X_u = \{x^u_1, \dots, x^u_n\}$[2] (with $X_\lambda = \emptyset$). The variables x^u_i are used as markers indicating the leaves where the substitution operation takes place. Given a tree t in $CT_{\Sigma \cup X_u}$ and an n-tuple $(t_1, \dots, t_n)$ of trees in CT_Σ with each tree t_i a tree of sort u_i, the result of composing $(t_1, \dots, t_n)$ with t denoted $(t_1, \dots, t_n) \circ t$ is the tree obtained by substituting the tree t_i for each leaf labeled x^u_i in t.

Algebraic theories. We explain the notion of an algebraic theory based on a set of sorts, S (an S-theory). Such a structure T is a set of vectors of operations ϕ, where each vector ϕ has a finite number of "scalar" components $\phi_1, \dots, \phi_p$ (for some $p \geq 1$), each component ϕ_i having some common "input sort" $u \in S^*$ and some "output sort" $v_i \in S$ (not necessarily the same for each ϕ_i). Every vector ϕ is considered as an "arrow" with some source u and some target $v = v_1 \dots v_p$ and is usually denoted

1. The empty string is denoted λ.

2. $n = |u|$.

$\phi : u \rightarrow v$. The components ϕ_i are denoted $\phi_i : u \rightarrow v_i$. For technical reasons, there is a unique arrow denoted $0_u : u \rightarrow \lambda$ for every $u \in S^*$. In addition, there exists a composition operation o, an operation [ ] called tupling which allows the creation of vector arrows from scalar arrows, and projection arrows $x_i^u : u \rightarrow u_i$ which extract the scalar components of vector arrows. More precisely, given any two arrows $\phi : u \rightarrow v$ and $\psi : v \rightarrow w$ where the source of ψ is the target of ϕ, $\phi \circ \psi : u \rightarrow w$ is the the arrow obtained by composing ϕ and ψ. The composition operation o is associative and has identities I_u for all $u \in S^*$. Also, for any p scalar arrows $\phi_i : u \rightarrow v_i$ ($u \in S^*$, $v_i \in S$), $[\phi_1, \ldots, \phi_p] : u \rightarrow v$ (with $v = v_1 \ldots v_p$) is the arrow from u to v having the ϕ_i as components, and for any vector arrow $\phi : u \rightarrow v$ ($v = v_1 \ldots v_p$), $\phi \circ x_i^v = \phi_i$ is the i-th component of ϕ. In summary, the following two identifies hold: $[\phi_1, \ldots, \phi_p] \circ x_i^v = \phi_i$ and $[\phi \circ x_1^v, \ldots, \phi \circ x_p^v] = \phi$. (In an axiomatic definition, these identities are taken as axioms.) The set of all arrows from u to v ($u, v \in S^*$) is denoted $T(u,v)$.

We will actually be interested in algebraic theories equipped with a partial ordering.

Ordered algebraic theories. An algebraic theory T is ordered if each set $T(u,v)$ is partially ordered and has a least element $\bot_{u,v}$, and composition and tupling are monotonic. It is required that for all $u, v \in S^*$, $0_u \circ \bot_{\lambda,v} = \bot_{u,v}$. This implies that for all $\phi : u \rightarrow v$, we have $\phi \circ \bot_{v,w} = \bot_{u,w}$.

ω-continuous algebraic theories. An ordered algebraic theory T is ω-continuous if each $T(u,v)$ is ω-complete and composition is ω-continuous. Continuity of tupling follows from the other axioms.

There is an obvious notion of a homomorphism of algebraic theories. If T_1 and T_2 are algebraic theories, a homomorphism $h : T_1 \rightarrow T_2$ maps every arrow $\phi : u \rightarrow v$ in T_1 onto an arrow $h(\phi) : u \rightarrow v$ in T_2 and preserves composition, tupling, identities and projections. In addition, for ordered algebraic theories, h is monotonic on each $T(u,v)$ and preserves least elements, and for ω-continuous theories, h is ω-continuous on each $T(u,v)$.

One of the reasons for being interested in algebraic theories comes from the fact that "free algebraic theories generated by an S-ranked alphabet" exist, and that they consist of trees. Furthermore, free algebraic theories are characterized by a universal extension property which proves to be a very useful tool, as we shall see in the next section. Without giving details, the set of n-tuples of Σ-trees can be made into the free ω-continuous algebraic theory $\underline{\underline{CT}}_\Sigma$, and similarly for the set of n-tuples of partial and total finite trees and the set of n-tuples of total finite trees, yielding the free ordered algebraic theory $\underline{\underline{FT}}_\Sigma$ and the free algebraic theory $\underline{\underline{T}}_\Sigma$. (In the rigorous definition, we actually deal with trees possibly labeled with variables and with tuples of trees of the form $(t_1, \ldots, t_p)$, where each t_i is a tree of sort v_i in $CT_{\Sigma \cup X_u}$.) The composition operation is tree-composition extended to tuples of trees.

The following theorem expresses the "freeness" of the algebraic theory $\underline{\underline{CT}}_\Sigma$ (and we have similar theorems for $\underline{\underline{FT}}_\Sigma$ and $\underline{\underline{T}}_\Sigma$).

Theorem [15,16,26]. For every ω-continuous algebraic theory T, for every function $h : \Sigma \to T$ assigning an arrow $h(f) : u \to s$ to each symbol $f \in \Sigma_{u,s}$, there exists a unique homomorphism of ω-continuous algebraic theories $\bar{h}$ extending h as in the following diagram:

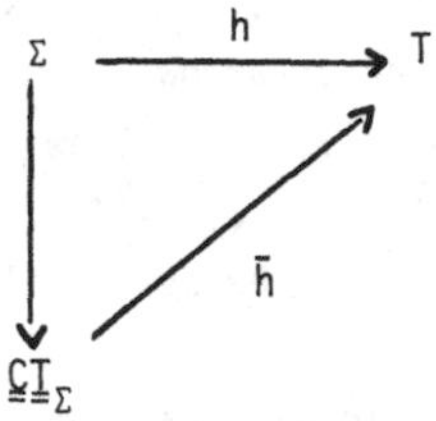

REFERENCES

1. Arnold, A., Systemes d'equations dans le magmoide. Ensembles Rationels et algebriques d'arbres, These d'Etat, Universite de Lille, (March 1977).

2. Arnold, A. and Dauchet, M., Theorie des Magmoides, Publications du Laboratoire de Calcul, Universite de Lille I, (January 1977).

3. Arnold, A. and Nivat, M., Nondeterministic Recursive Program Schemes. IRIA Technical Report No. 262, Domaine de Voluceau, Le Chesnay, France (November 1977).

4. Arnold, A. and Nivat, M., Algebraic semantics of nondeterministic recursive program schemes, Technical Report no. 78-4, Universite Paris VII, (Feb. 1978).

5. Burstall, R.M., and Thatcher, J.W., The algebraic theory of recursive program schemes, Symposium on Category Theory Applied to Computation and Control. Lecture Notes in Computer Science, Vol. 25, Springer-Verlag, New York, 1975, 126-131.

6. Courcelle, B., A Representation of trees by Languages, Part I and Part II, Theoretical Computer Science. Part I: Vol. 6, pp. 255-279; Part II: Vol. 7, pp. 25-55, (1978).

7. Courcelle, B., On the Definition of Classes of Interpretations, IRIA Technical Report No. 236, Domaine de Voluceau, Le Chesnay, France (May 1977).

8. Courcelle, B. and Nivat, M., Algebraic families of interpretations, Proc. 17th IEEE Symp. on Foundations of Comp. Sci., Houston, Texas (October 1976), 137-146.

9. Eilenberg, S. and Wright, J.B., Automata in general algebras, Inf. and Cont. 11 (1967), 452-470.

10. Elgot, C.C., Monadic computation and iterative algebraic theories. In H.E. Rose and J.C. Shepherdson (Eds.), Logic Colloquium '73, Studies in Logic, Vol. 80, North-Holland, Amsterdam, 1975, 175-230.

11. Elgot, C.C., Algebraic Theories and Program Schemes. Symposium on Semantics of Algorithmic Languages, (Ed. E. Engeler), Springer-Verlag (1971), 71-88.

12. Elgot, C.C., Structured programming with and without GOTO statements. IBM Research Report, RC-5626 (1975); IEEE Transactions on Software Engineering SE1 (1976), 41-53.

13. Ginali, S., Iterative Algebraic Theories, Infinite Trees and Program Schemata. Ph.D. Thesis, Department of Mathematics, University of Chicago, Chicago, Illinois, June 1976.

14. Goguen, J.A., Thatcher, J.W., Wagner, E.G., and Wright, J.B. An Introduction to Categories, Algebraic Theories and Algebras. IBM Report RC-5369, Yorktown Heights, New York (1975).

15. Goguen, J.A., Thatcher, J.W., Wagner, E.G., and Wright, J.B. Rational algebraic theories and fixed point solutions. Proc. 17th IEEE Symp on Foundations of Comp. Sci., Houston, Texas (October 1976). 147-158.

16. Goguen, J.A., Thatcher, J.W., Wagner, E.G., and Wright, J.B. Initial algebra semantics and continuous algebras, JACM 24 (1977), 68-95.

17. Guessarian, I. Schemas de Programmes Recursif Polyadiques: Equivalence Semantiques et Classes d'Interpretations. These d'Etat, Universite de Paris VII, 1975.

18. Manes, E.G. Algebraic Theories. Graduate Texts in Mathematics, Vol. 26, Springer-Verlag, New York, 1976.

19. Mezei, J. and Wright, J.B. Algebraic automata and context-free sets, Inf. and Cont. 11 (1967), 3-29.

20. Nivat, M. On the interpretation of recursive polyadic program schemes, Symposia Mathematica, Vol. 15, Academic Press, New York, 1975, 255-281.

21. Nivat, M. and Arnold, A., Calculs infinis, interpretations metriques et plus grands points fixes, Technical Report no. 78-19, Universite Paris VII, (May 1978).

22. Scott, D. Outline of a Mathematical Theory of Computation. Technical Monograph PRG-2, Oxford University Computing Laboratory, Programming Research Group (1970).

23. Scott, D. The Lattice of Flow Diagrams. Technical Monograph PRG-3, Oxford University Computing Laboratory, Programming Research Group (1971).

24. Scott, D. Continuous Lattices. Technical Monograph PRG-7, Oxford University Computing Laboratory, Programming Research Group (1971).

25. Scott, D. Data types as lattices, SIAM J. Comp. 5 (1976), 522-587.

26. Thatcher, J.W., Wagner, E.G. and Wright, J.B., Programming languages as mathematical objects, to appear in Mathematical Foundations of Computer Science, '78.

27. Thatcher, J.W., Wagner, E.G. and Wright, J.B., Free continuous theories, Technical Report RC 6906, IBM T.J. Watson Research Center, Yorktown Heights, New York, (December 1977).

28. Wagner, E.G. Languages for defining sets in arbitrary algebras: Proceedings, 12th IEEE Symposium on Switching and Automata Theory, East Lansing, Michigan (1971).

29. Wagner, E.G. An algebraic theory of recursive definitions and recursive languages. Proceedings, 3rd Annual ACM Symposium on Theory of Computing, Shaker Heights, Ohio (1971).

---

* This research has been partially supported by the National Science Foundation under Grant #MCS77-11360.

A RATIONAL THEORY OF AFLS*

Jonathan Goldstine
Department of Computer Science
The Pennsylvania State University
University Park, PA 16802 USA

1. INTRODUCTION

Doctrina AFL est omnis divisa in partes duo.

One part of AFL theory is a fairly clean study of abstract families of languages closed under certain operations. The other part is a very dirty study of abstract families of acceptors (AFAs) and their relation to abstract families of languages. This part of the theory is so complex and ugly that it has been dormant for some time, and its results are seldom used. There is in fact a widespread belief that abstract families of acceptors are of at most historical interest and that AFL theory will survive without them.

This belief is based on a fallacy. It is not true that the concept of an abstract family of acceptors is a complicated one. It is only the particular formalization of this concept used in the literature that is excessively complicated. With hindsight, one can see that the original formulation of an AFA, although it arose independently in essentially identical form in two different places [6,9], was a poor one; and that the source of this problem was the earlier choice, also poor, for formalizing such specific automata as the pushdown automaton as a 7-tuple with a transition function. This notation, more in the style of engineering than mathematics, was abstracted in the definition of an AFA to the point where its deficiencies placed an overwhelming burden on the theory.

We have discussed elsewhere the benefits that accrue from a clean and simple definition of the pushdown automaton, and have shown that when such a definition is abstracted to define an abstract family of acceptors, the concept remains clean and simple [7]. In the present paper, we shall indicate how this concept can be used in the development of AFL theory. For the purpose of this demonstration, we shall take Ginsburg's book [5] as the authoritative description of AFL theory, but we shall omit all discussion of AFLs and semiAFLs that are not full (i.e. not closed under erasing). Such families are indeed important since they correspond to acceptors that operate in realtime. They should be considered, along with the entire spectrum of time- and space-restricted acceptors. While their theory is not quite as elegant as in the unrestricted case, it too can be developed within our framework. However, to do so here would only obscure and lengthen the exposition.

The organization of Ginsburg's book [5] is as follows: Chapters 1 and 2 contain preliminaries, Chapter 3 treats families of languages, Chapter 4 treats families of acceptors, Chapter 5 treats generators for families, Chapter 6 treats substitution,

*This research was supported in part by the National Science Foundation under Grant MCS 76-10076A01.

and Chapter 7 treats bounded generators. In the present paper, we shall omit the material from Chapters 6 and 7 and ignore families that are not full. Furthermore, generators arise so naturally in our development that a separate section discussing them is unnecessary. Consequently, the remainder of this paper contains just two sections, one on families of languages, the other on families of acceptors. (In this shortened version of the paper, each section is represented by just a few illustrative results.)

We believe that the central spine of AFL theory should be the duality between families of (one-way nondeterministic) acceptors and families of languages closed under certain operations. A principal goal of the theory should be to make it as easy as possible to switch viewpoints, so that a problem can be conceptualized one moment in terms of automata, the next in terms of languages. The principal tool in the theory should be the concept of a rational set and its use in describing rational transductions and acceptors with auxiliary storage. In this sense, at least, our development of AFL theory is a "rational" one.

It is a simple matter to develop the theory for unsophisticated audiences without mentioning rational sets at all except for the special case of regular sets (i.e. rational subsets of a free monoid), but at the cost of a slight loss of elegance. Some of the ingredients used in our development of the theory may be found in [2,3,4, 11]. Additional motivation may be found in [7].

2. FAMILIES OF LANGUAGES

A monoid M is a set with an associative binary operation $\cdot$ and a two-sided identity 1. If S is an abstract set, let S^* denote the free monoid generated by S. If S is a subset of a monoid M, let S^* denote the submonoid of M generated by S, and let $\langle S\rangle^*$ denote the free monoid generated by S. Thus, if S is a subset of M then $\langle S\rangle^*$ is not the same as S^* and is not even a subset of M. For example, if $\Sigma = \{a,b\}$ and $L = \{a,b,ab\} \subseteq \Sigma^*$, then L^* has its usual meaning as the Kleene closure of the language L, which in this case equals Σ^*; whereas $\langle L\rangle^*$ is isomorphic to $\{a,b,c\}^*$, which is quite different. For $s \in S$, it is convenient to write $\langle s\rangle$ for the same element in $\langle S\rangle^*$. There is a natural projection from $\langle S\rangle^*$ to $S^* \subseteq M$:

$$\hat{}\,: \quad \langle s_1\rangle \dots \langle s_n\rangle \mapsto s_1 \dots s_n.$$

If $A \subseteq \langle S\rangle^*$ then $\hat{A} \subseteq S^* \subseteq M$ is called the <u>trace</u> of A.

If M is any monoid, then the collection of <u>rational</u> subsets of M, denoted $\mathrm{RAT}(M)$, is the smallest collection $\mathcal{C}$ of subsets of M such that:

(1) All finite subsets of M are in $\mathcal{C}$.

(2) If A and B are in $\mathcal{C}$ then $A \cup B$ is in $\mathcal{C}$.

(3) If A and B are in $\mathcal{C}$ then $A \cdot B = \{a \cdot b \mid a,b \in M\}$ is in $\mathcal{C}$.

(4) If A is in $\mathcal{C}$ then A^* is in $\mathcal{C}$.

Let Σ_∞ be a fixed countably infinite set of symbols. If X is a symbol, possibly embellished with subscripts or primes, denoting a subset of Σ_∞^*, then the symbol Σ_X denotes the smallest set $\Sigma \subseteq \Sigma_\infty$ such that $X \subseteq \Sigma^*$, called the alphabet of X. The set of all languages is $\text{LANG} = \{L \mid L \subseteq \Sigma_\infty^*, \Sigma_L \text{ finite}\}$. The set of all regular languages is $\text{REG} = \text{RAT}(\Sigma_\infty^*) = \cup\{\text{RAT}(\Sigma^*) \mid \Sigma \subseteq \Sigma_\infty, \Sigma \text{ finite}\} \subseteq \text{LANG}$. A set of languages $\mathcal{L} \subseteq \text{LANG}$ is nontrivial if there is a language $L \neq \emptyset$ in $\mathcal{L}$.

A (binary rational) transducer is an element of the set

$$\mathcal{T} = \text{RAT}(\langle\Sigma_\infty^* \times \Sigma_\infty^*\rangle^*).$$

If T is a transducer, then its trace $\hat{T} \subseteq \Sigma_\infty^* \times \Sigma_\infty^*$ is a transduction or a binary rational (or birational) relation, and for $S \subseteq \Sigma_\infty^*$, $\hat{T}(S) = \{v \mid (u,v) \in \hat{T} \text{ for some } u \in S\}$.

It is easily seen that $\text{RAT}(\Sigma_\infty^* \times \Sigma_\infty^*)$ is the set of all birational relations. It is also easy to establish that if R_1 and R_2 are in REG then $R_1 \times R_2 \subseteq \Sigma_\infty^* \times \Sigma_\infty^*$ is a birational relation.

2.1. Example. For finite $\Sigma \subseteq \Sigma_\infty$, the identity relation I_Σ on Σ is birational since it is finite; hence the identity on Σ^* is birational since it equals $I_\Sigma^* \subseteq \Sigma_\infty^* \times \Sigma_\infty^*$. (Recall that multiplication in a product monoid is performed coordinatewise.)

2.2. Example. For $L \in \text{LANG}$ and $R \in \text{REG}$, let $B = I_{\Sigma_L}^* \cdot (\{1\} \times R) \subseteq \Sigma_\infty^* \times \Sigma_\infty^*$. Then B is a birational relation and $B(L) = L \cdot R$.

Any $T \in \text{RAT}(\langle\Sigma_\infty^* \times \Sigma_\infty^*\rangle^*)$ is built up from a finite number of elements in $\langle\Sigma_\infty^* \times \Sigma_\infty^*\rangle$, and hence is a set of strings over a finite alphabet. Except for the technicality that this alphabet need not lie in Σ_∞, it would follow that T is a language in LANG. However, since Σ_∞ is infinite, we can identify such a finite alphabet with a subset of Σ_∞. Thus, each transducer will be considered to be a regular language in REG.

Let $\hat{\mathcal{T}}(\mathcal{L}) = \{\hat{T}(L) \mid T \in \mathcal{T}, L \in \mathcal{L}\}$; $\mathcal{L}$ is birationally closed if $\hat{\mathcal{T}}(\mathcal{L}) \subseteq \mathcal{L}$. If M_1, M_2, M_3 are monoids, and $X \in \text{RAT}(M_1 \times M_2)$ and $Y \in \text{RAT}(M_2 \times M_3)$ then the composition $Y \circ X$ of these two relations is in $\text{RAT}(M_1 \times M_3)$, provided that M_2 is free [3, Th. IX, 4.1, p. 245]. Thus, the composition of birational relations is a birational relation, so $\hat{\mathcal{T}}(\mathcal{L})$ is birationally closed for any $\mathcal{L} \subseteq \text{LANG}$.

A BFL (for "Birationally-closed Family of Languages," and pronounced, appropriately enough, "baffle") is a birationally-closed countable nontrivial family of languages which is closed under finite union. It is a BFL* if it is closed under $*$, i.e. if L^* is in the family whenever the language L is. The smallest BFL or BFL* containing each language in $\mathcal{L}$ is denoted $\mathcal{B}(\mathcal{L})$ or $\mathcal{B}_*(\mathcal{L})$, respectively. A BFL (or BFL*) is principal if it has the form $\mathcal{B}(L)$ (or $\mathcal{B}_*(L)$) for some language L; L is called a generator. (We frequently identify elements and singletons; thus, $\mathcal{B}(L)$ means $\mathcal{B}(\{L\})$.) The countability requirement is convenient and does not exclude any families of interest. Except for this requirement, a BFL is what in [5] is called a full semiAFL and a BFL* is called a full AFL. (We would call a semiAFL a "realtime BFL" and require it always to contain {1} if we were discussing such families here.)

The following analogues of results from Chapter 3 of [5] are obtained more easily here because we treat transducers as rational sets. This approach is not original; it may be found, for example, in [2]. Unfortunately, it has not become widespread. What is original, so far as we know, is the continuation of this same approach in treating acceptors in the next section.

2.3. Proposition. A BFL is closed under post-concatenation with regular sets.

Proof. If $\mathcal{L}$ is a BFL, L is in $\mathcal{L}$, and R is in REG, then $L \cdot R = B(L)$ is in $\mathcal{L}$, where B is as in 2.2. □

2.4. Proposition. A BFL* is closed under concatenation.

Proof. Let $\mathcal{L}$ be a BFL*. For L and L' in $\mathcal{L}$, let ¢ and \$ be new symbols. Then L¢ and L'\$ are in $\mathcal{L}$ by 2.3. Hence, $LL' = B((L¢ \cup L'\$)^*)$ is in $\mathcal{L}$, where $B = (I^*_{\Sigma_L} \cdot (¢ \times 1) \cdot I^*_{\Sigma_{L'}} \cdot (\$ \times 1))$. □

2.5. Proposition. For each transducer T, there is a regular set R and homomorphisms h_1 and h_2 such that

$$\hat{T}(S) = h_2(h_1^{-1}(S) \cap R)$$

for all $S \subseteq \Sigma_\infty^*$.

Proof. Let π_i be the projection of $\Sigma_T^* \times \Sigma_T^*$ onto the i-th coordinate for $i = 1,2$. Let

$$\hat{\pi}_i: \ <\Sigma_T^* \times \Sigma_T^*>^* \to \Sigma_T^* \times \Sigma_T^* \xrightarrow{\pi_i} \Sigma_T^*$$

be the trace function composed with π_i. Then

$$\begin{aligned}\hat{T}(S) &= \{v \mid u \in S,\ (u,v) \in \hat{T}\} \\ &= \{\pi_2(\hat{t}) \mid \pi_1(\hat{t}) \in S,\ \hat{t} \in \hat{T}\} \\ &= \{\hat{\pi}_2(t) \mid \hat{\pi}_1(t) \in S,\ t \in T\} \\ &= \hat{\pi}_2(\hat{\pi}_1^{-1}(S) \cap T)\end{aligned}$$

where T, $\hat{\pi}_1$ and $\hat{\pi}_2$ are as required. □

2.6. Corollary. If $\mathcal{L}$ is a nontrivial family of languages then $\mathcal{R}(\mathcal{L})$ is the closure of $\mathcal{L}$ under homomorphism, inverse homomorphism, and intersection with regular sets.

Proof. Since each of these mappings is obviously birational, this result follows from 2.5. (Note: By convention, the range and domain of a homomorphism are required to be of the form Σ_1^* and Σ_2^*, where Σ_1 and Σ_2 are finite.) □

2.7. Proposition. A family $\mathcal{L}$ is a BFL or a BFL* iff $\mathcal{L} = \hat{\mathcal{T}}(S)$ or $\mathcal{L} = \hat{\mathcal{T}}((S¢)^*)$, respectively, for some S, $\emptyset \neq S \subseteq \Sigma_\infty^*$, and ¢ a new symbol. The family is principal iff S can be chosen to be a language.

Proof. If $\mathcal{L}$ is a BFL then let $S = L_1 \cup L_2 \cup \ldots$, where $L_1, L_2, \ldots$, are isomorphic copies of the languages in $\mathcal{L}$ taken over pairwise disjoint alphabets. For any transducer T there is an n such that

$$\hat{T}(S) = \hat{T}(L_1 \cup \ldots \cup L_n) \in \hat{\mathcal{T}}(L_1 \cup \ldots \cup L_n) \subseteq \mathcal{L},$$

so $\hat{\mathcal{T}}(S) \subseteq \mathcal{L}$. Since $L_i = I^*_{\Sigma_i}(S) \in \hat{\mathcal{T}}(S)$, $\mathcal{L} \subseteq \hat{\mathcal{T}}(S)$. Hence, $\mathcal{L} = \hat{\mathcal{T}}(S)$. If, in addition, $\mathcal{L}$ is closed under $*$, then let ¢ be a new symbol. For any transducer T there is an n such that $\hat{T}((S¢)^*) = \hat{T}((L¢)^*)$, where $L = L_1 \cup \ldots \cup L_n$, so that $(L¢)^*$ is in $\mathcal{L}$. Thus, $\hat{\mathcal{T}}((S¢)^*) \subseteq \mathcal{L}$. Since

$$L_i = (I^*_{\Sigma_i} \cdot (¢ \times 1))((S¢)^*) \in \hat{\mathcal{T}}((S¢)^*),$$

$\mathcal{L} \subseteq \hat{\mathcal{T}}((S¢)^*)$. Hence, $\mathcal{L} = \hat{\mathcal{T}}((S¢)^*)$.

If $\mathcal{L} = \hat{\mathcal{T}}(S)$, $\emptyset \neq S \subseteq \Sigma^*_\infty$, then $\mathcal{L}$ is a birationally-closed countable nontrivial family. Since $\hat{T}_1(S) \cup \hat{T}_2(S) = (\hat{T}_1 \cup \hat{T}_2)(S)$, $\mathcal{L}$ is closed under union and hence is a BFL.

If $\mathcal{L} = \hat{\mathcal{T}}((S¢)^*)$ then $\mathcal{L}$ is a BFL by the preceding paragraph, so to show $\mathcal{L}$ is a BFL* it suffices to show that it is closed under $*$. Suppose L is in $\mathcal{L}$. Then $L = \hat{T}((S¢)^*) = \hat{T}((L'¢)^*)$, where $(L'¢)^*$ is in $\mathcal{L}$. (Here, L' can be chosen to be that part of S that lies over the alphabet that $\hat{T}$ actually uses.) Let \$ be a new symbol, and let I be the identity relation on $\Sigma^*_{L'}$. Then the language

$$((L'¢)^*\$)^* = [(I \cdot (¢ \times ¢))^* \cdot (1 \times \$)]^*((L'¢)^*)$$

is in $\mathcal{L}$. Hence, the language

$$[\hat{T} \cdot (\$ \times 1)]^*(((L'¢)^*\$)^*) = (\hat{T}((L'¢)^*))^* = L^*$$

is in $\mathcal{L}$, as required.

Finally, it is easy to see that the family $\mathcal{L}$ is principal iff S can be chosen to be a language. □

3. FAMILIES OF ACCEPTORS

If D is any set, let Rel(D) be the set of all binary relations on D. Then Rel(D) is a monoid under the operation of composition defined by

$$X \cdot Y = \bigcup_{z \in D} \{(x,y) \mid (x,z) \in X,\ (z,y) \in Y\}.$$

If F is a set of binary relations on D and if D_0 and D_1 are subsets of D, then we write $F\colon D_0 \mapsto D_1$ if $(x,y) \in f$ for some $x \in D_0$, $y \in D_1$, $f \in F$.

3.1. Definition. A data store is a triple $\mathcal{D} = (D_0, \iota, D_1)$, where

$\iota\colon I \to \mathrm{Rel}(D)$ is a function, called the interpreter;

I is a countable set, called the set of instructions;

D is an arbitrary set, called the set of storage configurations; and

D_0 and D_1 are subsets of D, called the sets of initial and terminal configurations.

Since I^* is a free monoid, ι extends uniquely to a homomorphism $\iota\colon I^* \to \mathrm{Rel}(D)$, and we further require that $\iota(I^*)\colon D_0 \mapsto D_1$. If I is finite then $\mathcal{D}$ is a principal data store. The set $\mathcal{A}$ of $\mathcal{D}$-automata is

$\mathscr{A} = \mathrm{RAT}(<\Sigma_\infty^* \times I^*>^*)$.

The language defined by an automaton A in $\mathscr{A}$ is

$$L(A) = \{u \in \Sigma_\infty^* \mid \iota(\hat{A}(u)): D_0 \mapsto D_1\}, \text{ and } \mathscr{L}(\mathscr{D}) = \{L(A) \mid A \in \mathscr{A}\}.$$

Recall that $\hat{A}$ is the trace of A, so that $\hat{A} \subseteq \Sigma_\infty^* \times I^*$; hence, $\hat{A}$ can be considered a relation from Σ_∞^* to I^*. Then $\hat{A}(u) = \{v \mid (u,v) \in \hat{A}\} \subseteq I^*$ and $\iota(\hat{A}(u)) \subseteq \mathrm{Rel}(D)$. In words, L(A) consists of all inputs u to computations of A whose "outputs" are instruction sequences that can carry the storage from an initial to a terminal configuration. Note that L(A) is a language, i.e. its alphabet is finite, since A is rational.

(The requirement that $\iota(I^*): D_0 \mapsto D_1$ insures that some sequence of instructions can map an initial storage configuration to a terminal one. This excludes the trivial case in which the instructions are essentially useless and all of the corresponding automata only define the empty language $\emptyset$. We rule this case out for the same reason that earlier we required all families of languages to be nontrivial.)

It is often convenient to encode each storage configuration in D as a string of symbols from Σ_∞. If this is done, then D can be identified with Σ_∞^*.

3.2. Example. Let $\mathscr{D} = (1,\iota,1)$, or more formally, $(\{1\},\iota,\{1\})$, where $\iota: I \to \mathrm{Rel}(\Sigma_\infty^*)$, $I = \{x, x^{-1} \mid x \in \Sigma_\infty\}$, and

$$\iota(x): \Sigma_\infty^* \to \Sigma_\infty^*: w \mapsto wx;$$

$$\iota(x^{-1}): \Sigma_\infty^* \to \Sigma_\infty^*: wx \mapsto w.$$

Then $\mathscr{D}$ is a pushdown store, and $A = <a,a>^* <b,a^{-1}>^*$ is an example of a pushdown store automaton. (One could write A less cryptically as $A = <\text{read } a, \text{push } a>^* <\text{read } b, \text{pop } a>^*$.) Note that $L(A) = \{a^n b^n \mid n \geq 0\}$.

If $\mathscr{D} = (D_0,\iota,D_1)$, $\iota: I^* \to \mathrm{Rel}(D)$, is a data store, then its set of storage tracks is defined to be

$$S(\mathscr{D}) = \{v \in I^* \mid \iota(v): D_0 \to D_1\}.$$

Note that this need not be a language unless I is finite, i.e. unless $\mathscr{D}$ is principal. In defining $S(\mathscr{D})$, we assume that I is, or has been identified with, a subset of Σ_∞.

3.3. Theorem. If $\mathscr{D}$ is a data store and S is its set of storage tracks, then $\mathscr{L}(\mathscr{D}) = \hat{\mathscr{T}}(S)$.

Proof. For any $\mathscr{D}$-automaton A,

$$L(A) = \{u \in \Sigma_\infty^* \mid \iota\hat{A}(u): D_0 \mapsto D_1\}$$

$$= \{u \in \Sigma_\infty^* \mid \hat{A}(u) \cap S \neq \emptyset\}$$

$$= \hat{A}^{-1}(S),$$

where $\hat{A}^{-1}$ is the inverse of the relation $\hat{A}$. Hence,

$$\mathcal{L}(\mathcal{D}) = \{\hat{A}^{-1}(S) \mid A \in RAT(<\Sigma_\infty^* \times I^*>^*)\}$$
$$= \{\hat{T}(S) \mid T \in RAT(<I^* \times \Sigma_\infty^*>^*)\}$$
$$= \hat{\mathcal{T}}(S). \quad \square$$

A <u>reset</u> instruction in a data store $\mathcal{D} = (D_0, \iota, D_1)$ is an instruction v such that $\iota(v) = D_1 \times D_0$. Let $\mathcal{D}¢$ denote the data store resulting from $\mathcal{D}$ when the new symbol ¢ is added to the instruction set and $\iota(¢)$ is defined to be $D_1 \times D_0$. If $\mathcal{D}$ has a reset instruction then obviously $\mathcal{L}(\mathcal{D}) = \mathcal{L}(\mathcal{D}¢)$. In any case, the set of storage tracks of $\mathcal{D}¢$ is clearly $(S¢)^*S$, where S is the set of storage tracks of $\mathcal{D}$. Finally, note that it is easy to show that $\hat{\mathcal{T}}((S¢)^*) = \hat{\mathcal{T}}((S¢)^*S)$.

In the standard treatment of AFAs [5], $D = \Sigma_\infty^*$ and $D_0 = \{1\}$. For acceptance by final state, $D_1 = \Sigma_\infty^*$. For acceptance by final state and empty store, $D_1 = \{1\}$. In the latter case, what we have called a reset instruction is simply an instruction v with $\iota(v) = \{1\} \times \{1\}$, i.e. an instruction that checks that the store is empty. Since AFAs always have such instructions, the family of automata corresponding to a data store with a reset instruction can be viewed as a generalization of an AFA accepting by final state and empty store. Consequently, we would expect such families to correspond to BFL*'s rather than to BFL's.

<u>3.4. Theorem</u>. A family $\mathcal{L}$ is a BFL iff $\mathcal{L} = \mathcal{L}(\mathcal{D})$ for some data store $\mathcal{D}$. The family is a BFL* iff it equals $\mathcal{L}(\mathcal{D})$ for some data store $\mathcal{D}$ with a reset instruction. Furthermore, the family is principal iff $\mathcal{D}$ can be chosen to be principal, in which case the set of storage tracks is a generator.

<u>Proof</u>. Suppose $\mathcal{L} = \mathcal{L}(\mathcal{D})$ for a data store $\mathcal{D}$ with storage tracks S. Then $\mathcal{L} = \hat{\mathcal{T}}(S)$ by 3.3, which is a BFL by 2.7. If $\mathcal{D}$ has a reset instruction, then $\mathcal{L} = \mathcal{L}(\mathcal{D}¢) = \hat{\mathcal{T}}((S¢)^*S) = \hat{\mathcal{T}}((S¢)^*)$, and $\mathcal{L}$ is BFL* by 2.7. If $\mathcal{D}$ is principal then S is a language, so $\mathcal{L} = \hat{\mathcal{T}}(S)$ is principal with generator S.

Suppose $\mathcal{L}$ is a BFL. Then by 2.7, $\mathcal{L} = \hat{\mathcal{T}}(S)$ for some S, $\emptyset \neq S \subseteq \Sigma_\infty^*$. Let ¢ be a new symbol and define a data store $\mathcal{D} = (1, \iota, ¢)$ with storage configurations $D = \Sigma_\infty^*$ and

$$\iota(a): \; w \mapsto wa \quad (\text{for } a \in \Sigma_S),$$
$$\iota(¢): \; w \mapsto ¢ \quad \text{if } w \in S.$$

Then the set of storage tracks is $S¢$, so $\mathcal{L}(\mathcal{D}) = \hat{\mathcal{T}}(S¢) = \hat{\mathcal{T}}(S) = \mathcal{L}$.

Finally, if $\mathcal{L}$ is a BFL*, then by 2.7, $\mathcal{L} = \hat{\mathcal{T}}((S¢)^*)$ for some S, $\emptyset \neq S \subseteq \Sigma_\infty^*$, with ¢ a new symbol. Define $\mathcal{D} = (1, \iota, 1)$,

$$\iota(a): \; w \mapsto wa \quad (\text{for } a \in \Sigma_S),$$
$$\iota(¢): \; w \mapsto 1 \quad \text{if } w \in S.$$

The set of storage tracks is $(S¢)^*$, so $\mathcal{L}(\mathcal{D}) = \hat{\mathcal{T}}((S¢)^*) = \mathcal{L}$.

In both of the preceding cases, if $\mathcal{L}$ is a principal then S can be chosen to be a language, in which case $\mathcal{D}$ will be principal. $\square$

Note that the Dyck language D_2 on two generators is precisely the set of storage tracks of a binary (i.e. a two-symbol) pushdown store. Hence, it follows from 3.4 that D_2 generates the context-free languages. This result can be obtained from the usual development of AFL theory only with excruciating difficulty (see Section 5.3 of [5]).

If $\mathcal{L}$ and $\mathcal{L}'$ are families of languages, then $\mathcal{L}\wedge\mathcal{L}'$ is defined to be the family $\{L \cap L' | L\in\mathcal{L}, L'\in\mathcal{L}'\}$. We now define as analogues to this operation an operation $\wedge$ (wedge) on data stores and on operation $ш$ (shuffle) on languages. But first we prove a technical lemma.

Let $\hat{\mathcal{H}}(\mathcal{L})$ be the family of all homomorphic images of languages in $\mathcal{L}$.

3.5. Lemma. For any sets S_1 and S_2 of words,

$$\hat{\mathcal{T}}(\hat{\mathcal{T}}(S_1) \wedge \hat{\mathcal{T}}(S_2)) = \hat{\mathcal{H}}(\hat{\mathcal{T}}(S\ ) \wedge \hat{\mathcal{T}}(S_2)).$$

Proof. It suffices to show that $\hat{\mathcal{T}}(\hat{\mathcal{T}}(S_1) \wedge \hat{\mathcal{T}}(S_2)) \subseteq \hat{\mathcal{H}}(\hat{\mathcal{T}}(S_1) \wedge \hat{\mathcal{T}}(S_2))$, the reverse inclusion being trivial. If L is a language in the former family then by 2.5, with notation having the obvious meaning,

$$\begin{aligned} L &= h_2(h_1^{-1}(\hat{T}_1(S_1) \cap \hat{T}_2(S_2)) \cap R) \\ &= h_2(h_1^{-1}(\hat{T}_1(S_1)) \cap h_1^{-1}(\hat{T}_2(S_2)) \cap R) \\ &= h_2(\hat{T}_3(S_1) \cap \hat{T}_4(S_2) \cap R) \\ &= h_2(\hat{T}_3(S_1) \cap \hat{T}_5(S_2)) \\ &\in \hat{\mathcal{H}}(\hat{\mathcal{T}}(S_1) \wedge \hat{\mathcal{T}}(S_2)). \quad \square \end{aligned}$$

3.6. Definition. If $\mathcal{D} = (D_0, I \xrightarrow{\iota} Rel(D), D_1)$ and $\mathcal{D}' = (D_0', I' \xrightarrow{\iota'} Rel(D'), D_1')$ are data stores, where we assume that I' is relabelled if necessary to insure that $I \cap I' = \emptyset$, then

$$\mathcal{D}\wedge\mathcal{D}' = (D_0 \times D_0', I \cup I' \xrightarrow{\iota\times 1 \cup 1\times\iota'} Rel(D \times D'), D_1 \times D_1').$$

3.7. Example. If $\mathcal{D}$ and $\mathcal{D}'$ are pushdown stores, then $\mathcal{D}\wedge\mathcal{D}'$ is a data store having two pushdown stacks, and a given instruction in $I \cup I'$ operates on either the first stack (if the instruction is unprimed) or the second stack (if the instruction is primed). Thus, the $\mathcal{D}\wedge\mathcal{D}'$-automata have free use of both stacks.

The shuffle of two sets of words S_1 and S_2 is

$$S_1 ш S_2 = \{x_1\bar{y}_1 \dots x_n\bar{y}_n | x_1 \dots x_n \in S_1,\ y_1 \dots y_n \in S_2,\ x_i, y_i \in \Sigma_\infty^*\},$$

where the overbar indicates a relabelling of the letters in S_2's alphabet if necessary in order to force them to lie in an alphabet disjoint from S_1's. From the definition of $\mathcal{D}\wedge\mathcal{D}'$, it is obvious that $S_{\mathcal{D}\wedge\mathcal{D}'} = S_{\mathcal{D}} ш S_{\mathcal{D}'}$.

3.8. Lemma. $\hat{\mathcal{T}}(S_1 ш S_2) = \hat{\mathcal{H}}(\hat{\mathcal{T}}(S_1) \wedge \hat{\mathcal{T}}(S_2))$.

Proof. In general, if $\mathcal{L}_S = \{S \cap \Sigma^* | \Sigma \subseteq \Sigma_\infty \text{ finite}\}$, so that $\mathcal{L}_S$ is a set of languages whose union is S, then $\hat{\mathcal{T}}(S) = \cup\{\hat{\mathcal{T}}(L) \mid L \in \mathcal{L}_S\}$. Therefore, it is not hard to see that it suffices to prove the lemma in the case where S_1 and S_2 are languages. Furthermore, we may assume that their alphabets Σ_1 and Σ_2 are disjoint.

Let $h_1 : (\Sigma_1 \cup \Sigma_2)^* \to \Sigma_1^*$ and $h_2 : (\Sigma_1 \cup \Sigma_2)^* \to \Sigma_2^*$ be the obvious projections. Then

$$S_1 ш S_2 = h_1^{-1}(S_1) \cap h_2^{-1}(S_2) \in \hat{\mathcal{T}}(S_1) \wedge \hat{\mathcal{T}}(S_2).$$

Hence,

$$\hat{\mathcal{T}}(S_1 ш S_2) \subseteq \hat{\mathcal{T}}(\hat{\mathcal{T}}(S_1) \wedge \hat{\mathcal{T}}(S_2)) = \hat{\mathcal{H}}(\hat{\mathcal{T}}(S_1) \wedge \hat{\mathcal{T}}(S_2)).$$

Let L_1 and L_2 be languages in $\hat{\mathcal{T}}(S_1)$ and $\hat{\mathcal{T}}(S_2)$ respectively. Then $L_1 = \hat{T}_1(S_1)$ and $L_2 = \hat{T}_2(S_2)$, where we can assume that the transducers T_1 and T_2 print at most one output symbol per move, i.e. $T_i \in \text{RAT}(<\Sigma_\infty^* \times (\Sigma_\infty \cup \{1\})>^*)$. Let $T = T_1 ш T_2$. Since T_1 and T_2 are regular languages, so is T; hence, T is a transducer. Since T_1 and T_2 print at most one output symbol per move and since S_1 and S_2 have disjoint alphabets, it is a routine matter to verify that

$$L_1 ш L_2 = \hat{T}_1(S_1) ш \hat{T}_2(S_2) = \hat{T}(S_1 ш S_2) \in \hat{\mathcal{T}}(S_1 ш S_2).$$

But $L_1 \cap L_2 = \hat{T}_0(L_1 ш L_2)$, where $T_0 = \{<x\bar{x}, x> \mid x \in \Sigma_1^*\}^*$. Hence, $L_1 \cap L_2 \in \hat{\mathcal{T}}(S_1 ш S_2)$. So $\hat{\mathcal{H}}(L_1 \cap L_2) \in \hat{\mathcal{T}}(S_1 ш S_2)$, and

$$\hat{\mathcal{H}}(\hat{\mathcal{T}}(S_1) \wedge \hat{\mathcal{T}}(S_2)) \subseteq \hat{\mathcal{T}}(S_1 ш S_2). \quad \Box$$

<u>3.9. Theorem</u>. If $\mathcal{D}$ and $\mathcal{D}'$ are data stores, then

$$\mathcal{L}(\mathcal{D} \wedge \mathcal{D}') = \hat{\mathcal{T}}(S_{\mathcal{D}} ш S_{\mathcal{D}'}) = \hat{\mathcal{H}}(\mathcal{L}(\mathcal{D}) \wedge \mathcal{L}(\mathcal{D}')).$$

<u>Proof</u>.
$$\begin{aligned}\mathcal{L}(\mathcal{D} \wedge \mathcal{D}') &= \hat{\mathcal{T}}(S_{\mathcal{D} \wedge \mathcal{D}'}) \\ &= \hat{\mathcal{T}}(S_{\mathcal{D}} ш S_{\mathcal{D}'}) \\ &= \hat{\mathcal{T}}(\hat{\mathcal{T}}(S_{\mathcal{D}}) \wedge \hat{\mathcal{T}}(S_{\mathcal{D}'})) \\ &= \hat{\mathcal{H}}(\mathcal{L}(\mathcal{D}) \wedge \mathcal{L}(\mathcal{D}')). \quad \Box\end{aligned}$$

<u>3.10. Example</u>. If M is any Turing machine making an even number of moves, let

$$L_1 = \{d_1 ¢ d_3 ¢ \ldots d_{2n-1} \$ d_{2n}^t \ldots ¢ d_4^t ¢ d_2^t \mid d_1 \in \text{Start}, d_{2i-1} \vdash d_{2i}\},$$

$$L_2 = \{d_1 ¢ d_3 ¢ \ldots d_{2n-1} \$ d_{2n}^t \ldots ¢ d_4^t ¢ d_2^t \mid d_{2n} \in \text{Accept}, d_{2i} \vdash d_{2i+1}\},$$

where the d_i are instantaneous descriptions (id's) of M, w^t denotes the transpose (left-to-right reversal) of the word w, Start and Accept are the sets of starting and accepting id's, $\vdash$ is the move relation, and ¢ and \$ are new symbols. Then L_i is in Lin, the family of linear languages, and $L_1 \cap L_2$ is the set of all valid computations of M. If T is the transducer that erases everything but the input to the starting id of a computation of M, then $\hat{T}(L_1 \cap L_2)$ is the language accepted by M. Hence, if RE is the family of recursively enumerable languages and L is the language consisting of all binary palindromes,

$$RE = \hat{\mathcal{T}}(L \sqcup\!\sqcup L) = \hat{\mathcal{R}}(\mathrm{Lin} \wedge \mathrm{Lin}) \quad [1].$$

3.11. Example. A Turing machine can be simulated by an automaton with two counters in such a way that each counter changes from an increasing mode to a decreasing mode only once between two adjacent zeros. (See [10].) Letting a stand for "add 1", b for "subtract 1", and ¢ for "test for zero", it follows from the preceding results that

$$RE = \hat{\mathcal{T}}(L \sqcup\!\sqcup L), \quad L = (\{a^n b^n \mid n \geq 0\} \cdot ¢)^* \quad \text{(cf. [8].)}$$

4. CONCLUSION

The results we have derived are known. It is the method of derivation that is important. We believe that AFL theory should be organized around the duality between transducers operating on a language and acceptors operating on a data store. The theory should make it as easy as possible to switch from one point of view to the other. Operations on languages have as their duals operations on acceptors. Thus, we can generate families using * in addition to transduction, or we can work with acceptors having reset operations. The two points of view are equivalent. In terms of storage tracks, and hence in terms of generators, reset operations show up as a "marked *" operation, $(S¢)^*$. Similarly, intersection of languages corresponds to wedging data stores or shuffling generators.

This duality is very clear in the original development of AFL theory. However, the definition of an AFA is so complex that interest in it has almost died out, and many researchers think of AFL theory as essentially just the study of families of languages closed under certain operations, with no place for automata. They would not use the theory to derive such results as that D_2 generates CFL or that $RE = \hat{\mathcal{R}}(\mathrm{Lin} \wedge \mathrm{Lin})$, because they believe it is so awkward to do so. But to us, it is the quintessential role of the theory to permit the easy and conceptually clear derivation of results such as these.

5. REFERENCES

[1] B. S. Baker and R. V. Book, Reversal-bounded multipushdown machines, Inf. and Contr. 24 (1979), 231-246.

[2] J. H. Conway, Regular Algebra and Finite Machines, Chapman and Hall, London, 1971.

[3] S. Eilenberg, Automata, Languages, and Machines, Vol. A, Academic Press, New York, 1974.

[4] C. C. Elgot and J. E. Mezei, On relations defined by generalized finite automata, IBM J. Res. and Dev. 9 (1965), 47-68.

[5] S. Ginsburg, Algebraic and Automata-Theoretic Properties of Formal Languages, North-Holland, Amsterdam, 1975.

[6] S. Ginsburg and S. A. Greibach, Abstract families of languages, in "Studies in Abstract Families of Languages," Memoirs of the Am. Math. Soc., No. 87 (1969), 1-32.

[7] J. Goldstine, Automata with data storage, Proc. Conf. on Theoretical Computer Science, Univ. of Waterloo, Ontario, Canada (August, 1977), 239-246.

[8] J. Hartmanis and J. Hopcroft, What makes some language theory problems undecidable, J. Comp. Sys. Sci. (1970), 368-376.

[9] J. E. Hopcroft and J. D. Ullman, An approach to a unified theory of automata, Bell System Tech. J. 46 (1967), 1793-1829.

[10] M. Minsky, Recursive unsolvability of Posts' problem of "tag" and other topics in the theory of Turing machines, Ann. Math. 74 (1961), 437-455.

[11] M. Nivat, Transductions des langages de Chomsky, Ph.D. thesis, Paris, 1967.

ON THE SUCCINCTNESS OF DIFFERENT REPRESENTATIONS OF LANGUAGES†

J. Hartmanis

Department of Computer Science
Cornell University
Ithaca, NY 14853

Abstract

The purpose of this paper is to give simple new proofs of some interesting recent results about the relative succinctness of different representations of regular, deterministic and unambiguous context-free languages and to derive some new results about how the relative succinctness of representations change when the representations contain a formal proof that the languages generated are in the desired subclass of languages.

Introduction

It has been shown recently that there exist dramatic compressions of the length of representations of languages in subclasses of context-free languages as we go from restricted to unrestricted representations of these languages [3,5,6]. For example, when we consider the representation of deterministic context-free languages by deterministic versus nondeterministic pushdown automata, then there is no recursive function which can bound the size of the minimal deterministic pushdown automaton as a function of the size of the equivalent minimal nondeterministic pushdown automaton [6]. It is well known that we cannot recursively decide whether a given pushdown automaton has an equivalent deterministic pushdown automaton, but the above result makes a considerably stronger statement: even if we would know (or be given) which pushdown automata describe deterministic languages, we still could not effectively write down the corresponding deterministic pushdown automata because of their enormous size which grows nonrecursively in the size of the nondeterministic pushdown automata. Therefore we see that though nondeterminism is not needed in the description of nondeterministic context-free languages its use in the description permits nonrecursively bounded shortening of infinitely many representations.

Similar results hold for the relative succinctness of the description of unambiguous context-free languages by unambiguous and ambiguous context-free grammers [5], and the description of finite or regular sets by finite automata and pushdown automata [3].

Some of the original proofs of these results are quite hard and they require special results about context-free languages. In the first part of this paper we give a very simple, elementary proof that the relative succinctness of representing deterministic context-free languages by deterministic or nondeterministic pushdown automata is not recursively bounded, and using a result about inherently ambiguous context-free languages and Turing machine computations [4], derive an equally simple proof for the representation of unambiguous context-free languages by unambiguous or ambiguous context-free grammars. The results about the representation of finite and regular sets can be easily proven by the same methods.

We observe that in the representation of deterministic context-free languages by deterministic pushdown automata we can easily check whether a given pushdown automaton is deterministic, on the other hand, for a nondeterministic pushdown automaton

†This research has been supported in part by National Science Foundation Grants DCR75-09433 and MCS 78-00418.

we have no uniform way of verifying that it accepts a deterministic context-free language. Therefore the question arises whether the relative succinctness of the two representations is caused by the fact that in one representation we can prove what we are accepting but that no such proofs are possible in the other representation.

Indeed a close inspection of the original proof [6] reveals that it does not hold when we represent deterministic context-free languages by deterministic pushdown automata and pushdown automata with attached proofs that they accept deterministic context-free languages.

In the second part of this paper we show that our proof techniques furthermore prove that, for example, the relative succinctness results hold for the representation of deterministic context-free languages by deterministic pushdown automata and nondeterministic pushdown automata with attached proofs that they accept deterministic context-free languages.

Finally, to gain further insight how the inclusion of formal proofs or correctness in representations of languages affects their succinctness, we consider the representation of finite sets. We show that there is no recursive bound in the relative succinctness of the representation of finite sets by finite automata or Turing machines (even if we attach proofs that the Tm accepts a finite set). On the other hand, we show that the relative succinctness is recursively bounded for the representation of finite sets by finite automata or Turing machines with proofs which explicitly give the cardinality of the finite set accepted.

It follows from the results that the relative succinctness is not recursively bounded for the representation of finite sets by finite automata (or tables) or Turing machines which accept them, but that there is a recursive bound for the representation of finite sets by finite automata (or tables) and Turing machines which list them and halt.

It is interesting to observe that the succinctness results discussed in this paper do not directly follow from Blum's well known Size of Machines Theorem [1]. This theorem asserts that for any infinite, recursively enumerable set S of Turing machines one can effectively exhibit Turing machines in S which are arbitrarily (by any given recursive function) bigger than other equivalent Turing machines. This is actually not a succinctness result, in the sense used in this paper, since there is no guarantee that the shorter descriptions are not in S itself. One can derive a succinctness result between restricted and unrestricted Turing machine descriptions from Blum's Theorem if the minimal machines in S can be recursively enumerated (for example, if the machines in S are total). Even then the results in this paper do not follow from this general theorem because they deal with succinctness between two restricted representations and furthermore, in several cases the class of machines (or grammars) considered in this paper is not recursively enumerable, for example the class of unambiguous context-free grammars.

Succinctness Results about CFL's

We first establish notation and summarize some well known facts about context-free languages (cfl's).

We denote pushdown automata (pda) by A_i and deterministic pushdown automata (dpda) by D_j. Let $|A_i|$ denote the length of the description of the automaton A_i over some finite alphabet and $L(A_i)$ the language accepted by A_i. We consider only one-tape Turing machines, denoted by M_i, and for technical reasons we assume (without any loss of generality) that M_i can halt only after an even number of moves, M_i accepts by halting and that it makes at least two moves before halting, finally assume that M_i cannot print a blank. An instananeous description of M_i depicts the symbols written on the tape, indicates the tape square scanned by M_i and its state; they are strings of the following form:

$$-\Sigma^*(a,q)\Sigma^*-,-(-,q)\Sigma^*- \text{ or } -\Sigma^*(-,q)-,$$

where - denotes a blank tape square, Σ is the finite alphabet of symbols M_i can print, $a \in \Sigma$ and q is a state of M_i. For Tm M_i $ID_0(x)$ denotes the instantaneous description of the starting configuration on input x and $ID_1(x), ID_2(x), \ldots$ denote the successive instantaneous descriptions of M_i on input x. If $x = a_1a_2\ldots a_n$ then $x^T = a_na_{n-1}\ldots a_2a_1$. Let VALC[$M_i$] denote the set of valid computations of M_i in which every second instantaneous description is reversed, i.e.

$$\text{VALC}[M_i] = \{\#ID_0(x)\#[ID_1(x)]^T\#ID_2(x)\ldots\#[ID_{2k-1}(x)]^T\#ID_{2k}(x)\# \mid x \in \Sigma^* \text{ and } ID_{2k}(x) \text{ is a halting configuration}\}.$$

Let

$$\text{INVALC}[M_i] = \Gamma^* - \text{VALC}[M_i].$$

It is well known that INVALC[M_i] can be accepted by a nondeterministic pda and therefore it is a cfl [2]. On the other hand, VALC[M_i] is a cfl iff $L(M_i)$ is a finite set, since otherwise for arbitrarily large inputs x the three first instantaneous descriptions must be related and the cfl pumping lemma does not hold. This yields the well known auxiliary result.

Lemma 1: INVALC[M_i] is a deterministic cfl iff $L(M_i)$ is finite.

Proof: If $L(M_i)$ is finite then INVALC[M_i] is a regular set and therefore a dcfl. If $L(M_i)$ is infinite then VALC[M_i] is not a cfl and therefore INVALC[M_i] cannot be a dcfl. ∎

Lemma 2: The set $R = \{A_i \mid L(A_i) \text{ is not a dcfl}\}$ is not recursively enumerable.

Proof: Since INVALC[M_i] is a deterministic cfl iff $L(M_i)$ is finite, a recursive enumeration of R would yield a recursive enumeration of the set $\{M_i \mid L(M_i) \text{ is infinite}\}$, which is seen not to be possible by Rices's theorem. ∎

For two representations, such as the representation of deterministic cfl's by deterministic and nondeterministic pda's, we will say that their relative succinctness is not recursively bounded, if there does not exist a recursive function F such that for any pda, A, that accepts a deterministic cfl, there exists an equivalent deterministic pda, D, for which $|D| \le F(|A|)$.

Theorem 3: The relative succinctness of representing deterministic cfl's by deterministic and nondeterministic pda's is not recursively bounded.

Proof: If such a recursive function F exists then for any pda A we can compute $F(|A|)$ and effectively list the dpda's whose length of description does not exceed $F(|A|)$, say $D_{i_1}, D_{i_2}, \ldots, D_{i_s}$. Then L(A) is a nondeterministic cfl iff none of the D_{i_j}, $1 \le j \le s$, is equivalent to A, but if this is so then we can detect it by comparing the D_{i_j} and A on successive inputs from Σ^*. Therefore the existence of F implies that the set

$$\{A \mid L(A) \text{ is not a dcfl}\}$$

is recursively enumerable, which we know is not the case by Lemma 2. Therefore, F does not exist as was to be shown. ■

Next we consider the relative succinctness between the representation of unambiguous cfl's by unambiguous and ambiguous cfg's.

We exploit a recent result, which is given in a somewhat different formulation in in [4]. For any Tm, M_i, let

$$A_S(M_i) = \{\#ID_0(x)\#([ID_j]^T\# \; ID_{j+1} \; \#)^* \mid ID_{j+1} \text{ follows from } ID_j \text{ by one operation of } M_i,\ x \in \Sigma^*\}$$

$$A_E(M_i) = \{\#(ID_j \#[ID_{j+1}]^T\#)^* \; ID_{2k}\# \mid ID_{j+1} \text{ follows from } ID_j \text{ in one operation of } M_i \text{ and } ID_{2k} \text{ is a halting configuration.}\}$$

and define

$$A(M_i) = A_S(M_i) \cup A_E(M_i).$$

It is easily seen that $A(M_i)$ is a context-free language and it links the ambiguity question for $A(M_i)$ to finiteness of sets accepted by the Turing machine M_i.

<u>Theorem 4</u>: $A(M_i)$ is an inherently ambiguous cfl iff $L(M_i)$ is infinite.

<u>Proof</u>: See [4]. ■

<u>Theorem 5</u>: The relative succinctness of representing unambiguous cfl's by unambiguous and ambiguous cfg's is not recursively bounded.

<u>Proof</u>: If a recursive bound F exists, then the set

$$AMB = \{G \mid G \text{ cfg and } L(G) \text{ is inherently ambiguous}\}$$

is rucursively enumerable. To see this note that we can list for any cfg G all cfg's whose representations are shorter than $F(|G|)$ and then cross off those grammars which are found to be ambiguous or not equivalent to G as we test them on successive strings from Σ^*. L(G) is inherently ambiguous iff eventually all grammars from the list are crossed off. Thus the set AMB is recursively enumerable and therefore, (by Theorem 4) so is the set

$$\{M_i \mid L(M_i) \text{ is infinite}\},$$

which leads to a contradiction. Therefore the recursive bound F does not exist. ■

By the same method we can give an easy proof for the next result [3].

<u>Theorem 6</u>: The relative succinctness of the representation of cofinite sets by finite automata and pushdown automata is not recursively bounded. Therefore the relative succinctness of the representation of regular sets by finite automata and pushdown automata is also not recursively bounded.

<u>Proof</u>: Similar to the proof of Theorem 3, by using the set

$$R = \{A_i \mid L(A_i) \text{ is not cofinite}\}.$$ ■

The same reasoning shows that there is no recursive bound between the size of context-free grammars (which generate cfl's whose complements are also cfl's) and the size of the cfg's generating the complements.

Theorem 7: There is no recursive function F such that for any cfg G for which $\Sigma^* - L(G)$ is a cfl, there exists a cfg, G', with $L(G') = \Sigma^* - L(G)$ and $|G'| \le F(|G|)$.

Proof: Similar to the proof of Theorem 3. ∎

Succinctness Results about Verified Representations

In the representation of deterministic cfl's by deterministic and nondeterministic pda's we can easily verify that a given automaton is indeed deterministic, but for an equivalent nondeterministic pda we have no fixed way of verifying that it will accept a deterministic cfl. This lack of symmetry in our representations suggests that we should consider only representations by nondeterministic pda's with attached proofs that they accept a deterministic language and add the length of the proof to the length of the representation of the pda.

A close inspection of the original proofs [3,5,6] reveals that they do not extend to representations with added proofs. On the other hand our proof techniques show that the previous succinctness results can be extended to representations with attached verifications that they accept the desired type of language.

More precisely, let FS be an axiomatizable, sound formal mathematical system which is powerful enough to express and prove elementary facts about Turing machines, context-free languages and pushdown automata. Since FS is axiomatizable we know that we can recursively enumerate the set of provable theorems and soundness assures us that the provable theorems are true. Instead of specifying FS in detail we will describe what must be easily provable in FS.

a) Let $M_{\sigma(r)}$ be a simply and uniformly constructed Tm which for each input x computes and saves the length of x, $|x| = n$; then enumerates all one-tape Tm's up to length r, i.e. $|M_i| \le r$, and simulates in a dowe-tail manner the computations of this finite set of machines on blank tape. $M_{\sigma(r)}$ halts (and thus accepts) iff some M_i, $|M_i| \le r$, halts after performing n or more steps. From this construction we see that for all r, $r \ge 1$, $M_{\sigma(r)}$ accepts a finite set. We assume that FS is sufficiently powerful that we can prove in FS that $L(M_{\sigma(r)})$ is finite and that the length of these proofs is recursively bounded in r.

b) We furthermore assume that there is a simple and uniform construction ρ which yields for each Tm M_i a pda $A_{\rho(i)}$ such that

$$L(A_{\rho(i)}) = \text{INVALC}[M_i]$$

and that it can be proven in FS (by a proof whose length is recursively bounded in i) that:

if $L(M_i)$ is finite then $L(A_{\rho(i)}) = \text{INVALC}[M_i]$ is a deterministic cfl.

From these assumptions it follows that we can prove (easily) in FS that:

$A_{\rho(\sigma(r))}$ accepts a deterministic cfl.

It should be observed that in any logic designed to reason about computations we should be able to formulate and prove easily the above result. Furthermore, to any given sound formal system we can add the above assertions as an axiom scheme to obtain the desired FS.

A nondeterministic pda with an attached proof in FS that it accepts a deterministic cfl is called a <u>verified</u> pda or <u>vpda</u>.

Theorem 8: The relative succinctness of representing dcfl's by dpda's and vpda's is not recursively bounded.

Proof: For r, $r \geq 1$, let $M_{\sigma(r)}$ be a Tm which accepts all inputs up to length N_r, where N_r is the maximal running time before halting achieved by a Tm of size r on blank tape. Let $A_{\rho(i)}$ be a non-deterministic pda which accepts INVALC$[M_i]$. It is assumed that $\sigma(r)$ and $\rho(r)$ are simple enough to compute and that FS is sufficiently rich that there exist short proofs (whose length is recursively bounded in r) that $L[M_{\sigma(r)}]$ is finite and therefore $L[A_{\rho(\sigma(r))}]$ is a deterministic cfl.

If there exists a recursive bound F between $|A_{\rho(\sigma(r))}|$ and the shortest equivalent dpda, then we can list all the dpda's

$$D_{i_1}, D_{i_2}, \ldots, D_{i_s}, \text{ such that } |D_{i_j}| \leq F[|A_{\rho(\sigma(r))}|], \; 1 \leq j \leq s.$$

From this list of dpda's we can effectively construct a list of dpda's which accept the complements of these languages. From this new list we can effectively select the dpda's which accept finite sets and compute the longest string accepted by these dpda's. Clearly the length of this string is bigger than N_r and therefore N_r is recursively bounded in r, which is a contradiction. ■

By exploiting the fact that we can recursively enumerate the vpda's we can prove the next result.

Corollary 9: There is no recursive succinctness bound between the representation of dcfl's by verified pda's and pda's.

By assuming that we can easily prove in FS relations between $A(M_i)$ and ambiguous cfl's (i.e. Theorem 4) we obtain the next result.

Corollary 10: There is no recursive succinctness bound between the representation of unambiguous cfl's by unambiguous cfg's and ambiguous cfg's with proofs that they accept unambiguous cfl's.

Representation of Finite Sets

The situation changes drastically if we consider representation of finite sets and finite sets of known size.

Theorem 11: a) There is no recursive succinctness bound for the representation of finite sets by finite automata and by Tm's with proofs that they accept finite sets.

b) There is a recursive succinctness bound for the representation of finite sets by finite automata (or tables) and Tm's with proofs which explicitly give the size of the finite set accepted.

c) There is a recursive bound for the relative succinctness of representing finite sets by finite automata (or lists) and Tm's with proofs that they print a list and halt.

Proof: a) Let $M_{\sigma(r)}$ be the Tm constructed for the proof of Theorem 8 and recall that we have assumed that our formal system FS is sufficiently rich to prove, by proofs whose length is recursively bounded in r, that $L(M_{\sigma(r)})$ is finite. Therefore the length of $M_{\sigma(r)}$ plus the length of the proof in FS that $L(M_{\sigma(r)})$ is finite is recursively bounded in r. On the other hand, since $L(M_{\sigma(r)})$ is finite the number of states of any finite automaton accepting $L(M_{\sigma(r)})$ must be no less than the length of the longest string in $L(M_{\sigma(r)})$, which by construction of $M_{\sigma(r)}$ is not recursively bounded in r. Therefore, the relative succinctness of these two representations cannot be recursively bounded.

b) The relative succinctness bound F can be constructed as follows. For n construct all proofs of "M_i accepts a set of size k", i,k = 1,2,..., such that $|M_i|$ plus the length of the proof is less or equal to n. For the M_i with such proofs let k_n be the cardinality of the largest set accepted and a_n the length of the longest string accepted. Clearly k_n and a_n are effectively computable and

$$F(n) = a_n \cdot k_n + 2$$

is such a recursive bound.

c) For any n we can effectively list the finite set of Tm's, $M_{i_1}, M_{i_2}, \ldots, M_{i_k}$, such that

$$|M_{i_j}| + |\text{proof that } M_{i_j} \text{ prints a list and halts}| \leq n.$$

Therefore we can run all the Tm's on this list, which are guaranteed to halt because FS is sound, and determine the length of the longest string printed, n_m. Clearly n_m is recursively computable from n, by the above procedure, and, furthermore, the size of the largest minimal finite automaton accepting the sets $L(M_{i_1})$, $L(M_{i_2})$,..., $L(M_{i_k})$ is recursively bounded in n_m. Therefore the size of the finite automata representation of these sets is recursively bounded to n and therefore to the size of the Tm representation with proofs.

■

References

[1] Blum, M. "On the Size of Machines", Information and Control, Vol. 11 (1967), 257-265.

[2] Hartmanis, J. "Context-Free Languages and Turing Machine Computations", Proceedings of Symposia in Applied Mathematics, Vol. 19, Mathematical Aspects of Computer Science, pp. 42-51, Amer. Math. Soc. 1967.

[3] Meyer, A.R. and M.J. Fischer. "Economy of Description by Automata, Grammars and Formal Systems", Conference Record, IEEE 12th Annual Symposium on Switching and Automata Theory (1971), 188-190.

[4] Reedy, H. and W.J. Savitch. "The Turing Degree of the Inherent Ambiguity Problem for Context-Free Languages", Theoretical Computer Science, Vol. 1 (1975), 77-91.

[5] Schmidt, E.H. and T.G. Szymanski. "Succinctness of Descriptions of Unambiguous Context-Free Languages", SIAM J. Computing, Vol. 6 (1977), 547-553.

[6] Valiant, L.G. "A Note on the Succinctness of Descriptions of Deterministic Languages", Information and Control, Vol. 32 (1976), 139-145.

A FIXED-POINT THEOREM FOR RECURSIVE-ENUMERABLE LANGUAGES AND SOME CONSIDERATIONS ABOUT FIXED-POINT SEMANTICS OF MONADIC PROGRAMS

Sorin Istrail
Computer Center, University "Al.I.Cuza"
Iaşi 6600, Romania

ABSTRACT

This paper generalizes the ALGOL-like theorem showing that every λ-free context-sensitive (recursive-enumerable) language is a component of the minimal solution of a system of equation $X=F(X)$, where $X=(X_1,\dots,X_t)$, $F=(F_1,\dots,F_t)$, $t \geqslant 1$ and F_i, $1 \leqslant i \leqslant t$ are regular expressions over the alphabet of operations:{concatenation, reunion, kleene "+" closure, nonereasing finite substitution (arbitrary finite substitution), intersection}.

In the second part is presented a method which constructs for a monadic program a system of equations (in the above form) so that one of the components of the minimal solution of the system gives the partial function f computed by the program in a language form:

$$\left\{ a^{n+1} \# b^{f(n)+1} \mid n \in \mathrm{Dom}\, f \right\} .$$

1. PRELIMINARIES

Let V be a finite set of symbols, V^* the free monoid generated by V, λ the unit of V^*, $V^+ = V^* \setminus \{\lambda\}$

The elements of V^* are called words and the subsets of V^* are called languages. We suppose the reader familiar with the basic facts about formal language theory [7] and developmental systems [2]. Let us denote by R, CF, CS, CS_λ, RE the classes of regular, context-free, context-sensitive, λ-free context-sensitive and recursive-enumerable languages.

DEFINITION. A OL-system is a triple $S = \langle V,P,w \rangle$ where P is a finite set of pairs, $P \subset V \times V^*$ with the property that for every $a \in V$, there exists $u \in V^*$ so that $(a,u) \in P$; the elements of P are called rules and are usually denoted by $p \longrightarrow q$, for $(p,q) \in P$; w is a word from V^*, called the axiom. The set P is called table, and the pair $S' = \langle V,P \rangle$ is sometimes called OL-scheme.

The binary relation $\underset{S}{\Longrightarrow} \subset V^* \times V^*$ is defined by $w_1 \underset{S}{\Longrightarrow} w_2$ if $w_1 = a_1 \dots a_t$, $w_2 = u_1 \dots u_t$, $t \geqslant 0$, $a_j \in V$, $u_j \in V^*$, $1 \leqslant j \leqslant t$ and for every i, $1 \leqslant i \leqslant t$, $a_i \to u_i \in P$.

The relation $\overset{*}{\underset{S}{\Longrightarrow}}$ denotes the reflexive transitive closure of $\underset{S}{\Longrightarrow}$.

A language L is called <u>OL language</u> if there exists an OL-system S so that L(S) = L.

A generative device, which is a derivational restricted OL system is introduced in the following lines.

<u>DEFINITION</u>. A <u>perturbant configuration</u> for the OL-scheme $S = \langle V,P \rangle$ is a family $\Pi = (\pi_a)_{a \in V}$ where for every $a \in V$, $\pi_a = \langle n(a), E_a, F_a \rangle$ and

i) $n(a) \geqslant 1$

ii) $E_a = \{ E_a^{(1)}, \dots, E_a^{(n(a))} \}$, $\bigcup_{i=1}^{n(a)} E_a(i) = V^+$,

$$E_a^{(i)} \cap E_a^{(j)} = \emptyset \text{ , } i \neq j, \ 1 \leqslant i, \ \ j \leqslant n(a)$$

iii) $F_a = \{ F_a^{(1)}, \dots, F_a^{(n(a))} \}, \emptyset \neq F_a^{(i)} \subset (P \cap \{a\} \times V^*)$
$1 \leqslant i \leqslant n(a)$

Let be $\mathcal{L}$ a family of languages. A perturbant configuration is called <u>$\mathcal{L}$-perturbant configuration</u> for an OL scheme S if $\Pi = (\pi_a)_{a \in V}$ and for every $a \in V$ and i, $1 \leqslant i \leqslant n(a)$ we have $E_a^{(i)} \in \mathcal{L}$.

<u>DEFINITION</u>. A <u>SICK-OL system</u> is a triple $\mathcal{S} = (S, \Pi, w)$ where:

i) $S = \langle V,P,w \rangle$ is an OL-system

ii) Π is a perturbant configuration for the scheme $S' = \langle V,P \rangle$.

iii) w is the axiom of $\mathcal{S}$, $w \in V^*$.

We define now the following binary relation $\underset{\mathcal{S}}{\Longrightarrow}$, for $w = a_1 \dots a_t$, $u = u_1, \dots, u_t$ with $a_k \in V$, $u_k \in V^*$, $1 \leqslant k \leqslant t$ we put $w \underset{\mathcal{S}}{\Longrightarrow} u$ iff for every j, $1 \leqslant j \leqslant t$, $a_j \to u_j \in F_{a_j}^{(s)}$, where "s" is defined by $w \in E_{a_j}^{(s)}$. (In words, we can apply for a letter "a" occuring in a word w_1 rules from those set in F_a corresponding to those set in E_a which contains w_1).

Let $\overset{*}{\underset{\mathcal{S}}{\Longrightarrow}}$ be the reflexive transitive closure of $\underset{\mathcal{S}}{\Longrightarrow}$.

<u>The language generated</u> by the SICK-OL system $\mathcal{S} = (S, \Pi, w)$ is defined by $L(\mathcal{S}) = \{ u \mid u \in V^*, w \overset{*}{\underset{\mathcal{S}}{\Longrightarrow}} u \}$, where $S' = \langle V,P \rangle$.

A language L is called <u>SICK-OL language</u> if there exists a SICK-OL system $\mathcal{S}$ so that $L(\mathcal{S}) = L$.

<u>DEFINITION</u>. An <u>extended SICK-OL system</u> is a 4-tuple $\mathcal{S}' = (S, \Pi, w, Z)$,

where $\mathcal{S} = (S, \Pi, w)$ is a SICK-OL system, $S' = \langle V, P \rangle$ and $Z \subset V$.

The language generated by the extended SICK-OL system $\mathcal{S}' = (S, \Pi, w, Z)$ is given by $L(\mathcal{S}') = L(S, \Pi, w) \cap Z^*$.

Let us denote by SICK-OL the class of SICK-OL languages. If $\mathcal{L}$ is a family of languages, $\mathcal{L}$ SICK-OL denotes the class of languages obtained from those SICK-OL system with $\mathcal{L}$-perturbant configurations.

If the rules of a certain type of L systems do not erase, the L-system is called propagating.

We add the letters P and E (or both) to the abreviation of L-systems to denote the classes of corresponding Propagating and Extended L-systems.

2. TWO FIXED-POINT THEOREMS

In this section we present two fixed-point theorems, one for CS_λ and another for RE. They are generalizations of the well known ALGOL-like theorem.

In the following we are interested in P SICK-OL systems with R-perturbant configurations.

THEOREM 1. For every λ-free context-sensitive language L, there exists a propagating extended R SICK-OL system $\mathcal{S}'$ so that $L(\mathcal{S}') = L$.

PROOF. Let $G = (I_N, I_T, x_o, F)$ be a context-sensitive grammar so that $L(G) = L$ and suppose that $\lambda \notin L$. The rules of the grammars are in the form $pxq \rightarrow puq$ where $p, q \in V^*$, $x \in I_N$, $u \in V^+$ and $V = I_N \cup I_T$. Thus no rules in the form $x_o \rightarrow \lambda$, belongs to F.

Let us consider a new alphabet $I_N = \{\bar{a} \mid a \in I_N\}$. We need some preliminary notations:

$$F(x) = \{x \rightarrow u \mid p, q \in V^*, \quad u \in V^+, \quad pxq \rightarrow puq \in F\}$$

If t_x is the number of elements of $F(x)$ then:

$$T_x = \{(p_i^x, r_i^x) \mid p_i^x \, x \, r_i^x \rightarrow p_i^x \, u \, r_i^x \in F, \; 1 \leqslant i \leqslant t_x\}$$

(the set of all contexts for x, used in the rules of G).

$$Z(i,x) = \{\bar{x} \rightarrow u \mid p_i^x \, x \, r_i^x \rightarrow p_i^x \, u \, r_i^x \in F\} \cup \{\bar{x} \rightarrow \bar{x}\}$$

$$F(i,x) = \bigcup \{Z(j,x) \mid p_i^x = v p_j^x, \; r_i^x = r_j^x \, z, v, z \in V^*\}$$

$$E(i,x) = V^* p_i^x \, x \, r_i^x V^* \setminus \bigcup \{V^* p^x \, x \, r_j^x \, V^* \mid p_j^x = v \, p_i^x, \; r_j^x = r_i^x z, \quad v, z \in V^*, \quad vz \neq \lambda\}.$$

We notice that for $i \neq j$, $1 \leqslant i, j \leqslant t_x$, $E(i,x) \cap E(j,x) = \emptyset$.

We intend to construct a propagating extended SICK-OL system $\mathcal{S}' = (S, \Pi, x_0, I_T)$. So that $L(\mathcal{S}') = L(G)$.

We define $S = \langle V \cup \bar{I}_N, D \rangle$, where

$$D = \Big(\bigcup_{\substack{x \in I_N \\ 1 \leq i \leq t_x}} Z(i,x) \Big) \cup \{ x \longrightarrow x, \bar{x} \longrightarrow \bar{x}, x \longrightarrow \bar{x} \mid x \in I_N \} \cup \{ a \longrightarrow a \mid a \in I_T \}$$

We define a $\underline{R}$-perturbant configuration $\Pi = (\pi_y)_{y \in V \cup \bar{I}_N}$ by

1) for $x \in I_N$, $\pi_x = \langle 2, E_x, F_x \rangle$, where

$E_x^{(1)} = V^+, E_x^{(2)} = (V \cup \bar{I}_N)^+ \setminus V^+$, $F_x^{(1)} = \{ x \longrightarrow x, x \longrightarrow \bar{x} \}$,

$F_x^{(2)} = \{ x \longrightarrow x \}$.

2) for $\bar{x} \in \bar{I}_N$, $\pi_{\bar{x}} = \langle t_x + 1, E_x, F_x \rangle$, where

$E_{\bar{x}}^{(i)} = E(i,x)$, $F_{\bar{x}}^{(i)} = F(i,x)$, $1 \leq i \leq t_x$

$E_{\bar{x}}^{(t_x+1)} = V^+ \setminus \bigcup_{i=1}^{t_x} E_{\bar{x}}^{(i)}$, $F_{\bar{x}}^{(t_x+1)} = \{ \bar{x} \longrightarrow \bar{x} \}$

3) for $a \in I_T$, $\pi_a = \langle 1, (V \cup \bar{I}_N)^+, \{ a \rightarrow a \} \rangle$.

<u>DEFINITION.</u> A <u>Self-controled Tabled OL system</u> (SC-TOL) is a 5-tuple $\mathcal{C} = (V, m(\mathcal{C}), D, C, w)$ where

i) V is <u>the alphabet</u> of $\mathcal{C}$;

ii) $m(\mathcal{C})$ is a positive integer;

iii) $D = \{ D_i \}_{i=1}^{m(\mathcal{C})}$, $D_i \cap D_j = \emptyset$, $i \neq j$, $1 \leq i,j \leq n$ $(\mathcal{C})$ $\bigcup_{i=1}^{m(\mathcal{C})} D_i = V^+$

iv) $C = \{ C_i \}_{i=1}^{m(\mathcal{C})}$, $C_i \subset V \times V^*$, is a table, $1 \leq i \leq m$ $(\mathcal{C})$

If $\mathcal{C}$ is a SC-TOL system, the following binary relation is introduced: for $w = a_1 \ldots a_t$, $u = u_1 \ldots u_t$ with the property that $a_k \in V$ and $u_k \in V^*$, $1 \leq k \leq t$ we put $w \underset{\mathcal{C}}{\Longrightarrow} u$ iff for every $j, 1 \leq j \leq t$, $a_j \longrightarrow u_j \in C_s$, where "s" is defined by $w \in D_s$. (In words, we can apply to w rules from a table C_s iff $w \in D_s$).

The definitions of $\overset{*}{\underset{\mathcal{C}}{\Longrightarrow}}$, language generated by $\mathcal{C}$, SC-TOL language, E SC-TOL, $\mathcal{L}$ SC-TOL can be obtained similarly.

Let us denote by $\hat{T}$ the finite substitution generated by a table T.

<u>THEOREM 2.</u> For every SC-TOL system $\mathcal{C}$ there is a SICK-OL system $\mathcal{S}$ so

that $L(\mathcal{C}) = L(\mathcal{S})$.

PROOF. Let us suppose that we have an SC-TOL $\mathcal{C} = (V, m(\mathcal{C}), C, D, w)$. Then we define a perturbant configuration $\Pi = (\pi_a)_{a \in V}$ by

$$\pi_a = (m(\mathcal{C}), D, \{C_i \cap (a \times V^*)\}_{i=1}^{m(\mathcal{C})})$$

The SICK-OL system $\mathcal{S} = (V, \Pi, w)$ generates exactly $L(\mathcal{C})$.

The converse of Theorem 2 is also true.

THEOREM 3. For every SICK-OL system $\mathcal{S} = (S, \Pi, w)$ there exists an equivalent SC-TOL system $\mathcal{C} = (V, m(\mathcal{C}), D, C, w)$, i.e. $L(\mathcal{C}) = L(\mathcal{S})$.

PROOF. Let be $V = \{a_1, \ldots, a_s\}$ and Π detailed by

$$E_{a_j}^{(i)}, \quad F_{a_j}^{(i)}, \quad 1 \leqslant i \leqslant n(a_j), \quad 1 \leqslant j \leqslant s.$$

For k_j variyng in $\{1, \ldots, n(a_j)\}$, $1 \leqslant j \leqslant s$, let us consider the sets:

$$E_{a_1}^{(k_1)} \cap E_{a_2}^{(k_2)} \cap \ldots \cap E_{a_s}^{(k_s)} = T(k_1, \ldots, k_s)$$

Now we have a partition of V^* given by the collection

$$\Delta = \{T(k_1, \ldots, k_s) \mid T(k_1, \ldots, k_s) \neq \emptyset,$$
$$k_j \in \{1, \ldots, n(a_j)\}, \quad 1 \leqslant i \leqslant s\}.$$

If m_o is the number of sets in Δ we define a SC-TOL

$$\mathcal{C} = (V, m_o, \{T(k_k, \ldots, k_s) \mid T(k_1, \ldots, k_s) \neq \emptyset\},$$
$$\{Z(k_1, \ldots, k_s) \mid T(k_1, \ldots, k_s) \neq \emptyset\}, w), \text{ where}$$
$$Z(k_1, \ldots, k_s) = \bigcup_{i=1}^{s} F_{a_i}^{(k_i)}$$

It is easy to see that

$$L(\mathcal{S}) = L(\mathcal{C}).$$

COROLLARY 1. SICK-OL = SC-TOL

$$\text{EP } \underline{R} \text{ SICK-OL} = \text{EP } \underline{R} \text{ SC-TOL} \supseteq \underline{CS}_\lambda$$

The inclusion presented in the Corollary 1 is in fact equality.

THEOREM 4. Every propagating $\underline{R}$ SC-TOL system generates a context-sensitive language.

COROLLARY 2.

$$\text{EP } \underline{R} \text{ SICK-OL} = \text{EP } \underline{R} \text{ SC - TOL} = \underline{CS}_\lambda$$

THEOREM 5. For every SC-TOL system $\mathcal{C} = (V, m(\mathcal{C}), P, Q, w)$ there exists a system of equations

$$(*)\qquad \begin{cases} X_1 = F_1(X_1,\dots,X_t) \\ \dots\dots\dots\dots\dots\dots \\ X_t = F_t(X_1,\dots,X_t) \end{cases}$$

so that $L(\mathcal{C}) = \bigcup_{n=1}^{t} X_n^{MIN}$ where $(X_1^{MIN},\dots,X_t^{MIN})$ is the minimal solution of $(*)$.

PROOF. Let be the system of equations

$$(1)\qquad \begin{cases} X_1 = \hat{Q}_1\ (P_1 \cap (X_1 \cup \dots \cup X_t \cup \{w\})) \\ \dots\dots\dots\dots\dots\dots\dots\dots\dots\dots \\ X_t = \hat{Q}_t\ (P_t \cap (X_1 \cup \dots \cup X_t \cup \{w\})) \end{cases}$$

with $t = m(\mathcal{C})$ and let us denote $F_i(X_1,\dots,X_t)=\hat{Q}_1(P_i \cap (X_1 \cup \dots$ $\dots \cup X_t \cup \{w\}))$.

The minimal solution of the system (1) $(X_1^{MIN},\dots, X_t^{MIN})$ is given by

$$X_1^{MIN} = \bigcup_{n=o}^{\infty} X_i^{(n)}, \qquad 1 \leqslant i \leqslant t$$

and

$$X_i^{(n+1)} = F_i(X_1^{(n)},\dots,X_t^{(n)}), \quad n \geqslant o,$$

We observe that $X_i^{(n)}$ is the set of all words from $L(\mathcal{C})$ with the property that are obtained in n steps of derivation in $\mathcal{C}$, and the last table used is Q_i. Of course X_i^{MIN} is the set of all words in $L(\mathcal{C})$ with the property that the last table used is Q_i.

Now it is manifest that

$$L(\mathcal{C}) = \bigcup_{i=1}^{t} X_i^{MIN}$$

THEOREM 6. Every E SC-TOL L is a component of the minimal solution of a system of equations in the form $(*)$.

PROOF. Let us consider $\mathcal{C}'=(V,m(\mathcal{C}'),P,Q,w,M)$ and a copy of $\mathcal{C}'$ with all letters a in V in the form $\bar{a}$: $\bar{\mathcal{C}}' = (\bar{V},m(\mathcal{C}'),\bar{P},\bar{Q},\bar{w},\bar{M})$.

Let us define now a SC-TOL $\mathcal{C}_1$.

We consider an alphabet $V' = \bar{V} \cup M \cup \{\sigma\}$, σ a new symbol.

Let us define a finite substitution h on V' by $h(a) = \{a,\bar{a}\}$, $\bar{a} \in \bar{M}$; $h(\bar{b}) = \{b\}$, $b \in \bar{V}-\bar{M}$; $h(c) = \{c\}$, $c \in M \cup \{\sigma\}$

1) For i, $1 \leqslant i \leqslant m(\mathcal{C})$ take

$$R_i = h(\bar{P}_i) \setminus M^+ \quad \text{and}$$

$$T_i = \{u \to v \mid u \in h(\bar{a}),\ v \in h(\bar{z}),\ \bar{a} \to \bar{z} \in \bar{Q}_i\} \cup \{\sigma \to \sigma\}$$

2) $R_{m(\mathcal{C}')+1} = M^+$, $T_{m(\mathcal{C}')+1} = \{x \to x \mid x \in V'\}$

3) $R_{m(\mathcal{G}')+2} = \{\sigma\}$, $T_{m(\mathcal{G}')+2} = \{\sigma \to u \mid u \in h(\overline{w})\} \cup \{x \to x \mid x \in V' - \{\sigma\}\}$

4) $(V')^+ - \bigcup_{i=1}^{m(\mathcal{G}')+2} R_i = R_{m(\mathcal{G}')+3}$

$T_{m(\mathcal{G}')+3} = \{x \to x \mid x \in V'\}$

We define the SC-TOL $\mathcal{G}_1$ by

$$\mathcal{G}_1 = (V', m(\mathcal{G}')+3, R, T, \sigma)$$

and we associate to $\mathcal{G}_1$ the system of equations:

$$\begin{cases} X_1 = \hat{T}_1(R_1 \cap (X_1 \cup \ldots \cup X_t \cup \{\sigma\})) \\ \ldots\ldots\ldots\ldots\ldots\ldots \\ X_t = \hat{T}_t(R_t \cap (X_1 \cup \ldots \cup X_t \cup \{\sigma\})) \end{cases}$$

where $t = m(\mathcal{G}')+3$.

We have

$$X_{t-2}^{MIN} = X_{m(\mathcal{G}')+1}^{MIN} = \left(\bigcup_{i=1}^{t} X_i^{MIN}\right) \cap R_{m(\mathcal{G}')+1}$$

(because $\hat{T}_{m(\mathcal{G}')+2}$ is the identity) $= \left(\bigcup_{i=1}^{t} X_i^{MIN}\right) \cap M^+ = L(\mathcal{G}_1) \cap M^+$.

It is easy to see that $\overline{u} \in L(\overline{\mathcal{G}}')$ iff $u \in L(\mathcal{G}')$ iff $u \in L(\mathcal{G}_1) \cap M^+$.

<u>THEOREM 7</u>. Let us consider the following data:

i) V an alphabet;

ii) $T_1, \ldots, T_p$, λ-free tables on V;

iii) $R_1, \ldots, R_p$, a partition of V^+ with each R_i regular;

iv) w a word over V.

Then, each component of the minimal solution of the system

$$\begin{cases} X_1 = \hat{T}_1(R_1 \cap (X_1 \cup \ldots \cup X_p \cup \{w\})) \\ \ldots\ldots\ldots\ldots\ldots\ldots \\ X_p = \hat{T}_p(R_p \cap (X_1 \cup \ldots \cup X_p \cup \{w\})) \end{cases}$$

is a context-sensitive language.

<u>PROOF</u>. The system of equations defines a SC-TOL $\mathcal{G} = (V, p, \{R_1, \ldots, R_p\}, \{T_1, \ldots, T_p\}, w)$ and we have that $L(\mathcal{G}) = \bigcup_{i=1}^{p} X_i^{MiN}$, where $X^{MiN} = (X_1^{MiN}, \ldots, X_t^{MiN})$ is the minimal solution of the system.

It can be proved that $X_i^{MiN} = \hat{T}_i(L(\mathcal{G}) \cap R_i)$, for all i, $1 \leq i \leq p$.

By theorem 4 it follows that $L(\mathcal{G})$ is in $\underline{CS_\lambda}$, and so is

$\hat{T}_i(L(\mathcal{C}) \cap R_i) = X_i^{MIN}$, $1 \leq i \leq p$.

<u>COROLLARY 3</u>. A language $L \subseteq V^+$ is in <u>CS</u> if and only if it is a component of the minimal solution of a system of equations in the form fulfiling the conditions i) - iv) from Theorem 7.

<u>COROLLARY 4</u>. Every <u>CS</u> language $L \subseteq V^+$ is a component of the minimal solution of a system of equations in the form:

$$(\ast_\ast) \quad \begin{cases} X_1 = F_1(X_1,\ldots,X_t) \\ \cdots\cdots\cdots\cdots\cdots\cdots \\ X_t = F_t(X_1,\ldots,X_t) \end{cases}$$

where $F_1,\ldots,F_t$ are regular espressions over the alphabet $\{$".", "$\cup$", "+", "h_λ", "$\cap$"$\} \cup V \cup \{), (\}$. (h_λ denotes the λ-free finite substitution).

<u>CONJECTURE 1</u>. The converse of the Corollary 4 is also true.

If the above conjecture holds, we have a fixed-point characterization of $\underline{CS}_\lambda$ languages using the set of operations: $\{\cdot, \cup, h_\lambda, \cap, +\}$.

The essential point seems to be the use of intersection, because without "$\cap$" a system of equations of type $(\ast_\ast)$ has <u>CF</u> languages as components of the minimal solution.

<u>CONJECTURE 2</u>. A language is in $\underline{CS}_\lambda$ iff it is a component of the minimal solution of a system $(\ast_\ast)$ using only $\{\cdot, \cup, \cap\}$.

<u>THEOREM 8</u>. A language $L \subseteq V^*$ is recursive-enumerable iff is a component of the minimal solution of a system of equations in the form

$$\begin{cases} X_1 = F_1\ (X_1,\ldots,X_t) \\ \cdots\cdots\cdots\cdots\cdots\cdots \\ X_t = F_t\ (X_1,\ldots,X_t) \end{cases}$$

where $F_1,\ldots,F_t$ are regular expressions over the alphabet: $\{$".", "$\cup$", "$\ast$", "h", "$\cap$"$\} \cup \{), (\} \cup V \cup \{\wedge\}$ where $\wedge$ stands for the empty word λ.

<u>REMARK 1</u>. The result of the Theorem 8 can be extended to the case when instead of letters of the alphabet V we consider a finite set of recursive-enumerable languages over V.

3. <u>SOME CONSIDERATIONS ABOUT FIXED-POINT SEMANTICS OF MONADIC PROGRAMS</u>

We work in this section with programs in the formalism presented by J.A. Goguen in [1].

Speaking heuristically now, in this section we consider programs consisting of operation and tests, each performed directly on values stored in memory. These tests and operations will appear as (labels) of edges in a graph, with all of the partial functions representing the several alternatives of a test emanating from the same node. Thus a path in this graph represents an execution sequence for the instructions of the program. It should be noted that these flow diagram programs are not purely syntactic entities: a specific interpretation is assumed to be already given for each operation and test instruction.

One of the question of greatest interest for such a program is semantic: What function does it compute?

We give now the formal definitions.

A (directed) graph is a pair, $G = (V,E)$ where V is a finite set of nodes, E is a set of edges $E \subset V \times V$.

An exit node v' is a node with the property that there are no edges in G with source v'.

We denote by $\mathcal{N}$ the class of sets in the form N^r, $r \geqslant 0$, and $\mathcal{PFN}$ the class of partial functions between sets in $\mathcal{N}$.

A program is a pair (G,P) where $|P| : V \longrightarrow \mathcal{N}$,

$P : E \longrightarrow \mathcal{PFN}$ with the property that for every $(v_1,v_2) \in E$,

$P(v_1,v_2) : |P|(v_1) \rightarrow |P|(v_2)$

A program (G,P) is called deterministic if whenever e,e' are edges with same source node, the partial functions Pe, Pe' have disjoint sets of definition.

If we denote by $Pa(G) = \{(v,v') \mid$ there exists a path in G from v to $v'\}$ we can define the behavior of a program. We can extend the functions $P : E \rightarrow \mathcal{PFN}$ to $\hat{P} : Pa(G) \rightarrow \mathcal{PFN}$. In fact, if $(v_0,v_1, \ldots,v_t)$ is the sequence of nodes which describes a path in G from v_0 to v_t we have

$$\hat{P}(v_0,\ldots,v_t) = P(v_0,v_1)\circ\ldots\circ P(v_{t-1},v_t).$$

Also we have the following result stated as Proposition 5 in [1] : If (G,P) is a deterministic program and if f, f' are path in G with same source, such that neither is an initial segment for the other, then $P(f)$ and $P(f')$ have disjoint sets of definition.

DEFINITION. The behavior or complete partial function computed by the program (G,P) with entry at v and exit at v' is

$$\hat{P}(v,v') = \bigcup \{\hat{P}(f) \mid f \text{ a path from } v \text{ to } v' \text{ in } G\}.$$

It is easy to see that if (G,P) is deterministic and v' is an exit node, then P(v,v') is also a partial function (Corollary 6 [1]).

Let us consider RelN the class of relations over N. We use three symbols "a", "b", " # " in order to define the function $S: \mathrm{Rel}\,N \longrightarrow \mathcal{P}(a^+ \# b^+)$ given by $S(R) = \{a^{n+1} \# b^{m+1} \mid (n,m) \in R\}$. (Note that $\mathcal{P}(A)$ is the power-set of A).

For a partial function $f: N \longrightarrow N$, if Dom f is the definition domain of f, we have

$$S(f) = \{a^{n+1} \# b^{f(n)+1} \mid n \in \mathrm{Dom} f\}$$

We notice that the language S(f) encodes the association realized by f.

Our intention is to work with such type of languages instead of functions, in the definition of <u>monadic programs</u>, i.e. programs which use only one-variable functions.

In fact, if (G,P) is a monadic deterministic program we can consider the diagram

$$E \xrightarrow{P} N \xrightarrow{S} \mathcal{P}(a^+ \# b^+)$$

We observe that the function S is bijective, and its reverse $F: \mathcal{P}(a^+ \# b^+) \longrightarrow \mathrm{Rel}\,N$ can be interpreted as a "forgetful" operator, i.e. forgets the language encoding of relations over N.

If "o" stands for the relation composition, we have:

$$S(R_1 \circ R_2) = S(FS(R_1) \circ FS(R_2)).$$

The above equality defines an operator which beginning with two languages $S(R_1)$ and $S(R_2)$ gives a new languages $S(R_1 \circ R_2)$.

More formally, the operation can be expressed with classical operators.

Let be c, $\#_1$ new symbols, and the languages:

$L_1 = \{a^m \# b^n \mid (m-1,n-1) \in R_1\}$, $L_2 = \{b^k \#_1 c^s \mid (k-1,s-1) \in R_2\}$.

We consider the language $L_3 = L_1 \#_1 c^+ \cap a^+ \# L_2$.

We have:

$$L_3 = \{a^m \# b^n \#_1 c^t \mid (m-1,\ n-1) \in R_1,\ \ (n-1,\ t-1) \in R_2\}.$$

The homomorphism h, defined by $h(b) = h(\#_1) = \lambda$, $h(a)=a$, $h(c)=b$ maps L_3 into $S(R_1 \circ R_2)$, i.e.

$$h(L_3) = \{a^m \# b^n \mid (m-1,\ n-1) \in R_1 \circ R_2\} = S(R_1 \circ R_2)$$

Therefore, if h' is a new homomorphism given by $h'(a)=b$, $h'(\#)=\#_1$, $h'(b)=c$ we have the following representation

(I) $$S(R_1 \circ R_2) = h(L_1 \#_1 c^+ \cap a^+ \# L_2) = h(S(R_1) \#_1 c^+ \cap a^+ \# h'(S(R_2))$$

We denote by φ this new operator, i.e.

$$\varphi : \mathcal{P}(a^+ \# b^+) \times \mathcal{P}(a^+ \# b^+) \longrightarrow \mathcal{P}(a^+ \# b^+)$$

given by

$$\varphi(E_1, E_2) = S(F(E_1) \circ F(E_2))$$

The operator can be extended for any $t \geqslant 2$ to

$$\underbrace{\mathcal{P}(a^+ \# b^+) \times \ldots \times \mathcal{P}(a^+ \quad b^+)}_{t}$$

Suppose that we have already defined the operator for s; now the extension to s+1 is defined by

$$\varphi(E_1, \ldots, E_{s+1}) = \varphi(\varphi(E_1, \ldots, E_s), E_{s+1})$$

In the rest of this section we consider monadic deterministic programs with one memory location only.

The extension to monadic nondeterministic programs with a finite number of locations requires a little bit more complicated notational apparatus.

Let (G,P) be a monadic deterministic program with one location. If G = (V,E), for every $e \in E$, by the way of P and S we have associate a language, i.e.

$$P(e) : |P|(v_1) \longrightarrow |P|(v_2), \quad e = (v_1, v_2)$$

and $S(P(e)) \in \mathcal{P}(a^+ \# b^+)$.

To a path from Pa(G), say $\mu : (v_{i_1}, v_{i_2}, \ldots, v_{i_k})$ we associate the language

$$S(\mu) = S(P(v_{i_1}, v_{i_2}) \circ P(v_{i_2}, v_{i_3}) \circ \ldots \circ P(v_{i_{k-1}}, v_{i_k}))$$

$$= \varphi(P(v_{i_1}, v_{i_2}), \ldots, P(v_{i_{k-1}}, v_{i_k}))$$

<u>EXAMPLE</u>

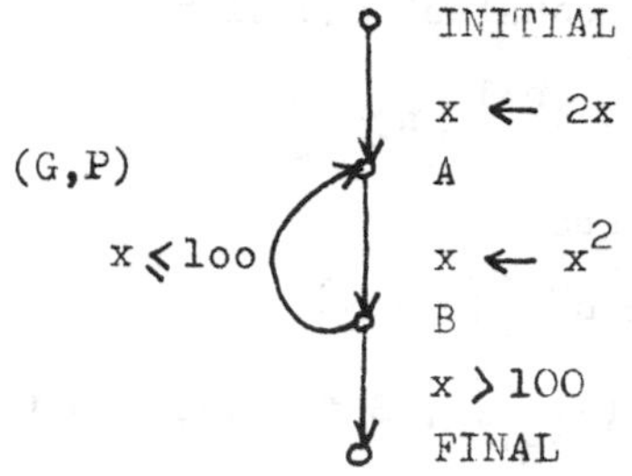

x the location

We have

$$S(x \leftarrow 2x) = \{a^{n+1} \# b^{2n+1} \mid n \geqslant o\}$$
$$S(x \leftarrow x^2) = \{a^{n+1} \# b^{n^2+1} \mid n \geqslant o\}$$
$$S(x \leqslant loo) = \{a^{n+1} \# b^{n+1} \mid n \leqslant loo\}$$
$$S(x > loo) = \{a^{n+1} \# b^{n+1} \mid n > loo\}$$

Let us consider the path μ: (A, B, A).

We have

$$S(\mu) = S((x \leftarrow x^2) \circ (x \leqslant loo)) =$$
$$= S(F(\{a^{n+1} \# b^{n^2+1} \mid n \geqslant o\}) o \quad F(\{a^{n+1} \# b^{n+1} \mid n \leq loo\}))$$
$$= \{a^{n+1} \# b^{n^2+1} \mid n^2+1 \leqslant loo\}.$$

Now, for such a program we intend to construct a system of equations with variables in the power-set of a finite generated free monoid so that one of the components of its minimal solution gives its behavior as a function encoded with S.

Let be (G,P) a program with the location x, and G=(V,E).Suppose that v_I and v_F are the entry and the exit nodes.

If $V = \{v_I = v_o, v_1, \ldots, v_t = v_F\}$ then we associate a variable X_i (varying in $\mathcal{P}(a^+ \# b^+)$) to each node v_i, $o \leqslant i \leqslant t$.

For a node v_i, let be $(v_{j_1,1}, v_1), \ldots, (v_{j_{k(i)},i}, v_i)$ the collection of all edges in G which enter in v_i, and $f_1^{(i)}, \ldots, f_{k(i)}^{(i)}$ the corresponding partial functions associated by P.

For every i, $1 \leqslant i \leqslant t$ we consider the equation

$$X_i = \bigcup_{s=1}^{k(i)} S(F(X_{j_s,i}) \circ f_s^{(i)}) =$$
$$\bigcup_{s=i}^{k(i)} \varphi(X_{j_s,i}, S(f_s^{(i)}))$$

To the node $v_I = v_o$ we associate a constant equation

$$X_o = \{a^{n+1} \# b^{n+1} \mid n \geqslant o\}$$

Putting together, we obtain the system

$$(+) \quad \begin{cases} X_o = \{a^{n+1} \# b^{n+1} \mid n \geqslant o\} \\ X_i = \bigcup_{s=1}^{k(i)} \varphi(X_{i_s,i}, S(f_s^{(i)})), \quad 1 \leqslant i \leqslant t \end{cases}$$

which plays a major role in the sequel.

Because of the representation of φ given in the formula (!), the equations of X_i, $1 \leq i \leq t$ have the form presented in the Theorem 9 with the addition of Remark 1.

So, at this moment, such a system has a minimal solution, with all components recursive - enumerable languages: $X^{MiN} = (X_o^{MiN}, \ldots, X_t^{MiN})$.

We intend to show the following

THEOREM 9.

$$S(\hat{P}(v_I, v_F)) = X_t^{MiN}$$

I.e., for every monadic deterministic program with one location, there exists a system of equations in the form (+) so that its semantics - in some encoded form - is a component of the minimal solution of the system.

PROOF. We have $\hat{P}(v_I, v_F) = \bigcup \{ \hat{P}(\mu) \mid \mu \text{ path in G from } v_I \text{ to } v_F \}$ and

$$S(\hat{P}(v_I, v_F)) = \bigcup \{ S(\hat{P}(\mu)) \mid \mu \text{ path in G from } v_I \text{ to } v_F \}.$$

On the other side, $X_t^{MiN} = \bigcup_{n=o}^{\infty} X_t^{(n)}$, where $X_t^{(n+1)} = F_t(X_o^{(n)}, \ldots$ $\ldots X_t^{(n)})$ and

$$F_t(X_o, \ldots, X_t) = \bigcup_{s=1}^{k(i)} \varphi\,(X_{j_s,i}, S(f_s^{(i)}))$$

We intend to show that for every i and p, with $1 \leq i \leq t$, $p \geq 1$ we have

(A) $\quad X_i^{(p)} = \bigcup \{ S(\hat{P}(\mu)) \mid \mu \text{ path in G of length p from } v_I \text{ to } v_i \}$.

We denote by Path $(v_i, v_j; m)$ the set of all paths of length m in G from v_i to v_j, and by Path $(v_i, v_j; -)$ the set of all path in G from v_i to v_j.

For p=o, $X_i^{(p)} = \emptyset$, $1 \leq i \leq t$.

We take first p=1. If $a^m \# b^n \in X_i^{(1)}$, we have for

$$X_i^{(1)} = \bigcup_{s=1}^{k(i)} \varphi(X_{j_s,i}^{(o)}, S(f_s^{(i)}))$$

a number r, so that $X_{j_r,i}^{(o)} = X_o^{(o)}$ and $a^m \# b^n \in S(f_r^{(i)})$.

Hence $(v_{j_r,i}, v_i)$ is the edge (v_I, v_i), and it follows that $a^m \# b^n$ $S(\hat{P}(v_I, v_i))$ and so the inclusion $X_i^{(1)} \subset \bigcup \{ S(\hat{P}(\mu)) \mid \mu \in \text{Path}(v_I, v_i; 1) \}$ holds.

Conversely, $S(P(v_I, v_i)) = S(F(X_o^{(o)}) \circ F(S(P(v_I, v_i)))) = \varphi\,(X_o^{(o)}, S(P(v_I, v_i))) \subset X_i^{(1)}$, because $(v_I, v_i) \in E$ implies that in the equation of X_i there exists a r so that $X_{j_r,1} = X_o$.

Now it is manifest that (A) holds for p=1. Suppose that it is true for $p \leq q$. Then we have

$$X_i^{(q+1)} = \bigcup_{s=1}^{k(i)} S(F(X_{j_s,i}^{(q)} \circ f_s^{(i)}) =$$

$$= \bigcup_{s=1}^{k(i)} S(F[\bigcup\{S(\hat{P}(\mu))|\mu \in Path(v_I, v_{j_s,i};q)\}] \circ f_s^{(i)})$$

$$= \bigcup_{s=1}^{k(i)} S(\bigcup\{FS(\hat{P}(\mu))|\mu \in Path(v_I, v_{j_s,i};q)\} \circ f_s^{(i)})$$

$$= \bigcup_{s=1}^{k(i)} S(\bigcup\{\hat{P}(\mu)|\mu \in Path(v_I, v_{j_s,i};q)\} \circ f_s^{(i)}$$

$$= \bigcup_{s=1}^{k(i)} S(\bigcup\{\hat{P}(\mu) \circ f_s^{(i)}|\mu \in Path(v_I, v_{j_s,i};q)\})$$

$$= \bigcup_{s=1}^{k(i)} S(\bigcup\{\hat{P}(\mu')|\mu' \in Path(v_I, v_i : q+1)\})$$

$$= \bigcup_{s=1}^{k(i)} (\bigcup S(\hat{P}(\mu'))|\mu' \in Path(v_I, v_i, q+1)\}).$$

Because of the simple observation that

$$\hat{P}(v_I, v_F) = \bigcup\{\hat{P}(\mu)|\mu \in Path(v_I, v_F: -)\}$$

$$= \bigcup_{m=o}^{\infty}\{\hat{P}(\mu)|\mu \in Path(v_I, v_F;m)\}$$

it follows that $S(\hat{P}(v_I, v_F)) = X_t^{MiN}$.

REFERENCES

1. J.A.G o g u e n - "On Homomorphism, Correctness, Termination, Unfoldments and Equivalence of Flow Diagram Programs". Journal of Comp.System Sci., vol.8, nr.3 (1974).
2. G.T.H e r m a n , G.R o z e n b e r g - "Developmental Systems and Languages" North-Holland (1975).
3. S.I s t r a i l - "Context-sensitive Languages: Recursivity, Fixed-point theorems and applications to program semantics and number theory".Ph.D.Thesis,Univ. Bucharest, March 1979.
4. S.I s t r a i l - "A fixed-point approach of context-sensitive languages using context-free grammars with choice" (submitted for publication).

5. S.I s t r a i l - "On the weak equivalence problem of SICK-OL systems with some generative devices". Annalles Univ.Iaşi, T.XXIII, S.I.a, f.2 (1977).

6. S.I s t r a i l - "SICK OL systems and simulating ability" (submitted for publication).

7. A.S a l o m a a - "Formal Languages" Academic Press, New York and London (1973).

HIERARCHIC INDEX SEQUENTIAL SEARCH WITH OPTIMAL VARIABLE BLOCK SIZE AND ITS MINIMAL EXPECTED NUMBER OF COMPARISONS

Wolfgang Janko
University of Karlsruhe, W-Germany

Summary. Multilevel indexes are intensively used for accessing records in files. The search costs can considerably be reduced by selecting the number of levels and the size of the index at each level optimally. In this paper a multilevel and variable size index design strategy is developed which minimizes the expected number of comparisons. Its performance is evaluated in dependence of the number of levels for unsuccessful and successful search. A method to determine the number of levels which minimizes the expected number of comparisons is presented. The number of index entries and index files is given. The relevance of the results for jump searching is indicated. As an asymptotic upper bound for the minimal number of comparisons in an index sequential search the expression $\log_2 n + 0.5 \log_2 \log_2 n$ is derived for $n = \binom{2i}{i}$.

I. INTRODUCTION.

A major problem with data files is the addressing problem: how to find a record with a given key (successful search) or to determine its absence from the file (unsuccessful search). Two types of processing may be used: random processing or sequential processing. The amount of sequential processing versus random processing done, affects the choice of the file organisation technique. For sequentially organized files, which are sorted by a key field, a variety of search algorithms is applicable. If applicable, interpolation search and related methods are extremely efficient in terms of necessary comparisons. But general performance is uneven and the necessary computations are costly [5]. Binary search is of very good performance and can be used if the file storage is allocated contiguously. For small files, or parts of files, sequential search can be used. This even if the records are not placed in a random access memory. If files are not stored in random access memory, or if sequential processing shall be supported efficiently, binary search techniques may be unsuited. A search technique called m-way-search, jump searching, block search or index sequential search may be well suited in such situations [2,4,6,8]. (Further applications of jump searching are described by Shneiderman, B., [4]). Several variants of the jump search method can be distinguished with regard to the block size and the number of levels of the search.

The well known simple jump searching jumps over portions of the sorted file until the portion or "block" of the file is localized, which contains the insertion place or the record with the key searched for. This block is then scanned sequentially. If these blocks are each of the same size, jump searching is said to be fixed in contrary to variable block length jump searching. Simple jump searching is called one level fixed jump searching. Jump searching may be performed within a block, with the blocks of a block, and so on; this leads to two level jump searching, three level jump searching, etc. If the blocks in a multilevel jump searching are always of the same size - and not only in each level of the search - it is called fixed jump searching with constant block length. Multilevel jump searching can also be done using blocks of variable size within each level of the search. This is called variable jump searching [4].

The average expected cost of the search is frequently given using the number of comparisons as simplified measure of time complexity and assuming equal probabilities of request. Similarly we will concentrate here on the problem of minimization of the expected number of comparisons. Optimal block lengths for jump searching with constant block length and for fixed jump searching assuming equal probabilities and equal or different costs of access at each level of search have been investigated by Shneiderman, B., [4,6]. Variable jump searching requires usually less comparisons than fixed jump searching. Simple variable jump searching was - as far as the author knows - first analysed by Six [7]. A simple and short proof of the optimal block lengths, their number, an algorithm for optimal variable jump searching, and its analysis is given in Janko [1]. (The optimal block lengths and the expected number of comparisons are independently given by Shneiderman, B. [4]).

Regarding the necessary number of comparisons searching in index sequentially organized files using multiple levels of index and admitting a variable block size at each level is equivalent to variable jump searching if we admit stopping in the last level sequential search of jump searching only. In successful variable jump searching we can stop searching at each level as soon as we have recognized equality between the target key and the key found. There is almost no difference between unsuccessful index sequential search and unsuccessful variable jump searching.

II. THE PROBLEM.

In this paper we analyse multilevel index sequential search with variable block size. We shall use in our analysis the concepts from jump searching remembering that the search can be stopped only in the last phase's sequential search. We shall denote the m block lengths of an i-level jump searching by the block length tuple

$$(n_1^{i+1}, n_2^{i+1}, \dots, n_m^{i+1}) \ , \quad \sum_{j=1}^{m} n_j^{i+1} = n \ ; \quad n \text{ is the number of records of the block}$$

or file searched.

For example in an i-level search and in a file of n records sorted in ascending order the n_1^{i+1}-th, $(n_1^{i+1} + n_2^{i+1})$-th,...,$(\sum_{j=1}^{m} n_j^{i+1})$-th record keys are examined until the target key value is reached or exceeded. Then in an (i-1)-level search the n_1^i-th, $(n_1^i + n_2^i)$-th,...,$(\sum_{j=1}^{q_i} n_j^i)$-th $(q_i \in \{1,2,\ldots,m\})$ record keys of the block located at the i-th level search are examined, and so on. Finally in a 0-level search the n_1^1-th, $(n_1^1 + n_2^1)$-th,...,$(\sum_{j=1}^{q_o} n_j^1)$-th record keys of the block q_o $(q_o \in \{1,2,\ldots,m\})$ are examined. The 0-level search is equal to sequential scanning and $(n_1^1, n_2^1,\ldots,n_{q_o}^1) = (1, 1,\ldots,1)$. (We shall see that if we localize the j-th block containing the key and determined by n_j^{i+1} in an i-level search, the optimal block length tuple for the (i-1)-level search is equal to $(n_j^i, n_{j+1}^i,\ldots,n_m^i)$.)

In an i-level search we can use (i+1)-tuples with each record to count in the (j+1)-th component the number of comparisons needed in the j-th level of search to locate the block containing the target key (j=1,2,...,i+1). i-tuples with positive integer components can be interpreted as coordinate tuples of an i-dimensional square lattice. Such assigning each record an i-tuple one-to-one is equivalent to a mapping of the jump searching tree of (i-1)-level jump searching into an i-dimensional lattice with coordinates out of {1,2,...}. We shall therefore call an (i-1)-level search simply an i-dimensional search.

Example: Set of keys: S = {3,6,8,11,16,17,21,35,38,45}

Optimal block length tuples for a two-dimensional search:

$$(n_1^2, n_2^2, n_3^2, n_4^2) = (4,3,2,1)$$

$$(n_1^1, n_2^1, n_3^1, n_4^1) = (1,1,1,1)$$

Search tree:

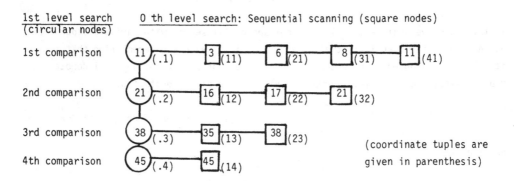

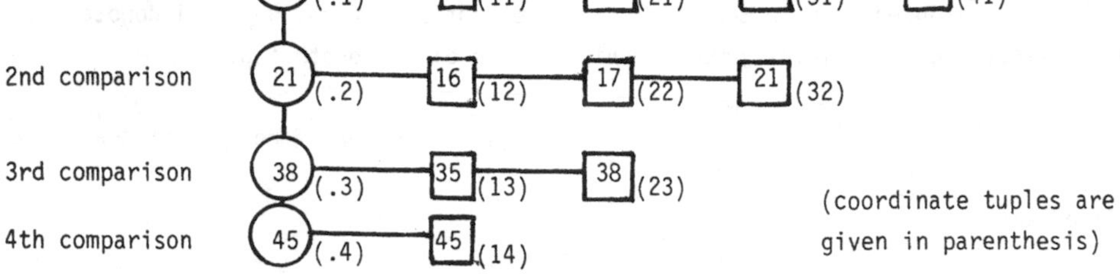

Minimizing the number of comparisons searching in a file of n records by i-dimensional search is therefore equivalent to the following problem:

> How shall we select n points in an i-dimensional square lattice with coordinates out of the set of positive integers such that we minimize the sum of the n sums of the coordinate values of the points selected?

III. THE PROBLEM'S SOLUTION AND ITS OPTIMAL BLOCK LENGTH TUPLES.

Before Theorem 1 is given we state two elementary lemmas which will be used in the theorem's proof. (Furtheron we call a square lattice simply a lattice. By N we denote the set of natural numbers including zero; by N^+ we denote the set of natural numbers.)

Lemma 1: There are exactly $p_i(h) = \binom{h-1}{i-1}$ points in an i-dimensional lattice having a coordinate sum of h with coordinates out of N^+ and $h \geq i$.

Lemma 2: The number of points in an i-dimensional lattice having a coordinate sum of exactly h is equal to the number of points in the (i-1)-dimensional sublattice having the coordinate sum of at most h-1 using (i-1) coordinates with values out of N^+; that means

$$p_i(h) = \sum_{j=i}^{h} p_{i-1}(j-1) \quad .$$

Theorem 1:

Case A: $n = \binom{h}{i}$ $\quad (i,h \in N^+;\ h \geq i)$

The optimal block length tuples of an i-dimensional search are:

$$n_j^i = \binom{h-j}{i-1} \quad (j=1,2,\ldots,h+1-i)$$

Case B: $\binom{h}{i} < n < \binom{h+1}{i}$ $\quad (i,h \in N^+;\ h \geq i)$

Let $(n_1^i, n_2^i, \ldots, n_{h+2-i}^i)$ be the optimal block length tuple for $n = \binom{h+1}{i}$ and let us define ℓ by the following relation:

$$\ell = \binom{h+1}{i} - n \quad ;$$

we get an optimal block length tuple for the first phase of search by applying the following procedure:

1) Reduce the values of n_j^i $(j=h+2-i,\ h+1-i,\ldots,2,1)$ by n_j^{i-1} starting with n_{h+2-i}^{i-1},

$n^{i-1}_{h+1-i}, \ldots$ until the relation

$$\sum_{k=i}^{m} n^{i-1}_{h+2-k} < \ell \leq \sum_{k=i}^{m+1} n^{i-1}_{h+2-k} \qquad (i \leq m < h+1-i)$$

is valid. Such we get the modified tuple

$$(n^i_1, n^i_2, \ldots, {}^*n^i_{h+2-m}, \ldots, {}^*n^i_{h+2-i}) \quad .$$

2) Subtract $\ell - \sum_{k=i}^{m} n^{i-1}_{h+2-k}$ from n^i_{h+1-m} getting $'n^i_{h+1-m}$.
The tuple derived

$$(n^i_1, n^i_2, \ldots, {}'n^i_{h+1-m}, {}^*n^i_{h+2-m}, \ldots, {}^*n^i_{h+1-i})$$

is the optimal block length tuple for the first phase; (${}^*n^i_{h+2-i}$ is zero).

Proceeding according to Theorem 1/B if the key searched for is in the block determined by $'n^i_{h+1-m}$ and according to Theorem 1/A if the key searched for is in one of the other blocks gives the optimal block length tuple for the (i-1)-dimensional search problem and so on.

Theorem 2:

Let $\binom{h}{i} < n < \binom{h+1}{i}$ be a valid relation.
Then the number v of optimal block length tuples in an i-dimensional search is given by

$$v = \binom{\binom{h}{i-1}}{r} \quad \text{with } r = n - \binom{h}{i} \quad .$$

Proof of Theorem 1 and Theorem 2:

We have to draw n points of an i-dimensional lattice minimizing the total of their coordinate sums. We have $p_i(k)$ points having a coordinate sum of k ($k \in N^+$ and $k \geq i$). If $n = \binom{h}{i}$ we draw the points with a coordinate sum of i, i+1,...,h as

$$\sum_{j=0}^{h-i} p_i(i+j) = \binom{h}{i} \quad .$$

If $\binom{h}{i} < n < \binom{h+1}{i}$, ($i,h \in N^+$; $h \geq i$), we finally choose sufficient points with a coordinate sum of h+1 to have n points selected. There are

$$\binom{p_i(h+1)}{n - \binom{h}{i}} = \binom{\binom{h}{i-1}}{n - \binom{h}{i}}$$

such selections of point sets. This proofs Theorem 2.

To proof the correctness of Theorem 1 we have to show that the tuples given are determined by coordinate values of at least one of the sets of points representing an optimal selection. Let us first consider Case A of Theorem 1. Each point of the set of points determined by the j-th block has j as the i-th coordinate value. The sum of the values of the (i-1) other coordinates of the points in the j-th block must be smaller or equal to h-j, integer and positive (j=1,2,...,h+1-i). There are exactly $p_i(h-j+1)$ such coordinate tuples by Lemma 2; but by definition $p_i(h-j+1)$ is equal to n_j^i. Recognizing that $n_j^i = \sum_{k=j}^{h+i-1} n_k^{i-1}$ and applying similar considerations for the (i-1)-th, (i-2)-th,... coordinate the correctness of Theorem 1/A is established.

The procedure described in Case B of Theorem 1 is only one way to select $n - \binom{h}{i}$ points with a coordinate sum of h+1 out of $\binom{h}{i-1}$ possible points. To select the block size optimally we start assuming n to be equal to $\binom{h+1}{i}$. This is equal to Case A and the optimal block length tuple would be $(n_1^i, n_2^i, \ldots, n_{h+2-i}^i)$. The number of points in block j having exactly a coordinate sum of h+1 in i coordinates is equal to n_j^{i-1}. Subtracting now successively n_j^{i-1} from n_j^i (j=h+2-i, h+1-i,...,2,1) until we finally subtract a rest $z < n_k^{i-1}$ for some k such that

$$z + \sum_{j=k+1}^{h+2-i} n_j^{i-1} = \binom{h+1}{i} - n \quad \text{we get}$$

the optimal block length tuple for the highest level of search. (This because we have exactly reduced the blocks by that point sets which have the highest values of coordinate sums within the block.) Applying similar considerations if the target key belongs to the k-th block and considerations according to Case A if the target key belongs to one of the other blocks shows the correctness of Theorem 1/B.

IV. THE EXPECTED NUMBER OF COMPARISONS, ITS VARIANCE, THE SPACE REQUIRED FOR INDEX FILES AND THE OPTIMAL DIMENSION OF SEARCH.

Assuming uniformly distributed request, successful search and a given dimension i for searching in a file of n records the expected number of comparisons E(C) using optimal block length tuples and its variance is given by Theorem 3.

Theorem 3:

Case A: $E(C) = \frac{(h+1)i}{i+1}$;

$$\sigma_C^2 = E(C)\left(\frac{(i+1)(h+2)}{(i+2)} - E(C) - 1\right) \quad ;$$

Case B:

$$E(C) = \frac{i\binom{h+1}{i+1} + (n - \binom{h}{i})(h+1)}{n} \quad ;$$

$$nE(C^2) = i(i+1)\binom{h+2}{i+2} - i\binom{h+1}{i+1} + (n - \binom{h}{i})(h+1)^2 \quad ;$$

using $\sigma_C^2 = E(C^2) - E^2(C)$ we get the variance.

Proof:

To minimize the total of coordinate sums for $n = \binom{h}{i}$ we have taken all tuples having a coordinate sum of i, i+1,...,h in i coordinates with values from {1,2,...}. The sum of coordinates is equal to the number of comparisons:

$$nE(C) = \sum_{k=i}^{h} k\binom{k-1}{i-1} = i\binom{h+1}{i+1} \quad .$$

In Case B we have to add $(n - \binom{h}{i})(h+1)$ to $i\binom{h+1}{i+1}$ to get the sum of comparisons nE(C).

To get the variance we evaluate

$$nE(C^2) = \sum_{k=i}^{h} k^2\binom{k-1}{i-1}$$

getting

$$nE(C^2) = (i+1)i\binom{h+2}{i+2} - i\binom{h+1}{i+1} \quad .$$

Using this expression and the fact that $\sigma_C^2 = E(C^2) - E^2(C)$ the variance for Case A can be derived. In Case B we have to add to the formula given above the value of $(n - \binom{h}{i})(h+1)^2$ to get $nE(C^2)$.

So far we have considered the problem of successful search assuming that each of the n keys is searched for equally likely; let us consider now the average number of comparisons of an unsuccessful search assuming that each of the n+1 insertion places is searched for equally likely. We locate each insertion place only during the last phase of the search scanning the records within the blocks sequentially. We stop searching the first time the key found is larger than the target key. Such we recognize the first n insertion places. Only if the key searched for is larger than the largest key of the key set we have to recognize this by the end of file condition. The total number of comparisons searching for each of the (n+1) insertion places is therefore equal to the number of comparisons searching successfully plus the number of comparisons necessary to find the insertion place for a key larger than the largest key so far. From this considerations the following theorem can be derived.

Theorem 4:

The expected number of comparisons in an unsuccessful i-dimensional search is given by:

$$E_u(C) = \frac{nE(C)+h}{n+1} \quad .$$

The variance σ_C^2 (= $E_u(C^2) - E_u^2(C)$) can be calculated using $(n+1)E_u(C^2) = nE(C^2) + h^2$.

Corollary:

The number of comparisons in an unsuccessful i-dimensional jump searching of variable block size is minimized using optimal block length tuples for index sequential search. The expected number of comparisons and its variance is approximately equal to the expected number of comparisons in an unsuccessful index sequential search.

Proof:

The correctness of this corollary follows as also in jump searching we can recognize insertion places only in the last phase's sequential search. Only if the key to be inserted is larger than the largest key in the file, the insertion place is recognized when we reach the last block in the first phase of search. In this case we need only h-i+1 comparisons.

Before we proceed in giving further results we want to draw the reader's attention on the relation between the block length tuples given and Pascal's triangle. Let us consider the values of n_k^i as components of an infinite symmetric matrix A. Each row begins with the smallest block size followed by the second smallest block size and so on. The row number equals the dimension of search. It can be seen that $a_{ij} = \binom{i+j-2}{i-1}$. The tuple $a_{i+j-1,1}, a_{i+j-2,2}, \ldots, a_{1,i+j-1}$ of components is equal to the (i+j-1)-th row of Pascal's triangle. Furthermore a_{ij} is equal to the number of points in an i-dimensional lattice having (i+j-1) as their coordinates sum:

Dimension	Number of blocks (j)									
of search (i)	1	2	3	4	5	6	7	8	9	...
1	1	1	1	1	1	1	1	1	1	...
2	1	2	3	4	5	6	7	8	9	...
3	1	3	6	1o	15	21	28	36	45	...
4	1	4	1o	2o	35	56	84	12o	165	...
5	1	5	15	35	7o	126	21o	33o	495	...
6	1	6	21	56	126	252	462	792	1287	...
7	1	7	28	84	21o	462	924	1716	3oo3	...
8	1	8	36	12o	33o	792	1716	3432	6435	...
9	1	9	45	165	495	1287	3oo3	6435	1287o	...
1o	1	1o	54	22o	715	2oo2	5oo5	1144o	2431o	...
⋮	⋮	⋮	⋮	⋮	⋮	⋮	⋮	⋮	⋮	⋮

The coefficients a_{ij} of the matrix A can be considered as values of n fulfilling the condition of Case A of Theorem 1. For a value of n equal to a_{ij} the optimal block length tuple is given by

$$(a_{i-1,j},\ a_{i-1,j-1},\ a_{i-1,j-2},\dots,\ a_{i-1,1}) \quad .$$

Theorem 5:

For $n = \binom{h}{i}$ the number of index files in an optimal i-dimensional index sequential search is equal to $\binom{h-2}{i-2}$. The total number of entries in these files is equal to $\binom{h-1}{i-1}$.

For simplicity we use the properties of the matrix A in this proof.

Proof:

Let n be equal to a_{ij} and let us consider an (i-1)-dimensional search. The optimal block length tuple consists of j components. Therefore for this stage we need one index file for j entries. In the (i-2)-dimensional search we need j index files to store j(j+1)/2 entries. But this is clearly equal to $a_{2,j}$ and $a_{3,j}$. We can proceed in this way getting finally that the number of index files is equal to $a_{i-2,j} = \binom{i+j-4}{i-3}$ with a total of $a_{i-1,j} = \binom{i+j-3}{i-2}$ entries. Translating this in our original terminology defining n to be equal to $\binom{h}{i}$ and considering h to be equal to i+j-2 and the dimension of search to be equal to i-1 we get the theorem.

A further interesting question is: Can we determine the optimal dimension of search for an arbitrary value of n?

Theorem 6:

By k_i let us denote that value of j for each row of A for which the inequality

$$\sum_{j=1}^{k_i-1} a_{ij} < n \le \sum_{j=1}^{k_i} a_{ij}$$

is valid; (a_{ij} is a coefficient of the matrix A). The optimal dimension of search is determined by that value of i which minimizes the total number of comparisons:

$$\min_{i\in N^+} \left\{ \sum_{j=1}^{k_i-1} (i-1+j)a_{ij} + \left(n - \sum_{j=1}^{k_i-1} a_{ij}\right)(i + k_i - 1)\right\} \tag{6.1}$$

Proof:

Choosing i such that the expression in formula (6.1) is minimized means to choose the dimension of the lattice such that the sum of coordinate totals is minimized using an optimal selection of points. This can be verified as a_{ij} is equal to the number of points in an i-dimensional lattice having (i+j-1) as their coordinate sum.

What seems interesting is a comparison of the efficiency of variable index sequential search and binary search techniques. We confine our considerations for reasons of simplicity on the special Case A with $n = \binom{2i}{i}$.

Theorem 7:

> Let the relation $n = \binom{2i}{i}$ be valid. If we increase or decrease the dimension i of search, the expected number of comparisons using block length tuples according to Theorem 1 cannot be reduced. i is an optimal dimension of search.

Proof:

The values of n which are equal to $\binom{2i}{i}$ are in the main diagonal of the matrix A. If we want to change the dimension of search in case $n = \binom{2i}{i}$ we can rise the dimension of search at least by one or we can diminuish the dimension of search at least by one. Rising the dimension: We assume that n is equal to $a_{i,i}$. As $a_{i+1,i-1} < a_{i,i}$ we must apply Theorem 1/B for the case $a_{i+1,i-1} < n < a_{i+1,i}$. The block length tuples are determined for $n = a_{i,i}$ by the row $(a_{i-1,i}, a_{i-1,i-1},\ldots,a_{i-1,1})$ and are determined by the number of points having a coordinate sum of i+j-1 (j=1,2,...,i-1) in i coordinates. As we can easily verify from the definition of the matrix A, the number of points determined by $a_{i,j-1}$ and $a_{i-1,j}$ have the same sum of their coordinate values. As $a_{i,j-1} < a_{i-1,j}$ is valid for components below the main diagonal of A, the difference

$$\sum_{m=2}^{i} a_{i-1,m} - \sum_{m=1}^{i-1} a_{i,m}$$

is taken from the points with increased coordinate values. Though we increase the total number of comparisons by an amount which is greater than zero. Similar arguments hold for increasing the dimension by more than one.

An analog method of proof can be used to show the lowering the dimension also increases the number of comparisons in a successful search. That these results are valid for the unsuccessful search can be seen using the relation expressed in Theorem 4.

Theorem 8:

For $n = \binom{2i}{i}$ an asymptotic upper bound for the expected number of comparisons for a successful search is given by

$$E(C) \lesssim \log_2 n + 0.5 \cdot \log_2 \log_2 n \quad .$$

Proof:

Using Stirling's formula we derive $n \sim 2^{2i}/\sqrt{\pi i}$ or equivalently $0.5 \cdot \log_2 n \sim i - 0.25 \cdot \log_2 i - 0.25 \cdot \log_2 \pi$. Substituting for $0.5 \cdot \log_2 n$ in the asymptotic inequality

$$(8.1) \qquad i \lesssim 0.5 \cdot \log_2 n + 0.25 \cdot \log_2 \log_2 n + 0.25 \cdot \log_2 \pi$$

we get: $i \lesssim i - 0.25 \cdot \log_2 i + 0.25 \cdot \log_2 (2i - 0.5 \cdot \log_2 i - 0.5 \cdot \log_2 \pi)$; that means that inequality (8.1) is asymptotically true for $n = \binom{2i}{i}$. Substituting now the value on the right side of the inequality (8.1) for values of i arising in E(C) we establish the correctness of above theorem:

$$E(C) = \frac{(2i+1)i}{i+1} = 2i - 1 + \frac{1}{i+1} \lesssim \log_2 n + 0.5 \cdot \log_2 \log_2 n \quad .$$

V. CONCLUDING REMARKS.

Using an index sequential file organisation with a multilevel index of variable size, successful and unsuccessful searching can be done with a small number of comparisons and accesses. A comparison minimal index sequential file organisation combines the advantages of a sequential file organisation with the advantages of a random file organisation using only a comparatively small number of index entries in comparison to an organisation using a dense index. The results given for the case of unsuccessful search are almost entirely valid for variable jump searching. In successful jump searching the number of comparisons is less than in index sequential search. Variable jump searching requires such asymptotically for $n = \binom{2i}{i}$ less comparisons like some other binary search methods using $c \cdot \log_2 n$ $(c > 1)$ comparisons. (In particular it needs for large n less comparisons than Fibonacci search [3].) Multilevel variable index sequential search and variable jump searching are therefore useful techniques compared to binary search techniques. Further attention should be given to the problem of index maintenance and the problem of record insertion and deletion. Problems like batched searching and the optimal design of index structures if the probabilities of request are not equal should be studied. Other potential applications are traversing pointer linked lists, list merging, searching through index blocks and compressed key searches [4].

REFERENCES.

[1] Janko,W. Zur optimalen Blocklänge beim m-Weg-Suchverfahren, Angew. Informatik, Heft 11, 1976, pp. 487-489.

[2] Martin,J. Computer Data-Base Organisation, Prentice-Hall, Englewood Cliffs, N.Y., 2nd Ed., 1977.

[3] Overholt,K.J. Efficiency of the Fibonacci Search Method, BIT, Nordisk Tidskr. Inform.-behandl., Vol. 13 (1973), pp. 92-96.

[4] Shneiderman,B. Jump Searching : A Fast Sequential Search Technique, Commun. ACM, Vol. 21 (1978), No. 1o, pp. 831-834.

[5] Shneiderman,B. Polynomial Search, Software-Practice and Experience, Vol. 3 (1973), pp. 5-8.

[6] Shneiderman,B. A Model for Optimizing Indexed File Structures, Intern. J. Computer Inform. Sci., Vol. 3 (1974), No. 1, pp.93-1o3.

[7] Six,H.W. Verbesserung des m-Weg-Suchverfahrens, Angew. Informatik, Heft 2, 1973, pp. 79-83.

[8] Wagner,R.E. Indexing Design Considerations, IBM Syst. J., Vol. 1o (1973), No. 4, pp. 351-367.

[9] Wedekind,H. Datenorganisation, Walter de Gruyter & Co., Berlin, 197o.

A Unique Termination Theorem for a Theory with Generalised Commutative Axioms

Hans-Josef Jeanrond
Computer Science Department
University of Edinburgh

Abstract: The procedures for deciding the unique termination property of rewriting systems by Knuth and Bendix [1], and Lankford and Ballantyne [2] are generalised to allow for permutative axioms of the form

$$F(F(t,e_1),e_2) = F(F(t,e_2),e_1)$$

(t,e_1,e_2 are variable symbols).
These can be thought of as many sorted commutative axioms as they might appear in axiomatic specifications of abstract data types.
A method is presented for deciding the unique termination property of a set of "permutative rewrite rules" having the finite termination property. It relies on "confluence" results of Gerard Huet [4].

0. Introduction:

In axiomatic specifications of abstract data types one might want axioms like

($\wp$) $\quad F(F(t,e_1),e_2) = F(F(t,e_2),e_1)$

in the following cases:
Let t be a term denoting a value of a type T, and F a function
F: T*ELEMENT -> T , such that F(t,e) denotes a new value of T "constructed" from t and some e∈ELEMENT. Then ($\wp$) expresses the fact that the order in which such "constructive operations" are performed is irrelevant. The most prominent example is, of course, the type SET of finite sets of ELEMENTs with an INSERT operation:
INSERT: SET*ELEMENT -> SET , one of its axioms being

INSERT(INSERT(s,e1),e2) = INSERT(INSERT(s,e2),e1)

Trying to establish the consistency of an axiomatic (equational) specification we would like to adopt the following approach: Regard the axioms as (left to right) rewriting rules and decide the Finite Termination Property (FTP) and the Unique Termination Property (UTP) of the resulting rewriting system. (Here we shall assume that all rewriting systems considered have the FTP.)

Allowing permutative axioms (such as ($\wp$) above) introduces of course infinite derivations in a trivial way. This difficulty can sometimes be overcome by dealing with equivalence classes of terms rather than simple terms, and by generalising the notion of a derivation accordingly.

Unfortunately there is no theory dealing with these "permutative derivations" in a uniform way, but each permutative axiom introduces a new problem which has to be tackled separately. Lankford and Ballantyne have shown how to cope with ordinary commutative axioms [2]: $f(x,y) = f(y,x)$, and with and with commutativity plus associativity, [3], but both methods fail to cope with axioms like ($\wp$). Basically this is because the presence of two function symbols on each side of the equation makes things much messier than in the case of ordinary commutativity, and because the equivalence classes under ($\wp$) are smaller than under ordinary commutativity plus associativity (i.e. more cases have to be distinguished).

In [4] Huet proves a whole range of "confluence" results that can be used as a basis for approaching UTP-problems. It seems that the approach of the present paper is fairly straightforward and can be adapted to deal with a variety of permutative derivations.

The amount of detail involved in algorithms and proofs in this field makes their presentation unfortunately rather unwieldy, and it is easy to lose confidence in intuitive and informal arguments. Thus formal definitions and proofs are presented here, but it is hoped that the gist of the argument (and the causes of difficulties) can be understood from the intuitive reasoning. In order to keep the amount of detail as small as possible the theory is presented for the axiom $\wp$ above instead of the more general axiom $F(G(t,e_1),e_2) = G(F(t,e_2),e_1)$. The necessary generalisations in chapter 3 are straightforward and do not demand nor, in fact, provide any deeper insight.

1. Basic Definitions:

Let $T = [\mathcal{C}, \mathcal{F}]$ be a many sorted algebra with a finite set of carriers $\mathcal{C}$ containing EL and T (allowing the usual ambiguity between the name of an algebra and its "principal carrier" or "type of interest"), and a set of function symbols, $\mathcal{F}$, containing F;

$$F: T*EL \rightarrow T$$

Let $t, t_1, t_2, \ldots$ be variables ranging over T,

$e, e_1, e_2, \ldots$ be variables ranging over EL.

Let X be a set of such (sorted) variables.

Let L(T) be the <u>word algebra</u> of T,

L(T,X) the set of words of L(T) where variables are allowed on argument positions.

For $w \in L(T,X)$ let <u>V(w)</u> be the set of all variables occurring in w.

Let $\approx$ be an equivalence relation on L(T,X) , $\approx(w) = \{ w' \mid w' \approx w\}$ for $w \in L(T,X)$

Let $u \vdash\!\dashv v$ denote the fact that v results from u by one application of $\mathcal{P}$.
Let $\vdash^{*}\dashv$ denote the reflexive transitive closure of $\vdash\!\dashv$,
$\vdash^{\varepsilon}\dashv$ the reflexive closure of $\vdash\!\dashv$

Our main interest will focus on the case where $\approx\ =\ \vdash^{*}\dashv$, even though not all of the results presented depend on this.
For the rest of this paper let us assume that $\approx$ has the following property:
If $u, u', v \in L(T,X)$ and $v = v_1 u v_2$ then $u \approx u'$ implies $v \approx v_1 u' v_2$
(Substitution of equivalent subwords results in equivalent words.)

A <u>permutative rewrite rule</u> is an expression $\approx(L) \to \approx(R)$ where $L, R \in L(T,X)$ and $V(R) \subseteq V(L)$.

Let $\mathcal{R}$ be a set of permutative rewriting rules. $\approx(v)$ is an <u>immediate reduction</u> of $\approx(u)$ by $\mathcal{R}$ if there exists a rule $\approx(L) \to \approx(R)$ in $\mathcal{R}$ and a substitution Θ, $u' \in \approx(u)$, $v' \in \approx(v)$, L' (L), substrings u_1, u_2 of u' such that

$$u' = u_1 \Theta(L') u_2 \qquad \text{and}$$
$$v' = u_1 \Theta(R') u_2$$

We use $\underset{\mathcal{R}}{=>}$ for the immediate reduction relation and $\underset{\mathcal{R}}{=>}^{*}$ for its reflexive and transitive closure, and $\underset{\mathcal{R}}{=>}c$ for "complete"derivations, i.e. if $\approx(u) \underset{\mathcal{R}}{=>}c \approx(v)$ then there is no rewrite rule applicable to $\approx(v)$. We write => instead of $\underset{\mathcal{R}}{=>}$ if the relevant $\mathcal{R}$ is understood from the context.

A set of rewrite rules $\mathcal{R}$ has the <u>Finite Termination Property</u>, (FTP), if there is no infinite derivation with respect to $\mathcal{R}$ from any $w \in L(T,X)$:
$w \Rightarrow w_1 \Rightarrow w_2 \Rightarrow \ldots\ldots$
It has the <u>Unique Termination Property</u> , (UTP), if for any $w \in L(T,X)$ such that $w \Rightarrow c\ u$ and $w \Rightarrow c\ v$, $u = v$

The definitions for permutative rewriting systems are analogous, replacing terms by equivalence classes of terms.

$u \updownarrow v$ denotes the fact that there exist w and w', $w \approx w'$, such that
$u \Rightarrow^{*} w$ and $v \Rightarrow^{*} w'$

$\mathcal{R}$ has the <u>UTP modulo $\approx$</u> if for all $u \in L(T,X)$: $u \Rightarrow c\ v$ and $u \Rightarrow c\ w$ implies $v \approx w$.

2. A strategy for coping with permutative axioms

The following technique seems adaptable to a variety of permutative rewriting systems, offering a fairly unified approach for dealing with those systems.

Let us try to "transport" the problems connected with permutative derivations to the better known ground of ordinary derivations:
Consider a rewriting system with the FTP,

$\mathcal{R} = \{ \approx(L_i) \to \approx(R_i) \mid 1 \leq i \leq n \}$

Form from this

$\mathcal{R}' = \{ L_i' \to R_i \mid L_i' \in \approx(L_i) \ , \ 1 \leq i \leq n \}$

Try to show that

(EQ) $\approx(u) \underset{\mathcal{R}}{\Rightarrow}^* \approx(v)$ iff $u \underset{\mathcal{R}'}{\Rightarrow}^* v'$ for some $v' \in \approx(v)$

i.e. for __any__ $u' \in \approx(u)$ there exists some $v' \in \approx(v)$ s.t. $u' \underset{\mathcal{R}'}{\Rightarrow}^* v'$.
(We shall see that this approach has to be refined to become applicable to our particular equivalence relation generated by $\mathcal{P}$.)

Then try then to establish the UTP modulo $\approx$ for $\mathcal{R}'$. The most important tool for doing so is the following lemma:

__Lemma (G.Huet)__: Let $\mathcal{R}'$ have the FTP (i.e. $\underset{\mathcal{R}'}{\Rightarrow}$ be a "noeterian" relation on L(T,X) in the terms of [4]).Let (α) and (β) be the following conditions:

(α) For all $u \in L(T,X)$ the following holds:
If $u \Rightarrow v'$ and $u \Rightarrow w'$ then there exist $v,w \in L(T,X)$, $v \approx w$, s.t. $v' \Rightarrow^* v$ and $w' \Rightarrow^* w$

(β) For all $u_1,u_2 \in L(T,X)$, $u_1 \approx u_2$, the following holds:
If $u_2 \Rightarrow w'$ then there exist $v,w \in L(T,X)$, $v \approx w$, s.t. $w' \Rightarrow^* w$ and $u_1 \Rightarrow^* v$

Illustration:

(α) 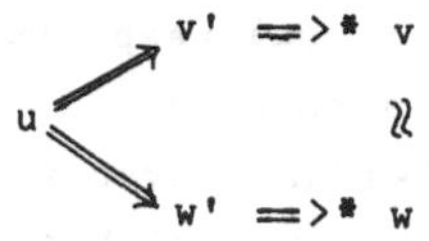 (β) 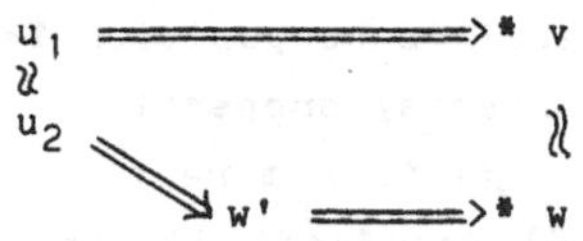

If $\Rightarrow$ fulfills (α) and (β) then (γ) holds:

(γ) For all $u_1,u_2 \in L(T,X)$, $u_1 \approx u_2$, s.t. $u_1 \Rightarrow^* v'$ and $u_2 \Rightarrow^* w'$ there exist $v,w \in L(T,X)$, $v \approx w$, s.t $v' \Rightarrow^* v$ and $w' \Rightarrow^* w$.

Illustration:

(γ) 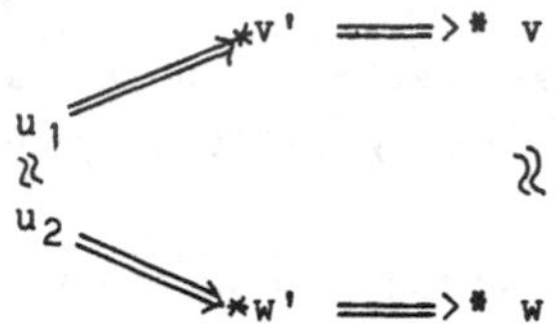

See [4] for the proof.

There are two weaker forms of this lemma which it might sometimes be convenient to use:

<u>Lemma</u>: Let $\mathcal{R}'$ have the FTP. Let (α') be the following condition:

(α') For all $u \in L(T,X)$ s.t. $u \Rightarrow v'$ and $u \Rightarrow w'$ there are <u>terminal</u> $v, w \in L(T,X)$, $v \approx w$, s.t. $v' \Rightarrow^* v$ and $w' \Rightarrow^* w$

(α') implies (γ') where (γ') is the following condition:

(γ') For all $u \in L(T,X)$ such that $u \Rightarrow^* v'$ and $u \Rightarrow^* w'$ there are $v, w \in L(T,X)$, $v \approx w$, such that $v' \Rightarrow^* v$ and $w' \Rightarrow^* w$.

The (rather technical) proof is not presented here for considerations of space.

<u>Lemma</u>: Let $\mathcal{R}'$ have the FTP, $\approx$ be such that if $u_1 \approx u_2$ and u_1 is terminal then so is u_2. Let ($\alpha\beta$) be the following condition:

($\alpha\beta$) For all $u_1, u_2 \in L(T,X)$, $u_1 \approx u_2$, s.t. $u_1 \Rightarrow v'$ and $u_2 \Rightarrow w'$ there exist $v, w \in L(T,X)$, $v \approx w$, s.t. $v' \Rightarrow^* v$ and $w' \Rightarrow^* w$.

($\alpha\beta$) implies (γ).

<u>Proof</u>: ($\alpha\beta$) implies (α) and (β):
It implies (α) since $u \approx u$ for all $u \in L(T,X)$.
It implies (β) since $u_2 \Rightarrow w'$ implies that u_1 is not terminal.
Hence there is a $v' \in L(T,X)$ s.t. $u_1 \Rightarrow v'$, and thus a $v \approx w$ such that $v' \Rightarrow^* v$, i.e. $u_1 \Rightarrow^* v$. q.e.d.

To decide whether $\mathcal{R}'$ has property (α) one can use a generalised form of the Knuth-Bendix Superposition Test [1]. (In case of (α') resp. ($\alpha\beta$) one has to take special properties of $\mathcal{R}'$ resp. $\approx$ into account.)

To decide (β) is a more tricky affair. Huet [4] has given a method to decide (β) for "left linear" rewriting systems (no variable occurs more than once on the left hand side of a rewrite rule). The restriction of left linearity seems too harsh for axiomatisations of abstract data types. E.g., in the example of SET one wants to be able to include an axiom like INSERT(INSERT(s,i),i) = INSERT(s,i).

Thus we shall have to pay special attention to (β). (In fact, we shall choose for any $\mathcal{R}$ an $\mathcal{R}''$ which is guaranteed to have property (β).)

3. Adaptations for the particular permuative axiom $\mathcal{P}$

Efforts to prove (EQ) focus on the following situation:

(D)

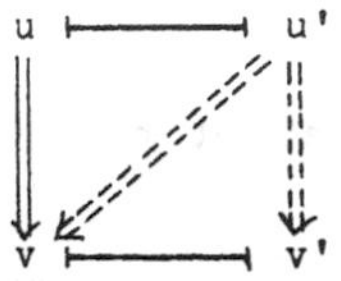

v is derived from u by some rule L -> R in $\mathcal{R}'$, u' results from u by one application of $\mathcal{P}$.

We would like to "close" this diagram by either finding a rule L' -> R in $\mathcal{R}'$ which derives v from u', or by deriving some v' from u' s.t. v $\mapsto$ v'.

This endeavour fails because of two reasons:

(1) $\mathcal{R}'$ is not "rich enough": There is no rule in $\mathcal{R}'$ to allow the derivation of v or v' from u'.

E.g. let $\mathcal{R}$ = { ≈(F(F(t,e),e)) -> ≈(F(t,e)) }

then $\mathcal{R}'$ = $\mathcal{R}$, identifying singletons with their only member.

Let u = F(F(F(E,2),1),1) then u $\mapsto$ u' for

u'= F(F(F(E,1),2),1) (some E L(T))

u $\underset{\mathcal{R}'}{\Rightarrow}$ F(F(E,2),1) but no rule of $\mathcal{R}'$ is applicable to u'.

(2) Since we abandoned left linearity we might encounter the following situation:

Let $\mathcal{R}$ = { ≈(U(t,t)) -> ≈(t) }; then $\mathcal{R}'$ = $\mathcal{R}$, as in (1).

Let u = U(F(F(E,1),2), F(F(E,1),2)),

u'= U(F(F(E,2),1), F(F(E,1),2)). Then u $\mapsto$ u'.

u $\underset{\mathcal{R}'}{\Rightarrow}$ F(F(E,1),2) but no rule of $\mathcal{R}'$ is applicable to u'.

To deal with (1) we shall "pad out" the rules of $\mathcal{R}'$ to one more level of nesting of F's.

To deal with (2) we shall introduce more general derivations. At the basis of those is the idea of a "relaxed" substitution which allows to substitute different occurrences of the same variable by different but equivalent (under ≈) terms.

3.1. Padding of Rewrite Rules

Remember that for every permutative rewriting system $\mathcal{R} = \{ \approx(L_i) \to \approx(R_i) \mid 1 \le i \le n \}$ we defined

$\mathcal{R}' = \{ L_i' \to R_i \mid L_i' \in \approx(L_i),\ 1 \le i \le n \}$

Define $\mathcal{R}''$ by the following steps:

(1) Set $\mathcal{R}'' = \mathcal{R}'$

(2) For all $L_i' \to R_i$ in $\mathcal{R}'$ for which $L_i' = F(\ldots)$ add the following set of rules to $\mathcal{R}''$:

$\{ L_i'' \to R_i'' \mid L_i'' \in \approx(F(L_i', e_{new})),\ R_i'' = F(R_i, e_{new}) \}$

where e_{new} is a variable that does not occur in either L_i' or R_i. ("Padding on the outside")

E.g. for the axiom $F(F(t,e),e) = F(t,e)$ the following set of padded rules is introduced:

$\{ F(F(F(t,e),e),e_{new}) = F(F(F(t,e),e_{new}),$
$F(F(F(t,e),e_{new}),e) = F(F(F(t,e),e_{new}),$
$F(F(F(t,e_{new}),e),e) = F(F(F(t,e),e_{new}) \}$

(3) For all $L_i' \to R_i$ in $\mathcal{R}'$ for which $L_i' = g(\ldots F(t,e)\ldots)$, ($t,e$ variables, $g \in \mathcal{F}$) add the following set of rules to $\mathcal{R}''$:

$\{ L_i'' \to R_i'' \mid L_i'' \in (\Theta(L_i')),\ R_i'' = (R_i)$, where Θ is a substitution s.t. $\Theta(t) = F(t',e')$; t',e' are variables that do not occur in either L_i' or R_i $\}$

("Padding on the inside")

E.g. for the same axiom as in (2) the following set of padded axioms is now introduced:

$\{ F(F(F(t_{new},t_{new}),e),e) = F(F(t_{new},t_{new}),e)$
$F(F(F(t_{new},e),e_{new}),e) = F(F(t_{new},e_{new}),e),$
$F(F(F(t_{new},e),e),e_{new}) = F(F(t_{new},e_{new}),e) \}$

<u>Notice</u> that L_i' might be of the form $g(\ldots F(t_1,e_1)\ldots\ldots F(t_m,e_m)\ldots)$ in which case we introduce m padded rules, one for each $F(t_j,e_j)$. Notice also that t might occur several times in L_i', e.g. L_i' might be of the form $g(\ldots t\ldots F(t,e)\ldots)$ in which case L_i'' is of the form $g(\ldots F(t',e')\ldots F(F(t',e')\ldots)$.

3.2. Generalised Derivations

For every substitution $\Theta: X \to L(T,X)$ let $\tilde{\Theta}: X \to L(T,X)/_\approx$ be defined by

$\tilde{\Theta}(x) = \approx(\Theta(x))$

Extend $\tilde{\Theta}$ homomorphically to L(T,X): For all w in L(T): $\tilde{\Theta}(w) = w$;
if $w \in L(T,X)$ and $w = f(w_1,\ldots,w_n)$ then
$\tilde{\Theta}(w) = \{ f(t_1,\ldots,t_n) \mid t_i \in \tilde{\Theta}(w_i),\ 1 \leq i \leq n \}$

Let $\mathcal{R}$ be a rewriting system: $\mathcal{R} = \{L_i \to R_i \mid 1 \leq i \leq n\}$
Definition: For $u,v \in L(T,X)$, $u \underset{\mathcal{R}}{\approx\!\!>} v$ if there is a substitution Θ, $L \to R$ in $\mathcal{R}$, $l \in \tilde{\Theta}(L)$ s.t. $u = v_1 l v_2$ and $v = v_1 \Theta(R) v_2$.

Facts: (i) If $u \underset{\mathcal{R}}{\approx\!\!>} v$ then there exists $u' \approx u$ s.t. $u' \underset{\mathcal{R}}{=>} v$
(ii) If $\mathcal{R}$ is left linear then $\underset{\mathcal{R}}{=>}$ and $\underset{\mathcal{R}}{\approx\!\!>}$ are the same.

Warning and apology: When this paper had already gone to the publishers Gerard Huet pointed out to me that the following paragraph contains a rather primitive but fundamental error which I have unfortunately no means of rectifying other than by this notice.

The paddings introduced above do not endow $\mathcal{R}''$ with the properties claimed below. Case 3b (ii) in the proof of the first lemma assumes implicitly iterated padding, which leads in general to infinite sets of rewrite rules. So the question of how to find an $\mathcal{R}''$ with properties (α) and (β) and equivalent to $\mathcal{R}$ in the sense of (EQ) is still open. Thus chapter 4 can only be regarded as hypothetical.

3.3. Equivalence of $\mathcal{R}$ and $\mathcal{R}''$

We shall now prove that $\mathcal{R}''$ satisfies diagram (D) above, and has property (EQ).

Notation: Let $Pl = F(F(t,e_1),e_2)$, $Pr = F(F(t,e_2),e_1)$

Lemma: Let $\mathcal{R}$ be a permutative rewriting system, $\mathcal{R}''$ be a padded version of $\mathcal{R}$ as described in 3.1. Let $u \underset{\mathcal{R}''}{\approx\!\!>} v$.
Then for any u' with $u \mapsto u'$ there exists a v', $v \vdash\!\mathcal{E}\!\dashv v'$, s.t. $u' \underset{\mathcal{R}''}{\approx\!\!>} v'$.

See (D) for an illustration (=> is now replaced by $\approx\!\!>$).

Proof: Let $L \to R \in \mathcal{R}''$ s.t. $u \underset{\mathcal{R}''}{\approx\!\!>} v$ by $L \to R$; i.e. there exists a substitution Θ and $l \in \tilde{\Theta}(L)$ s.t. $u = v_1 l v_2$ and $v = v_1 \Theta(R) v_2$.

Let furthermore λ be a substitution s.t.
$u = w_1 \lambda(Pl) w_2$ and $u' = w_1 \lambda(Pr) w_2$

Distinguish three cases:

Case 1: l and $\lambda(Pl)$ do not overlap.
Case 2: $\lambda(Pl)$ occurs in l
(a) on a position that corresponds to a variable in L.

(b) on a position that does not correspond to a variable in L.

Case 3: l occurs in $\lambda(Pl)$

(a) on a position that corresponds to a variable in Pl.

(b) on a position that does not correspond to a variable in Pl.

Notice: Case (2a) forced us to introduce the generalised derivations, if we wanted to drop the condition of left linearity. Cases (2b) and (3b) make difficulties because of the occurrence of two function symbols on each side of the permutative axiom $\mathcal{P}$. To overcome these, i.e. to guarantee that there are "enough"rules with permuted lefthand sides, the padded rules were introduced.

Case 1: $u = u_1 l u_2 \lambda(Pl) u_3$ (or $u = u_1 \lambda(Pl) u_2 l u_3$) for some strings u_1, u_2, u_3

$v = u_1 r u_2 \lambda(Pl) u_3$

$u' = u_1 l u_2 \lambda(Pr) u_3$. Applying L -> R to u' results in

$v' = u_1 r u_2 \lambda(Pr) u_3$ and clearly $v \mapsto v'$

Case 2a: $L = L_1 x L_2$ for some variable x, (remember: $l \in \tilde{\Theta}(L)$)

$l = l_1 p \lambda(Pl) q l_2$ where $p\lambda(Pl)q \in \tilde{\Theta}(x)$.

Thus $p\lambda(Pr)q \in \tilde{\Theta}(x)$.

Thus $l' = l_1 p \lambda(Pr) q l_2 \in \tilde{\Theta}(L)$, and $u' = v_1 l' v_2 \underset{(L\to R)}{\widetilde{\Longrightarrow}} v = v_1 r v_2$.

Notice that in the case of ordinary reductions one needs a substitution Θ' s.t. $\Theta'(x) = p\lambda(Pr)q$; but then it might happen that $\Theta'(L) \neq l'$ if x occurs more than once in L.

Illustration:

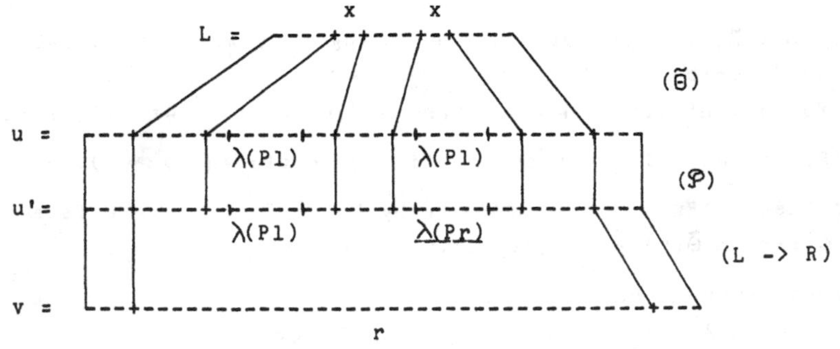

Case 3a: $Pl = P_1 x P_2$, where x is one of the variables t, e_1, or e_2;

$\lambda(Pl) = p_1 olq p_2$ where $olq = \lambda(x)$.

If $Pl = P_1 x P_2$ then $Pr = P_1' x P_2'$ for some P_1', P_2'.

Hence

$\lambda(Pr) = p_1'\underline{olq}p_2'$ for some p_1', p_2' ,

$u' = w_1 p_1'\underline{olq}p_2' w_2$

Let $\quad v' = w_1 p_1'\underline{orq}p_2' w_2$

Then $\quad u' \underset{(L\to R)}{\Longrightarrow} v'$ and $v' \longmapsto v$

__Case 2b__: Let $\lambda(Pl) = F(F(T_0,E_1),E_2)$ for some $T_0,E_1,E_2 \in L(T,X)$. Then

$$l = l_1 F(F(T_0,E_1),E_2) l_2$$

and one occurrence of F, or both, occurs also in L; there are two possible forms of L:

(i) $L = L_1 F(F(T_0',E_1'),E_2') L_2$ where $T_0',E_1',E_2' \in L(T,X)$ and $T_0 \in \tilde{\Theta}(T_0')$, $E_i \in \tilde{\Theta}(E_i')$, $i = 1,2$.

(ii) $L = L_1 F(t,E_2') L_2$ where $t \in X$, $E_2' \in L(T,X)$, $F(T_0,E_1) \in \tilde{\Theta}(t)$, $E_2 \in \tilde{\Theta}(E_2')$

Illustration:

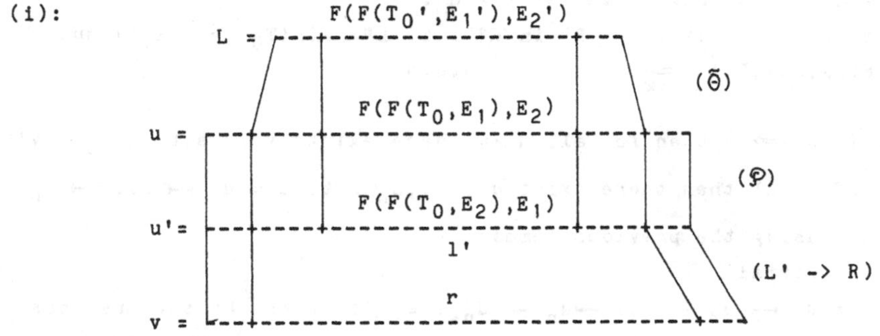

The picture for (ii) is the same as for (i), changing the inscriptions from $F(F(T_0',E_1'),E_2')$ to $F(t,E_2')$, from r to r', and from L' -> R to L" -> R'.

Case (i): If L ->R is in $\mathcal{R}''$ then for every $L' \approx L$: L'-> R is in $\mathcal{R}''$. Hence there is a rule L'-> R in $\mathcal{R}''$ such that $L' = L_1 F(F(T_0',E_2'),E_1') L_2$. Hence $\quad u' = v_1 l_1 F(F(T_0,E_2),E_1) l_2 v_2 \underset{\mathcal{R}''}{\Longrightarrow} v$.

Case (ii): There exist padded (on the inside) rules L'-> R and L"-> R' in $\mathcal{R}''$ and a substitution Θ' s.t.

$L' = L_1 F(\underline{F(t',e_1')},E_2') L_2$, $\quad L'' = L_1 F(\underline{F(t',E_2')},e_1') L_2$,

$\Theta'(t') = T_0$, $\Theta'(e_1') = E_1$, and $\Theta'(x) = \Theta(x)$ for all variables occurring in L or R. Then $u' = v_1 l_1 F(F(T_0,E_2),E_1) l_2 v_2 \underset{(L'\to R)}{\Longrightarrow} v$

Notice again that t might occur several times in L, e.g. $L = g(\ldots t \ldots F(t,E_2')\ldots)$. In that case we get $L' = g(\ldots F(t',e_1')\ldots F(F(t',e_1'),E_2')\ldots)$ and $L'' = g(\ldots F(t',e_1')\ldots F(F(t',E_2'),e_1')\ldots)$. Since $\Theta(t) = F(T_0,E_1)$ and $\Theta'(t') = T_0$, and $\Theta'(e_1') = E_1$ we can indeed be sure that $L'' \to R'$ is applicable to u' whenever $L \to R$ is applicable to u.

Case 3b: If l occurs in $\lambda(Pl)$ on a position that does not correspond to a variable in Pl, there are only two possible forms of l:

(i) $l = \lambda(Pl)$

(ii) $l = F(T_0,E_1)$ (assuming that $\lambda(Pl) = F(F(T_0,E_1),E_2)$)
$L = F(T_0',E_1')$, $\Theta(T_0') = T_0$, $\Theta(E_1') = E_1$

In the first case there is a permuted rule $L' \to R$ in $\mathcal{R}''$ such that $\Theta(L') = F(F(T_0,E_2),E_1)$ and thus $u' = \lambda(Pr) \underset{(L'\to R)}{\Longrightarrow} v$.

In the second case there is a padded (on the outside) rule $L' \to R'$ in $\mathcal{R}''$ and a substitution Θ' s.t. $L' = F(F(T_0',E_1'),e')$, $\Theta'(e') = E_2$, $\Theta'(x) = \Theta(x)$ for all variables $x \neq e'$.
There is also a rule $L'' \to R'$ in $\mathcal{R}''$ s.t. $L'' = F(F(T_0',e'),E_1')$ and $u' = F(F(T_0,E_2),E_1) \underset{(L''\to R')}{\Longrightarrow} v$. q.e.d.

Lemma: If $u \underset{\mathcal{R}'}{\Longrightarrow} v$ then for all $u' \approx u$ there exists $v' \approx v$ s.t. $u' \underset{\mathcal{R}''}{\Longrightarrow} v'$

Proof: If $u \approx u'$ then there exist $u_1,\ldots,u_n$ s.t. $u = u_1 \vdash\!\dashv \ldots \vdash\!\dashv u_n = u'$

Induction using the previous lemma:

- n = 1: trivial
- Let $u = u_1 \vdash\!\dashv u_2 \vdash\!\dashv \ldots \vdash\!\dashv u_n \vdash\!\dashv u_{n+1} = u'$; then, by the previous lemma, there exists v' s.t. $v \vdash_{\varepsilon}\!\dashv v'$ and $u_2 \underset{\mathcal{R}''}{\Longrightarrow} v'$, and, by induction hypothesis, there exists v'' s.t. $v'' \approx v'$, hence $v'' \approx v$, and $u_{n+1} \underset{\mathcal{R}''}{\Longrightarrow} v''$. q.e.d.

Notice that this lemma implies that $\mathcal{R}''$ has property (β).

Now we can finally prove a refined version of (EQ):

Theorem: Let $\mathcal{R}$ be a permutative rewriting system, $\approx\ = \vdash^*\!\dashv$, $\mathcal{R}''$ as defined in 3.1.

$\approx(u) \underset{\mathcal{R}}{\Rightarrow} \approx(v)$ iff for all $u' \in \approx(u)$ there exists $v' \in \approx(v)$ such that $u' \underset{\mathcal{R}''}{\Longrightarrow} v'$.

Proof: Obvious from the previous lemma and the definition of permutative reduction.

Corollary: If $\mathcal{R}$ has the FTP then so does $\mathcal{R}''$.

4. The Unique Termination Theorem

We would now like to use the Knuth-Bendix Superposition Test (see [1], or [4] for a version generalised to cover unique termination modulo some equivalence relation) to verify the UTP modulo $\approx$ for $\mathcal{R}''$, and use the theorem above to infer the result for $\mathcal{R}$. But since we have introduced non-standard notions for substitution and derivation, we have to adapt the methods of [1] to cover this more general case. In particular we have to modify the notions of unification and critical pairs, and to prove a corresponding "crititical pairs lemma".

Definition: Let $t_1, t_2 \in L(T,X)$. A substitution Θ: $X \rightarrow L(T,X)$ is a unifier of t_1 and t_2 if $\tilde{\Theta}(t_1) \cap \tilde{\Theta}(t_2) \neq \emptyset$.
Notation: $t_1 \bigtriangledown t_2$

(Notice that we do not distinguish between terms of L(T,X) that are identical up to consistent renaming of variables, and can thus assume that $V(t_1) \cap V(t_2) = \emptyset$)
This definition differs from the standard one only in case some variable occurs more than once in t_1 or t_2.

μ is the most general unifier for terms t_1, t_2 if for all unifiers Θ there exists a substitution λ s.t. $\Theta = \lambda \circ \mu$
(In fact μ is unique up to consistent renaming of variables.) Robinson's algorithm (see [5] pp.32)to determine the most general unifier can be generalised in a straightforward way to cope with the above definition of unification. (Basically, there are no difficulties because the equivalence classes of terms are finite.)

Definition: $\langle t_1, t_2 \rangle$ is a critical pair of a (ordinary) rewriting system $\mathcal{R}$ if there exist rules $L_1 \rightarrow R_1$, $L_2 \rightarrow R_2$ in $\mathcal{R}$ such that L_2 unifies with a subword t of L_1: $L_1 = v_1 t v_2$, $t \notin X$, $L_2 \bigtriangledown t$, and

$$t_1 = v_1 \mu(R_2) v_2 \quad \text{and} \quad t_2 = \mu(R_1)$$

where μ is chosen such that $\mu(R_2)$ has no variables in common with v_1 and v_2.

Lemma (Critical Pairs): Let $\mathcal{R}$ be a permutative rewriting system, $\approx = \vdash^{*}\dashv$, $\mathcal{R}''$ constructed as above. Let C be the set of all critical pairs of $\mathcal{R}''$.
Then $\mathcal{R}''$ has property (α) iff for all $\langle t_1, t_2 \rangle$ in C: $t_1 \updownarrow t_2$

Proof: (i) Assume that $\mathcal{R}''$ has property (α):
Let $\langle t_1, t_2 \rangle \in C$, then there exists a $L \rightarrow R \in \mathcal{R}''$ and a substitution Θ s.t. $\Theta(L) \underset{\mathcal{R}''}{\approx\!\Rightarrow} t_1$, $\Theta(L) \underset{\mathcal{R}''}{\approx\!\Rightarrow} t_2$ and hence, by (α): $t_1 \updownarrow t_2$.

(ii) Assume that for every $\langle t_1,t_2\rangle \in C$ we have $t_1 \downarrow t_2$. Let $t \underset{\mathcal{R}''}{\Rrightarrow} t'$ and $t \underset{\mathcal{R}''}{\Rrightarrow} t''$ for some $t,t',t'' \in L(T,X)$.

Then there exist $L_1 \to R_1$, $L_2 \to R_2 \in \mathcal{R}''$, substitutions Θ_1, Θ_2, $l_i \in \tilde{\Theta}_i(L_i)$, $i = 1,2$ and

$$t = r_1 l_1 r_2 \qquad t = s_1 l_2 s_2$$
$$t' = r_1 \Theta_1(R_1) r_2 \qquad t'' = s_1 \Theta_2(R_2) s_2$$

Distinguish two cases:

(a) l_1 and l_2 do not overlap in t:

$t = u_1 l_1 u_2 l_2 u_3$ or $t = u_1 l_2 u_2 l_1 u_3$ for some u_1,u_2,u_3.
Then, trivially, t' and t" both derive to $u_1\Theta_1(R_1)u_2\Theta_2(R_2)$ resp. $u_1\Theta_2(R_2)u_2\Theta_1(R_1)u_3$, i.e. ($\alpha$) holds.

(b) l_2 occurs in l_1 or vice versa.
Without loss of generality assume that l_2 occurs in l_1:
$l_1 = h_1 l_2 h_2$, $t = r_1 h_1 l_2 h_2 r_2$, $t' = r_1\Theta_1(R_1)r_2$,
$t'' = r_1 h_1 \Theta_2(R_2) h_2 r_2$ $\quad (s_1 = r_1 h_1$, $s_2 = h_2 r_2)$

Show that there exist t_3,t_4 s.t. $t_3 \approx t_4$, $\Theta_1(R_1) \Rrightarrow^* t_3$ and $h_1\Theta_2(R_2)h_2 \Rrightarrow^* t_4$ then the desired result follows.

Distinguish two cases again:

(b1) l_2 occurs in l_1 on a position that corresponds to a variable in L_1:

Here we have to pay special attention to the effects of replacing $\Rightarrow$ by $\Rrightarrow$.

Illustration:

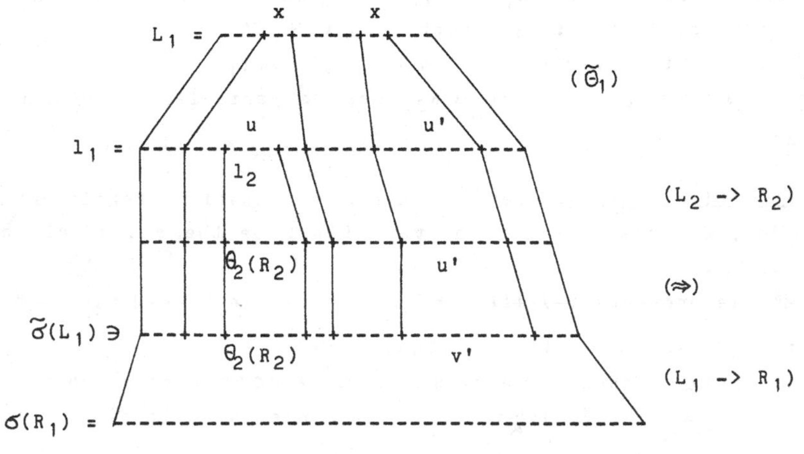

Assume x occurs n times in L_1: $L_1 = W_1 x W_2 x W_3 \ldots W_n x W_{n+1}$.

These occurrences of x are replaced in l_1 by some $u_1, \ldots, u_n \in \Theta_1(x)$, $l_1 = w_1 u_1 \ldots w_n u_n w_{n+1}$ and l_2 is a subword of some u_i: $u_i = p l_2 q$ and $u_i \underset{\mathcal{R}''}{\Longrightarrow} p\Theta_2(R_2)q$.

Let $p\Theta_2(R_2)q = v_i$ then we know from the previous theorem that for every $u_j \in \Theta_1(x)$ there exists a v_j s.t.

$$u_j \underset{\mathcal{R}''}{\Longrightarrow} v_j \text{ and } v_j \approx v_i \quad (\text{since } u_i \approx u_j)$$

Thus $l_1 \underset{\mathcal{R}''}{\Longrightarrow} h_1\Theta_2(R_2)h_2 \underset{\mathcal{R}''}{\Longrightarrow}{}^* w_1 v_1 w_2 \ldots w_n v_n w_{n+1}$.

Let σ be a substitution s.t. $\sigma(x) = v_i$ and $\sigma(x') = \Theta_1(x')$ for all $x' = x$; then $v_j \in \tilde{\sigma}(x)$ for all $j = 1,2,\ldots,n$, $l_1' = w_1 v_1 \ldots w_n v_n w_{n+1} \in \tilde{\sigma}(L_1)$ and $l_1' \underset{\mathcal{R}''}{\Longrightarrow} \sigma(R_1)$

Furthermore, we have $\Theta_1(x) \Longrightarrow \sigma(x)$ and hence $\Theta_1(R_1) \Longrightarrow^* \sigma(R_1)$.

Summing up, we have $h_1\Theta_2(R_2)h_2 \Longrightarrow \sigma(R_1)$, $\Theta_1(R_1) \Longrightarrow^* \sigma(R_1)$ and hence $t' \Longrightarrow^* \sigma(R_1)$ and $t'' \Longrightarrow^* \sigma(R_1)$

(b2) l_2 occurs in l_1 on a place that does not correspond to a variable in L_1:

Then there exists a critical pair $\langle t_1, t_2 \rangle$ and a substitution ρ s.t. $h_1\Theta_2(R_2) = \rho(t_1)$ and $\Theta_1(R_1) = \rho(t_2)$.

Then, by assumption, there exist t_3, t_4, $t_3 \approx t_4$, s.t.

$$t_1 \Longrightarrow^* t_3 \quad \Big| \quad \rho(t_1) \Longrightarrow^* \rho(t_3)$$

$$t_2 \Longrightarrow^* t_4 \quad \Big| \quad \rho(t_2) \Longrightarrow^* \rho(t_4)$$

Then $t' = r_1\rho(t_2)r_2 \Longrightarrow^* r_1\rho(t_3)r_2$ and

$t'' = r_1\rho(t_1)r_2 \Longrightarrow^* r_1\rho(t_4)r_2$ and $r_1\rho(t_3)r_2 \approx r_1\rho(t_4)r_2$

q.e.d.

<u>Theorem (Unique Termination)</u>:

Let $\mathcal{R}$ be a permutative rewriting system, $\approx\ = \vdash^*\dashv$, $\mathcal{R}''$ defined as in chapter 3. Assume $\mathcal{R}$ has the FTP (and hence $\mathcal{R}''$ too). Let C be the set of critical pairs of $\mathcal{R}''$.

Then $\mathcal{R}$ has the UTP modulo $\approx$ iff for all $\langle t_1, t_2 \rangle \in C$ there exist t_3, t_4 s.t. $t_3 \approx t_4$ and $t_1 \underset{\mathcal{R}''}{\Longrightarrow}{}^* t_3$, $t_2 \underset{\mathcal{R}''}{\Longrightarrow}{}^* t_4$.

<u>Proof</u>: From the critical pairs lemma we know that $\mathcal{R}''$ has property (α) under the assumption of the theorem; we have seen that $\mathcal{R}''$ has property (β) for any $\mathcal{R}$.

So we know from Huet's lemma that $\mathcal{R}''$ has the UTP. Thus, by the theorem in chapter 3 , $\mathcal{R}$ has the UTP. q.e.d.

References:

[1] D.E.Knuth & P.B.Bendix: Simple Word Problems in Universal Algebras in Computational Problems in Abstract Algebra
Ed. J.Leech, Pergamon Press 1970, pp.263-297

[2] D.S.Lankford & A.M.Ballantyne: Decision Procedures for Simple Equational Theories with a Commutative Axiom: Complete Sets of Commutative Reductions
Automatic Theorem Proving Project, Depts. Math. and Comp. Science, University of Texas at Austin; Report #ATP-35

[3] D.S.Lankford & A.M.Ballantyne: Decision Procedures for Simple Equational Theories with Commutative-Associative Axioms: Complete Sets of Commutative-Associative Reductions
As [2], Report #ATP-39

[4] G.Huet: Confluent Reductions: Abstract Properties and Applications to Term Rewriting Systems
IRIA-LABORIA, Domaine de Voluceau, F-78150 Rocquencourt France. Preliminary version in 18th IEEE Symposium on Foundations of Computer Science, Oct 1977

[5] J.A.Robinson: A Machine-Oriented Logic Based on the Resolution Principle. JACM Vol.12, No.1; January 1965; pp.23-41

DAGS AND CHOMSKY HIERARCHY

(extended abstract)

Tsutomu Kamimura
Giora Slutzki

University of Delaware
Newark, DE 19711 USA

1. Introduction. The notion of a tree automaton is extended to that of an automaton operating on special directed acyclic graphs, called dags. Dags model derivations of phrase-structure grammars analogously to the way that trees model derivations of context-free grammars, and we show how the dag automata may be used to prove properties of the generated languages.

Several attempts to generalize tree automata theory have already been reported [1,2,3, 6,9]. However, it is our concern that the extension (at least at the definitional level) should be straightforward and natural relatively to the tree case. We first introduce the definitions of dags and dag automata. Then, after presenting several basic results in section 3, we use these to illustrate how dag automata can be used to prove properties of phrase-structure grammars. For example, by extending the proof technique of Rounds [11], from trees to dags, we show (the well-known result) that the (Chomsky) class of languages of type-i is closed under intersection with regular sets, i=1,2,3. A more interesting result (Theorem 4.4) presents a dynamic restriction on a phrase-structure grammar G which forces L(G) to be context-free. Together with a result of [5] this yields the following corollary: if there exists a bound K such that every word of a language generated by a type-0 grammar can be generated by a derivation in which at most K non-type-i rules are used, then the language is still of type i, i=1, 2,3.

Finally we present some recent results and also some suggestions for future work.

2. Basic Definitions. For basic graph terminology the reader is referred to [13]. Dags are graphs having (but not characterized by) the following properties: they are labeled, directed, acyclic, ordered, planar and connected. The labels are symbols out of a doubly ranked alphabet which is a set $\Sigma = \bigcup_{i,j} \Sigma_{ij}$ where each Σ_{ij} is a finite set and only for a finite number of i and j $\Sigma_{ij} \neq \emptyset$. An element $\sigma \in \Sigma_{ij}$ has head-rank i and tail-rank j. Also we define $\Sigma_{*j} = \bigcup_i \Sigma_{ij}$ and $\Sigma_{i*} = \bigcup_j \Sigma_{ij}$. Then (rooted) dags are defined inductively (as in the tree case) along with the concept of "leaves."

2.1. Definition. Let Σ be a doubly ranked alphabet. The set of partial dags over Σ, denoted by P_Σ, is defined as follows.

(i) If $a \in \Sigma_{0*}$ then $a \in P_\Sigma$; leaves(a)=a (when convenient we will identify the node with its label).

(ii) Let $d \in P_\Sigma$ with leaves(d)=$a_1 \dots a_n$ and $a_i \in \Sigma_{*m}$; let $b_1, \dots, b_m \in \Sigma_{1*}$. Then d' of Fig. 1(a) is in P_Σ, and leaves(d')=$a_1 \dots a_{i-1} b_1 \dots b_m a_{i+1} \dots a_n$.

(iii) Let $d \in P_\Sigma$ with leaves(d)=$a_1 \dots a_n$ and $a_i, a_{i+1}, \dots, a_j \in \Sigma_{*1}$ for some $1 \le i \le j \le n$. Let $b \in \Sigma_{(j-i+1)*}$ then d' of Fig. 1(b) is in P_Σ with leaves(d')=$a_1 \dots a_{i-1} b a_{j+1} \dots a_n$.

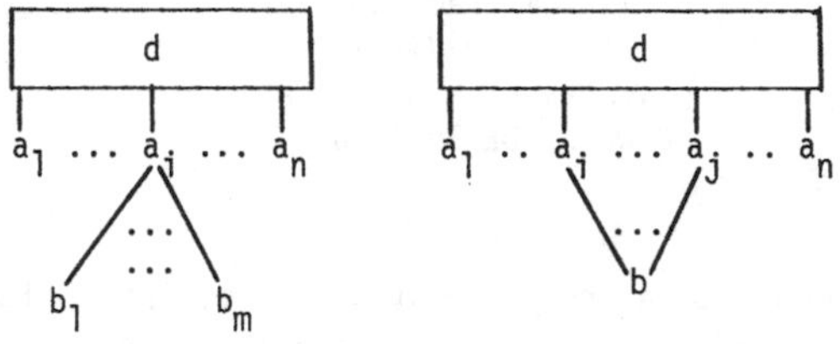

(a) (b)

Fig. 1. ⊠

The set of dags over Σ is then $D_\Sigma = \{d \in P_\Sigma \mid \text{leaves}(d) \in \Sigma^*_{*0}\}$.
We now define dag automata. For a doubly ranked alphabet Σ we define a companion alphabet $\Sigma' = \{\sigma' \mid \sigma \in \Sigma\}$ such that σ and σ' have precisely the same head and tail ranks.

2.2. Definition. A finite dag automaton is a construct $A=(Q,\Sigma,R)$ where Q is a finite set of states, Σ is a doubly ranked alphabet and R is a finite set of rules of the form r: $\alpha \to \beta$. α and β are respectively the left-hand side and the right-hand side of r. A is deterministic if two different rules have different left-hand sides; otherwise A is nondeterministic. A being top-down or bottom-up depends on the form of α and β above as follows.

(a) A is top-down if the rules in R are of the form

$$[p_1 \dots p_n]\sigma \to \sigma'(q_1 \dots q_m)$$

(b) A is bottom-up if the rules in R are of the form

$$\sigma(q_1 \dots q_m) \to [p_1 \dots p_n]\sigma'$$

for some $\sigma \in \Sigma_{nm}$ and $p_1, \dots, p_n, q_1, \dots, q_m \in Q$. ⊠

The reason for introducing the primes in the right-hand sides of rules is to signify that σ has been processed and to prevent repeated reprocessing of the same dag.
A configuration of the finite dag automaton $A=(Q,\Sigma,R)$ is a dag over the doubly ranked alphabet $\Delta = \Sigma \cup \Sigma' \cup Q$ with $Q \subseteq \Delta_{11}$. Let d_1 and d_2 be two configurations of A. Then the (direct computation) relation $\vdash_A$ is defined as follows:

(i) If A is top-down, then $d_1 \vdash_A d_2$ if d_1 contains a subdag of Fig. 2(a), R contains the rule $[p_1 \dots p_n]\sigma \to \sigma'(q_1 \dots q_m)$ and d_2 is obtained from d_1 by replacing the subdag of Fig. 2(a) by the subdag of Fig. 2(b).

(ii) If A is bottom-up, then $d_1 \vdash_A d_2$ if d_1 contains a subdag of Fig. 2(c), R has a rule $\sigma(q_1 \ldots q_m) \to [p_1 \ldots p_n]\sigma'$ and d_2 is obtained from d_1 by replacing the subdag of Fig. 2(c) by the subdag of Fig. 2(d).

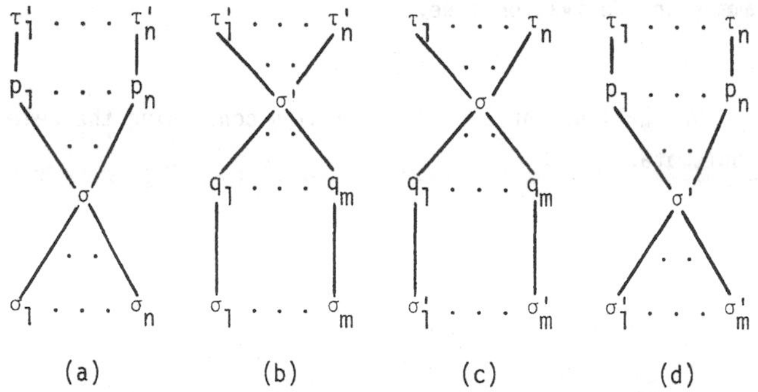

Fig. 2.

Given $\vdash_A$, $\vdash_A^*$ is the reflexive-transitive closure of $\vdash_A$. The dag language recognized by A is $L(A)=\{d \in D_\Sigma \mid d \vdash_A^* d'\}$ where $d' \in D_{\Sigma'}$ is the dag resulting from $d \in D_\Sigma$ by priming all the labels of d.

NT and DT denote respectively the set of all nondeterministic and deterministic top-down automata and similarly NB and DB in the bottom-up case. For a class K of dag automata $\mathcal{L}(K)=\{L(A) \mid A \in K\}$ is the class of dag languages defined by automata in K. Languages in $\mathcal{L}(NB)$ are said to be recognizable, and $\mathcal{L}(NB)$ will also be denoted by $RECOG_D$.

If a dag automaton instead of priming the labels of the processed dag consistently relabels them by symbols of another doubly ranked alphabet then we obtain a device called finite state relabeling, cf. [4]. The easy formal definition is left to the reader. Let T be a finite state relabeling (from Σ to Δ) and let $L \subseteq D_\Sigma$; then $T(L)=\{g \in D_\Delta \mid d \vdash_T^* g$ for some $d \in L\}$. A relabeling is just a (total) single state relabeling.

The next concept to be defined is derivation dag. Consider a phrase-structure grammar $G=(N,T,P,S)$ which has a set S of initial nonterminals instead of just a single nonterminal and such that for every rule $\alpha \to \beta$ in P, $\alpha, \beta \in (N \cup T)^+$ (for simplicity we exclude rules with empty right-hand sides) $|\alpha|=1$ or $|\beta|=1$ ($|w|$ denotes the length of the word w). Such grammars will be called simple type-0 grammars. It is easy to see that every non-empty type-0 language which does not contain the null string can be generated by some simple type-0 grammar.

Let $G=(N,T,P,S)$ be a simple type-0 grammar. A dag d over $N \cup T$ (the reader should easily figure out the head and tail ranks of terminals and nonterminals) is said to be a derivation dag of G if the following conditions are satisfied: (i) the root of d is labeled by an element of S, (ii) leaves(d) is in T^+, (iii) whenever step (ii) of Definition 2.1 is used for d, $a_i \to b_1 \ldots b_m$ is a production in P, (iv) whenever step (iii) of Definition 2.1 is used for d, $a_i \ldots a_j \to b$ is a rule in P. The set of derivation dags of a simple type-0 grammar G is denoted by D_G.

Compare these definitions to similar ones in [2,3,6,9].
The reader should notice the analogy between the notions: dag, dag automaton, simple type-0 grammar, derivation dag and the respective tree concepts: tree, tree automaton, context-free grammar and derivation tree.

3. Some Results. We shall now present some results concerning the relative power of the various dag automata.

3.1. Theorem. $\mathcal{L}(DT)\subsetneq\mathcal{L}(DB)=\mathcal{L}(NT)=\mathcal{L}(NB)(=RECOG_D)$. ⊠

Further discussion and more results are presented in [7].
The next result states two closure properties of $RECOG_D$.

3.2. Theorem. $RECOG_D$ is closed under intersection and finite state relabelings. ⊠

The relation between derivation dags of simple type-0 grammars and our dag automata is given in the next two theorems.

3.3. Theorem. Given a simple type-0 grammar G, there is a bottom-up dag automaton A such that $D_G=L(A)$. ⊠

3.4. Theorem. Given $L\in RECOG_D$ there is a simple type-0 grammar G and a relabeling h such that $L=h(D_G)$. ⊠

These two theorems reduce to well-known results [4,12] in the tree case and similar results for the "dag" case can be found in [2,6] although the graphs considered there were slightly less general than ours.
In the next theorem we characterize the context-sensitive languages in terms of special kind of recognizable dag languages. The proof is left to the reader.

3.5. Theorem. A (string) language K is context-sensitive if and only if there is $L\in RECOG_D$, $L\subseteq D_\Sigma$, such that $i>j>0$ implies $\Sigma_{ij}=\emptyset$, and $K=leaves(L)$. ⊠

4. Application. In this section, we apply dag automata to prove a couple of properties of phrase-structure languages. The first application deals with the closure property of intersection with regular sets. Our method extends the idea of [11] which treated the case of context-free languages.

4.1. Lemma. Given a doubly ranked alphabet Σ, let $R\subseteq\Sigma_{*0}^{+}$ be a regular set. Then $leaves^{-1}(R)=\{d\in D_\Sigma \mid leaves(d)\in R\}$ is recognizable. ⊠

4.2. Corollary. The class of languages of type-i is closed under intersection with regular sets, $i=0,1,2,3$. ☒

Proof. For the type-1 case, let K and R be context-sensitive and regular languages respectively. Consider L of Theorem 3.5. Then $K \cap R = \text{leaves}(L \cap \text{leaves}^{-1}(R))$. Since by Theorem 3.1 and Lemma 4.1, $L \cap \text{leaves}^{-1}(R)$ is recognizable, $K \cap R$ is context-sensitive by Theorem 3.5. The other cases are similar. ☒

Next, we discuss a particular type of phrase-structure grammars which generates no more than context-free languages. First, we need some definitions.

4.3. Definition. Let $G=(N,T,P,S)$ be a simple type-0 grammar and $X \stackrel{*}{\Longrightarrow} \alpha = A_1 \ldots A_n \stackrel{*}{\Longrightarrow} w \in T^*$ a derivation of G with $X \in S$ and $A_1, \ldots, A_n \in N \cup T$. A_i and A_{i+1} in α are said to be cooperative if the nodes corresponding to these occurrences of A_i and A_{i+1} in the derivation dag of this derivation have a common descendant. A cooperative subsequence $A_s \ldots A_t$ in α is a subsequence of α such that for every i, $s \leq i < t$, A_i and A_{i+1} are cooperative. The derivation has k-bounded cooperation if the length of the cooperative subsequence in every sentential form α of the derivation is bounded by k. The grammar G has k-bounded cooperation if for every $w \in L(G)$ there is the derivation of w which has k-bounded cooperation. G has bounded cooperation if there is such a k. ☒

Note that every context-free grammar has 1-bounded cooperation.

4.4. Theorem. Let G be a simple type-0 grammar which has bounded cooperation. Then L(G) is context-free. ☒

Proof. We construct a recognizable tree language T_G in which the labels represent the maximal cooperative subsequences in the sentential forms of derivations of G. Suppose G has k-bounded cooperation. We define a (bottom-up) tree automaton $A'=(Q',\Sigma',R')$ from the (bottom-up) dag automaton $A=(Q,\Sigma,R)$ recognizing D_G. Let r be the maximal head-rank of Σ. The states of A' are $Q'=\{<p_1 \ldots p_n> \mid p_i \in Q \text{ for } 1 \leq i \leq n \text{ and } 0 \leq n \leq k \cdot r\}$. The (ranked) alphabet Σ' is $\{<\sigma_1 \ldots \sigma_n> \mid \sigma_i \in \Sigma \text{ for } 1 \leq i \leq n \text{ and } 1 \leq n \leq k\}$. The head (tail) rank of $<\sigma_1 \ldots \sigma_n>$ is the sum of the head (tail) ranks of the σ_i's, $1 \leq i \leq n$. R' consists of all rules of the form

$$<\sigma_1 \ldots \sigma_n>(<\xi_1> \ldots <\xi_m>) \to [<p_1 \ldots p_\ell>]<\sigma_1 \ldots \sigma_n>'$$

where for each $1 \leq i \leq n$, $\sigma_i(<\zeta_i>) \to [w_i]\sigma_i$ is in R with $\zeta_1 \ldots \zeta_n = \xi_1 \ldots \xi_m$, $w_1 \ldots w_n = p_1 \ldots p_\ell$ and $|\xi_i|, \ell \leq k \cdot r$, $p_i \in Q$ and ξ_i, ζ_i, w_i are sequences of elements of Q. Define $T_G = L(A')$. Then $L(G) = h(\text{leaves}(T_G))$ where $h(<\sigma_1 \ldots \sigma_n>) = \sigma_1 \ldots \sigma_n$ is a homomorphism. It follows that L(G) is context-free. ☒

Before stating further results we need some terminology. A rule $\alpha \to \beta$ of a phrase-structure grammar $G=(N,T,P,S)$ is said to be non-type-i if: (a) i=1 then $|\alpha| > |\beta|$, (b) i=2 then $\alpha \notin N$, (c) i=3 then either $\alpha \notin N$ or $\beta \notin TN \cup T$; we will also use non-context-sensitive, non-context-free and non-right-linear respectively. The next corollary follows immediately from Theorem 4.4.

4.5. Corollary. Let G be a phrase-structure grammar. Let K be a constant such that for every $w \in L(G)$ there is a derivation of w in G which uses at most K non-context-free rules. Then L(G) is context-free. ⊠

Applying some additional dag transformations we also obtain

4.6. Corollary. Let G be a phrase-structure grammar. Let K be a constant such that for every $w \in L(G)$ there is a derivation of w in G which uses at most K non-right-linear rules. Then L(G) is regular. ⊠

Regarding the context-sensitive version of the above corollaries there is a more powerful result by Ginsburg and Greibach [5]. We may now summarize

4.7. Corollary. Let G be a phrase-structure grammar. If there exists a constant K such that for every $w \in L(G)$ there is a derivation of w in G which uses at most K non-type-i rules, then L(G) is a language of type-i, i=1,2,3. ⊠

5. Future Work. One possible topic of interest is dag-to-tree transformations. In fact, a restricted type of such transformations (called "unfolding") was introduced in [1]. We can discuss these concepts more generally by introducing dag-to-tree transducers [8]. In particular, we can show that the leaves (also called the yield) of a tree language obtained by "unfolding" a recognizable dag language is deterministic context-sensitive.

Another topic of interest is (string) dag expressions. The usual prefix notation with parentheses provides a convenient way to represent trees. We can define a fairly natural dag expression using two types of parentheses. Then we can show that the sets of dag expressions obtained from languages in $RECOG_D$ are accepted by two-way deterministic pushdown automata (2DPDA). But if the dag language is D_G for some phrase structure grammar G, then two-way deterministic counter (2DC) is sufficient. It is not known whether the inclusion $2DC \subseteq 2DPDA$ is proper. On the other hand we were, so far, unable to prove that the dag expressions resulting from $RECOG_D$ can be recognized by 2DC (or even 2NC).

Acknowledgement. We wish to thank Professor Joost Engelfriet for his insightful remarks on the first version of this paper.

6. References.

[1] Arbib, M. A. and Give'on, Y. - Algebra Automata I: Parallel Programming as a Prelogomena to the Categorical Approach; Information and Control 12 (1968), 331-345.

[2] Buttelmann, H. W. - On the Syntactic Structure of Unrestricted Grammars, I and II; Information and Control 29(1975), 29-101.

[3] Eickel, J. and Loeckx, J. - The Relation Between Derivations and Syntactical Structures in Phrase-Structure Grammars; JCSS 6(1972), 267-282.

[4] Engelfriet, J. - Tree Automata and Tree Grammars; Lecture Notes DAIMI, FN-10, University of Aarhus, Denmark, 1975.

[5] Ginsburg, S. and Greibach, S. A. - Mappings Which Preserve Context-Sensitive Languages; Information and Control 9(1966), 563-582.

[6] Hart, J. M. - Acceptors for the Derivation Language of Phrase-Structure Grammars; Information and Control 25(1974), 75-92.

[7] Kamimura, T. and Slutzki, G. - Parallel and Two-way Recognizers of Directed Acyclic Graphs; to appear in MFCS '79, Olomouc, Czechoslovakia.

[8] Kamimura, T. and Slutzki, G. - Dag Transductions, in preparation.

[9] Loeckx, J. - The Parsing of General Phrase-Structure Grammar; Information and Control 16(1970), 443-464.

[10] Ogden, W. F. and Rounds, W. C. - Compositions of n Tree Transducers; Proc. of 4th Annual ACM STOC, Denver, Colorado, 1972, 198-206.

[11] Rounds, W. C. - Tree-oriented Proofs of some Theorems on Context-free and Indexed Languages; Proc. of 2nd Annual ACM STOC, Northampton, Mass., 1970, 109-116.

[12] Thatcher, J. - Characterizing Derivation Trees of Context-Free Grammar through a Generalization of Finite Automata Theory; JCSS 1(1967), 317-322.

[13] Wilson, R. - Introduction to Graph Theory; Oliver and Boyd, Edinburgh, 1972.

RECENT ADVANCES IN THE PROBABILISTIC ANALYSIS[†] OF GRAPH-THEORETIC ALGORITHMS

Richard M. Karp
University of California
Berkeley, CA 94720/USA

Abstract

This talk is a survey of a research area at the interface between concrete complexity theory and the theory of random graphs. It concerns the construction of graph-theoretic algorithms which are efficient on the average, when presented with inputs drawn from a well-defined probability distribution. We present such algorithms for the following problems:

1) putting a graph in canonical form with respect to isomorphism;
2) computing a maximum flow in a network;
3) finding a Hamiltonian circuit in a graph or digraph;
4) computing the connected and biconnected components of a graph;
5) computing the strongly connected components and the reachability relation of a digraph;
6) computing a perfect matching of minimum weight in a bipartite graph;
7) obtaining a good approximate solution to the directed traveling-salesman problem.

We then observe that no fast-average-time algorithms are known for constructing minimum colorings or maximum cliques, and we discuss some of the impediments to constructing such algorithms.

References:

1. Angluin, D. and L.G. Valiant, Fast Probabilistic Algorithms for Hamiltonian Circuits and Matchings. Proc. Ninth ACM Symposium on Theory of Computing (1977)
2. Apers, P., The Expected Number of Phases of the Dinic-Karzanov Network Flow Algorithm. Informatica Rapport IR 27. Vrije Universiteit, Amsterdam (1978)
3. Chvátal, V., Determining the Stability Number of a Graph. SIAM J. Comp 6 (1977) 643-662.
4. Erdös, P. and A. Rényi., On Random Graphs I, Publicationes Mathematicae 6 (1959) 290-297.
5. Erdös, P. and A. Rényi, On the Evolution of Random Graphs, Publ. Math. Inst. Hung. Acad. Sci. 5A (1960), 17-61.

[†]Research supported by the National Science Foundation under Grant MCS 77-09906

6. Erdös, P. and A. Rényi, On Random Matrices, Publ. Math. Inst. Hung. Acad. Sci., 8A (1963), 455-461.
7. Erdös, P. and A. Rényi, On the Existence of a Factor of Degree One of a Connected Random Graph, Acta Math. Acad. Sci. Hung. 17 (1966), 359-368.
8. Grimmett, G. R. and C. J. H. McDiarmid, On Coloring Random Graphs, Math. Proc. Camb. Phil. Soc. 77 (1975), 313-324.
9. Hamacher, H., Numerical Investigations on the Maximal Flow Algorithm of Karzanov. Report 78-7, Mathematisches Institut, Universität zu Köln, (1978)
10. Karp, R. M., The Probabilistic Analysis of Some Combinatorial Search Algorithms. Algorithms and Complexity: New Directions and Recent Results (Ed. J. Traub), Academic Press (1976).
11. Karp, R. M., A Patching Algorithm for the Nonsymmetric Traveling-Salesman Problem. To appear in SIAM J. Comp. (1979).
12. Karp, R. M. Probabilistic Analysis of a Canonical Numbering Algorithm for Graphs. Proc. AMS Symposia in Applied Mathematics 34 (1979).
13. Karp, R. M., An Algorithm to Solve the m x n Assignment Problem in Expected Time O (mn log n), Memorandum No. UCB/ERL M78/67, Electronics Research Laboratory, University of California, Berkeley (1978)
14. Lueker, G. S., Maximization Problems on Graphs with Edge Weights Chosen From a Normal Distribution. Proc. Tenth ACM Symposium on Theory of Computing (1978)
15. McDiarmid, C., Determining the Chromatic Number of a Graph, SIAM J. Comp. 8 (1979) 1-14.
16. Posa, L., Hamiltonian Circuits in Random Graphs, Discrete Math. 14 (1976) 359-364.
17. Schnorr, C. P., An Algorithm for Transitive Closure with Linear Expected Time. SIAM J. Comp. 7 (1978) 127-133.

ON THE AVERAGE STACK SIZE OF REGULARLY DISTRIBUTED BINARY TREES

R. Kemp
Universität des Saarlandes, Fachbereich 10

Summary. The height of a tree with n nodes, that is the number of nodes on a maximal simple path starting at the root, is of interest in computing because it represents the maximum size of the stack used in algorithms that traverse the tree. In the classical paper of de Bruijn, Knuth and Rice, there is computed the average height of planted plane trees with n nodes assuming that all n-node trees are equally likely. The first section of this paper is devoted to the computation of the cumulative distribution function of this problem; we give an asymptotic equivalent in terms of familiar functions (Theorem 1). Then we derive an explicit expression and an asymptotic equivalent for the sth moment about origin of this distribution (Theorem 2). In the last section we compute the average stack size after t units of time during postorder-traversing of a binary tree with n leaves. Thereby, in one unit of time, a node is stored in the stack or is removed from the top of the stack.

I. THE CUMULATIVE DISTRIBUTION FUNCTION

Let $T(n)$, $n \in \mathbb{N}$, be the number of all *extended binary trees* (|9|, p. 399) with n leaves and $T \in T(n)$. The *stack size* $S(T)$ is recursively defined by

$$S(T) := \text{IF } |T| = 1 \text{ THEN } 1 \text{ ELSE IF } S(T_1) > S(T_2) \text{ THEN } S(T_1) \text{ ELSE } S(T_2)+1;$$

where $|T|$ is the number of nodes of the tree T and T_1 (resp. T_2) is the left (resp. right) subtree of T. $S(T)$ is the maximum number of nodes stored in the stack during postorder-traversing of $T \in T(n)$. The set of all trees $T \in T(n)$ with a stack size $S(T) \leq k$ is denoted by $T(n,k)$, the cardinality of $T(n,k)$ by $t(n,k)$.

LEMMA 1.

(a) $$t(n+1,n+1) = \frac{1}{n+1}\binom{2n}{n}$$

(b) $$t(n+1,k-1) = t(n+1,n+1) - \sum_{j\geq 1}\left[\binom{2n}{n+1-jk} - 2\binom{2n}{n-jk} + \binom{2n}{n-1-jk}\right]$$

for $k \geq 2$.

Proof. Let

$$F_k(z) := \sum_{n\geq 1} t(n,k)\, z^n$$

be the generating function of the numbers $t(n,k)$. Obviously, $F_0(z)=0$ because $t(n,0)=0$ for all $n\geq 1$. Since $T \in T(n,\lambda) \setminus T(n,\lambda-1)$ iff T has a left (resp. right) subtree $T_1 \in T(n-m,j)$ (resp. $T_2 \in T(m,i)$) with $j=\lambda$ and $1\leq i\leq \lambda-1$ or $1\leq j\leq \lambda-1$ and $i=\lambda-1$, $1\leq m\leq n-1$, we obtain all trees $T \in T(n,k)$ by taking

(i) the one-point-tree $T \in T(1,1)$, giving the contribution z and

(ii) all trees $T \in T(n,\lambda) \setminus T(n,\lambda-1)$, $2\leq\lambda\leq k$, giving the contribution

$$\sum_{\lambda=2}^{k}\{F_\lambda(z) - F_{\lambda-1}(z)\}F_{\lambda-1}(z) + \sum_{\lambda=2}^{k} F_{\lambda-1}(z)\{F_{\lambda-1}(z) - F_{\lambda-2}(z)\}$$

The sum of all contributions in (i) and (ii) leads to the recursion

$$F_0(z) = 0$$
$$F_k(z) = z + F_k(z)F_{k-1}(z) \quad \text{for } k\geq 1$$

An inspection of formula (2) in |5| shows that $F_k(z)$ is the generating function of the number of planted plane trees with n nodes and height less than or equal to k. Using formula (4),(21), (22) in |5| we obtain part (a) and part (b) of our lemma. ////

Considering all binary trees $T \in T(n)$ equally likely, the cumulative distribution function $V_n(x)$ is defined by $V_n(x) = t(n,x)/t(n,n)$. With Lemma 1 we find immediately

$$V_n(x) = 1 - \sum_{1\leq j\leq \lfloor n/(x+1)\rfloor} H_2(j(x+1)/\sqrt{n}) \frac{\binom{2n}{n-j(x+1)}}{\binom{2n}{n}} \tag{1}$$

where $H_2(t) = 4t^2-2$ is the second Hermite polynomial.

LEMMA 2. *Let* $t=(x+1)^2/\pi n$, $\Theta(z) := \sum_{j\geq 1} \exp(-j^2\pi z)$ *and* $\beta>0$ *a constant. We have*

$$V_n(x) = 1 + 2\left[\Theta(t) + 2t\Theta'(t)\right]\left[1 + O\left(\frac{\log^*(n)}{\sqrt{n}}\right)\right] + O(\exp(-\beta\log^2(n)))$$

where $O(n^*)$ *is to be interpreted as* $O(n^k)$ *for some* $k \in \mathbb{N}$.

Proof. Using the well-known approximation by Gaussian distribution (|6|)

$$\frac{\binom{2n}{n-k}}{\binom{2n}{n}} = \begin{cases} \{1 + O(\frac{\log^*(n)}{\sqrt{n}})\} \exp(-k^2/n) & \text{for } 0\leq k\leq \sqrt{n}\log(n) \\ O(\exp(-\log^2(n))) & \text{for } k > \sqrt{n}\log(n) \end{cases}$$

we obtain with (1)

$$V_n(x) = 1 - \{1 + O(\frac{\log^*(n)}{\sqrt{n}})\}\{\phi_2(n) - \phi_1(n)\} - G(n) \tag{2}$$

where

$$G(n) = O(\exp(-\log^2(n))) \sum_{\sqrt{n}\,\log(n)/(x+1) \leq j \leq \lfloor n/(x+1)\rfloor} H_2(j(x+1)/\sqrt{n}) =$$

$$= O(\exp(-\beta_1 \log^2(n))) \quad \text{with fixed } \beta_1 > 0$$

and

$$\phi_1(n) = \sum_{j > \sqrt{n}\,\log(n)/(x+1)} H_2(j(x+1)/\sqrt{n})\ \exp(-j^2(x+1)^2/n)$$

$$= O(\exp(-\beta_2 \log^2(n))) \quad \text{with fixed } \beta_2 > 0$$

and

$$\phi_2(n) = \sum_{j\geq 1} H_2(j(x+1)/\sqrt{n})\ \exp(-j^2(x+1)^2/n) = -2\Theta(t) - 4t\Theta'(t)$$

Returning to (2) we obtain our lemma with $\beta := \mathrm{MIN}(\beta_1, \beta_2)$. ////

THEOREM 1. *The distribution function $V_n(x)$ is given by*

$$V_n(x) = 1 - \sum_{j\geq 1}\left[4j^2\ \frac{(x+1)^2}{n} - 2\right] \exp(-j^2(x+1)^2/n) + O\left(\frac{\log^*(n)}{\sqrt{n}}\right)$$

Proof. With Lemma 2 we have for some $\beta > 0$

$$V_n(x) = 1 - \Lambda_n(x)\ \{1 + O(\frac{\log^*(n)}{\sqrt{n}})\} + O(\exp(-\beta \log^2(n)))$$

where $\Lambda_n(x) = -2\Theta(t) - 4t\Theta'(t)$ with $t = (x+1)^2/n\pi$.
Choosing $x+1 = c\sqrt{n}$ with a constant c we obtain immediately

$$\Lambda_n(x) = \sum_{j\geq 1} H_2(jc)\ \exp(-j^2c^2)$$

and therefore

$$V_n(x) = 1 - \sum_{j\geq 1} H_2(jc)\ \exp(-j^2c^2) + O(\frac{\log^*(n)}{\sqrt{n}})$$

This expression is equivalent to our proposition. ////

Using the "Theta-relation" (|4|)

$$\Theta(t) = \frac{1}{\sqrt{t}}\,\Theta(\frac{1}{t}) + \frac{1}{2\sqrt{t}} - \frac{1}{2}$$

we obtain another expression for $V_n(x)$ given in the following

COROLLARY 1. *The distribution function $V_n(x)$ is given by*

$$V_n(x) = 4\pi\left[\frac{\sqrt{\pi n}}{(x+1)}\right]^3 \sum_{j\geq 1} j^2 \exp(-\frac{j^2\pi^2 n}{(x+1)^2}) + O(\frac{\log^*(n)}{\sqrt{n}})$$

////

Numerical results

Some distribution results are summarized in Table 1 and Table 2. Table 1 shows, that the asymptotic expression of $V_n(x)$ given in Theorem 1 is a good approximation of the exact value of $V_n(x)$. Some values of $V_n(x)$ with $x = c\sqrt{n}-1$, c fixed, are given in Table 2. For example, 74.53% of all trees T with 100 leaves have a stack size $S(T) \leq 19$ and 99.62% of all trees have a stack size less than or equal to 29. In the asymptotic case, 74.36% of all trees with n leaves can be recognized with a stack of length $2\sqrt{n}-1$ and 99.58% with a stack of length $3\sqrt{n}-1$.

n \ x	5	10	15	20	25	30	35	40	45	50	100
10	.675 .661	1 .999									
20	.110 .120	.956 .948	.999 .999	1 .999							
30	.011 .014	.756 .750	.995 .994	.999 .999	.999 .999	1 .999					
40	.001 .001	.510 .509	.964 .961	.999 .999	.999 .999	.999 .999	.999 .999	1 .999			
50	.000 .000	.312 .315	.894 .890	.996 .995	.999 .999	.999 .999	.999 .999	.999 .999	.999 .999	1 .999	
100	.000 .000	.014 .015	.361 .362	.812 .810	.972 .971	.998 .998	.999 .999	.999 .999	.999 .999	.999 .999	1 .999

Table 1. Some values of the distribution function $V_n(x)$. For each n, the first row represents the exact value of $V_n(x)$, computed by formula (1). The corresponding asymptotic value (Theorem 1) is given in the second row.

n \ c	0.5	1	1.5	2	2.5	3
9		.0007		.7650		.9993
16	.0000	.0017	.2467	.7550	.9653	.9980
25		.0023		.7507		.9972
36	.0000	.0027	.2532	.7485	.9598	.9968
49		.0029		.7471		.9966
100	.0000	.0033	.2563	.7453	.9571	.9962
∞	.0000	.0036	.2580	.7436	.9556	.9958

Table 2. Some values of $V_n(c\sqrt{n}-1)$. The last row represents the asymptotic value for $n \to \infty$.

II. THE sth MOMENT ABOUT ORIGIN

Considering all binary trees $T \in T(n)$ equally likely, the quotient

$$p(n,k) = \{t(n,k)-t(n,k-1)\}/t(n,n)$$

is the probability, that a tree $T \in T(n)$ has a stack size $S(T)=k$. The

s^{th} moment about origin is defined by

$$m_s(n) = \sum_{k=1}^{n} k^s \; p(n,k)$$

Using the definition of $p(n,k)$ and $t(n,0)=0$ for $n\geq 1$, this expression can be easily transformed into

$$m_s(n) = n^s - t^{-1}(n,n) \; R_s(n)$$

where

$$R_s(n) = \sum_{k=1}^{n-1} \{(k+1)^s - k^s\} \; t(n,k)$$

Now, an application of Lemma 1(a) leads to

$$m_s(n+1) = 1 + \frac{1}{t(n+1,n+1)} \sum_{k=1}^{n} \{(k+1)^s - k^s\} \; \Psi(n,k) \tag{3}$$

where $\quad \Psi(n,k) = \psi_1(n,k) - 2\psi_0(n,k) + \psi_{-1}(n,k)$

and

$$\psi_a(n,k) = \sum_{j\geq 1} \binom{2n}{n+a-j(k+1)}$$

LEMMA 3. *Let $a \in \mathbb{Z}$ and $\psi_a(n,k)$ be the function defined in (3). We have*

$$m_s(n+1) = \frac{1}{t(n+1,n+1)} \sum_{R\geq 1} \delta_s(R) \left[\binom{2n}{n+1-R} - 2\binom{2n}{n-R} + \binom{2n}{n-1-R}\right]$$

where $\delta_s(n)$ is the arithmetical function defined by

$$\delta_s(n) = \sum_{d|n} \{d^s - (d-1)^s\}$$

Proof. Let $a \in \{-1,0,1\}$. Since $\psi_a(n,k)=0$ for $k>n$ we have

$$\Xi_a^{(s)}(n) := \sum_{k=1}^{n} \{(k+1)^s - k^s\} \; \psi_a(n,k) =$$

$$= \sum_{k\geq 1} \{(k+1)^s - k^s\} \sum_{j\geq 1} \binom{2n}{n+a-j(k+1)} =$$

$$= \sum_{k\geq 1} \{k^s - (k-1)^s\} \sum_{j\geq 1} \binom{2n}{n+a-jk} - \sum_{j\geq 1} \binom{2n}{n+a-j} =$$

$$= \sum_{R\geq 1} \binom{2n}{n+a-R} \sum_{d|R} \{d^s - (d-1)^s\} - \psi_a(n,0)$$

Hence with (3) and the definition of $\delta_s(n)$

$$m_s(n+1) = 1 + t^{-1}(n+1,n+1)\{\Xi_1^{(s)}(n) - 2\Xi_0^{(s)}(n) + \Xi_{-1}^{(s)}(n)\} =$$

$$= 1 + t^{-1}(n+1,n+1)\sum_{R\geq 1}\delta_s(R)\left[\binom{2n}{n+1-R} - 2\binom{2n}{n-R} + \binom{2n}{n-1-R}\right]$$

$$- t^{-1}(n+1,n+1)\ \{\psi_1(n,0) - 2\psi_0(n,0) + \psi_{-1}(n,0)\}$$

Since

$$\psi_1(n,0) - 2\psi_0(n,0) + \psi_{-1}(n,0) = \sum_{j\geq 1}\underset{j}{\Delta}\left[\binom{2n}{n-j} - \binom{2n}{n+1-j}\right]$$

where $\underset{j}{\Delta}$ is the difference operator defined by $\underset{x}{\Delta}f(x)=f(x+1)-f(x)$, we obtain with Lemma 1(a)

$$\psi_1(n,0) - 2\psi_0(n,0) + \psi_{-1}(n,0) = -\left[\binom{2n}{n-1} - \binom{2n}{n}\right] = t(n+1,n+1)$$

Using this expression in the above formula for $m_s(n+1)$ we get our proposition. ////

Setting s=1 in Lemma 3 we obtain a formula for the first moment $m_1(n+1)$, that is the average stack size of a tree $T \in T(n+1)$. This expression is the same as in |5| for the average height of planted plane trees with (n+1) nodes, because in this case $\delta_1(m)=d(m)$, where d(m) is the number of the positive divisors of the natural number m.

THEOREM 2. *For all ε>0 we have*

(a) $m_1(n+1) = \sqrt{\pi n} - \frac{1}{2} + \frac{11}{24}\sqrt{\pi/n} + O(\frac{\log(n)}{n^{1-\varepsilon}})$

(b) $m_2(n+1) = \frac{1}{3}n\pi^2 - \sqrt{\pi n} + \frac{1}{3} + \frac{5}{18}\pi^2 - \frac{11}{24}\sqrt{\pi/n} + O(n^{-0.5+\varepsilon})$

(c) $m_s(n+1) = 2\binom{s}{2}\zeta(s)\Gamma(\frac{1}{2}s)\ n^{0.5s} - 3\binom{s}{3}\zeta(s-1)\Gamma(\frac{1}{2}(s-1))\ n^{0.5(s-1)}$
$+ O(n^{0.5(s-2)})$ *for* $s\geq 3$

Γ(z) is the complete gamma function and ζ(z) Riemann's zeta function.

Proof. A similar computation as in |5;p.20| leads to the following approximation with a smaller O-term

$$\frac{\binom{2n}{n+a-k}}{\binom{2n}{n}} = \begin{cases} \exp(-k^2/n)\ f_a(n,k) & \text{iff } k<n^{0.5+\varepsilon}+a \\ O(\exp(n^{-2\varepsilon})) & \text{iff } k\geq n^{0.5+\varepsilon}+a \end{cases}$$

for all fixed ε>0.

Here

$$f_a(n,k) = 1 - \frac{a^2+a^4}{2n^2} - \frac{a^2}{n} + \{\frac{2a}{n} - \frac{2a^3+a}{n^2}\}k + \{\frac{4a^2+1}{2n^2} - \frac{12a^4+21a^2+1}{6n^3}\}k^2 +$$

$$+ \frac{4a^3+5a}{3n^3} k^3 + \{\frac{16a^4+60a^2+9}{24n^4} - \frac{1}{6n^3}\}k^4 - \frac{a}{3n^4} k^5 - \frac{20a^2+9}{60n^5} k^6 + \frac{1}{72n^6} k^8 +$$

$$+ O(n^{-2.5+\varepsilon})$$

With $a \in \mathbb{Z}$ we define the functions

$$\phi_a^{(s)}(n) := \sum_{j\geq 1} \delta_s(j) \frac{\binom{2n}{n+a-j}}{\binom{2n}{n}}$$

and

$$g_a^{(s)}(n) := \sum_{j\geq 1} \delta_s(j)\, j^a \exp(-j^2/n)$$

where $\delta_s(n)$ is the arithmetical function given in Lemma 3. It is not hard to show, that in both sums the terms for $j \geq n^{0.5+\varepsilon}+a$ are negligible. Using the above approximation and the definition of $g_a^{(s)}(n)$ we obtain immediately

$$\phi_1^{(s)}(n) - 2\phi_0^{(s)}(n) + \phi_{-1}^{(s)}(n) =$$

$$= \{\frac{2}{n^2} - \frac{2}{n}\}g_0^{(s)}(n) + \{\frac{4}{n^2} - \frac{11}{n^3}\}g_2^{(s)}(n) + \frac{19}{3n^4} g_4^{(s)}(n) -$$

$$- \frac{2}{3n^5} g_6^{(s)}(n) + O(g_0^{(s)}(n)n^{-2.5+\varepsilon})$$

and therefore with Lemma 1(a) and Lemma 3

$$m_s(n+1) = (n+1)\{\phi_1^{(s)}(n) - 2\phi_0^{(s)}(n) + \phi_{-1}^{(s)}(n)\} =$$

$$= \frac{n+1}{n}\{(\frac{2}{n} -2)g_0^{(s)}(n) + (\frac{4}{n} - \frac{11}{n^2})g_2^{(s)}(n) + \frac{19}{3n^3} g_4^{(s)}(n) -$$

$$- \frac{2}{3n^4} g_6^{(s)}(n) + O(g_0^{(s)}(n)n^{-1.5+\varepsilon})\} \quad (4)$$

We now turn to the asymptotic behaviour of the function $g_a^{(s)}(n)$. Since

$$\sum_{j\geq 1} j^{-z} \sum_{d|j} d^b = \zeta(z)\zeta(z-b)$$

we obtain

$$\sum_{j\geq 1} \delta_s(j)\, j^{-z} = \sum_{j\geq 1} j^{-z} \sum_{d|j} \left[d^s - \sum_{\lambda=0}^{s} \binom{s}{\lambda} (-1)^{s-\lambda} d^\lambda \right] =$$

$$= -\zeta(z) \sum_{\lambda=0}^{s-1} \binom{s}{\lambda} (-1)^{s-\lambda} \zeta(z-\lambda)$$

An application of this expression and of the well-known formula

$$\exp(-x) = \frac{1}{2\pi i} \int_{c-i\infty}^{c+i\infty} \Gamma(z)\, x^{-z}\, dz \qquad x>0,\ c>0,\ i^2=-1$$

leads to

$$g_a^{(s)}(n) = -\sum_{\lambda=0}^{s-1} \binom{s}{\lambda} (-1)^{s-\lambda} I_{a,\lambda}^{(s)}(n)$$

where

$$I_{a,\lambda}^{(s)}(n) = \frac{1}{2\pi i} \int_{c-i\infty}^{c+i\infty} n^z \Gamma(z)\zeta(2z-a)\zeta(2z-a-\lambda)\, dz$$

Now, let $\psi(z)$ be the psi-function $\Gamma'(z)/\Gamma(z)$ and γ Euler's constant. We regard the integral $I_{a,\lambda}^{(s)}(n)$, $0 \leqslant \lambda \leqslant s-1$, $a \geqslant 0$. It can be shown by a well-known method, that we can shift the line of integration to the left as far as we please if we only take the residues into account. If $\lambda=0$, there is a double pole at $z=\frac{1}{2}(a+1)$ with the residue

$$n^{\frac{1}{2}(a+1)} \Gamma(\tfrac{1}{2}(a+1)) \{\tfrac{1}{4} \ln(n) + \tfrac{1}{4}\psi(\tfrac{1}{2}(a+1)) + \gamma\}$$

and possibly simple poles at $z=-k$, $k \in \mathbb{N}_0$, with the residues

$$n^{-k}(-1)^k \zeta^2(-2k-a)/k! \quad ,$$

which are zero for $2k+a$ even. If $\lambda \geqslant 1$, there are simple poles at $z=\frac{1}{2}(a+1)$, $z=\frac{1}{2}(a+\lambda+1)$ and possibly $z=-k$, $k \in \mathbb{N}_0$, with the residues

$$\tfrac{1}{2} n^{\frac{1}{2}(a+1)} \Gamma(\tfrac{1}{2}(a+1))\zeta(1-\lambda) \quad , \quad \tfrac{1}{2} n^{\frac{1}{2}(a+\lambda+1)} \Gamma(\tfrac{1}{2}(a+\lambda+1))\zeta(1+\lambda)$$

and

$$n^{-k}(-1)^k \zeta(-2k-a)\zeta(-2k-a-\lambda)/k! \quad ,$$

which are zero for $2k+a$ or $2k+a+\lambda$ even. Hence, we get for all $m>0$

$$\begin{aligned} g_a^{(s)}(n) = {} & (-1)^{s+1}\left[n^{\frac{1}{2}(a+1)} \Gamma(\tfrac{1}{2}(a+1))(\tfrac{1}{4}\ln(n) + \tfrac{1}{4}\psi(\tfrac{1}{2}(a+1)) + \gamma)\right] + \\ & + (-1)^{s+1} \sum_{k \geqslant 0} \frac{\zeta^2(-2k-a)}{n^k k!} (-1)^k + \\ & + \sum_{\lambda=1}^{s-1} (-1)^{s-\lambda+1} \binom{s}{\lambda} \tfrac{1}{2} n^{\frac{1}{2}(a+1)} \Gamma(\tfrac{1}{2}(a+1))\zeta(1-\lambda) + \\ & + \sum_{\lambda=1}^{s-1} (-1)^{s-\lambda+1} \binom{s}{\lambda} \tfrac{1}{2} n^{\frac{1}{2}(a+\lambda+1)} \Gamma(\tfrac{1}{2}(a+\lambda+1))\zeta(1+\lambda) + \\ & + \sum_{\lambda=1}^{s-1} (-1)^{s-\lambda+1} \binom{s}{\lambda} \sum_{k \geqslant 0} \frac{\zeta(-2k-a)\zeta(-2k-a-\lambda)}{n^k\, k!} (-1)^k + O(n^{-m}) \end{aligned}$$

Using this approximation and some known special values of $\zeta(z)$, $\Gamma(z)$ and $\psi(z)$ (comp. |1|) we get with (4) for all $\varepsilon>0$

$$m_1(n+1) = \frac{n+1}{n} \{\sqrt{\pi n} - \tfrac{1}{2} - \tfrac{13}{24}\sqrt{\pi/n} + O(\ln(n)/n^{-1+\varepsilon})\}$$

$$m_2(n+1) = \frac{n+1}{n}\{\tfrac{1}{3}n\pi^2 - \sqrt{\pi n} - \tfrac{1}{18}\pi^2 + \tfrac{1}{3} + \tfrac{13}{24}\sqrt{\pi/n} + O(n^{-0.5+\varepsilon})\}$$

$$m_s(n+1) = \frac{n+1}{n}\{2\binom{s}{2}\zeta(s)\Gamma(\tfrac{1}{2}s)n^{0.5s} - 3\binom{s}{3}\zeta(s-1)\Gamma(\tfrac{1}{2}(s-1))n^{0.5(s-1)} + $$
$$+ O(n^{0.5(s-2)})\} \qquad \text{for } s\geq 3.$$

These expressions are equivalent to our proposition. ////

Since the variance is given by $\sigma^2(n+1) = m_2(n+1)-m_1^2(n+1)$, an application of Theorem 2 leads to

COROLLARY 2. *The variance* $\sigma^2(n+1)$ *is for all* $\varepsilon>0$

$$\sigma^2(n+1) = (\tfrac{\pi}{3} - 1)\pi n + \tfrac{1}{12} + \tfrac{5}{18}\pi^2 - \tfrac{11}{12}\pi + O(n^{-0.5+\varepsilon})$$

////

Numerical results

An inspection of corollary 2 shows, that the variance is very large and therefore the deviation of the stack size of a tree from the expected value. Using Theorem 1, we find, that only 54.32% of all trees have a stack size less than or equal to the average value $m_1(n)$ in the asymptotic case. For some n, the exact (Lemma 3(a)) and the asymptotic (Theorem 2, Corollary 2) values of the average stack size and the variance are summarized in Table 3 and Table 4.

n	exactly	asymptoticly
1	1.0000	-
2	2.0000	2.0848
3	2.5000	2.5810
4	3.0000	3.0390
5	3.4286	3.4511
8	4.4849	4.4965
10	5.0802	5.0882
12	5.6176	5.6235
14	6.1114	6.1160

Table 3. The average stack size $m_1(n)$.

n	exactly	asymptoticly
1	0.0000	-
2	0.0000	0.0934
3	0.2500	0.2416
4	0.4000	0.3900
5	0.5306	0.5382
8	0.9817	0.9830
10	1.2782	1.2796
12	1.5743	1.5761
14	1.8712	1.8727

Table 4. The variance $\sigma^2(n+1)$

III. THE AVERAGE STACK SIZE AFTER t UNITS OF TIME

Traversing a binary tree $T \in T(n)$ in postorder we assume that in one unit of time a node is stored in the stack or is removed from the top of the stack. Considering all binary trees with n leaves equally likely, in this section we shall compute the average number of nodes $R(n,t)$ stored in the stack after t units of time. We regard the diagram given in Figure 1. Obviously, each path from $(t,k)=(1,1)$ to $(t,k)=(2n-1,1)$ corresponds to the

traversing of a binary tree $T \in T(n)$ in postorder; for example, the marked path in Figure 1 corresponds to the following tree $T \in T(6)$

If we reach the point (i,j) then we have exactly j nodes in the stack after i units of time.

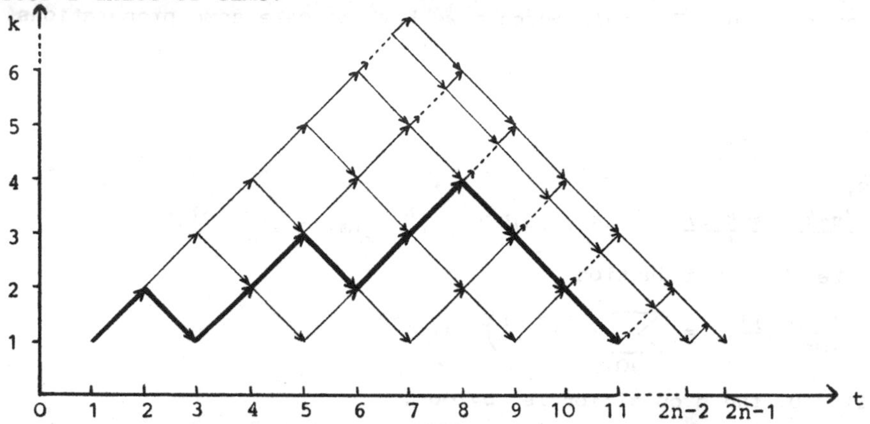

Figure 1. Path diagram corresponding to the trees $T \in T(n)$. (k is the number of nodes in the stack, t represents the units of time)

Now, let H(n,k,t) be the number of binary trees $T \in T(n)$ having exactly k nodes in the stack after t units of time. Regarding the above diagramm this number is the product of

(i) the number of paths from (1,1) to (t,k), which is $\frac{k}{t}\binom{t}{(t+k)/2}$

and

(ii) the number of paths from (t,k) to (2n-1,1), which is $\frac{k}{2n-t}\binom{2n-t}{n-(t+k)/2}$

These enumeration results of the number of paths are well-known. (for example |3|)

Hence

$$H(n,k,t) = \frac{k^2}{t(2n-t)}\binom{t}{(t+k)/2}\binom{2n-t}{n-(t+k)/2}$$

Obviously, we have the conditions $k \leq t \leq 2n-1$ and (k+t) even. Now, our expected value R(n,t) is given by

$$R(n,t) = t^{-1}(n,n)\sum_{k=1}^{t} k\, H(n,k,t)$$

where t(n,n) is the number of trees $T \in T(n)$ given in Lemma 1(a). Using the above formula for H(n,k,t) we get finally

$$\text{(i)}\quad R(n,2\tau) = \frac{1}{4\tau(n-\tau)t(n,n)} \sum_{k\geq 0} (2k)^3 \binom{2\tau}{\tau-k} \binom{2n-2\tau}{n-\tau+k} \qquad (5a)$$

$$\text{(ii)}\quad R(n,2\tau+1) = \frac{1}{(2\tau+1)(2n-2\tau-1)t(n,n)} \sum_{k\geq 0} (2k+1)^3 \binom{2\tau+1}{\tau-k} \binom{2n-2\tau-1}{n-\tau+k} \qquad (5b)$$

In order to compute $R(n,t)$ we have to examine the sums on the right side of (5a) and (5b). Indeed, it is possible to transform these sums into closed expressions. For this purpose we have to make some preparations. In order to simplify the proofs of the following propositions we use the Blissard calculus (comp. |11|). Thus, for example $(1+x)^n, x^n \equiv x_n$ is a shorthand for $\sum_{0\leq i\leq n} \binom{n}{i} x_i$.

LEMMA 4.

$$\frac{(n-k)!(m+k-1)!}{(m+n)!} = x^k (1-x)^{n-k} , \quad x^k \equiv x_k(m) = (k+m)^{-1}$$

Proof. We show by induction

$$\frac{n!\ (m-1)!}{(m+n)!} = \sum_{j\geq 0} (-1)^j \binom{n}{j} (j+m)^{-1}$$

1. If $n=0$, the proposition is obvious.
2. We have: $\frac{(n+1)!\ (m-1)!}{(m+n+1)!} = \frac{n+1}{m+n+1} \sum_{j\geq 0} (-1)^j \binom{n}{j} (j+m)^{-1} =$

$$= \sum_{j\geq 0} (-1)^j \binom{n+1}{j} \frac{n+1-j}{m+n+1} (j+m)^{-1} =$$

$$= \sum_{j\geq 0} (-1)^j \binom{n+1}{j} \left[\frac{1}{m+j} - \frac{1}{m+n+1}\right] =$$

$$= \sum_{j\geq 0} (-1)^j \binom{n+1}{j} (m+j)^{-1}$$

Setting $m:=m+k$ and $n:=n-k$ in the proved formula we get

$$\frac{(n-k)!(m+k-1)!}{(m+n)!} = \sum_{j\geq 0} (-1)^j \binom{n-k}{j} (j+m+k)^{-1}$$

which is the same as

$$\frac{(n-k)!(m+k-1)!}{(m+n)!} = \sum_{j\geq 0} (-1)^j \binom{n-k}{j} x^{k+j} , \quad x^k \equiv x_k(m) = (k+m)^{-1}$$

This expression is equivalent to our proposition. ////

LEMMA 5. *Let $s \in \mathbb{N}_0$. We have*

$$A_n(s,x) = \sum_{j\geq 0} \binom{n+j+s}{2j+s} \binom{2j+s}{j+s} x^j \Leftrightarrow A_n(s,x) = \sum_{j\geq 0} \binom{n}{j} \binom{n+s}{j+s} x^j (1+x)^{n-j}$$

Proof. Let $a\leq 0$. In this case, the Gauss hypergeometric series $F(a,b;c;x)$ is the polynomial

$$F(a,b;c;x) = \sum_{j=0}^{-a} \frac{(a)_j\ (b)_j}{(c)_j} \frac{x^j}{j!}$$

where $(z)_n$ is Pochhammer's symbol defined by $(z)_0=1$ and $(z)_n=z(z+1)\ldots$ $\ldots(z+n-1)$ for $n\geq 1$. Since (|1|;p.561)

$$P_n^{(\alpha,\beta)}(1+2x) = \frac{1}{n!}(\alpha+1)_n\ F(-n,\alpha+\beta+n+1;\alpha+1;-x)$$

where $P_n^{(\alpha,\beta)}(x)$ is a Jacobi polynomial, we obtain immediately

$$P_n^{(\alpha,\beta)}(1+2x) = \sum_{j=0}^{n} \frac{(\alpha+n)!(\alpha+\beta+n+j)!}{(n-j)!(\alpha+j)!(\alpha+\beta+n)!j!} x^j =$$

$$= \sum_{j\geq 0} \binom{\alpha+\beta+n}{\alpha+n}^{-1} \binom{2j+\alpha+\beta}{2j+\alpha}\binom{n+\alpha+\beta+j}{2j+\alpha+\beta}\binom{2j+\alpha}{j+\alpha} x^j$$

On the other hand we have for $\alpha,\beta>-1$ (|1|;p.775)

$$P_n^{(\alpha,\beta)}(z) = 2^{-n}\sum_{j=0}^{n}\binom{n+\alpha}{j}\binom{n+\beta}{n-j}(z-1)^{n-j}(z+1)^j$$

or with $z=1+2x$

$$P_n^{(\alpha,\beta)}(1+2x) = \sum_{j=0}^{n}\binom{n+\alpha}{j}\binom{n+\beta}{n-j} x^{n-j}(1+x)^j$$

which is equivalent to

$$P_n^{(\alpha,\beta)}(1+2x) = \sum_{j\geq 0}\binom{n+\alpha}{j+\alpha}\binom{n+\beta}{j} x^j(1+x)^{n-j}$$

A comparison of this expression with the above formula for $P_n^{(\alpha,\beta)}(1+2x)$ implies for $\alpha,\beta>-1$

$$\sum_{j\geq 0}\binom{\alpha+\beta+n}{\alpha+n}^{-1}\binom{2j+\alpha+\beta}{2j+\alpha}\binom{n+\alpha+\beta+j}{2j+\alpha+\beta}\binom{2j+\alpha}{j+\alpha} x^j = \sum_{j\geq 0}\binom{n+\alpha}{j+\alpha}\binom{n+\beta}{j} x^j(1+x)^{n-j}$$

Using this expression for $(\alpha,\beta) = (s,0)$, $s\in\mathbb{N}_0$, we get our lemma 5. ////

LEMMA 6. *Let $s\in\mathbb{N}_0$ and $d_n(s,m)$ be a sequence defined by*

$$d_0(s,m) = m^{-1}$$

$$d_n(s,m) = \sum_{j\geq 0}\frac{2n+s}{n+j+s}\binom{n+j+s}{2j+s}\binom{2j+s}{j+s}\frac{(-1)^j}{j+m} \qquad \text{for } n\geq 1$$

We have

$$(a)\ \frac{1}{n+m}\binom{2n+s}{n+s} = \sum_{j\geq 0}(-1)^j\binom{2n+s}{n-j} d_j(s,m)$$

$$(b)\ d_n(s,m) = \begin{cases} m^{-1} & \text{iff } n=0 \\ (-1)^{n-1}(2n+s)\binom{m-s-1}{n-1}\frac{(m-1)!(n-1)!}{(m+n)!} & \text{iff } n\geq 1 \end{cases}$$

Proof.

(a) The following pair of equations

$$a_n = \sum_{j=0}^{n}\binom{n+p+j}{2j+p}\frac{2n+p}{n+p+j}\, b_j \iff b_n = \sum_{j=0}^{n}(-1)^{n+j}\binom{2n+p}{n-j}\, a_j$$

is known as inverse relations of Legendre. Using this relation for p=s and

$$b_j = \binom{2j+s}{j+s}\frac{(-1)^j}{j+m}$$

we get $a_n = d_n(s,m)$ and therefore

$$\frac{1}{n+m}\binom{2n+s}{n+s} = \sum_{j=0}^{n}(-1)^j\binom{2n+s}{n-j}\, d_j(s,m)$$

This completes the proof of part (a) of our lemma.

(b) Let $A_n(s,x)$ be the polynomial of Lemma 5 and $Q_n(s,x)$ be defined by $Q_n(s,x)=A_n(s,x)+A_{n-1}(s,x)$. With the definition of $A_n(s,x)$ we get immediately

$$Q_n(s,x) = \sum_{j\geq 0}\frac{2n+s}{n+j+s}\binom{n+j+s}{2j+s}\binom{2j+s}{j+s}\, x^j$$

Since $Q_0(s,x)=x^0$, a comparison with the definition of $d_n(s,m)$ leads to

$$d_n(s,m) = Q_n(s,-x)\,,\quad x^k \equiv x_k(m) = (k+m)^{-1}$$

On the other hand we get with Lemma 5

$$Q_n(s,x) = \sum_{j\geq 0}\binom{n}{j}\binom{n+s}{j+s}x^j(1+x)^{n-j} + \sum_{j\geq 0}\binom{n-1}{j}\binom{n-1+s}{j+s}x^j(1+x)^{n-1-j} =$$

$$= \sum_{j\geq 0}\left[\binom{n}{j}\binom{n+s}{j+s} + \binom{n-1}{j}\binom{n-1+s}{j+s} - \binom{n-1}{j-1}\binom{n-1+s}{j-1+s}\right]x^j(1+x)^{n-j} =$$

$$= \frac{2n+s}{n}\sum_{j\geq 0}\binom{n}{j}\binom{n+s-1}{j+s}\, x^j(1+x)^{n-j}$$

and therefore

$$d_n(s,m) = Q_n(s,-x) = \frac{2n+s}{n}\sum_{j\geq 0}\binom{n}{j}\binom{n+s-1}{j+s}(-1)^j x^j(1-x)^{n-j},\quad x^k \equiv x_k(m) = (k+m)^{-1}$$

Now, an application of Lemma 4 leads to

$$d_n(s,m) = \frac{2n+s}{n}\sum_{j\geq 0}\binom{n}{j}\binom{n+s-1}{j+s}(-1)^j\frac{(n-j)!\,(m+j-1)!}{(m+n)!} =$$

$$= (2n+s)\ \frac{(m-1)!\,(n-1)!}{(m+n)!} \sum_{j\geq 0} \binom{n+s-1}{j+s} \binom{m+j-1}{j} (-1)^j =$$

$$= (2n+s)\ \frac{(m-1)!\,(n-1)!}{(m+n)!}\ (-1)^{n-1} \binom{m-s-1}{n-1}$$

This expression is equivalent to our proposition. ////

LEMMA 7.

$$(a)\ \sum_{k\geq 0} (2k)^3 \binom{2n}{n-k}\binom{2m}{m+k} = 4\ \frac{m^2 n^2}{(m+n)(m+n-1)} \binom{2m}{m}\binom{2n}{n}$$

$$(b)\ \sum_{k\geq 0} (2k+1)^3 \binom{2n+1}{n-k}\binom{2m-1}{m+k} = w(n,m) \binom{2m-2}{m-1}\binom{2n}{n}$$

with

$$w(n,m) = \frac{(2n+1)(2m-1)}{(n+m)(n+m-1)} \{(2n+1)(2m-1)-(n+m)\}$$

Proof.

(a) Define the sequence

$$X_n(m) := 4m^2 \binom{2m}{m}\left[\binom{2n}{n} + \sum_{k\geq 0} (-1)^k \binom{2n}{n-k}\{(m-1)^2 d_k(0,m-1) - m^2 d_k(0,m)\}\right]$$

with the numbers $d_n(s,m)$ given in Lemma 6. Using the explicit expression for $d_k(0,m)$ given in Lemma 6(b) an elementary computation shows

$$X_n(m) = \sum_{k\geq 0} (2k)^3 \binom{2n}{n-k}\binom{2m}{m+k}$$

On the other hand, an application of Lemma 6(a) for s=0 leads directly to

$$X_n(m) = 4\ \frac{m^2 n^2}{(m+n)(m+n-1)} \binom{2m}{m}\binom{2n}{n}$$

This completes the proof of part (a).

(b) Define the sequence

$$Y_n(m) := \frac{1}{2}(m-1)\binom{2m}{m}\left[(4m+1)\binom{2n+1}{n} + m\sum_{k\geq 0}(-1)^k\binom{2n+1}{n-k}\,\partial_k(m)\right]$$

with $\partial_k(m) = 4(m-1)(m-2)d_k(1,m-1) - (2m-1)^2 d_k(1,m)$

where the numbers $d_n(s,m)$ are given in Lemma 6. With the explicit expression for $d_k(1,m)$ given in Lemma 6(b) we get

$$Y_n(m) = \sum_{k\geq 1} (2k+1)^3 \binom{2n+1}{n-k}\binom{2m-1}{m+k}$$

On the other hand, an application of Lemma 6(a) for s=1 leads to

$$Y_n(m) = \frac{1}{2}(m-1)\binom{2m}{m}\binom{2n+1}{n}\left[4m + 1 + \frac{7nm + 3m^2 + m - 8nm^2 - 4m^3}{(m+n)(m+n-1)}\right]$$

Adding the term $\binom{2n+1}{n}\binom{2m-1}{m}$ to the preceding two expressions for $Y_n(m)$, a comparison yields to part (b) of our Lemma. ////

Now, we can give an explicit expression for the average number of nodes R(n,t) stored in the stack after t units of time during postorder-traversing of a binary tree $T \in T(n)$. Using Lemma 7 with $n:=\tau$ and $m:=n-\tau$ we get with (5a) and (5b) the

THEOREM 3.

$$(a)\quad R(n,2\tau) = \tau\frac{n-\tau}{n-1}\binom{2\tau}{\tau}\binom{2n-2\tau}{n-\tau}\binom{2n-2}{n-1}^{-1}$$

$$(b)\quad R(n,2\tau+1) = \frac{(2\tau+1)(2n-2\tau-1)-n}{(n-1)}\binom{2\tau}{\tau}\binom{2n-2\tau-2}{n-\tau-1}\binom{2n-2}{n-1}^{-1}$$

////

Notice, that the arithmetical mean of R(n,2τ) and R(n,2τ+2) is R(n,2τ+1); but R(n,2τ) is not the arithmetical mean of R(n,2τ-1) and R(n,2τ+1). Now, setting x:=t/2n, x fixed, and making use of Stirling's approximation we get with Theorem 3 by an elementary computation

$$R(n,t) = 4\sqrt{n/\pi}\sqrt{x(1-x)} + O(n^{-0.5})$$

Therefore, we have the following

THEOREM 4. *The average number of nodes R(n,t) stored in the stack after t units of time during postorder-traversing of a binary tree $T \in T(n)$ is asymptoticly given by*

$$R(n,t) = \frac{2}{\sqrt{\pi n}}\sqrt{t(2n-t)} + O(n^{-0.5})$$

////

Numerical results

Obviously, R(n,t) is symmetric to t=n, that is R(n,n+t)=R(n,n-t); in the average, the maximum number of nodes is stored in the stack after t=n units of time. This number is asymptoticly $2\sqrt{n}/\sqrt{\pi}$ and is less than the average stack size given in Theorem 2(a). In Table 5, we give some values of R(n,t) for some n. In the first column appears the exact value of R(n,t) (Theorem 3), in the second column the asymptotic value (Theorem 4). Figure 2 shows the graph of R(n,t) as a function of the proportion of the units of time t to the whole number of units of time 2n needed to traverse a tree $T \in T(n)$.

t \ n	10		20		30		40	
1	1.000	1.555	1.000	1.576	1.000	1.582	1.000	1.586
2	2.000	2.141	2.000	2.200	2.000	2.219	2.000	2.228
3	2.412	2.548	2.460	2.658	2.474	2.694	2.481	2.712
4	2.824	2.855	2.919	3.028	2.947	3.083	2.961	3.111
5	3.059	3.090	3.233	3.338	3.282	3.416	3.307	3.455
6	3.294	3.270	3.544	3.604	3.617	3.708	3.652	3.759

Table 5. The average number R(n,t) of nodes after t units of time.

t \ n	10		20		30		40	
7	3.421	3.404	3.777	3.835	3.879	3.968	3.927	4.033
8	3.548	3.496	4.010	4.037	4.141	4.202	4.202	4.282
9	3.588	3.550	4.188	4.215	4.354	4.414	4.432	4.510
10	3.628	3.568	4.366	4.370	4.567	4.607	4.661	4.720
15	3.059	3.090	4.906	4.886	5.342	5.352	5.540	5.571
20	0.000	0.000	5.083	5.046	5.842	5.827	6.176	6.180
25			4.906	4.886	6.115	6.094	6.622	6.616
30			4.366	4.370	6.209	6.180	6.927	6.910
40			0.000	0.000	5.842	5.827	7.161	7.137

Table 5. Continuation

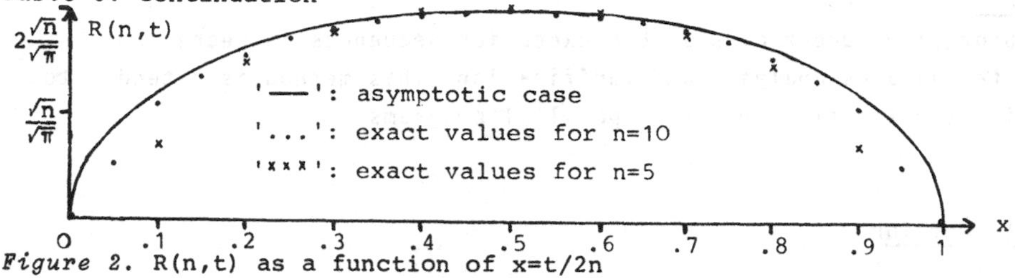

Figure 2. R(n,t) as a function of x=t/2n

REFERENCES

|1| ABRAMOWITZ,M., STEGUN,I.A., Handbook of Mathematical Functions, Dover, New York, 1970

|2| APOSTOL,T.M., Introduction to Analytic Number Theory, Springer-Verlag, New York, 1976

|3| CARLITZ,L., ROSELLE,D.P., SCOVILLE,R.A., 'Some Remarks on Ballot-Type Sequences of Positive Integers', J. Comb. Theory, Ser.A, 11, 258-271, 1971

|4| CHANDRASEKHARAN,K., Arithmetical Functions, Die Grundlehren der Mathematischen Wissenschaften, Band 167, Springer-Verlag,1970

|5| DE BRUIJN,N.G., KNUTH,D.E., RICE,S.O., 'The Average Height of Planted Plane Trees', in: Graph Theory and Computing, (R.C.Read, Ed.), 15-22, New York, London, Ac. Press, 1972

|6| FELLER,W., An Introduction to Probability Theory and Its Application, vol. 1, 2.nd ed., Wiley, New York, 1957

|7| FLAJOLET,PH., RAOULT,J.C., VUILLEMIN,J., 'On the Average Number of Registers Required for Evaluating Arithmetic Expressions',IRIA, Rapport de Recherche, No. 228, 1977

|8| KEMP,R., 'The Average Number of Registers Needed to Evaluate a Binary Tree Optimally', appears in Acta Informatica, 1977

|9| KNUTH,D.E., The Art of Computer Programming, vol. 1, second ed., Addison-Wesley, Reading, 1973

|10| KREWERAS,G., 'Sur les éventails de segments', Cahiers du B.U.R.O., 15, Paris, pp. 1-41, 1970

|11| RIORDAN,J., An Introduction to Combinatorial Analysis, Wiley, New York, 1958

|12| RIORDAN,J , Combinatorial Identities, Wiley, New York, 1968

ON REDUCTIONS OF PARALLEL PROGRAMS

Wolfgang Kowalk
Rüdiger Valk
Universität Hamburg, Fachbereich Informatik
Schlüterstraße 70, D-2000 Hamburg 13

Abstract: By a reduction of a parallel program, as informally introduced by Lipton, the number of possible execution sequences is decreased, which facilitates analysis and verification. This method is extended to simplify verification proofs of parallel programs.

1. Introduction

By the reduction of a program consisting of a number of cooperating processes, sequences of statements are replaced by a single and indivisible instruction. By this the number of possible execution sequences can be considerably decreased. Analysis and correctness proofs are simplified, if the investigated properties are unchanged by the reduction.
This will be done by extending a method introduced by Lipton /Li/. Whereas the presentation in /Li/ was rather informal and limited to special situations, a more formal treatment of reduction was given by Kwong /Kw/. But Kwong uses the notation of a transition system as a model to describe all execution sequences of a parallel system. This model is very general and allows to formulate many important properties of reductions, but applicationsto verification proofs of parallel programs are not given in a precise way.

In this paper we show, how these results can be applied directly to parallel programs. We give new reduction theorems, which are formulated for parallel programs. This is done by keeping results as general as possible. Furthermore we give a classification of movers, and investigate their different properties. This leads to a deeper understanding of movers and facilitates proofs about them. It is shown how correctness proofs as given by Owicki and Gries /OG/ are simplified by reductions, which demonstrates the usefullness of this approach.

2. Transitions systems

Many properties of reductions can be derived on the very abstract level of transition systems. In the forth section it will be shown how to apply them to parallel programs. In this section we briefly recall the notions of transition systems and reductions as given in /Kw/.

A transition system is a quadrupel $S = (Q,T,tr,Q^o)$, where Q is a set of states, T is a set of transitions, $tr \subseteq Q\times T\times Q$ is the state transitions relation and $Q^o \subseteq Q$ is the set of initial states. The relation tr is recursively extended to $tr^* \subseteq Q\times T^*\times Q$ by $(q,\lambda,q')\in tr^*$ iff $q=q'$, where λ is the empty sequence, and $(q,wt,q')\in tr^*$ iff $\exists q''\in Q: (q,w,q'')\in tr^* \wedge (q'',t,q')\in tr$ for all $w\in T^*$, $t\in T$. Let be $tr^+ := tr^* - Q\times\{\lambda\}\times Q$. If $(q,w,q')\in tr^*$ for some $q,q'\in Q$, $w\in T^*$, we also write $q\ w\ q'$ or $q\ tr\ q'$ and say, that w is fireable in q and that q' is reachable from q by a firing of w. $Reach(q) := \{q' \mid \exists w\in T^*: q\ w\ q'\}$ denotes the set of all reachable states from q and $Q^d := \bigcup_{q\in Q^o} Reach(q)$ is the reachability set of S or the dynamical state set of S. The set $\mathcal{F}_S$ of all (firable) sequences of S is the set of all sequences $w\in T^*$, which are firable in some initial state.

We now recall some properties of transition systems /Kw/.

For $q\in Q$ and $t\in T$ we have:

live(q,t) $:\Leftrightarrow \exists q'\in Reach(q)$: t is firable in q'

dead(q) $:\Leftrightarrow \forall t\in T: \neg live(q,t)$

S can halt $:\Leftrightarrow \exists q\in Q^d: dead(q)$

A transition system is determinate, if

$$\forall q,q'\in Q^d: \quad dead(q) \wedge dead(q') \Rightarrow \quad q = q'$$

S is Church-Rosser, if

$$\forall q\in Q^d, \forall q',q''\in Reach(q): Reach(q') \cap Reach(q'') \neq \emptyset$$

A state $q\in Q$ is a home state of S, if

$$\forall q'\in Q^d: q\in Reach(q')$$

Let $S_i = (Q_i,T_i,tr_i,Q_i^o)$ be transition systems and Q_i^d the reachability set of S_i. Then S_1 reduces to S_2 provided that the following conditions hold:

(1) $Q_2 \subseteq Q_1$ and $Q_2^o = Q_1^o$

(2) $\forall q_o\in Q_1^o\ \forall q\in Reach(q_o)\ \exists q'\in Q_2$: $q\ tr_1\ q' \ \wedge\ q_o\ tr_2\ q'$

(3) $\forall q,q'\in Q_2^d\ \forall t\in T_2$: $q\ t\ q' \ \Rightarrow\ q\ tr_1^+\ q'$

(4) $\forall\, q,q' \in Q_2^d$: $q\ tr_1\ q'$ => $q\ tr_2\ q'$

If condition (4) can be replaced by the following stronger condition:

(4') $\forall\, q,q' \in Q_2^d$: $q\ tr_1^+\ q'$ => $q\ tr_2^+\ q'$

then we say, that S_1 strictly reduces to S_2.

Theorem 2.1 /Kw/

If S_1 reduces to S_2, then

a) $Q_2^d \subseteq Q_1^d$

b) There is a home state in S_1 iff there is a home state in S_2.

c) S_1 is Church-Rosser iff S_2 is Church-Rosser.

If S_1 strictly reduces to S_2, then

d) S_1 can halt iff S_2 can halt.

e) S_1 is determinate iff S_2 is determinate.

We introduce the following property of transition systems, which is fundamental in the case of parallel programs. A transition system $S = (Q,T,tr,Q_0)$ is unambigous or deterministic, if

$\forall\, q,q',q'' \in Q$ $\forall t \in T$: $q\ t\ q' \wedge q\ t\ q''$ => $q' = q''$

3. Programs

We now formalize the notion of a (parallel) program. To describe the state of a program we distinguish memory states from control states.

A (parallel) program $P = (V,M,\mathcal{O},Act,\mathcal{L}^0)$ is defined by a set $V = \{v_1,\dots,v_n\}$ of variables, which habe values in a domain $M = M_1 \times .. \times M_n$. of memory states, a set of statements $\mathcal{O}$, a map Act and a set of initial states $\mathcal{L}^0$.

$\mathcal{L}^t := M \times \mathcal{P}(\mathcal{O})$ is the total set of states of the program, hence $\mathcal{L}^0 \subseteq \mathcal{L}^t$. ($\mathcal{P}(\mathcal{O})$ denotes the set of subsets of $\mathcal{O}$). If $\alpha = (x,A) \in \mathcal{L}^t$, then x is the memory state and A is called control state or ready set (of statements). Act : $\mathcal{L}^t \to \mathcal{P}(\mathcal{O})$ gives for any state $\alpha = (x,A) \in \mathcal{L}^t$ a set Act(x,A) of active instructions, which is supposed to be a subset of the control state A of α. With each statement $a \in \mathfrak{A}$ two mappings M_a and R_a are given, which describe an execution of a: $M_a: M \to M$ gives the change of memory and $R_a: \mathcal{L}^t \to \mathcal{P}(\mathfrak{A})$ with $A-\{a\} \subseteq R_a(x,A)$ for all $(x,A) \in \mathcal{L}^t$ gives the new control state. The first and second projection on $\mathcal{L}^t = M \times \mathcal{P}(\mathfrak{A})$ is denoted by Mem and Ready, respectively.

To summarize some properties of our model of a parallel program, we can say that in any state $\alpha = (x,A) \in \mathcal{L}^t$ we have a memory state Mem(α) = x and a ready set of statements Ready(α) = A. The ready set A contains a subset Act(α) of active statements, which can be executed. The statements in A and A - Act(α) are said to be ready and blocked, respectively.

The execution of a statement $a \in \mathfrak{A}$ is defined as follows. For states $\alpha = (x,A)$ and $\alpha' = (x',A')$ we define $\alpha \; a \; \alpha'$ if $a \in \text{Act}(\alpha)$ and $x' = M_a(x)$ and $A' = R_a(\alpha)$. Then a is executable in α and α' is the result of the execution. By $\alpha \; \lambda \; \alpha$ and $\alpha \; wa \; \alpha' \iff \exists \beta: \alpha \; w \; \beta \wedge \beta \; a \; \alpha'$ this relation ist extended to all finite sequences over $\mathfrak{A}^*$.

Reach(α) := $\{\beta \mid \exists \; w: \alpha \; w \; \beta\}$ is the set of reachable states from α. $\mathcal{L}^d$:= Reach($\mathcal{L}^o$) ist the reachability set or the set of dynamical states of P. If $\beta \in \text{Reach}(\alpha)$ we also write $\alpha * \beta$.

$\mathcal{F}_P := \{w \in \mathfrak{A}^* \mid \exists \; \alpha \in \mathcal{L}^o, \exists \; \beta: \alpha w \beta\}$ is the set of execution sequences of P.

In many applications the set of dynamical states is very difficult to compute whereas the total set of states is too large. But for many programs an intermediate set of states can be given. Any such set $\mathcal{L}^s$, that has the property $\mathcal{L}^d \subseteq \mathcal{L}^s \subseteq \mathcal{L}^t$ will be called a static state set of P.

In investigating properties of parallel programs we are interested in statements, that can be executed in parallel. Therefore we define the following mapping for any $r \in \{s,t,d\}$ by $\text{Par}^r: \mathfrak{A} \to \mathcal{P}(\mathfrak{A})$
$\text{Par}^r(a) := \{b \in \mathfrak{A}-\{a\} \mid \exists \; \alpha \in \mathcal{L}^r: \{a,b\} \subseteq \text{Ready}(\alpha)\}$. A statement b is said to be parallel with a (with respect to $\mathcal{L}^r$) if $b \in \text{Par}^r(a)$.

4. Transition systems and programs

In this section we show, that programs as defined in the previous section correspond to deterministic transition systems. By this many definitions and theorems made for transition systems can also be used for programs.

Let be $S = (Q,T,tr,Q^0)$ a deterministic transition system and $P = (V,M,\mathfrak{A},Act,\mathfrak{L}^0)$ a program. Then S and P are equivalent, if there is a bijection $\phi: Z \to \mathfrak{L}^s$ to a static state set $\mathfrak{L}^s$ of P and a bijection $\psi: T \to \mathfrak{A}$ such that $\psi^*(\mathfrak{F}_S) = \mathfrak{F}_P$ and $\forall w \in T^* \forall q,q' \in Q$: $q\ w\ q'$ $<=>$ $\phi(q)\ \psi^*(w)\ \phi(q')$. ($\psi^*$ is the homomorphism generated by ψ).

Theorem 4.1: For every program P there is an equivalent deterministic transition system and vice versa.

proof: For a program $P = (V,M,\mathfrak{A},Act,\mathfrak{L}^0)$ an equivalent deterministic transition system $S = (\mathfrak{L}^t, \mathfrak{A}, tr, \mathfrak{L}^0)$ is constructed, where $\mathfrak{L}^t$ is the total set of states of P, $(\alpha,a,\alpha') \in tr :<=> \alpha\ a\ \alpha'$. Conversely, if $S = (Q,T,tr,Q^0)$ is a deterministic transition system, then $P = (\{x\},Q,T,Act,Q^0)$ is an equivalent program, if we define $\mathfrak{L}^s := Q \times \{T\}$, $Act(q,T) := \{t \in T \mid \exists\ q' \in Q: (q,t,q') \in tr\}$, and for all $t \in T$: $M_t(q)$:= if $(q,t,q') \in tr$ then q' else q and $R_t(q,T) := T$.

The proof that the constructions have the required properties is omitted here.

By the theorem the definitions of 'live', 'dead', 'can halt', 'determinate', 'Church-Rosser' and 'home states' are also valid for programs. Furthermore all theorems of /Kw/ about transition systems hold for programs.

5. Movers and blockers

The concept of movers was introduced by Lipton /Li/. A mover is a statement that has the property, that the order of execution with respect to parallel statements is unimportant. By this property a sequence of statements can be replaced by a new indivisible statement representing it. Such reductions of programs are very useful for program verification and analysis, as the number of possible execution sequences can be considerably decreased.

In this chapter we introduce a number of different classes of movers. In this way some properties of a mover can better be understood and proofs are simplified. A special class of movers as defined here is a mover as defined in /Li/.

We now define the following classes of movers:

A mover can be

$$\left\{\begin{array}{ll}\text{permanent} & (P)\\ \text{total} & (T)\\ \text{static} & (S)\\ \text{dynamical} & (D)\end{array}\right\} \quad \left\{\begin{array}{ll}\text{right} & (R)\\ \text{left} & (L)\\ \text{left-right} & (LR)\end{array}\right\} \quad \left\{\begin{array}{ll}\text{value} & (V)\\ \text{active} & (A)\\ \text{value-active} & (VA)\end{array}\right\} \text{ mover}$$

In the following definitions we refer to a set of states $\mathcal{L}^r$. If this set is the total set of states of a program P, we call the defined objects <u>total</u> (with respect to P). If that set is a static set of states of P, we call the defined object <u>static</u> (with respect to P). If the set $\mathcal{L}^r$ is the dynamical set of states of P, we call the defined objects <u>dynamical</u> (with respect to P). If $\mathcal{L}^r$ is any set of states of any program P, we call the defined objects <u>permanent</u>.

A statement $a \in \mathfrak{A}$ is called a <u>right (left) active mover</u> (or <u>RA-mover (LA-mover)</u>), if $\forall\, \beta \in \mathcal{L}^r$ and $\forall\, b \in Ready(\beta)$ in P:

$\beta\, ab\, \gamma \;\Rightarrow\; \beta\, ba\, \delta \qquad (\,\beta\, ba\, \gamma \;\Rightarrow\; \beta\, ab\, \delta\,)$

A statement $a \in \mathfrak{A}$ is called a <u>right (left) value mover (RV-mover (LV-mover)</u>), if $\forall\, \beta \in \mathcal{L}^r$ and $\forall\, b \in Ready(\beta)$ in P:

$\beta\, ab\, \gamma \wedge \beta\, ba\, \delta \;\Rightarrow\; \gamma = \delta \qquad (\,\beta\, ba\, \gamma \wedge \beta\, ab\, \delta \;\Rightarrow\; \gamma = \delta\,)$

A mover is called <u>value-active (VA-mover</u>), if it is a value mover and an active mover. It is called a <u>left-right mover (LR-mover</u>), if it is a left mover and a right mover.

A DRVA-mover (that is a dynamical right value-active mover) is a right mover as defined in /Li/. A DLVA-mover is a left mover in /Li/.

In this paper not all of these classes of movers are used, but their usefullness should be evident.

By the definitions above the following corollary is obvious.

<u>Corollary 5.1</u>: Let be $a \in \mathfrak{A}$ a statement of a program P.

a) a is a P-mover => a is a T-mover => a is a S-mover => a is a D-mover.

b) a is a RV-mover <=> a is a LV-mover <=> a is a RLV-mover

By this corollary the distinction between right, left and right-left movers is important only in the case of active movers. The following definition of blockers and deblockers leads to a deeper understanding of this property. We again use the set $\mathcal{L}^r$ to distinguish between permanent, total, static and dynamical blockers and deblockers.

A statement a of a program is called a blocker, if there is a statement b and a state $\beta \in \mathcal{L}^r$, and we have $\beta\ a\ \gamma$ and $\beta\ b\ \delta$ and b is blocked in γ. The statement a is called a deblocker, if there is a statement b and a state $\beta \in \mathcal{L}^r$, and we have $\beta\ ab\ \gamma$ and b is blocked in β.

Corollary 5.2: Given a statement $a \in \mathfrak{A}$, then
a is a D-blocker => a is a S-Blocker => a is a T-blocker => a is a P-blocker.
The same holds for deblockers.

Theorem 5.3: Let be $a \in \mathfrak{A}$ a statement of P, that is not blocked in $\mathcal{L}^r$.
a) a is a deblocker <=> a is not an RA-mover.
b) a is a blocker <=> a is not an LA-mover.

In part a) of the theorem the inclusion from the left to the right hand side is valid without the assumption, that a cannot be blocked. This theorem illustrates the difference between right and left active movers. For instance the V(s)-operation on semaphores is a P-deblocker but not a P-blocker. Therefore it is a PLA-mover but not an PRA-mover. Since it is a value mover, it is a PLVA-mover, or a left mover as defined in /Li/. Since a P(s)-operation can be blocked, the theorem cannot be used to proof, that it is a right mover.

A statement $a \in \mathfrak{A}$ is called a symmetrical blocker, if
(1) a is a blocker and can be blocked in a state of $\mathcal{L}^r$ and
(2) for all states $\beta \in \mathcal{L}^r$:
$\beta\ a\ \gamma \wedge \beta\ b\ \delta \Rightarrow$ (a is blocked in $\delta \Leftrightarrow$ b is blocked in γ)

Using theorem 5.3 we can proof the following theorem.

Theorem 5.4: Let be $a \in \mathfrak{A}$ a statement, that cannot be blocked in any state of $\mathcal{L}^r$ or that is a symmetrical blocker. Then
a is a deblocker <=> a is no RA-mover

As an example it follows that P(s) is a PRVA-mover, that is a right mover as defined in /Li/.

The corresponding theorem for blockers and LA-movers does not hold. This can be proved by a simple example.

6. Reduction of parallel programs

We now introduce a formal definition of reduction of programs in such a way that the results obtained in /Kw/ for transition systems can be applied.

Let be $w \in \mathcal{F}_P$ an execution sequence of a program $P = (V, M, \mathfrak{A}, Act, \mathcal{L}^0)$, that can be decomposed to $w = w_0\, a_1\, \beta_1\, w_1\, a_2\, \beta_2\, w_2 \ldots a_n\, \beta_n$, where no w_i $(1 \le i \le n-1)$ contains an a_j $(1 \le j \le n)$. (The states β_i are not members of the sequence w, but indicate the states reached after the execution of the previous part of the sequence.) Then $a_1\, a_2 \ldots a_n$ is called a <u>ready sequence</u> in w, if for all $i \in \{1, .., n-1\}$ $a_{i+1} \in Ready(\beta_i)$. For convenience in the sequel we apply set-theoretical operations to sequences $y_1 \ldots y_k \in \mathfrak{A}^*$, that are interpreted as sets $\{y_1, \ldots, y_k\} \subseteq \mathfrak{A}$. In the following movers are assumed to be at least dynamical value-active movers(DVA-mover).

Let be $R \subseteq \mathfrak{A}$ a set of statements, that are pairwise not parallel. Let $a_0 \in R$ be a statement, and let no $a \in R - \{a_0\}$ be blocked in any state $\beta \in \mathcal{L}^S$. Then we say that a sequence $w \in \mathcal{F}_P$ is <u>(a_0, R)-reducible</u> in P, iff

$w \cap R = \emptyset$ or

$w = w'\ \beta\ v\ \gamma\ v'$ where

(1) w' is (a_0, R)-reducible

(2) $v' \cap R = \emptyset$ and $a_0 \in Ready(\beta)$ and $R \cap Ready(\gamma) = \emptyset$

(3) $v = u_0\, a_0\, u_1\, a_1 \ldots u_n\, a_n$ where

$R \cap \bigcup_{i=0}^{n} u_i = \emptyset$ and

$\exists\, k \in \{1, \ldots n\}$:

$a_0, \ldots, a_{k-1}$ are right movers and $a_{k+1}, \ldots, a_n$ are L-movers

$a_0, \ldots, a_n$ is a ready sequence in w and

$\{a_1, \ldots, a_n\} \subseteq R - \{a_0\}$ and $\bigcup_{i=0}^{n} u_i \subseteq Par^S(R - \{a_k\})$

R is called a <u>reduction set of P with initial element a_0</u> and $a_0 a_1 \ldots a_n$ is called a <u>reduction sequence of R in P</u>.

In this definition it is important, that the initial element a_0 is unique and that after the execution of an reduction sequence no statement of R is ready, i.e. the reduction sequence must terminate.

A program P is <u>(a_0, R)-reducible</u> for $a_0 \in R \subseteq \mathfrak{A}$ if $\forall w \in \mathcal{F}_P\ \exists\, w' \in \mathfrak{A}^*$: $w\,w' \in \mathcal{F}_P$ and $w\,w'$ is (a_0, R)-reducible in P.

We now come to the definition of the new statement [R] that will replace the statements of R in a reduction P/R of P. For a (a_0, R)-reducible program P with a total set of states $\mathcal{L}^t$ we define the predicate Red on $\mathcal{L}^t \times \mathcal{O}\!\mathcal{l}^* \times \mathcal{L}^t$ by $Red(\beta, a_0 a_1 \dots a_n, \gamma)$ = true iff there is an execution sequence $w = w' \; \beta \; a_0 \; a_1 \dots a_n \; \gamma \; w''$ in P, such that $a_0 \; a_1 \dots a_n$ is (a_0, R)-reducible in P. For $A \subseteq \mathcal{O}\!\mathcal{l}$ and $\beta = (x, A)$ we write $A/R :=$ if $a_0 \notin A$ then A else $(A - \{a_0\}) \cup [R]$ and $\beta/R := (x, A/R)$.

<u>Lemma 6.1</u>: a) If $Red(\beta, a_0 a_1 \dots a_n, \gamma)$ is true in P, then the reduction sequence and the state γ are uniquely determined by β.

b) The mapping $/R: \mathcal{P}(\mathcal{O}\!\mathcal{l}) \to \mathcal{P}((\mathcal{O}\!\mathcal{l} - \{a_0\}) \cup \{[R]\})$ is a bijection.

The lemma justifies the following definition of a reduction. Let $P = (V, M, \mathcal{O}\!\mathcal{l}, Act, \mathcal{L}^0)$ be a (a_0, R)-reducible program. Then we say that $P/R = (V, M, \mathcal{O}\!\mathcal{l}', Act', \mathcal{L}^{0\prime})$ is a <u>(a_0, R)-reduction</u> of P if

(1) $\mathcal{O}\!\mathcal{l}' := (\mathcal{O}\!\mathcal{l} - R) \cup \{[R]\}$ with $[R] \notin \mathcal{O}\!\mathcal{l}$.

(2) $Act'(\beta/R) := Act(\beta)/R$.

(3) The mappings M_a' and R_a' of P/R are defined by:

$$M_a'(\beta/R) := \begin{cases} Mem(\gamma) & \text{if } a = [R] \text{ and } Red(\beta, a_0 \dots a_n, \gamma) \\ M_a(\beta) & \text{if } a \in \mathcal{O}\!\mathcal{l} - R \\ Mem(\beta/R) & \text{otherwise} \end{cases}$$

$$R_a'(\beta/R) := \begin{cases} Ready(\gamma) & \text{if } a = [R] \text{ and } Red(\beta, a_0 \dots a_n, \gamma) \\ R_a(\beta)/R & \text{if } a \in \mathcal{O}\!\mathcal{l} - R \\ Ready(\beta/R) & \text{otherwise} \end{cases}$$

(4) $\mathcal{L}^{0\prime} := \{\beta/R \mid \beta \in \mathcal{L}^0\}$.

The following lemma states some properties of the reduction P/R.

<u>Lemma 6.2</u>: Let P be a program, P/R it's (a_0, R)-reduction.

a) $\beta/R \in \mathcal{L}^d_{P/R} \Rightarrow \beta \in \mathcal{L}^d_P$

b) $\forall \beta/R, \gamma/R \in \mathcal{L}^d_{P/R} \; \forall w \in (\mathcal{O}\!\mathcal{l} - R)^*: \; \beta \; w \; \gamma \Leftrightarrow \beta/R \; w \; \gamma/R$

c) If $\beta, \gamma \in \mathcal{L}^d_P$, $w \in \mathcal{O}\!\mathcal{l}^+$, $Ready(\beta) \cap (R - \{a_0\}) = \emptyset$ and $Ready(\gamma) \cap (R - \{a_0\}) = \emptyset$ then $\beta \; w \; \gamma \Rightarrow \exists v \in \mathcal{O}\!\mathcal{l}'^+: \beta/R \; v \; \gamma/R$

d) $\forall \beta/R, \gamma/R \in \mathcal{L}^d_{P/R}, w \in \mathcal{O}\!\mathcal{l}'^+: \; \beta/R \; w \; \gamma/R \Rightarrow \exists v \in \mathcal{O}\!\mathcal{l}^+: \beta \; v \; \gamma$.

We now come to our main result.

<u>Theorem 6.3</u>: If P/R is a (a_0, R)-reduction of a program P, then there are transition systems S_1 and S_2, equivalent to P and P/R, respectively, such that S_1 strictly reduces to S_2.

proof: We first have to find transition systems S_1 and S_2, that are equivalent to P and P/R, respectively. We define $S_1 := (\mathcal{L}_P^t, \mathcal{A}, tr, \mathcal{L}^o)$ by $(\beta,a,\gamma) \in tr$ iff $\beta\ a\ \gamma$ in P and $S_2 := (\mathcal{L}, (\mathcal{A}-R) \cup \{a_o\}, tr_2, \mathcal{L}^{o\prime})$, where $\mathcal{L} := \Phi(\mathcal{L}^d_{P/R})$ is defined by the mapping $\Phi(x,A/R) := (x,A)$, that is a bijection. To show that S_1 strictly reduces to S_2, we have to check the four conditions of the definition in section 2. This can be done using lemma 6.2.

By theorem 6.2 and 2.1 it follows:

Theorem 6.4: If P/R is a (a_o,R)-reduction of P, then

a) P/R has a home state iff P has a home state
b) P/R is Church-Rosser iff P is Church-Rosser
c) P/R can halt iff P can halt
d) P/R is determinate iff P is determinate.

7. Applications and examples

In the previous section the reduction of a program is formulated using the set of execution sequences. This allows great generality, but cannot be used for effective reductions. Therefore in this section as an application a reduction of a parallel program will be derived, that uses the program listing itself.

The parallelism of the program is expressed by a statement **cobegin** P_1 // P_2 // ... // P_n **coend**. By this statement the subprograms P_1, .., P_n are executed in parallel. By a *jump* from a statement b to a statement c we mean a goto statement or a conditional statement, by which the control can be transfered from b to c.

Theorem 7.1: Let be P a program

```
P:  begin w0; cobegin w1; a0; a1; ... ; an; w2
                // w3 // ... // wn
              coend; wn+1
    end.
```

where all w_i are arbitrary sequences of statements not containing **cobegin** or **coend**, and where $R := \{a_o,a_1,...,a_n\}$ has the following properties:

(1) no a_i $(1 \le i \le n)$ can be blocked in $\mathcal{L}_P^s$.

(2) there is a $k \in \{0,...,n\}$, such that $a_o,...,a_{k-1}$ are DRVA-movers and

$a_{k+1},\dots,a_n$ are DLVA-movers.
(3) none of the statements $a_1,\dots,a_n$ can be reached by a jump from outside of R and a_0 cannot be reached by a jump from R.
(4) inside of R no jumps from $\{a_k,\dots,a_n\}$ to $\{a_1,\dots,a_k\}$ are possible where k is the k from (2).
proof: We have to show first, that P is (a_0,R)-reducible. Let $w\in\mathcal{F}_P$ be any execution sequence of P and let be α w β in P. If there is no statement of $R-\{a_0\}$, that is ready in β (i.e. $R-\{a_0\}\cap Ready(\beta) = \emptyset$), then define u := w and continue with the next section. If there is a statement $a\in R-\{a_0\}\cap Ready(\beta)$, this statement cannot be blocked because of (1). Since there is no nonterminating loop of statements belonging to $R-\{a_0\}$ in P, there is a sequence $v\in\mathcal{O}\!\ell^*$ with α w β v γ and $Ready(\gamma)\cap R-\{a_0\} = \emptyset$. Let be u := w v.

We now prove, that u is (a_0,R)-reducible in P by inspecting the conditions in the definition. If $u\cap R = \emptyset$ there is nothing to show. Otherwise it follows from (3), that there at least one statement a_0 in u. Let us decompose u = w' u' v' in such a way that
α' w' β' u' γ' v', where the first statement of u' is the last occurence of a_0 in u. By (3) the state γ' and the sequence v' can be taken in such a way, that neither $Ready(\gamma')$ nor v' contain a statement of R.

By induction assume, that w' is (a_0,R)-reducible. From the construction follows $v'\cap R = \emptyset$, $a_0\in Ready(\beta')$ and $Ready(\gamma)\cap R = \emptyset$. We decompose $u' = a_0\ u_0\ a_{i_1}\ u_1\ a_{i_2}\ u_2\ \dots\ a_{i_m}\ u_m$ such that there is no statement of R in any u_i^1.

Since a_0 ist not in $\{a_{i_1},\dots,a_{i_m}\}$, by (3) the sequence $a_{i_1}a_{i_2}\dots a_{i_m}$ is a ready sequence. By (2) and (4) $a_0,a_{i_1},\dots a_{i_{r-1}}$ are DRVA-movers and $a_{i_{r+1}},\dots,a_{i_m}$ are DLVA-movers. Finally, using the definition of (a_0,R)-reduction and the definition of the statement [R], the substitution of the statements in R by [R] is the (a_0,R)-reduction of P.

This theorem is more general than the D-reduction of /Li/, where no jumps within R are allowed. As an example consider the solution of a consumer-producer-problem in Fig. 1 given by Owicki and Gries /OG/ (with a little modification that will be disdussed later).

By theorem 7.1 this program can be reduced to a program P/R, where all sequences of statements in brackets [and] are assumed to be one indivisible instruction. The program P/R is much easier to verify.

```
P: const m,n : integer;
   var   i=j=1 : integer;
         full = 0, empty = n : semaphore;
         buffer : array(o..n-1) of item;
         A, B : array (o..m) of item;
         x, y : item;

   cobegin  a1: if i>m then goto aend;
           [a2: wait(empty);
            a3: x := A(i);
            a4: buffer(i mod n) := x;
            a5: signal (full);
            a6: i := i+1;
            a7: goto a1;]
            aend: skip
      //
            b1: if j>m then goto bend;
           [b2: wait(full);
            b3: y := buffer (j mod n);
            b4: signal(empty);
            b5: B(j) := y;
            b6: j := j+1;
            b7: goto b1;]
            bend: skip
   coend.
```

Figure 1

The following invariant ist true for all reachable states of P/R:

$$I := i>0 \wedge j>0 \wedge n-(i-j)=empty \wedge i-j=full \wedge$$
$$buffer(k \bmod n)=A(k) \text{ for } k=j-i-1 \wedge B(k)=A(k) \text{ for } k=1..j-1$$

By this invariant I it is not difficult to prove, that the program P/R is non blocking and determinate. In the only halting state of P/R we have A=B. By theorem 6.3 and theorem 6.4 also the original program P has these properties, which proves the correctness of the program P.

Comparing this proof to that of Owicki and Gries in /OG/ we observe that this proof is much shorter and easier to find. Especially we do not need any auxiliary variables and the number of assertions needed in this proof is considerably decreased.

The next theorem shows how the number of execution sequences can be reduced by shifting statements out of the cobegin-coend statement.

Theorem 7.2: Let be P a program

P: **begin** w_o; a_o;
cobegin a_1; a_2; ... ; a_n; w_1
// w_2 // ... // w_m
coend; w_{m+1}
end.

where all w_i are arbitrary sequences of statements. Let be $a_1,\ldots,a_n$ left movers (that are DLVA-movers), which cannot be reached by jumps and which cannot be blocked. Then with R := $\{a_o,\ldots,a_n\}$ the program P is (a_o,R)-reducible to the program:

P/R: **begin** w_o; [R];
cobegin w_1 // w_2 // ... // w_n **coend**;
w_{n+1}
end.

Another application of movers are 'permutations' which are introduced now.

Let P be a program of the form

P: ... **cobegin** ... a; b ... **coend** ...

with two statements a and b, which are assumed not to be in parallel. Permutating a and b we obtain the program P/ab/:

P/ab/: ... **cobegin** ... b; a ... **coend** ...

a and b are said to be permutable iff for all states $\beta \in \mathcal{S}^s$ and some $\dot{\gamma}$: β a b γ holds in P iff β b a γ holds in P/ab/. The following theorem states, that P and P/ab/ behave in almost the same way.

Theorem 7.3: Let P: ... **cobegin** ... a; b ... **coend** be a program, where a and b are statements, that are permutable and not in parallel. If in P and in P/ab/ holds:

1. (a is a DRVA-mover and does not block) or
(b is a DLVA-mover and does not block)

and

2. (a is a DLVA-mover and does not block) or
(b is a DRVA-mover and does not block)

then P blocks iff P/ab/ blocks. Furthermore the sets of states where a and b are not ready are identical for P and P/ab/.

We now demonstrate the usefullnes of this theorem. If statements a2 and a3 in the program P of Fig. 1 are exchanged, we obtain a program P_1, that is identical to the program given by Owicki and Gries /GO/. A reduction of the program P_1 can never include the statement a3 since a2 can block. Since P equals P_1/a3 a2/ we can apply theorem 7.3. (It is easy to prove that a3 and a2 are permutable in P_1). Hence P is determinate and blocks iff P_1 is determinate and blocks. Thus the correctness of P_1 follows from the proof for P, which has been discussed earlier in this paper. This shows how some limitations of the method of reduction can be dropped by the concept of permutations.

References:

/Kw/ KWONG, Y. S., On Reduction of Asynchronous Systems, Theoretical Computer Science 5(1977),25-50

/Li/ LIPTON,R. J., Reduction: A Method of Proving Peoperties of Parallel Programs, Comm. ACM 18(1975)12,717-721

/OG/ OWICKI,S,, GRIES,P., An Axiomatic Proof Techniques for Parallel Programs I, Acta Informatica 6(1976),319-340

ON THE HEIGHT OF DERIVATION TREES

Werner Kuich, Helmut Prodinger, Friedrich J. Urbanek
Institut für Mathematische Logik und Formale Sprachen
Technische Universität Wien, Wien

ABSTRACT

Derivation trees generated by context-free grammars with regular parallel control language are considered. The generating function of the derivation trees counted according to height and length of yield is rational and the asymptotic behaviour of the average height is of the form g(n).n, g(n) periodic and bounded.

INTRODUCTION

According to Knuth [4,p.316], the three principal ways used to traverse a binary tree are to visit the nodes in preorder, postorder or endorder. These ways can be generalized in an obvious way to n-ary trees, $n \geq 2$.

The height of a tree i. e. the maximal length of a path from the root to the leaves equals the maximum size of a stack used in the following algorithm traversing the tree in endorder:

> If tree to be traversed consists of a node only then
> visit that node.
> If tree to be traversed has subtrees $t_1, t_2, \ldots, t_n$
> then push down root onto stack;
> for $1 \leq i \leq n$ traverse tree t_i;
> pop up stack and visit that node.

The word visit means to do what ever activity is intended.

De Bruijn, Knuth, Rice [2] have computed the asymptotic value of the average height of planted plane trees with n nodes, considering all such trees to be equally likely.

Kemp [3] has computed the average size of the stack that is needed to traverse the derivation trees of linear context-free grammars.

In our paper we consider derivation trees generated by context-free grammars with regular parallel control language, which implies that each level of a derivation tree contains only a bounded number of nodes.

In the first part of the paper we show that the family of languages generated by these grammars is identical to a well-known family of languages considered in detail by Rozenberg, Vermeir [8].

In the second part of the paper we compute the generating function of the derivation trees counted according to height and length of yield. It turns out that the generating functions are rational and hence the powerful theory of rational functions as developed in Salomaa, Soittola [10] comes into play. We then examine the asymptotic behaviour of the average height of the derivation trees generated by a context-free grammar with regular parallel control language and show that the average height has an asymptotic representation of the form g(n).n, where g(n) is a bounded periodic function.

PRELIMINARIES

It is assumed that the reader is familiar with the basic definitions concerning formal grammars and languages as stated in Salomaa [9] and formal power series as stated in Salomaa, Soittola [10]. Additional definitions will be given whenever needed.

Let $G = (\Phi,\Sigma,P,S)$ be a context-free grammar. Then define $\alpha \xRightarrow[p_{i_1},\ldots,i_n]{} \beta$ iff $\alpha = x_1A_1x_2\ldots x_nA_nx_{n+1}$, $\beta = x_1\alpha_1x_2\ldots x_n\alpha_nx_{n+1}$ and $p_{i_j} : A_j \to \alpha_j \in P$, where $x_j \in \Sigma^*$, $1\le j\le n+1$, $A_j \in \Phi$, $1\le j\le n$.

Let $\sigma : (\Phi \cup \Sigma)^* \to \Phi^*$, $\tau : (\Phi \cup \Sigma)^* \to \Sigma^*$ be the homomorphisms defined by $\sigma(A) = A$, $\tau(A) = \varepsilon$ if $A \in \Phi$ and $\sigma(a) = \varepsilon$, $\tau(a) = a$ if $a \in \Sigma$.

Let $\Phi_k = \{\alpha \in (\Phi \cup \Sigma)^* \mid |\sigma(\alpha)| \le k\}$. Then $P_k = \{p_{i_1,\ldots,i_r} \mid \alpha_{i_1}\alpha_{i_2}\ldots\alpha_{i_r} \in \Phi_k$, $r\le k$, $p_{i_j} : A_{i_j} \to \alpha_{i_j} \in P$, $1\le j\le r\}$, $k>0$ and for $k>0$

$$\psi_\alpha^k : P_k^* \to \Phi_k,\ \alpha \in \Phi_k$$

are the mappings defined by $\psi_\alpha^k(\pi) = \beta$ iff

(i) $\pi = \varepsilon$ and $\alpha = \beta$, or

(ii) $\pi = p^{(1)}\ldots p^{(t)}$, $(t\ge 1)$ and there exist $\gamma_1,\ldots,\gamma_{t+1} \in \Phi_k$, such that $\gamma_1 = \alpha$, $\gamma_{t+1} = \beta$ and $\gamma_i \xRightarrow[p^{(i)}]{} \gamma_{i+1}$, $1\le i\le t$.

The mapping ψ_α^k will be undefined if no such β exists. Let ψ_S^k be denoted by ψ^k. Then

$$PL^k(G) = \{\pi \mid \psi^k(\pi) = w \in \Sigma^*\}$$

is called <u>parallel label language of degree k of G</u>.

Given a language $C \subseteq PL^k(G)$, the language

$$L_C^k(G) = \{w \mid \psi^k(\pi) = w,\ \pi \in C\}$$

is called the <u>language generated by G with parallel control language C of degree k</u>.

The language $L_C^k(G)$ is generated <u>k-unambiguously</u> by G with parallel control language C iff the restricted mapping

$\psi^k : C \to L_C^k(G)$

is bijective.

Lemma 1. Let $G = (\Phi,\Sigma,P,S)$ be a context-free grammar and $k>0$. Then $PL^k(G)$ is regular.

Proof. Let $K = \{\alpha \mid |\alpha| \le k,\ \alpha \in \Phi^*\}$ and $M = (K,P_k,\delta,S,\{\varepsilon\})$ be the incomplete finite deterministic automaton where $\delta(\alpha,p_{i_1,\ldots,i_r}) = \sigma(\psi_\alpha^k(p_{i_1,\ldots,i_r}))$. Then $\delta(\alpha,\pi) = \sigma(\psi_\alpha^k(\pi))$, $\pi \in P_k^*$ and $\pi \in T(M)$ iff $\delta(S,\pi) \in F$ iff $\sigma(\psi^k(\pi))=\varepsilon$ iff $\pi \in PL^k(G)$.

Lemma 2. Let $G = (\Phi,\Sigma,P,S)$ be a context-free grammar and $C \subseteq PL^k(G)$ be a context-free language. Then the Parikh mapping of $L_C^k(G)$ is semilinear.

Proof. Let $\rho_1 : P_k^* \to \mathbb{N}^{|P_k|}$ and $\rho_2 : \Sigma^* \to \mathbb{N}^{|\Sigma|}$, ($\mathbb{N}$ denotes the nonnegative integers) be Parikh mappings. Let $h : \mathbb{N}^{|P_k|} \to \mathbb{N}^{|\Sigma|}$ be the homomorphism defined by $h(\rho_1(p_{i_1,\ldots,i_r})) = \rho_2(\tau(\alpha_1\alpha_2\ldots\alpha_r))$ if $p_{i_j} : A_j \to \alpha_j \in P$. Then $h(\rho_1(\pi)) = \rho_2(\psi^k(\pi))$. Since the restricted mapping $\psi^k : C \to L_C^k(G)$ is surjective and $\rho_1(C)$ is semilinear, the lemma is proved.

Tree controlled grammars were introduced by Culik, Maurer [1] and are defined to be a pair (G,R), where $G = (\Phi,\Sigma,P,S)$ is a context-free grammar and $R \subseteq (\Phi \cup \Sigma)^*$ is regular. The language generated by (G,R) is denoted by $L(G,R)$ and defined by

$L(G,R) = \{w \in L(G) \mid$ there exists a derivation tree of w such that each word obtained by concatenating all symbols at any level from left to right is in R$\}$.

The original definition of Culik, Maurer [1] is slightly changed for technical reasons but yields the same family of languages.

A tree controlled grammar with finite control is a tree controlled grammar (G,R), where R is a finite language.

Rozenberg, Vermeir [8] introduced ETOL systems of uncontrolled index k. Let $G = (\Phi\cup\Sigma,\mathbf{P},S,\Sigma)$ be an ETOL system. A symbol $A \in \Phi\cup\Sigma$ is called active in G if there exist a table P and a word α in $(\Phi \cup \Sigma)^*$ such that $A \to \alpha$ is in P and $A \neq \alpha$. Then $A(G) = \{A \in \Phi\cup\Sigma \mid A$ is active in G$\}$.

The ETOL system G is of uncontrolled index k, if for every word $w \in L(G)$ whenever $\beta_1,\ldots,\beta_n$ is the trace of a derivation of w then the number of active symbols in each β_j, $1 \le j \le n$, is not greater than k. An ETOL system $G = (\Phi \cup \Sigma, \mathbf{P},S,\Sigma)$ is in active normal form, if $A(G) = \Phi$. Rozenberg, Vermeir [8] show that given an ETOL system of uncontrolled index k there always exists an equivalent ETOL system of uncontrolled index k in active normal form.

Lemma 3. Let (G,R) be a tree controlled grammar with finite control. Then there exist $k>0$ and a regular $C \subseteq PL^k(G)$ such that $L_C^k(G) = L(G,R)$.

Proof. Let $k = \max\{|\sigma(\alpha)| \mid \alpha \in R\}$, $K = \sigma(R)$ and $M = (K,P_k,\delta,S,\{\varepsilon\})$ (if $L(G,R) \neq \emptyset$, then $S \in R$ and $R \cap \Sigma^* \neq \emptyset$) be the incomplete finite deterministic automaton where

$$\delta(\alpha,p_{i_1,\ldots,i_r}) = \sigma(\psi_\alpha^k(p_{i_1,\ldots,i_r}) \cap R).$$

Let $S = \beta_0,\beta_1,\ldots,\beta_n$ be the levels of a derivation tree with yield w, $\beta_i \in R$, $0 \le i \le n$, and $p_{i_1}^{(j)},\ldots,p_{i_{m_j}}^{(j)}$ the productions applied to the variables of β_j to yield β_{j+1}. Then $\delta(\sigma(\beta_j),p_{i_1^{(j)},\ldots,i_{m_j}^{(j)}}) = \sigma(\beta_{j+1})$. Since $\beta_n \in \Sigma^*$ the controlword $v = p_{i_1^{(0)},\ldots,i_m^{(0)}} p_{i_1^{(1)},\ldots,i_{m_1}^{(1)}} \ldots p_{i_1^{(n-1)},\ldots,i_{m_{n-1}}^{(n-1)}}$ is in T(M). Since $\psi^k(v) = w$, the word w is in $L_C^k(G)$.

The second part of the proof is left to the reader.

Lemma 4. Let $G = (\Phi,\Sigma,P,S)$ be a context-free grammar, $k>0$ and $C \subseteq PL^k(G)$ regular. Then there exists a tree controlled grammar with finite control (G_1,R) such that $L(G_1,R) = L_C^k(G)$.

Proof. Let $M = (K,P_k,\delta,q_0,F)$ be an incomplete finite deterministic automaton without dead states and $T(M) = C$. We note the following facts:

(i) $q \in F$ iff $\delta(q,p)$ is undefined for all $p \in P_k$.

(ii) if $\delta(q,p_{i_1,\ldots,i_n})$ and $\delta(q,p_{\ell_1,\ldots,\ell_m})$ are both defined, then $n = m$ and $A_1\ldots A_n = B_1\ldots B_m$ if $p_{i_j} : A_j \to \alpha_j$, $1 \le j \le n$, $p_{\ell_j} : B_j \to \beta_j$, $1 \le \ell \le m$.

(iii) If $\delta(q_0,p_{i_1,\ldots,i_n})$ is defined, then $n = 1$ and $p_{i_1} : S \to \alpha$.

The context-free grammar $G_1 = (\Phi_1,\Sigma,P_1,S)$ and the finite set R are constructed as follows:

(a) $\Phi_1 = \{(q,p_{i_1,\ldots,i_n},1,A_1),\ldots,(q,p_{i_1,\ldots,i_n},n,A_n) \mid q \in K-F$, $\delta(q,p_{i_1,\ldots,i_n})$ defined and $p_{i_j} : A_j \to \alpha_j$, $1 \le j \le n\} \cup \{S\}$.

(b) (i) $S \in R$.

(ii) Let $\delta(q_0,p_i) = q_1$.

If $q_1 \in F$ and $p_i : S \to w$, $w \in \Sigma^*$. Then $S \to w \in P_1$ and $w \in R$.

If $q_1 \notin F$ and $p_i : S \to x_1B_1x_2\ldots x_mB_mx_{m+1}$, $m \ge 1$, $x_j \in \Sigma^*$, $B_j \in \Phi$, then for all $p_{j_1,\dots,j_m}$ where $\delta(q_1,p_{j_1,\dots,j_m})$ is defined (there exists at least one $p_{j_1,\dots,j_m}$) $S\to x_1(q_1,p_{j_1,\dots,j_m},1,B_1)x_2..x_m(q_1,p_{j_1,\dots,j_m},m,B_m)x_{m+1}\in P_1$ and $x_1(q_1,p_{j_1,\dots,j_m},1,B_1)x_2..x_m(q_1,p_{j_1,\dots,j_m},m,B_m)x_{m+1} \in R$.

(iii) Let $\delta(q,p_{i_1,\dots,i_n}) = q_1$, $p_{i_j} : A_{i_j} \to \alpha_{i_j}$, $1\le j\le n$.

If $q_1 \in F$, then $\alpha_{i_1}\alpha_{i_2}\dots\alpha_{i_n} \in \Sigma^*$ and $(q,p_{i_1,\dots,i_n},j,A_{i_j}) \to \alpha_{i_j} \in P_1$, $1\le j\le n$, and $\alpha_{i_1}\alpha_{i_2}\dots\alpha_{i_n} \in R$.

If $q_1 \notin F$ and $\alpha_{i_1}\dots\alpha_{i_n} = x_1B_1x_2\dots x_mB_mx_{m+1}$, $m\ge 1$, $x_j \in \Sigma^*$, $B_j \in \Phi$, then for all $p_{j_1,\dots,j_m}$ where $\delta(q_1,p_{j_1,\dots,j_m})$ is defined $(q,p_{i_1,\dots,i_n},j,A_{i_j}) \to \overline{\alpha}_{i_j} \in P_1$, $1\le j\le n$, and $\overline{\alpha}_{i_1}\overline{\alpha}_{i_2}\dots\overline{\alpha}_{i_n} \in R$. The words $\overline{\alpha}_{i_j}$ result from α_{i_j} by replacing each variable B in α_{i_j} by the variable $(q_1,p_{j_1,\dots j_m},\ell,B)$ such that $\overline{\alpha}_{i_1}\overline{\alpha}_{i_2}\dots\overline{\alpha}_{i_n} = x_1(q_1,p_{j_1,\dots,j_m},1,B_1)x_2\dots$ $\dots x_m(q_1,p_{j_1,\dots j_m},m,B_m)x_{m+1}$.

(1) Proof of $L_C^k(G) \subseteq L(G_1,R)$.

Let $w \in L_C^k(G)$, i.e. there exists a $\pi \in C$ such that $\psi^k(\pi) = w$. If $\pi = p_i$ the proof is trivial.

Let $\pi = p_ip_{i_1^{(1)},\dots,i_{n_1}^{(1)}}\dots p_{i_1^{(m)},\dots,i_{n_m}^{(m)}}$, $m\ge 1$, i.e. $\delta(q_0,p_i) = q^{(1)}$, $\delta(q^{(r)},p_{i_1^{(r)},\dots,i_{n_r}^{(r)}}) = q^{(r+1)}$, $1\le r<m$ and $\delta(q^{(m)},p_{i_1^{(m)},\dots,i_{n_m}^{(m)}}) \in F$.

Let $p_i : S \to x_1^{(1)}B_1^{(1)}\dots x_{n_1}^{(1)}B_{n_1}^{(1)}x_{n_1+1}^{(1)}$, $n_1\ge 1$, $x_j^{(1)} \in \Sigma^*$, $B_j^{(1)} \in \Phi$, and

$p_{i_j^{(r)}} : B_j^{(r)} \to \alpha_{i_j^{(r)}}$, $\alpha_{i_1^{(r)}}\dots\alpha_{i_{n_r}^{(r)}} = x_1^{(r+1)}B_1^{(r+1)}\dots x_{n_{r+1}}^{(r+1)}B_{n_{r+1}}^{(r+1)}x_{n_{r+1}+1}^{(r+1)}$, $n_r\ge 1$, $x_j^{(r+1)} \in \Sigma^*$, $B_j^{(r+1)} \in \Phi$, $1\le j\le n_r$, $1\le r<m$, and $p_{i_j^{(m)}}:B_j^{(m)}\to x_j\in\Sigma^*$, $1\le j\le n_m$.

Then the construction of P_1 yields the following productions:

$S\to x_1^{(1)}(q^{(1)},p_{i_1^{(1)},\dots,i_{n_1}^{(1)}},1,B_1^{(1)})\dots x_{n_1}^{(1)}(q^{(1)},p_{i_1^{(1)},\dots,i_{n_1}^{(1)}},n_1,B_{n_1}^{(1)})x_{n_1+1}^{(1)}$,

$(q^{(r)},p_{i_1^{(r)},\dots,i_{n_r}^{(r)}},j,B_j^{(r)}) \to \overline{\alpha}_{i_j^{(r)}}$, $1\le j\le n_r$, $1\le r<m$, and

$(q^{(m)},p_{i_1^{(m)},\dots,i_{n_m}^{(m)}},j,B_j^{(m)}) \to x_j \in \Sigma^*$, $1\le j\le n_m$.

Hence the levels of the derivation tree with yield w are S, β_1, $\beta_2,\dots\beta_m$, $x_1x_2\dots x_{n_m}$, where

$\beta_r = x_1^{(r)}(q^{(r)},p_{i_1^{(r)},\ldots,i_{n_r}^{(r)}},1,B_1^{(r)})\ldots x_{n_r}^{(r)}(q^{(r)},p_{i_1^{(r)},\ldots,i_{n_r}^{(r)}},n_r,B_{n_r}^{(r)})x_{n_r+1}^{(r)}$,

$1 \leq r \leq m$. By construction of R, $\{S,\beta_1,\beta_2,\ldots,\beta_m,x_1x_2\ldots x_{n_m}\} \subseteq R$.
Hence $w \in L(G_1,R)$.

(2) Proof of $L(G_1,R) \subseteq L_C^k(G)$.
Let $w \in L(G_1,R)$ with levels of the derivation tree with yield w being $S,\beta_1,\beta_2,\ldots,\beta_m,x$. Let

$\beta_r = x_1^{(r)}(q^{(r)},p_{i_1^{(r)},\ldots,i_{n_r}^{(r)}},1,B_1^{(r)})\ldots x_{n_r}^{(r)}(q^{(r)},p_{i_1^{(r)},\ldots,i_{n_r}^{(r)}},n_r,B_{n_r}^{(r)})x_{n_r+1}^{(r)}$.

Then by construction, the automaton M and the set of productions P have the following properties:

(i) There exists a $p_i \in P_k$, such that $\delta(q_0,p_i)=q^{(1)}$, $\delta(q^{(1)},p_{i_1^{(1)},\ldots,i_n^{(1)}})$ is defined and $p_i : S \to x_1^{(1)}B_1^{(1)}x_2^{(1)}\ldots x_{n_1}^{(1)}B_{n_1}^{(1)}x_{n_1+1}^{(1)}$.

(ii) $\delta(q^{(r)},p_{i_1^{(r)},\ldots,i_{n_r}^{(r)}}) = q^{(r+1)}$, $\delta(q^{(r+1)},p_{i_1^{(r+1)},\ldots i_{n_{r+1}}^{(r+1)}})$ is defined and $p_{i_j^{(r)}} : B_j^{(r)} \to \alpha_{i_j}^{(r)}$, $1 \leq j \leq n_r$, such that $\alpha_{i_1}^{(r)}\alpha_{i_2}^{(r)}\ldots\alpha_{i_{n_r}}^{(r)} =$
$= x_1^{(r+1)}B_1^{(r+1)}x_2^{(r+1)}\ldots x_{n_{r+1}}^{(r+1)}B_{n_{r+1}}^{(r+1)}x_{n_{r+1}+1}^{(r+1)}$, $1 \leq r < m$.

(iii) $\delta(q^{(m)},p_{i_1^{(m)},\ldots,i_{n_m}^{(m)}}) \in F$ and $p_{i_j^{(m)}} : B_j^{(m)} \to x_j$, $1 \leq j \leq n_m$, such that $x_1x_2\ldots x_{n_m} = x$.

Let $\pi = p_ip_{i_1^{(1)},\ldots,i_{n_1}^{(1)}}p_{i_1^{(2)},\ldots,i_{n_2}^{(2)}}\ldots p_{i_1^{(m)},\ldots,i_{n_m}^{(m)}}$. Then $\pi \in C$, $\psi^k(\pi) = w$ and hence $w \in L_C^k(G)$.

Let $h : (\Phi_1 \cup \Sigma)^* \to (\Phi \cup \Sigma)^*$ be the homomorphism defined by $h(a) = a$, $a \in \Sigma$, $h((q,p_{i_1,\ldots,i_n},j,A)) = A$ otherwise. Then the construction of the proof yields an isomorphism between the derivation trees of G_1 and G, such that corresponding nodes are labelled by A and h(A) and the concatenation of all symbols of corresponding levels yields α and $h(\alpha)$.

<u>Lemma 5.</u> Let $G = (\Phi\cup\Sigma,\mathbf{P},S,\Sigma)$ be an ETOL system of uncontrolled index $k>0$ in active normal form. Then there exists a tree controlled grammar with finite control (G_1,R) such that $L(G_1,R) = L(G)$.

<u>Proof.</u> Let $\mathbf{P} = \{P_1,\ldots,P_n\}$. Then $G_1 = (\Phi_1,\Sigma,P,S)$ is constructed as follows:

$\Phi_1 = (\Phi \times \{1,2,\ldots,n\}) \cup \{S\}$

$P = \{(A,i) \to x_1(B_1,j)\ldots x_m(B_m,j)x_{m+1} \mid A \to x_1B_1\ldots x_mB_mx_{m+1} \in P_i, 1 \leq i,j \leq n\} \cup$

$\cup \{S \to x_1(B_1,j)x_2..x_m(B_m,j)x_{m+1} \mid S \to x_1B_1x_2..x_mB_mx_{m+1} \in P_i,\ 1 \le i,j \le n\}$.

Let $\ell = \max\{|\alpha| \mid A \to \alpha \in P_i,\ 1 \le i \le n\}$. Then $S \overset{*}{\Longrightarrow} x_1A_1x_2...x_mA_mx_{m+1} \Longrightarrow$ $\Longrightarrow x_1\alpha_1x_2...x_m\alpha_mx_{m+1}$, $x_i \in \Sigma^*$, $A_i \in \Phi$ implies $|\alpha_1\alpha_2...\alpha_m| \le k\ell$.

Hence R needs only to contain words of length not greater than $k\ell$ and R is finite. Each word of R contains only variables whose second components are identical. This guarantees the application of productions of one table in going from one level of the derivation tree to the next level. Hence

$$R = \bigcup_{j=0}^{k\ell} \left[(\Phi \times \{1\} \cup \Sigma)^j \cup \ldots \cup (\Phi \times \{n\} \cup \Sigma)^j\right]$$

is a possible choice for controlling the levels of the derivation tree.

Lemma 6. Let (G,R) be a tree controlled grammar with finite control. Then there exists an EDTOL system G_1 of uncontrolled finite index, such that $L(G_1) = L(G,R)$.

Proof. If $L(G,R) = \emptyset$ the lemma is trivial. Hence let $S \in R$. Label the words of $R - \Sigma^*$. The EDTOL system $G_1 = (\Phi_1 \cup \Sigma, \mathbf{P}, S, \Sigma)$ is constructed as follows:

(1) $\Phi_1 = \{(\ell,1,A_1),\ldots,(\ell,m,A_m) \mid x_1A_1x_2...x_mA_mx_{m+1} \in R$ with label $\ell\} \cup$ $\cup \{S,X\}$, where X is a new symbol.

(2) (i) Let $S \to \alpha \in P$ and $\alpha \in R$.

If $\alpha \in \Sigma^*$, then $\{S\to\alpha\} \cup \{B\to X \mid B\in\Phi_1-\{S\}\} \cup \{a\to a \mid a\in\Sigma\}$ is a table in $\mathbf{P}$.

If $\alpha = x_1A_1x_2...x_mA_mx_{m+1}$ and α is labelled by ℓ, then $\{S \to x_1(\ell,1,A_1)x_2...$ $...x_m(\ell,m,A_m)x_{m+1}\} \cup \{B \to X \mid B \in \Phi_1 - \{S\}\} \cup \{a \to a \mid a \in \Sigma\}$ is a table in $\mathbf{P}$.

(ii) Let $x_1A_1x_2...x_mA_mx_{m+1} \in R$ with label ℓ and $A_j \to \alpha_j \in P$, $1 \le j \le m$, such that $\alpha_1\alpha_2...\alpha_m \in R$.

If $\alpha_1\alpha_2...\alpha_m \in \Sigma^*$, then $\{(\ell,j,A_j) \to \alpha_j \mid 1\le j\le m\} \cup \{B\to X \mid B\in\Phi_1 - \{(\ell,j,A_j) \mid 1\le j\le m\}\}$ $\cup \{a \to a \mid a \in \Sigma\}$ is a table in $\mathbf{P}$.

If $\alpha_1\alpha_2...\alpha_m = y_1B_1y_2...y_rB_ry_{r+1}$ and is labelled by ℓ_1 then $\{(\ell,j,A_j) \to \bar{\alpha}_j \mid 1\le j\le m\} \cup \{B \to X \mid B \in \Phi_1-\{(\ell,j,A_j) \mid 1\le j\le m\}\} \cup \{a \to a \mid a \in \Sigma\}$ is a table in $\mathbf{P}$ where $\bar{\alpha}_j$ results from α_j by replacing each variable B in α_j by (ℓ_1,k,B) in such a way that $\bar{\alpha}_1\bar{\alpha}_2...\bar{\alpha}_m = y_1(\ell_1,1,B_1)..y_r(\ell_1,r,B_r)y_{r+1}$.

The derivations in G and G_1 correspond to each other in the following way: The level $\alpha = x_1A_1x_2...x_mA_mx_{m+1} \in R$ with label ℓ corresponds to $S \overset{*}{\Longrightarrow} \beta = x_1'(\ell,1,A_1)x_2'...x_m'(\ell,m,A_m)x_{m+1}'$. The productions $A_j \to \alpha_j$, $1 \le j \le m$

can be applied to α, $\alpha_1\alpha_2\ldots\alpha_m = y_1B_1y_2\ldots y_rB_ry_{r+1} \in R$ labelled by ℓ_1 iff a table constructed in (ii) can be applied to β with result $y_1'(\ell_1,1,B_1)y_2'\ldots y_r'(\ell_1,r,B_r)y_{r+1}'$. Any other table not corresponding to ℓ_1 contains the productions $(\ell,j,A_j) \to X$, $1 \le j \le m$. Applying such a table would yield a word which can not derive a word over the terminal alphabet.

Theorem 1. The families of languages

(i) $\{L_C^k(G) \mid G$ context-free grammar, $C \subseteq PL^k(G)$ regular, $k>0\}$

(ii) $\{L(G,R) \mid (G,R)$ tree controlled grammar with finite control$\}$

(iii) $\{L(G) \mid G$ ETOL system of uncontrolled index k, $k>0\}$

coincide.

Hence Theorem 1 yields two more characterizations of the family of languages considered in Rozenberg, Vermeir [8], (see Theorem 10 (1)).

THE HEIGHT OF DERIVATION TREES

Let $G = (\Phi,\Sigma,P,S)$ be a context-free grammar, $C \subseteq PL^k(G)$ regular, $k>0$ fixed. The set of derivation trees generated by G with parallel control language C is denoted by $T^k(G,C)$. The height $h(t)$ of a tree t is defined to be the maximal length of a path from the root to the leaves. The yield $r(t)$ of a tree t is defined to be the word resulting from going around the tree in positive direction and concatenating the labels of the leaves. Note that $h(t) \ge 1$ and $r(t) \in \Sigma^*$, if $t \in T^k(G,C)$.

Let $\chi : P_k^* \to \mathbb{N}$ be the homomorphism defined by $\chi(p) = |\tau(\alpha)|$ if $p = p_{i_1,\ldots,i_n} \in P_k$, $p_{i_j} : A_{i_j} \to \alpha_j$, $1 \le j \le n$, and $\alpha = \alpha_1\alpha_2\ldots\alpha_n$. Hence $\chi(\pi)$, $\pi \in C$, yields the number of terminal symbols generated by π, i.e. $\chi(\pi) = |\psi^k(\pi)|$.

Let $\rho : C \to T^k(G,C)$ be the natural bijective mapping between controlwords and derivation trees. Then $\chi(\pi) = |r(\rho(\pi))|$ and $|\pi| = h(\rho(\pi))$.

Let $T^k_{m,n}(G,C) \subseteq T^k(G,C)$ be the finite set of trees of height m and length of yield n. Let $a_{m,n} = |T^k_{m,n}(G,C)|$ be the number of trees t with $h(t)=m$ and $|r(t)| = n$, and let $f(y,z) = \sum_{n=0}^{\infty} \sum_{m=1}^{\infty} a_{m,n} y^m z^n$, y,z complex variables, be the generating function of the numbers $a_{m,n}$. If $\sum_{m=1}^{\infty} a_{m,n}$ exists, let $a_n = \sum_{m=1}^{\infty} a_{m,n}$. If $f(y,z)$ is analytic then

$f(1,z) = \sum_{n=0}^{\infty} a_n z^n$ is the generating function of the numbers a_n. If $L_C^k(G)$ is generated k-unambiguously, then $f(1,z)$ is the structure generating function of $L_C^k(G)$ as defined in Kuich [5] (see also Kuich, Maurer [6], and Kuich, Shyamasundar [7]).

Define the average height s_n of derivation trees with yield of length n, considering all such trees to be equally likely, to be

$$s_n = \frac{\sum_{m=1}^{\infty} m a_{m,n}}{a_n} \qquad \text{if } a_n>0$$

and

$$s_n = 0 \qquad \text{if } a_n=0.$$

If $f(y,z)$ is analytic, then

$$f_y(y,z) = \sum_{n=0}^{\infty} \sum_{m=1}^{\infty} m a_{m,n} y^{m-1} z^n$$

and hence

$$f_y(1,z) = \sum_{n=0}^{\infty} b_n z^n, \quad b_n = \sum_{m=1}^{\infty} m a_{m,n} \text{ if } a_n,\ n\geq 0 \text{ exist.}$$

Our goal is to compute $f(y,z)$, s_n, $n\geq 0$ and the asymptotic behaviour of s_n with $n \to \infty$.

Let $M = (\{q_0,q_1,\ldots,q_\ell\},P_k,\delta,q_1,\{q_0\})$ be an incomplete finite deterministic automaton generating C. Without loss of generality M has exactly one final state and $\delta(q_0,p)$ is undefined for all $p \in P_k$.

According to Salomaa, Soittola [10] define the $(\ell+1)\times(\ell+1)$ matrices $A(p) = (a_{ij}(p))$, $p \in P_k$ by

$$a_{ij}(p) = \begin{cases} 1 \text{ if } \delta(q_i,p) = q_j \\ 0 \text{ otherwise} \end{cases} \qquad 0\leq i,j\leq \ell .$$

If $\pi = p^{(i_1)}\ldots p^{(i_r)} \in P_k^*$, define $A(\pi) = A(p^{(i_1)})\ldots A(p^{(i_r)})$.

Then the characteristic series of C is given by

$$\text{char } C = \sum_{\pi\in P_k^*} e_1^T A(\pi) e_0 \pi,$$

where e_i is the i-th $(\ell+1)$-column vector of unity.

Let $Q_1 = \sum_{p\in P_k} A(p)p$. Then by Salomaa, Soittola [10] char $C = e_1^T Q_1^+ e_0$.

Since $a_{0j}(p) = 0$ for $0\leq j\leq \ell$, $p \in P_k$, Q_1 has the form

$$Q_1 = \begin{pmatrix} 0 & 0 \\ q & Q \end{pmatrix}$$

where Q is an $\ell\times\ell$ matrix and 0 are zero matrices. Hence

$$Q_1^+ e_o = (I + \begin{pmatrix} 0 & 0 \\ 0 & Q^+ \end{pmatrix}) \begin{pmatrix} 0 \\ q \end{pmatrix},$$

where I is the matrix of unity, and

$$\text{char } C = e_1^T (I + Q^+) q$$

is a formal power series which equals the first component of the solution of the system

$$X = q + QX, \; X = \begin{pmatrix} x_1 \\ \vdots \\ x_\ell \end{pmatrix}.$$

Denote by $c(\{y,z\}^*)$ the free commutative monoid generated by $\{y,z\}$. Let

$$\varphi : \mathbb{N}\langle\langle P_k^* \rangle\rangle \to \mathbb{N}\langle\langle c(\{y,z\}^*) \rangle\rangle$$

be the homomorphism defined by

$$\varphi(p) = yz^{\chi(p)}, \; p \in P_k.$$

Then

$$\varphi(\pi) = y^{|\pi|} z^{\chi(\pi)} = y^{h(\rho(\pi))} z^{|r(\rho(\pi))|}, \; \pi \in C$$

and

$$\varphi(\text{char } C) = \sum_{n=0}^{\infty} \sum_{m=1}^{\infty} a_{m,n} y^m z^n.$$

Since $\text{char } C \in \mathbb{N}^{rat}\langle\langle P_k^* \rangle\rangle$ and $\varphi(\pi)$ is a quasiregular rational series for every $\pi \in P_k^+$, Theorem 4.2 of Salomaa, Soittola [10] implies that

$$f(y,z) \in \mathbb{N}^{rat}\langle\langle c(\{y,z\}^*) \rangle\rangle$$

and

$$f(y,z) = e_1^T (I + \varphi(Q^+)) \varphi(q).$$

Hence $f(y,z)$ is the first component of the solution of the system

$$X = yr(z) + yR(z)X,$$

where $\varphi(q) = yr(z)$ and $\varphi(Q) = yR(z)$, and

$$f(y,z) = e_1^T (I - yR(z))^{-1} yr(z).$$

Let $R(z) = (r_{ij}(z))$, $1 \le i,j \le \ell$ and $r(z) = (r_{io}(z))$, $1 \le i \le \ell$, then

$$f(y,z) = \det^{-1}(I - yR(z))\, y \begin{vmatrix} r_{1o}(z) & -yr_{12}(z) & \dots & -yr_{1\ell}(z) \\ r_{2o}(z) & 1-yr_{22}(z) & \dots & -yr_{2\ell}(z) \\ \vdots & \vdots & & \vdots \\ r_{\ell o}(z) & -yr_{\ell 2}(z) & \dots & 1-yr_{\ell\ell}(z) \end{vmatrix}$$

Since formally

$$\frac{\partial}{\partial y} \left[(I - yR(z))^{-1} y \right] = (I - yR(z))^{-2}$$

the methods of matrix analysis yield

$$f_y(y,z) = e_1^T (I - yR(z))^{-2} r(z).$$

Theorem 2. The generating function $f(y,z)$ of the derivation trees that are generated by a context-free grammar with regular parallel control language and counted according to height and length of yield is given by $f(y,z) = e_1^T(I - yR(z))^{-1}yr(z)$.

The language $L_C^k(G)$ is generated by a context-free grammar $G = (\Phi,\Sigma,P,S)$ with regular parallel control language C in non-cyclic form iff $\pi_1\pi_2^i\pi_3 \in C$ for infinitely many $i \geq 0$ and $\psi^k(\pi_1) = \alpha$, $\psi_\alpha^k(\pi_2) = \alpha$ imply $\pi_2 = \varepsilon$.

This definition makes sure that each word of $L_C^k(G)$ is the yield of only a finite number of derivation trees and hence the numbers a_n exist.

Lemma 7. Let $G = (\Phi,\Sigma,P,S)$ be a context-free grammar and $C \subseteq PL^k(G)$ be regular. Then there exists $C_1 \subseteq C$ such that

(i) C_1 is regular

(ii) $L_{C_1}^k(G) = L_C^k(G)$

(iii) $L_{C_1}^k(G)$ is generated by G with C_1 in non-cyclic form

(iv) each $\pi \in C$ has a factorization $\pi = \pi_0'\pi_1\pi_1'\ldots\pi_r\pi_r'$, where $\psi^k(\pi_0')=S=\alpha_0$, $\psi_{\alpha_j}^k(\pi_{j+1})=\alpha_{j+1}$, $\psi_{\alpha_{j+1}}^k(\pi_{j+1}')=\alpha_{j+1}$, $0 \leq j < r$, such that $\pi_1\pi_2\ldots\pi_r \in C_1$.

Proof. Let $M = (K,P_k,\delta,q_o,F)$ be an incomplete finite deterministic automaton accepting C. Let $D = \{\pi_1\pi_2\pi_3 \in C \mid \pi_2 \neq \varepsilon,\ \delta(q_o,\pi_1) = q,\ \delta(q,\pi_2)=q$ $\psi^k(\pi_1) = \alpha,\ \psi_\alpha^k(\pi_2) = \alpha\}$ and $C_1 = C - D$.

(1) Proof of C_1 is regular. It suffices to show D is regular.
Let $F : (\Phi\cup\Sigma)^* \to (\Phi\cup\{\$\})^*$ be defined by $F(x_1A_1x_2\ldots x_nA_nx_{n+1}) = A_1z_2\ldots z_nA_n$, where $z_i = \$$ if $x_i \neq \varepsilon$, $z_i = \varepsilon$ if $x_i = \varepsilon$, $2 \leq i \leq n$.

Then $F(\psi_{\alpha_1}^k(\pi)) = F(\psi_{\alpha_2}^k(\pi))$ if $F(\alpha_1) = F(\alpha_2)$.

Let $\overline{P}_k = \{p_{i_1,\ldots,i_n} \in P_k \mid p_{i_j} : A_{i_j} \to \alpha_j,\ \alpha_1\alpha_2\ldots\alpha_n \in \Phi^*,\ 1 \leq j \leq n\}$.

Then $\psi_\alpha^k(\pi) = \alpha$ implies $\pi \in \overline{P}_k^*$. Hence $\{\pi \in P_k \mid \psi_\alpha^k(\pi)=\alpha\} = \{\pi' \in \overline{P}_k \mid F(\psi_\alpha^k(\pi'))= =F(\alpha)\}$. Since all considered α are in Φ_k and $F(\Phi_k)$ is finite, a finite indeterministic automaton $M_1 = (K_1,P_k,\delta_1,q_1,F_1)$ with $T(M_1) = D$ is constructed as follows:

$K_1=K\cup\{A_{q,F(\alpha)} \mid q\in K,\alpha\in\Phi_k\}\cup\{B_{q,F(\alpha)}^{p,F(\gamma)} \mid p,q\in K,\alpha,\gamma\in\Phi_k\}$, $q_1=A_{q_o,S}$, $F_1=F$ and

δ_1 is defined by

(a) if $\delta(q,p_{i_1,\ldots,i_n}) = r$ and $\psi_\alpha^k(p_{i_1,\ldots,i_n}) = \beta$, $q\in K$, $\alpha,\beta\in\Phi_k$, $p_{i_1,\ldots,i_n}\in P_k$ then $A_{r,F(\alpha)}\in\delta_1(A_{q,F(\alpha)},p_{i_1,\ldots,i_n})$, $r\in\delta_1(q,p_{i_1,\ldots,i_n})$, $r\in\delta_1(B^{q,F(\alpha)}_{q,F(\alpha)},p_{i_1,\ldots,i_n})$.

(b) if $\delta(q,p_{i_1,\ldots,i_n}) = r$ and $\psi_\alpha^k(p_{i_1,\ldots,i_n}) = \beta$, $q\in K$, $\alpha,\beta\in\Phi_k$, $p_{i_1,\ldots,i_n}\in\overline{P}_k$ then $B^{q,F(\alpha)}_{r,F(\beta)}\in\delta_1(A_{q,F(\alpha)},p_{i_1,\ldots,i_n})$, $B^{p,F(\gamma)}_{r,F(\beta)}\in\delta_1(B^{p,F(\gamma)}_{q,F(\alpha)},p_{i_1,\ldots,i_n})$ for all $p\in K$, $\gamma\in\Phi_k$.

M accepts the words of D as follows:

Let $\pi_1\pi_2\pi_3\in D$, i.e. $\pi_2\neq\varepsilon$, $\delta(q_o,\pi_1)=q$, $\delta(q,\pi_2)=q$, $\delta(q,\pi_3)=r\notin F$, $\psi^k(\pi_1)=\alpha$ and $\psi_\alpha^k(\pi_2)=\alpha$. Then $A_{q,F(\alpha)}\in\delta_1(A_{q_o,S},\pi_1)$ by rules (a), $B^{q,F(\alpha)}_{q,F(\alpha)}\in\delta_1(A_{q,F(\alpha)},\pi_2)$ by rules (b) and $r\in\delta_1(B^{q,F(\alpha)}_{q,F(\alpha)},\pi_3)$ by rules (a). Since $r\in\overline{F}=F_1$, $\pi_1\pi_2\pi_3\in T(M_1)$. The proof of $T(M_1)\subseteq D$ is left to the reader.

(2) Proof of (iv).
Let $\pi\in C$ have a factorization $\pi=\pi_o'\pi_1\pi_1'\ldots\pi_r\pi_r'$ such that: $\delta(q_o,\pi_o')=q_o$, $\delta(q_j,\pi_{j+1})=q_{j+1}$, $\delta(q_{j+1},\pi_{j+1}')=q_{j+1}$, $0\leq j\leq r$, and $\pi_1\pi_2\ldots\pi_r$ has no factorization $\eta_1\eta_2\eta_3$, $\eta_2\neq\varepsilon$, $\delta(q_o,\eta_1)=q$, $\delta(q,\eta_2)=q$. Then $\pi_1\pi_2\ldots\pi_r\in C_1$.

(3) Proof of (ii).
Let π and π_j, $1\leq j\leq r$ as in (2). Since $\psi^k(\pi_1\ldots\pi_r)=\psi^k(\pi)$, $L^k_C(G)\subseteq L^k_{C_1}(G)$ is implied. Since $C_1\subseteq C$, $L^k_{C_1}(G)\subseteq L^k_C(G)$ is implied.

(4) Proof of (iii).
If $L^k_{C_1}(G)$ is generated by G with C_1 not in non-cyclic form, then there would exist π_1,π_2,π_3, such that $\pi_2\neq\varepsilon$, $\pi_1\pi_2^i\pi_3\in C_1$ for infinitely many i and $\psi^k(\pi_1)=\alpha$, $\psi_\alpha^k(\pi_2)=\alpha$. Let $n=|K|$ and $\delta(q_o,\pi_1)=q$. Then there exist ℓ,m with $1\leq\ell<m\leq n+1$, such that $\delta(q,\pi_2^\ell)=\delta(q,\pi_2^m)=q_1$. Choose $i_o\geq m$ such that $\pi_1\pi_2^{i_o}\pi_3\in C_1$. Then $\pi_1\pi_2^{i_o}\pi_3=\pi_1\pi_2^\ell\pi_2^{m-\ell}\pi_2^{i_o-m}\pi_3$, $m-\ell>0$, $\delta(q_o,\pi_1\pi_2^\ell)=q_1$, $\delta(q_1,\pi_2^{m-\ell})=q_1$, $\psi^k(\pi_1\pi_2^\ell)=\alpha$, $\psi_\alpha^k(\pi_2^{m-\ell})=\alpha$. Hence $\pi_1\pi_2^{i_o}\pi_3\in D$, contradicting $\pi_1\pi_2^{i_o}\pi_3\in C_1$.
Intuitively, the set D contains a "minimal" set of controlwords to be excluded, such that the generated language remains unchanged and by (iv) each derivation tree of $L^k_C(G)$ has a "similar" derivation tree of $L^k_{C_1}(G)$.

<u>Lemma 8.</u> Let s_n be the average height of derivation trees with yield of length n generated by a context-free grammar G with regular infinite parallel control language C in non-cyclic form. Then there exist constants c_1, c_2 with $0<c_1<c_2$ such that if $s_n>0$

$$c_1 n \le s_n \le c_2(n+1).$$

<u>Proof.</u> Let $M = (K, P_k, \delta, q_1, F)$ be an incomplete finite deterministic automaton accepting C. Let $\pi = p^{(1)}p^{(2)}\ldots p^{(m)} \in C$ with

$$S = \gamma_0 \underset{p^{(1)}}{\Longrightarrow} \gamma_1 \underset{p^{(2)}}{\Longrightarrow} \cdots \underset{p^{(m)}}{\Longrightarrow} \gamma_m = w \in \Sigma^*.$$

Consider any t consecutive steps of the derivation, $t \ge |K|$,

$$\gamma_s \underset{p^{(s+1)}}{\Longrightarrow} \gamma_{s+1} \underset{p^{(s+2)}}{\Longrightarrow} \cdots \underset{p^{(s+t)}}{\Longrightarrow} \gamma_{s+t}, \quad 0 \le s \le m-t.$$

Then there exist i,j, $0 \le i<j \le t$ such that $\sigma(\gamma_{s+i}) = \sigma(\gamma_{s+j})$ and $|\tau(\gamma_{s+j})| \ge |\tau(\gamma_{s+i})|+1$. Hence $m \le c_2(|\tau(\gamma_m)|+1)$, $c_2=|K|$.
Let $c_1^{-1} = \max\{|\tau(\alpha_1\alpha_2\ldots\alpha_r)| \mid$ there exist q and $p_{i_1,\ldots,i_r}$, such that $\delta(q,p_{i_1,\ldots,i_r})$ is defined and $p_{i_j} : A_{i_j} \to \alpha_j$, $1 \le j \le r\}$.
Hence $|\tau(\gamma_{s+1})| \le |\tau(\gamma_s)|+c_1^{-1}$, $0 \le s \le m-1$, and $|\tau(\gamma_m)| \le mc_1^{-1}$.
Hence $c_1 r(\rho(\pi)) \le h(\rho(\pi)) \le c_2(r(\rho(\pi))+1)$ and

$$a_n c_1 n \le \sum_{r(\rho(\pi))=n} h(\rho(\pi)) \le a_n c_2(n+1).$$

Since $\sum_{r(\rho(\pi))=n} h(\rho(\pi)) = \sum_{m=1}^{\infty} m a_{m,n}$, the lemma is proven.

In the sequel only derivation trees are considered that are generated by context-free grammars with regular <u>infinite</u> parallel control language in non-cyclic form.

According to the properties of context-free grammars with regular parallel control languages in non-cyclic form, the matrix R(O) is nilpotent and hence $f(1,z)$ and $f_y(1,z)$ exist and are given by

$$f(1,z) = e_1^T(I - R(z))^{-1} r(z)$$

and

$$f_y(1,z) = e_1^T(I - R(z))^{-2} r(z).$$

Furthermore, $f(1,z)$ and $f_y(1,z)$ are in $\mathbb{N}^{rat}\langle\langle z^*\rangle\rangle$.

Let $\alpha_1^{-1},\ldots,\alpha_s^{-1}$ and $\alpha_{s+1}^{-1},\ldots,\alpha_{s+r}^{-1}$ be the distinct poles of $f(1,z)$ and $f_y(1,z)$. Then Lemma 9.7 of Salomaa, Soittola [10] implies

$$a_n = \sum_{i=1}^{s} P_i(n)\alpha_i^n, \quad b_n = \sum_{i=1}^{r} Q_i(n)\alpha_{s+i}^n$$

for large values of n, where $P_i(n)$, $Q_i(n)$ are polynomials.

Applying Corollary 10.3 of Salomaa, Soittola [10], there exist p_1, p_2 such that

$$a_{j+np_1} \sim c'_j n^{\ell'_j} \beta'^n_j \;, \quad 0 \le j < p_1,\; c'_j > 0,\; \ell'_j \ge 0,\; \beta'_j \ge 0$$

and

$$b_{j+np_2} \sim d'_j n^{m'_j} \gamma'^n_j \;, \quad 0 \le j < p_2,\; d'_j > 0,\; m'_j \ge 0,\; \gamma'_j \ge 0.$$

Let p be the least common multiple of p_1 and p_2. Then

$$a_{j+np} \sim c_j n^{\ell_j} \beta^n_j \;, \quad b_{j+np} \sim d_j n^{m_j} \gamma^n_j \;,$$

$0 \le j < p$, $c_j, d_j > 0$, $\ell_j, m_j \ge 0$, $\beta_j, \gamma_j \ge 0$.

If $\beta_j \ne 0$ then $\gamma_j \ne 0$ and Lemma 8 implies

$$c_1 n \lesssim s_{j+np} \sim \frac{d_j n^{m_j} \gamma^n_j}{c_j n^{\ell_j} \beta^n_j} \le c_2 n.$$

This implies $\beta_j = \gamma_j$, $m_j = \ell_j + 1$. Hence $s_{j+np} \sim \frac{d_j}{c_j} n = e_j n \sim \frac{e_j}{p}(j+np)$, where $e_j = \frac{d_j}{c_j}$. If $\beta_j = 0$ then $\gamma_j = 0$. In this case define $e_j = 0$.

Define $g(j+np) = \frac{e_j}{p}$, then $s_n \sim g(n)n$.

<u>Theorem 3.</u> The average height s_n of derivation trees that are generated by a context-free grammar with regular infinite parallel control language in non-cyclic form is given by

$$s_n \sim g(n)n,$$

where g(n) is a bounded periodic function.

<u>EXAMPLE</u>

Let $G = (\Phi, \Sigma, P, S)$, where $\Phi = \{S,A,C,D\}$, $\Sigma = \{a,b,c,d\}$ and $P = \{p_1: S \to ACD,$ $p_2: A \to aAb, p_3: A \to ab, p_4: C \to cC, p_5: C \to c, p_6: D \to dD, p_7: D \to d\}$ and $C = p_1 p^*_{2,4,6}(p_{3,5,7} + p_{3,5,6} p^*_6 p_7 + p_{2,4,7} p^*_{2,4} p_{3,5})$. Then $L_C(G) = \{a^n b^n c^n \mid n \ge 1\} d^+$.

This yields

$$R(z) = \begin{pmatrix} 0 & 1 & 0 & 0 \\ 0 & z^4 & z^4 & z^4 \\ 0 & 0 & z^3 & 0 \\ 0 & 0 & 0 & z \end{pmatrix} \qquad r(z) = \begin{pmatrix} 0 \\ z^4 \\ z^3 \\ z \end{pmatrix}$$

Hence

$$f(y,z) = \frac{y^2z^4-y^4z^8}{(1-yz)(1-yz^3)(1-yz^4)}$$

and

$$f(1,z) = \frac{z^4}{(1-z)(1-z^3)}\ ,\quad f_y(1,z) = \frac{2z^4+3z^5+4z^6+4z^7+z^8-z^{10}}{(1-z^3)^2(1-z^4)}\ .$$

This yields $a_o=0$ and $a_{3k}=a_{3k-1}=a_{3k-2}=k-1$ for $k\geq 1$, $b_{12k-j}=26k^2+c_jk+d_j$ for $k\geq 1$, $0\leq j\leq 11$, and $s_n \sim \frac{13}{24}n$.

REFERENCES.

[1] CULIK,K. and MAURER,H.A., Tree Controlled Grammars, Computing 19 (1977), 129-139.

[2] DE BRUIJN,N.G., KNUTH,D.E. and RICE,S.O., The average height of planted plane trees, in Graph Theory and Computing (R.C.Read, ed.), Academic Press, 1972, 15-22.

[3] KEMP,R., The average height of a derivation tree generated by a linear grammar in a special Chomskynormalform, Technical Report A78/01, 1978, Universität des Saarlandes.

[4] KNUTH,D.E., The Art of Computer Programming, Vol.1: Fundamental Algorithms, Addison-Wesley, 1972.

[5] KUICH,W., On the entropy of context-free languages, Information and Control 16 (1970), 173-200.

[6] KUICH,W. and MAURER,H.A., On the structure generating function and entropy of tuple languages, Information and Control 19 (1971),195-203

[7] KUICH,W. and SHYAMASUNDAR,R.K., The structure generating function of some families of languages, Information and Control 32(1976),85-92.

[8] ROZENBERG,G. and VERMEIR,D., On the Effect of the Finite Index Restriction on Several Families of Grammars. Information and Control 39(1978), 284-302.

[9] SALOMAA,A., Formal Languages, Academic Press, 1973.

[10] SALOMAA,A. and SOITTOLA,M., Automata-Theoretic aspects of Formal Power Series, Springer, 1978.

THE MODAL LOGIC OF PROGRAMS

by

Zohar Manna
Stanford University and Weizmann Institute

and

Amir Pnueli
Tel-Aviv University

ABSTRACT

We explore the general framework of Modal Logic and its applicability to program reasoning. We relate the basic concepts of Modal Logic to the programming environment: the concept of "world" corresponds to a program state, and the concept of "accessibility relation" corresponds to the relation of derivability between states during execution. Thus we adopt the Temporal interpretation of Modal Logic. The variety of program properties expressible within the modal formalism is demonstrated.

The first axiomatic system studied, the sometime system, is adequate for proving total correctness and 'eventuality' properties. However, it is inadequate for proving invariance properties. The stronger nexttime system obtained by adding the next operator is shown to be adequate for invariances as well.

I. THE GENERAL CONCEPTS OF MODAL LOGIC

In the hierarchic development of logic as a formalization tool, we can observe different levels of variability. Propositional Calculus was developed to express constant or absolute truth stating basic facts about the universe of discourse. This framework mainly deals with the question of how does the truth of a composite sentence depend on the truth of its constituents. In Predicate Calculus we deal with variable or relative truth by distinguishing the statement (the predicate) from its arguments. It is understood that the statement may be true or false according to the individuals it is applied to. Thus we may regard predicates as parameterized propositions. The Modal Calculus adds another dimension of variability to the description by predicates. If we contemplate a major transition in which not only

---

This is a preliminary abridged version of a forthcoming Technical Report, Computer Science Department, Stanford University.

This research was supported in part by the National Science Foundation under Grant MCS76-83655 and by the Advanced Research Projects Agency of the Department of Defense under Contract MDA903-76-C-0206.

individuals are changed, but possibly the complete structure of basic premises and meaning of predicates, then the Modal Calculus suggests a special notation to denote this major change. Thus any chain of reasoning which is valid on Earth may become invalid on Mars because some of the basic concepts naturally used on Earth may assume completely different meanings (or become meaningless) on Mars. Conceptually, this calls for a partition of the universe of discourse into worlds of similar structure. Variability within a world is handled by changing the arguments of predicates, while changes between worlds are expressed by the special modal formalism.

Consider for example the statement: "It rains today". Obviously, the truth of such a statement depends on at least two parameters: The date and location at which it is stated. Given a specific date t_0 and location ℓ_0, the specific statement: "It rains at ℓ_0 on t_0" has propositional character, i.e., it is fully specified and must either be true or false. We may also consider the fully variable predicate rain(ℓ,t): "It rains at ℓ on t" which gives equal priority to both parameters. The modal approach distinguishes two levels of variability. In this example, we may choose time to be the major varying factor, and the universe to consist of worlds which are days. Within each day we consider the predicate rain(ℓ) which, given the date , depends only on the location. Alternately, one can choose the location to be the major parameter and regard the raining history of each location as a distinct world.

As is seen from this example the transition from Predicate Logic to Modal Logic is not as pronounced as the transition from Propositional Logic to Predicate Logic. For one thing it is not absolutely essential. We could manage quite reasonably with our two parameter predicate. Secondly, the decision as to which parameter is chosen to be the major one may seem arbitrary. It is strongly influenced by our intuitive view of the situation.

In spite of these qualifications there are some obvious advantages in the introduction and use of modal formalisms. It allows an explicit discrimination of one parameter as being appreciably more significant than all the others, and makes the dependence on that parameter implicit. Nowadays, when increasing attention is paid to the clear correspondence between syntax and natural reasoning (as is repeatedly stressed by the discipline of Structured Programming), it seems only appropriate to introduce extra structure into the description of varying situations. Thus a clear distinction is made between variation within a state, which we express using predicates and quantifiers, and variation from one state to another, which we express using the modal operators.

The general modal framework considers therefore a universe which consists of many similar states (or worlds) and a basic accessibility relation between the states, R(s,s') , which specifies the possibility of getting from one state s into another state s' .

Consider again the example of the universe of rainy days. There, each state is a day. A possible accessibility relation might hold between two days s and s' if s' is in the future of s .

The main notational idea is to avoid any explicit mention of either the state parameter (date in our example) or of the accessibility relation. Instead we introduce two special operators which describe properties of states which are accessible from a given state in a universe.

The two <u>modal</u> operators introduced are $\Box$ (called the <u>necessity</u> operator) and $\Diamond$ (called the <u>possibility</u> operator). Their meaning is given by the following rules of interpretation, informally expressed, in which we denote by $|w|_s$ the truth value of the formula w in a state s .

$$|\Box w|_s = \forall s'[R(s,s') \supset |w|_{s'}]$$

$$|\Diamond w|_s = \exists s'[R(s,s') \wedge |w|_{s'}] \ .$$

Thus, $\Box w$ is true at a state s if the formula w is true at all states R-accessible from s . Similarly, $\Diamond w$ is true at a state s if w is true in at least one state R-accessible from s .

A <u>modal formula</u> is a formula constructed from proposition symbols, predicate symbols, function symbols, individual constants and individual variables, the classic logic operators (including equality) and quantifiers, and the modal operators. The truth value of a modal formula at a state in a universe is found by a repeated use of the rules above for the modal operators and evaluation of any classic (non-modal) subformula on the state itself. It is of course assumed that every state contains a full interpretation for all the predicates in the formula.

For example, the formula $rain(\ell) \supset \Diamond \sim rain(\ell)$ is interpreted in our model of rainy days as stating: For a given day and a given location ℓ , if it rains on that day at ℓ then there exists another day in the future on which it will not rain at ℓ ; thus any rain will eventually stop. Similarly, $rain(\ell) \supset \Box rain(\ell)$ claims that if it rains on that day it will rain everafter. Note that any modal formula is always considered with respect to some fixed reference state, which may be chosen arbitrarily. In our example it has the meaning of 'today'.

Consider the general formula $\Diamond \sim w \equiv \sim \Box w$. As we can see from the definitions this claims that there exists an accessible state satisfying $\sim w$ if and only if it is not the case that all accessible states satisfy w . This formula is true in any state for any universe with an arbitrary R .

Giving a more precise definition, a <u>universe</u> consists of a set of <u>states</u> (or <u>worlds</u>), on which a relation R , called <u>accessibility relation</u>, is defined. Each state provides a domain and a first-order interpretation over the domain to all the proposition symbols, predicate symbols, function symbols, individual constants, and individual variables in the vocabulary under consideration. A formula which is true in <u>all states</u> of every universe is called <u>valid</u>. Thus the above formula $\Diamond \sim w \equiv \sim \Box w$ is a valid formula.

Following is a list of some valid formulas:

A1*. $\Diamond \sim w \equiv \sim \Box w$.

This establishes the connection between "necessity" and "possibility".

A2*. $\Box(w_1 \supset w_2) \supset (\Box w_1 \supset \Box w_2)$

i.e., if in all accessible states $w_1 \supset w_2$ holds and also w_1 is true in all accessible states, then w_2 must also be true in all of these states.

The formulas A1* and A2* are valid for any accessibility relation. If we agree to place further general restrictions on the relation R , we obtain additional valid formulas which are true for any model with a restricted relation. According to the different restrictions we may impose on R we obtain different modal systems. In our discussion we stipulate that R is always <u>reflexive</u> and <u>transitive</u>.

A3*. $\Box w \supset w$ (equivalently $w \supset \Diamond w$) .

This formula is valid for any reflexive model. It claims for a state s that if all states accessible from s satisfy w, then w is satisfied by s itself. This is obvious since s is accessible from itself (by reflexivity).

A4*. $\Box w \supset \Box\Box w$ (equivalently $\Diamond\Diamond w \supset \Diamond w$) .

This formula is valid for transitive models. The equivalent form claims that if there exists an s_2 accessible from s_1 which is accessible from s such that s_2 satisfies w ; then there exists an s_3 accessible from s which satisfies w . By transitivity s_2 is also accessible from s and we may take $s_3 = s_2$.

Having a list of valid formulas, it is natural to look for an axiomatic system in which we take some of these formulas as basic axioms and provide a set of sound inference rules by which we hope to be able to prove other valid formulas as theorems. In order to denote the fact that a formula w is a theorem derivable in our logical system we will write $\vdash w$. This will be the case if w is an axiom or derivable from the axioms by a <u>proof</u> using the inference rules of the system.

<u>Axioms:</u>

A1. $\vdash \Diamond \sim w \equiv \sim \Box w$

A2. $\vdash \Box(w_1 \supset w_2) \supset (\Box w_1 \supset \Box w_2)$

A3. $\vdash \Box w \supset w$

A4. $\vdash \Box w \supset \Box\Box w$

The inference rules are:

R1. If w is an instance of a propositional tautology then $\vdash w$. (Tautology Rule)

R2. If $\vdash w_1 \supset w_2$ and $\vdash w_1$ then $\vdash w_2$. (Modus Ponens)

R3. If $\vdash w$ then $\vdash \Box w$. (Modal Generalization)

All these rules are sound. The soundness of R1 and R2 is obvious. Note that in R1 we also include modal instances of tautologies, e.g., $\Box w \supset \Box w$. To justify R3 we recall that validity of w means that w is true in <u>all</u> states of every universe, hence $\Box w$ is also valid.

This system provides a logical basis for propositional reasoning. In the Modal Logic circles this system is known as S4 (see, e.g., [H&C]).

Some theorems which can be derived in that system are:

T1. $\vdash w \supset \Diamond w$

T2. $\vdash \Box(w_1 \wedge w_2) \equiv \Box w_1 \wedge \Box w_2$

T3. $\vdash \Box(w_1 \supset w_2) \supset (\Diamond w_1 \supset \Diamond w_2)$

T4. $\vdash \Diamond(w_1 \vee w_2) \equiv \Diamond w_1 \vee \Diamond w_2$

Note that because of the universal character of $\Box$ it commutes with $\wedge$, while $\Diamond$ which is existential commutes with $\vee$.

T5. $\vdash \Diamond(w_1 \wedge w_2) \supset \Diamond w_1 \wedge \Diamond w_2$

T6. $\vdash (\Box w_1 \vee \Box w_2) \supset \Box(w_1 \vee w_2)$

T7. $\vdash \Box w_1 \wedge \Diamond w_2 \supset \Diamond(w_1 \wedge w_2)$

T8. $\vdash \Box w \equiv \Box\Box w$

T9. $\vdash \Diamond w \equiv \Diamond\Diamond w$.

Because of these last two theorems we can collapse any string of consecutive identical modalities such as $\Box \ldots \Box$ or $\Diamond \ldots \Diamond$ into a single modality of the same type.

Since we intend to use predicates in our reasoning we have to extend our system to include some axioms and rules involving quantifiers and their interaction with modalities:

P1. $\vdash (\forall x w(x)) \supset w(t)$

where t is any term "free for x" in w.

P2. $\vdash (\forall x \Box w) \supset (\Box \forall x w)$ (Barcan's Formula).

The last implies the commutativity of $\forall$ with $\Box$, both having universal character with one quantifying over individuals while the other quantifying over states.

An additional rule of inference is:

R4. If $\vdash w_1 \supset w_2$ then $\vdash w_1 \supset \forall x w_2$

provided w_1 does not contain free occurrences of x .

Some theorems of the predicate modal system are:

T10. $\vdash (\forall x \Box w) \equiv (\Box \forall x w)$

T11. $\vdash (\exists x \Diamond w) \equiv (\Diamond \exists x w)$.

The system consisting of axioms A1-A4, P1, P2, and rules R1-R4 has been shown to be complete (see [H&C]).

In the next section we consider the application of the general modal framework to the analysis of programs. For the class of universes which are used there, the states in a given universe all share the same domain D and may differ by at most the values assigned to proposition symbols and individual variables. Such restricted universes are called D-universes. Since in such universes the assignment to all the other symbols is common to all states, we may associate this common part of the interpretation with the universe itself rather than with each state. Thus, a D-universe can be defined to consist of: The domain D , a common partial D-interpretation, a set of states each of which gives an assignment to the rest of the proposition symbols and individual variables, and an accessibility relation on the states. Typical D domains are the domain N of natural numbers, the domain Z of integers, the domain R of real numbers, the domain L of lists, the domain T of trees, etc.

A formula w over a domain D is any partially interpreted modal formula which may contain concrete predicates, functions, and individual elements over D , as well as uninterpreted predicate symbols, function symbols, individual constants and individual variables. A formula which is true in all states of all D-universes for a fixed D is called a D-valid formula.

The following are some examples of D-valid formulas for different D 's :
Each instance of the formula schema:

$$A(0) \wedge \forall n[A(n) \supset A(n+1)] \supset A(k)$$

is an N-valid formula. This partially interpreted formula schema represents the induction principle over the natural numbers.

Similarly, each instance of the schema:

$$\forall t[(\forall t' \prec t)A(t') \supset A(t)] \supset A(t)$$

is a T-valid formula, where '$\prec$' denotes the subtree relation between trees. This states the complete induction principle over trees.

II. MODAL LOGIC APPLIED TO PROGRAM ENVIRONMENT

In this section we apply the general concepts of Modal Logic to situations generated by the execution of programs. To simplify the presentation we will only consider deterministic programs. The power and elegance of the modal method are even more pronounced in dealing with nondeterministic and parallel programs.

For the concept of a state we will take an "execution state" which consists of the current values of all program variables at a certain stage in the execution. The accessibility relation between execution states will represent derivability by the program's execution. We will use predicates and quantifiers to describe properties of a single state and modalities to describe properties of the execution leading from one state to another.

Let us consider some particular program A with n program variables $\bar{y} = y_1, \ldots, y_n$. Assume that the program operates over a domain D . Let $\ell_0, \ell_1, \ldots, \ell_e$ be a set of labels, labeling every statement of the program. ℓ_0 is the single entry point and ℓ_e the single exit point. An <u>execution state</u> has the general structure $s = \langle \ell, \bar{\eta} \rangle$ with $\ell \in \{\ell_0, \ldots, \ell_e\}$ and $\bar{\eta} \in D^n$. For every input $\bar{\xi}$, the program generates an <u>execution sequence</u>:

$$\sigma = s^0, s^1, \ldots$$

where $s^0 = \langle \ell^0, \bar{\xi} \rangle$, and each s^i is an execution state.

The basic accessibility relation R holds between two states $\langle \ell, \bar{\eta} \rangle$ and $\langle \ell', \bar{\eta}' \rangle$ if there exists a computation path from ℓ to ℓ' which transforms $\bar{\eta}$ at ℓ to $\bar{\eta}'$ at ℓ' .

With these conventions we will proceed to express meaningful properties of programs and their executions. Remember that under our rules of the game we are never to mention R explicitly.

The formulas we will consider will use a basic vocabulary which includes a set of special propositions:

$$at\ell_0,\ at\ell_1, \ldots, at\ell_e,$$

each corresponding to one of the labels. In addition we will allow arbitrary predicates over the $\bar{y}$ (program variables) and additional auxiliary variables $\bar{u}$. We assume that only the $\bar{y}$'s change from one state to another, while the $\bar{u}$'s , being external, remain fixed. Let $\bar{\zeta}$ denote the fixed values of the auxiliary variables. The truth value of an atomic formula at a state $s = \langle \ell, \bar{\eta} \rangle$ is given as follows:

$at\ell_i$ is true at s iff $\ell_i = \ell$.

$p(\bar{y}, \bar{u})$ is true at s iff $p(\bar{\eta}, \bar{\zeta}) =$ <u>true</u>.

The truth value of a non-atomic formula, possibly containing modalities, is determined by the classic rules and the rules for interpreting modalities given above.

Note that our definition of a state here conforms with the general convention of D-universes. The specification of a state only specifies the elements by which one state may differ from another, namely, propositions $(at\ell_0, at\ell_1, \ldots, at\ell_e)$ and the values assigned to some of the individual free variables $(y_1, \ldots, y_n)$.

1. Invariance Properties

Consider first the class of program properties which are expressible by formulas of the form

$$w_0 \supset \Box w .$$

In the general modal context such a formula claims that w holds true in all states R-accessible from any state satisfying w_0. In our programming context we will often take w_0 as $at\ell_0 \wedge \bar{y}=\bar{\xi}$, which exactly characterizes the initial state, and then we have

$$(at\ell_0 \wedge \bar{y}=\bar{\xi}) \supset \Box w .$$

This then states that w is true for all states arising during execution. A formula of this form therefore expresses an invariance property.

Samples of important properties which fall under this category are:

A. Partial Correctness. Let $\varphi(\bar{x})$ be a precondition which restricts the set of inputs for which the program is supposed to be correct, and $\psi(\bar{x},\bar{y})$ the statement of its correctness, i.e., the relation which should hold between the input values $\bar{x}$ and the output values $\bar{y}$. Then in order to state partial correctness w.r.t. (φ,ψ) we can write:

$$(at\ell_0 \wedge \bar{y}=\bar{x} \wedge \varphi(\bar{x})) \supset \Box(at\ell_e \supset \psi(\bar{x},\bar{y})) .$$

This claims that if the initial state satisfies the restricting precondition then in any state accessible from the initial state: If that state happens to be the exit state ℓ_e then $\psi(\bar{x},\bar{y})$ holds between the input values $\bar{x}$ and the current $\bar{y}$ values. Thus this formula states that all convergent φ-sequences terminate in a state satisfying ψ, but it does not guarantee termination itself.

Let us consider a concrete example (a program computing $x!$ over the natural numbers):

Program P1:

ℓ_0: $y_2 \leftarrow 1$;

ℓ_1: if $y_1 > 0$ then

begin ℓ_2: $(y_1, y_2) \leftarrow (y_1 - 1, y_1 \cdot y_2)$;

ℓ_3: goto ℓ_1

end ;

ℓ_e: Halt.

The statement of its partial correctness is

$$(at\ell_0 \wedge y_1 = x \wedge x \geq 0) \supset \Box(at\ell_e \supset y_2 = x!) .$$

This is indeed an inherently invariant property since it is actually only a part of a bigger global invariant which represents the "network of invariants" normally used in the Invariant-Assertion Method (see [FLO]), namely:

$$\Box(at\ell_0 \wedge y_1 = x \wedge x \geq 0) \supset$$
$$[(at\ell_1 \supset y_1 \geq 0 \wedge y_2 \cdot y_1! = x!) \wedge$$
$$(at\ell_2 \supset y_1 > 0 \wedge y_2 \cdot y_1! = x!) \wedge$$
$$(at\ell_3 \supset y_1 \geq 0 \wedge y_2 \cdot y_1! = x!) \wedge$$
$$(at\ell_e \supset y_1 = 0 \wedge y_2 = x!)] .$$

B. Clean Behavior. For every location in a program we can formulate a cleanness condition which states that the statement at this location will execute successfully and generate no fault. Thus if the statement contains division, the cleanness condition will include the clause that the divisor is nonzero or not too small to avoid arithmetic overflow. If the statement contains an array reference, the cleanness condition will imply that the subscript expressions do not exceed the declared range. Denoting the cleanness condition at location i by α_i, the statement of clean behavior is:

$$(at\ell_0 \wedge \varphi(\bar{y})) \supset \Box(\bigwedge_i (at\ell_i \supset \alpha_i)) .$$

The conjunction is taken over all "potentially dangerous" locations in the program.

For example, the program P1 above should produce only natural number values during its computation. A cleanness condition at ℓ_2, which is clearly a critical point, is:

$$(at\ell_0 \wedge y_1 \geq 0) \supset \Box(at\ell_2 \supset y_1 > 0) ,$$

guaranteeing that the subtraction at ℓ_2 always yields a natural number.

C. Global Invariants. Very frequently, cleanness conditions are not related to any particular location. More generally, some other properties may be "truly" invariant independent of the location. In these cases we speak of global invariants unattached to any particular location. The expression of global invariance is even more straightforward. Thus to claim for the example above that y_1 is always a natural number, we may write:

$$(at\ell_0 \wedge y_1 \geq 0 \wedge \text{integer}(y_1)) \supset \Box(y_1 \geq 0 \wedge \text{integer}(y_1)) .$$

Another global invariant valid for this example is:

$$(at\ell_0 \wedge (y_1, y_2) = (x, 1)) \supset \Box(y_2 \cdot y_1! = x!) ,$$

which states that everywhere in the execution $y_2 \cdot y_1! = x!$.

Similarly, to ensure subscript cleanness we may claim global invariants of the form:

$$(at\ell_0 \wedge \varphi(\bar{y})) \supset \Box(0 \leq I \leq N) .$$

Another example of the usage of invariants is in the context of a program whose output is not necessarily apparent at the end of the execution; for example, a program whose output is printed on an external file during the computation. Consider a program for printing a sequence of prime numbers. Let ℓ be any location which contains a "print" instruction of form:

$$\ell: \text{ print}(y) .$$

Then a part of the correctness statement for such a program is:

$$w_0 \supset \Box(at\ell \supset \text{prime}(y))$$

for all print locations ℓ . It indicates that nothing but primes is printed.

Note that this property may specify the partial correctness even of continuous programs, i.e., programs which are not supposed to terminate but to operate continuously.

Even though our main interest in this paper is in deterministic programs, we cannot resist illustrating the efficacy of the modal formalism for parallel programs.

A state in the execution of two parallel processes will be structured as: $s = \langle \ell_1, \ell_2; \bar{\eta} \rangle$, i.e., it will contain references to locations in both processes. These references are tested by the propositions $at\ell_1$, $at\ell_2$ for all locations ℓ_1 and ℓ_2 in the two processes.

D. Mutual Exclusion. Let us consider first the property of Mutual Exclusion. Let two processes P_1 and P_2 execute in parallel. Assume that each process contains a section C_i , $i = 1,2$, which includes some task critical to the cooperation of the two processes. For example, it might access a shared device (such as a disk) or a shared variable. If the nature of the task is such that it must be done exclusively by one process or the other, but never by both of them simultaneously, we call these sections critical sections. The property that states that the processes are never simultaneously executing in their respective critical sections is called Mutual Exclusion with respect to this pair of critical sections.

The property of mutual exclusion for C_1 and C_2 can be described by:

$$w_0 \supset \Box(\sim(at\ell_1 \wedge at\ell_2))$$

for every pair of labels $\ell_1 \in C_1$ and $\ell_2 \in C_2$. This states that it is never the case that the joint execution of the processes reaches ℓ_1 and ℓ_2 simultaneously. Hence, mutual exclusion is implied. In practice, one does not have to actually consider all possible pairs $\ell_i \in C_i$.

E. Deadlock Freedom. A standard synchronization device in concurrent systems is the semaphore which is implemented by the atomic instructions:

$$p(x): \quad x > 0 \rightarrow [x \leftarrow x-1]$$

$$v(x): \quad x \leftarrow x+1 \quad .$$

A process reaching a $p(x)$ instruction will proceed beyond it only if $x > 0$ and then it will decrement x by 1, usually setting it to 0. No further process may go beyond a $p(x)$ instruction until somebody (in all probability the process that has just decremented x) will perform a $v(x)$ operation, increasing x to 1.

A concurrent system consisting of n parallel processes is said to be deadlocked if none of the processes can execute any further step. If we assume that the only synchronization choice in a system is semaphores then the only possibility for a deadlock is the situation:

$$\begin{array}{ccc} \vdots & & \vdots \\ \ell_1 : p(x^1) & & \ell_n : p(x^n) \\ \vdots & & \vdots \end{array}$$

for some locations $\ell_1, \ldots, \ell_n$ (ℓ_i belonging to process i), where all n of the processes in the system are currently waiting for 'p' operations on the semaphore variables $x^1, \ldots, x^n$ (not necessarily distinct) while $x^1 = x^2 = \ldots = x^n = 0$.

To exclude this possibility we can require:

$$w_0 \supset \Box\left(\bigwedge_{i=1}^{n} at\ell_i \supset \bigvee_{i=1}^{n} (x^i > 0)\right) .$$

This requires that whenever all the processes are each at the ℓ_i: $p(x^i)$ operation, $i = 1, \ldots, n$, at least one of the x^i's must be positive. The corresponding process can then proceed.

In order to completely eliminate the possibility of deadlock in the system, we must impose a similar requirement for every n-tuple of 'p' locations.

2. Eventuality Properties

A second category of properties are those expressible by formulas of the form:

$$w_1 \supset \Diamond w_2 \quad .$$

In the general context this means that if at any state s_1 , w_1 is true, there exists a state s_2 , R-accessible from s_1 , in which w_2 is true. In the programming context it means that if w_1 ever arises during execution, it will eventually be followed by another state in which w_2 is true. A formula of this form therefore expresses an eventuality property. Following are some samples of properties expressible by formulas of this form.

A. Total Correctness. A program is said to be totally correct w.r.t. a specification (φ,ψ) , if for every input $\bar{\xi}$ satisfying $\varphi(\bar{\xi})$, termination is guaranteed, and the final values $\bar{y} = \bar{\eta}$ upon termination satisfy $\psi(\bar{\xi},\bar{\eta})$. Once more, let ℓ_0 denote the entry location and ℓ_e the exit location of the program. Total correctness w.r.t. (φ,ψ) is expressible by:

$$(at\ell_0 \wedge \bar{y}=\bar{x} \wedge \varphi(\bar{x})) \supset \Diamond(at\ell_e \wedge \psi(\bar{x},\bar{y})) \quad .$$

This says that if we have an execution sequence which begins in a state which is at location ℓ_0 and has values $\bar{y}=\bar{x}$ satisfying φ , then later in that execution sequence we are guaranteed to have a state which is at ℓ_e and satisfies $\psi(\bar{x},\bar{y})$.

For example, the statement of total correctness for the program P1 for the computation of x! is:

$$(at\ell_0 \wedge y_1=x \wedge x\geqslant 0) \supset \Diamond(at\ell_e \wedge y_2=x!) \quad .$$

B. General Eventualities. Eventuality formulas enable us to express a causality relation between any two events, not only between program initialization and termination but also between events arising during the execution. This becomes especially important when discussing continuously executing programs, i.e., where termination is not expected. The general form of such an eventuality is:

$$(at\ell_1 \wedge \varphi_1) \supset \Diamond(at\ell_2 \wedge \varphi_2)$$

and it claims that whenever φ_1 arises at ℓ_1 we are guaranteed of eventually reaching ℓ_2 with φ_2 true. This is the exact formalization of the basic Intermittent-Assertion statement (see [M&W]):

"If sometimes φ_1 at ℓ_1 then sometimes φ_2 at ℓ_2 " .

Consider for example the program for printing successive prime numbers. Under the invariance properties we expressed the claim that nothing but primes are printed. Here we can state that the proper sequence of primes is produced. Let

$$\ell\text{: print(y)}$$

be the only printing instruction in the program. Then the following two clauses ensure the desired property:

$$at\ell_0 \supset \Diamond(at\ell \wedge y=2)$$

$$(at\ell \wedge y=x) \supset \Diamond(at\ell \wedge y=nextprime(x)) .$$

The first statement assures arrival at ℓ with y being the first prime. The second claim ensures that after any prime is printed the next prime in sequence will eventually be printed.

Note that these statements do not guarantee that some primes are not printed more than once or out of sequence, but they do guarantee that all printed results are primes, and that a subsequence of the printed results is the ascending sequence of primes.

Again, let us allow ourselves a short excursion into the world of parallel programs.

C. Accessibility. Consider again a process which has a critical section C. In the previous discussion we have shown how to state exclusion or protection for that section. A related property is that of accessibility, that if a process wishes to enter its critical section it will eventually get there and will not be indefinitely held up by the protection mechanism.

Let ℓ_1 be a location just before the critical section. The fact that the process is at ℓ_1 indicates an intention to enter the critical section. Let ℓ_2 be a location inside the critical section. The property of accessibility can then be expressed by:

$$at\ell_1 \supset \Diamond at\ell_2 \quad ;$$

namely, whenever the program is at ℓ_1, it will eventually get to ℓ_2.

A correct construction of critical sections should ensure these two complementary properties: that of protection (exclusiveness) and that of accessibility.

D. Responsiveness. Consider an example of a program modeling an operating system. Assume that it serves a number of customer programs by scheduling a shared resource between them. Let the customer programs communicate with the operating system concerning a given resource via a set of boolean variables $\{r_i, g_i\}$. r_i is set to true by customer program number i to signal a request for the resource. g_i is set to true by the operating system to signal that customer i is granted the use of the resource. The statement that the operating system fairly responds to user requests -- responsiveness -- is given by:

$$r_i \supset \Diamond g_i$$

i.e., whenever r_i becomes <u>true</u> eventually g_i will turn <u>true</u>.

Note that since these events are global and not attached to any specific location they can model external events such as interrupts and unsolicited signals.

III. PROOF SYSTEMS

After giving some evidence of the power of the modal notation in expressing interesting program properties, we should search next for proof systems in which these properties can be formally established. Obviously, the basis for all such systems will be the general S4 framework introduced above. However, this basis must be augmented by additional axioms and rules, reflecting the properties of the domain and the structure of the program under consideration. These additional conditions will constrain the accessibility relation $R(s,s')$ to represent the relation of s' being derivable from s by an execution of the program. This releases us from the need to express program text syntactically in the system; instead all necessary information is captured by the constraints on the accessibility relation as expressed by the additional axioms.

Our proof systems will therefore consist of three parts: a <u>general part</u> which contains S4-like axioms, elaborating the general properties of the relation R; a <u>proper part</u> which gives an axiomatic description of the domain; and a <u>local part</u> consisting of axiom schemata which generate a set of local axioms for any particular program. The local axioms constrain the state sequences to those considered to be execution sequences of the program under study.

1. <u>The sometime system.</u>

Our simpler system, called here the <u>sometime system</u>, is based on S4.

A. <u>General part:</u> The general part consists of the following S4 axioms:

A1. $\vdash \Diamond \sim w \equiv \sim \Box w$

A2. $\vdash \Box(w_1 \supset w_2) \supset (\Box w_1 \supset \Box w_2)$

A3. $\vdash \Box w \supset w$

A4. $\vdash \Box w \supset \Box\Box w$

P1. $\vdash (\forall x\ w(x)) \supset w(t)$
where t is "free for x" in w.

P2. $\vdash (\forall x \Box w) \supset (\Box \forall x w)$.

The rules of inference are:

R1. If w is an instance (possibly modal) of a tautology then $\vdash w$.

R2. If $\vdash w_1 \supset w_2$ and $\vdash w_1$, then $\vdash w_2$.

R3. If $\vdash w$ then $\vdash \Box w$.

R4. If $\vdash w_1 \supset w_2$ then $\vdash w_1 \supset \forall x w_2$ provided w_1 does not contain free occurrences of x .

This system generally constrains R to be reflexive (A3) and transitive (A4).

B. Proper part: The next part of the system contains a set of proper axioms and axiom schemata. These axioms specify all the needed properties of the domain of interest. Thus, to reason about programs manipulating natural numbers, we need the set of Peano axioms. To reason about trees we need a set of axioms giving the basic properties of trees and of the basic operations defined on them. An essential axiom schema for every domain should be the induction axiom schema. This (and all other schemata) should be formulated to admit modal instances as subformulas. Thus the induction principle for natural numbers is:

$$\vdash A(0) \wedge \forall n[A(n) \supset A(n+1)] \supset A(k) \ .$$

A modal instance of this principle which will be used later is:

Induction Theorem:

$$\vdash \Box(P(0) \supset \Diamond \psi) \wedge \forall n[\Box(P(n) \supset \Diamond \psi) \supset \Box(P(n+1) \supset \Diamond \psi)] \supset \Box(P(k) \supset \Diamond \psi) \ .$$

Similar induction theorems will exist for any other set of proper axioms which depend on natural well-founded orderings existing in the domain.

C. Local part: The axioms and rules above represent the general framework needed for our reasoning. Next we introduce a set of local axioms which depend on the particular program to be analyzed.

The first axiom depends only on the identity of the program variables. Let w be any formula which does not contain any program variables, then the following is an axiom:

Frame Axiom: $\vdash w \supset \Box w$.

The justification hinges on the fact that R-related states may differ from one another only in the assignments to program variables.

A second generic axiom states that every state s has exactly one label ℓ_i such that $at\ell_i$ is true.

<u>Location Axiom:</u> $\vdash \sum_{i=0}^{e} at\ell_i = 1$.

We use here the abbreviation $\Sigma p_i = 1$ or $p_1 + \ldots + p_n = 1$ meaning that exactly one of the p_i 's is true.

The other axioms are local to each program. For these axiom schemata we make the following simplifying assumptions about the program:

Assume that the program is represented as a directed graph whose nodes are the program locations or labels, and whose edges represent transitions between the labels. A transition is an instruction of the general form

$$c(\bar{y}) \rightarrow [\bar{y} \leftarrow \bar{f}(\bar{y})] \ .$$

$c(\bar{y})$ is a condition (may be the trivial condition <u>true</u>) under which the transition replacing $\bar{y}$ by $\bar{f}(\bar{y})$ should be taken. $\bar{y} = y_1, \ldots, y_n$ is the vector of program variables. We assume that all the conditions $c_1, \ldots, c_k$ on transitions departing from any node are mutually exclusive and exhaustive (i.e., $\Sigma c_i = 1$) .

The role of the local axioms is to introduce our knowledge about the program into the system. Since the system does not provide direct tools for speaking about programs (such as Hoare's formalism), the local axioms represent the program by characterizing the possible state transitions under the program control.

For any transition:

$$\textcircled{\ell} \xrightarrow[\alpha]{c(\bar{y}) \ \rightarrow \ [\bar{y} \leftarrow f(\bar{y})]} \textcircled{\ell'}$$

we can generate an axiom F_α . This axiom corresponds to a "forward" propagation (derivation of the strongest postcondition) across the transition α :

$$F_\alpha: \ \vdash \ [at\ell \wedge c(\bar{y}) \wedge \bar{y}=\bar{\eta}] \supset \Diamond(at\ell' \wedge \bar{y}=\bar{f}(\bar{\eta})) \ .$$

This axiom states: If at any state, execution is at ℓ , $c(\bar{y})$ hold, and the current values of $\bar{y}$ are $\bar{\eta}$, then sometime later we will be at ℓ' with the variables $\bar{y} = \bar{f}(\bar{\eta})$.

A different approach which suggests an alternate axiom schema is obtained by "backward" substitution (derivation of the weakest precondition):

$$B_\alpha: \ \vdash \ [at\ell \wedge c(\bar{y}) \wedge P(\bar{f}(\bar{y}))] \supset \Diamond(at\ell' \wedge P(\bar{y})) \quad ,$$

where $P(\bar{f}(\bar{y}))$ denotes the substitution of $\bar{f}(\bar{y})$ for all free occurrences of $\bar{y}$ in $P(\bar{y})$. This form of the axiom expresses the effect of the transition on an arbitrary predicate P (predicate transformer). It says that if $at\ell \wedge c(\bar{y})$ and $P(\bar{f}(\bar{y}))$ hold, then we are guaranteed to eventually reach ℓ' with $P(\bar{y})$. F_α and B_α are equivalent and can be derived from each other.

Note that both forms ignore the fact that the 'sometime' guaranteed is actually in the immediately next instance. This is a consequence of the fact that we can only guarantee things eventually and have no way to formulate properties of the next instance.

Consider for example the following program over the integers which raises a number x_1 to an integral power $x_2 \geqslant 0$, assuming that (x_1,x_2) are the initial values of the variables (y_1,y_2).

Program P2:

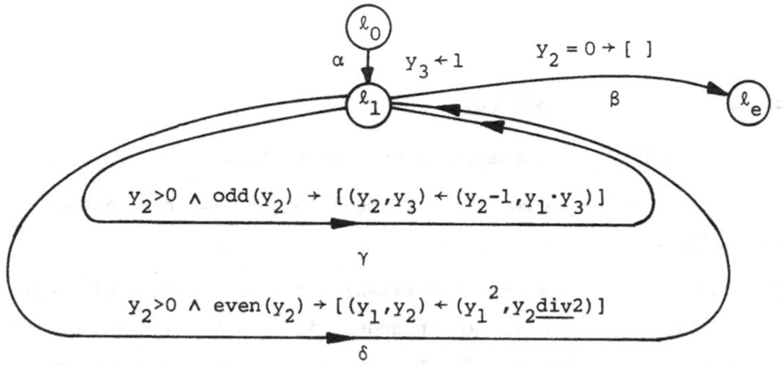

The local backward axiom schemata corresponding to this program are:

B_α : $\vdash$ [$at\ell_0 \wedge P(y_1,y_2,1)] \supset \Diamond(at\ell_1 \wedge P(y_1,y_2,y_3))$

B_β : $\vdash$ [$at\ell_1 \wedge y_2=0 \wedge P] \supset \Diamond(at\ell_e \wedge P)$

B_γ : $\vdash$ [$at\ell_1 \wedge y_2>0 \wedge odd(y_2) \wedge P(y_1,y_2-1,y_1\cdot y_3)] \supset \Diamond(at\ell_1 \wedge P(y_1,y_2,y_3))$

B_δ : $\vdash$ [$at\ell_1 \wedge y_2>0 \wedge even(y_2) \wedge P(y_1^2,y_2\underline{div}2,y_3)] \supset \Diamond(at\ell_1 \wedge P(y_1,y_2,y_3))$

D. Derived rules: Before demonstrating a proof in the system we will develop several useful derived rules:

$\Box\Box$-Generalization: $\dfrac{\vdash P \supset Q}{\vdash \Box P \supset \Box Q}$.

This is obtained by application of modal generalization R3 and the use of A2.

By substituting in the above $\sim Q$ for P and $\sim P$ for Q, we obtain:

$\Diamond\Diamond$-Generalization: $\dfrac{\vdash P \supset Q}{\vdash \Diamond P \supset \Diamond Q}$.

The following additional rules correspond to proof rules existent in most axiomatic verification systems. (In these rules interpret $P \supset \Box Q$ and $P \supset \Diamond Q$ as stating the partial and total correctness of some program segment respectively.)

Consequence: $\dfrac{\vdash P \supset Q,\ \vdash Q \supset \Diamond R,\ \vdash R \supset S}{\vdash P \supset \Diamond S}$.

From $\vdash R \supset S$ (using $\Diamond\Diamond$-Gen.) we obtain $\vdash \Diamond R \supset \Diamond S$ which can be combined with the other premises to lead to the result.

Concatenation: $\dfrac{\vdash P \supset \Diamond Q,\ \vdash Q \supset \Diamond R}{\vdash P \supset \Diamond R}$.

Here we derive $\vdash \Diamond Q \supset \Diamond\Diamond R$ by the $\Diamond\Diamond$-Gen. rule. We then use Theorem T9 ($\vdash \Diamond\Diamond R \supset \Diamond R$) to obtain $\vdash \Diamond Q \supset \Diamond R$. The conclusion follows by propositional reasoning.

A derived frame rule more appropriate to step-by-step transitions is given by:

Frame Rule: $\dfrac{\vdash P \supset \Diamond Q}{\vdash (P \wedge w) \supset \Diamond (Q \wedge w)}$

provided w contains no program variables.

This rule is a simple consequence of the Frame Axiom $\vdash w \supset \Box w$ and of Theorem T7 ($\vdash \Diamond Q \wedge \Box w \supset \Diamond (Q \wedge w)$) .

We will also need some rules for establishing the convergence of loops. These rules will of course depend on the domain under discussion and the induction principle provided in that domain. For the domain of natural numbers we already mentioned the Induction Theorem:

$$\Box[P(0) \supset \Diamond \psi] \wedge \forall n[\Box(P(n) \supset \Diamond \psi) \supset \Box(P(n+1) \supset \Diamond \psi)] \supset \Box[P(k) \supset \Diamond \psi] .$$

Using this induction theorem we can derive the following rule:

Induction Rule 1: $\dfrac{\vdash P(0) \supset \Diamond \psi,\ \ \vdash \Box(P(n) \supset \Diamond \psi) \supset \Box(P(n+1) \supset \Diamond \psi)}{\vdash (\exists k P(k)) \supset \Diamond \psi}$.

This rule says that if $P(0)$ eventually guarantees ψ , and if for any n , the fact that $P(n)$ guarantees ψ implies that $P(n+1)$ guarantees ψ , then if $P(k)$ is true for some k , ψ is eventually guaranteed. This rule is useful for proving convergence of a loop, if for example we have a P such that $P(0) \supset \Diamond \psi$ and across the loop's body $P(n+1) \supset \Diamond P(n)$, implying the second premise of the rule.

From this rule we can derive a more liberal form of the induction rule.

Induction Rule 2: $\dfrac{\vdash P(0) \supset \Diamond \psi,\ \vdash P(n+1) \supset \Diamond (\psi \vee P(n))}{\vdash (\exists k P(k)) \supset \Diamond \psi}$

Rule 2 is more liberal than Rule 1 since it does not require us to give an exact estimate of the number of repetitions of the loop, but allows instead an estimate of an upper bound. We can see this by observing that in the previous case we required that $P(n+1)$ leads to $P(n)$ across the loop's body, and only $P(0)$ ensures ψ . Thus to start the argument we have to state $P(k)$ where we expect the loop to be executed k times. In Rule 2 we claim that for each n , either

$P(n+1)$ implies $P(n)$ across the loop, or that it establishes ψ and no further execution is necessary. Thus $P(k)$ ensures that either the loop is executed at most k times and ψ is established on the last iteration or earlier.

2. Total Correctness - Example and Discussion

Let us use this system to establish the correctness of the example program P2 computing $x_1^{x_2}$. We will prove that

$$\vdash [at\ell_0 \wedge (y_1,y_2)=(x_1,x_2) \wedge x_2 \geq 0] \supset \Diamond(at\ell_e \wedge y_3 = x_1^{x_2}) \quad ,$$

namely: If we are in any state at ℓ_0 with $\bar{y}=\bar{x}$ then there exists a state in which we are at ℓ_e and $y_3 = x_1^{x_2}$.

In the proof below we use the backward form of the axioms. The proof proceeds as follows:

1. $\vdash [at\ell_0 \wedge (y_1,y_2)=(x_1,x_2) \wedge x_2 \geq 0] \supset$

   $[at\ell_0 \wedge y_2 \geq 0 \wedge y_1^{y_2} = x_1^{x_2}]$ A Z-valid formula.

2. $\vdash [at\ell_0 \wedge y_2 \geq 0 \wedge 1 \cdot y_1^{y_2} = x_1^{x_2}] \supset$

   $\Diamond[at\ell_1 \wedge y_2 \geq 0 \wedge y_3 \cdot y_1^{y_2} = x_1^{x_2}]$

   By B_α with $P(y_1,y_2,y_3) = (y_2 \geq 0 \wedge y_3 \cdot y_1^{y_2} = x_1^{x_2})$.

3. $\vdash [at\ell_0 \wedge (y_1,y_2)=(x_1,x_2) \wedge x_2 \geq 0] \supset$

   $\Diamond[at\ell_1 \wedge y_2 \geq 0 \wedge y_3 \cdot y_1^{y_2} = x_1^{x_2}]$ By Consequence 1,2.

Denote now:

$Q(n,\bar{y})$: $at\ell_1 \wedge 0 \leq y_2 \leq n \wedge y_3 \cdot y_1^{y_2} = x_1^{x_2}$.

Using Induction Rule 2, we will establish

(*) $\vdash (\exists k Q(k,\bar{y})) \supset \Diamond(at\ell_e \wedge y_3 = x_1^{x_2})$,

where we take $\psi = (at\ell_e \wedge y_3 = x_1^{x_2})$.

Applying the Consequence Rule to 3, we have:

4. $\vdash [at\ell_0 \wedge (y_1,y_2)=(x_1,x_2) \wedge x_2 \geq 0] \supset \Diamond Q(y_2,\bar{y})$

   which establishes $\exists k Q(k,\bar{y})$ by taking $k = y_2$.

In order to use the Induction Rule 2, we show first $Q(0,\bar{y}) \supset \Diamond\psi$: Note that $Q(0,\bar{y})$ implies $y_2 = 0$.

5. $\vdash Q(0,\bar{y}) \supset \Diamond[at\ell_e \wedge y_3=x_1^{x_2}]$, hence $\Diamond\psi$, by B_β and Consequences.

We now proceed to show by case analysis that

$$\vdash Q(n+1,\bar{y}) \supset \Diamond[\psi \vee Q(n,\bar{y})] \ .$$

6. $\vdash [Q(n+1,\bar{y}) \wedge y_2=0] \supset \Diamond[at\ell_e \wedge y_3=x_1^{x_2}]$, hence $\Diamond\psi$, by B_β and Consequences.

7. $\vdash [Q(n+1,\bar{y}) \wedge y_2>0 \wedge odd(y_2)] \supset \Diamond Q(n,\bar{y})$

   by B_γ , logic and Consequences.

8. $\vdash [Q(n+1,\bar{y}) \wedge y_2>0 \wedge even(y_2)] \supset \Diamond Q(n,\bar{y})$

   by B_δ , logic and Consequences.

In the proof of 8 we use the fact that $0<y_2\leq n+1$ implies $0\leq y_2\underline{div}2\leq n$.

9. $\vdash Q(n+1,\bar{y}) \supset \Diamond[[at\ell_e \wedge y_3=x_1^{x_2}] \vee Q(n,\bar{y})]$

   by taking the "or" of 6, 7, 8, propositional reasoning and T4.

By the Induction Rule 2 we get from 5 and 9 :

10. $\vdash \exists k Q(k,\bar{y}) \supset \Diamond[at\ell_e \wedge y_3=x_1^{x_2}]$.

Combining 4 and 10 with Concatenation and Consequences, we get:

11. $\vdash [at\ell_0 \wedge (y_1,y_2)=(x_1,x_2) \wedge x_2\geq 0] \supset \Diamond[at\ell_e \wedge y_3=x_1^{x_2}]$.

This concludes the proof of total correctness of our example program.

Clearly, a statement of the form

$$[at\ell \wedge P] \supset \Diamond[at\ell' \wedge P']$$

is exactly a formalization of the typical "intermittent assertion" :

"If <u>sometime</u> P at ℓ then <u>sometime</u> P' at ℓ' " .

Thus we are justified in regarding this modal system as the most appropriate formalization of the Intermittent-Assertion method.

When we investigate the "power" of the system we find that it is adequate for proving valid eventualities, i.e., properties of the form:

$$P \supset \Diamond Q$$

which are valid for programs over the given domain. For this reason we named this system the "sometime" system.

Unfortunately this system is inadequate for proving invariance properties such as partial correctness or global properties. This deficiency is not a flaw in the logic formalism itself, but in the failure of the local axioms to capture exactly the execution sequences of the given program and nothing more. While $[at\ell \wedge P] \supset \Diamond[at\ell' \wedge P']$ guarantees that ℓ' will be reached sometime in the future, we have no way to specify that ℓ' is actually reached in the next immediate state. This does not hurt us when we prove eventualities since we do not care about intermediate states other than those explicitly mentioned. But in order to claim invariance, we have to keep track of all intermediate states, and then we must be able to describe what happens in the next immediate state.

3. The Nexttime System

In order to correct this deficiency we introduce an additional modal operator into our system. This is the next instance operator, denoted by $\bigcirc$.

A semantic model for the extended system will now consist of a set of states and an immediate accessibility relation ρ connecting some of these states. ρ corresponds to the next or immediate future relation. In any such universe (model) we define R to be the reflexive transitive closure of ρ which therefore gives it the meaning of "present or eventual future". Semantic truth in a state s in such a universe is now defined (extending the previous definition) as:

$$|\Box w|_s \equiv \forall s'[R(s,s') \supset |w|_{s'}]$$

$$|\Diamond w|_s \equiv \exists s'[R(s,s') \wedge |w|_{s'}]$$

$$|\bigcirc w|_s \equiv \exists s'[\rho(s,s') \wedge |w|_{s'}]$$

This extended system is aptly called the nexttime system.

Following we present an axiomatic system for the 'nexttime' logic. Where it differs very little from the 'sometime' system, we will only mark the differences.

A. General Part:

Axioms:

C1. $\vdash \Diamond\sim w \equiv \sim\Box w$

C2. $\vdash \Box(w_1 \supset w_2) \supset (\Box w_1 \supset \Box w_2)$

C3. $\vdash \Box w \supset w$

C4. $\vdash \bigcirc(\sim w) \equiv \sim\bigcirc(w)$

C5. $\vdash \bigcirc(w_1 \supset w_2) \supset (\bigcirc w_1 \supset \bigcirc w_2)$

C6. $\vdash \square w \supset \bigcirc w$

C7. $\vdash \square w \supset \bigcirc \square w$

C8. $\vdash \square (w \supset \bigcirc w) \supset (w \supset \square w)$

P1. $\vdash [\forall x w(x)] \supset w(t)$ where t is "free for x" in w

P2. $\vdash (\forall x \square w) \supset (\square \forall x w)$.

C1-C3, P1, P2 are the same as A1-A3, P1, P2 in the 'sometime' system. C4 claims the uniqueness of the next instance. C5 is the analogue of C2 for the $\bigcirc$ operator. C6 claims that the next state is one of the reachable states. It also guarantees that each state has a successor. (In order to satisfy this requirement in the programming context we stipulate that each exit label in the program's graph is connected to itself by a trivial transition.) C7 is a weaker version of A4 ($\vdash \square w \supset \square \square w$) in the 'sometime' system and can be used together with C8 to prove this as a theorem in the 'nexttime' system. C8 is the "computational induction" axiom; it states that if a property is inherited over one step transition, it is invariant over any path.

Rules of Inference: Identical to R1-R4 of the 'sometime' system.

A simple theorem of this system is:

T12: $\vdash \bigcirc w \supset \lozenge w$

obtained by negation of C6 and applications of C1 and C4.

B. **Proper part:** Since the proper part consists solely of first-order axioms, it is identical with the proper part of the 'sometime' system.

C. **Local part:** The Frame and Location axioms remain the same. The main difference is in the local axioms which now describe transitions between a state and its immediate successor. For a transition

$$ \textcircled{\ell} \xrightarrow{\frac{c(\bar{y}) \; \to \; [\bar{y} \leftarrow \bar{f}(\bar{y})]}{\alpha}} \textcircled{\ell'} $$

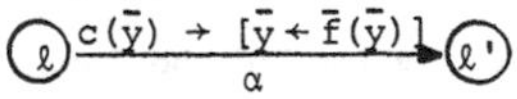

we generate the "forward" axiom $\tilde{F}_\alpha$:

$\tilde{F}_\alpha$: $\vdash [at\ell \wedge c(\bar{y}) \wedge \bar{y}=\bar{\eta}] \supset \bigcirc (at\ell' \wedge \bar{y}=\bar{f}(\bar{\eta}))$,

and similarly the "backward" axiom schema:

$\tilde{B}_\alpha$: $\vdash [at\ell \wedge c(\bar{y}) \wedge P(\bar{f}(\bar{y}))] \supset \bigcirc (at\ell' \wedge P(\bar{y}))$.

By the theorem $\vdash \bigcirc w \supset \lozenge w$, we have that $\vdash \tilde{F}_\alpha \supset F_\alpha$. Therefore any proof in the 'sometime' system is automatically carried over to the 'nexttime' system. Consequently the 'nexttime' system is also adequate for proving total correctness and other eventualities. In addition it is also adequate for proving invariance properties.

4. Proof of Invariance

Let us consider now a typical proof of invariance. Let Q be an inductive program property. Intuitively this means that Q is true of the initial state and is preserved under any program step. Thus we have

(a) $\vdash \varphi \supset Q$

for the input predicate φ .

Also for any transition $\alpha\colon c(\bar{y}) \rightarrow [\bar{y} \leftarrow \bar{f}(\bar{y})]$, we have

(b) $\vdash c(\bar{y}) \wedge Q(\bar{y}) \supset Q(\bar{f}(\bar{y}))$.

Let ℓ be any label in the program and let its outgoing transitions be α_i leading to ℓ_i respectively. Assume each transition to be $\alpha_i\colon c_i(\bar{y}) \rightarrow [\bar{y} \leftarrow \bar{f}_i(\bar{y})]$. We have already assumed that $\bigvee_i c_i(\bar{y}) = \underline{\text{true}}$.

For any i we have

$\vdash [\text{at}\ell \wedge c_i(\bar{y}) \wedge Q(\bar{y})] \supset [\text{at}\ell \wedge c_i(\bar{y}) \wedge Q(\bar{f}_i(\bar{y}))]$

by the inductiveness of Q , i.e., (b).

$\vdash [\text{at}\ell \wedge c_i(\bar{y}) \wedge Q(\bar{f}_i(\bar{y}))] \supset \bigcirc (\text{at}\ell_i \wedge Q(\bar{y}))$

by the local backward axiom $\tilde{B}_{\alpha_i}$.

Combining the last two we get:

$$\vdash [\text{at}\ell \wedge c_i(\bar{y}) \wedge Q(\bar{y})] \supset \bigcirc (\text{at}\ell_i \wedge Q(\bar{y})) ,$$

from which, by Consequence, we get:

$$\vdash [\text{at}\ell \wedge c_i(\bar{y}) \wedge Q(\bar{y})] \supset \bigcirc Q(\bar{y}) .$$

Since the above was obtained for an arbitrary i we can take the logical 'or' of all these statements over all i 's. Using the fact that $\bigvee_i c_i = \underline{\text{true}}$, we obtain:

$$\vdash [\text{at}\ell \wedge Q(\bar{y})] \supset \bigcirc Q(\bar{y}) .$$

Taking the disjunction over all program labels $\ell \in \{\ell_0,\ldots,\ell_e\}$ and using the location axiom which states that $\bigvee_\ell \text{at}\ell = \underline{\text{true}}$, we get:

$$\vdash Q(\bar{y}) \supset \bigcirc Q(\bar{y}) .$$

Hence by Generalization (R3)

$$\vdash \square Q(\bar{y}) \supset \bigcirc Q(\bar{y}) .$$

By the induction axiom C8 we get:

$$\vdash Q(\bar{y}) \supset \square Q(\bar{y}) .$$

Consider now an initial state at which we have $at\ell_0$ and φ true. By (a) φ implies Q , from which we conclude

$$\vdash [at\ell_0 \wedge \varphi] \supset \Box Q(\bar{y}) \quad ,$$

which establishes the invariance of Q .

* * * * *

Due to lack of space we could not discuss a number of closely related and relevant issues:

* Completeness and adequacy proofs for the systems.
* Relation and Comparison to other modal systems, notably Dynamic Logic (see [HAR]), Program Logic ([CONS]), etc.
* The treatment of nondeterminism and parallelism under the same framework (see (PNU]).
* A complete reference list.

ACKNOWLEDGEMENTS: We wish to thank Bill Scherlis for his critical reading of the manuscript.

REFERENCES

[BUR] Burstall, R.M. "Formal Description of Program Structure and Semantics of First-Order Logic", in Machine Intelligence 5, B. Meltzer and D. Michie (eds.), Edinburgh Press, pp. 79-98 (1970).

[CON] Constable, R.L. "On the Theory of Programming Logic", Proceedings of the 9th Annual Symposium on Theory of Computing, Boulder, Colorado (May 1977).

[HAR] Harel, D. "Logic of Programs: Axiomatic and Descriptive Power", Ph.D. Thesis, Laboratory of Computer Science, M.I.T. (May 1978).

[HOA] Hoare, C.A.R. "An Axiomatic Basis of Computer Programming", CACM, Vol.12, No. 10 (October 1969).

[H&C] Hughes, G.E. and Cresswell, M.J. "An Introduction to Modal Logic", Methuess & Co., London (1968).

[M&W] Manna, Z. and Waldinger, R. "Is 'Sometime' Sometimes Better Than 'Always'?: Intermittent Assertions in Proving Program Correctness", CACM, Vol. 21, No. 2 (February 1978), pp. 159-172.

[PNU] Pnueli, A. "The Temporal Semantics of Concurrent Programs", Technical Report, Tel-Aviv University (1978).

A COMPARISON BETWEEN TWO VARIATIONS OF A PEBBLE GAME ON GRAPHS

by

Friedhelm Meyer auf der Heide

Faculty of mathematics, University of Bielefeld, W-Germany

Abstract:

We study the relation between the number of pebbles used in the black and the black-white pebble game and show that the additional use of white pebbles cannot save more than a square-root and give an example in which it does save a factor $\frac{1}{2}$.

(1) Introduction:

This paper deals with two kinds of pebble games:

- the "black pebble game" which was used to exhibit a space efficient simulation for time-bounded Touring machines. ($\mathrm{DTIME}(t(n)) \subseteq \mathrm{DTAPE}(t(n)/\log t(n))$) [5] .

- the "black-white pebble game" which was used to show that there is a language $SP \in P$ which uses at least $\Omega(n^{1/4})$ space in a special model of machines (Sound-Path-Machines) [3] .

(2) Description of the games:

Let G always be a directed acyclic graph with vertex set V and edge set E , $\Gamma_G^{-1}(x)$ the set of all direct predecessors of the vertex x and $\Gamma_G^{\stackrel{*}{-}1}(x)$ the set of all predecessors of x , i.e. the set of all vertices, from which there is a directed path to x in G . If it is clear which graph is concerned, we only write $\Gamma^{-1}(x)$, $\Gamma^{\stackrel{*}{-}1}(x)$. For $x \in V$ let V_x be the set $\Gamma_G^{\stackrel{*}{-}1}(x) \cup \{x\}$ and G_x the induced subgraph of G with vertex set V_x .

(2.1) The black-white pebble game is played on a DAG G by placing black or white pebbles on some vertices of G according to certain rules which are implicit in the following description:

A configuration of G is a pair (B,W) with $B,W \subset V$ and $B \cap W = \emptyset$. B is the set of vertices, on which black pebble are lying, W that one for white pebbles.

We say "(B,W) directly derives (B', W') using k pebbles" and write

"$(B,W) \Rightarrow_k (B', W')$" iff $B \cup W \subset B' \cup W'$ or $B' \cup W' \subset B \cup W$ and

either (i) $W=W'$, $\#(B \setminus B')=1$

or (ii) $W=W'$, $B' \setminus B=\{x\}$ and $\Gamma^{-1}(x) \subset W \cup B$ for some $x \in V$

or (iii) $B=B'$, $\#(W' \setminus W)=1$

or (iv) $B=B'$, $W \setminus W'=\{x\}$ and $\Gamma^{-1}(x) \subset W \cup B$ for some $x \in V$

or (v) $B=B'$, $W=W'$

and $\# W + \# B \leq k$, $\# W' + \# B' \leq k$

where for some set A , $\# A$ is the number of element of A . A sequence $[(B_i, W_i), i = 1...n]$ is called a b/w-k-strategy from (B,W) to (B',W') in G , iff (B_i, W_i) are configurations of G and $(B_i, W_i) \Rightarrow_k (B_{i+1}, W_{i+1})$ for all i and $(B_1, W_1) = (B,W)$, $(B_n, W_n) = (B',W')$.

(2.2) The black pebble game is a special kind of the black-white pebble game: A b/w-k-strategy $[(B_i,W_i), i = 1...n]$ in G is called a b/w-k-strategy from D to D' in G iff $W_i = \emptyset$ for all i and $B_1 = D$, $B_n = D'$. In this case we write $[D_i, i = 1...n]$ for the strategy.

(2.3) The object of both games is to find a strategy which begins with the empty configuration and ends with one black pebble on a distinguished vertex and no white pebbles using a number of pebbles as small as possible.

Notations: $Opt(G,r)$ = number of pebbles used in an optimal b/w-strategy (i.e. in a strategy which uses a minimal number of pebbles) from $(\emptyset,\emptyset)$ to $(\{r\}, \emptyset)$. We define $Opt_b(G,r)$ for b-strategies analogously.

Remark: In [3] and [4], the object of the game is defined in an other way, but optimal strategies in the sense of [3] and [4] and in the sense of (2.3) differ by at most one pebble.

(2.4) Intuitively, we can think of the black-white pebble game as a model of a proof:
The sources (vertices without predecessors) are the axioms, known theorems

etc., a distinguished vertex r is the theorem which shall be proved and the other vertices are lemmas. Each lemma and the theorem can be deduced from its predecessors. Placing a black pebble on a vertex corresponds to proving the lemma (theorem) by its predecessors, placing a white pebble on a vertex corresponds to assuming this lemma (theorem) to be true, intending later to justify it by its predecessors. The maximal number of pebbles used in some configuration corresponds to the maximal number of lemmas, one must have "in mind" at one time.

(2.5) The <u>black pebble game</u> can be looked upon as a model for an evaluation of a (for example boolean) expression by a register machine:
A vertex is an operator, its predecessors are its operands, the sources are the variables and the pebbles the registers. Placing a pebble on a vertex x corresponds to computing the value of the subexpression in the register (Notice that all predecessors of x are pebbled, i.e. all operands are available). Removing a pebble from a vertex corresponds to freeing the register. Thus, the number of pebbles used in the game corresponds to the number of registers used in the computation.

(3) <u>Some known results about pebble games</u>

(3.1) For both games, it is known that if G is a DAG with indegree 2 (i.e. $\#(\Gamma^{-1}(x)) \leq 2$ for all $x \in V$) and n vertices, then an optimal strategy from $(\emptyset, \emptyset)$ to $(\{r\}, \emptyset)$ for some $r \in V$ uses less or equal to $\Omega(n/\log n)$ pebbles and there exists a family of graphs which needs this number of pebbles [1], [2], [6].

(3.2) If S_m is a pyramid with m levels and sink r (S_5 is shown in figure 1) then $\mathrm{Opt}_{b/w}(S_m,r) \geq \sqrt{\frac{m}{2}} - 1$ [3] .

(3.3) $\mathrm{Opt}_b(S_m,r) = m + 1$ [4] .

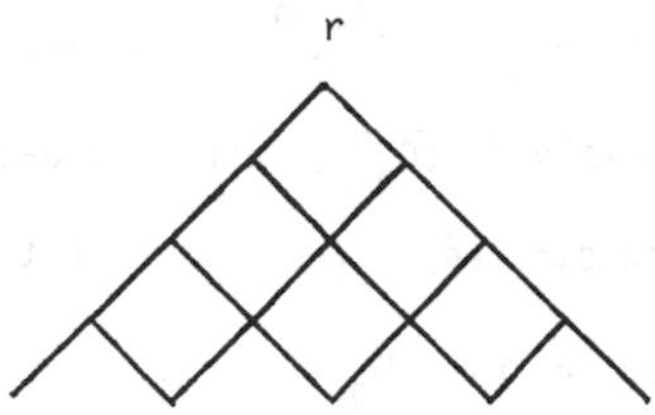

<u>Figure 1:</u> The pyramid S_5

(4) We state without proof 3 simple, technical lemmas:

(4.1) <u>Lemma 1:</u> Let $[(B_i, W_i), i = 1...n]$ be a b/w-k-strategy in G, then $[(W_{n-i+1}, B_{n-i+1}), i = 1...n]$ is a b/w-k-strategy in G. Let us call this strategy the <u>contra-strategy of $[(B_i, W_i), i = 1...n]$</u>.

(4.2) <u>Lemma 2:</u> Let $[(B_i, W_i), i = 1...n]$ be a b/w-k-strategy in G, H an induced subgraph of G with vertex set $V(H)$, then $[(B_i \cap V(H), W_i \cap V(H)), i = 1...n]$ is a b/w-k-strategy in H. If $H = G_x$ for some x, then $[B_i \cap V(H), W_i \cap V(H)), i = 1...n]$ is also a b/w-k-strategy in G.

(4.3) <u>Lemma 3:</u> If G is a DAG, (B,W) a configuration in G, $\overline{G}$ the induced subgraph of G with vertex set $V \setminus (B \cup W)$ and $[(B_i, W_i), i = 1...n]$ is a b/w-k-strategy in $\overline{G}$, then $[(B_i \cup B, W_i \cup W), i = 1...n]$ is a b/w-$(k + \#(B \cup W))$-strategy in G.

In the first theorem we shall see that for the family of pyramids, the b/w-pebble game does save at least a factor $\frac{1}{2}$.

(5) <u>Theorem 1:</u> $Opt(S_m, r) \leq \lceil \frac{m}{2} \rceil + 2$ for $m \geq 2$.

<u>Proof</u> by induction on m.

Obviously, $Opt(S_1, r) = 1$, $Opt(S_2, r) = 3$, $Opt(S_3, r) = 4$.

Let $m \geq 4$ and $[C_{n-2}]$ be the $(\lceil \frac{m-2}{2} \rceil + 2)$ - strategy for S_{m-2}, given by induction hypothesis and $[\overline{C_{n-2}}]$ the contra-strategy of $[C_{n-2}]$.

Then consider the following strategy: (We use the notations of figure 2).

1) place a black pebble on a by $[C_{n-2}]$,

2) place a black pebble on c by $[C_{n-2}]$,

3) place a white pebble on b,

4) go on as shown in figure 2,

5) remove the white pebble from b by $[\overline{C_{n-2}}]$.

This strategy needs $\max\{(\lceil\frac{m-2}{2}\rceil + 2) + 1, 4\}$ pebbles. As $m \geq 4$, we need $\lceil\frac{m-2}{2}\rceil + 2 + 1 = \lceil\frac{m}{2}\rceil + 2$ pebbles.

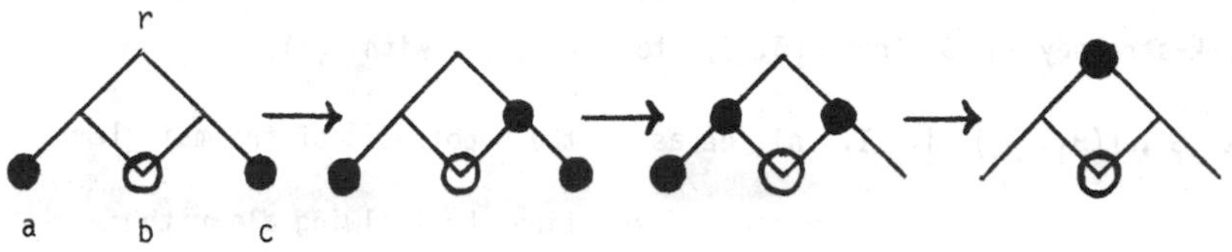

Figure 2: The top of S_m

The following theorem gives a method to change b/w-strategies into b-strategies. As a corollary we improve the lower bound in (3.2) by a factor of 2.

(6) Theorem 2: Let $G = (V,E)$ be a DAG, $r \in V$, $Opt(G,r) = k$ then $Opt_b(G,r) \leq \frac{k^2-k}{2} + 1$, i.e. $Opt(G,r) \geq \frac{1}{2} + \sqrt{2 \cdot Opt_b(G,r) - 1\frac{3}{4}}$.

(6.1) Cor: $Opt(S_m) \geq \frac{1}{2} + \sqrt{2 \cdot (m+1) - 1\frac{3}{4}}$.

The idea of the proof is to replace a move of a b/w-strategy in which a white pebble is placed on a vertex by a b-strategy which places a black pebble on it. The observation that it is not useful to place a white pebble on a vertex x, if $Opt(G_x, x) = Opt(G,r)$ yields the recursion: if $F(k) = \max\{Opt_b(G,r), G,r$ chosen such that $Opt(G,r) \leq k\}$ then $F(1) = 1$ and $F(k) \leq F(k-1) + k - 1$ which implies the theorem.

(6.2) Main lemma: Let G be a DAG, $[(B_i, W_i), i = 1...n]$ a b/w-k-strategy from $(\emptyset, \emptyset)$ to $(\{r\}, \emptyset)$ in G, then there exists a b/w-k-strategy from $(\emptyset, \emptyset)$ to $(\{r\}, \emptyset)$ - $[(B_i^*, W_i^*), i = 1...m]$ - with the property:

(*) For all ℓ, if $W_\ell^* \setminus W_{\ell-1}^* = \{x\}$ for some x and $S_x^{\ell-1}$ is the induced subgraph of G with vertex set $V_x \setminus (B_{\ell-1}^* \cup W_{\ell-1}^*)$, then there is a b/w-

(k - 1)-strategy from $(\emptyset, \emptyset)$ to $(\{x\}, \emptyset)$ in $S_x^{\ell-1}$.

Proof:

We construct a new sequence $[(B_i^*, W_i^*), i = 1...n]$ and show that it is a b/w-k-strategy in G from $(\emptyset, \emptyset)$ to $(\{r\}, \emptyset)$ with (*) .

Let G , $[(B_i, W_i), i = 1...n]$ be as in the hypothesis of the main lemma. Transform it into a new sequence by executing the follwing algorithm:

(6.2.1) Begin:

Let $\{\ell_1...\ell_p\}$ be the set of indices such that

(**) $W_{\ell_i} \setminus W_{\ell_{i-1}} = \{x_i\}$ for some x_i and there is a $j \geq \ell_i : \#((W_j \cup B_j) \cap V_{x_i}) = k$. Let j_i be the maximal such j and $t_i = \max \{h | x_i \in W_{\ell_i} ... W_h\}$.

Loop:

For $i = 1$ until p do
if $j_i < t_i$

Comment: One move after k pebbles are the last time in V_{x_i} , the white pebble is still on x_i ;

then $[(B_i, W_i), i = 1...n] \leftarrow [(B_1 \cap \Gamma^{*1}(x_i), W_1 \cap \Gamma^{*1}(x_i)),...,$
$(B_{j_i+1} \cap \Gamma^{*1}(x_i), W_{j_i+1} \cap \Gamma^{*1}(x_i)), (B_{j_i+1} \cap \Gamma^{*1}(x_i) ,$
$(W_{j_i+1} \cap \Gamma^{*1}(x_i)) \cup \{x_i\}), (B_{j_i+2}, W_{j_i+2}),...,(B_n, W_n)]$;

else

Comment: $t_i \leq j_i$, i.e., the white pebble on x is removed in the last move which reduces the number of pebbles in V_x from k to (k - 1) or earlier;

$[(B_i, W_i), i = 1...n] \leftarrow [(B_1 \cap \Gamma^{*1}(x_i), W_1 \cap \Gamma^{*1}(x_i)),...,$
$(B_{t_i} \cap \Gamma^{*1}(x_i), W_{t_i} \cap \Gamma^{*1}(x_i)), (B_{t_i+1} \cap V_{x_i}, W_{t_i+1} \cap V_{x_i}),...,$
$(B_{j_i} \cap V_{x_i}, W_{j_i} \cap V_{x_i}), (B_{j_i+1}, W_{j_i+1}),...,(B_n, W_n)]$;

End;

We conclude the main lemma from the following 3 propositions:

Let $[(B_i, W_i), i = 1...n]$ be the input sequence for some pass of the loop and ℓ, x, j, t the actual values of ℓ_i, x_i, j_i and t_i then:

(6.2.2) - the output sequence of the pass of the loop is a b/w-k-strategy from $(\emptyset, \emptyset)$ to $(r, \emptyset)$,

(6.2.3) - if a configuration (B,W) is inserted in the "then-clause" between (B_{j+1}, W_{j+1}) and (B_{j+2}, W_{j+2}) , then $\#(B \cup W) \leq k - 1$ and after the pass of the loop, $\#((B_q \cup W_q) \cap V_x) \leq k - 1$ for all $q \geq j + 2$,

(6.2.4) - if for some y and q $[(B_q \cap V_y, W_q \cap V_y),...,(B_m \cap V_y, W_m \cap V_y)]$ is a b/w-(k - 1)-strategy, then it is still one after the pass.

If we have this, it follows that the output-sequence of the algorithm - $[(B_i^*, W_i^*), i = 1...m]$ - is a b/w-k-strategy in G from $(\emptyset, \emptyset)$ to $(\{r\}, \emptyset)$ with the property:

For all ℓ , if $W_\ell^* \setminus W_{\ell-1}^* = \{x\}$ for some x , then the sequence $[(B_i^* \cap V_x, W_i^* \cap V_x), i = \ell...m]$ is a b/w-(k - 1)-strategy in G_x . By Lemma 2, (4.5), it follows, that

$[((B_i^* \cap V_x) \setminus (B_{\ell-1}^* \cup W_{\ell-1}^*)), (W_i^* \cap V_x) \setminus (B_{\ell-1}^* \cup W_{\ell-1}^*)), i = \ell...m]$

is a b/w-(k - 1)-strategy in $S_x^{\ell-1}$.

Notice that $(B_\ell^* \cap V_x) \setminus (B_{\ell-1}^* \cup W_{\ell-1}^*) = \emptyset$, $(W_\ell^* \cap V_x) \setminus (B_{\ell-1}^* \cup W_{\ell-1}^*) = \{x\}$, $(W_m^* \cap V_x) \setminus (B_{\ell-1}^* \cup W_{\ell-1}^*) = \emptyset$ and

$$(B_m^* \cap V_x) \setminus (B_{\ell-1}^* \cup W_{\ell-1}^*) = \begin{cases} \emptyset, & x \neq r \\ \{r\}, & x = r \quad (***) \end{cases} .$$

In the case (***) remove the black pebble from r in a new move. Now we have a b/w-(k - 1)-strategy in $S_x^{\ell-1}$ from $(\emptyset, \{x\})$ to $(\emptyset, \emptyset)$ and with the help of Lemma 1 (4.1), the main lemma follows.

It remains to prove (6.2.2), (6.2.3), (6.2.4) .

Proof of (6.2.2):

Case 1: The "then-clause" is executed.

- $[(B_1 \cap \Gamma^{*1}(x), W_1 \cap \Gamma^{*1}(x)),\ldots,(B_{j+1} \cap \Gamma^{*1}(x), W_{j+1} \cap \Gamma^{*1}(x))]$ is a b/w-k-strategy because of Lemma 2 (4.2) .

- $(B_{j+1} \cap \Gamma^{*1}(x), W_{j+1} \cap \Gamma^{*1}(x)) \Rightarrow_k$ $(B_{j+1} \cap \Gamma^{*1}(x), (W_{j+1} \cap \Gamma^{*1}(x)) \cup \{x\}))$, because it is always allowed to place a white pebble and because of the following:

  As $\#((B_j \cup W_j) \cap V_x) = k$, it follows that $B_j \cup W_j \subset V_x$ and that in the next move, one pebble will be removed (j maximal!) .

  Therefore, $\#(B_{j+1} \cup W_{j+1}) \leq k - 1$ and as $x \in W_{j+1}$:

  $\#((B_{j+1} \cap \Gamma^{*1}(x)) \cup (W_{j+1} \cap \Gamma^{*1}(x))) \leq k - 2$ and

(6.2.5) $\#((B_{j+1} \cap \Gamma^{*1}(x)) \cup (W_{j+1} \cap \Gamma^{*1}(x)) \cup \{x\}) \leq k - 1$.

- $(B_{j+1} \cap \Gamma^{*1}(x), (W_{j+1} \cap \Gamma^{*1}(x)) \cup \{x\}) \Rightarrow_k (B_{j+2}, W_{j+2})$, because $B_{j+1} \cap \Gamma^{*1}(x) = B_{j+1}$ and $W_{j+1} \cap \Gamma^{*1}(x)) \cup \{x\} = W_{j+1}$.

- $[(B_{j+2}, W_{j+2}),\ldots,(B_m, W_m)]$ is b/w-k-strategy in G .

Case 2: The "else-clause" is executed.

- $[(B_1 \cap \Gamma^{*1}(x), W_1 \cap \Gamma^{*1}(x)),\ldots,(B_t \cap \Gamma^{*1}(x), W_t \cap \Gamma^{*1}(x))]$ and $[(B_{t+1} \cap V_x, W_{t+1} \cap V_x),\ldots,(B_j \cap V_x, W_j \cap V_x)]$ are b/w-k-strategies because of Lemma 2 (4.2) .

- $(B_t \cap \Gamma^{*1}(x), W_t \cap \Gamma^{*1}(x)) \Rightarrow_k (B_{t+1} \cap V_x, W_{t+1} \cap V_x)$, because $B_t \cap \Gamma^{*1}(x) = B_{t+1} \cap V_x$ and $W_t \setminus W_{t+1} = \{x\}$, therefore: $W_{t+1} \cap V_x = W_t \cap \Gamma^{*1}(x)$.

- $(B_j \cap V_x, W_j \cap V_x) \Rightarrow_k (B_{j+1}, W_{j+1})$, because $B_j, W_j \subset V_x$.

- $[(B_{j+1}, W_{j+1}),\ldots,(B_m, W_m)]$ is a b/w-k-strategy.

Proof of (6.2.3):

$\#(B \cup W) \leq k - 1$, because $(B,W) = (B_{j+1} \cap \Gamma^{*1}(x),(W_{j+1} \cap \Gamma^{*1}(x))\cup\{x\})$ and because of (6.2.5).

$\#(B_q \cup W_q) \leq k - 1$ for all $q \geq j + 2$, because none of these configurations is manipulated by the pass and j was chosen maximally.

Proof of (6.2.4):

The algorithm inserts new configurations only in the "then-clause", and in (6.2.5) we have seen, that these new configurations always use less than k pebbles. If the algorithm manipulates some configuration, it never enlarges it. (6.2.4) follows by Lemma 2 (4.2) and (6.2.2).

Proof of theorem 2:

By induction on k we prove:

(6.3) On every DAG, on which we have a b/w-k-strategy from $(\emptyset, \emptyset)$ to $(\{r\}, \emptyset)$, we have a b-$(\frac{k^2-k}{2} + 1)$-strategy from $\emptyset$ to $\{r\}$.

For $k = 1$, (6.3) is obvious.

Let $k \geq 1$ and G be a DAG, $[(B_i, W_i), i = 1\ldots n]$ a b/w-$(k + 1)$-strategy in G from $(\emptyset, \emptyset)$ to $(\{r\}, \emptyset)$. Then by the main lemma, there is a b/w-$(k + 1)$-strategy in G from $(\emptyset, \emptyset)$ to $(\{r\}, \emptyset)$ with property (*). Let this strategy be $[(B_i^*, W_i^*), i = 1\ldots m]$.

Let $\{\ell_1\ldots\ell_p\}$ be the set of numbers such that $W_{\ell_i}^* \setminus W_{\ell_i-1}^* = \{x_i\}$ for some x_i. Then for every i, there is a b/w-k-strategy $[(B_j^i, W_j^i), i = 1\ldots n_i]$ in $S_{x_i}^{\ell_i-1}$ from $(\emptyset, \emptyset)$ to $(x_i, \emptyset)$. From the induction hypothesis we know that there is a b-$(\frac{k^2-k}{2} + 1)$-strategy from $\emptyset$ to $\{x_i\}$ in $S_{x_i}^{\ell_i-1}$ for each $i = 1\ldots p$.

The induction hypothesis for $k + 1$ follows immediately from the following

(6.3.1) <u>Lemma:</u> Let $[(B_i, W_i), i = 1\ldots n]$ be a b/w-k-strategy in G. If a white pebble is placed on x in (B_ℓ, W_ℓ) and removed in (B_{t+1}, W_{t+1}), $\#(B_{\ell-1} \cup W_{\ell-1}) = d$ and there is a b-k_1-strategy $[D_i, i = 1\ldots p]$ in $S_x^{\ell-1}$ from $\emptyset$ to $\{x\}$ and $\bar{k} = \max\{d + k_1, k\}$, then $[(B_1, W_1),\ldots,(B_{\ell-1}, W_{\ell-1}), (B_{\ell-1} \cup D_1, W_{\ell-1}),\ldots,(B_{\ell-1} \cup D_p, W_{\ell-1})$, $(B_{\ell+1} \cup \{x\}, W_{\ell+1} \setminus \{x\}),\ldots,(B_t \cup \{x\}, W_t \setminus \{x\})$, $(B_{t+1}, W_{t+1}),\ldots,(B_n, W_n)]$ is a b/w-$\bar{k}$-strategy in G.

Now for all ℓ_i we have:

$\#(B^*_{\ell_i-1} \cup W^*_{\ell_i-1}) \le k$, because in the next move a pebble is placed on the graph. By the lemma and the induction hypothesis it follows that there is a b - $(\frac{k^2-k}{2} + 1 + k)$-strategy from $\emptyset$ to $\{r\}$ in G.

As $\frac{k^2-k}{2} + 1 + k = \frac{(k+1)^2 - (k+1)}{2} + 1$, the theorem follows.

It remains to prove the lemma:

<u>Proof of the lemma:</u>

It is clear, that the maximal number of pebbles used in some configuration is $\bar{k}$.

- $[(B_1, W_1),\ldots,(B_{\ell-1}, W_{\ell-1})]$ and $[(B_{t+1}, W_{t+1})\ldots(B_n, W_n)]$ are b/w-$\bar{k}$-strategies in G.
- $(B_{\ell-1}, W_{\ell-1}) \Rightarrow_{\bar{k}} (B_{\ell-1} \cup D_1, W_{\ell-1})$, because $D_1 = \emptyset$.
- $[(B_{\ell-1} \cup D_1, W_{\ell-1}),\ldots,(B_{\ell-1} \cup D_p, W_{\ell-1})]$ is a b/w-$\bar{k}$-strategy because of Lemma 3 (4.3).
- $(B_{\ell-1} \cup D_p, W_{\ell-1}) \Rightarrow_{\bar{k}} (B_{\ell+1} \cup \{x\}, W_{\ell+1} \setminus \{x\})$ because $D_p = \{x\}$ and therefore $B_\ell \cup W_\ell = B_{\ell-1} \cup D_p \cup W_{\ell-1}$.
- $[(B_{\ell+1} \cup \{x\}, W_{\ell+1} \setminus \{x\}),\ldots,(B_t \cup \{x\}, W_t \setminus \{x\})]$ is a b/w-$\bar{k}$-strategy

because $B_{\ell+i} \cup W_{\ell+i} = (B_{\ell+i} \cup \{x\}) \cup (W_{\ell+i} \setminus \{x\})$.

- $(B_t \cup \{x\}, W_t \setminus \{x\}) \Rightarrow_k (B_{t+1}, W_{t+1})$, because $W_t \setminus \{x\} = W_{t+1}$, $B_{t+1} = B_t$ and it is always allowed to remove a black pebble.

Conclusion:

We have seen that, if we have an optimal b-strategy in G with k pebbles, then every b/w-strategy needs at least $\Omega(k^{1/2})$ pebbles, but no example is known in which the b/w pebble game saves more than a constant factor.

References:

[1] W. Paul, R.E. Tarjan, J.R. Celoni: Space bounds for a game on graphs, Math. Systems Theory 10 (1976/77), 239-251.

[2] J.R. Gilbert, R.E. Tarjan: Variations of a pebble game, preprint, Stanford, 1978.

[3] S. Cook, R. Sethi: Storage requirements for deterministic polynomial time recognizable languages, Journal Comp. and Syst. Sc. 13 (1976), 25-37.

[4] S. Cook: An observation on time-storage trade off, Proceedings of the Fifth Annual ACM Symp. on Theory of Computing (1973), 29-33.

[5] J. Hopcroft, W. Paul, L. Valiant: On time versus space and related problems, Sixteenth Annual Symposium on Foundations of Computer Science (1975), 57-64.

LL(k) Parsing for Attributed Grammars

D. R. Milton

Bell Laboratories

Naperville, IL 60540

C. N. Fischer†

Computer Sciences Department

University of Wisconsin-Madison

Madison, WI 53706

1. Introduction

It is well-known that many aspects of programming language syntax cannot be expressed with a context-free grammar. However, context-free methods are particularly attractive to language implementors, since they are of proven value in organizing translations. Accordingly, numerous efforts have been made to extend the power of context-free grammars. Examples include matrix grammars, time-varying grammars, programmed grammars, and van Wijngaarden grammars ([Sal 73], [Wij 75]). A major problem with these grammars is that they were designed primarily as generative and definitional devices — no efficient techniques for their recognition or parsing are known.

The approach we have taken to the problem of providing a readable and parsable programming language specification mechanism involves the use of attributed grammars. Previous work has established attributed grammars as an effective tool for semantic specification and for the implementation of the translation phase of compilers (*e.g.*, [Wil 71], [Fan 72], [LRS 74], [Bra 76], [LRS 76]). We will investigate a class of attributed grammars, called ALL(k), for which efficient top-down parsers can be generated, and which is sufficiently powerful to handle the context-sensitive aspects of programming language syntax. In addition, we will find that ALL(k) grammars can often provide a more succinct specification than equivalent context-free grammars.

† Work supported in part by NSF grant #MCS 78-02570.

2. Attributed Grammars

Informally, an attributed grammar is a context-free grammar where attributes may be associated with each non-terminal and terminal symbol. In addition, attribute evaluation functions may be attached to each production. Each such function defines the value of an attribute of a symbol as a function of attributes of symbols appearing in the same production. Attributes are segregated into two disjoint sets: a synthesized attribute of a symbol is a function of the attributes of the symbol's immediate descendants; an inherited attribute of a symbol is a function of the symbol's immediate parent or siblings. A (fully-evaluated) derivation tree for a sentence in the language of an attributed grammar has the same form as a context-free derivation tree. Each node is, however, additionally decorated with the values of the attributes of the respective symbols. For the "standard", formal definition of an attributed grammar, the reader is directed to [Knu 68], [Wil 71], or [Mil 77].

In order to clarify the concept of an attributed derivation, we augment the standard definition with the concept of *contextual predicates*. Contextual predicates may be attached to a production and are predicates on the attribute values of the symbols in that production (they are similar the primitive predicates defined by Koster for affix grammars [Kos 71], [Wat 77]). An attributed derivation is only valid when all of the contextual predicates associated with all of the applied productions evaluate to *true* on the corresponding attribute instances.

As an example, consider the following grammar fragment for an assignment statement:

assignment → leftside := rightside
CP: leftside.type = rightside.type

The contextual predicate requires that for a proper assignment the types of the leftside and rightside be identical.

Contextual predicates can be implemented within the standard framework of attribute evaluation with the addition of "error" attributes ([Wil 71]). The predicate would be replaced by an attribute evaluation rule that would evaluate a lefthand-side symbol attribute to *error* if the remaining attributes in the production violated a context-sensitive constraint.

Many typical context-sensitive restrictions in programming languages can be easily and naturally expressed with contextual predicates. Examples include restricting variables to be declared before they are used, checking the number and type of the actual arguments in procedure calls, and, as above, insisting on type-compatibility between the source and destination of assignments.

Formally, the class of attributed grammars is equivalent to the class of Type-0 grammars, but this is not a particularly interesting result since a Turing Machine can be embodied in a contextual predicate. It is more useful to look at attributed grammars as a semi-formal technique for *structuring* a language specification, rather than as a self-contained specification mechanism (in competition with, say, van Wijngaarden grammars). It is precisely this semi-formality that we exploit in the development of a *practical* parser.

3. Attributed ALL(k) Grammars

Top-down processing has particular advantages from the point of view of attribute handling. These result from the fact that a top-down parser constructs a derivation tree from left to right in a depth-first manner. At every point in the parse, there exists a partial derivation tree, and attribute evaluation rules can communicate context across this tree for use in further expansion. Since we are interested in efficiency and practicality, the class of LL(k) grammars immediately presents itself as a basis for attributed parsing ([LS 68], [RS 70]).

For a context-free grammar G = (N,T,P,S) (where N, T, and P are respectively the sets of nonterminals, terminals, and productions, and S is the start symbol), the standard LL(k) parsing function is a mapping:

$$M: (N \cup T) \times T^{*k} \rightarrow \{\textit{predict } i, \textit{pop}, \textit{error}, \textit{accept}\} .$$

That is, the parser uses the top stack symbol, $A \in N \cup T$, and the k-symbol lookahead, $u \in T^{*k}$, to determine the next move. The central idea behind *attributed* LL(k) parsing is to permit the parsing function to be a function not only of A and u but also of the evaluated attributes of A and u.

Since LL parsing proceeds left-to-right without backup, we need to constrain the attribute evaluation rules so that the attribute values needed by the parser will be available at the right time. There is no problem with the attributes of the lookahead, since the lookahead consists entirely of terminal symbols whose attributes are constrained (by definition) to be synthesized (*e.g.*, supplied by the scanner). If the stack symbol is a terminal, there is also no problem: its synthesized attributes will assume the values of the attributes of the input symbol it matches. The attributes of a nonterminal stack symbol present a greater difficulty. Its synthesized attributes cannot be available to the parser, since they are computed as a function of righthand-side attributes, and the righthand-side has yet to be predicted. The inherited attributes *may* be available, but only if they are strictly a function of previously evaluated attributes. Restricting all inherited attributes to depend only on their left context result in an *L-attributed* grammar, as defined by Lewis, Rosenkrantz, and Stearns ([LRS 74]). The L-attributed restrictions assure that the inherited attributes of a nonterminal stack symbol will have been evaluated by the time they are needed to guide the parser in making a prediction. Further, such restrictions guarantee that all contextual predicates associated with a production can be evaluated by the time that production is fully expanded. This allows prompt identification of many context-sensitive errors.

We require some notation to describe attributed symbols. A vocabulary symbol X together with its attributes (evaluated or unevaluated) will be denoted by X". X^I is the set of X" with exactly the inherited attributes evaluated, and X^S is the set of X" with exactly the synthesized attributes evaluated.

In order to integrate attributes into the parsing function, we allow *disambiguating* predicates to be included with the grammar specification. These are based upon the usual definition of the FIRST and FOLLOW functions ([AU 72]), as well as an attributed counterpart of FIRST:

Definition 3.1. For an attributed grammar G with the underlying context-free grammar G′, and $x \in (N \cup T)^*$,

$$AFIRST_k^G(x) = \{ w \mid w = X_1"...X_n",\ X_1...X_n \in FIRST_k^{G'}(x),\ \text{where } X_i" \in X_i^S \}.$$

$AFIRST_k$ is thus determined by assigning all possible attribute values to all of the attributes of the strings in $FIRST_k$. It must be emphasized that AFIRST is based on derivation in the underlying context-free grammar. Such derivations, of course, will include the attributed derivations of the attributed grammar, and, in non-trivial cases the inclusion will be proper. In practice, only the "required" members of AFIRST will be computed.

Definition 3.2. For each production $p_i = (X \rightarrow x)$ in an attributed grammar G, a d^k*-predicate* for p_i is a total predicate:

$$d_i^k\colon X^I \times AFIRST_k(x \cdot FOLLOW_k(X)) \rightarrow \{\mathit{true}, \mathit{false}\}\ .$$

The d^k-predicates will be used as follows: with the partially evaluated non-terminal X" on top of the parsing stack, and the attributed k-symbol lookahead u", production p_i may be predicted if and only if $d_i^k(X",u") = \mathit{true}$.

Definition 3.3. A d^k*-predicated attributed grammar* is a pair (G,D^k) where G is an attributed grammar, and D^k is a function that assigns to each $p_i \in P$ a predicate d_i^k.

Again, in practice, d^k-predicates need only be specified for those productions and lookaheads where LL(k) conflicts exist. If a d^k-predicate is not supplied for a production, a "default" predicate returning a constant *true* is assumed. If a d^k-predicate is supplied for only a subset of the possible lookahead strings, the predicate is assumed to be augmented to return *true* for the lookaheads not considered.

Definition 3.4. A strong ALL(k) grammar is a d^k-predicated attributed grammar such that for every pair of productions of the form:

$$p_1 = (X \rightarrow x_1)$$
$$p_2 = (X \rightarrow x_2)\ ,$$

if $u \in FIRST_k(x_1 \cdot FOLLOW_k(X)) \cap FIRST_k(x_2 \cdot FOLLOW_k(X))$
then for all $u" \in u^S$, and all $X" \in X^I$: $d_1(X",u")$ *and* $d_2(X",u") = \mathit{false}$.

That is, the attributes of the top stack symbol along with the attributes of the lookahead will be sufficient to resolve all strong LL(k) conflicts.

We can contrast the use of contextual and disambiguating predicates. Contextual predicates determine the validity of a production application based on the attributes of the symbols in that production. Given an attributed grammar G, z" $\in (T^S)^*$ is in L(G) when all contextual predicates associated with all applied productions in a derivation of z" evaluate to *true*. The d^k-predicates, on the other hand, are designed specifically to disambiguate the choices of a strong LL(k) parser. We can thus characterize the leftmost derivations of a strong ALL(k) grammar as follows: z" $\in L((G,D^k))$ exactly when z" $\in$ L(G) and each step in the associated leftmost derivation

$$w"A"y" \Rightarrow w"x"y" \Rightarrow^* z" \quad (w,z \in T^*,\ A \in N,\ x,y \in (N \cup T)^*),$$

has the following property:

$$\text{let } z" = w"v" \text{ and } p_t = (A \rightarrow x), \text{ then } d_t(A",u") = \textit{true}, \text{ where } u" = AFIRST_k(v").$$

From this concept of a strong ALL(k) derivation, and from the strong ALL(k) condition of Definition 3.4, we can obtain:

Theorem 3.5. No strong ALL(k) grammar is ambiguous.

4. The ALL(k) Parser

The strong ALL(k) parser may be thought of as a strong LL(k) parser which uses disambiguating predicates to determine the prediction move. *Predict* entries in the strong LL(k) table are computed as follows: *predict i* $\in$ M(A,u) whenever production i is $A \rightarrow x_i$ and $u \in FIRST_k(x_i \cdot FOLLOW_k(A))$. If for some A and u, $|M(A,u)| > 1$, then the grammar is not strong LL(k). If, however, the grammar is strong ALL(k), we can use the d^k-predicates to produce a single-valued *attributed* parsing function. In particular, production i is predicted for stack symbol A" and lookahead u" if and only if d_i(A",u") = *true*. By Definition 3.4, such moves are always uniquely predicted.

This parsing strategy can be readily incorporated into an attributed pushdown automaton ([LRS 74]) that will perform the required attribute evaluations in step with the parse. The automaton will also be responsible for evaluating the contextual predicates. Whenever a predicate evaluates to *false* the parse terminates in error.

In order to present the parsing algorithm, we will use a modification of the above automaton designed for efficient implementation ([LRS 76]). The essential difference is that each attribute evaluation rule and contextual predicate will be represented as a symbol in the righthand-side of the associated production. The symbol is stacked along with the righthand-side on a prediction, and the corresponding rule or predicate is executed when it reaches the top of the stack. A configuration of the parser is a triple, (x,Xw,m), where x is the unused portion of the input string, Xw is the contents of the stack with X on top, and m is the output string of production indices. m is initially ϵ, upon acceptance m will constitute the leftmost parse of the input. Let u = $AFIRST_k(x)$. The stack is initialized with S$, and the input string is terminated with the endmarker $.

Algorithm 4.1.

1. $(x,Xw,m) \vdash (x,zw,mi)$ if *predict i* $\in M(X,u)$ and $d_i(X'',u'') = $ *true*, where production i is $(X \rightarrow z)$.

2. $(x,Xw,m) \vdash (x,w,m)$ if X is an attribute evaluation rule.

3. $(x,Xw,m) \vdash (x,w,m)$ if X is a contextual predicate evaluating to *true*.

4. $(ax,aw,m) \vdash (x,w,m)$.

5. $(\$,\$,m) \vdash$ *accept* .

6. $(x,Xw,m) \vdash$ *error* if X is a contextual predicate evaluating to *false*.

7. $(x,Xw,m) \vdash$ *error* if $d_i(X'',u'') = $ *false* for all *predict i* $\in M(X,u)$.

As a simple example, consider the following grammar for arithmetic expressions with two levels of operator precedence (superscripts will be used to distinguish multiple instances of a symbol in a production):

1) $S \rightarrow E$

   $E.prec \leftarrow 1$

2) $E \rightarrow id$

   $d(E'',id)$: $(E.prec = 3)$

3) $E^1 \rightarrow E^2\ EL$

   $d(E^1'',id)$: $(E^1.prec \neq 3)$

   $E^2.prec \leftarrow E^1.prec + 1$

   $EL.prec \leftarrow E^1.prec + 1$

4) $EL^1 \rightarrow op\ E\ EL^2$

   $d(EL^1'',op'')$: $(EL^1.prec = op.prec)$

   $E.prec \leftarrow EL^1.prec$

   $EL^2.prec \leftarrow EL^1.prec$

5) $EL \rightarrow \epsilon$

   $d(EL'',op'')$: $(EL.prec \neq op.prec)$

The disambiguation will be done on the basis of the precedence level (the attribute "prec") of the current expression being parsed, along with the precedence of the operator. We adopt the convention that op<2> will represent "+" and op<3> will represent "*". Note that this grammar can be modified to handle any number of precedence levels *without* increasing number of productions. For expressions in ALGOL 60, which allows ten precedence levels, the strong ALL(1) grammar is about 1/5 the size of the equivalent LL(1) grammar, and uses many fewer vocabulary symbols.

The unattributed parsing table, M, appears below (we use an endmarker, $, to initialize the parse stack and to terminate the input). Since the underlying grammar is not LL(1), the entries for M(EL,op) and M(E,id) are multi-valued and will need to rely on the d-predicates for disambiguation.

	op	id	$
S		1	
E		2,3	
EL	4,5		5
op	*pop*		
id		*pop*	
$			*accept*

The grammar is strong ALL(1) since it is L-attributed and an exhaustive examination of the d-predicates reveals no conflicts.

We will trace the stack history of the parser on the input string, "id + id * id", which, after scanner preprocessing, will appear as:

id op<2> id op<3> id $.

stack	input	action
$ S	id op<2> id op<3> id $	*predict 1*
$ E<1>	id op<2> id op<3> id $	*predict 3*
$ EL<2> E<2>	id op<2> id op<3> id $	*predict 3*
$ EL<2> EL<3> E<3>	id op<2> id op<3> id $	*predict 2*
$ EL<2> EL<3> id	id op<2> id op<3> id $	*pop*
$ EL<2> EL<3>	op<2> id op<3> id $	*predict 5*
$ EL<2>	op<2> id op<3> id $	*predict 4*
$ EL<2> E<2> op<2>	op<2> id op<3> id $	*pop*
$ EL<2> E<2>	id op<3> id $	*predict 3*
$ EL<2> EL<3> E<3>	id op<3> id $	*predict 2*
$ EL<2> EL<3> id	id op<3> id $	*pop*
$ EL<2> EL<3>	op<3> id $	*predict 4*
$ EL<2> EL<3> E<3> op<3>	op<3> id $	*pop*
$ EL<2> EL<3> E<3>	id $	*predict 2*
$ EL<2> EL<3> id	id $	*pop*
$ EL<2> EL<3>	$	*predict 5*
$ EL<2>	$	*predict 5*
$	$	*accept*

5. Correctness and Linearity of the Parser

Informally, the "correctness" of a parser is the property that it accepts exactly those strings which are generated by the given grammar, (conditions sufficient to guarantee that the ALL(k) parser will halt announcing *error* for illegal strings will be discussed below). The correctness theorem for the strong ALL(k) parser is a straightforward analog of the similar result for the LL(k) parser

([AU 72]):

Theorem 5.1. Given a strong ALL(k) grammar, (G,D^k), there exists a disambiguated leftmost derivation:

$$S'' \Rightarrow_{m_1} z_1'' \Rightarrow_{m_2} \ldots \Rightarrow_{m_t} z_t'' , z_t'' \in L((G,D^k)),$$

if and only if the strong ALL(k) parser for (G,D^k) halts accepting on input z_t'' after making the predictions $m_1, m_2, \ldots, m_t$.

The number of moves executed by the strong LL(k) parsing algorithm on an input of length n is O(n) ([AU 72]). This is a direct result of the fact that LL(k) grammars cannot be left-recursive. A similar result can be obtained for the strong ALL(k) parser. Of course, if an ALL(k) grammar has an underlying LL(k), and hence non-left-recursive, grammar, linearity follows immediately. However, the ALL(k) definition does not require that the underlying grammar be LL(k), and even left-recursion is permitted (see the example in the previous section). But there is an attributive form of left-recursion which must be proscribed:

Definition 5.2. An ALL(k) grammar is *attributively left-recursive* if and only if there is an attributed leftmost derivation:

$$S'' \Rightarrow^* w''A''y'' \Rightarrow^+ w''A''x''y'' \Rightarrow^* \ldots$$

(Conditions which enable a grammar to be tested for attributive left-recursion are discussed in [Mil 77]).

Theorem 5.3. Given a strong ALL(k) grammar which is not attributively left-recursive, and which has finite attribute value sets for all attributes examined by the d^k-predicates, the number of moves performed by the corresponding strong ALL(k) parser on an input of length n in O(n).

The proof is virtually identical to the proof of linearity for the LL(k) parser. That is, the number of *predict* moves before a *pop* must be executed is bounded by the length of the longest partial derivation $A'' \Rightarrow^+ B''x''$, $A'' \neq B''$, which is bounded by the number of distinct attributed symbols, a grammar-dependent constant.

6. Conclusions

We have defined a parser which makes efficient use of the wealth of syntactic information available in the attributes of an attributed grammar. Moreover, we have found that, with contextual predicates, ALL(k) grammars can naturally express context-sensitive syntax, and, with disambiguating predicates, can significantly reduce the size of context-free grammars.

A compiler generator (the Aparse system) based on ALL(k) grammars has now been implemented. In combining the traditional usage of attributed grammars as a method for organizing translations) with their new role as a technique for structuring syntactic analysis, Aparse has been found to be a system of considerable flexibility and power ([MKR 79]).

References

[AU 72] Aho, A. V., and J. D. Ullman. *The Theory of Parsing, Translation, and Compiling, Volume 1: Parsing*, Prentice-Hall, Englewood Cliffs, N. J., 1972.

[Bra 76] Branquart, P., J.-P. Cardinael, J. Lewi, J.-P. Delescaille, and M. Vanbegin. *An Optimized Translation Process and its Application to ALGOL 68*, Springer-Verlag, Berlin, 1976.

[Fan 72] Fang, I. "FOLDS, A Declarative Formal Language Definition System," Ph.D. Thesis, Stanford Univ., 1972.

[Knu 68] Knuth, D. E. "Semantics of Context-free Languages," *Mathematical Systems Theory*, Vol. 2, No. 2, June 1968, pp. 127-146.

[Kos 71] Koster, C. H. A. "Affix Grammars," in: *ALGOL 68 Implementation* (J. E. Peck, ed.), North-Holland, Amsterdam, 1971.

[LRS 74] Lewis, P. M. II, D. J. Rosenkrantz, and R. E. Stearns. "Attributed Translations," *Journal of Computer and System Sciences*, Vol. 9, No. 3, Dec. 1974, pp. 279-307.

[LRS 76] Lewis, P. M. II, D. J. Rosenkrantz, and R. E. Stearns. *Compiler Design Theory*, Addison-Wesley, Reading, Mass., 1976.

[LS 68] Lewis, P. M. II, and R. E. Stearns, "Syntax-Directed Transduction," *Journal of the ACM*, Vol. 15, No. 3, July 1968, pp. 465-488.

[Mil 77] Milton, D. R. "Syntactic Specification and Analysis with Attributed Grammars," Ph.D. Thesis, University of Wisconsin-Madison, Comp. Sci. Dept. Tech. Rept. #304, 1977.

[MKR 79] Milton, D. R., L. W. Kirchhoff, and B. R. Rowland. "An ALL(1) Compiler Generator," *Conference Record of the SIGPLAN Symposium on Compiler Construction*, Aug. 1979 (to appear).

[RS 70] Rosenkrantz, D. J., and R. E. Stearns. "Properties of Deterministic Top-down Grammars," *Information and Control*, Vol. 17, No. 3, Oct. 1970, pp. 226-256.

[Sal 73] Salomaa, A. *Formal Languages*, Academic Press, New York, 1973.

[Wat 77] Watt, D. A. "The Parsing Problem for Affix Grammars," *Acta Informatica*, Vol. 8, 1977, pp. 1-20.

[Wij 75] Wijngaarden, A. van, B. J. Mailloux, J. E. L. Peck, C. H. A. Koster, M. Sintzoff, C. H. Lindsey, L. G. L. T. Meertens, and R. G. Fisher. "Revised Report on the Algorithmic Language ALGOL 68," *Acta Informatica*, Vol. 5, 1975.

[Wil 71] Wilner, W. T. "Declarative Semantic Definition," Ph.D. Thesis, Stanford Univ., 1971.

On eliminating nondeterminism from Turing machines which use less than logarithm worktape space.

by

Burkhard Monien[1] and Ivan Hal Sudborough*[2]

(1) Fachbereich 17
Gesamthochschule Paderborn
4790 Paderborn
West Germany

(2) E.E./C.S. Dept.
Northwestern University
Evanston, Illinois 60201
U. S. A.

* the work of this author was supported in part by NSF Grant No. MCS 77-02494 and was performed in part while visiting the Gesamthochschule Paderborn in Paderborn, Germany.

Abstract

A family of problems $\{GAP(2^{dS(n)})\}_{d>0}$ is described that is log space complete for NSPACE(S(n)), for functions S(n) which grow less rapidly than the logarithm function. An algorithm is described to recognize $GAP(2^{dS(n)})$ deterministically in space S(n) x log n. Thus, we show for constructible functions S(n), with log log n ≤ S(n) ≤ log n, that:

(1) NSPACE(S(n)) ⊆ DSPACE(S(n) x log n), and

(2) NSPACE(S(n)) ⊆ DSPACE(log n) iff

$\{GAP(2^{dS(n)})\}_{d>0} \subseteq$ DSPACE(log n)

In particular, when S(n) = log log n, we have: (1) NSPACE(log log n) ⊆ DSPACE(log n x log log n), and (2) NSPACE(log log n) ⊆ DSPACE(log n) iff $\{GAP(\log n)^d)\}_{d>0} \subseteq$ DSPACE(log n). In addition it is shown that the question of whether NSPACE(S(n)) is identical to DSPACE(S(n)), for sublogarithmic functions S(n), is closely related to the space complexity of the graph accessibility problem for graphs with bounded bandwidth.

Introduction

In 1969, Walter Savitch described a method for eliminating nondeterminism from L(n) space bounded Turing machines at a cost of the square of the tape bound, for all L(n) that grow at least as rapidly as the logarithm function [1,2]. That is, for all L(n) ≥ log n, $NSPACE(L(n)) \subseteq DSPACE(L(n)^2)$. Savitch also described a problem, the <u>graph accessibility problem</u> (GAP) or, as it is also called, the <u>threadable maze problem</u>, which is complete for NSPACE(log n) [2]. It follows from results about log space reduciblilities [3] that GAP is in DSPACE(log n) iff NSPACE(log n) = = DSPACE(log n). In addition, Savitch has shown that if NSPACE(log n) = DSPACE(log n), then NSPACE(L(n)) = DSPACE(L(n)), for all L(n) ≥ log n.

Here we consider the amount of space required by a deterministic Turing machine to simulate a nondeterministic L(n) space bounded Turing machine, when L(n) grows less rapidly than the logarithm function. An early result of Stearns, Hartmanis, and Lewis has shown that DSPACE(L(n)) = NSPACE(L(n)) is the family of regular sets, for all functions L(n) that grow less rapidly than any constant multiple of log log n [4]. Thus, we shall consider the NSPACE(L(n)) classes, for log log n ≤ L(n) ≤ log n.

For functions L(n), with log log n ≤ L(n) ≤ log n, we show that graph accessibility problems restricted to graphs with bandwidth $2^{dL(n)}$, for some d>0, denoted by GAP($2^{dL(n)}$), are log space complete for NSPACE(L(n)). (In [5], Papadimitriou has shown that the <u>bandwidth minimization problem</u> is log space complete for NP.) It is shown also that membership in GAP($2^{L(n)}$) can be determined deterministically in space L(n) x log n. It follows that NSPACE(L(n)) ⊆ DSPACE(log n x L(n)), for certain constructible functions L(n), where log log n ≤ L(n) ≤ log n. In particular, we show that NSPACE(log log n) ⊆ DSPACE(log n × log log n). This represents a considerable improvement over results previously described in the literature. That is, NSPACE(log log n) ⊆ NSPACE(log n) yields NSPACE(log log n) ⊆ DSPACE($(\log n)^2$) from Savitch's theorem [2] and no better result seems to have been known.

In particular, it follows from the fact that $\{GAP((\log n)^d)\}_{d>0}$ is log space complete for NSPACE(log log n) that NSPACE(log log n) ⊆ DSPACE(log n) iff $\{GAP((\log n)^d)\}_{d>0}$ is in DSPACE(log n). However, log space reducibility is not a particularly good tool for studying the question of whether NSPACE(log log n) = DSPACE(log log n), since DSPACE(log log n) is not closed under log space reducibilities. For this reason we consider L(n)-tape reducibility, for functions L(n), where log log n ≤ L(n) ≤ log n. It is observed that every language in NSPACE(L(n)) is L(n) tape reducible to one of the languages in $\{\widetilde{GAP}(2^{cL(n)})\}_{c=1,2,3,...}$

<u>Section 1</u>. Restricted Graph Accessibility Problems

Let G = (V,E) be a finite directed graph. We shall assume, for convenience that V is the set consisting of the first k natural numbers, for some k ≥ 1. We shall say that G has <u>bandwidth</u> m if (i,j) ∈ E implies |i-j| ≤ m. For example, the graph of Figure 1.1 has bandwidth three but not bandwidth two.

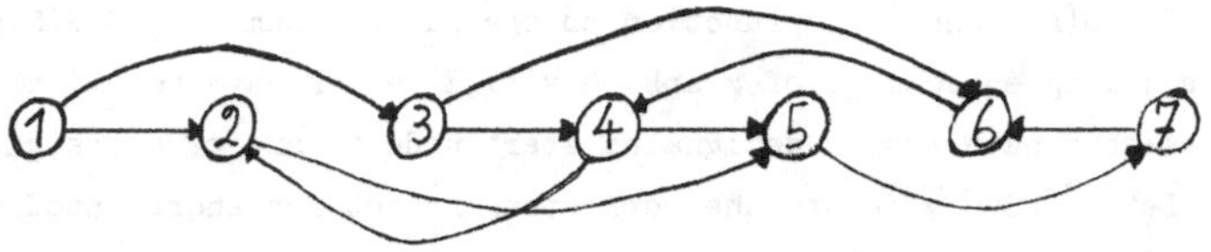

Figure 1.1   A graph with bandwidth three.

Let S(n) be a function on the natural numbers. A family of graphs $\{G_i\}_{i=1,2,3,\ldots}$ has bandwidth S(n), if each graph G_i in the family has bandwidth $S(|V_i|)$, where V_i is the set of vertices of G_i. It is, of course, true that the family of all finite graphs has bandwidth I(n), where I(n) is the identity function.

We shall need to fix on some convenient encoding of finite directed graphs. Let G = (V,E) be such a graph, where V = {1,2,...,k}, for some k ≥ 1. We shall actually not settle on just one encoding; instead, we shall describe two separate encodings. The long encoding of G, denoted by x_G, is the string:

$$\left[\text{bin}(1)\#\text{bin}\left(n_1^{(1)}\right)\#\text{bin}\left(n_2^{(1)}\right)\ldots\#\text{bin}\left(n_{t(1)}^{(1)}\right)\right]$$

$$\left[\text{bin}(2)\#\text{bin}\left(n_1^{(2)}\right)\#\text{bin}\left(n_2^{(2)}\right)\ldots\#\text{bin}\left(n_{t(2)}^{(2)}\right)\right]$$

$$\ldots$$

$$\left[\text{bin}(k)\#\text{bin}\left(n_1^{(k)}\right)\#\text{bin}\left(n_2^{(k)}\right)\ldots\#\text{bin}\left(n_{t(k)}^{(k)}\right)\right]$$

where bin(j) denotes the binary representation of the integer j (with no leading zeros, the first bit indicating whether the number is positiv or negativ), and, for 1 ≤ i ≤ k, $\{j \mid (i,j) \in E\} = \{i+n_l^{(i)} \mid 1 \le l \le t(i)\}$. That is, (1) there is a block for each node in G(a "block" is a string of the form $[x_1\#x_2\ldots\#x_t]$, where x_i is a string of 0's and 1's, for 1 ≤ i ≤ t), (2) each block begins with the number of the node in the graph it corresponds to, and (3) the numbers following the first number i in block i indicate how much needs to be added to i to get the numbers of nodes to which an edge enters from node i (these numbers can be positive or negative).

A short encoding of G, denoted by $\tilde{x}_G$, is a string identical to that described above for the long encoding of G except that the first number in each block is deleted. That is, the i-th block in $\tilde{x}_G$ is

$$\left[\text{bin}\left(n_1^{(i)}\right)\#\text{bin}\left(n_2^{(i)}\right)\ldots\#\text{bin}\left(n_{t(i)}^{(i)}\right)\right] \quad \text{and not}$$

$$\left[\text{bin}(i)\#\text{bin}\left(n_1^{(i)}\right)\#\text{bin}\left(n_2^{(i)}\right)\ldots\#\text{bin}\left(n_{t(i)}^{(i)}\right)\right].$$

Definition 1.1. Let $S(n)$ denote any function on the natural numbers. $GAP(S(n))$ denotes the set of all long endcodings of graphs $G = (V,E)$ which have bandwidth $S(|V|)$ and which possess a path from a designated start node to one of a designated set of goal nodes. Let $\widetilde{GAP}(S(n))$ denote the corresponding set for short endodings.

It needs to be indicated how certain nodes are designated as start nodes or goal nodes in the encoding strings. We shall stipulate that (1) if a node is a goal node, then the block corresponding to that node in the encoding will be immediately preceded by the symbol +, and (2) if a node is a start node, then the block corresponding to that node in the encoding will be immediately preceded by the symbol -.

Lemma 1.1. Let $f(n)$ be any constructible function such that $f(n) \geq n$. Let $S(n)$ be the function on the natural numbers defined by $S(n) = f(\log \log n)$. Then, $GAP(2^{S(n)})$ is in $NSPACE(S(n))$.

Proof. We construct a Turing machine that does the following steps in sequence on input x_G:

(1) mark off $S(n)$ worktape cells,

(2) check that the graph has bandwidth $2^{S(n)}$,

(3) determine whether there is a path from the start node to a goal node.

The Turing machine can mark off $S(n)$ worktape cells by first laying off $\log n$ worktape cells. This is possible since the successive first strings in the blocks of the encoding form the sequence: bin(1), bin(2),..., bin(n) and $\log \log n$ is known to be constructible on such a sequence [4]. The Turing machine can then mark off $S(n) = f(\log \log n)$ worktape cells, without using more than $S(n)$ worktape cells, using the fact that $f(n)$ is constructible.

The Turing machine can then perform step (2) and check that the graph has bandwidth $2^{S(n)}$. If this is the case, then every string in each block of the encoding except for the first string in each block, which is used for describing which mode the block corresponds to, has length at most $S(n)$. This can be checked by simply comparing the lengths of such strings on the input tape to the length of the marked off space on the worktape. Thus, checking whether the graph has bandwidth $2^{S(n)}$ can be done in space $S(n)$.

The Turing machine will perform step (3) nondeterministically by executing the following, with the start node chosen initially:

(a) Is the chosen node a goal node? If yes, stop and accept; otherwise, proceed to step (b)

(b) Choose a new node from the list of nodes to which an edge is directed from the current node and go to (a).

It should be noted that step (b) above is performed by selecting one of the strings $\text{bin}\left(n_j^{(i)}\right)$ from block i, when node i is the current node, writing this string into the worktape, and then subtracing one from this number for each block passed as the input head moves right (left) if $n_j^{(i)}$ is positive (negative) until the number is zero. The input head is then on the block corresponding to the next node. The procedure for step (3) is basically the same as in Savitch [2]. □

Lemma 1.2. Let S(n) be any constructible function on the natural numbers such that $\log\log n \le S(n) \le \log n$. Every language in NSPACE(S(n)) is log space reducible to $GAP(2^{dS(n)})$, for some $d > 0$.

Proof. Let M be a nondeterministic Tm and let w be an input string of length n. We describe a graph, denoted by G(M,w), which has bandwidth $2^{dS(n)}$, for some constant $d > 0$, and possesses a path from its start node to one of its goal nodes iff M accepts w within space S(n). That is, G(M,w) is in $GAP\left(2^{dS(n)}\right)$ iff M accepts w within space S(n).

Furthermore, for a fixed Tm M the process of producing on an output tape G(M,w), when given w of length n on the input, requires at most log n worktape cells.

The nodes of G(M,w) are instantaneous descriptions (ID's) of M on input w. That is, each node may be thought of as a triple $(s,i,w_1{\uparrow}w_2)$, where s is an internal state of M,i is an input head position, w_1w_2 is the content of M's worktape, and the leftmost symbol of w_2 is currently scanned by M's worktape head. The nodes of G(M,w) will be enumerated in such a way that all ID's with head position j occur before any ID with head position j+1, for $1 \le j < n$. We note that there are at most $pS(n)t^{S(n)} \le 2^{dS(n)}$, for some constant $d > 0$, ID's with a fixed head position, where t is the number of worktape symbols of M and p is the number of internal states.

The edges of G(m,w) correspond to transitions of M on input w. Since any transition of M moves its head from a cell to one on the immediate right or left of that cell, no edge goes from an ID with head position i to one with head position $i + \delta$, unless $\delta = \pm 1$. Since the nodes are enumerated (numbered) by consecutive head positions, this means that all edges are between nodes at most $2^{dS(n)}$ apart. In other words, G(M,w) has bandwidth $2^{dS(n)}$.

Let the start node of G(m,w) be the initial ID of M on input w. Let the goal nodes be the ID's with a final state. It follows that G(M,w) is in $GAP\left(2^{dS(n)}\right)$ iff M accepts w within space S(n). The proof is identical to that described by Savitch [2]. It is quite straightforward to verify that G(M,w) can be produced using at most $\log(|w|)$ worktape cells. (The constructibility condition on S(n), however, seems to be needed here to ensure that the log space machine can construct successive ID's of the S(n) space bounded Tm M.) Thus, every L in NSPACE(S(n)) is log space reducible to $GAP\left(2^{dS(n)}\right)$. □

Theorem 1.3. Let f be any constructible function with $n \leq f(n) \leq 2^n$. Let $S(n) = f(\log \log n)$. Then, $\{GAP(2^{dS(n)})\}_{d>0}$ is log space complete for NSPACE(S(n)).

Proof. Follows immediately from Lemma 1.1. and Lemma 1.2. □

Corollary 1.4. $\{GAP((\log n)^d)\}_{d>0}$ is in DSPACE(log n) iff NSPACE(log log n) $\subseteq$ DSPACE(log n).

Although we are unable, as yet, to show GAP(log n) is in DSPACE(log n), we are able to show that GAP($(\log n)^d$)is in DSPACE($\log n \times \log \log n$). This means, of course, that NSPACE(log log n) $\subseteq$ DSPACE($\log n \times \log \log n$). In fact, we show that GAP(S(n)) is in DSPACE($\log n \times \log (S(n))$), for all S(n), where $\log n \leq S(n) \leq n$.

The basic idea of the algorithm is a divide-and-conquer concept. The question of whether or not a path exists from a node s_1 to a node s_2 is divided into a fixed number of smaller questions. The division of the path questions is handled in such a way that at each step either the length of the path searched for is divided in half or the region of the graph in which the path is looked for is divided in half. This means that c log n blocks are sufficient to record information about these successively smaller path questions, for some constant $c > 0$. That is , the original path question is one of whether or not a path exists in the whole graph of length at most n, where n is the number of nodes of the graph, from the start node to a goal node. At each step either the path length or portion of the graph investigated is divided by two, so that on the order of log n steps are required before the path question has been divided into one of length at most one. (Note that if the portion of the graph investigated has k nodes, then the maximum length path we need to look for is of length k. Thus, dividing the portion of the graph investigated decreases the maximum length of non-looping paths as well.)

The economy in our algorithm over the basic divide-and-conquer algorithm described by Savitch [2] is in the lengths of the blocks. For graphs of bandwidth S(n) we show that the process can be arranged so that each block has length d log S(n), for some constant $d > 0$. This is done by indicating the position of a node within a certain set of S(n) nodes, called a window, rather than the position of this node in the whole graph. Furthermore, the windows are chosen in an easily computable manner so that one can obtain the position of a node in the whole graph from the history of division steps recorded on the worktape and the recorded position of that node within a window. For example, for graphs of bandwidth log n, the blocks will have length log log n, which represents a considerable improvement over the basic divide-and-conquer algorithm [2] with blocks of length log n.

Let x_G be a long encoding of a graph G. The sequence of blocks in x_G consisting of blocks j, j+1,..., j+i-1 will be called a window of size i starting at block j. A window of size i is any of the various windows of size i starting at block j, for j ≥ 1. Let G = (V,E) be a graph with bandwidth m and let W be any window of size m. If P is a path from node s_1 to node s_2 in G, then P must either pass through a node in the window W or P must be pass only through nodes to the left or right of W in x_G. This follows simply from the fact that G has bandwidth m and W is a window of size m; hence, no edge can be from a node to the left (right) of W to a node to the right (left) of W.

If P is a path in a graph G = (V,E), then |P| will denote the length of the path, i.e. the number of edges traversed. The following lemma describes how the division process of a given path question will take place in our algorithm. That is, it justifies our assertion that one can divide up a given path question into at most three smaller path questions with the intermediate nodes being chosen from a suitable window.

Lemma 1.5. Let x_G be the long encoding of a graph G = (V,E) with n vertices with bandwidth S(n). Let W be a window of size S(n) in x_G. If x , y are any two nodes of G and there is a path P from x to y , then either:

(a) there are nodes z_1 and z_2, both in the window W or one in W and the other either x or y , such that z_1 and z_2 are nodes entered in the path P and each of the following three conditions is satisfied:

(1) the path P_1, the portion of the path P from x to z_1, is of length at most one half the length of P,

(2) the path P_2, the portion of the path P from z_1 to z_2, is completely to the left or right of the window W,

(3) the path P_3, the portion of the path P from z_2 to y , is of length at most one half the length of P.

(b) the path P is entirely to the left or right of the window W.

Proof. Our assumption is that a path P exists from node x to node y. Suppose this path does not pass through any node in the window. Then both x and y must be on one side of the window, either the left or the right, since paths in a S(n) bounded graph cannot have edges which connect nodes more than S(n) apart. Thus, if the path does not pass through the window, condition (b) of the lemma is satisfied and we are finished. Thus, let us assume that the path P from x to y passes through the window.

Let z be a node in the window such that z is in the path P. Let Q_1 denote that part of the path P from x to z and let Q_2 denote that part of the path P from z to y. If both $|Q_1|$ and $|Q_2|$ are less than or equal to one-half |P|, then condition (a) is satisfied with $z=z_1=z_2$. Thus, we shall assume that either

$|Q_1| > \frac{1}{2}|P|$ or $|Q_2| > \frac{1}{2}|P|$. The situation is symmetrical; we shall assume that $|Q_1| > \frac{1}{2}|P|$. The other case, when $|Q_2| > \frac{1}{2}|P|$, is handled similarly. Without loss of generality we shall assume that z isthe first node along the path P that is in the window and is such that the length of the path from x to z is greater than $\frac{1}{2}|P|$. (It follows, of course, that if $|Q_1| > \frac{1}{2}|P|$, then $|Q_2| < \frac{1}{2}|P|$.) Suppose that the path Q_1 does not pass through the window. Then condition (a) of the lemma is satisfied with $z_1 = x$ and $z_2 = z$, since Q_1 must be a path completely to the left or right of the window. Thus, we shall assume that Q_1 does pass through the window.

Let z' be the last node along the path Q_1 that is in the window. Let P_1 denote that part of the path Q_1 from x to z' and P_2 denote the part of Q_1 from z' to z. It follows that $|P_1| \leq \frac{1}{2}|P|$, since the node z was chosen to be the first node along the path P in the window with path length greater than $\frac{1}{2}|P|$. Furthermore, P_2 is a path that is completely to the left or right of the window, since there can be no node in P_2, other than the endpoints, in the window. (That is, z' was selected to be the last such node in the window before z.) It follows that condition (a) of the lemma is satisfied with $z_1 = z'$ and $z_2 = z$. □

We shall choose successive windows in an easily computed manner. In fact, the windows will be chosen always to be in the center of the portion of the graph currently under investigation for a path. Each time the portion of the graph under investigation is restricted to the last half or first half of the current portion this fact is recorded in the current block on the Turing machine's worktape. Thus, by reading through the previous blocks recorded on the worktape, we can determine the position of a window in the encoding.

Let e_1 and e_2 be the indices of two blocks in the encoding x_G of G, with $e_2 > e_1$. By <u>mid</u>(e_1,e_2), we mean the block with index $\max\{e_1, \lfloor \frac{1}{2}(e_2 + e_1 - S(n))\rfloor\}$. That is, by choosing a window W of size S(n) starting at mid(e_1,e_2) we are choosing a window of size S(n) centered in the middle of the portion of x_G between block e_1 and block e_2. For a given window W, let FIRST(W) denote the index of the first node in W and let LAST(W) denote the index of the last node in W. The following recursive boolean procedure PATH(s_1,s_2,e_1,e_2,t) is designed so that PATH(s_1,s_2,e_1,e_2,t) is true iff there is a path from node s_1 to node s_2 in the portion of the graph between the nodes with indices e_1 and e_2, respectively, of length at most t. The correctness of the algorithm follows from Lemma 1.5. The fact that the windows are always chosen to be of size S(n) starting at mid(e_1,e_2) guarantees that the portion of the graph to the right (left) of the window has at most one-half the number of nodes between e_1 and e_2.

```
Boolean procedure PATH(s1,s2,e1,e2,t)
if t ≤ 1 or e2 - e1 ≤ 1 then if (s1,s2) ∈ E or s1 = s2 then return true
                                                          else return false
                    else
                    begin
                        choose W to be a window of size S(n)
                        starting at mid(e1,e2);
                        for all z1 in WU{s1} and z2 in WU{s2} do
                        if PATH(s1,z1,e1,e2,⌈t/2⌉) and
                           (PATH(z1,z2,e1,FIRST(W),t)
                           or PATH(z1,z2,LAST(W),e2,t))
                           and PATH(z2,s2,e1,e2,⌈t/2⌉)
                        then return true;
                        if PATH(s1,s2,e1,FIRST(W),t) or PATH(s1,s2,LAST(W),e2,t)
                                                          then return true;
                        return false
                    end
```

Figure 1.2. The boolean procedure PATH

Theorem 1.6. $GAP(S(n)) \in DSPACE(\log n \times \log S(n))$

Proof. Let x_G be the encoding of a graph $G = (V,E)$ of bandwidth $S(n)$. We construct a Turing which implements the recursive boolean procedure PATH in order to determine whether or not a path exists from the start node to one of the goal nodes in the graph G. The Turing machine will accept x_G iff G has such a path.

The worktape of the Turing machine is divided into 2 log n blocks; each block is of length $c \log S(n)$, for some constant $c > 0$. Thus, the worktape space is bounded in length by $O(\log n \times \log S(n))$. Each block is used to record at most three calls to the procedure PATH. The nodes s_1 and s_2 in such a call to the procedure are recorded by indicating their position within a window of size $S(n)$. Thus, using binary notation to represent their positions in the windows, at most $\log S(n)$ space is required to record the position of the nodes s_1 and s_2. The positions of the windows that contain s_1 and s_2, furthermore, can be computed, as will be indicated, from the fact that we always choose a window in the middle of the portion of the graph currently under investigation. The position of a current window will be determined by looking in sequence at the previous blocks. That is, if the portion of the graph under investigation is restricted to the nodes to the right of the current window, then the symbol R will appear in the block. If the portion of the graph investigated for a path is restricted to the nodes to the left of the current window, then the symbol L will appear. Hence, the Turing machine can determine the portion of the graph currently under investigation by looking through blocks and reading the sequence of R's and L's. For example, if it starts with two pointers at the left and right ends, respectively, then it can compute the portion of the graph currently investigated by: (1) moving the left pointer to the last node of the current window when an R appears in a block, and (2) moving the right pointer to the first node of the current window when an L appears in a block. The current window is always the sequence of S(n) consecutive blocks in the middle of the portion of x_G currently between the left and right pointers.

In addition to the two nodes s_1 and s_2 in a call to the procedure PATH, as indicated in Figure 1.2, are the elements e_1, e_2, and t indicating, respectively, the leftmost node of the portion of the graph currently considered, the rightmost node of the portion of the graph currently considered, and the maximum length of the path in question. None of these quantities, however, need be included in the blocks contained in the worktape. The value of e_1 and e_2 can be determined, as outlined above, from a sequential scan of the earlier blocks. The maximum length of the path need not be physically written on the worktape as the procedure will continue to divide the question about the existence of a path until the rightmost, i.e. last, block is encountered. At that time the procedure will assume that the path in question is of length at most one and check to see if either $s_1 = s_2$ or $(s_1,s_2) \in E$. It should be noted that the Turing machine can fill in arbitrary many blocks by choosing $z_1 = s_1$ and $z_2 = s_2$. That is, in effect, by simply repeating the same question again and again the Turing machine can pad out any remaining blocks to get to the last block. Furthermore, the number of blocks on the worktape, namely 2 log n, is sufficiently large so that any path question can be divided sufficiently often to reduce it to one involving the existence of a path of length one (or zero) in the last block. That is, in each successive block either the length of the path is divided in half or the portion of the graph investigated is divided in half. Thus, 2 log n blocks are sufficient.

The procedure is one that tries all possibilities in a systematic order. It begins by writing PATH(-,+) in the first block. This simply represents the question: "Is there a path from the source node to one of the terminal nordes?" In general, let us suppose that the Tm is attempting to verify the existence of a path from s_1 to s_2 in the portion of the graph's encoding between two pointers e_1 and e_2 because of some item of the form PATH(s_1,s_2) in block i. (In the beginning, s_1 is -, s_2 is +, the pointers are at the beginning and end of the encoding, respectively, and the block number is one.) If the item PATH(s_1,s_2) in block i is followed by an R, indicating that the path form s_1 to s_2 is to be found only in the nodes to the right of the current window, then the left end pointer e_1 is advanced to the node immediately to the right of the current window before writing items in block i + 1. If the item in block i is followed by an L, then the right end pointer is moved to the node immediately to the left of the current window before writing items in block i + 1. If the item in block i is not followed by either R or L, then the TM proceeds directly to write items in block i + 1.

The items written in block i + 1 are: PATH(s_1,z_1), PATH(z_1,z_2)X, where X is either R or L, and PATH(z_2,s_2), where z_1 and z_2 are numbers between 1 and S(n), represented in binary notation, and are to be interpreted as denoting the positions of two nodes in the current window. The choice of z_1 and z_2 and the choice of whether X is R or L, is determined by choosing z_1 and z_2 to both be 1 and X to be R initially. The other choices for z_1,z_2 and X will be tried in the backtracking process in some easily computed order. For example, after trying both X = R and X = L for a given z_1 and z_2, the Tm may try z_1,z_2+1, and X = R. When z_2 reaches S(n), then the Tm tries z_1+1, 1, and X = R, etc. (When all of these possibilities have been attempted the Tm also tries PATH(s_1,s_2) in block i + 1 in order to include the possibility of padding out the remaining blocks and trying for an immediate path.) If none of these possibilities are found to be successful, then the Tm backtracks to block i and tries the next possibilities there. If any choice is found to be successful, in that all path questions are verified, then the Turing machine attempts to verify the next item in block i, if there is one, and checks off the current item in block i as successful. If all items in block i have been checked as being successful, then the Tm returns to block i-1 and checks off the current item there as successful.

In this manner the Turing machine tries all possibilities to find a path from a start node to a goal node. The procedure divides at each step the current path question into at most three smaller path questions involving nodes chosen from a window in the middle of the portion of the graph currently investigated. By Lemma 1.5 , if there is such a path, then we must be able to find it in the number of blocks allowed by choosing new windows successively as indicated. The only thing that remains to be seen, then, is how the Turing machine can compute which window a given node is in. This is, of course, required when the Turing machine has to verify in the rightmost block whether two nodes are identical or there is an edge from one to the other.

Let us suppose that the rightmost block contains the items PATH(s_1,s_2), PATH(s_2,s_3)X, and PATH(s_3,s_4). As indicated, nodes s_2 and s_3 are chosen from the current window, which is just the sequence of S(n) nodes in the middle of the portion of the encoding between the left and right pointers. Nodes s_1 and s_4, on the other hand, need not be from the current window. In order to answer the indicated path questions, we must recompute the windows that contain s_1 and s_4. This can be done as follows. By moving backwards through the previous blocks, one can determine the last block, preceeding the rightmost block, that indicates either the second or third item is currently under investigation. Let this be block j. (If all previous blocks indicate that the first item is currently under investigation, then let j = 1.) The window containing s_1 is the window that was current at the time the items were written in this block j. The window current at the time items were written in block j can be computed, as previously indicated, by scanning sequentially the previous blocks and reading the R's and L's indicated on the items listed as being currently investigated. Similarly, the window containing s_4 is that one which was current for the last block in which the first or second item were expanded. (If all blocks indicate the third item was expanded, then the block is chosen to be the first block).

	PATH(-,s)	PATH(s_1,s_3)	PATH(s_1,s_5)	PATH(s_5,s_7)	PATH(s_8,s_9)
PATH(-,+)	PATH(s_1,s_2)R	PATH(s_3,s_4)L	PATH(s_5,s_6)L	PATH(s_7,s_8)R	PATH(s_9,s_{10})R
	PATH(s_2,+)	PATH(s_4,s_2)	PATH(s_6,s_3)	PATH(s_8,s_6)	PATH(s_{10},s_6)

Figure 1.3. Sample worktape contents

For example, see Figure 1.3. Here the items checked in each block represent the items currently under investigation. It follows that the nodes s_9 and s_{10} of the rightmost block (block 6) are from the window centered in the region between $1/2|x_G|$ and $3/4\ |x_G|$, since the previous blocks indicate first that a current item, in block 2, is followed by R and secondly that a current item, in block 4, is followed by an L. Furthermore, node s_8 in the rightmost block is from the same window. That is, block 5 is the last block indicating item 2 or 3 is current and the window for block 5 is the same as for the rightmost window (block 6). Node s_6, on the other hand, is from the window centered in the region between $1/2\ |x_G|$ and $|x_G|$which was current at the time of block 4.

Finally, it should be noted that the Turing machine has more than log n worktape space. Hence, once the positions of the nodes listed in the rightmost block are computed, the Turing machine can represent this position on its worktape. It can then look into the description of the graph to see whether two nodes are the same or whether there is an edge from one to the other. □

Corollary 1.7. NSPACE(S(n)) $\subseteq$ DSPACE(log n × S(n)).

Proof. This follows directly from the fact that $\{GAP(2^{dS(n)})\}_{d>0}$ is log space complete for NSPACE(S(n)), Theorem 1.6, and the fact that DSPACE(log n×S(n)) is closed under log space reducibilities.

Examples.

NSPACE(log log n) $\subseteq$ DSPACE(log n × log log n)

NSPACE(log n/log log n) $\subseteq$ DSPACE($(\log n)^2$/log log n)

It is known that NSPACE(log log n) and NSPACE(log n/log log n), for example, are not closed under log space reducibilities. It is conceivable, therefore, that every language in NSPACE(log n) is log space reducible to languages in some such slow growing tape complexity class. If one could show, for example, that

NSPACE(log n) $\leq_{\log}$ NSPACE(log log n), then one would have as a corollary NSPACE(S(n)) $\subseteq$ DSPACE(S(n) $\times$ log S(n)), for all S(n) $\geq$ log n [5]. Although this does not seem particularly likely, we are unable to show, for example, that GAP is not log space reducible to GAP(log n).

Section 2. Restricted Reducibilities

As indicated in Section 1, $\{\mathrm{GAP}((\log n)^d)\}_{d>0} \subseteq$ DSPACE(log n) iff NSPACE(log log n) $\subseteq$ DSPACE(log n). It is not known that NSPACE(log log n) $\neq$ DSPACE(log log n). Even if one were able to show that GAP(log n) is in DSPACE(log log n), it need not follow that NSPACE(log log n) = DSPACE(log log n). This is true because DSPACE(log log n) is not closed under log space reducibilities and we have only shown in Section 1 that $\{\mathrm{GAP}((\log n)^d)\}_{d>0}$ is log space complete for NSPACE(log log n). (That DSPACE(log log n) is not closed under log space reducibilities follows from the fact that there is a hierarchy of complexity classes between log log n space and log n space [4,5,6].) In this section we shall strengthen the results of Section 1 by showing that every language in NSPACE(S(n)) is S(n)-tape reducible to one of the languages $\widetilde{\mathrm{GAP}}(2^{dS(n)})$, for some d > 0. For example, every language in NSPACE(log log n) is log log n tape reducible to one of the languages $\widetilde{\mathrm{GAP}}([\log n]^d)$, for some d > 0. Furthermore, every one of the languages $\widetilde{\mathrm{GAP}}(2^{dS(n)})$, for d > 0, can be recognized by a nondeterministic Tm that uses only S(n) space provided that S(n) squares are marked off on its worktape in advance of its computation. Let $\widetilde{\mathrm{DSPACE}}$(S(n)) and $\widetilde{\mathrm{NSPACE}}$(S(n)) denote the family of languages recognized, respectively, by deterministic and nondeterministic S(n)-tape bounded Turing machines that have S(n) preset worktape cells, i.e. marked off in advance of their computation. We show that $\widetilde{\mathrm{DSPACE}}$(S(n)) is closed under S(n) tape reducibilities. Thus, for example, $\widetilde{\mathrm{NSPACE}}$(log log n) = $\widetilde{\mathrm{DSPACE}}$(log log n) iff $\widetilde{\mathrm{GAP}}((\log n)^k)$ is in $\widetilde{\mathrm{DSPACE}}$(log log n), for all k $\geq$ 1.

It should be noted that $\widetilde{\mathrm{GAP}}(2^{S(n)})$ is in $\widetilde{\mathrm{NSPACE}}$(S(n)), for all functions S(n), where 1 $\leq$ S(n) $\leq$ log n. In particular, $\widetilde{\mathrm{GAP}}$(log log n) is in $\widetilde{\mathrm{NSPACE}}$(log log log n). Since GAP(log log n) is not a regular set, the class $\widetilde{\mathrm{NSPACE}}$(log log log n) does not contain only regular sets. In particular, it cannot be true that for all functions S(n), $\widetilde{\mathrm{NSPACE}}$(S(n)) = NSPACE(S(n)), since NSPACE(S(n)) contains only regular sets for all S(n) growing less rapidly than log log n [4]. It follows that allowing Turing machines to have a pre-set amount of tape to work with changes considerably the class of languages they can recognize for slow growing tape bounds. For fully constructible [8] tape bounding functions S(n) it is, of course, true that $\widetilde{\mathrm{NSPACE}}$(S(n)) = NSPACE(S(n)).

Lemma 2.1. For any functions S(n) on the natural numbers and any d > 0, $\widetilde{\mathrm{GAP}}(2^{dS(n)})$ is in $\widetilde{\mathrm{NSPACE}}$(S(n)).

Proof. The algorithm is the same as described in the proof of Lemma 1.1 except that the first step may be eliminated since our Tm now has a pre-set worktape with S(n) marked cells. □

Definition 2.2. Let S(n) be a function on the natural numbers. A function f from Σ^* to Δ^* , where Σ and Δ are arbitrary finite alphabets, is S(n)-decomposable if there exists a function $F : \mathbb{N} \times \Sigma \to \Delta^*$, where $\mathbb{N}$ is the set of natural numbers, such that for any string $x = a_1a_2 \ldots a_n$ in Σ^*, $f(a_1a_2\ldots a_n) = F(S(n),a_1) F(S(n),a_2)\ldots F(S(n),a_n)$.

A function f is S(n)-decomposable if, for any string $x = a_1a_2\ldots a_n$ of length n, f(x) can be written as $y_1y_2\ldots y_n$, where y_i depends only upon a_i and the value of S(n), for $1 \le i \le n$.

Definition 2.3. Let f be a function from Σ^* to Δ^* and S(n) be a function on the natural numbers such that f is S(n)-decomposable. Let $F : \mathbb{N} \times \Sigma \to \Delta^*$ be such that, for any string $x = a_1a_2\ldots a_n$ in Σ^*, $f(a_1a_2\ldots a_n) = F(S(n),a_1)F(S(n),a_2)\ldots F(S(n),a_n)$. We shall say that f is S(n)-tape computable if there is a Turing machine with a read-write worktape and a one-way output tape which when presented with a symbol a in Σ and S(n) cells marked off on its worktape will eventually halt having produced F(S(n),a) on its output tape without having used more than the S(n) marked worktape cells.

The following notion of reducibility is similar to the tape reducibilities considered by Neil Jones [3] and the more recent one-way log space reducibility considered by Hartmanis et al. in [9].

Definition 2.4. Let S(n) be any function on the natural numbers. Let A,B be two languages. We shall say that A is S(n)-tape reducible to B, denoted by $A \le_{S(n)} B$, if there is a S(n)-tape computable function f such that, for all x, x is in A iff f(x) is in B.

Lemma 2.2. Let S(n) be any function such that, for some c and all k, $S(n^k) \le c(S(n))$. If $A \le_{S(n)} B$ and B is in $\widetilde{DSPACE}(S(n))$, then A is in $\widetilde{DSPACE}(S(n))$.

Proof. Let M be a Tm that recognizes B using only its pre-marked S(n) worktape cells. Let f(n) be an S(n)-tape computable function such that x is in A iff f(x) is in B. It is not difficult to construct a Tm M' that with input $x = a_1a_2\ldots a_n$ and with S(n) pre-marked worktape cells simulates M on input f(x).

The worktape space used by M on input f(x) is $S(|f(x)|) \le S(n2^{dS(n)})$. Since $S(n^k) \le cS(n)$, it follows that $S(n) \le \log n$. Hence, $S(n2^{dS(n)}) \le S(n^k)$, for some $k \ge 1$, and, therefore, $S(n2^{dS(n)}) \le S(n^k) \le cS(n)$. Thus, M' need not use more than the S(n) marked cells on its worktape to simulate M on input f(x). □

Lemma 2.3. For every L in $\widetilde{NSPACE}(S(n))$ there is some d > 0 such that $L \le_{S(n)} \widetilde{GAP}(2^{dS(n)})$.

Proof. The proof is essentially the same as in Lemma 1.2. Here the encoding of the graph G(M,x) must be the short encoding, since a Tm with only S(n) worktape cells cannot, in general, compute the successive node numbers. □

<u>Theorem 2.4.</u> Let $S(n)$ be any function such that, for some c and all k, $S(n^k) \leq cS(n)$. Then, the following statements are equivalent:

(1) $\widetilde{NSPACE}(S(n)) = \widetilde{DSPACE}(S(n))$,

(2) for all $d > 0$, $\widetilde{GAP}(2^{dS(n)})$ is in $\widetilde{DSPACE}(S(n))$.

<u>Proof.</u> That (1) implies (2) follows from Lemma 2.1. That (2) implies (1) follows from Lemma 2.2 and Lemma 2.3. □

<u>Corollary 2.5.</u> $\widetilde{NSPACE}(\log \log n) = \widetilde{DSPACE}(\log \log n)$ iff $\widetilde{GAP}([\log n]^d)$ is in $\widetilde{DSPACE}(\log \log n)$, for all $d > 0$.

It should be noted that our construction in Section One works also for the $\widetilde{NSPACE}(S(n))$ classes, so that $\widetilde{NSPACE}(S(n)) \subseteq DSPACE(\log n \times \log S(n))$ is known to be true.

<u>References</u>

(1) W. J. Savitch, "Deterministic simulation of nondeterministic Turing machines", <u>ACM Symposium on Theory of Computing</u> (1969), 247-248.

(2) W. J. Savitch, "Relationships between nondeterministic and deterministic tape complexities", <u>JCSS</u> 4(1970), 177-192.

(3) N. D. Jones, "Space bounded reducibility among combinatorial problems", <u>JCSS</u> 11(1975), 68-75.

(4) R. E. Stearns, J. Hartmanis, and P. M. Lewis, "Hierarchies of memory limited computations", <u>IEEE Conf. Record on Switching Circuit Theory and Logical Design</u> (1965), 191-202.

(5) C. Papadimitriou, "The NP-completeness of the bandwidth minimization problem", <u>Computing</u> 16(1976), 263-270.

(6) M. Sipser, "Halting space bounded computations", <u>IEEE Conf. Record on Foundations of Computer Science</u> (1978), 73-74.

(7) J. E. Hopcroft and J. D. Ullman, "Some results on tape bounded Turing machines", <u>J. ACM</u> (1969), 168-188.

(8) J. Seiferas, "Techniques for separating space complexity classes", <u>JCSS</u> 14(1977), 73-99.

(9) J. Hartmanis, M. Immerman, and S. Mahaney, "One-way log-tape reductions", <u>IEEE Conf. Record on Foundations of Computer Science</u> (1978), 65-72.

STRUCTURE PRESERVING TRANSFORMATIONS ON NON-LEFT-RECURSIVE GRAMMARS

(preliminary version)

Anton Nijholt
Vrije Universiteit
Department of Mathematics
P.O.-Box 7161, Amsterdam
The Netherlands

1. INTRODUCTION AND PRELIMINARIES

If a context-free grammar is transformed to another context-free grammar in most of the cases it is quite obvious to demand *weak equivalence* for these two grammars. Transformations on context-free grammars can be defined for several reasons. Dependent on these reasons one may be interested in stronger relations of grammatical similarity.

Instead of arbitrary context-free grammars one can consider context-free grammars which conform to some requirements on, for example, the form of the productions. It is natural to ask whether each context-free language has a context-free grammar in this form and, if possible, how to transform a context-free grammar to a context-free grammar of this special form.

One of the reasons to consider normal forms may be the mathematical interest in how to generate a class of languages with a so simple possible grammatical description. Moreover, normal forms can simplify descriptions and proofs. Some normal form descriptions of the context-free grammars or their subclasses can be particularly amenable for parsing and this can be a strong motivation to transform grammars. Transformations can be applied to obtain grammars for which smaller sized parsers or faster parsing methods can be constructed. For such transformations stronger relations than weak equivalence are desirable.

A slightly stronger relation is obtained if we demand that the language preserving transformation is such that each sentence has the same number of parse trees in each grammar, that is, the transformation is also *ambiguity preserving*.

Another relation which has been defined is *structural equivalence*, in which case it is demanded that the parse trees of the one grammar are the same, except for a relabeling of the internal nodes, as the trees of the other grammar.

Our interest is in the semantic equivalence of context-free grammars which are syntactically related. It is assumed that semantic rules are associated with each production of a grammar and, quite obvious, it follows that we will be interested in the correspondence of the derivations of related grammars. Such a correspondence should be formalized.

Some rather independent developments can be distinguished.

a. In the older literature one can find ideas and examples which come close to later formal concepts, for example Griffiths and Petrick [15], Kurki-Suonio [27], Kuno [26] and Foster [8]. Transformations have been defined in practically oriented situations of compiler construction. In such cases no general definitions of the syntactic relation between the grammars are presented.

b. *Grammar functors* (X-functors) were introduced by Hotz [20,21] as special functors on categories associated with (general) phrase structure grammars. These syntax categories originate from work on switching circuits. The main concern has been to find an algebraic framework for describing general properties of phrase structure grammars. Only recently functors have been considered from a more "practical" point of view. See for example Bertsch [3], Benson [2], Walter, Keklikoglou and Kern [42] and Hotz [22].

c. *Grammar covers,* in the sense that we will use them here, were introduced about 1969 by Gray and Harrison [11]. A practical reason to consider covers concerns compiler construction. In such a case we consider a parse as the argument of a semantic mapping. In case a context-free grammar G' covers a context-free grammar G we can use the original semantic mapping, corresponding to G, and do the parsing according to G'.

d. In the case of attribute grammars (see Knuth [24]) attributes are associated with the nodes of a parse tree. These attributes (which contain semantic information) are obtained from attributes associated with the symbols which appear in the productions and from attribute evaluation rules. If an attribute grammar is transformed to, for example, some normal form attribute grammar, we have not only the question of language equivalence but also the question of semantic equivalence. Such an equivalence is explored in Bochman [4,5].

We will be concerned with grammar covers. The first part of this paper presents a general framework for covers. The second part introduces a transformation from non-left-recursive grammars to grammars in Greibach normal form. An investigation of the structure preserving properties of this transformation, which serves also as an illustration of our framework for covers, is presented.

Preliminaries

We shortly review some definitions and concepts of formal language theory. It is assumed that the reader is familiar with the basic results concerning context-free grammars and with parsing, otherwise see Aho and Ullman [1].

Let V be an *alphabet* and let $\alpha \in V^*$, then $|\alpha|$ denotes the *length* of string α. The *empty* string is denoted by ε. If $|\alpha| \geq k$ then $\alpha : k$ denotes the *suffix* of α with

length k, otherwise $\alpha : k = \alpha$. For *prefixes* the notation $k : \alpha$ is used. The number of elements in any set V is denoted by $|V|$; the empty set by $\emptyset$. $\mathbb{N}$ stands for the set of positive integers.
Consider two alphabets V en W. A *homomorphism* $h : V^* \to W^*$ is obtained by defining $h : V \to W^*$, $h(\varepsilon) = \varepsilon$ and $h(\alpha\beta) = h(\alpha).h(\beta)$ for all $\alpha, \beta \in V^*$. Let Σ and Δ be disjoint alphabets. Homomorphism $h_\Sigma : (\Sigma \cup \Delta)^* \to \Delta^*$ is defined by $h_\Sigma(X) = X$ if $X \in \Delta$, and $h_\Sigma(X) = \varepsilon$ if $X \in \Sigma$. Homomorphism h_Σ is called the Σ-*erasing homomorphism.*
A *context-free grammar* (CFG) will be denoted by the four-tuple $G = (N,\Sigma,P,S)$ where $N \cap \Sigma = \emptyset$, N is the set of *nonterminals,* Σ is the set of *terminals,* $N \cup \Sigma$ is denoted by V, $S \in N$ is the *start symbol* and P is the set of *productions,* $P \subseteq N \times V^*$. Elements of N will generally be denoted by the Roman capitals A,B,C,...,S,...; elements of Σ by the smalls a,b,c,... from the first part of the Roman alphabet; X, Y and Z will usually stand for elements of V, elements of Σ^* will be denoted by u,v,w,x,y and z and Greek smalls $\alpha,\beta,\gamma,\ldots$ will usually stand for elements of V^*. It will be convenient to provide the productions in P with a label. In general these labels will be in a set Δ_G (or Δ if G is understood) and we always take $\Delta_G = \{i \mid 1 \le i \le |P|\}$; we often identify P and Δ_G. We write $i.\ A \to \alpha$ if production $A \to \alpha$ has label (or number) i.
We have the usual notations $\Rightarrow$, $\overset{+}{\Rightarrow}$ and $\overset{*}{\Rightarrow}$ for *derivations* and we use subscripts L and R for leftmost and rightmost derivations, respectively. The notation $\overset{\pi}{\Rightarrow}$ will be used to denote that the derivation is done according to a specific sequence $\pi \in \Delta_G^*$ of production numbers. A *left parse* of a sentence $w \in L(G)$ (the language of G) is a sequence of productions used in a leftmost derivation from S to w. The reverse of a sequence used in a rightmost derivation is called a *right parse* of w.
The number of different leftmost derivations from S to w is called the *degree of ambiguity* of w (with respect to G), written $\langle w,G\rangle$.
The set of *parse trees* of G (with roots labeled with S and frontiers in Σ^*) is denoted by PTR(G). If $t \in PTR(G)$ then fr(t) denotes its frontier.

DEFINITION 1.1. A CFG $G = (N,\Sigma,P,S)$ is
a) *proper,* if G is ε-free, cycle-free and G has no useless symbols.
b) *left-recursive,* if there exist $A \in N$ and $\alpha \in V^*$ such that $A \overset{+}{\Rightarrow} A\alpha$.
c) in *Greibach normal form* (GNF), if $P \subseteq N \times \Sigma N^* \cup \{(S,\varepsilon)\}$.

It is rather natural to start with a CFG $G = (N,\Sigma,P,S)$ and generalize it to a *simple syntax directed translation scheme* (simple SDTS) $T = (N,\Sigma,\Delta,R,S)$, where Δ(the output alphabet) contains the production numbers and R contains rules of the form $A \to \alpha,\alpha'$ where $A \to \alpha$ is in P and α' is a word over $(N \cup \Delta)^*$ which satisfies $h_\Delta(\alpha') = h_\Sigma(\alpha)$.

In such a case we say that T is defined on G. The *translation* defined by such a scheme T is denoted by $\tau(T)$.

DEFINITION 1.2. A simple SDTS is *semantically unambiguous* if there are no two distinct rules of the form $A \to \alpha,\beta$ and $A \to \alpha,\gamma$.

2. GRAMMAR COVERS

This section is devoted to building a general framework for grammar covers.
Let $G = (N,\Sigma,P,S)$ be a CFG with production numbers in Δ_G. The following definition is also in Brosgol [6].

DEFINITION 2.1. A relation $f_G \subset \Sigma^* \times \Delta_G^*$ is said to be a *parse relation* for G provided that

(i) if $(w,\pi) \in f_G$ and $(w',\pi) \in f_G$ then $w = w'$, and

(ii) for each $w \in \Sigma^*$, $|\{\pi \mid (w,\pi) \in f_G\}| = |\{t \in PTR(G) \mid w = fr(t)\}|$.

If f_G is a parse relation and $(w,\pi) \in f_G$ then π is said to be an f_G-parse of w. Our following definitions will be based on parse relations. Index G of f_G will be omitted whenever it is clear from context for which grammar f_G is the parse relation.

DEFINITION 2.2. Let $G = (N,\Sigma,P,S)$ and $G' = (N',\Sigma',P',S')$ be CFGs. Let $f_{G'} \subseteq \Sigma'^* \times \Delta_{G'}^*$, and $h_G \subset \Sigma^* \times \Delta_G^*$ be parse relations. For a given $f_{G'}$ and h_G a *parse homomorphism* $g : f_{G'} \to h_G$ is defined by two homomorphisms $\phi : \Sigma'^* \to \Sigma^*$ and $\psi : \Delta_{G'}^* \to \Delta_G^*$ such that $(w,\pi) \in f_{G'}$ implies $(\phi(w),\psi(\pi)) \in h_G$. If $\Sigma' = \Sigma$ and ϕ is the identity homomorphism then g is said to be externally fixed. We use the notation $g = \langle\phi,\psi\rangle$.

DEFINITION 2.3. A parse homomorphism $g : f_{G'} \to h_{G'}$ with $g = \langle\phi,\psi\rangle$, is said to be a *cover homomorphism* if it is surjective, that is, for all $(w,\pi) \in h_G$ there exists $(w',\pi') \in f_{G'}$ such that $(w,\pi) = (\phi(w'),\psi(\pi'))$.

Notice that in the case of a cover homomorphism $\langle w,G'\rangle$ and $\langle\phi(w),G\rangle$ are incomparable. In case ϕ is the identity homomorphism then $L(G) = L(G')$ and $\langle w,G'\rangle \geq \langle\phi(w),G\rangle$. Notice that $\langle w,G'\rangle = |\{\pi \mid (w,\pi) \in f_{G'}\}|$.

DEFINITION 2.4. A parse homomorphism $g : f_{G'} \to h_G$ with $g = \langle\phi,\psi\rangle$, is said to be *properly injective* if its restrictions to Σ'^* and $\Delta_{G'}^*$ are injective, that is,

(i) if $(w,\pi) \in f_{G'}$ and $(w,\pi') \in f_{G'}$ then $\psi(\pi) = \psi(\pi')$ implies $\pi = \pi'$, and

(ii) if $(u,\pi) \in f_{G'}$ and $(v,\pi') \in f_{G'}$ then $\phi(u) = \phi(v)$ implies $u = v$.

EXAMPLE 2.1

Let G' be defined (In our example grammars only the productions are listed.) by

0./1.	$S \to aA \mid cB$	and G by	0./1.	$S \to Ab \mid Bb$
2./3.	$A \to aA \mid b$		2./3.	$A \to Aa \mid a$
4./5.	$B \to cB \mid d$		4./5.	$B \to Ba \mid a$

Let $f_{G'} = \{(a^{n+1}b, 02^n3) \mid n \geq 0\} \cup \{(c^{n+1}d, 14^n5) \mid n \geq 0\}$

and $h_G = \{(a^{n+1}b, 32^n0) \mid n \geq 0\} \cup \{(a^{n+1}b, 54^n1) \mid n \geq 0\}$.

Homomorphism $g = \langle\phi,\psi\rangle$ is defined by

$\phi(a) = a$ $\phi(c) = a$ $\psi(0) = 3$ $\psi(2) = 2$ $\psi(4) = 4$

$\phi(b) = b$ $\phi(d) = b$ $\psi(1) = 5$ $\psi(3) = 0$ $\psi(5) = 1$.

It follows that g is a parse homomorphism which is surjective, hence g is a cover homomorphism. A parse homomorphism is said to be a *proper bijection* if it is both properly injective and surjective.

The results in the following table are immediate from the definitions given above.

surjection	-	$\phi(L(G')) = L(G)$
proper injection	$\langle w,G'\rangle \leq \langle\phi(w),G\rangle$	$\phi(L(G')) \subseteq L(G)$
proper bijection	$\langle w,G'\rangle = \langle\phi(w),G\rangle$	$\phi(L(G')) = L(G)$

Table I. Properties of parse homomorphisms.

In the following diagram the definition of a parse homomorphism is illustrated.

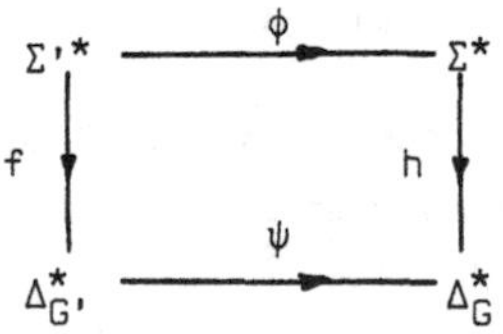

Figure 1. Diagram for the parse homomorphism.

Notice, if g is a cover homomorphism and ϕ is the identity homomorphism, then $L(G') = L(G)$ and $\langle w,G'\rangle \geq \langle w,G\rangle$.

DEFINITION 2.5. Let $G' = (N',\Sigma',P',S')$ and $G = (N,\Sigma,P,S)$ be two CFGs. Let $f \subseteq \Sigma'^* \times \Delta_{G'}^*$ and $h \times \Sigma^* \to \Delta_G^*$ be parse relations. G' *f-to-h covers* G if a cover homomorphism $g : f \to h$ can be defined.

Most of the time one will be satisfied with a cover homomorphism $g = \langle\phi,\psi\rangle$ such that $\phi : \Sigma'^* \to \Sigma^*$ is the identity homomorphism. In such cases there is only one homomorphism to consider, namely $\psi : \Delta^*_{G'} \to \Delta^*_G$ and we will simply speak of cover homomorphism ψ.
Examples of often used parses are left parses, right parses and left-corner parses (Rosenkrantz and Lewis [37]. These parses are examples of 'production directed' parses. In the following definition $h_\Sigma : (N \cup \Sigma \cup \Delta)^* \to (N \cup \Delta)^*$ is the Σ-erasing homomorphism.

DEFINITION 2.6. Let $G = (N,\Sigma,P,S)$ be a CFG. A parse relation $f \subseteq \Sigma^* \times \Delta^*$ is said to be a *production directed parse relation* for G if there exists a simple SDTS T = $= (N,\Sigma,\Delta,R,S)$ where R is defined by : if $A \to \alpha$ is the ith production in P then R contains exactly one rule of the form $A \to \alpha, h_\Sigma(\alpha_1 i \alpha_2)$ with $\alpha_1\alpha_2 = \alpha$, R does not contain other rules, and $f = \tau(T)$.

It is a well-known trick to insert special symbols (standing for production numbers or, more generally, marking the place for semantical information) in the right-hand sides of productions to obtain special parses (for example, see Aho and Ullman [1]). In fact this has been done by Kurki-Suonio [27] who adds a symbol to the right of the righthand sides of the productions and Kuno [25] who adds a symbol to the left of the right-hand sides. Related ideas are in the definitions of parenthesis and bracketed grammars (see McNaughton [29] and Ginsburg and Harrison [10], respectively).
The special symbols can sometimes be considered as newly introduced nonterminal symbols which are left-hand sides of ε-productions.
For instance, this is done by Soisalon-Soininen [39] to convert the Kurki-Suonio idea to the cover formalism. Also Demers [7] does this to define generalized left corner parsing. A slightly restricted version of Brosgol's parse specifying translation grammar coincides with the simple SDTS of Definition 2.6. Demers uses Brosgol's definition. Following Demers, if we have a rule $A \to \alpha, h_\Sigma(\alpha_1 i \alpha_2)$ then α_1 is called the left corner or leading part of the rule and α_2 is its trailing part.

The following table lists a few names of parses which have been introduced before. Conform Demers [7] all production directed parses should be called *generalized left corner parses*. Notice that left part parses are defined as the opposite of left corner parse. Left part parses come close to being right parses.

i.A → α, $h_\Sigma(i\alpha)$	left parses
i.A → α, $h_\Sigma(\alpha i)$	right parses
i.A → α, $h_\Sigma(\alpha_1 i \alpha_2)$ where $\alpha_1\alpha_2 = \alpha$ and $\|\alpha_1\| = 1$	left corner parses (Rosenkrantz, Lewis [37])
i.A → α, $h_\Sigma(\alpha_1 i \alpha_2)$ where $\alpha_1\alpha_2 = \alpha$ and $\alpha \in \Sigma^*$ or $\alpha_1 \in \Sigma^* N$	extended left corner parses (Brosgol [6])
i.A → α, $h_\Sigma(\alpha_1 i \alpha_2)$ where $\alpha_1\alpha_2 = \alpha$ and $\|\alpha_2\| = 1$	left part parses (Nijholt [29])

Table II. Parses

The following table lists a few names and notations for covers according to Definition 2.5. We use $\bar{r}$ to denote right parses (or parse relations).

parse relations		notation	name
f	h	G'[f/h]G	f-to-h cover
left	left	G'[l/l]G	left cover
left	right	G'[l/$\bar{r}$]G	left-to-right cover
right	left	G'[$\bar{r}$/l]G	right-to-left cover
right	right	G'[$\bar{r}$/$\bar{r}$]G	right cover

Table III. Covers

It will be convenient to have the possibility to talk about positions in the right-hand sides of productions. Therefore we have the following notation.

<u>NOTATION 2.1.</u> Let $j.A \to X_1X_2 \ldots X_n$ be a production of a CFG G. The positions in the right-hand side are numbered according to the following scheme:

$$j.A \to [1]X_1[2]X_2 \ldots [n]X_n[n+1]$$

For a given production directed parse relation each production has a fixed position in which its number is inserted, conform Definition 2.6. We use $\Gamma_G(j)$ (or simply $\Gamma(j)$) to denote this position. Hence, $\Gamma_G : \Delta_G \to \mathbb{N}$.

We conclude this section with a few remarks on our definition of cover. Assume that $g : f_{G'} \to h_G$ is a cover homomorphism with $g = \langle\phi,\psi\rangle$. We have defined g in such a way that for any $i \in \Delta_{G'}$, $\psi(i) \in \Delta_G^*$. It is possible to introduce restrictions, for example,

(a) $\psi(i) \in \Delta_G \cup \{\varepsilon\}$, or (b) $\psi(i) \in \Delta_G$.

The definition of *complete cover* in Gray and Harrison [12] can be compared with our definition of cover if we have for ϕ the identity and ψ is defined according to restriction (a). We do not include Gray and Harrison's notion of (not necessarily complete) *cover* in our formalism. Obviously it is possible to do so but since we already allow $\psi(i) \in \Delta_G^*$ we do not see useful applications.
It is also possible to include the notion of weak cover (Ukkonen [ ]). In that case one should allow homomorphisms to be defined on a subset of $f_{G'}$. For some other concepts of grammatical similarity the reader is referred to Hunt and Rosenkrantz [24].

3. THE LEFT PART TRANSFORMATION TO GREIBACH NORMAL FORM.

Now that we have presented the general framework, we come to the second aim of this paper: its application for a relevant transformation. We consider a transformation from *non-left-recursive grammars* to *Greibach normal form* (GNF) grammars. A few historical notes are in order. Greibach [13] introduced this normal form and she showed that each context-free language has a context-free grammar in this normal form.
In Greibach [14] a more simple method is introduced to obtain the same result. Some of the structure preserving properties of the latter method have been investigated in Hotz [19,22]. Rosenkrantz [36] uses a matrix equation method to show that each context-free language has a CFG in GNF. Both Greibach and Rosenkrantz start with an -except for a few minor conditions- arbitrary CFG and transform it into a weakly equivalent CFG in GNF.
Often such a transformation is done in two steps (for example, see Hopcroft and Ullman [18] and Aho and Ullman [1]). The first step is a transformation from an arbitrary CFG to a non-left-recursive grammar. The second step transforms the non-left-recursive grammar to a CFG in GNF. This second step (Aho and Ullman's Algorithm 2.14, attributed by them to M.Paull) will be referred to as the usual method. This usual method has been used in Wood [43] (see also Wood [44] and some of its structure preserving properties have been discussed in Kuno [25], Hotz and Claus [23], Benson [2] and for an adapted version, Nijholt [30].
There are some important subclasses of the non-left-recursive grammars for which more or less adapted versions of this usual method have been introduced. For example, the *LL(k) grammars* (Rosenkrantz and Stearns [38]) and the *strict deterministic grammars* (Geller, Harrison and Havel [9]).
The algorithm which will be considered in this section is a generalized version of a transformation which has been used in Nijholt [29,31].

Before we can introduce the algorithm we have to define a few less familiar concepts.

DEFINITION 3.1. Let $G = (N,\Sigma,P,S)$ be a CFG. Define a relation $CH \subseteq V \times N^*\Sigma$ as follows:
If $X_0 \in N$ then $CH(X_0)$, the set of *chains* of X_0, is defined by

$$CH(X_0) = \{X_0X_1\ldots X_n \in N^*\Sigma \mid X_0 \underset{L}{\Rightarrow} X_1\psi_1 \underset{L}{\Rightarrow} \ldots \underset{L}{\Rightarrow} X_n\psi_n, \psi_i \in V^*, 1 \leq i \leq n\}.$$

and for $c \in \Sigma$, $CH(c) = \{c\}$.

The left part transformation which we display below is an one-step transformation, in the sense that each production of the new grammar is obtained in one step from the productions of the original grammar. Another example of such a transformation is that of strict deterministic grammars to their GNF-version (Geller, Harrison and Havel [9]). Chains will be used for the construction of the right-hand sides of the productions of the new grammar.
Consider the following example grammar G with productions $S \to A|B$, $A \to a$ and $B \to a$. *Any* transformation of G into GNF yields a CFG with only production $S \to a$. Since a cover homomorphism is surjective it follows that no such homomorphism can be defined. However, it can be shown that any ε-free non-left-recursive CFG G can be given an equivalent ε-free non-left-recursive CFG G' without single productions (i.e., productions of the form $A \to B$, where $A,B \in N$). If we introduce a special production $S_0 \to S\bot$, where S is the start symbol of G and $\bot$ is an endmarker, then this can be done in such a way that G'[l/l]G (cf.Nijholt [30]).
In what follows we assume that, if necessary, first the single productions are eliminated. Hence, the input grammar will be a *very proper* (that is, no useless symbols, ε-free, no single productions) and non-left-recursive CFG.
The transformation is such that the new grammar left-to-x covers G, where, intuitively, x may 'run' from left to left part in the production directed parse relations.

DEFINITION 3.2. Let $G = (N,\Sigma,P,S)$ be a CFG. Define $[N] = \{[Ai\alpha] \mid i.\ A \to \alpha\beta$ is in P, for some $\beta \in V^*\}$ and define a homomorphism $\xi : [N]^* \to [N]^*$ by letting $\xi([Ai\alpha])$ is
(i) ε if $i.\ A \to \alpha$ is in P,
(ii) $[Ai\alpha]$ if $i.\ A \to \alpha\beta$ is in P, where $\beta \neq \varepsilon$.

DEFINITION 3.3. Let $G = (N,\Sigma,P,S)$ be a CFG. Define relation $LP \subseteq N^*\Sigma \times \Delta^*$ as follows:
Let $\pi = X_0X_1\ldots X_n \in N^+\Sigma$. $LP(\pi)$, the set of *left production chains* of π, is defined by

$$LP(\pi) = \{i_0i_1\ldots i_{n-1} \in \Delta^* \mid X_0 \overset{i_0}{\underset{L}{\Rightarrow}} X_1\psi_1 \overset{i_1}{\underset{L}{\Rightarrow}} \ldots \overset{i_{n-1}}{\underset{L}{\Rightarrow}} X_n\psi_n, \psi_j \in V^*, 1 \leq j \leq n\}.$$

If $\pi \in \Sigma$ then $LP(\pi) = \{\varepsilon\}$.

In the algorithm we use Notation 2.1.

ALGORITHM 3.1. (*Left Part Transformation*)

Input. A very proper, non-left-recursive CFG $G = (N,\Sigma,P,S)$ such that for each production $j.\ A \to \alpha$ in P we have that $\Gamma(j)$ satisfies $1 \le \Gamma(j) \le |\alpha|$.

Output. A weakly equivalent CFG $G' = (N',\Sigma,P',[S])$ in GNF.

Method. P' is the set of all productions introduced below. N' will contain [S] and all symbols of [N] which appear in the productions.

(i) For each pair (π,ρ), $\pi = SX_1 \ldots X_n \in CH(S)$ and $\rho = i_o i_1 \ldots i_{n-1} \in LP(\pi)$, add $[S] \to X_n \xi([X_{n-1} i_{n-1} X_n] \ldots [S i_o X_1])$ to P'.

(ii) Let $i.\ A \to \alpha X_o \phi$ be in P, $\alpha \neq \varepsilon$; for each pair (π,ρ), where

$\pi = X_o X_1 \ldots X_n \in CH(X_o)$

and

$\rho = i_o i_1 \ldots i_{n-1} \in LP(\pi)$

add

$[Ai\alpha] \to X_n \xi([X_{n-1} i_{n-1} X_n] \ldots [X_o i_o X_1][Ai\alpha X_o])$ to P'. □

THEOREM 3.1.

Let $G = (N,\Sigma,P,S)$ be a very proper, non-left recursive CFG. Assume, for each production $j.\ A \to \alpha$ in P, $1 \le \Gamma(j) \le |\alpha|$.

Algorithm 3.1 yields a CFG G' in GNF such that $G'[l/x]G$, where x denotes the parse relation defined by Γ.

Proof. (Sketch) Let $T = (N,\Sigma,\Delta,R,S)$ be the simple SDTS defined on $G = (N,\Sigma,P,S)$ which performs the translation x. Define $T' = (N',\Sigma,\Delta,R',[S])$ on $G' = (N',\Sigma,P',[S])$ by the rules:

(1) $[S] \to X_n \xi([X_{n-1} i_{n-1} X_n] \ldots [S i_o X_1]),$

$\quad j_o j_1 \ldots j_{n-1}\ \xi([X_{n-1} i_{n-1} X_n] \ldots [S i_o X_1])$

for each corresponding production introduced in step (i) of the algorithm.

The j_k's are defined by, for $0 \le k \le n-1$, $j_k = i_k$ if $\Gamma(i_k) = 1$, and $j_k = \varepsilon$ otherwise.

(2) $[Ai\alpha] \to X_n \xi([X_{n-1} i_{n-1} X_n] \ldots [X_o i_o X_1][Ai\alpha X_o]),$

$\quad j j_o j_1 \ldots j_{n-1} \xi([X_{n-1} i_{n-1} X_n] \ldots [X_o i_o X_1][Ai\alpha X_o])$

for each corresponding production introduced in step (ii) of the algorithm.

The j_k's and j are defined by, for $0 \le k \le n-1$,

$j_k = i_k$ if $\Gamma(i_k) = 1$, and $j_k = \varepsilon$ otherwise, and

$j = i$ if $|\alpha X_o| = \Gamma(i)$, and $j = \varepsilon$ otherwise.

Cover homomorphism ψ is defined by mapping each production of P' on the string $j_o j_1 \ldots j_{n-1}$ or $j j_o j_1 \ldots j_{n-1}$ of its corresponding rule in R', obtained in (1) or (2), respectively. Clearly, T' is semantically unambiguous and therefore ψ is a function. The main task is now to prove that $\tau(T') = \tau(T)$. Then, if $(w,\pi') \in l_{G'}$ it follows immediately that $(w,\psi(\pi')) \in x_G$. Moreover, by the definitions of T' and ψ it follows also that if $(w,\pi) \in x_G = \tau(T)$ then there exists $(w,\pi') \in l_{G'}$ such that $(w,\psi(\pi') = (w,\pi)$. Thus we may conclude that G'[l/x]G. The proof that $\tau(T') = \tau(T)$ is omitted here. □

Because of the condition $1 \le \Gamma(j) \le |\alpha|$ the parse relations defined by such Γ are the left parses, the left part parses and 'everything in between'. We can slightly weaken this condition by defining $\Gamma(j) \le |\alpha|$ if $\alpha : 1 \in N$ and $\Gamma(j) \le |\alpha| + 1$ if $\alpha : 1 \in \Sigma$.
However, the condition prevents that the theorem says anything about a left-to-right cover. We return to this problem in the following section.

We conclude this section with a result on (ε-free) *strict deterministic grammars* (Harrison and Havel [16]). Strict deterministic grammars are non-left-recursive. Hence the question arises whether our transformation preserves strict determinism. This is indeed the case. Since strict deterministic grammars are unambiguous it is sufficient to demand that the input grammar is ε-free and it does not have useless symbols.

<u>COROLLARY 3.1.</u> (Left part transformation for strict deterministic grammars.)
Let G be strict deterministic under partition π. Then G' is strict deterministic under a partition π' which is defined as follows:

(i) $\Sigma \in \pi'$ and $\{[S]\} \in \pi'$

(ii) $[Ai\alpha] \equiv [Bj\beta] \pmod{\pi'}$ iff $A \equiv B \pmod{\pi}$ and $\alpha = \beta$

It follows that Theorem 3.1 can be used for strict deterministic grammars.
Note: It can be shown that partition π' as defined above is the minimal strict partition of G'. Moreover, when the left part transformation is applied to a *real-time* strict deterministic grammar (Harrison and Havel [17]) the resulting grammar is also real-time strict deterministic.

4. OTHER COVERS

There remain some interesting questions. Firstly, in the preceeding section we obtained l/x-covers where (in an informal notation) $l \le x \le lp$. One can ask whether it is possible to replace lp by $\bar{r}$. This can not be done. That is, if we do not introduce restrictions on the (ε-free and non-left-recursive) grammars which we consider then lp is as far as we can go. In Ukkonen [41] an example of an ε-free and non-left-recursive grammar is given for which no left-to-right cover in GNF can be obtained.

Another question is whether 1 can be replaced by $\bar{r}$. This can be done. From the transitivity of the cover relation and from the following algorithm it follows that for any proper CFG G one can find a GNF-grammar G' such that $G'[\bar{r}/x]G$, with $1 \le x \le lp$.

ALGORITHM 4.1.

Input. A CFG $G = (N,\Sigma,P,S)$ in GNF.

Output. A CFG $G' = (N',\Sigma,P',S)$ in GNF such that $G'[\bar{r}/1]G$.

Method. In this algorithm each production in P' will be followed by its image under the cover homomorphism. If $A \in N$ then rhs(A) denotes its set of right hand sides. Initially set $P' = \{A \to a \ \langle i\rangle \mid i.A \to a \in P,\ a \in \Sigma\}$ and $N' = N$. The indexed symbols H which are introduced below are added to N'.

(i) For each production of the form $i.A \to a\alpha$ in P, $\alpha \ne \varepsilon$, the following is done.
Assume $\alpha = B\gamma$, $\gamma \in N^*$.
For any $j_k.B \to b_k\gamma_k$ in P, $1 \le k \le |\text{rhs}(B)|$
add

$$A \to aH_{ij_k}\gamma_k\gamma \ \langle\varepsilon\rangle$$

and

$$H_{ij_k} \to b_k \ \langle ij_k\rangle$$

to P'.

(ii) Remove all useless symbols. □

In the following corollary we collect the results of Algorithm 3.1, Algorithm 4.1 and the observation on the elimination of single productions.

COROLLARY 4.1.

Any proper non-left-recursive CFG G can be transformed to a CFG G' in GNF such that with $1 \le x \le lp$,

(i) $G'[1/x]G$, and

(ii) $G'[\bar{r}/x]G$.

In [33] a complete overview of cover results for 1/1, $1/\bar{r}$, $\bar{r}/1$ and $\bar{r}/\bar{r}$-covers is given. For example, in (ii) we may drop the condition that G is non-left-recursive if we take $x = \bar{r}$. If we use non-right-recursive instead of non-left-recursive then we may take $x = \bar{r}$ in (i). A similar result (for unambiguous grammars) has been obtained by Ukkonen [40].

REFERENCES.

[1] AHO, A.V. and ULLMAN, J.D., *The Theory of Parsing, Translation and Compiling,* Vol.1 and 2, Prentice Hall, Englewood Cliffs, N.J. 1972 and 1973.

[2] BENSON, D.B. *Some preservation properties of normal form grammars,* SIAM J. Comput. 6 (1977), pp. 381-402.

[3] BERTSCH, E., *An observation on relative parsing time,* J.Assoc.Comput. Mach. 22 (1975), pp. 493-498.

[4] BOCHMAN, G.V., *Semantic equivalence of covering attribute grammars,* Publication #218, december 1975, Université de Montreal.

[5] BOCHMAN, G.V., *Semantic attributes for grammars with regular expressions,* Publication #195, Université de Montreal.

[6] BROSGOL, B.M., *Deterministic translation grammars,* Proc.Eight Princeton Conference on Information Sciences and Systems, 1974, pp. 300-306.

[7] DEMERS, A.J., *Generalized left corner parsing,* Conf. Record of the Fourth ACM Symposium on Principles of Programming Languages, 1977, pp. 170-182.

[8] FOSTER, J.M., *A syntax improving program,* Computer Journal 11 (1968), pp.31-34.

[9] GELLER, M.M., HARRISON, M.A. and HAVEL, I.M., *Normal forms of deterministic grammars,* Discrete Mathematics 16 (1976), pp.313-322.

[10] GINSBURG, S. and HARRISON, M.A., *Bracketed context-free languages,* J.Comput. System Sci. 1 (1967), pp. 1-23.

[11] GRAY, J.N. and HARRISON, M.A., *Single pass precedence analysis,* IEEE Conf.Record of the 10 th Annual Symposium on Switching and Automata Theory, 1969, pp. 106-117.

[12] GRAY, J.N. and HARRISON, M.A., *On the covering and reduction problems for context-free grammars,* J. Assoc.Comput.Mach. 19 (1972), pp. 385-395.

[13] GREIBACH, S.A., *A new normal-form theorem for context-free phrase structure grammars,* J. Assoc.Comput.Mach. 12 (1965), pp. 42-52.

[14] GREIBACH, S.A. *Erasable context-free languages,* Information and Control 29 (1975), pp. 301-326.

[15] GRIFFITHS, T.V., and PETRICK, S.R., *On the relative efficiencies of context-free grammar recognizers,* Comm. ACM 8 (1965), pp. 289-300.

[16] HARRISON, M.A., and HAVEL, I.M., *Strict deterministic grammars,* J.Comput. System Sci. 7 (1973), pp. 237-277.

[17] HARRISON, M.A., and HAVEL, I.M., *Real-time strict deterministic languages,* SIAM J. of Comput. 4 (1972), pp. 333-349.

[18] HOPCROFT, J.E., and ULLMAN, J.D. *Formal Languages and Their Relation to Automata,* Addison Wesley Publishing Co., Reading, Mass., 1969.

[19] HOTZ, G., *Normal-form transformations of context-free grammars,* to appear in Acta Kybernetica.

[20] HOTZ, G., *Eine Algebraisierung des Syntheseproblem von Schaltkreisen, I und II,* Elektr. Inform. und Kybernetik 1 (1965), pp. 185-231.

[21] HOTZ, G., *Eindeutigkeit und mehrdeutigkeit formaler Sprachen,* Elektr. Inform. und Kybernetik 2 (1966), pp. 235-246.

[22] HOTZ, G., *LL(k)-und LR(k) Invarianz von kontextfreien Grammatiken unter einer Transformation auf Greibachnormalform,* manuscript, 1978.

[23] HOTZ, G., and CLAUS, V., *Automaten-Theorie und Formale Sprachen III*, Bibliographisches Institut Mannheim, West Germany 1971.

[24] HUNT, H.B., and ROSENKRANTZ, D.J., *Complexity of grammatical similarity relations*, Proc. of the Conference on Theoretical Computer Science, Waterloo 1977, pp. 139-145.

[25] KNUTH, D.E., *Semantics of context-free languages*, Math. Systems Theory 2 (1968) pp. 127-145.

[26] KUNO, S., *The augmented predictive analyzer for context-free languages-Its relative efficiency*, Comm. ACM 9 (1966), pp. 810-823.

[27] KURKI-SUONIO, R., *On the top-to-bottom recognition and left recursion*, Comm. ACM 9 (1966), pp. 527-528.

[28] McNAUGHTON, R., *Parenthesis grammars*, J. Assoc.Comput.Mach. 14 (1967), pp.490-500.

[29] NIJHOLT, A., *On the parsing and covering of simple chain grammars*, in: Automata, Languages and Programming, G.Ausiello and C.Böhm (eds.), Lect.Notes in Comp.Sci.62 (Springer, Berlin, 1978), pp.330-344.

[30] NIJHOLT, A., *Grammar functors and covers: From non-left-recursive to Greibach normal form grammars*, to appear in BIT 19 (1979).

[31] NIJHOLT, A., *A left part theorem for grammatical trees*, Discrete Mathematics 25 (1979), pp. 51-64.

[32] NIJHOLT, A., *From left regular to Greibach normal form grammars*, unpublished manuscript.

[33] NIJHOLT, A., *A survey of normal form covers for context-free grammars*, IR-49, February 1979, Vrije Universiteit, Amsterdam.

[34] REYNOLDS, J.C., *Grammatical covering*, Argonne National Laboratory, T.M. No. 96, 1968.

[35] REYNOLDS, J.C. and HASKELL, R., *Grammatical coverings, unpublished manuscript*, Syracuse University, 1970.

[36] ROSENKRANTZ, D.J., *Matrix equations and normal forms for context-free grammars*, J.Assoc.Comput.Mach. 14 (1967), pp. 501-507.

[37] ROSENKRANTZ, D.J. and LEWIS, P.M. *Deterministic left-corner parsing*, IEEE Conf. Record of the 11th Annual Symposium on Switching and Automata Theory, 1970, pp. 139-152.

[38] ROSENKRANTZ, D.J. and STEARNS, R.E., *Properties of deterministic top-down grammars*, Information and Control 17 (1970), pp. 226-256.

[39] SOISALON-SOININEN, E., *On the covering problem for left-recursive grammars*, to appear in Theor.Comput.Science.

[40] UKKONEN, E., *Transformations to produce certain covering grammars*, in: Mathematical Foundations of Computer Science, J.Winkowski (ed.), Lect. Notes in Comp.Sci.64 (Springer, Berlin, 1978), pp. 516-525.

[41] UKKONEN, E., *Remarks on the nonexistence of some covering grammars*, to appear in Proc. 4th G.I.Conference on Theoretical Computer Science, 1979.

[42] WALTER, H.K.G. KEKLIKOGLOU, J. and KERN, W., *The behaviour of parsing time under grammar morphisms*, RAIRO-Theor.Comput.Science 12 (1978), pp.83-97.

[43] WOOD, D., *The normal form theorem - another proof*, Computer Journal 12 (1969), pp. 139-147.

[44] WOOD, D., *A generalized normal form theorem for context-free grammars*, Computer Journal 13 (1970), pp. 272-277.

The Complexity of Restricted Minimum Spanning Tree Problems

(Extended Abstract)

Christos H. Papadimitriou*
Laboratory for Computer Science
M.I.T.
Cambridge, MA 02139/USA

Mihalis Yannakakis
Bell Laboratories
Murray Hill, NJ 07974/USA

ABSTRACT

We examine the complexity of finding in a given finite metric the shortest spanning tree which satisfies a property P. Most problems discussed in the mathematical programming literature--including the minimum spanning tree problem, the matching problem, matroid intersection, the travelling salesman problem, and many others--can be thus formulated. We study in particular *isomorphism* properties--those that are satisfied by at most one tree with a given number of nodes. We show that the complexity of these problems is captured by the rate of growth of a rather unexpected--and easy to calculate--parameter.

1. Introduction

Most of the research effort in the field of combinatorial optimization during the 1960's was directed toward developing polynomial-time algorithms for some special cases of the following general class of problems

MST(P)

"Given an n×n distance matrix $[|d_{ij}|]$, find the shortest spanning tree satisfying a property P."

The principal results in this area can be paraphrased as follows:

THEOREM 1. ([Pr],[Kr]). If P=∅ (the trivial property satisfied by all trees) MST(P) can be solved in polynomial time. □

THEOREM 2. ([Ed1]). If P = "isomorphic to a 2-star" (see Figure 1b), MST(P) can be solved in polynomial time. □

It is not hard to verify that Theorem 2 is equivalent to saying that there is a polynomial-time algorithm for weighted matching.

THEOREM 3. ([Ed2],[La1]). If P is a matroidal property (definition follows) then MST(P) can be solved in polynomial time. □

A property is matroidal essentially if the corresponding optimization problem can be solved by the greedy algorithm (see [La2], [PS]). It is assumed that the property P is given by an algorithm that can uniformly

* Research supported by NSF Grant MCS77-01193.

recognize independent sets of edges in polynomial time. Theorem 3 is, therefore, a weak version of the matroid intersection algorithm. Theorems 2 and 3 are in many ways the most general and non-trivial problems in the area that are solved by known efficient algorithms. Other examples are shown in Table 1 (entries 1 through 6).

More recently, negative results were proven concerning problems in this class. The principal one is the one concerning the travelling salesman problem (TSP):

THEOREM 4. [Ka]. If P = "isomorphic to a path" (see Figure 1d) MST(P) is NP-complete. □

We show in Table 1, rows 7 through 12, more examples of NP-complete problems in this class. Until very recently, it was not known whether MST(P) is polynomial or NP-complete when P is the <u>parity</u> property: "an edge appears in the tree if and only if its prescribed mate does." The parity problem for general matroids is a common generalization of matroid intersection and matching [La2]. A polynomial-time algorithm for this problem was discovered by Lovász [Lo].

In this paper we attempt to understand the reasons that make some of these problems hard and others easy. We restrict ourselves to the cases in which P is an <u>isomorphism</u> property; that is, P is satisfied by at most one tree with n nodes, for all n. For example, the properties of Theorems 2 and 4 are ismorphism properties. In Section 2 we show that if the diameter of the trees satisfying P grows as a power of the number of nodes--in other words, if the problem bares the slightest resemblance to the TSP--we have an NP-complete problem. This was first conjectured by Shen Lin [Li]. In Section 3 we generalize this to show that the growth of the <u>dissociation number</u> of the trees satisfying P--i.e., the smallest number of nodes whose removal reduces the tree to isolated points and lines--is sufficient to make MST(P) NP-complete. In Section 4, we present a polynomial-time algorithm for a generalization of matching, and explain why a further generalization is not solvable by the same algorithm. In Section 5 we use these ideas to prove our main result, stating that the complexity of MST(P) for isomorphic properties P is captured exactly by the growth of a rather unexpected parameter of the trees satisfying P: the dissociation number, plus the second largest degree after the deletion of the leaves. MST(P) is NP-complete if and only if this parameter grows as a power of the order of the tree--assuming two very likely conjectures.

2. A Lower Bound Based on Diameter

To formalize our notion of an isomorphism property P, we consider a sequence of trees $<T_0,T_1,...>$ such that

1. $<T_j>$ is infinite.
2. $|T_j|<|T_{j+1}|<p(|T_j|)$ for some polynomial p; $|T_j|$ is the number of vertices in T_j.
3. Given n, the smallest tree in $<T_j>$ with $|T_j|>n$ can be generated in polynomial time (in n).

Let $P(<T_j>)$ be the property "isomorphic to some tree in the sequence $<T_j>$". If T is a tree, diam(T) is its diameter.

THEOREM 5. If $\mathrm{diam}\,(T_j) = \Omega(|T_j|^{\varepsilon})$ for some $\varepsilon>0$ $\mathrm{MST}(P(<T_j>))$ is NP-complete.

The idea in the proof of Theorem 5 is quite simple, only it doesn't work without the assistance of some non-trivial graph theory. Ideally, we would like to reduce Hamilton path to our problem as follows: Let G=(V,E) be an instance of Hamilton path; let T_j be the tree in $<T_j>$ with $|T_j|>|V|^{1/\varepsilon}$ (ignoring constants for a moment). We would like to construct a $|T_j|\times|T_j|$ distance matrix such that we have a cheap tree that looks like T_j if and only if G is Hamiltonian. T_j has a path of length $|V|$ in it; the nodes of this path will correspond to nodes of G. Subtrees "hanging" from this path (see Figures 2a, b) will be formed at no cost, and they will be connected to all nodes of G at some substantial cost M. The costs among vertices of G reflect the structure of G, and all other costs are partically ∞. The reason that this does not work is because certain tree automorphisms can create a non-path arrangement of the nodes of G (Figure 2c).

The correct reduction works as follows:

1. Find T_j such that (a) $|T_j|^{\varepsilon}/|V|^2>\log|T_j|$, and (b) $|V|>\log|T_j|$. For the finitely many Hamilton path instances for which this is impossible use table lookup.

2. Call a leaf <u>critical</u> if it is the endpoint of a diameter. Call a node a <u>branching point</u> if more than two components of the forest resulting from its removal contain critical leaves. Start from the center of the tree T_j and follow a diameter. Whenever a branching point is met, follow the subtree with the least number of critical leaves.

Claim. It follows from (a) above that this procedure will eventually find a path of length $|V|^2$ without branching points, lying on a diameter. □

3. Among the $|V|$ possible paths of length $|V|$ that we isolated in step

(2) above, we shall select one with the following property: The subtree starting at the furthest endpoint of the path is not isomorphic to any subtree hanging from this path (note: this pathology hurt the validity of our original argument, see Figure 1a, 1c). We do this by solving $O(|V|)$ tree isomorphism problems. Suppose that there is no such choice. Then, we can argue that T_j contains the homeomorph of a full binary tree of depth $|V|$, which is impossible by (b) above.

4. After this careful choice of the location of the path of length $|V|$, our original argument is applicable. □

Despite its apparent generality, however, Theorem 5 fails to explain the following:

THEOREM 6. [PY]. If T_j is the full binary tree (Figure 1e) of depth j, $MST(P(<T_j>))$ is NP-complete. □

As is well-known, these trees have a diameter growing as the logarithm of the number of nodes, and hence Theorem 5 does not apply. More surprisingly, there are classes with constant diameter that are NP-complete:

THEOREM 7. [JL]. If $<T_j>$ is one of the classes shown in Figures 1c,1d, then $MST(P(<T_j>))$ is NP-complete. □

The next section is devoted to explaining these phenomena. One of our tools in doing so is Theorem 5.

3. The Dissociation Number

The dissociation number of a graph G, dis (G), is the smallest number of nodes that one has to delete in order to reduce G to single points and lines. dis(G) is NP-complete to determine for general graphs, but easy in trees. Remarkably, it is a crucial parameter for determining the complexity of a class of trees.

One can compute the dissociation number of a tree as the number of nodes deleted by the following algorithm:

```
begin
loop:while |T|>4 do
for all critical leaves v of T do
if deg(father*(v)) ≠ 2 then delete father(v) else delete father
 (father(v));
if 3 ≤|T|≤4  then delete one appropriate node
end
```

* father(v) is a non-leaf neighbor of v; father (·) will always be used unambiguously.

A flower (a term long overdue in graph theory after Edmonds' article ([Ed1]) is a tree with dissociation number 1 (See Figure 1f).
A d-bouquet is a tree consisting of a single point connected with the centers of d flowers (see Figure 1g).

We now prove the following characterization:

THEOREM 8. If $<T_j>$ has dis $(T_j) = \Omega(|T_j|^{\varepsilon})$ for $\varepsilon>0$, then there is either a subsequence $<T_j'>$ - satisfying the requirements 1-3 of Section 2--with diam $(T_j') = \Omega(|T_j'|^{\delta_1})$ for some $\delta_1>0$, or a subsequence $<T_j''>$ of trees that are homeomorphs of d_j-bouquets for $d_j = \Omega(|T_j|^{\delta_2})$, $\delta_2>0$.

Sketch. Each iteration of the loop of the algorithm above reduces the diameter of T_j by at least 4. Since T_j has a large* dissociation number, then it either has a large diameter or there is a large number of points deleted in one execution of the loop. In the latter case, we can exhibit a large number of flowers. □

THEOREM 9. If $\mathrm{dis}(T_j) = \Omega(|T_j|^{\varepsilon})$ for $\varepsilon>0$, then $\mathrm{MST}(P(<T_j>))$ is NP-complete.

Sketch. If $<T_j>$ has a large diameter, we are done by Theorem 5. So assume that $<T_j>$ is a sequence of large bouquets, where the centers of the bouquets have been replaced by arbitrary trees. We distinguish among two cases, depending on whether among the flowers of the bouquet those of diameter 2 or those of diameter 3 or 4 predominate. In each case, we observe that either there is a large number of isomorphic flowers, or a large number of pairwise non-isomorphic flowers. In each of the four subcases, we apply a reduction from the exact cover problem [GJJ.] □

4. α-β Matching

A class of trees that Theorem 9 fails to capture is the one in Figure 1h. Certainly $\mathrm{dis}(T_j) = 2$, but no efficient algorithm is apparent. Consider even the case in which the two centers are fixed, the graph is unweighted, and the neighborhoods of the centers exhaust the vertices. This is equivalent to

α-β Matching

Given $G = (V,E)$ and $\alpha,\beta \subseteq V$ with $\alpha\cup\beta = V$, find a matching $M \subseteq E$ with $|\{e\in M: e\cap\alpha \neq \emptyset\}| > a$, $|\{e\in M: e\cap\beta\neq \emptyset\}| > b$.

This is a nontrivial generalization of matching, solvable by the following $O(|V|^3)$ algorithm:

* By "large" we mean here $\Omega(|T_j|^{\delta})$ for some $\delta>0$.

1. Find a complete matching. If none, no α-β matching exists.

2. Without loss of generality, $|\{e \in M: e \ \alpha\neq \emptyset\}| < a$. Repeat the following steps, until this condition is no longer met.

3. Construct a weighted digraph (V,A,w) by the rules
   a. $(u,v) \in A$ if and only if $[u, mate(v)] \in E$.
   b. $w(u,v) = 1$ if $u \in \alpha-\beta$; $v, mate(v) \in \beta-\alpha$
      -1 if $u \in \beta-\alpha$; $v, mate(v) \in \alpha-\beta$
      0 otherwise.

4. Find a positive cycle in (V,A,w) and "augment" (details omitted).

Unfortunately, the algorithm above fails to solve the problem with the $V-\alpha\cup\beta=i=\emptyset$ assumption removed. The reason is that in the $i \neq \emptyset$ case we may have positive cycles like the one in Figure 3, which augments the α-edges by considerably decreasing the β-edges. This counterexample will be used in the next section to characterize the complexity of the general α-β matching or, equivalently, the $MST(P(<T_j>))$ for the trees of Figure 1h.

5. The Main Result

Consider the following problem

EXACT CYCLE SUM

"Given a digraph (V,A) and $k > 0$ is there a set of disjoint cycles of total length exactly k?"

CONJECTURE 1. Exact cycle sum is NP-complete. □

LEMMA 1. Exact cycle sum reduces to $MST(P(<T_j>))$ for the trees T_j of Figure 1h.

Idea. Substitute each arc (u,v) by the path from u to v in Figure 3. □

LEMMA 2. Let a(n) be the dissociation number of T_j ($|T_j| = n$) and b(n) be the second largest degree in T_j after the removal of leaves. Then $MST(P(<T_j>))$ can be solved in

$O(2^{3\ a(n)\log n\ +\ (2\ \log n+1)b(n)\ +\ 3\ \log n})$ arithmetic operations.

Sketch. We iterate the construction for all possible dissociation trees (induced subtree by the dissociation points), and this is the $n^{3a(n)}$ factor. For all dissociation points except for the one with the largest degree we solve exhaustively the matching problems by trying out all possible free points. This can be done in $O([n^{2b(n)} \cdot 2^{b(n)}]^{a(n)})$ time. Finally we solve matching in $O(n^3)$ time for the remaining dissociation point. □

Let us define for any tree T (T) to be the sum of dis (T) plus the second largest degree of T after the removal of T's leaves, also, for a family T_j of trees, let us define the complexity of T_j to be

$$\mathrm{Comp}\,(T_j) = \max_{i \le j} c\,(T_i)$$

Consider the complexity class

$$\mathrm{SUBEXP} = \bigcup_{f \in \bigcap_{\varepsilon > 0} o(n^{\varepsilon})} \mathrm{DTIME}(2^{f(n)})$$

The following is widely accepted:

CONJECTURE 2. $\mathcal{NP} \nsubseteq$ SUBEXP.

We now state:

THEOREM 10. Assuming Conjectures 1 and 2 the MST(P(<T_j>)) is NP-complete if and only if comp(T_j) = $\Omega(|T_j|^{\varepsilon})$ for some $\varepsilon > 0$.

Sketch. If: Since comp(T_j) = $\Omega(|T_j|^{\varepsilon})$, either dis($T_j$) is large, or T_j contains copies of the trees in Figure 1h. In the first case, we have NP-completeness by Theorem 9; in the latter by Lemma 1 and Conjecture 1.

Only if: Follows from Lemma 2 and Conjecture 2.

6. Discussion

Conjecture 2 is stronger than $\mathcal{P} \neq \mathcal{NP}$ but Conjecture 1 certainly seems provable by standard methodology.

Several generalizations could be considered.

a. The underlying system is a general matroid, instead of a graph. Possibly similar results can be shown, but the exact parameter is not obvious.

b. The sequence <T_j> of prototypes consists of graphs, instead of trees. This seems more difficult, since "Treeness" was used in essential parts of our proof.

c. More importantly, extend the results to non-isomorphism properties P. This appears to be very challenging. For one thing, exact characterizations, such as the one of Theorem 10, cannot be brought about without understanding the currently gray area of the parity constraint. Still, sufficient conditions for NP-completeness may be very valuable to our understanding of combinatorial optimization.

REFERENCES

[Ed1] J. Edmonds "Paths, Trees, and Flowers," Canad. J. Math., 17, pp. 449-467, [65].

[Ed2] J. Edmonds "Matroids and the Greedy Algorithm," Math. Programming, 1, pp. 127-136, [71].

[GJ] M.R. Gar D.S. Johnson, Computers and Intractability: A Guide to the Theory of NP-Completeness, Freeman, 1979.

[JL] D.S. Johnson, S. Lin, private communication, Feb. 1976.

[Ka] R.M. Karp "Reducibility among Combinatorial Problems," in Complexity of Computer Computations, R.E. Miller and J.W. Thatcher (eds.), Plenum, NY, pp 85-103, 1972.

[Kr] J.B. Kruskal "On the Shortest Spanning Subtree of the Graph and the Traveling Salesman Problem," Proc. Am. Math Soc. 2, pp. 48-50, [56].

[La1] E.L. Lawler "Matroid Intersection Algorithms," Math. Programming, 9, pp. 31-56, [75].

[La2] E.L. Lawler Combinatorial Optimization: Networks and Matroids, Holt-Rhinehart-Winston, 1977.

[Li] Shen Lin, private communication, Feb. 1976.

[Lo] L. Lovász "The Matroid Parity Problem", manuscript, University of Waterloo, 1979.

[Pa] C.H. Papadimitriou "The Complexity of the Capacitated Tree Problem," Networks Aug. 1978.

[Pr] R.C. Prim "Shortest Connection Networks and some Generalizations", BSTJ pp. 1389-1401, 1957.

[PS] C.H. Papadimitriou, K. Steiglitz Combinatorial Optimization Algorithms, in preparation [79].

[PY] C.H. Papadimitriou, M. Yannakakis, unpublished, [77].

	Property P	Complexity	Comments
1		$0(n^2)$	Minimum spanning tree tree [Kr,Pr]
2	"isomorphic to the star"	$0(n^2)$	
3	"isomorphic to the 2-star"	$0(n^3)$	matching [Edl, La2, PS]
4	Matroidal property	$0(n^3 C(n^2))$	matroid intersection [La1]
5	$L \supseteq S$	$0(n^2)$	
6	$\deg(v_0) = k$	$0(n^2)$	
7	"isomorphic to a path"	NP-complete	TSP [Ka]
8	"isomorphic to a 3-star"	"	[JL]
9	"isomorphic to a full binary tree"	"	[PY]
10	$L \subseteq, = S$; $\lvert L\rvert =, \le, \ge k$	"	
11	$Cap[v_0,k]$	"	Capacitated Tree Problem [Pa]
12	$\deg(v) \le k$ for all v	"	

<u>Notes</u>

2,3,7,8,9 Fig. 1 contains examples of special kinds of trees.

5,10 L is the set of leaves.

6,12 deg(v) is the degree of v.

5,6,10,11,12 k is an integer parameter, S is a set parameter, v_0 is a fixed node.

11 $Cap[v_0,k]$ states that the removal of v_0 results in a forest with components of size k or less.

TABLE 1

(a)

(b)

cost of edges

● —— ● : 0

○ —— ○ : 1

○   ○ : 2

● ——○ : M

all others: M^2

(c)

Figure 2

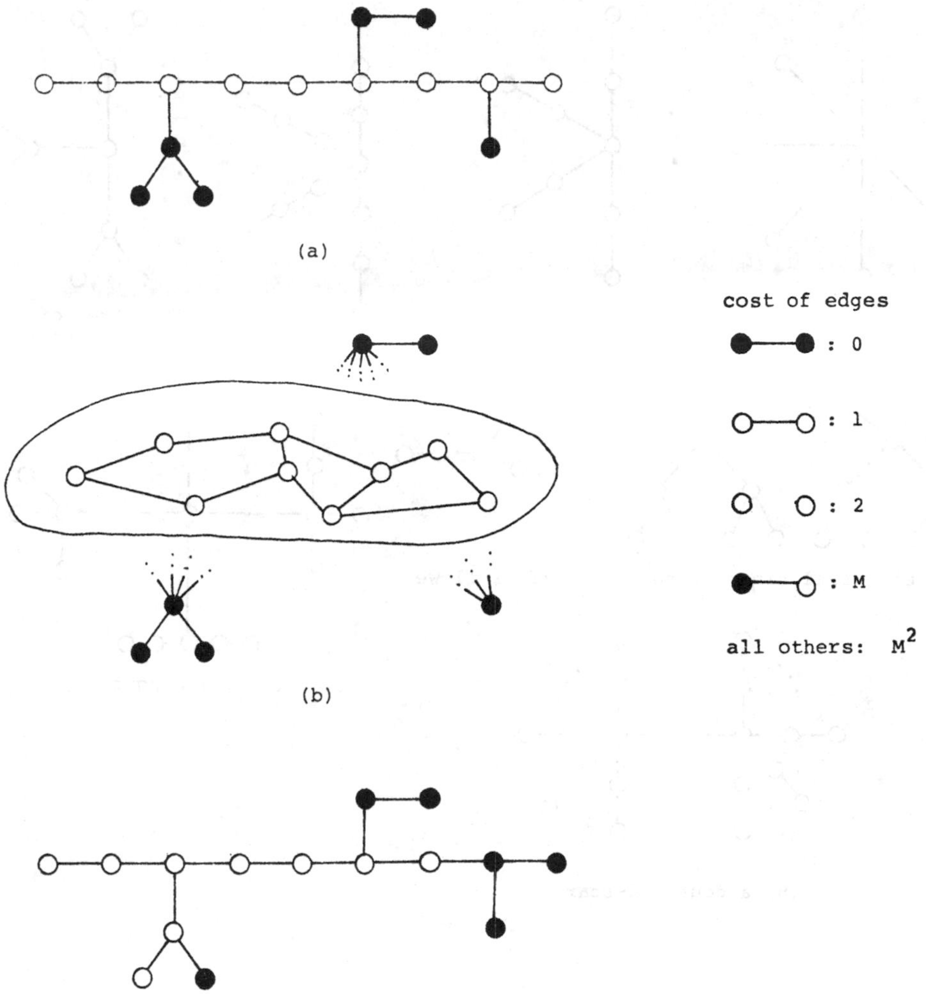

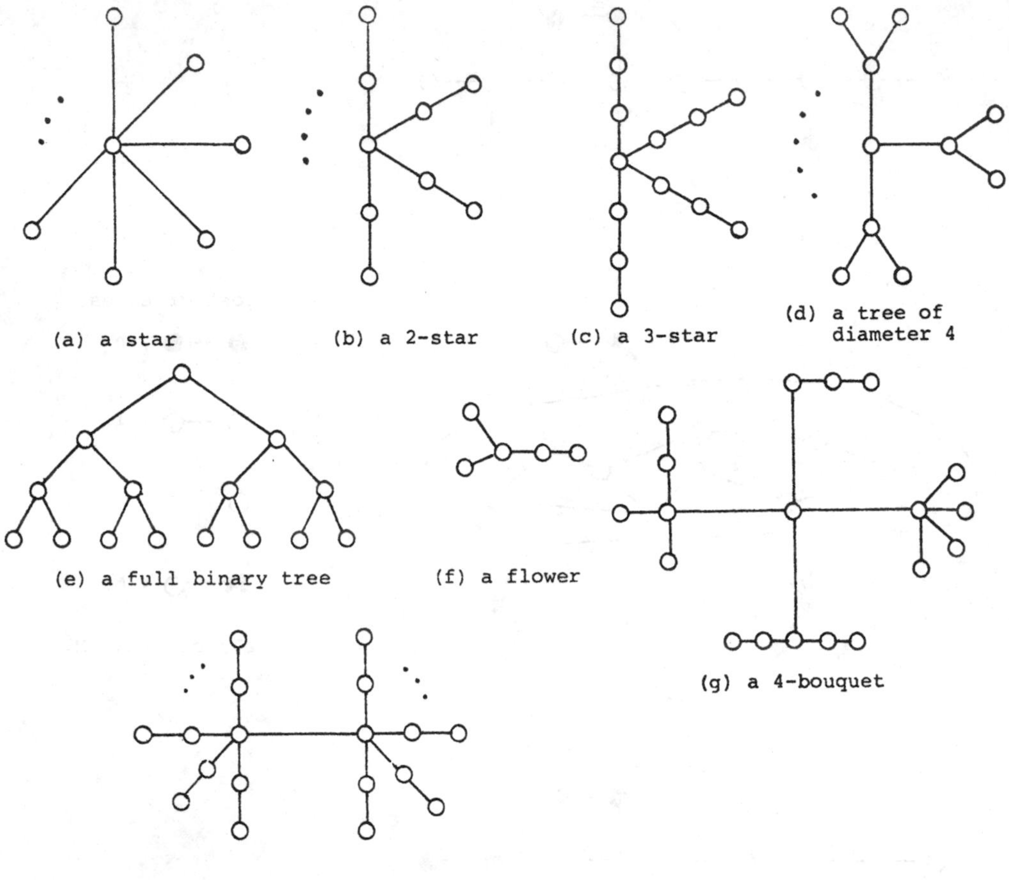

(a) a star (b) a 2-star (c) a 3-star (d) a tree of diameter 4

(e) a full binary tree (f) a flower (g) a 4-bouquet

(h) a double 2-star

Figure 1

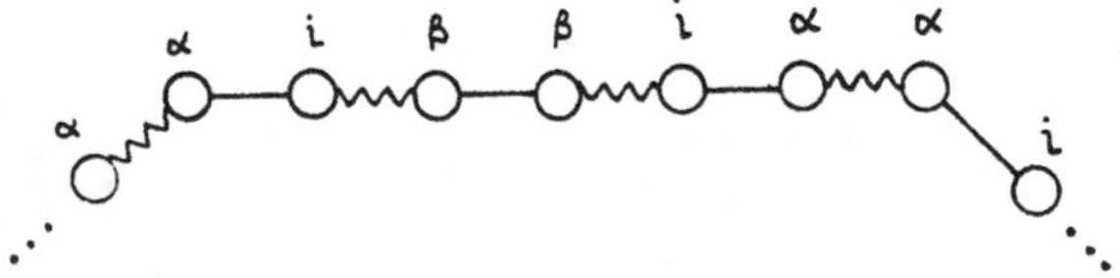

Figure 3

A SYSTEMATIC APPROACH TO FORMAL LANGUAGE THEORY THROUGH PARALLEL REWRITING

G. Rozenberg
Dept. of Applied Math. and Computer Science
University of Leiden
Leiden, Holland

INTRODUCTION

L systems were introduced by Aristid Lindenmayer in connection with biological considerations in 1968. From that time on the research in the theory of L systems was very active indeed and it has led to a theory rich in original results and novel techniques. The theory of L systems constitutes today a considerable body of mathematical knowledge and it has not only enriched the theory of formal languages but has also been able to put the latter theory in a totally new perspective.

An outstanding feature of the theory of L systems is that its core fits into a very systematic and basic mathematical framework. Since most of the significant research areas from formal language theory are well represented within this framework, the theory of L systems might take a central place within the theory of formal languages. One can also study in this way various traditional classes of languages since quite a number of them, e.g., context free, context sensitive and recursively enumerable languages, have their natural counterparts within the framework of L systems.

The aim of this paper is to outline the systematic construction of (a part of) the theory of L systems and to indicate at the same time how various traditional research areas of formal language theory are extensively represented within the theory of L systems. Because of restrictions on the size of this paper we have chosen to survey only that part of the theory which is referred to as the theory of L systems without interactions. For the same reason our survey is very sketchy. We do not credit results quoted here since they are referenced in one of the two monographs listed in the references.

We use mostly standard terminology and notation. For a word x we use $|x|$ to denote its length and $\#_B x$ to denote the number of occurrences of letters from B in x, Λ denotes the empty word. For a language K, $Length(K) = \{n : n = |x| \text{ for some } x \in K\}$. Given an alphabet Σ and $\Delta \subseteq \Sigma$, $Pres_\Delta$ is a homomorphism from Σ^* into Σ^* defined by $Pres_\Delta(a) = a$ for $a \in \Delta$ and $Pres_\Delta(a) = \Lambda$ for $a \in \Sigma \setminus \Delta$.

I. SINGLE HOMOMORPHISMS ITERATED

The most basic construct of L systems theory is a DOL system which is defined as a triple $G = (\Sigma,h,\omega)$ where Σ is a finite alphabet, $h : \Sigma^* \to \Sigma^*$ is a homomorphism and $\omega \in \Sigma^+$. The sequence of G, denoted E(G), is defined by $E(G) = \omega_0, \omega_1, \ldots$ where $\omega_0 = \omega$ and $\omega_{i+1} = h(\omega_i)$ for $i \geq 0$. The language of G, denoted L(G), is defined by $L(G) = \{h^n(\omega) : n \geq 0\}$. The length sequence of G, denoted LS(G), is defined by $LS(G) = |\omega_0|, |\omega_1|, \ldots$. The growth function of G, denoted f_G, is the function from nonnegative integers into nonnegative integers defined by $f_G(n) = |h^n(\omega_0)|$, $n \geq 0$. E(G) is referred to as a DOL sequence, L(G) as a DOL language, LS(G) as a DOL length sequence and f_G as a DOL growth function.

A DOL system represents thus a very basic mathematical structure - the iteration of a single homomorphism on a free monoid. The theory of DOL systems brought to formal language theory a totally new topic - the theory of sequences of words, rather than their sets (languages). We shall survey now quickly several research areas concerning DOL sequences.

I.1. DOL growth functions.

The theory of growth functions of DOL systems forms today a well understood area. Its basic mathematical framework is that of formal power series in noncommuting variables. One may safely say that the theory of formal power series and the theory of DOL growth functions have mutually contributed to each others development. The relationship between DOL length sequences and Z-rational sequences of numbers is by now sufficiently understood. Here are two typical results.

Theorem. Assume that an N-rational sequence of numbers has a matrix representation $u(n) = \pi M^n \eta$, $n = 0,1,2,\ldots$ with either only positive entries in π or only positive entries in η. Then u(n) is a DOL length sequence. ∎

Theorem. Every Z-rational sequence can be expressed as the difference of two DOL sequences. ∎

Generating functions form a very useful tool in investigating DOL growth functions. The following result is typical in characterizing generating functions of DOL growth functions.

Theorem. A rational function F(x) with integral coefficients and written in lowest terms is the generating function of a DOL growth function not identical to the zero function if and only if either $F(x) = a_0 + a_1x + \ldots + a_nx^n$ where $a_0, a_1, \ldots, a_n$ are positive integers, or else F(x) satisfies each of the following conditions :

(i) The constant term of its denominator equals 1.

(ii) The coefficients of the Taylor expansion $F(x) = \sum_{n=0}^{\infty} a_n x^n$ are positive integers and, moreover, the ratio a_{n+1}/a_n is bounded by a constant.

(iii) Every pole x_0 of F(x) of the minimal absolute value is of the form $x_0 = r\varepsilon$ where $r = |x_0|$ and ε is a root of unity. ∎

I.2. Locally catenative DOL systems.

A very natural way to generalize linear homogeneous recurrence relations to words is as follows. A locally catenative formula (LCF for short) is an ordered k-tuple $v = (i_1,\dots,i_k)$ of positive integers where $k \geq 1$ (we refer to k as the width of v and to $\max\{i_1,\dots,i_k\}$ as the depth of v). An infinite sequence of words $\omega_0,\omega_1,\omega_2,\dots$ satisfies v with a cut $p \geq \max\{i_1,\dots,i_k\}$ if, for all $n \geq p$, $\omega_n = \omega_{n-i_1}\dots\omega_{n-i_k}$. A sequence of words satisfying some LCF v with some cut is called (v-) locally catenative. A DOL system G is called (v-) locally catenative. if E(G) is (v-) locally catenative. We say that G is locally catenative of depth (width) d if G is v-locally catenative for some LCF v with depth (width) of v equal to d.

First of all we get the following correspondence between locally catenative DOL sequences and languages.

Theorem. A DOL system G is locally catenative if and only if $L(G)^*$ is a finitely generated monoid. ∎

An important research area within the theory of DOL systems (and indeed within the general theory of L systems) is that of connections between the global properties of a sequence (language) generated by a system and the local properties of a system itself (that is properties of the underlying mapping of a system). A locally catenative property of a DOL sequence is a typical example of a global property (its definition does not depend on a particular system that defines the sequence). The following result illustrates the relationship between a locally catenative property of a DOL sequence and a local property of the underlying DOL system. Let $G = (\Sigma,h,\omega)$ be a DOL system with $\omega \in \Sigma$ where for no a in Σ, $h(a) = \Lambda$. The graph of G, denoted $\mathcal{G}(G)$, is a directed graph the nodes of which are elements of Σ and, for $a,b \in \Sigma$, (a,b) is an edge in $\mathcal{G}(G)$ if and only if $h(a) = \alpha b \beta$ for some $\alpha,\beta \in \Sigma^*$.

Theorem. If there exists $a \in \Sigma$ such that $h^n(\omega) = a$ for some $n \geq 0$ and every cycle in $\mathcal{G}(G)$ goes through a then G is locally catenative. ∎

The most important open problem concerning locally catenative DOL systems is decidability status of the question : "Is an arbitrary DOL system locally catenative?" The best known result in this direction is :

Theorem. (1) It is decidable whether or not an arbitrary DOL system is locally catenative of depth d, where d is an arbitrary positive integer. (2) It is decidable whether or not an arbitrary DOL system is locally catenative of width d, where d is an arbitrary positive integer. ∎

I.3. DOL equivalence problem.

One of the more challenging problems in the theory of DOL systems has been the DOL sequence (respectively language) equivalence problem : "Given two arbitrary DOL systems G_1,G_2 is it decidable whether or not $E(G_1) = E(G_2)$(respectively $L(G_1) = L(G_2)$)?"

Theorem. The DOL sequence and language equivalence problems are decidable. ∎

Various efforts to solve the above mentioned problems created quite a number of notions and results that are of interest on its own and which in fact opened quite new research areas within formal language theory. One of these topics - equality and fixed point languages - will be discussed later on. Another such topic is that of elementary homomorphisms and elementary languages. A homomorphism $h:\Sigma^* \to \Delta^*$ is simplifiable if there is an alphabet Θ with $\#\Theta < \#\Sigma$ and homomorphisms $f:\Sigma^* \to \Theta^*$ and $g:\Theta^* \to \Delta^*$ such that $h = gf$. Otherwise h is called elementary. A finite language K is elementary if there is no language K_1 such that $\#K_1 < \#K$ and $K \subseteq K_1^*$. Clearly elementary homomorphisms and elementary languages are very closely connected : if a homomorphism h defined on Σ is elementary then so is the language $\{h(a) : a \in \Sigma\}$; conversely if the language $\{h(a) : a \in \Sigma\}$ is elementary and consists of $\#\Sigma$ words then h is elementary.

The basic result on elementary languages (and homomorphisms) is the following one.

Theorem. Let $L = \{u_1, \ldots, u_k\}$ be an elementary language over the alphabet Σ. Assume that $u_i x \gamma = u_j y$ for some $i \neq j, \gamma \in \Sigma^*$ and $x, y \in L^*$. Then $|u_i x| \leq |u_1 \ldots u_k| - k$. ■

As an immediate corollary we get the following result.

Theorem. Every elementary language is both, a code with a bounded delay from left to right and a code with a bounded delay from right to left. ■

In this way DOL systems contributed an interesting research area within the coding theory.

II. SINGLE FINITE SUBSTITUTIONS ITERATED

A natural way to generalize DOL systems is to consider the iteration of a finite substitution rather than the iteration of a homomorphism. Since in such a case the generated language (rather than the sequence) becomes the primary concept, one considers (as usual in formal language theory) an additional (terminal) alphabet.

An EOL system is a construct $G = (\Sigma, h, \omega, \Delta)$ where Σ, Δ are finite alphabets, $\Delta \subseteq \Sigma$, $\omega \in \Sigma^+$ and h is a finite substitution from Σ^* into 2^{Σ^*}. The language of G is defined by $L(G) = \{x \in \Delta^* : x \in h^n(\omega) \text{ for some } n \geq 0\}$. L(G) is referred to as an EOL language. (If $\Sigma = \Delta$ then G is referred to as a OL system and L(G) is referred to as a OL language).

The following results illustrate the combinatorial structure of EOL languages. They are especially useful for proving in general that various "concrete" languages are not EOL languages (which is often a difficult task). Let K be a language over Σ and let B be a nonempty subset of Σ. Let $N(K,B) = \{n : (\exists x)_K (\#_B x = n)\}$. We say that B is numerically dispersed in K if N(K,B) is infinite and, for every natural number k, there exists a natural number n_k such that whenever u_1 and u_2 are in N(K,B) and $u_1 > u_2 > n_k$ then $u_1 - u_2 > k$. B is clustered in K if N(K,B) is infinite and there exist natural numbers k_1, k_2 both larger than 1 such that whenever a word x in K satisfies $\#_B x \geq k_1$ then x contains at least two occurrences of letters from B, which lie at a distance smaller than k_2 from each other.

Theorem. Let K be an EOL language over Σ and B a nonempty subset of Σ. If B is numerically dispersed in K then B is clustered in K. ■

Let K be a language over an alphabet Σ and let B be a nonempty subset of Σ. We say that K is B-determined if for every positive integer k there exists a positive integer n_k such that for every x,y in K if $|x|,|y| > n_k$, $x = x_1ux_2$, $y = x_1vx_2$ and $|u|,|v| < k$ then $Pres_B(u) = Pres_B(v)$. ■

Theorem. Let K be a B-determined EOL language. There exist positive integer constants c and d such that, for every $x \in K$, if $\#_B x > c$ then $|x| < d^{\#_B x}$. ■

Theorem. Let K be an EOL language over an alphabet Σ. If K is Σ-determined then there exists a constant c such that, for every nonnegative integer n, $\pi_n(K) \leq c.n^3$. ■

The theory of EOL systems and languages constitutes today quite well understood fragment of L systems theory. It also provides quite natural representations of the class of context free languages. For example we have the following result. The adult language of a OL system $G = (\Sigma,h,\omega)$ is defined by $L_A(G) = \{w \in L(G) : x \in h(w)$ implies $w = x$ for all words $x\}$.

Theorem. A language K is the adult language of a OL system if and only if K is a context free language. ■

III. SEVERAL HOMOMORPHISMS ITERATED.

The language of a DOL system is obtained by applying to a fixed word an arbitrary homomorphism from the semigroup generated by a single homomorphism. Semigroups generated by a finite number of homomorphisms form a natural next step.

A DTOL system is a construct $G = (\Sigma,H,\omega)$ where Σ is a finite alphabet, $\omega \in \Sigma^+$ and H is a finite set of homomorphisms from Σ^* into Σ^*. The language of G is defined by $L(G) = \{x \in \Sigma^* : x = h_n \ldots h_1(w)$ for $n \geq 0$, $h_i \in H\}$.

A useful way of looking at the combinatorial structure of a DTOL language is to investigate the structure of its set of subwords. The basic result in this direction is the following one. (For a language K and a positive integer ℓ, $\pi_\ell(K)$ denotes the number of different subwords of length ℓ occurring in words of K).

Theorem. Let Σ be a finite alphabet such that $\#\Sigma = n \geq 2$. If K is a DTOL language over Σ then $\lim_{\ell \to \infty} \frac{\pi_\ell(K)}{n^\ell} = 0$. ■

As a matter of fact it turns out that various structural restrictions imposed on a DTOL system influence considerably the richness of its set of subwords. So we have for example the following result.

Theorem. (1) For every DOL language K there exists a constant c such that, for every $\ell > 0$, $\pi_\ell(K) \leq c.\ell^2$. (2) For every positive integer c there exists a DOL language K such that $\pi_\ell(K) \geq c\ell^2$ for infinitely many positive integers ℓ. ■

If we restrict ourselves to languages generated by DOL systems in which every letter is rewritten as a word of length 2 (we call them growing DOL systems) then the resulting systems become even more restricted in their subword generating capacity.

Theorem. (1) For every growing DOL language K there exists a positive integer constant c such that, for every $\ell > 0$, $\pi_\ell(K) \leq c\,\ell \log \ell$. (2) For every positive integer c there exists a growing DOL language K such that $\pi_\ell(K) \geq c\,\ell \log \ell$ for infinitely many positive integers ℓ. ▪

Adding an extra (terminal) alphabet one can define a richer class of languages. An EDTOL system is a construct $G = (\Sigma, H, \omega, \Delta)$ where (Σ, H, ω) is a DTOL system and $\Delta \subseteq \Sigma$. The language of G is defined by $L(G) = \{x \in \Delta^* : x = h_n \dots h_1(\omega)$ for $n \geq 0$, $h_i \in H\}$; it is referred to as an EDTOL language.

The following two results are very useful results on the combinatorial structure of EDTOL languages.

A function f from $\mathbb{R}_+$ into $\mathbb{R}_+$ is called slow if for every $\alpha \in \mathbb{R}_+$ there exists $n_\alpha \in \mathbb{R}_+$ such that for every $x \in \mathbb{R}_+$ if $x > n_\alpha$ then $f(x) < x^\alpha$.

Let Σ be a finite alphabet and let $f : \mathbb{R}_+ \to \mathbb{R}_+$. A word w over Σ is called f-random if every two disjoint subwords of w which are longer than $f(|w|)$ are different.

Theorem. For every EDTOL language K and for every slow function f there exists a constant s such that for every f-random word x in L(G) longer than s there exist a positive integer t and words $x_0, \dots, x_t$, $\sigma_1, \dots, \sigma_t$ with $\sigma_1 \dots \sigma_t \neq \Lambda$ such that $x = x_0 \dots x_t$ and, for every nonnegative integer n, $x_0 \sigma_1^n x_1 \sigma_2^n \dots \sigma_t^n x_t$ is in K. ▪

Theorem. Let K be an EDTOL language over an alphabet Σ, where $\#\Sigma = n \geq 2$. If Length(K) does not contain an infinite arithmetic progression then $\lim_{\ell \to \infty} \frac{\#\{w \in K : |w| = \ell\}}{n^\ell} = 0$. ▪

IV. SEVERAL FINITE SUBSTITUTIONS ITERATED.

In the same way as one generalizes DOL systems to EOL systems one extends DTOL systems to obtain ETOL systems.

An ETOL system is a construct $G = (\Sigma, H, \omega, \Delta)$ where Σ is a finite alphabet, $\omega \in \Sigma^+$, $\Delta \subseteq \Sigma$ and H is a finite set of finite substitutions from Σ^* into 2^{Σ^*}. The language of G is defined by $L(G) = \{x \in \Delta^* : x \in h_n \dots h_1(\omega)$ for $n \geq 0$, $h_i \in M\}$.

Here are two typical results concerning combinatorial structure of ETOL languages.

Theorem. Let K be an ETOL language over an alphabet Σ. Then for every nonempty subset Δ of Σ there exists a positive integer k such that for every x in K either (i) $|Pres_\Delta x| \leq 1$, or (ii) there exist a,b in Δ and w in Σ^* such that $x = x_1 awb x_2$ for some x_1, x_2 in Σ^* with $|awb| \leq k$ or (iii) there exist an infinite subset M of K such that, for every y in M, $|Pres_{\Delta}y| = |Pres_{\Delta}x|$. ■

Before stating our next result we need the following definition. Let K be a language over Σ and let Δ be a nonempty subset of Σ. Then : (1) Δ is called nonfrequent in K if there exists a constant c such that, for every x in K, $\#_{\Delta}x < c$; (2) Δ is called rare in K if for every positive integer ℓ there exists a positive integer m such that, for every n greater than m, if a word x in K contains n occurrences of letters from Δ then each two such occurrences are of distance not smaller than k.

Theorem. If K is an ETOL language over Σ and Δ is a nonempty subset of Σ which is rare in K, then B is nonfrequent in K. ■

The following result is a typical "bridging" result. It allows one to construct examples of non ETOL languages providing that one has examples of languages that are not EDTOL.

Theorem. Let Σ_1, Σ_2 be two disjoint alphabets and let $K_1 \subseteq \Sigma_1^*$, $K_2 \subseteq \Sigma_2^*$. Let f be a surjective function from K_1 into K_2 and let $K = \{wf(w) : w \in K_1\}$. Then

(1) If K is an ETOL language then K_2 is an ETOL language.

(2) If f is a bijection, then also K_1 is an EDTOL language (if K is an ETOL language). ■

V. EQUALITY LANGUAGES AND FIXED POINT LANGUAGES

As we have already pointed out various efforts to solve the DOL equivalence problem activated research in the area that could be called "similarity of basic mappings in language theory". A way to measure similarity of mappings is through equality languages and fixed point languages. Given two mappings h,g of Σ^* the equality language of h and g (denoted Eq(h,g)) consists of all elements of Σ^* on which h and g are equal. The fixed point language of h (denoted Fp(h)) consists of all elements from Σ^* that h maps into itself (hence the fixed point language of h measures its similarity with the identity mapping on Σ^*).

It turns out that the theory of equality languages and fixed point languages of homomorphisms and finite substitutions provides quite a number of surprisingly simple representations of recursively enumerable languages. For example we can represent recursively enumerable languages through homomorphisms as follows.

Let for an alphabet Σ, $\overline{\Sigma} = \{\overline{a} : a \in \Sigma\}$ and then let for $w \in \Sigma^*$, $\overline{w}$ be the word obtained from w by replacing every letter a in w by $\overline{a}$. The complete twin shuffle over Σ is the language $L_{\Sigma} = \{w \in (\Sigma \cup \overline{\Sigma})^* : \overline{Pres_{\Sigma}(w)} = Pres_{\overline{\Sigma}}(w)\}$. Clearly L_{Σ} is an equality language of two homomorphisms.

Theorem. For every recursively enumberable language K there exist an alphabet Σ and a regular language M such that $K = Pres_{\Sigma}(L_{\Sigma} \cap M)$. ■

Theorem. For every recursively enumerable language K there exist an alphabet Σ and homomorphisms h,g such that $K = Pres_{\Sigma}(pref(Eq(h,g)))$, where $pref(K) = \{x \in K : x \neq \Lambda$ and no proper prefix of x different from Λ is in K$\}$. ■

Fixed point languages of homomorphisms are too weak to represent recursively enumerable languages (they are finite star events). However fixed point languages of finite substitutions represent recursively enumberable languages as follows.

Theorem. For every recursively enumberable language K there exist an alphabet Σ, a finite substitution h and a regular language M such that $K = Pres_{\Sigma}(F_p(h) \cap M)$. ■

Whereas a finite substitution is a nondeterministic extension of the notion of a homomorphism, a deterministic generalized sequential machine with final states (abbreviated as a dgsm) mapping, is a context-dependent but still deterministic extension of the notion of a homomorphism. Dgsm mappings provide very simple representations of recursively enumerable languages.

Theorem. For every recursively enumberable language K over an alphabet Σ there exists a dgsm mapping h such that $K = Pres_{\Sigma}(F_p(h))$. ■

Theorem. For every recursively enumberable language K there exists a dgsm mapping h such that $K = h(L_{\{0,1\}})$. ■

VI. CONCLUDING REMARKS

In this survey we have tried, within a very limited space, to present to the reader the flavour of the theory of L systems. In particular we have tried to demonstrate how the core of this theory is constructed in a very systematic way within a very basic and natural mathematical framework. We have tried to give examples of areas that are very novel to the theory of formal languages (as for example the theory of sequences of words) as well as to illustrate how various very important research areas of formal language theory (as for example investigation of combinatorial structure of languages) are well represented within the theory of L systems. Because of the limitations on the size of this paper we could not indicate how various other significant research areas (e.g. complexity theory, theory of machine models or theory of grammatical similarity) have been successfully developed in the theory of L systems. We have also tried to indicate how various important classical classes of languages (like for example the class of context free languages and the class of recursively enumerable languages) are easily representable within the framework of L systems.

Altogether, the above points should make it quite clear to the reader that the theory of L systems occupies today a central place in formal language theory.

REFERENCES

[1] G.T. Herman and G. Rozenberg, Developmental systems and languages, North Holland Publ. Co., Amsterdam, 1975.

[2] G. Rozenberg and A. Salomaa, The mathematical theory of L systems, Academic Press, London, to appear.

EXTENDING THE NOTION OF FINITE INDEX

G. Rozenberg
Dept. of Mathematics
University of Antwerp UIA
Universiteitsplein 1
B 2610 Wilrijk, BELGIUM

D. Vermeir
Dept. T.E.W.
University of Leuven
Dekenstraat 2
B 3000 Leuven, BELGIUM

0. INTRODUCTION

This paper is concerned with extensions of the classical notion of finite index (see, e.g. [5]).

The finite index restriction can be imposed on both the sequential rewriting systems yielding e.g. context free grammars of finite index and on the parallel rewriting systems yielding e.g. ETOL systems of finite index (see, e.g., [2]). One of the reasons to investigate ETOL systems of finite index is to have a "bridge" between parallel and sequential rewriting. However, for several reasons the restriction to finite index seems to be too strong in that it loses several important features of (totally) parallel rewriting.

This paper presents an approach to extending the notion of finite index so as to make it closer to (total) parallel rewriting. We introduce and investigate two extensions of ETOL systems of finite index: ETOL systems of finite rank and ETOL systems of finite tree rank. We demonstrate that they form a proper extension of the finite index case and that they give rise to a quite interesting (structural) theory. Moreover, it turns out that these notions are intrinsic to parallel rewriting, because in the case of context free grammars they coincide with the notion of finite index. We believe that this may be one of the most essential differences between parallel and sequential rewriting.

We end this section by listing some basic concepts and notations to be used in the sequel.

(1) Let V be an alphabet and let Δ be a subset of V;

(i) The homomorphism $\underline{Pres}_\Delta$ is defined by $\underline{Pres}_\Delta(a)=a$ if $a \in\Delta$ and $\underline{Pres}_\Delta(a)= \Lambda$ otherwise;

(ii) For a language L in V* we use $\underline{Length}_\Delta$ L to denote the set $\{|\underline{Pres}_\Delta\ x|:x \in L\}$ (where $|x|$ is the length of x).

(2) An unlabeled tree T is called a <u>parallel full binary</u> tree, abbreviated p.f.b. tree, if every node which is not a leaf has precisely two sons and all paths from the root to a leaf have the same length.

(3) Let $G = \langle V, P, S, \Sigma \rangle$ be an ETOL system.

(i) A symbol A from V is called active if there exists a production $A \to \alpha$ in some table from P such that $\alpha \neq A$.

(ii) G is said to be of <u>finite index</u> if there exists a constant $k \geq 1$ such that every word in L(G) has a derivation which is such that no intermediate word in this derivation contains more than k occurrences of active symbols.

(iii) G is said to be <u>uncontrolled finite index</u> if there exists a constant $k \geq 1$ such that for every word in L(G), every derivation of it is such that no intermediate word in this derivation contains more than k occurrences of active symbols.

For a detailed study of ETOL systems of finite index, we refer the reader to [2].

1. ETOL SYSTEMS WITH FINITE RANK

Roughly speaking, an ETOL system G is of finite rank if its alphabet V has an ordered partition $R_0, \ldots, R_t$ which allows one to view derivations in G as if they were of finite index in the following sense. If a symbol a is in R_i then by erasing all symbols of $\bigcup_{j<i} R_j$ from every string derived from a in G, then one obtains a finite language. This, as we shall see, imposes a nice hierarchical structure on the system. Formally, we define it as follows.

<u>DEFINITION 1</u>.

Let $G = \langle V, P, S, \Sigma \rangle$ be an ETOL system.

We define $\underline{rank}_G$ to be a (partial) function from V into the set of nonnegative integers defined inductively as follows.

(1)(i) Let $Z_0 = V$. Then for a in V, $\underline{rank}_G(a)=0$ if and only if $\{\underline{Pres}_{Z_0} x : a \Rightarrow^* x \Rightarrow^* w, w \in \Sigma^*\}$ is a finite set.

(ii) Let $Z_{i+1} = V - \{a \in V : \underline{rank}_G(a) \leq i\}$. Then for a in Z_{i+1}, $\underline{rank}_G(a) = i+1$ if and only if $\{\underline{Pres}_{Z_{i+1}} x : a \Rightarrow^* x \Rightarrow^* w, w \in \Sigma^*\}$ is a finite set.

(2) We say that G is an <u>ETOL system with rank</u> if and only if $\underline{rank}_G$ is a total function on V. Moreover, we say that G is of rank m, denoted $\underline{rank}\ G=m$, if every letter in V is of rank not larger than m and at least one letter from V is of rank m.

We will use $R_i(G)$ to denote the set of all letters which have rank i in G. Also, we use $(ETOL)_{RAN(i)}$ and $(ETOL)_{RAN}$ to denote the class of all ETOL systems of rank i and the class of all ETOL systems with rank respectively.

It is useful to note here that the above definition, when restricted to the case of DOL systems, coincides with the corresponding notion of the rank of a DOL system from [1]. However, perhaps the most interesting fact is that the notion of an ETOL system with rank can be regarded as an extension of the concept of an ETOL system of finite index (see, e.g. [3]). Indeed, the set of symbols of rank 0 contains the set of nonactive symbols (those are symbols a which are such that $a \Rightarrow^* \alpha$ implies $\alpha = a$) and moreover, even if a symbol of rank 0 is active, it is still not very active as it can be rewritten only into a finite number of words during a successful derivation. Thus the definition of an ETOL system of rank 1 closely resembles the definition of an ETOL system of (uncontrolled) finite index. As a matter of fact, the classes of languages generated by those classes of systems coincide.

THEOREM 1.

$L(\text{ETOL})_{FIN} = L(\text{ETOL})_{RAN(1)}$

As it was pointed out above, the notion of an ETOL system with rank is a proper extension of the concept of an ETOL system of finite index. It is then natural to investigate which properties of ETOL systems of finite index are preserved by ETOL systems with rank. For example, in [3] it was shown that every ETOL language of finite index can be generated by a deterministic ETOL system of finite index, i.e. $L(\text{ETOL})_{FIN} = L(\text{EDTOL})_{FIN}$. Although we can prove a normal form theorem which implies that every ETOL language of rank k can be generated by an ETOL system G' of rank k which is deterministic in $R_k(G')$, it follows from the next result that the deterministic restriction is a proper one in the case of ETOL systems with rank greater than one.

THEOREM 2.

There exists a OL language of rank 2 which is not an EDTOL language.

Next we show that the notion of rank of an ETOL system gives rise to an infinite hierarchy of classes of languages. This is proved using a result which is interesting on its own.

THEOREM 3.

Let $K \subseteq \Sigma^*$ be an ETOL language of rank m. Let $\Delta \subseteq \Sigma$ be such that $\underline{\text{Length}}_\Delta$ K is infinite. Then there exists a strictly growing polynomial f of degree not larger than m such that $\underline{\text{Range}}$ f $\subseteq$ $\underline{\text{Length}}_\Delta$ K.

Theorem 3 can be used to show that, e.g., $\{a^{(n^2+n)/2} : n \geq 1\} \in L(\text{ETOL})_{RAN(2)} - L(\text{ETOL})_{RAN(1)}$ and $\{a^{2^n} : n \geq 0\} \notin L(\text{ETOL})_{RAN}$. In this way one obtains the following.

THEOREM 4.

$L\text{FIN} = L(\text{ETOL})_{RAN(0)} \subsetneq L(\text{ETOL})_{RAN(1)} \subsetneq L(\text{ETOL})_{RAN(2)} \subsetneq \ldots \subsetneq L(\text{ETOL})_{RAN} \subsetneq L\text{ETOL}$.

As for the closure properties of the corresponding classes of languages, we have the following result.

THEOREM 5.

(1) For every $i \geq 1$, $L(ETOL)_{RAN(i)}$ is a non-full-principal full AFL which is closed under substitution with ETOL languages of finite index.

(2) $L(ETOL)_{RAN}$ is a non-full-principal full substitution closed AFL.

As the above hierarchy is proved by spanning it on a sequence of 'polynomial' DOL languages with rank, it follows that it properly extends the corresponding hierarchy within $L(DOL)_{RAN}$ which was proved in [1]. In the same paper it was also shown that a DOL system G is of finite rank if and only if its growth function μ_G is bounded by some polynomial P (with positive coefficient at the highest power). This result can be extended as follows. First we define the maximal growth function of a FTOL system as follows. (Recall that an FTOL system is a TOL system which may have a finite set of axiom words instead of a single one.)

DEFINITION 2.

Let $G = \langle V,P,AX \rangle$ be an FTOL system.

The M-growth function of G, where M stands for 'maximal' is a function of N denoted as μ_G and defined by $\mu_G(n) = \max\{|x| : \alpha \overset{\rho}{\Rightarrow} x, \alpha \in AX, \rho \in P^n\}$. Thus $\mu_G(n)$ is the length of the longest word which can be derived from an axiom in exactly n steps. Note that in the case of a DOL system, the M-growth function coincides with its growth function while, in general, it represents the fastest possible growth in the system. We then have the following result.

THEOREM 6.

An FTOL system G is of rank k $(k \geq 0)$ if and only if there exist polynomials P and Q of degree k (with positive coefficients at the highest power) such that $P \leq \mu_G \leq Q$.

In [4], the class of ETOL systems of finite index and some of its subclasses have been characterized by forbidding symbols with a particular type of recursion. The following theorem provides a similar characterization for the class of ETOL systems with rank. First we need a definition.

DEFINITION 3.

Let $G = \langle V,P,S,\Sigma \rangle$ be an ETOL system. A symbol a from V is called expansive if $a \overset{*}{\Rightarrow} \alpha_0 a \alpha_1 a \alpha_2$ for some $\alpha_0 \alpha_1 \alpha_2 \in V^*$. An ETOL system is called non-expansive if it does not have any expansive symbols.

THEOREM 7.

An ETOL language has a rank if and only if it can be generated by a nonexpansive ETOL system.

Note that this theorem also extends a result from [1], which states a similar characterization for DOL systems with rank.

In establishing the above results we have mainly focussed our investigation of ETOL systems with rank on the properties of the associated length sets or the M-growth functions of such systems. As a matter of fact, most of the results obtained so far use in some way languages with 'polynomial length sets' as 'typical' languages in $\mathcal{L}(ETOL)_{RAN}$.

One can also prove results on the structure of the languages (rather than their length sets) that can be generated by ETOL systems with rank. An example of a step in this direction is an investigation of copying possibilities of ETOL systems with rank. Particularly useful in this respect will be a "copy operator" c^{∞}. Intuitively, the application of c^{∞} to a language L yields another language consisting of words which are a catenation of an arbitrary number of 'copies' of a single word from L. Formally, it is defined as follows.

DEFINITION 4.

Let L be a language and let # be a new symbol. The language $c^{\infty}(L)$ is defined by $c^{\infty}(L) = \{(\#w)^n : w \in L, n \geq 1\}$.

Then we can prove the following.

THEOREM 8.

For $i \geq 1$, if L is a language in $\mathcal{L}(EDITOL)_{RAN(i)} - \mathcal{L}(ETOL)_{RAN(i-1)}$ then $c^{\infty}(L)$ is in $\mathcal{L}(EDTOL)_{RAN(i+1)} - \mathcal{L}(ETOL)_{RAN(i)}$.

The above theorem allows us to prove the hierarchy in $\mathcal{L}(ETOL)_{RAN}$ in a way that is fundamentally different from the method used in the proof of Theorem 4. Indeed, we can now span the hierarchy on an infinite sequence $L_1, L_2, \ldots$ of languages which are such that the length set of each language L_i $i \geq 1$, contains the range of strictly growing polynomial of degree one.

COROLLARY 1.

Let $L_1, L_2, \ldots$ be a sequence of languages inductively defined by

(i) $L_1 = \{a\}^+$ and

(ii) $L_{i+1} = c^{\infty}(L_i)$ for every $i \geq 1$.

Then, for all $i \geq 1$, $L_i \in \mathcal{L}(ETOL)_{RAN(i)} - \mathcal{L}(ETOL)_{RAN(i-1)}$ and the length set of L_i contains the range of a strictly growing polynomial of degree one.

Thus the method of Theorem 3 cannot be used to show that L_i is of rank i and not of rank i-1. On the other hand: Theorem 8 seems to be useless when one wants to prove that, e.g., the language $\{a^{(n^2+n)/2}: n\geq 1\}$ is in $\mathcal{L}(ETOL)_{RAN(2)}$ but not in $\mathcal{L}(ETOL)_{RAN(1)}$ which is easily shown using Theorem 3.

2. ETOL SYSTEMS OF FINITE TREE RANK

One can interpret both the finite index restriction and the finite rank property in terms of 'complexity' of derivation trees: one can imagine the 'index' of an ETOL system as a horizontal complexity measure (we count the number of 'branching points' at a level in a derivation tree) while the notion of rank is more vertical: it says something about the depth-structure of a derivation tree. In this sense, the research on ETOL systems of finite index and their extension to ETOL systems of finite rank is concerned with the structure of derivations. A very basic representation of derivations in an ETOL system is provided by the set of its derivation trees stripped from their labels. Those trees will be investigated in this section and surprisingly enough, it will turn out that this very basic structure provides means to characterize ETOL languages of finite rank.

First, we introduce a bottom-up complexity measure for unlabeled trees, called the 'rank' of a tree. Intuitively, the rank of a tree represents the structure of its branching pattern, i.e. the total number of branching points and their relative positions in the tree. Here is a formal definition.

DEFINITION 5.

Let $T = (A,R)$ be a tree with root r.

(1) The tree rank function of T, denoted Dr_T is a mapping from A into the nonnegative integers which is defined as follows.

(i) If $a\in A$ is a leaf, then $Dr_T(a) = 0$.

(ii) If $a\in A$ is not a leaf, then we consider the number $M_T(a) = \max\{Dr_T(b)\colon b$ is a son of $a\}$. Then

$$Dr_T(a) = \begin{cases} M_T(a) & \text{if there is but one son } b \text{ of } a \text{ with } Dr_T(b) = M_T(a)\text{, and} \\ M_T(a)+1 & \text{otherwise.} \end{cases}$$

(2) The rank of T, denoted Drank T, is defined by $Drank(T) = Dr_T(r)$.

Obviously, the rank of a pfb tree equals its height. This observation is generalized in the following theorem which provides a characterization of trees of rank k.

THEOREM 9.

A tree has rank k if and only if it contains a parallel full binary tree of height k and it does not contain a parallel full binary tree of height bigger than k.

Next we introduce the notion of an ETOL system of finite tree rank.

DEFINITION 6.

Let G = <V,P,S,Σ> be an ETOL system.

(1) We say that G is of tree rank k for some k≥0, denoted as Drank G=k, if every (unlabeled) derivation tree of G has rank not exceeding k and at least one (unlabeled) derivation tree of G has rank k.

(2) We say that G is of finite tree rank if Drank G=k for some k≥0.

We use $(ETOL)_{DR(k)}$ and $(ETOL)_{DR}$ to denote the class of ETOL systems of tree rank not exceeding k and the class of ETOL systems of finite tree rank repsectively.

The notion of tree rank gives rise to an infinite hierarchy of classes of languages strictly included in $\mathcal{L}$ETOL, as is demonstrated by the following theorems.

Theorem 10.

$$\mathcal{L}(ETOL)_{DR(0)} \subsetneqq \mathcal{L}(ETOL)_{DR(1)} \subsetneqq \cdots \subsetneqq \mathcal{L}(ETOL)_{DR(k)} \cdots \subsetneqq \mathcal{L}ETOL$$

THEOREM 11.

(1) For every k≥1, $\mathcal{L}(ETOL)_{DR(k)}$ is a full principal full semi-AFL

(2) $\mathcal{L}(ETOL)_{DR}$ is a non-full-principal full substitution closed AFL.

The notion of an ETOL system of finite tree rank was defined using the set of its unlabeled derivation trees. However, the class of ETOL systems of finite tree rank can also be chracterized by their sets of labeled derivation trees.
First we need a definition.

DEFINITION 7.

(1) A labeled tree T is called expansive if there exist three distinct nodes a,b and c with the same label such that a is an ancestor of both b and c, and b(c) is not an ancestor of c(b).

(2) An ETOL system G is called strongly nonexpansive if none of its derivation trees is expansive.

Note that the notion of a strongly nonexpansive ETOL system can indeed be regarded as an extension of the concept of a nonexpansive ETOL system (see Definition 3) : a strongly nonexpansive TOL system is nonexpansive but the converse is not always true.

THEOREM 12.

An ETOL language has a finite tree rank if and only if it can be generated by a strongly nonexpansive ETOL system.

In the remainder of this section we will concentrate on the relationship between the finite rank and the finite tree rank restrictions.

First of all, it turns out (quite surprisingly) that the hierarchies corresponding to both restrictions have the same 'limit'.

THEOREM 13.

$\mathcal{L}(\text{ETOL})_{RAN}=\mathcal{L}(\text{ETOL})_{DR}$.

On the otherhand one can also prove that for every k≥1, there exists an ETOL language of finite index which is not in $\mathcal{L}(\text{ETOL})_{DR(k)}$ and so we obtain the following result.

THEOREM 14.

For every k≥0, $\mathcal{L}(\text{ETOL})_{DR(k)} \subsetneq \mathcal{L}(\text{ETOL})_{RAN(k)}$.

Next we will characterize the class of ETOL systems of tree rank (not exceeding) k in terms of a special type of ETOL systems of rank (not bigger than) k. To do this we introduce the notion of an ETOL system of 'linear rank' k.

Intuitively, an ETOL system G with rank is of 'linear rank' if for every i≥1, every production of every symbol A in $R_i(G)$ is 'linear' in $R_i(G)$.

DEFINITION 8.

Let G = $\langle V,P,S,\Sigma\rangle$ be an ETOL system.

(1) We say that G is of linear rank k, k≥0, if rank(G) = k and for every 0≤i≤k, $A\in R_i(G)$, if $A\rightarrow\alpha$ then α contains at most one occurrence of a symbol from $R_i(G)$.

(2) We say that G is of linear rank if G is of linear rank k for some k≥0.

We use $(\text{ETOL})_{RAN\ell(k)}$ and $(\text{ETOL})_{RAN\ell}$ to denote the class of all ETOL systems of linear rank k and the class of all ETOL systems of linear rank respectively.

ETOL systems of linear rank can be regarded as extensions of metalinear ETOL systems (see [2]) in the following way. First, let us do away with the special status of the axiom letter in a metalinear ETOL system and instead, let us allow for a finite number of axiom words. Clearly, this does not alter the generating power of metalinear ETOL systems nor their fundamental feature : only linear productions (linear in the set of active symbols) are available. Let us also extend the notion of linear rank to EFTOL systems, i.e., we allow for a finite set of axiom words.

But then there is a strong correspondence between our modified metalinear ETOL systems and EFTOL systems of linear rank not exceeding 1.

Indeed, it has been pointed out already that active symbols in ETOL systems of uncontrolled finite index correspond to symbols of rank 1 in ETOL systems with rank. Similarly, nonactive symbols correspond to symbols of rank 0.

Thus the modified metalinear ETOL systems are practically the same as EFTOL systems of linear rank not exceeding 1 : both have only 'linear' productions, in the set of active (nonactive) symbols or in the set of symbols of rank 1 (rank 0).

As a matter of fact, it is a straightforward matter to show the following.

THEOREM 15.

$L(\mathrm{ETOL})_{m\ell} = L(\mathrm{EFTOL})_{\mathrm{RAN}\ell(1)}$.

Note the analogy of Theorem 15. and Theorem 1.

The following result shows that ETOL systems of tree rank (not larger than) k can be characterized by ETOL systems of linear rank (not exceeding) k.

THEOREM 16.

(1) For every $k \geq 0$, $L(\mathrm{ETOL})_{\mathrm{RAN}\ell(k)} = L(\mathrm{ETOL})_{\mathrm{DR}(k)}$.

(2) $L(\mathrm{ETOL})_{\mathrm{RAN}\ell} = L(\mathrm{ETOL})_{\mathrm{DR}}$.

From Theorem 1, Theorem 15 and Theorem 16 it follows that ETOL systems of finite tree rank relate to ETOL systems with rank as do metalinear ETOL systems to ETOL systems of finite index (see [2]), thus establishing a tight connection between the first and the second part of this paper.

We want to conclude with the following observation. The notion of finite rank (and finite tree rank) that we have presented here forms the most natural (in our opinion) extension of the classical notion of finite index as applied to ETOL systems. Clearly one can define in completely analogous way those notions for context-free grammars. Then we can prove the following result.

THEOREM 17.

$L(\mathrm{CF})_{\mathrm{DR}} = L(\mathrm{CF})_{\mathrm{RAN}} = L(\mathrm{CF})_{\mathrm{FIN}}$.

This theorem compared with the results presented in this paper is quite remarkable. We believe that it points to one of the most essential differences between parallel and sequential rewriting systems. It is the parallel nature of rewriting that allows meaningful structural extensions of the notion of finite index, the point that we have tried to illustrate in our paper.

REFERENCES

[1] Ehrenfeucht, A. and Rozenberg, G., 1974. On DOL systems with rank, in Lecture Notes in Computer Science N° 15, 136-141. Springer Verlag, Heidelberg.

[2] Rozenberg, G. and Vermeir, D., 1977. On L systems of finite index, in Lecture Notes in Computer Science N° 52, 430-440. Springer Verlag, Heidelberg.

[3] Rozenberg, G. and Vermeir, D., 1978, On ETOL systems of finite index, Information and Control, 38, 103-133.

[4] Rozenberg, G. and Vermeir, D., 1977, On recursion in ETOL systems, Journal of Computer and System Sciences, to appear.

[5] Salomaa, A., 1973. Formal languages, Academic Press, New York.

ON THE COMPLEXITY OF GENERAL CONTEXT-FREE LANGUAGE PARSING AND RECOGNITION*

(Extended Abstract)

Walter L. Ruzzo
Department of Computer Science
University of Washington
Seattle, Washington 98195/USA

ABSTRACT

Several results on the computational complexity of general context-free language parsing and recognition are given. In particular we show that parsing strings of length n is harder than recognizing such strings by a factor of only $O(\log n)$, at most. The same is true for linear and/or unambiguous context-free languages. We also show that the time to multiply $\sqrt{n} \times \sqrt{n}$ Boolean Matrices is a lower bound on the time to recognize all prefixes of a string (or do on-line recognition), which in turn is a lower bound on the time to generate a particular convenient representation of all parses of a string (in an ambiguous grammar). Thus these problems are solvable in linear time only if $n \times n$ Boolean matrix multiplication can be done in $O(n^2)$.

1. Introduction

This paper presents several results on the time complexity of some recognition and parsing problems for general context-free grammars. General context-free grammars provide a powerful "pattern matching" capability which is useful for a variety of problems including natural language and speech processing. While more efficient algorithms are known for special cases, the general case is still of practical importance since the special cases impose constraints which render them unsuitable for many applications.

Our first result concerns the relative difficulty of recognizing a context-free language, i.e., deciding if given strings are in the language, versus parsing the language, i.e., constructing parse trees for those strings which are in the language. Parsing is clearly the harder of the two problems. How much harder is it? All recognizers known to the author, e.g. the algorithms of Cocke-Kasami-Younger [Hays 1962, Kasami 1965, Younger 1967], Earley [Earley 1970], Valiant [1975], or [Graham, Harrison, Ruzzo 1976; Ruzzo 1978], are easily converted to parsers with at most a constant factor loss in speed. Is it true in general that "good recognizers make good parsers"? Or is it possible that every parser is significantly slower than the best recognizer? We will answer the latter question in the negative in section two, where we show that any recognizer can be turned into a parser at a cost of a factor of only about

*This research supported by an IBM pre-doctoral fellowship and by NSF grants GJ-474 and MCS77-02474.

$O(\log n)$ (n is the length of the input). The same is true of recognizers for unambiguous and/or linear context-free languages.

In section three we consider the problems of recognizing all prefixes of the input and generating a convenient representation for all of the parses of the input (in an ambiguous grammar). These problems are interesting since all of the algorithms mentioned in section 1 are prefix recognizers and also can be made to solve the "all-parses" problem. The all-parse problem is also interesting since many practical applications require that some consideration of multiple parses be made. Since these problems are at least as hard as recognition, there is some possibility that we can prove better lower bounds on them. This in turn might lead to better upper bounds by indicating features which must be absent from any improved recognition algorithm. In section 3 we present a small step in these directions by showing that the problems mentioned above are at least as hard (for inputs of length n) as multiplying $\sqrt{n} \times \sqrt{n}$ Boolean matrices, even for unambiguous linear languages. Thus these problems are solvable in linear time only if $n \times n$ Boolean matrix multiplication is solvable in time n^2 . (Many researchers feel that this is unlikely.)

2. Complexity of Parsing Versus Recognition

Every context-free language parser is implicitly a recognizer for the same language, so it's clear that parsing is "harder" than recognition. More precisely, $R(n) \le P(n)$ for all n , where $R(n)$ and $P(n)$ are the times required for recognition and parsing, respectively, of strings of length n . A natural question is "how much harder is parsing?".

For all of the recognizers mentioned in the introduction, it turns out that the information constructed during recognition allows parsing to be done in less time than it took to do the recognition. This seems possible that some very fast recognition algorithm may be discovered which can't be easily modified to allow parsing. In this section we will show that this is not the case. We will show how to construct from any recognizer a parser which is only about $\log n$ times slower than the recognizer (on strings of length n). It is quite possible that the recognition time required for linear and/or unambiguous grammars is less than for arbitrary grammars. Our construction also shows that an analogous relation holds between parsing and recognition times for these restricted classes of grammars.

Theorem 1

Let $R'(n)$ be any suitably "well behaved" upper bound on $R(n)$. Precise conditions on the form of $R'(n)$ are that $R(n) = O(R'(n))$ and that $R'(n) = n^{\gamma}h(n)$ for some $\gamma > 1$ and some function $h(n)$ which is positive and monotonically increasing for all sufficiently large n . Then there is a constant c such that for all sufficiently large n , $R(n) \le P(n) \le cR'(n)\cdot\log n$. Furthermore, this relation also holds between the recognition and parsing times for unambiguous and/or linear languages.

Notice that $R'(n)$ may equal $R(n)$ in many cases, e.g., if $R(n)$ is of the form $n^{\alpha}\log^{\beta}n$ for $\alpha > 1$, $\beta \geq 0$. (The analysis could also be extended to more slowly growing functions, e.g., $\alpha = 1$.)

<u>Proof Sketch</u>

Let $G = (V,\Sigma,P,S)$ be a Chomsky Normal Form grammar. There is no loss of generality since every grammar is covered by a CNF grammar [Gray & Harrison 1972]. Let $a_1a_2 \ldots a_n$ be the input, a_i in Σ, and let $w_{i,j} = a_{i+1} \ldots a_j$. We locate some node A in the parse tree for $S \Rightarrow^* w_{0,n}$, spanning, say $w_{i,j}$, then we repeat the procedure on the parse trees for $A \Rightarrow^* w_{i,j}$ and $S \Rightarrow^* w_{0,i}Aw_{j,n}$. The complete parse is obtained by combining the parses of the two substrings. The key is (1) to pick a node which spans a string which is about 1/2 of the input, so both subproblems are of approximately the same size, and (2) to locate such a node using only a context-free recognizer.

Locating a node spanning about 1/2 of the input is easy. Suppose we divide the input into 4 segments of (approximately) equal length of "marking" the 5 input letters a_1, a_{d+1}, a_{2d+1}, a_{3d+1}, and a_n, where $d = \lfloor \frac{n}{4} \rfloor$. If we insist that the subtree rooted at the selected node A must include exactly 2 of the marked letters, then we will be sure that A spans between 1/4 and 3/4 of the input. We can use recognizers to locate such a node as follows.

Let $\hat{V}$ be the new alphabet $\{X^{(m)} \mid X \in V,\ 0 \leq m \leq 5\}$, i.e., we have 6 distinct copies of each letter of V. We will call a letter $X^{(m)}$ "marked by m" if $m > 0$, unmarked if $m = 0$. "Marking" the input as above will be done by replacing $a_1, a_{d+1}, a_{2d+1}, \ldots$ by $a_1^{(1)}, a_{d+1}^{(2)}, a_{2d+1}^{(3)}, \ldots$ and all other letters a_i by $a_i^{(0)}$. Define $h: \hat{V} \to V$ such that $h(X^{(i)}) = X$. We will use the following languages: for all $B,A \in V$, $1 \leq m \leq 4$ let $L_{B,A,m}$ be the set of all $\hat{\alpha} \in \hat{V}^*$ such that

(i) $\hat{\alpha}$ has exactly 5 marked letters, one of each kind, and occurring in order (i.e., $X^{(1)}$ is to the left of $Y^{(2)}$, etc.),

(ii) $S \Rightarrow_G^* \alpha$ where $\alpha = h(\hat{\alpha})$, and

(iii) in the parse tree for some derivation $B \Rightarrow_G^* \alpha$, A (labels the node which) is the lowest common ancestor of the letters marked by m and $m+1$, and is an ancestor of no other marked letters.

It is not hard to show that the $L_{B,A,m}$ are CFL's using tree automata [Thatcher 1967, Thatcher & Wright 1968]. Further, they are unambiguous and/or linear if F is.

Given recognizers for these languages, we can implement the "divide and conquer" parsing strategy outlined above. First, form the "marked" string $\hat{w}$ corresponding to the input w as described above. Then find $A \in V$ and $1 \leq m \leq 4$ such that

$w \in L_{S,A,m}$. By the definition of $L_{S,A,m}$ we know there exist i,j such that $A \Rightarrow^* w_{ij}$ and $S \Rightarrow^* w_{0,i}Aw_{j,n}$. Further, by the positioning of the marks in $\hat{w}$, we know that the length of $w_{i,j}$ is between 1/4 and 3/4 the length of w . Since $m-1$ is not a descendant of A , the leftmost descendant of A , i.e., a_{i+1} , must lie between marks $m-1$ and m . Its exact position can be found by moving mark m between these two extremes using a binary search strategy in $O(\log n)$ calls on the recognizer for $L_{S,A,m}$. (Of course, $i = 0$ in case $m = 1$.) Leaving mark m on a_{i+1} , we can find j similarly. Thus in $O(\log n)$ calls on the recognizer we will obtain the desired decomposition of the problem into $S \Rightarrow^* w_{0,i}Aw_{j,n}$ and $A \Rightarrow^* w_{i,j}$. The running time of this parser thus satisfies the recurrence

$$P(n) \le \begin{cases} c_1 & \text{for } n \le c_2 \text{, otherwise} \\ c_3R(n) \log n + \max \{P(n') + P(n - n' + 1) \mid \frac{1}{4} n \le n' \le \frac{3}{4} n\} \end{cases}$$

which has the solution given in the statement of the theorem. This may be shown by induction. □

3. Some Lower Bounds.

In this section we will give a lower bound on the time complexities of prefix and online recognition, and two variants of the "all parses" problem. These problems are defined below.

A prefix recognizer for a context-free language L is a procedure which reads an input $a_1 \ldots a_n$ and generates a string $r_0r_1 \ldots r_n$ of 0's and 1's where $r_i = 1$ if and only if $a_1 \ldots a_i$ is in L . An online recognizer has the same behavior, except that it is additionally required to generate r_i before reading a_{i+1} .

Recall that a parser as defined above outputs (any) one parse of the input. The all-parses problem is to output (a convenient representation of) all possible parses of the input. The choice of the "convenient representation" critically affects the complexity of the problem. Since the number of distinct parses of an input of length n may grow exponentially with n , a simple enumeration of all possible parses may be prohibitively expensive. At the other extreme, the input itself in some sense represents all parses, but for most purposes, not very conveniently! At a minimum, it would seem that a convenient representation would describe the phrase structure of the input, i.e., give the set of triples (A,i,j) such that $A \Rightarrow^* w_{ij}$ (as part of some parse). This suggests use of a matrix $t_{i,j}$ $(0 \le i \le j \le n)$ of sets, where $t_{i,j} = \{A \in N \mid S \Rightarrow^* w_{0,i}Aw_{j,n} \text{ and } A \Rightarrow^* w_{i,j}\}$. We will define the all-parses problem to be the generation of this matrix. A variety of other encodings of this information, e.g. a list of triples (A,i,j) , would be just as good since they can easily be interconverted. Many applications will require more detailed information than these representations provide, but lower bounds on our problem will still apply. Of course, we should not dismiss the possibility that some radically different data structure may be found which is at least as convenient, yet more easily generated.

The <u>weak all-parses</u> problem is like the all-parses problem in that we want a representation of all possible parses of the input, but we also allow representations of parses of proper substrings of the input. For reasons similar to those above, we will use the matrix $t_{i,j} = \{A \mid A \Rightarrow^* w_{i,j}\}$ as the representation.

The all-parses problems are interesting since most practical applications of general context-free recognition actually require that all parses be examined. The representations chosen above seem to be convenient in practice for such applications. The prefix recognition problem is interesting since it will give us a lower bound on the all-parses problems. The prefix and online restrictions are also of interest since it is sometimes possible to prove sharper lower bounds on more restricted classes of algorithms. This may help in finding better algorithms by indicating features which must be absent if better performance is to be achieved. Also, note that all of the recognizers discussed in the introduction are (or can easily be converted to) prefix recognizers, and all but Valiant's method are online. Further, the weak all-parses problem is solved by the Cocke-Kasami-Younger and Valiant algorithms, referenced above.

Let $R(n)$ be the time required to recognize context-free languages, as a function of the length, n, of the input string. Likewise, $R_{ol}(n)$, $R_{pre}(n)$, $P(n)$, $AP(n)$ and $AP_w(n)$ will be the times required for the online recognition, prefix recognition, parsing, all-parses, and weak all-parses problems respectively. Similarly, $BM(n)$ will be the time required to multiply two Boolean matrices having n entries, e.g., $\sqrt{n} \times \sqrt{n}$ matrices. (<u>Note</u>: It is more usual to parametrize matrix operations by the dimension of the matrix, e.g. "BM(n)" for $n \times n$ matrices. We prefer to parametrize by the length of the input since we will be relating matrix operations to context-free recognition, where the latter convention is more common. Thus, in our notation $BM(n) = O(n^{1.39+}) = O(n^{2.79+/2})$ [Strassen 1969, Furman 1970, Fischer & Meyer 1971, Munro 1971, Pan 1978].† We will say a Boolean matrix multiplication algorithm computing $A \cdot B = C$ is <u>online</u> if it reads all of A; then for $j = 1,2,\ldots$ it outputs the jth column of C immediately after reading the jth column of B. Let $BM_{ol}(n)$ denote the time required for online Boolean matrix multiplication. (Online multiplication may have higher complexity than offline multiplication. Note that the methods of [Strassen 1969, Pan 1978] are not online). Let $CHBM(n)$ be the time required for checking Boolean matrix multiplication; i.e., given 3 Boolean matrices A, B and C, deciding if $A \cdot B = C$.

---

†Actually, for a log cost RAM (see [Aho et al., 1974] for definition) the best known result is $O(n^{\alpha/2}(\log n)^{1-\alpha/4}(\log \log n)^{\alpha/2} - 1)$ where $\alpha = \log_{70} 143640 = 2.79+$ [Adleman, Booth, Preparata & Ruzzo 1978]. For simplicity, we will use the result given above.

Figure 1 summarizes the known complexity relationships between the various problems defined above. In the figure, a line from "a" down to "b" means that "b"(n) = O("a"(n)) . Relations shown with heavy lines are presented herein. The others were previously known or are trivial. References to the n^3 and $n^{2.79}$ upper bounds, and for $AP_w(n) = \Omega(P(n))$ may be found in e.g. [Harrison 1978]. The n^2 lower bound on AP_w follows trivially from the fact that the problem generates output of length n^2 . The CHBM lower bound on R is from [Harrison & Havel 1974, Harrison 1978, probl. 12.7 #7]. In fact, their lower bound holds even for linear cfl's. Our new lower bounds on R_{pre} and R_{ol} use a similar argument, and also hold for linear cfl's, and in fact for unambiguous ones as well. The construction appears below, as do the bounds on the all-parses problems. The new upper bound on P was given in Section 2.

[Gallaire 1969] gives the $n^2/\log n$ lower bound for online recognition on a multitape Turing machine.* For Turing machines, this bound is better than our BM_{ol} bound. However, on a random access machine Gallaire's language is known to be recognizable in linear time [Weiner 1973], whereas ours in not known to be. Further, many researchers believe it unlikely that Boolean matrix multiplication (or even the possible simpler problem of checking Boolean matrix multiplication) can be done in linear time. Thus, these results strongly suggest a non-linear lower bound on the three recognition problems even for (unambiguous and/or) linear context-free languages. Of course, even if the best known upper bounds on CHBM , BM and BM_{ol} were proved optimal, there would still be a considerable gap between these lower bounds on the recognition problems and the $n^{2.79}$ or n^3 upper bounds we currently know.

Our new results are presented below.

<u>Theorem 2</u>

(i) $AP(n) = \Omega(AP_w(n))$,

(ii) $AP_w(n) = \Omega(R_{pre}(n))$, and

(iii) $AP_w(n) = O(n \cdot R_{pre}(n))$.

<u>Proof</u>. Omitted; details are in [Ruzzo 1978].

<u>Theorem 3</u>

$$R_{pre}(n) = \Omega(BM(n))$$

$$R_{ol}(n) = \Omega(BM_{ol}(n))$$

Further, these results hold even for the recognition of unambiguous, linear context-free languages.

<u>Proof Sketch</u>.

We will use the following unambiguous linear CFL defined over the alphabet $\Sigma = \{0,1,\$,¢\}$.

---

*Gallaire's language is also a linear cfl, and hence is recognizable in time $O(n^2)$ on a Turing machine, so his lower bound is very close to optimal.

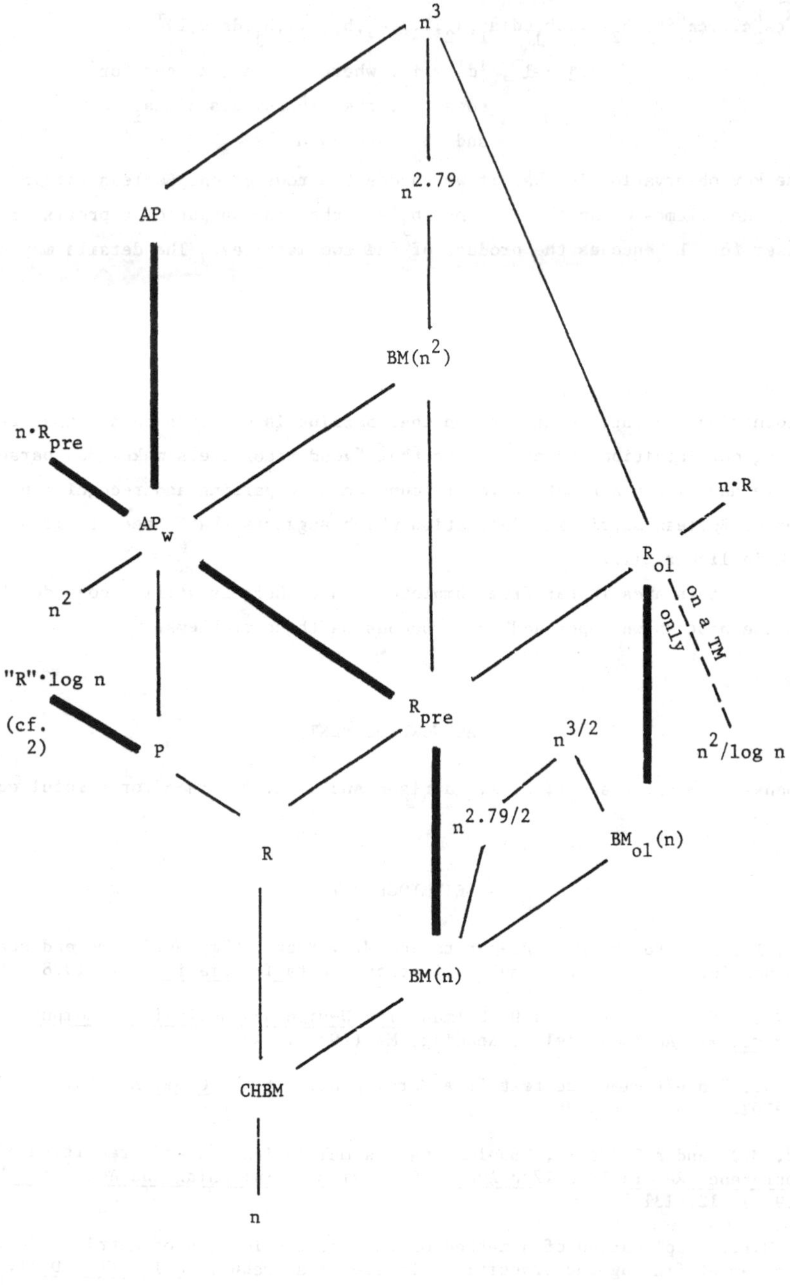

Figure 1. Relative Complexities of Recognition and Parsing Problems.

$$L = \{a_1^{R\dagger}¢a_2^R¢\ldots¢a_\ell^R\$b_1¢b_2¢\ldots¢b_j¢d \mid a_1,a_2,\ldots,a_\ell,b_1,\ldots,b_j,d\in\{0,1\}^+ ,$$
$$\ell,j \geq 1 ,\ |d| = i ,\ \text{where } 1 \leq i \leq \ell \text{ and for some } k \text{, the } k^{th} \text{ sumbols of } a_i \text{ and } b_j \text{ are both 1's}\} .$$

The key observation is that if we encode the rows of one Boolean matrix as the a_i's and the columns of another as the b_j's , then the output of a prefix or online recognizer for L encodes the product of the two matrices. The details may be found in [Ruzzo 1978].

4. Conclusion

We have presented two principle results on general context-free language parsing and recognition. First, we have shown that parsing is not much harder than recognition, confirming our intuition and experience that "good recognizers make good parsers". Second, we have given a relative lower bound on some parsing and recognition problems in terms of Boolean matrix multiplication which suggests that these problems are not solvable in linear time.

Work in this area is far from complete, since there is still a considerable gap between the best known upper and lower bounds on these problems.

ACKNOWLEDGEMENT

Thanks to M. J. Fischer, M. A. Harrison and G. L. Peterson for helpful comments.

BIBLIOGRAPHY

Adleman, L., K.S. Booth, F.P. Preparata and W.L. Ruzzo, "Improved time and space bounds for Boolean matrix multiplication", Acta Informatica, 11 (1978), 61-70.

Aho, A.V., J.E. Hopcroft and J.D. Ullman, The Design and Analysis of Computer Algorithms, Addison-Wesley, Reading, MA (1974).

Earley, J., "An efficient context-free parsing algorithm", Comm. ACM 13:1 (1970), 94-102.

Fischer, M.J. and A.R. Meyer, "Boolean matrix multiplication and transitive closure", Conference Record IEEE 12th Annual Symposium on Switching and Automata Theory (1971), 129-131.

Furman, M.E., "Application of a method of fast multiplication of matrices in the problem of finding the transitive closure of a graph", Soviet Math Dokl. 11:5 (1970), 1252.

$^\dagger x^R$ is the reversal of x .

Gallaire, H., "Recognition time of context free languages by on-line Turing machines", Information and Control 15 (1969), 288-295.

Graham, S.L., M.A. Harrison and W.L. Ruzzo, "Online context free language recognition in less than cubic time", Proc. 8th Annual ACM Symposium on Theory of Computing (1976), 112-120.

Gray, J. and M.A. Harrison, "On the covering and reduction problems for context-free grammars", JACM 19 (1972), 675-698.

Harrison, M.A., Introduction to Formal Language Theory, Addison-Wesley, Reading, MA (1978).

Harrison, M.A. and I. Havel, "On the parsing of strict deterministic languages", JACM 21 (1974), 525-548.

Hays, D.G., "Automatic language-data processing", in Computer Applications in the Behavioral Sciences, H. Borko (ed.), Prentice-Hall, Englewoods Cliffs, NJ (1962), 394-423.

Kasami, T., "An efficient recognition and syntax analysis algorithm for context free languages", Science Report AF CRL-65-758, Air Force Cambridge Research Laboratory, Bedford, MA (1965).

Munro, J.I., "Efficient determination of the transitive closure of a directed graph", Information Processing Letters 1:2 (1971), 56-58.

Pan, V.Ya.,"Strassen's algorithm is not optimal: Trilinear technique of aggregating, uniting and cancelling for constructing fast algorithms for matrix operations", IEEE 19th Annual Symposium on Foundations of Computer Science, (1978), 166-176.

Ruzzo, W.L., "General Context-Free Language Recognition". Ph.D. Dissertation, U. C. Berkeley (1978).

Strassen, V., "Gaussian elimination is not optimal", Numerische Mathematik 13 (1969), 354-356.

Thatcher, J.W., "Characterizing derivation trees of context-free grammars through a generalization of finite automata theory", JCSS 1:4 (1967) 317-322.

Thatcher, J.W. and J.B. Wright, "Generalized finite automata theory with an application to a decision problem of second-order logic", Math. Sys. Th. 2:1 (1968) 57-81.

Valiant, L., "General context free recognition in less than cubic time", J. Computer and System Sciences 10 (1975), 308-315.

Weiner, P., "Linear pattern matching algorithms", Conference Record IEEE 14th Annual Symposium on Switching and Automata Theory (1973), 1-11.

Younger, D.H., "Recognition of context-free languages in time n^3", Information and Control 10:2 (Feb. 1967), 189-208.

SPACE-TIME TRADEOFFS FOR OBLIVIOUS INTEGER MULTIPLICATION**

by

John E. Savage
Sowmitri Swamy*

Department of Computer Science
Brown University
Providence, Rhode Island, U.S.A.

ABSTRACT

An extension of a result by Grigoryev is used to derive a lower bound on the space-time product required for integer multiplication when realized by straight-line algorithms. If S is the number of temporary storage locations used by a straight-line algorithm on a random-access machine and T is the number of computation steps, then we show that $(S+1)T \geq \Omega(n^2)$ for binary integer multiplication when the basis for the straight-line algorithm is a set of Boolean functions.

1. INTRODUCTION

Storage space and computation time are two important parameters that reflect, at least in part, the real cost of computing. In selecting an algorithm for a problem, it could be very useful to have knowledge of lower limits on values of space and time that can be achieved simultaneously. In this paper we derive such results for binary integer multiplication when realized by oblivious algorithms, namely, algorithms in which the sequence of computations is data independent.

Oblivious algorithms can be directly transformed into straight-line algorithms without increasing the number of operations performed or the number of storage locations (or registers) used. We assume that straight-line algorithms are to be employed for integer multiplication and we assume that these algorithms are to be executed on machines which have a limited number of storage locations (or *space* S) for temporary results. We also assume that the instructions available on these machines are Boolean functions, and we define T (*time*) to be the number of instructions executed. We explicitly allow straight-line programs to be read as input, as well as from storage locations, and we explicitly permit partial results of the computation to be generated as output. Thus, in principle, the temporary storage S which a

---

INDEX TERMS: space-time tradeoffs, pebble game, integer multiplication, straight-line algorithm.

* *Present address: Coordinated Sciences Laboratory, University of Illinois at Urbana-Champaign, Urbana, Illinois 61801.*

** *This work was supported in part by the National Science Foundation under Grant MCS 76-20023.*

program uses may in fact be the maximum amount of storage which is used to complete the computation.

The essence of this model has been captured in the *pebble game* played on the graphs of straight-line algorithms. When a pebble is placed on a node of such graphs, it indicates that the value of the function associated with that node has been computed and resides in a temporary storage location. The pebble game was introduced by Paterson and Hewitt [1] and studied by several authors. Hopcroft, Paul and Valiant [2] have shown that a graph on nodes can be pebbled using space $O(N/\log N)$, where the constant of proportionality depends on the maximum in-degree of the vertices. Paul, Tarjan and Celoni [3] have also shown the existence of arbitrarily large graphs for which every pebbling strategy uses space $\Omega(N/\log N)$.

An early result in space-time tradeoffs is due to Savage [4] who demonstrated a hyperbolic lower bound for the computation of general functions. Savage and Swamy [5] obtain the results $ST \geq \Omega(n^2)$ for the n-input Fast-Fourier Transform. Their result was extended by Tompa [6] to apply to straight-line algorithms whose structure could be described by concentrators and grates [7].

Pippenger [8] exhibits a graph of N vertices for which the pebble game takes time proportional to $\omega(N)$ for space less than $o(N)$. Swamy and Savage [9], Paterson and Hewitt [1], and Chandra [10] have obtained space-time tradeoffs for linear recursion. Moreover, in [9] algorithms that achieve a given optimal space time tradeoff are described. Paul and Tarjan [11] have shown the existence of graphs on N nodes such that a reduction in S by a constant factor causes T to expand from $O(N)$ to $2^{\Omega(\sqrt{N})}$.

In this paper we present new results on space-time tradeoffs for binary integer multiplication and in doing so, introduce extensions of a method due to Grigoryev [12] to derive space-time tradeoffs for straight-line algorithms. We show that $(S+1)T \geq \Omega(n^2)$ for any oblivious algorithm for binary integer multiplication when the instructions are Boolean functions.

Section 2 describes the extension of Grigoryev's method and incidentally introduces the method to English speaking audiences. The lower bound for binary integer multiplication is described in Section 3. Section 4 concludes the discussion.

2. AN EXTENSION OF GRIGORYEV'S METHOD

We describe below a method to obtain lower bounds on the space-time product of straight-line algorithms that compute sets of Boolean functions. The method is a simple extension of that due to Grigoryev [12] and is useful in cases where a direct application of Grigoryev's method does not yield significant results. Grigoryev's method is important because the derivation of a lower bound on the space-time product is based entirely on the properties of the Boolean functions being computed and hence is valid for any straight-line program that computes the set of functions. A weakness of the method is that the property that the functions must possess in order to obtain a significant lower bound may be difficult to establish. Our extension of Grigoryev's result makes it easier to establish the property that allows the method to be applied.

Let $\{y_i:\{0,1\}^n \to \{0,1\} \mid 1 \leq i \leq m\}$ be a set of Boolean functions which are computed by a straight-line algorithm A, over some basis of Boolean functions. (A basis is said to have *fan-in* r if no function in the basis depends upon more than r variables.) The algorithm uses space S (registers or storage locations) and time T (number of operations). The object is to derive a lower bound on achievable S and T.

DEFINITION 1. Let $F = \{f:\{0,1\}^n \to \{0,1\}^p \mid 1 \leq n,p\}$ be the set of all binary functions. Then $R:F \to N$ $(N = 0,1,2,\cdots)$ is a function defined on $f \in F$ by

$$R(f) = |\{f(x)|x \in \{0,1\}^n\}|$$

that is, R(f) is the number of distinct points in the range of f.

DEFINITION 2. A function $f:\{0,1\}^n \to \{0,1\}^m$, $f = \{y_1,y_2,\cdots,y_m\}$, $y_i:\{0,1\}^n \to \{0,1\}$, is (α,ℓ)-*independent* for $\alpha \geq 1$ and integer $\ell \geq 1$ if

$$\forall k < \ell,\ \ \forall 1 \leq i_1,i_2,\cdots,i_k \leq n,\ \ \forall 1 \leq j_1,j_2,\cdots,j_{\ell-k} \leq m,\ \ \exists\, c_1,\cdots,c_k \in \{0,1\}$$

such that

$$R\left((y_{j_1}, y_{j_2},\cdots, y_{j_{\ell-k}}) \left| \begin{matrix} x_{i_r} = c_r \\ 1 \leq r \leq k \end{matrix} \right. \right) \geq 2^{\lfloor(\ell-k)/\alpha\rfloor -1} + 1$$

where $(y_{j_1},\cdots,y_{j_{\ell-k}}) \left| \begin{matrix} x_{i_r} = c_r \\ 1 \leq r \leq k \end{matrix} \right.$ is a subfunction of $(y_{j_1}, y_{j_2},\cdots, y_{j_{\ell-k}})$, obtained by substituting the value c_r for the variable x_{i_r}, $1 \leq r \leq k$.

NOTE: If $f:\{0,1\}^n \to \{0,1\}^m$ is (α,ℓ)-independent, then it is (α,ℓ')-independent for $\ell' \leq \ell$. Also, $\ell \leq m$ since $\ell-k \leq m$ for all $0 \leq k \leq \ell$.

THEOREM 1. If $f:\{0,1\}^n \to \{0,1\}^m$ is (α,ℓ)-independent for $\alpha \geq 1$, then

$$\alpha(S+1)T \geq \frac{m(\ell-4)}{2(r_o-1)}$$

where S and T are the (temporary) space and time used by straight-line algorithms over Boolean bases of fan-in r_o.

PROOF: If $\alpha(S+1) \geq \ell/2$, then the above is true because $T \geq m$. Thus assume that $\alpha(S+1) < \ell/2$.

Let the steps in the algorithm A used to compute f, be numbered and let y_i be computed at step $a(i)$. Let $x_{i_1}, x_{i_2}, \ldots, x_{i_p}$ be the inputs which occur in algorithm A between steps $a(i)$ and $a(i+t-1)$, where $t = \lceil \alpha(S+1) \rceil$. We show that $p + t \geq \ell + 1$, by contradiction.

Suppose that $p + t \leq \ell$. Since f is (α,ℓ)-independent, it is also $(\alpha,(p+t))$-independent. Therefore $\exists c_1, c_2, \cdots, c_p \in \{0,1\}$, such that

$$R\left((y_i, y_{i+1}, \cdots, y_{i+t-1}) \middle| \begin{matrix} x_{i_r} = c_r \\ \\ 1 \leq r \leq p \end{matrix}\right) \geq 2^{\lfloor t/\alpha - 1 \rfloor} + 1 > 2^S \tag{1}$$

(We assume without loss of generality that the components of f are computed in the order $y_1, y_2, \cdots, y_m$.)

Now let $A_1, A_2, \cdots, A_S$ be the values contained in the S registers at the time that y_i is computed. These values plus the values of the inputs $x_{i_1}, x_{i_2}, \cdots, x_{i_p}$, that occur between $a(i)$ and $a(i+t-1)$, determine the values of $y_i, y_{i+1}, \cdots, y_{i+t-1}$. However, when $x_{i_1}, x_{i_2}, \cdots, x_{i_p}$ have their values fixed, $(y_i, y_{i+1}, \cdots, y_{i+t-1})$ have their values determined by $A_1, A_2, \cdots, A_S$ and can thus have at most 2^S values. That is

$$\forall\, c_1, c_2, \cdots, c_p \in \{0,1\} \quad , \quad R\left((y_i, y_{i+1}, \cdots, y_{i+t-1}) \middle| \begin{matrix} x_{i_r} = c_r \\ \\ 1 \leq r \leq p \end{matrix}\right) \leq 2^S$$

contradicting (1). Therefore, $p + t \geq \ell + 1$.

If $y_1, y_2, \cdots, y_m$ are computed in this order, at least $p \geq \ell + 1 - t \geq \ell + 1 - \alpha(S+1) \geq \ell/2$ inputs are called by the algorithm for f between steps $a(i)$ and $a(i+t-1)$. Therefore, between steps $a(1)$, $a(\lceil \alpha(S+1) \rceil)$, $a(2\lceil \alpha(S+1) \rceil - 1), \cdots,$ $a(k\lceil \alpha(S+1) \rceil - k + 1)$ there must be $k\ell/2$ inputs invoked or at least this many inputs are needed to compute the m outputs. Here k is the largest integer satisfying $k(\lceil \alpha(S+1) \rceil - 1) \leq m-1$ or $k = \left\lfloor \frac{m-1}{\lceil \alpha(S+1) \rceil - 1} \right\rfloor \geq \frac{m-1}{\alpha(S+1)} - 1$. It is easy to demonstrate that any straight-line algorithm with n inputs and m outputs over a basis of fan-in r_o has at least $(n-m)/(r_o-1)$ computation steps. Thus, the time T to execute a straight-line algorithm satisfies the following inequality.

$$T \geq \frac{(k\ell/2)-m}{r_o-1} \geq \frac{m(\ell-4)/2}{\alpha(S+1)(r_o-1)}$$

since $\ell \leq m$ and $\alpha(S+1) \geq 1$.

□

Grigoryev's original result [12] assumes the value of α to be 1. He stated the following results without proof.

THEOREM 2. (Grigoryev [12]) The space-time product for Boolean $(n\times n)$ matrix multiplication (mod 2) and Boolean polynomial multiplication (mod 2) of polynomials of degree n are bounded below by $c_1 n^3$ and $c_2 n^2$, where c_1 and c_2 are positive constants.

3. A LOWER BOUND FOR BINARY INTEGER MULTIPLICATION

We provide an interesting application of the result derived in Section 2, by deriving a lower bound on the space-time product for binary integer multiplication. The proof is based on a combinatorial argument. To apply the result of the previous section, we show that there is a set of $n/2$ outputs of any straight-line algorithm for binary integer multiplication that are (α,ℓ)-independent for $\alpha = 2$, $\ell = n/2$, where n is the number of bits in each operand.

Let $\underline{x} = (x_{n-1}, x_{n-2}, \cdots, x_o)$ and $\underline{y} = (y_{n-1}, y_{n-2}, \cdots, y_o)$ be two n-bit binary integers and let $\underline{z} = (z_{2n-1}, z_{2n-2}, \cdots, z_o)$ represent their product in binary. Let $Z^* = \{z_{n-1}, z_{n-2}, \cdots, z_{n/2}\}$. (We assume without loss of generality that 2 divides n).

LEMMA 1. The set of $n/2$ functions in Z^* is $(2, n/2)$-independent.

PROOF: Choose $Z' = \{z_{j_t}, z_{j_{t-1}}, \cdots, z_{j_1}\}$, $n-1 \geq j_t \geq j_{t-1} \cdots \geq j_1 \geq n/2$, to be any subset of Z^* of t functions, and let $V = \{v_{i_1}, v_{i_2}, \cdots, v_{i_p}\}$ be any subset of p inputs, where $p+t \leq \ell = n/2$.

Define

$$D = \{d_{t-1}, \cdots, d_2, d_1\}$$

where $d_i = j_{i+1} - j_1$, $t-1 \geq i \geq 1$.

We construct sets $\{x[i]\}$, $\{y[i]\}$ as follows:

$$x[i] = \{x_{i+d_{t-1}}, \cdots, x_{i+d_1}, x_i\}, \qquad 0 \leq i \leq n/2$$

$$y[i] = \{y_{i+d_{t-1}}, \cdots, y_{i+d_1}, y_i\}, \qquad 0 \leq i \leq n/2$$

Let $C_i = |x[i] \cap V|$ and $C_i' = |y[i] \cap V|$. We prove, by contradiction, that $\exists i \ni C_i \leq \lfloor t/2 \rfloor$ or $C_i' \leq \lfloor t/2 \rfloor$. If not, $\forall i$, $0 \leq i \leq n/2$, $C_i > \lfloor t/2 \rfloor$ and $C_i' > \lfloor t/2 \rfloor$. That is,

$$\sum_{i=o}^{n/2} C_i' + \sum_{i=o}^{n/2} C_i \geq 2\left(\frac{n}{2} + 1\right)\left(\lfloor t/2 \rfloor + 1\right)$$

We observe that each of the p elements of the set V can appear in at most t elements of $\{x[i], y[i] \mid 0 \leq i \leq n/2\}$

Thus,

$$pt \geq \sum_{i=o}^{n/2} C_i' + \sum_{i=o}^{n/2} C_i \geq 2(n/2+1)\left(\lfloor t/2 \rfloor + 1\right)$$

or

$$pt > 2(n/2+1)\frac{t}{2}$$

or

$$p > n/2 .$$

However, $p \leq n/2$, since $p \leq \ell \leq m$ and we have only $m = n/2$ functions in the set Z^*. Therefore, $\exists\, i_o \ni C_{i_o} \leq \lfloor t/2 \rfloor$ or $C'_{i_o} \leq \lfloor t/2 \rfloor$. Without loss of generality, we assume $C_{i_o} \leq \lfloor t/2 \rfloor$. We now assign the following values to the inputs:

1. All inputs in the set $\{x_{n-1}, x_{n-2}, \cdots, x_o\}$, except those in $x[i_o] - V$ are assigned the value 0.
2. All inputs in the set $\{y_{n-1}, y_{n-2}, \cdots, y_o\}$, except $y_{(j_1 - i_o)}$, are assigned the value 0. $y_{(j_1-i_o)}$ is assigned the value 1.

We observe that by this assignment of values, at least $t - \lfloor t/2 \rfloor$ outputs of the set Z' have the inputs in the set $x[i_o] - V$ mapped onto them. Thus, the number of distinct output values in the range of the functions $Z' = \{z_{i_1}, z_{i_2}, \cdots, z_{i_t}\}$ is at least $2^{|x[i_o]-V|} \geq 2^{t-\lfloor t/2 \rfloor} \geq \frac{2^{\lfloor t/2 \rfloor}}{2} + 1$ for all $t \geq 1$. Thus the set Z^* is (2, n/2)-independent. □

THEOREM 3. The space and time required for binary integer multiplication must satisfy the following inequality.

$$(S+1)T \geq \left(\frac{n^2}{16} - \frac{n}{2}\right)/(r_o - 1)$$

An upper bound of $O\left((n\log n)^2\right)$ on $(S+1)T$ follows from a simple modification of the standard multiplication algorithm.

4. CONCLUSION

We have described an extension of Grigoryev's result which we have applied to the problem of obtaining space-time tradeoffs for integer multiplication. The extension is necessary because a straightforward application of Grigoryev's result does not seem to produce significant results. A simple combinatorial argument is used to demonstrate the property of (2, n/2)-independence for a set of $n/2$ outputs. The definition of independence used above is somewhat less restrictive than the definition given by Grigoryev. It has been used to show that the space-time products required to perform binary integer multiplication of n-bit numbers with oblivious algorithms must grow as the square of n.

REFERENCES

1. Paterson, M. S. and C. E. Hewitt, "Comparative Schematology," *Proj. MAC Conf. on Concurrent Systems and Parallel Computation*, Woods Hole, Massachusetts, pp. 119-127, June 2-5, 1970.

2. Hopcroft, J. E., W. J. Paul, and L. G. Valiant, "On Time Versus Space," *JACM*, Vol. 24, No. 2, pp. 332-337, 1977.

3. Paul, W. J., R. E. Tarjan, and J. R. Celoni, "Space Bounds for a Game on Graphs," *Eighth Ann. Symp. on Theory of Computing*, Hershey, Pennsylvania, pp. 149-160, May 3-5, 1976.

4. Savage, J. E., "Computational Work and Time on Finite Machines," *JACM*, Vol. 19, No. 4, pp. 660-674, 1972.

5. Savage, J. E. and S. Swamy, "Space-Time Tradeoffs on the FFT Algorithm," *IEEE Transactions on Information Theory*, Vol. IT-24, No. 5, pp. 563-568, Sept. 1978.

6. Tompa, M., "Time-Space Tradeoffs for Computing Functions Using Connectivity Properties of their Circuits," *Proceedings of the Tenth Annual ACM Symp. on Theory of Computing*, pp. 196-204, May 1-3, 1978.

7. Valiant, L. G., "Graph-Theoretic Properties in Computational Complexity," *Journal of Computer and System Sciences*, Vol. 13, pp. 278-285, 1976.

8. Pippenger, N., "A Time-Space Tradeoff," IBM preprint, May 1977, to appear in *JACM*.

9. Swamy, S. and J. E. Savage, "Space-Time Tradeoffs for Linear Recursion," Brown University, Computer Science Technical Report No. CS-36, June 1978.

10. Chandra, A. K., "Efficient Compilation of Linear Recursive Programs," IBM Research Report RC4517, 10 pp., August 29, 1973, *14th SWAT Conference*.

11. Paul, W. J. and R. E. Tarjan, "Time-Space Tradeoffs in a Pebble Game," Stanford University Technical Report STAN-CS-77-619, July 1977, *Fourth Colloq. on Auto. Langs. and Progr.*, Turku, Finland.

12. Grigoryev, D. Yu., "An Application of Separability and Independence Notions for Proving Lower Bounds on Circuit Complexity," *Notes of Scientific Seminars*, Steklov Math. Inst., Leningrad, Vol. 60, 1976.

jbf

INVESTIGATING PROGRAMS IN TERMS OF PARTIAL GRAPHS

Gunther Schmidt

Institut für Informatik der Technischen Universität München

ABSTRACT

A common feature of most theoretical investigations on semantics, correctness, and termination is a strict distinction between one descriptional tool used for the flow of control of the program and another for single program steps. This paper exhibits a unified approach to the presentation of these concepts in terms of TARSKI's and RIGUET's relational algebra. Partial graphs and programs are introduced and formally manipulable relational notions of semantics, correctness, and termination are obtained.

1. INTRODUCTION

In many papers on the theoretical foundations of programming, flow of control of the program is described in a completely different form than single program steps, e.g. flow diagrams versus partial functions or sequencing and conditional branching versus axiomatized assignment operations. This leads in turn to different methods which are difficult to handle where a cooperation of the two is necessary. It is very hard to apply mathematical operations to the objects obtained, because their definition does not support further formal manipulation. A simpler "linear" nature of these concepts which makes them easier to handle for some formal theoretical investigations - whether directed towards control flow or termination problems or towards questions of correctness - is exhibited here. Following [3,1,7], this is achieved using linear relational algebra, amended, however, by the notion of a partial graph which in turn is introduced in terms of relational algebra.

After an explanation of the basic concepts of relational algebra in Section 2, partial graphs and programs are defined in Section 3. The investigation of unfolding and covering properties in Section 4 extends results that GOGUEN [6] obtained in categorical context. A contraction theorem is proved in Section 5, which is interpreted as the most immediate form of FLOYD's inductive assertion method in terms of relational algebra. In Section 6, termination and total correctness are investigated in the context developed here, giving notions of termination explicitly as algebraic transformations of postconditions which fulfill the laws invented by DIJKSTRA [4,5].

As a general reference for the results of this paper, we give the report [8], where more details are presented.

2. RELATIONAL ALGEBRA

The subsequent sections are formulated in terms of relational algebra. This means, that a relation R is not conceived as a subset of the Cartesian product X x Y of two sets X and Y, writing R(x,y) or xRy if the relation holds for certain elements $x \in X$ and $y \in Y$. Instead, a component-free formulation is used throughout this paper. We do not restrict ourselves to total relational algebras. In addition, we include Axiom 2.1.v, which is sometimes omitted by other authors.

DEFINITION 2.1 A *relational algebra* $\mathcal{L}$ is a set of elements, called relations, in which operations and axioms are declared which we informally present as follows:

(i) Every relation R belongs to a subset $\mathcal{L}_R$ of $\mathcal{L}$, containing those relations with a shape congruent to that of R, which constitutes an atomistic complete Boolean algebra. Inside each of these Boolean algebras we have, therefore, the 2-ary operations union "$\vee$" and conjunction "$\wedge$", the 1-ary operation negation "$\overline{\ }$" and the 0-ary operations consisting of the universal element L and the null element 0. As usual, inclusion of relations is denoted by "$\subset$".

(ii) For every relation R there exists a transposed relation R^T and $(R^T)^T = R$ is always fulfilled.

(iii) Given two relations R, S of fitting shape, the product RS is declared. The multiplication is associative. There exist right and left identities for every set $\mathcal{L}_R$ of relations, which for simplicity are all denoted by I. For null elements $0R = R0 = 0$ is always valid.

(iv) The DEDEKIND rule $(QR \wedge S) \subset (Q \wedge SR^T)(R \wedge Q^TS)$ holds whenever one of the three parenthetical expressions is defined.

(v) $LSL = L$ holds for every relation $S \neq 0$.

If union, conjunction, and product are always defined, $\mathcal{L}$ is called *total*. ■

The most important model of a relational algebra is the set of relations on a given set. Other examples include the set $\{0,I,\overline{I},L\} \subset \mathbb{B}^{2x2}$ of Boolean matrices, which as a consequence of its cardinality is not isomorphic to the set $\mathbb{B}^{XxX}$ of relations on a set X. In addition, if $\mathcal{L}$ is a total relation algebra, then the matrices with coefficents from $\mathcal{L}$ constitute again a relational algebra.

Two immediate consequences can be derived from (2.1.iv), namely

$$PQ \subset R \Leftrightarrow P^T\overline{R} \subset \overline{Q} \quad \text{and} \quad PQ \subset R \Leftrightarrow \overline{R}Q^T \subset \overline{P},$$

from which by elementary reasoning the well-known rules of relational calculus are obtained:

$$(PQ)^T = Q^TP^T, \qquad \overline{P^T} = \overline{P}^T, \qquad P \subset Q \Leftrightarrow P^T \subset Q^T, \qquad (R \vee S)^T = R^T \vee S^T,$$

$$P \subset Q \Rightarrow RP \subset RQ, \qquad Q(R \vee S) = QR \vee QS, \qquad Q(R \wedge S) \subset QR \wedge QS.$$

As in every complete Boolean lattice, the infinite distributive laws are valid in relational algebras as well as the infinite forms of the last two formulae.

We can now transfer familiar definitions to a relational algebra. A relation R will be called *total*, if one of the following three equivalent conditions is fulfilled: $I \subset RR^T$, $\overline{R} \subset R\overline{I}$, $RL = L$. R is *unique*, if $R^TR \subset I$. If the transpose R^T of R is unique (total), R will be said to be *injective* (*surjective*, respectively). A *mapping* R is a total and unique relation. The following theorem contains all the rules we are going to use in addition to the basic ones already mentioned.

<u>THEOREM 2.2</u> If the following constructs are defined, we have

(i)	R unique	$\Rightarrow$	$R(S \wedge T) = RS \wedge RT$;
(ii)	$R \subset S$, S unique, $RL \supset SL$	$\Rightarrow$	$R = S$;
(iii)	R unique	$\Rightarrow$	$(S \wedge TR^T)R = SR \wedge T$;
(iv)	R mapping	$\Rightarrow$	$R\overline{S} = \overline{RS}$;
(v)	$(R \wedge SL)T = RT \wedge SL$;		$(R \wedge (SL)^T)T = R(SL \wedge T)$.

We include <u>proofs</u> of (ii) and of the first part of (v) using the DEDEKIND formula:

(ii) $S = SL \wedge S \subset RL \wedge S \subset (R \wedge SL^T)(L \wedge R^TS) \subset RR^TS \subset RS^TS \subset R$.

(v) $(R \wedge SL)T \subset RT \wedge SLT \subset RT \wedge SL \subset (R \wedge SLT^T)(T \wedge R^TSL) \subset (R \wedge SL)T$. ■

In addition to $\vee$-distributivity, $\wedge$-distributivity holds at least for unique relations multiplied from the left, (i). In (ii) it is assured, that a relation R being contained in a unique relation S but "having a greater domain" is necessarily equal to S. Equations (v) can easily be interpreted by matrix-multiplication in connection with screening of some rows or columns.

Of course, the letter L has just been used for universal relations "of different shape"; this will cause no confusion. If a relation r is row-constant, $r = rL$, it may be unterstood as a *point set*, a *Boolean vector* or a *predicate* depending on the respective application. With $r = rL \neq 0$ a nonempty set may be characterized, which is a point, if in addition injectivity $rr^T \subset I$ holds.

As a *transitive closure* we term $R^+ := \bigvee_{n=1}^{\infty} R^n$, whereas $R^* := I \vee R^+$ is called the reflexive transitive closure, (provided R^2 is defined). A relation X will be said to contract a relation R if $R^TX \subset X$.

3. PARTIAL GRAPHS AND PROGRAMS

A (directed) *graph* is usually defined on a given set V of vertices and a set A of arcs specifying a source relation $S \subset A \times V$ in connection with a target relation $T \subset A \times V$. S and T are assumed to be mappings. $M := S \vee T \subset A \times V$ is called the *incidence relation*; the *associated relation* is defined as $B := S^TT \subset V \times V$, which indicates that a vertex is joined by an arc to another vertex.

Some parts of graph theory can be studied without the assumption of S and T being total, using only that S and T are unique. Putting this as a definition, we introduce as a *(partial) graph* G (later classical graphs will be distinguished by calling them total graphs) a pair $G = (S,T)$ of relations with the properties that $S^TS \subset I$ and $T^TT \subset I$ and that the associated relation $B := S^TT$ exists as well as the incidence $S \vee T$. Furthermore, we introduce as a *homomorphism* from graph $G = (S,T)$ into graph $G' = (S',T')$ a pair $\phi = (\phi_V,\phi_A)$ of relations, where ϕ_V is a mapping of the vertices and ϕ_A is a mapping of the arcs subject to

$$S\phi_V \subset \phi_A S', \quad T\phi_V \subset \phi_A T'.$$

In the case of total graphs, these homomorphism conditions specialize to $S\phi_V = \phi_A S'$, $T\phi_V = \phi_A T'$, as a consequence of Theorem 2.2.ii. If ϕ is a homomorphism from G into G', the associated relations B and B' fulfill $B\phi_V \subset \phi_V B'$.

We are accustomed to saying that the vertex y of a graph is reachable from a vertex x of the graph, if there exists at least one directed path from x to y, i.e. if $xy^T \subset B^*$. We define *reachability* of a graph with associated relation B to be the reflexive transitive closure B^* of B.

Expressed in terms of relational algebra, the set of *terminal vertices* is characterized by $\overline{BL}$. A *root* is defined as a point x fulfilling the exhaustion condition $L \subset x^TB^*$, which may be expressed by $xL \subset B^*$ as well. As a *rooted graph* we will denote a pair $R = (G,x)$ consisting of a total G and a root x of G. Of special interest among these rooted graphs are *rooted trees*, which are in addition characterized by being circuit-free, $B^+ \subset \overline{I}$, and having an injective target relation, $TT^T \subset I$. Homomorphisms $\phi = (\phi_V,\phi_A)$ of rooted graphs shall always map the root onto the root, $\phi_V^Tx = x'$.

In the definitions concerning graphs given so far, only axiomatic relational algebra has been employed. We are, therefore, free to use these defintions in a n y relational algebra fulfilling the axioms given in Section 2. Our interest mainly concentrates on two types. The first one is the algebra of relations between sets. It allows, for instance, to introduce an associated relation $B_F \in \mathbb{B}^{V\times V}$ describing a flow graph F on a set V of vertices. An example of the second relational algebra is that of matrices with coefficents which belong to a total relational algebra. Taking a machine with a set Z of machine states, we have the total relational algebra $\mathbb{B}^{Z\times Z}$ of all relations and state transitions on Z. We are going to consider elements $B \in (\mathbb{B}^{Z\times Z})^{V\times V}$ assigning a state transition to each pair of vertices of a flow graph. Nevertheless, our exposition will at no stage make explicit use of these special relational algebras.

In the following definition we have a (partial) state graph G with associated relation B which is homomorphically mapped onto a total flow graph F with associated relation B_F.

<u>DEFINITION 3.1</u> The 5-tuple $\mathcal{P} = (G,F,\theta,\alpha,\omega)$ will be called a *program*, if

(i) $G = (S,T)$ is a graph describing state transitions,

(ii) $F = (S_F,T_F)$ is a total graph describing flow of control,

(iii) $\theta = (\theta_V,\theta_A)$ is a surjective homomorphism from G onto F, giving raise to talk about "states assumed at a vertex" and "state transitions along an arc",

(iv) α is an input relation characterized by $\alpha^T\alpha = I$, $\alpha\alpha^T \subset I$, $\alpha L = \theta_V\theta_V^T\alpha L$ and $\theta_V^T\alpha = \theta_V^T\alpha L$,

(v) ω is an output relation characterized by $\omega^T\omega = I$, $\theta_V\theta_V^T \wedge \omega\omega^T \subset I$ and $\omega L = \theta_V\theta_V^T\omega L$.

By $\alpha_F := \theta_V^T\alpha L = \theta_V^T\alpha$ a begin vertex and by $\omega_F := \theta_V^T\omega L$ a set of end vertices is selected from the flow graph F. If the associated relation $B := S^TT$ is unique, the program will be called *deterministic*. If $R := (F,\alpha_F)$ is a rooted tree, $\mathcal{P}$ is said to be a *rooted tree program*. ∎

The domain of the surjective 1 : 1 relation α consists exactly of the states over the begin vertex α_F; therefore α^T is an inclusion of input states into the state graph. There is only one begin vertex, since $\alpha_F\alpha_F^T = \theta_V^T\alpha\alpha^T\theta_V \subset \theta_V^T\theta_V \subset I$. However, it is not correct to admit only one single end vertex, since we are going to study tree programs. To consider these cases, the restriction of ω to states over each of the end vertices should be a surjective and 1 : 1 mapping onto the output states. State and flow graph, input and output relation of a small program are shown in Fig. 3.1.

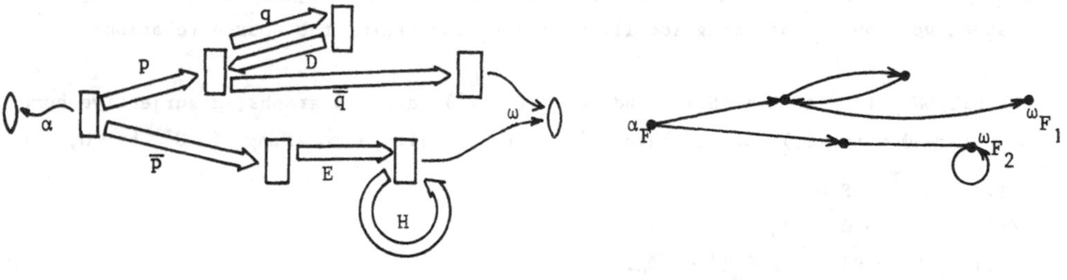

Fig. 3.1 Stategraph and flow graph of the program
if p *then while* q *do* D *else* E; *repeat* H *fi*.

Having defined the program as a new structure, we need an appropriate notion of homomorphism. It decomposes into homomorphisms of the flow graph and of the state graph.

<u>DEFINITION 3.2</u> The pair (ϕ,η) of relations will be called a *homomorphism* from the program $\mathcal{P} = (G,F,\theta,\alpha,\omega)$ into the program $\mathcal{P}' = (G',F',\theta',\alpha',\omega')$ if

(i) $\phi = (\phi_V,\phi_A)$ is a homomorphism from G into G',

(ii) $\eta = (\eta_V,\eta_A)$ is a homomorphism from F into F',

(iii) $\phi_V^T\alpha \subset \alpha'$, $\omega \subset \phi_V\omega'$,

(iv) $\phi_V^T\theta_V = \theta_V'\eta_V^T,\quad \phi_A^T\theta_A = \theta_A'\eta_A^T.$ ■

The two analogous conditions in (iii) are written differently with respect to the Definition 4.3. From (iv), $\phi\theta' = \theta\eta$ may easily be deduced. Now, we are in a position to define semantics of such programs. If the program $\mathcal{P} = (G,F,\theta,\alpha,\omega)$ is given, where the graph G has B as its associated relation, we define the relation B^* to be the *action* of the program. Since we are primarily interested in terminating computation sequences of a program, we call $C := B^* \wedge \overline{BL}^T$ the *terminating action* of $\mathcal{P}$. Termination of these computation sequences will not necessarily occur in states over an end vertex. Such cases of abortion are suppressed if we define $\Sigma := \alpha^T C\omega$ to be the *semantics* of the program $\mathcal{P}$.

Since the begin vertex need not be initial and the end vertices need not be terminal in the flow graph, cf. Fig. 3.1, our definition of a flow diagram is more general than those given elsewhere. Admitting end vertices which are no longer terminal, necessarily presumes the ability of expressing termination of a computation by other means which allow a natural extension to the recursive case.

4. COVERING THEORY OF FLOW EQUIVALENCE

The notions we are now going to introduce will strongly resemble a concept in algebraic topology, in particular, in the covering theory of Riemann surfaces. Among surjective homomorphisms of graphs and programs we will distinguish those, having the respective property of being locally topologic concerning the source relation.

DEFINITION 4.1 If $G = (S,T)$ and $G' = (S',T')$ are two graphs, a surjective homomorphism $\phi = (\phi_V,\phi_A)$ of G onto G' will be called a *covering* of G' by G, if

(i) $\phi_V S'^T \subset S^T\phi_A$,

(ii) $SS^T \wedge \phi_A\phi_A^T \subset I$,

(iii) $\phi_A S' \subset S\phi_V,\qquad \phi_A T' \subset T\phi_V$. ■

We will explain this definition: Given an arc p' of G' together with its source x' and an arbitrary vertex x over x', then by (ii) there is at most one arc p over p' starting from x. On the other hand, (i) guaranties that there is at least one such arc. Putting these two assertions together, we might say that ϕ behaves locally topologic concerning the source relation.

As a consequence of (iii), an arc of G is mapped onto an arc of G' with initial (terminal) vertex only, if an initial (terminal) vertex is defined for the arc itself. In the case of total graphs, condition (iii) of the definition becomes obsolete and may therefore be omitted. It can easily be proved that composition of two coverings again constitutes a covering.

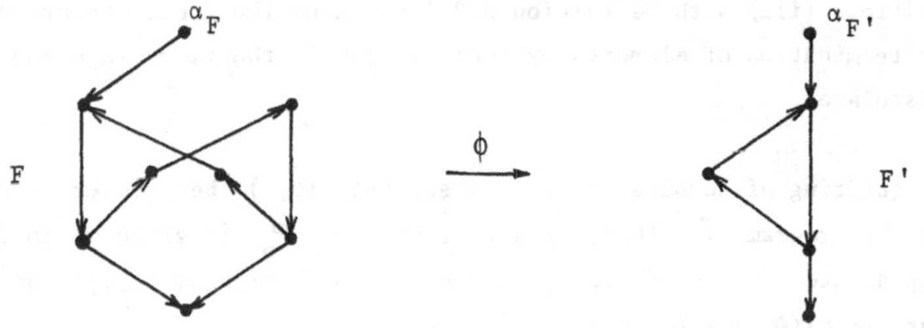

Fig. 4.1 Graph F' covered by graph F.

Before we consider programs, it shall be shown that the above notion of covering is sufficient to model the path lifting property.

<u>THEOREM 4.2</u> (Lifting of paths) Let ϕ be a covering of the total graph F' by the total graph F and let in either graph a vertex α_F resp. $\alpha_{F'}$ be distinguished such that $\phi_V^T\alpha_F = \alpha_{F'}$. Then, given any rooted tree $R = (F_o, \alpha_{Fo})$ which by ψ' is homomorphically mapped into F' so that $\psi'^T_V\alpha_{Fo} = \alpha_{F'}$, there exists a homomorphism ψ of F_o into F such that $\psi_V^T\alpha_{Fo} = \alpha_F$ and that ψ' factorizes to $\psi' = \psi\phi$. ■

A strictly relational <u>proof</u> is given in [8]. The construction of the relations ψ_V, ψ_A, is easily interpreted: We map the root α_{Fo} onto α_F and then exhaust R in the following way. The arc p_o, the source of which had obtained an image shortly before, is mapped to an arc emerging at the image of its source in F and covering the image of p_o in F'. Every vertex x_o ($\neq \alpha_{Fo}$) of the rooted tree R is the target of exactly one arc, the image of which has been determined earlier. Vertex x_o is mapped to the target of the image of this arc.

It should be pointed out that F need not be the unfoldment (i.e. the covering rooted tree) of F'. Therefore this theorem is more general than other results of this kind which lift homomorphisms only to the unfoldment of a graph.

Following our general theme of showing that programs can be treated as partial graphs, it should now be possible to prove a similar lifting theorem for programs. First, we have to define those program homomorphisms that will be coverings. These coverings correspond to GOGUEN's notion of flow equivalence.

<u>DEFINITION 4.3</u> A homomorphism (ϕ,η) of the program $\mathcal{P} = (G,F,\theta,\alpha,\omega)$ into the program $\mathcal{P}' = (G',F',\theta',\alpha',\omega')$ is called a *covering* of $\mathcal{P}'$ by $\mathcal{P}$, if

(i) $\phi = (\phi_V, \phi_A)$ is a graph covering of G' by G,

(ii) $\eta = (\eta_V, \eta_A)$ is a graph covering of F' by F,

(iii) $\alpha' \subset \phi_V^T\alpha$, $\phi_V\omega' \subset \omega$,

(iv) $\theta_V\theta_V^T \wedge \phi_V\phi_V^T \subset I$, $\theta_A\theta_A^T \wedge \phi_A\phi_A^T \subset I$. ■

Compare conditions (iii) with Definition 3.2.iii and notice their difference. In (iv) the unique determination of elements by their images in the flow graph and their ϕ-images is postulated.

THEOREM 4.4 (Lifting of computation sequences) Let (ϕ,η) be a covering of the program $\mathcal{P}'$ by the program $\mathcal{P}$. Then, if a tree program $\mathcal{P}_o$ is given which is homomorphically mapped into $\mathcal{P}'$ by (ψ',ϱ'), there is a homomorphism (ψ,ϱ) of $\mathcal{P}_o$ into $\mathcal{P}$, such that $(\psi,\varrho)(\phi,\eta) = (\psi',\varrho')$.

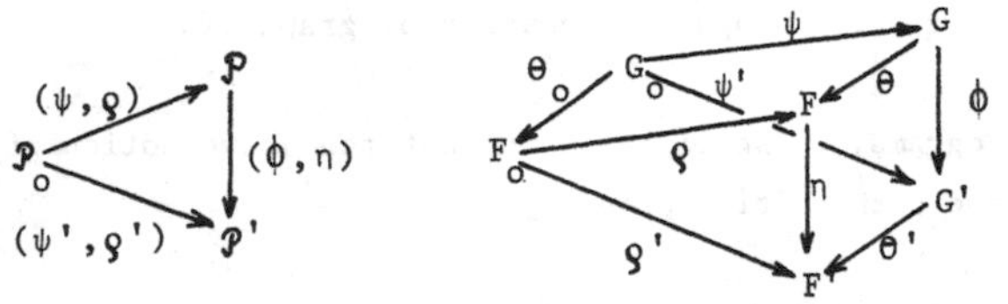

Fig. 4.2 Lifting of the program homomorphism (ψ',ϱ').

The formal proof in [8] is based on the preceding theorem, from which we deduce that a rooted graph homomorphism ϱ of the desired type exists. So ψ is obtained as

$$\psi_V := \psi'_V\phi_V^T \wedge \theta_{oV}\varrho_V\theta_V^T, \qquad \psi_A := \psi'_A\phi_A^T \wedge \theta_{oA}\varrho_A\theta_A^T,$$

intersecting the two approximations of ψ obtained from the top and the rear side of the diagram. ■

If the flow graphs of $\mathcal{P}$ and $\mathcal{P}'$ are rooted graphs and if (ψ',ϱ') is a covering, then (ψ,ϱ) will again be a covering. Therefore a covering tree program is uniquely determined up to an isomorphism, and it is correct to talk about the covering tree program, sometimes called universal covering or unfoldment.

In a given relational algebra, a universal covering does not necessarily exist; however, its existence can easily be shown by construction if only graphs in the classical sense are considered. It is therefore worth noting, that our following theorem can be proved directly, not using the universal covering.

THEOREM 4.5 (Flow equivalence theorem) If the program $\mathcal{P}$ is a covering of the program $\mathcal{P}'$ by (ϕ,η), then the respective semantics coincide.

Proof: Firstly, we conclude from Definition 4.1.i,iii that $\phi_V B' = \phi_V S'^T T' = S^T\phi_A T' = S^T T\phi_V = B\phi_V$ so that $\phi_V B'^* = B^*\phi_V$. Furthermore, we have by Theorem 2.2.iv

$$\phi_V\overline{B'L}\phi_V^T = \overline{\phi_V B'L\phi_V^T} = \overline{B\phi_V L\phi_V^T} = \overline{BL\phi_V^T} = \overline{BL}.$$

With this, we prove

$$\phi_V C' = \phi_V(B'^*\wedge\overline{B'L}^T) = \phi_V B'^*\wedge\phi_V\overline{B'L}^T = B^*\phi_V\wedge\phi_V\overline{B'L}^T = (B^*\wedge\phi_V\overline{B'L}^T\phi_V^T)\phi = (B^*\wedge\overline{BL}^T)\phi_V = C\phi_V.$$

Using Definition 4.3.iii, we get $\Sigma' = \alpha'^T C'\omega' = \alpha^T\phi_V C'\omega' = \alpha^T C\phi_V\omega' = \alpha^T C\omega = \Sigma$. ■

Thus we have the possibility of transforming programs depending on purely graph-theoretic considerations. We demonstrate this with two very simple loop constructions. (Always read $I \wedge pL$ for a matrix coefficient denoted by a predicate p.)

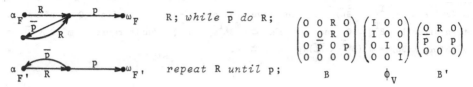

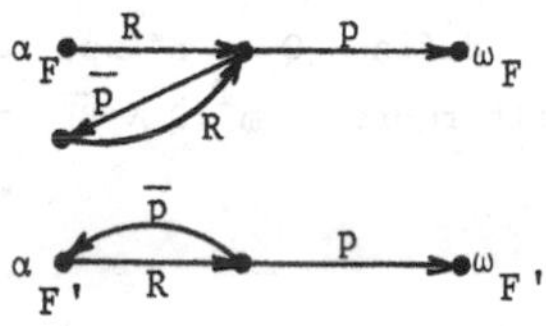

R; *while* $\overline{p}$ *do* R;

repeat R *until* p;

$$B = \begin{pmatrix} 0 & 0 & R & 0 \\ 0 & 0 & R & 0 \\ 0 & \overline{p} & 0 & p \\ 0 & 0 & 0 & 0 \end{pmatrix} \quad \phi_V = \begin{pmatrix} I & 0 & 0 \\ I & 0 & 0 \\ 0 & I & 0 \\ 0 & 0 & I \end{pmatrix} \quad B' = \begin{pmatrix} 0 & R & 0 \\ \overline{p} & 0 & p \\ 0 & 0 & 0 \end{pmatrix}$$

Fig. 4.3 A covering of programs.

Since we easily verify that there is a graph homomorphism of the while flow graph onto the repeat flow graph which fulfills the covering conditions, and since obviously $\phi_V B' = B\phi_V$, we can directly conclude that the semantics coincide.

5. CONTRACTION THEORY OF PARTIAL CORRECTNESS

The action B^* of a program connects a state with all subsequent states, whereas the terminating action $C = B^* \wedge \overline{BL}^T$ associates only subsequent terminal states to a given state. Screening those relations that hold between input states and output states from the latter, we obtain semantics $\Sigma = \alpha^T(B^* \wedge \overline{BL}^T)\omega$.

Usually, one is only interested in a certain subset of all the computation sequences of a program. The subset is characterized by a precondition p and a postcondition q. To reflect this, a program $\mathcal{P}$ with semantics Σ is defined to be *partially correct* with respect to precondition p and postcondition q, if $\Sigma^T p \subset q$. In absence of a relational calculus, often $\{p\}\mathcal{P}\{q\}$ is written to denote partial correctness symbolically.

Having in mind that this definition resembles only full computation sequences beginning in an input state and terminating in an output state which neither abort nor loop forever, it can easily be interpreted: Every full computation sequence originating in an input state fulfilling p leads to an output state fulfilling q. The definition is equivalent to $\Sigma\overline{q} \subset \overline{p}$, which can be read as: A full computation sequence leading to a state violating q necessarily orginates in a state violating p.

In the above definition of partial correctness, p and q are related to semantics Σ. Of course, it is desirable to check partial correctness directly from the program, i.e. using the associated relation B. We have, therefore, the problem of taking the condition $\Sigma^T p \subset q$ and tracing it back to a condition concerning p,q, and B.

<u>THEOREM 5.1</u> (Contraction theorem) Let $\mathcal{P}$ be a program with associated relation B

and semantics Σ and let p and q be given pre- and postconditions. Then $\mathcal{P}$ is partially correct with respect to p and q, if and only if there is a predicate Q with $B^T Q \subset Q$, $p \subset \alpha^T Q$, and $\omega^T(Q \wedge \overline{BL}) \subset q$.

<u>Proof:</u> The if-direction is shown by $\Sigma^T p \subset \Sigma^T \alpha^T Q = \omega^T(B*^T \wedge \overline{BL})\alpha\alpha^T Q \subset \omega^T(B*^T \wedge \overline{BL})Q$ $= \omega^T(B*^T Q \wedge \overline{BL}) = \omega^T(Q \wedge \overline{BL}) \subset q$. To prove the only-if-part, we define $Q := B*^T \alpha p$ to obtain directly $B^T Q \subset Q$ and $p = \alpha^T \alpha p \subset \alpha^T B*^T \alpha p = \alpha^T Q$. Furthermore, $\omega^T(Q \wedge \overline{BL}) =$ $= \omega^T(B*^T \alpha p \wedge \overline{BL}) = \omega^T(B*^T \wedge \overline{BL})\alpha p = \Sigma^T p \subset q$. ∎

This contraction theorem resembles FLOYD's approach expressing inductive assertions in terms of relational algebra; it should however be noted that the output nodes of the flow graph need not be terminal nodes of that flow graph. The ability to handle partial correctness if nonterminal output nodes occur, is prerequisite for dealing with recursion. In [8] this has been shown in full detail, thereby giving an extremely short and clear new proof of the difficult DE BAKKER-MEERTENS completeness theorem, which asserts the validity of FLOYD's method even in the case of systems of recursive programs.

We will now show how verification rules can systematically be derived from the contraction theorem. In Fig. 5.1.a the simple concatenation of two program steps D and E is shown as a flow diagram together with the associated relation B. The input relation is α and the output relation is ω. This program is partially correct with respect to p and q, $\{p\}D;E\{q\}$, if and only if a predicate Q, assumed to be given as $Q^T = (x,y,z)$, exists with $p \subset x$, $z \subset q$ and $D^T x \subset y$, $E^T y \subset z$. Therefore, $D;E$ is partially correct with respect to p and q precisely when there is an intermediate condition y, such that D is partially correct with respect to p and y, and E is partially correct with respect to y and q.

a)

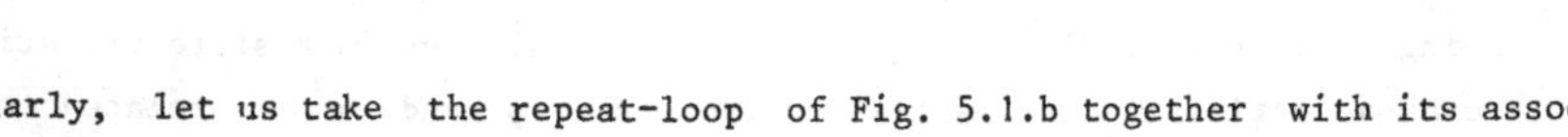

$$B = \begin{pmatrix} 0 & D & 0 \\ 0 & 0 & E \\ 0 & 0 & 0 \end{pmatrix} \qquad \alpha = \begin{pmatrix} I \\ 0 \\ 0 \end{pmatrix} \quad \omega = \begin{pmatrix} 0 \\ 0 \\ I \end{pmatrix} \qquad B = \begin{pmatrix} 0 & R & 0 \\ \overline{r} & 0 & r \\ 0 & 0 & 0 \end{pmatrix}$$

Fig. 5.1 Concatenation and repeat-loop as partial graphs.

Similarly, let us take the repeat-loop of Fig. 5.1.b together with its associated relation B. Following the contraction theorem, *repeat* R *until* r is partially correct with respect to p and q if and only if there is a predicate Q, assumed to be given as $Q^T = (x,y,z)$, such that $\overline{r} \wedge y \subset x$, $R^T x \subset y$, and $r \wedge y \subset z$, which means that there exists a (possibly larger) precondition $x \supset p$ and an intermediate condition y with $r \wedge y \subset q$ and $\overline{r} \wedge y \subset x$, such that R is partially correct with respect to x and y.

6. TOTAL CORRECTNESS AND TERMINATION

Partial correctness has been introduced as a statement concerning semantics Σ of a program in connection with a precondition p and a postcondition q. Semantics as defined formally in Section 3 does not express information about loops and abortion of computation sequences. Semantics cannot, therefore, be used to define total correctness. Other constructs are needed.

DEFINITION 6.1 Let G be a graph with associated relation B.

(i) G is called *progressively bounded* if $L = \bigvee_{h=0}^{\infty} \overline{B^h L}$.

(ii) The *initial part* of the graph G is $I(G) := \min \{X \mid \overline{X} \subset B\overline{X}\}$.

(iii) G is called *progressively finite* if $I(G) = L$. ∎

Interpreted for graphs in the classical sense, a graph is progressively bounded if for every vertex x there is a natural number h_x such that none of the paths starting from x is longer than h_x. However, there are progressively unbounded graphs in which every path starting from an arbitrary vertex has finite length. Quantifying over all subsets of vertices of the graph we formulate such a finiteness property.

If a vertex is starting point of a path of infinite length, then at least one of its successors has the same property. The set Y of all starting vertices of paths of infinite length, therefore, is the maximum set with $Y \subset BY$. The other way around, the set of vertices from which only paths of finite length emerge is given by the initial part $I(G) = \min \{X \mid \overline{X} \subset B\overline{X}\}$. If every vertex belongs to the initial part, $I(G) = L$, the graph is said to be progressively finite. HITCHCOCK and PARK [7] gave the equivalent definition $I(G) := \underline{\min} \{X \mid \overline{X} = B\overline{X}\}$ of the initial part as minimal fixed point of the functional $\tau(X) := \overline{B\overline{X}}$ (which is not continuous).

The following theorem asserts that a vertex x with a common bound h_x for the lengths of all paths emerging from x is not the initial vertex of an infinite path. Furthermore, it is possible to reach a terminal vertex from x.

THEOREM 6.2 If B is the associated relation of the graph G, we have

(i) $\bigvee_{h=0}^{\infty} \overline{B^h L} \subset I(B) \subset B^*\overline{BL}$;

(ii) $B^T B \subset I \Rightarrow \bigvee_{h=0}^{\infty} \overline{B^h L} = I(B) = B^*\overline{BL}$;

(iii) G progressively bounded $\Rightarrow L = \bigvee_{h=0}^{\infty} \overline{B^h L} = I(B) = B^*\overline{BL}$;

(iv) G progressively finite $\Rightarrow \bigvee_{h=0}^{\infty} \overline{B^h L} \subset I(B) = B^*\overline{BL} = L$.

Proof: (i) The set $X_o := B^*\overline{BL}$ fulfills $\overline{X_o} \subset B\overline{X_o}$, since $B^*\overline{BL} \vee \overline{BB^*\overline{BL}} = (\overline{BL} \vee BB^*\overline{BL}) \vee \overline{BB^*\overline{BL}} = \overline{BL} \vee BL = L$, giving the right inclusion. Furthermore, for every X with $B\overline{X} = \overline{X}$, $\bigwedge_{h=0}^{\infty} B^h L \supset \overline{X}$ is valid, since $B^o L = L \supset \overline{X}$ and by induction

$B^hL \supset \overline{X}$ implies $B^{h+1}L \supset B\overline{X} = \overline{X}$. (ii) If $B^TB \subset I$, we have for all $h \geq 0$ $(B^h)^T B^{h+1}L \subset (B^{h-1})^T B^h L \subset \ldots \subset BL$ so that $B^h\overline{BL} \subset \overline{B^{h+1}L}$. ■

If the associated relation B is unique, it is obvious that a vertex from which a terminal vertex can be reached is the starting point of exactly one maximal path, the length of which is therefore a common upper bound for all paths emerging from that vertex.

We will now apply these notions directly to partial state graphs of programs. DIJKSTRA investigated deterministic nonrecursive programs [4] and nondeterministic nonrecursive programs [5] using predicate transformers applied to postconditions. If a program $\mathcal{P}$ is given, such a predicate transformer specifies for every postcondition q the weakest precondition $wp(\mathcal{P},q)$ such that every computation sequence starting therefrom necessarily terminates in an output state which fulfills q. In the following definition three transformations of postconditions are explicitly given in terms of relational algebra.

DEFINITION 6.3 Let the program $\mathcal{P} = (G,F,\theta,\alpha,\omega)$ be given with associated relation B, terminating action $C := B^* \wedge \overline{BL}^T$, initial part $I(B)$ and semantics $\Sigma := \alpha^T C\omega$. If p is a precondition and q is a postcondition, we will say that the program is *totally correct* with respect to p and q of

type 1, if $p \subset \alpha^T \bigvee_{n=0}^{\infty} \overline{B^hL} \wedge \alpha^T\overline{C\omega\overline{q}}$

type 2, if $p \subset \alpha^T I(B) \wedge \alpha^T\overline{C\omega\overline{q}}$

type 3, if $p \subset \Sigma q = \alpha^T C\omega q$.

$\mathcal{P}$ *terminates* of type i for precondition p, if $\mathcal{P}$ is totally correct of type i with respect to p and L. ■

$\mathcal{P}$ is totally correct of type 1 with respect to p and q, if from none of the input states fulfilling p there are computation sequences of arbitrary lengths, and if it is impossible to reach with C a terminal state of computation which doesn't, after output with ω, fulfill q (whether this is a consequence of an abortion or of reaching an output state with $\overline{q}$). In type 2 it is no longer necessary that the lengths of computation sequences from an input state x have a common bound h_x. It suffices that they all be finite.

For total correctness of type 3 it is sufficient that from every input state with precondition p at least one computation sequence leads to a terminal output state with q. Obviously, ΣL is the domain of semantics of the program considered as a relation. Total correctness of type 1 implies that of type 2 which in turn implies that of type 3. If the program is deterministic, the three variants of total correctness coincide. Using Theorem 6.2.ii, we only have to show that $C\omega q \subset B^*\overline{BL} \wedge \overline{C\omega\overline{q}}$.

Of course, in the deterministic case we would prefer to use type 3 as the simplest of the three equivalent conditions. However, it behaves entirely different in the nondeterministic case. For instance, only total correctness of type 1 or 2 is equivalent to partial correctness and termination of the respective type.

It is now easy to check DIJKSTRA's postulates

(i) $wp(\mathit{skip},q) = q$;

(ii) $wp(\mathit{abort},q) = 0$;

(iii) $wp(\mathcal{P},0) = 0$;

(iv) $wp(\mathcal{P},q_1) \wedge wp(\mathcal{P},q_2) = wp(\mathcal{P},q_1 \wedge q_2)$;

(v) $wp(\mathcal{P},q_1) \vee wp(\mathcal{P},q_2) \subset wp(\mathcal{P},q_1 \vee q_2)$ with equality in the deterministic case;

(vi) $q_1 \subset q_2 \Rightarrow wp(\mathcal{P},q_1) \subset wp(\mathcal{P},q_2)$.

Defining $wp_3(\mathcal{P},q) := \Sigma q$ if the program is deterministic and accordingly interpreting semantics of *skip* and *abort* to be I and O respectively, we have the immediate meaning of the postulates in terms of relational algebra. It is as easy to verify that $wp_1(\mathcal{P},q) := \alpha^T \bigvee_{h=0}^{\infty} \overline{B^h L} \wedge \alpha^T \overline{C\overline{\omega q}}$ and $wp_2(\mathcal{P},q) := \alpha^T \overline{I(B)} \wedge \alpha^T \overline{C\overline{\omega q}}$ satisfy the postulates even in the nondeterministic case. This means that we have established two different notions of total correctness fulfilling DIJKSTRA's postulates.

We will show that both these notions of total correctness may coexist. To achieve this, we recall the intention of Section 5 of establishing partial correctness as a condition on p, q, and the program B. Following these lines, we will now for either type of total correctness exhibit a condition on p, q, and B.

<u>THEOREM 6.4</u> (Theorem of exhaustion) The program $\mathcal{P} = (G,F,\theta,\alpha,\omega)$ is totally correct of type 1 with respect to the precondition p and the postcondition q, if and only if there is a sequence of predicates Q_i such that $p \subset \alpha^T \bigvee_{i=0}^{\infty} Q_i$ and that, beginning with $\overline{Q_{-1}} = L$, $\overline{Q_{i+1}} := B\overline{Q_i} \vee \overline{\omega q \vee BL}$ is valid for $i \geq -1$. ■

We omit the proof of this theorem. Total correctness of type 1 of a program $\mathcal{P}$ with respect to a precondition p and a postcondition q is equivalent to the possibility of exhausting the states in the state graph starting from output states which fulfill q. In every step of the exhaustion $Q_{i+1} := \overline{B\overline{Q_i}} \wedge (\omega q \vee BL)$ every state is added from which a step of the program can not lead to the complement of the set Q_i already obtained, paying attention to the fact that terminal states are added only if they are output states with q.

One would of course, like to work with the limit value $Q := \bigvee_{i=0}^{\infty} Q_i$ and obtain the formula $\overline{Q} = B\overline{Q} \vee \overline{\omega q \vee BL}$. However, this is not correct since the functional $\tau_1(X) := \overline{B\overline{X}} \wedge (\omega q \vee BL)$ is not continuous. Considering the fixed points of $X = \tau_1(X)$ necessarily requires talking about total correctness of type 2. Consequently, we prove the following theorem with entirely different - second order - methods. The close relationship with Theorem 5.1 should be noticed, which stems from the equivalence of $B^T Q \subset Q$ and $B\overline{Q} \subset \overline{Q}$.

<u>THEOREM 6.5</u> (Second order theorem of total correctness) The program $\mathcal{P}$ with associated relation B is totally correct of type 2 with respect to the precondition p and the postcondition q if and only if $p \subset \alpha^T \min \{Q \mid \overline{Q} \subset B\overline{Q} \vee \overline{\omega q \vee BL}\}$.

<u>Proof:</u> Using the abbreviation $F := \overline{\omega q \vee BL}$, we show that $\min \{X \mid \overline{X} \subset B\overline{X}\} \wedge \overline{C\overline{\omega q}} = \min \{Q \mid \overline{Q} \subset B\overline{Q} \vee F\}$. For every $\overline{X} \subset \overline{BX}$, $Q := X \wedge C\overline{\omega q} = X \wedge \overline{B^*F}$ is contained in X and, furthermore, fulfills $B\overline{Q} \vee F = B\overline{X} \vee BB^*F \vee F \supset \overline{X} \vee B^*F = \overline{Q}$, thus showing "$\supset$". On the other hand, we find to every $\overline{Q} \subset B\overline{Q} \vee F$ the $X := B^*(\overline{Q} \wedge \overline{B^*F})$ for which

$$\begin{aligned}\overline{X} &= B^*(\overline{Q} \wedge \overline{B^*F}) = (\overline{Q} \wedge \overline{B^*F}) \wedge BB^*(\overline{Q} \wedge \overline{B^*F}) \\ &\subset ((B\overline{Q} \vee F) \wedge \overline{B^*F}) \vee B\overline{X} = (B\overline{Q} \wedge \overline{B^*F}) \vee B\overline{X} \\ &= ((B(\overline{Q} \wedge \overline{B^*F}) \vee B(\overline{Q} \wedge B^*F)) \wedge \overline{B^*F}) \vee B\overline{X} \\ &\subset (BB^*(\overline{Q} \wedge \overline{B^*F}) \wedge \overline{B^*F}) \vee (B^+F \wedge \overline{B^*F}) \vee B\overline{X} \\ &\subset BB^*(\overline{Q} \wedge \overline{B^*F}) \vee 0 \vee B\overline{X} = B\overline{X}\end{aligned}$$

is valid. Showing that $X = \overline{B^*(\overline{Q} \wedge \overline{B^*F})} \subset \overline{I(\overline{Q} \wedge \overline{B^*F})} = Q \vee B^*F$, we obtain $X \wedge C\overline{\omega q} = X \wedge \overline{B^*F} \subset Q$; hence "$\subset$". ∎

Let us consider the simplest case, namely a single program step D. Then $B = \begin{pmatrix} 0 & D \\ 0 & 0 \end{pmatrix}$ is the associated relation of the state graph. Assuming Q to be given as $Q^T = (x,y)$, we obtain

$$\begin{aligned}wp(D,q) &= \alpha^T \min \{Q \mid \overline{Q} \subset B\overline{Q} \vee \overline{\omega q \vee BL}\} \\ &= (I\ 0) \min \{\begin{pmatrix} x \\ y \end{pmatrix} \mid \begin{pmatrix} \overline{D\overline{y}} \wedge DL \\ q \end{pmatrix} \subset \begin{pmatrix} x \\ y \end{pmatrix}\} \\ &= (I\ 0)\begin{pmatrix} \overline{D\overline{q}} \wedge DL \\ q \end{pmatrix} = \overline{D\overline{q}} \wedge DL.\end{aligned}$$

As one would expect, the program step D is totally correct of type 2 with respect to precondition p and postcondition q, if it is defined for every state with p, i.e. $p \subset DL$, and if it is not the case that D leads to a state for which q is not valid, i.e. $p \subset \overline{D\overline{q}}$.

As another example, we investigate the nondeterministic-choice-construct. We agree, that Fig. 6.1 gives the corresponding flow diagram program, which is totally correct with respect to p and q precisely when $p \subset \alpha^T \min\{Q \mid \overline{Q} \subset B\overline{Q} \vee \overline{\omega q \vee BL}\}$. Assuming

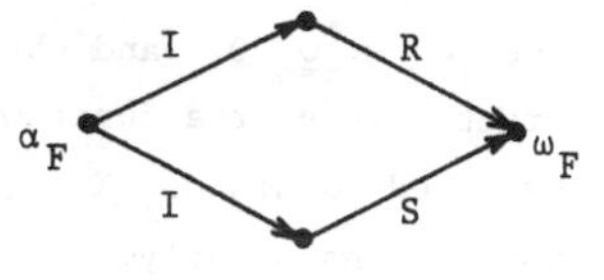

$$B = \begin{pmatrix} 0 & I & I & 0 \\ 0 & 0 & 0 & R \\ 0 & 0 & 0 & S \\ 0 & 0 & 0 & 0 \end{pmatrix} \quad \alpha = \begin{pmatrix} I \\ 0 \\ 0 \\ 0 \end{pmatrix} \quad \omega = \begin{pmatrix} 0 \\ 0 \\ 0 \\ I \end{pmatrix}$$

Fig. 6.1 Nondeterministic choice.

Q to be given as $Q^T := (u,v,x,y)$, the inclusion reads as follows

$$\overline{\begin{pmatrix} u \\ v \\ x \\ y \end{pmatrix}} \subset \begin{pmatrix} O & I & I & O \\ O & O & O & R \\ O & O & O & S \\ O & O & O & O \end{pmatrix} \cdot \overline{\begin{pmatrix} u \\ v \\ x \\ y \end{pmatrix}} \vee \overline{\begin{pmatrix} O \\ O \\ O \\ q \end{pmatrix} \vee \begin{pmatrix} L \\ RL \\ SL \\ O \end{pmatrix}}$$

This leads to $\bar{u} \subset \bar{v} \vee \bar{x}$, $\bar{v} \subset R\bar{y} \vee \overline{RL}$, $\bar{x} \subset S\bar{y} \vee \overline{SL}$, $\bar{y} \subset \bar{q}$. Minimisation therefore produces $y = q$, $x = wp(S,q)$, $v = wp(R,q)$ and finally

$$wp(\text{nondeterministic choice between } R \text{ and } S,q) = wp(R,q) \wedge wp(S,q).$$

7. CONCLUSION

An approach to the theory of semantics, correctness, and termination of flow diagram programs has been made in terms of relational algebra. First partial graphs were defined, i.e. graphs where source and target of one arc are allowed to be partially defined. Using this concept, programs were introduced. Semantics, correctness, and termination were obtained in terms of linear relational algebra. Coverings of programs turned out to be flow equivalences, and it has been shown how the microscopic correctness rules of a while-loop and a nondeterministic choice can be deduced from our macroscopic point of view. As a main feature we would like to emphasize that the method extends to systems of recursive programs.

REFERENCES

[1] DE BAKKER, J.W., DE ROEVER, W.P.: A calculus for recursive program schemes. In: Nivat, M. (ed.): Automata, languages and programming. Proc. of a Symp. organized by IRIA, 3. - 7. Juli 1972, Rocquencourt, North-Holland, Amsterdam, 1973, p. 167-196

[2] DE BAKKER, J.W., MEERTENS, L.G.L.T.: On the completeness of the inductive assertion method. J. Comput. Syst. Sci. 11, 323-357 (1975)

[3] COOPER, D.C.: Programs for mechanical program verification. In: Meltzer, B., Michie, D. (eds.): Machine Intelligence 6, Edinburgh Univ. Press, 1971, p. 43-59

[4] DIJKSTRA, E.W.: A simple axiomatic basis for programming language constructs. Indag. math. 36, 1-15 (1974)

[5] DIJKSTRA, E.W.: Guarded commands, nondeterminacy and formal derivation of programs. Comm. ACM 18, 453-457 (1975)

[6] GOGUEN, J.A.: On homomorphisms, correctness, termination, unfoldments and equivalence of flow diagram programs. J. Comput. Syst. Sci. 8, 333-365 (1974)

[7] HITCHCOCK, P., PARK, D.: Induction rules and termination proofs. In: Nivat, M. (ed.): Automata, languages and programming. Proc. of a Symp. organized by IRIA, 3.-7. Juli 1972, Rocquencourt, North-Holland, Amsterdam, 1973, p. 225-251

[8] SCHMIDT, G.: Programme als partielle Graphen. Inst. für Informatik der Techn. Univ. München, Habilitationsschrift 1977 und Bericht 7813, 1978

ON THE POWER OF RANDOM ACCESS MACHINES

Arnold Schönhage
Mathematisches Institut der Universität Tübingen, Germany

Abstract. We study the power of deterministic successor RAM's with extra instructions like $+, *, \div$ and the associated classes of problems decidable in polynomial time. Our main results are $\mathrm{NP} \subseteq \mathrm{PTIME}(+,*,\div)$ and $\mathrm{PTIME}(+,*) \subseteq \mathrm{RP}$, where RP denotes the class of problems randomly decidable (by probabilistic TM's) in polynomial time.

1. Random Access Machines

All RAM models considered here have countably many storage locations with addresses $0,1,2,\ldots,n,\ldots$ each of which can store a natural number denoted by $\langle n \rangle$, and an extra accumulator register with current contents z. Initially, $z = 0$ and $\langle n \rangle = 0$ for all n. For input and output the alphabet $\{0,1\}$ is used. The finite control is always given by a deterministic program written as a sequence of labels and instructions.

All RAM's will have the following common instructions:

goto λ ;	control is transferred to label λ ;
input λ_0, λ_1 ;	the next input symbol β is read and causes branching to λ_β ; if the input string is exhausted, the next instruction is performed;
output α ;	$\alpha \in \{0,1\}$ is output;
halt;	the RAM halts;
a-load n ;	$z := n$;
load n ;	$z := \langle n \rangle$;
i-load n ;	$z := \langle\langle n \rangle\rangle$;
store n ;	$\langle n \rangle := z$;
i-store n ;	$\langle\langle n \rangle\rangle := z$;
equal n ;	if $z = \langle n \rangle$ then $z := 0$ else $z := 1$;
skip;	the next instruction is skipped iff $z = 0$;
suc;	$z := z + 1$;

This list describes the class of the so-called <u>successor</u> RAM's , denoted by $\mathcal{M}_0$. Their relationship to Turing machines and storage modification machines is thoroughly investigated in [4] . Now we are interested in the additional power of RAM's having some <u>extra instructions</u> from the following list:

<u>less</u>	n ;	$<$	if $z < \langle n \rangle$ then $z := 0$ else $z := 1$;
<u>add</u>	n ;	$+$	$z := z + \langle n \rangle$;
<u>sub</u>	n ;	$\dot{-}$	$z := \max\{0, z - \langle n \rangle\}$;
<u>mult</u>	n ;	$*$	$z := z * \langle n \rangle$;
<u>div</u>	n ;	$\div$	$z := \lfloor z/\langle n \rangle \rfloor$; <u>halt</u>, if $\langle n \rangle = 0$;
<u>shift</u>	n ;	$\leftarrow$	$z := \lfloor z/2^{\langle n \rangle} \rfloor$;
<u>and</u>	n ;	$\wedge$	$z := z \wedge \langle n \rangle$, where both operands are considered as binary strings.

Observe that (in contrast to other authors in this field) we prefer to consider general comparisons like <u>less</u> as extra instructions, whereas the instruction <u>equal</u> belongs to the basic features of our RAM's , since it can be simulated in real-time by means of indirect addressing (see [4]).

2. Simulations

Let $\mathcal{M}(Q)$ denote the class of all RAM's with the common instructions (as listed in 1.) and the extra instructions belonging to Q ; thus, for instance, $\mathcal{M}(+,\dot{-},*)$ contains all RAM's with the extra instructions <u>add</u>, <u>sub</u>, <u>mult</u>; and $\mathcal{M}(\emptyset) = \mathcal{M}_0$.

A RAM M_2 is said to simulate M_1 in polynomial (linear, real) time, denoted by $M_1 \xrightarrow{p} M_2$ ($M_1 \xrightarrow{l} M_2$, $M_1 \xrightarrow{r} M_2$), if there exists a constant c such that for every input $x = x_1x_2 \ldots x_n$ the following holds: if x causes M_1 to read an input symbol, or to print an output symbol, or to halt at time steps $0 = s_0 < s_1 < \ldots < s_\ell$, respectively, then x will cause M_2 to act in the very same way with regard to those external instructions at time steps $0 = t_0 < t_1 < \ldots < t_\ell$, where $t_\ell \le c s_\ell^c$ (rsp. $t_\ell \le c \cdot s_\ell$ for linear time, $t_j - t_{j-1} \le c(s_j - s_{j-1})$ for $1 \le j \le \ell$ in the real time case).

For machine classes $\mathcal{M}_1$, $\mathcal{M}_2$ we define <u>polynomial reducibility</u> $\mathcal{M}_1 \xrightarrow{p} \mathcal{M}_2$ by the condition that for each $M_1 \in \mathcal{M}_1$ there exists a machine $M_2 \in \mathcal{M}_2$ such that $M_1 \xrightarrow{p} M_2$. $\mathcal{M}_1 \xrightarrow{l} \mathcal{M}_2$ and $\mathcal{M}_1 \xrightarrow{r} \mathcal{M}_2$ are defined similarly. For the class $\mathcal{T}_1$ of all multitape Turing machines we know

$$\mathcal{T}_1 \xrightarrow{r} \mathcal{M}_0 \xrightarrow{r} \mathcal{M}(+,\dot{-},<,\wedge) \xrightarrow{p} \mathcal{T}_1 , \tag{2.1}$$

which yields the equivalences

$$\mathcal{T}_1 \xleftrightarrow{p} \mathcal{M}_0 \xleftrightarrow{p} \mathcal{M}(+,\dot{-},<,\wedge) . \tag{2.2}$$

On the other hand the speed-up theorem in [2, p. 63] shows that $\mathcal{M}(+) \xrightarrow{\ell} \mathcal{T}_1$ is not true.

Sometimes it will be possible to simulate an instruction directly without changing the internal representation of numbers; so we have $\mathcal{M}(<,F) \xrightarrow{r} \mathcal{M}(\dot{-},F)$ for arbitrary instruction sets F by observing that less n can be replaced by the instruction sequence suc; sub n; skip; a-load 1; in general, however, it is by no means clear whether $\mathcal{M}(Q_1) \xrightarrow{p} \mathcal{M}(Q_2)$ implies $\mathcal{M}(Q_1 \cup F) \xrightarrow{p} \mathcal{M}(Q_2 \cup F)$.

3. Polynomial classes

From the work on vector machines [1,3] it is known that

$$\mathrm{PSPACE}(\mathcal{T}_1) = \mathrm{PTIME}(\mathcal{M}(+,\dot{-},*,\wedge)) , \tag{3.1}$$

and that on this level non-determinism does not make any difference. Here we are mainly interested in classes below this level.

Theorem 1. $\mathrm{NPTIME}(\mathcal{T}_1) \subseteq \mathrm{PTIME}(\mathcal{M}(+,*,\leftarrow))$.

The proof is by constructing a machine $M \in \mathcal{M}(+,*,\leftarrow)$ which decides the satisfiability of propositional formulae in conjunctive normal form in polynomial time. Consider a conjunction $C \equiv D_1 \wedge D_2 \wedge \ldots \wedge D_m$ of disjunctions D_k in boolean variables $x_0, x_1, \ldots, x_{n-1}$ and their complements $\bar{x}_j$. We may assume that it is presented as a binary input of length L by some suitable encoding such that each atom x or $\bar{x}$ ocurring in one of the D's requires at least one bit. By thoroughly applying the or-and distributive law to $D_1 \wedge \ldots \wedge D_m$ a disjunctive expansion $C \equiv C_1 \vee C_2 \vee \ldots \vee C_R$ is obtained, i.e. the C_r are conjunctions in the x's and their complements. Assuming that D_k has d_k atoms and binary length L_k we get

$$R = \prod_k d_k \leq \prod_k L_k < \prod_k 2^{L_k} \leq 2^L . \tag{3.2}$$

Now the main idea is to simulate this expansion by means of the add-mult distributive law arithmetically.

After having read the input the machine M chooses minimal numbers β and λ such that

$$b = 2^{\beta} > m , \ \ell = 2^{\lambda} \geq L . \tag{3.3}$$

For each disjunction D_k it computes an arithmetic representation

$$A_k = \sum_{j=o}^{n-1} (\xi_{k,j} 2^{\ell b^{2j}} + \eta_{k,j} 2^{\ell b^{2j+1}}) , \tag{3.4}$$

where the ξ's and η's are chosen as zero or one according to

$$\begin{aligned} \xi_{k,j} &= 1 \quad \text{iff} \quad x_j \text{ occurs in } D_k , \\ \eta_{k,j} &= 1 \quad \text{iff} \quad \overline{x}_j \text{ occurs in } D_k . \end{aligned} \tag{3.5}$$

This requires (by means of successive squaring) not more than $\lambda + 2n\beta = O(L \log L)$ multiplications and $O(L)$ other steps. Then $m-1$ further multiplications yield the product

$$B = A_1 * A_2 * \dots * A_m = \sum_{p=o}^{b^{2n}-1} w_p 2^{\ell p} , \tag{3.6}$$

which is closely related to the disjunctive expansion mentioned above. By (3.2) and (3.3) we have

$$\sum_p w_p = R < 2^{\ell} . \tag{3.7}$$

If p has the b-ary expansion

$$p = \sum_{j=o}^{n-1} (u_{p,j} b^{2j} + v_{p,j} b^{2j+1}) \qquad (0 \le u_{p,j}, v_{p,j} < b) ,$$

then there are precisely w_p many conjunctions C_r which contain exactly $u_{p,j}$ times the variable x_j and $v_{p,j}$ times $\overline{x}_j$, so for $0 \le j < n$. Since C is satisfiable iff in the disjunctive expansion there is at least one C_r not containing x_j and $\overline{x}_j$ simultaneously for any j, we introduce the set of indices

$$S = \{p < b^{2n} \mid u_{p,j} v_{p,j} = 0 \quad \text{for all} \quad j \}$$

and arrive at the <u>criterion</u>:

$$C \text{ satisfiable} \quad \text{iff} \quad W = \sum_{p \in S} w_p > 0 . \tag{3.8}$$

In order to extract this sum from the expansion (3.6) we exploit the convolution property of multiplication by forming the product

$$G = B * F = \sum_s g_s 2^{\ell s} \qquad (0 \le g_s < 2^{\ell}) \tag{3.9}$$

where the "filter" number F is defined and computed as

$$F = \sum_{p \in S} 2^{\ell(nh-p)} = F_o * F_1 * \dots * F_{n-1} ,$$

with $h = b + b^2 + \ldots + b^{2n}$ and

$$F_j = 2^{\ell h} + \sum_{k=1}^{b-1} \left(2^{\ell(h-kb^{2j})} + 2^{\ell(h-kb^{2j+1})} \right) . \tag{3.10}$$

By means of

$$2^{\ell(h-kb^q)} = \left(\prod_{\substack{t=o \\ t\neq q}}^{2n-1} 2^{\ell b^{t+1}} \right) \cdot \left(2^{\ell b^q} \right)^{b-k}$$

these computations require at most $O(L^2)$ steps.
The binary expansion of G contains the test quantity $W = g_{nh}$ as a substring (see (3.9); inequality (3.7) excludes improper overflow). Therefore the machine finally computes

$$G' = \lfloor G/2^{nh\ell} \rfloor$$

and performs the test $W > 0$ by checking whether

$$\lfloor G'/2^{\ell} \rfloor * 2^{\ell} \neq G' .$$

This completes our proof of Theorem 1. The reader will have observed that it is only this final extraction of W, where the instruction shift ($\leftarrow$) is used. In order to compare the result of Theorem 1 with (3.1) we like to state several polynomial reducibilities among machine classes with different sets of extra instructions.

Theorem 2.

$$\begin{array}{ccccc}
 & & \mathcal{M}(+,\dot{-},*,\wedge) & \underset{(1)}{\overset{p}{\longleftrightarrow}} & \mathcal{M}(+,*,\wedge) \\
 & & (2)\uparrow p & & \uparrow p \\
\mathcal{M}(+,\dot{-},*,\div) & \underset{(3)}{\overset{p}{\longleftrightarrow}} & \mathcal{M}(+,\dot{-},*,\leftarrow) & \underset{(4)}{\overset{p}{\longleftrightarrow}} & \mathcal{M}(+,*,\leftarrow) .
\end{array}$$

Similar reductions have been given by others. One has to be very careful, however, since in our setting comparisons like less are not always available and indirect addressing cannot be eliminated in general.

By means of $\wedge$ and $\dot{-}$ all bitwise boolean operations can be implemented (after time t the masks $m_\ell = 2^\ell - 1$ can be computed for any $\ell \leq 2^t$ in time $O(t)$, even without $\dot{-}$ by use of $+$ and $*$ and $m_{2k} = m_k*(m_k+2)$, $m_{2k+1} = 2m_{2k} + 1$). The proof of (1) is based upon the observation that by $[m_\ell \wedge u = u$ iff $u < 2^\ell]$ the binary length of any number u can be determined economically. Now, for $u, v < 2^\ell$, proper subtraction $u \dot{-} v$ is achieved by computing $w = m_\ell \wedge ((m_\ell * v) + u)$, provided $v \leq u$. Otherwise we have $v > u$ and $u \dot{-} v = 0$. These two cases can be distinguished simply by checking whether $v+w = u$ holds.

The proof of (3) is by Newton iteration essentially, where $\leftarrow$ is used to furnish some kind of floating point arithmetic. So far direct simulations could be used, i.e. without changing the internal representation of numbers. For the reductions (2) and (4) we need a different technique which will be described in the next section; therefore we postpone the corresponding proofs.

We do not know whether the vertical arrows in Theorem 2 can be reversed (if so, then Theorem 1 would become a simple corollary of (3.1)). This question is closely related to the problem $NP \stackrel{?}{=} PSPACE$.

4. Further polynomial reducibilities

In view of Theorem 1 we are interested in the complexity levels below the second line of Theorem 2, i.e. we would like to answer the question-marks in

$$\mathcal{M}(+,*,\leftarrow) \underset{p}{\overset{?}{\longrightarrow}} \mathcal{M}(+,*) \underset{p}{\overset{?}{\longrightarrow}} \mathcal{M}_0 \,. \tag{4.1}$$

At first we discuss the second one. We consider straight line programs which begin with the instruction $x_0 := 0$ followed by computational steps of the form $x_k := x_i + 1$ or $x_k := x_i \;\underline{op}\; x_j$ (or $x_k := \underline{op}\; x_i$), where $0 \le i,j < k$, and $\underline{op}$ is any binary (or unary) operation in some finite set Q of extra instructions, so for $1 \le k \le n$; finally some index $r \le n$ is stated. (In this particular case we have to deal with $Q = \{+,*\}$). Such data are considered as generic descriptions for natural numbers like x_r or x_n. Let $COMP_=(+,*)$ or, more generally $COMP_=(Q)$ ($COMP_{\neq}(Q)$ resp.) denote the language of all such straight line programs (with given r) which fulfil $x_r = x_n$ ($x_r \neq x_n$, resp.). Beyond its own appeal the corresponding decision problem is linked to our previous discussion by

<u>Theorem 3.</u> $\mathcal{M}(Q_1) \xrightarrow{p} \mathcal{M}(Q_2)$ iff $COMP_=(Q_1) \in PTIME(\mathcal{M}(Q_2))$, in particular, $\mathcal{M}(+,*) \xrightarrow{p} \mathcal{M}_0$ iff $COMP_=(+,*) \in PTIME(\mathcal{M}_0)$.

A very similar result has been obtained by J. Simon ([5], Lemma 3.1). His proof, however, does not work in our case; it ignores the extra problems encountered with indirect addressing. We restrict our proof to the non-trivial part for the special case $Q_1 = \{+,*\}$, $Q_2 = \emptyset$, i.e. we assume that $COMP_=(+,*)$ is decidable in polynomial time by some machine $M_0 \in \mathcal{M}_0$ (or by some Turing machine, equivalently) and describe how to simulate any given machine $M \in \mathcal{M}(+,*)$ by a suitable $M' \in \mathcal{M}_0$ in polynomial time. (In view of (2.1) such an M' can be designed as to have all the string handling capabilities of a multi-tape Turing machine.)

When simulating M the machine M' generates a straight line program P (with current length k) such that all numbers produced by M internally are described by some initial segment of P. In addition a "contents" function c with domain D is maintained dynamically. D contains indices of those variables in P which are used (or have been used) as the address of a storage location of M. More precisely, $c(p)=q$ means $\langle x_p \rangle = x_q$, and for $p,s \in D$, $p \neq s$ shall always imply $x_p \neq x_s$. Similarly, an extra index r will indicate that x_r is the current accumulator value of M.

Initially, M' creates P as the straight line program

$$x_o := 0;\ x_1 := x_o + 1;\ \ldots\ x_m := x_{m-1} + 1;$$

where m denotes the maximum of 1 and all n's that occur as an explicit address in the program of M, and sets $k := m+1$; $r := 0$; $D := \{0,1,\ldots,m\}; c(p) := 0$ for all $p \in D$. Then M' simulates the steps of M as follows (we omit goto, ..., halt, which cause no problems here): a-load n is simulated by r:= n; load n by r := c(n); store n by c(n) := r; equal n by [q := c(n); if $x_r = x_q$ then r := 0 else r := 1]. In case of skip, M' skips the simulation of the next M-instruction iff $x_r = x_o$. With suc the straight line program P is prolonged by $x_k := x_r+1$; correspondingly for add n, or mult n, after q := c(n), P is prolonged by $x_k := x_r+x_q$, or $x_k := x_r*x_q$ resp.; then in all three cases M' does r := k; k := k+1.

The crucial point is, of course, the simulation if indirect addressing, namely i-load n by

[q := c(n); r := 0; for p ∈ D do if $x_p = x_q$ then r := c(p)],

and i-store n by

[q := c(n); for p ∈ D do if $x_p = x_q$ then goto fin ;
D := D ∪{q}; p := q ; fin: c(p) := r].

In order to perform the various comparisons $x_i \overset{?}{=} x_j$ used in the preceding simulations M' has to apply the decision procedure of M_o to corresponding segments of P. This will require a number of steps polynomial in the length of P, hence polynomial in the number of M-steps simulated, which (up to a constant) also bounds the current size of D. This completes our proof of Theorem 3.

For the subsequent discussion we need the following

Lemma. There exists a constant $c > 0$ such that for any numbers $x_r \neq x_n$ generated by some $(+,*)$-straight line program of length n there are more than $2^{cn}/cn$ numbers $m < 2^{cn}$ with $x_r \not\equiv x_n \bmod m$.

Proof. The number of primes $m < 2^{cn}$ not dividing $|x_r - x_n| < 2^{2^n}$ is at least $\pi(2^{cn}) - 2^n > 2^{cn}/cn$, so for all n with suitable $c > 0$.

As an immediate corollary we get

Theorem 4. $\mathrm{COMP}_{\neq}(+,*) \in \mathrm{NP}$.

The corresponding TM simply guesses an appropriate number $m < 2^{cn}$ and verifies $x_r \not\equiv x_m \bmod m$ (hence $x_r \neq x_m$) in polynomial time by executing the straight line program mod m.

We did not succeed in proving $\mathrm{COMP}_{=}(+,*) \in \mathrm{NP}$. This together with Theorem 4 would supplement Theorem 1 with the inclusion $\mathrm{PTIME}(\mathcal{M}(+,*)) \subseteq \mathrm{NP}$, as the proof of Theorem 3 shows. We are able, however, to establish an important relationship to the class RP of problems which are randomly decidable by probabilistic TM's in polynomial time (a paradigm for this type of problem is given in the pioneer paper [6]).

Theorem 5. For any $\varepsilon > 0$ there is a polynomial f such that for every $M \in \mathcal{M}(+,*)$ there exists a probabilistic Turing machine M' which simulates t steps of M in time $f(t)$ correctly with probability greater than $1 - \varepsilon$; therefore $\mathrm{PTIME}(\mathcal{M}(+,*)) \subseteq \mathrm{RP}$.

The proof is the same as for Theorem 3, except for the tests $x_i \stackrel{?}{=} x_j$. Here M' performs the k-th test, say $x_r \stackrel{?}{=} x_n$, by randomly choosing v_k many values of m, independently and equally distributed in $1 \leq m < 2^{cn}$. Then for each of these the n-th segment of the straight line program P is executed mod m; if $x_r \not\equiv x_n \bmod m$ is observed, then certainly $x_r \neq x_n$. Otherwise M' assumes $x_r = x_n$. By our lemma this assumption can be wrong only with probability less than

$$(1 - \frac{1}{cn})^{v_k} < \exp(-v_k/cn) < \varepsilon \cdot 2^{-k} \quad ,$$

if M' chooses $v_k = \lceil cn(k + \lg \frac{1}{\varepsilon}) \rceil$. Thus M' simulates M correctly with overall probability greater than $\prod_k (1 - \varepsilon/2^k) > 1 - \varepsilon$, and the running time of M' grows only polynomially in the number of M-steps (and in $\lg \frac{1}{\varepsilon}$).

Now we are able to appreciate the left-hand reduction in (4.1): if $\leftarrow$ could be eliminated at polynomial cost, then our Theorems 1 and 5 would imply $\mathrm{NP} \subseteq \mathrm{RP}$, a relationship of rather great significance. We see that the classes NP and RP are intimately related to the complexity levels induced by the extra instructions $+, *, \leftarrow, \wedge$.

Finally we have to append the proofs for (2) and (4) in Theorem 2, which will be based on Theorem 3 in its general form. With respect to (2) we consider a straight line program with instructions suc, $+$, $\dot{-}$, $*$, $\leftarrow$ and show that it can be simulated in polynomial time by a machine $M \in \mathcal{M}(+,\dot{-},*,\wedge)$ which represents each x_k by a pair (y_k, z_k) such that z_k is a power of 2 and $x_k z_k = y_k$ (a similar idea was used in [1]). M starts with $y_o := 0$, $z_o := 1$; then it simulates

$$x_k := x_i + 1 \quad \text{by} \quad z_k := z_i \; ; \qquad y_k := y_i + z_i \; ;$$

$$x_k := x_i + x_j \quad \text{by} \quad z_k := z_i * z_j \; ; \quad y_k := z_j * y_i + z_i * y_j \; ;$$

$$x_k := x_i \dot{-} x_j \quad \text{by} \quad z_k := z_i * z_j \; ; \quad y_k := z_j * y_i \dot{-} z_i * y_j \; ;$$

$$x_k := x_i * x_j \quad \text{by} \quad z_k := z_i * z_j \; ; \quad y_k := y_i * y_j \; ;$$

for $x_k := \lfloor x_i / 2^{x_j} \rfloor$ at first $x_j \geq 2^i$ is checked: if $2^i * z_j \dot{-} y_j = 0$ then $y_k := 0$; $z_k := 1$ (since $x_i < 2^{2^i}$) ; otherwise 2^{x_j} is determined by an extra computation within $O(i)$ steps and then
$z_k := z_i * 2^{x_j}$; $y_k := (2^{2^k} \dot{-} z_k) \wedge y_i$.

Finally $x_r = x_n$ can be answered by checking whether $z_n * y_r = z_r * y_n$.
With respect to the reduction (4) we show at first that for numbers $u \neq v$, $u, v < 2^{2^t}$ the comparison $u < v$ can be achieved in the following way (by means of $+, *, \leftarrow$): $O(t)$ steps of binary search yield the unique w such that $u' = \lfloor u/2^w \rfloor \neq \lfloor v/2^w \rfloor = v'$, but $\lfloor u/2^{w+1} \rfloor = \lfloor v/2^{w+1} \rfloor$; then $u < v$ iff $u' + 1 = v'$. Now it is fairly obvious how to simulate a straight line program with instructions suc, $+$, $\dot{-}$, $*$, $\leftarrow$ by representing each x_k as a pair (y_k, z_k) with $x_k + z_k = y_k$, except for the simulation of $x_k := \lfloor x_i / 2^{x_j} \rfloor$ which is a bit more delicate. Again it suffices to deal with the case $x_j < 2^i$, i.e. $y_j < 2^i + z_j$. Then x_j and 2^{x_j} are determined explicitly by $O(i)$ steps of binary search. The naive $y_k := \lfloor y_i / 2^{x_j} \rfloor$, $z_k := \lfloor z_i / 2^{x_j} \rfloor$ (computed by means of $\leftarrow$) does not always yield the desired result. After $y' := y_k * 2^{x_j}$, $z' := z_k * 2^{x_j}$ the correction $z_k := z_k + 1$ has to be applied iff $y_i + z' < y' + z_i$.
Finally $x_r = x_n$ can be answered by checking whether $z_n + y_r = z_r + y_n$.

References

[1] J. Hartmanis and J. Simon, On the power of multiplication in random access machines. IEEE Conf. Rec. 15th Symp. Switching Automata Theory (1974) 13-23.

[2] J. E. Hopcroft, W. J. Paul and L. G. Valiant, On time versus space and related problems. Proc. 16th Ann. IEEE Symp. Foundations Comp. Sci., Berkeley (1975) 57-64.

[3] V. Pratt, L. Stockmeyer, M. O. Rabin, A characterization of the power of vector machines. Proc. 6th Ann. ACM Symp. Theor. Comp. (1974) 122-134.

[4] A. Schönhage, Storage modification machines. Preprint, Universität Tübingen (1978), submitted to SIAM J. Comput.

[5] J. Simon, On feasible numbers. Proc. 9th ACM Symp. Theor. Comp., Boulder (1977) 195-207.

[6] R. Solovay, V. Strassen, A fast Monte-Carlo test for primality. SIAM J. Comput. 6 (1977), 84-85.

An Axiomatic Treatment of ALGOL 68 Routines

Richard L. Schwartz*

Department of Applied Mathematics
The Weizmann Institute of Science
Rehovot, Israel

Abstract

An axiomatic treatment of ALGOL 68 routines (procedures and functions) is presented. An approach to axiomatically defining the semantics of an expression-oriented language is first introduced. Using this, rules of inference for routines are given. The rules contain no aliasing restrictions, allow parameters of arbitrary modes including routines, treat full static scoping of identifiers, and allow side-effects to global variables. Attendant issues in language design and verification are also discussed.

1. Introduction

Recently completed dissertation research [Sch 78] by this author gives a formal axiomatic semantic definition of a major subset of ALGOL 68 [vWi 75, Tan 76, ScB 79]. This definition, roughly the same length as the axiomatic definition of EUCLID [Lam 77] defines an extraordinarily expressive language. At the same time, the axiomatic definition imposes no restrictions on the language. The elegant composition of semantics in ALGOL 68 makes it possible to handle, with very little additional effort, many features that have not been previously treated. The orthogonal design of the language permits a relatively small set of very general rules of inference to govern the semantics.

This paper focuses on the treatment of routines (the ALGOL 68 concept unifying the notions of "procedure" and "function"). Two forms of rules of inference for routines are given: a copy-rule [vWi 69] style rule for non-recursive routines and a rule of adaptation for potentially mutually recursive routines. In both cases, the rules allow unrestricted aliasing of names and routines as parameters. In addition, the rules treat full static binding of identifiers and allow assignment to global variables.

Before giving the rules of inference for routines, it is necessary to present background material on the axiomatic approach taken. Section two of this paper summarizes the variant of the axiomatic approach which is required to handle the

*This work was supported in part by an IBM Doctoral Fellowship at the University of California at Los Angeles, and in part by a Weizmann Post-Doctoral Fellowship at the Weizmann Institute of Science.

expression-oriented nature of ALGOL 68. Section three discusses several of the data type domains found in ALGOL 68. The general form of the axioms and rules of inference is introduced in Section four, followed by several axioms and rules of inference given in Section five for the fundamental ALGOL 68 constructs. Having provided a foundation for discussion of the axiomatic treatment of routines, the rules of inference for routines appear in Section six. A discussion of the treatment of aliasing within the rules of inference is found in Section seven. The paper concludes with some general remarks about language design and verification.

A less technical higher-level look at the ALGOL 68 axiom system and its treatment of routines appears in [Sch 79b].

2. Axiomatic Semantics for Expression-Oriented Languages

ALGOL 68 is an *expression-oriented* language resulting as a generalization of *statement-oriented* languages such as ALGOL 60 [Nau 63]. As a consequence of the ALGOL 68 design philosophy, centered around goals of generality and orthogonality of concepts, the distinction between statements and expressions has disappeared. Each "statement-construct" has been defined to return a value as a result of its *elaboration*, or execution. Thus the conventional notion of expression has been extended to include the embedding of IFTHENELSE, BEGINEND, assignments, etc. Those effects known as "side-effects" in other languages occur in a very natural way in ALGOL 68, namely, as secondary effects during elaboration of an expression.

Because of these secondary effects, the property of *referential transparency* of expressions, meaning that an expression in the language is fully characterized by the value which it denotes, does not hold in ALGOL 68. As a consequence, the commonly used axioms and rules of inference cannot be applied to ALGOL 68 programs. A variant of the Hoare-style axiomatic approach [Hoa 69] is therefore developed to serve as a basis for the definition of ALGOL 68.

The axiomatic approach presented here describes the semantics of a program by regarding the program as a composite expression, built up by embedding expressions within expressions. In order to do this, a syntactic translation is performed from normal program notation to a prefix notation. Such notation may be viewed as a linear representation of an *abstract syntax tree*.

Corresponding to Hoare's notion of a pre- and post-condition associated with each statement, we associate a pre- and post-condition with the application of each expression layer, that is, with each step in the evaluation of an expression. This is necessary since a change of state may result from the evaluation of an expression. Associated with *each occurrence of each expression* in the program there is a corresponding unique special variable $ב_i$ (the Hebrew letter vet) an element of an infinite indexed set of special variables $ב_N$.* An element of this set, $ב_i$,

*See footnote on the following page.

represents the value yielded by the evaluation of the i-th expression. In the abstract syntax tree, this corresponds to a unique association of each node in the tree with some element of $\beth$.

The association of an assertion about program variables and elements of $\beth$ with the application of each expression layer may be thought of as producing a *tagged abstract syntax tree*, in contrast to Floyd's notion [Flo 67] of a tagged flowchart.

As a small example, the prefix format for the assignment expression x:=a+b, together with its associated elements of $\beth$ are shown in Figure 1. Figure 2 then illustrates the corresponding tagged abstract syntax tree.

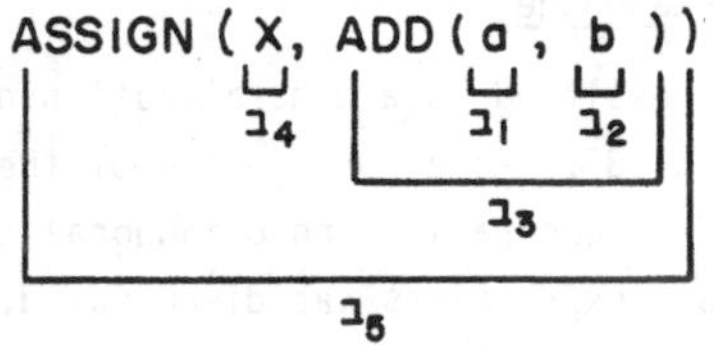

Fig. 1

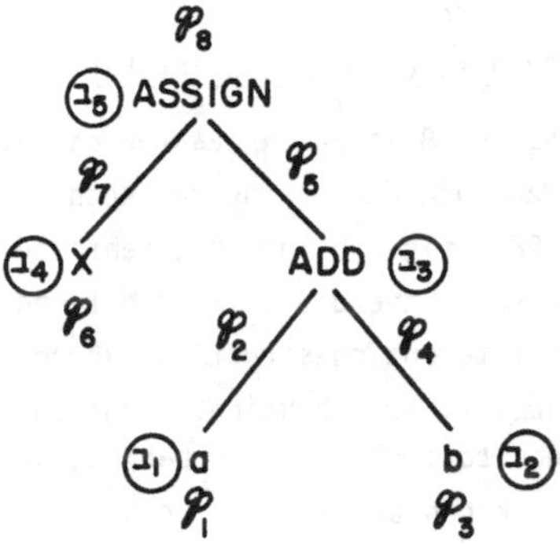

Fig. 2

3. Domain of Values

A unique set of values is defined to be associated with each *mode*, or data type, in ALGOL 68. For the sake of brevity, only the reference and routine modes are introduced.

3.1 References

Associated with each mode M occurring in the program is a unique infinite indexed domain

$P_{REF\ M} = \{d_{n,REF\ M} \mid n \in N\}$

where **N** is the set of non-negative integers.

Now REF M is defined by

Mode REF M = $P_{REF\ M} \cup \{NIL_{REF\ M}\}$

---

*Any suitable indexing domain may be used; for illustrative purposes we use the set of natural numbers here, and will use other domains as convenient. The particular association of the embedded expressions with the elements of $\beth$ is unimportant, as long as there is a unique correspondence between each expression in the program and an element of $\beth$.

where $NIL_{REF\ M}$ is the special variable for each mode M that does not refer to anything.

Furthermore, it is assumed that, for each mode M, there exists a unique logical variable

$$\tau_{REF\ M} \in [REF\ M \rightarrow M]$$

ranging over the set of all partial functions from REF M to M.

Intuitively, a mode REF M is (or is associated with) a set of *locations*, or *names*, each containing a value of mode M. The function $\tau_{REF\ M}$ maps the set of currently defined locations into their contents.

The dereferencing operation will be defined later as a rule of inference.

3.2 Routines

A routine value, a storable value in ALGOL 68, is characterized simply as a routine text rather than in a completely functional manner as a mapping from parameters and an environment to a resultant value and a new environment. Treating a routine value as a syntactic object will allow working completely within an axiomatic framework.

For a PROC mode with the n parameter-modes $M_1,\ldots,M_n$, and the (possibly VOID) return-value mode M_{n+1}:

$PROC(M_1,\ldots,M_n)M_{n+1}$ =

$$\{"(M_1\ i_1,\ldots,M_n\ i_n)M_{n+1}:e" \mid i_1,\ldots,i_n \in id \wedge e \in expr\}$$

where id is the set of all identifiers and expr is the set of all expressions.

3.4 Conditional and Formal Values

In order to produce a normal form for assertions about elements of ℶ, the domain of values is enlarged to include *conditional values* of the forms

$$(P \mid v)$$

and

$$v_1 \oplus v_2$$

where P is some predicate in the underlying logic, and v, v_1, and v_2 are *formal values*, being either denotations for values in our original domain or themselves conditional values.

Intuitively, $(P \mid v)$ is the value v when P is true and is undefined otherwise, while $v_1 \oplus v_2$ is either the value v_1 or the value v_2. Thus, one can read "$(P \mid v)$" as "IF P THEN v FI", and "$v_1 \oplus v_2$" as "v_1 or v_2".

More formally, these conditional values are introduced by means of the following definition:

(1) $op(v_1,\ldots,v_{i1} \oplus v_{i2},\ldots,v_n) = op(v_1,\ldots,v_{i1},\ldots,v_n) \oplus op(v_1,\ldots,v_{i2},\ldots,v_n)$

(2) $pred(v_1,\ldots,v_{i1} \oplus v_{i2},\ldots,v_n) = pred(v_1,\ldots,v_{i1},\ldots,v_n) \vee pred(v_1,\ldots,v_{i2},\ldots,v_n)$

(3) $pred(v_1,\ldots,(P \mid v_i),\ldots,v_n) = P \wedge pred(v_1,\ldots,v_i,\ldots,v_n)$

(4) $op(v_1,\ldots,(P|v_i),\ldots,v_n) = (P \mid op(v_1,\ldots,v_i,\ldots,v_n))$

where op and pred are n-ary operator and predicate symbols, for some $n \geq 1$.

The use of formal values allows assertions concerning values of elements of ℶ

to be expressed in the normal form $\beth_i$=v, where v is a formal value. This normal form is exploited to provide automatic simplification of assertions about $\beth$ within the rules of inference.

One additional value is added to the set of formal values: $\perp$ is used as an internal undefined value of no mode. This value resides solely in the proof system and has no interpretation in the program domain.

4. Assertions and Statements

Two types of predicates are distinguished. Predicate symbols P, Q, R, and S, with or without subscripts, denote predicates in the underlying theory and may not contain free occurrences of elements of $\beth$. Predicate symbols $\mathcal{P}, \mathcal{Q}, \mathcal{R}$ and $\mathcal{S}$ may contain free occurrences of elements of $\beth$.

Assertions in the language are of the form

$$N/\mathcal{Q}$$

where N∈NESTLS (see below) and $\mathcal{Q}$ is some formula in the extended logic. N/$\mathcal{Q}$ is defined to be true if $\mathcal{Q}$ is true in the standard first-order definition of truth for $\mathcal{Q}$, and N/$\mathcal{Q}$ is vacuously true for states inconsistent with the mode algebra derived from N. N/$\mathcal{Q}$ can be read as "$\mathcal{Q}$ being true with respect to N".

Sentences in the extended logic are of the form

$$N/P\{e\}\mathcal{Q}$$

where N∈NESTLS, while P and $\mathcal{Q}$ are formulas in the extended logic, and e is an expression in the considered ALGOL 68 subset. The statement is to be interpreted as "If P is true with respect to N and if the elaboration of the expression e halts, then $\mathcal{Q}$ is true with respect to N after elaboration of e."

A NESTL N is used to provide a correspondence between identifiers and modes and between derived modes and their definitions. This information can be used by a theorem prover to determine a mode algebra needed to establish properties to be associated with values and operations in the assertions.

A NESTL functions in much the same manner as the environment E component of the axiom systems of Gorelick [Gor 75], Clarke [Cla 77], and Fokkinga [Fok 77]. In the present system as well as in the previous systems, the additional "environment"* component has been brought in to contain the *static* properties of programs necessary for the proof. There is however an important distinction. In the languages explored by Gorelick, Clarke, and Fokkinga, the procedure type specification includes the body of the procedure. This allows them to statically link the procedure body with its name in the "environment". This cannot be done in ALGOL 68, since the routine

---

*There is a deliberate avoidance of naming such a concept in the present system an "environment". The use of the term would seem to be inconsistent with the notion of an environment in both denotational semantics and ALGOL 68 terminology where an environment is a mapping from identifiers to locations. It is therefore preferable to use NESTL, an invented term close to the ALGOL 68 concept of a NEST, a layered correspondence of identifiers with modes at each nesting level (leaving out a few details...).

value referred to by a variable ranging over routine values is not constant. Similarly, the bounds of an array (multiple value) are part of the value and not of the type.

A copy-rule style of renaming is used in order to formalize rules of scope. One of the goals of this research is to define an explicit careful treatment of the *full static scoping rules*. As recent papers exploring consistency and completeness issues have discovered, formalizing the correspondence between declaration and reference within the proof system is important. Furthermore, it was not considered desirable to formalize static scope rules by adding sufficient constraints to the language to cause static scoping and dynamic scoping to be coincident.

Following Clarke [Cla 76], the copy-rule of the present system renames all locally declared identifiers with fresh identifiers upon encountering a block.* The renaming extends into inner ranges; fortunately, ALGOL 68 scope rules guarantee that proper renaming of locally declared identifiers in inner ranges occurs before they are encountered. Clarke's results have been generalized to handle the semantic issues present in ALGOL 68.

5. Preliminary Rules of Inference

In this section we introduce axioms and rules of inference for several of the fundamental ALGOL 68 constructs.

5.1 Denotations

$N \;/\; P \;\{c\}\; P \wedge \beth = c$

where c is a denotation (constant) defined by the Report.

5.2 Identifiers

The elaboration of an identifier *yields*, or returns, the value which has been *ascribed*, or bound, to the identifier. Thus:

$N \;/\; P \wedge \mathrm{ascribed}(x,v) \;\{x\}\; P \wedge \mathrm{ascribed}(x,v) \wedge \beth = v$

where v is a formal value, and ascribed(x,v) is a predicate asserting that the identifier x is ascribed the value v.

5.2.1 Ascription. The following property is assumed to be true of ascribed(x,v):

$$\mathrm{ascribed}(x,v_1) \wedge \mathrm{ascribed}(x,v_2) \supset v_1 = v_2 \;.$$

5.3 Dereferencing

$$\frac{N \;/\; P \;\{e\}\; Q \wedge \beth_e = d_M}{N \;/\; P \;\{\mathrm{DEREF}(e)\}Q \wedge \beth = \tau_M(d_M)}$$

where d_M is a formal reference value of mode M.

---

*Clarke's approach is altered to prohibit assertions about identifiers outside the range in which they are declared.

5.4 Identity Declarations

$$\frac{N \,/\, P \,\{e\}\, Q \wedge \beth_e = v}{N \,/\, P \,\{M \,i{=}e\}\, Q \wedge \mathrm{ascribed}(i,v) \wedge \beth = \bot}$$

where v is a formal value.

The relationship between identifiers and values (including variables) is established via an identity declaration of the form M i=e. The effect of the elaboration of the identity declaration is to ascribe (for the duration of the enclosing block) the yield of the elaboration of e to the identifier i. We define the identity declaration to yield the internal undefined value $\bot$, of no mode. Such a declaration unifies the notions of constant declaration, variable declaration, procedure declaration, and function declaration which occur in other languages.

5.5 Closed Clauses

A closed clause BEGIN expression-sequence END, or equivalently BEGINEND(e) in the abstract syntax, has the following rule of inference:

$$\frac{N' \,/\, P \,\{e[\mathrm{LIDS}(e) \leftarrow \mathrm{LIDS}'(e)]\}\, Q \wedge \beth_e = v}{N \,/\, P \,\{\mathrm{BEGINEND}(e)\}\, Q \wedge \beth = v}$$

where LIDS'(e) is a set (described below) of identifiers which do not appear in P, e, Q, or N, and N' = N ∪ LAYER(e) [LIDS(e) ← LIDS'(e)] .

The set LIDS(e) contains all identifiers declared at the outermost nesting level of e; LIDS'(e) is a corresponding set of fresh (with respect to the specified context) identifiers. LAYER(e) then contains the mapping from the locally declared renamed identifiers to their declared modes. The notations e[y←t] and s[y←t] are used to mean the proper substitution of the term t for the logical variable y in the expression e and set s, respectively.

The premise in the rule of inference asserts that, with precondition P, after the elaboration of e, with all locally declared identifiers renamed with unique (for that context) names, the post-condition $Q \wedge \beth_e = v$ is true. This is to be true with respect to the context surrounding the BEGINEND, updated with the identifier and mode correspondence for the newly declared and renamed identifiers in e.

6. Rules of Inference for Routines

6.1 Copy-Rule Semantics

Two copy-rule style rules of inference are given for routine calls where it can be determined that there is no possibility of a recursive call.

In the simplest case, where the expression yielding a routine value is an identifier which is ascribed a routine text (i.e., a routine constant), the rule is:

(Routine Copy-Rule)

$N \,/\, P \,\{\mathrm{COLLAT}(e_1,\ldots,e_n)\}\, R \wedge \beth_{e_1} = v_1 \wedge \ldots \wedge \beth_{e_n} = v_n$

$$N \;/\; R\ \{\text{BEGIN } M_1\ i_1 = v_1,\ldots,M_n\ i_n = v_n;e \text{ END}\}\ Q \wedge \beth_1 = v$$

$$N \;/\; P \wedge \text{ascribed}(p,w)\ \{p(e_1,\ldots,e_n)\}\ Q \wedge \beth = v$$

where w is a non-conditional routine value of the form "$(M_1\ i_1,\ldots,M_n\ i_n)M_{n+1}$:e", and v is a formal value.

COLLAT($e_1,\ldots,e_n$) specifies the *collateral elaboration* of its n component expressions, resulting in the treatment of the expressions as asynchronous parallel processes. (For brevity, a treatment of collaterality has been omitted here; a formal treatment appears in [Sch 78, Sch 79a].)

The above rule expresses the fact that a routine call, with expressions $e_1,\ldots,e_n$ yielding the values $v_1,\ldots,v_n$ of the actual parameters, is equivalent to the elaboration of the closed clause in which n identity declarations are collaterally elaborated (indicated in the second premise by the separation of the expressions by commas), causing the values $v_1,\ldots,v_n$ to be ascribed to formal parameter identifiers $i_1,\ldots,i_n$, with the subsequent elaboration of the routine body.* Thus, the effect is to copy the routine body into the program text at the point of every call, after ascribing actual parameter values to formal parameter identifiers. There is no restriction that the expressions $e_1,\ldots,e_n$ yield distinct values or that global identifiers may not be passed as actual parameters. Additionally, the notions of "passing by value," "passing by reference," and "passing by name," are all possible in ALGOL 68, and are handled by modification of the modes of the formal parameters. This is discussed more fully in Section 7.

In the more general case, where an arbitrary expression yields the routine value rather than an identifier-ascribed routine constant, the following rule holds:

(Routine Copy-Rule)

$$N \;/\; P\ \{\text{COLLAT}(e,e_1,\ldots,e_n)\}\ ((P_1 \wedge \beth_e = w_1) \vee \ldots \vee (P_m \wedge \beth_e = w_m)) \wedge \beth_{e_1} = x_1 \wedge \ldots \wedge \beth_{e_n} = x_n$$

$$N \;/\; P_1\{\text{BEGIN } M_1\ i_{11} = x_1,\ldots,M_n\ i_{1n} = x_n;b_1 \text{ END}\}\ Q_1 \wedge \beth_1 = v_1,$$

$$\vdots$$

$$N \;/\; P_m\ \{\text{BEGIN } M_1\ i_{m1} = x_1,\ldots,M_n\ i_{mn} = x_n;b_m \text{ END}\}\ Q_m \wedge \beth_m = v_m$$

$$N \;/\; P\ \{e(e_1,\ldots,e_n)\}\ (Q_1 \vee \ldots \vee Q_m) \wedge \beth = (Q_1|v_1)\oplus\ldots\oplus(Q_m|v_m)$$

where w_j, for $1 \le j \le m$, is a non-conditional routine value of the form "$M_1\ i_{j1},\ldots, M_n\ i_{jn})M_{n+1}:b_j$", where b_j is an expression, and $v_1,\ldots,v_m$, $x_1,\ldots,x_n$ are formal values.

It is necessary to force a disjunction of non-conditional values for $w_1,\ldots,w_m$ in order to prove different properties in each case. One must prove an assertion

---

*For those well versed in ALGOL 68: we have chosen to consider the cast, converting the yield of e to mode M_{n+1} as part of e rather than being applied to the entire entire closed clause, as implied in the Report.

related to the effect of each routine value which could be yielded by the elaboration of e. This leads to the m proofs in the premise, showing the effect of each of the m possible routine values resulting from the elaboration of e.

Recall that while the modes of the formal parameter identifiers are part of the mode of the routine, the identifiers themselves are not. Thus each of the m routine values could have different formal parameter identifiers.

6.2 Rule of Adaptation Semantics

We now introduce rules of inference which use a rule of adaptation to define the semantics of routine calls. The approach taken here is different from previous adaptation style rules (e.g., [Hoa 71, Gut 78, Car 78]) in several ways; the most important being that the present abstract characterization of a routine assumes dummy *values* for formal parameters rather than dummy identifiers. Thus the abstract characterization must be sufficiently strong to show the effect of the routine with all possible combinations of parameter values of the appropriate modes. It is shown later how this characterization, in conjunction with the parameter binding mechanism present in ALGOL 68, causes aliasing of parameters not to be a problem.

The first rule is an induction rule, allowing derivation of abstract characterizations $w_i(\bar{x}_i)$ for a system of mutually recursive routines:

(Induction Rule)

$$N_1/P_1\ \{w_1(x_{11},\dots,x_{1n_1})\}\ Q_1 \wedge \beth_1 = v_1,\dots,N_m/P_m\ \{w_m(x_{m1},\dots,x_{mn_m})\}\ Q_m \wedge \beth_m = v_m$$

$\vdash$

$$N_1/P_1\ \{\text{BEGIN } M_{11}\ i_{11} = x_{11},\dots,M_{1n_1}\ i_{1n_1} = x_{1n_1}; e_1 \text{ END}\}\ Q_1 \wedge \beth_1 = v_1\ ,$$

$\vdots$

$$N_m/P_m\ \{\text{BEGIN } M_{m1}\ i_{m1} = x_{m1},\dots,M_{mn_m}\ i_{mn_m} = x_{mn_m}; e_m \text{ END}\}\ Q_m \wedge \beth_m = v_m$$

$$N_1/P_1\ \{w_1(\bar{x}_1)\}\ Q_1 \wedge \beth_1 = v_1,\dots,N_m/P_m\ \{w_m(\bar{x}_m)\}\ Q_m \wedge \beth_m = v_m$$

where each w_j, for $1 \le j \le m$, is a non-conditional routine value of the form "$(M_{j1}\ i_{j1},\dots,M_{jn_j}\ i_{jn_j})M_{jn_j+1}:e_j$", $\bar{x}_j$ are vectors of logical variables ranging over formal values of the modes determined by the parameter mode declarations in w_j, and $v_1,\dots,v_m$ are formal values.

For non-recursive routines, the above rule reduces to:

(Induction Rule)

$$N/P\ \{\text{BEGIN } M_1\ i_1 = x_1,\dots,M_n\ i_n = x_n; e \text{ END}\}\ Q \wedge \beth_1 = v$$

$$N/P\ \{w(\bar{x})\}\ Q \wedge \beth = v$$

where w is a non-conditional routine value of the form "$(M_1\ i_1,\dots,M_n\ i_n)M_{n+1}:e$" and $\bar{x}$ is a vector of logical variables ranging over formal values of the modes determined by the parameter declaration in w, and v is a formal value.

The induction rule is similar in intent to that of Clarke [Cla 77], with the principal difference being that the present rule deals with proving properties of routines with arbitrary *values* for parameters rather than with the routine's formal parameter identifiers. In addition, the effect of the routine is defined in terms of the effect caused by the constructed BEGINEND closed clause. The rule thus uses the identity declarations to implement the linkage between the actual values and formal parameter identifiers.

The abstract characterization derived via the above rules is referred to as an *in situ* characterization in distinction to the more commonly used *in vacuo* characterization, since the characterization is to be true with respect to a particular NESTL.

Given a routine characterization derived using the above rules, several rules are now given which can be used to transform the characterization obtained via the Induction Rule to fit the desired proof.

First a substitution rule:

(Substitution)

$$\frac{N/P\ \{e\}\ Q \wedge \beth = v}{N/P\theta\ \{e\theta\}\ Q\theta \wedge \beth = v\theta}$$

for *any* substitution θ, of a logical term for a free logical variable in P, Q, e, and v, where modes are preserved.

Note that there are *no* restrictions concerning the choice of the logical terms to be substituted for the logical variables in P, Q, e, and v. The concepts of a *free set* introduced by Cook [Coo 76] and *active terms* introduced by Clarke [Cla 77] are not necessary in the present formulation. Arbitrary substitution of terms for variables is allowed – leaving open the possibility of aliased names and overlapping actual parameters. Ramifications of this possibility are discussed in Section 7.

The following rule allows enlarging the NESTL N with new identifiers and modes.

(NESTL Enlargement)

$$\frac{N_1/P\ \{e\}\ Q \wedge \beth = v}{N/P\ \{e\}\ Q \wedge \beth = v}$$

where N_1 is a subset of N and the relation N is a function.

The next rule expresses the fact that ascription of a value to an identifier is a permanent relationship (for a given block activation) and is unmodifiable.

(Ascription Invariance)

$$\frac{N/P\ \{e\}\ Q \wedge \beth = v}{N/P \wedge \mathrm{ascribed}(x,w)\ \{e\}\ Q \wedge \mathrm{ascribed}(x,w) \wedge \beth = v}$$

where v,w are formal values, and x is an identifier in N.

This rule can be justified on the basis of ALGOL 68 syntax rules, since ascription to the same identifier in the same reach more than once is syntactically disallowed.

The following rule is similar to the rules of adaptation given in [Gut 78] and [Car 78], but is used only to transform one in situ characterization into another.

(Transformation Consequence)

$$N/P\ \{w(\bar{v})\}\ Q \wedge \beth_1 = x$$

$$N/\forall\bar{z}((P \supset (Q \wedge \beth_1 = x)[mod(\bar{v},w,Q \wedge \beth_1 = x) \leftarrow mod'(\bar{v},w,Q \wedge \beth_1 = x)]) \supset$$
$$(R \supset (S \wedge \beth_1 = y)[mod(\bar{v},w,Q \wedge \beth_1 = x) \leftarrow mod'(\bar{v},w,Q \wedge \beth_1 = x)]))$$

$$N/R\ \{w(\bar{v})\}\ S \wedge \beth = y$$

where w is a non-conditional routine value, x, $\bar{v}$, and y are formal values, $\bar{z}$ is the set of free logical variables in P, Q, and x, $N'=N[mod(\bar{v},w,Q\wedge\beth_1=x)\leftarrow mod'(\bar{v},w,Q\wedge\beth_1=x)]$, and $mod(\bar{v},w,Q\wedge\beth_1=x)$ and $mod'(\bar{v},w,Q\wedge\beth_1=x)$ are the sets defined below.

The above rule basically allows the conclusion of $N/R\{w(\bar{v})\}S\wedge\beth=y$ provided that $N/P\{w(\bar{v})\}Q\wedge\beth_1=x$ and that the relationship between P and $Q\wedge\beth_1=x$ implies the desired relationship between R and $S\wedge\beth=y$. In order to have a consistent rule, it is necessary (in the usual manner) to rename in Q and S all variables (not identifiers) which could be modified by the procedure call. It is this set that is specified as $mod(\bar{v},w,Q\wedge\beth_1=x)$.

Intuitively, the set $mod(\bar{v},w,Q\wedge\beth_1=x)$ is a set of names (i.e., elements of REF M, for some M) which must include all names which could be modified by the routine call. This set consists of all names passed within the possibly conditional parameter values $\bar{v}$, as well as any names accessible via global identifiers present within the body of w. In order to have a consistent rule, it is necessary that all modifiable names free in $(Q\wedge\beth_1=x)$ be renamed with fresh names. The set $mod'(\bar{v},w,Q\wedge\beth_1=x)$ is then a set of fresh names corresponding to $mod(\bar{v},w,Q\wedge\beth_1=x)$ which do not appear in **N**, P, Q, or x.

More formally, the set $mod(\bar{v},w,Q\wedge\beth_1=x)$ is constructed as follows:

$mod(\bar{v},w,\mathcal{Q}) = parmod(v_1) \cup \ldots \cup parmod(v_n) \cup globmod(w,\mathcal{Q})$

where $\bar{v} = v_1,\ldots,v_n$

and

```
parmod(v) =
     if v is of the form (P | v1) for some P and v1
       then parmod(v1)
       else
         if v is of the form v1 ⊕ v2 for some v1 and v2
           then parmod(v1) ∪ parmod(v2)
           else
             if v∈REF M for some M
               then {v}
               else {}
```

and

$globmod(w,\mathcal{Q})$ = a set of names such that each name d_i appearing in $\mathcal{Q}$ that was created in a range enclosing w is included in the set.

The function parmod has been defined to return all names modifiable via actual parameter values, while globmod has been defined to return a set containing, at minimum, all names modifiable via global identifiers which appear in the assertion $\mathcal{Q}$.

The final rule of inference adapts an in situ characterization to a particular routine call. In the simple case, where an identifier yields a non-conditional routine value to be applied, the rule is:

(Routine Expression Adaptation)

$$N/P\ \{COLLAT(e_1,\ldots,e_n)\}\ Q \wedge \beth_{e_1} = v_1 \wedge \ldots \wedge \beth_{e_n} = v_n$$

$$N/Q\ \{w(\bar{v})\}\ R \wedge \beth_1 = x$$

$$N/P \wedge ascribed(p,w)\ \{p(e_1,\ldots,e_n)\}\ R \wedge \beth = x$$

where w is a non-conditional routine value of the form "$(M_1\ i_1,\ldots,M_n\ i_n)M_{n+1}:e$", and $v_1,\ldots,v_n$ and x are formal values.

The first premise to the rule expresses the effect of evaluating the actual parameter expressions to obtain actual parameter values. The second premise then asserts that the routine value applied to *those* parameter values has the desired post-condition. The previous rules of inference for routines would be used to prove the second premise.

In the general case, where an arbitrary expression yielding a routine value is used, the rule is:

(Routine Expression Adaptation)

$$N/P\ \{COLLAT(e,e_1,\ldots,e_n)\}\ ((Q_1 \wedge \beth_e = w_1) \vee \ldots \vee (Q_m \wedge \beth_e = w_m))$$

$$\wedge\ \beth_{e_1} = v_1 \wedge \ldots \wedge \beth_{e_n} = v_n$$

$$N/Q_1\ \{w_1(\bar{v})\}\ R_1 \wedge \beth_1 = x_1,\ldots,N/Q_m\ \{w_m(\bar{v})\}\ R_m \wedge \beth_1 = x_m$$

$$N/P\ \{e(e_1,\ldots,e_n)\}\ (R_1 \vee \ldots \vee R_m) \wedge \beth = (R_1|x_1) \oplus \ldots \oplus (R_m|x_m)$$

where w_j, for $1 \leq j \leq m$, is a non-conditional routine value of the form "$(M_1\ i_{j1},\ldots,M_n\ i_{jn})M_{n+1}:e_j$", and $\bar{v}=v_1,\ldots,v_n$ and $x_1,\ldots,x_m$ are formal values.

Thus, one must show the effect of each possible routine value that is yielded by the elaboration of e on the actual parameter values $\bar{v}$.

The basic strategy for proving an assertion involving a routine call $e(e_1,\ldots,e_n)$ is as follows. First establish an in situ characterization for each of the routines possibly involved in the call. Then, using Substitution, substitute actual parameter values for dummy parameter values in the in situ characterizations. Following this, using NESTL Enlargement and Ascription Invariance, enlarge the NESTL N from that present at each routine declaration to the NESTL present at the call, and add ascription relationships for identifiers visible at the point of the call and not visible at the declarations. The next step is to use Transformation Consequence to attempt to reconcile the previously proved behavior with the desired behavior. Having done that, Routine Expression Adaptation can be used to conclude the desired post-condition (if it is a valid conclusion).

7. The Treatment of Aliasing

The existence of more than one name for a given location, known as *aliasing*, has traditionally led to the failure of axiomatic proof techniques. In a language such as PASCAL [Wir 71], aliasing can occur by passing an overlapping set of actual by-reference parameters, or by passing an accessed global variable as an actual parameter. In order to obtain a consistent rule of inference for procedures, most rules simply state that actual parameters passed by reference must themselves be distinct and must be different from the set of global variables visible from within the procedure body. In general, of course, such a restriction requires a transitive closure algorithm and run-time checks to enforce. The programming language EUCLID was the first to take steps to prohibit aliasing as part of the language definition rather than as a requirement for proving properties of the program. In the case where aliasing cannot be ruled out by the compiler, a *legality assertion* is inserted into the object code, causing a run-time validation to occur.

Such a treatment is unnecessary and in fact will not work for ALGOL 68. *Aliasing is a natural integral part of ALGOL 68.* The simplest way to create an alias in ALGOL 68 is via an identity declaration such as

REF INT x = y .

The effect of this is for the name ascribed to the identifier y to be ascribed to the identifier x. Thus, x becomes an alias for y.

In ALGOL 68, unlike PASCAL and other languages, a strict distinction is made between identifiers and variables. An identifier is an *external object* appearing in the program text. A variable is an *internal value* of mode REF M for some mode M, that refers to another value. There is no assumption that a variable, or any other value, is ascribed to only one identifier — thus there is no opportunity for the programmer to be "misled".

The generalized identity declaration leads to a simple and powerful mechanism for the declaration of identifiers and the binding of routine parameters. We have already pointed out that the notions of constant declaration, variable declaration, procedure declaration and function declaration are all subsumed by the identity declaration. In addition, using the same mechanism for parameter binding, one gets a general capability for passing values by value, by reference, by name or at any other level in the reference hierarchy. The method of parameter passing is indicated via the declared modes of the formal parameter identifiers *not* merely via a keyword in the procedure heading as in PASCAL or EUCLID. Thus the method of parameter passing manifests itself as a different semantic domain, allowing an integrated solution.

As a result of the binding of actual parameter values to formal parameter identifiers being accomplished via the elaboration of identity declarations, there is no problem caused by ascribing the same actual parameter value to more than one formal parameter identifier. Aliasing is neatly handled by the construction of underlying domains, together with a suitable definition of the *update* function.

This solution to the aliasing issue, outlined herein and described more fully in [Sch 78, 79b] handles unrestricted aliasing without any addition to either the proof theory or to the language. The characterization of the effect of a routine now explicitly includes the situation in which one or more aliased names exist.

Two other approaches for handling aliasing have been suggested. Cartwright and Oppen [Car 78] propose proof rules for modified PASCAL-like procedures which allow aliasing. They do this by introducing two additional notions in the verification theory and a change in the PASCAL procedure parameter mechanism. The verification change consists of the addition of an *access sequence* as a value and the use of an *updated formula*, denoting a possibly non-disjoint "simultaneous" substitution.

A set of rather complex rules is given to convert updated formulas into formulas in the standard logic. In addition, they conclude that PASCAL syntax for passing procedure parameters by reference is misleading and conflicts with their intended treatment of aliased reference parameters. They propose that each reference parameter be modified to use pointer syntax and semantics. Such semantics are, of course, already an integral part of ALGOL 68.

The other approach, presently under investigation [Lon 78] by the ALPHARD [Wul 76] group, is to keep the standard verification rules but to carry out separate proofs for each possible combination of aliased names. They propose verification of a set of modified routine bodies where, in each case, some number of identifiers are textually substituted for their aliases. Such a solution, while allowing verification with existing software verification systems, seems to be somewhat inelegant and unwieldy. In addition, the proof system outlined herein has as an upper-bound the work required by the ALPHARD approach.

8. Final Comments

There seems to be a trend in the past few years toward programming language design centered around large numbers of special case rules, each designed to provide one particular capability or feature, while at the same time attempting to eliminate those unpleasant synergistic effects which arise as a result of the interaction of the set of rules. Such a design policy leads to complex unwieldy languages such as the recent four DOD1 language proposals [DOD 78 abcd]. The ALGOL 68 design goal of orthogonality, with a small number of very general rules governing the semantics, seems to be a valuable paradigm to keep in mind in the design of future languages. Indeed, while there are some valid criticisms which one can level at both the ALGOL 68 committee and the Revised Report on ALGOL 68, there are also a great number of lessons in the area of programming language design that can be learned from ALGOL 68.

Acknowledgments

The author wishes to thank Daniel M. Berry, Ralph London, Dave Musser, Shaula Yemini and Susan Schwartz for discussions concerning this work.

References

[Car 78] Cartwright, R., D. Oppen. "Unrestricted Procedure Calls in Hoare's Logic," *Proceedings of the Fifth Annual ACM Symposium on Principles of Programming Languages*, Tuscon, Arizona, January 1978.

[Cla 76] Clarke, E. "Pathological Interaction of Programming Language Features," Computer Science Department, Duke University, Report CS-1976-15, September 1976.

[Cla 77] Clarke, E. "Programming Language Constructs for which it is Impossible to Obtain Good Hoare-like Axiom Systems," *Proceedings of the Fourth ACM Symposium on Principles of Programming Languages*, Los Angeles, January 1977.

[Coo 76] Cook, S.A. "Soundness and Completeness of an Axiom System for Program Verification," Computer Science Department, University of Toronto, Report 95, June 1976.

[DOD 78a] Department of Defense. *Blue Programming Language Specification*, February 1978.

[DOD 78b] Department of Defense. *Green Programming Language Specification*, February 1978.

[DOD 78c] Department of Defense. *Red Programming Language Specification*, February 1978.

[DOD 78d] Department of Defense. *Yellow Programming Language Specification*, February 1978.

[Flo 67] Floyd, R.W. "Assigning Meanings to Programs," *Proceedings of the Symposium of Applied Mathematics*, 19, in J.T. Schwartz, Editor, *Mathematical Aspects of Computer Science*, pp. 19-32, American Mathematical Society, Providence, Rhode Island, 1967.

[Fok 77] Fokkinga, M. "Axiomatization of Declarations and the Formal Treatment of an Escape Construct," IFIP Technical Committee 2 Meeting, Toronto Canada, August 1977.

[Gor 75] Gorelick, G. "A Complete Axiomatic System for Proving Assertions about Recursive and Non-Recursive Programs," Computer Science Department, University of Toronto, Report 75, January 1975.

[Gut 78] Guttag, J., J. Horning, R. London. "A Proof Rule for EUCLID Procedures," in E. Neuhold, Editor, *Formal Description of Programming Concepts*, North Holland Publishing Company, 1978.

[Hoa 69] Hoare, C.A.R. "An Axiomatic Basis for Computer Programming," *Communications of the ACM*, 12:10, October 1969.

[Hoa 71] Hoare, C.A.R. "Procedures and Parameters: An Axiomatic Approach," *Symposium on Semantics of Algorithmic Languages*, E. Engeler, Editor, Springer Verlag, pp. 102-116, 1971.

[Lam 77] Lampson, B., et al. "Report on the Programming Language EUCLID," *SIGPLAN Notices*, 12:2, 1977.

[Lon 78] London, R., private communication, August 1978.

[Nau 63] Naur, P., Editor. "Revised Report on the Algorithmic Language ALGOL 60," *Communications of the* ACM, 6:3, March 1963.

[Owi 75] Owicki, S. *Axiomatic Proof Techniques for Parallel Programs*, Ph.D. Dissertation, Cornell University, Ithaca, New York, 1975.

[Sch 78] Schwartz, R. "An Axiomatic Semantic Definition of ALGOL 68," Computer Science Department, University of California at Los Angeles, UCLA-34-P214-75, August 1978 (Ph.D. Dissertation).

[Sch 79a] Schwartz, R. "An Axiomatic Treatment of Asynchronous Parallel Processes in ALGOL 68," submitted for publication, January 1979.

[Sch 79b] Schwartz, R. "On Axiomatizability as a Language Design Tool," January 1979.

[ScB 79] Schwartz, R., D. Berry. "A Semantic View of ALGOL 68," *Journal of Computer Languages*, Vol. 4, No. 1, 1979.

[Tan 76] Tanenbaum, A. "A Tutorial on ALGOL 68," ACM *Computing Surveys*, Vol. 8, No. 2, June 1976.

[vWi 69] van Wijngaarden, A., Editor. "Report on the Algorithmic Language ALGOL 68," *Numerische Mathematik*, 14, pp. 79-218, 1969.

[vWi 75] van Wijngaarden, A., et al., Editor. "Revised Report on the Algorithmic Language ALGOL 68," *Acta Informatica*, 5, 1975.

[Wir 71] Wirth, N. "The Programming Language PASCAL," *Acta Informatica*, 1, pp. 35-63, 1971.

[Wul 76] Wulf, W., R.L. London, M. Shaw. "Abstraction and Verification in ALPHARD: Introduction to Language and Methodology," Information Sciences Institute Technical Report ISI/RR-76-46, Marina del Rey, California, June 1976.

P-SELECTIVE SETS, TALLY LANGUAGES, AND THE BEHAVIOR OF POLYNOMIAL TIME REDUCIBILITIES ON NP[1]

(Preliminary Report)

Alan L. Selman

Computer Science Department
Iowa State University
Ames, Iowa 50011

Abstract

The notion of p-selective sets, and tally languages, are used to study polynomial time reducibilities on NP. P-selectivity has the property that a set A belongs to the class P if and only if both $\bar{A} \le_m^P A$ and A is p-selective. We prove that for every tally language set in NP there exists a polynomial time equivalent set in NP that is p-selective. From this result it follows that if NEXT ≠ DEXT, then polynomial time Turing and many-one reducibilities differ on NP.

1. Introduction

In Ladner, Lynch, and Selman [13] it is shown that various deterministic polynomial time reducibilities differ on the sets computable in 2^n time. For example, there exists an infinite, coinfinite set A such that $\bar{A} \not\le_m^P A$ and A is computable in 2^n time. We would like to know whether polynomial time reducibilities differ on NP. If there exists a set $A \in NP$ with the above stated properties, then, of course, $P \neq NP$. It is conjectured in [13] that $P \neq NP$ implies $\le_T^P$ and $\le_m^P$ differ on NP. This question has also motivated the work of Simon and Gill [15]. Relationships between the behavior of polynomial time reducibilities and the question of how sets in NP-P can be deterministically computed are herein further explored. We prove, in particular, that for each tally language set A in NP, there exists a polynomial time equivalent set $B \in NP$ such that $\bar{B} \not\le_m^P B$. Book has shown [3] that there exist tally languages in NP-P if and only if the deterministic and nondeterministic exponential time complexity classes differ. We conclude that if either $NP \not\subseteq DEXT$ or $NEXT \neq DEXT$, then there exists an infinite, coinfinite set A in NP such that $\bar{A} \not\le_m^P A$. Some related questions are settled, more are raised, and some approaches for further work are suggested.

The role of tally languages in comparing complexity classes is reviewed in Section 2 below. Section 3 contains some results which relate the open problem of whether

[1] This research was supported in part by the National Science Foundation under grant MCS77-23493

NP is closed under complements to the issue of whether there exist sets in NP which are $\leq_m^P$ -reducible to their complements. P-selective sets are defined in Section 4. They are most important to the development, for they provide the means by which polynomial time reducibilities are shown to differ on NP. The principal results are contained in Sections 4 and 5.

Unless otherwise stated, all sets are assumed to be over the finite alphabet $\Sigma = \{0,1\}$. Our notation for polynomial time reducibilities is that of [13]. In particular, a set A is <u>polynomial time Turing reducible to</u> a set B , $A \leq_T^P B$, if there is a deterministic oracle Turing machine which accepts A within polynomial time with B as its oracle; A is <u>polynomial time many-one reducible to</u> B , $A \leq_m^P B$, if there is a function f computable in polynomial time such that $x \in A$ if and only if $f(x) \in B$.

We introduce one new reducibility here.

<u>Definition 1.</u> A set A is <u>positive reducible in polynomial time to</u> a set B , $A \leq_{pos}^P B$, if A is polynomial time Turing reducible to B by a machine M with the following property: If M accepts a string x with an oracle B and if $B_0 \supseteq B$ then M accepts x with oracle B_0 .

If M accepts x with oracle B and if $B_0 \supseteq B$ then queries to the oracle B which have negative answers may very well have positive answers when made to the oracle B_0 . Suppose x is accepted by M and suppose that w is a query to the oracle set with a negative response. According to the above definition, the query w cannot affect the outcome of the computation if the oracle set is enlarged to include the string w . This reducibility is a generalization of the polynomial time positive truth-table reducibility found in [13]. We will require $\leq_{pos}^P$ reductions in the following development. The usefulness of $\leq_{pos}^P$ arises from the following easily proved property.

<u>Lemma 1.</u> $B \in NP$ and $A \leq_{pos}^P B$ implies $A \in NP$.

Consistent with common usage, if $\leq_r^P$ is any polynomial time reducibility, a set A is $\leq_r^P$ -<u>complete</u> if $A \in NP$ and for all B , $B \in NP$, $B \leq_r^P A$.

2. <u>Complexity classes and tally languages</u>

Let f be a Turing machine time bounding function. For a Turing acceptor M , L(M) is the set of strings accepted by M . DTIME(f) = {L(M) | M is a deterministic Turing acceptor which operates within time bound f} and NTIME(f) = {L(M) | M is a nondeterministic Turing acceptor which operates within time f} .

The specific classes we are concerned with are:

(i) the class of sets accepted by deterministic Turing machines which operate in polynomial time, $P = \bigcup\{DTIME(p) \mid p \text{ is a polynomial}\}$, and the corresponding nondeterministic class, $NP = \bigcup\{NTIME(p) \mid p \text{ is a polynomial}\}$;

(ii) the class of sets accepted by Turing machines which operate in exponential time, $DEXT = \bigcup_{c=1}^{\infty} DTIME(2^{cn})$, and the corresponding nondeterministic class $NEXT = \bigcup_{c=1}^{\infty} NTIME(2^{cn})$;

(iii) the class of sets $TIME(2^{P}) = \bigcup\{DTIME(2^{p}) \mid p \text{ is a polynomial}\}$.

The importance of the classes P and NP by this time requires no further justification. DEXT is characterized in [7] as the class of sets accepted by auxiliary push-down machines which operate within tape bound n . In [9] NEXT is characterized as the class of spectra of formulae of first-order logic with equality. $TIME(2^{P})$ is mentioned because the standard, and only known, deterministic simulation of sets in NP gives $NP \subseteq TIME(2^{P})$. It is not known whether $NP \subseteq DEXT$. Computational experience suggests that this is unlikely. The relationships between the classes NP and other complexity classes is naturally of interest, and has been studied chiefly by Book [2,4]. We begin by recalling some of the known results.

Facts. (i) [4,9]. $NEXT \not\subseteq DEXT$ implies $NP \not\subseteq P$.

(ii) $NP \not\subseteq DEXT$ implies $NEXT \not\subseteq DEXT$ and $NP \not\subseteq P$.

These relationships can be further drawn out with the use of tally languages (cf. [3] and[5]) and tally languages will be used in the later development. A tally language is a subset of $\{1\}^*$. If Σ is a 2 letter alphabet, then the symbols of Σ may be identified with the digits 1 and 2, and each word $w \in \Sigma^*$ may be identified with a number n(w) in dyadic notation. For $L \subseteq \Sigma^*$, Tally(L) is defined as $\{1^{n(w)} \mid w \in L\}$. The following facts pinpoint the distinction between the hypotheses $NEXT \not\subseteq DEXT$ and $NP \not\subseteq DEXT$.

Facts. (iii) [3]. Every tally language in NP belongs to P if and only if $NEXT \subseteq DEXT$.

(iv) For every $A \in NP$, $Tally(A) \in P$ if and only if $NP \subseteq DEXT$.

A proof of (iv) follows from the same padding argument used to prove (iii). For each set A , $Tally(A) \leq_m^P A$. Thus, $A \in NP$ implies $Tally(A) \in NP$. Observe therefore that the left hand side of (iii) trivially implies the left hand side of (iv).

3. Sets reducible to their complements

Before showing (with the hypothesis $NEXT \neq DEXT$) that there exist sets $A \in NP$ such that $\bar{A} \not\leq_m^P A$, we digress in this section to give some results which suggest that the opposite can also occur. Let $co\text{-}NP = \{A \mid \bar{A} \in NP\}$. No results are known about $NP \cap co\text{-}NP$. Karp [11] and Pratt [14], show that there are difficult (i.e., probably not in P) problems in NP whose complements are also in NP. No positive reduction of any of these problems to its complement is known. Since NP is closed under complements if and only if there is a $\leq_T^P$ -complete set A in NP such that $\bar{A}$ in NP, it is likely that none of the Karp, Pratt problems is complete. Also, NP is closed under complements if and only if there exists an $\leq_m^P$ -complete set A in NP such that $\bar{A} \leq_m^P A$. (Some of these observations have previously been made in [12].) In any case, we show that if A and $\bar{A}$ both belong to NP, then there is a set B in NP so that A and B are $\leq_T^P$ -equivalent and $\bar{B} \leq_m^P B$. Thus, there exist problems of the same difficulty as the Karp and Pratt problems that are $\leq_m^P$-reducible to their complements.

The following lemma is probably well known.

Lemma 2. $A \in NP$ and $\bar{A} \in NP$ and $B \leq_T^P A$ implies $B \in NP$ and $\bar{B} \in NP$.

Theorem 1. For every set A ($\neq \Sigma^*$) there exists a set B such that

(i) $B \leq_T^P A$,

(ii) $A \leq_m^P B$,

(iii) $\bar{B} \leq_m^P B$, and

(iv) $A \in NP$ and $\bar{A} \in NP$ implies $B \in NP$.

We need to construct B so that (i) through (iii) are satisfied. (iv) follows from the lemma. As a corollary to Theorem 1, note that there exist NP-hard sets B such that $\bar{B} \leq_m^P B$.

Proof. Let $A \subseteq \{0,1\}^*$. Define $A1 = \{\sigma 1 \mid \sigma \in A\}$. It is very easy to see that $A1 \equiv_m^P A$. Construct B from $A1$ as follows: If σ is of the form $\beta 1$, then place σ into B if and only if σ belongs to $A1$. (It follows that $A1 \leq_m^P B$.) Next, inductively close B up under the following operations.

(1) Place $\alpha 0$ into $\bar{B}$, for each α in B .

(2) Place $\alpha 0$ into B , for each α in $\bar{B}$.

Then, $\alpha \in \bar{B} \leftrightarrow \alpha 0 \in B$. So, $\bar{B} \leq_m^P B$. A straightforward recursive procedure can be used for testing membership in B with $A1$ as an oracle. Namely, to determine whether a string of the form $\alpha 0$ belongs to B , test whether α belongs to $\bar{B}$; to determine whether $\alpha 0$ belongs to $\bar{B}$, test whether α belongs to B : a string of the form $\alpha 1$ belongs to B if and only if $\alpha 1$ belongs to $A1$. Each recursive call can be accomplished in constant time, and the number of calls is bounded by the length of the input string α . Thus, $B \leq_T^P A1$, from which it follows that $B \leq_T^P A$. □

4. P-selectivity

We now introduce the concept that will enable us to distinguish polynomial time reducibilities on NP.

Definition 2. Let Σ be a finite alphabet. A set A , $A \subseteq \Sigma^*$, is p-selective if there is a function $f: \Sigma^* \times \Sigma^* \to \Sigma^*$ so that

(i) f is computable in polynomial time,

(ii) $f(x,y) = x$ or $f(x,y) = y$, and

(iii) $x \in A$ or $y \in A \to f(x,y) \in A$.

The analogue of this concept in recursive function theory is due to Jockusch [8], where it has been used successfully to distinguish reducibilities on the recursively enumerable sets. In fact, our principal construction borrows heavily from the technique due to McLaughlin and Martin that appears in [8].

The function f is a selector for A . The selector is a choice function. Yet, p-selectivity is not the same as non-determinism. The reader, when first confronted with this notion, may suspect that a set A must belong to P in order for there to exist a polynomial time computable function which when given any two input values always chooses the right one. We will prove, however, that there exist arbitrarily complex p-selective sets. Conversely, assuming $P \neq NP$, there exist sets in NP-P that are not p-selective. The following theorem gives some basic properties of p-selectivity.

Theorem 2.

(i) For all sets A, $A \neq \Sigma^*$ and $A \neq \emptyset$, $A \in P$ if and only if $\bar{A} \leq^P_m A$ and A is p-selective.

(ii) If A is p-selective and $B \leq^P_m A$, then B is p-selective.

If there exists an $A \in NP$ so that A is not p-selective, then, by Theorem 2(i), $P \neq NP$. To show the existence of a set $A \in NP$ such that $\bar{A} \not\leq^P_m A$ it would suffice to construct a set in NP-P that is p-selective. More generally, to show the existence of a set $A \in NP$ such that $B \leq^P_T A$ does not imply $B \leq^P_m A$, by use of Theorem 2(ii), it would suffice to construct sets A and B so that $A \in NP$, $B \leq^P_T A$, A is p-selective, but B is not p-selective. We will proceed in this manner. In the remainder of this section we will obtain (assuming $NP \neq P$) sets in NP-P that are not p-selective. In the next section we will construct (with suitable hypothesis, as said before) sets in NP-P that are p-selective.

Let SAT denote the set of all formulas of propositional logic in conjuctive normal form. SAT is a well-known $\leq^P_m$-complete set in NP [6, 10].

Theorem 3. If SAT is p-selective, then SAT can be recognized deterministically in polynomial time.

Proof. Suppose that f is a selector for SAT. Note that, for any two formulas of propositional logic, ϕ and ψ, $f(\phi,\psi) \in SAT \leftrightarrow (\phi \vee \psi) \in SAT$.

Let ϕ be in conjunctive normal form. Then, $\phi = C_1 \wedge \ldots \wedge C_n$, $n \geq 1$, and each $C_i = L_{i1} \vee \ldots \vee L_{im_i}$, $i = 1,\ldots,n$, where each L_{ij} is a literal. To determine in polynomial time whether $\phi \in SAT$ proceed as follows:

$$\begin{aligned} \text{Write } \phi &= C_1 \wedge \ldots \wedge C_n \\ &= (L_{11} \vee \ldots \vee L_{1m_1}) \wedge C_2 \wedge \ldots \wedge C_n \\ &= (L_{11} \wedge C_2 \wedge \ldots \wedge C_n) \vee (L_{12} \wedge C_2 \wedge \ldots \wedge C_n) \\ &\qquad \vee \ldots \vee (L_{1m_1} \wedge C_2 \wedge \ldots \wedge C_n), \end{aligned}$$

i.e., distribute the first set of disjuncts. Let $D_j = L_{1j} \wedge C_2 \wedge \ldots \wedge C_n$, $j \leq m_1$. Compute $f(D_1, D_2 \vee \ldots \vee D_{m_1})$. If the answer is D_1 then ϕ is satisfiable only if D_1 is satisfiable, so proceed with D_1. Otherwise, compute $f(D_2, D_3 \vee \ldots \vee D_{m_1})$. Continue in this manner until some D_j is obtained with which to proceed.

$$\begin{aligned} \text{Recalling that } D_j &= L_{1j} \wedge C_2 \wedge \ldots \wedge C_n \\ &= L_{1j} \wedge (L_{21} \vee \ldots \vee L_{2m_2}) \wedge C_3 \wedge \ldots \wedge C_n, \end{aligned}$$

next distribute C_2 across and proceed as above. Eventually obtain a conjunction of literals (one literal from each C_i). ϕ is satisfiable if and only if this conjunction of literals is satisfiable. Check to see whether or not this is so. The result is a polynomial time algorithm. □

Corollary 1. If $P \neq NP$, then every $\leq_m^P$-complete set in NP is not p-selective.

This corollary appears to be similar to P. Berman's result [1] that if $P \neq NP$, then there are no $\leq_m^P$-complete tally languages in NP. However, in spite of Theorem 6 to follow, neither result seems to directly imply the other. Corollary 1 is also obtainable as a direct consequence of the next theorem, but the direct proof via SAT provides useful insight for further construction of sets in NP that are not p-selective.

Theorem 4. For every set $A \in NP - P$ there exists a set B such that:

(i) $B \in NP - P$,

(ii) $A \leq_m^P B$, and

(iii) B is not p-selective.

Proof. Let $A \in NP$. Let M be an NP acceptor for A and assume that each state of M allows at most two possible next actions. Define a computation of M to be a string σ such that $\sigma = x\#\rho$, where x is an input word to M, $\#$ is a marker, and ρ is a standard string encoding (as a sequence of instantaneous descriptions) of a computation of M on input x. Since $A \in NP$, there is a polynomial p such that $|\sigma| \leq p(|x|)$, for each accepting computation σ. Define $B = \{x\#\mu \mid x\#\mu$ is an initial segment of an accepting computation of $M\}$. Thus, $x\#\mu$ belongs to B if and only if $x \in \{0,1\}^*$ and there exists a string η such that $x\#\mu\eta$ is an accepting computation of M. Define $f(x) = x\#$. It is not hard to see that f and B (suitably encoded into $\{0,1\}^*$) satisfy the properties required. If B were p-selective, then that could be used in place of nondeterminism to recognize B in polynomial time, in much the same way as in the previous theorem. □

Since B in general seems to be "close" to A, the construction just given suggests that there may be sets in NP-P which are not p-selective and which are not $\leq_m^P$-complete. Our next result shows that this is indeed the case.

Theorem 5. If B is computable and B is not p-selective, then there exists a set D in P such that $A = D \cap B$ is not p-selective and such that $B \not\leq_T^P A$.

Proof. The proof is based directly on the proof techniques of Ladner [12]. □

Corollary 2. If $B \in NP - P$ is not p-selective, then there exists $A \in NP - P$ such that A is not p-selective, $A \leq_m^P B$, and $B \not\leq_T^P A$.

Corollary 3. If $P \neq NP$, then there exist sets in NP-P which are not $\leq_T^P$-complete (hence not $\leq_m^P$-complete) and which are not p-selective.

To prove Corollary 3, apply Corollary 2 to any $\leq_m^P$-complete set B. By Corollary 1, B is not p-selective.

5. Existence theorems

Our principal results are corollaries to the following theorem.

Theorem 6. For every tally language set A there exist sets B and C such that

(i) $B \leq^P_{pos} A$,

(ii) $A \leq^P_T B$,

(iii) $C \leq^P_T B$ and $C \leq^P_T A$,

(iv) $B \leq^P_{pos} C$,

(v) B is p-selective, and

(vi) if C is p-selective, then $C \in P$.

<u>Proof.</u> Let A be a tally language. Define $C \in \{0,1\}^*$ so that for each $n \geq 1$, C contains exactly one string of length n : The string $x = x_1 \ldots x_n$ is to belong to C , if and only if:

$x_i = 1$, if $1^i \in A$, and

$x_i = 0$, otherwise $(i = 1,\ldots,n)$.

Define $B = \{x \mid \exists y[y \in C \ \& \ x \leq y]\}$, where $\leq$ is the dictionary ordering of binary strings with $0 < 1$. If $x \in B$ and $y \leq x$, then $y \in B$, because dictionary ordering is transitive. To prove (v), define

$$f(x,y) = \begin{cases} x, \text{ if } x \leq y \\ y, \text{ if } y < x . \end{cases}$$

It is easy to see that f is a selector function for B , which proves part (v).

The following algorithm demonstrates that $B \leq^P_{pos} A$. Let $x \in \{0,1\}^*$ be written $x = x_1 \ldots x_n$.

```
i = 1;
repeat
    if x_i = 1 and 1^i ∉ A
        then reject input x and halt;
    if x_i = 0 and 1^i ∈ A
        then accept input x and halt;
    i = i + 1 ;
until (accept or reject or i = n );
if x_n = 0 or 1^n ∈ A
    then accept else reject;
```

The computation is clearly polynomial time in A . Moreover if x is accepted with A as the oracle and if $A_0 \supseteq A$, then x is accepted by the algorithm with A_0 as the oracle. In fact, rejection is only possible if a symbol $x_i = 1$ and the corresponding string 1^i does not belong to the oracle set. So, the addition of strings 1^i to the oracle set cannot cause previously accepted strings x to become rejected. Thus, $B \leq^P_{pos} A$.

A minor alteration to the above algorithm yields part (iv), $B \leq^P_{pos} C$.

We can prove (ii) by the following algorithm. "Let 1^n be input. Generate the largest string x of length n in B . Accept 1^n if and only if the rightmost symbol of x is 1 ."

$C \leq^P_T A$ is immediate from the definition. $A \leq^P_T B$ and $C \leq^P_T A$ yields $C \leq^P_T B$.

Hence, (iii) is proved.

We show next that if C is p-selective, then $C \in P$. Assume that f is a selector function for C. Determine in polynomial time whether $x \in C$, where $|x| = n$, as follows. Compute $f(0,1)$. Exactly one of 0 or 1 belongs to C. So, $f(0,1) \in C$. Let $a_1 = f(0,1)$. Compute $f(a_1 0, a_1 1)$. Since exactly one of the strings $a_1 0$ or $a_1 1$ belongs to C, the result $f(a_1 0, a_1 1) \in C$. Let $a_1 a_2 = f(a_1 0, a_1 1)$. Continue in this manner until $a_1 a_2 \ldots a_n$ is obtained. $x \in C$ if and only if $x = a_1 \ldots a_n$. The theorem is proved. □

Corollary 4. If $NEXT \neq DEXT$, then there exist infinite, coinfinite sets B and C so that

(i) $B \in NP - P$,

(ii) $C \leq_T^P B$ and $B \leq_{pos}^P C$,

(iii) $C \nleq_m^P B$, and

(iv) $\bar{B} \nleq_m^P B$.

Proof. By use of fact (iii), if $NEXT \neq DEXT$, then there exists a tally language set A in NP-P. (A is easily seen to be infinite and coinfinite.) Use the theorem to construct B and C from A. By parts (i) and (ii) of the theorem, together with Lemma 1, $B \in NP - P$. Since B is p-selective and C is not p-selective, $C \nleq_m^P B$ follows by use of Theorem 2 (ii). $\bar{B} \nleq_m^P B$ follows by use of Theorem 2 (i). □

For any polynomial time reducibility $\leq_r^P$, an $\leq_r^P$-degree is defined to be an equivalence class given by the equivalence relation $\equiv_r^P$ which is defined over the class of all recursive sets. An $\leq_r^P$-degree is said to be an NP $\leq_r^P$-degree if it contains a set in NP.

Corollary 5. If $NEXT \neq DEXT$, then there exists an NP $\leq_T^P$-degree not equal to P which consists of at least two distinct $\leq_m^P$-degrees.

Proof. Let $\underset{\sim}{d}$ be the $\leq_T^P$-degree which contains the set B constructed in the theorem. Then, B and $\bar{B}$ both belong to $\underset{\sim}{d}$, but B and $\bar{B}$ belong to distinct $\leq_m^T$-degrees. □

Corollary 6. If $NP \not\subseteq DEXT$, then there exist sets A_0, B, and C so that

(i) $A_0 \in NP - DEXT$,

(ii) $B \in NP - P$,

(iii) $B \leq_{pos}^P A_0$,

(iv) $B \equiv_T^P C$,

(v) B is p-selective, hence $\bar{B} \leq_m^P B$, and

(vi) C is not p-selective, hence $C \nleq_m^P B$.

Proof. By use of fact (iv), choose $A_0 \in NP - DEXT$, so that $Tally(A_0) \in NP - P$. Then apply the theorem with $A = Tally(A_0)$. The remainder of the proof of Corollary 6 follows from the same reasoning as the proof of Corollary 5. □

Corollary 7. If every p-selective set in NP belongs to P, then $NP \subseteq DEXT$ and $NEXT = DEXT$.

Corollary 8. There exist arbitrarily complex p-selective sets. Hence there exist p-selective sets that do not belong to NP.

Proof. Let A be an arbitrarily complex tally language and apply the theorem to A. □

Corollary 9. If NP is closed under complements and NEXT ≠ DEXT then there exist sets B_1 and B_2 so that B_1 and B_2 both belong to NP-P, $B_1 \equiv_T^P B_2$, and B_1 and B_2 are $\leq_m^P$-incomparable.

Proof. Apply Corollary 4. Let $B_1 = B$ and $B_2 = \bar{B}$. If NP is closed under complements, then both B and $\bar{B}$ belong to NP. □

6. Open problems

In this section we list some open problems and further directions.

1. Show that $P \neq NP$ implies there exists a tally language in NP-P. This is equivalent to the downward translation problem, $P \neq NP$ implies NEXT ≠ DEXT. More generally, obtain the conclusions of Corollary 2 as a consequence of $P \neq NP$, rather than NEXT ≠ DEXT.
2. By use of Theorem 4, for each set $A \in NP - P$ there exist sets higher in NP (i.e., sets B so that $A \leq_T^P B$ and B in NP) which are not p-selective. In contrast, Corollary 4 and Theorem 2(ii) give us low sets in NP-P that are p-selective. Bridge the gap! That is, find sets B and C in NP which belong to the same $\leq_T^P$-degree so that B is p-selective and C is not p-selective. We would then have sets B and C in NP so that $C \leq_T^P B$ but $C \not\leq_m^P B$.
3. Is every p-selective set in NP $\leq_T^P$-equivalent to a tally language set in NP? It would be useful to obtain techniques for constructing p-selective sets in NP other than the one given in Theorem 6. This knowledge would have some bearing on discerning whether there exist other techniques for obtaining p-selective sets. In particular, if we could construct a $\leq_T^P$-complete p-selective set, we could conclude that $\leq_T^P$-complete ≠ $\leq_m^P$-complete. (If there exists a $\leq_T^P$-complete tally language, then these same results could be derived. It is known that there are no $\leq_m^P$-complete tally languages unless $P = NP$ [1]).
4. Consider the set C constructed in the proof of Theorem 6. If it can be shown that C belongs to NP, then sets B and C in NP are obtained so that $B \leq_T^P C$ and $B \not\leq_m^P C$. However, if it can be shown that C does not belong to NP, then the conclusion we can draw is even more interesting. Namely, in this case, we would have NEXT ≠ DEXT implies NP is not closed under complements. In fact, $B \in NP$, $C \leq_T^P B$, and $C \notin NP$ imply $C \in \Delta_2^P - \Sigma_1^P$, from which it follows that $\Pi_1^P \neq \Sigma_1^P$.

References

1. P. Berman, Relationships between density and deterministic complexity of NP-complete languages, Fifth International Colloquium on Automata, Languages and Programming, Lecture Notes in Computer Science 62(1978), 63-71.

2. R. Book, On languages accepted in polynomial time, SIAM J. Comput. 1(1972), 281-287.

3. R. Book, Tally languages and complexity classes, Information and Control 26(1974), 186-193.

4. R. Book, Comparing complexity classes, J. Computer System Sci. 9(1974), 213-229.

5. R. Book, C. Wrathall, A. Selman, and D. Dobkin, Inclusion complete tally languages and the Hartmanis-Berman conjecture, Math. Systems Theory 11(1977), 1-8.

6. S. Cook, The complexity of theorem-proving procedures, Third annual ACM Symposium on Theory of Computing (1971), 151-158.

7. S. Cook, Characterizations of pushdown machines in terms of time-bounded computers, J. Assoc. Comput. Mach. 18(1971), 4-18.

8. C. Jockusch, Semirecursive sets and positive reducibility, Trans. Amer. Math. Soc. 131(1968), 420-436.

9. N. Jones and A. Selman, Turing machines and the spectra of first-order formulas, J. Symbolic Logic 29(1974), 139-150.

10. R. Karp, Reducibility among combinatorial problems, Complexity of Computer Computations, R. Miller and J. Thatcher, eds., Plenum Press, New York, 1972, 85-103.

11. R. Karp, Combinatories = ? linear programming + number theory, Project MAC Workshop on Complexity Computations, 1973.

12. R. Ladner, On the structure of polynomial time reducibility, J. Assoc. Comput. Mach. 22(1975), 155-171.

13. R. Ladner, N. Lynch, and A. Selman, A comparison of polynomial time reducibilities, Theoretical Computer Sci. 1(1975), 103-123.

14. V. Pratt, Every prime has a succinct certificate, SIAM J. Comput. 4(1975), 214-220.

15. I. Simon and J. Gill, Polynomial reducibilities and upward diagonalizations, Ninth annual ACM Symposium on Theory of Computing (1977), 186-194.

Constructing call-by-value continuation semantics

Ravi Sethi

Bell Laboratories
Murray Hill, New Jersey 07974

Adrian Tang

Department of Computer Science
The University of Kansas
Lawrence, Kansas 66045

ABSTRACT

The primary motivation behind this paper is an interest in transforming one semantic description for a language into another related description of the same language. Since direct and continuation semantics have been studied in some detail, they are obvious test-beds for suggesting the problems that might be encountered in the process. One of the problems is that the semantic objects in two descriptions of a language may be quite dissimilar. For example, function values of procedures in direct semantics are quite different from function values in continuation semantics. Milne and Reynolds have defined predicates which can be used to relate the two kinds of function values. Starting with such predicates we define transformations and then show that the transformations preserve the predicates. The transformations are used to construct continuation semantics, starting from a direct semantics of a language with procedures called by value.

1. Introduction

1.1. *purpose.* Even within the denotational approach to the semantics of programming languages [3,6,9,12], quite distinct semantic descriptions can be given for the same language. Denotational semantics of realistic programming languages are given using *continuations,* which were introduced in [4,11] to handle jumps like **goto** commands, or error exits during the evaluation of an expression. If such jumps do not occur, then a more intuitive (at least for the uninitiated) *direct* semantics can be given for the language.

Since the programming language remains the same, there must be a close relationship between the various descriptions of the language. Milne [3], Reynolds [5], and more recently Stoy [10] have shown the congruence of pairs of descriptions by carefully setting up predicates that these descriptions satisfy. Using this approach, both descriptions of a language have to be specified before it can be shown that they are congruent.

Once we can define predicates which express the congruence between two semantic descriptions, it is natural to wonder if, instead of having to specify both descriptions independently, we might perhaps be able to *construct* one description, starting with the other. For a very simple language without procedures it was shown in [8] that a direct semantic description can be transformed into a continuation semantic description. The exclusion of procedures allowed the underlying semantic objects in both direct and continuation semantics to be essentially the same. In a more general setting, the semantic objects in two descriptions for the same language may be quite dissimilar.

Take the case of procedures that are called by value and return values. If $\mathbf{V}$ is the domain of values in the direct semantics, then the meaning of a procedure is a function from $\mathbf{V}$ to $\mathbf{V}$. In Algol 60, procedures may take themselves as parameters, so $\mathbf{V}$ will in general be a reflexive domain. The programming language C [2] passes functions through the device of passing pointers to functions: in particular, a function can be passed a pointer to itself as a parameter.

In continuation semantics the domain of values $\mathbf{V}'$ will be quite different from $\mathbf{V}$ since we shall see that functions will not be elements of $\mathbf{V}' \rightarrow \mathbf{V}'$, but some other domain that need not concern us just yet.

Since both **V** and **V**′ are reflexive domains, given an element a in **V**, the best we can do is point to one of possibly many related elements a' in **V**′. Following Milne, Stoy [10] defines a predicate which we call **pe**, relating elements in **V** and **V**′, and a predicate **ps** relating domain **V** with a domain **[K→A]** which will soon be motivated.

a calculus. Let term T represent a value a in domain **V**. We will define transformations to derive a term T' from T, where T' represents an element a' in **[K→A]**. The derivation of T' from T will be done in small steps. Using an auxiliary operator δ as a syntactic placeholder we will start with $\delta(T)$ and push δ down onto smaller and smaller subexpressions of T using the transformations.

It will be shown that the transformations "preserve" predicates like **pe** and **ps**. It immediately follows that the value a' of T' must be such that $\mathbf{ps}(a,a')$ holds, where a is the value of T.

One contribution of this paper is the construction of a congruent continuation semantics from a direct semantic description. A potentially more interesting contribution is the calculus that is used to do the construction, since congruence of the two semantic descriptions follows from the formal manipulations rather than from a direct proof.

On a more technical level, we feel that the notion of "replacements" in section 5.2 is of independent interest. Starting with $\delta(T)$ the transformations push δ down onto subexpressions of T. Treating a term as a tree, the subtree below a δ operator represents values from one semantic world, while the rest of the tree represents values from another semantic world. "Replacements" will be used to give meanings to terms with δ operators in them. It seems that any time we seek to transform objects in one semantic world into objects in another semantic world we will need a mechanism related to "replacements".

The eager reader may now proceed directly to section 2.

1.2. *syntax and informal semantics.* Consider a programming language in which functions are defined and applied using the following syntax

$$E ::= \mathbf{proc}(I){:}E \mid E_1(E_2)$$

We will use the term "procedure" for any user defined functions so that they may easily be distinguished from any semantic functions that may be floating around.

The intent is that call-by-value will be used. Consequently, given some environment ρ (which provides values for the free identifiers) the expression $E = (\mathbf{proc}(I){:}E_0)(E_2)$ is evaluated by first determining a_2 the value of E_2: the value of the entire expression E is then the result of evaluating E_0 with a_2 for I i.e. the value of E_0 in the modified environment $\rho[a_2/I]$ which yields a_2 for I, and agrees with ρ everywhere else. If the evaluation of E_2 does not terminate, then we write $a_2{=}\bot$, and require that the value of E be $\bot$ as well.

The major difference between the above syntax and the syntax for procedure definition in most programming languages is that procedures are defined in-line here. One advantage of an in-line definition is that it minimizes the size of the language under discussion, without at the same time eliminating the issues we wish to study. In fact, the in-line syntax allows procedures to be passed as parameters, as well as allowing nested procedure definitions.

The remainder of section 1 reviews direct and continuation semantics.

1.3. *background.* Some idea of the distinction between direct and continuation semantics for expressions can be gained just by looking at the meaning of an identifier. We use an environment ρ to keep track of the current value of an identifier I.

In direct semantics we might use a function **ed** to map an expression and an environment to a value. For identifier I, the value of I in ρ, written $\mathbf{ed}[\![I]\!]\rho$ will be just $\rho[\![I]\!]$. The special parentheses $[\![$ and $]\!]$ enclose syntactic objects. Function application associates to the left.[1] If **Exp**, **U** and **V** are domains of expressions, environments and values, respectively, then $\mathbf{ed}[\![E]\!]$ is a function that maps an environment to a value:

$$\mathbf{ed} : \mathbf{Exp} \to [\mathbf{U} \to \mathbf{V}]$$

Thus $\mathbf{ed}[\![I]\!]\rho$ is the same as $(\mathbf{ed}[\![I]\!])(\rho)$. As might be expected, $\mathbf{ed}[\![-E]\!]\rho$ is $\ominus(\mathbf{ed}[\![E]\!]\rho)$, where $\ominus$ represents the unary negation operator.

Functions like **ed** which map syntactic objects to semantic objects are sometimes called *valuations.*

Informally, an expression continuation κ represents the "context" in which an expression E is evaluated. Think of κ representing the remainder of the computation following E. Once the value of E is known, κ will be able to tell us the final result of the program.

[1] A proliferation of parentheses will be avoided by consistently associating function application to the left. For example, given $f \in \mathbf{D} \to [\mathbf{D}' \to \mathbf{D}'']$, $a \in \mathbf{D}$, and $b \in \mathbf{D}'$, both fab and $f(a)b$ are equivalent to $(f(a))(b)$.

In continuation semantics we might use a valuation **ec** whose functionality is indicated by

$$\mathbf{ec} : \mathbf{Exp} \rightarrow [\mathbf{U} \rightarrow [\mathbf{K} \rightarrow \mathbf{A}]]$$

where $\mathbf{K} = \mathbf{V} \rightarrow \mathbf{A}$ is a domain of *expression continuations* mapping values in **V** to *answers* in some domain **A**. It makes intuitive sense to view $\mathbf{ec}[\![E]\!]\rho\kappa$ as determining the "value" of E in environment ρ and then applying κ to this "value".[2]

The meaning of an identifier I, $\mathbf{ec}[\![I]\!]\rho\kappa$ is an answer in **A**: the continuation κ is applied to the value $\rho[\![I]\!]$ to yield an answer $\kappa(\rho[\![I]\!])$. Treating $\ominus$ again as a function negating values, the semantic equations for **ec** might include

$$\mathbf{ec}[\![I]\!]\rho\kappa = \kappa(\rho[\![I]\!])$$

$$\mathbf{ec}[\![-E]\!]\rho\kappa = \mathbf{ec}[\![E]\!]\rho[\lambda a.\ \kappa(\ominus(a))]$$

As an example, for the expression $-I$ we get

$$\begin{aligned}\mathbf{ec}[\![-I]\!]\rho\kappa &= \mathbf{ec}[\![I]\!]\rho[\lambda a.\kappa(\ominus(a))] \\ &= [\lambda a.\ \kappa(\ominus(a))](\rho[\![I]\!]) \\ &= \kappa(\ominus(\rho[\![I]\!]))\end{aligned}$$

1.4. *procedures.* Let us now see how the valuations **ed** and **ec** might behave with procedure definitions and applications.

direct semantics. First consider $\mathbf{ed}[\![\mathbf{proc}(I){:}E]\!]\rho$. The informal semantics of section 1.2 suggest that the expression E be evaluated in a modified environment $\rho[a/I]$, so we might write something like

$$\lambda a.\ \mathbf{ed}[\![E]\!]\rho[a/I]$$

If $a \in \mathbf{V}$ then clearly $\lambda a.\ \mathbf{ed}[\![E]\!]\rho[a/I]$ is a function from **V** to **V** as we might expect. Procedure application is straightforward as well. The only detail we have neglected is how we ensure that $\perp$ as an argument yields $\perp$ as a result.

functions with continuations. In continuation semantics, the meaning of $\mathbf{proc}(I){:}E$ will be built up using the valuation **ec** applied to the expression E in some environment. Recall that

$$\mathbf{ec}:\ \mathbf{Exp} \rightarrow [\mathbf{U} \rightarrow [\mathbf{K} \rightarrow \mathbf{A}]]$$

So given E and a modified environment we get

$$\lambda a.\mathbf{ec}[\![E]\!]\rho[a/I] \in \mathbf{V} \rightarrow [\mathbf{K} \rightarrow \mathbf{A}]$$

In the presence of continuations, the meaning of a function called by value is often taken to be an element of the following domain [3,10,12]:

$$\mathbf{V} \rightarrow [\mathbf{K} \rightarrow \mathbf{A}]$$

There is some intuitive justification for taking a function value to be an element of $\mathbf{V} \rightarrow [\mathbf{K} \rightarrow \mathbf{A}]$. This domain allows for the possibility of a jump out of a function evaluation. Since evaluation of a function f on an argument a may not return, an expression continuation κ is supplied as an additional parameter to f. The function f now takes charge: if evaluation proceeds normally, then the continuation κ is used and an answer determined; otherwise, if a jump occurs, the continuation κ is disregarded, and the continuation appropriate to where the jump lands is used.

simple functions. Expression continuations serve two purposes: they may be supplied as arguments to functions, or applied to values (which include function values). These uses of continuations can be illustrated by considering a restricted class of expressions in which all procedures map basic values from some domain **B** to basic values in **B**. This simple case will be discussed primarily to build up the reader's intuition about the use of continuations.

Since procedures return basic values, the continuation argument of a function will, intuitively, be applied to a basic value, so let $\mathbf{K}_b = \mathbf{B} \rightarrow \mathbf{A}$. The domain **F** of functions will be

$$\mathbf{F} = \mathbf{B} \rightarrow [\mathbf{K}_b \rightarrow \mathbf{A}]$$

We will also need a domain $\mathbf{K}_f$ of continuations applied to function values. An example will clarify that the arguments in **B** to which functions are applied will sometimes be remembered within elements of $\mathbf{K}_f$.

[2] In [8] we used a *state* to map an identifier to a value, and the functionality of the continuation valuation was $\mathbf{Exp} \rightarrow [\mathbf{K} \rightarrow [\mathbf{S} \rightarrow \mathbf{A}]]$. Moreover an expression continuation was an element of $\mathbf{V} \rightarrow [\mathbf{S} \rightarrow \mathbf{A}]$. The syntax and semantics here are close to that in [10].

$$K_f = F \to A$$

Under call-by-value, we compute $E_1(E_2)$ by first computing E_2 and then applying the function for E_1 to the computed value. If we "model" this computation using expression continuations (which after all represent "the rest of the computation"), then $\mathbf{ec}[\![E_1(E_2)]\!]\rho\kappa$ will be something like

$$\mathbf{ec}[\![E_2]\!]\rho\kappa'$$

where we expect κ' to be applied to the "value" of E_2. Once E_2 is computed, we will compute E_1, so the computation of E_1 must be "modeled" within κ':

$$\kappa' = \lambda a \in \mathbf{B}.\mathbf{ec}[\![E_1]\!]\rho\kappa''$$

Here κ' takes an argument a and sets up a continuation κ'' so that when E_1 is evaluated, the function application takes place.

Once again, if we view $\mathbf{ec}[\![E_1]\!]\rho\kappa''$ as evaluating E_1 and then applying κ'' to its "value", we want

$$\kappa'' = \lambda f \in \mathbf{F}.f(a)\kappa$$

where a is the argument of κ' and κ is the original continuation κ in $\mathbf{ec}[\![E_1(E_2)]\!]\rho\kappa$. Putting it all together

$$\mathbf{ec}[\![E_1(E_2)]\!]\rho\kappa = \mathbf{ec}[\![E_2]\!]\rho[\ \lambda a \in \mathbf{B}.\mathbf{ec}[\![E_1]\!]\rho[\lambda f \in \mathbf{F}.f(a)\kappa]\ ]$$
$$\mathbf{ec}[\![\mathbf{proc}(I){:}E]\!]\rho\kappa = \kappa(\lambda a \in \mathbf{B}.\lambda\kappa' \in \mathbf{K}_b.\mathbf{ec}[\![E]\!]\rho[a/I]\kappa')$$

In the simple case we have been dealing with, the continuation argument of a function belongs to $\mathbf{K}_b$, and a continuation applied to a function belongs to $\mathbf{K}_f$. The distinction between the two types of continuations disappears when reflexive value domains are considered.

2. Relating the Semantic Domains

2.1. *the domains.* Let **B** be a domain of *basic* values, which include constants like *true* and *false*, and let **F** be the domain of *function* values, given by

$$\mathbf{V} = [\mathbf{B}+\mathbf{F}]$$

$$\mathbf{F} = [\mathbf{V}\to\mathbf{V}]$$

The reflexive domains **V** and **F** will be used to give direct semantics for expressions.

When continuations are present, the following semantic domains are often used to give the semantics of functions called by value [3,9,10,12] (the exception is our use of strict continuations). Note that function values are now elements of $\mathbf{F}' = \mathbf{V}' \to [\mathbf{K}\to\mathbf{A}]$, which is quite unlike $\mathbf{F} = \mathbf{V} \to \mathbf{V}$.

$\mathbf{B}$	basic values
$\mathbf{F}' = \mathbf{V}' \to [\mathbf{K}\to\mathbf{A}]$	function values
$\mathbf{V}' = \mathbf{B} + \mathbf{F}'$	
$\mathbf{A}$	answers
$\mathbf{K} = \mathbf{V}' \to_{\perp} \mathbf{A}$	expression continuations

The problem we must contend with here is that of relating the two domains of values **V** and **V'**. We cannot inductively proceed by first relating basic values, and then working outwards from "simpler" to more "complex" function values, since **V** and **V'** are both reflexive domains.

2.2. *predicates relating* **V** *and* **V'**. The solution by Milne [3] and Reynolds [5] has been to define predicates relating reflexive domains. The predicates we will use are similar to the ones employed by Stoy [10]. The reader is referred to [3,5] for techniques for demonstrating the existence of these predicates.

2.2.1. **pe**. Predicate $\mathbf{pe}(a,a')$ will test if $a \in \mathbf{V}$ and $a' \in \mathbf{V}'$ are "equivalent". Informally, $\mathbf{pe}(a,a')$ is true if and only if both a and a' are $\perp$ (or both $\top$), or both a and a' are the same basic value, or a and a' are functions related by predicate **pf**.[3]

[3] Let $\mathbf{D} = \mathbf{A} + \mathbf{B}$. For d in **D**, we write $d \,\mathrm{E}\, \mathbf{A}$ (read d is "squarely" in **A**) for the predicate, "Does d correspond to an element of **A**?" For d in **D**, when $d \,\mathrm{E}\, \mathbf{A}$ is true, we write $d|\mathbf{A}$ to represent the element of **A** that d corresponds to. Similarly, given a in **A**, we write "a **in D**" to represent the element of **D** that corresponds to a in **A**.

$$
\begin{aligned}
\mathbf{pe}(a,a') \text{ iff } & (a{=}\bot \vee a'{=}\bot) \rightarrow (a{=}\bot \wedge a'{=}\bot),\\
& (a{=}\top \vee a'{=}\top) \rightarrow (a{=}\top \wedge a'{=}\top),\\
& (a \,\mathrm{E}\, \mathbf{B}) \rightarrow (a' \mathrm{E}\, \mathbf{B} \wedge (a|\mathbf{B}{=}a'|\mathbf{B})),\\
& (a \,\mathrm{E}\, \mathbf{F}) \rightarrow (a' \mathrm{E}\, \mathbf{F}' \wedge \mathbf{pf}(a|\mathbf{F}, a'|\mathbf{F}')),\\
& \mathit{false}
\end{aligned}
$$

2.2.2. *informal discussion.* We will informally discuss the role of predicate **pf** before defining it.

Suppose function $g \in \mathbf{F}$ maps a basic value a to a basic value $g(a)$. Recall that $\mathbf{F} = \mathbf{V} \rightarrow \mathbf{V}$ and $\mathbf{V} = \mathbf{B} + \mathbf{F}$ so we have carefully picked $g \in \mathbf{F}$ and $a \in \mathbf{V}$ so that $a \,\mathrm{E}\, \mathbf{B}$ and $ga \,\mathrm{E}\, \mathbf{B}$. Consider function $g' \in \mathbf{F}'$, which we suspect is "equivalent" to $g \in \mathbf{F}$. Since $\mathbf{V}' = \mathbf{B} + \mathbf{F}'$, g' can also be applied to basic values (provided they are first injected into $\mathbf{V}'$). Let a' be an element of $\mathbf{V}'$ corresponding to $a \in \mathbf{V}$:

$$a' = (a|\mathbf{B}) \text{ in } \mathbf{V}'$$

What domain is $g'a'$ an element of? We know that $\mathbf{F}' = \mathbf{V}' \rightarrow [\mathbf{K} \rightarrow \mathbf{A}]$, so $g'a'$ must be an element of $[\mathbf{K} \rightarrow \mathbf{A}]$.

We expect "equivalent" functions to map "equivalent" arguments to "equivalent" results. So we are left with relating $ga \in \mathbf{V}$ with $g'a' \in [\mathbf{K} \rightarrow \mathbf{A}]$. In this simple example, we have chosen g and a such that $ga \,\mathrm{E}\, \mathbf{B}$ so $ga \in \mathbf{V}$ corresponds to the following element of $\mathbf{V}'$:

$$(ga|\mathbf{B}) \text{ in } \mathbf{V}'$$

Quite obviously, $(ga|\mathbf{B})$ **in** $\mathbf{V}'$ and $g'a' \in [\mathbf{K} \rightarrow \mathbf{A}]$ must also somehow be related.

Let κ be an expression continuation. We can do two things with κ: supply κ as one of the arguments to a function; or κ itself can be applied to a value to produce an answer. In other words, we can supply κ as an argument to $g'a' \in [\mathbf{K} \rightarrow \mathbf{A}]$ and get an element of $\mathbf{A}$; or we can apply κ to $(ga|\mathbf{B})$ **in** $\mathbf{V}'$ and get an element of $\mathbf{A}$.

For $g \in \mathbf{F}$ and $g' \in \mathbf{F}'$ to be related we would like

$$\kappa(ga|\mathbf{B} \text{ in } \mathbf{V}') = g'a'\kappa \tag{2.1}$$

We will reexpress equation (2.1) using notation closer to that in the definition of **pf** and **ps**. Let $b{=}ga$, and let $b'{=}ga|\mathbf{B} \text{ in } \mathbf{V}'$. From the definition of **pe**, $\mathbf{pe}(b,b')$ must be true. From equation (2.1) we get

$$\mathbf{pe}(b,b') \wedge g'a' = \lambda\kappa.\kappa(b')$$

In general, function $g \in \mathbf{F} = [\mathbf{V} \rightarrow \mathbf{V}]$ will map some $a \in \mathbf{V}$ to some $b \in \mathbf{V}$.

2.2.3. **pf** *and* **ps**. Predicates **pf** and **ps** are defined by

$\mathbf{pf}(g,g')$ if and only if $\mathbf{ps}(ga,g'a')$ holds whenever $\mathbf{pe}(a,a')$ holds.

$$
\begin{aligned}
\mathbf{ps}(b,c) \text{ iff } & (b{=}\bot \vee c{=}\bot) \rightarrow (b{=}\bot \wedge c{=}\bot),\\
& (b{=}\top \vee c{=}\top) \rightarrow (b{=}\top \wedge c{=}\top),\\
& (\exists b'.\mathbf{pe}(b,b') \wedge c{=}\lambda\kappa.\kappa(b')),\\
& \mathit{false}^{4}
\end{aligned}
$$

Since values in direct and continuation semantics are drawn from different domains, we need two domains of environments $\mathbf{U} = \mathbf{Ide} \rightarrow \mathbf{V}$ and $\mathbf{U}' = \mathbf{Ide} \rightarrow \mathbf{V}'$, where **Ide** is the domain of *identifiers*. Environments will be related by the predicate **pu**:

$\mathbf{pu}(\rho,\rho')$ if and only if $\mathbf{pe}(\rho[\![I]\!],\rho'[\![I]\!])$ holds for all I in **Ide**

Based on the predicates **pe**, **pf**, **ps** and **pu**, we will define transformations that will take an element $b \in \mathbf{V}$ into an element $c \in \mathbf{K} \rightarrow \mathbf{A}$ such that $\mathbf{ps}(b,c)$ holds.

[4] There is no *a priori* guarantee that an appropriate b' exists. It has however been shown [3, pp. 615-616] that an appropriate b' can indeed be found, so that the predicates are directed complete [5] or inclusive [3].

3. Transforming V into V′

The transformations in this section will be applied to the semantic description of a sample language, consisting of rules like the following:

$$\mathbf{ed}[\![E_1(E_2)]\!]\rho = (\mathbf{ed}[\![E_1]\!]\rho|\mathbf{F})(\mathbf{ed}[\![E_2]\!]\rho)$$

Consider the right hand side of the above equation. Suppose $\mathbf{ed}[\![E_1]\!]\rho = g$ and $\mathbf{ed}[\![E_2]\!]\rho = a$. From the definition of **ed**, both g and a are elements of **V**. Starting with g and a, the right hand side constructs an element of **V** by first projecting g from **V** into **F**, and then applying the function to a.

3.1. *terms.* The operations used in constructing semantic descriptions include:

O1. Project an element of a domain like $\mathbf{V}=\mathbf{B}+\mathbf{F}$ into one of the summand domains, e.g., if $g \in \mathbf{V}$ and $g \,\varepsilon\, \mathbf{F}$, then $g|\mathbf{F}$ is an element of **F**. Given an appropriate summand domain **D**, "$|\mathbf{D}$" will be treated as a unary operator.

O2. Inject an element of a summand domain into the sum, e.g., $g = (g|\mathbf{F})$ **in** **V**. Given an appropriate sum domain **D**, "**in D**" will be treated as a unary operator.

O3. Conditionals. The ternary operator "$\rightarrow$" tests if its first operand is true: if it is, the second operand is returned; otherwise the third operand is returned. The second and third arguments must represent elements of the same domain. The tests we will be interested in are (a) $X=X'$ where X and X' are variables representing identifiers, and (b) $a \,\varepsilon\, \mathbf{D}$, where **D** is an appropriate summand domain.

O4. Apply a function to an argument. When required, we use the binary operator "$\downarrow$" as in $\downarrow(g,a)$ to represent $g(a)$.

O5. Lambda abstraction. For example, if $a \in \mathbf{V}'$, then $\lambda\kappa.\kappa(a)$ is an element of $[\mathbf{K}\rightarrow\mathbf{A}]$. "$\lambda$" is a binary operator with the bound variable being the first argument.

O6. If g is a function in $\mathbf{D}\rightarrow\mathbf{D}'$, then *strict*$(g)$ is a function that maps $\bot \in \mathbf{D}$ to $\bot' \in \mathbf{D}'$, $\top \in \mathbf{D}$ to $\top' \in \mathbf{D}'$, and agrees with g everywhere else.

A *term* is a tree in which nonleaf nodes are labeled with one of the operators (O1-O6). Since the injection and projection operators cancel each other, we will assume that such cancellations are performed whenever possible. Leaves are labeled with variables. Variables are either free or bound, following the usual rules for lambda expressions.

In section 3.2 we will add an auxiliary unary operator δ to terms. Valuations **ed** and **ec** will be introduced in section 4. For any expression E, we will allow $\mathbf{ed}[\![E]\!]\rho$ and $\mathbf{ec}[\![E]\!]\rho'$ to appear where a free variable representing an element of **V** and $\mathbf{K}\rightarrow\mathbf{A}$, respectively, might appear in a term. Note that variables representing environments and identifiers are allowed in terms.

The only domain that occurs both in the direct and continuation semantic domains is **B**. We wish to keep the two kinds of semantic domains quite separate and wish to prevent interaction between them through **B**. When constructing terms, we will therefore pretend that $\mathbf{V}'=\mathbf{B}'+\mathbf{F}'$, where $\mathbf{B}'$ is a domain of basic values distinct from **B**. That **B** and $\mathbf{B}'$ are in fact the same domain will not be exploited until later.

Each node in a term must represent an element of a particular domain. If node x represents an element of domain **D** we say that x has *type* **D**. The *type* of a term T is the type of the root of T.

Having defined a term as a syntactic object of a particular type, say **D**, it is now time to show how an element of domain **D** can be associated with the term. The meaning of operators (O1-O6) is fixed and is well defined. As usual, free variables can be mapped to elements of appropriate domains by an *interpretation* **i**. For term T of type **D**, an interpretation **i** determines a unique element $\mathbf{i}[\![T]\!]$ in **D**.

3.2. *bridging the direct and continuation worlds.* Starting with a term T of type **V** we want to gradually transform T into T' of type $\mathbf{K}\rightarrow\mathbf{A}$. In the process there will be intermediate terms that must encompass elements of both direct and continuation semantic domains.

The auxiliary operator δ will serve as a syntactic placeholder separating nodes representing elements of the direct domains from the continuation domains.

Definition. If A is a term of type **B**, **F**, **V** or **U**, then $\delta[A]$ is a term of type $\mathbf{B}'$, $\mathbf{F}'$, $\mathbf{V}'$ or $\mathbf{U}'$, respectively. □

Since there is no sequence of operations which maps an element of the continuation domains to an element of the direct domains (within terms we use $\mathbf{B}'$ as the summand domain of $\mathbf{V}'$), we conclude:

REMARK. Instances of δ may not be nested. Thus if $\delta[A]$ is a subterm of some term T, then A has no instances of δ, and has type **B**, **F**, **V** or **U**. □

We will not attempt to give meaning for terms like δA until section 5.2. δA is a placeholder for some b that is related under the predicates to the interpreted value $\mathbf{i}[\![A]\!]$.

3.3. *the transformations.* The basic idea is to start with a term T containing instances of δ and "push" δ down towards the leaves as far as possible. All the transformations are based on the predicates.

transformation T1. When distributing δ over the conditional operator "$\rightarrow$", a test of the form $X=X'$, where X and X' represent identifiers, is unaffected. Since $\mathbf{V} = \mathbf{B}+\mathbf{F}$, $\mathbf{V}' = \mathbf{B}'+\mathbf{F}'$ and an element $a\epsilon\mathbf{F}$ can only be related under **pe** to $a'\epsilon\mathbf{F}'$ a test of the form $a\epsilon\mathbf{B}$ or $a\epsilon\mathbf{F}$ is easy to handle. This transformation relies on the fact that $\perp$ is related only to $\perp'$ and $\top$ is related only to $\top'$ under both **pe** and **ps**.

T1. In the following, either $\mathbf{D}=\mathbf{B}$ and $\mathbf{D}'=\mathbf{B}'$, or $\mathbf{D}=\mathbf{F}$ and $\mathbf{D}'=\mathbf{F}'$.

$$\delta[X=X'\rightarrow B,C] \Rightarrow X=X'\rightarrow\delta B,\delta C$$
$$\delta[A\,\epsilon\mathbf{D}\rightarrow B,C] \Rightarrow \delta A\,\epsilon\mathbf{D}'\rightarrow\delta B,\delta C$$

transformation T2. The next transformation allows δ to be distributed over a function application, and is based on the predicate **pf**. The definition of **pf** allows us to relate $ga\,\epsilon\mathbf{V}$ with $g'a'\epsilon\mathbf{K}\rightarrow\mathbf{A}$. (See also section 2.2.2.) Since transformations must preserve types, we will apply a continuation to $\delta[G(A)]$ to get an element of **A**.

T2. $\kappa(\delta[GA]) \Rightarrow (\delta G)(\delta A)\kappa$

Before transformation T2 can be applied, "factoring", which is explained in section 3.4, may be necessary.

transformation T3. A strict function $g\epsilon\mathbf{F}$ maps $\perp$ to $\perp$. If for some g', $\mathbf{pf}(g,g')$ holds, then $\mathbf{ps}(g\perp,g'\perp)$ must be true. Since $g\perp$ is $\perp$, from predicate **ps**, $g'\perp=\perp$ as well. $\top$ is treated similarly. Thus g' must also be strict, thereby motivating transformation T3.

T3. $\delta[\mathit{strict}\ G] \Rightarrow \mathit{strict}(\delta G)$

transformation T4. Given an element a in **V**, if $a\epsilon\mathbf{B}$, then it is easy to transform a into an element of $\mathbf{V}'$ since $\mathbf{B}=\mathbf{B}'$ is a summand domain of $\mathbf{V}'$. The next transformation allows $g\epsilon\mathbf{F}$ to be transformed to an element of $\mathbf{V}'$

Since T4 is defined recursively, we need a minor amount of notation. We write $T \Rightarrow^i U$ if U is derived from T by i applications of (T1-T6). We write $T \Rightarrow^* U$ if $i\geqslant 0$ and $T \Rightarrow^+ U$ if $i\geqslant 1$. U is said to be *irreducible* if U cannot be transformed under (T1-T6). If $T \Rightarrow^* U$ and U is irreducible, then we write $T \Rightarrow^{-} U$.

T4. Let G be a term $\lambda Y.B$ of type **F** and let X be a new variable. Let H be the term $B\{X/Y\}$ i.e. H is formed from $G(X)$ by beta conversion. Let $\kappa(\delta H) \Rightarrow^* H'(\kappa)$ where all instances of X in H' are in subterms of the form δX, and let $G' = \lambda Y.H'\{Y/\delta X\}$. Then $\delta[G] \Rightarrow G'$

transformation T5. The next transformation affects environments.

T5. $\delta[\rho[\![X]\!]] \Rightarrow (\delta\rho)[\![X]\!]$

If $\lambda X.B$ has type **U** then $\delta[\lambda X.B] \Rightarrow \lambda X.\delta B$

transformation T6. Finally, δ distributes over injections and projections.

T6. In the following, either $\mathbf{D}=\mathbf{B}$ and $\mathbf{D}'=\mathbf{B}'$, or $\mathbf{D}=\mathbf{F}$ and $\mathbf{D}'=\mathbf{F}'$.

$$\delta[A|\mathbf{D}] \Rightarrow (\delta A)|\mathbf{D}'$$
$$\delta[A\ \mathbf{in}\ \mathbf{V}] \Rightarrow (\delta A)\ \mathbf{in}\ \mathbf{V}'$$

We can measure the extent to which a term remains to be transformed by defining the "rank" of a term. Let $\delta U_1,\delta U_2,\cdots,\delta U_k$ be all the subterms of T that have roots labeled δ. The *rank* of T is defined to be the sum of the operators in $U_1,U_2,\cdots,U_k$.

Remark. Since each transformation decreases the rank of a term, for each term T there is a limit l such that if $T \Rightarrow^i U$ for any U, then $i<l$. It therefore makes sense to talk of the irreducible elements that can be derived from a starting term.[5] □

[5] The irreducible elements derived from a given starting term need not be unique. The intuitive reason is that direct semantics does not specify the order of evaluation of E_1 and E_2 in $E_1(E_2)$, but in continuation semantics we must decide which of E_1 and E_2 is to be computed first. Thus starting with the same direct semantic description we can construct two distinct but related semantic descriptions, so we cannot expect to have the Church-Rosser property as in [1,7].

3.4. *factoring.* When applying transformations T2 and T4 we will permit controlled use of "factoring" which was also used in [8]. Let T and S be terms and let X be a new variable. We write $T\{X/S\}$ to represent the term formed by uniformly substituting X for the subexpression S in T. The usual notion of substitution which eliminates clashes of bound variables is intended. The term $[\lambda X.T\{X/S\}](S)$ is said to be formed by *factoring S from T*.

The following restriction lays out our use of factoring.

RESTRICTION. The only uses of factoring will be:

(a) If T is a term of type **A** and S is $\delta[GA]$ then $\kappa' = \lambda X.T\{X/\delta GA\}$ is an expression continuation. This use of factoring must be followed by the application of transformation T2 to $\kappa'(\delta[GA])$.

(b) In transformation T4, let T' be such that $\kappa(\delta H) \Rightarrow^* T'$ and all instances of X in T' are in subterms of the form δX. The term T' may not be of the form $U'(\kappa)$, but factoring may be used to convert T' to $H'(\kappa)$.

(c) In section 4.2, the transformations will be augmented by a transformation that allows instances of **ed** to be eliminated in favor of instances of **ec**. Factoring will be permitted while applying this transformation.

These uses of factoring will become clear in section 5.1 where we show essentially that instances of δ can be "pushed" all the way down to the leaves.

4. Call by Value Semantics

4.1. *direct semantics.* The starting point in this section is the semantic description in Figure 1. Since call-by-value is intended, the value of $E_1(E_2)$ must be $\bot$ if the value of E_2 is $\bot$. This requirement can be met in one of two ways: (1) we can make the meaning of a procedure a strict function to start with; or (2) the meaning of a procedure need not be strict, but when a procedure is applied we use

$$\mathbf{ed}[\![E_1(E_2)]\!]\rho = \mathit{strict}(\mathbf{ed}[\![E_1]\!]\rho|\mathbf{F})(\mathbf{ed}[\![E_2]\!]\rho)$$

We prefer to make the meaning of a procedure a strict function, since we would rather build the parameter passing mechanism into the meaning of a procedure than toy with the notion of function application. (After all, the meaning of a procedure definitely has to take call-by-name into account if that mechanism is used.)

Syntactic Domains

I:	**Ide**	identifiers
E:	**Exp**	expressions
$-$:		operator

Syntax

$E ::= I \mid -E \mid E(E) \mid \mathbf{proc}(I){:}E$

Semantic Domains

	B	basic values
	F	function values
	V	expression values
ρ:	**U**	environments

Valuation

$\mathbf{ed}{:}\mathbf{Exp} \to [\mathbf{U} \to \mathbf{V}]$

Semantic Equations

$$\mathbf{ed}[\![I]\!]\rho = \rho[\![I]\!]$$
$$\mathbf{ed}[\![-E]\!]\rho = \ominus(\mathbf{ed}[\![E]\!]\rho)$$
$$\mathbf{ed}[\![E_1(E_2)]\!]\rho = (\mathbf{ed}[\![E_1]\!]\rho|\mathbf{F})(\mathbf{ed}[\![E_2]\!]\rho)$$
$$\mathbf{ed}[\![\mathbf{proc}(I){:}E]\!]\rho = \mathit{strict}\ \lambda a.\mathbf{ed}[\![E]\!]\rho[a/I]\ \mathbf{in}\ \mathbf{V}$$

Figure 1: Expressions and their direct semantics. $\ominus \in \mathbf{V} \to \mathbf{V}$ is the negation function.

4.2. *continuation semantics.* Starting with the direct semantic description in Figure 1 we will construct the continuation semantic description in Figure 2, using the transformations from section 3 and the following

$$\kappa(\delta[\mathbf{ed}[\![E]\!]\rho]) \Rightarrow \mathbf{ec}[\![E]\!](\delta\rho)\kappa \qquad (4.1)$$

As discussed in section 1.3, it makes intuitive sense to view $\mathbf{ec}[\![E]\!]\rho'\kappa$ as determining the "value" of E in environment ρ' and then applying κ to this "value". This "value" will be related under predicate **pe** to

Semantic Domains

	$\mathbf{B}$	basic values
	$\mathbf{F}' = \mathbf{V}' \to [\mathbf{K} \to \mathbf{A}]$	function values
	$\mathbf{V}' = \mathbf{B} + \mathbf{F}'$	expression values
ρ':	$\mathbf{U}' = \mathbf{Ide} \to \mathbf{V}'$	environments
	$\mathbf{A}$	answers
κ:	$\mathbf{K} = \mathbf{V}' \to_{\perp} \mathbf{A}$	continuations

Valuation

$$\mathbf{ec}: \quad \mathbf{Exp} \to [\mathbf{U}' \to [\mathbf{K} \to \mathbf{A}]\,]$$

Semantic Equations

$$\begin{aligned}
\mathbf{ec}[\![I]\!]\rho'\kappa &= \kappa(\rho'[\![I]\!]) \\
\mathbf{ec}[\![-E]\!]\rho'\kappa &= \mathbf{ec}[\![E]\!]\rho'[\lambda a.\ominus' a\kappa] \\
\mathbf{ec}[\![E_1(E_2)]\!]\rho'\kappa &= \mathbf{ec}[\![E_2]\!]\rho'[\,\lambda a.\mathbf{ec}[\![E_1]\!]\rho'[\lambda g.(g|\mathbf{F}')a\kappa]\,] \\
\mathbf{ec}[\![\mathbf{proc}(I){:}E]\!]\rho'\kappa &= \kappa(\mathit{strict}(\,\lambda a.\mathbf{ec}[\![E]\!]\rho'[a/I])\ \mathbf{in}\ \mathbf{V}')
\end{aligned}$$

Figure 2: The transformation $\kappa(\delta[\mathbf{ed}[\![E]\!]\rho]) \twoheadrightarrow \mathbf{ec}[\![E]\!](\delta\rho)\kappa$ constructs the above semantic equations from the equations for **ed** in Figure 1.

$\mathbf{ed}[\![E]\!]\rho$, where environments ρ and ρ' are related under **pu**. The patterns in (4.1) are a formalization of this intuitive view.

We illustrate the process of constructing the description in Figure 2 by considering the semantic equations for $E_1(E_2)$ in Figure 1. Start by applying δ and then κ to the right hand side of the equation:

$$\kappa(\,\delta[(\mathbf{ed}[\![E_1]\!]\rho|\mathbf{F})(\mathbf{ed}[\![E_2]\!]\rho)]\,)$$

This term is of the form $\kappa(\delta[GA])$ so T2, the only applicable transformation yields

$$(\delta[\mathbf{ed}[\![E_1]\!]\rho|\mathbf{F}])(\delta[\mathbf{ed}[\![E_2]\!]\rho])\kappa$$

δ can now be distributed over the projection onto $\mathbf{F}$:

$$(\delta[\mathbf{ed}[\![E_1]\!]\rho]|\mathbf{F}')(\delta[\mathbf{ed}[\![E_2]\!]\rho])\kappa$$

Since the direct semantics does not specify which of $\mathbf{ed}[\![E_1]\!]\rho$ and $\mathbf{ed}[\![E_2]\!]\rho$ is to be computed first, we have a choice of where pattern (4.1) is to be applied. Let us choose $\delta[\mathbf{ed}[\![E_2]\!]\rho]$ and use factoring to get

$$[\lambda a.(\delta[\mathbf{ed}[\![E_1]\!]\rho]|\mathbf{F}')a\kappa](\delta[\mathbf{ed}[\![E_2]\!]\rho])$$

This term is of the form $\kappa'(\delta[\mathbf{ed}[\![E_2]\!]\rho])$ so from (4.1) we get

$$\mathbf{ec}[\![E_2]\!](\delta\rho)[\lambda a.(\delta[\mathbf{ed}[\![E_1]\!]\rho]|\mathbf{F}')a\kappa]$$

Similar manipulations lead to

$$\mathbf{ec}[\![E_2]\!](\delta\rho)[\,\lambda a.\mathbf{ec}[\![E_1]\!](\delta\rho)[\lambda g.(g|\mathbf{F}')a\kappa]\,]$$

A different choice while applying pattern (4.1) leads to the equivalent term

$$\mathbf{ec}[\![E_1]\!](\delta\rho)[\,\lambda g.\mathbf{ec}[\![E_2]\!](\delta\rho)[\lambda a.(g|\mathbf{F}')a\kappa]\,]$$

In the semantic equations in Figure 2 the environment ρ' appears instead of $\delta\rho$. When we relate **ed** and **ec** we expect ρ and ρ' to be related under predicate **pu**. It is worth pointing out that the negation function $\ominus'$ is now an element of $\mathbf{V}' \to [\mathbf{K} \to \mathbf{A}]$, the domain of function values.

THEOREM 4.1. *The semantic equations for* **ec** *in Figure 2 can be generated from the semantic equations for* **ed** *in Figure 1 using transformations (T1-T6) and pattern (4.1).*

PROOF: The interesting case is the semantic equation for $\mathbf{proc}(I){:}E$. Start with

$$\kappa(\delta[\mathit{strict}\ \lambda a.\mathbf{ed}[\![E]\!]\rho[a/I]\ \mathbf{in}\ \mathbf{V}])$$

Transformations T6 and then T3 yield

$$\kappa(\mathit{strict}(\,\delta[\,\lambda a.\mathbf{ed}[\![E]\!]\rho[a/I]\,]\,)\ \mathbf{in}\ \mathbf{V}') \tag{4.2}$$

Since we have a subexpression of the form $\delta[\lambda Y.B]$, let us attempt to use transformation T4 by starting the auxiliary derivation

$$\kappa'(\,\delta[\mathbf{ed}[\![E]\!]\rho[X/I]\,]\,) \twoheadrightarrow \mathbf{ec}[\![E]\!](\delta[\,\rho[X/I]\,])\kappa' \tag{4.3}$$

Recall that $\rho[X/I]$ is just $\lambda I'.I'{=}I \to X,\ \rho[\![I']\!]$, so transformations T5 and T1 yield

$\delta[\ \rho[X/I]\ ] \Rightarrow^* \lambda I'.I'=I \rightarrow \delta X,\ (\delta\rho)[\![I']\!]$

which abbreviates to

$(\delta\rho)[\delta X/I]$

Going back to (4.3) we get

$\mathbf{ec}[\![E]\!](\ (\delta\rho)[\delta X/I]\ )\kappa'$

Since all instances of X are in subterms of the form δX, transformation T2 applied to (4.2) yields

$\kappa(\ \mathit{strict}(\lambda a'.\mathbf{ec}[\![E]\!](\ (\delta\rho)[a'/I]\ )\ \mathbf{in}\ \mathbf{V}'\ )$

□

The proof that valuations **ed** and **ec** are related by predicate **ps** follows in section 5 from a consideration of the properties of the transformations.

5. Results about the Transformations

Given a term T of type **V**, we will generally want to construct a related term T' of type **K→A**. Since the transformations preserve types, we will start with $\lambda\kappa.\kappa(\delta T)$. There are two parts to showing that $\lambda\kappa.\kappa(\delta T)$ can indeed be transformed to a related term T'. We must first show that the transformations can continue to be applied until T' is derived, and secondly we must show that T' is related to the term T under predicate **ps**.

The transformations are based on the predicates **pe**, **pf**, **ps** and **pu**, so if a term represents an element of a domain that is not related by one of the predicates we cannot expect the transformations to do very much with the term. We may not for example construct a very complex function and then apply it repeatedly, yielding functions of lower type, until an element of a domain that can be related is reached.

In sections 5.1-5.3 we require that each node in a term represent an element of one of the domains **B**, **B'**, **F**, **F'**, **V**, **V'**, **Ide**, **U**, **U'**, **K**, **A**, **K→A**. Results for such terms will be useful when terms with occurrences of $\mathbf{ed}[\![E]\!]$ and $\mathbf{ec}[\![E]\!]$ are considered in section 5.4.

5.1. *adequacy of the transformations.* Given the term $\delta[GA]$, there is no transformation that will distribute δ over the function application, but in $\kappa(\delta[GA])$, we can distribute δ. The question of the "completeness" of the transformations naturally arises. One consequence of Theorem 5.1 is that given a term T of type **V**, starting with $\kappa(\delta T)$ we can "push" δ down to the leaves.

THEOREM 5.1. *Let T be a term of type* **A** *and let the types of nodes in T be chosen from the domains listed above. If $T \Rightarrow^{-} W$ then W has rank 0.*

PROOF: Suppose the theorem is false and there exist T and W such that $T \Rightarrow^{-} W$, but the rank of W is greater than 0. Then W must contain a subterm δU with rank greater than 0. We assume that among all terms of its kind, T has least rank.

Looking over the operators, if the root of U is a projection, an injection, a conditional or *strict* then δU cannot be irreducible, so these cases cannot occur. The only cases to be considered are for function application and lambda abstraction.

Case 1. function application. If U is $\rho[\![I]\!]$ then δU will not be irreducible, so U must be of the form GA where G has type **F**.

Note that the types of nodes that are ancestors of the term δU must represent elements of the domains in continuation semantics, while all nodes in U represent elements of the domains in direct semantics. Thus any free variables in δU must remain free in the entire term T.

Here is where we use the property that the starting term T has type **A**. Let V with subterm δU be of type **A**. Then $\lambda B'.V\{B'/\delta U\}$ is a continuation and using $U = GA$, V factors (see section 3.4) to

$[\lambda B'.V\{B'/\delta GA\}](\delta GA)$

Since $[\lambda B'.V\{B'/\delta GA\}]$ is a continuation, transformation T2 is applicable, so this case cannot occur.

Case 2. lambda abstraction. Given the allowable types, U must have type **F** or **U**. From transformation T5 δ easily distributes over a term of type **U** so the case of interest is type **F**. Using renaming if necessary, let the bound variable in this abstraction be unique and let U be $\lambda X.B$.

Since B has fewer operators than U, $\kappa(\delta B)$ of type **A** has smaller rank than T. Thus $\kappa(\delta B)$ transforms to a term C of rank 0. All transformations except T2 can affect only the subterms below a δ operator. T2 can alter the position of a continuation κ, but κ itself must still exist in the derived term. Since copies cannot be made of κ, there must be exactly one instance of κ in C. If C is not already of the form $D(\kappa)$ then factoring can be used to factor C to $D(\kappa)$. From the definition of rank, D will also have rank 0, so all instances of X in D must therefore be in subterms of the form δX. Transformation T4 is therefore applicable to δU after all, so this case cannot occur either.

Since all cases have been considered, we have contradicted the assumption that W with $rank(W)>0$ is irreducible. The theorem must therefore be true. □

5.2. *replacements.* Starting with a term T of type **V**, let $\lambda\kappa.\kappa(\delta T) \to^* W$. We expect W to contain instances of δ, as shown in Figure 3, so merely specifying an interpretation **i** is not enough to associate an element of **K→A** with W: we need to do something with the δ-subterms of W as well.

5.2.1. *musings on replacements.* Consider the subterm δA of type **V** in Figure 3, and suppose that an interpretation **i** is given. The terms "replace" and "replacements" will be used informally in this subsection.

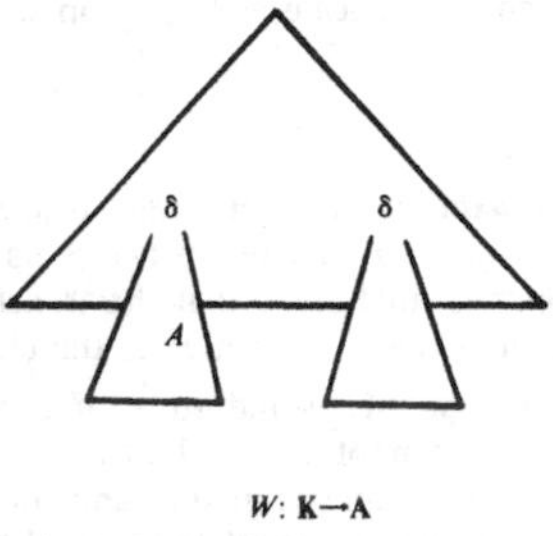

Figure 3: The term W of type **K→A** contains a subterm δA where A has type **V**. Within the term W, subterms below a δ operator represent elements of the direct domains, while other nodes represents elements of the continuation domains. A "replacement" is used to bridge the two kinds of domains.

A first, inadequate, cut at defining replacements is to use **i** to determine $\mathbf{i}[\![A]\!] = a \in \mathbf{V}$ and then pick some $a' \in \mathbf{V}'$ for δA, such that $\mathbf{pe}(a,a')$ holds. Similar choices can be made for δ-subterms of other types. Once we replace each δ-subterm by an element of one of the continuation semantic domains it is easy to determine a value in **K→A** for W: all that needs to be done is to interpret using **i** the remaining nodes representing elements of the continuation domains.

The problem with this approach is that all terms with value $a \in \mathbf{V}$ will be replaced by the same $a' \in \mathbf{V}'$. After all there may be another $a'' \in \mathbf{V}'$ such that $\mathbf{pe}(a,a'')$ is also true. As an example, let X and Y be distinct variables of type **V**. Purely by coincidence, it is possible that $\mathbf{i}[\![X]\!] = \mathbf{i}[\![Y]\!] = a \in \mathbf{V}$, but under some other interpretation **i'**, $\mathbf{i}'[\![X]\!] \neq \mathbf{i}'[\![Y]\!]$. We would like the freedom of replacing δX by a' but δY by a'', since X and Y are quite distinct terms.

The definition of replacements will parallel that of interpretations. First, let us tend to variables. Let X be a variable of type **V**, and let $\mathbf{i}[\![X]\!] = a \in \mathbf{V}$. Since we want to replace X by some $a' \in \mathbf{V}'$ such that $\mathbf{pe}(a,a')$ holds, we will supply *both* **i** and X as arguments to replacement **r**. **r** maps interpretation **i** to a function **ri** from variables to values in **V'**, such that $\mathbf{pe}(\mathbf{i}[\![X]\!],\mathbf{ri}[\![X]\!])$ holds.

Once continuation values have been determined for all the free variables in a term, we will extend replacements to apply to all terms by suitably replacing operator symbols by functions.

5.2.2. *Definition.* A function **r** is a *replacement* if and only if **r** maps an interpretation **i** to a function **ri** from variables X of type **B**, **F**, **V**, or **U** to elements of **B'**, **F'**, **V'**, or **U'** as follows:

Let X be a variable of type **V**. For all **i** such that $\mathbf{i}[\![X]\!] = a \in \mathbf{V}$, $\mathbf{ri}[\![X]\!]$ is a particular element of $a' \in \mathbf{V}'$ such that $\mathbf{pe}(a,a')$ is true. For variables X of type **F** or **U** we want **pf** or **pu** to hold on $\mathbf{i}[\![X]\!]$ and $\mathbf{ri}[\![X]\!]$. For variables X of type **B**, $\mathbf{ri}[\![X]\!]$ is $\mathbf{i}[\![X]\!] \mid \mathbf{B}$ **in** **V'**. □

As an immediate consequence of the above definition, for all **i** and **i'** if $\mathbf{i}[\![X]\!] = \mathbf{i}'[\![X]\!]$ the $\mathbf{ri}[\![X]\!] = \mathbf{ri}'[\![X]\!]$.

Replacements are extended to all terms as follows. Intuitively, for each operator that normally takes arguments in the direct semantic domains, a corresponding operator taking related arguments in the continuation semantic domains will be used.

Definition. For a term T of type **B**, **F**, **V** or **U**, $\mathbf{ri}[\![T]\!]$ is constructed by looking at the structure of T.

1. If T is $I=I' \to B,C$ then $\mathbf{ri}[\![T]\!]$ is $\mathbf{i}[\![I]\!] = \mathbf{i}[\![I']\!] \to \mathbf{ri}[\![B]\!],\mathbf{ri}[\![C]\!]$. If T is $G \in \mathbf{D} \to B,C$ then $\mathbf{ri}[\![T]\!]$ is $\mathbf{ri}[\![G]\!] \in \mathbf{D}' \to \mathbf{ri}[\![B]\!],\mathbf{ri}[\![C]\!]$, where again **D** is either **B** or **F** and **D**′ is **B**′ and **F**′ as needed.
2. If T is a term $G(A)$ of type **V**, let $\mathbf{ri}[\![G]\!]$ be g' and $\mathbf{ri}[\![A]\!]$ be a'. Then $\mathbf{ri}[\![T]\!]$ is a particular element $b' \in \mathbf{V}'$ such that $g'a' = \lambda\kappa.\kappa b'$ and $\mathbf{pe}(\mathbf{i}[\![GA]\!],b')$ holds. It follows from predicate **ps** that such a b' exists.
3. If T is $strict(G)$ then $\mathbf{ri}[\![T]\!]$ is $strict(\mathbf{ri}[\![G]\!])$. Theorem 5.2 justifies this case.
4. If T of type **F** is $\lambda Y.B$ then $\mathbf{ri}[\![T]\!]$ is $\lambda a'.\lambda\kappa.\kappa(\{\mathbf{ri}[a'/Y]\}[\![B]\!])$. Here $\mathbf{ri}[a'/X]$ is a function that agrees with **ri** at all arguments except X, where it has value a'.
5. If T is $\rho[\![I]\!]$ then $\mathbf{ri}[\![T]\!]$ is $(\mathbf{ri}[\![\rho]\!])(\mathbf{i}[\![I]\!])$. If T is $\lambda I.B$ of type **U** then $\mathbf{ri}[\![T]\!]$ is $\lambda x.\mathbf{ri}[\![B]\!]$.
6. If T is $A|\mathbf{D}$ then $\mathbf{ri}[\![T]\!]$ is $\mathbf{ri}[\![A]\!]|\mathbf{D}'$, where **D** is either **B** or **F** and **D**′ is **B**′ or **F**′. If T is A **in V** then $\mathbf{ri}[\![T]\!]$ is $\mathbf{ri}[\![A]\!]$ **in V**′.

If T is a term δU then $\mathbf{ri}[\![T]\!] = \mathbf{ri}[\![U]\!]$. The extension of **ri** to all other types chosen from the continuation domains is the natural one of first applying **ri** to all subterms with root δ and then interpreting the modified term normally. □

Theorem 5.2. *Let T be a term of type* **B**, **F**, **V**, *or* **U**. *For all* **i** *and* **r**, $\mathbf{i}[\![T]\!]$ *and* $\mathbf{ri}[\![T]\!]$ *are related under* **pf**, **pe** *or* **pu**, *as appropriate.*

Proof: We prove the theorem by structural induction on the term T. The basis, T being a variable, follows from the definition of replacements.

For the inductive step we have a case for each operator which might be the root of T. The only cases which are not immediate are when the root is *strict* or λ.

Case 1. strict. We need to prove that

$$\mathbf{pf}(g,g') \text{ implies } \mathbf{pf}(strict\ g,\ strict\ g')$$

We know that

$$\mathbf{pf}(g,g') \text{ if and only if } \mathbf{ps}(ga,g'a') \text{ holds whenever } \mathbf{pe}(a,a') \text{ holds.}$$

By examining the cases for a and a' under which $\mathbf{pe}(a,a')$ is true, if $a=\perp$ or $a'=\perp$ then both must be $\perp$. In this case both $g(\perp)$ and $strict\ g'(\perp)$ are $\perp$ by definition, and by definition $\mathbf{ps}(\perp,\perp)$ is true. The case for $\top$ is similar. At all other values for a and a', $strict\ g$ agrees with g and $strict\ g'$ agrees with g', so $\mathbf{pf}(strict\ g,\ strict\ g')$ must be true.

Case 2. lambda abstraction. The case of interest is when T is of type **F** and is of the form $\lambda Y.B$.

Suppose that under **i** and **r**, $\mathbf{i}[\![T]\!] = g \in \mathbf{F}$ and $\mathbf{ri}[\![T]\!] = g' \in \mathbf{F}'$. We seek to show that g and g' are related under **pf**. In order to do so we must show that if $\mathbf{pe}(a,a')$ holds for any a and a', then $\mathbf{ps}(ga,g'a')$ must also hold.

Using renaming of bound variables if necessary, suppose that all bound variables in $T = \lambda Y.B$ are distinct, and that Y does not appear free in T. From the definitions,

$$ga = (\mathbf{i}[\![T]\!])(a) = \{\mathbf{i}[a/Y]\}[\![B]\!]$$

$$g'a' = (\mathbf{ri}[\![T]\!])(a') = \lambda\kappa.\kappa(\{\mathbf{ri}[a'/Y]\}[\![B]\!])$$

Let $\mathbf{i}' = \mathbf{i}[a/Y]$. Since $\mathbf{pe}(a,a')$ holds, the function $\mathbf{r}'$ such that $\mathbf{r}'\mathbf{i}'$ agrees with **ri** on all variables except Y and $\mathbf{r}'\mathbf{i}'[\![Y]\!] = a'$ is a replacement. Since Y is bound in T, $\mathbf{r}'\mathbf{i}'[\![T]\!] = g'$ as well. Moreover, from the definition of $\mathbf{r}'$ and $\mathbf{i}'$, $\mathbf{r}'\mathbf{i}'[\![B]\!] = \{\mathbf{ri}[a'/Y]\}[\![B]\!]$. From the inductive hypothesis $\mathbf{i}'[\![B]\!]$ and $\mathbf{r}'\mathbf{i}'[\![B]\!]$ are related under **pe**. Thus $\mathbf{i}'[\![B]\!] = ga$ and $\lambda\kappa.\kappa(\mathbf{r}'\mathbf{i}'[\![B]\!]) = g'a'$ are related under **ps**, finishing the proof of this case. □

5.3. *transformations preserve predicates.* Consider a term T of type **V**, and let $\lambda\kappa.\kappa(\delta T)$ transform to W under (T1-T6). Given an interpretation **i**, term T represents $\mathbf{i}[\![T]\!]$ in **V**. We expect term W to contain instances of δ, so a replacement **r** will be needed to associate a value in $\mathbf{K} \to \mathbf{A}$ with W. The result we would like to show is that for any interpretation **i** and replacement **r**, $\mathbf{i}[\![T]\!]$ is related under **ps** to $\mathbf{ri}[\![W]\!]$:

$$\forall\mathbf{i}\ \forall\mathbf{r}\ \mathbf{ps}(\mathbf{i}[\![T]\!],\mathbf{ri}[\![W]\!]) \tag{5.1}$$

The result (5.1) follows immediately from Theorem 5.2 and the next theorem.

Theorem 5.3. *If $T \twoheadrightarrow^* W$ then*

$$\forall\mathbf{i}\ \forall\mathbf{r}\ \mathbf{ri}[\![T]\!] = \mathbf{ri}[\![W]\!]$$

Proof: The proof proceeds by induction on the number of steps in the derivation of W from T. We note in passing that an inductive proof is necessitated by the fact that for T4 the number of steps in the auxiliary derivation are also counted.

The basis, zero steps, is trivial since $T = W$. For the inductive step we have a case for each transformation.

Suppose the last term before W is U: $T \Rightarrow^* U \Rightarrow^+ W$. For all transformations except T4, U will transform to W in one step. We just need to show that $\mathbf{ri}[\![U]\!] = \mathbf{ri}[\![W]\!]$. The theorem will then follow from the inductive hypothesis.

Most of the cases in the proof are straightforward. We will give the proofs for T2 and T4.

Case 1. W is derived from U by $\kappa(\delta[GA]) \Rightarrow (\delta G)(\delta A)\kappa$. Since the subterm $\kappa(\delta[GA])$ in U is transformed to yield W, if we can show that $\mathbf{ri}[\![\kappa(\delta[GA])]\!] = \mathbf{ri}[\![(\delta G)(\delta A)\kappa]\!]$, it will follow that $\mathbf{ri}[\![U]\!] = \mathbf{ri}[\![W]\!]$.

Let $\mathbf{ri}[\![G]\!] = g'$ and let $\mathbf{ri}[\![A]\!] = a'$. In this case, $\mathbf{ri}[\![GA]\!] = b'$, where $g'a' = \lambda\kappa.\kappa b'$. Clearly, $g'a'\kappa = \kappa b'$ so the desired equality $\mathbf{ri}[\![U]\!] = \mathbf{ri}[\![W]\!]$ follows.

Case 2. Let $\delta[\lambda X.B]$ be a subterm of U, where the variable X is unique to this bound instance. Furthermore, let $\kappa(\delta B) \Rightarrow^* C\kappa$ where all instances of X in C are in subterms of the form δX. Then, from the definition of transformation T4, $\delta[\lambda X.B] \Rightarrow^+ \lambda Y.C\{Y/\delta X\}$. From the definition of replacements,

$$\mathbf{ri}[\![\lambda X.B]\!] = \lambda a'.\lambda\kappa.\kappa(\{\mathbf{ri}[a'/X]\}[\![B]\!])$$

Since $\lambda Y.C\{Y/\delta X\}$ has rank 0,

$$\mathbf{ri}[\![\lambda Y.C\{Y/\delta X\}]\!] = \lambda a'.\{\mathbf{ri}[a'/Y]\}[\![C\{Y/\delta X\}]\!]$$

Since X and Y do not occur elsewhere

$$\mathbf{ri}[\![\lambda Y.C\{Y/\delta X\}]\!] = \lambda a'.\{\mathbf{ri}[a'/X]\}[\![C]\!]$$

From the inductive hypothesis applied to the derivation $\kappa(\delta B) \Rightarrow^* C\kappa$ we have $\mathbf{r'i'}[\![\kappa(\delta B)]\!] = \mathbf{r'i'}[\![C\kappa]\!]$ for all $\mathbf{i'}$ and $\mathbf{r'}$. Note that $\mathbf{r'i'}[\![\kappa(\delta B)]\!] = \kappa(\mathbf{r'i'}[\![B]\!])$ and $\mathbf{r'i'}[\![C\kappa]\!] = (\mathbf{r'i'}[\![C]\!])\kappa$. Therefore $\lambda a'.\lambda\kappa.\kappa(\mathbf{r'i'}[\![B]\!]) = \lambda a'.\mathbf{r'i'}[\![C]\!]$. If we choose $\mathbf{r'i'} = \mathbf{ri}[a'/X]$ we immediately get $\mathbf{ri}[\![\lambda X.B]\!] = \mathbf{ri}[\![\lambda Y.C\{Y/\delta X\}]\!]$, from which the desired equality $\mathbf{ri}[\![U]\!] = \mathbf{ri}[\![W]\!]$ follows. □

A useful corollary of the last two theorems is the following.

COROLLARY 5.1. *If* $\lambda\kappa.\kappa(\delta T) \Rightarrow^* W$ *then*

$$\forall \mathbf{i}.\ \forall \mathbf{r}.\ \mathbf{ps}(\mathbf{i}[\![T]\!], \mathbf{ri}[\![W]\!])$$

PROOF: It follows from Theorem 5.2 that for all $\mathbf{i}$ and $\mathbf{r}$, $\mathbf{ps}(\mathbf{i}[\![T]\!], \mathbf{ri}[\![\lambda\kappa.\kappa(\delta T)]\!])$ holds. From Theorem 5.3, $\mathbf{ri}[\![\lambda\kappa.\kappa(\delta T)]\!] = \mathbf{ri}[\![W]\!]$ so the corollary must be true. □

5.4. *relating* **ed** *and* **ec**. When the direct and continuation semantic domains were related in section 5.3, the pattern (4.1) used to construct the equations for **ec** was not in the picture. We need to show that Corollary 5.1 can be used even when (4.1) is allowed.

The semantic equation for $\mathbf{ed}[\![I]\!]\rho$ does not have **ed** on the right hand side. In fact, for any expression E, proceeding in a syntax directed manner, we can construct a term free of **ed** which represents the meaning of $\mathbf{ed}[\![E]\!]\rho$. Thus, we do not expect much difficulty in proving that (4.1) can be integrated into the transformations.

Direct proofs of theorems like the following have appeared in [3,5,10].

THEOREM 5.4. *For all expressions E and pairs of environments* ρ *and* ρ' *where* $\mathbf{pu}(\rho,\rho')$ *holds,*

$$\mathbf{ps}(\mathbf{ed}[\![E]\!]\rho, \mathbf{ec}[\![E]\!]\rho')$$

must be true.

PROOF: Starting with $\mathbf{ed}[\![E]\!]\rho$ we can use syntax directed methods to construct a term T_E in which all instances of **ed** have been eliminated. Similarly, starting with $\mathbf{ec}[\![E]\!](\delta\rho)$ we can construct a term U_E in which all instances of **ec** have been eliminated.

A structural induction on E establishes that $\lambda\kappa.\kappa(\delta T_E) \Rightarrow^* U_E$. The basis involves expressions for which the right hand side has no instance of **ed**. In this case $\lambda\kappa.\kappa(\delta T_E) \Rightarrow^* U_E$ follows by construction of the equations for **ec**. For the inductive step, consider the right hand side of the equation for $\mathbf{ed}[\![E]\!]\rho$. Mimic the construction of $\mathbf{ec}[\![E]\!](\delta\rho)$ except that whenever (4.1) would be applied to $\mathbf{ed}[\![E']\!]\rho$, use the derivation $\lambda\kappa.\kappa(\delta T_{E'}) \Rightarrow^* U_{E'}$ that must exist by the inductive hypothesis.

From Corollary 5.1, $\mathbf{ps}(\mathbf{i}[\![T_E]\!], \mathbf{ri}[\![U_E]\!])$ must be true, for all $\mathbf{i}$ and $\mathbf{r}$. The only free variable in T_E is for the environment ρ so pick $\mathbf{i}$ so that ρ is used and $\mathbf{r}$ so that ρ' is used. It follows that $\mathbf{ps}(\mathbf{ed}[\![E]\!]\rho, \mathbf{ec}[\![E]\!]\rho')$ must be true. □

Notice that the proof of Theorem 5.4 does not need to look at the exact structure of pattern (4.1) which was used to construct **ec** from **ed**.

Finally, we need to show that the analogue of Theorem 5.1 holds even when $\mathbf{ed}[\![E]\!]\rho$ and $\mathbf{ec}[\![E]\!]\rho'$ are allowed to appear in terms and (4.1) may be applied. Recall that we allow $\mathbf{ed}[\![E]\!]\rho$ and $\mathbf{ec}[\![E]\!]\rho'$ for some E, ρ, and ρ' to appear where free variables of type **V** and **K→A**, respectively, might appear.

Suppose that in term $\kappa(\delta T)$ we wish to substitute $\mathbf{ed}[\![E]\!]\rho$ for a free variable X. From Theorem 5.1, if $\kappa(\delta T) \Rightarrow^{*} U$, then U has rank 0. In this case all instances of X in U appear in subterms of the form δX. Let V be formed by substituting $\mathbf{ed}[\![E]\!]\rho$ for X in U. Since V has type **A**, using factoring, we can construct a term of the form $\kappa'(\delta[\mathbf{ed}[\![E]\!]\rho])$ from V. (4.1) converts this term to $\mathbf{ec}[\![E]\!](\delta\rho)\kappa'$. If there were a term of type **U** instead of ρ, Theorem 5.1 could again be invoked to derive a rank 0 term.

The above discussion shows that even when $\mathbf{ed}[\![E]\!]\rho$ is allowed in a term, using (4.1) and the transformations, all instances of δ can be "pushed" down to the leaves, and all instances of **ed** can be eliminated.

6. Discussion

The meaning of a procedure is a function value. Let **F** and **F**′ be the domains of function values in direct and continuation semantics. **F** and **F**′ have a quite different structure since a function in continuation semantics takes a continuation as a parameter. The problem of relating **F** and **F**′ is complicated by the fact that both domains are recursively defined. Milne [3] and Reynolds [5] solve this problem using predicates.

Let a term T represent an element of **F**. Our first step was to define transformations which derive T' from T, where T' represents an element of **F**′. Since the number of transformations is small, but terms like T can be arbitrarily large, the derivation of T' was done in small stages. Using an auxiliary operator δ as a syntactic placeholder, we started with δT and pushed δ down onto smaller and smaller subexpressions of T using the transformations.

The interesting part was showing that T and T' represent related values. As usual, an interpretation was used to map a term with no instances of δ to an element of **F** or **F**′ as appropriate. But what about terms that contain δ? In showing that T and T' represent related values, it was convenient to show that the intermediate terms in the derivation also represent related values. Therefore meaning had to be given to terms with δ in them.

Treating a term as a tree, the subterm below δ represents values from the direct domains, while the rest of the term represents values from the continuation domains. The definition of replacements in section 5.2 which give meaning for terms like δT was arrived at after several false starts. It seems that any time we seek to transform objects in one semantic world into objects in another semantic world we will need a mechanism playing the role of replacements.

Predicates, transformations and replacements are very closely related. Can the construction of replacements from transformations be automated so that separate proofs that the transformations preserve the predicates will not be necessary? Can the transformations be derived automatically from the predicates? The next step is clearly to apply the methods of this paper to construct other semantic descriptions.

References

1. G. Huet, "Confluent reductions: abstract properties and applications to term rewriting systems," *Eighteenth Annual IEEE Symposium on Foundations of Computer Science*, pp. 30-45 (October 1977).
2. B. W. Kernighan and D. M. Ritchie, *The C Programming Language*, Prentice-Hall, Englewood Cliffs, NJ (1978).
3. R. E. Milne and C. Strachey, *A Theory of Programming Language Semantics, 2 Vols.*, Chapman and Hall, London, and John Wiley, New York (1976).
4. F. L. Morris, "The next 700 programming language descriptions," unpublished manuscript (1970).
5. J. C. Reynolds, "On the relation between direct and continuation semantics," pp. 141-156 in *2nd Colloquium on Automata, Languages and Programming*, Lecture Notes in Computer Science 14, Springer-Verlag, Berlin (1974).
6. D. Scott and C. Strachey, "Towards a mathematical semantics for computer languages," pp. 19-46 in *Proceedings of the Symposium on Computers and Automata*, Polytechnic Press, Brooklyn, N. Y. (April 1971).
7. R. Sethi, "Testing for the Church-Rosser property," *J. ACM* **21**(4), pp. 671-679, Errata in *J. ACM* **22**(3) p. 424 (July 1975). (October 1974).
8. R. Sethi and A. Tang, "Transforming direct into continuation semantics for a simple imperative language," unpublished manuscript, Bell Laboratories, Murray Hill, NJ (1978).
9. J. E. Stoy, *Denotational Semantics: The Scott-Strachey Approach to Programming Language Theory*, MIT Press, Cambridge, MA (1977).
10. J. E. Stoy, "The congruence of two programming language definitions," unpublished manuscript (1976).

11. C. Strachey and C. Wadsworth, "Continuations: a mathematical semantics which can deal with full jumps," Technical Monograph PRG-11, Programming Research Group, Oxford University (1974).

12. R. D. Tennent, "The denotational semantics of programming languages," *Comm. ACM* **19**(8), pp. 437-453 (August 1976).

A FORMAL SEMANTICS FOR CONCURRENT SYSTEMS

M.W. Shields and P.E. Lauer
Computing Laboratory,
University of Newcastle upon Tyne,
Claremont Tower, Claremont Road,
Newcastle upon Tyne, NE1 7RU, England.

1. Introduction

It is important, in the discussion of concurrent systems, to have a firm formal basis for their analysis, since in such cases intuition is even more inadequate and misleading than is the case for sequential systems. For this reason it is important to be able formally to define the 'meaning' of any synchronisation mechanism in order to be able to define systems properties involving such mechanisms and to analyse them properly. However, to reduce the great complexity arising from the interaction of processes in concurrent system, it is important to abstract from irrelevant details of particular mechanisms. The COSY notation and its accompanying system theory, which is discussed in this paper, was designed to satisfy the requirements of formality and appropriate abstractness. Moreover, the accompanying system theory has been developed sufficiently to permit the application of formal results to discover deep (non obvious) properties of concurrent systems such as absence of deadlock and starvation and degree of concurrency and distribution.

In this paper we look at one synchronisation mechanism, the extended semaphore primitives (ESPs) of Agerwala, and give a formal meaning for a class of programs involving these primitives. We then sketch out a concurrency preserving translation of such programs into the COSY notation. COSY is a formalism for describing and analysing synchronic properties of systems, those properties which have to do with the relationship between event occurrences. A program in the COSY notation is a collection of statements, essentially regular expressions, each of which describes, for a subset of the set of events associated with a system, how these are related sequentially. A collection of such statements relates elements of the whole set of events either sequentially or concurrently. With each such program is associated a set of n-tuples of strings, called vector firing sequences, which formally describe possible 'histories' of the system being specified, in terms of the component histories of the subsystems into which the system is decomposed. COSY has associated with it a formal theory which is concerned with the relationship between properties of descriptions, that is COSY programs, and the properties of their possible histories such as deadlock and starvation. The advantage of translation of ESP programs into COSY is that a formal theory for defining and analysing system properties is associated with the former

Vector firing sequences are one of a number of possible ways of formally describing the set of behaviours or histories specified by a COSY program. The principal semantics of COSY are those given in [Lauer 75] and modified in [Lauer 78a], which map COSY programs to marked labelled transition nets [Petri 76]. In the papers cited we point out that there are standard ways in this semantics for associating with a COSY program a set of either firing sequences, or of labelled causal nets which may be said to define the behaviour of the corresponding system. In [Lauer 75] a notion of behaviour based on labelled posets and in [Shields 78] a notion of behaviour based on firing sequences, in both cases defined directly in terms of COSY programs without the mediation of the net semantics, were given and used as the basis for the development of general theorems concerning the relationship between systems definition and system behaviour - mostly concerning deadlock problems. Vector firing sequences themselves may be considered as means for modelling concurrent behaviour which have the advantages both of the firing sequence and of the labelled poset model. They may be treated as strings, while labelled posets are clumsy to manipulate. At the same time they are formally equivalent to labelled causal nets and do represent concurrency. In fact, a set of vector firing sequences of a COSY program may be regarded as a trace language in the sense of Mazurkiewicz [Mazurkiewicz 77].

In the present paper, section 2 serves to give a brief introduction to the basic COSY notation. We explain how vector firing sequences may be considered as describing histories of a concurrent system. We then show how a basic COSY program determines a set of vector firing sequences, which may be considered as formally modelling the set of all possible histories of the system specified by the program. Section 3 deals with ESP programs in preparation for the translation to COSY programs in section 4. In order to show that our translation rules are 'correct', that is, preserve meaning, it is necessary to give the ESPs, which were introduced informally and by example in [Agerwala 77], a precise meaning. In section 3 we explicate this 'meaning' in terms of the notion of vector firing sequences referred to above. We may then formally define the translation to be correct iff, for a given ESP program E and its corresponding COSY program COSY(E), E and COSY(E) have the same set of vector firing sequences.

In section 4, we introduce this translation, using some of the macro notation of COSY, and sketch a proof of its correctness in the case in which the semaphores are bounded. In section 5 we indicate how the translation may be extended to deal with the unbounded case.

2. Introduction to the COSY notation and its vector firing sequence semantics

In this section we present the COSY (COncurrent SYstem) notation. COSY is a language whose terminal objects (programs) constitute abstract descriptions of systems in terms of their synchronic properties. The notation itself is a development of the path expressions of Campbell and Habermann [Campbell 74] and of the path-process notation of Lauer and Campbell [Lauer 75]. Essentially, the COSY notation adds generators to the path-process notation so that systems can be specified as path and process patterns (templates) from which instances of paths and processes can be generated in an orderly manner.

A system, from the COSY point of view, consists of a collection of resources and of sequential but nondeterministic processes. A resource is represented by a set of atomic actions (operations) together with a collection of statements expressing constraints on the order of activation of these operations (paths). A process is represented by an expression (process expression) which describes the pattern of usage of resources required by the process. Formally a process expression determines a collection of sequences of activations of operations. Distinct processes are notionally parallel; however, the paths determine a set of usages of resources of the system as a whole and thereby achieve a co-ordination of the processes.

A program in the basic notation is a string derived from the following BNF-type production rules.

```
     <program> = begin <programbody> end
     <programbody> = <path>|<process>|<path><programbody>|<process><programbody>
     <path> = path <sequence> end
(PR) <process> = process <sequence> end
     <sequence> = <orelement>|<orelement>;<sequence>
     <orelement> = <element>|<element>,<orelement>
     <element> = <operation>|<element>*|(<sequence>)
```

where the nonterminals are included between < and > and we assume a set of terminals called operations disjoint from the set {begin, end, , , ; , path, process, *, (,)}.

The following is an example of a program in this notation.

```
     begin
        process request_a1_a2; use_a1_a2; release_a1_a2 end
(1)     process request_a2_a3; use_a2_a3; release_a2_a3 end
        path (request_a1_a2;release_a1_a2),(request_a2_a3;release_a2_a3) end
     end
```

Intuitively, this program describes a pair of sequential processes progressing through cycles of requests, usages and releases of pairs of resources, the ai. Semicolon may be thought of as specifying sequentialization. The path effects mutual exclusion of requests and releases of the two sets of resources since comma denotes exclusive choice. It binds more strongly than the semicolon, hence the need for parentheses. Paths and processes are cyclic.

To illustrate the use of the star, which denotes iteration zero or more times, we give the following program fragment:

```
(2) path push;(push;(push;pop)*;pop)*;pop end
```

which defines the behaviour of a three-frame stack which is initially empty. The star binds more strongly than the comma (and hence the semicolon), whence the need for parentheses.

We shall see these two examples again when we show how to translate ESP programs into COSY programs.

The 'formal meaning' of a basic program will be obtained here by associating with each program P, an object called VFS(P), the vector firing sequences of P, a set of n-tuples whose coordinates are strings of operations of P.

The intuitive basis of the VFS semantics is the notion of a system composed of a finite number n of (sequential) subsystems, each of which can only 'observe' that part of a behaviour of the system which consists of sequences of occurrences of events belonging to the subsystem in question. If E_i is the set of events belonging to the i-th subsystem, then the set of events E belonging to the whole system is $E_1 \cup \ldots \cup E_n$. If $a \in E$, then let $\underline{a}$ denote the n-tuple $(a_1, \ldots, a_n)$, where $a_i = a$ if $a \in E_i$ and $a_i = \epsilon$ (the null string) otherwise. $\underline{a}$ may be considered to represent the event:

"for all i for which $a \in E_i$, subsystem i observes a occur".

Let $V = \{\underline{a} \mid a \in E\}$. Let V^* be the smallest set such that $\underline{\epsilon} = (\epsilon, \ldots, \epsilon) \in V^*$, $V \subseteq V^*$ and that if $(x_1, \ldots, x_n), (y_1, \ldots, y_n) \in V^*$, then $(x_1, \ldots, x_n)(y_1, \ldots, y_n) = (x_1y_1, \ldots, x_ny_n) \in V^*$. V^* is clearly a semigroup with identity $\underline{\epsilon}$.

If $\underline{x} \in V^*$ then $\underline{x}$ can be regarded as a behaviour in which for each i, the i-th subsystem observes the sequence $[\underline{x}]_i$, the i-th coordinate of $\underline{x}$. If $a, b \in E$ and $\underline{ab} \neq \underline{ba}$, then for some i $a, b \in E_i$. Every i-th subsystem with $a, b \in E_i$ will in fact observe in $\underline{ab}$ an occurrence of a precede an occurrence of b. In this sense, we may interpret the fact that a and b both belong to some E_i as meaning that orderings of occurrences of a and b in behaviours is objective; any pair of subsystems capable of observing both a and b will always agree on the order in which they have occurred. In contrast, if $\underline{ab} = \underline{ba}$, then for no i will $a, b \in E_i$ be the case. Orderings of occurrences of a and b are not objective. a and b are concurrent. Note that no subsystem may actually 'observe concurrency', but that the concurrency of two event occurrences in a behaviour $\underline{x}$ may be deduced from the set $\{[\underline{x}]_i \mid i \in \{1, \ldots, n\}\}$ of observations of $\underline{x}$ by the subsystems of the system. Concurrency is 'social'.

Suppose, now, that we define a system by associating with each E_i a constraint regarding permitted sequences of occurrences of the events in E_i. We may think of E_i as corresponding to some system component whose well-functioning is defined by this constraint and which it is the i-th subsystems duty to observe. The constraint determines a subset $B_i \subseteq E_i^*$, B_i is the set of permitted behaviours of the i-th subsystem. The set of behaviours of a system obeying precisely these constraints will thus be $(B_1 \times \ldots \times B_n) \cap V^*$. This is the set of behaviours $\underline{x}$ of the system such that the view $[\underline{x}]_i$ of $\underline{x}$ of the i-th subsystem is consistent both with its own associated constraint and with the views $[\underline{x}]_j$ of all the other subsystems.

It should be pointed out that there is an intended conceptual difference between the VFS semantics and descriptions of behaviours such as firing sequences, in that vector firing sequences are not to be thought of as being generated step by step according to some 'firing rule'. As abstract mathematical objects, they are, indeed, obtained by a sequence of concatenations, but a particular history thus obtained is not in general generated by a sequence of events.

We may now see how such n-tuples of strings, which we call <u>vector firing sequences</u> may be used to describe histories of systems specified by COSY or ESP programs. In the former case, each path or process may be considered to be 'observing' a sequence of activations of operations mentioned in it; paths and processes themselves define constraints on orderings of occurrences - by the use of the separators comma, semicolon and star. In the case of ESP programs, the observers are sequential processes and individual semaphores. The notion of vector firing sequence was introduced by Shields in 1977 under the name of <u>congreeable vectors</u> and used to obtain criteria for absence of deadlock in path programs of a certain restricted kind.

Let us first consider the set of permitted orderings of occurrences determined by a single path or process, its set B_i, in the terminology of the preceding discussion. To do this, consider a string of terminal symbols e generated from one of the nonterminals <element>,<orelement> or <sequence> by the rules (PR). We define a set Cyc(e) as follows:

a) If a is an operation, then $Cyc(a) = \{a\}$
b) If e is a string of type element, then $Cyc(e^*) = Cyc(e)^*$
c) If e is a string of type element and e' is string of type orelement then $Cyc(e,e') = Cyc(e) \cup Cyc(e')$
d) If e is a string of type orelement and e' is a string of type sequence then $Cyc(e;e') = Cyc(e)Cyc(e') = \{xx' \mid x \in Cyc(e) \wedge x' \in Cyc(e')\}$ where juxtaposition denotes concatenation of strings as usual.
e) If e is a string of type sequence then Cyc(<u>process</u> e <u>end</u>) = Cyc(<u>path</u> e <u>end</u>) = Cyc((e)) = Cyc(e)

Intuitively, each path or process loops through a number of cycles in using its component operations. The <u>history</u> of a given path or process P may thus be defined to be $Pref(Cyc(P)^*)$, where for a string set X, Pref(X) is defined to be the set $\{x \mid \exists y : xy \in X\}$.

If we now have a program P = <u>begin</u> $P_1 \ldots P_n$ <u>end</u>, where each P_i is a single path, then each P_i 'observes' operations from $Ops(P_i)$, which is defined to be the set of operations mentioned in P_i. Exactly as in the preceding discussion, we form $Ops(P) = \bigcup Ops(P_i)$ and <u>vector operations</u> $\underline{a_P} = (a_1, \ldots, a_n)$, where $a_i = a$ if $a \in Ops(P_i)$ and $a = \epsilon$ otherwise. We let $Vops(P) = \{\underline{a_P} \mid a \in Ops(P)\}$ and construct $Vops(P)^*$ as above. We may now define the set of histories of P, VFS(P), to be

$$VFS(P) = (FS(P_1) \times \ldots \times FS(P_n)) \cap Vops(P)^*$$

We cannot apply this semantics directly to programs involving paths and processes. This is because the process semantics of [Lauer 75] entails an implicit distinction between two operations with the same name occurring in different processes. For example, in the program begin process a end process a end end, one has two processes which may concurrently be activating a; there are two 'a's; an a-in-process-1 and an 'a-in-process-2'. If we were to insert into this program path a end then the 'observer' associated with the path would have to see a sequence of 'a's in order that his constraint hold, that is, the path enforces mutual exclusion between occurrrneces of 'a-in-process-1' and 'a-in-process-2'. This suggests the following transformation, which makes the semantics of processes explicit and permits one to define VFS(P) for any program. Let Pr = begin $P_1 \ldots P_m$ end, where each P_i is either a path or a process. If P_i is a process, then replace every operation $a \in Ops(P_i)$ by an operation a&i ('a-in-P_i'). Do this for every process. Then we make the mutually excluding effect of paths on process operations with the same name explicit. Suppose a is an operation occurring in processes $P_{i_1}, \ldots, P_{i_n}$, if a belongs to a path P_i, then replace a in P_i by the orelement a&i_1,...,a&i_n. Finally, replace each 'process' by 'path'. We shall denote the resulting program by Path(Pr). Path(Pr) consists exclusively of paths, we may thus define VFS(Pr) = VFS(Path(Pr)).

We illustrate this construction by the following example. 'rq' and 'rl' stand for 'request resource' and 'release resource' respectively.

begin
(2) process rq; rl end process rq; rl end path rq;rl end
end

This translates as follows:

begin
(3) path rq&1; rl&1 end path rq&2; rl&2 end path rq&1,rq&2; rl&1, rl&2 end
end

This has the following set of vector firing sequences:

Pref({(rq&1 rl&1, ϵ, rq&1 rl&1), (ϵ, rq&2 rl&2, rq&2 rl&2)}*).

where 'Pref' is defined in analogy with the string case, that is for $X \subseteq Vops(P)^*$, $Pref(X) = \{\underline{x} \in Vops(P)^* \mid \exists \underline{y} \in Vops(P)^*: \underline{xy} \in X\}$

For example, (rq&1,rq&2 rl&2,rq&2 rl&2 rq&1) = rq&2 rl&2 rq&1 is a history of this system. Note that each process coordinate consists of a sequence of alternating requests and releases and that only one process may be active at any one time, for if not, we may have, say rq&1 and rq&2 concurrently active. But this is not possible, since rq&1 rq&2 = (rq&1,rq&2,rq&1 rq&2) $\neq$ (rq&1,rq&2,rq&2 rq&1) = rq&2 rq&1.

3. A vector firing sequence semantics for extended semaphore primitives

The extended semaphore primitives (ESPs) pe and ve are assumed indivisible and each operates on a set of semaphores which must be initialised to non-negative integer values [cf. Agerwala 77] pe($S_1,\ldots,S_k,\bar{S}_{k+1},\ldots,\bar{S}_{k+l}$)

  <u>if</u> <u>for</u> <u>all</u> i, $1 \leq i \leq k, S_i > 0$ <u>and</u> <u>for</u> <u>all</u> j, $1 \leq j \leq l, S_{k+j} = 0$

    <u>then</u> <u>for</u> <u>all</u> i, $1 \leq i \leq k S_i := S_i - 1$

    <u>else</u> the process is blocked

ve($S_1,S_2,\ldots,S_k$)

  <u>for</u> <u>all</u> i, $1 \leq i \leq k$, $S_i := S_i + 1$

ESPs are used, of course, to co-ordinate concurrent processes in order to satisfy some general desideratum associated with the system being designed. The desideratum may be of a synchronic nature, for example, that the system be free from deadlock. Formal verification of deadlock-freeness in a program using ESPs requires that such synchronic notions be precisely defined and hence it is necessary to have a formal notion of a possible history of an ESP program. No such notion was offered in [Agerwala 77] so we will have to do it ourselves. We use the vector firing sequence method of modelling behaviour as described in the last section.

Agerwala says nothing about the kind of programming language in which ESPs might be embedded or might have constructed around them. His examples however deal with situations in which ESPs are the only means of process co-ordination. We shall define, therefore, an ESP program to be a collection of cyclic, sequential processes without jumps or conditional statements, using ESPs as their only means of synchronisation. By an ESP program, therefore, we mean something of the form

(4)

<u>semaphore</u> $S_1,\ldots,S_n$ <u>initial</u>($S_1,\ldots,S_n$) = ($M_1,\ldots,M_n$)

<u>loop</u> $a^1_1;\ldots;a^1_{f_1}$ <u>end</u> ... <u>loop</u> $a^m_1;\ldots;a^m_{f_m}$ <u>end</u>

which we shall call E, where the a^i_j are either ESP operations or are in some sense local to the process containing them. Thus, if an operation a occurs in two distinct processes of E, then the two processes may be activating a concurrently, unless prevented from doing so by the semaphores. We are accordingly in the same situation as that concerning operations in distinct COSY processes. As in that case, we make a distinction between identically named operations in distinct processes. Our vector firing sequences $\underline{x} \in VFS(E)$, will thus contain operations of the form $a^i_j\&i$ as in the COSY case. Note that we are implicitly assuming the indivisibility of pe and ve operations by representing each instance of one of these operations in a process by a single symbol. Let us denote <u>loop</u> $a^i_1;\ldots;a^i_{f_i}$ <u>end</u> by Q_i, and define FS(Q_i)
$FS(Q_i) = Pref(\{a^i_1\&i\ldots a^i_{f_i}\&i\}^*)$.

For the given program E, we define VFS(E) and $eval_E: VFS(E) \to Z^n$ as follows. (Z is the set of integers).

1) $(\varepsilon,\ldots,\varepsilon)$ (n+m times) = $\underline{\varepsilon}_E \in VFS(E)$ and $eval[(\underline{\varepsilon}_E)]_i = M_i$ for each i. ($[z]_i$ denotes the i'th co-ordinate of the n-tuple z).

2) Now suppose $\underline{x} \in VFS(E)$ and a is some a_j^i appearing in Q_i, such that $[\underline{x}]_i a\&i \in FS(Q_i)$.

a) If a is not an ESP then $\underline{y} \in VFS(E)$, where $\underline{y}$ is defined by $[\underline{y}]_j = [\underline{x}]_j a\&i$ if $j = i$, $[\underline{y}]_j$ otherwise, and $eval_E(\underline{y}) = eval_E(\underline{x})$.

b) If $a = ve(S_{i_1},\ldots,S_{i_k})$ and a belongs to Q_i, then $\underline{y} \in VFS(E)$, where $[\underline{y}]_j = [\underline{x}]_j a\&i$ if $j=i$ or if $j = m+i_h$, $h = 1,\ldots,k$ and $[\underline{y}]_j = [\underline{x}]_j$ otherwise, and we set $[eval_E(\underline{y})]_j = [eval_E(\underline{x})]_j + 1$ if $j \in \{i_1,\ldots,i_k\}$ and $[eval_E(\underline{y})]_j = [eval_E(\underline{x})]_j$ otherwise.

c) If $a = pe(S_{i_1},\ldots,S_{i_k},S_{i_{k+1}},\ldots,S_{i_{k+1}})$ belongs to Q_i and for $j = 1,\ldots,k$ $[eval_E(\underline{x})]_{i_j} > 0$ and for $j = 1,\ldots,l$ $[eval_E(\underline{x})]_{i_{k+j}} = 0$, then $\underline{y} \in VFS(E)$, where $[\underline{y}]_j = [\underline{x}]_j a\&i$ if $j = i$ or if $j \in \{m+i_1,\ldots,m+i_{k+l}\}$ and $[\underline{y}]_j = [\underline{x}]_j$ otherwise, and we define $[eval_E(\underline{y})]_j = [eval_E(\underline{x})]_j - 1$ if $j \in \{i_1,\ldots,i_k\}$ and $[eval_E(\underline{y})]_j = [eval_E(\underline{x})]_j$ otherwise.

VFS(E) contains only the n+m-tuples determined by (1) and (2).

Thus, if $\underline{x} \in VFS(E)$, $[\underline{x}]_i$, $i \in \{1,\ldots,m\}$ is a history of the process Q_i and $\underline{x}_{m+i}$, $i \in \{1,\ldots,n\}$, is a sequence of activations of pe and ve operations involving the semaphore S_i. $[eval_E(\underline{x})]_i$ gives the value of the semaphore S_i after the history $\underline{x}$ has happened. (a), (b) and (c) reflect the manner in which ESPs determine how occurrences of the operations belonging to E may be partially ordered.

4. Proof of correctness of a concurrency preserving translation from ESP programs to COSY programs with bounded semaphores.

In this section we define a construction which takes a program of the type (4) and produces a program in COSY with the same 'behaviour'. In the process of doing so, we introduce some of the macro notation associated with COSY. This allows one to write long programs containing iteratively definable structure in a succinct manner.

Let us first consider the case of a semaphore S with test for zero initialised to M and capable of taking values from 0 to N>M≥0. The semaphore will have a sequential history and may be described by a single path. This path will be of the form <u>path</u> I(N-M),D(M) <u>end</u>, where I(N-M) concerns that part of S's history concerning increments of S within the range M to N and D(M), that part of S's history concerning decrements in the range M to 0 and a test for zero, $P(\overline{S})$. Let us see what I(k) should be, for k>0. Since we are concerned with increments, the first thing that may happen is an operation v(S), after which comes a history of a semaphore which may perform up to k-1 increments, after which comes a decrement, p(S). It is thus sensible to define I(k) = (v(S);I(k-1);p(S))* with I(1) = (v(S);p(S))*. In a similar fashion, for k>0, we would have D(k) = (p(S);D(k-1);v(S))* with D(0) = $p(\overline{S})$*. The path describing the semaphore may thus be written:-

$$\underline{\text{path}}\ \underbrace{(v(S);(\ldots;(v(S)}_{N-M};\underbrace{p(S))*;\ldots)*;p(S))}_{N-M}*,$$
$$\underbrace{(p(S);(\ldots;(p(S)}_{M};p(\overline{S})*;\underbrace{v(S))*;\ldots)*;v(S))}_{M}*\underline{\text{end}}$$

The macro notation associated with COSY contains facilities for the definition of such iterative structures, specifically the replicator. One version of the replicator is $[p\boxed{i}q|\ k,n,m]$ where $k>0$, $n>0$, $m \neq 0$ and p and q are strings, which is expanded as follows

$$[p\ \boxed{i}\ q|\ k,n,m] = \begin{cases} p\ [p\ \boxed{i}\ q\ |\ k+m,n,m]q, & \text{if } 0<k+m\leq n \\ pq, & \text{if } k\leq n<k+m \\ \epsilon & \text{otherwise} \end{cases}$$

The "@" in a replicator of the form $[p@;\boxed{i}\ q|\ k,n,m]$ indicates that ";" is a seperator not a terminator and

$$[p@;\ \boxed{i}\,q|\ k,n,m] = \begin{cases} p;[p@;\ \boxed{i}\ q|\ k+m,n,m]q, & \text{if } 0<k+m\leq n \\ pq, & \text{if } k\leq n<k+m \\ \epsilon & \text{otherwise} \end{cases}$$

We shall not go into detail here - an extensive treatment of the COSY macro facilities may be found in [Lauer 78b] - but merely give macro definitions of the structures we need in the sequel. In terms of this notation, I(k) would be written

$$[(v(S)@;\boxed{i};p(S))^*|\ 1,k,1]$$

and the formal definition of the replicator ensures that $I(0) = \epsilon$. D(k) would be written

$$[(p(S);\boxed{i}\ |\ 1,k,1]\ p(\overline{S})^*\ [;v(S))^*\boxed{i}\ |\ 1,k,1\ ].$$

We may thus define a path P(S,M,N) describing a semaphore S with test for zero, initialised to M and bounded by N as follows. If N>M, then P(S,M,N) = path I(N-M),D(M) end. If N = M, then P(S,M,N) = path D(M) end.

We now extend this argument to give a COSY description of a collection of extended semaphores in an ESP program E of the form (4). The COSY version of E will be a program of the form

$$\underline{\text{begin}}\ Q_1\cdots Q_m\ P_1\cdots P_n\ \underline{\text{end}} \text{ where each } Q_i \text{ is a process}$$
$$Q_i = \underline{\text{process}}\ a_1^i;\ldots;a_{f_i}^i\ \underline{\text{end}}$$

and each P_i is a path corresponding to the semaphore S_i.

Let us see what P_i ought to be. IN P(S,M,N), a p(S) operation has the effect of decreasing the value of S by 1. In the program E, this may be effected by any operation pe(...,S,...), and wherever a p(S) is valid a pe(...,S,...) is valid provided it is so for the other semaphores mentioned.

This suggests the following construction. For each S_i define N_i to be the maximal value taken by S_i over all possible histories of E and define:

a) $PS_i = PS_i^1,\ldots,PS_i^{h_i}$ where the PS_i^j are all the $pe(\ldots,S_i,\ldots)$ operations mentioned in E.

b) $VS_i = VS_i^1,\ldots,VS_i^{g_i}$ where the VS_i^j are all the $ve(\ldots,S_i,\ldots)$ mentioned in E.

c) $\overline{PS}_i = \overline{PS}_i^1, \ldots, \overline{PS}_i^{f_i}$ where the $\overline{PS}_i^j$ are all the pe(...,$\overline{S}_i$,...) occurring in E.

We assume that every semaphore is used somewhere in the program, and that thus all the orelements PS_i and VS_i are non-null.

In order to construct P_i, first form $P(S_i,M_i,N_i)$. Next, replace each $p(S_i)$ by PS_i, each $v(S_i)$ by VS_i. If $\overline{PS}_i$ is not null, replace $p(\overline{S}_i)$ by it, otherwise delete ";$p(\overline{S}_i)$*" from the path. Call the COSY program derived from E by this procedure COSY(E).

We illustrate this construction by translating Agerwala's ESP solution to the second reader-writer problem:

semaphore A,R,M; initial(A,R,M) = (0,0,1)
(6) (reader) loop pe(M,$\overline{A}$);ve(M,R);read;pe(R) end
(writer) loop ve(A);pe(M,$\overline{R}$);write;ve(M);pe(A) end

We assume that there are r readers and w writers. It may be seen that the maximum value that can be attained by A,R and M is, respectively, w,r and 1. Applying the above construction, we obtain the following COSY program.

begin
[process pe(M,$\overline{A}$);ve(M,R);read;pe(R) end $\boxed{i}$ |1,r,1]
[process ve(A);pe(M,$\overline{R}$);write;ve(M);pe(A) end $\boxed{i}$ |1,w,1]
(7) path [(ve(A)@;$\boxed{i}$;pe(A))* |1,w,1],pe(M,$\overline{A}$)* end
path [(ve(M,R)@;$\boxed{i}$;pe(R))* |1,r,1],pe(M,$\overline{R}$)* end
path (pe(M,$\overline{A}$),pe(M,$\overline{R}$);ve(M,R),ve(M))* end
end

The COSY version (7) of the ESP program (6) is slightly longer than (6). Note, however, that the synchronisation properties implicit in (6) have been made explicit in (7).

An ESP program E is an object which defines synchronic relationships between its operations indirectly via a functional interpretation of the pe and ve operations contained in it. COSY(E) is an object which defines synchronic relationships between its operations directly; we shall now show that the pe and ve operations in COSY(E) may be given a functional interpretation. This, indeed, is central to the proof that the translation from E to COSY(E) is correct. For E as in (4), we define a function $eval_{COSY(E)}: VFS(COSY(E)) \rightarrow Z^n$ as follows:

1) $[eval_{COSY(E)}(\underline{\varepsilon})]_i = M_i$ for each i.

2) Suppose $\underline{x} \in VFS(COSY(E))$ and a is some a_j^i appearing in a process Q_i and that $\underline{xa\&i} = \underline{y} \in VFS(COSY(E))$

a) If a is not an ESP, then $eval_{COSY(E)}(\underline{y}) = eval_{COSY(E)}(\underline{x})$

b) If $a = \underline{ve}(S_{i_1},\ldots,S_{i_k})$ then we set $[\text{eval}_{COSY(E)}(\underline{y})]_j = [\text{eval}_{COSY(E)}(\underline{x})]_j + 1$, for $j\in\{i_1,\ldots,i_k\}$ and $[\text{eval}_{COSY(E)}(y)]_j = [\text{eval}_{COSY(E)}(\underline{x})]_j$ otherwise.

c) If $a = pe(S_{i_1},\ldots,S_{i_k},\overline{S}_{i_{k+1}},\ldots,\overline{S}_{i_{k+l}})$, then we set $[\text{eval}_{COSY(E)}(\underline{y})]_j = [\text{eval}_{COSY(E)}(\underline{x})]_j - 1$ for $j\in\{i_1,\ldots,i_k\}$ and $[\text{eval}_{COSY(E)}(\underline{y})]_j = [\text{eval}_{COSY(E)}(\underline{x})]_j$ otherwise.

It is important to note that $\text{eval}_{COSY(E)}$ is well defined, which is not immediately apparent, since some of the elements of Vops(COSY(E)) commute. To see that it is well defined, consider $\underline{x}\in$VFS(COSY(E)) and look at $[\underline{x}]_{m+i}$, $i\in\{1,\ldots,n\}$. This is the coordinate corresponding to the semaphore S_i. If nopes is the number of operations $pe(\ldots,S_i,\ldots)$ and noves is the number of operations $ve(\ldots,S_i,\ldots)$ occurring in $[\underline{x}]_{m+i}$, then it may be shown that $[\text{eval}_{COSY(E)}(\underline{x})]_i = M_i$ + noves − nopes.

We may now state

<u>Theorem</u>

With the above terminology VFS(E) = VFS(COSY(E)) and $\text{eval}_E = \text{eval}_{COSY(E)}$

<u>Proof</u> (sketch)

We have $\underline{\varepsilon}\in$VFS(E)$\cap$VFS(COSY(E)) and $\text{eval}_E(\underline{\varepsilon}) = \text{eval}_{COSY(E)}(\underline{\varepsilon})$ by definition. A comparison of the definition of VFS(E) with that of $\text{eval}_{COSY(E)}$ shows that if $\underline{x}\in$VFS(E)$\cap$VFS(COSY(E)) with $\text{eval}_E(\underline{x}) = \text{eval}_{COSY(E)}(\underline{x})$ then for all $\underline{a}\in$ Vops(COSY(E)), $\underline{xa}\in$ VFS(E) $\Leftrightarrow$ $\underline{xa}\in$ VFS(COSY(E)) and that $\text{eval}_E(\underline{xa}) = \text{eval}_{COSY(E)}(\underline{xa})$. From these remarks the theorem follows by induction on the length of vector firing sequences.

Note that this result shows that the translation 'preserves concurrency'. It also permits one to use concepts, developed in terms of the COSY formalism, in connection with ESP programs. For example, we may now formally define an ESP program E to be deadlock-free iff $\forall \underline{x}\in$ VFS(E) $\exists\, \underline{a}\in$Ops(E): $\underline{xa}\in$ VFS(E). A definition as succinct is hardly possible without such a semantics and we have not only given bounded ESP programs such a semantics, but have shown that they may be reformulated in such a way as to be susceptible to treatment by the formal theory associated with COSY programs [Shields 78, Lauer 78a].

5. <u>Extensions to unbounded semaphores</u>

We have so far dealt only with the case in which the values that semaphores in an ESP program E may take are bounded, that is, the case in which the set $\text{Val}(E) = \{[\text{eval}_E(\underline{x})]_i \mid \underline{x}\in \text{VFS}(E) \wedge i\in\{1,\ldots,n\}\}$ is finite. Programs E for which Val(E) is infinite (e.g. for which $0\in$ Val(E) and $i\in$ Val(E) $\Rightarrow$ $i+1\in$Val(E) which implies of course that Val(E) is the set of natural numbers) are clearly unimplementable on anything other than a Turing machine and are therefore useless from a practical point of view. Indeed, an attempt to implement such a program could well lead to a systems failure; the problem of boundedness is as important, in such a context, as the problem of deadlock or starvation. Strangely enough, this subject is not discussed in [Agerwala 77], instead the author talks about a property he calls 'completeness'; a mechanism is complete if it can simulate the action of an arbitrary Turing machine. ESPs are complete, in this sense; that is, it is possible to write programs using this mechanism which are incapable of being implemented. Such programs are precisely those for which there is no possible translation into COSY, as it stands, which seems to argue well for the notation, but out of theoretical interest, we here intimate how the notation might be extended to deal with semaphores in the general, unbounded case.

To obtain a complete translation of a given ESP program, which may contain unbounded semaphores, requires a real extension of the descriptive power of the COSY notation. COSY may only describe finite systems. In order to describe infinite counters, one would need to be able to write things like

(8) path $p(\overline{S})$, $[(v(S)@;\boxed{i};p(S))* \mid 1,\infty,1]$ end

which 'intuitively' defines the behaviour of infinite counters with a test for zero; it is the 'path' $P(S,0,\infty)$.

Unfortunately, this is not something that could be generated by the production rules PR nor could it be expanded using the definition of the expansion of a replicator expression. It is not a path in a strict sense. It is a kind of least upper bound 'lub' of the 'sequence' $P(S,0,n)$, $n = 1,2,\ldots$. To put it another way, the expression to the right of the comma in (8) is a 'fixed point' of the function: $F(s) = (v(S);s;p(S))*$. It is likely that the words 'lub', 'sequence' and 'fixed point' could be made formally meaningful, say by defining an ordering relation on the finite paths and then introducing a set FPATH of equivalence classes of directed sets of finite paths, much as in the construction of the reals from the rationals, hoping that the result would be a domain with the finite paths as finite elements, in which fixed-point results hold. The ordering relation should be such that $P \sqsubset Q$, P and Q finite, implies $FS(P) \subseteq FS(Q)$, as in the case of $P(S,0,n)$ and $P(S,0,m)$ with $n<m$. If OPS denotes the set of operations then we would have a function $FS{:}FPATHS \to 2^{OPS*}$, where FPATHS is the set of all finite paths. Regarding 2^{OPS*} as being partially ordered with respect to inclusion, one could then define for a directed set of paths $\{P_1,P_2,\ldots\} = X$, $FS(\sqcup X) = \text{lub } FS(P_i)$, which, with the assumption that $P \sqsubset Q \Rightarrow FS(P) \subseteq FS(Q)$, would ensure that $FS'{:}PATH \to 2^{OPS*}$ agrees with FS on FPATHS and is continuous.

The purpose of these statements is to justify the following definition. Suppose n is some integer. We define

$$Cyc(P(S,m,\infty)) \text{ to be } \lim_{i \to \infty} Cyc(P(S,m,i))$$

With this definition, we have given a 'meaning' to $P(S,m,\infty)$. We may now carry out the construction of a COSY program for every ESP program as in section 4, but starting with paths $P(S_i,m_i,\infty)$ as opposed to paths $P(S_i,m_i,n_i)$. The justification for the correctness of the translation in the finite case may be extended to deal with the infinite case.

6. Summary

We have introduced the reader to the COSY notation and one of its accompanying semantic formalisms. Other semantic formalisms such as Petri Nets and firing sequences were introduced in [Lauer 75] and [Lauer 78a]. We have indicated how such a formalism can be used to formalise the meaning of a synchronisation mechanism such as the ESPs. The COSY notation is a way to program which makes the vector firing sequence semantics quite explicit whereas such a semantics is very implicit in programs involving specific synchronisation mechanisms. Hence, we indicated how a translation from programs involving mechanisms into COSY programs not only makes the concurrent semantics of the former explicit but immediately makes formal results applicable for a deep study of properties of programs using such mechanisms.

ACKNOWLEDGEMENTS

The research reported in this paper was supported by a grant from the Science Research Council of Great Britain. We would like to express our gratitude to Mrs. J. Armstrong for her patience and efficiency in preparing the manuscript.

REFERENCES

[Agerwala 77] Agerwala, T.: Some extended semaphore primitives, Acta Informatica 8, pp. 201-220, 1977.

[Campbell 74] Campbell, R.H., and Habermann, A.N.: The specification of process synchronization by path expressions. Lecture Notes in Computer Science (Ed. G. Goos and J. Hartmanis) pp. 89-102, V16 Springer Verlag, 1974.

[Lauer, 75] Lauer, P.E., and Campbell, R.H.: Formal semantics for a class of high level primitives for coordinating concurrent processes. Acta Informatica 5, pp. 297-332, 1975.

[Lauer 78a] Lauer, P.E., Shields, M.W. and Best, E.: On the design and certification of asynchronous systems of processes. Final Report Period 1976-1977. ASM/45 Part 2: Formal Theory of the Basic COSY Notation. March 1978. ASM/49 Part 1: COSY - a system specification language based on paths and processes. June, 1978. Computing Laboratory, University of Newcastle upon Tyne.

[Lauer, 78b] Lauer, P.E., and Torrigiani, P.R.: Towards a system specification language based on paths and processes. Tech. Report 120, Computing Laboratory, University of Newcastle upon Tyne, 1978.

[Mazurkiewicz 77] Mazurkiewicz, A.: Concurrent program schemes and their interpretation. Presented at the Arhus Workshop on Verification of Parallel Processes, June 13-24. 1977, Arhus, Denmark.

[Petri 76] Petri, C.A.: General Net Theory, Proceedings of the Joint IBM University of Newcastle upon Tyne Seminar on Computing Systems Design, 7th-10th September 1976, (Ed. B. Shaw), Computing Laboratory, University of Newcastle upon Tyne, England, 1977.

[Shields 78] Shields, M.W., Lauer, P.E.: On the abstract specification and formal analysis of synchronization properties of concurrent systems, In Proceedings of the International Conferences on Mathematical Studies of Information Processing, 1978 Kyoto, Springer-Verlag.

ON CONSTRUCTING LL(k) PARSERS
(extended abstract)

Seppo Sippu and Eljas Soisalon-Soininen

Department of Computer Science, University of Helsinki
Tukholmankatu 2, SF-00250 Helsinki 25, Finland

ABSTRACT. A method for constructing canonical LL(k) parsers for context-free grammars is presented. This method can be regarded as a dual of the well-known LR(k) parser construction technique involving so-called LR(k) items and viable prefixes. The counterparts of LR(k) items and viable prefixes are called LL(k) items and viable suffixes, respectively. Modifications of the basic method give rise to subclasses of the canonical LL(k) grammars corresponding to the LALR(k) and SLR(k) grammars. The duals of LALR(k) grammars are called LALL(k) grammars and they form a proper subclass of the canonical LL(k) grammars when k > 1. The duals of SLR(k) grammars, called SLL(k) grammars, in turn coincide with the so-called strong LL(k) grammars and form a proper subclass of the LALL(k) grammars when k > 1.

1. INTRODUCTION

The construction method for LR(k) parsers, which is based on the construction of different collections of sets of so-called LR(k) items, is widely accepted in the literature [1,2,8]. The advantages of the approach are that the method itself can be compactly defined by closures of certain relations, and that different types of construction techniques are described by small variations in the basic method applicable to canonical LR(k) grammars [9]. The classes of grammars that correspond to these variations are SLR(k) grammars [4,5] and LA(k)LR(m) grammars [3,10]. Here the LA(k)LR(0) grammars are known as LALR(k) grammars [4], whereas the LA(k)LR(k) grammars are known as canonical LR(k) grammars.

Although the LL(k) grammars are defined as duals of LR(k) grammars in the sense that rightmost derivations are replaced by leftmost derivations, no dual construction method has been devised for LL(k) parsers. Construction techniques for general LL(k) parsers and for so-called strong LL(k) parsers are given in [1] and [11], but later attention is given in the literature usually only to strong LL(k) parsers, the construction of which is particularly easy. Considering only strong LL(k) parsers may be regarded as practically motivated, since if k = 1, i.e. the length of the lookahead string is 1, the class of strong LL(k) grammars equals the class of LL(k) grammars. However, the strong LL(k) parser even for k = 1 detects errors later than the true LL(k) parser, and recent developments in error recovery techniques for LL(k) parsing require very early error detection [6,7,12].

In this paper, a technique for constructing LL(k) parsers is presented which can be regarded as a dual of that commonly used for constructing LR(k) parsers. The technique given makes use of the so-called LL(k) items of a context-free grammar G and the so-called viable suffixes of G, that is, viable prefixes needed in the LR(k) construction of the reversal of G (obtained by replacing the right-hand sides of productions by their reversals). The construction method gives rise to a hierarchy of different LL(k) grammars in the same way as the LR(k) parser construction method gives rise to a hierarchy of different LR(k) grammars, i.e. LA(k)LR(m) and SLR(k) grammars. In this hierarchy of LL(k) grammars, for example, the duals of LALR(k) grammars, called LALL(k) grammars, form a subclass of the canonical LL(k) grammars. The duals of SLR(k) grammars, called SLL(k) grammars, in turn coincide with strong LL(k) grammars and are included in the class of LALL(k) grammars. The inclusions are proper in the case $k > 1$.

2. LL(k) PARSING

We make free use of the notation and definitions given in [1] concerning strings and (context-free) grammars. We recall the convention that (1) A, B and C denote nonterminals, (2) a, b, c and d denote terminals, (3) X, Y and Z denote either nonterminals or terminals, (4) terminal strings are represented by u, v,..., z, whereas general strings are represented by α, β,..., ω, and (5) the empty string is denoted by ε. As usual, we assume that every nonterminal can be used in the derivation of some terminal string. A grammar $G = (N,\Sigma,P,S)$ is said to be *LL(k)*, if $\mathrm{FIRST}_k(\omega_1\delta) \cap \mathrm{FIRST}_k(\omega_2\delta) = \emptyset$ whenever $xA\delta$ is a left sentential form of G and $A \to \omega_1$ and $A \to \omega_2$ are different productions in P. Further, G is said to be *strong LL(k)*, if $\mathrm{FIRST}_k(\omega_1\mathrm{FOLLOW}_k(A)) \cap \mathrm{FIRST}_k(\omega_2\mathrm{FOLLOW}_k(A)) = \emptyset$ whenever $A \to \omega_1$ and $A \to \omega_2$ are different productions in P.

We begin by defining dual concepts for viable prefixes and LR(k) items of a grammar. We say that a string γ is a *viable suffix* of a grammar $G = (N,\Sigma,P,S)$, if either $\gamma = S$ or $\gamma = \varepsilon$ or there exists a terminal string x, a production $A \to \alpha\beta$ and a string δ such that

$$(1) \qquad S \underset{lm}{\overset{*}{\Rightarrow}} xA\delta \underset{lm}{\Rightarrow} x\alpha\beta\delta = x\alpha\gamma^R$$

holds in G. (Here γ^R denotes the reversal of γ defined as follows: $\varepsilon^R = \varepsilon$, $(\gamma X)^R = X\gamma^R$ for X in $N \cup \Sigma$.) It is clear that the set of viable suffixes of G equals the set of viable prefixes of the *reversal* G^R of G. (The set of productions of G^R consists of all productions $A \to \omega^R$ such that $A \to \omega$ is a production of G.)

A pair $[A \to \alpha.\beta, u]$ is an *LL(k) item* (or an *item* for short) of the grammar G, if $A \to \alpha\beta$ is a production of G and u is a string in $\mathrm{FIRST}_k(\beta\mathrm{FOLLOW}_k(A))$. (Recall that

$[A \to \alpha.\beta,\ u]$ is an *LR(k) item*, if u is in $FOLLOW_k(A)$; e.g. [8].) If (1) holds for a production $A \to \alpha\beta$ and a viable suffix γ and, in addition, u is in $FIRST_k(\gamma^R)$, then we say that the item $[A \to \alpha.\beta,\ u]$ is *valid* for γ. We denote by $[\gamma]_k$ the set of all those LL(k) items of G which are valid for γ. Since the set of all LL(k) items of G is finite for every non-negative integer k, then there exists, for a fixed k, only a finite number of different sets $[\gamma]_k$, where γ is a viable suffix of G. The finite collection of all classes $[\gamma]_k$ of G is denoted by $[G]_k$. We say that two viable suffixes γ_1 and γ_2 of G are *LL(k) equivalent* if $[\gamma_1]_k = [\gamma_2]_k$. The LL(k) equivalence is clearly an equivalence relation on the set of viable suffixes of G, and the sets $[\gamma]_k$ can be regarded as finite representations for the corresponding equivalence classes.

Now let k and p, $k \geq p$, be non-negative integers and let the vertical bar | denote a symbol not in $N \cup \Sigma$. Further, let β be a general string, A a nonterminal, and for each $i = 1,\ldots,n$, $n \geq 0$, X_i a symbol in $N \cup \Sigma$ such that βA is a viable suffix of G and $A \to X_1 \ldots X_n$ is a production of G. Clearly, then, $\beta X_n \ldots X_1$ is also a viable suffix of G for each $i = 1,\ldots,n$. Let y be a terminal string in $FIRST_k(X_1 \ldots X_n \gamma^R)$ for some string γ such that γA is a viable suffix and $\gamma X_n \ldots X_1$ is LL(p) equivalent to $\beta X_n \ldots X_1$. We then say that the rule

(a) $\qquad [\beta A]_p | y \to [\beta X_n]_p \ldots [\beta X_n \ldots X_1]_p | y$

is an *LA(k)LL(p) produce action* of G. (If n = 0, i.e. $X_1 \ldots X_n = \varepsilon$, we stipulate throughout this paper that $[\beta X_n]_p \ldots [\beta X_n \ldots X_1]_p$ also means ε.) Let y be a terminal string, β a general string and let a be a terminal such that βa is a viable suffix of G. If ay is in $FIRST_{max(k,1)}(a\gamma^R)$ for some viable suffix γ such that γa is a viable suffix LL(p) equivalent to βa, then we say that the rule

(b) $\qquad [\beta a]_p | ay \to | y$

is an *LA(k)LL(p) shift action* of G. A quadruple $P = ([G]_p, \Sigma \cup \{|\}, R_{kp}, [S]_p)$ is called the *LA(k)LL(p) parser* of G, if R_{kp} is the set of all LA(k)LL(p) produce and shift actions of G. The LA(k)LL(k) parser is called the *canonical LL(k) parser* of G and the LA(k)LL(0) parser is called the *LALL(k) parser* of G. A quadruple $P = ([G]_0, \Sigma \cup \{|\}, R_k, [S]_0)$ is called the *SLL(k) parser* of G, if R_k consists of (1) all produce actions of the form (a) where p = 0 and y is any string in $FIRST_k(X_1 \ldots X_n FOLLOW_k(A))$, and (2) all shift actions of the form (b) where p = 0 and ay is any string in $FIRST_{max(k,1)}(a\Sigma^*)$.

If $P = ([G]_q, \Sigma \cup \{|\}, R, [S]_q)$ is the LA(k)LL(p) or SLL(k) parser of G we stipulate that $\vdash_P$ ($\vdash$ for short) is the relation on $[G]_q^* | \Sigma^*$ defined as follows: $\psi\varphi_1 | y_1 z \vdash \psi\varphi_2 | y_2 z$ if $FIRST_k(y_1 z) = y_1$ and $\varphi_1 | y_1 \to \varphi_2 | y_2$ is an action in R. The parser P is *deterministic* if $\vdash$ is a partial function. In terms of the corresponding actions in R, P is deterministic if and only if its produce actions are *consistent*; i.e., for each string β, nonterminal A and terminal string y in $FIRST_k(\Sigma^*)$, there is at most one action in R of the form (a). Notice that no inconsistencies arise from shift actions, since for any LL(q) equivalent viable suffixes γ_1 and γ_2 the last symbol of γ_1 equals the last symbol of γ_2. The parser P *accepts* a terminal string w if $[S]_q|w \vdash^* |$ holds in P. The set of terminal strings accepted by P is called the *language* accepted by P and is denoted by $L(P)$.

Theorem 2.1. The language generated by a grammar G equals the language accepted by the LA(k)LL(p) or by the SLL(k) parser of G.

Theorem 2.2. Let G be a grammar which has no left recursive nonterminals (e.g.[1]). If $P = ([G]_q, \Sigma\cup\{|\}, R, [S]_q)$ is the LA(k)LL(p) or SLL(k) parser of G, then P *detects an error* in any terminal string not in L(G). That is, if w is not in L(G), then there is a string $\varphi|w'$ in $[G]_q^*|\Sigma^*$ such that $[S]_q|w \vdash^* \varphi|w'$ holds in P and $\vdash(\{\varphi|w'\}) = \emptyset$.

It turns out that the behaviour of the LA(k)LL(p) parser P of a grammar is not affected if the class $[\beta a]_p$ in a shift action of P is replaced by the terminal a and the class $[\beta X_n \ldots X_i]_p$ in a produce action of P is replaced by X_i whenever X_i is a terminal. In fact, this procedure leads (in the case k = p) to the conventional canonical LL(k) parser presented in [1]. The LA(k)LL(p) parser could, without loss of generality, be further simplified by allowing the lookahead string ay in a shift action be any string in $FIRST_{max(k,1)}(a\Sigma^*)$. However, the error detection capability of the parser would then be affected. The conventional strong LL(k) parser [11] is in turn obtained from the SLL(k) parser by replacing every produce action of the form (a) by the action $A|y \to X_n \ldots X_1|y$ and every shift action of the form (b) by the action $a|ay \to |y$. It is clear that the strong LL(k) parser and the SLL(k) parser operate exactly in the same way. Because the size of the SLL(k) parser can be exponential with respect to the size of the grammar, the SLL(k) parser thus cannot be regarded as practically motivated. (Note that the strong LL(k) parser is only of polynomial size.) In this paper we have, however, deviated from the conventional definitions in order to more clearly demonstrate the dualism between the LL(k) and LR(k) theories.

Theorem 2.3. A grammar G is LL(k) if and only if G is a *canonical LL(k)* grammar, that is, the canonical LL(k) parser of G is deterministic.

Theorem 2.4. A grammar G is strong LL(k) if and only if G is *SLL(k)*, that is, the SLL(k) parser of G is deterministic.

We say that a grammar G is *LA(k)LL(p)* if the LA(k)LL(p) parser of G is deterministic. In particular, G is *LALL(k)* if its LALL(k) parser is deterministic. By definition, the SLL(k) grammars are LALL(k) grammars, which in turn are LA(k)LL(p) grammars. Furthermore, the LA(k)LL(p) grammars are all canonical LL(k) grammars. These inclusions are proper if k > 1 and p > 0. To see that for k > 1 the LALL(k) grammars are properly included in the class of canonical LL(k) grammars and the SLL(k) grammars are properly included in the class of LALL(k) grammars consider first the grammar G_1 with productions [1]

$$S \to aAaa \mid bAba$$
$$A \to b \mid \varepsilon$$

The actions of the canonical LL(2) parser of G_1 are

$[S]_2|ab \to [a]_2[aa]_2[aaA]_2[aaAa]_2|ab$
$[S]_2|aa \to [a]_2[aa]_2[aaA]_2[aaAa]_2|aa$
$[S]_2|bb \to [a]_2[ab]_2[abA]_2[abAb]_2|bb$
$[aaA]_2|ba \to [aab]_2|ba$
$[aaA]_2|aa \to \ |aa$
$[abA]_2|bb \to [abb]_2|bb$
$[abA]_2|ba \to \ |ba$
$[abAb]_2|bb \to \ |b$
$[aaAa]_2|ab \to \ |b$
$[aaAa]_2|aa \to \ |a$
$[a]_2|a \to \ |$
$[aa]_2|aa \to \ |a$
$[ab]_2|ba \to \ |a$
$[aab]_2|ba \to \ |a$
$[abb]_2|bb \to \ |b$

Clearly all the produce actions are consistent so that G_1 is LL(2). In addition to the actions obtained from those above by replacing the subscript 2 by 0, the LALL(2) parser contains also the following actions (since $[aab]_0 = [abb]_0$ we denote this class by the corresponding regular expression $[aab|abb]_0$):

$[aaA]_0|bb \to [aab|abb]_0|bb$
$[abA]_0|ba \to [aab|abb]_0|ba$

Now since the actions $[abA]_0|ba \to \ |ba$ and $[abA]_0|ba \to [aab|abb]_0|ba$ are not consistent we conclude that G_1 is not LALL(2). More generally, if the productions $A \to b \mid \varepsilon$ are replaced by $A \to b^{k-1} \mid b^{k-2}$ we get a grammar which is LL(k) but not LALL(k).

Consider then the grammar G_2 with productions

$$S \to aAaa \mid bAba \mid cbba$$
$$A \to b \mid \varepsilon$$

(This is a slight modification of G_1.) The actions of the LALL(2) parser of G_2 are

$[S]_0|aa \to [a]_0[aa]_0[aaA]_0[aaAa]_0|aa$
$[S]_0|ab \to [a]_0[aa]_0[aaA]_0[aaAa]_0|ab$
$[S]_0|bb \to [a]_0[ab]_0[abA]_0[abAb]_0|bb$
$[S]_0|cb \to [a]_0[ab]_0[abb]_0[abbc]_0|cb$
$[aaA]_0|ba \to [aab]_0|ba$
$[aaA]_0|aa \to \ |aa$
$[abA]_0|bb \to [abb]_0|bb$
$[aaAa]_0|ab \to \ |b$
$[aaAa]_0|aa \to \ |a$
$[abbc]_0|cb \to \ |b$
$[aab]_0|ba \to \ |a$
$[abb]_0|bb \to \ |b$
$[aa]_0|aa \to \ |a$
$[ab]_0|ba \to \ |a$

$[abA]_0|ba \rightarrow \ |ba$ $\qquad$ $[a]_0|a \rightarrow \ |$

$[abAb]_0|bb \rightarrow \ |b$

Clearly all the produce actions are consistent so that G_2 is LALL(2). Note that the parser does not contain the action

$$[abA]_0|ba \rightarrow [abb]_0|ba$$

because $[aab]_0 \neq [abb]_0$ in G_2. This action is, however, present in the SLL(2) parser of G_2. Since it is not consistent with the action $[abA]_0|ba \rightarrow \ |ba$, we can conclude that G_2 is not an SLL(2) grammar. More generally, if the production $S \rightarrow cbba$ of G_2 is replaced by $S \rightarrow cb^ka$ and the productions $A \rightarrow b \mid \varepsilon$ are replaced by $A \rightarrow b^{k-1} \mid b^{k-2}$ we get a grammar which is LALL(k) but not SLL(k).

Since the class of strong LL(1) grammars equals the class of LL(1) grammars (e.g.[1]), we conclude that the classes of SLL(1), LALL(1) and canonical LL(1) grammars are all equal. However, the LALL(1) parser may detect errors later than the canonical LL(1) parser, and the SLL(1) parser may detect errors later than the LALL(1) parser. To see these differences in the error detection capability consider the LL(1) grammar G_3 with productions

$S \rightarrow aABb \mid Ac$

$A \rightarrow B$

$B \rightarrow \varepsilon$

The canonical LL(1) parser of G_3 has the actions

$[S]_1|a \rightarrow [b]_1[bB]_1[bBA]_1[bBAa]_1|a$ $\qquad$ $[cA]_1|c \rightarrow [cB]_1|c$

$[S]_1|c \rightarrow [c]_1[cA]_1|c$ $\qquad$ $[cB]_1|c \rightarrow \ |c$

$[bB]_1|b \rightarrow \ |b$ $\qquad$ $[b]_1|b \rightarrow \ |$

$[bBA]_1|b \rightarrow [bBB]_1|b$ $\qquad$ $[bBAa]_1|a \rightarrow \ |$

$[bBB]_1|b \rightarrow \ |b$ $\qquad$ $[c]_1|c \rightarrow \ |$

In addition to the actions obtained from those above by replacing the subscript 1 by 0, the LALL(1) parser of G_3 has the actions

$[bBA]_0|c \rightarrow [bBB|cB]_0|c$

$[cA]_0|b \rightarrow [bBB|cB]_0|b$

In addition to the actions of the LALL(1) parser, the SLL(1) parser of G_3 has, among others, the action

$$[bB]_0|c \rightarrow \ |c$$

The error detection capabilities of these parsers are different, as is seen by considering the erroneous string ac. In the case of the canonical LL(1) parser

$$[S]_1|ac \vdash [b]_1[bB]_1[bBA]_1[bBAa]_1|ac$$
$$\vdash [b]_1[bB]_1[bBA]_1|c$$

and no next move is possible, but for the LALL(1) parser

$$[S]_0|ac \vdash [b]_0[bB]_0[bBA]_0[bBAa]_0|ac$$
$$\vdash [b]_0[bB]_0[bBA]_0|c$$
$$\vdash [b]_0[bB]_0[bBB|cB]_0|c$$
$$\vdash [b]_0[bB]_0|c$$

before the error is detected. The SLL(1) parser of G_3 detects the error even later than the LALL(1) parser, since for the SLL(1) parser

$$[b]_0[bB]_0|c \vdash [b]_0|c$$

is possible.

3. CONSTRUCTION OF LL(k) PARSERS

We now present a method for constructing LL(k) parsers, i.e. the actions of the parser; the method can be regarded as a dual of that commonly used for constructing LR(k) parsers. Since the actions of an LL(k) parser are constructed using the equivalence classes of LL(k) equivalent viable suffixes, we should have a vehicle for determining the equivalence class for each viable suffix. Corresponding to the "descendant" relation defined on the set of LR(k) items, we begin by defining the relation D_k on the set of all LL(k) items of a grammar G as follows:

$$[A \rightarrow \alpha B.\beta,\ u]\ D_k\ [B \rightarrow \omega.,\ u]$$

for all productions $A \rightarrow \alpha B\beta$ and $B \rightarrow \omega$ of G and u in $FIRST_k(\beta FOLLOW_k(A))$. (Notice that, unlike in the LR(k) case, the dot is *after* the string ω and the lookahead symbol u is *the same* in both items.)

The GOTO function for sets of LL(k) items is defined as follows. If q is a set of LL(k) items and X is a nonterminal or a terminal, then we denote by $GOTO_k(q,X)$ the closure of the set

$$\{[A \rightarrow \alpha.X\beta,\ v] \mid [A \rightarrow \alpha X.\beta,\ u] \in q,\ v \in FIRST_k(Xu)\}$$

under the relation D_k. (Notice that, again unlike in the LR(k) case, the dot is moved to the *left* and the lookahead symbol is *changed*.) The $GOTO_k$ function is extended on general strings by the conditions $GOTO_k(q,\varepsilon) = q$ and $GOTO_k(q,\gamma X) = GOTO_k(GOTO_k(q,\gamma),X)$.

Further, we define the "successor" relation S_k on the sets of LL(k) items of the grammar G as follows: $q_1 \; S_k \; q_2$, if there exists a nonterminal or terminal X of G such that $q_2 = \text{GOTO}_k(q_1,X)$. Now if q_0 denotes the *initial* set of LL(k) items, i.e. the closure of the set $\{[S \to \omega., \varepsilon] | S \to \omega$ is a production of G$\}$ under the relation D_k, then we call the closure of the set $\{q_0\}$ under the relation S_k the *canonical collection* of sets of LL(k) items for the grammar G. The following theorems ensure that the equivalence classes of LL(k) equivalent viable suffixes of a grammar G are obtained from the canonical collection of sets of LL(k) items for G.

Theorem 3.1. The initial set of LL(k) items equals $[\varepsilon]_k$, the set of valid LL(k) items for the viable suffix ε.

Theorem 3.2. If γ is a viable suffix of the grammar G, then $[\gamma]_k = \text{GOTO}_k([\varepsilon]_k,\gamma)$.

Corollary 3.3. The canonical collection of sets of LL(k) items for the grammar G equals the collection $[G]_k$.

The canonical collections $[G_1]_2$, $[G_2]_2$ and $[G_3]_1$ for our example grammars G_1, G_2 and G_3 are found in Figures 1, 2 and 3, respectively, where the GOTO functions for these collections are given as directed graphs.

Finally, we define the actual construction of parsers, i.e. the construction of produce and shift actions. Let, therefore, k and p, $k \geq p$, be non-negative integers, q a set of items in $[G]_p$ and $A \to X_1 \ldots X_n$ a production of G such that either $q = q_0$ and $A = S$ or $\text{GOTO}_p(q,A) \neq \emptyset$. Further let y be a string in $\text{FIRST}_k(\Sigma^*)$ such that $[A \to .X_1 \ldots X_n, y]$ is an item in some q' in $[G]_k$ for which the set

(1) $\quad \{[B \to \alpha.\beta, \text{FIRST}_p(u)] | [B \to \alpha.\beta, u] \in q'\}$

equals $\text{GOTO}_p(q,X_n \ldots X_1)$. In this case

$$\text{GOTO}_p(q,A)|y \to \text{GOTO}_p(q,X_n) \ldots \text{GOTO}_p(q,X_n \ldots X_1)|y$$

is an LA(k)LL(p) produce action of the grammar G. Now let q be a set of items in $[G]_p$ and let a be a terminal such that $\text{GOTO}_p(q,a) \neq \emptyset$. Further let y be a terminal string such that there is an item of the form $[C \to \delta.a\gamma, ay]$ in some q' in $[G]_k$ for which the set (1) equals $\text{GOTO}_p(q,a)$. Then

$$\text{GOTO}_p(q,a)|ay \to \; |y$$

is an LA(k)LL(p) shift action of G.

It is obvious by Corollary 3.3 that the above rules really give the LA(k)LL(p) produce and shift actions of the grammar. A few observations may, however, be necessary. In constructing the produce actions we use the fact that for any viable suffix γ the

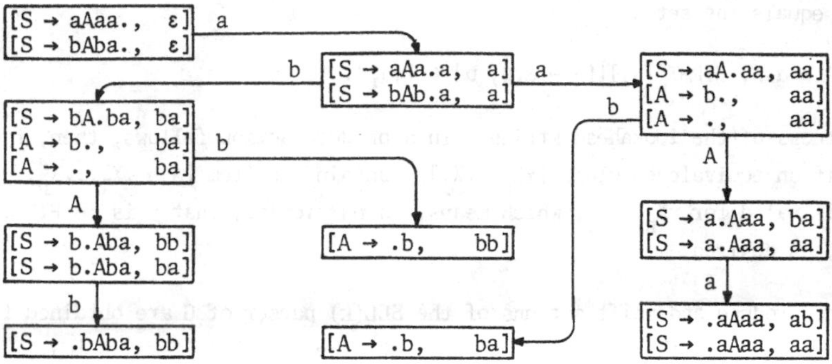

Figure 1. The GOTO graph of the collection $[G_1]_2$ for the grammar G_1 with productions S → aAaa | bAba, A → b | ε.

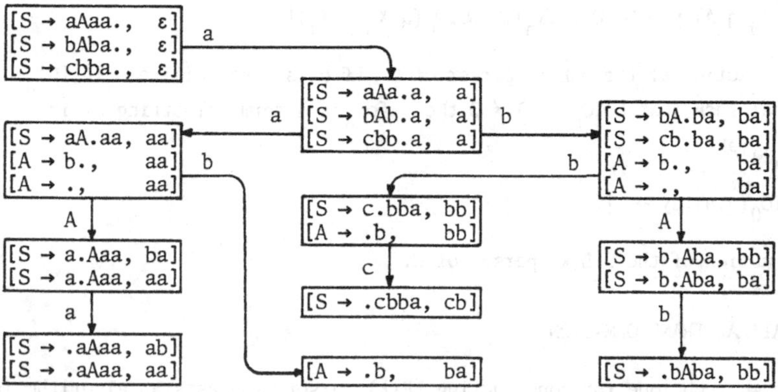

Figure 2. The GOTO graph of the collection $[G_2]_2$ for the grammar G_2 with productions S → aAaa | bAba | cbba, A → b | ε.

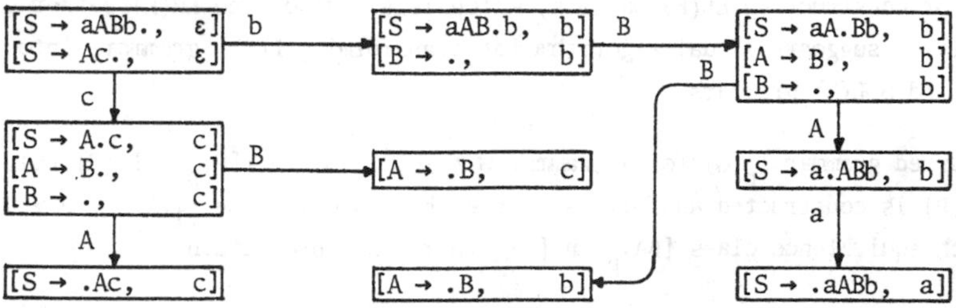

Figure 3. The GOTO graph of the collection $[G_3]_1$ for the grammar G_3 with productions S → aABb | Ac, A → B, B → ε.

class $[\gamma]_p$ equals the set

$$\{[A \to \alpha.\beta,\ FIRST_p(u)] \mid [A \to \alpha.\beta,\ u] \in [\gamma]_k\}.$$

The correctness of the lookahead string y in a produce action follows, then, from the fact that if an equivalence class $[\gamma X_n \ldots X_1]_k$ contains an item $[A \to .X_1 \ldots X_n,\ y]$ then this item is valid for $\gamma X_n \ldots X_1$, which means, in particular, that y is in $FIRST_k(X_1 \ldots X_n \gamma^R)$, as desired.

Finally, the produce and shift actions of the SLL(k) parser of G are obtained from the collection $[G]_0$ in the following manner. Let q be a set of items in $[G]_0$, $A \to X_1 \ldots X_n$ a production of G such that either $q = q_0$ and $A = S$ or $GOTO_0(q,A) \neq \emptyset$, and let y be a terminal string in $FIRST_k(X_1 \ldots X_n FOLLOW_k(A))$. Then

$$GOTO_0(q,A) \mid y \to GOTO_0(q,X_n) \ldots GOTO_0(q,X_n \ldots X_1) \mid y$$

is a produce action of the SLL(k) parser of G. If q is a set of items in $[G]_0$ and a is a terminal such that $GOTO_0(q,a) \neq \emptyset$ then, for each terminal string ay in $FIRST_{max(k,1)}(a\Sigma^*)$,

$$GOTO_0(q,a) \mid ay \to \ \mid y$$

is a shift action of the SLL(k) parser of G.

4. A GRAMMATICAL TRANSFORMATION

The well-known technique for constructing LR(k) parsers suggests an algorithm for transforming LR(k) grammars into LA(k)LR(p) and SLR(k) grammars such that the resulting grammars cover (and are even structurally equivalent to) the original grammar. Our technique for constructing LL(k) parsers, which is a dual of the LR(k) parser construction technique, suggests a dual algorithm for transforming LL(k) grammars into LA(k)LL(p) and SLL(k) grammars.

The transformed grammar $T_p(G)$ for a grammar $G = (N,\Sigma,P,S)$ is $([G]_p,\Sigma,T_p(P),[S]_p)$ where the set $T_p(P)$ is constructed as follows. For each production $A \to X_1 \ldots X_n$, $n \geq 0$, of G and for each equivalence class $[\beta A]_p$ in $[G]_p$ there is a production

$$[\beta A]_p \to Y_1 \ldots Y_n$$

in $T_p(P)$ where each Y_i, $i = 1,\ldots,n$, equals the class $[\beta X_n \ldots X_i]_p$ if X_i is a nonterminal, and X_i otherwise.

Theorem 4.1. The transformed grammar $T_p(G)$ is LA(k)LL(p) (resp. SLL(p)) if and only if the given grammar G is LL(k) (resp. LL(p)), and $T_p(G)$ is structurally equivalent to G.

As an example, consider the LL(2) grammar G_1 given in Section 2. The transformed grammar $T_2(G_1)$ for G_1 has the following productions:

$$[S]_2 \rightarrow a[aaA]_2aa \mid b[abA]_2ba$$
$$[aaA]_2 \rightarrow b \mid \varepsilon$$
$$[abA]_2 \rightarrow b \mid \varepsilon$$

Clearly, $T_2(G_1)$ is an SLL(2) grammar and structurally equivalent to G_1.

Finally we wish to point out that this transformation is related to that given in [11]; the advantages of the given transformation are that its correctness is easily verified and that it can be regarded as a dual of the corresponding transformation in the LR(k) case.

ACKNOWLEDGEMENTS

Financial support from the Emil Aaltonen Foundation and the Finnish Cultural Foundation is gratefully acknowledged.

REFERENCES

1. Aho,A.V., and J.D.Ullman, *The Theory of Parsing, Translation and Compiling, Vol. I: Parsing*. Englewood Cliffs, N.J.: Prentice-Hall, 1972.
2. Aho,A.V., and J.D.Ullman, *Principles of Compiler Design*. Reading, Mass.: Addison-Wesley Publishing Co., 1977.
3. Anderson,T., Syntactic Analysis of LR(k) Languages, Ph.D. Thesis, Computing Lab., University of Newcastle upon Tyne, 1972.
4. DeRemer,F.L., Practical Translators for LR(k) Languages, Ph.D. Thesis and Project MAC Technical Report TR-65, Mass. Inst. of Tech., 1969.
5. DeRemer,F.L., Simple LR(k) Grammars, *Comm. ACM 14*, 453-460, 1971.
6. Fischer,C.N., D.R.Milton and S.B.Quiring, An Efficient Insertion Only Error-Corrector for LL(1) Parsers, in *Conference Record of the Fourth ACM Symposium on Principles of Programming Languages*, 97-103, 1977.
7. Ghezzi,C., LL(1) Grammars Supporting an Efficient Error Handling, *Information Processing Letters 3*, 174-176, 1975.
8. Harrison,M.A., *Introduction to Formal Language Theory*. Reading, Mass.: Addison-Wesley Publishing Co., 1978.
9. Knuth,D.E., On the Translation of Languages from Left to Right, *Information and Control 8*, 607-639, 1965.
10. LaLonde,W.R., On Directly Constructing LA(k)LR(m) Parsers without Chain Productions, Technical Report No. SE & CS 76-9, Department of Systems Engineering and Computing Science, Carleton University, 1976.
11. Rosenkrantz,D.J., and R.E.Stearns, Properties of Deterministic Top-Down Grammars, *Information and Control 17*, 226-256, 1970.
12. Wood,D., Lecture Notes on Top-Down Syntax Analysis, Computer Science Technical Report 78-CS-12, Department of Applied Mathematics, McMaster University, 1978.

MORE ON ADVICE ON STRUCTURING COMPILERS AND PROVING THEM CORRECT

James W. Thatcher, Eric G. Wagner and Jesse B. Wright

Mathematical Sciences Department
IBM Thomas J. Watson Research Center
Yorktown Heights, New York 10566
USA

The purpose of this paper is to affirm and applaud the advice given by F. L. Morris (1973) at the Second SIGACT/SIGPLAN Symposium on Principles of Programming Languages and to correct, refine, and complete the example he gave there.

The goal, first announced by McCarthy, is to make compilers for high level programming languages completely trustworthy by proving their correctness. Morris (1973) stated his belief (shared by many) that the compiler correctness problem is much less general and better structured than the unrestricted program correctness problem.

The essence of Morris' advice was that a proof of compiler correctness should be a proof that a diagram of the form[†].

(★)

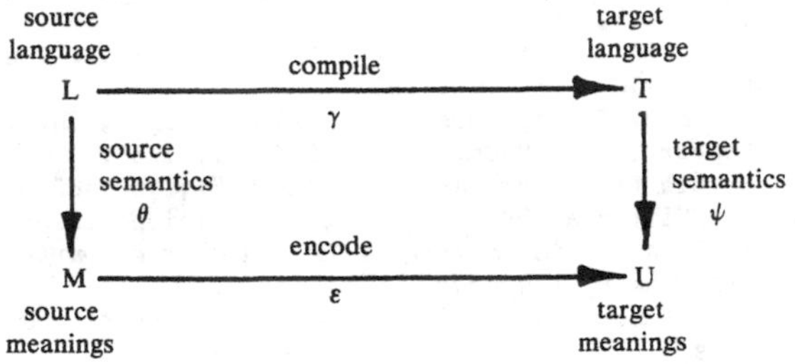

commutes; that the corners of the diagram are not just sets but are many-sorted (heterogeneous) algebras and that the arrows are homomorphisms.

This paper can be seen as the fourth in the sequence: McCarthy and Painter (1967), Burstall and Landin (1970) and Morris (1973). At each step the content of (★) has become more algebraic and the example source language richer. Although our example language is similar to that of Milner and Weyrauch (1972)[‡] and Milner (1976), our approach is different because we are explicitly avoiding the lambda calculus (and thus LCF, Milner (1972)) and because their target semantics is interpretive.

---

† Morris' diagram had $\delta: U \to M$ along the bottom, though in the text he uses $\varepsilon: M \to U$.

‡ Milner [personal communication] commented on the Milner and Weyrauch (1972) proof: "... we could only think clearly enough to do our proof at all on the machine by structuring it algebraically." (See page 58 of their paper.)

Morris observed that the source language, being described by a context free grammar, determined an initial many-sorted (heterogeneous) algebra. This correspondence is discussed in detail in ADJ (1975); if G is the grammar and N is its set of non-terminals, then G is viewed as an N-sorted operator domain where the productions are the operator symbols. T_G is the initial G-algebra and its carrier of sort $A \in N$ is the set of all parse trees from non-terminal A.

Recall that T_G being initial means that there is a unique homomorphism from it to any other algebra with operator domain G. This is how the top and left side of the diagram (★) are determined; L is T_G and M and T are G-algebras -- then γ and θ are unique homomorphisms. Initiality is also the method of correctness proof, for if ψ and ε are also homomorphisms, then $\gamma \circ \psi = \theta \circ \varepsilon$ by uniqueness. This is an extremely powerful methodology; no "structural induction" is required for the definition of the arrows or the proof.

So to describe the source semantics (the left side of the diagram) we need only define a G-algebra M, that is, carriers corresponding to the non-terminals and operations corresponding to the productions. Morris, "as a concession to readability," combined the specification of θ and M's operations in a "conventional style of recursive function definition, following the notation of Scott and Strachey (1970)." However we claim the result is *not* more readable for two reasons; first, combining with the definition of θ is just more notation -- θ is uniquely determined, and, second, the algebraic operations (composition, tupling, product, etc.) have not been separated out from the "local" operations, those involved with manipulating environments or "adding numbers." For example, for assignment, our semantic line is (see (M2)):

$$(\alpha)x{:=}_M = \alpha \circ \mathrm{assign}_x$$

where $\alpha{:}E \to E \times V$ and assign_x is the obvious function from $E \times V$ to E (environments). In contrast Morris writes:

$$\theta[\![x{:=}r]\!] = (\lambda a \lambda e.\lambda w.w{=}\theta[\![x]\!] \to a,e(w)) * \theta[\![r]\!]$$

where $p*q = \lambda x.p(q(x)_1)(q(x)_2)$!

Besides these relatively minor points, our treatment differs radically from that of Morris in that we have succeeded in making the right-hand side of (★) algebraic. This is what Morris wanted to do, but his algebraic model of flow charts was too unwieldy. In particular, we do not see the justification for his claim that a semantic homomorphism is determined by specifying the effect of the homomorphism on the individual instructions. Recognizing fundamental operations for building up flow charts (Section 5) and uniqueness of interpretation (Section 7) are crucially important contributions of Elgot (1973).

Thus, we take for the target language, an algebra T_0 of flow charts (actually a category) whose operations are things like parallel and serial composition and iteration, and whose individual instructions manipulate a stack and a "memory." The semantics of this category of flow charts is uniquely determined by the interpretations of the flow chart primitives. And the semantic target (U_0) is a category of meanings for those flow charts (actually an algebraic theory in the sense of Lawvere (1963)).

Then we extract from T_0 a G-algebra T, defining the operations of T in terms of the operations of T_0. This, by initiality, gives the compile function $\gamma{:}L \to T$ and it also *immediately* determines an algebra U, extracted from U_0, and a homomorphism ψ from T to U. These arrows are each uniquely determined by the interpretations of certain primitives. All that is left is the "bottom line," $\varepsilon{:}M \to U$. Given the (simple) definition of ε from the carrier of M to the carrier of U we have to prove that ε is a homomorphism, that is, that it preserves all the operations of M. Once this is done, the compiler correctness proof is complete for, by initiality, $\gamma \circ \psi = \theta \circ \varepsilon$.

As Barry Rosen has pointed out to us, commuting of (★) is not, in itself, "compiler correctness." T and U could be one-point algebras and γ, ψ, and ε, the unique homomorphisms to those one-point algebras resulting in a commuting square. One possibility around this degenerate case, suggested by Rosen, would be to require the encoding (ε) to be injective (it is in our case) and that condition is certainly sufficient. We are just not sure at this time that it is necessary.

Our treatment differs from Morris (1973) in one other less significant respect. We make the advice that the starting point for the semantic definition should be an abstract data type in the sense of ADJ (1976,1976a).

This paper presumes familiarity with many-sorted algebras, categories, and algebraic theories, but we hope that it can be read without detailed knowledge of those concepts. It is our intention that the example will prove potent enough to convince the reader of the importance of the algebraic ideas; that they are worth the investment of time and energy to obtain even better understanding.

2. THE UNDERLYING DATA TYPE

Let Σ be the following $\{int,Bool\}$-sorted signature for integer and Boolean valued expressions.

$$\Sigma_{int,\lambda}=\{0,1\} \qquad \Sigma_{int,int}=\{\,^{-},Pr,Su\} \qquad \Sigma_{int,int\ int}=\{+,-,\times\}$$

$$\Sigma_{Bool,\lambda}=\{tt,ff\} \qquad \Sigma_{Bool,Bool}=\{\neg\} \qquad \Sigma_{Bool,Bool\ Bool}=\{\wedge\}$$

$$\Sigma_{Bool,int}=\{even\} \qquad \Sigma_{Bool,int\ int}=\{\leq,\geq,EQ\} \qquad \Sigma_{int,Bool\ int\ int}=\{cond\}.$$

All other $\Sigma_{s,w}$ are empty. $T_{\Sigma,int}$ is the set (or algebra) of integer valued expressions and $T_{\Sigma,Bool}$ is the set of Boolean valued expressions. The underlying data type (an $\{int, Bool\}$-sorted algebra S) for our simple programming language is the abstract data type[†] determined by the signature Σ together with axioms E consisting of at least (the correctness of these axioms is not at issue for this paper) axioms E1-E17 below. Assuming those axioms *are* correct (in the strong sense of ADJ (1976a)), we can take $S_{int} = \mathbb{Z}$ (the integers) and (for technical reasons) $S_{Bool} = [2] = \{1,2\}$ (with $tt_S = 2$).

(E1) $Pr(Su(x)) = x$ (E2) $Su(Pr(x)) = x$ (E3) $Su(0) = 1$

(E4) $\neg(tt) = ff$ (E5) $\neg(ff) = tt$

(E6) $b\wedge tt = b$ (E7) $b\wedge ff = ff$ (E8) $b' = \neg(\neg b\wedge\neg b')$

(E9) $x+0 = x$ (E10) $x+Su(y) = Su(x+y)$

(E11) $x-0 = x$ (E12) $x-Su(y) = Pr(x-y)$

(E13) $x\times 0 = 0$ (E14) $x\times Su(y) = (x\times y)+x$ (E15) $^{-}(x) = 0-x$

(E16) $cond(tt,x,y) = x$ (E17) $cond(ff,x,y) = y$

(E18) $x\leq x = tt$ (E19) $1\leq 0 = ff$ (E20) $x\leq y = Su(x)\leq Su(y)$

(E21) $x\leq y=tt \Rightarrow x\leq Su(y)=tt$ (E22) $x\leq y=ff \Rightarrow S(x)\leq y=ff$

(E23) $EQ(x,y) = (x\leq y)\wedge(y\leq x)$ (E24) $x\geq y = EQ(x,y)(x\leq y)$

(E25) $even(0) = tt$ (E26) $even(1) = ff$ (E27) $even(x) = \neg even(Su(x))$

---

† See, for instance, Zilles (1974), Guttag (1975) or ADJ (1976a).

3. THE LANGUAGE L

Our programming language is essentially the one employed by Morris (1973). As such, it is a slight enrichment of the language used as an example by Milner (1976). Our grammar will have non-terminals {<st>,<ae>,<be>} for "statements", "arithmetic expressions" and "Boolean expressions." The terminals include the symbols in the signature Σ above, plus those other letters in boldface occurring in the productions below. Further, we assume given a set X of variables or identifiers.

We list the productions of G giving each a name which we can use in defining the semantic algebra. Thus, for example, when G is viewed as an operator domain, ifthenelse is an operator symbol to denote a function that takes three arguments of sorts <be>,<st>,<st>, respectively, and yields a result of sort <st>. Similarly result takes two arguments of sort <st> and <ae> and yields a result of sort <ae>.

(L1)	continue	<st> ::= **continue**	
(L2)	x:=	<st> ::= **x:=**<ae>	For x ∈ X
(L3)	ifthenelse	<st> ::= **if**<be>**then**<st>**else**<st>	
(L4)	;	<st> ::= <st>;<st>	
(L5)	whiledo	<st> ::= **while**<be>**do**<st>	
(L6)	c	<ae> ::= **c**	For $c \in \Sigma_{int,\lambda}$
(L7)	x	<ae> ::= **x**	For x ∈ X
(L8)	aop1	<ae> ::= **aop1**<ae>	For $aop1 \in \Sigma_{int,int}$
(L9)	aop2	<ae> ::= <ae>**aop2**<ae>	For $aop2 \in \Sigma_{int,int\ int}$
(L10)	cond	<ae> ::= **if**<be>**then**<ae>**else**<ae>	
(L11)	result	<ae> ::= <st>**result**<ae>	
(L12)	letx	<ae> ::= **letxbe**<ae>**in**<ae>	For x ∈ X
(L13)	bc	<be> ::= **bc**	For $bc \in \Sigma_{Bool,\lambda}$
(L14)	prop	<be> ::= **prop**<ae>	For $prop \in \Sigma_{Bool,int}$
(L15)	rel	<be> ::= <ae>**rel**<ae>	For $rel \in \Sigma_{Bool,int\ int}$
(L16)	bop1	<be> ::= **bop1**<be>	For $bop1 \in \Sigma_{Bool,Bool}$
(L17)	bop2	<be> ::= <be>**bop2**<be>	For $bop2 \in \Sigma_{Bool,Bool\ bool}$

4. SOURCE LANGUAGE SEMANTICS, THE ALGEBRA M.

Now we define the semantic algebra M. For this we need the set Env of "environments," Env = $[X \rightarrow \mathbb{Z}]$. Then the three carriers are:

$$M_{<st>} = [Env \rightharpoonup Env] \quad M_{<ae>} = [Env \rightharpoonup Env \times \mathbb{Z}] \quad M_{<be>} = [Env \rightharpoonup Env \times [2]].$$

Here $[A \rightarrow B]$ is the set of (total) functions from A to B and $[A \rightharpoonup B]$ is the (po)set of partial functions from A to B.

Even for partial functions $f \in [A \rightharpoonup B]$ we will write $f{:}A \rightarrow B$ to designate source and target, function arguments will *usually* be written on the left as in (a)f, and we will explicitly write $\circ$ for the operation of function composition whose arguments are written in diagrammatic order: if $f{:}A \rightarrow B$ and $g{:}B \rightarrow C$ then $f \circ g{:}A \rightarrow C$. 1_A is the identity function on the set A (for $f{:}A \rightarrow B$, $1_A \circ f = f = f \circ 1_B$).

The definitions of the seventeen operations on M (corresponding to the grammar's seventeen productions) involve certain primitive operations on M's carriers along with standard (and some not so standard) combining forms.

We first list the primitive operations:

$$\mathrm{assign}_x : E\times V \to E \qquad (z)\langle e,v\rangle \mathrm{assign}_x = \begin{cases} v \text{ if } z=x \\ (z)e \text{ if } z\neq x \end{cases}$$

$$\mathrm{fetch}_x : E \to E\times V \qquad (e)\mathrm{fetch}_x = \langle e,(x)e\rangle$$

We also have available all the operations σ_S, for $\sigma\in\Sigma$, from Section 2; e.g., $+_S$ is addition on the integers.

Given two (partial) functions, $f_i:A\to B$, define the *source tuple*, $(f_1,f_2):A\times[2]\to B$, by

$$\langle a,i\rangle(f_1,f_2) = (a)f_i.$$

Define the *sum*, $f_1+f_2:A\times[2]\to B\times[2]$, of functions $f_i:A\to B$ for $i\in[2]$ by:

$$\langle a,i\rangle(f_1+f_2) = \langle (a)f_i,i\rangle.$$

If $\iota_i:B\to B\times[2]$ is the injection sending $b\in B$ to $\langle b,i\rangle$, for $i\in[2]$, then $f_1+f_2=(f_1\circ\iota_1,f_2\circ\iota_2)$. $B\times[2]$ is the disjoint union, sum or coproduct of B with itself, and more generally $B\times[n]$ is the coproduct of B with itself n times (n disjoint "copies" of B); $\iota_i:B\to B\times[n]$ sends b to $\langle b,i\rangle$, for $i\in[n]$. Context will usually distinguish the source of an injection and for this paper, the target will always be clear. When necessary to distinguish sources, we will write $\iota_j^B:B\to B\times[n]$.

Given a partial function $f:A\to A\times[2]$, define the *iterate*, $f^\dagger:A\to A$, to be the least upper bound (i.e. union) of the sequence $f^{(k)}$ defined by:

$$f^{(0)} = \emptyset$$
$$f^{(k+1)} = f\circ(f^{(k)},1_A),$$

where $\emptyset$ is the empty partial function from A to A.

Given (partial) functions $f_i:A\to B_i$, define the *target tuple*, $[f_1,f_2]:A\to B_1\times B_2$, by:

$$(a)[f_1,f_2] = \langle (a)f_1,(a)f_2\rangle.$$

Note that if either f_1 or f_2 is undefined at a, then $[f_1,f_2]$ is undefined at a. The projection function $\pi_i:A_1\times\ldots\times A_n\to A_i$ takes $\langle a_1,\ldots,a_n\rangle$ to a_i. Given functions $f_i:A_i\to B_i$, define their *product*, $f_1\times f_2:A_1\times A_2\to B_1\times B_2$, by:

$$\langle a_1,a_2\rangle(f_1\times f_2) = \langle (a_1)f_1,(a_2)f_2\rangle.$$

Paralleling the sum case above, the product of functions is defined in terms of target tupling and projections: $f_1\times f_2=[\pi_1\circ f_1,\pi_2\circ f_2]$.

Now for the definitions of M's operations; τ,τ_1,τ_2, range over $M_{\langle st\rangle}$; α,α_1,α_2 range over $M_{\langle ae\rangle}$; and, β,β_1,β_2 range over $M_{\langle be\rangle}$.

(M1) $\mathrm{continue}_M = 1_{Env}$

(M2) $(\alpha)x{:=}_M = \alpha\circ\mathrm{assign}_x$

(M3) $(\beta,\tau_1,\tau_2)\mathrm{ifthenelse}_M = \beta\circ(\tau_1,\tau_2)$

(M4) $(\tau_1,\tau_2);_M = \tau_1\circ\tau_2$

(M5) $(\beta,\tau)\text{whiledo}_M = (\beta\circ(\tau+1_{Env}))^{\dagger}$

(M6) $c_M = 1_{Env}\times c_S$

(M7) $x_M = \text{fetch}_x$

(M8) $(\alpha)\text{aop1}_M = \alpha\circ(1_{Env}\times \text{aop1}_S)$

(M9) $(\alpha_1,\alpha_2)\text{aop2}_M = \alpha_1\circ(\alpha_2\times 1_{\mathbb{Z}})\circ[\pi_1,\pi_3,\pi_2]\circ(1_{Env}\times \text{aop2}_S)$

(M10) $(\beta,\alpha_1,\alpha_2)\text{cond}_M = \beta\circ(\alpha_1,\alpha_2)$

(M11) $(\tau,\alpha)\text{result}_M = \tau\circ\alpha$

(M12) $(\alpha_1,\alpha_2)\text{letx}_M = \text{fetch}_x\circ[(\alpha_1\circ \text{assign}_x\circ\alpha_2)\times 1_{\mathbb{Z}}]\circ[\pi_1,\pi_3,\pi_2]\circ(\text{assign}_x\times 1_{\mathbb{Z}})$

(M13) $bc_M = 1_{Env}\times bc_S$

(M14) $(\alpha)\text{prop}_M = \alpha\circ(1_{Env}\times \text{prop}_S)$

(M15) $(\alpha_1,\alpha_2)\text{rel}_M = \alpha_1\circ(\alpha_2\times 1_{\mathbb{Z}})\circ(1_{Env}\times \text{rel}_S)$

(M16) $(\beta)\neg_M = \beta\circ(\iota_2,\iota_1)$

(M17a) $(\beta_1,\beta_2)\wedge_M = \beta_1\circ(\iota_1,\beta_2)$

(M17b) $(\beta_1,\beta_2)\vee_M = \beta_1\circ(\beta_2,\iota_2)$

The Boolean expressions are treated differently from the arithmetic expressions. In the definition of $\wedge_M$, for example, β_1 can give the value false (1) and β_2 will not be evaluated, i.e., could be non-terminating: if $(e)\beta_1=\langle e',1\rangle$ (false with new environment e'), then $(e)\beta_1\circ(\iota_1,\beta_2)=\langle e',1\rangle$ independent of β_2.

Calling our grammar above, G, we have made $M = \langle M_{\langle st\rangle}, M_{\langle ae\rangle}, M_{\langle be\rangle}\rangle$ into a G-algebra with the seventeen definitions, (M1-M17). The algebraic semantics for G is the unique homomorphism $\theta:T_G\rightarrow M$.

5. THE TARGET LANGUAGE, T_0, THE (ENRICHED) CATEGORY OF FLOW CHARTS

In what follows Ω is an arbitrary *one-sorted* signature or operator domain, i.e. an indexed family of disjoint sets, $\langle\Omega_i\rangle_{i\in\omega}$. Viewing Ω as the union of the Ω_i, we associate with the operator domain a ranking function, $r_\Omega:\Omega\rightarrow\omega$ where $(\sigma)r_\Omega = k$ iff $\sigma\in\Omega_k$. $\Omega_\perp$ is the operator domain Ω with $\perp$ adjoined as a symbol of rank zero, i.e., $(\Omega_\perp)_0=\Omega_0\cup\{\perp\}$. Below we will fix on a specific operator domain Ω for our language T_0.

We now define flow charts, identity charts, and the operations of composition, pairing and iteration on flow charts. That these are the essential operations on charts is a key contribution of Elgot (1973). We obtain an enriched category of flow charts which is small (a set of objects instead of a proper class) by using the various [n], $n\in\omega$, as the sets of vertices. Elgot (1977) and Elgot and Shepherdson (1977) define an equivalent large category and consider the skeletal small category determined by isomorphism classes of flow charts.

In addition to the combining forms used in Section 4 (composition, iteration, etc.), we need the following: $0_A:[0]\rightarrow A$ is the unique function from $[0]=\emptyset$ to A; and, $I_A:A\rightarrow A^*$ is the set injection of A into the underlying set of the free monoid A^*.

Definition 5.1. A (*normalized*) $\Omega_\perp$*-flow chart from* n *to* p *of weight* s consists of a triple $\langle b,\tau,\ell\rangle$ where:

begin function	$b:[n]\rightarrow[s+p]$
underlying graph	$\tau:[s]\rightarrow[s+p]^*$
labeling function	$\ell:[s]\rightarrow\Omega_\perp$,

satisfying the requirement that $|(i)\tau| = ((i)\ell)r_{\Omega_\perp}$.

(i)b is called a *begin vertex*, $i \in [s]$ is an *internal vertex*, $i \in s+[p]$ is an *exit* and in particular, s+j is the jth *exit vertex*. $(i)\ell$ is the operation symbol labeling the ith internal vertex; by the above requirement it must have rank $|(i)\tau|$. Let $Flo_{\Omega_\perp}(n,p)$ be the set of $\Omega_\perp$-flow charts from n to p. □

This definition of flow chart employs the convenient definition of directed ordered graph introduced by Arbib and Giveon (1968). To relate to more familiar notions of flow charts, say the function $\tau:[s]\to[s+p]^*$ takes $k \in [s]$ to $k_1...k_u \in [s+p]^*$. This says that there is an edge from vertex k to *each* of the vertices k_i ($i \in [u]$) and the natural ordering on [u] induces the (local) ordering on the edges leaving vertex k. This ordering is essential to distinguish between, for example, the "true" and "false" branches of a (binary) test node.

Definition 5.2. The *identity* $\Omega_\perp$-flow chart from n to n, denoted 1_n, has weight 0 and:

begin function	$1_{[n]}:[n]\to[n]$
underlying graph	$0_{[n]^*}:[0]\to[n]^*$
labeling function	$0_{\Omega_\perp}:[0]\to\Omega_\perp$. □

Informally the identity chart from n to n has n begin vertices which are also exits and thus there is no labeling.

Definition 5.3. The *composite* of $\Omega_\perp$-flow charts, $F=\langle b,\tau,\ell\rangle$ from n to p of weight s and $F'=\langle b',\tau',\ell'\rangle$ from p to q of weight s' is $F \circ F'$ from n to q of weight s+s' with:

begin function	$bf:[n]\to[s+s'+q]$
underlying graph	$(\tau f^*,\tau' g^*):[s+s']\to[s+s'+q]^*$
labeling function	$(\ell,\ell'):[s+s']\to\Omega_\perp$

where f and g are the following functions,

$$f=1_{[s]}+b':[s+p]\to[s+s'+q]$$

$$g=0_{[s]}+1_{[s'+q]}:[s'+q]\to[s+s'+q]. \quad \square$$

Informally $F \circ F'$ is obtained by identifying the p exits of F with the q begin vertices of F'. At the same time the vertices of F' are "translated" by s, i.e., a vertex j of F' becomes s+j in $F \circ F'$.

Theorem 5.4. For each $n,p \in \omega$, let $\mathbf{Flo}_{\Omega_\perp}(n,p)$ be the set of $\Omega_\perp$-flow charts from n to p (i.e., $Flo_{\Omega_\perp}(n,p)$). Then $\mathbf{Flo}_{\Omega_\perp}$ is a category with the nonnegative integers as objects, with composition given by Definition 5.3, and with identities given by Definition 5.2. □

Without identifying it as such, Elgot (1973) describes a category of *normal descriptions over* Ω which is essentially the same as $\mathbf{Flo}_{\Omega_\perp}$, and it is also equipped with the operations of pairing and iteration which we now proceed to define.

Definition 5.5. The *pairing* or *coalesced sum* of two $\Omega_\perp$-flow charts $F=\langle b,\tau,\ell\rangle$ from n to p of weight s and $F'=\langle b',\tau',\ell'\rangle$ from n' to p of weight s' is (F,F') from n+n' to p of weight s+s' where

begin function	$(bf,b'g):[n+n']\to[s+s'+p]$
underlying graph	$(\tau f^*,\tau' g^*):[s+s']\to[s+s'+p]^*$
labeling function	$(\ell,\ell'):[s+s']\to\Omega_\perp$

where

$$f = 1_{[s]} + 0_{[s']} + 1_{[p]} : [s+p] \to [s+s'+p]$$

$$g = 0_{[s]} + 1_{[s'+p]} : [s'+p] \to [s+s'+p].$$ □

Informally, the effect of pairing is to put the two charts F and F′ next to each other identifying the p exits of F with those of F′.

Proposition 5.6. Pairing of $\Omega_\perp$-flow charts is associative, i.e.,

$$(F_1,(F_2,F_3)) = ((F_1,F_2),F_3)$$

for F_1, F_2, F_3 where the pairing is defined. □

Definition 5.7. For any function $f:[n] \to [p]$ we define an associated $\Omega_\perp$-flow chart $f^\wedge$ from n to p of weight 0; $f^\wedge = \langle f, 0_{[p]^*}, 0_{\Omega_\perp} \rangle$. □

Using the charts corresponding to maps (Definition 5.7) and coalesced sum (Definition 5.5) we define *the separated sum* of F_i from n_i to m_i $(i \in [2])$ to be the chart

$$F_1 \oplus F_2 = (F_1 \circ f_1{}^\wedge, F_2 \circ f_2{}^\wedge)$$

where $f_i:[s_i+m_i] \to [s_1+s_2+m_1+m_2]$ are the obvious injections for $i = 1,2$.

We want special notation for the flow charts corresponding to certain maps (injections); this is notation used for the corresponding morphisms in algebraic theories. First, $x_{(i)}^{n_1+\ldots+n_r}:n_i \to n_1+\ldots+n_r$ is $f^\wedge$, where

$$f:[n_i] \to [n_1+\ldots+n_r]$$

is the injection sending $j \in [n_i]$ to $n_1+\ldots+n_{i-1}+j$. Next (actually a special case) $x_i^n:1 \to n$ is $f^\wedge$ where $f:[1] \to [n]$ sends 1 to i. In general we will not distinguish between the maps (f, above) and the corresponding charts, $x_{(i)}^{n_1+\ldots+n_r}$ and x_i^n.

The last operation is perhaps the most important operation; it is the only one that employs '$\perp$'. Thus all the definitions above apply to Ω-flow charts with arbitrary Ω replacing our special $\Omega_\perp$. The idea is that for an $\Omega_\perp$-flow chart from n to n+p of weight s, the "iterate" of F, denoted $F^\dagger$, identifies the ith exit with the ith begin node, thus introducing 'loops,' the result has p exits and weight s. The construction is more complicated than that, however, because the ith exit might be the ith begin (for example) and this iteration has to yield an nonterminating loop ($\perp$).

Definition 5.8. Let $F = \langle b, \tau, \ell \rangle$ be a $\Omega_\perp$-flow chart from n to n+p of weight s. Further, let $f = (x_{(1)}^{s+n+p}, b, x_{(3)}^{s+n+p}):[s+n+p] \to [s+n+p]$ and factor f^n to

$$f^n = h \circ (1_s + g + 1_p):[s+n+p] \to [s+n+p],$$

where $h:[s+n+p] \to [s+u+p]$ and $g:[u] \to [n]$ and u is the smallest natural number yielding such a factorization. The *iterate* of F is the flow chart $F^\dagger$ from n to p of weight s+u with:

begin function	$b \circ h:[n] \to [s+u+p]$
underlying graph	$(\tau \circ h^*, \lambda^u)):[s+u] \to [s+u+p]^*$
labeling function	$(\ell, \perp^u):[s+u] \to \Omega_\perp$,

where $\lambda^u:[u] \to [s+u+p]^*$ sends each $i \in [u]$ to $\lambda \in [s+u+p]^*$ and $\perp^u$ sends each $i \in [u]$ to $\perp \in \Omega_\perp$.

Flow charts will be interpreted in Section 7. Once the operations and tests (Ω) have been interpreted in a (rational or continuous) algebraic theory, the interpretation of the flow charts is uniquely determined by certain natural preservation properties.

We present a signature (ranked alphabet) Ω which we use to construct $\Omega_\perp$-flow charts. In that alphabet we include some of the symbols from the $\{int,Bool\}$-sorted signature Σ of Section 2.

$$\Omega_1 = \{\text{load}_x, \text{store}_x \mid x \in X\} \cup \{\text{switch}\} \cup \bigcup_{w \in \{int\}^*} \Sigma_{int,w}$$
$$\Omega_2 = \bigcup_{w \in \{int\}^*} \Sigma_{Bool,w}$$
$$\Omega_n = \emptyset, \quad n = 0,3,4,\ldots\ .$$

This signature determines the category $\mathbf{Flo}_{\Omega_\perp}$ of $\Omega_\perp$-flow charts via Definition 5.1 and Theorem 5.4. This *is* T_0!

So as not to keep the excited reader in a cloud of mystery we immediately provide an interpretation of Ω in $\mathbf{Sum}_A$ where $A = \text{Stk} \times \text{Env}$ (stacks cross environments):

$$\text{Stk} = [\omega \to \mathbb{Z}] \qquad \text{Env} = [X \to \mathbb{Z}].$$

For any set A, $\mathbf{Sum}_A$ is the algebraic theory whose morphisms from n to p consist of all *partial* functions from $A \times [n]$ to $A \times [p]$. U_0 is $\mathbf{Sum}_{\text{Stk} \times \text{Env}}$; the reader will find the target language semantics in Section 7. (See ADJ (1976b) or Elgot (1973) where this theory is denoted [A].) Composition in $\mathbf{Sum}_A$ is function composition, identities are identities from **Set**, and tupling of n functions, $f_i{:}A \to a \times [p]$ gives $(f_1,\ldots,f_n){:}[n] \to [p]$ which takes $<a,i>$ to $(a)f_i$. For distinguished morphisms,

(S1) $$x_i^n = \iota_i^A{:}A \to A \times [n].$$

Note that we have taken stacks to be infinite to make the definitions simpler. For example we will write $v_1 \bullet v_2 \bullet \ldots \bullet v_n \bullet \rho$ where $v_i \in \mathbb{Z}$ and $\rho \in \text{Stk}$ to denote the stack whose first n elements are $v_1,\ldots,v_n$, and whose "rest" is ρ. The usual functions are associated with stacks: push:Stk $\times\, \mathbb{Z} \to$ Stk; and, pop:Stk $\to$ Stk $\times\, \mathbb{Z}$.

(S2) $<\rho,v>\text{push} = v \bullet \rho$

(S3) $(v \bullet \rho)\text{pop} = <\rho,v>$.

With the identification of A with $A \times [1]$, the interpretation, $I{:}\Omega \to \mathbf{Sum}_A$ $(A = \text{Stk} \times \text{Env})$, is given as follows.

(I1)	$<\rho, e>(\text{load}_x I)$	$= <(x)e \bullet \rho, e>$	For $x \in X$
(I2)	$<v \circ \rho, e>(\text{store}_x I)$	$= <\rho, e[x/v]>$	
(I3)	$<v_1 \bullet v_2 \bullet \rho, e>(\text{switch}I)$	$= <v_2 \bullet v_1 \bullet \rho, e>$	
(I4)	$<\rho, e>(cI)$	$= <c_S \bullet \rho, e>$	For $c \in \Sigma_{int,\lambda}$
(I5)	$<v \bullet \rho, e>(\text{aop1}I)$	$= <(v)\text{aop1}_S \bullet \rho, e>$	For $\text{aop1} \in \Sigma_{int,int}$
(I6)	$<v_2 \bullet v_1 \bullet \rho, e>(\text{aop2}I)$	$= <(v_1,v_2)\text{aop2}_S \bullet \rho, e>$	For $\text{aop2} \in \Sigma_{int,int\ int}$
(I7)	$<\rho, e>(\text{bc}I)$	$= <<\rho, e>, \text{bc}_S>$	For $\text{bc} \in \Sigma_{Bool,\lambda}$
(I8)	$<v \bullet \rho, e>(\text{prop}I)$	$= <<\rho, e>, (v)\text{prop}_S>$	For $\text{prop} \in \Sigma_{Bool,int}$
(I9)	$<v_1 \bullet v_2 \bullet \rho, e>(\text{rel}I)$	$= <<\rho, e>, (v_1,v_2)\text{rel}_S>$	For $\text{rel} \in \Sigma_{Bool,int\ int}$

6. THE TARGET ALGEBRA OF FLOW CHARTS, T.

Now take $T_{<ae>}=T_{<st>}=\mathbf{Flo}_{\Omega_\perp}(1,1)$ and $T_{<be>}=\mathbf{Flo}_{\Omega_\perp}(1,2)$, where Ω is the ranked alphabet introduced at the end of the last section. We will make T into a G-algebra where G is the context-free grammar of Section 3, and we do that by defining operations on $\Omega_\perp$-flow charts corresponding to each of the seventeen productions of G. F, F_1, F_2 range over $T_{<ae>}=T_{<st>}=\mathbf{Flo}_{\Omega_\perp}(1,1)$ and P, P_1, P_2 range over $T_{<be>}=\mathbf{Flo}_{\Omega_\perp}(1,2)$.

(T1)	$\mathsf{Continue}_T = 1_1$
(T2)	$(F)x{:=}_T = F \circ \mathsf{store}_x$
(T3)	$(P,F_1,F_2)\mathsf{ifthenelse}_T = P \circ (F_1,F_2)$
(T4)	$(F_1,F_2){;}_T = F_1 \circ F_2$
(T5)	$(P,F)\mathsf{whiledo}_T = (P \circ (F \oplus 1_1))^\dagger$
(T6)	$c_T = c$
(T7)	$x_T = \mathsf{load}_x$
(T8)	$(F)\mathsf{aop1}_T = F \circ \mathsf{aop1}$
(T9)	$(F_1,F_2)\mathsf{aop2}_T = F_1 \circ F_2 \circ \mathsf{aop2}$
(T10)	$(P,F_1,F_2)\mathsf{cond}_T = P \circ (F_1,F_2)$
(T11)	$(F_1,F_2)\mathsf{result}_T = F_1 \circ F_2$
(T12)	$(F_1,F_2)\mathsf{letx}_T = \mathsf{load}_x \circ F_1 \circ \mathsf{store}_x \circ F_2 \circ \mathsf{switch} \circ \mathsf{store}_x$
(T13)	$bc_T = bc$
(T14)	$(F)\mathsf{prop}_T = F \circ \mathsf{prop}$
(T15)	$(F_1,F_2)\mathsf{rel}_T = F_1 \circ F_2 \circ \mathsf{rel}$
(T16)	$(P)\neg_T = P \circ (x_2^2, x_1^2)$
(T17a)	$(P_1,P_2)\wedge_T = P_1 \circ (P_2, x_2^2)$
(T17b)	$(P_1,P_2)\vee_T = P_1 \circ (x_1^2, P_2)$

7. SEMANTICS FOR FLOW CHARTS, THE TARGET THEORY U_0

We already have defined the target theory, U_0, to be the algebraic theory $\mathbf{Sum}_{\mathrm{Stk}\times\mathrm{Env}}$; we need the interpretation functor. Rather than going directly from $\mathbf{Flo}_{\Omega_\perp}$ to $\mathbf{Sum}_{\mathrm{Stk}\times\mathrm{Env}}$ it is convenient to factor that interpretation through the continuous algebraic theory freely generated by Ω, $\mathbf{CT}_\Omega$ (c.f. ADJ 1975, 1976b, 1976c, 1977). Recall that $\mathbf{CT}_\Omega(n,p)$ consists of all n-tuples of countable partial trees on the ranked alphabet Ω and variables, $x_1,\ldots,x_p$; the composition operation is simultaneous substitution. The following is a variation of an important theorem first proved by Elgot (1973).

Theorem 7.1. There is a unique functor Un (for *un*folding) from $\mathbf{Flo}_{\Omega_\perp}$ to $\mathbf{CT}_\Omega$ that preserves maps, pairing, iteration, $\perp$, and the primitives Ω. □

Theorem 7.2. (ADJ 1977) For any ω-continuous algebraic theory **T** and any interpretation $I{:}\Omega\to\mathbf{T}$ there exists a unique ω-continuous functor $I^\#{:}\mathbf{CT}_\Omega\to\mathbf{T}$ that preserves maps, pairing, iteration, $\perp$ and the interpretation (I) of the primitives Ω □

The combination of Un from Theorem 7.1 and $I^\#$ from Theorem 7.2 (with the interpretation I of Section 5) gives us an interpretation (unique subject to certain conditions) of all Ω-flow charts; the composite $\mathrm{Un}\circ I^\#$ goes from $\mathbf{Flo}_{\Omega_\perp}$ to $\mathbf{Sum}_{\mathrm{Stk}\times\mathrm{Env}}$. It is now a simple matter to describe the algebra U for the interpretation of the algebra of flow charts because each of the operations of T (Section 6) is defined in terms of operations preserved by the composite $Un \circ I^{\#}$.

8. THE SEMANTIC ALGEBRA FOR FLOW CHARTS, U

Take $U_{<ae>}=U_{<st>}=\mathbf{Sum}_{Stk\times Env}(1,1)$ and $U_{<be>}=\mathbf{Sum}_{Stk\times Env}(1,2)$. We make U into a G-algebra (one operation of appropriate arity for each production of the G) by translating the definition of T in Section 6. This translation is possible because each of the operations used in the definitions in Section 6 (on right-hand sides) is preserved by the composite $Un \circ I^{\#}$. In the displayed equations below defining U, ϕ, ϕ_1, and ϕ_2 range over $U_{<ae>}=U_{<st>}$ while ρ, ρ_1 and ρ_2 range over $U_{<be>}$.

(U1) $\mathsf{Continue}_U = 1_1 = 1_{Stk\times Env}$

(U2) $(\phi)\mathsf{x}{:=}_U = \phi \circ (\mathrm{store}_x I)$

(U3) $(\rho,\phi_1,\phi_2)\mathsf{ifthenelse}_U = \rho \circ (\phi_1,\phi_2)$

(U4) $(\phi_1,\phi_2);_U = \phi_1 \circ \phi_2$

(U5) $(\rho,\phi)\mathsf{whiledo}_U = (\rho \circ (\phi + 1_1))^{\dagger}$

(U6) $\mathsf{c}_U = \mathrm{c}I$

(U7) $\mathsf{x}_U = \mathrm{load}_x I$

(U8) $(\phi)\mathsf{aop1}_U = \phi \circ (\mathrm{aop1}I)$

(U9) $(\phi_1,\phi_2)\mathsf{aop2}_U = \phi_1 \circ \phi_2 \circ (\mathrm{aop2}I)$

(U10) $(\rho,\phi_1,\phi_2)\mathsf{cond}_U = \rho \circ (\phi_1,\phi_2)$

(U11) $(\phi_1,\phi_2)\mathsf{result}_U = \phi_1 \circ \phi_2$

(U12) $(\phi_1,\phi_2)\mathsf{letx}_U = (\mathrm{load}_x I) \circ \phi_1 \circ (\mathrm{store}_x I). \circ \phi_2 \circ (\mathrm{switch}I) \circ (\mathrm{store}_x I)$

(U13) $\mathsf{bc}_U = \mathrm{bc}I$

(U14) $(\phi)\mathsf{prop}_U = \phi \circ (\mathrm{prop}I)$

(U15) $(\phi_1,\phi_2)\mathsf{rel}_U = \phi_1 \circ \phi_2 \circ (\mathrm{rel}I)$

(U16) $(\rho)\neg_U = \rho \circ (x^2_2, x^2_1)$

(U17a) $(\rho_1,\rho_2)\wedge_U = \rho_1 \circ (\rho_2, x^2_2)$

(U17b) $(\rho_1,\rho_2)\vee_U = \rho_1 \circ (x^2_1, \rho_2)$

Let ψ be the restriction of the composite $Un \circ I^{\#}$ to the carriers of T. Then ψ is a G-homomorphism because of the way U was defined (and the preservation properties of $Un \circ I^{\#}$) which gives algebraic semantics to the algebra T of flow charts.

9. THE ENCODING FROM PROGRAM MEANINGS TO FLOW CHART MEANINGS

As the final step before the proof of the correctness of the compiler (commuting of ★) we must define the function ε from M to U. In particular we must define ε_s for $s \in \{<ae>, <st>, <be>\}$. The proof that ★ commutes then amounts to proving that ε is in fact a homomorphism. This is accomplished in the next section. We recall the types of ε:

$$\varepsilon_{<st>}: M_{<st>} = [Env \multimap Env] \to U_{<st>} = [Stk\times Env \multimap Stk\times Env]$$

$$\varepsilon_{<ae>}: M_{<ae>} = [Env \multimap Env\times \mathbb{Z}] \to U_{<ae>} = [Stk\times Env \multimap Stk\times Env]$$

$\varepsilon_{<be>}: M_{<be>} = [\mathrm{Env} \multimap \mathrm{Env} \times [2]] \rightarrow U_{<be>} = [\mathrm{Stk} \times \mathrm{Env} \multimap \mathrm{Stk} \times \mathrm{Env} \times [2]]$

The definition of the bottom line is now given by the following.

(B1) $(\tau)\varepsilon_{<st>} = 1_{\mathrm{Stk}} \times \tau$

(B2) $(\alpha)\varepsilon_{<ae>} = (1_{\mathrm{Stk}} \times \alpha) \circ [\pi_1,\pi_3,\pi_2] \circ (\mathrm{push} \times 1_{\mathrm{Env}})$

(B3) $(\beta)\varepsilon_{<be>} = 1_{\mathrm{Stk}} \times \beta.$

10. THE CORRECTNESS PROOF: ε IS A HOMOMORPHISM

To emphasize again the main point made by Morris in 1973 and, we believe, carried to fruition here, the correctness proof for the compiler (★ commutes) now reduces to seventeen little proofs or lemmas; one lemma for each operation ξ of G (Section 3). We must prove that ε is a homomorphism, i.e., that

$$((\gamma_1,\ldots,\gamma_n)\xi_M)\varepsilon = ((\gamma_1)\varepsilon,\ldots,(\gamma_n)\varepsilon)\xi_U$$

for each of the seventeen instances of ξ as given in M1-M17.

This proof process has some very intriguing aspects. The proofs of the lemmas are all equational, each line being justified by some previous line, some definition (M1-M17, U1-U17, and B1-B3) or some fact about the operations involved in those definitions. We divide these latter facts into three groups.

(E) Properties of the underlying data type.

(F) Properties of the "storage" operations (push, access_x, etc).

(G) Properties of the set-theoretic operators like composition, identities, tupling, sum and product.

Even though we make the advice that all properties of the underlying data type(s) be included in the specification of the language (E1-E27), we will have no need for these facts in connection with the compiler correctness. Presumably program correctness and program transformation in the proposed style would use properties of this first kind.

The second kind of justification will depend on the particular kind of mathematical semantics given for the languages (source and target). In our case we must relate functions like access_x, push and store_x. Each of these assertions itself has a simple set-theoretic proof, depending, in part, on properties of the third kind.

(F1) $\mathrm{load}_x\mathrm{I} = (1_{\mathrm{Stk}} \times \mathrm{fetch}_x) \circ [\pi_1,\pi_3,\pi_2] \circ (\mathrm{push} \times 1_{\mathrm{Env}})$

(F2) $\mathrm{store}_x\mathrm{I} = (\mathrm{pop} \times 1_{\mathrm{Env}}) \circ [\pi_1,\pi_3,\pi_2] \circ (1_{\mathrm{Stk}} \times \mathrm{assign}_x)$

(F3) $\mathrm{switchI} = (\mathrm{pop} \times 1_{\mathrm{Env}}) \circ (\mathrm{pop} \times 1_{\mathbb{Z} \times \mathrm{Env}}) \circ [\pi_1,\pi_3,\pi_2,\pi_4] \circ (\mathrm{push} \times 1_{\mathbb{Z} \times \mathrm{Env}}) \circ (\mathrm{push} \times 1_{\mathrm{Env}})$

(F4) $\mathrm{cI} = (1_{\mathrm{Stk}} \times c_S \times 1_{\mathrm{Env}}) \circ (\mathrm{push} \times 1_{\mathrm{Env}})$

(F5) $\mathrm{aop1I} = (\mathrm{pop} \times 1_{\mathrm{Env}}) \circ (1_{\mathrm{Stk}} \times \mathrm{aop1}_S \times 1_{\mathrm{Env}}) \circ (\mathrm{push} \times 1_{\mathrm{Env}})$

(F6) $\mathrm{aop2I} = (\mathrm{pop} \times 1_{\mathrm{Env}}) \circ (\mathrm{pop} \times 1_{\mathbb{Z}} \times 1_{\mathrm{Env}}) \circ (1_{\mathrm{Stk}} \times \mathrm{aop2}_S \times 1_{\mathrm{Env}}) \circ (\mathrm{push} \times 1_{\mathrm{Env}})$

(F7) $\mathrm{bcI} = 1_{\mathrm{Stk} \times \mathrm{Env}} \times \mathrm{bc}_S$

(F8) $\mathrm{propI} = (\mathrm{pop} \times 1_{\mathrm{Env}}) \circ [\pi_1,\pi_3,\pi_2] \circ (1_{\mathrm{Stk} \times \mathrm{Env}} \times \mathrm{prop}_S)$

(F9) $\mathrm{relI} = (\mathrm{pop} \times 1_{\mathrm{Env}}) \circ (\mathrm{pop}. \times 1_{\mathbb{Z} \times \mathrm{Env}}) \circ [\pi_1,\pi_3,\pi_2,\pi_4] \circ (1_{\mathrm{Stk} \times \mathrm{Env}} \times \mathrm{rel}_S)$

(FX) $\mathrm{push} \circ \mathrm{pop} = 1_{\mathrm{Stk} \times \mathbb{Z}}$

(FXa) $[\pi_1,\pi_3,\pi_2] \circ (\mathrm{push} \times 1_{\mathrm{Env}}) \circ (\mathrm{pop} \times 1_{\mathrm{Env}}) \circ [\pi_1,\pi_3,\pi_2] = 1_{\mathrm{Stk} \times \mathbb{Z} \times \mathrm{Env}}$

The last are the most interesting properties for they are general and, in effect, category theoretic. Presumably the set of these equations is pretty small and will not keep changing with different languages or styles. This suggests the plausibility of Mosses' approach to "making denotational semantics less concrete," (Mosses (1977, 1978)).

(G0) $1_A \circ f = f = f \circ 1_B$

(G1) $(f \circ g) \circ h = f \circ (g \circ h)$

(G2) $(f \times g) \times h = f \times (g \times h)$

(G3) $1_A \times 1_B = 1_{A \times B}$

(G4) $1_A \times (f \circ g) = (1_A \times f) \circ (1_A \times g)$

(G5) $(f \times g) \circ (h \times k) = (f \circ h) \times (g \circ k)$

(G6) $(f \times 1_C) \circ (1_B \times g) = f \circ g = (1_A \times g) \circ (f \times 1_D)$

(C1) $1_A \times \iota_j^B = \iota_j^{A \times B}$

(C2) $1_A \times (f,g) = (1_A \times f, 1_A \times g)$

(C3) $1_A \times (f+g) = (1_A \times f) + (1_A \times g)$

(C4) $1_A \times f^\dagger = (1_A \times f)^\dagger$

(C5) $(f,g) \circ h = (f \circ h, g \circ h)$

The following identities are necessary for permuting arguments for functions, i.e., manipulating tuples of projection functions.

(P1) $[\pi_1, \pi_2, \ldots, \pi_n] = 1$

Let q,r:[n]→[n] be permutations of [n].

(P2) $[\pi_{1q}, \pi_{2q}, \ldots, \pi_{nq}] \circ [\pi_{1r}, \pi_{2r}, \ldots, \pi_{nr}] = [\pi_{1rq}, \pi_{2rq}, \ldots, \pi_{nqr}]$

(P3) $1_A \times [\pi_{1q}, \pi_{2q}, \ldots, \pi_{nq}] = [\pi_1, \pi_{1q+1}, \pi_{2q+1}, \ldots, \pi_{nq+1}]$

For monadic functions $f_i: A_i \to B_i$ there is a convenient general rule for permuting arguments:

(P4) $(f_1 \times \ldots \times f_n) \circ [\pi_{1q}, \ldots, \pi_{nq}] = [\pi_{1q}, \ldots, \pi_{nq}] \circ (f_{1q} \times \ldots \times f_{nq})$.

But when the functions involved have cartesian products for sources and/or targets, then the corresponding scheme has a very complicated statement. Below we list the special cases of that general scheme which we will need in proofs to follow. Assume $f_i: A_i \to B_i$, $c: \to C$, $g: C_1 \times C_2 \to D$ and $h: C \to D_1 \times D_2$.

(P4a) $(f_1 \times f_2 \times c) \circ [\pi_1, \pi_3, \pi_2] = f_1 \times c \times f_2$

(P4b) $(g \times f_1 \times f_2) \circ [\pi_1, \pi_3, \pi_2] = [\pi_1, \pi_2, \pi_4, \pi_3] \circ (g \times f_1 \times f_2)$

(P4c) $(f_1 \times g \times f_2) \circ [\pi_1, \pi_3, \pi_2] = [\pi_1, \pi_4, \pi_2, \pi_3] \circ (f_1 \times f_2 \times g)$

(P4d) $(f_1 \times f_2 \times g) \circ [\pi_1, \pi_3, \pi_2] = [\pi_1, \pi_3, \pi_4, \pi_2] \circ (f_1 \times g \times f_2)$

(P4e) $[\pi_1, \pi_3, \pi_2] \circ (h \times f_1 \times f_2) = (h \times f_2 \times f_1) \circ [\pi_1, \pi_2, \pi_4, \pi_3]$

(P4f) $[\pi_1, \pi_3, \pi_2] \circ (f_1 \times h \times f_2) = (f_1 \times f_2 \times h) \circ [\pi_1, \pi_4, \pi_2, \pi_3]$

(P4g) $[\pi_1, \pi_3, \pi_2] \circ (f_1 \times f_2 \times h) = (f_1 \times h \times f_2) \circ [\pi_1, \pi_3, \pi_4, \pi_2]$

To save space in displaying the proofs we will abbreviate the isomorphism $[\pi_{1q}, \ldots, \pi_{nq}]$ with the sequence [1q...nq] which will not need commas since n<10 (thank goodness). In addition we will abbreviate Stk, Env and ℤ by S, E and Z respectively. Use of associativity of ∘ (G1) and of × (G2) will not be mentioned explicitly in the proofs.

Now we proceed with the 17 (actually 18 because $\wedge$ and are treated separately.) proofs. Each proof will be a line-by-line proof with justifications (on the right) coming from previous facts and definitions. Observe the form; they begin with the definition in M, the definition of ε (B1,2,3), and then the various facts. In the middle we are justifying what at times seem to be tediously manipulative steps; this is particularly true in proofs (9), (12) and (15), and in them, in applications of (FX), (FXa) and (P4a-P4g). The proofs conclude with the definition (again) of ε and of operations in U.

(1) $(\text{continue}_M)\varepsilon_{<st>} = (1_E)\varepsilon_{<st>}$ (M1)
$= 1_S \times 1_E$ (B1)
$= 1_{S\times E}$ (G3)
$= \text{continue}_U$ (U1)

(2) $((\alpha)x{:=}_M)\varepsilon_{<st>} = (\alpha \circ \text{assign}_x)\varepsilon_{<st>}$ (M2)
$= 1_S \times (\alpha \circ \text{assign}_x)$ (B1)
$= (1_S \times \alpha) \circ [132] \circ [132] \circ (1_S \times \text{assign}_x)$ (G4)
$= (1_S \times \alpha) \circ [132] \circ (\text{push} \times 1_E) \circ (\text{pop} \times 1_E) \circ [132] \circ (1_S \times \text{assign}_x)$ (FXa)
$= (1_S \times \alpha) \circ [132] \circ (\text{push} \times 1_E) \circ (\text{store}_x I)$ (F2)
$= (\alpha)\varepsilon_{<ae>} \circ (\text{store}_x I)$ (B2)
$= ((\alpha)\varepsilon_{<ae>})x{:=}_U$ (U2)

(3) $((\beta,\tau_1,\tau_2)\text{ifthenelse}_M)\varepsilon_{<st>} = (\beta \circ (\tau_1,\tau_2))\varepsilon_{<st>}$ (M3)
$= 1_S \times (\beta \circ (\tau_1,\tau_2))$ (B1)
$= (1_S \times \beta) \circ (1_S \times (\tau_1,\tau_2))$ (G4)
$= (1_S \times \beta) \circ (1_S \times \tau_1, 1_S \times \tau_2)$ (C2)
$= (\beta)\varepsilon_{<be>} \circ ((\tau_1)\varepsilon_{<st>}, (\tau_2)\varepsilon_{<st>})$ (B1,B3)
$= ((\beta)\varepsilon_{<be>}, (\tau_1)\varepsilon_{<st>}, (\tau_2)\varepsilon_{<st>})\text{ifthenelse}_U$ (U3)

(4) $((\tau_1,\tau_2);_M)\varepsilon_{<st>} = (\tau_1 \circ \tau_2)\varepsilon_{<st>}$ (M4)
$= 1_S \times (\tau_1 \circ \tau_2)$ (B1)
$= (1_S \times \tau_1) \circ (1_S \times \tau_2)$ (G4)
$= (\tau_1)\varepsilon_{<st>} \circ (\tau_2)\varepsilon_{<st>}$ (B1)
$= ((\tau_1)\varepsilon_{<st>}, (\tau_2)\varepsilon_{<st>});_U$ (U4)

(5) $((\beta,\tau)\text{whiledo}_M)\varepsilon_{<st>} = ((\beta \circ (\tau + 1_E))^{\dagger})\varepsilon_{<st>}$ (M5)
$= 1_S \times (\beta \circ (\tau + 1_E))^{\dagger}$ (B1)
$= (1_S \times (\beta \circ (\tau + 1_E)))^{\dagger}$ (C4)
$= ((1_S \times \beta) \circ (1_S \times (\tau + 1_E)))^{\dagger}$ (G4)
$= ((1_S \times \beta) \circ ((1_S \times \tau) + (1_S \times 1_E)))^{\dagger}$ (C3)
$= ((1_S \times \beta) \circ ((1_S \times \tau) + 1_{S\times E}))^{\dagger}$ (G3)
$= ((\beta)\varepsilon_{<be>} \circ ((\tau)\varepsilon_{<st>} + 1_{E\times S}))^{\dagger}$ (B1,3)
$= ((\beta)\varepsilon_{<be>} \circ ((\tau)\varepsilon_{<st>} + 1_1))^{\dagger}$ (U1)
$= ((\beta)\varepsilon_{<be>}, (\tau)\varepsilon_{<st>})\text{whiledo}_U$ (U5)

(6) $(c_M)\varepsilon_{<ae>} = (1_E \times c_S)\varepsilon_{<ae>}$ (M6)
$= (1_S \times 1_E \times c_S) \circ [132] \circ (\text{push} \times 1_E)$ (B2)
$= (1_S \times c_S \times 1_E) \circ (\text{push} \times 1_E)$ (P4a)
$= cI$ (F3)

$= c_U$ (U6)

(7) $(x_M)\varepsilon_{<ae>} = (\mathrm{fetch}_x)\varepsilon_{<ae>}$ (M7)

$= (1_S\times \mathrm{fetch}_x)\circ[132]\circ(\mathrm{push}\times 1_E)$ (B2)

$= \mathrm{load}_x I$ (F1)

$= x_M$ (U7)

(8) $((\alpha)\mathrm{aop1}_M)\varepsilon_{<ae>} = (\alpha\circ(1_E\times \mathrm{aop1}_S))\varepsilon_{<ae>}$ (M8)

$= (1_S\times(\alpha\circ(1_E\times \mathrm{aop1}_S)))\circ[132]\circ(\mathrm{push}\times 1_E)$ (B2)

$= (1_S\times\alpha)\circ(1_S\times 1_E\times \mathrm{aop1}_S)\circ[132]\circ(\mathrm{push}\times 1_E)$ (G4)

$= (1_S\times\alpha)\circ[132]\circ(1_S\times \mathrm{aop1}_S\times 1_E)\circ(\mathrm{push}\times 1_E)$ (P4)

$= (1_S\times\alpha)\circ[132]\circ(\mathrm{push}\times 1_E)\circ(\mathrm{pop}\times 1_E)\circ(1_S\times \mathrm{aop1}_S\times 1_E)\circ(\mathrm{push}\times 1_E)$ (F2)

$= (\alpha)\varepsilon_{<ae>}\circ(\mathrm{pop}\times 1_E)\circ(1_S\times \mathrm{aop1}_S\times 1_E)\circ(\mathrm{push}\times 1_E)$ (B2)

$= (\alpha)\varepsilon_{<ae>}\circ(\mathrm{aop1I})$ (F6)

$= ((\alpha)\varepsilon_{<ae>})\mathrm{aop1}_U$ (U8)

(9) $((\alpha_1,\alpha_2)\mathrm{aop2}_M)\varepsilon_{<ae>} = (\alpha_1\circ(\alpha_2\times 1_Z)\circ[132]\circ(1_E\times \mathrm{aop2}_S))\varepsilon_{<ae>}$ (M9)

$=(1_S\times(\alpha_1\circ(\alpha_2\times 1_Z)\circ[132]\circ(1_E\times \mathrm{aop2}_S)))\circ[132]\circ(\mathrm{push}\times 1_E)$ (B2)

$=(1_S\times(\alpha_1\circ(\alpha_2\times 1_Z)))\circ(1_S\times[132])\circ(1_S\times 1_E\times \mathrm{aop2}_S)\circ[132]\circ(\mathrm{push}\times 1_E)$ (G4)

$=(1_S\times(\alpha_1\circ(\alpha_2\times 1_Z)))\circ[1243]\circ(1_S\times 1_E\times \mathrm{aop2}_S)\circ[132]\circ(\mathrm{push}\times 1_E)$ (P3)

$=(1_S\times(\alpha_1\circ(\alpha_2\times 1_Z)))\circ[1243]\circ[1342]\circ(1_S\times \mathrm{aop2}_S\times 1_E)\circ(\mathrm{push}\times 1_E)$ (P4d)

$=(1_S\times(\alpha_1\circ(\alpha_2\times 1_Z)))\circ[\pi_1,\pi_4,\pi_3,\pi_2]\circ(1_S\times \mathrm{aop2}_S\times 1_E)\circ(\mathrm{push}\times 1_E)$ (P2)

$=(1_S\times(\alpha_1\circ(\alpha_2\times 1_Z)))\circ[\pi_1,\pi_4,\pi_3,\pi_2]\circ(\mathrm{push}\times 1_Z\times 1_E)\circ(\mathrm{pop}\times 1_Z\times 1_E)\circ$
$(1_S\times \mathrm{aop2}_S\times 1_E)\circ(\mathrm{push}\times 1_E)$ (FX)

$=(1_S\times(\alpha_1\circ(\alpha_2\times 1_Z)))\circ[\pi_1,\pi_4,\pi_3,\pi_2]\circ(\mathrm{push}\times 1_Z\times 1_E)\circ(\mathrm{push}\times 1_E)\circ(\mathrm{pop}\times 1_E)\circ$
$(\mathrm{pop}\times 1_Z\times 1_E)\circ(1_S\times \mathrm{aop2}_S\times 1_E)\circ(\mathrm{push}\times 1_E)$ (FX)

$=(1_S\times(\alpha_1\circ(\alpha_2\times 1_Z)))\circ[\pi_1,\pi_4,\pi_3,\pi_2]\circ(\mathrm{push}\times 1_Z\times 1_E)\circ(\mathrm{push}\times 1_E)\circ(\mathrm{aop2I})$ (F6)

$=(1_S\times\alpha_1)\circ(1_S\times\alpha_2\times 1_Z)\circ[\pi_1,\pi_4,\pi_3,\pi_2]\circ(\mathrm{push}\times 1_Z\times 1_E)\circ(\mathrm{push}\times 1_E)\circ(\mathrm{aop2I})$ (G4)

$=(1_S\times\alpha_1)\circ[132]\circ(1_{S\times Z}\times\alpha_2)\circ[1243]\circ(\mathrm{push}\times 1_Z\times 1_E)\circ(\mathrm{push}\times 1_E)\circ(\mathrm{aop2I})$ (P4g,G3)

$=(1_S\times\alpha_1)\circ[132]\circ(1_{S\times Z}\times\alpha_2)\circ[1243]\circ(\mathrm{push}\times 1_Z\times 1_E)\circ(\mathrm{push}\times 1_E)\circ(\mathrm{aop2I})$ (P2)

$=(1_S\times\alpha_1)\circ[132]\circ(1_S\times 1_Z\times\alpha_2)\circ(\mathrm{push}\times 1_E\times 1_Z)\circ[132]\circ(\mathrm{push}\times 1_E)\circ(\mathrm{aop2I})$ (P4b)

$=(1_S\times\alpha_1)\circ[132]\circ(\mathrm{push}\times 1_E)\circ(1_S\times\alpha_2)\circ[132]\circ(\mathrm{push}\times 1_E)\circ(\mathrm{aop2I})$ (G6)

$=((\alpha_1)\varepsilon_{<ae>})\circ((\alpha_2)\varepsilon_{<ae>})\circ(\mathrm{aop2I})$ (B2)

$=((\alpha_1)\varepsilon_{<ae>},(\alpha_2)\varepsilon_{<ae>})\mathrm{aop2}_U$ (U9)

(10) $((\beta,\alpha_1,\alpha_2)\mathrm{cond}_M)\varepsilon_{<ae>} = (\beta\circ(\alpha_1,\alpha_2))\varepsilon_{<ae>}$ (M10)

$= (1_S\times(\beta\circ(\alpha_1,\alpha_2)))\circ[132]\circ(\mathrm{push}\times 1_E)$ (B2)

$= (1_S\times\beta)\circ(1_S\times(\alpha_1,\alpha_2))\circ[132]\circ(\mathrm{push}\times 1_E)$ (G4)

$= (1_S\times\beta)\circ(1_S\times\alpha_1,1_S\times\alpha_2)\circ[132]\circ(\mathrm{push}\times 1_E)$ (C2)

$= (1_S\times\beta)\circ((1_S\times\alpha_1)\circ[132]\circ(\mathrm{push}\times 1_E),(1_S\times\alpha_2)\circ[132]\circ(\mathrm{push}\times 1_E))$ (C5)

$= (\beta)\varepsilon_{<be>}\circ((\alpha_1)\varepsilon_{<ae>},(\alpha_2)\varepsilon_{<ae>})$ (B2,B3)

$= ((\beta)\varepsilon_{<be>},(\alpha_1)\varepsilon_{<ae>},(\alpha_2)\varepsilon_{<ae>})\mathrm{cond}_U$ (U10)

(11) $(\tau,\alpha)\mathrm{result}_M = (\tau\circ\alpha)\varepsilon_{<ae>}$ (M11)

$= (1_S\times(\tau\circ\alpha))\circ[132]\circ(\mathrm{push}\times 1_E)$ (B2)

$= (1_S\times\tau)\circ(1_S\times\alpha)\circ[132]\circ(\mathrm{push}\times 1_E)$ (G4)

$= (\tau)\varepsilon_{<st>}\circ(\alpha)\varepsilon_{<ae>}$ (B1,B2)

$= ((\tau)\varepsilon_{<st>},(\alpha)\varepsilon_{<ae>})\mathrm{result}_U$ (U11)

(12) $((\alpha_1,\alpha_2)\mathrm{letx}_M)\varepsilon_{<ae>}$

$$= (\mathrm{fetch}_x \circ ((\alpha_1 \circ \mathrm{assign}_x \circ \alpha_2)\times 1_Z)\circ[132]\circ(\mathrm{assign}_x\times 1_Z))\varepsilon_{<ae>} \qquad \text{(M12)}$$

$$= 1_S\times(\mathrm{fetch}_x\circ((\alpha_1\circ\mathrm{assign}_x\circ\alpha_2)\times 1_Z)\circ[132]\circ(\mathrm{assign}_x\times 1_Z))\circ[132]\circ (\mathrm{push}\times 1_E) \qquad \text{(B2)}$$

$$= (1_S\times\mathrm{fetch}_x)\circ(1_S\times(\alpha_1\circ\mathrm{assign}_x\circ\alpha_2)\times 1_Z)\circ[1243]\circ(1_S\times\mathrm{assign}_x\times 1_Z))\circ[132]\circ (\mathrm{push}\times 1_E) \qquad \text{(G4,P3)}$$

$$= (1_S\times\mathrm{fetch}_x)\circ(1_S\times(\alpha_1\circ\mathrm{assign}_x\circ\alpha_2)\times 1_Z)\circ[1243]\circ[1423]\circ(1_{S\times Z}\times\mathrm{assign}_x)\circ (\mathrm{push}\times 1_E) \qquad \text{(P4c,G3)}$$

$$= (1_S\times\mathrm{fetch}_x)\circ(1_S\times(\alpha_1\circ\mathrm{assign}_x\circ\alpha_2)\times 1_Z)\circ[1324]\circ(1_{S\times Z}\times\mathrm{assign}_x)\circ(\mathrm{push}\times 1_E) \qquad \text{(P2)}$$

$$= (1_S\times\mathrm{fetch}_x)\circ(1_S\times(\alpha_1\circ\mathrm{assign}_x\circ\alpha_2)\times 1_Z)\circ[1324]\circ(\mathrm{push}\times 1_{E\times Z})\circ(1_S\times\mathrm{assign}_x) \qquad \text{(G6)}$$

$$= (1_S\times\mathrm{fetch}_x)\circ(1_S\times(\alpha_1\circ\mathrm{assign}_x\circ\alpha_2)\times 1_Z)\circ[1324]\circ (\mathrm{push}\times 1_{E\times Z})\circ[132]\circ(\mathrm{push}\times 1_E)\circ(\mathrm{pop}\times 1_E)\circ[132]\circ(1_S\times\mathrm{assign}_x) \qquad \text{(G0,FXa)}$$

$$= (1_S\times\mathrm{fetch}_x)\circ(1_S\times(\alpha_1\circ\mathrm{assign}_x\circ\alpha_2)\times 1_Z)\circ[1324]\circ(\mathrm{push}\times 1_{E\times Z})\circ[132]\circ (\mathrm{push}\times 1_E)\circ(\mathrm{store}_x\mathrm{I}) \qquad \text{(F2)}$$

$$= (1_S\times\mathrm{fetch}_x)\circ(1_S\times(\alpha_1\circ\mathrm{assign}_x\circ\alpha_2)\times 1_Z)\circ[1324]\circ[1243]\circ(\mathrm{push}\times 1_{Z\times E})\circ (\mathrm{push}\times 1_E)\circ(\mathrm{store}_x\mathrm{I}) \qquad \text{(G3,P4b)}$$

$$= (1_S\times\mathrm{fetch}_x)\circ(1_S\times(\alpha_1\circ\mathrm{assign}_x\circ\alpha_2)\times 1_Z)\circ[1324]\circ(\mathrm{push}\times 1_{Z\times E})\circ (\mathrm{push}\times 1_E)\circ(\mathrm{store}_x\mathrm{I}) \qquad \text{(P2)}$$

$$= (1_S\times\mathrm{fetch}_x)\circ[132]\circ(\mathrm{push}\times 1_E)\circ(\mathrm{pop}\times 1_E)\circ[132]\circ(1_S\times(\alpha_1\circ\mathrm{assign}_x\circ\alpha_2)\times 1_Z) \circ[1324]\circ(\mathrm{push}\times 1_{Z\times E})\circ(\mathrm{push}\times 1_E)\circ(\mathrm{store}_x\mathrm{I}) \qquad \text{(G0,FXa)}$$

$$= (\mathrm{load}_x\mathrm{I})\circ(\mathrm{pop}\times 1_E)\circ[132]\circ(1_S\times(\alpha_1\circ\mathrm{assign}_x\circ\alpha_2)\times 1_Z)\circ[1324]\circ (\mathrm{push}\times 1_{Z\times E})\circ(\mathrm{push}\times 1_E)\circ(\mathrm{store}_x\mathrm{I}) \qquad \text{(F1)}$$

$$= (\mathrm{load}_x\mathrm{I})\circ(\mathrm{pop}\times 1_E)\circ(1_{S\times Z}\times(\alpha_1\circ\mathrm{assign}_x\circ\alpha_2))\circ[1324]\circ[1324]\circ (\mathrm{push}\times 1_{Z\times E})\circ(\mathrm{push}\times 1_E)\circ(\mathrm{store}_x\mathrm{I}) \qquad \text{(P4f)}$$

$$= (\mathrm{load}_x\mathrm{I})\circ(\mathrm{pop}\times 1_E)\circ(1_{S\times Z}\times(\alpha_1\circ\mathrm{assign}_x\circ\alpha_2))\circ[1423]\circ (\mathrm{push}\times 1_{Z\times E})\circ(\mathrm{push}\times 1_E)\circ(\mathrm{store}_x\mathrm{I}) \qquad \text{(P2,P1)}$$

$$= (\mathrm{load}_x\mathrm{I})\circ(1_S\times(\alpha_1\circ\mathrm{assign}_x\circ\alpha_2))\circ(\mathrm{pop}\times 1_{E\times Z})\circ[1423]\circ (\mathrm{push}\times 1_{Z\times E})\circ(\mathrm{push}\times 1_E)\circ(\mathrm{store}_x\mathrm{I}) \qquad \text{(G6)}$$

$$= (\mathrm{load}_x\mathrm{I})\circ(1_S\times\alpha_1)\circ(1_S\times\mathrm{assign}_x)\circ(1_S\times\alpha_2)\circ(\mathrm{pop}\times 1_{E\times Z})\circ[1423]\circ (\mathrm{push}\times 1_{Z\times E})\circ(\mathrm{push}\times 1_E)\circ(\mathrm{store}_x\mathrm{I}) \qquad \text{(G4)}$$

$$= (\mathrm{load}_x\mathrm{I})\circ(1_S\times\alpha_1)\circ[132]\circ(\mathrm{push}\times 1_E)\circ(\mathrm{pop}\times 1_E)\circ[132]\circ (1_S\times\mathrm{assign}_x)\circ(1_S\times\alpha_2)\circ(\mathrm{pop}\times 1_{E\times Z})\circ[1423]\circ (\mathrm{push}\times 1_{Z\times E})\circ(\mathrm{push}\times 1_E)\circ(\mathrm{store}_x\mathrm{I}) \qquad \text{(FXa)}$$

$$= (\mathrm{load}_x\mathrm{I})\circ(\alpha_1)\varepsilon_{<ae>}\circ(\mathrm{store}_x\mathrm{I})\circ(1_S\times\alpha_2)\circ(\mathrm{pop}\times 1_{E\times Z})\circ [1423]\circ(\mathrm{push}\times 1_{Z\times E})\circ(\mathrm{push}\times 1_E)\circ(\mathrm{store}_x\mathrm{I}) \qquad \text{(B2,F2)}$$

$$= (\mathrm{load}_x\mathrm{I})\circ(\alpha_1)\varepsilon_{<ae>}\circ(\mathrm{store}_x\mathrm{I})\circ(1_S\times\alpha_2)\circ [132]\circ(\mathrm{push}\times 1_E)\circ(\mathrm{pop}\times 1_E)\circ[132]\circ(\mathrm{pop}\times 1_{E\times Z})\circ [1423]\circ(\mathrm{push}\times 1_{Z\times E})\circ(\mathrm{push}\times 1_E)\circ(\mathrm{store}_x\mathrm{I}) \qquad \text{(FXa)}$$

$$= (\mathrm{load}_x\mathrm{I})\circ(\alpha_1)\varepsilon_{<ae>}\circ(\mathrm{store}_x\mathrm{I})\circ(\alpha_2)\varepsilon_{<ae>}\circ(\mathrm{pop}\times 1_E)\circ[132]\circ (\mathrm{pop}\times 1_{E\times Z})\circ[1423]\circ(\mathrm{push}\times 1_{Z\times E})\circ(\mathrm{push}\times 1_E)\circ(\mathrm{store}_x\mathrm{I}) \qquad \text{(B2)}$$

$$= (\mathrm{load}_x\mathrm{I})\circ(\alpha_1)\varepsilon_{<ae>}\circ(\mathrm{store}_x\mathrm{I})\circ(\alpha_2)\varepsilon_{<ae>}\circ(\mathrm{pop}\times 1_E)\circ (\mathrm{pop}\times 1_{Z\times E})\circ[1243]\circ[1423]\circ(\mathrm{push}\times 1_{Z\times E})\circ(\mathrm{push}\times 1_E)\circ(\mathrm{store}_x\mathrm{I}) \qquad \text{(P4e)}$$

$$= (\mathrm{load}_x\mathrm{I})\circ(\alpha_1)\varepsilon_{<ae>}\circ(\mathrm{store}_x\mathrm{I})\circ(\alpha_2)\varepsilon_{<ae>}\circ(\mathrm{pop}\times 1_E)\circ (\mathrm{pop}\times 1_{Z\times E})\circ[1324]\circ(\mathrm{push}\times 1_{Z\times E})\circ(\mathrm{push}\times 1_E)\circ(\mathrm{store}_x\mathrm{I}) \qquad \text{(P2)}$$

$= (\mathrm{load}_x\mathrm{I}) \circ (\alpha_1)\varepsilon_{\langle ae\rangle} \circ (\mathrm{store}_x\mathrm{I}) \circ (\alpha_2)\varepsilon_{\langle ae\rangle} \circ (\mathrm{switchI}) \circ (\mathrm{store}_x\mathrm{I})$ (F3)

$= ((\alpha_1)\varepsilon_{\langle ae\rangle},(\alpha_2)\varepsilon_{\langle ae\rangle})\mathrm{letx}_U$ (U12)

(13) $(\mathrm{bc}_M)\varepsilon_{\langle be\rangle} = (1_E \times \mathrm{bc}_S)\varepsilon_{\langle be\rangle}$ (M13)

$= 1_S \times 1_E \times \mathrm{bc}_S$ (B3)

$= 1_{S\times E} \times \mathrm{bc}_S$ (G3)

$= \mathrm{bcI}$ (F7)

$= \mathrm{bc}_U$ (U13)

(14) $((\alpha)\mathrm{prop}_M)\varepsilon_{\langle be\rangle} = (\alpha \circ (1_E \circ \mathrm{prop}_S))\varepsilon_{\langle be\rangle}$ (M14)

$= 1_S \times (\alpha \circ (1_E \times \mathrm{prop}_S))$ (B3)

$= (1_S \times 1\alpha) \circ (1_S \times 1_E \times \mathrm{prop}_S)$ (G4)

$= (1_S \times 1\alpha) \circ [132] \circ [132] \circ (1_S \times 1_E \times \mathrm{prop}_S)$ (P2,P1)

$= (1_S \times 1\alpha) \circ [132] \circ (\mathrm{push} \times 1_E) \circ (\mathrm{pop} \times 1_E) \circ [132] \circ (1_S \times 1_E \times \mathrm{prop}_S)$ (FXa)

$= (\alpha)\varepsilon_{\langle ae\rangle} \circ (\mathrm{pop} \times 1_E) \circ [132] \circ (1_S \times 1_E \times \mathrm{prop}_S)$ (B2)

$= (\alpha)\varepsilon_{\langle ae\rangle} \circ (\mathrm{propI})$ (F8)

$= ((\alpha)\varepsilon_{\langle ae\rangle})\mathrm{prop}_U$ (U14)

(15) $((\alpha_1,\alpha_2)\mathrm{rel}_M)\varepsilon_{\langle be\rangle} = (\alpha_1 \circ (\alpha_2 \times 1_Z) \circ [132] \circ (1_E \times \mathrm{rel}_S))\varepsilon_{\langle be\rangle}$ (M15)

$= 1_S \times (\alpha_1 \circ (\alpha_2 \times 1_Z) \circ [132] \circ (1_E \times \mathrm{rel}_S))$ (B2)

$= (1_S \times (\alpha_1 \circ (\alpha_2 \times 1_Z))) \circ (1_S \times [132]) \circ (1_{S\times E} \times \mathrm{rel}_S)$ (G4)

$= (1_S \times (\alpha_1 \circ (\alpha_2 \times 1_Z))) \circ [1243] \circ (1_{S\times E} \times \mathrm{rel}_S)$ (P3)

$= (1_S \times \alpha_1) \circ (1_S \times \alpha_2 \times 1_Z) \circ [1243] \circ (1_{S\times E} \times \mathrm{rel}_S)$ (G4)

$= (1_S \times \alpha_1) \circ [132] \circ (\mathrm{push} \times 1_E) \circ (\mathrm{pop} \times 1_E) \circ [132] \circ (1_S \times \alpha_2 \times 1_Z) \circ$
$[1243] \circ (1_{S\times E} \times \mathrm{rel}_S)$ (FXa)

$= (\alpha_1)\varepsilon_{\langle ae\rangle} \circ (\mathrm{pop} \times 1_E) \circ [132] \circ (1_S \times \alpha_2 \times 1_Z) \circ [1243] \circ (1_{S\times E} \times \mathrm{rel}_S)$ (B2)

$= (\alpha_1)\varepsilon_{\langle ae\rangle} \circ (\mathrm{pop} \times 1_E) \circ (1_{S\times Z} \times \alpha_2) \circ [1423] \circ [1243] \circ (1_{S\times E} \times \mathrm{rel}_S)$ (P4f)

$= (\alpha_1)\varepsilon_{\langle ae\rangle} \circ (\mathrm{pop} \times 1_E) \circ (1_{S\times Z} \times \alpha_2) \circ [1324] \circ (1_{S\times E} \times \mathrm{rel}_S)$ (P2)

$= (\alpha_1)\varepsilon_{\langle ae\rangle} \circ (1_S \times \alpha_2) \circ (\mathrm{pop} \times 1_{E\times Z}) \circ [1324] \circ (1_{S\times E} \times \mathrm{rel}_S)$ (G6)

$= (\alpha_1)\varepsilon_{\langle ae\rangle} \circ (1_S \times \alpha_2) \circ [132] \circ (\mathrm{push} \times 1_E) \circ (\mathrm{pop} \times 1_E) \circ [132] \circ$
$(\mathrm{pop} \times 1_{E\times Z}) \circ [1324] \circ (1_{S\times E} \times \mathrm{rel}_S)$ (FXa)

$= (\alpha_1)\varepsilon_{\langle ae\rangle} \circ (\alpha_2)\varepsilon_{\langle ae\rangle} \circ (\mathrm{pop} \times 1_E) \circ [132] \circ (\mathrm{pop} \times 1_{E\times Z}) \circ [1324] \circ (1_{S\times E} \times \mathrm{rel}_S)$ (B2)

$= (\alpha_1)\varepsilon_{\langle ae\rangle} \circ (\alpha_2)\varepsilon_{\langle ae\rangle} \circ (\mathrm{pop} \times 1_E) \circ (\mathrm{pop} \times 1_{Z\times E}) \circ [1243] \circ [1324] \circ (1_{S\times E} \times \mathrm{rel}_S)$ (P4e)

$= (\alpha_1)\varepsilon_{\langle ae\rangle} \circ (\alpha_2)\varepsilon_{\langle ae\rangle} \circ (\mathrm{pop} \times 1_E) \circ (\mathrm{pop} \times 1_{Z\times E}) \circ [1423] \circ (1_{S\times E} \times \mathrm{rel}_S)$ (P2)

$= (\alpha_1)\varepsilon_{\langle ae\rangle} \circ (\alpha_2)\varepsilon_{\langle ae\rangle} \circ (\mathrm{relI})$ (F9)

$= ((\alpha_1)\varepsilon_{\langle ae\rangle},(\alpha_2)\varepsilon_{\langle ae\rangle})\mathrm{rel}_U$ (U15)

(16) $((\beta)\neg_M\varepsilon_{\langle be\rangle} = (\beta \circ (\iota_2,\iota_1))\varepsilon_{\langle be\rangle}$ (M16)

$= 1_S \times (\beta \circ (\iota_2,\iota_1))$ (B2)

$= (1_S \times \beta) \circ 1_S \times (\iota_2,\iota_1)$ (G2)

$= \beta\varepsilon_{\langle be\rangle} \circ ((1_S \times \iota_2),(1_S \times \iota_1))$ (B2,C2)

$= \beta\varepsilon_{\langle be\rangle} \circ (x_2^2,x_1^2)$ (C1,S1)

$= (\beta\varepsilon_{\langle be\rangle})\neg_U$ (U16)

(17a) $((\beta_1,\beta_2)\wedge_M)\varepsilon_{\langle be\rangle} = (\beta_1 \circ (\iota_1,\beta_2))\varepsilon_{\langle be\rangle}$ (M17a)

$= 1_S \times (\beta_1 \circ (\iota_1,\beta_2))$ (B2)

$= (1_S \times \beta_1) \circ 1_S \times (\iota_1,\beta_2)$ (G2)

$= (\beta_1)\varepsilon_{\langle be\rangle} \circ (1_S \times \iota_1, 1_S \times \beta_2)$ (B2,C2)

$$= (\beta_1)\varepsilon_{\langle be\rangle} \circ (1_S \times \iota_1, (\beta_2)\varepsilon_{\langle be\rangle}) \qquad \text{(B2)}$$
$$= (\beta_1)\varepsilon_{\langle be\rangle} \circ (x^2_1, (\beta_2)\varepsilon_{\langle be\rangle}) \qquad \text{(S1,C1)}$$
$$= ((\beta_1)\varepsilon_{\langle be\rangle}, (\beta_2)\varepsilon_{\langle be\rangle})^{\wedge}{}_U \qquad \text{(U17a)}$$

$$\text{(17b)} \quad ((\beta_1,\beta_2)_M)\varepsilon_{\langle be\rangle} = (\beta_1 \circ (\beta_2,\iota_2))\varepsilon_{\langle be\rangle} \qquad \text{(M17b)}$$
$$= 1_S \times (\beta_1 \circ (\beta_2,\iota_2)) \qquad \text{(B2)}$$
$$= (1_S \times \beta_1) \circ 1_S \times (\beta_2,\iota_2) \qquad \text{(G2)}$$
$$= (\beta_1)\varepsilon_{\langle be\rangle} \circ (1_S \times \beta_2, 1_S \times \iota_2) \qquad \text{(B2,C2)}$$
$$= (\beta_1)\varepsilon_{\langle be\rangle} \circ ((\beta_2)\varepsilon_{\langle be\rangle}, 1_S \times \iota_2) \qquad \text{(B2)}$$
$$= (\beta_1)\varepsilon_{\langle be\rangle} \circ ((\beta_2)\varepsilon_{\langle be\rangle}, x^2_2) \qquad \text{(S1,C1)}$$
$$= ((\beta_1)\varepsilon_{\langle be\rangle}, (\beta_2)\varepsilon_{\langle be\rangle})_U \qquad \text{(U17b)}$$

11. CONCLUSION

The eighteen proofs, yielding the homomorphism property of ε, turned out to be considerable longer and more cumbersome than we had expected. But they are equational and we believe that we have isolated the properties used for the correctness proof. That list of properties is itself somewhat of a motley assortment and we feel that it can and should be cleaned up. We hope, however, that the reader will recognize that something very different is going on in that the compiler correctness is being developed in a machine checkable equational framework despite those rough edges.

Perhaps it is typical of detailed and exhaustive correctness efforts, but the process of carrying out the 18 proofs with unflinching detail uncovered several errors in the preceding definitions. This was particularly true of the more difficult (more lengthy) proofs involving the more complex definitions: 9, 12, and, 15. These proofs pointed to errors in the source definition of binary arithmetic operation evaluation (M9), of the block construct (M12), and in the definition of "switchl" in terms of pop and push (F9).

Note also the important fact that the 18 proofs are independent; that is, each programming feature is analyzed independent of the others. So long as the language can be extended within the semantic definition of Section 4, that extension can be checked without consideration of the rest of the correctness proof.

We hope, in the future, to carry out such extensions; even to classify what extensions are possible. Also, if the extension requires new semantic domains for the denotational semantics of the language (the carriers of M) we hope that there will be a uniform way to carry over the proofs already done.

Finally, we hope to carry out the same kind of algebraic arguments with alternative semantic definitions; alternatives to ψ (compile) and alternatives to θ (source semantics). One would hope also to find translations of the flow chart language so that correctness of a composite translation would be obtained by "pasting" commuting squares together.

ACKNOWLEDGEMENTS

We have had a continuing interest in the "complier correctness problem." In the spring of 1974 that interest was active; Susanna Ginali did a thorough study of the McCarthy and Painter (1967) and Burstall and Landin (1969) papers while visiting IBM. There were several fruitful discussions with Joe Goguen and Susanna Ginali at that time. An important discussion with Calvin Elgot occurred during the summer of 1978 at which time we realized that T_0 should be the category of flow charts, rather than the quotient rational theory or the continuous algebraic theory of countable trees. We are deeply indebted to Susanna Ginali, Joe Goguen and Calvin Elgot for their help and encouragement in general and for their contributions to our progress on this problem in particular.

This work on compiler correctness was initiated following a series of lectures on algebraic semantics for the Summer School on Foundations of Artificial Intelligence and Computer Science, Pisa, Italy, 19-30 June 1978, by JWT. We were seeking a significant and informative example employing many of the algebraic concepts. This example (though not developed to the point it is here) was used for the 3rd Advanced Course on Foundations of Computer Science, Amsterdam, The Netherlands, 21 August - 1 September, 1978. We are grateful to the organizers and sponsors of those summer schools for the opportunity to discuss and promote our ideas on algebraic semantics.

We are very grateful to Calvin Elgot, Robin Milner, Barry Rosen and the ICALP '79 referee for specific suggestions and corrections based on earlier drafts of this paper.

BIBLIOGRAPHY

ADJ (Authors: J. A. Goguen, J. W. Thatcher, E. G. Wagner and J. B. Wright)

(1975) (JAG, JWT, EGW, JBW) "Initial algebra semantics and continuous algebras," IBM Research Report RC-5701. November 1975. *JACM 24* (1977) pp. 68-95.

(1976) (JWT, EGW, JBW) "Specification of abstract data types using conditional axioms," IBM Research Report RC-6214, September 1976.

(1976a) (JAG, JWT, EGW) "An initial algebra approach to the specification, correctness, and implementation of abstract data types," IBM Research Report RC-6487, October 1976. To appear, *Current Trends in Programming Methodology, IV: Data Structuring* (R. Yeh, Ed.) Prentice Hall, New Jersey.

(1976b) (EGW, JBW, JAG, JWT) "Some fundamentals of order algebraic semantics," *Lecture Notes in Computer Science 45* (Mathematical Foundations of Computer Science 1976), Springer-Verlag, pp153-168; IBM Research Report RC 6020, May 1976.

(1976c) (JBW, JWT, EGW, JAG) "Rational algebraic theories and fixed-point solutions," *Proceedings* 17th IEEE Symposium on Foundations of Computing, Houston, Texas, October, 1976, pp. 147-158.

(1977) (EGW, JWT, JBW) "Free continuous theories," IBM Research Report RC 6906, December, 1977.

Arbib, M.A. and Giveon, Y.

(1968) "Algebra automata I: Parallel programming as a prolegomena to the categorical approach," *Information and Control 12* (1968) 331-345.

Birkhoff, G. and Lipson, J.D.

(1970) "Heterogeneous algebras," *J. Combinatorial Theory 8* (1970) 115-133.

Burstall, R.M. and Landin, P.J.

(1969) "Programs and their proofs: an algebraic approach," *Machine Intelligence 4*, 1969.

Elgot, C.C.

(1973) "Monadic computation and iterative algebraic theories," IBM Research Report RC 4564, October 1973. *Proceedings*, Logic Colloquium 1973, North Holland (1975)175-230.

(1977) "Some geometrical categories associated with flow chart schemes," IBM Research Report RC 6534, May 1977. *Proceedings*, Conference on Fundamentals of Computation Theory, Poznan-Kornik, Poland, 1977.

Elgot, C.C. and Shepherdson, J.C.

(1977) "A semantically meaningful characterization of reducible flow chart schemes," IBM Research Report RC 6656, July, 1977.

Fiebrich, Rolf-Dieter

(1978) "Generation of correct compiler parts from formal language descriptions," LRZ-Bericht Nr. 7802/1, Institut für Informatik der LudwigMaximilians-Universität, Müchen, 1978.

Guttag, J. V.

(1975) "The specification and application to programming of abstract data types," Univ. of Toronto, Computer Systems Research Group, Techical Report CSRG-59, September, 1975.

Lawvere, F.W.

(1963) "Functorial semantics of algebraic theories," *Proceedings*, Nat'l Acad. Sci. *50* (1963) 869-872.

McCarthy, J. and Painter, J.

(1967) "Correctness of a compiler for arithmetic expressions," *Mathematical Aspects of Computer Science*, Proceedings of Symposia in Applied Mathematics, Vol. 19 (J.T. Schwartz, Ed.) American Math. Soc., Providence R.I. (1967) 33-41.

Milner, R.

(1972) "Inplementation and application of Scott's logic for computable functions," *Proceedings*, ACM Conference on Proving Assertions about Programs, Las Cruces, New Mexico, January, 1972, pp. 1 - 6.

(1976) "Program semantics and mechanized proof," Mathematical Centre Tracts 82 (K.R. Apt and J.W. de Bakker (Eds.), Mathematisch Centrum, Amsterdam, 1976, pp. 3-44.

Milner, R. and Weyrauch, R

(1972) "Proving compiler correctness in a mechanized logic," *Machine Intelligence 7* (B. Meltzer and D. Michie, Eds.), Edinburgh University Press (1972) 51-72.

Morris, F. L.

(1972) "Correctness of translations of programming languages," Stanford Computer Science Memo CS 72-303 (1972).

(1973) "Advice on structuring compilers and proving them correct," *Proceedings*, ACM Symposium on Principles of Programming Languages, Boston (1973) 144-152.

Mosses, P.

(1977) "Making denotational semantics less concrete," manuscript, Aarhus University, August, 1977.

(1978) "Modular denotational semantics," Draft paper, 1978-11-11, Department of Computer Science, Institute of Mathematics, Aarhus University, 1978.

Schmeck, Hartmut

(1975) "Korrektheit von Übersetzungen," Bericht Nr. 3/75 des Institut für Infromatik und Praktische Mathematik, Christian-Albrechts-Universität Kiel, 1975.

Scott, D. and Strachey, C.

(1971) "Toward a mathematical semantics for computer languages," Technical Monograph PRG-6, Oxford University Computing Laboratory, Programming Research Group, 1971.

Zilles, S. N.

(1974) "Algebraic specification of data types," Computation Structures Group Memo 119, MIT, Cambridge, Mass. (1974) 28-52.

LANGUAGES OF NILPOTENT AND SOLVABLE GROUPS (extended abstract)

Denis Thérien
School of Computer Science
McGill University
Montreal, Quebec.

1. INTRODUCTION

There is a deep relationship between the theory of regular languages and the theory of finite monoids. In fact, to each regular language we can associate its syntactic monoid, necessarily finite, and conversely, looking at a finite monoid as a semiautomaton, we can associate to it the set of languages, necessarily regular, which it can recognize for some choice of final states (the initial state being fixed as the unit of the monoid).

The importance of the relationship above can be seen in the fact that many families of regular languages have been characterized by the corresponding families of monoids. A most interesting result of this kind is certainly the correspondance between the family of star-free languages and the family of group-free monoids (Schutzenberger [65]).

An approach commonly used is to define some family of congruences on A*, the free monoid generated by a finite alphabet A, and then investigate the set of languages which are unions of congruence classes for some congruence in the family. Among the interesting families of monoids that have been characterized completely by corresponding families of congruences are: "locally testable" monoids (Brzozowski & Simon [72], McNaughton [74]), J-trivial monoids (Simon [72]), p-groups (Eilenberg [76]) and recently R-trivial and L-trivial monoids (Brzozowski & Fish [78]).

In this paper, we define by congruence the family of modulo languages and we establish the correspondence of this family with the set of finite nilpotent groups. Modulo languages can be defined by the sole operation of counting subwords modulo an integer. This serves as a basis step in the recursive definition of a family of languages which we call counting languages; this family is shown to correspond to finite solvable groups. Furthermore, the congruences we are using are powerful enough to characterize some important structural properties of the corresponding groups. Using different techniques, Straubing [78] was able to give a language characterization for these families of groups; his main result was a classification of the languages corresponding to solvable groups according to the derived length of their syntactic monoids. The results that we obtain by using congruences include this classification as a special case; other natural classifications for the same family of languages are also derived. This extended abstract presents the main results from Thérien [78]. Many technical proofs have been omitted.

Let A be a finite set and $A^* = \bigcup_{i\geq 0} A^i$ be the free monoid generated by A with the empty word λ acting as unit. The length of $w \in A^*$ is defined by $|w| = i$ iff $w \in A^i$; note that the set of all words of length $\leq i$ is given by $(A \cup \lambda)^i$. A language is a subset of A^*. The word x is a segment of the word w iff $w = uxv$, for some u, v in A^*. The word $x = a_1 \ldots a_m$, $a_i \in A$, is a subword of w iff $w = w_0 a_1 w_1 \ldots a_m w_m$ for some $w_0, \ldots, w_m \in A^*$. We use the convention that $a_i \ldots a_j = \lambda$ if $j < i$; we extend this notation to sequences over arbitrary sets, i.e. the sequence $(x_i, \ldots, x_j)$ of elements of X is empty whenever $j < i$.

A congruence α on A^* is an equivalence relation having the property that $x \,\alpha\, y$ implies $uxv \,\alpha\, uyv$ for all $u,v,x,y \in A^*$. The set $\{y : y \,\alpha\, x\}$ is denoted by $[x]_\alpha$: the set $A^*/\alpha = \{[x]_\alpha : x \in A^*\}$ is a monoid. If there exists an integer n such that $x^n \,\alpha\, \lambda$ for all x in A^*, then A^*/α is a group: we denote by x^{-1} any word such that $xx^{-1} \,\alpha\, \lambda$. The language L is an α language iff it is the union of congruence classes of α: any language L is an α_L language where $x \,\alpha_L\, y$ iff ($uxv \in L$ iff $uyv \in L$ for all $u,v \in A^*$). L is regular iff $M_L = A^*/\alpha_L$ is finite.

A semiautomaton is a triple $\mathcal{A} = \langle S_{\mathcal{A}}, A_{\mathcal{A}}, \delta_{\mathcal{A}} \rangle$; we use the notation S, A and δ when it is clear which semiautomaton is involved. S is the finite set of states, A is a finite alphabet and δ: $S \times A \to S$ is the transition function. We extend δ to all pairs (s,x) in $S \times A^*$ by defining

$$\delta(s,x) = \begin{cases} s & \text{if } x = \lambda \\ \delta(\delta(s,x'),a) & \text{if } x = x'a. \end{cases}$$

By choosing an initial state $s_0 \in S$ and a set of final states $S' \subseteq S$ we get an automaton $\mathcal{A} = \langle S, A, \delta, s_0, S' \rangle$ which accepts the regular language $L = \{x \in A^* : \delta(s_0,x) \in S'\}$.

With any semiautomaton $\mathcal{A} = \langle S, A, \delta \rangle$ we associate a monoid $\mathcal{A}^\tau = A^*/\sim$ where $\sim$ is the congruence of finite index defined by

$$x \sim y \text{ iff for all } s \in S,\ \delta(s,x) = \delta(s,y).$$

$\mathcal{A}^\tau$ is a group iff there exists an integer n such that $x^n \sim \lambda$ for all $x \in A^*$.

Conversely any finite monoid M determines a unique semiautomaton <M, M, δ> where δ is the monoid multiplication: we call such a semiautomaton a monoid (or group) semiautomaton.

Let $A_i = \langle S_i, A_i, \delta_i \rangle$ for i = 1, 2. A_1 is a subsemiautomaton of A_2 iff $S_1 \subseteq S_2$, $A_1 \subseteq A_2$ and δ_1 is the restriction of δ_2 to $S_1 \times A_1$. A_1 is a homomorphic image of A_2 iff $A_1 = A_2$ and there exists an epimorphism $\phi\colon\ S_2 \to S_1$ with the property that for all $s \in S_2$, for all $a \in A_2$, $\phi(\delta_2(s,a)) = \delta_1(\phi(s),a)$. A_1 is covered by A_2, $A_1 \prec A_2$ iff A_1 is a homomorphic image of a subsemiautomaton of A_2. If $A_i = \langle M_i, M_i, \delta_i \rangle$ is a monoid semiautomaton for i = 1, 2, this coincides with the notion of M_1 being a homomorphic image of a submonoid of M_2. Also if L is an α language then $M_L \prec A^*/\alpha$. The cross product of A_1, and A_2 is defined as

$$A_1 \times A_2 = \langle S_1 \times S_2,\ A_1 \cap A_2,\ \delta \rangle$$

where $\delta((s_1,s_2),a) = (\delta_1(s_1,a),\ \delta_2(s_2,a))$. If $A_2 = S_1 \times A_1$, we define the cascade connection of A_1 and A_2 to be

$$A_1 \circ A_2 = \langle S_1 \times S_2,\ A_1,\ \delta \rangle$$

where $\delta((s_1,s_2),a) = (\delta_1(s_1,a),\ \delta_2(s_2,(s_1,a)))$; if $x = a_1 \ldots a_m$, this extends to

$$\delta((s_1,s_2),x) = (\delta_1(s_1,x),\ \delta_2(s_2,\omega(x)))$$

where $\omega(x) = (t_1,a_1)(t_2,a_2)\ldots(t_m,a_m)$, $t_i = \delta_1(s_1,a_1\ldots a_{i-1})$ for i = 1,...,m. For more details on these concepts, see Ginzburg [68].

Finally we recall some elementary notions of modular arithmetic. Let N be the set of nonnegative integers; we write $m \mid n$ for m divides n. For m, n, $q \in N$, $q > 0$, $m \equiv n \pmod q$ iff $q \mid m - n$; in particular $m \equiv n \pmod 1$ for all integers m, n. If K is a finite subset of N, lcm K is the least common multiple of the integers in K; if $K = \phi$, lcm K = 1; if $K' \subseteq K$ then lcm $K' \mid$ lcm K. Also $m \equiv n \pmod{q_1}$ and $m \equiv n \pmod{q_2}$ iff $m \equiv n \pmod{\mathrm{lcm}\{q_1,q_2\}}$. If $q_2 \mid q_1$, $m \equiv n \pmod{q_1}$ implies $m \equiv n \pmod{q_2}$ We will denote by Z_q the set of equivalence classes of the integers mod q.

2. ELEMENTS OF GROUP THEORY

All groups considered are finite. A group G is abelian iff $gh = hg$ for all g, h ε G. A subset H of G is subgroup iff it forms a group under the multiplication of G; the right (left) cosets Hg (gH) are either equal or disjoint and $|H| \mid |G|$. H is normal in G, $H \triangleleft G$, iff $g^{-1}hg \in H$ for all $g \in G$, $h \in H$. The set of all right cosets then form a group under the multiplication $(Hg_1)(Hg_2) = H(g_1g_2)$ and we denote this group by G/H. If G has normal subgroup H such that G/H is isomorphic with K, which we denote $G/H \cong K$, we say that G is an extension of H by K.

A normal series of G is a sequence of nested subgroups of G such that

$$G_0 = G \triangleright G_1 \triangleright G_2 \triangleright \dots .$$

For a given prime integer p, G is a p-group iff each element is of order p^α for some $\alpha > 0$, i.e. $g^{p^\alpha} = 1$; if $|G| = p^\alpha q$ with p, q relatively prime, G has a subgroup of order p^α; any such subgroup is called a Sylow p-subgroup of G.

The center of a group G is the normal subgroup $Z(G) = \{h: gh = hg \text{ for all } g \in G\}$. A normal series

$$Z_0 = \{1\} \triangleleft Z_1 \triangleleft \dots \triangleleft Z_m = G$$

is a central series iff $Z_i/Z_{i-1} \subseteq Z(G/Z_{i-1})$ for $i = 1,\dots,m$. G is said to be nilpotent if such a series exists; it is said to be of class m, if no shorter central series exists. If $H \subseteq Z(G)$ is a normal subgroup of G and G/H is nilpotent of class m-1, then G is nilpotent of class $\leq m$. Also G is nilpotent iff it is the direct product of a set of representatives of its Sylow p-subgroups.

The commutator of g and h is $[g,h] = g^{-1}h^{-1}gh$. The derived subgroup $G_1 = [G,G]$ is the normal subgroup of G generated by the set of all commutators; it is always the case that G/G_1 is abelian. Get $G_0 = G$ and $G_i = [G_{i-1}, G_{i-1}]$ for $i \geq 1$, G_i is the ith derived subgroup of G. G is solvable of derived length n iff

$$G_0 \triangleright G_1 \triangleright \quad \dots \triangleright G_n = \{1\},$$

that is if the nth derived subgroup is trivial. Alternatively, G is solvable of fitting length k iff there exists a normal series

$$F_0 = \{1\} \triangleleft F_1 \triangleleft \dots \triangleleft F_k = G$$

such that F_{i+1}/F_i is nilpotent.

Let $\mathcal{G}_{ab}$, $\mathcal{G}_p$ for arbitrary prime p, $\mathcal{G}_{nil}$ and $\mathcal{G}_{sol}$ denote respectively the family of abelian groups, p-groups, nilpotent groups and solvable groups; the following chains of inclusions hold

$$\mathcal{G}_{ab} \subsetneq \mathcal{G}_{nil} \subsetneq \mathcal{G}_{sol}$$

$$\mathcal{G}_{p} \subsetneq \mathcal{G}_{nil} \subsetneq \mathcal{G}_{sol} .$$

Also each one of these families is closed under homomorphism, finite direct product and the operation of taking subgroups, i.e. each one is a variety in Eilenberg's sense (Eilenberg [76]).

An important result linking the structure of a group G and the structure of the group semiautomaton $<G, G, \delta>$ is the following.

Lemma 2.1: If $H \triangleleft G$, then $<G, G, \delta> \prec <G_1, G_1, \delta_1> \circ <G_2, G_2, \delta_2>$ with $G_1 \simeq G/H$ and $G_2 \simeq H$.

Proof. See Ginzburg [68] or Eilenberg [76]. □

Thus for any normal series

$$G = G_0 \triangleright G_1 \triangleright \dots \triangleright G_n = \{1\}$$

we have

$$<G, G, \delta> \prec <H_1, H_1, \delta_1> \circ \dots \circ <H_n, H_n, \delta_n>$$

where $H_i \simeq G_{i-1}/G_i$. From this follows the fact that any solvable-group semiautomaton can be constructed with abelian-group semiautomata (or nilpotent-group semiautomata) provided cascade product and covering are available.

If $A^*_\alpha = A^*/\alpha$ is a group, normal subgroups have a particularly simple form.

Lemma 2.2: a) Let $\beta \supsetneq \alpha$ be congruences on A^*, $H = \{[x]_\alpha : x\beta\lambda\}$: then $H \triangleleft A^*_\alpha$ and $A^*_\alpha/H \simeq A^*_\beta$;
b) let $\gamma \supsetneq \beta \supseteq \alpha$ be congruences on A^*; $H_1 = \{[x]_\alpha : x \beta \lambda\}$, $H_2 = \{[x]_\alpha : x \gamma \lambda\}$, $H_3 = \{[x]_\beta : x \gamma \lambda\}$; then $H_1 \triangleleft H_2$ and $H_2/H_1 \simeq H_3$.

In practice, we often make no distinction between a group and the corresponding group semiautomaton; we extend this identification to the case where a group G is given on a set of generators A, this corresponding naturally to a semiautomaton $<G, A, \delta>$ where δ is the group multiplication.

3. MODULO LANGUAGES AND NILPOTENT GROUPS

In this section, we introduce a family of congruences on A*. These congruences are defined by counting the number of times that subwords appear in words, modulo some integer. These congruences define a family of regular languages, which we call the family of modulo languages. A characterization of these languages is given in terms of their syntactic monoids: L is a modulo language iff M_L is a finite nilpotent group.

The following definition and proposition are borrowed from Eilenberg [76]. Let $u = a_1 \ldots a_m$, $x \in A^*$;

$$\binom{x}{u} = \begin{cases} 1 \text{ if } u = \lambda \\ \text{the number of factorizations of } x \text{ in the form} \\ x = x_0 a_1 x_1 \ldots a_m x_m \text{ otherwise} \end{cases}$$

<u>Lemma 3.1</u>: Let $u, x, y \in A^*$, $a \in A$. Then

a)
$$\binom{xy}{u} = \sum_{u=u_1u_2} \binom{x}{u_1} \binom{y}{u_2}$$

b)
$$\binom{a}{u} = \begin{cases} 1 & \text{if } u = \lambda \text{ or } u = a \\ 0 & \text{otherwise;} \end{cases}$$

c)
$$\binom{\lambda}{u} = \begin{cases} 1 & \text{if } u = \lambda \\ 0 & \text{otherwise.} \end{cases}$$

For example, $\binom{abbab}{ab} = 4$ and $\binom{abbab}{ba} = 2$.

For any $m \geq 0$, $q \geq 1$, the relation $\alpha_{m,q}$ is defined on A* by

$$x \;\alpha_{m,q}\; y \text{ iff for all } u \in (A \cup \lambda)^m,\ \binom{x}{u} \equiv \binom{y}{u} \pmod{q}.$$

<u>Lemma 3.2</u>: For all $m \geq 0$, $q \geq 1$, $\alpha_{m,q}$ is a congruence of finite index.

Proof: Left to the reader. □

The family of all $\alpha_{m,q}$ languages, $m \geq 0$, $q \geq 1$, is called the family of modulo languages: if m is fixed, we use the term modulo languages of class m. The rest of this section is devoted to the characterization of this family in terms of syntactic monoids.

Lemma 3.3: Modulo languages of class m form a boolean algebra.
Proof: Closure under complementation is obvious. Also suppose $L = L_1 \cup L_2$ where L_1 is a α_{m,q_1} language, L_2 is a α_{m,q_2} language. Then L is a $\alpha_{m,q}$ language where $q = \mathrm{lcm}\{q_1,q_2\}$ and L is a modulo language of class m. □

We denote $A^*/\alpha_{m,q}$ by $A_{m,q}$.

Lemma 3.4 $A_{m,q}$ is a finite group for any $m \geq 0$, $q \geq 1$.
Proof: $A_{m,q}$ is a finite monoid since $\alpha_{m,q}$ is a congruence of finite index. It is not difficult to show that $x^{q^m}\ \alpha_{m,q}\ \lambda$ and from this follows that $A_{m,q}$ is a group. □

Corollary 3.1: A_{m,p^c} is a p-group for all $m \geq 1$, p prime, $c \geq 1$.
Proof: Immediate from the proof of lemma 3.4. □

Let m be a fixed integer ≥ 1: denote by $H = \{[x]_{m,q} : x\ \alpha_{m-1,q}\lambda\}$

Lemma 3.5: $H \subseteq Z(A_{m,q})$.
Proof: Clearly $\alpha_{m-1,q} \supseteq \alpha_{m,q}$. By lemma 2.2, H is a normal subgroup of $A_{m,q}$. Moreover

$$\binom{xy}{u} = \binom{x}{u} + \binom{y}{u} + \sum_{\substack{u=u_1u_2\\ u_1\neq\lambda\\ u_2\neq\lambda}} \binom{x}{u_1}\binom{y}{u_2}\ ;$$

but if $x\ \alpha_{m-1,q}\ \lambda$, $\binom{x}{u_1} \equiv 0 \pmod q$, whenever $u_1 \neq \lambda$.
Thus $\binom{xy}{u} \equiv \binom{x}{u} + \binom{y}{u} \pmod q$.
Similarly $\binom{yx}{u} \equiv \binom{y}{u} + \binom{x}{u} \pmod q$ and $xy\ \alpha_{m,q}\ yx$. Hence $H \subseteq Z(A_{m,q})$. □

Lemma 3.6: $A_{m,q}$ is nilpotent of class $\leq m$.
Proof: By induction on m.

Basis $m = 0$

$A_{0,q} = \{1\}$ is nilpotent of class 0.

Induction step $m > 0$

By lemma 3.5 $H \subseteq Z(A_{m,q})$; by lemma 2.2 $A_{m,q}/H \simeq A_{m-1,q}$; by induction hypothesis $A_{m-1,q}$ is nilpotent of class $\leq m-1$. Thus $A_{m,q}$ is the extension of a nilpotent group of class $\leq m-1$ by a group included in its center. Hence $A_{m,q}$ is nilpotent of class $\leq m$. □

It can be shown that if $|A| = 1$, $A_{m,q}$ is nilpotent of class 1 (i.e. abelian) and that if $|A| > 1$, $A_{m,q}$ is nilpotent of class exactly m, for all $m > 0$, $q > 1$.

Lemma 3.7 (Eilenberg): If L is a language such that M_L is a p-group, then L is a modulo language. Moreover L is a $\alpha_{m,p}$ language.

Theorem 3.1: L is a modulo language iff M_L is a finite nilpotent group.

Proof: If L is a modulo language, L is a union of classes of $\alpha_{m,q}$ for some $m \geq 0$, $q \geq 1$. M_L is then a homomorphic image of $A_{m,q}$. By lemma 3.6 $A_{m,q}$ is nilpotent, hence M_L is nilpotent. Conversely suppose that M_L is nilpotent. Then $M_L \simeq G_1 \times \ldots \times G_n$ where G_i is a p_i-group. If L is over the alphabet $A = \{a_1,\ldots,a_k\}$, each element $[a_j]_{\equiv_L}$ has a unique representation $(g_{j1},\ldots,g_{jn}) \in G_1 \times \ldots \times G_n$ and G_i is generated by $A_i = \{g_{1i},\ldots,g_{ki}\}$. By lemma 3.7 there exists m_i, c_i such that each language accepted by the automaton (G_i, A_i, δ_i) is a $\alpha_{m_i,p_i^{c_i}}$ language. Let $m = \max\{m_i\}$, $q = \mathrm{lcm}\{p_i^{c_i}\}$. Let $\theta_i : A^* \to (A_i)^*$ be the ith projective morphism. Then $x \ \alpha_{m,q}\ y$ implies $\theta_i(x)\ \alpha_{m_i,p_i^{c_i}}\ \theta_i(y)$ for $i = 1,\ldots,n$. This establishes that $x \equiv_L y$ and that L is a modulo language. □

It follows from lemma 3.6 that to a modulo language of class m corresponds a nilpotent group of class m. Theorem 3.1 does not give such a strong converse, i.e. if M_L is nilpotent of class m, the theorem does not say that L is a modulo language of class m. This stronger converse holds for $m \leq 1$ and the conjecture is that this is true for all m.

As an example to the notions discussed in this section, consider the dihedral group D_4, which is nilpotent of class 2. One possible set of defining relations over two generators is $a^2 = b^2 = (ab)^4 = 1$. This corresponds to the representation of Fig. 1a. The group D_4 is a homomorphic image of $A_{2,2}$: it can be verified that it counts $\binom{x}{a}$, $\binom{x}{b}$ and $\binom{x}{ab}$ (mod 2). The center consists of those elements which have an even number of a and an even number of b and this corresponds to the elements 0 and 4. The resulting quotient group can be verified to be the abelian group $Z_2 \times Z_2$ of Fig. 1b where we have identified the cosets by enumerating their elements.

D_4 also has the defining relations $a^4 = b^2 = (ab)^2 = 1$ and this representation is pictured in Fig. 2. Of course, this is again a homomorphic image of $A_{2,2}$: this time $\binom{x}{a}$, $\binom{x}{b}$ and $\binom{x}{aa} + \binom{x}{ba}$ are counted mod 2. The center is {0,2} and it corresponds again to those elements having an even number of a and an even number of b.

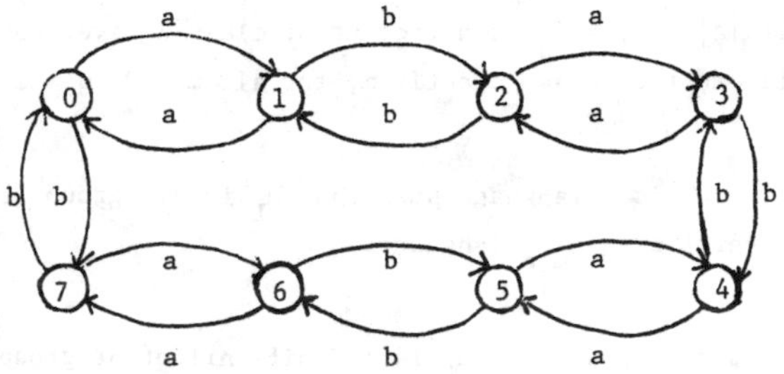

Fig. 1a

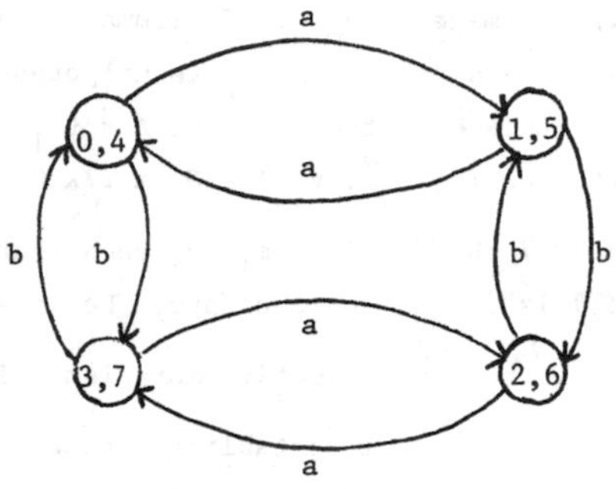

Fig. 1b

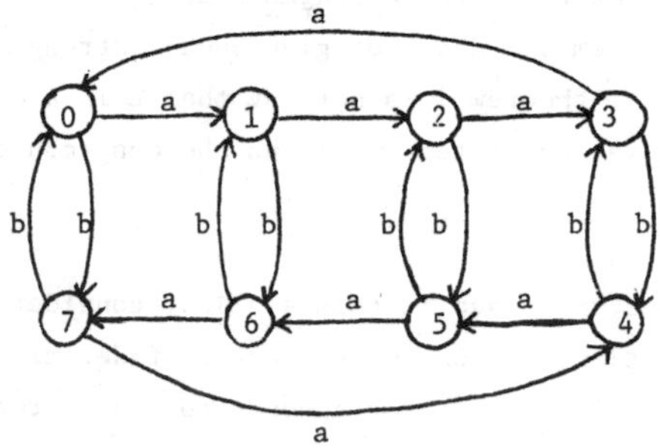

Fig. 2

4. COUNTING LANGUAGES AND SOLVABLE GROUPS

In the previous section, we have considered factorizations of x in the form $x = x_0a_1x_1\ldots a_mx_m$ without taking the x_i's into account. Introducing the notion of counting in context, we are able to define other hierarchies of families of congruences; this is essentially done by taking into consideration the intermediate segments $x_0,x_1,\ldots,x_m$ in the factorization above. The corresponding languages are called counting languages, and modulo languages will be seen to occur as the first nontrivial level of this hierarchy. The name counting languages is motivated by the fact that this family also corresponds to the closure of cyclic counters under the operation of cascade connection. The main result of this section asserts that L is a counting language iff M_L is a solvable group; the structure of M_L is also related to the hierarchy.

We say that $u = a_1\ldots a_m$ appears in context $X = (x_0,\ldots,x_m)$ in x iff $x = x_0a_1x_1\ldots a_mx_m$. For any pair of contexts $V_1 = (v_{01},\ldots,v_{m1})$, $V_2 = (v_{02},\ldots,v_{n2})$, we define their product V_1V_2 to be $V = (v_0,\ldots,v_{m+n})$ where $v_i = v_{i1}$, for $i = 0,\ldots,m-1$, $v_m = v_{m1}v_{02}$, and $v_j = v_{j-m2}$ for $j = m+1,\ldots,m+n$. Any congruence $\sim$ on A* induce a congruence on contexts: we say that $V \sim V'$ iff $V = (v_0,\ldots,v_m)$, $V' = (v'_0,\ldots,v'_m)$ and $v_i \sim v'_i$, $i = 0,\ldots,m$. We also define the following symbol

$$\binom{x}{u}_{[V]_\sim} = \begin{array}{l}\text{the number of factorizations of x in the form}\\ x = x_0a_1x_1\ldots a_mx_m \text{ with } X \sim V\end{array}$$

Observe that this notion is defined only in the case where V is a vector of length $|u| + 1$; in what follows, we always assume that the lengths of u and V are correctly related. Note the special case $u = \lambda$; λ always appears in context $X = (x)$ in x and $\binom{x}{\lambda}_{[V]_\sim}$ is 1 iff $x \sim v$, where $V = (v)$, and it is 0 otherwise. Finally it is clear that when $\sim$ is the universal congruence $\binom{x}{u}_{[V]_\sim} = \binom{x}{u}$. We write [V] for $[V]_\sim$ when it is understood which relation $\sim$ is intended.

As an example of the notions introduced above, let $\sim$ be the congruence on {a,b}* defined by

$$x \sim y \text{ iff } |x| \equiv |y| \pmod 2.$$

Clearly any context V is equivalent to some $(v_0,\ldots,v_m)$ where $v_i = a$ or $v_i = \lambda$ for

$i = 0,\ldots,m$. The reader may verify that, taking x = babaaa, we have $\binom{x}{a}_{(a,\lambda)} = 3$, $\binom{x}{a}_{(\lambda,a)} = 1$, $\binom{x}{ab}_{(a,\lambda,a)} = 1$.

Lemma 4.1: Let $\sim$ be a congruence on A^*, V a context, $u, x, y \in A^*$, $a \in A$; then

i) $$\binom{xy}{u}_{[V]_\sim} = \sum_{\substack{u=u_1u_2 \\ [V]=[V_1V_2]}} \binom{x}{u_1}_{[V_1]} \binom{x}{u_2}_{[V_2]} ;$$

ii) $$\binom{a}{u}_{[V]_\sim} = \begin{cases} 1 & \text{if } (u = a \text{ and } V \sim (\lambda,\lambda)) \text{ or } (u = \lambda \text{ and } V \sim (a)) \\ 0 & \text{otherwise;} \end{cases}$$

iii) $$\binom{\lambda}{u}_{[V]_\sim} = \begin{cases} 1 & \text{if } u = \lambda \text{ and } V \sim (\lambda) \\ 0 & \text{otherwise.} \end{cases}$$

Proof: Clear. □

For any $m \geq 0$, $q \geq 1$, $n \geq 0$, we define recursively the following relations:

$n = 0$ $\quad x \; \alpha_{m,q,0} \; y$ for all $x, y \in A^*$

$n > 0$ $\quad x \; \alpha_{m,q,n} \; y$ iff for all $u \in (A \cup \lambda)^m$ and for all contexts V of length $|u|+1$

$$\binom{x}{u}_{[V]_{\alpha_{m,q,n-1}}} \equiv \binom{y}{u}_{[V]_{\alpha_{m,q,n-1}}}$$

The case $n=1$ thus yields the $\alpha_{m,q}$ of last section.

Lemma 4.2: Let $m, n \geq 0$, $q \geq 1$; $\alpha_{m,q,n}$ is a congruence of finite index.

Proof: easily verified, by induction on n. □

For the rest of this section, we investigate the languages corresponding to this new family of congruences. If we restrict ourselves to the case m = 1, the construction of the congruence $\alpha_{1,q,n}$ uses the same idea as the operation on languages that appeared in Straubing [78].

Let C_n = {L: L is a $\alpha_{m,q,n}$ language, $m \geq 0$, $q \geq 1$}. It is clear that $C_0 = \{\phi, A^*\}$ and that C_1 is the family of modulo languages. Moreover, $C_n \subseteq C_{n+1}$ for n = 0,1,... . We denote by $C = \bigcup_{n=0} C_n$ and we call C the family of counting languages.

We extend the notation of the last section to the following: we use $A_{m,q,n}$ for $A^*/\alpha_{m,q,n}$: clearly we then have $\alpha_{m,q,n}$ implies $\alpha_{m',q',n'}$, whenever $m' \leq m$, $n' \leq n$, $q' | q$.

We now proceed to give a characterization of counting languages in terms of their syntactic monoids.

<u>Lemma 4.3</u>: For any m, n $\geq$ 0, q $\geq$ 1, $A_{m,q,n}$ is a finite group.

Proof: $A_{m,q,n}$ is a finite monoid since $\alpha_{m,q,n}$ is a congruence of finite index. Also, it can be proved that $x^{q^{mn}} \; \alpha_{m,q,n} \; \lambda$. □

<u>Corollary 4.1</u>: For any m, n > 0, p prime, c > 1, $A_{m,p^c,n}$ is a p-group.

Proof: Clear. □

Let m, n, q be fixed and define $H = \{[x]_{m,n,q} : x \; \alpha_{m,q,n-1} \; \lambda\}$

<u>Lemma 4.4</u>: H is nilpotent of class m.

Proof: We establish by induction on i the following stronger result: let β_i be the congruence defined by

$$x \ \beta_i \ y \ \text{ iff } \ \text{for all } u \in (A \cup \lambda)^i$$
$$\text{for all } V \text{ of length } |u| + 1$$
$$\binom{x}{u}_{[V]_{m,q,n-1}} \equiv \binom{y}{u}_{[V]_{m,q,n-1}} \pmod q$$

Then $H_i = \{[x]_{\beta_i} : x \ \alpha_{m,q,n-1} \ \lambda\}$ is nilpotent of class i.

<u>Basis</u> i = 0

$\beta_i = \alpha_{m,q,n-1}$ and $H_i = \{1\}$.

<u>Induction step</u> i > 0

Clearly $\alpha_{m,q,n-1} \supseteq \beta_{i-1} \supseteq \beta_i$: by lemma 2.2, $H' = \{[x]_{\beta_i} : x \ \beta_{i-1} \ \lambda\} \triangleleft H_i$ and $H_i/H' \simeq H_{i-1}$. H_{i-1} is nilpotent of class i-1 by induction hypothesis and to show that H_i is nilpotent of class i, it is thus sufficient to prove $H' \subseteq Z(H_i)$. Let $x \in H'$, $y \in H_i$:

$$\binom{xy}{u}_{[V]_{m,q,n-1}} = \sum_{\substack{u=u_1u_2 \\ V=V_1V_2}} \binom{x}{u_1}_{[V_1]} \binom{y}{u_2}_{[V_2]}$$

But $x \in H'$ implies that $\binom{x}{u_1}_{[V_1]} = 0 \pmod q$ for all $u_1 \in (A \cup \lambda)^{m-1}$. Also $\binom{y}{\lambda}_{[V_2]} = 1$ iff $V_2 = (y)$ and similarly $\binom{x}{\lambda}_{[V_1]} = 1$ iff $V_1 = (x)$. Using the fact that $y \ \alpha_{m,q,n-1} \ \lambda$ and $x \ \alpha_{m,q,n-1} \ \lambda$ we get

$$\binom{xy}{u}_{[V]_{m,n-1,q}} \equiv \binom{x}{u}_{[V][(y^{-1})]} + \binom{y}{u}_{[(x^{-1})][V]}$$

$$\equiv \binom{x}{u}_{[V]} + \binom{y}{u}_{[V]}$$

$$\equiv \binom{yx}{u}_{[V]}$$

which was to be proved. □

<u>Theorem 4.1</u>: L is a counting language iff M_L is a solvable group.

Proof: If L is a counting language, $M_L \prec A_{m,q,n}$ for some $m,n \geq 0$, $q \geq 1$. If $n = 0$, $A_{m,q,0} = \{1\}$ is solvable. If $n = 1$, $A_{m,q,1}$ is nilpotent, hence solvable. For the general case, we have that $A_{m,q,n} \prec A_{m,q,n-1} \circ H$, where $A_{m,q,n-1}$ is solvable by induction hypothesis and H is nilpotent by lemma 4.4 Hence $A_{m,q,n}$ is covered by a solvable group, since the extension of a solvable group by a nilpotent group is solvable. Thus $A_{m,q,n}$ is solvable and M_L is solvable. Conversely let L be a language such that M_L is a solvable group. Let $H_0 = M_L \rhd H_1 \rhd \ldots \rhd H_n = \{1\}$ be the fitting series of M_L. If $n = 0$, $M_L = \{1\}$ and L is a $\alpha_{m,q,0}$ language; if $n = 1$, M_L is nilpotent and L is a $\alpha_{m,q,1}$ language. For the general case, $M_L \prec G_1 \circ G_2$ where G_1 is solvable of fitting length n-1 and G_2 is nilpotent. By induction hypothesis $G_1 \prec A_{m_1,q,n-1}$ for some $m_1 > 0$, $q_1 > 1$, and $G_2 \prec (G_1 \times A)_{m_2,q_2,1}$ for some $m_2 > 0$, $q_2 > 1$. Let $m = \max \{m_1,m_2\}$, $q = \text{lcm}\,\{q_1,q_2\}$, and suppose $x \, \alpha_{m,q,n} \, y$: then $x \, \alpha_{m_1,q_1,n-1} \, y$ and $\delta_1(\lambda,x) = \delta_1(\lambda,y)$ since $G_1 \prec A_{m_1,q,n-1}$. Also each factorization of x as $x = x_0 a_1 x_1 \ldots a_m x_m$ corresponds to a factorization of $\omega(x)$ as $\omega(x) = \omega_0 \, (g_1,a_1) \, \omega_1 \ldots (g_m,a_m) \omega_m$, $\omega_i \in (G_1 \times A)^*$ where $g_i \, \alpha_{m,q,n-1} \, x_0 \, a_1 \, x_1 \ldots a_{i-1} \, x_{i-1}$ and similarly for y. Since $\binom{x}{u}_{[V]_{m,q,n-1}} \equiv \binom{y}{u}_{[V]_{m,q,n-1}} \pmod q$ it follows that $\binom{\omega(x)}{u'} \equiv \binom{\omega(y)}{u'} \pmod q$ where $u' = (g_1,a_1)\ldots(g_m,a_m)$; this establishes that $\delta_2(\lambda,\omega(x)) = \delta_2(\lambda,\omega(y))$ since $G_2 \prec (G_1 \times A)_{m,q,1}$. Altogether, it shows that $M_L \prec A_{m,q,n}$ and that L is a $\alpha_{m,q,n}$ language. □

<u>Corollary 4.2</u>: $L \in \mathcal{C}_n$ iff M_L is a solvable group of fitting length $\leq n$.

Proof: Clear from the proof of the theorem. □

This last result shows a close connection between the operation of couting sub-words in recursively-defined contexts and the operation of "dividing" a solvable group by a nilpotent subgroup; this extends the results of section 3 which said that counting subwords without context is closely related to nilpotent groups. Moreover if we count only words of length one in recursively-defined contexts, this corresponds to "dividing" G by an abelian subgroup just like counting subwords of length 1 was observed in section 3 to correspond to abelian groups. Let $\mathcal{D}_n = \{L:$ L is a $\alpha_{1,q,n}$ language; then $\mathcal{D}_0 \subseteq \mathcal{D}_1 \subseteq \ldots$; let $\mathcal{D} = \bigcup_{n \geq 0} \mathcal{D}_n$.

<u>Theorem 4.2</u>: $L \in \mathcal{D}_n$ iff M_L is a solvable group of derived length $\leq n$.

Proof: The proof is essentially a replica of the proof of theorem 4.1.

This result appeared in a different form in Straubing [78]. He had also shown the equivalence of D with the family of languages recognized by cascade connection of cyclic counters.

A more general result is at hand; let $E_{m,n}$ = {L: L is a $\alpha_{m,q,n}$ language}.

Lemma 4.5: If $L \in E_{m,n}$ then M_L has a normal series of length n where each factor is nilpotent of class m.

Proof: Clear. □

Also, by an argument exactly similar to the one used in theorem 4.1, it is seen that is the conjecture stated in section 3 is true, then the converse of lemma 4.5 holds as well.

As an example consider the groups S_3 of all permutations of three objects. It has two different representations on two generators. The first one can be pictured as in Fig. 3; it can be checked to be isomorphic to the cascade connection of Fig. 4 with all the inputs not shown in the tail machine being identities. For this representation, $S_3 \prec A_{1,6,2}$; the front machine determines the length (mod 2) and the tail machine counts mod 3 occurrences of b which arrives after an odd-length prefix (counted as 1) or an even-length prefix (counted as 2).

The other representation can be pictured as in Fig. 5; this one is isomorphic to the cascade connection of Fig. 6 again with the inputs not shown in the tail machine being identities. For this representation, the front machine counts occurrences of b mod 2 and the tail machine counts mod 3 occurences of a after prefixes containing an even number of b (each such a is counted as 1) or an odd number of b (each such a is counted as 2). Again $S_3 \prec A_{1,6,2}$.

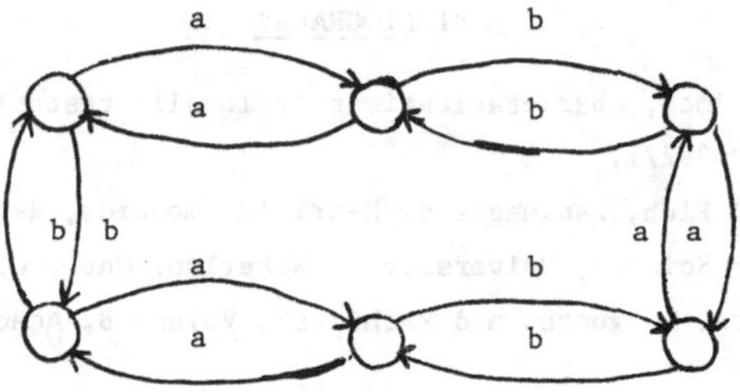

Fig. 3

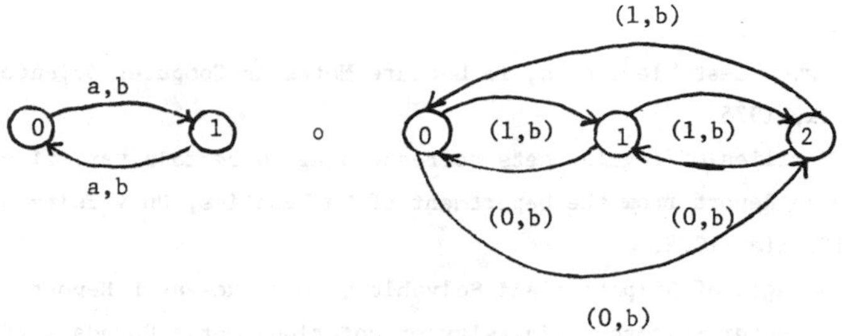

Fig. 4

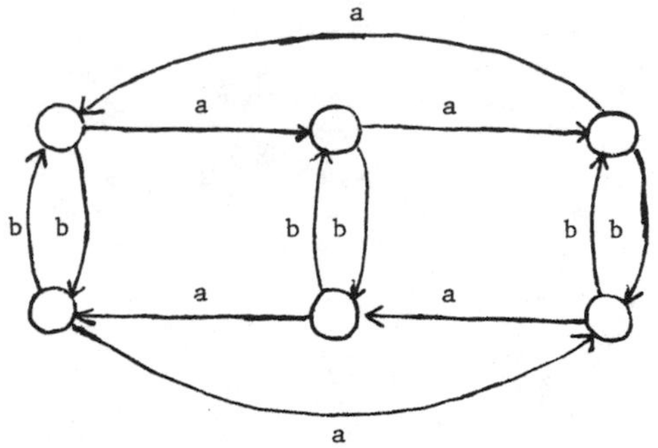

Fig. 5

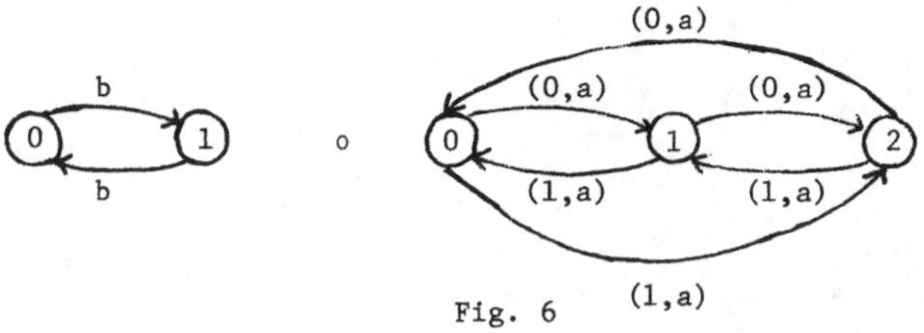

Fig. 6

BIBLIOGRAPHY

J.A. Brzozowski & I. Simon, Characterizations of locally testable events, Discrete Mathematics 4 (1973) 243-271.

J.A. Brzozowski & F.E. Fich, Languages of R-trivial monoids, Research Report CS-78-32, Department of Computer Science, University of Waterloo, Ont., Canada, 1978.

S. Eilenberg, "Automata, Languages and Machines", Volume B, Academic Press, New York, 1976.

A. Ginzburg, "Algebraic Theory of Automata", Academic Press, New York, 1968.

R. McNaughton, Algebraic decision procedures for local testability, Mathematical Systems Theory 8 (1974), 60-76.

M.P. Schützenberger, On finite monoids having only trivial subgroups, Information and Control 8 (1965), 190-194.

I. Simon, Piecewise testable events, in Lecture Notes in Computer Science 33, Springer-Verlag, New York, 1975.

H. Straubing, Families of regular sets corresponding to certain varieties of finite monoids, Research Report from the Department of Mathematics, University of California, Berkeley, California, 1978.

D. Thérien, Languages of Nilpotent and Solvable Groups, Research Report CS-78-44, Department of Computer Science, University of Waterloo, Ont., Canada 1978.

UNIQUE FIXED POINTS VS. LEAST FIXED POINTS

/extended abstract/

Jerzy Tiuryn

RWTH Aachen, Lehrstuhl für Informatik II

and

Warsaw University, Institute of Mathematics

0. Introduction

There are known two approaches to the semantics of programming languages, which are using fixed points. Historically the first approach is based on the existence of least fixed points of ω-continuous mappings defined on ω-complete posets (cf. [2,8,9,]) The second approach, dealing with unique fixed points of certain maps, was originated by C.C. Elgot [4] . While the first approach seems to be more intuitive, due to the possibility of generating those fixed points by increasing sequences of "finite pieces of information", nevertheless there exist structures where the order relation is somehow unnatural and superfluous, and where the unique-fixed-Point approach can be applied, as this is the case for example, with trees (cf. [3]).

Those two approaches have been studied independently. The original motivation for this paper is to compare them in the sense we are going to describe now briefly.

The least-fixed-point approach is represented here by regular algebras. These are, roughly speaking, all those algebras with ordered carriers where one can get least solution of an algebraic system of equations by taking the least upper bound of the ω-chain of iterations. The notion of a regular algebra has been introduced in [10]. The equivalence of this notion to the notion of a rational algebraic theory (cf.[1]) is shown in [12] . The application of regular algebras to the semantics of nondeterministic recursive procedures, where the ω-continuous algebras cannot be applied, the reader may find in [13].

The unique-fixed-point approach is represented here by iterative algebras. Informally, these are all algebras with the property that every "ideal" (i.e. nontrivial)) algebraic system of fixed point equations has a unique solution. The notion of an iterative algebra is introduced in this paper, and it is shown here that it corresponds to the notion of iterative algebraic theory.

Let $k,n \in \omega$, and let $p = (p_o,\dots,p_{n-1})$ be a vector of $n+k$-ary polynomial symbols (i.e. finite trees) over the signature Σ .Assume moreover that none of p_i's is a variable (i.e. p is ideal). In a given iterative Σ-algebra $\underline{A}$, for every vector of parameters $a \in A^k$ one may solve the system of equations.

$$x_o = p_{o_{\underline{A}}} (x_o \ldots, x_{n-1}, a)$$

(0.1) $$\ldots\ldots\ldots\ldots\ldots$$

$$x_{n-1} = p_{n-1_{\underline{A}}} (x_o, \ldots, x_{n-1}, a)$$

getting the unique solution: $(p_{\underline{A}})^+(a)$.

Similarly, in a given regular Σ-algebra $\underline{B}$, for every vector of parameters $b \in B^k$ one may solve the system

$$x_o = p_{o_{\underline{B}}} (x_o, \ldots, x_{n-1} cb)$$

(0.2) $$\ldots\ldots\ldots\ldots$$

$$x_{n-1} = p_{n-1_{\underline{B}}} (x_o, \ldots, x_{n-1}, b)$$

getting the least solution: $(p_{\underline{B}})^{\Delta}$ (b).

In both cases it gives rise to functions $(p_{\underline{A}})^+ : A^k \to A^n$, and $(p_{\underline{B}})^{\Delta} : B^k \to B^n$. The following definition is a basic one for this paper.

An iterative Σ-algebra $\underline{A}$ is said to <u>admit a regular extension</u> iff there is a regular algebra $\underline{A}_R$ and a map $\varphi_A : A \to \underline{A}_R$ such that:

(0.3) for any vector p of polynomial symbols as above,

$$\varphi_{\underline{A}} (p_{\underline{A}})^+ = (p_{\underline{A}_R})^{\Delta} \varphi_{\underline{A}}$$

(0.4) for any regular Σ-algebra $\underline{B}$ and for any map $f : A \to B$ satisfying

$$f(p_{\underline{A}})^+ = (p_{\underline{B}})^{\Delta} f, \text{ for all p's,}$$

there is exactly one regular homomorphism

$$f^* : \underline{A}_R \to \underline{B} \text{ with } f^* \varphi_{\underline{A}} = f$$

(f^* is a regular homomorphism means: for all polynomial vectors p's

$$f^*(p_{\underline{A}_R})^{\Delta} = (p_{\underline{B}})^{\Delta} f^*).$$

In (0.3) and (0.4) we use the same notation for a function and for its extension to vectors (componentwise).

Condition (0.3) states that $\varphi_{\underline{A}}$ "translates" results, i.e. interpretation of the unique solution of fixed point equations with parameters, in the iterative algebra $\underline{A}$ is the same as least solution of the same system with interpreted parameters in the regular algebra $\underline{A}_R$. Condition (0.4) states that the construction $\underline{A} \mapsto (\varphi_{\underline{A}}, A_R)$ is universal (cf. [7]).

The aim of this paper is to prove the existence and provide the construction of a regular extension for every iterative algebra. It is shown that every iterative algebra admits exactly one (up to isomorphism) regular extension. It is also shown that there exists an iterative algebra $\underline{A}$ which cannot be "freely embedded" into any regular algebra, i.e. there is no regular extension $(\varphi_{\underline{A}}, \underline{A}_R)$ with injective $\varphi_{\underline{A}}$.

In the author's opinion the above-mentioned construction is quite hard to carry due to unsatisfactory development of combinatorial methods for infinite trees.

The paper is divided into seven sections. Sections 1 to 3 are of preliminary character. They collect basic definitions and results to be used in the sequel. Section 1 fixes some notations and definitions. In section 2 we introduce the notion of an iterative algebra, show its connection with Elgot's iterative thories, and give a construction of free iterative algebras by using the result of S. Ginali (cf. [5]) relating free iterative theories with free rational theories. In section 3 we state some basic results on regular algebras, that are used in section 5.

In section 4 we formulate the problem which was described above. Section 5 contains basic steps of the solution of this problem. In section 6 we give some examples illustrating our construction. Some open problems are stated in section 7.

Due to space limitations all proofs in this paper are omited. The interested reader may find complete proofs of these results in [14] .

1. Preliminary notations and definitions

Let X be a set, n-vectors over X (or simply vectors), i.e. elements of X^n wiil be treated as functions from $n = \{o,\dots,n-1\}$ into X. If $x \in X^n$, and $i < n$, then X_i denotes the i-th component of x. The map that associates with each vector its i-th component is called the i-th projection and will be denoted by e_i^n. We denote by ω the set of all finite ordinals.

If X,Y,Z are sets, and $f\colon X \to Y$, $g\colon Y \to Z$ are functions, then the composition of f and g will be denoted by $gf\colon X \to Z$.

Each function $f\colon X \to Y$ can be naturally extended (componentwise), for every $n \in \omega$, to n-vectors. We will not introduce a special notation for this extension, as it will not cause misunderstanding. Thus f(x) means either the value of f at x, if $x \in X$, or the vector $(f(X_o),\dots,f(X_{n-1}))$, if $x \in X^n$.

If Σ is a signature (i.e. a ranked alphabet) and $n \in \omega$, then by $T_\Sigma(n)$ we denote the Σ-algebra of all finite terms over Σ, with at most n variables. A rector $p \in T_\Sigma(n)^k$ is called an ideal vector of terms if none of its components is a variable. Finite Terms over Σ with at most n variables will be called sometimes n-ary (Σ-)polynomial symbols.

A category T is an algebraic theory (cf. [6]) if Objects (T) = ω, for each $n \in \omega$, there are basic morphisms $\{e_o^n,\dots,e_{n-1}^n\} \subseteq T(1,n)$, For each $n,k \in \omega$ there is defined a source tupling operation: $\alpha_o,\ldots,\alpha_{n-1} \in T(1,k) \rightarrow (\alpha_o,\ldots,\alpha_{n-1}) \in T(n,k)$. Moreover, the above notions are supposed to satisfy the following axioms, for any $n,k \in \omega, \alpha \in T(n,k), \alpha_o,\ldots,\alpha_{n-1} \in T(1,k)$:

(1.1) $(e^n_o\alpha,\ldots,e^n_{n-1}\alpha) = \alpha$;

(1.2) $\alpha(e^k_o,\ldots e^k_{k-1}) = \alpha$;

(1.3) $e^n_i(\alpha_o,\ldots,\alpha_{n-1}) = \alpha_i$, for all $i<n$

We compose morphisms in algebraic theories in converse order to that for functions, i.e. if $\alpha \in T(n,k)$, $\beta \in T(k,p)$, then $\alpha\beta \in T(n,p)$ denotes the composition of α and β.

An algebraic theory T is said to be ideal (cf. [4]) if for every $n \in \omega$ and for every non-base morphism $\alpha \in T(1,n)$, $\alpha\beta$ is non-base for every morphism $\beta \in T(n,k)$, $k \in \omega$.

An ideal theory T is said to be iterative (cf. [4]) if for any $n,k \in \omega$ and for any ideal morphism $\alpha \in T(n,n+k)$ the equation $x = \alpha(x,e^k_o,\ldots,e^k_{k-1})$ has unique solution in $T(n,k)$. This solution will be denoted by α^+.

A theory morphism between iterative theories is a functor between underlying and preserves: basic morphisms, the property of "being ideal morphism", and $^+$ operation.

If Σ is a signature and X is a set, then by $\Sigma(X)$ we denote the extension of by "constants" from X, i.e. $\Sigma(X)$ is a signature with $\Sigma(X)_o = \Sigma_o \sqcup X$ ($\sqcup$ denotes disjoint set-union), and $\Sigma(X)_n = \Sigma_n$ for $n<o$.

Suppose Σ is a signature. By a Σ-tree t we mean a partial function $t: \omega^* \multimap \bigcup \Sigma_n$ (here ω^* denotes the set of all finite words $n \in \omega$ over ω, by Λ we will denote the empty word), such that for all $w \in \omega^*$, $i \in \omega$:

(1.4) if $w\,i \in Dom(t)$, then $w \in Dom(t)$;

(1.5) if $w \in Dom(t)$ and $t(w) \in \Sigma_n$, then $w\,i \in Dom(t)$ for all $i<n$;

(1.6) $\Lambda \in Dom(t)$.

A tree t is finite if Dom(t) is finite. In particular $T_\Sigma(o)$ is the set of all finite Σ-trees. Denote by T^∞_Σ the set of all Σ-trees.

Let $t \in T^\infty_\Sigma$, and $w \in Dom(t)$. By $t \upharpoonright w$ we denote a subtree of t determined by the path w, i.e. $Dom(t) \upharpoonright w) = \{u \in \hat{\omega}^*: w\,u \in Dom(t)\}$ and for $u \in Dom(t \upharpoonright w)$, $t \upharpoonright w\,(u) = T(wu)$

A tree $t \in T_\Sigma^\infty$ is said to be of finite index if $\{t\ w : w\ \mathrm{Dom}(t)\}$ is finite. Trees of finite index are known also as regular trees (cf. [3]).

If $n \in w$, $t \in T_{\Sigma(n)}^\infty$ (t as a $\Sigma(n)$-tree can be also treated in obvious way as a Σ-tree with at most n variables), and $p \in (T_\Sigma^\infty)^n$, then $t[p]$ denotes the result of substituting of n-vector p into the tree t (cf. [2]) .

On the set ω^* we define a partial order $\leqslant$ by: $w \leqslant u$ iff $u = wv$ for some $v \in \omega^*$. We shall write $w \lessdot u$ to indicate that $w \leqslant u$ and $w \neq u$.

If P is a set, $R \subseteq P \times P$ ist a binary relation on P and $X, Y \subseteq P$, then we write XRY iff for every $x \in X$ there exists $y \in Y$ with $(x,y) \in R$. In particular, if $\leq$ is a partial order on P, then $X \leq \{a\}$ means that a is an upper bound of X.

If $R \subseteq P \times P$ is an equivalence relation on P and $a \in P$, then $|a|_R = \{x \in P : (a,x) \in R\}$. We will omit the subscript R when it will be clear from the context what relation R is meant. Since $|\ |_R : P \to P/R = \{|x|_R : x \in P\}$ is a function, $|A|_R$ will denote the set $\{|a|_R : a \in A\}$, for any set $A \subseteq P$.

2. Iterative algebras and iterative algebraic theories

A Σ-algebra $\underline{A}$ is said to be iterative if for any $n, k \in \omega$ and for any ideal vector $p \in T_\Sigma(n+k)^n$ the following hold:

(2.1) For any $a \in A^k$ the equation $x = P_{\underline{A}}(x,a)$ has unique solution in A^n. Denote this solution by $(P_{\underline{A}})^+(a)$;

(2.2) There is $a \in A^k$ such that $a_o \neq ((P_{\underline{A}})^+(a))_o$.

Remarks: Condition (2.1) guarantee that for ideal P the map $(P_{\underline{A}})^+ : A^k \to A^n$ is well defined and $P_{\underline{A}}((P_{\underline{A}})^+(x),x) = (P_{\underline{A}})^+(x)$ for $x \in A^k$. Condition (2.2) says that $(P_{\underline{A}})^+_o$ ist not a projection.

With each iterative algebra we associate a set of maps one can get solving equation (2.1) and treating a as a vector of parameters. Suppose $\underline{A}$ is an iterative Σ-algebra. A map $f : A^k \to A$ is called an (k-ary) iterative polynomial if either it is a projection, or if for some $n \in \omega$ and ideal $p \in T_\Sigma(n+k)^n$, $f = (P_{\underline{A}})^+_o$. Denote by $k\mathrm{IP}(\underline{A})$ the set of all k-ary iterative polynomials in $\underline{A}$.

The following result is an immediate consequence of our definitions.

Proposition 2.1. If $\underline{A}$, $\underline{B}$ are iterative Σ-algebras and $h : A \to B$ is a Σ-homomorphism, then for every ideal vector $p \in T_\Sigma(n+k)^n$, $h(P_{\underline{A}})^+ (P_{\underline{B}})^+h$, i.e. every Σ-homomorphism between iterative algebras preserves all interative polynomials.

With a given iterative algebra $\underline{A}$ we associate an algebraic theory $I(\underline{A})$, where for $k \in \omega$, $I(\underline{A})(1,k) = k\mathrm{IP}(\underline{A})$. Composition of morphisms is just usual composition of functions, basic morphisms are projections, and source tupling is just an ordinary tupling of functions. The following result relates iterative algebras with iterative algebraic theories. The full proof can be found in [14] .

Theorem 2.2

(i) For any iterative algebra $\underline{A}$, $I(\underline{A})$ is an iterative algebraic theory.

(ii) For any iterative algebraic theory T there is a signature Σ and an iterative Σ-algebra $\underline{A}_T$ with $T \cong I(\underline{A}_T)$ (here isomorphism means an isomorphism of iterative theories).

The above result indicates that iterative algebraic theories are categorical counterparts of "iterative clones" of iterative algebras. One may also prove that iterative algebraic theories play the same role for "varietes" of iterative algebras (i.e. for classes of iterative algebras definable by certain equations between iterative polynomials) as ordinary algebraic theories (cf. [6]) play for varieties of universal algebras.

Let Σ be a signature, for any set X denote by $\bar{R}_\Sigma(X)$ the Σ-algebra of $\Sigma(X)$-trees of a finite index (this is a Σ-subalgebra of $T^\infty_\Sigma(X)$). For $X = \phi$ the above algebra is denoted by $\bar{R}_\Sigma$. The next result provides free iterative theories as well as free iterative algebras.

Theorem 2.3

(i) for any X, $\bar{R}_\Sigma(X)$ is an iterative Σ-algebra.

(ii) $I(\bar{R}_\Sigma)$ is an iterative algebraic theory freely generated by Σ i.e. for any iterative theory T and for any function $f : \Sigma \to T$ such that $f(\Sigma n) \subseteq T(1,n) \setminus \{e^n_o, \ldots, e^n_{n-1}\}$ for $n \in \omega$, there exists exactly one extension of f to a theory morphism $F : I(\bar{R}_\Sigma) \to T$.

(iii) For any X, $\bar{R}_\Sigma(X)$ is an iterative algebra freely generated by X, i.e. for any iterative Σ-algebra $\underline{A}$ and for any function $f : X \to A$ there is exactly one extension $\bar{f} : \bar{R}_\Sigma(X) \to \underline{A}$ to a Σ-homomorphism.

Part (ii) of the above result is due to S. Ginali [5] and S. Bloom, C. Elgot, R. Tindell [3] ($I(\bar{R}_\Sigma)$ is called there ΣTr). Parts (i) and (iii) are proved in [14] .

In particular part (iii) provides a natural way to define derived operations in an arbitrary iterative Σ-algebra $\underline{A}$: each $t \in \bar{R}_\Sigma(X)$ determines in $\underline{A}$ a function (called derived operation) $t_{\underline{A}} : A^X \to A$ defined by $t_{\underline{A}}(a) = \bar{a}(t)$, where $a \in A^X$ and $\bar{a} : \bar{R}_\Sigma(X) \to \underline{A}$ is the unique extension of a to a Σ-homomorphism. Because in each $t \in \bar{R}_\Sigma(X)$ appears only a finite number of elements of X, so in fact, we may only define finitary derived operations in iterative algebras. On the other hand, because of an obvious isomorphism $nIP(\bar{R}_\Sigma) \cong \bar{R}_\Sigma(n)$, one can easily deduce that both notions of iterative polynomial and derived operation coincide in every iterative algebra.

3. Basic results on regular algebras

In this section we recall basic definitions and results concerning regular algebras. Full exposition of these results the reader may find in [10,11] . Throughout this section we assume that all algebras have ordered carrier with least element, denoted by $\perp$. Moreover we assume that all operations are monotonic (the last assumption can be replaced by weaker one, as it is done in [10] , by for simplicity of exposition we are dealing here exclusively with monotone operations). We call such structures <u>ordered algebras</u>.

Let $\underline{A}$ be an ordered Σ-algebra. Let $n,k \in \omega$, $p \in T_\Sigma(n+k)^n$, $a \in A^k$. Denote by $f: A^n \to A^n$ the map $f(x) = p_{\underline{A}}(x,a)$. Maps obtained in this way are called <u>algebraic (vector) maps</u> in $\underline{A}$. Let $L_f = \{ f^i(\perp,\ldots,\perp) : i \in \omega \}$. A subset $X \subseteq A$ is called an <u>iteration</u> if there is $n \in \omega$ and an algebraic map $f: A \to A$ such that $X = e_o^n(L_f)$. Subsets of iterations play essentially the same role for regular algebras as directed sets for Δ-continuous algebras (cf. [2])

An ordered Σ-algebra $\underline{A}$ is said to be a <u>regular algebra</u> if for any $n \in \omega$ and for any algebraic map $f: A^n \to A^n$ the following conditions hold:

(3.1) the set L_f has least upper bound in A^n;

(3.2) $f(\sup L_f) = \sup L_f$.

In other words, regular algebras are all those ordered algebras where every finite system of fixed-point polynomial equations with arbitrary parameters can be solved by taking a least upper bound of a ω-chain of iterations. It can be easily shown that $\sup L_f$ is the least solution of the equation $x = p_{\underline{A}}(x,a)$. Denote this solution by $(p_{\underline{A}})^\nabla(a)$. This gives rise to a map $(p_{\underline{A}})^\nabla : A^k \to A^n$. Call each map f of the form $\overline{f} = (p_{\underline{A}})^\nabla_o$ for some $p \in T_{\Sigma(\perp)}(n+k)^n$, $n,k \in \omega$, a <u>regular polynomial</u> in $\underline{A}$.

Condition (3.1) expresses a weaker notion of completeness of the carrier (weaker than, for example, chain-completeness), while condition (3.2) expresses a weaker notion of continuity of operations (weaker than, for example, chain-continuity). This definition, in our opinion, links much better *algebraic* and *order aspects* of algebras in question, and is more suitable for computer science purposes as there are natural examples of regular algebras (defined on infinite trees) where the stronger notion of completeness of the carrier fails (cf. [10]) as well as examples where the stronger notion of continuity of operations fails (cf. [13]). There are also natural examples (connected with semantics of nondeterministic recursive procedures, (cf.[13]) where arbitrary finite systems of fixed-point polynomial equations *without* parameters can be solved within of ω-steps of iterations, while allowing parameters causes usually more than ω-steps.

Let $\underline{A}$, $\underline{B}$ be regular Σ-algebras. A map $h: A \to B$ is said to be a <u>regular homomorphism</u> if it is strict (i.e. $h(\perp) = \perp$) Σ-homomorhism that preserves lub's of iterations (i.e. if $E \subseteq A$ is an iteration, then $h(\sup E) = \sup h(E)$ ($\sup h(E)$ exists because $h(E)$ is an iteration in $\underline{B}$).

Now we will give an important class of examples of regular algebras. Let Σ be a signature and X a set. Let $R_\Sigma(X) = R_\Sigma(X \cup \{\perp\})$ (we assume that $\perp \notin X$).

We define a partial order on $R_\Sigma(X)$ in the following way:

$t \leq t'$ iff one obtains t' replacing some occurences of $\perp$ in t by some elements of $R_\Sigma(X)$

$R_\Sigma(X)$ is an obvious way a Σ-algebra (isomorphic, as algebra, to $\overline{R}_\Sigma(X \cup \{\perp\})$. It is also an ordered algebra with least element $\perp$. One can easily check that the carrier usually is not chain-complete.

Theorem 3.1 ([10])

$R_\Sigma(X)$ is a regular Σ-algebra freely generated by X, i.e. for any regular Σ-algebra $\underline{A}$ and for any map $f: X \to A$, there is exactly one extension of f to a regular homomorphism $\overline{f} : R_\Sigma(X) \to \underline{A}$.

Having free regular algebras one can define derived operations in a regular algebra, in the same way as it was done in section 2 for iterative algebras. In [11] it is shown that this notion coincides with the notion of a regular polynomial.

It also turns out (cf. [12]) that there are close connections between regular algebras and rational algebraic theories [1] , similar to those between iterative algebras and iterative theories, presented in section 2.

4. Formulation of problem

We are interested in a relationship between unique fixed points and least fixed points. The following problem arises naturally. Given an iterative Σ-algebra $\underline{A}$, is it possible to extend the carrier A to A_R and to define on A_R a partial order and a structure of Σ-algebra so that $\underline{A}_R$ becomes a regular algebra, and any solution of ideal system of equations in A is also the least solution of the same system in $\underline{A}_R$? Moreover, it is natural to require the construction $\underline{A} \to \underline{A}_R$ to be universal (cf.[7]), This leads to the following formulation.

An iterative Σ-algebra $\underline{A}$ is said to admit a regular extension if there is a regular algebra $\underline{A}_R$ and a map $\varphi_{\underline{A}} : A \to A_R$ such that

(4.1) for any $n,k \in \omega$, and for any ideal

$p \in T_\Sigma(n+k)^n$, $\varphi_{\underline{A}}\ (p_{\underline{A}})^+ = (p_{\underline{A}_R})^\nabla\ \varphi_{\underline{A}}$;

(4.2) for any regular Σ-algebra $\underline{B}$ and for any map $f: A \to B$ satisfying

$f(p_{\underline{A}})^+ = (p_{\underline{B}})^\nabla f$ for all ideal $p \in T_\Sigma(n+k)^n$, $n,k \in \omega$,

there is exactly one regular homomorhism

$f^* : \underline{A}_R \to \underline{B}$ with $f^* \varphi_A = f$

The pair $(\varphi_{\underline{A}}, \underline{A}_R)$ is called a regular extension of $\underline{A}$.

An iterative algebra $\underline{A}$ is said to admit a faithful regular extension if there is a regular extension $(\varphi_{\underline{A}}, \underline{A}_R)$ with $\varphi_{\underline{A}}$ being injective.

We consider in this paper the following questions.

(4.3) Does every iterative algebra admit a faithful regular extension? (this was our original motivation).

(4.4) Does every iterative algebra admit a regular extension?

We will see in the next section that the answer to (4.3) is negative, while the main result of this paper solves (4.4) in affirmative. The following standard result (cf. [7]) shows that every iterative algebra admits *at most one* (up to isomorphism) regular extension.

Proposition 4.1

If $(\varphi_{\underline{A}}, \underline{A}_R)$ and $(\Psi_{\underline{A}}, \underline{A}'_R)$ are regular extension of an iterative algebra $\underline{A}$, then there is a regular isomorphism $\xi : \underline{A}_R \to \underline{A}'_R$ with $\xi \varphi_{\underline{A}} = \Psi_{\underline{A}}$.

5. Regular extensions of iterative algebras

The construction of a regular extension for an arbitrary iterative algebra will be given in four steps. We sketch here only basic steps; the full construction is given in [14].

Let $\underline{A}$ be an arbitrary iterative Σ-algebra.

5.1 (*the congruence* $\equiv \underline{A}$).

For $n \in \omega$, $p \in \overline{R}_\Sigma(A)^n$ let $p^{\underline{A}} \in A^n$ be a vector defined by $p_i^{\underline{A}} = f(p_i)$ (for $i < n$), where $f: \overline{R}_\Sigma(A) \to \underline{A}$ is the unique extension of $id_A : A \to A$ to a Σ-homomorphism (cf. Theorem 2.3 (iii)).

On the set $R_\Sigma(A)$ (notice: without overbar) we define a binary relation $\equiv \underline{A}$ in the following way: for $t, t' \in R_\Sigma(A)$, $t \equiv_{\underline{A}} t'$ iff there are $n \in \omega$, $q \in R_\Sigma(n)$, $p, p' \in \overline{R}_\Sigma(A)^n$ such that

(5.1.1) $t = q[p]$, $t' = q[p']$;

(5.1.2) $p^{\underline{A}} = p'^{\underline{A}}$.

Proposition 5.1.1

$\equiv_{\underline{A}}$ is a Σ-congruence on $R_\Sigma(A)$.

5.2 (*quasi-order relations* $\leqslant_\alpha, \alpha \in \underline{\text{Ord}}$).

Let $\underline{A}^* = R_\Sigma(A)/_{\equiv_{\underline{A}}}$. On A^* we define a sequence of binary relations

$\leq_{\alpha}$, $\alpha \in$ Ord. For $t \in R_{\Sigma}(A)$, $|t|$ denotes the $\equiv$ equivalence class determined by t.

(0.) $\leq_{0} = \leq$, i.e. we extend partial order $\leq$ in $R_{\Sigma}(A)$ to subsets (cf. section 1).

(α+1.) If $\alpha \in$ Ord and $t, t' \in R_{\Sigma}(A)$ then we define $|t| \leq_{\alpha+1} |t'|$ iff there exist $n \in \omega$ and iterations $E_{0},\dots,E_{n}$ in $R_{\Sigma}(A)$ such that

(5.2.1) $\sup E_{0} \equiv_{A} t$;

(5.2.2) for every $i < n$ and for every $x \in E_{i}$, $|x| \leq_{\alpha} |\sup E_{i+1}|$;

(5.2.3) for every $x \in E_{n}$, $|x| \leq_{\alpha} |t'|$.

(α-limit.) If $0 < \alpha$ is a limit ordinal then $\leq_{\alpha} = \bigcup_{\beta<\alpha} \leq_{\beta}$

The next result collects the basic properties of $\leq_{\alpha}$'s.

Proposition 5.2.1

(i) For each $\alpha \in$ Ord, $\leq_{\alpha}$ is reflexive and transitive.

(ii) If $\alpha < \beta$ then $\leq_{\alpha} \subseteq \leq_{\beta}$.

(iii) For each $\alpha \in$ Ord, all Σ-operations of A^* are $\leq_{\alpha}$-monotone.

(iV) For each $\alpha \in$ Ord, and for each $t \in R_{\Sigma}(A)$, $|\bot| \leq_{\alpha} |t|$.

5.3 (*the congruence* $\sim$).

It turns out that the first good candidate for a partial order to make A^* into a regular algebra is the quasi-order $\leq \omega_{1}$ (cf. remarks below), where ω_{1} is the first uncountable ordinal. This is suggested by the following result.

Proposition 5.3.1

Let $\tilde{E}$ be an arbitrary iteration in A^* .
There is an iteration E in $R_{\Sigma}(A)$ such that

(i) $|E| = \tilde{E}$;

(ii) for any $t \in R_{\Sigma}(A)$, if $|x| \leq_{\omega_{1}} |t|$ for all $x \in E$,
then $|\sup E| \leq_{\omega_{1}} |t|$;

(iii) for any $x \in E$, $|x| \leq_{\omega_{1}} |\sup E|$.

Remark: to prove part (ii) of the above result we essentially need the property of ω_{1} to be the least uncountable ordinal. For example, for $A = \langle R, f \rangle$, where R stands for reals and $f(x) = \frac{1}{2}x$, one easily proves that $\leq_{0}$ does not satisfy (ii).

In general $\leq\omega_{1}$ is not antisymetric (this point is connected with faithful extensions, (cf. remarks in 5.4) so we have to take a quotient of $\underline{A}^*$ by the relation $\sim$ defined as follows: for $t, t' \in R_\Sigma(A)$, $|t| \sim |t'|$ iff $|t| \leqslant_{\omega_1} |t'|$ and $|t'| \leqslant_{\omega_1} |t|$.

By Proposition 5.2.1 (iii), $\sim$ is a congruence relation on A^*. Denote by $\underline{A}_R$ the quotient algebra $\underline{A}^*/\sim$. For any $t \in R_\Sigma(A)$, denote by $||t||$ the $\sim$-equivalence class determined by $|t|$. The carrier, A_R is ordered by relation $\sqsubseteq$ defined as follows: for $t, t' \in R_\Sigma(A)$, $||t|| \sqsubseteq ||t'||$ iff $|t| \leqslant_{\omega_1} |t'|$.

Propositions 5.2.1 and 5.3.1 imply the following result.

<u>Proposition 5.3.2</u>

$\underline{A}_R$ is a regular Σ-algebra with bottom element $||\bot||$.

<u>5.4</u> (*the main result*).

<u>Theorem 5.4</u>

(i) $(\varphi_{\underline{A}}, \underline{A}_R)$ is a regular extension of $\underline{A}$, where $\varphi_{\underline{A}}(a) = ||a||$ for $a \in A$.

(ii) $\underline{A}$ admits a faithful regular extension iff $\sim$ restricted to the set $\{|a| : a \in A\}$ is equality relation.

(iii) $\underline{A}$ admits a faithful regular extension iff $\leqslant_{\omega_1}$ is a partial order; and in this case $\underline{A}^*$ and $\underline{A}_R$ are isomorphic.

<u>6. Examples</u>

(6.1) One can easily check that the regular extension of $\overline{R_\Sigma(X)}$ is isomorphic to $R_\Sigma(X)$.

(6.2) Let $\underline{A} = \langle R, f \rangle$, where R stands for reals and $f(x) = \frac{1}{2}x$ (cf. remark following Proposition 5.3.1). It can be shown that $\underline{A}$ admits a faithful regular extension, and $\underline{A}_R$ can be presented pictorially as follows:

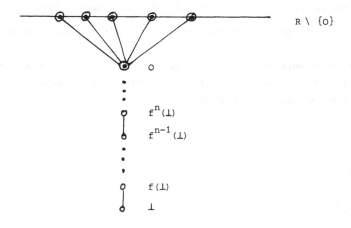

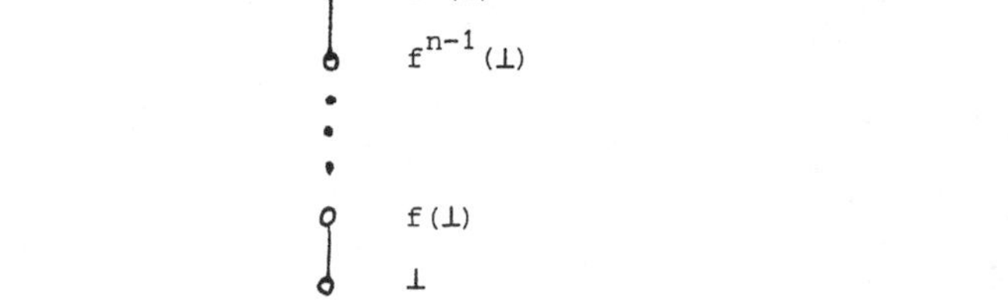

Operation f is defined in $\underline{A}_R$ naturally.

(6.3) Let $\underline{A} = < R,f,g, >$, where R and f are as before, and

$g(x) = \frac{1}{2}x + \frac{1}{2}$.

Theorem 6.1

The algebras $\underline{A}$ defined in (6.3) does not admit a faithful regular extension. More exactly, in each regular extension the elements 0 and 1 have to be collapsed.

Proof. By showing that $|0| \leqslant_1 |1|$ and $|1| \leqslant_1 |0|$.

7. Concluding remarks

The following problems seem to be worth of solving, as answers to them should throw a bit more light on relationships between unique and least fixed points.

7.1 We conjecture that for any iterative algebra $\underline{A}$ the regular extension $(\varphi_{\underline{A}}, \underline{A}_R)$ is such that $\underline{A}_R$ is still an iterative algebra. If this is true, then it would mean that the category of iterative regular Σ-algebras with regular homomorphisms is a *reflexive* subcategory of the catogory of iterative Σ-algebras with Σ-homomorphisms.

7.2 Is the algebra $\underline{A}^*$ iterative? This question is connected with 7.1 since for an iterative algebra $\underline{A}$ admiting faithful regular extension, $\underline{A}^* \cong \underline{A}_R$ (cf. Theorem 5.4 (iii)).

7.3 Observe that algebras $\underline{A}^*$ and $\underline{A}_R$ are quotient algebras of $R_\Sigma(A)$. Thus the following problem seems to be natural. Characterize those congruences $\sim$ on $R_\Sigma(X)$ for which $R_\Sigma(X)/\sim$ becomes an iterative algebra.

7.4 Necessary and sufficient conditions on an iterative algebra to admit a faithful regular extension, found in Theorem 5.4 are not satisfactory. Find simpler conditions. One possible way to achieve this would be as follows.

7.5 Define on A^* a sequence of equivalence relations $(\sim_\alpha, \alpha \in \underline{\text{Ord}})$ by $|t| \sim_\alpha |t'|$ iff $|t| \leqslant_\alpha |t'|$ and $|t'| \leqslant_\alpha |t|$.

Theorem 5.4 (iii) states that $\underline{A}$ admits a faithful regular extension iff $\sim_{\omega_1}$ is that $\sim_1 = \sim_{\omega_1}$? If it is, then it would provice a simpler characterization mentioned in 7.4.

7.6 Find concrete representations of regular extensions of various known iterative theories (like: theories of sequacious functions, and various matricial thories, (cf. [4]). Do they admit faithful extensions?

References

[1] ADJ (Authors: Goguen, J.A. / Thatcher, J.W. / Wagner, E.G. /Wright, J.B.) *Some fundamentals of order-algebraic semantics* Proceedings MFCS '76, Lecture Notes in Computer Science, No. 45, ed. Mazurkiewicz, A., Springer Verlag, 1976

[2] ADJ *Initial algebra semantics and continuous algebras* J.A.C.M. 24, (68-95), 1977

[3] Bloom, S.L. / Elgot, C.C. / Tindell, R. *The algebraic structure of rooted trees* J.C.S.S. 16, (362-399), 1978

[4] Elgot, C.C. *Monadic computation and iterative algebraic theories* Logic Colloquium '73 eds. Rose, H.E. / Shepherdson, J.C.,North-Holland Publishing Company, 1975

[5] Ginali, S. Ph. D. Dissertation, University of Chicago, 1976

[6] Lawvere, F.W. *Functional semantics of algebraic theories* Proc. Nat. Acad. Sci. 50, (869-872), 1963

[7] MacLane, S. Categories for the working mathematician Springer Verlag, 1971

[8] Nivat, M. *Languages algebraic sur le magma libre et semantique des schemas de programme* Automata Languages and Programming (293-308), ed. Nivat, M. North-Holland Publishing Company, 1973

[9] Scott, D. *The lattice of flow diagrams* Lecture Notes in Mathematics, No. 188, Springer Verlag, 1971

[10] Tiuryn, J. *Fixed points and algebras with infinitely long expressions Part I. Regular algebras* Proceedings MFCS '77, Lecture Notes in Computer Science No. 53, ed. Gruska, J., Springer Verlag, 1977 The full version will appear in Fundamente Informaticae

[11] Tiuryn, J. *Fixed points and algebras with infinitely long expressions Part II. μ-clones of regular algebras* Proceedings FCT '77, Lecture Notes in Computer Science No. 56, ed. Karpiński, M., Springer Verlag, 1977 The full version will appear in Fundamenta Informaticae

[12] Tiuryn, J. *On a connection between regular algebras and rational algebraic theories* Proceedings of the second Workshop on Categorical and Algebraic Methods in Computer Science and System Theory, Dortmund, 1978

[13] Tiuryn, J. *Continuity problems in the power-set algebra of infinite trees* To be presented at the Forth Workshop on Trees in Algebra and Programming, Lille, February 1979

[14] Tiuryn, J. *Unique fixed points vs. least fixed points* Schriften zur Informatik und Angewandten Mathematik, RWTH Aachen, Bericht Nr. 49, November 1978

A MODIFICATION OF THE LR(k) METHOD FOR CONSTRUCTING COMPACT BOTTOM-UP PARSERS

(Extended Abstract)

Esko Ukkonen

Department of Computer Science, University of Helsinki
Tukholmankatu 2, SF-00250 Helsinki 25, Finland

Abstract. A subclass of context-free grammars properly between the PLR(k) and the LR(k) grammars is defined. Grammars in this class, called the weak PLR(k) grammars, generate the LR(k) languages. A construction of a deterministic bottom-up parser for weak PLR(k) grammars is given based on the same collection of sets of LR(k) items as the standard construction of LR(k) parsers. The resulting parsers use the parsing stack in a way which resembles LL(k) parsing and simplifies the optimization of the parser. Finally some optimization methods are described.

1. Introduction

The original algorithm by Knuth [10] for the construction of a parser for an LR(k) grammar produces parsers that are often too large for practical use. Several modified techniques have therefore been proposed to produce parsers of practical size. The SLR(k) and LALR(k) methods given by DeRemer [5] are the best-known techniques.

In addition, much effort has been devoted to developing transformations on sets of LR(k) tables that make the parser smaller and faster. Such methods include the merging of compatible states, the use of default actions in parsing, and the elimination of reductions by single productions; see e.g. [2,3] and the references in [4, p. 244].

In this extended abstract we present a deterministic bottom-up parsing technique which is applicable to a subclass of context-free grammars properly between the PLR(k) grammars [12] and the LR(k) grammars. These grammars, called the weak PLR(k) grammars, are LR(k) grammars satisfying an additional condition. The condition is rather insignificant since the LR(k) grammars used in practice usually satisfy it. Moreover, there is a simple method for transforming all LR(k) grammars into the weak PLR(k) form. Hence the parsable grammars generate all the deterministic languages when $k > 0$.

Our parsing technique, the weak PLR(k) parsing, is a modification of the LR(k) methods (the canonical LR(k), SLR(k), and LALR(k) methods) in the sense that the construction of the parsing tables can be based on the same collection of sets of LR(k) items as the construction of the usual LR(k) tables. It is therefore easy to modify an LR(k) parser generator such that it produces a weak PLR(k) parser.

The main difference between the new method and the conventional LR(k) methods is in the parsing algorithm, i.e. in the way the parsing tables direct the parsing process. Generally speaking, in weak PLR(k) parsing the parsing stack is used as in the LL(k) parsing - the well-known deterministic top-down parsing method. This means that the parsing algorithm is not as natural as the usual LR(k) parsing algorithm for bottom-up parsing. On the other hand, the optimization of a weak PLR(k) parser is in many cases an essentially simpler task than that of LR(k) parsers since the optimization techniques of LL(k) parsing can be used. In fact, some simple and effective optimizations should always be included in the parser construction. Although the unoptimized version of a weak PLR(k) parser is rather slow and large, the elimination of redundant states and reductions by single productions often leads to parsers which seem competitive with optimized LR(k) parsers.

In Section 2 we first informally describe the parsing method and its background. Grammatical conditions specifying the parsable grammars for the method will be given in Section 3. Then in Section 4 we define the parsing algorithm and give the parser construction. Finally in Section 5 we present different optimizations and demonstrate their use in examples.

We presume that the reader is familiar with the LR(k) and LL(k) parsing as described in [1,2], and make free use of the notations and definitions given in these references concerning strings, grammars, and LR(k) parsing. We recall that (1) $G = (N,\Sigma,P,S)$ denotes a (context-free) grammar where N is the set of nonterminals, Σ is the set of terminals, P is the set of productions, S is the start symbol, (2) A, B, C denote nonterminals, (3) a, b, c, d denote terminals, (4) X, Y, Z denote nonterminals or terminals, (5) x, y, z, u, v, w denote terminal strings and α, β, γ general strings, and (6) ε denotes the empty string.

2. Informal description of the parsing method

When a move *reduce i* is encountered in LR(k) parsing, the right-hand side of production i or the *handle* is guaranteed to be a suffix of the string of grammar symbols on the parsing stack. The symbols corresponding to the right-hand side are removed from the stack, leaving an LR(k) table T on the top. Then the left-hand side A of production i and a new table g(T,A) are inserted on the top. Here g denotes the *goto* function of the parser.

Thus the depth of the reduction of the stack is not a constant, but depends on the length of the right-hand side of the production. We feel that this irregularity often makes the optimization of LR(k) parsers difficult. The purpose of this paper is to develop a parser in which the depth of reductions is *constantly one*. This is achieved if the parser is always able to represent with only one symbol all the tables which will be removed from the stack in the same reduction step.

To this end the parser must be able to decide whether the symbol on the top of of the stack represents the first symbol or the *left corner* in a handle in which it will finally be removed. (Thus at this stage it is not needed decide for the left corner the corresponding production or its left-hand side. Hence the method is more general than the left corner parsing [11] or the PLR(k) parsing [12].) As in the LR(k) parsing, the parser must also be able to decide whether or not the top symbol represents the last symbol of a handle and which is the left-hand side of the reduction to be done next. The above decisions are made deterministically based on the current stack and the k symbol lookahead.

As an illustration consider the action of the method when the length of the lookahead is one and the grammar has between the start symbol S and a right sentential form AaBEbcd a parse tree of the form

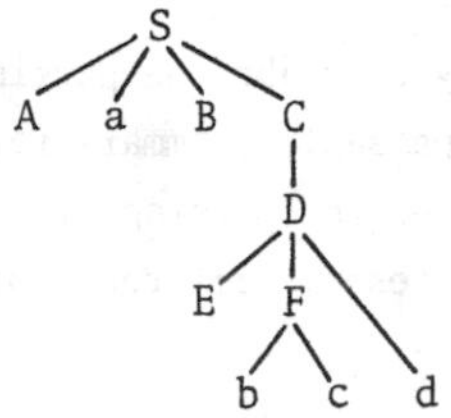

Before scanning b, the parsing stack contains symbols [{D,D',D''},E] and [{S},AaBΔ] with [{D,D',D''},E] on the top, corresponding to the "incomplete handles" E and AaB. (This representation, which is convenient for illustration, is not precisely the same as that used in the formal definitions in Section 4.) Notation {S} indicates in [{S},AaBΔ] that after recognizing A the parser has decided on the basis of the stack and the lookahead a that A will be a left corner of S. Similarly, {D,D',D''} indicates in [{D,D',D''},E] that E must in this context be a left corner and the set of possible left-hand sides is {D,D',D''}. Thus the parser does not know the left-hand side precisely. The same thing is also indicated by Δ in [{S},AaBΔ]. Intuitively, Δ denotes the place reserved for D.

In this configuration of parsing, the next move is to replace [{D,D',D''},E] by string b [{D,D',D''},Eb]. Thereafter the parser scans b and removes the top symbol b from the stack in the same time.

A step characteristic of our method follows. The parser decides that the scanned symbol b is a left corner. Suppose that the possible left-hand sides for left corner b in this context are F and F'. Then the next move is to split the current top symbol [{D,D',D''},Eb] into [{F,F'},b][{D,D',D''},EΔ]. The parser then replaces the new top symbol [{F,F'},b] by c [{F,F'},bc], scans c, and removes c from the top.

The next step is a reduction because bc is a handle. The parser decides that the left-hand side is F, announces production F → bc, removes [{F,F'},bc] from the stack, and finally replaces the top symbol [{D,D',D''},EΔ] by [{D,D',D''},EF]. This replacement in which Δ is fixed to be F corresponds to the use of the goto function in the usual LR parsing. Next, [{D,D',D''},EF] will be replaced by d [{D,D',D''},EFd], and so on.

It is often possible to avoid some moves corresponding to the use of the goto function. In terms of the above example, if we can already decide in the splitting phase of [{D,D',D''},Eb] that the left-hand side of the production with left corner b is F, then [{D,D',D''},Eb] may be replaced by [{F},b][{D,D',D''},EF] instead of [{F,F'},b] [{D,D',D''},EΔ]. Hence the parser avoids the later replacement of [{D,D',D''},EΔ] by [{D,D',D''},EF].

There are some bottom-up parsing methods resembling the method described, particularly in their way of using the stack. We mention only the production prefix parsing [6], the multiple stack parsing [7,8], the strict deterministic parsing [9], and the PLR(k) parsing [12]. Our approach is, however, more general than these methods.

3. Weak PLR(k) grammars

In this section the weak PLR(k) grammars will be grammatically defined and analyzed. First some preliminary definitions are given.

For a grammar $G = (N,\Sigma,P,S)$, the *augmented grammar* is the grammar $G' = (N \cup \{S'\}, \Sigma \cup \{\perp\}, P \cup \{S' \to \perp S\}, S')$ where S' is not in N and $\perp$ is not in Σ. Notation $\underline{\alpha}\beta \overset{*}{\Rightarrow}_{rm} \underline{\alpha}\gamma$ means that $\alpha\beta \overset{*}{\Rightarrow}_{rm} \alpha\gamma$ and $\beta \overset{*}{\Rightarrow}_{rm} \gamma$.

We shall now define the class of the weak PLR(k) grammars. A grammar $G = (N,\Sigma,P,S)$ is *weak PLR(k)*, $k \geq 0$, if it is LR(k) [1] and if in the augmented grammar G' for each production $A \to X\beta$, $X\beta \neq \varepsilon$, the conditions

(1) $S' \overset{*}{\Rightarrow}_{rm} \alpha A w \Rightarrow_{rm} \underline{\alpha X}\beta w \overset{*}{\Rightarrow}_{rm} \underline{\alpha X}yw$

(2) $S' \overset{*}{\Rightarrow}_{rm} \alpha' B w' \Rightarrow_{rm} \underline{\alpha\alpha'' X}\gamma w' \overset{*}{\Rightarrow}_{rm} \underline{\alpha'\alpha'' X}y'w'$

(3) $\alpha'\alpha'' = \alpha$ and $FIRST_k(yw) = FIRST_k(y'w')$

always imply that $\alpha = \alpha'$.

The parsing method described in Section 2 suggests the above definition for parsable grammars as follows. A parsable grammar must be LR(k) in order that the parser is able to decide the reductions deterministically. The additional condition in the definition of weak PLR(k) grammars guarantees that the parser is able to recognize the left corners deterministically.

The definition of the weak PLR(k) grammars is an extension of the definition of the PLR(k) grammars [12]. A grammar G is said to be PLR(k), $k \geq 0$, if it is LR(k) and if in the augmented grammar G' the conditions (1), (2), (3) always imply that $\alpha = \alpha'$ and $A = B$. We evidently have:

Theorem 1. PLR(k) grammars $\subsetneq$ weak PLR(k) grammars $\subsetneq$ LR(k) grammars. □

The next theorem gives some idea of the extent of the class of the weak PLR(k) grammars.

Theorem 2. (i) Every LR(k) grammar such that the length of each right-hand side of the productions is ≤ 2 is weak PLR(k).

(ii) Every LR(k) grammar in Greibach normal form is weak PLR(k). □

Corollary. The weak PLR(k) grammars generate the LR(k) languages. In particular, if $k > 0$, then weak PLR(k) grammars generate all the deterministic languages. □

Theorem 2 (i) implies that an LR(k) grammar in Chomsky normal form is always weak PLR(k). In addition, every LR(k) grammar G is easily transformed into an equivalent weak PLR(k) grammar. For each production $A \to X_1X_2\ldots X_n$ of G the new grammar contains production $A \to X_1X_2\ldots X_n$ if $n \leq 2$, and otherwise the productions $A \to X_1[X_2\ldots X_n]$, $[X_2\ldots X_n] \to X_2[X_3\ldots X_n]$, ... , $[X_{n-2}X_{n-1}X_n] \to X_{n-2}[X_{n-1}X_n]$, $[X_{n-1}X_n] \to X_{n-1}X_n$, where each $[X_i\ldots X_n]$ is a new nonterminal symbol. For example, a grammar with productions

$$S \to A \qquad A \to xxA \qquad B \to xB$$
$$S \to B \qquad A \to a \qquad B \to b$$

is LR(1) but not weak PLR(k) for any $k \geq 0$. The above transformation yields for this grammar an equivalent weak PLR(1) grammar with productions

$$S \to A \qquad A \to x[xA] \qquad B \to xB$$
$$S \to B \qquad [xA] \to xA \qquad B \to b$$
$$A \to a$$

4. Parser construction

In this section we present the weak PLR(k) parsing algorithm and a method for constructing the parsing tables. The construction is illustrated by an example.

The *configurations* of the weak PLR(k) parsing algorithm are presented by triples $(x, X\alpha, \pi)$ where x in Σ^* is the unused portion of the input string, $X\alpha$ the string on the pushdown stack (with X on top), and π the string on the output tape. The pushdown alphabet contains symbols:

(1) the terminals Σ of the grammar,

(2) the production numbers of the grammar ($\langle A \to \alpha \rangle$ denotes the number of a production $A \to \alpha$), and

(3) the states.

The set of the states consists of disjoint sets of the *open* states K_o and the *closed* states K_c. The output alphabet consists of the production numbers.

The actions of the parsing algorithm are determined by the *parsing table* M and the *goto table* M_g. For a grammar $G = (N, \Sigma, P, S)$ and for an integer $k \geq 0$, M_g is a mapping from $K_o \times N$ to strings of pushdown stack symbols, and M is a mapping from $K_c \times \Sigma^{*k}$ to a set containing:

(1) all strings of pushdown stack symbols,

(2) *accept*, and

(3) *error*.

As usual, we shall represent the *moves* of the weak PLR(k) parsing algorithm in terms of a relation $\vdash$ on the set of configurations. We have the possibilities:

(P1) $(x, a\alpha, \pi) \vdash (x', \alpha, \pi)$ if $x = ax'$,

(P2) $(x, X\alpha, \pi) \vdash (x, \beta\alpha, \pi)$ if X is a closed state and $\beta = M(X, FIRST_k(x))$, and

(P3) $(x, \langle A\to\gamma\rangle X\alpha, \pi) \vdash (x, \beta\alpha, \pi\langle A\to\gamma\rangle)$ if X is an open state and $\beta = M_g(X,A)$ or X is not an open state and $\beta = X$.

The parsing algorithm *accepts* a terminal string x if $(x, X_0, \varepsilon) \vdash^* (\varepsilon, accept, \pi)$ holds for some π. Here the closed state X_0 is a designated *initial state* and π is the right parse of x. If $(x, X_0, \varepsilon) \vdash^* (x', \alpha, \pi)$ such that $(x', \alpha, \pi) \neq (\varepsilon, accept, \pi)$ and the next configuration is not defined by rules (P1), (P2) or (P3), then parsing ceases and an error is reported. Usually in this case the top symbol of α is *error*.

Next, an algorithm is presented which computes tables M and M_g. The construction is based on the same collections of sets of LR(k) items as the usual construction of LR(k), SLR(k) or LALR(k) tables. The canonical collection of sets of LR(k) items for a grammar G and integer $k \geq 0$ can be computed as described in [1,2]. By the SLR(k) collection of sets of LR(k) items for G we mean a collection which is obtained from S_0, the canonical collection of sets of LR(0) items for G, by replacing every item $[A \to \alpha.\beta, \varepsilon]$ in each set of S_0 by items $[A \to \alpha.\beta, u]$ for all u in $FOLLOW_k(A)$. By the LALR(k) collection of sets of LR(k) items for G we mean a collection which is obtained from the canonical collection of sets of LR(k) items by merging the sets with identical cores.

Algorithm 1. Let S be the canonical or the SLR(k) or the LALR(k) collection of sets of LR(k) items, $k \geq 0$, for a grammar $G = (N,\Sigma,P,S)$. To compute weak PLR(k) parsing tables M and M_g for G the following method can be used.

1. Parsing table M is defined on $K_c \times \Sigma^{*k}$ and goto table M_g is defined on $K_o \times N$ using steps 2, 3 and 4. Initially, K_c contains a state T for each set of items $\tilde{T}$ in S, and K_o is empty. In steps 2 and 3 some new closed states of the form [T,X] where X is in $N \cup \Sigma$ are added into K_c and open states of the form $[T,\Delta]$ are added into K_o.
2. For each state T in K_c with a corresponding set of items $\tilde{T}$ in S and for each u in Σ^{*k} set

$$M(T,u) = \begin{cases} a[T,a] & \text{if an item } [A \to \alpha.a\beta, v] \text{ is in } \tilde{T} \text{ and } u \text{ is in } FIRST_k(a\beta v);\\ & \text{add } [T,a] \text{ to } K_c.\\ \langle A\to\gamma\rangle & \text{if } [A \to \gamma., u] \text{ is in } \tilde{T} \text{ and } \gamma \neq \varepsilon.\\ \langle A\to\varepsilon\rangle[T,A] & \text{if } [A \to ., u] \text{ is in } \tilde{T}\text{; add } [T,A] \text{ to } K_c.\\ accept & \text{if } [S' \to S., \varepsilon] \text{ is in } \tilde{T} \text{ and } u = \varepsilon. \end{cases}$$

   Then repeat step 3 until no changes are possible.
3. For each state [T,X] in K_c where T corresponds to a set of items $\tilde{T}$ in S and for each u in Σ^{*k} set

$$M([T,X],u) = \begin{cases} T' & \text{if } \tilde{T}' = GOTO(\tilde{T},X) \text{ in } S \text{ and } \tilde{T}' \text{ contains an item } [A \to \alpha X.\beta,v] \\ & \text{such that } \alpha \neq \varepsilon \text{ and } u \in FIRST_k(\beta v)\text{, or } \tilde{T}' \text{ contains item} \\ & [S' \to S.,\varepsilon] \text{ and } u = \varepsilon. \\ T'[T,Y] & \text{if } \tilde{T}' = GOTO(\tilde{T},X) \text{ in } S \text{ and } Y \text{ is the only element of set } L = \\ & \{Z \mid [Z \to X.\beta,v] \in \tilde{T} \text{ and } u \in FIRST_k(\beta v)\}\text{; add } [T,Y] \text{ to } K_c. \\ T'[T,\Delta] & \text{if } \tilde{T}' = GOTO(\tilde{T},X) \text{ in } S \text{ and the above set L contains at least} \\ & \text{two elements. Then add the open state } [T,\Delta] \text{ to } K_o \text{ and for} \\ & \text{each Z in L, define } M_g([T,\Delta],Z) = [T,Z] \text{ and add } [T,Z] \text{ to } K_c. \end{cases}$$

4. If some entry of M or M_g is not defined by step 2 or 3 make it *error*. The initial state is the closed state T_0 which corresponds to the unique set of items $\tilde{T}_0$ containing the item $[S' \to .S,\varepsilon]$. □

The validity of the weak PLR(k) parsing is considered in the following theorems.

Theorem 3. If tables M and M_g are uniquely determined by Algorithm 1 then they are valid parsing tables of the weak PLR(k) parsing algorithm for G, that is, the parsing algorithm with tables M and M_g defines $(x,X_0,\varepsilon) \vdash^* (\varepsilon, accept, \pi)$ if and only if π is a right parse of x in G. □

Theorem 4. A grammar G is weak PLR(k) if and only if Algorithm 1 determines unique tables M and M_g from the canonical collection of sets of LR(k) items for G.

Proof outline. Grammar G is LR(k) if and only if step 2 of Algorithm 1 produces unique entries, and G satisfies the special weak PLR(k) condition if and only if step 3 of Algorithm 1 produces unique entries in tables M and M_g. □

By Theorems 3 and 4, weak PLR(k) parsing is a valid bottom-up parsing method for weak PLR(k) grammars. A similar result is also true for SLR(k) or LALR(k) grammars satisfying the special weak PLR(k) condition. That is, Algorithm 1 produces from the SLR(k) or, respectively, LALR(k) collection of sets of LR(k) items for such grammars valid weak PLR(k) parsing tables.

Example 1. As an illustration of the construction of a weak PLR(1) parser consider a grammar G_1 with productions

1. $S \to A$	4. $A \to a$
2. $S \to B$	5. $B \to cBc$
3. $A \to cAc$	6. $B \to b$

To construct tables M and M_g for G_1 we first compute the LALR(1) collection of sets of LR(1) items for G_1. The resulting collection with the GOTO graph is shown in Fig. 1. From this collection we construct tables M and M_g, shown in Figures 2 and 3. The blank spaces in tables are supposed to be filled with *error*. There are 24 closed and two open states for G_1.

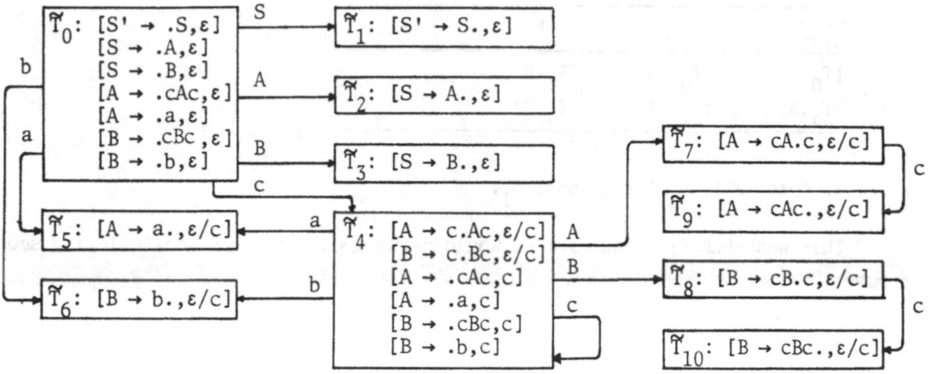

Figure 1. The GOTO graph of the LALR(1) collection of sets of LR(1) items for G_1.

closed state	a	b	c	ε
T_0	$a[T_0,a]$	$b[T_0,b]$	$c[T_0,c]$	
$[T_0,a]$			$T_5[T_0,A]$	$T_5[T_0,A]$
$[T_0,b]$			$T_6[T_0,B]$	$T_6[T_0,B]$
T_5			$\langle A \to a\rangle$	$\langle A \to a\rangle$
T_6			$\langle B \to b\rangle$	$\langle B \to b\rangle$
$[T_0,A]$				$T_2[T_0,S]$
$[T_0,B]$				$T_3[T_0,S]$
T_2				$\langle S \to A\rangle$
T_3				$\langle S \to B\rangle$
$[T_0,S]$				T_1
T_1				*accept*
$[T_0,c]$	$T_4[T_0,A]$	$T_4[T_0,B]$	$T_4[T_0,\Delta]$	
T_4	$a[T_4,a]$	$b[T_4,b]$	$c[T_4,c]$	
$[T_4,a]$			$T_5[T_4,A]$	$T_5[T_4,A]$
$[T_4,b]$			$T_6[T_4,B]$	$T_6[T_4,B]$
$[T_4,c]$	$T_4[T_4,A]$	$T_4[T_4,B]$	$T_4[T_4,\Delta]$	
$[T_4,A]$			T_7	
$[T_4,B]$			T_8	
T_7			$c[T_7,c]$	
T_8			$c[T_8,c]$	
$[T_7,c]$			T_9	T_9
$[T_8,c]$			T_{10}	T_{10}
T_9			$\langle A \to cAc\rangle$	$\langle A \to cAc\rangle$
T_{10}			$\langle B \to cBc\rangle$	$\langle B \to cBc\rangle$

Figure 2. Parsing table M for grammar G_1.

open state	A	B	S
$[T_0,\Delta]$	$[T_0,A]$	$[T_0,B]$	
$[T_4,\Delta]$	$[T_4,A]$	$[T_4,B]$	

Figure 3. Goto table M_g for grammar G_1.

This weak PLR(1) parser for G_1 would parse input ccacc in the following sequence of moves.

$$
\begin{aligned}
(\text{ccacc},T_0,\varepsilon) &\vdash (\text{ccacc},\ c[T_0,c],\ \varepsilon)\\
&\vdash (\text{cacc}\ ,\ [T_0,c],\ \varepsilon)\\
&\vdash (\text{cacc},\ T_4[T_0,\Delta],\ \varepsilon)\\
&\ \ \vdots\\
&\vdash (\varepsilon,\ T_9[T_0,\Delta],\ \langle A\to a\rangle\langle A\to cAc\rangle)\\
&\vdash (\varepsilon,\ \langle A\to cAc\rangle[T_0,\Delta],\ \langle A\to a\rangle\langle A\to cAc\rangle)\\
&\vdash (\varepsilon,\ [T_0,A],\ \langle A\to a\rangle\langle A\to cAc\rangle\langle A\to cAc\rangle)\\
&\vdash (\varepsilon,\ T_2[T_0,S],\ \langle A\to a\rangle\langle A\to cAc\rangle\langle A\to cAc\rangle)\\
&\vdash (\varepsilon,\ \langle S\to A\rangle[T_0,S],\ \langle A\to a\rangle\langle A\to cAc\rangle\langle A\to cAc\rangle)\\
&\vdash (\varepsilon,\ [T_0,S],\ \langle A\to a\rangle\langle A\to cAc\rangle\langle A\to cAc\rangle\langle S\to A\rangle)\\
&\vdash (\varepsilon,\ T_1,\ \langle A\to a\rangle\langle A\to cAc\rangle\langle A\to cAc\rangle\langle S\to A\rangle)\\
&\vdash (\varepsilon,\ \mathit{accept},\ \langle A\to a\rangle\langle A\to cAc\rangle\langle A\to cAc\rangle\langle S\to A\rangle).
\end{aligned}
$$

5. Optimization of the parser

It is obvious that the parser with tables produced by Algorithm 1 is relatively large and slow. Therefore we now give some effective optimizations to save space and time. The optimizations, in particular the substitution methods in Algorithms 2 and 3 and the elimination of reductions by single productions, are so simple that they should always be carried out.

Optimizations may result in a postponement of error checking. However, the optimized parser always has the correct prefix property that the shifted portion of the input is a prefix of some string in the language.

The first two optimizations are simple substitution methods. The "LL(k) nature" of weak PLR(k) parsers makes them possible. (The optimization of LL(k) parsers has been given little consideration in the literature. Hammer [7], however, analyzes the matter in detail. His optimizations seem more complicated than ours, the reason for this being that Hammer minimizes the underlying LL(k) grammar and we minimize the parsing tables.)

Algorithm 2. (*Substitution*) Given tables M and M_g produced by Algorithm 1 this algorithm eliminates closed states having identical non-error entries on the corresponding row in M. The optimized tables are denoted M' and M_g'.

1. Initially set $M' = M$ and $M'_g = M_g$. Then repeat step 2 until no changes are possible.
2. If there is a closed state C different from the initial state such that all the non-error entries on the corresponding row of M' have identically the same value, δ, then remove C from K_c and the corresponding row from M' and replace every occurrence of C in M' and M'_g by δ. □

When Algorithm 2 is applied on tables M and M_g shown in Figures 2 and 3, we obtain optimized tables in Figures 4 and 5, respectively. (In these figures the coding $<S \to A> = 1$, $<S \to B> = 2$, ... , is used.)

closed state	a	b	c	ε
T_0	a 4 1 *accept*	b 6 2 *accept*	$c[T_0,c]$	
$[T_0,c]$	T_4 1 *accept*	T_4 2 *accept*	$T_4[T_0,\Delta]$	
T_4	a 4 c 3	b 6 c 5	$c[T_4,c]$	
$[T_4,c]$	T_4 c 3	T_4 c 5	$T_4[T_4,\Delta]$	

Figure 4. Optimized parsing table M' for grammar G_1.

open state	A	B	S
$[T_0,\Delta]$	1 *accept*	2 *accept*	
$[T_4,\Delta]$	c 3	c 5	

Figure 5. Optimized goto table M'_g for grammar G_1.

The next optimization can be used to improve the result of Algorithm 2.

Algorithm 3. (*Lookahead substitution*) Given tables M' and M'_g produced by Algorithm 2 this algorithm transforms M' such that if $\gamma a \delta$ is an entry where a is a terminal of G, then γ contains only production numbers. The resulting table is denoted M". Table M'_g does not change.

1. Initially, M" = M'. Then repeat step 2 until no changes are possible, and then repeat step 3 until no changes are possible.
2. If there is in M" an entry M"(C,u) of the form $<A_1 \to \alpha_1>\ldots<A_n \to \alpha_n>C'\delta$, where $n \geq 0$ and C' is a closed state, then replace this occurrence of C' by the string in entry M"(C',u).
3. If C is a closed state different from the initial state such that C does not appear in the entries of M" and M'_g, except possibly in the entries of the row corresponding to C in M", then remove C from K_c and the corresponding row from M". □

Figure 6 shows the resulting table M" for G_1.

closed state	a	b	c	ε
T_0	a 4 1 *accept*	b 6 2 *accept*	c$[T_0,c]$	
$[T_0,c]$	a 4 c 3 1 *accept*	b 6 c 5 2 *accept*	c$[T_4,c][T_0,\Delta]$	
$[T_4,c]$	a 4 c 3 c 3	b 6 c 5 c 5	c$[T_4,c][T_4,\Delta]$	

Figure 6. Optimized parsing table M' for grammar G_1.

Finally we consider the use of default entries in parsing tables and the elimination of reductions by single productions. The use of default actions in parsing, a well-known optimization useful in list representation of parsers, can also be applied in weak PLR(k) parsers. The elimination of reductions by single productions (those of the form $A \to X$) has for usual LR(k) parsers received much attention [4, p.244]. For weak PLR(k) parsers we shall provide a straightforward solution.

Default entries. Since a weak PLR(k) parser checks every input symbol by comparing it with the top symbol of the stack in step (P1) of the parsing algorithm, every *error* entry in tables M and M_g (or in M' and M'_g) is redundant and can be replaced by some non-error entry, called the *default entry*, on the same row. The resulting parser still has the correct prefix property. To decrease the postponement of error detection it is advantageous to choose for the default entry an entry with a terminal of G as the first symbol.

Elimination of reductions by single productions. For each production $A \to X$ to be eliminated, replace every occurrence of $\langle A \to X \rangle$ in optimized tables M' and M'_g by the empty string. The replacement can also be made in unoptimized tables M and M_g. Then the only optimization effect is that the parser does not report reductions by single productions. To avoid also the related state transitions Algorithms 2 and 3 must then be applied.

We conclude with an example on parsing arithmetic expressions. The above optimizations and also a technique not considered so far, the merging of compatible states will be illustrated.

Example 2. Consider the grammar G_0 of [2] with productions

1. $E \to E + T$	4. $T \to F$
2. $E \to T$	5. $F \to (E)$
3. $T \to T * F$	6. $F \to a$

Starting from the SLR(1) collection of sets of LR(1) items given e.g. in [2, pp. 623-625] we arrive at optimized table M' for G_0 shown in Figure 7. Goto table M_g for G_0 is empty because G_0 is in fact a PLR(1) grammar.

The reductions by productions $E \to T$ and $T \to F$ are eliminated next. In the resulting table the entries for states $[T_0,E]$ and $[T_5,E]$ on input * are *don't care*

closed state	a	+	*	(	)	ε
T_0	a 6 4 $[T_0,T]$			(T_5 4 $[T_0,T]$		
$[T_0,T]$		2 + T_6 $[T_0,E]$	* T_7 $[T_0,T]$			2 *accept*
$[T_0,E]$		+ T_6 $[T_0,E]$				*accept*
T_6	a 6 4 $[T_6,T]$			(T_5 4 $[T_6,T]$		
$[T_6,T]$		1	* T_7 $[T_6,T]$		1	1
T_7	a 6 3			(T_5 3		
T_5	a 6 4 $[T_5,T]$			(T_5 4 $[T_5,T]$		
$[T_5,T]$		2 + T_6 $[T_5,E]$	* T_7 $[T_5,T]$		2) 5	
$[T_5,E]$		+ T_6 $[T_5,E]$			) 5	

Figure 7. Optimized parsing table M' for grammar G_0.

entries [2], that is, they are never consulted by the parser. Hence we may replace the former entry by * T_7 $[T_0,T]$ and the latter entry by * T_7 $[T_5,T]$ without destroying the validity of the table. Now states $[T_0,T]$ and $[T_0,E]$ as well as states $[T_5,T]$ and $[T_5,E]$ are identical. They can be merged, and so we finally obtain the table shown in Fig. 8 with 7 closed states and 18 non-error entries. (An optimized SLR(1) parser for G_0 is given in [3, p.120]. When comparing the weak PLR(1) parser constructed here to the SLR(1) parser it should be noted, that the entries of the weak PLR(1) parsing tables are strings while the entries of the usual LR(1) tables are single symbols.)

closed state	a	+	*	(	)	ε
T_0	a 6 $[T_0,T]$			(T_5 $[T_0,T]$		
$[T_0,T]$		+ T_6 $[T_0,T]$	* T_7 $[T_0,T]$			*accept*
T_6	a 6 $[T_6,T]$			(T_5 $[T_6,T]$		
$[T_6,T]$		1	* T_7 $[T_6,T]$		1	1
T_7	a 6 3			(T_5 3		
T_5	a 6 $[T_5,T]$			(T_5 $[T_5,T]$		
$[T_5,T]$		+ T_6 $[T_5,T]$	* T_7 $[T_5,T]$		) 5	

Figure 8. Optimized parsing table M' with two merged states for grammar G_0.

Acknowledgement. I am indebted to Eljas Soisalon-Soininen for useful remarks on earlier drafts of this paper.

References

1. Aho,A.V. and J.D.Ullman: The Theory of Parsing, Translation and Compiling, Vol. I: Parsing. Prentice-Hall, Englewood Cliffs, N.J., 1972.

2. Aho,A.V. and J.D.Ullman: The Theory of Parsing, Translation and Compiling, Vol. II: Compiling. Prentice-Hall, Englewood Cliffs, N.J., 1973.

3. Aho,A.V. and J.D.Ullman: A technique for speeding up LR(k) parsers. SIAM J. Computing 2 (1973), 106-127.

4. Aho,A.V. and J.D.Ullman: Principles of Compiler Design. Addison-Wesley, Reading, Mass., 1977.

5. DeRemer,F.L.: Simple LR(1) grammars. Comm. ACM 14:7 (1971), 435-460.

6. Geller,M.M. and S.L.Graham and M.A.Harrison: Production prefix parsing (extended abstract). In: Automata, Languages and Programming, Second Colloquium (ed. J. Loeckx), Lecture Notes in Computer Science 14, pp. 232-241, Springer-Verlag, 1974.

7. Hammer,M.: A new grammatical transformation into deterministic top-down form. Project MAC Technical Report TR-119, MIT, Mass., 1974.

8. Hammer,M.: A new grammatical transformation into LL(k) form. In: Proc. of Sixth Annual ACM Symposium on Theory of Computing (1974), 266-275.

9. Harrison,M.A. and I.M.Havel: On the parsing of deterministic languages. J. Assoc. Comput. Mach. 21 (1974), 525-548.

10. Knuth,D.E.: On the translation of languages from left to right. Information and Control 8:6 (1965), 607-639.

11. Rosenkrantz,D.J. and P.M.Lewis: Deterministic left corner parsing. In: IEEE Conf. Record of 11th Annual Symp. on Switching and Automata Theory (1970), 139-152.

12. Soisalon-Soininen,E. and E.Ukkonen: A characterization of LL(k) languages. In: Automata, Languages and Programming, Third Colloquium (eds. S.Michaelson, R.Milner), pp. 20-30, Edinburgh University Press, Edinburgh, 1976.

OPTIMAL DECOMPOSITION OF LINEAR AUTOMATA

László Úry
Research Institut for Applied Computer Science
Budapest, P.O.Box 227 H-1536/Hungary

INTRODUCTION

In the theory of automata the question of decomposition is very important but is hasn't been solved yet. From both theoretical and pragmatical point of view it would be interesting whether a given automaton can be decomposed by using automata that are irreducible in a certain sense. It seems to be true that the better categories are within the automata considered the better decomposition theorems hold. We conjuct that for the automata defined in an Abelian category an appropriate optimal decomposition theorem hold, but we can prove this statement only for linear machines. The elementary facts of the decomposition theory of linear machines can be found in Eilenberg's book. Thus the aim of this paper is only to prove an optimal decomposition theorem for linear machines.

1. PRELIMINARY NOTIONS

As a background we recall the most important notions of the theory of linear machines. All notions and theorem recalled here can be found in Eilenberg's book.

First let us fix a commutative ring with unit, say R. Let us denote Mod-R the category of right R-modules. An R-*linear machine* or R-*linear automaton* is a tuple $M = (Q,A,B;F,G,H,J)$ where Q,A,B are R-modules; F,G,M and J are R-linear maps corresponding to the following diagram:

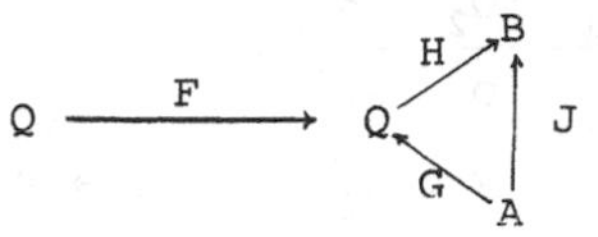

Q is called the state-module of M denoted by M_Q. We often write an R-linear machine M as a diagram:

$$M = \begin{array}{c|cc} & Q & B \\ \hline Q & F & M \\ & & \\ A & G & J \end{array} : A \to B$$

Any R-linear machine generates *the machine map of* M $f_M : A[z] \to B[[z]]$ defined by the following way. For $\vec{a} \in A[z]$ let $q_o = 0$, $q_{n+1} = q_n G + a_n F$ and $b_n = q_n H + a_n J$. Then $\vec{b} = \vec{a} f_M$ per definitionem. A trivial computation shows that this f_M is $R[z]$-linear. Thus

$$f_M \in \mathrm{Hom}_{R[z]}(A[z]\ ,\ B[[z]]) \approx \mathrm{Hom}_R(A,B)[[z]]\ .$$

Let $f \in \mathrm{Hom}_R(A,B)[[z]]$ be arbitrary. An R-linear automaton M *realise* f iff $f_M = f$.

THEOREM 1.1.
For any $f \in \mathrm{Hom}_R(A,B)[[z]]$ there is a canonical automaton M that realises f. I.e. M is both reachable and observable. ●

DEFINITION 1.2.
An $f \in \mathrm{Hom}_R(A,B)[[z]]$ is called *sequential* iff there is an automaton M that realises f and its state-module is finitely generated. ●

DEFINITION 1.3.
For R-linear automata

$$M_i = \begin{array}{c|cc} & Q_i & B \\ \hline Q_i & F_i & H_i \\ & & \\ A & G_i & J_i \end{array} : A \to B \qquad (i=1,2)$$

let us denote M_1+M_2 (with state-module Q_1+Q_2) the parallel composition of linear automaton M_1 and M_2, where

$$M_1+M_2 = \begin{array}{c|ccc} & Q_1 & Q_2 & B \\ \hline Q_1 & F_1 & 0 & H_1 \\ Q_2 & 0 & F_2 & H_2 \\ A & G_1 & G_2 & J_1+J_2 \end{array} : A \to B$$

Similarly for R-linear automata

$$M_1 = \begin{array}{c|cc} & Q_1 & B \\ \hline Q_1 & F_1 & H_1 \\ A & G_1 & J_1 \end{array} : A \to B$$

$$M_2 = \begin{array}{c|cc} & Q_2 & C \\ \hline Q_2 & F_2 & H_2 \\ B & G_2 & J_2 \end{array} : B \to C$$

let us denote M_1M_2 (with state-module Q_1+Q_2) the serial composition of M_1 and M_2 where

$$M_1M_2 = \begin{array}{c|ccc} & Q_2 & Q_1 & C \\ \hline Q_2 & F_2 & O & H_2 \\ Q_1 & H_1G_1 & F_1 & H_1J_1 \\ A & J_1G_2 & G_1 & J_1J_2 \end{array} : A \to B$$

●

If M is an R-linear automaton then its state-module Q can be considered as an $R[z]$-module. The $R[z]$-module structure is given by $q\cdot z \overset{d}{=} q\cdot F$. In the following if we speak about Q as an $R[z]$-module we think about this module structure.

THEOREM 1.4.
Let

$$M = \begin{array}{c|cc} & Q & B \\ \hline Q & F & H \\ A & G & J \end{array} : A \to B$$

be any R-linear automaton.

(i) Let us suppose that $Q = Q_1+Q_2$ in Mod-$R[z]$. There are such linear automata M_1, M_2 that $M = M_1+M_2$ and

$$Q_{M_i} = Q_i \quad (i=1,2)$$

(ii) Let us suppose that $0 \to Q_2 \to Q \to Q_1 \to 0$ is an exact sequence in Mod-$R[z]$.

There are such linear automata M_1, M_2 that $M = M_1M_2$ and $Q_{M_i} = Q_i$ $(i=1,2)$. ●

REMARK 1.5.
Similarly to the aboves the parallel and serial composition can be defined for the other kinds of automata. Several times, for instan((i) and (ii) of Theorem 1.4. can be modified in such a way that a corresponding decomposition theorem hold. Yet in most cases the modified theorem are useless to give a *general* and *simple* theory of decomposition.

2. SOME LEMMAS

For the linear machines there is no good decomposition theorem in general unless module R is a field. In the case of field $R[z]$ is a Noetherian ring and this fact is enough for the theory. The assumption that R is a field perhaps decreases the possibilities of applications, but not much. Thus in the following consideration we suppose that R is a field. So every $R[z]$-module Q is in the form

$$Q \approx Q_1 + \dots + Q_n \tag{1}$$

where Q_i's are irreducible. Moreover for any $i \in [1,n]$

$$Q_i \approx R[z] \big/ \left(p_i{}^{u_i}\right) \tag{2}$$

where p_i is prime in $R[z]$.(See this fact in Jacobson [1953].) First of all we need some technical lemmas. Their proof can be omitted at first reading.

DEFINITION 2.1.
Let $p \in R[z]$ be prime and let Q be an arbitrary $R[z]$-module. p *occours in* Q iff in (1) and (2) there is such i that $p_i = p$ and $u_i > 0$. *The range of* Q *w.r.t.* p denoted by rg_pQ is the sum $\sum_{p=p_i} u_i$.

The p-*part of* Q is

$$Q^p = \{x \in Q \mid m \in \mathbb{N} \quad x \cdot p^m = 0\} \qquad ●$$

LEMMA 2.2.
$Q^p = \prod_{p=p_i} Q_i$ and thus $\dim_R Q^p / \deg p = rg_p Q$.

Proof:

Let $Q^* = \prod_{p=p_i} Q_i$ and $m = rg_p Q$. It is clear that for any $x \in Q^*$ $x \cdot p^m = 0$ and so $Q^* \subset Q$. In order to prove that $Q \subset Q^*$ let $q=(q_1,\ldots,q_n) \in Q_1+\ldots+Q_n$ be such that $q \cdot p^u = 0$ for an appropriate $u \in \mathbb{N}$. This means that $q_i \cdot p^u=0$ $(i\in[1,n])$. Since $q_i \in R[z]/(p_i^{u_i})$ so there is such a $\bar{q}_i \in R[z]$ that $\deg \bar{q}_i < u_i \cdot \deg p_i$ and $q_i \equiv \bar{q}_i \mod (p_i^{u_i})$. Hence $\bar{q}_i p^u = \ell_i p_i$ in $R[z]$ for an appropriate $\ell_i \in R[z]$. We prove that if $p_i \neq p$, then $\bar{q}_i = 0$. Indeed let p_i and p be coprime. Since $p_i^{u_i} | q_i$ and $\deg \bar{q}_i < u_i \cdot \deg p_i$ so $\bar{q}_i = 0$. Thus $q \in Q^*$. ●

LEMMA 2.3.

Let $p \in R[z]$ be prime and let $0 \to Q_2 \overset{\alpha}{\to} Q \overset{\beta}{\to} Q_1 \to 0$ be exact in Mod-$R[z]$. We have

$$rg_p Q_2 + rg_p Q_1 = rg_p Q.$$

Proof:

Let $\alpha_p = \alpha \restriction Q_2^p$ and $\beta_p = \beta \restriction Q^p$. It is enough to prove that the sequence

$$0 \to Q_1^p \overset{\alpha_p}{\to} Q^p \overset{\beta_p}{\to} Q_2 \to 0 \tag{3}$$

is also exact. First we must prove that $Q_1^p \alpha_p \subset Q^p$ and $Q^p \beta_p \subset Q_2^p$. Let $x \in Q_1^p$. There is an $m \in \mathbb{N}$ such that $xp^m = 0$. Hence $0 = (xp^m)\alpha_p = (x\alpha_p) \cdot p^m$ and thus $x\alpha_p \in Q^p$. Similarly $Q^p \beta_p \subset Q_2^p$.

Since α is mono so α_p is also mono. Since $\beta = \bigoplus_{rg_p Q>0} \beta_p$ and β is epi so β_p's must be epi too.

Now we prove that if $q \in \operatorname{Ker} \beta$ then there is such a $q_1 \in Q_1^p$ that $q_1\alpha_p = q$. Since the original sequence is exact there is a $q^* \in Q_1$ such that $q^*\alpha = q$. But for an appropriate n $gp^n = 0$ and thus $0 = q^*\alpha p^n = q^* p^n \alpha$. α is mono and so $q^* p^n = 0$ i.e. $q^* \in Q_1^p$. In the end (3) is exact in Mod-R too. Since R is a field so (3) splits in Mod-R and thus

$$\dim Q^p = \dim Q_1^p + \dim Q_2^p.$$

Using 2.2 we have

$$rg_p Q_2 + rg_p Q_1 = rg_p Q. \quad ●$$

DEFINITION 2.4.

Let S, Q be $R[z]$-module. S is a *subfactor of* Q (written by $S < Q$)

iff there are two morphisms $\varphi : M \to S$, $\psi : M \to Q$ in Mod-R[z] such that φ is epi and ψ is mono.
The following is a wellknown theorem.

THEOREM 2.5.
For any R-linear automaton M the state-module of the canonical realization of f_M is a subfactor of Q_M , i.e. $Q_{f_M} < M_Q$. ●

COROLLARY 2.6.
For any $S < Q$ and any prime p we have $rg_p S \le rg_p Q$.

Proof:
Let $Q' \subset Q'' \subset Q$ be such that $Q''/Q' \approx S$. Then $0 \to Q' \to Q \to S \to 0$ is an exact sequence and from 2.4 $rg_p Q' + rg_p S = rg_p Q$. Thus $rg_p S \le rg_p Q$. ●

LEMMA 2.7.
Let $0 \to Q_2 \overset{\alpha}{\to} Q \overset{\beta}{\to} Q_1 \to 0$ be any exact sequence in Mod-R[z] and let S be such an R[z]-module that $S < Q$ and $S^p = S$. Then there are such R[z]-modules S_1, S_2 that $S_i < Q_i$ (i=1,2) and $rg_p S_1 + rg_p S_2 = rg_p S$.

Proof:
Let $M \subset Q$ and let $\varphi : M \to S$ be any epimorphism. Let $M_1 = M\beta$, $M_2 = M\alpha^{-1}$, $\alpha' = \alpha \restriction M_2$ and $\beta' = \beta \restriction M$. It is clear that $\cdot \overset{\alpha'}{\to} \cdot \overset{\beta'}{\to} \cdot$ is a short exact sequence in Mod-R[z]. Let $\alpha'\varphi = \varphi_1\alpha_1$ be the epi-mono factorization of $\alpha'\varphi$. Let $\beta_1 : S \to S/S_2 \overset{d}{\cong} S_1$. Summarizing these definitions we get the following diagram:

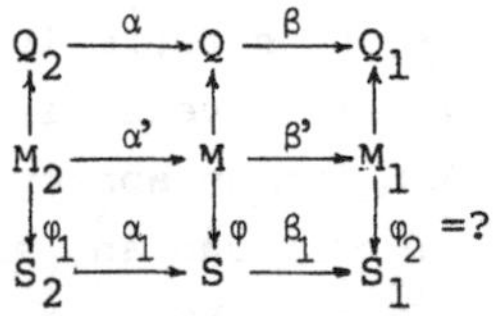

Of course $\cdot \xrightarrow{\alpha_1} \cdot \xrightarrow{\beta_1} \cdot$ is also exact.
There is an epimorphism $\varphi_2 : M_1 \to S_1$ such that the above diagram commutes. Indeed, for any $m \in M_1$ let $x,y \in M$ be such that $x\beta' = y\beta' = m$. Let us define $m\varphi_2$ as $x\varphi\beta_1$. In order to prove that $x\varphi\beta_1 = y\varphi\beta_1$ let $m_2 \in M_2$ be such that $m_2\alpha' = x-y$. Since $x-y \in \mathrm{Ker}\,\beta'$ such m_2 exists. Hence

$$x\varphi - y\varphi = (x-y)\varphi = m_2\alpha'\varphi = m_2\varphi_1\alpha_1 .$$

Using the exactness of the midle row $x\varphi\beta_1 - y\varphi\beta_1 = m_2\varphi_1\alpha_1\beta_1 = 0$. Thus φ_2 is well-deined. Since $\varphi\beta_1 = \beta'\varphi_2$ so φ_2 is epi and since φ, β_1, β' are in Mod-R[z] thus φ_2 is also R[z]-linear. In the end $S_i < Q_i$ and using 2.3 we have $rg_p S_1 + rg_p S_2 = rg_p S$. ◉

3. ON THE OPTIMAL DECOMPOSITION

The question of optimal decomposition can be considered at least from two different points of view:

- there is given an automaton $M = (\Omega,A,B,F,H,J)$ and M has to be built up from as few "little","irreducible" or "indecomposable" automata as possible,
- a sequential map $f \in Hom_R(A,B)[\![z]\!]$ is given and we should like to constmet this f as a machine map of an automaton M which is built up from as few irreducible machines as possible. (The case is similar when a given Boolean function is built up from $\wedge$- and $\vee$-gates./

Further an optimal building up means such a construction where the number of prime-machines is as few as possible.
According to the above mentioned first point of view the optimal decomposition is as follows.

THEOREM 3.1.
If an R-linear automation M is built up from finitely many prime machines by using serial and parallel composition then the number K of automata in use is greater than or equal to $\sum_p rg_p Q$.

Proof:
By 2.3 and 1.3 if M is built up from serial or parallel decomposition of M_1, M_2 then their range w.r.t. any p will be summed up. Since the range of a p-prime machine w.r.t. p is 1 and w.r.t. any other p^* is 0 we must use at most $\sum_p rg_p\Omega$ machines to get M. ◉

We note that $\sum_p rg_p\Omega$ machines will do. Let M be such that its state--module M_Ω is finitely generated. Then $M_\Omega \approx \Omega_1+\ldots+Q_n$, where $Q_i \approx R[z]/(p_i^{u_i})$. Using 1.4 (i) $M = M_1+\ldots+M_n$, where state-module of M_i is Q_i $(i=[1,n])$. For a fixed i there is a long exact sequence

$$0 = \frac{(p_i^{u_i})}{(p_i^{u_i})} \subset \frac{(p_i^{u_i-1})}{(p_i^{u_i})} \subset \ldots \frac{(p_i^{0})}{(p_i^{u_i})} = R[z] \big/ (p_i^{u_i})$$

Let us apply 1.4 (ii) u_i-1 times and we have that $M_i=M_{i_1}\dots M_{iu_i}$ where M_{ij}'s are p_i-prime machines.
Thus

$$M = \sum_{i=1}^{n} \prod_{j=1}^{u_i} M_{ij}$$

Of course $K = \sum_{i=1}^{n} u_i = \sum_{p} rg_p M_Q$.
Let us fix an $f\in Hom_R(A,B)[[z]]$. In the followings we would like to realize f as the composition of prime machines using as few ones as possible. In order to do this let us take the followings.

DEFINITION 3.2.
A *prime* polinome $p\in R[z]$ occurs in f iff p occurs in Q_f ; $rg_p f=rg_p Q_f$.
f is called (p-) prime or primer iff Q_f is (p-) prime or primer respectively.
From 3.1 immediately follows:
THEOREM 3.3.
For any sequential f there are such functions f_{ij} that ($i\in[1,n]$, $j\in[1,u_i]$)

$$f = \sum_{i=1}^{n} \prod_{j=1}^{u_i} f_{ij}$$

and f_{ij}'s are prime.

LEMMA 3.4.
For any prime p and sequential f_1,f_2 we have
a/ $rg_p f_1 + rg_p f_2 \geq rg_p(f_1+f_2)$,
b/ $rg_p f_1 + rg_p f_2 \geq rg_p(f_1\cdot f_2)$.
Proof:
Let M_{f_i} (i=1,2) be the canonical realisation of f_i. By 2.5 $Q_f<Q_{f_1}+Q_{f_2}$.
Applying 2.7 for the sequence $0 \to Q_{f_2} \to Q_{f_1}+Q_{f_2} \to Q_{f_1} \to 0$ and for $S = Q_f^{\,p}$ there are such $S_i<Q_{f_i}$ that $rg_p S_1+rg_p S_2 = rg_p S = rg_p Q_f^{\,p} = rg_p f$.
From 2.6 $rg_p S_i \leq rg_p f_i$ and thus $rg_p f_1+rg_p f_2 \geq rg_p(f_1+f_2)$. The proof of a/ is similar and we omit it. ●

THEOREM 3.5 (On Optimal Decomposition)
Let M realise f and be built up from K linear machine by using serial and parallel decomposition. Then $K \geq \sum_p rg_p f$. Moreover there are such prime machines M_{ij} that for the linear automaton

$$N = \sum_{i=1}^{n} \prod_{j=1}^{u_i} M_{ij}$$

realises f and

$$\sum_{i=1}^{n} u_i = \sum_{p} rg_p f.$$

These M_{ij} can be obtained in such a way that we decompose M_f.

Proof:

It is immediate from 3.4 and 3.1. ◉

REFERENCES

[1] Eilenberg, S.:
Automata and languages, Volume A, Academic Press.

[2] Jacobson, N.:
Lectures in Abstract Algebra Volume II,
Lineare algebra, Van Nostrand, 1953.

BRACKETED TWO-LEVEL GRAMMARS - A DECIDABLE AND PRACTICAL APPROACH TO LANGUAGE DEFINITIONS

Lutz Wegner
Institut für Angewandte Informatik
und Formale Beschreibungsverfahren
Universität Karlsruhe (TH), D-7500 Karlsruhe
W.Germany

Abstract. Bracketed two-level grammars are not a variation of two-level grammars (van Wijngaarden grammars) but consitute a restriction within the general scheme. The resulting grammars give rise to an effective top-down analysis, where the replacement of metanotions is governed by rules similar to the evaluation dependencies in attribute grammars. Supplemented by the formalized concept of predicates, the class of languages is shown to be decidable and includes EXSPACE. Moreover it has been demonstrated by a description of PASCAL-S, that the grammars are versatile enough to yield quite readable formal definitions of programming languages. To allow a critical comparison, a grammar for the syntax of ASPLE is given in an Appendix.

1. Introduction.

Marcotty, Ledgard and Bochmann compared in their excellent survey paper 'A Sampler of Formal Definitons' [8] W-Grammars (van Wijngaarden Grammars, two-level grammars), Production Systems and the axiomatic approach, VDL, and Attribute Grammars. As a test case they used the language ASPLE which was introduced by Cleaveland and Uzgalis [2].

In their ratings two-level grammars (TLGs) fared well in the categories 'completeness' and 'simplicity of model' but did not score any points for 'clarity of defined syntax' and other criteria. In contrast, Attribute Grammars did well with 'clarity of defined syntax' but rated low on everything else, including 'completeness' and 'simplicity of model'.

This paper introduces "bracketed two-level grammars" which look like two-level grammars in the ordinary sense but permit an "attribute grammar interpretation". It is the author's opinion that the presented model combines the strong points of both methods. An informal introduction into the problems of restricting TLGs to be generally decidable is given first together with an informal description of the new method. Formal definitions and some results follow. In an Appendix, a formal description of ASPLE (syntax only) is given by means of a bracketed TLG. The author would also like to draw the attention to a paper by Dembinski and Małuszyński [3], presented in Zakopane, in which "generalized attribute grammars" are introduced. In going the opposite way as described here, they can construct, in general, the attribute version of a TLG.

2. Decidable Two-Level Grammars

When aiming towards decidable TLGs two fundamental problems arise:

a) if in a top-down derivation step, a hyperrule is employed which contains on the right-hand side (rhs) a metanotion which does not occur on the left-hand side (lhs) then its replacement has to be "guessed" (bottom-up analogously);

b) hyperrules which produce the empty word and cyclic hyperrules (i.e. rules of the form $<H_0> \rightarrow <H_1>$) exclude an a-priori upper bound on the length of a derivation.

Three approaches to solve these problems are known to the author. The first by John L. Baker [1] introduces context-sensitive TLGs. The requirement is that the length of the rhs of any strict rule is not less than the length of the lhs. As to (a), this limits the "guessing" to a finite number of possible replacements of length not greater than a terminal word w under consideration. In the same manner the length of w is a limit to (b).

The more general solution by Peter Deussen [4,5] deals with (a) and (b) straightforwardly. Metanotions may not occur on the rhs unless they also occur on the lhs; ε-hyperrules and shrinking cyclic rules are forbidden.

The third approach, which was investigated by the author in his Ph.D. thesis recently [9], also requires the Deussen restriction as to (a). Point (b) is solved by constructing a context-free skeleton grammar from the cross-reference of the TLG. Under certain restrictions it can be shown that there exists a derivation in the TLG iff there exists a derivation in the skeleton grammar. If the skeleton grammar is unambiguous then there is an upper bound on the length of any derivation in the TLG.

When inspecting any of the known TLG-language reports (see [6] for a bibliographie of TLGs) one finds that none of the grammars used are generally decidable by any of the three criteria above. However, what is even worse is that no effort will produce a nondegenerate TLG fulfilling (a) for even a toy language like ASPLE.

To realize this, consider the familiar context-free production

<stmts>::= <stmt> ; <stmts>|< stmt >.

If (a) is to be fulfilled for a top-down approach, the corresponding hyperrule has the form

<TABLE stmts> → <TABLE stmt> ; <TABLE stmts>|<TABLE stmt>.

Whatever information has been gathered in TABLE is passed down both branches. However, anything occurring in the 'stmt-subtree' will not become known in the 'stmts-subtree'. Thus if 'stmt' becomes a 'block' with unresolved labels in goto-statements, there is no way to check for their label occurrences in stmts.

Similarly a bottom-up approach yields a hyperrule of the form

<TABLE 1 TABLE 2 stmts> → <TABLE 1 stmt>;<TABLE 2 stmts>|
<TABLE 1 TABLE 2 stmt>

making it impossible to see immediatly whether an applied identifier is declared in a surrounding block.

3. Bracketed Two-level Grammars.

The new method which we introduce here will solve this problem. It uses a very "human technique": if you cannot solve a subproblem immediately, set it aside for the moment. The German term for such a policy is "ausklammern" (to bracket) which is exactly what we shall do. Two new, otherwise not used syntactic marks "(" and ")" are introduced. Using a top-to-bottom-to-top leftmost derivation, we bracket any rhs metanotion which does not occur on the lhs. The brackets uniquely determine the position of the metanotion(s) which act as placeholders. Their replacement is ignored when deriving the subtree top-down and is not undertaken until the subtree is completed and their values become available in returning from the leaves of the subtree.

Those familiar with attribute grammars will recognize bracketed metanotions as synthesized attributes and unbracketed metanotions as derived (inherited) attributes. The previously mentioned hyperrule then becomes

<T 1 (T 2 T 3)stmts> → <T 1 (T 2) stmt>;<T 1 T 2 (T 3) stmts> |
<T 1 (T 2 T 3) stmt>.

As compared to attribute grammars, this method does not introduce a new mechanism into the system (such as "evaluation of attributes" by means of arithmetic). Rather any "bracketed TLG" is just a TLG, written in a way such that a particular effective interpretation is possible for a user, but which may also be ignored by anybody not interested in the technique. We give now an example and leave the formal results to Section 4.

Example:

Consider a TLG to generate words of the form a+b=c, where a,b,c, $\in \{1\}\{o,1\}^*$ and c is the obvious result of adding the binary numbers a and b. Although this could be achieved by various types of TLGs, including some which satisfy known decidability criteria, one can see already, how a 'bracketed two-level grammar' preserves the underlying context-free structure.

As usual for every metavariable X with following index i there is an implicit metarule $Xi \rightarrow X$ (see [1o]).

Metarules

```
    VALUE : n VALUE | ε.
```

Hyperrules

```
   <start> → <term (VALUE 1)> + <term (VALUE 2)> =
             <result VALUE 1  VALUE 2>
 <term (n)> → 1
 <term (VALUE VALUE n)> → <term (VALUE)>1
 <term (VALUE VALUE)> → <term (VALUE)>O
 <result n> → 1
 <result VALUE VALUE n> → <result VALUE>1
 <result VALUE VALUE> → <result VALUE>O.
```

Consider 101 + 100 = 1001.
Picture 1 shows the derivation tree after having derived "term a" with synthesized values not yet filled in. The rhs-hypernotions appear on top of the lhs-hypernotions which they have to match.

The derivation for "term b" is analogue to "term a". The result, however, is generated with derived values only. The complete tree is shown in Picture 2.

4. Formal Definitions and Results.

We assume basic knowledge of TLGs and include the following formal definition of a TLG only to establish our terminology.

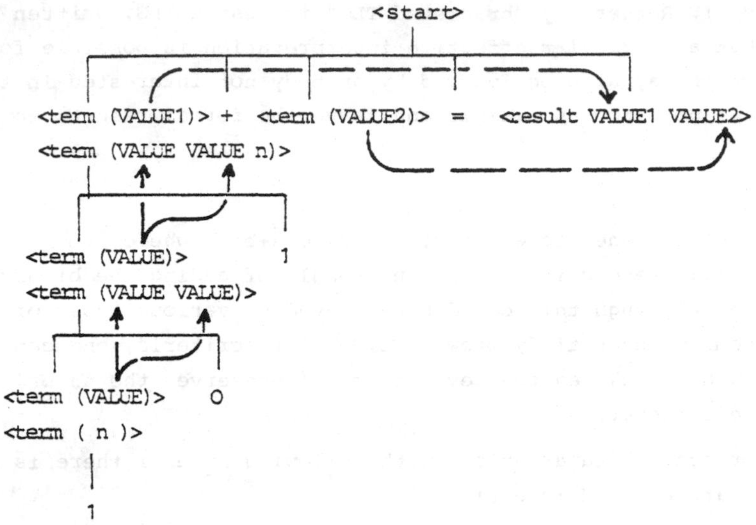

Picture 1.

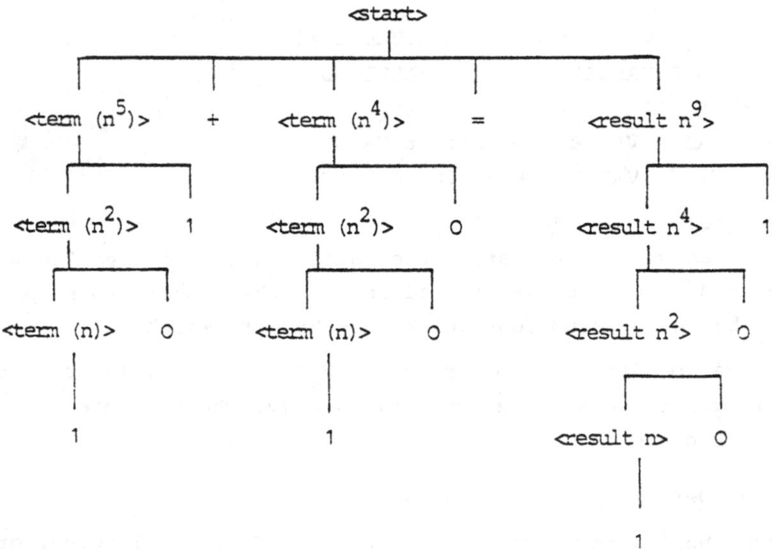

Picture 2

Definition 1. A *two-level grammar* (TLG, van Wijngaarden grammar, W-Grammar) is an ordered 7-tuple (M,V,N,T,R_M,R_V,S), where

M is a finite set of *metanotions*;

V is a finite set of *syntactic variables*, $M \cap V = \phi$;

N $= \{<H> \mid H \in (M \cup V)^+\}$, the finite set of *hypernotions*;

T is a finite set of *terminals*;

R_M is a finite set of *metaproduction rules* $X \to Y$, where $X \in M$, $Y \in (M \cup V)^*$, s.t. for all $W \in M$: (M,V,R_M,W) is a context-free grammar;

$R_V \subseteq N \times (N \cup T)$, the finite set of *hyperproduction rules* $<H_o> \to h_1h_2...h_m$, $h_i \in (T \cup N \cup \{\varepsilon\})$ $(1 \leq i \leq m)$;

S $= <s> \in N, s \in V^+$, the *start notion*.

Derivation steps $\alpha_i => \alpha_{i+1}$ in TLGs are defined by means of strict rules which are obtained from the hyperrules through a homomorphic replacement of metanotions. In particular a terminal derivation D in G is a sequence of sentential forms, $D = \alpha_o, \alpha_1, ..., \alpha_n$ with $\alpha_o = S$, start-symbol of G, $\alpha_n = w \in T^*$ and $\alpha_i \underset{G}{\Rightarrow} \alpha_{i+1} (i \leq o \leq n-1)$.

Analogously to CFGs one has leftmost derivations in TLGs and it is important to note that there is a terminal derivation of w in G iff there is a leftmost terminal derivation of w in G, i.e. this property of CF-Grammars carries over.

Furthermore we call a sequence of hyperrules $E = r_{i_1}, r_{i_2}, ..., r_{i_n}$ a *parse* of some sentential form α_n if there exists a derivation $D = \alpha_o, \alpha_1, ..., \alpha_n$ s.t. for all $0 \leq j \leq n-1$: $\alpha_j \Rightarrow \alpha_{j+1}$ by use of hyperrule r_{i_j}. We say D is *induced* by E. If E induces a lm derivation, then E is a *left parse*.

Note that a parse may induce several derivations and also that a single derivation may be induced by several parses. For details see [9].

We now define "bracketed two-level grammars".

Definition 2. We call a TLG $G = (M,V,N,T,R_M,R_V,S)$ a *bracketed two-level grammar (BTLG)* if (i) - (iii) holds:

(i) there are two distinguished symbols - called *brackets* - $(,) \in V$, $(,)$ not subword of any word derivable from a metanotion;

(ii) if in a hyperrule $<H_o> \to h_1h_2...h_m$ there is a metanotion W in brackets in H_o, then either W appears also outside brackets in

H_o or inside brackets in at least one h_i, $1 \leq i \leq m$.

(iii) if in a hyperrule $\langle H_o \rangle \rightarrow h_1 h_2 \ldots h_m$ there is a metanotion W outside of brackets in h_i ($1 \leq i \leq m$) then either W appears outside of brackets in H_o or inside brackets in at least one h_j with $1 \leq j < i \leq m$.

The underlying concept of a BTLG is an attempt to carry over the well-formed conditions of simple attribute grammars and we state its effect on derivations in a Theorem. First we need the property of "metadeterminism" which takes care of problem (a) mentioned in the informal introduction above.

Definition 3. A TLG is called *metadetermined* if there exists an effective procedure P s.t. for all left sentential froms α_i, α_j and every left parse E of α_j from α_i the procedure P computes all derivations induced by E.

Intuitively "metadetermined" means that in tracing out a derivation using a given left parse, i.e. a hyperrule sequence, we do not have to guess the replacement of metavariables.

Theorem 4. *If G is a BTLG then G is metadetermined.*

Proof. Note first that given a strict notion v and a hypernotion H there are only finitely many ways of assigning v to H ("matching v and H").

Consider then any given sentential forms α_i, α_j and left parse E. P works as follows (sketch only):

Successively the next hyperrule $\langle H_o \rangle \rightarrow h_1 h_2 \ldots h_m$ indicated by E is applied to the leftmost nonterminal in α_i. The following cases may arise:

case a: A metavariable W appears in a nonbracketed position in h_i ($1 \leq i$). By Definition 2, the replacement of W is determined by W occuring outside brackets in H_o (case a1) or by W in brackets in h_j, $j < i$ (case a2). Since we look at lm derivations, h_j is derived before h_i.

case b: A metavariable W appears in a bracketed position in h_j. By ignoring its replacement we continue the left parse and derive h_j using a hyperrule $\langle H_o' \rangle \rightarrow h_1' h_2' \ldots h_n'$. Because of the use of the distinguished symbols "(" and ")", H_o' which matches h_j must contain a term over $(V \cup M)^*$ in brackets.

case b1: If this term is just a notion (i.e. a word over V*), then the replacement of W in h_j is determined. If the term in H_o' contains a metanotion, say W', then by Def. 2, H_o' may also contain W' outside a bracketed position (see a1) which then also determines the replacement of W' in brackets; or (case b2) W' occurs in brackets in some h_k' on the rhs which recursively leads us to the situation in case b.

Case c: The recursion ends whenever a rhs consists entirely of terminals (case c1) which, of course, do not contain anything in brackets.

The process of ignoring replacements must then end by the situation described in cases a1 and b1.

Otherwise (case c2) in replacing a nonterminal using the last indicated hyperrule $<H_o''> \rightarrow h_1'', h_2'' \ldots h_k''$ in E, we arrive at the given sentential form α_j. In matching $h_i''(1 \leq i \leq k)$ with its corresponding strict notions in α_j we learn the replacement of a bracketed metavariable W in h_i'' which in turn determines the replacement of W in H_o'', etc. □

One can see that the derivation tree of a word $w \in T^*$ is constructed alternatively top-down and bottom-up. We shall call this procedure P used in BTLG's the "two-directional tracing method".

From the proof above the following corollary is obvious since if there is a derivation for a $w \in T^*$ at all then there is a lm derivation of w in G as well.

Corollary 5. *Let G be a BTLG. For all $w \in T^*$ there is a derivation D of w in G iff the two-directional tracing method P computes a lm derivation D' of w in G.*

What Corollary 5 says, is that given a bracketed two-level grammar, it is sufficient to try to construct derivation trees in the two directional way described above.

5. Predicative BTLGs

To avoid misunderstandings, we do not claim that BTLGs are generally decidable without further restrictions (problem (b) from above has not been touched yet). Clearly there are many ways to avoid the almost looping situations caused by ε-hyperrules and circular hyperrules. In a Master's Thesis presently written by G. Jungkind in Karlsruhe, a quite readable BTLG description of PASCAL-S is given [7]. To solve problem (b) a rather pragmatic, yet provable approach has been taken.

Since predicates, which are essentially ε-hyperrules, were considered indispensable, two additional symbols "{" and "}" were introduced. The set of hyperrules was then divided into "skeleton rules", which may not have an ε-rhs, and "predicate rules" marked by "{" and "}", which either have a nonterminal or empty rhs. Furthermore skeleton rules of the form $<H_o>\to<H_1>$ had the length restriction $|H_o| \geq |H_1|$ known from the Deussen Type R-criterion.

Bracketed two-level grammars which are of the form just described, have been called "predicative bracketed two-level grammars of Type R", short: PBTLGs of Type R. We now give the formal definition.

We shall use $|\varphi(H_i)|$ to denote the length of hypernotion H_i in terms of syntactic variables under some homomorphic replacement φ, i.e. the length of a strict notion which H_i may yield.

Definition 6. A two-level grammar $G=(M,V,N,T,R_M,R_V,S)$ is a *predicative bracketed two-level grammar of type R (PBTLG of type R)* if

a) G is a bracketed two-level grammar;

b) the set of hypernotions N is the disjoint union of N', N" where
$N' = \{<H> \mid H \in (M \cup V)^+\}$, the finite set of *skeleton hypernotions*,
$N'' = \{\{H\} \mid H \in (M \cup V)^+\}$, the finite set of *predicative hypernotions;*

c) the set of hyperrules R_V is the disjoint union of R_p, R_s, where

$R_p \subseteq N'' \times (N'' \cup \{\varepsilon\})$ and $\{H_o\} \to \{H_1\}\ldots\{H_m\} \in R_p$

implies for all replacements φ:

$|\varphi(H_o)| > |\varphi(H_i)| \qquad (1 \leq i \leq m)$, the *predicates;*

$R_s \subseteq N' \times (N' \cup N'' \cup T)$ and $<H_o> \to h_1h_2\ldots h_m \in R_s$

implies for at least one i: $h_i \notin N''$ and if

$h_1h_2\ldots h_m = h' <H_i> h'' \in (N'')^*N'(N'')^*$ then

$|\varphi(H_o)| \geq |\varphi(H_i)| \qquad (1 \leq i \leq m)$,

the *nonpredicative hyperrules.*

The rather lengthy definition is easily perceived with the following motivation in mind.

The introduction of N" is a slight abuse of notation. Rather than extending V to $V' = V \cup \{\#\}$, $\# \notin V$, and defining N" as a set of hypernotions $\{<\#H> \mid H \in (M \cup V)^+\}$, we use curly brackets to distinguish the disjoint sets.

Once a predicative notion has been introduced, it can only be derived further by the predicates and must ultimately lead to the empty word ("the predicate holds").

The requirement, that each rhs predicative hypernotion is strictly shorter than the lhs, is a very simple method to guarentee decidability. All Algol 68 predicates [10] can be rewritten to satisfy the criterion by "padding" them sufficiently at the point of introduction in R_s.

As for the latter set, we neither allow an empty rhs nor may the rhs consist entirely of predicative hypernotions, which avoids implicit empty right-hand sides.

If in ignoring predicative hypernotions, the remaining "skeleton hyperrule" is of the form $<H_o> \rightarrow <H_1>$, then H_1 is of at most the length of H_o. But this is the R-criterion of Deussen and again decidability is guaranteed.

Thus Theorem is easily obtained from the preceding definition.

Theorem 7. *For PBTLGs G of Type R it is generally decidable whether* $w \in L(G)$.

Proof. Since G is a BTLG we shall try to apply the two directional method of Theorem 4. This is done by successively extending left parses. The proof is complete if we can show that there are only finitely many left parses, each of which we can trace out since G is metadetermined. Of course we trace out and extend the parse simultaneously.
Consider what may happen:

Each skeleton strict notion can either (i) derive $n \geq 2$ new strict notions giving rise to a process that is bound by the terminal word w (a skeleton notion cannot disappear(!)), or (ii) it may in cyclic rules permute its syntactic variables and possibly shrink until a terminal is derived or a derivation step (i) occurs again.

Similarly each predicative strict notion $\underline{h}$ will yield the empty word in at most $k^{|\underline{h}|}$ steps, where $k \in \mathbb{N}$ is the greatest number of predicative hypernotions on the rhs of a predicate rule.

Clearly these restrictions limit the length of left parses and we are done. □

We close with the following Theorem. It uses a result by P. Deussen and K. Mehlhorn [5] which shows the equivalence of L_R, L_L, and EXSPACE, where L_R [L_L] is the class of languages generated by type L [type R] TLGs [4], and EXSPACE is the class of languages whose space complexity is C^n. Let L_{PBTLGR} denote the class of languages generated by predicative bracketed two-level grammars of type R.

Theorem 8. $EXSPACE \subseteq L_{PBTLGR}$.

Proof. In [5], EXSPACE is shown to equal L_R.
But any Deussen type R TLG is a PBTLG of type R without metanotions in

brackets and predicates (see Definitions 2 and 6). □

The other direction is open and it is not immediately clear, how to simulate predicates within the Deussen type R framework.

6. Conclusion

We leave it to the reader to judge the practicability of BTLGs, e.g. by looking at ASPLE in the Appendix.

Disadvantages are, that hyperrules become slightly longer and that languages which are not tailored to 1-Pass-Compilers do not directly suit BTLGs.

Advantages are, that the description mechanism is uniform, decidable and elegant enough to yield readable language descriptions. The syntax analysis parts of experimental compilers based on BTLGs are easy to write but are at present prohibitively inefficient. Further research in this direction is needed and might eliminate some of the current bad feelings about formal descriptions of programming languages.

APPENDIX: A bracketed two-level grammar of ASPLE.

Metarules

ALPHA ::= a | b | ... | z .
BOOL ::= true | false .
EMPTY ::= .
INTBOOL :: = int | bool .
LOC ::= loc TAG has MODE .
LOCS ::= LOC | LOC LOCS .
LOCSETY ::= LOCS | EMPTY .
MODE ::= INTBOOL | ref MODE .
NOTETY ::= NOTION | EMPTY .
NOTION ::= ALPHA | ALPHA NOTION .
TABLE ::= LOCS .
TAG ::= letter ALPHA | letter ALPHA TAG .
TAGETY ::= TAG | EMPTY .

Hyperrules

1. Start Rule

a) <program> ::= begin <dcl train of (TABLE)>
{TABLE restrictions} <TABLE statement train> end.

2. Declarations

a) <dcl train of (LOCS LOCSETY)> ::= <(MODE) declarer> <ref MODE definitions of (LOCS)> ; {where (LOCSETY) is} | <(MODE) declarer> <ref MODE definitions of (LOCS)> ; <dcl train of (LOCSETY)>.

b) <(MODE1) declarer> ::= ref <(MODE2) declarer> {where (MODE1) is ref MODE2} | int {where (MODE1) is int} | bool {where (MODE1) is bool}.

c) <MODE definitions of (loc TAG has MODE LOCSETY)> ::= <create (TAG) id> {where (LOCSETY) is} | <create (TAG) id> , <MODE definitions of (LOCSETY)>.

3. TABLE restrictions

a) {LOCSETY loc TAG has MODE restrictions} ::= {where TAG is not in LOCSETY} {LOCSETY restrictions}.

b) {EMPTY restrictions} ::= .

c) {where TAG1 is not in loc TAG2 has MODE LOCSETY} ::= {where TAG1 differs from TAG2} {where TAG1 is not in LOCSETY}.

d) {where TAG is not in EMPTY} ::= .

4. Statements

a) <TABLE statement train> ::= <TABLE statement> ; <TABLE statement train> | <TABLE statement>.

b) <TABLE statement> ::= <TABLE asgt stmt> | <TABLE cond stmt> | <TABLE loop stmt> | <TABLE transput>.

c) <TABLE asgt stmt> ::= <TABLE (ref MODE1 TAG) ident> : = <TABLE (MODE2 TAGETY) value> {where MODE2 derefs to MODE1}.

d) <TABLE cond stmt> ::= if <TABLE (MODE TAGETY) value> {where MODE derefs to bool} then <TABLE statement train> <TABLE else end>.

e) <TABLE else end> ::= fi | else <TABLE statement train> fi.

f) <TABLE loop stmt> ::= while <TABLE (MODE TAGETY) value> {where MODE derefs to bool} do <TABLE statement train> end.

g) <TABLE transput> ::= input <TABLE (MODE TAG) ident> |
output <TABLE (MODE TAGETY) value>.

5. Expressions

a) <TABLE (MODE1 TAGETY1) value> ::= <TABLE (MODE1 TAGETY1) factor> | <TABLE (MODE2 TAGETY2) value> + <TABLE (MODE3 TAGETY3) factor> {where MODE2 yields (INTBOOL)} {where MODE3 yields (INTBOOL)} { where (MODE1) is INTBOOL} {where (TAGETY1) is}.

b) <TABLE (MODE1 TAGETY1) factor> ::= <TABLE (MODE1 TAGETY1) primary> | <TABLE (MODE2 TAGETY2) factor> * <TABLE (MODE3 TAGETY3) primary> {where MODE2 yields (INTBOOL)} {where MODE3 yields (INTBOOL)} {where (MODE1) is INTBOOL} {where (TAGETY) is}.

c) <TABLE (MODE TAGETY) primary> ::= <(MODE) denotation> {where (TAGETY) is} | **(** <TABLE (MODE TAGETY) value> **)** <TABLE (MODE TAGETY) ident> | **(** <TABLE compare> **)** {where (MODE) is bool} {where (TAGETY) is}.

d) <TABLE compare> ::= <TABLE (MODE1 TAGETY1) value> <relate token> <TABLE (MODE2 TAGETY2) value> {where MODE1 derefs to int} {where MODE2 derefs to int}.

e) <relate token> ::= = | ≠ .

f) <(MODE) denotation> ::= true {where (MODE) is bool} | false {where (MODE) is bool} | <number> {where (MODE) is int}.

6. Identifiers

a) <TABLE (MODE TAG) ident> ::= <create (TAG) id> {where TABLE contains loc TAG has (MODE)}.

b) <create (letter ALPHA NOTETY) id> ::= <letter (ALPHA) token> {where (NOTETY) is} | <letter (ALPHA) token> <create (NOTETY) id>.

c) <letter (ALPHA) token> ::= a {where (ALPHA) is a} | ... | z {where (ALPHA) is z}.

d) <number> ::= <digit> | <digit> <number>.

e) <digit> ::= 0 | 1 | ... | 9 .

7. MODE checking

a) {where INTBOOL derefs to INTBOOL} ::= .

b) {where ref MODE1 derefs to INTBOOL} ::=
{where MODE1 derefs to INTBOOL}.

c) {where ref MODE1 derefs to ref MODE2} ::=
{where MODE1 derefs to MODE2}.

d) {where ref MODE yields (INTBOOL)} ::=
{where MODE yields (INTBOOL)}.

e) {where INTBOOL yields (INTBOOL)} ::= .

8. General Predicates

a) {where (NOTETY) is NOTETY} ::= .

b) {where NOTETY is NOTETY} ::= .

c) {where NOTETY1 NOTION NOTETY2 contains NOTION} ::= .

d) {where NOTETY1 ALPHA1 differs from NOTETY2 ALPHA2} ::=
{where NOTETY1 differs from NOTETY2} |
{where ALPHA1 precedes ALPHA2 in abc...xyz} |
{where ALPHA2 precedes ALPHA1 in abc...xyz}.

e) {where ALPHA1 precedes ALPHA2 in NOTETY1 ALPHA1 NOTETY2 ALPHA2 NOTETY3} ::= .

f) {where LOCSETY1 loc TAG has MODE LOCSETY2 contains loc TAG has (MODE)} ::= .

References

[1] Baker, J.L.: Grammars with Structured Vocabulary: a Model for the Algol 68 Definition, Information and Control 20:4, 351-395 (1972)

[2] Cleaveland, J.C., Uzgalis, R.: What Every Programmer Should Know about Grammar, Dept. of Computer Science, School of Engineering and Applied Science, UCLA (1973), also; American Elsevier Publ., Co., New York, 1976

[3] Dembiński, P., Małuszyński, J.: Attribute grammars and two-level grammars; a unifying approach, MFCS 1978, Zakopane, LNCS 64, 143-154 (1978)

[4] Deussen, P.: A Decidability Criterion for van Wijngaarden Grammars, Acta Informatica 5, 353-375 (1975)

[5] Deussen, P., Mehlhorn, K.: Van Wijngaarden Grammars and Space Complexity Class EXSPACE, Acta Informatica 8, 193-199 (1977)

[6] Deussen, P., Wegner, L.: A Bibliographie of van Wijngaarden Grammars, Bulletin of the European Ass. for Theoretical Computer Science (EATCS), No. 6, 1978

[7] Jungkind, G.: Geklammerte zweischichtige Grammatiken, Master's Thesis, Institut für Angewandte Informatik und Formale Beschreibungsverfahren, Universität Karlsruhe, October 1978

[8] Marcotty, M., Ledgard, H.F., Bochmann, G.V.: A Sampler of Formal Definitions, Computing Surveys, 8/2 (1976)

[9] Wegner, L.: Analysis of Two-Level Grammars, Ph.D.thesis, Stuttgart: Hochschul-Verlag 1977

[10] Wijngaarden, A. van, et al. (eds.): Revised Report on the Algorithmic Language ALGOL 68, Berlin-Heidelberg-New York: Springer 1976.

INDEX OF AUTHORS